Contents

©The National Gardens Scheme 1994

All rights reserved. No part of this publication may be reproduced or transmitted in any form by any means electronic or mechanical including photocopying, recording or any other information storage and retrieval system without prior written permission from the publisher.

Published by the National Gardens Scheme, Hatchlands Park, East Clandon, Guildford, Surrey GU4 7RT

Editor: Lt Col D G Carpenter (Retd.)

Designed by Jonathan Newdick.

Cover illustration of Redisham Hall, Suffolk by Val Biro

A catalogue record for this book is available from the British Library.

Typeset in Linotron Bell Centennial by Land & Unwin (Data Sciences) Limited, Bugbrooke.

Text printed and bound by Wm Clowes Ltd, Beccles.

Cover and colour section printed by George Over Limited, Rugby.

ISBN 0-900558-26-1 ISSN 0141-2361

WHY CARR SHEPPARDS ARE SUPPORTING THE NATIONAL GARDENS SCHEME

The name Carr Sheppards is probably unfamiliar to you, but the two stockbroking firms from which we sprang in May last year are among the oldest-established in London; W.I. Carr was founded in 1825 and Sheppards in 1827.

Our French parent company, Banque Indosuez, is also an unfamiliar name to many in this country, although most school children have heard of their distinguished antecedent, Ferdinand de Lesseps, who founded Compagnie de Suez in 1858 to dig and operate the Suez Canal. Compagnie de Suez, of which Banque Indosuez is today a major part, is one of Europe's largest companies.

This unfamiliarity with our name, in spite of our deep and strong roots, is obviously one of the reasons why we are so pleased to have been given the opportunity to support the National Gardens Scheme and its associated charities.

Another reason for supporting the Scheme is that in many ways our activities are similar, in that the care and long term commitment that show their results in the gardens resemble the nature of the service we strive to give our private clients.

Finally, we cannot think of a more revered and worthwhile organisation with whom to be associated.

We look forward to a long and mutually beneficial relationship.

Fred Carr

Fred Carr, Chief Executive

CARR SHEPPARDS
Banque Indosuez Group

Carr Sheppards Limited, No1 London Bridge, London SE1 9TJ. Tel: 071-378 7050 Fax: 071-403 0755
A member of the Securities and Futures Authority and the London Stock Exchange.

The National Gardens Scheme Charitable Trust

'The Gardens Scheme' was started at the suggestion of Miss Elsie Wagg, a member of the council of the Queen's Nursing Institute, as part of a national memorial to Queen Alexandra whose deep and sympathetic interest in district nursing was well known.

Although this country was renowned for its gardens, few people had the opportunity to see them, so that when 600 were opened in 1927 the response was such that the experiment became an English institution. The Scheme, now called the **National Gardens Scheme Charitable Trust**, has continued and expanded ever since, in 1993 raising more than £1.500,000 from over 3,000 gardens.

The National Gardens Scheme helps many deserving causes, the first call on its funds being in support of its original beneficiary, the **Queen's Nursing Institute** and, with them, the **Nurses Welfare Service** for the relief of district and other nurses in need – be this caused by old age, difficulties through illness or the stress and pressure of their work.

Since 1949 a contribution has been made to the **Gardens Fund of The National Trust** to help maintain gardens of special historic or horticultural interest. In 1984 the increasing popularity of the Scheme made it possible to extend further its charitable work by assisting the **Cancer Relief Macmillan Fund** with funds for training **Macmillan Nurses** in the continuing care of the terminally ill. In 1986 the Scheme took on the charitable work previously organised by Gardeners' Sunday in aid of the **Gardeners' Royal Benevolent Society** and the **Royal Gardeners' Orphan Fund**.

Many other national and local charities also benefit from the Scheme, since garden owners may, if they so wish, allocate an agreed proportion of the proceeds of an opening for the National Gardens Scheme to another charity. The names of these additional charities are published in the descriptive entries for the gardens.

We wish to emphasise that the majority of the gardens listed are privately owned and are only opened on the dates shown in the text through the generosity of the owners wishing to support this charity. These gardens are **NOT OPEN** to the public on other dates except by prior agreement.

The Chairman and Council wish to express their deep gratitude to all those whose generous support of the National Gardens Scheme makes it possible to help these most worth-while charities. We hope that you will enjoy visiting as many of these gardens as you can – so helping us to help others.

Thank you for your support.

Chairman of Council

Patron, President and Council of The National Gardens Scheme Charitable Trust

Famous for fine Jewellery
and an incomparable service

Member of
THE NATIONAL ASSOCIATION
OF GOLDSMITHS

Member of
THE BRITISH ANTIQUE DEALERS
ASSOCIATION

Richard Ogden

International Jeweller

28 & 29 Burlington Arcade Piccadilly London W1
Telephones: 071-493 9136/7 & 6239

On request: Brochure £1 – refundable with purchase

Relevant organisations and publications

Historic Houses Castles and Gardens in Great Britain and Ireland, 1994 edition
Published by Professional Publications, Reed Information Services, Windsor Court, East Grinstead House, East Grinstead, West Sussex RH19 1XA. Price £7.70 at W.H. Smith, National Trust Shops and all leading booksellers in Great Britain and Ireland. Published annually in February in full colour throughout, it contains details of over 1,300 famous historic properties and beautiful gardens open to the general public.

The National Trust
Certain gardens opened by The National Trust are opened in aid of the National Gardens Scheme on the dates shown in this book. Information about the regular opening of these gardens is given in the 1994 *Handbook for Members and Visitors* (issued free to members), published by The National Trust (Enterprises) Ltd (£4.50 plus 70p for postage; subject to alteration) and obtainable from 36 Queen Anne's Gate, London SW1H 9AS or from any National Trust Property. The National Trust Gardens Handbook (£3.95) provides more detailed information on the Trust's gardens, sold in bookshops & National Trust shops.

Scotland's Gardens Scheme
Raises funds through the opening of gardens for the Queen's Nursing Institute (Scotland), the Gardens Fund of The National Trust for Scotland and over 160 other charities nominated by the garden owners. Handbook with all details of openings published mid-February. Tours: two six-day coach tours. Free brochure available. Handbook (£3.00 inc. p & p) from Scotland's Gardens Scheme, 31 Castle Terrace, Edinburgh EH1 2EL Telephone 031-229 1870, Fax 031-243 9302

The National Trust for Scotland
Established in 1931. In its care are over 100 properties. As well as castles, cottages, mountains, islands and historic sites, the Trust has in its care 24 major Scottish gardens. The National Trust for Scotland, 5 Charlotte Square, Edinburgh EH2 4DU Telephone 031-226 5922 Fax 031 243 9302

The Ulster Gardens Scheme
A list of the private gardens open to the public under the Ulster Gardens Scheme can be obtained from: The Public Affairs Manager, The National Trust, Rowallane, Saintfield, Co. Down, BT24 7LH. Telephone Saintfield (0238) 510721

The Automobile Association Guide to Britain
Days out in Britain gives details of more than 2,000 places of interest in England, Wales, Scotland, Channel Islands and Northern Ireland together with location maps & 1994 calendar of events. Available from AA bookshops and all good booksellers. Price £7.99.

The Historic Houses Association
Represents over 1,300 private owners of historic houses and outstanding gardens. The HHA is particularly concerned with the problem of funding gardens. It runs the Christie's/HHA Garden of the Year Award; helps administer a scheme for training gardeners and organises periodic seminars. A quarterly magazine is available to members and friends of the Historic Houses Association and on subscription. HHA, 2 Chester Street, London SW1X 7BB. Telephone 071-259 5688.

Irish Heritage Properties (HITHA)
Publishes annually an illustrated booklet with information on over 60 properties. Available from Irish Heritage Properties, 3a Castle Street, Dalkey, Co. Dublin. Telephone Dublin 2859633.

The Automobile Association
The AA has kindly arranged for information on gardens open for the Scheme to be available from their local offices.

The Royal Automobile Club
The RAC has kindly arranged that their RAC Touring Information Department (081-686 0088) can provide details of locations of gardens open for the Scheme.

The Garden History Society
This international society campaigns to protect our garden heritage. Members receive the Society's acclaimed Journal and Newsletter. The Garden History Society, 5 The Knoll, Hereford HR1 1RU.

THE ROYAL HORTICULTURAL SOCIETY

Get the best out of your garden with the help of Britain's top gardening experts

THE BEAUTY OF GARDENING is that no matter how experienced you are, there are always new ideas to try out and discoveries to make.

For thousands of gardeners The Royal Horticultural Society is the best inspiration of all.

A gardener's needs are many and varied and a visit to your local garden centre is unlikely to solve all your problems. But membership of The Royal Horticultural Society is like having a panel of experts on hand whenever you need advice or ideas. From inspirational Shows and Gardens to practical courses and a free advisory service, there's no other organisation that pulls together all Britain's top gardening brains specially for you.

A special invitation to join The Royal Horticultural Society

Your membership helps us protect Britain's gardening heritage

THE RHS has been promoting horticultural excellence all over the globe since 1804. Today, gardening is Britain's most popular hobby. With its extensive programme of education, conservation and scientific research, the RHS is dedicated to ensuring that future generations can enjoy our gardening heritage too.

As a registered charity, we rely entirely on the money we can raise ourselves – and your subscription is a vital contribution.

Join today, or introduce a friend - and save £5

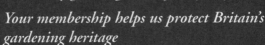

NORMALLY the first year of RHS membership costs £30 (£23 plus a £7 enrolment fee). But, as a special introduction to the Society for readers of the National Garden Scheme's *Gardens of England and Wales*, you can join or, if your are already a Member, enrol a friend, for just £25.

All you have to do is complete and return the form below. If you are enrolling a friend, please complete the form with your own name and address and enclose a separate sheet with the new Member's details.

RHS

membership brings many delightful privileges

- *The Garden*, the gardener's magazine, sent to you every month
- Privileged tickets and Members' days at the Chelsea and Hampton Court Palace Flower Shows
- Free entry to monthly flower shows at Westminster Privileged admission to BBC Gardeners' World Live, the Harrogate Spring and Autumn Flower Shows and the Malvern Spring Gardening Show.
- Free entry for yourself and a guest to the RHS Gardens at Wisley, Rosemoor and Hyde hall, plus seven others all over Britain
- Privileged admission to over 250 lectures and demonstrations
- Free advice on gardening problems from RHS experts
- Free seeds from Wisley Garden
- Use of the Lindley Library

Apply today and save £5

TO: The Royal Horticultural Society, Membership Department, PO Box 313, London SW1P 2PE.   Tel: 071-821 3000

If you would prefer not to cut this coupon, please write to us with your details, quoting code 314 and mentioning that you are a *Gardens of England and Wales* reader.

❑   I would like to join the Society at the special introductory rate of £25 for the year.

❑   I would like to enrol a friend as a Member. I enclose their name and address on a separate sheet.

Name ....

Address ....

Postcode ....Daytime Tel. No. ....

Please make your cheque payable to The Royal Horticultural Society. If you have enrolled a friend, the new Member's pack and card will be sent to you to pass on.   Code 314

Royal Gardens

SANDRINGHAM HOUSE AND GROUNDS Norfolk
By gracious permission of Her Majesty The Queen, the House and grounds at Sandringham will be open (except when Her Majesty The Queen or any members of the Royal Family are in residence) on the following days:
From 1st April to 2nd October inclusive daily.
Please note that the **house only** will be **closed** to the public from 19 July to 4th August inclusive and that the house and grounds will be closed from 23rd July to 3rd August inclusive. Coach drivers and visitors are advised to confirm these closing and opening dates nearer the time.

Hours
Sandringham House: 11 (12 noon on Sundays and Good Friday) to 4.45; Sandringham grounds: 10.30 (11.30 on Sundays and Good Friday) to 5.

Admission Charges
House, grounds and museum: adults £3.50, OAPs £2.50, children £2.00. Grounds only: adults £2.50, OAPs £2.00; children £1.50. It is not possible to purchase a ticket to visit the house only. Admission to the museum is free.
Advance party bookings will be accepted. There are no reductions in admission fees for parties. Picnicking is not permitted inside the grounds. Dogs are not permitted inside the grounds. Free car and coach parking.

Sandringham Church
This will be open as follows, subject to weddings, funerals and special services: when the grounds are open as stated above, hours 11-5 April to September, 1-5 during October. At other times of the year the church is open by appointment only.

Enquiries
The Public Enterprises Manager, Estate office, Sandringham or by telephone 9-1, 2-4.30 Monday to Friday inclusive on King's Lynn 772675.

Sandringham Flower Show
This will be held on Wednesday 27th July.

FROGMORE GARDENS Berkshire
By gracious permission of Her Majesty The Queen, the Frogmore Gardens, Windsor Castle, will be open from 10.30-7 on the following days:
Wednesday May 4 and Thursday May 5.
Coaches by appointment only: apply to the National Gardens Scheme, Hatchlands Park, East Clandon, Guildford, Surrey, GU4 7RT (Telephone 0483 211535) stating whether May 4 or 5, and whether morning or afternoon. Admission £1.50 accompanied children free. Dogs not allowed. Royal mausoleum also open, free of charge, both days. Entrance to gardens and mausoleum through Long Walk gate. Visitors are requested kindly to refrain from entering the grounds of the Home Park. Light refreshments will be available at the free car park (near the outer gate to the gardens).

FROGMORE HOUSE Berkshire
Also open but not for NGS. Entrance only from Frogmore Gardens. Admission Adults £2.50, over 60's £2, under 17 £1.50, children under age of 8 not admitted.

BARNWELL MANOR Northamptonshire
By kind permission of Their Royal Highnesses Princess Alice Duchess of Gloucester and the Duke and Duchess of Gloucester, the gardens at Barnwell Manor will be open from 2.30-6 on:
Sundays 8th and 22nd May. Admission £1, children free.

General Information

‡ following a garden name in the Dates of Opening list indicates that those gardens sharing the same symbol are nearby and open on the same day. ‡‡ indicates a second series of nearby gardens open on the same day.

¶ Opening for the first time.
❀ Plants/produce for sale if available.
♿ Gardens with at least the main features accessible by wheelchair.
✕ No dogs except guide dogs but otherwise dogs are usually admitted, provided they are kept on a lead. Dogs are not admitted to houses.
● Gardens marked thus, which open throughout the season, give a guaranteed contribution from their takings to the National Gardens Scheme.
▲ Where this sign appears alongside dates in the *descriptive* entry for a garden it denotes that this garden is *also open* regularly to the public on days other than those for the NGS. Details of National Trust gardens can also be found in the *National Trust Gardens Handbook;* see page 9.

Children All children must be accompanied by an adult.

Additional charities nominated by owner Where the owners of 'private' gardens (not normally open to the public) have nominated some other cause to receive an agreed share from an opening for the National Gardens Scheme, the name of the other cause is included in the descriptive entry as (Share to ....) with an ® or © to indicate whether it is a Registered Charity or a Charitable Cause.

Distances and sizes In all cases these are approximate.

Open by appointment Please do not be put off by this notation. The owner may consider his garden too small to accommodate the numbers associated with a normal opening or, more often, there may be a lack of car parking space. It is often more rewarding than a normal opening as the owner will usually give a guided tour of the garden. The minimum size of party can be found out when making the appointment; usually 2.

Coach parties Please, by appointment only unless stated otherwise.

Houses Not open unless this is specifically stated; where the house or part-house is shown an additional charge is usually made.

Tea When this is available at a garden the information is given in capitals, e.g. TEAS (usually with home-made cakes) or TEA (usually with biscuits). There is, of course, an extra charge for any refreshments available at a garden. Any other information given about tea is a guide only to assist visitors in finding somewhere in the area for tea.

Buses Continuance of many bus services is a matter of considerable uncertainty, especially on Sundays. It is strongly recommended that any details given in this guide be checked in advance.

National Trust Members are requested to note that where a National Trust property has allocated an opening day to the National Gardens Scheme which is one of its normal opening days, members can still gain entry on production of their National Trust membership card (although donations to the Scheme will be welcome). Where, however, the day allocated is one on which the property would *not* normally be open, then the payment of the National Gardens Scheme admission fee will be required.

Professional photographers Photographs taken in a garden may not be used for sale or reproduction without the prior permission of the garden owner.

Lavatories Private gardens do not normally have outside lavatories. Regretably, for security reasons, owners have been advised not to admit visitors into their houses to use inside toilets.

ENTERPRISE TRAVEL ♥

P.O. BOX 1
BRADFORD BD1 2QE

Dear Friends

Join us on a tour of Britain's best **HOMES & GARDENS** combined with fine hospitality and first class company!
Apply for our **FREE** colour brochure and you'll be spoilt for choice.

Shirley

CHELSEA FLOWER SHOW

HARROGATE SPRING & AUTUMN FLOWER SHOWS

HAMPTON COURT PALACE FLOWER SHOW

THESE ARE ONLY A SELECTION AND MANY INCLUDE COACH TRAVEL TO OUR HOTELS FROM NATIONWIDE PICK UP POINTS TOO!

Complete the coupon or phone our BROCHURE LINE for a PRIORITY copy today.

(0756) 710507

1994 PRIORITY BROCHURE REQUEST

NAME ....

ADDRESS ....

....

....

FRIEND'S NAME ....

ADDRESS ....

....

Send to: ENTERPRISE TRAVEL
PO BOX 1 BRADFORD BD1 2QE

Cornwall & the Scilly Isles
1994

HOMES & GARDENS of Gloucestershire
19. 1994

BBC Gardeners World Live
19. 1994

BUXTON & the Devonshires
19. 1994

Homes & Gardens of SHROPSHIRE
19.

LAKES, LOWLANDS & BORDERS
1994 19. 1994

HEVER CASTLE & 'Garden of England'
19. 1994

Treasure Houses of WESSEX
19. 1994 19. 1994 19. 1994

THE INTERNATIONAL MAGAZINE
FOR THE GARDEN CONNOISSEUR

GARDENS
ILLUSTRATED

ROSEMARY VEREY
IN A PAINTER'S
GARDEN

GERTRUDE JEKYLL'S
ANNIVERSARY
EXHIBITION

PLUS
ANNA PAVORD
PATRICK TAY
JAMIE CO

£2.95 AT ALL GOOD
NEWSAGENTS

"The most enjoyable gardening magazine...glossy, well-written, and droolingly
well illustrated" –ALAN TITCHMARSH, DAILY MAIL

GARDENS
OF ENGLAND & WALES

1994

**A GUIDE TO NEARLY 3,500 GARDENS
THE MAJORITY OF WHICH ARE NOT NORMALLY
OPEN TO THE PUBLIC**

THE NATIONAL GARDENS SCHEME CHARITABLE TRUST
HATCHLANDS PARK, EAST CLANDON, GUILDFORD, SURREY GU4 7RT
TEL 0483 211535   FAX 0483 211537
Reg Charity No: 279284

ENGLAND

Avon

Hon County Organiser:	Mrs Mary Bailey, Quakers, Lower Hazel, Rudgeway, Bristol BS12 2QP Tel 0454 413205
Assistant Hon County Organisers:	Dr Margaret Lush, Hazel Cottage, Lower Hazel, Rudgeway, Bristol BS12 2QP Tel 0454 412112
	Mrs Amanda Osmond, Church Farm House, Hawkesbury, nr Badminton, Avon GL9 1BN Tel 0454 238533
Avon Leaflet:	Mrs Jean Damey, 2 Hawburn Close, Bristol BS4 2PB Tel 0272 775587
Hon County Treasurer:	J K Dutson Esq., The Firs, Rockhampton, Nr Berkeley, Glos GL13 9DY Tel 0454 413210

DATES OF OPENING

By appointment
For telephone numbers and other details see garden descriptions. Private visits welcomed

Algars Manor, Iron Acton
Alwih Cottage, Alveston
Brewery House, Southstoke
Church Farm, Lower Failand
Jasmine Cottage, Clevedon
Madron, Ostlings Lane, Bathford
The Manor House,
    Walton-in-Gordano
Pearl's Garden, Coalpit Heath
Sherborne Garden (Pear Tree
    House) Litton
Stanton Prior Gardens, nr Bath
The Urn Cottage, Charfield
University of Bristol Botanic Gardens
Vine House, Henbury
Windmill Cottage, Backwell

Regular openings
For details see garden descriptions

Jasmine Cottage, Clevedon. Every
    Thurs April 14 to Aug 25
The Manor House,
    Walton-in-Gordano. Every Weds
    and Thurs April 13 to Sept 15 &
    Oct 19 to Nov 3
Sherborne House, (Pear Tree
    House), Litton. Suns, Mons June
    6 to Sept 26
Stanton Prior Gardens, nr Bath.
    Every Wed April 6 - Sept 7

February 28 Monday
The Urn Cottage, Charfield
March 19 Saturday
Old Down House, Tockington
March 20 Sunday
Old Down House, Tockington
March 27 Sunday
Jasmine Cottage, Clevedon
March 28 Monday
The Urn Cottage, Charfield
April 3 Sunday
Algars Manor & Algars Mill,
    Iron Acton
Bedford House, Clevedon
Brook Cottage, Upper
    Langford
Sherborne Garden (Pear Tree
    House) Litton
Vine House, Henbury
April 4 Monday
Algars Manor & Algars Mill, Iron
    Acton
Bedford House, Clevedon ‡
Brook Cottage, Upper Langford
The Manor House,
    Walton-in-Gordano ‡
Vine House, Henbury
April 17 Sunday
Algars Manor & Algars Mill,
    Iron Acton
Coley Court, East Harptree & The
    Little Manor, Farrington Gurney
April 23 Saturday
Brackenwood Garden Centre,
    Portishead
April 24 Sunday
Brackenwood Garden Centre,
    Portishead
Burwalls House and Garden,
    Leigh Woods, Bristol
Crowe Hall, Widcombe

Jasmine Cottage, Clevedon
April 25 Monday
Brackenwood Garden Centre,
    Portishead
The Urn Cottage, Charfield
April 26 Tuesday
Brackenwood Garden Centre,
    Portishead
April 27 Wednesday
Brackenwood Garden Centre,
    Portishead
May 1 Sunday
Coombe Dingle Gardens, Bristol
The Manor House,
    Walton-in-Gordano
Sherborne Garden (Pear Tree
    House) Litton
May 2 Monday
Coombe Dingle Gardens, Bristol
The Manor House,
    Walton-in-Gordano
May 8 Sunday
Severn View, Thornbury
May 11 Wednesday
Windmill Cottage, Backwell
May 15 Sunday
Goldney Hall, Bristol
Hill House, Wickwar
Severn View, Thornbury
May 21 Saturday
Parsonage Farm, Publow
May 22 Sunday
Algars Manor & Algars Mill, Iron
    Acton
Barrow Court, Barrow Gurney
Jasmine Cottage, Clevedon
Parsonage Farm, Publow
Severn View, Thornbury
May 23 Monday
Algars Manor & Algars Mill, Iron
    Acton

May 28 Saturday
Lower Failand Gardens
May 29 Sunday
Bedford House, Clevedon ‡
Lower Failand Gardens
The Manor House,
    Walton-in-Gordano ‡
Pearl's Garden, Coalpit Heath
Severn View, Thornbury
Vine House, Henbury
May 30 Monday
Bedford House, Clevedon ‡
The Manor House,
    Walton-in-Gordano ‡
Pearl's Garden, Coalpit Heath
Vine House, Henbury
The Urn Cottage, Charfield
June 5 Sunday
Clifton Gardens, Bristol
Crowe Hall, Widcombe
Severn View, Thornbury
Sherborne Garden (Pear Tree
    House) Litton
June 8 Wednesday
Windmill Cottage, Backwell
June 11 Saturday
Tranby House, Whitchurch, Bristol
June 12 Sunday
Harptree Court, Harptree
Hazel Cottage, Lower Hazel ‡
Severn View, Thornbury ‡
Tranby House, Whitchurch, Bristol
The Urn Cottage, Charfield
June 18 Saturday
Gatcombe Court, Flax Bourton

June 19 Sunday
Gardener's Cottage, Upton
    Cheyney
Gatcombe Court, Flax Bourton
The Manor House,
    Walton-in-Gordano
June 26 Sunday
Badminton House, Badminton
Brooklands, Burnett
Doynton House, Doynton
Jasmine Cottage, Clevedon
June 29 Wednesday
Brooklands, Burnett
Windmill Cottage, Backwell
July 2 Saturday
Bryncrug, 23 Charnhill Ridge,
    Mangotsfield
West Tyning, Beach
July 3 Sunday
Stanton Drew Gardens
West Tyning, Beach
July 13 Wednesday
Windmill Cottage, Backwell
July 10 Sunday
University of Bristol Botanic
    Gardens
July 16 Saturday
Bellevue, Publow
July 17 Sunday
Brewery House, Southstoke
July 24 Sunday
Jasmine Cottage, Clevedon
July 30 Saturday
Tranby House, Whitchurch,
    Bristol

July 31 Sunday
Stanton Prior Gardens, nr Bath
Tranby House, Whitchurch, Bristol
August 7 Sunday
Dyrham Park
August 10 Wednesday
Windmill Cottage, Backwell
August 28 Sunday
Jasmine Cottage, Clevedon ‡
The Manor House,
    Walton-in-Gordano ‡
August 29 Monday
The Manor House,
    Walton-in-Gordano
September 11 Sunday
Bourne House, Burrington
University of Bristol Botanic
    Gardens
September 14 Wednesday
Windmill Cottage, Backwell
September 17 Saturday
Old Down House, Tockington
September 18 Sunday
Old Down House, Tockington
September 26 Monday
The Urn Cottage, Charfield
October 2 Sunday
Sherborne Garden (Pear Tree
    House) Litton
October 31 Monday
The Urn Cottage, Charfield

DESCRIPTIONS OF GARDENS

Algars Manor & Algars Mill ❀ Iron Acton 9m N of Bristol. 3m W of Yate Sodbury. Turn S off Iron Acton bypass B4059, past village green, 200yds, then over level Xing (Station Rd). TEAS **Algars Manor**. *Combined adm £1.50 Chd 20p. Easter Sun, Mon April 3, 4; Suns, Mon April 17, May 22, 23 (2-6)*
    Algars Manor ❀ (Dr & Mrs J M Naish) 3-acre woodland garden beside R Frome; mill-stream; native plants mixed with azaleas, rhododendrons, camellias, magnolias, eucalyptus. Picnic areas. Early Jacobean house (not open) and old barn. *Private visits also welcome* Tel 0454 228372
    Algars Mill (Mr & Mrs J Wright) entrance via Algars Manor. 2-acre woodland garden beside R Frome; spring bulbs, shrubs; early spring feature of wild Newent daffodils. 300-400 yr old mill house (not open) through which mill-race still runs

Alwih Cottage ⅃❀ (Y E Buckoke) Shellards Lane Alveston. 3m SE of Thornbury, 10m N of Bristol. Take 'The Street' leading to Shellards Lane off the A38 immediately opp The Alveston House Hotel. Signposted Itchington. 1.7m down the lane. ⅓-acre landscaped garden with interesting trees, shrubs, herbaceous borders and a gravel garden planted with herbs. TEAS by arrangement. *Adm*

£1 OAP's 50p Chd free. Open April to Sept. Private visits and parties welcome, maximum 4 cars, please Tel 0454 412124

Badminton ⅃❀ (The Duke & Duchess of Beaufort) 5m E of Chipping Sodbury. Large garden designed eight years ago. Still in the process of being created. Mixed and herbaceous borders; many old-fashioned and climbing roses; conservatories and orangery; walled kitchen garden recreated in Victorian style ¼m from house with a new glass house. TEAS. *Adm £1.50 OAPs/Chd £1 under 10 free (Share to Meningitis Trust®). Sun June 26 (2-6)*

Barrow Court ❀ Barrow Gurney 5m SW Bristol. From Bristol take A370 and turn E onto B3130 towards Barrow Gurney; immediate right, Barrow Court Lane, then ½m, turn R through Lodge archway. 2 acres of formal gardens, designed by Inigo Thomas in 1890. Architectural garden, with sculpture and pavilions; arboretum; on going renovations to paths; stonework, replanted yew hedging and parterres. C17 E-shaped house (not open). Parking limited. TEAS. *Adm £1 Chd 50p. Sun May 22 (2-6)*

By Appointment Gardens. Avoid the crowds. Good chance of a tour by owner. See garden description for telephone number.

Bedford House ⚹⚘ (Mrs M D Laverack) 16 Wellington Terrace, Clevedon. 12m W of Bristol (Junction 20 off M5). Follow signs to seafront and Pier. From Pier, turn N up Marine Parade into Wellington Terrace (B3124). No 16 is on L (sea) side. A terraced cliff garden overlooking the Bristol Channel, designed to suit steep contours and its setting in a splendid seascape; also illustrates gardening in sea winds. Steep steps down to each terrace, also enjoyable from above. Featured on HTV. TEAS. *Adm £1 Chd free. Easter Sun, Mon, April 3, 4; Sun, Bank Hol Mon, May 29, 30 (2-6). Parties welcome April to July, please* Tel 0275 874872/871128

Bellevue ⚹⚹⚘ (Mr & Mrs J A Heaford) Publow. 7m S of Bristol, A37 Bristol-Wells to Pensford Bridge. Turn L off A37 and L again into Publow Lane and ½m on to Publow Church. Mature 1¼-acre garden in lovely setting with brook below steep bank; wide variety of plants; trees, shrubs and vegetables, extensively replanted by present owners since 1980. Some streamside and bank planting with moisture-loving and drought tolerant plants. TEAS in aid of All Saints, Publow. *Adm £1 Chd free. Sat, Sun July 16, 17 (2-5)*

Bourne House ⚹⚹⚘ (Mr & Mrs Christopher Thomas) 12m S Bristol. N of Burrington. Turning off A38 signposted Blagdon-Burrington; 2nd turning L. 4 acres, and 2 paddocks. Stream with waterfalls & lily pond; mature trees, and shrubs. Herbaceous border, roses; bulbs; large area of cyclamen 'neapolitanum'. TEAS. *Adm £1 Chd free. Sun Sept 11 (2-6)*

Brackenwood Garden Centre Woodland Garden ⚹⚘ (Mr & Mrs John Maycock) 131 Nore Rd, Portishead. From Bristol A369 (10m). M5 Junc 19. Walk lies behind Brackenwood Garden Centre, open daily 9-5. Tel 0275 843484, 1m from Portishead on coast rd to Clevedon. 8-acre woodland garden featured on the cover of 'Beautiful Gardens of Britain' Calendar 1994. Rhododendrons, camellias, Japanese maples and pieris; secluded woodland pools with black swans; many rare trees and shrubs; abundant wild flowers, birds and mammals with magnificent views of the Bristol Channel to Wales and the Severn Bridge. New Restaurant/Tea-Room, lunches and refreshments all day. *Adm £1.30 Chd 60p. Sat, Sun, Mon, Tues, Wed April 23, 24, 25, 26, 27 (10-5)*

Brewery House ⚹⚘ (John and Ursula Brooke) 2½m S of Bath off A367, L onto B3110, take 2nd R to Southstoke or bus to Cross Keys. House is ¼m down Southstoke Lane. Please park where signed and walk down. ⅔-acre garden on 2 levels. Fine views; top garden walled. Many unusual plants. Vegetable garden with raised beds. Water garden. All organic. Partly suitable for wheelchairs. Plants for sale. TEAS in aid of Southstoke Village Hall. *Adm £1 Chd free. Sun July 17 (2-6). Private visits welcome, please* Tel 0225 833153

Regular Openers. Too many days to include in diary. Usually there is a wide range of plants giving year-round interest. See head of county section for the name and garden description for times etc.

Brook Cottage ⚹⚹⚘ (Mr & Mrs J S Ledbury) Upper Langford. 13m S Bristol on A368 NW of Burrington Combe, adjacent to the Blagdon Water Garden Centre. Mature garden of 2½ acres with stream. Interesting collection of trees, shrubs and spring bulbs. Walled garden with good selection of fruit trees. TEAS in aid of St John's Church. *Adm £1 Chd free. Sun April 3 (2-5), Mon April 4 (11-5)*

Brooklands ⚹⚘ (Mr & Mrs Patrick Stevens) Burnett. 2m S Keynsham on B3116. Turn R into Burnett Village. 1½-acre garden; mature trees and variety of ornamental shrubs; rose garden; herbaceous border; extensive planting of shrub roses and clematis; fine views of distant Mendip Hills. Ploughman lunches and TEAS in aid of St Michael's Church, Burnett. *Adm £1 Chd free. Sun June 26 (10-6), Wed June 29 (2-7)*

¶**Bryncrug** ⚹⚘ (Mrs Margaret Jones) Mangotsfield. ½m from Staplehill on the Mangotsfield Rd B4465 and at the bottom of the hill turn R into Charnhill Drive and in 30yds turn L to Charnhill Ridge. Small town garden, densely planted with interesting trees and shrubs, many in dry shade; pond; conservatory and unusual front garden. Featured in Nov 93 Practical Gardening. TEAS in aid P.D.S.A. *Adm £1 Chd 20p. Sat July 2 (12-6)*

Burwalls House and Garden ⚹⚹ (University of Bristol) 1st house on L immed after crossing Clifton Suspension Bridge from Clifton into Leigh Woods on B3129. Entrance on L through small wooden door in wall behind lay-by, just beyond main entrance to Burwalls House. 4-5 acres terraced garden on edge of Avon Gorge, rich in British native flowers, shrubs and trees; also natural woodland containing remains of Iron Age Fort. Leaflet providing map and names of plants available. Ground floor of Burwalls House (former home of Sir George A Wills Bt) also open. TEAS. *Adm £1.50 Chd free (Share to BRACE®). Sun April 24 (2.30-6)*

Church Farm ⚹⚘ (Mr & Mrs N Slade) Lower Failand, 6m SW Bristol. Take B3128 out of Bristol to Clevedon Rd via Clerk-Combe Hill, turn R down Oxhouse Lane opp garage; or turn off M5 at junction 19 towards Bristol. 1st R through Portbury, turn L into Failand Lane. L past Church then R into private rd. House is 1st R. Parking adj to Church. 3-acre small holding garden started in 1974; run on organic principles; large collection clematis, unusual plants and trees. TEAS May 28, 29 only. *Adm £1 Chd 25p (Share to Failand Church®). Sat, Sun May 28, 29 (2-5). Private visits welcome Weds June 1 to end of Sept, please* Tel 0275 373033

Clifton Gardens Bristol. Close to Clifton Suspension Bridge. *Combined adm £1.50 Chd 25p. Sun June 5 (2-6)*
  9 Sion Hill ⚹⚘ (Mr & Mrs R C Begg) Entrance from Sion Lane. Small walled town garden, densely planted; climbing & herbaceous plants; herb garden; old roses
  16 Sion Hill ⚹⚹ (Drs Cameron and Ros Kennedy) Entrance via green door in Sion Lane, at side of No 16. Small pretty town garden with pond, several interesting shrubs and trees
  17 Sion Hill ⚹⚹⚘ (Mr & Mrs Philip Gray) Entrance from Sion Lane. Town garden with trees and shrubs. TEAS

Coley Court & The Little Manor ✍ Teas at **Manor Farm**. *Adm £1.50 Chd free. Sun April 17 (2-6)*
   Coley Court ❀ (Mrs M J Hill) East Harptree, 8m N of Wells. Take B3114 through East Harptree turn L signed Coley and Hinton Blewitt. From A39 at Chewton Mendip take B3114 2m, sign on R, Coley, Hinton Blewitt, follow lane 400yds to white house on L before bridge. 1-acre garden, open lawn, stone walls, spring bulbs; 1-acre old Somerset orchard. Early Jacobean house (not open)
   The Little Manor (Lt Col & Mrs K P P Goldschmidt) Farrington Gurney on A39. Turn E in village on to A362 towards Radstock-600yds turn L. ¾-acre spring garden; many varieties of bulbs, flowering trees, many rare shrubs; rose garden. Early C17 house with attractive courtyard

Coombe Dingle Gardens ⅃ 4m NW of Bristol centre. From Portway down Sylvan Way, turn left into the Dingle and Grove Rd. From Westbury-on-Trym, Canford Lane sharp right at beginning of Westbury Lane. From Bristol over Downs, Parrys Lane, Coombe Lane; turn left and sharp right into the Dingle and Grove Rd. TEAS **Hillside**. *Combined adm £1 Chd free. Sun, Mon May 1, 2 (2-6)*
   Hillside ⅃ (Mrs C M Luke) 42 Grove Rd. 2 acres late Georgian lay-out. Victorian rose garden; fine trees, shrubs. Walled kitchen garden
   Pennywell ❀ (Mr & Mrs D H Baker) Grove Rd. 2 acres; varied collection trees and shrubs inc 50ft span flowering cherry; rockery, organic kitchen garden. Views over adjoining Blaise Castle Estate, Kingsweston Down and the Trym Valley. Exhibition of sculpture by Mary Donington. Plant stall (in aid of Friends of Blaise)

Crowe Hall (John Barratt Esq) Widcombe. 1m SE of Bath. L up Widcombe Hill, off A36, leaving White Hart on R. Large varied garden; fine trees, lawns, spring bulbs, series of enclosed gardens cascading down steep hillside. Italianate terracing and Gothick Victorian grotto contrast with park-like upper garden. Dramatic setting, with spectacular views of Bath. Featured in NGS gardens video 2, see page 344. DOGS welcome. TEAS. *Adm £1.50 Chd 30p. Suns Mar 20; May 15; June 26; Aug 14, for NGS Suns April 24, June 5 (2-6)*

Doynton House ⅃❀ (Mrs C E Pitman) Doynton. 8m E of Bristol, ¾m NE of A420 at E end of Wick. Mature, old-fashioned 2-acre garden with herbaceous borders, shrubs and lawns. TEAS by W.I. *Adm £1 Chd 20p. Sun June 26 (2-6)*

Dyrham Park ✍❀ (The National Trust) 8m N of Bath. 12m E of Bristol. Approached from Bath-Stroud Road (A46), 2m S of Tormarton interchange with M4, exit 18. Situated on W side of late C17 house. Herbaceous borders, yews clipped as buttresses, ponds and cascade, parish church set on terrace. Niches and carved urns. Long lawn to old west entrance Deer Park. TEAS. *Adm incl house £4.80 Chd £2.40. Sun Aug 7 (12-5)*

By Appointment Gardens. These owners do not have a fixed opening day usually because they do not like crowds or have insufficient parking space. Owner will often give guided tour.

Gardener's Cottage ✍❀ (Mr & Mrs M J Chillcott) Wick Lane, Upton Cheyney. 6m NW of Bath; 8m SE of Bristol off A431, turn L near Bitton signposted Upton Cheyney; ¾m up Brewery Hill, first turning L after Upton Inn, parking at Upton Inn. 1-acre part walled garden, formerly kitchen garden of early C18 manor house, redesigned by present owners within the last 6 yrs with shrubs, herbaceous borders, pergolas, clematis and roses. Also large pond and rock garden, bog area and other water features. TEAS. *Adm £1 Chd free. Sun June 19 (2-6)*

¶**Gatcombe Court** ✍❀ (Mr & Mrs Charles Clarke) Flax Bourton. 5m as the crow flies W of Bristol. Take A370 towards Weston-super-Mare, at B3130 intersection go N towards Nailsea for 200yds, turn R (E) and after 100yds follow small lane L down through the trees. Approx 2 acres of ornamental garden, terraced with stone walls on which climbing roses grow, with lawns, borders, herb garden and old yew hedges, set on a wooded hillside. TEAS. *Adm £1 Chd 50p (Share to Flax Bourton Church®). Sat, Sun June 18, 19 (2-5)*

Goldney Hall ✍ (University of Bristol) Lower Clifton Hill, Bristol. At top of Constitution Hill, Clifton. 9-acre Grade II Outstanding Garden, developed 1731-68 by Thomas Goldney, Bristol merchant; fine period grotto; terrace, bastion, tower, orangery and parterre; old-world garden with many species of the period. Cream TEAS in orangery. *Adm £1.50 OAPs/Chd 75p (Share to Goldney Restoration Fund). Sun May 15 (2-6)*

Harptree Court ⅃❀ (Mr & Mrs Richard Hill) East Harptree, 8m N of Wells via A39 Bristol Rd to Chewton Mendip; then B3114 to East Harptree, gates on left. From Bath via A368 Weston-super-Mare Rd to West Harptree. Large garden; fine old trees in lovely setting; woodland walks; handsome stone bridge; subterranean passage, Doric temple, lily pond and paved garden. TEAS. *Adm £1 Chd free. Sun June 12 (2-6)*

Hazel Cottage ✍❀ (Dr & Mrs Brandon Lush) Lower Hazel 700yds W of Rudgeway from A38; 10m N of Bristol. ½-acre cottage garden in rural setting with wide variety of plants and shrubs including alpines and some unusual varieties. TEAS. *Adm £1 Chd free (Share to BRACE®). Sun June 12 (2-6)*

¶**Hill House** ⅃✍❀ (Dr & Mrs Richard Adlam) 4m N of Chipping Sodbury on B4060. Through Wickwar, L by wall signed to M5; then 200yds on L. 7 acres of land, of which 4 acres of gardens originally designed and planted by Sally, Duchess of Westminster. Gold/silver plantings in gravel; pleached lime walk; wild flowers and bulbs; owls and pheasant aviaries, peacocks, flock of Southdown sheep. TEAS. *Adm £1.50 Chd 50p. Sun May 15 (2-6)*

Iford Manor see Wiltshire

Jasmine Cottage ✍❀ (Mr & Mrs Michael Redgrave) 26 Channel Rd, Clevedon. 12m W of Bristol (junction 20 off M5). Follow signs to seafront and Pier, continue N on B3124, past Walton Park Hotel, turn R at St Mary's Church. Medium-sized garden created by owners from a wooded shelter belt for interest in all seasons. Old-fashioned roses; clematis, pergola; mixed shrub borders;

island beds; gravel beds, pond and potager. Many unusual herbaceous, tender perennials and climbers. Featured in HTV News and BBC Points West. Tea Thurs in April and May, TEAS Thurs in June to Aug and Suns. *Adm £1 Chd free. Suns March 27, April 24, May 22, June 26, July 24, Aug 28, (2-6). Every Thurs April 14 to Aug 25 (2.30-5.30). Private visits welcome all the year, please* **Tel Clevedon (0275) 871850**

Lower Failand Gardens &❀ Lower Failand, 6m SW of Bristol. Take B3128 out of Bristol to Clevedon Rd. Via Clerk-Combe Hill, turn right down Oxhouse Lane opp garage; or turn off M5 Junc 19 towards Bristol. 1st R through Portbury, turn left into Failand Lane

    Church Farm (Mr & Mrs N Slade) L past Church then R into private rd. House is 1st R. Parking adj to Church. 3-acre small holding garden started in 1974; run on organic principles; large collection clematis, unusual plants and trees. TEAS May 28, 29 only. *Adm £1 Chd 25p (Share to Failand Church®). Sat, Sun May 28, 29 (2-5). Private visits welcome Weds June 1 to end of Sept, please* **Tel 0275 373033**

    Failand Court (Mr & Mrs B Nathan) 1m along Oxhouse Lane. Park in Oxhouse Lane and at church. 1¼-acre mature garden originally landscaped by Sir Edward Fry. Further developed by Miss Agnes Fry. Interesting trees, shrubs and vegetable garden. TEAS. *Adm £1 Chd 25p. Sat, Sun May 28, 29 (2-5.30)*

Madron ❀❀ (Mr & Mrs Martin Carr) Ostlings Lane, Bathford. Approx 3½m, E of Bath close to A4. At Batheaston roundabout take A363 Bradford-upon-Avon Rd; then 1st turning L, Ostlings Lane is immediately on R alongside Crown Inn. At top of short rise 100yds stone pillars on L are entrance to Madron - 2nd house on L along drive. 1¼-acre garden created over 10 yrs on site overlooking the Avon valley and surrounding hills. Borders and banks with shrubs, hardy and tender perennials, with particular emphasis on plant and colour associations and water garden, all set amidst fine lawns with conifer and deciduous trees. Featured in Practical Gardening, April 1992. TEAS. *Adm £1 Chd free. Thurs June 9 to Aug 11 by prior appt only (2.30-5) other times possible by arrangement, please* **Tel 0225 859792**

The Manor House &❀❀ (Mr & Mrs Simon Wills) Walton-in-Gordano, 2m NE of Clevedon. Entrance on N side of B3124, Clevedon to Portishead Rd, just by houses on roadside nearest Clevedon. Clevedon-Portishead buses stop in Village. 4-acres; plantsman's garden, featured in 'Country Life' 1989, trees, shrubs, herbaceous and bulbs mostly labelled. Coaches by appt only. TEAS (Suns, Mons only) (in aid of St Peters Hospice Bristol). *Adm £1.50, Acc. chd under 14 free (Share to St Peter's Hospice, Bristol®). April 13 to Sept 15 and Oct 19 to Nov 3 every Wed & Thurs (10-4); Mon April 4; Suns, Mons May 1, 2; 29, 30; Sun June 19, Sun, Mon Aug 28, 29 (2-6). Private visits welcome all year, please* **Tel 0275 872067**

Regular Openers. Too many days to include in diary. Usually there is a wide range of plants giving year-round interest. See head of county section for the name and garden description for times etc.

Old Down House & (Mr & Mrs Robert Bernays) Tockington, 10m N of Bristol. Follow brown Tourist Board signs to Old Down from A38 at Alverston. 5 acres divided into small formal and informal gardens by hedges and walls; topiary, shrubs; azaleas, rhododendrons, camellias; extensive lawns; rock garden; fine trees (weeping beeches, etc). Herbaceous borders, semi-wild areas; fine views to Severn and Welsh hills. TEAS. *Adm £1 Chd free (Share to Bristol Age Care Concern®). Sat, Sun March 19, 20; Sept 17, 18 (2-6)*

Parsonage Farm ❀❀ (Andrew Reid Esq) Publow. 9m S of Bristol. A37 Bristol-Wells; at top of Pensford Hill, almost opp B3130 to Chew Magna, take lane which runs down side of row of houses; 250yds on R. 3½-acre woodland garden with large collection of trees and shrubs incl rhododendrons, azaleas and conifers; tuffastone rockery and heather garden. Partly suitable for wheelchairs. TEAS in aid of All Saints, Publow. *Adm £1 Chd free. Sat, Sun May 21, 22 (2-5)*

¶**Pearl's Garden** &❀❀ (Mr & Mrs D Watts) Coalpit Heath. NE Bristol. Take Downend (Westerleigh Rd) to Tomarton Rd past "Folly" public house over motorway and garden is 500yds on L. From junction 18 on M4, turn N on the A46 and almost immed L signposted Pucklechurch. After 5½m the garden is on R shortly before bridge over the motorway. 2 acres developed since 1966; mixed trees, flowering shrubs with 100 varieties of hollies; herb and water gardens, peafowl and aviaries. Good views over Bristol from outside stairs. TEAS. *Adm £1.50 Chd free. Sun, Mon May 29, 30 (2-6). Also private visits welcome May and June, please* **Tel 0272 562953**

Severn View ❀❀ (Mr & Mrs Eric Hilton) Grovesend, 1½m E of Thornbury. On A38 on Bristol side of Wye Vale Nurseries. (Grovesend is postal address, but ignore signpost to it) 1-acre; notable for large rock garden with wide range of alpine plants, many rare, grown in screes, raised beds, troughs, rock walls, peat beds etc. Also shrubs, herbaceous borders; 3 alpine houses and many frames. Fine views of Severn Valley. *Adm 80p Acc chd free (Share to Thornbury Hospital®). Suns May 8, 15, 22, 29, June 5, 12 (2-6)*

Sherborne Garden (Pear Tree House) &❀ (Mr & Mrs John Southwell) Litton. 15m S of Bristol, 7m N of Wells. On B3114 Litton to Harptree, ½m past Ye Olde Kings Arms. 3½ acres landscaped into several gardens of distinctive character; cottage garden; rock garden; large ponds with moisture gardens; pinetum; mixed wood. Collection of hollies (190 varieties); grasses, birches; species roses. Featured on TV 'Gardeners World'. Picnic area. TEA. *Adm £1.50 Chd free. Suns, Mons June 6 to Sept 26. For NGS Suns, April 3; May 1 Homemade TEAS on Suns June 5, Oct 2 (11-6.30). Private visits welcome; parties by arrangement, please* **Tel 0761 241220**

Stanton Drew Gardens &❀❀ 7m S Bristol A37 Bristol-Wells; at top of Pensford Hill take B3130 to Chew Magna. After 1m turn towards Stanton Drew at thatched round house. Cautiously negotiate humpbacked bridge and the gardens are just after the bridge. Parking is supervised. TEAS in aid of Village Funds. *Combined adm £1.50 Chd free. Sun July 3 (12-6)*

Rectory Farm House (Dr & Mrs J P Telling) ½-acre garden surrounding C15 Church House later used as a farmhouse. Garden completely redesigned and replanted over the past 18 mths. Trees, shrubs, mixed borders, pond and new rock garden

Stanton Court (Dr R J Price & Partners) A new garden established from 1986 to complement the recreational needs of a Nursing Home. Ideal for disabled visitors. Access for elderly persons a priority. Our aim is minimal maintenance with maximum variety. The wide range of plants have been largely donated by the locality. Pond; terrace garden; patio; large sweeping borders; cut flower beds and fruits in season. Mature copper beech and cedars

Stanton Prior Gardens ✿✿✿ 6m from Bath on A39 Wells Rd; at Marksbury turn L to Stanton Prior; gardens either side of Church set in beautiful countryside in unspoilt village. Ploughmans lunch & cream TEAS. *Combined adm £2 Chd free. Every Wed April 6 to Sept 7 (12-5) for NGS Sun July 31 (11-5); also private visits welcome all year, please* **Tel 0761 470384/471942**

Church Farm (Mr & Mrs L Hardwick) Herbaceous borders, rock garden, scree garden; shrub roses, many unusual plants, wild area with ¼-acre pond; ducks and geese

The Old Rectory (Lt Col & Mrs Patrick Mesquita) 1-acre garden incl mediaeval pond. Landscaped and replanted since 1983, with unusual shrubs and plants, apple and pear arches and pergola with white roses and clematis; a newly-created knot garden

9 Stanton Prior (Mrs J Groom) Small cottage garden created in 1987. Rockeries, mixed borders, pond and species clematis

Tranby House ✿✿ (Paul & Jan Barkworth) Norton Lane, Whitchurch. ½m S of Whitchurch Village. Leave Bristol on A37 Wells Rd, through Whitchurch Village 1st turning on R, signposted Norton Malreward. Parking in field at junction of A37 and Norton Lane. Garden is 200yds along Norton Lane. 1¼-acre informal garden, designed and planted to encourage wildlife. Includes trees, shrubs, flower borders, ponds and meadow area; flowers from the garden are pressed and used to create pressed flower pictures. Partly suitable for wheelchairs. TEA. *Adm £1 Chd free. Sats, Suns June 11, 12; July 30, 31 (2-5.30)*

University of Bristol Botanic Garden ✿✿✿ Bracken Hill, North Rd, Leigh Woods, 1m W of Bristol via Clifton. Cross suspension bridge, North Rd is 1st R. As featured on Gardeners World 1993, Superintendent Nicholas Wray, (presenter). 5-acre garden supporting approx 4,500 species; special collections incl cistus, hebe, ferns, salvia and sempervivum, plus many native plants. Range of glasshouses and large Pulhams rock garden. TEAS. *Adm £1 Chd 50p (Share to Friends of Bristol University Botanic Garden®).* ▲*Suns July 10 (11-5), Sept 11 (2-5) also private visits welcome all year, please* **Tel 0272 733682**

The Urn Cottage ✿✿ (Mr A C & Dr L A Rosser) 19 Station Road, Charfield. 3m W of Wotton-under-edge and 3m E of M5 exit 14. In Charfield turn off main road at the The Railway Tavern, then 400 yds on L: short walk from car park. ¾-acre cottage gdn made from scratch by owners since 1982 and still developing. Natural materials used throughout to compliment stone built cottage and country setting. Wide variety and profusion of plants in mixed borders of differing character, incl, small streamside gardens. TEAS. *Adm £1 Chd 10p. Mons Feb 28, March 28, April 25, May 30, Sept 26, Oct 31, (2-4) Sun June 12 (12-6) Parties by appt all year* **Tel 0453 843156**

Vine House ✿✿ (Prof & Mrs T F Hewer) Henbury Rd, Henbury, 4m N of Bristol. Bus stop: Salutation, Henbury, 50yds. 2-acres; trees, shrubs, water garden, bulbs, naturalised garden landscaped and planted by present owners since 1946. TEAS. *Adm £1 OAPs/Chd 50p (Share to Friends of Blaise®).* Suns, Mons April 3, 4; May 29, 30 (2-6); also private visits welcome all year, please* **Tel Bristol 0272 503573**

West Tyning ✿✿✿ (Mr & Mrs G S Alexander). Beach. From Bath (6m) or Bristol (7m) on A431. From Bitton village turn N up Golden Valley, signposted Beach. Continue up lane for 2m to Wick–Upton Cheyney Crossroads, turn R up Wick Lane for 200 yds. Parking in adjacent field. 1¼-acre garden, much altered through the years. Since 1986 aiming for a more informal woodsey look, easy plants. New shrubs, trees, roses, geraniums and other ground cover. Rock garden, curved mixed borders, woodland garden with stone paths and circular beds, planting continuing in newly cleared copse. TEAS. *Adm £1 Chd free. Sat, Sun July 2, 3 (2-6). Also by appt for groups of 10 or more. Please* **Tel 0272 322294**

Windmill Cottage ✿✿ (Alan & Pam Harwood) Hillside Rd, Backwell. 8m SW of Bristol. Take A370 out of Bristol to Backwell, ½m past Xrds/traffic lights, turn L into Hillside Rd. Parking available in Backwell recreation area, on R hand side of main rd (10 min walk). Hillside Rd is single track lane with no parking (unless by prior arrangement or special reasons). Parking also at New Inn. Into a 2-acre plot put a plentiful variety of plants, add to this a pinch of knowledge and a sprinkling of wildflowers, together with a reasonable amount of ground cover; blend in some colour and a generous dash of fragrance. Bind the whole thing together with a large collection of clematis, balanced with a proportion of vegetables. A good supply of enthusiasm to be added at regular intervals, allow to develop over a period of 8 to 10 yrs, adjusting quantities as the ingredients mature and set into a rocky outcrop. TEAS. *Adm £1 Chd 50p. Weds May 11, June 8 (2-5.30); June 29, July 13 (2-8); Aug 10, Sept 14 (2-5.30). Groups welcome by appt, please* **Tel 0275 463492**

Bedfordshire

Hon County Organiser: Mrs S Whitbread, The Mallowry, Riseley, Bedford MK44 1EF

DATES OF OPENING

By appointment
For telephone numbers and other details see garden descriptions. Private visits welcomed

88 Castlehill Road, Middle End, Totternhoe
Seal Point, Luton

Regular opening
For details see garden descriptions

Toddington Manor, Toddington

April 3 Sunday
King's Arms Path Gardens, Ampthill
April 17 Sunday
Woburn Abbey, Woburn

April 24 Sunday
Howard's House, Cardington
May 8 Sunday
The Old Stables, Hockcliffe
May 15 Sunday
Odell Castle, nr Bedford
May 22 Sunday
Aspley Guise Gardens, Bletchley, Bucks
May 29 Sunday
88 Castlehill Rd, Middle End, Totternhoe
The Manor, Yielden
Milton House, nr Bedford
Woodleys Farm House, Melchbourne
June 5 Sunday
Southhill Park, nr Biggleswade
June 12 Sunday
Woburn Abbey, Woburn
June 19 Sunday
Deepdale Lodge, Potton
Grove Lodge, Potton

Odell Castle, nr Bedford
June 26 Sunday
Toddington Manor, Toddington
July 3 Sunday
Luton Hoo Gardens, Luton
The Manor, Yielden
The Old Stables, Hockliffe
July 10 Sunday
47 Hexton Raod, Barton-le-Clay
The Rectory, Barton-le-Clay
July 17 Sunday
88 Castlehill Rd, Middle End, Totternhoe
Dean and Shelton Gardens
July 23 Saturday
Broadfields, Keysoe Row East
July 24 Sunday
Broadfields, Keysoe Row East
August 7 Sunday
The Old Stables, Hockliffe

DESCRIPTIONS OF GARDENS

Aspley Guise Gardens 2m SW of M1 (Exit 13) towards Woburn Sands. Entrance from Church Rd. *Combined adm £2 Chd ½ price. Sun May 22 (2-6)*
   Aspley House ⚹✿ (Mr & Mrs C I Skipper) House on E side of village. 5 acres; shrubs and lawns. William and Mary house (not open). TEA
   The Rookery ⚹ (C R Randall Esq) 5 acres; rhododendrons and woodland

Broadfields ⅍ (Mr & Mrs Izzard) Keysoe, Row East. Leave Bedford on Kimbolton Rd B660 approx 8½m. Turn R at Keysoe Xrds by White Horse public house ½m on right. 3 acres of herbaceous borders; mature trees; shrubs; vegetable and fruit gardens. TEAS. *Adm £1.50 Chd 50p. Sat July 23 (2-6) Sun July 24 (10-2)*

88 Castlehill Road ⚹✿ (Chris & Carole Jell) Middle End, Totternhoe. 2m W of Dunstable, R turn off B489 Aston-Clinton Rd. Fronting main rd approx ½m through village. Elevated position with fine views across Aylesbury Vale and Chilterns. Adjoining Totternhoe Knolls Nature Reserve. ½-acre, S sloping on limestone and clay, entirely created by owners. Plantsman garden for all seasons; designed as small gardens within a garden since 1986; shrubs; climbers and herbaceous. TEAS. *Adm £1 Chd free. Suns May 29, July 17 (2-6). Also private visits welcome, please* Tel 0525 220780

¶**Dean and Shelton Gardens** ⚹✿ N of Bedford on Northants/Cambs Border, 4m W of Kimbolton. Home-made TEAS. Tickets and maps in each village. Free car parks. No coaches. *Combined adm £2 Chd £1. Creche 50p. Sun July 17 (2-6).* **Tel 0234 708632**
Lower Dean
   ¶**Barnside** ⅍ (Mr Bill Baker) Approx ¾-acre. Recently established garden around old farm buildings. Some unusual plants and roses
   ¶**Inglenook House** ⅍ (Mr & Mrs Bill Ashby) ¾-acre, shrubs, trees, herbaceous, pond and water garden
   ¶**The Old Butcher's Shop** ⅍ (Mr & Mrs P Draper) ⅓-acre artist's garden with emphasis on form, texture and colour. Studio also open
Upper Dean
   ¶**Ashley** (Mr & Mrs William Cade) Established garden of approx ¾-acre. Interesting old stones and unusual clapper gate. Exceptional kitchen garden
   ¶**Dean House Farm** ⅍ (Mr & Mrs Paul Cook) C16 farmhouse with ½-acre garden being gradually rescued by owners. Pond with geese and ducks
   ¶**Francis House** (Mr & Mrs David Butter) Traditional garden recently established around restored C16 farmhouse. Many choice and unusual plants
   ¶**Highbank House** ⅍ (Mr & Mrs D J Gray) 1-acre garden interesting trees, shrubs, herbaceous borders. Pond and newly planted knot garden
Shelton
   ¶**Birwell Lodge** ⅍ (Mr & Mrs J Fenning) Large shrub garden
   ¶**The Little House** ⅍ (Mr & Mrs I W Burns) Cottage garden, herbaceous and shrub borders, vegetable garden
   ¶**The Old Rectory** ⅍ (Mr & Mrs J H Wells) Approx 6 acres. Sweeping lawns, herbaceous border, roses, orchard, kitchen garden

Grove Lodge ⚘ (Peter Wareing & Jean Venning) 6 Deepdale, Potton. 2m E of Sandy on 1042 towards Potton, past RSPB Reserve, downhill to Xrds. L at 'Locomotive' - lane to TV mast; first house on R. 1½-acre sandy hillside garden; conifers; heathers, shrubs, incl rhododendrons, climbing roses, herbaceous border, orchard with wild flowers, rockery banks with pond. **Deepdale Lodge** (Richard & Deanna Brawn) opposite; displays of hanging baskets; containers with colourful displays & new conservatory. TEAS in aid of R.A.T.S. *Combined adm £1.50 Chd 50p. Sun June 19 (2-6)*

47 Hexton Road ♿⚘ (Mrs S H Horsler) Barton-le-Clay. 6m N of Luton on the B655 Barton-le-Clay to Hitchin Rd (Hitchin 5m). Set in ¼ acre cottage garden with mixed borders. *Adm £1 Chd 50p. Sun July 10 (2-6)*

Howard's House ♿ (Humphrey Whitbread Esq) Cardington. 2m SE of Bedford. Walled and flower gardens; flowering cherries and clematis. Tea Bedford. *Adm £1 Chd 50p. Sun April 24 (2-6)*

King's Arms Path Gardens ♿⚘ Ampthill Town Council (Mrs N W Hudson) Ampthill. Free parking in town centre. Entrance opp. old Market Place, Ampthill, down Kings Arms Yard. Small woodland garden of about 1½ acres created by plantsman the late William Nowrish. Trees, shrubs, bulbs and many interesting collections. Maintained since 1987 by 'The Friends of the Garden.' Teas at adjacent Bowling Club or nearby tea shops. *Adm 50p Chd 25p. Suns Feb 13, (2-4). May 1, 29, June 26, Oct 16 (2.30-5). For NGS Sun April 3 (2.30-5). Private group visits welcome, please* **Tel 0525 402030**

Luton Hoo Gardens ♿⚘ (The Wernher Family) Luton; entrance at Park St gates. Bus: Green line 707, 717, 727 London-Luton Garage: London Country 321 Watford-Luton via St Albans to Luton Garage. Landscape garden by Capability Brown. House built by Robert Adam in 1767. Wernher Collection. Restaurant. NO DOGS. TEAS. *Adm gardens only £1.85 OAP £1.60 Chd 60p. ▲For NGS Sun July 3 (2-6)*

¶The Manor ♿⚘ (Mrs Anita Woolf) Yielden. N of Bedford, on A6 take turnoff through Riseley from Rushden, take Newton Rd through Newton Bromswold. Domestic garden of 2½ acres, formal rose garden surrounding fish pond 12' × 50'. Shrubbery leading to tennis court bordered by rockery and herbaceous border leading to swimming pool; at rear of house is ornamental vegetable garden and greenhouses; 9 acres divided into 4 fields, 1 devoted to flowers grown for drying, others for sheep. Bunched dried flower arrangements for sale, also organic vegetables and some plants. TEAS. *Adm £1.50 Chd 50p. Suns May 29, July 3 (2-6)*

¶Milton House ♿⚘ (Mr & Mrs Clifton Ibbett) nr Bedford. N of Bedford on the A6. The drive to the house is on the R, S of the village of Milton Ernest. Formal, terrace and sunken gardens set in large grounds with lakes and waterfall. TEAS in aid of All Saints Parish Church, Milton Ernest. *Adm £2 Chd 50p. Sun May 29 (2-6)*

Odell Castle (The Rt Hon Lord Luke) NW of Bedford. From A6 turn W through Sharnbrook; from A428, N through Lavendon and Harrold. Station: Bedford 10m. Terrace and lower garden down to R. Ouse. House built 1962 on old site, using original stone. TEAS. *Adm £1 Chd free. Suns May 15 June 19 (2-6)*

¶The Old Stables ♿⚘ (Mr & Mrs D X Victor) 3m N of Dunstable. From A5 in Hockliffe, W on A4012. Turn R after ¼m (signposted Church End), then L at Church. Follow lane for ½m and take field track on R. 2 acres incl walled garden. Alpines, mixed herbaceous and shrub borders. Wide range of plants incl hardy geraniums, erodiums, dianthus, saxifrages, euphorbias, deutzias and clematis. National collections of alpine dianthus and oxalis. *Adm £1.50 Chd 50p. Suns May 8, July 3, Aug 7 (10-6)*

The Rectory ♿ (Canon Peter Whittaker) Barton-Le-Clay. Barton-Le-Clay is 6m N of Luton. From A6 turn E on to B655 then to Church Rd. Bus Bedford to Luton. 2 acres with background of Chilterns; moat, rockery, mature trees, lawns; overlooked by C12 church. TEAS. *Adm £1.50 Chd 50p. Sun July 10 (2-6)*

Seal Point ⚘ (Mrs Danae Johnston) 7 Wendover Way. In NE Luton, turning N off Stockingstone Rd into Felstead Way. A small sloping most exciting town garden with many unusual herbaceous plants, climbers and trees; water features, topiary cats and bonsai; beds with oriental flavour representing yin and yang; original ornaments, grasses, ferns, architectural plants & much more. TEA. *Adm £1. Private visits welcome, also small groups, please* **Tel 0582 26841**

Southill Park ♿⚘ (Mr & Mrs S C Whitbread) 5m SW of Biggleswade. Large garden, rhododendrons, renovated conservatory. *Adm £1.50 Chd 50p. Sun June 5 (2-6)*

Toddington Manor ♿ (Sir Neville & Lady Bowman-Shaw) Exit 12 M1. Signs in village. House and gardens restored by present owners. Walled garden with greenhouses and herb garden; beautiful roses & shrubs; lakeside walks in the woods; rare breeds centre and vintage tractor collection. Cricket on pitch in front of house at weekends. Best months June & July. Refreshments. Shop. TEAS. *Adm £2.50 OAP's & Chd £1. Special rates for parties. Open Easter to end Sept daily (10-5) Closed July 4-10. For NGS Sun June 26 (10-5)*

Woburn Abbey ♿⚘ (The Marquess of Tavistock) Woburn. Woburn Abbey is situated 1½m from Woburn Village, which is on the A4012 almost midway from junctions 12 and 13 of the M1 motorway. 22 acres of private garden originally designed by Wyattville, with recent restoration of the The Duchess' rose garden. Unique hornbeam maze with C18 temple by Chambers. TEAS. *Adm £1 Chd free. Suns April 17, June 12 (11-5.30)*

Woodleys Farm House ♿⚘ (Hon Mrs Hugh Lawson Johnston) Melchbourne. Leave A6 10m N of Bedford, or 4m S of Rushden. House reached by lime avenue before reaching village of Melchbourne. Small garden 1½ acres, with roses, lawns, shrubs and herbaceous plants. TEAS. *Adm £1 Chd free. Sun May 29 (3-6)*

Regular Openers. See head of county section.

Berkshire

Hon County Organiser: Bob Avery Esq, 'Jingles', Derek Rd., Maidenhead, SL6 8NT
Asst Hon County Organisers: (Central) Mrs J Granville, Holly Copse, Goring Heath, Nr Reading
The Hon Mrs A Willoughby, Buckhold Farm, Pangbourne
(NW) Mrs C Povey, Bussock Mayne, Snelsmore Common, Newbury
(SW) Mrs P Meigh, Fishponds, West Woodhay, Nr Newbury
Mrs M A Henderson, 'Ridings', Kentons Lane, Wargrave, RG10 8PB
(Publicity & Brochures) Mrs J Bewsher, Arcturus, Church Road, Bray, Berks
SL6 1UR
Hon County Treasurer: Bob Avery Esq

DATES OF OPENING

By appointment
For telephone numbers and other details see garden descriptions. Private visits welcomed

Blencathra, Finchampstead
Fairing, Littlewick Green
Hurst Lodge, nr Reading
Jasmine House, nr Windsor
Meadow House, nr Newbury
Simms Farm House, Mortimer, nr
  Reading

Regular openings
For details see garden description

Englefield House, Theale. Tues,
  Weds, Thurs April 11 to May 30
  and every Mon all year
Meadow House, nr Newbury. Every
  Wed May 11 to Aug 10 (excl
  June 15)
The Old Rectory, Burghfield
Waltham Place, White Waltham.
  Weds April & Sept

February 23 Wednesday
The Old Rectory, Burghfield, nr
  Reading
February 27 Sunday
Old Rectory Cottage, Tidmarsh nr
  Pangbourne
March 13 Sunday
Foxgrove, Enborne, nr Newbury
March 27 Sunday
Welford Park, nr Newbury
March 30 Wednesday
The Old Rectory, Burghfield, nr
  Reading
April 4 Monday
Swallowfield Park, nr Reading
April 10 Sunday
Foxgrove, Enborne, nr Newbury
Kirby House, Inkpen ‡
Old Rectory Cottage, Tidmarsh nr
  Pangbourne

West Woodhay House, Inkpen ‡
April 17 Sunday
Blencathra, Finchampstead
Englefield House, Theale
Folly Farm, nr Reading
April 24 Sunday
The Old Rectory, Farnborough,
  Wantage
Scotlands, Cockpole Green, nr
  Wargrave
April 27 Wednesday
The Old Rectory, Burghfield, nr
  Reading
May 1 Sunday
Oakfield Gardens, nr Mortimer ‡
Simms Farm House, Mortimer, nr
  Reading ‡
May 4 Wednesday
Frogmore Gardens, Windsor
May 5 Thursday
Frogmore Gardens, Windsor
May 8 Sunday
Hurst Lodge, nr Reading ‡
Jasmine House, nr Windsor
Odney Club, Cookham
Old Rectory Cottage, nr
  Pangbourne
Reynolds Farm, nr Twyford ‡
Trunkwell Park, Beech Hill
May 15 Sunday
Alderwood House, Greenham
  Common
Bussock Wood, Snelsmore
  Common, nr Newbury
The Old Rectory, Farnborough,
  Wantage
Padworth Common Gardens
Silwood Park, Ascot
Waltham Place, White Waltham
Whiteknights, The Ridges,
  Finchampstead
May 21 Saturday
Inkpen House, Inkpen
May 22 Sunday
Aldermaston Park, Aldermaston ‡
Beenham House, Beenham ‡‡
Blencathra, Finchampstead
Englefield House, Theale ‡‡
Fox Steep, Crazies Hill
Silwood Park, Ascot ‡‡‡

Sunningdale Park, Ascot ‡‡‡
Wasing Place, Aldermaston ‡
May 25 Wednesday
The Old Rectory, Burghfield, nr
  Reading
May 29 Sunday
Bowdown House, Greenham
  Common
Little Bowden, Pangbourne
Stone House, Brimpton
May 30 Monday
Folly Farm, nr Reading
June 5 Sunday
Alderwood House, Greenham
  Common
Mariners, Bradfield, nr Reading
June 12 Sunday
Chieveley Gardens, nr Newbury
Foxgrove, Enborne, nr Newbury
Meadow House, nr Newbury
Old Rectory Cottage, nr
  Pangbourne
Padworth Common Gardens
The Priory, nr Reading
Sonning Lane Gardens
June 18 Saturday
Eton College, Windsor
June 19 Sunday
Basildon Park, Lower Basildon
Combe Manor, Newbury ‡
Fox Hill, Inkpen ‡
Peasemore Gardens
Summerfield House, Crazies Hill,
  nr Wargrave
June 26 Sunday
Alderwood House, Greenham
  Common
Folly Farm, nr Reading
The Old Rectory, Farnborough,
  Wantage ‡
West Woodhay House,
  Inkpen
Woolley Park, nr Wantage ‡
June 29 Wednesday
The Old Rectory, Burghfield, nr
  Reading
Rooksnest, Lambourn
July 3 Sunday
Old Rectory Cottage, nr
  Pangbourne

Stanford Dingley Village Gardens
July 10 Sunday
Chieveley Manor, nr Newbury
The Harris Garden, Whiteknights, Reading
Little Bowden, Pangbourne
Wasing Place, Aldermaston
July 24 Sunday
Ockwells Manor, Maidenhead ‡
The Old Mill, Aldermaston
Stone House, Brimpton
Waltham Place, White Waltham ‡

July 27 Wednesday
The Old Rectory, Burghfield, nr Reading
August 28 Sunday
Hurst Lodge, nr Reading
August 31 Wednesday
The Old Rectory, Burghfield, nr Reading
September 4 Sunday
Scotlands, Cockpole Green, nr Wargrave
Trunkwell Park, Beech Hill

September 28 Wednesday
The Old Rectory, Burghfield, nr Reading
October 2 Sunday
Foxgrove, Enborne, nr Newbury
October 9 Sunday
Silwood Park, Ascot
October 26 Wednesday
The Old Rectory, Burghfield, nr Reading

DESCRIPTIONS OF GARDENS

Aldermaston Park &❀ (Blue Circle Industries plc) Newbury 10m W; Reading 10m E; Basingstoke 8m S. 137-acres, surrounding Victorian Mansion (1849) with modern offices making interesting contrast of architecture. Fine trees; specimen rhododendrons and shrubs; large lawns; lakeside walk. TEA. *Adm £1 Chd 50p. Sun May 22 (10-4)*

Alderwood House ❀❀ (Mr & Mrs P B Trier) Greenham Common. S of Newbury take A 339 towards Basingstoke for approx 3m. Turn L towards the Main Gates of RAF Greenham Common. Turn R immediately before gate along gravel path to house. Interesting 2½-acre garden started in 1904. On many levels with a number of rare trees and shrubs. Old roses, herbaceous border, conservatory and fine vegetable garden. TEAS. *Adm £1 Chd 50p. Suns May 15, June 5, 26 (2-6)*

Basildon Park &❀ (Lord & Lady Iliffe; The National Trust) Lower Basildon, Reading. Between Pangbourne and Streatley, 7m NW of Reading on W of A329. Private garden designed and planted by Lady Iliffe with help of Lanning Roper. Mainly old roses but other interesting plants constantly being added by owner. TEAS in NT house. *Adm 50p Chd free.* ▲*For NGS Sun June 19 (2-6)*

Beenham House &❀ (Prof & Mrs Gerald Benney) Beenham. ½-way between Reading and Newbury, 1m N of A4; entrance off Webbs Lane. 21 acres of grounds and garden; old Lebanon cedars, oaks, hornbeams; recent plantings. Good views of park and Kennett Valley. Regency house (not open). Coach parties by appt. TEAS. *Adm £1 Chd free (Share to St Mary's Church, Beenham®). Sun May 22 (2-6)*

Blencathra &❀ (Dr & Mrs F W Gifford) Finchampstead. Entrance from private drive at the NW end of Finchampstead Ridges on B3348 between Finchampstead War Memorial and Crowthorne Station. Parking on joint private drive or The Ridges. Disabled passengers may alight near the house. 11-acre garden which present owners started in 1964, laid out and maintained with minimum of help. In 'Good Gardens Guide' since 1993. Many varied mature trees; lawns; heathers; rhododendrons; azaleas; wide range of conifers; three small lakes and stream; bog areas and spring bulbs. Interesting throughout year. TEAS. *Adm £1.60 Chd free. Suns April 17, May 22 (2-6) also private visits welcome - parties welcome, please* **Tel 0734 734563**

Bowdown House &❀ (Mr & Mrs M Dormer) Newbury. 3m Newbury, Greenham Common N. On Bury's Bank Rd 2m past Greenham Golf Club. Lutyen's parterre gardens in style of Gertrude Jekyll; fine trees and rare shrubs. 50 acres of ancient woodland, now a nature reserve in care of BBONT. House by Sir Oswald Partridge Miln. TEAS. *Adm £1.50 Chd free (Share to BBONT®). Sun May 29 (2-5.30)*

Bussock Wood ❀ (Mr & Mrs W A Palmer) Snelsmore Common. 3m N of Newbury. On B4494 Newbury-Wantage Rd. Bluebells, fine trees and views; sunken garden with lily pond. Early Briton Camp. TEAS. *Adm £1 Chd 10p (Share to Winterbourne Parish Church®). Sun May 15 (2-6)*

Chieveley Gardens &❀ 5m N Newbury. Take A34 N, pass under M4, then L to Chieveley. Follow rd into High St. Chieveley House on R, Maypole Cottage further on L. *Combined adm £1 Chd free. Sun June 12 (2-6)*
   Chieveley House ❀ (Lord & Lady Goff) Large walled garden containing substantial trees, yew hedges; herbaceous borders; sunken water garden. Listed house (not open). TEAS
   Maypole Cottage (The Misses B & R Hartas Jackson) Attractive small garden, owner maintained with shrubs and plants of botanical interest

Chieveley Manor &❀❀ (Mr & Mrs C J Spence) 5m N Newbury. Take A34 N pass under M4, then L to Chieveley. After ½m L up Manor Lane. Large garden with fine view over stud farm. Walled garden containing borders, shrubs and rose garden. Listed House (not open). TEAS. *Adm £1 Chd free (Share to St Mary's Church Chieveley®). Sun July 10 (2-6)*

Cobwood House, Newbury see Hampshire

Combe Manor (Lady Mary Russell) Combe. Approx 10m from Newbury or from Andover. From M4 in Hungerford, turn L after passing under railway bridge; over cattle grid onto Hungerford Common; turn R 400yds later and follow signs to Inkpen; pass The Swan on L, bear R at junction and then almost immediately L to Combe Gibbet and Combe. The Manor stands ½m from the village beside the church. 2 acres of lawns, borders, roses, shrubs and fruit trees. Walled garden with C17 gazebo. C11 church adjoining will be open. TEAS. *Combined adm with* **Fox Hill** *£1.50 Chd free. Sun June 19 (2-6)*

Englefield House &@ (Mr & Mrs W R Benyon) nr Theale. Entrance on A340. 7 acres of woodland garden with interesting variety of trees; shrubs; stream and water garden; formal terrace with fountain and borders. Commercial garden centre in village. Deer park. Part of garden suitable for wheelchairs. Home made TEAS Long Gallery NGS days only. Open every Mon all yr and Mons, Tues, Weds, Thurs from April 11 to May 30 (10-dusk). *Adm £2 Chd free (Share to St Mark's Church®).* ▲*For NGS Suns April 17, May 22(2-6)*

Eton College Gardens & (Provost & Fellows). Stations: Windsor ¾m Eton ½m. Bus: Green Line 704 & 705 London-Windsor 1m. Luxmoore's Garden is an island garden created by a housemaster about 1880; reached by beautiful new bridge; views of college and river. Provost's and Fellows' Gardens adjoin the ancient buildings on N and E sides. Parking off B3022 Slough to Eaton rd, signposted. TEAS in aid of Datchet PCC. *Combined adm £1 Chd 20p. Sat June 18 (2-6)*

¶**Fairing** &@ (Mr & Mrs M P Maine) Littlewick Green. Turn S into Littlewick Green off A4. 3m W of Maidenhead. 1-acre plant lover's garden developed since 1990. Colour-schemed borders give yr-round interest with large variety of hardy plants. Ornamental herb garden. TEA. *Adm £1 Chd free. Private visits welcome March to Sept, please* Tel 0628 822008

Folly Farm &@ (The Hon Hugh & Mrs Astor) Sulhamstead, 7m SW of Reading. A4 between Reading/Newbury (2m W of M4 exit 12); take rd marked Sulhamstead at Mulligans Restaurant 1m after Theale roundabout; entrance 1m on right, through BROWN gate marked 'Folly Farm Gardens'. One of the few remaining gardens where the Lutyens architecture remains intact. Garden, laid out by Gertrude Jekyll, has been planted to owners' taste, bearing in mind Jekyll and Lutyens original design. Raised white garden, sunken rose garden; spring bulbs; herbaceous borders; ilex walk; avenues of limes, yew hedges, landscaped lawn areas, formal pools. Some recent simplifications and new planting. House (not open). TEAS. *Adm £1.50 Chd free (Share to West Berkshire Marriage Guidance Trust®). Sun April 17, Mon May 30, Sun June 26 (2-6)*

Foxgrove &@ (Miss Audrey Vockins) Enborne, 2½m SW of Newbury. From A343 turn R at 'The Gun' 1½m from town centre. Bus: AV 126, 127, 128; alight Villiers Way PO 1m. Small family garden with adjoing nursery (Foxgrove Plants); interesting foliage plants, troughs, spring bulbs, naturalised in orchard; double primroses, snowdrop species and varieties; peat bed. Autumn opening for cyclamen, colchicums, nerines. TEAS. *Adm £1 Chd free. Suns March 13, April 10, June 12, Oct 2 (2-6)*

Fox Hill &@ (Mrs Martin McLaren) Inkpen. Between Hungerford and Newbury, turn off A4 at sign saying Kintbury & Inkpen. Drive into Kintbury. Turn L by shop onto Inkpen Rd. After approx 1m, turn R at Xrds. After passing village signpost saying Inkpen, turn 1st L down bridleroad. Garden 2nd on L. Car park in field. 3-acre garden, blossom, bulbs, many interesting shrubs. Newly planted. Small formal garden and duck pond. Teas at Combe Manor. *Combined adm with* **Combe Manor** *£1.50 Chd free. Sun June 19 (2-6)*

Fox Steep &@ (Juddmonte Farms) Crazies Hill. Midway between Henley-on-Thames and Wargrave. 2m E of Henley on A423; take turning at top of hill to Cockpole Green. From Knowl Hill on A4 and Wargrave follow Cockpole Green signs. Old well-established 4-acre garden provides pretty setting for Elizabethan timbered house, formerly an Inn; associated with Gertrude Jekyll. TEAS. *Adm £1 Chd free. Sun May 22 (2-6)*

Frogmore Gardens &@ (by gracious permission of Her Majesty The Queen) Windsor Castle; entrance via Park St gate into Long Walk (follow AA signs). Visitors are requested kindly to keep on the route to the garden and not stray into the Home Park. Station and bus stop; Windsor (20 mins walk from gardens); Green Line bus no 701, from London. Limited parking for cars only (free). Large garden with lake and lovely trees. The Royal Mausoleum, within the grounds, will also be open free of charge. Refreshment tent in car park on Long Walk (from where there is a 5 min walk to the gardens). **Coaches by appointment only** (apply to NGS, Hatchlands Park, East Clandon, Guildford, Surrey GU4 7RT enc. s.a.e. or Tel 0483 211535 stating whether May 4 or 5; am or pm). *Adm £1.50 Chd free. Wed May 4, & Thurs May 5 (10.30-7; last adm 6.30)*

The Harris Garden & Experimental Grounds &@ (University of Reading, School of Plant Sciences) Whiteknights, Reading RG6 2AS. Turn R just inside Pepper Lane entrance to University campus. 12-acre research and teaching garden extensively redeveloped since 1989. Rose gardens; shrub rose, herbaceous and annual borders, winter garden, bog garden, herb garden, walled garden etc. Gertrude Jekyll border new in 1993. Extensive glasshouses. Most plants labelled. TEAS. *Adm £1 Chd free. Sun July 10 (2-6)*

Highclere Castle, nr Newbury see Hampshire

Hurst Lodge &@ (Mr & Mrs Alan Peck) In Hurst village on A321 Twyford to Wokingham Rd. An old garden 5 acres, spring flowers and bulbs, camellias, magnolias, rhododendrons, hydrangeas. TEAS. *Adm £1 Chd 20p. Also open* **Reynolds Farm** *(May only) Suns May 8, Aug 28 (2-5.30). Private visits also welcome, please* Tel 0734 341088

¶**Inkpen House** (Sir Fred Warner) Inkpen. From Hungerford: Take the rd to Inkpen. After passing The Swan Inn on the L, turn R at T-junction. Take the 2nd lane on the L (sign to C13 church). Garden 200 yds on R above church. From Newbury: Take the A4 and turn off to Kintbury. In Kintbury Sq, turn L on Inkpen Rd. Continue for approx 2½m (STOP sign 63yds). Straight over Xrds. House on L. 4-acre garden laid out in approx 1715 in the French style with avenues and enclosures formed by hedges of mixed beech, yew and holly. Walled kitchen garden and a walk with many wild flowers in spring and summer; more recent lawns and plantings. *Adm £1 Chd free. Sat May 21 (2-6)*

By Appointment Gardens. See head of county section

Jasmine House ⚹ (Mr & Mrs E C B Knight) Hatch Bridge, 2m W of Windsor. Off A308 Windsor-Maidenhead opp Windsor Marina; follow signs from new roundabout by Jardinerie Garden Centre. ⅓-acre garden designed for all-yr interest with conifers (over 150 different), dwarf rhododendrons, heather beds; hostas; sink gardens; trees notable for decorative bark; ornamental pools; collection of Bonsai. Garden featured in RHS Journal (March 1979); 'The Gardens of Britain' & 'Mon Jardin et Ma Maison' (Feb 82). TEAS Country Gardens Garden Centre (1m). *Adm £1 Chd free. Sun May 8 (2-6). Private visits welcome May to August, please* Tel 0753 841595

Kirby House ⚹⚹ (Richard Astor Esq) Turn S off A4 to Kintbury; L at Xrds in Kintbury towards Combe. 2m out of Kintbury. Turn L immediately beyond Crown & Garter. House and garden at bottom of hill. 4 acres in beautiful setting; bulbs and blossom and many mature trees C18 brick house (not open). TEAS at **West Woodhay House.** *Combined adm with* **West Woodhay House** *£2 Chd free. Sun April 10 (2-6)*

Little Bowden ⚹⚹ (Geoffrey Verey Esq) 1½m W of Pangbourne on Pangbourne-Yattendon Rd. Large garden with fine views; woodland walk, azaleas, rhododendrons, bluebells. Heated swimming pool 20p extra. TEAS. *Adm £1 Chd free. Suns May 29, July 10 (2.30-6)*

Mariners ⚹⚹ (Mr & Mrs W N Ritchie) 7m W of Reading. From Theale (M4 exit 12 take A340) towards Pangbourne 1st L to Bradfield. Pass through wood and turn L by farm. 1st R after War Memorial into Mariners Lane. 1-acre charming well-designed garden, owner maintained; made from heavy clay field, now waterlogged; large variety of plants; herbaceous and shrub border; rose, clematis; silver leaved plants. TEAS & ice cream. *Adm £1 Chd 20p. Sun June 5 (2-6)*

Meadow House ⚹⚹⚹ (Mr & Mrs G A Jones) Ashford Hill is on the B3051 8m SE of Newbury. Take turning at SW end of village signposted Wolverton Common and Wheathold. Meadow House on R approx 300yds along lane. Approx 1½-acre plantsman's garden. Pond with waterside planting; mixed shrub and herbaceous borders. Many unusual plants. *Every Wed May 11 to Aug 10 (10-5) (excl June 15). For NGS TEAS. Adm £1.25 Chd free (Share to St Paul's Church, Ashford Hill®). Sun June 12 (2-6). Private visits also welcome, please* Tel 0734 816005 *(2-6)*

North Ecchinswell Farm, nr Newbury see Hampshire

Ockwells Manor ⚹⚹ (Mr & Mrs B P Stein) Maidenhead. Exit 8/9 off M4. A404M towards Henley. 1st slip rd to L to Cox Green and White Waltham. R at 1st roundabout. L at 2nd roundabout. Follow rd to end and turn R. 3½ acres of formal garden around mediaeval Manor House. Listed grade 1 (not open); walled garden; clipped yews; small maze; lime avenue; swimming pool; peacocks, ornamental ducks and geese; farm animals; woodland walk. TEAS. *Adm £1.50 Chd free. Sun July 24 (2-6)*

Odney Club ⚹⚹ (John Lewis Partnership) Cookham. Car park in grounds. 120 acres; lawns, garden and meadows on R. Thames; specimen trees. Cream TEAS River Room. *Adm £1.50 Chd free (Share to Sue Ryder Foundation®). Sun May 8 (2-6)*

The Old House, Silchester see Hampshire

The Old Mill ⚹ (Mrs E M Arlott) Aldermaston. On A4 between Reading and Newbury, take A340 then follow signs. 7 acres; lawns; walks; flower beds; shrubs; R Kennet flows through with sluices and hatches. Fine Old Mill House (not open). TEAS. *Adm £1 Chd free. Sun July 24 (2-6)*

Old Rectory Cottage ⚹⚹ (Mr & Mrs A W A Baker) Tidmarsh, ½m S of Pangbourne, midway between Pangbourne and Tidmarsh turn E down narrow lane; L at T-junction. 2-acre cottage garden and wild garden with small lake bordered by R Pang. Unusual plants, spring bulbs, roses climbing into old apple trees, ferns, hellebores and lilies. Featured on TV and in many gardening books. *Adm £1 Chd free (Share to BBONT®). Suns Feb 27, April 10, May 8, June 12, July 3 (2-6)*

The Old Rectory, Burghfield ⚹⚹⚹ (Mr & Mrs R R Merton), 5m SW of Reading. Turn S off A4 to Burghfield village; R after Hatch Gate Inn; entrance on R. Medium-sized garden; herbaceous and shrub borders; roses, hellebores, lilies, many rare and unusual plants collected by owners from Japan and China; old-fashioned cottage plants; autumn colour. Georgian house (not open). *Adm £1 Chd 50p (Share to Save the Children® & NCCPG Local Group®). The last Weds of every month except Nov-Dec & Jan (11-4)*

The Old Rectory, Farnborough ⚹⚹ (Mrs Michael Todhunter) 4m SE of Wantage. From B4494 Wantage-Newbury Rd, 4m from Wantage turn E at sign for Farnborough. Outstanding garden with unusual plants: fine view; old-fashioned roses; collection of small flowered clematis; herbaceous borders. Beautiful house (not open) built c.1749. Teas in village. *Adm £1.50 Chd free (Share to All Saints, Farnborough©). Suns April 24, May 15, June 26 (2-6)*

¶**Padworth Common Gardens** ⚹⚹⚹ Padworth Common. ½-way between Reading and Newbury. 1½m S of A4 take Padworth Lane at Padworth Court Hotel. TEAS. *Combined adm £1.50 Chd free. Suns May 15, June 12 (2-6)*
    ¶**Bloomsbury** (Mr & Mrs M J Oakley) Upper Lodge Farm. Medium-sized, with white garden; orchard garden with collection of old shrub roses; courtyard garden with pots; large polytunnel with specimen conservatory plants; unusual trees and shrubs; nursery. Field walk to C11 church
    ¶**Honeyhanger** (Mrs Jenny Martin) Rectory Rd. Medium-sized with unusual trees, shrubs. Courtyard with collection of Australian shrubs. Woodland, some mature and some new plantings. Tropical house, aviary, pond

---

By Appointment Gardens. These owners do not have a fixed opening day usually because they do not like crowds or have insufficient parking space. Owner will often give guided tour.

Regular Openers. Too many days to include in diary. Usually there is a wide range of plants giving year-round interest. See head of county section for the name and garden description for times etc.

Peasemore Gardens 7m N of Newbury on A34 to M4 junction 13. N towards Oxford then immed L signed Chievely. Through Chievely and onto Peasemore approx 3½m. TEAS. *Combined adm £1.50 Chd free. Sun June 19 (2-6)*

The Old Rectory, Peasemore ৬৯ (Mr & Mrs I D Cameron) Georgian house with fine trees in lovely setting. Shrub roses, peonies, large rose border and herbaceous border

Paxmere House ৬৯ (The Hon Mrs John Astor) Opp The Old Rectory. 2-acre cottage garden. Roses, shrubs, etc

Peasemore House ৬ (Mr & Mrs Richard W Brown) Past 3 thatched cottages on R entering Peasemore. Garden on R behind flint and brick wall. 2½ acres traditional garden with lovely trees, shrubs and roses with extensive views over arable downland

The Priory ৬৯৯ (O W Roskill Esq) Beech Hill, 9m S of Reading. Turn off at Spencers Wood PO Bus: 411, 412 from Reading. C14 Benedictine priory largely rebuilt 1648. Branch of Loddon flows through garden. Probably laid out in C17. Lawns, herbaceous borders, shrubs; kitchen garden. Teas in village in aid of Beech Hill Church. *Adm £1 Chd 30p. Sun June 12 (2-6)*

Reynolds Farm ৯৯ (Mr & Mrs Christopher Wells) Hurst, 3m S of Twyford. From Hurst Lodge turn L; after ¾m take 1st left; entrance 200yds on L. Twenty five yrs of careful planting by the present owners, mainly shrubs & bulbs but with some specialised and unusual plants, has resulted in a small paddock transformed into a secluded wild garden with hopefully an instant bog garden. Teas at **Hurst Lodge**. *Adm £1 Chd free. Sun May 8 (2-5.30)*

Rooksnest ৯ (Dr & Mrs M D Sackler) Earls Court Farm, Lambourn Woodlands. Situated approx 3m from the A338 (Wantage) Rd along the B4000. Nearest village, Lambourn. Rooksnest signposted on the B400 in both directions, ie whether approaching from Lambourn or from the A338. Approx 10-acre exceptionally fine traditional English garden. Recently restored with help from Arabella Lennox-Boyd. Includes terraces; rose garden; lilies; herbaceous borders; herb garden; many specimen trees and fine shrubs. TEA. *Adm £1.50 Chd 50p. Wed June 29 (2-5)*

Scotlands (Mr Michael & The Hon Mrs Payne) ৬৯ Cockpole Green. Midway between Henley-on-Thames and Wargrave. 2m E of Henley on A423; take turn at top of hill to Cockpole Green. 4 acres; clipped yews; shrub borders; grass paths through trees to woodland and pond-gardens with Repton design rustic summer house. Rocks with waterfall. Featured in 'New Englishwoman's Garden' by R Verey, 'English Gardens' by Peter Coats. TEAS. *Adm £1.50 Chd free. Suns April 24, Sept 4 (2-6). Private parties welcome, please* Tel 0344 23911

Silwood Park (Imperial College) Ascot. 1½m E of Ascot in the junction of A329 and the B383. Access from the B383 200 metres N of the Cannon Inn. 240 acres of parklands and natural habitats, surrounding fine C19 house by Waterhouse, architect of the Natural History Museum. Japanese garden under restoration; pinetum, young arboretum specialising in oaks and birches. Two nature walks (1m & 2m) through oak and beech woodland to lake. TEAS. *Adm £1 Chd 50p. Suns May 15, 22; Oct 9 (2-6). Parties by appt, please* Tel 0628 822648

Simms Farm House ৯৯ (H H Judge Lea & Mrs Lea) Mortimer, 6m SW of Reading. At T-junction on edge of village, from Grazeley, turn R uphill; L by church into West End Rd; at next Xrd L down Drury Lane; R at T-junction. 1-acre garden with mixed shrub borders, small rockery; Bog garden; formal pond; unusual plants. Lovely view. TEA. *Adm £1 Chd 50p. Sun May 1 (2-6); Private visits welcome, please* Tel 0734 332360

Sonning Lane Gardens ৯ 4m E of Reading in Sonning Lane off the A4 (9m W of Maidenhead off the A4), 400 metres heading N along Sonning Lane. School found on L. TEAS. *Combined adm £1.50 Chd free. Sun June 12 (2-5)*

Reading Blue Coat School (Headmaster) The school is in 45 acres of fields and woods with paths running down to the R Thames and Sonning Lock. The garden consist mainly of annual bedding, roses and shrubs mixed with trees eg magnolias in Magnolia Walk

South Hill (Mr & Mrs B Tomlinson) Entrance opp Reading Blue Coat School. 5 acres of lawns; specimen trees beautifully planted with shrubs; walled garden

Thatched Cottage ৬ (Dr & Mrs Grenfell Bailey) 3 acres well laid out; lawns, specimen trees, herbaceous border

Stanford Dingley Village Gardens ৯৯ Between Reading and Newbury. Pretty village with ancient Church and bridge over River Pang. Parking in field. TEAS at Bradfield Farm. *Combined adm £2 Chd free. Sun July 3 (2-6) including:*

Bradfield Farm (Mr & Mrs Newton) ½-acre. Wide variety of plants. Further 5-acres mixed broadleaf planting in 1990. TEAS

¶**Bridge Cottage** (Mr & Mrs M Ranwell) Pretty ½-acre cottage garden. Deep mixed borders. Interesting terrace and tub planting

The Manor House ৯ (Mr & Mrs Park) Close to church, 3-acre garden planted informally; water gardens

Roman Way (Mr & Mrs P Trentham) Thatched cottage, 5-acre garden with magnolias, walled vegetable garden, specimen shrubs, mixed borders

Saffron House (Mrs P Hobson) Large informal garden beside R Pang

Stone House ৯ (Mr & Mrs Nigel Bingham) Brimpton, 6m E of Newbury. Turn S off A4 at junction by Coach & Horses, signed Brimpton and Aldermaston. ½m W of T-junction by War Memorial signed Newbury. Medium-sized garden in attractive park; naturalised bulbs; rhododendrons; water garden; extensive collection plants and shrubs; walled kitchen garden; picnic area. TEA. *Adm £1 Chd free (Share to Brimpton Church©). Suns May 29, July 24 (2-6)*

Summerfield House ৯ (Mr & Mrs R J S Palmer) Crazies Hill. Midway between Henley-on-Thames and Wargrave. 2m E of Henley on A423, take turn at top of hill signed Cockpole Green, then turn R at Green. Garden opp village hall. 7 acres, herbaceous and shrub borders, many recently planted rare trees, large working greenhouse, 1½-

acre lake plus 20 acres parkland. House (not open) formerly Henley Town Hall, originally constructed in 1760 in centre of Henley and moved at end of C19. TEAS. *Adm £1.50 Chd under 12 free. Sun June 19 (2-6)*

Sunningdale Park &# (Civil Service College) Ascot. 1½m E of Ascot off A329 at Cannon Inn or take Broomhall Lane off A30 at Sunningdale. Over 20 acres of beautifully landscaped gardens reputedly laid out by Capability Brown. Terrace garden and victorian rockery designed by Pulham incl cave and water features. Lake area with paved walks; extensive lawns with specimen trees and flower beds; impressive massed rhododendrons. Beautiful 1m woodland walk. Cream TEAS. *Adm £1.75 Chd 75p. Sun May 22 (2-5)*

Swallowfield Park &# (Country Houses Association) 5m S between Reading and Wokingham on B3349 under M4; 2m then L to Swallowfield. Entrance by Village Hall. Landscaped garden, exceptionally fine trees including cedars; ancient yew tree walk, small lake, massed rhododendrons; distinguished house built 1689 (not open). TEAS. *Adm £1.50 Chd 50p (Share to Country House Association©). Mon April 4 (2-5)*

¶**Trunkwell Park** &# (Trunkwell Project) Beech Hill. From Reading: M4 junction 11 follow Basingstoke sign approx. ¼m at roundabout turn L and follow Three Mile Cross-Spencers Wood. Centre of Spencers Wood look for Beech Hill Rd on R and follow into Beech Hill Village (centre) and follow signs. From Basingstoke follow A33 to Wellington roundabout turn L following Beech Hill signs. At village turn R. Located in grounds of Trunkwell House Hotel. Parking and toilets. Conducted tours. 3-acre Victorian walled garden on Berkshire-Hampshire borders. The garden is being developed for use by people with a wide range of disabilities who love gardening. The site is designed for teaching and therapy and incl organic propagation, in very attractive surroundings. Part dedicated to wildlife and conservation, butterfly garden, pond and bog garden, wild garden, etc. TEA. *Adm £1 Chd free. Suns May 8, Sept 4 (2-6)*

Waltham Place &# White Waltham. 3½m S of Maidenhead. Exit 8/9 on M4, then A423(M) or M40 exit 4 then A404 to A4 Maidenhead exit and follow signs to White Waltham. 40 acres woodland, lake and gardens with magnificent trees, daffodils, bluebells, rhododendrons; interesting long borders; walled garden; kitchen garden; glasshouses. Plants well labelled. Organic farm and gardens. Home-made cream TEAS, plants and dried flowers (May 15 & July 24 only). *Adm £2 Chd 50p (Share to Thames Valley Adventure Playground®). Suns May 15, July 24 (2-7) Wednesdays during April and September (2-5)*

Wasing Place &# (Lady Mount) Aldermaston, SE of Newbury. Turn S off A4 at Woolhampton; or 3m E take A340 to Aldermaston. ½m drive. Large garden; unusual shrubs and plants, rhododendrons; azaleas; lawns, walled and kitchen garden; greenhouses, herbaceous borders, magnificent cedars. C12 church. TEAS in aid of St Nicholas Church, Wasing. *Adm £1 Chd free. Suns May 22, July 10 (2-6)*

Welford Park &# (Mrs J L Puxley) 6m NW of Newbury on Lambourn Valley Rd. Entrance on Newbury/Lambourn Rd (fine gates with boot on top). Spacious grounds; spring flowers; walk by R. Lambourn. Queen Anne house (not open). TEA. *Adm £1 Chd free (Share to Welford Church©). Sun March 27 (2- 4.30)*

West Silchester Hall, nr Reading see Hampshire

West Woodhay House &# (J R Henderson Esq) 6m SW of Newbury. From Newbury take A343. At foot of hill turn R for East Woodhay and Ball Hill. 3½m turn L for West Woodhay. Go over Xrds in village, next fork R past Church. Gate on L. Parkland; large garden with bulbs, roses, shrubs, lake, woodland garden. Large walled kitchen garden, greenhouses. TEAS. *Combined adm £2 Chd free (Share to West Woodhay Church). Sun April 10 (2-6) with **Kirby House**. **West Woodhay House** only Adm £1.50 Chd free. Sun June 26 (2-6)*

Whiteknights &# (Mr & Mrs P Bradly) Finchampstead. Midway along Finchampstead Ridges on B3348 between Finchampstead War Memorial and Crowthorne Station. 2½ acres, lawns, Japanese water garden, dwarf conifers, interesting plantings, small vegetable garden. Cream TEAS in aid of Guide Dogs for the Blind. *Adm £1 Chd free. Sun May 15 (2-5.30)*

Woolley Park &# (Mr & Mrs Philip Wroughton) 5m S of Wantage on A338 turn L at sign to Woolley. Large park, fine trees and views. Two linked walled gardens beautifully planted. Teas close to Old Rectory, Farnborough. *Adm £1. Sun June 26 (2-6)*

Buckinghamshire

Hon County Organiser: Mrs H Beric Wright, Brudenell House, Quainton, nr Aylesbury, Bucks HP22 4AW

Assistant Hon County Organisers: Mrs D W Fraser, The Old Butcher's Arms, Dark Lane, Oving, Aylesbury HP22 4HP Tel 0296 641026
Mrs C S Sanderson, Wellfield House, Cuddington, Aylesbury HP18 OBB Tel 0844 291626

Hon County Treasurer: Dr H Beric Wright

DATES OF OPENING

By appointment
For telephone numbers and other details see garden descriptions. Private visits welcomed

Blossoms, nr Great Missenden
Brill Gardens, nr Thame
Old Farm
14 The Square
Tramway Farm
56 Windmill St
Campden Cottage, Chesham Bois
Charlton, Dorney Reach, nr Maidenhead
Dadbrook House, Cuddington Gardens
Dorneywood Garden, Burnham
(By written appt only)
Garden Cottage, Farnham Royal
Gracefield, Lacey Green
Great Barfield, High Wycombe
Hall Barn, Beaconsfield
(By written appt only)
The Manor Farm, Little Horwood, nr Winslow
The Manor House, Bledlow, nr Aylesbury
6 Oldfield Close, Little Chalfont
Pasture Farm, Longwick, nr Princes Risborough
Peppers, Great Missenden
Sheredon, Longwick, nr Princes Risborough
Sprindrift, Jordans, nr Beaconsfield
Springlea, Seymour Plain, Marlow
Tramway Farm, see Brill Gardens, nr Thame
Turn End, Haddenham
Walmerdene, Buckingham
The Wheatsheaf Inn, Weedon

February 20 Sunday
Great Barfield, High Wycombe
March 6 Sunday
Campden Cottage, Chesham Bois
March 13 Sunday
Springlea, Seymour, Marlow
April 3 Sunday
Overstroud Cottage, Gt Missenden
Turn End, Haddenham
April 4 Monday
Spindrift, Jordans, Beaconsfield
Turn End, Haddenham
April 6 Wednesday
Turn End, Haddenham
April 9 Saturday
Kincora, Beaconsfield
April 10 Sunday
Ascott, nr Leighton Buzzard
Campden Cottage, Chesham Bois

Kincora, Beaconsfield
The Old Vicarage, Padbury ‡
Oving Gardens, nr Aylesbury ‡
Quoitings, Marlow
April 13 Wednesday
Turn End, Haddenham
April 17 Sunday
Chicheley Hall, Newport Pagnell ‡
Newton Longville Gardens, Milton Keynes ‡
Springlea, Seymour, Marlow
April 20 Wednesday
Turn End, Haddenham
April 24 Sunday
Great Barfield, High Wycombe
Long Crendon Gardens, nr Thame
April 27 Wednesday
Turn End, Haddenham
May 1 Sunday
Garden Cottage, Farnham Royal
The Manor House, Bledlow, nr Aylesbury ‡
Nether Winchendon House, nr Aylesbury
6 Oldfield Close, Little Chalfont ‡‡
Overstroud Cottage, Gt Missenden ‡‡
Pasture Farm, Longwick, nr Princes Risborough ‡
Winslow Hall, nr Buckingham
May 2 Monday
Garden Cottage, Farnham Royal
May 8 Sunday
Campden Cottage, Chesham Bois ‡
Cliveden, Taplow
Overstroud Cottage, Gt Missenden ‡
Quainton Gardens, nr Aylesbury
Spindrift, Jordons, Beaconsfield
May 15 Sunday
Chalfont St Giles Gardens ‡
Peppers, Great Missenden ‡
Springlea, Seymour, Marlow
The White House, Denham Village
May 17 Tuesday
Stowe Landscape Garden, Stowe, nr Buckingham
May 22 Sunday
The Edge, Chalfont St Giles
Oving Gardens, nr Aylesbury
May 29 Sunday
Brill Gardens, nr Thame
Garden Cottage, Farnham Royal
May 30 Monday
Garden Cottage, Farnham Royal
Gracefield, Lacey Green
Newton Longville Gardens, Milton Keynes
June 1 Wednesday
Spindrift, Jordans, Beaconsfield
June 5 Sunday
Campden Cottage, Chesham Bois ‡

The Claydons, nr Winslow
Overstroud Cottage, Gt Missenden ‡
Springlea, Seymour, Marlow
Turn End, Haddenham
June 12 Sunday
Turn End, Haddenham ‡
Tythrop Park, Kingsey, nr Thame ‡
Weir Lodge, Chesham
Whitchurch Gardens, nr Aylesbury
June 18 Saturday
Favershams Meadow, Gerrards Cross
The Old Vicarage, Padbury ‡
Walmerdene, Buckingham ‡
June 19 Sunday
Chalfont St Giles Gardens ‡
Cuddington Gardens, nr Thame
Faversham Meadow, Gerrards Cross ‡
Gipsy House, Gt Missenden ‡
Hillesden House, nr Buckingham ‡‡
Little Linford Gardens, nr Newport Pagnell
The Manor House, Bledlow, nr Aylesbury
The Old Vicarage, Padbury ‡‡
Walmerdene, Buckingham ‡‡
June 22 Wednesday
Cuddington Gardens, nr Thame
June 26 Sunday
Brill Gardens, nr Thame ‡
Cheddington Gardens, nr Leighton Buzzard
Dinton Gardens, nr Aylesbury ‡‡
The Edge, Chalfont St Giles
Long Crendon Gardens, nr Thame ‡
The Manor House, Hambleden
Old Manor Farm, Cublington ‡‡‡
The Old Rectory, Cublington ‡‡‡
Pasture Farm, Longwick, nr Princes Risborough ‡‡
June 29 Wednesday
Old Manor Farm, Cublington
July 3 Sunday
Ascott, nr Leighton Buzzard
Great Barfield, High Wycombe
The Manor Farm, Little Horwood, nr Winslow
Overstroud Cottage, Gt Missenden
The Thatched Cottage, Ludgershall, nr Aylesbury
Watercroft, Penn
The White House, Denham Village
July 9 Saturday
Bucksbridge House, Wendover
Kincora, Beaconsfield
July 10 Sunday
Bucksbridge House, Wendover ‡

Chearsley Gardens, nr Thame ‡‡
Flint House, Penn Street Village,
   nr Amersham ‡‡‡
Kincora, Beaconsfield ‡‡‡
Nether Winchendon House,
   nr Aylesbury ‡‡
Newton Longville Gardens,
   Milton Keynes
Prestwood Gardens,
   nr Gt Missenden ‡
Watercroft, Penn ‡‡‡

July 17 Sunday
Campden Cottage, Chesham Bois
Chilton Gardens, nr Thame ‡
Hughenden Manor, High Wycombe
Sheredon, Longwick

Springlea, Seymour, Marlow
The Thatched Cottage,
   Ludgershall, nr Aylesbury ‡

July 24 Sunday
14 Well Street, Buckingham

August 7 Sunday
Campden Cottage, Chesham Bois

August 21 Sunday
Peppers, Great Missenden

August 28 Sunday
Heron Path House, Wendover

August 29 Monday
Heron Path House, Wendover
Spindrift, Jordans, Beaconsfield

September 4 Sunday
Campden Cottage, Chesham Bois ‡

Cliveden, Taplow
Overstroud Cottage, Gt
   Missenden ‡
Quoitings, Marlow

September 11 Sunday
Pasture Farm, Longwick, nr
   Princes Risborough
Springlea, Seymour, Marlow

September 18 Sunday
Great Barfield, High Wycombe
Turn End, Haddenham

September 25 Sunday
West Wycombe Park

October 2 Sunday
Campden Cottage, Chesham
   Bois

DESCRIPTIONS OF GARDENS

Ascott &&& (Sir Evelyn and Lady de Rothschild; The National Trust) Wing, 2m SW of Leighton Buzzard, 8m NE of Aylesbury via A418. Bus: United Counties 141 Aylesbury-Leighton Buzzard. Beautiful surroundings and layout. Garden part formal, part natural; many specimen trees, shrubs, naturalised bulbs, sunken garden; lily pond. Tea Mentmore Village. *Adm £3 Chd £1.50 Under 5 free. Suns April 10, July 3 (2-6). Last adm 5pm*

Blossoms &&& (Dr & Mrs Frank Hytten) Cobblers Hill, 2½m NW of Great Missenden by Rignall Road (signed to Butlers Cross) to King's Lane (1½m) then to top of Cobblers Hill, R at yellow stone marker and in 50yds R at stone marked Blossoms. [Map ref SP874034]. 4-acre garden begun as hill-top fields in 1923, plus 1-acre beechwood. Lawns, trees, old apple orchard, small lake, water gardens, woodland, troughs, scree garden and several patios. Large areas of bluebells, wild daffodils, fritillaria and other spring bulbs. Flowering cherries and many interesting trees incl small collections of acer, eucalyptus and salix; foliage effects throughout the year. TEAS. *Adm £1.50. Private visits only, please* **Tel 0494 863140**

Brill Gardens & 7m N of Thame. Turn off B4011, Thame-Bicester or turn off A41 at Kingswood; both signed to Brill. C17 windmill open 2.30-5.30. Teas in village hall in aid of Brill WI. Plant & craft stalls at Old Vicarage. *Combined adm £2 Chd free*
Sun May 29 (2-6)
   Commoners & (Mr & Mrs R Wickenden) Tram Hill. Under ¼-acre, low walled old cottage garden; alpines, shrubs, herbaceous, many plants from seed and cuttings. Views in all directions
   Leap Hill && (Mr & Mrs R Morris-Adams) Thame Rd. 2 acres, roses, shrubs, herbaceous and spring bulbs; pond, new bog area & rockery; vegetable garden and new woodland area. Extensive views towards Chilterns. Sculptures by Fred Close
   The Old Vicarage &&& (Mr & Mrs P Toynbee) The Square. ¾-acre (partly walled) garden with small area of interest in sun and shade. Arches and ornamental features of special appeal to young children. Labour and money saving tips as seen on TV

56 Windmill Street && (Mr & Mrs C D Elliott) Pocket handkerchief walled clay garden featuring imaginative use of space; mixed borders in raised beds incl interesting foliage, uncommon plants; pergola, patio, many containers. Featured in Gardeners' World book. *Private visits welcome by appointment only April - Sept, please* **Tel 0844 237407**
Sun June 26 (2-6)
   Old Farm & (Dr & Mrs Raymond Brown) The Common. ½-acre established garden around 3 terraces of old shrub roses; secluded position with high open views over Otmoor; kitchen garden; soft fruit, mature and younger trees, interesting shrubs, small pond; conservatory added to C17 stone and brick cottage (not open). *Private visits welcome, please* **Tel 0844 238232**
   The Old Vicarage (description with May opening)
   14 The Square && (Mrs Audrey Dyer) Tiny paved garden with handmade pots. culinary and fragrant herbs and plants to attract wildlife. *Private visits welcome April - Sept, please* **Tel 0844 237148**
   ¶**1 Temple Farm** & (Mr & Mrs C Mockett) Temple St. New village garden established in 1989 on N facing slope designed to provide yr-round interest with minimum maintenance; spectacular views
   56 Windmill Street (description with May opening)
By appointment only April - Sept
   ¶**Tramway Farm** && (Mr & Mrs K Richardson) Ludgershall Rd. 1-acre clay garden in hidden valley along the banks of a stream with wildlife pond; herbaceous borders with long season of interest, vegetable plot and mature spinney with spring bulbs. *Adm £1. Private visits welcome April - Sept, please* **Tel 0844 238249**

Bucksbridge House &&& (Mr & Mrs J Nicholson) Heron Path, Wendover. ½m S of Wendover. Chapel Lane is 2nd turn on L off A413 towards Amersham. House is on L at bottom of lane. Georgian house with established 2-acre garden; large herbaceous border, unusual shrubs, roses, laburnum arches, an ornamental vegetable garden and 2 well stocked greenhouses. Also available pots and sculptures by Frances Levy. TEAS. *Adm £1.50 Chd free. Sat, Sun July 9, 10 (2-6)*

Campden Cottage ⚘❀ (Mrs P Liechti) 51 Clifton Rd, Chesham Bois, N of Amersham. From Amersham-on-the-Hill take A416; after 1m turn R (E) at Catholic Church. From Chesham take A416; and first turning L after beech woods. ½-acre derelict garden, restored by owner since 1971; plantsman's garden of yr-round interest; fine collection of unusual and rare plants. Hellebores in March. Featured on TV 'Gardeners' World' and in 'The New Englishwoman's Garden' 1987 and the 'Good Gardens Guide 1994'. Please use car park signed on main rd. Teas Old Amersham. No push chairs. *Adm £1 Chd free. Suns March 6, April 10, May 8, June 5, July 17, Aug 7, Sept 4, Oct 2, (2-6). Also by appt for parties with TEAS. No coaches. Please* **Tel 0494 726818**. *First opening in 1995 Sun March 5, subject to unforeseen events*

Chalfont St Giles Gardens Off A413. TEAS. *Combined adm £2 for 3 gardens or £1 per garden Chd free. Suns May 15, June 19 (2-6)*
 Concordia ⚘ (Mr & Mrs D E Cobb) 76 Deanway, Chalfont St Giles. Parking in Deanway. A small challenging garden on a difficult sloping site. Herbaceous and shrub borders; rock garden; fruit trees; collection of unusual orchids
 Halfpenny Furze ♿⚘❀ (Mr & Mrs R Sadler) Mill Lane, Chalfont St Giles. From London take A413 signed Amersham. Mill Lane is ¼m past mini roundabouts at Chalfont St Giles. Limited parking in Mill Lane, 1-acre plantsman's garden on clay: part woodland (rhododendrons, azaleas, acers, magnolias, cercis, cercidiphyllum) part formal (catalpa, cornus, clerodendrum unusual shrubs, roses and mixed borders). Plants for sale if available. TEAS
 ¶North Down ⚘ (Mr & Mrs J Saunders) From Halfpenny Furze, short uphill walk L into Dodds Lane. Garden is 250yds on R. Limited parking in Dodds Lane. Approx ¾-acre garden on N facing slope; stony, free-draining soil on gravel and flint. Interest throughout yr, some unusual plants, vistas. Mixed beds, shrubs, with rhododendrons, azaleas, acers; spring bulbs. Small bog garden; climbers; collection of sempervivums; patio with water feature

Charlton ❀ (Mrs L Rutterford) 5 Harcourt Rd, Dorney Reach, nr Maidenhead. Turn S off A4 approx 3m E of Maidenhead into Marsh Lane (signposted Dorney Reach) continue 1m; Harcourt Road is 2nd on R over motorway bridge. Approx ¾-acre garden on light free draining soil organically cultivated and designed to provide interest throughout the yr. Mixed borders with variety of shrubs, hardy perennials, climbers and annuals; small pond, vegetables, fruit and greenhouse. (Suitable for wheelchairs if dry). TEA. *Adm £1. Private visits only welcome all year, please* **Tel 0628 24325**

¶Chearsley Gardens 4m NE Thame turn E off B4011 at Long Crendon, or 7m SW of Aylesbury turn W off A418. Gardens and parking are signposted in village. Teas in Village Hall. *Combined adm £2 Chd free. Sun July 10 (2-6)*

┌───┐
Regular Openers. Too many days to include in diary. Usually there is a wide range of plants giving year-round interest. See head of county section for the name and garden description for times etc.
└───┘

¶The Cottage ⚘❀ (Mr & Mrs Tony Hall) Very small organic cottage garden kept in order with use of railway sleepers; unusual vegetables; wildlife pond; small but interesting herbaceous beds and alpines
¶Manor Farm ♿⚘ (Mr & Mrs Michael Heybrook) 1¼-acre walled garden adjoining old farmhouse and fruit farm. Unusual plants in mixed shrub and herbaceous borders; old roses, clematis and other climbers. Tranquil pond area, mature trees
¶4 Old Plough Close ⚘ (Mr & Mrs John Hillier) ¼-acre garden designed and planted by owners on 45 degrees slope. Terraces, rockeries and trellises; small pond; unusual conifers and ferns to create all yr interest. Small collection of bonsai

Cheddington Gardens 11m E of Aylesbury; turn off B489 at Pitstone. 7m S of Leighton Buzzard; turn off B488 at Cheddington Station. TEAS on the green. *Combined adm £2 Chd free (Share to Methodist Chapel and St Giles Church, Cheddington®). Sun June 26 (2-6)*
 Chasea (Mr & Mrs A G Seabrook) Small garden on clay; assorted tubs and baskets round pool on patio; shrubs and conifers; perennials and bedding
 Cheddington Manor ⚘ (Mr & Mrs H Hart) 3½-acres; small lake and moat in informal setting, roses, herbaceous border, and interesting mature trees
 ¶34 Gooseacre ⚘ (Mrs Barbara Smith) A well-designed partly paved small garden with magnificent views over the Chilterns. Delightful water feature, patio, mixed shrubs and climbers for all yr interest
 The Old Reading Room ♿⚘ (Mr & Mrs W P Connolley) ⅓-acre cottage garden; shrubs, perennials, bedding and small fern collection; trees incl ginkgo biloba
 Rose Cottage ♿⚘❀ (Mr & Mrs D G Jones) ¼-acre cottage garden planted for all year interest with accent on colour; old roses; small scree area with unusual plants and conservatory
 21 Station Road ♿ (Mr & Mrs P Jay) ½-acre informal garden with wildflower conservation area; herbaceous and shrub borders; herbs and kitchen garden
 Woodstock Cottage ⚘ (Mr & Mrs D Bradford) 42 High Street. Delightful cottage garden with rear courtyard and patio

Chicheley Hall ♿⚘ (The Trustees of the Hon Nicholas Beatty & Mrs John Nutting) Chicheley, on A422 between Bedford and Newport Pagnell; E of Newport Pagnell and 3m from junction 14 of M1. Georgian House (open) set in spacious lawns, herbaceous borders, roses on mellowed brick walls; woodland planted with bulbs; formal lake attributed to London & Wise 1709 after Hampton Court. TEAS. *Adm £1.50 Chd 50p.* ▲*Sun April 17 (2.30-5)*

Chilton Gardens 3m N of Thame. In Long Crendon turn off B4011 follow signs to Chilton; village has C18 mansion house C12-C16 church, parking available. TEAS in aid of church. *Combined adm £1.50 Chd free. Sun July 17 (2-6)*
 The Old School House ♿⚘ (Mr & Mrs John Rolfe) Working cottage garden; newly built pond; extensive views; new fruit garden
 The Old Vicarage ♿❀ (Mr & Mrs G Rosenthal) Approx ½-acre walled garden; mature trees, mixed borders, vegetables and plants for shady areas

Signpost Cottage &✿ (Mr & Mrs G Baker) Approx ⅔-acre colourful village garden reclaimed form meadowland 5 yrs ago behind C17 thatched cottage (not open); assorted bright containers on terrace

The Claydons ✿ 2½m SW of Winslow. Follow signs to Claydons. Mediaeval church, car parking. Teas in village hall in aid of WI. *Combined adm £1.50 Chd 20p. Sun June 5 (2-6)*

¶**Ashton** (Mr & Mrs G Wylie) Botyl Rd, Botolph Claydon. ⅓-acre plot on clay with superb views on site of former barnyard. Mixed beds of shrubs and herbaceous plants

Beech House (Mr & Mrs D Dow) Church Way, E Claydon. ¼-acre walled garden, derelict in 1977; mixed borders, shrubs, flowers; paved features, small alpine beds

¶**1 Emerald Close** (Mr & Mrs L B Woodhouse) E Claydon. Small garden with collection of deciduous and coniferous Bonsai

Pond Cottage & (Mr & Mrs Brian Kay) Botolph Claydon. ¼-acre garden framed by C17 cottage and C19 barn, developed on clay since 1975. Bulbs, shrubs, foliage and fruit trees; mixed borders, peat bed, troughs

The Pump House (Mr & Mrs P M Piddington) St. Mary's Rd, E Claydon. ¾-acre, trees, shrubs, borders, vegetable and herb garden, fish pools

Cliveden &✿❀ (The National Trust) 2m N of Taplow. A number of separate gardens within extensive grounds, first laid out in the C18 incl water garden, rose garden; herbaceous borders; woodland walks and views of the Thames. Suitable for wheelchairs only in part. TEAS. *Adm grounds only £3.80 Chd £1.90. Suns May 8; Sept 4 (11-6)*

Cuddington Gardens 3½m NE Thame or 5m SW Aylesbury off A418. Regional winners of Britain in Bloom 1993. Gardens signed in village. TEAS in aid of Darby & Joan and Village Hall Restoration Fund. Parking behind Dadbrook House. *Combined adm £2 Acc chd free. Sun, Wed June 19, 22 (2-6)*

Dadbrook House &✿❀ (Mr & Mrs G Kingsbury) 3-acre garden in process of being recreated by garden designer owner. Formal rose parterre, established knot garden lead to two newly planted herbaceous borders which frame vista over ha·ha; mown paths lead through mature trees to a small lake, focus of wildlife garden; behind house is a walled decorative herb and vegetable garden with pleached hornbeam and box edging. Stall in aid of Anti-M418 Action Group. *Private visits welcome May to July, please* **Tel 0844 290129**

1 Great Stone Cottages ✿ (Mr & Mrs P Wenham) Entry to garden is from the drive in Holly Tree Lane. Long, narrow cottage garden divided into several sections, each with its own character. They contain ponds and fountains with patio, shrub, alpine, herb, heather and vegetable areas

The Old Post & (Mr & Mrs Robert Fleming) ½-acre family garden planted for yr-round interest. Wisteria colonnade, wychert wall, shrub, herbaceous and mixed borders; shady beds and vegetables

The Platt & (The Misses Corby) Mixed herbaceous and annual border; roses, soft fruits; paved area with varieties of thyme

Tibby's Cottage & (Mrs Rosalind Squires) Cottage garden surrounding 400-yr-old picturesque thatched cottage. Natural stream running through to pool and bog garden; lovely views to Nether Winchendon

Tyringham Hall & (Mr & Mrs Ray Scott) Water and bog garden, patios and lawns surround mediaeval house. Dell with well and waterfall between Tyringham Hall and **Tibby's Cottage**

¶**Dinton Gardens** 4m SW Aylesbury or 4m NE Thame. Gardens signed in village. Teas in Village Hall in aid of Dubrovnik Appeal for Children. Parking at Perryfield and Haddenham Low House. *Combined adm £2 Acc chd free. Sun June 26 (2-6)*

¶**Appletree Cottage** ✿ (Mr & Mrs J K Mitchell) High St. A village centre garden begun from scratch in 1985. A blend of trees, shrubs, conifers and flowers on several levels designed to give privacy on an exposed site and good foliage colour whilst complementing neighbouring gardens

¶**Haddenham Low House** &✿❀ (Mr & Mrs P J Edwards) Oxford Rd. On A418 next to 'Shell' garage, this ½-acre garden has been created from field and farmyard since 1989. Many trees planted to exclude noise from increased traffic. 2 formal herbaceous beds; special interest, medicinal plants

¶**Hermits Cottage** &✿❀ (Mr & Mrs M Usherwood) Westlington. ¾-acre surrounding old thatched cottage at Westlington end of village. Front open with shrubs and trees; rear partially wychert-walled incl kitchen garden; mixed borders with open and shaded areas at rear adjacent to water features

¶**9 New Road** &✿ (Mr & Mrs B K J Tibbatts) Long, narrow garden with colourful bedding, roses and unusual varieties of fuchsia; good use of small space for vegetables

¶**Orchard Cottage** ✿ (Mr & Mrs H C Bingham) High St. 10-yr-old garden of ⅓-acre designed for minimum maintenance and all yr colour, variety and interest; sculpted lawns, hidden vistas, pergola and patios; shrubberies, ornamental and fruit trees, roses, mixed borders, plants for perfume ground cover and particularly to attract butterflies

¶**Perryfield** &✿ (Mr & Mrs J Gray) New Rd. ⅓-acre with mature trees and planted for colour contrast; small water garden; island beds, mainly herbaceous and shrubs; some bedding. Footpath from car park to Hermits Cottage

¶**Stonesfield** &✿❀ (Mr & Mrs W Turner) High St. Old-fashioned cottage garden with flowers, herbaceous borders and small pond; vegetable garden

Dorneywood Garden &✿❀ (The National Trust) Dorneywood Rd, Burnham. From Burnham village take Dropmore Rd, and at end of 30mph limit take R fork into Dorneywood Rd. Dorneywood is 1m on R. From M40 junction 2, take A355 to Slough then 1st R to Burnham, 2m then 2nd L after Jolly Woodman signed Dorneywood Rd. Dorneywood is about 1m on L. 6-acre country garden with shrubs, rose garden, mixed borders and dell. TEAS. *Adm £2.50 Chd free. Garden open by written appt only on Weds July 6, 13, Sats Aug 6, 13 (2-6). Apply to the Secretary, Dorneywood Trust, Dorneywood, Burnham, Bucks SL1 8PY*

The Edge ✿❀ (Mr & Mrs D Glen) London Rd, Chalfont St Giles. Garden is ¼m towards Chalfont St Peter from The Pheasant Xrds on A413 nr Kings Rd. Georgian cottage with landscaped garden of ¾ acre, created by owners. Partially enclosed with walls and yew hedges, interesting shrubs incl magnolias, wisterias, climbing and shrub roses. TEAS. *Adm £1 Chd free. Suns May 22, June 26 (2-6)*

Faversfams Meadow ♿✿ (Mr & Mrs H W Try) 1½m W of Gerrards Cross on A40. Turn N into Mumfords Lane opp lay-by with BT box. Garden ¼m on R. 1½-acre garden started in 1989. Mixed herbaceous, knot, parterre and rose gardens; separate blue and white garden with statue and gazebo; brick paved vegetable garden; views to Bulstrode Park. TEAS in aid of the Red Cross and The Wexham Gastrointestinal Trust. *Adm £1.50 Chd free. Sat, Sun June 18, 19 (2-6)*

Flint House ♿✿❀ (Mr & Mrs David White) Penn Street Village, 2m SW of Amersham. Turn S off A 404 into village opp church (open). Parking in church car park. 1½-acre garden surrounding C19 flint vicarage; herbaceous borders, shrubs and climbing roses, raised alpine bed, herb garden; urns and rose 'hoops' beside tennis court. Geraniums in garden room. TEA. *Adm £1 Chd 20p. Sun July 10 (2-6)*

Garden Cottage ♿❀ (Mrs Pauline Sheppey) Farnham Royal. 3m NW of Slough; on A355 turn W at Farnham Royal along Farnham Lane towards Burnham; then 2nd R and 1st L into East Burnham Lane. Informal 1-acre country garden. Wide range of plants particularly herbaceous. Yr-round colour, form and foliage. Yew hedges, mixed borders, raised beds, heather garden & ponds. Nursery adjoining. Cream TEAS by Thames Valley Hospice. Plants and local produce for sale. *Adm £1 Chd free. Suns, Mons May 1, 2; 29, 30 (11-5). Private group visits welcome all year, please* Tel 0753 642243

Gipsy House ♿✿❀ (Mrs F Dahl) Gt Missenden. A413 to Gt Missenden. From High St turn into Whitefield Lane, continue under railway bridge. Large Georgian house on R with family additions. York stone terrace, pleached lime walk to writing hut; shrubs, roses, herbs, small walled vegetable garden, orchard and gipsy caravan for children. Limited access for wheelchairs. Teas locally. *Adm £1.20 Chd 30p (Share to Roald Dahl Foundation®). Sun June 19 (2-5.30)*

Gracefield ♿❀ (Mr & Mrs B Wicks) Lacey Green. Take A4010 High Wycombe to Aylesbury Rd. Turn R by Red Lion at Bradenham, up hill to Walters Ash; L at T-junction for Lacey Green. Brick and flint house on main rd beyond church facing Kiln Lane. 1½-acre mature garden; many unusual plants, trees, mostly labelled; orchard, soft fruit, shrub borders, rockery; plants for shade, sink gardens. Two ponds. PLOUGHMAN'S LUNCHES, TEAS and plants in aid of local Macmillan Nurses Group. *Adm £1.50 Chd free. Bank Hol Mon May 30 (11.30-5). Parties by written appt May to Sept*

Great Barfield ♿✿❀ (Richard Nutt Esq) Bradenham, A4010 4m NW of High Wycombe 4m S of Princes Risborough. At Red Lion turn into village and turn R. Park on green. Walk down No Through Road. 1½-acre garden,

designed for views, lay out, contrast and colour, as background for unusual plants. Michael Gibson in 'The Rose Gardens of England' says that it is a plantsman's garden in the best possible sense of the term and not to be missed to see how all plants should be grown to the best advantage. Feb now not only famous for snowdrops and hellebores but willows and a variety of bulbs; drifts of crocus; May unique collections of Pulmonarias and Bergenias; also red Trilliums now naturalised. July old-fashioned and climbing roses, Lilies including naturalised. L. martagon. Sept considerable collection of colchicum, autumn colour and Sorbus berries. NCCPG national collection of leucojum (spring & late April); celandine (early May); iris unguicularis. Sales of unusual plants. TEAS. *Adm £1 Chd under 16 free (Share to Friends of St Botolphs Church®). Suns Feb 20 (2-5), April 24 (2-6), July 3 (2-6), Sept 18 (2-5). Private visits and parties welcome, please* Tel 0494 563741. *First opening in 1995 Sun Feb 19 (2-5), subject to unforeseen events*

Hall Barn ✿ (The Dowager Lady Burnham) Lodge gate 300yds S of Beaconsfield Church in town centre. One of the original gardens opening in 1927 under the National Gardens Scheme, still owned by the Burnham family. A unique landscaped garden of great historical interest, laid out in the 1680's. Vast 300-yr-old curving yew hedge. Extensive replanting in progress after severe gale damage. Formal lake. Long avenues through the Grove, each terminating in a temple, classical ornament or statue. Obelisk with fine carvings in memory of Edmund Waller's grandson who completed the garden about 1730. *Garden open* by written appointment only. *Applications to The Dowager Lady Burnham, Hall Barn, Beaconsfield, Buckinghamshire HP9 2SG*

Heron Path House ♿✿❀ (Mr & Mrs Bryan C Smith) Chapel Lane. ½m S of Wendover off A413. Chapel Lane 2nd turn on L; house at bottom. 2½-acre garden featuring immaculate lawns, brilliant bedding displays and hanging baskets of fuchsias, geraniums etc; shrub borders, rockery, pond and greenhouse. TEAS. *Adm £1.50 Chd 50p (Share to The Wendover Society© and RUKBA®). Sun, Mon Aug 28, 29 (2-6)*

Hillesden House ♿✿❀ (Mr & Mrs R M Faccenda) Hillesden, 3m S of Buckingham via Gawcott. Follow Hillesden signs after Gawcott on Calvert Rd. 6 acres developed since 1978 from virgin land on site of C16 Manor House by superb Perpendicular Church 'Cathedral in the Fields'; large lawns, shrubberies; rose, alpine and foliage gardens; interesting clipped hedges; conservatory; large lakes and deer park; commanding views over countryside. TEAS. *Adm £1.50 Chd under 12 free (Share to Hillesden Church®). Sun June 19 (2-6)*

Hughenden Manor ♿✿❀ (The National Trust) 1½m N of High Wycombe on W side of Great Missenden Rd A4128; [Grid ref: SU866955 on OS sheet 165]. 5 acres with lawns, terraced garden, herbaceous border, formal annual bedding, orchard and woodland walks. The Trust has undertaken restoration work in accordance with photographs taken at the time of Disraeli's death. Teas available from Hughenden Church House. *Adm House & Garden £3.50 Chd £1.75. Sun July 17 (12-6). Last adm 5.30*

Kincora ბ⚹❀ (Mr & Mrs J A K Leslie) 54 Ledborough Lane. Take M40 or A40 to Beaconsfield, then Amersham Rd (A355) 1m, turn L at sign for New Town and Model Village. Parking next turning L after 14th lamppost. 2-acre garden; borders, mixed bedding, wild area and containers surrounding swimming pool. TEAS. *Adm £1 Chd free (Share to Iaian Rennie Hospice®). Sats, Suns April 9, 10; July 9, 10 (2-6)*

Little Linford Gardens ბ⚹❀ 2m N of Newport Pagnell between Gayhurst & Haversham overlooking Great Ouse valley. Flower display in beautiful C13/14 village church. TEAS in aid of Little Linford Church. *Combined adm £1.50 Chd free (Share to Little Linford Church). Sun June 19 (2-6)*

    Elmwood House (Mr & Mrs Peter Tinworth) 1¾-acre country garden, sloping site on 3 levels. Collection of old roses; mature trees; shrubs; flower borders; orchard and vegetable garden; conservatory and small pond

    Hall Farm (Hon Richard & Mrs Godber) 3-acre hilltop farmhouse garden created over last 14 yrs. Mixed borders; trees and shrubs. Walled garden with converted barn and conservatory; secluded swimming pool with sun loving plants. Also kitchen garden, herbs; orchard and water garden

Long Crendon Gardens 2m N of Thame B4011 to Bicester. TEAS. *Combined adm £2 Chd free (Share to Long Crendon Charity®)*
Sun April 24 (2-6)

    Manor House ბ❀ (Sir William & Lady Shelton) turn R by church; house through wrought iron gates. 6-acres; lawns sweep down to 2 ornamental lakes; each with small island, willow walk along lower lake with over 20 varieties of willow; fine views towards Chilterns. House (not open) 1675. TEAS

    The Old Crown ❀ (Mr & Mrs R H Bradbury) 100yds past Chandos Inn. 1 acre on steep SW slope. Old-fashioned and other roses and climbers. Flowering shrubs, herbaceous plants. Spring bulbs, assorted colourful containers in summer; small vegetable patch

    Old Post House ❀ (Mr & Mrs Nigel Viney) In the picturesque High St at corner of Burts Lane. Attractive cottage garden. Interesting spring & summer shrubs, and planting. Small produce stall

    Springfield Cottage ბ❀ (Mrs Elizabeth Dorling) 6 Burts Lane. ⅓-acre planted for all yr colour and easy maintenance. Many flowering shrubs, spring bulbs, primroses, herbaceous borders
Sun June 26 (2-6)

    Barrys Close ბ (Mr & Mrs Richard Salmon) Lower End. 2 acre, interesting collection of trees and shrubs; herbaceous border. Spring-fed pools and water garden. Good views. TEAS

    Croft House ბ⚹ (Cdr & Mrs Peter Everett) Thame Rd. In square, white wrought iron railings. ½-acre walled garden; plants and shrubs of botanical interest especially to flower arrangers. TEAS

    8 Ketchmere Close ბ⚹❀ (Mr & Mrs A Heley) 1991, 1992 & 1993 award winner incl Booker Garden Centre Competition for the best kept garden under 100ft in Buckinghamshire. Colourful split level garden with extensive views. Wide range of shrubs, conifers, rockery and water feature

    The Old Crown ❀ (Mr & Mrs R H Bradbury) Description with April opening

Windacre ბ⚹❀ (Mr & Mrs K Urch) 62 Chilton Rd, next to Primary School. 1-acre; roses, interesting shrubs, herbaceous plants, orchard, main features sunken lawns, conifers and trees. Cream TEAS

The Manor Farm ბ⚹❀ (Mr & Mrs Peter Thorogood) Little Horwood sign-posted 2m NE Winslow off A413. 5m E Buckingham and 5m W Bletchley turning S off A421. Hilltop farmhouse garden on acid clay, laid out and re-planted 1986. Wide range of alpines and plantsman's plants for yr-round interest in colour, form and foliage; good roses, 100' hosta border, herbaceous, wild flower meadow, damp garden, lovely views. Cream TEAS and stalls. *Adm £1.50 Chd free (Share to National Lifeboat Institute®). Sun July 3 (2-6). Private visits welcome April to Sept, please* **Tel 029671 4758**

The Manor House, Bledlow ბ⚹ (The Lord & Lady Carrington) ½m off B4009 in middle of Bledlow village. Station: Princes Risborough, 2½m. Paved garden, parterres, shrub borders, old roses and walled kitchen garden. House (not open) C17 & C18. Water and species garden with paths, bridges and walkways, fed by 14 chalk springs. Also a new 2-acre garden with sculptures and landscaped planting. Partly suitable wheelchairs. TEA May, TEAS June only. *Adm £2 Chd free. Suns May 1, June 19 (2-6); also private visits welcome May to Sept (2-4.30)*

The Manor House, Hambleden ⚹ (Maria Carmela, Viscountess Hambleden) Hambleden. NE of Henley-on-Thames, 1m N of A4155. Conservatory; shrubs and old-fashioned rose garden. Teas at Hambleden Church. *Adm £1.50 Chd 20p. Sun June 26 (2-6)*

Nether Winchendon House ბ⚹ (Mr & Mrs R Spencer Bernard) Nether Winchendon, 5m SW of Aylesbury; 7m from Thame. Picturesque village, beautiful church. 5 acres; fine trees, variety of hedges; naturalised spring bulbs; shrubs; herbaceous borders. Tudor manor house (not open) home of Sir Francis Bernard, last British Governor of Massachusetts. TEA weather permitting. *Adm £1.30 Chd under 15 free.* ▲*Suns May 1, July 10 (2-5.30)*

Newton Longville Gardens ბ⚹❀ 1½m SW Bletchley off A421 Buckingham-Bletchley (Milton Keynes). TEAS and plants April and May. *Combined adm £1.50 Chd free*
Sun April 17 (2-6)

    ¶**Bucca's Ash** ბ⚹ (Mr & Mrs A Southard) 66 Westbrook End. 1-hectare garden, ⅕ lawns with flowering shrubs and herbaceous plants around house; remainder being long grass, wild flowers and hedgerows with mown paths leading to spiral viewing mound. 10-yr-old garden (& house) has been carefully planted to give maximum shelter and sustenance to wild creatures, birds, butterflies and fish. 50 species of birds have been seen in the garden since 1983, with 25 species of butterflies and dragonflies; 3 ponds with distinct character and species of fish, frogs, toads and newts

---

By Appointment Gardens. Avoid the crowds. Good chance of a tour by owner. See garden description for telephone number.

11a Drayton Road & (Mr & Mrs A Lay) ½-acre long narrow rear garden. Interesting lay-out. Herbaceous and shrub borders open into fruit and vegetable areas

69 Drayton Road (Mr & Mrs O Schneidau) Beautifully landscaped cottage garden with many interesting features. A large pond; shrubs, annuals and herbaceous perennials

The Old Rectory & (Mr & Mrs J Clarke) Garden of approx ½ acre created over last 11 yrs surrounding C18 house. Mature tulip tree supporting kiftsgate rose thought to be planted to commemorate the Battle of Waterloo. Shrub and herbaceous borders, series of small ponds leading to larger lily pond

Mon May 30 (2-6)

¶**5 Lilac Close** &✿❀ (Mr & Mrs R Robinson) Small to medium sized garden; mixed borders, lawn, shrubs, plants, bulbs in season

The Old Rectory (description with April opening)

¶**4 Stoke Road** &✿ (Mr & Mrs P McClaskey) Medium sized garden; lawns and mixed borders; large pond with bridge, small ornamental pond

Sun July 10 (2-6)

Flower and country craft festival in St Faith's Church. Craft stalls in village hall. *Combined adm £2 Chd free (Share to St Faith's Church®)*

11a Drayton Road (description with April opening)
69 Drayton Road (description with April opening)
¶**5 Lilac Close** (description with May opening)
The Old Rectory (description with April opening)
3 School Drive (Mr & Mrs Hand) Patio with water feature and steps leading to small garden and attractively shaped lawn with surrounding borders. Pergola with climbers; plants in containers. Winner of Best Kept part of Garden (Village) competition 1992
¶**4 Stoke Road** (description with May opening)

¶**6 Oldfield Close** ✿❀ (Mr & Mrs Jolyon Lea) Little Chalfont. 3m E of Amersham. Take A404 E through Little Chalfont, turn 1st R after railway bridge, then R again into Oakington Ave. From M25 junction 18 take A404 to Amersham. In 2m turn L at Xrds (Lodge Lane & Church Grove) then bear R into Oakington Ave. Plantsman's ⅙-acre garden of borders, peat beds, rock plants, troughs and small alpine house. Over 2,000 species and varieties of rare and unusual plants incl cassiopes, daphnes, fritillaries, alpines and bulbs. Plant stall in aid of Bethany Leprosy Village, in India. *Adm £1 Chd free. Sun May 1 (2-5). Private visits welcome all yr, please* Tel 0494 762384

¶**Old Manor Farm** &✿❀ (Mr & Mrs N R Wilson) Cublington. From Aylesbury take Buckingham Rd A413. At Whitchurch (4m) turn R to Cublington. At X-rds turn L. In 50yds turn R down Reads Lane, house is 100yds on R. Large garden in process of being redesigned; rose and 'yellow' gardens, herbaceous borders; swimming pool with collection of planted tubs; ha ha and walled vegetable garden. TEAS. *Adm £1.50 Chd free. Sun, Wed June 26, 29 (2-5)*

The Old Rectory, Cublington &❀ (Mr & Mrs J Naylor) 7m SW of Leighton Buzzard. From Aylesbury via A418 towards Leighton Buzzard; after 4½m turn L (W) at Xrds. Follow signs to Aston Abbots, then Cublington. 2-acre country garden with herbaceous border, rosebeds, shrubs and mature trees; vegetables; ponds, climbing plants. TEAS. *Adm £1.50 Chd free. Sun June 26 (2-5)*

The Old Vicarage, Padbury &✿❀ (Mr & Mrs H Morley-Fletcher) Padbury 2m S of Buckingham on A413 follow signs in village. 2½ acres on 3 levels; flowering shrubs and trees; rose garden, new parterre. Display collection of hebes; pond and sunken garden. Fine views. TEAS. *Adm £1.50 Chd free (Share to League of Friends of Buckingham Hospital®). Sun April 10 (2-5), Sat, Sun June 18, 19 (2-6). Open with* **Walmerdene**, *Buckingham 2m in June only*

Overstroud Cottage ✿❀ (Mr & Mrs J Brooke) The Dell, Frith Hill. Amersham 6m Aylesbury 10m. Turn E off A413 at Gt Missenden onto B485 Frith Hill to Chesham. White Gothic cottage set back in layby 100yds up hill on L. Parking on R at Parish Church. Cottage originally C16 hospital for Missenden Abbey. 1-acre garden on two levels carved from chalk quarry. Winter/spring garden with hellebores, bulbs and winter flowering shrubs; borders of different colour schemes; collection of old-fashioned and species roses and traditional cottage plants; herb and sink gardens. Not suitable for children or push chairs. Teas at Parish Church. *Adm £1 Chd 50p (Share to The Ralph Sutcliffe Fund for Meningitis Research®). Suns April 3, May 1, 8, June 5, July 3, Sept 4 (2-6)*

Oving Gardens 5m NW of Aylesbury signposted off A413 at Whitchurch. Also signposted 1m E of Waddesdon off A41. C13 church open. village stalls, pets corner and local exhibition (May only), garden pots by Julie Marr. Disabled parking in centre of village. *Combined adm £2 Chd free*

Sun April 10 (2-6)

Manor Close ✿ (Mr & Mrs R J Hawkins) Manor Rd. Mature, established garden of 1½ acres herbaceous borders; brick pathways, many spring bulbs, spectacular views over countryside

The Old Butchers Arms ✿❀ (Mr & Mrs Denys Fraser) ¼-acre sloping chalk garden featured in Gardener's World magazine. Hellebores, clematis, old roses, shrubs and herbaceous plants flank wide grass paths, paved, tiled and wood-chip areas. Ornamental brick and gravel rope-swagged walkways, all maturing over past 10 yrs

The Old School House & (Mr & Mrs M Ryan) Playground now a walled garden. Small courtyard with rockery; orchard with daffodils and lovely views. TEAS

Sun May 22 (2-6)

Village stalls and local exhibition in church

Manor Close (description under April. New book stall)

Milton Cottage ✿ (Mr & Mrs G Harrington) Small garden with wide steps dividing into 2 levels; pond and rock garden; interesting colour combinations of foliage and flowers

The Old Butchers Arms (description under April)

The Old School House (description under April) TEAS

Thatched Cottage ✿❀ (Mr & Mrs Brian Law) Typical ½-acre cottage garden of herbaceous borders, clematis and rose rustic walkway. Developing shade area with bulbs, hostas and foxgloves with old brick-floored folly; lawns and orchard provide perfect setting for 450-yr-old listed building

Pasture Farm &✿ (Mr & Mrs R Belgrove) Thame Rd. Longwick, nr Princes Risborough. 1m W of Longwick on the Thame Rd. A4129. 4m E of Thame. Farm entrance 50yds from layby. Garden at top of farm track. ½-acre labelled plantswoman's garden. Herbaceous border, rockery. White garden with shrubs, perennials, bulbs and annuals. Integral nursery with perennials incl unusual white varieties. TEAS. *Adm £1 Chd free. Suns May 1, June 26, Sept 11 (2-6). Also private visits welcome, please* Tel 0844 343651

Peppers &✿ (Mr & Mrs J Ledger) 4 Sylvia Close, Gt Missenden. A413 Amersham to Aylesbury Rd. At Great Missenden by-pass turn at sign Great & Little Kingshill (Chiltern Hospital). After 400yds turn L, Nags Head Lane. After 300yds turn R under railway bridge. Sylvia Close 50yds on R. Approx 1 acre. Wide variety of plants, shrubs, trees, inc uncommon conifers, collection of acers, unusual containers, spring and autumn colour. TEAS. Donation from plant sale and teas to local charities (workaid). *Adm £1 Chd free. Suns May 15, Aug 21 (10-5). Private visits welcome, please* Tel 0494 86 4419

Prestwood Gardens ✿ From Amersham or Aylesbury turn off A413 at Gt Missenden. Take A4128 to High Wycombe through Prestwood. At end of High St as rd bears L go straight on. Anchor Cottage is adjoining Pinecroft on R hand side in Honor End Lane. Parking in public car park in High St, 300yds. Teas at Hughenden Church House. *Combined adm £1 Chd free (Share to Save the Children Fund®). Sun July 10 (2-6)*
   Anchor Cottage (Group Captain & Mrs D L Edwards) ¼-acre garden with colour for all seasons. Pergola, pond, roses, shrubs and shade loving plants
   Pinecroft (Mrs B Checkley & Mr & Mrs P Smith) An enthusiast's very small and wide garden. Good use made of difficult shaped area with features

Quainton Gardens 7m NW of Aylesbury. Nr Waddesdon turn N off A41. *Combined adm £2 Chd free. Sun May 8 (2-6)*
   Brudenell House &✿ (Dr & Mrs H Beric Wright) Church St (opp. Church). 2-acre garden surrounding old rectory. Specimen trees planted between 1822–1885; good garden for children. Wide variety of flower shrubs, large herbaceous border; fruit and vegetables. TEAS
   Capricorner &✿ (Mr & Mrs A Davis) Small garden created in former stable yard since 1986, planted for yr-round interest with many scented plants; wild garden evolving
   Hatherways &✿ (Mr & Mrs D Moreton) A cottage garden which has gradually emerged from a near wilderness. Bog garden, many interesting shrubs, herbaceous plants and bulbs. Plant stall in aid of the NSPCC
   Thorngumbald &✿ (Mr & Mrs J Lydall) Cottage garden heavily planted with wide selection of old-fashioned plants, organically grown; small pond, conservatory; attempts to encourage wild life

Quoitings &✿ (Kenneth Balfour Esq) Oxford Rd, Marlow, 7m E of Henley, 3m S of High Wycombe; at Quoiting Sq, in Marlow turn N out of West St (A4155); garden 350yds up Oxford Rd on L. 2½-acres secluded garden

with wide range of conifers and magnificent trees incl tulip, lime and pomegranate. Grand display of self propagated tulips followed by colourful mixed flower and dahlia beds; lawns; ha-ha; vistas. C17/18 house (not open) formerly home of Historiographer Royal to William IV and Queen Victoria. Brass Band. TEAS. *Adm £2 Chd free. Suns April 10 (1-5), Sept 4 (1-6)*

Sheredon &✿ (Mr & Mrs G Legg) Thame Rd, Longwick. Between Princes Risborough and Thame on A4129 next to Longwick PO. Winner of "Bookers" Best large garden in Bucks 1993. ⅓-acre colourful garden, large pond with bog plants, many roses and unusual plants; organic vegetable garden with melon house. Large collection of fruits and orchard; chickens and aviary. TEAS. *Adm £1 Chd 20p. Sun July 17 (11-6). Also private visits welcome Suns only Aug to Sept, please* Tel 0844 346557

Spindrift &✿ (Mr & Mrs Eric Desmond) Jordans, 3m NE of Beaconsfield. From A40, midway between Gerrards Cross and Beaconsfield turn N into Potkiln Lane; after 1m turn L into Jordans village; at far side of green turn R. Park in school playground. Garden for all seasons on different levels full of surprises. Herbaceous border, variety of unusual hardy plants, fine hedges and specimen trees; hosta and hardy geraniums collection; dell with pond. Model terraced vegetable and fruit garden with greenhouses and vine. Inspired by Monet, nasturtium arches surrounded by iris poppies and peonies. Partly suitable for wheelchairs. Member of Wellesborne Vegetable Research Assoc. TEAS. *Adm £1.50 Chd under 12 20p. Mon April 4, Sun May 8, Wed June 1, Mon Aug 29 (2-5); also by appt for parties* Tel 0494 873172

Springlea &✿ (Mr & Mrs M Dean) Seymour Plain. 1m from Marlow, 2½m from Lane End off B482. From Lane End pass Booker airfield on L then in 1m pass Seymour Court, L at pillar-box on grass triangle. ⅓-acre secluded garden backed by beechwoods. Flower arrangers' garden for colour, foliage and all yr interest. Spring bulbs, azaleas, rhododendrons, unusual trees, shrubs. Rockery, pond, waterfall, bog garden. Hosta. Arched walkway with labelled clematis collection. 60' herbaceous border against high brick wall with many climbers, racing pigeon loft. Award winner of large garden 1991 and 1992 in Buckinghamshire. Small selection of unusual plants. TEAS in aid of PACE (not March or April). *Adm £1.50 Chd free. Suns March 13 (1-5), April 17, May 15, June 5, July 17, Sept 11 (2-6). Private visits and groups welcome March to October, please* Tel 0628 473366

Stowe Landscape Gardens ✿ (The National Trust) 3m NW of Buckingham via Stowe Ave. Follow brown NT signs. One of the supreme creations of the Georgian era; the first, formal layout was adorned with many buildings by Vanbrugh, Kent and Gibbs; in the 1730s Kent designed the Elysian Fields in a more naturalistic style, one of the earliest examples of the reaction against formality leading to the evolution of the landscape garden; miraculously, this beautiful garden survives; its sheer scale must make it Britain's largest work of art. TEAS. *Adm £3.60 Chd £1.80. Tues May 17 (10-5)*

Regular Openers. See head of county section.

The Thatched Cottage ✿❀ (Mr & Mrs D Tolman) Duck Lane, Ludgershall. 2m S A41 (Bicester 6m; Aylesbury 13m). An enchanting cottage garden crammed with rare and old-fashioned plants and surrounding a pretty thatched hovel, a type of building almost extinct but still inhabited by the owners. The garden contains many rare plants incl violets, primulas, old-fashioned pinks and geraniums; many summer flowering perennials; roses, clematis, unusual shrubs and herbs. Interesting features incl topiary, gnarled oak structures and stone paths all neatly fitted into ½-acre. Plants are labelled; garden and house are featured in several publications. Teas and plant sales at owners nearby nursery. *Adm £1.50 Chd free (Share to RSPCA®). Suns July 3, 17 (2-6)*

Turn End ✿❀ (Mr & Mrs Peter Aldington) Townside, Haddenham. From A418 turn to Haddenham between Thame (3m) and Aylesbury (6m). Turn at Rising Sun into Townside. BR Hadd and Tham Parkway. This acre seems much more. Through archways and round corners are several secret gardens. A sweeping lawn bounded by herbaceous beds and a wooded glade with snowdrops, narcissi and bluebells. Old roses, iris and climbers abound. A sunny gravel garden has raised beds, alpine troughs and sempervivum pans. The house designed and built by the owners encloses a courtyard and fish pool. Featured in 'Country Life', 'The Garden', 'Practical Gardening'. Homemade TEAS. *Adm £1.20 Chd 40p (Share to HDA Haddenham Helpline®). Sun, Mon April 3, 4; Suns June 5, 12; Sept 18 (2-6). Also open Weds during April (11-4) Collecting box, no teas. Groups by appt at other times, please* **Tel 0844 291383**

Tythrop Park ♿❀ (Mr & Mrs Jeremy Cotton) Kingsey 2m E of Thame, via A4129; lodge gates just before Kingsey. 4 acres. Replanting of wilderness. Walled kitchen garden, fully productive. Muscat and black (Muscat) d'Hamburg vine propagated from vine at Hampton Court 150yrs ago in vine house. Courtyard now planted as grey garden. Newly planted parterre to South of Carolean house (not open). TEA. *Adm £1.50 Chd free. Sun June 12 (2-6)*

Walmerdene ✿❀ (Mr & Mrs M T Hall) 20 London Rd Buckingham. From Town Centre take A413 (London Rd). At top of hill turn R. Park in Brookfield Lane. Cream House on corner. Small town garden, unusual plants mostly labelled; bulbs; herbaceous; euphorbias; climbing shrub and species roses; geraniums; clematis. Sink garden, rill garden, 2 ponds; white and yellow border; 2 greenhouses, small conservatory and grapehouse. TEAS. *Adm £1 Chd free. Private visits welcome, May, June, July please,* **Tel 0280 817466***. Open Sat, Sun June 18, 19 (2-6) with* **Old Vicarage, Padbury** *2m. Sun July 24 (2-5). TEAS at* **14 Well Street, Buckingham** *also open*

Watercroft ♿❀ (Mr & Mrs P Hunnings) Penn 3m N of Beaconsfield on B474, 600yds past Penn Church. Medium-sized garden on clay; white flowers, new herb garden planted 1993, rose walk, weeping ash; kitchen garden; pond, wild flower meadow. New planting in meadow, plants and honey for sale. C18 house, C19 brewhouse (not open). TEAS in aid of Abbeyfield Beaconsfield Society. *Adm £1.50 Chd 30p. Suns July 3, 10 (2-6)*

Weir Lodge ♿❀ (Mr & Mrs Mungo Aldridge) Latimer Rd Chesham. Approx 1m SE of Chesham. Turn L from A416 along Waterside at junction of Red Lion St and Amersham Rd. From A404 Rickmansworth Amersham Rd turn R at signpost for Chenies and Latimer and go for 4m. Parking at Weir House Mill (McMinns) dangerous turning. ¾-acre garden on bank of R. Chess. Recovered from dereliction in 1983 by owners. Stream and ponds with planted banks. Gravelled terrace with sun loving plants. Assorted containers; shrub and mixed beds; wild flowers. Mature trees incl fine beeches in adjoining paddock. TEAS in aid of Chesham Society. *Adm £1 Chd free. Sun June 12 (2-6)*

¶**14 Well Street** ♿❀ (Mr & Mrs P Bradley) Buckingham. Well St is off Town centre (S side). 14 is opp The Woolpack Public House. Small enclosed and private town garden; paved and walled with raised beds, troughs, pots and colourful annuals. Smaller secondary garden of shrubs and trees accessible through covered passageway; hanging baskets to front. TEAS. *Adm £1 Chd free. Sun July 24 (2-5). Also open* **Walmerdene** *20 London Rd, Buckingham (2-5)*

West Wycombe Park ✿❀ (Sir Francis Dashwood; The National Trust). West Wycombe. 3m W of High Wycombe on A40. Bus: from High Wycombe and Victoria. Landscape garden; numerous C18 temples and follies incl Temple of the Winds, Temple of Venus, Temple of Music. Swan-shaped lake, with flint bridges and cascade. *Adm (grounds only) £2.50 Chd £1.25. Sun Sept 25 (2-5)*

The Wheatsheaf Inn ♿✿❀ (Mrs W Witzmann) Weedon. 2m N of Aylesbury off A413 Buckingham-Aylesbury rd. Black and White thatched Tudor Inn opp 15' brick wall of 'Lilies'. Parking in courtyard and village. Since 1985 3 acres of field turned into a formal, flower and wild garden; with pond, roses, shrubs, perennials, spring bulbs, heather, conifers. Badminton and croquet lawn. Yr-round interest and fine views. Front has a preservation 400-yr-old walnut probably planted when the Old Wheatsheaf Coaching Inn was built. Many other old trees incl. hazel Grove for thatching. *Adm £1 Chd free. Private visits welcome, please* **Tel 0296 641 581**

Whitchurch Gardens 4m N of Aylesbury on A413. TEAS at Priory Court. combined *adm £1.50 Chd free. Sun June 12 (2-6)*

    Bay Cottage ❀ (Mr & Mrs J Crick) 50 High St. small secluded split-level garden with interesting patio, borders and colourful pots

    Church View Barn ❀ (Mr & Mrs J Manson) Beechtree Court. Converted barn with partly walled garden designed by owners in 1992. Many climbers, roses, rockery and herbaceous border. Good views

    ¶**Kempsons Farm** ♿ (Mr G Band & Miss S Wells) Church Headland Lane. Converted barn set in 1-acre garden established in 1993. Set high on outskirts of the village behind the church, surrounded by paddocks and far-reaching views towards Cresslow Manor, the garden features a large natural looking pond stocked with assorted fish incl Koi carp, cascading waterfall and Japanese bridge; young shrubs and continuing planting, with patio and stable courtyard

Priory Court &❀ (Mr & Mrs H Bloomer) 52 High St. ⅔-acre partly walled former C17 rectory garden. Herbaceous and mixed borders, roses and herbs. Wild shady areas, vegetables and fruit. TEAS in aid of church

¶**The White House** &❀ (Mr & Mrs P G Courtenay-Luck) Denham Village. Approx 3m NW of Uxbridge, off A40 between Uxbridge and Gerrards Cross. Denham Village is signposted from A40 or A412; nearest main line station Denham Green. Underground Uxbridge. Parking in village rd. The White House is opp the Norman church in centre of village. 17 acres comprising 6 acres formal garden and an 11 acre paddock. Old flagstone terrace surrounds 2 sides of C18/19 house, leading to new yorkstone terrace; garden being restored to former glory; rejuvenation of old yew hedges, reclamation of lawns and shrubberies. R

Misbourne meanders through lawns containing shrubberies, flower beds, orchard and developing rose garden. Large walled vegetable garden and restored Victorian greenhouses. Cream TEAS. *Adm £2 Acc chd free (Share to St Mary's Church, Denham Village®). Suns May 15, July 3 (2-5)*

Winslow Hall & (Sir Edward & Lady Tomkins) Winslow. On A413 10m N of Aylesbury, 6m S of Buckingham. Free public car park. Winslow Hall (also open), built in 1700, designed by Christopher Wren, stands in a beautiful garden with distant perspectives, planted with many interesting trees and shrubs. In spring, blossom, daffodils and the contrasting foliage of trees combine to make the garden particularly attractive. *Adm house & garden £3 garden only £1.50 Chd free. Sun May 1 (2-6)*

Cambridgeshire

Hon County Organisers:

South:	Lady Nourse, North End House, Grantchester CB3 9NQ Tel 071 439 0172
North:	Mrs M Thompson, Stibbington House, Wansford, Peterborough PE8 6JS Tel 0780 782043

Assistant Hon County Organisers:

South:	John Drake Esq., Hardwicke House, Highditch Road, Fen Ditton Tel 022 052 246
	Timothy Clark Esq, Nether Hall Manor, Soham, Ely CB7 5AB Tel 0353 720269

Hon County Treasurer (North Cambridgeshire): Michael Thompson Esq.

DATES OF OPENING

By appointment
For telephone numbers and other details see garden descriptions. Private visits welcomed

Chippenham Park, nr Newmarket
Docwra's Manor, Shepreth
Greystones, Swaynes Lane, Comberton
Hardwicke House, Fen Ditton
83 High Street, Harlton
Nuns Manor, Frog End, Shepreth
Padlock Croft, West Wratting
Rose Cottage, Upton, nr Peterborough
Scarlett's Farm, West Wratting
31 Smith Street, Elsworth
Tetworth Hall, nr Sandy
Weaver's Cottage, West Wickham

Regular opening
For details see garden descriptions

The Crossing House, Shepreth. Open daily
Docwra's Manor, Shepreth. Every Mon, Wed, Fri and selected Suns. Also Bank Hol Mons
Netherhall Manor, Soham, Ely. May 7 to 14, month of Aug

March 12 Saturday
   Burghley House, Stamford
March 13 Sunday
   Burghley House, Stamford
March 27 Sunday
   Barton Gardens, Cambridge
April 3 Sunday
   Chippenham Park, nr Newmarket
April 4 Monday
   Padlock Croft, West Wratting
   Scarlett's Farm, West Wratting
   Weaver's Cottage, West Wickham
April 8 Friday
   Wimpole Hall, Royston
April 9 Saturday
   Monksilver Nursery, Cottenham
April 10 Sunday
   King's College Fellows' Garden, Cambridge
   Trinity College Fellows' Garden, Cambridge
April 30 Saturday
   Padlock Croft, West Wratting
   Scarlett's Farm, West Wratting
   Weaver's Cottage, West Wickham
May 2 Monday
   Ely Gardens
   Waterbeach Gardens, nr Waterbeach
May 14 Saturday
   Monksilver Nursery, Cottenham

May 15 Sunday
Docwra's Manor, Shepreth
Thorpe Hall (Sue Ryder Home)
   Peterborough
May 22 Sunday
Tetworth Hall, nr Sandy
May 28 Saturday
Island Hall, Godmanchester
Padlock Croft, West Wratting
Scarlett's Farm, West Wratting
Weaver's Cottage, West Wickham
May 29 Sunday
Fen Ditton Gardens
83 High Street, Harlton
Tetworth Hall, nr Sandy
May 30 Monday
Padlock Croft, West Wratting
Scarlett's Farm, West Wratting
Weaver's Cottage, West
   Wickham
June 5 Sunday
Leckhampton, Cambridge
June 11 Saturday
Monksilver Nursery, Cottenham
June 12 Sunday
Ely Gardens ‡
Hardwicke Farm, Gt Gransden
The Lodge, Horningsea,
   Cambridge
Madingley Hall, Cambridge
Quanea, Quanea Drove, Ely ↓
June 18 Saturday
Padlock Croft, West Wratting
Scarlett's Farm, West Wratting
Weaver's Cottage, West Wickham

June 19 Sunday
Alwalton Gardens
Greystones, Swaynes Lane,
   Comberton
Inglethorpe Manor, nr Wisbech
31 Smith Street, Elsworth
June 23 Thursday
Peckover House, Wisbech
June 26 Sunday
The Close House, Barnack,
   Stamford ‡
Grantchester Gardens,
   Grantchester
Stibbington House, Wansford ‡
Sutton Gardens, nr Ely
West Wratting Park, nr
   Newmarket
July 3 Sunday
Bainton House, Stamford
Chippenham Park, nr
   Newmarket
Clare College, Fellows' Garden,
   Cambridge
Elton Hall, nr Peterborough
Hemingford Abbots Gardens
Melbourn Bury, Royston
Melbourn Lodge, Royston
Mill House, North End,
   Bassingbourn
July 9 Saturday
Christ's College, Cambridge
   University
Emmanuel College Garden &
   Fellows' Garden
Monksilver Nursery, Cottenham

July 10 Sunday
Nuns Manor, Frog End, Shepreth
July 16 Saturday
Padlock Croft, West Wratting
Scarlett's Farm, West Wratting
Weaver's Cottage, West Wickham
July 17 Sunday
Anglesey Abbey, Cambridge
Pampisford Gardens, nr
   Cambridge
July 24 Sunday
King's College Fellows' Garden,
   Cambridge
July 31 Sunday
Stibbington Gardens
August 6 Saturday
Conservatory Gallery, Cambridge
August 7 Sunday
Conservatory Gallery, Cambridge
Wytchwood, Great Stukeley
August 11 Thursday
Peckover House, Wisbech
August 13 Saturday
Monksilver Nursery, Cottenham
August 14 Sunday
Anglesey Abbey, Cambridge
August 28 Sunday
15 Latham Road,
   Cambridge
September 4 Sunday
Docwra's Manor, Shepreth
September 10 Saturday
Monksilver Nursery, Cottenham
October 8 Saturday
Monksilver Nursery, Cottenham

DESCRIPTIONS OF GARDENS

¶**Alwalton Gardens** ✗❀ Alwalton. 4m W of Peterborough, next to E of England showground. Parking at Village Hall. TEAS. *Combined adm £2 Chd free (Share to St Andrews Church®). Sun June 19 (2-6)*
   ¶**April Cottage** (Dr & Mrs I Mungall) Interesting mixture at this village garden. Flower borders, vegetable garden and hens
   ¶**14 Church Street** (Mr M Parker) Cottage garden with mature trees. Large vegetable plot
   ¶**The Forge** (Mr & Mrs M Watson) Large cottage garden. Deep bed vegetables
   ¶**Manor House** (Mr & Mrs M Holmes) 1½-acre garden, walled formal garden, topiary. Views over R Nene
   ¶**Oak Cottage** (Mr & Mrs J Wilson) Small garden, highly scented, roses, lilies
   ¶**The Old Rectory** (Mr & Mrs J Gooding) Walled garden with mature trees, lawns, borders
   ¶**9 Oundle Road** (Mr & Mrs C Leary) Medium-sized garden, mixed borders, pond, shrubs, rose arbour

> **Regular Openers.** Too many days to include in diary. Usually there is a wide range of plants giving year-round interest. See head of county section for the name and garden description for times etc.

Anglesey Abbey ᳖✗❀ (The National Trust) 6m NE of Cambridge. From A45 turn N on to B1102 through Stow-cum-Quy. 100 acres surrounding an Elizabethan manor created from the remains of an abbey founded in reign of Henry I. Garden created during last 50 years; avenues of beautiful trees; groups of statuary; hedges enclosing small intimate gardens; daffodils and 4,400 white and blue hyacinths (April); magnificent herbaceous borders (June). Lunches & TEAS. *Adm garden only £3.50 Chd £1.75. Suns July 17, Aug 14 (11-5.30)*

Bainton House ᳖✗ (Major W & Hon Mrs Birkbeck) Stamford. 4m E of Stamford on B1443 in Bainton Village. Turn N at Bainton Church. Entrance 400yds on the L. Approx 3 acres mature garden, shrubs, mixed borders, wild flowers and woodland. TEAS in aid of Macmillan Nurses. *Adm £1.50 Chd free. Sun July 3 (2-5.30)*

Barton Gardens 3½m SW of Cambridge. Take A603, in village turn R for Comberton Rd. TEA. *Combined adm £1.25 Chd 25p (Share to GRBS®). Sun March 27 (2-5)*
   Farm Cottage ✗ (Dr R Belbin), 18 High St. Cottage garden with water feature. Courtyard garden
   The Gables ᳖✗ (P L Harris Esq) 11 Comberton Rd. 2-acre old garden, mature trees, ha-ha, spring flowers

14 Haslingfield Road & (J M Nairn Esq) Orchard, lawns, mixed domestic
31 New Road (Dr D Macdonald) Cottage garden
Orchard Cottage, 22 Haslingfield Road &✂ (Mr J Blackhurst) Interesting mixed domestic. ½-acre garden with raised vegetable beds
The Seven Houses &✂✿ (GRBS) Small bungalow estate on L of Comberton Rd. 1½-acre spring garden; bulbs naturalised in orchard. Gift stall
Townsend & (B R Overton Esq) 15a Comberton Rd. 1-acre; lawns, trees, pond; extensive views. TEA

Burghley House &✂ (Lady Victoria Leatham) Stamford Lincs. 1½m SW of Stamford signposted. Large 'Capability' Brown garden with lake. Extensive new shrub plantings and naturalised spring bulb display. Thousands of spring flowers. House closed in March. TEAS. *Adm £1 Chd 50p (5 to 14). Sat, Sun March 12, 13 (1-5)*

Chippenham Park &✿ (Mr & Mrs Eustace Crawley) Chippenham. 5m NE of Newmarket 1m off A11. Walled parkland with mature and newly planted rare trees, large lake with 3 islands. 7 acres of gardens and woods containing roses, mixed borders of some rare shrubs and perennials and unusual trees. The spring gardens around the lake are dramatically beautiful and becoming more so after extensive replantings. The summer gardens too have been greatly extended and replanted in recent years. TEAS. *Adm £1.50 Chd free (Share to St Margaret's Church, Chippenham®). Suns April 3, July 3 (2-6). Also private visits welcome, please Tel 0638 720221*

Christ's College &✂ (Fellows) Cambridge. Large college garden near city centre; some form of garden since C16; present design from mid C19; 'Milton's Mulberry Tree'; large herbaceous borders and mature trees. *Adm £1 Chd free. Sat July 9 (2-6)*

Clare College, Fellows' Garden &✂ (Master & Fellows) Cambridge. The Master and Fellows are owners of the Fellows' Garden which is open; the Master's garden (nearby) is not open to the public. Approach from Queen's Rd or from city centre via Senate House Passage, Old Court and Clare Bridge. 2 acres; one of the most famous gardens on the Cambridge Backs. TEAS. *Adm £1 Chd under 13 free. Sun July 3 (2-6)*

¶**The Close House** &✂ (Mr & Mrs H Brassey) Barnack. 3m E of Stamford on B1443 to Barnack village. Turn R (S) at Xrds into Jack Haws Lane. 2nd gate on R. 2 acres mature garden, herbaceous borders, acacia trees, yew hedges, lawns and shrubs. TEAS. *Adm £1 Chd free. Sun June 26 (2-5.30)*

¶**Conservatory Gallery** ✂ (Mr & Mrs A W Barrell) 6 Hills Avenue, Cambridge. Southern outskirts of Cambridge. Hills Ave is off Hills Rd which is the main rd from railway station to Addenbrooke's Hospital. Once part of 5-acre Victorian estate, now ⅓-acre town garden with magnificent tree-line incl crataegus prunifolius. Rockery and borders incl jacobs ladder, carex pendula, macleaya cordata, 2 species ligularia, hepatica tribola etc and 2 small ponds provide interesting setting for exhibition of sculpture. TEA. *Adm £1 Chd over 10 50p. Sat, Sun Aug 6, 7 (10-5)*

The Crossing House & (Mr & Mrs Douglas Fuller and Mr John Marlar) Meldreth Rd, Shepreth, 8m SW of Cambridge. ½m W of A10. King's Cross-Cambridge railway runs alongside garden. Small cottage garden with many old-fashioned plants grown in mixed beds in company with modern varieties; shrubs, bulbs, etc, many alpines in rock beds and alpine house. *Collecting box. Private visits welcome any day of the year Tel 0763 261071*

Docwra's Manor &✂✿ (Mrs John Raven) Shepreth, 8m SW of Cambridge. ½m W of A10. Cambridge-Royston bus stops at gate opposite the War Memorial in Shepreth. 2½-acres of choice plants in series of enclosed gardens. Small nursery. TEA May 15, Sept 4 only, in aid of Shepreth Church Funds. *Adm £1.50 Chd free. All year Mon, Wed, Fri (10-4), Suns April 3, May 1, June 5, July 3, Aug 7, Oct 2 (2-5), also Bank Hol Mons (10-4). Proceeds for garden upkeep. Also private visits welcome, please Tel 0763 261473, 261557, 260235. For NGS Suns May 15, Sept 4 (2-6)*

Elton Hall &✂ (Mr & Mrs William Proby) Elton. 8m W of Peterborough, 5m N of Oundle off A605. 8 acres; rose garden, 1000 roses replanted, knot garden, herbaceous borders, sunken garden with lily pond. Arboretum planted 1983. House (Open). TEAS. *Adm garden only £1.50 Chd 75p. ▲Sun July 3 (2-5)*

Ely Gardens &✂✿ 16m N of Cambridge on A10. *Share to Old Palace Sue Ryder Home®*
Mon May 2 (2-5) *Combined adm £1 Chd 50p*
   Old Bishops Palace 1½ acres with small lake, iris walk and herbaceous border wonderfully restored by two expert volueners to its original C17. Famous for its plane tree - oldest and largest in country
   ¶**The Old Fire Engine House Restaurant and Gallery** (Mr & Mrs R Jarman) Walled country garden with wild flowers. Situated just W of the Cathedral. TEAS
Sun June 12 (2.30-5.30) *Combined adm £2.50 Chd 50p single garden £1*
   58 Barton Road (Mrs R Sadler) Small wildlife garden with pond and many interesting plants to attract bees, birds and butterflies
   Belmont House, 43 Prickwillow Rd (Mr & Mrs P J Stanning) Designed ½-acre garden with interesting and unusual plants
   The Bishops House To R of main Cathedral entrance. Walled garden, former cloisters of monastery. Mixed herbaceous, box hedge, rose and kitchen garden
   31 Egremont St (Mr & Mrs J N Friend-Smith) A10 Lyn Rd out of Ely. 2nd L. Approx 1 acre. Lovely views of cathedral, mixed borders, cottage garden. Ginkgo tree, tulip tree and many other fine trees
   Old Bishops Palace Description with May opening. TEAS
   The Old Guildhall, 48 St Mary's St (Mr & Mrs J Hardiment) Interesting walled garden with unusual plants
   ¶**Quanea** (Mr & Mrs John Green) Description and admission charges under **Quanea**

By Appointment Gardens. Avoid the crowds. Good chance of a tour by owner. See garden description for telephone number.

Emmanuel College Garden & Fellows' Garden ⅍✻ in centre of Cambridge. Car parks at Parker's Piece and Lion Yard, within 5 mins walk. One of the most beautiful gardens in Cambridge; buildings of C17 to C20 surrounding 3 large gardens with pools; also herb garden; herbaceous borders, fine trees inc Metasequoia glyptostroboides. On this date access allowed to Fellows' Garden with magnificent Oriental plane and more herbaceous borders. Teashops in Cambridge. *Adm £1 Chd under 16 free. Sat July 9 (2.30-5.30)*

Fen Ditton Gardens ✻✿ 3½m NE of Cambridge. From A45 Cambridge-Newmarket rd turn N by Borough Cemetery into Ditton Lane; or follow Airport sign from bypass. Teas in church hall. *Combined adm £1.50 Chd 50p (Share to Sue Ryder Foundation®). Sun May 29 (2-5.30)*

    Hardwicke House ✻✿ (Mr J Drake) 2 acres designed to provide shelter for plants on exposed site; divided by variety of hedges; species roses; rare herbaceous plants; home of national collection of aquilegias, collection of plants grown in this country prior to 1650. Please park in road opposite. Large sale of plants in aid of NGS; rare aquilegias from National Collection; foliage plants and rare herbaceous plants. **Exceptional rare plant sale for NGS.** *Also private visits welcome, please* **Tel 022 052 246**

    The Old Stables (Mr & Mrs Zavros) Large informal garden; old trees, shrubs and roses; many interesting plants, herbs and shrubs have been introduced. House (not open) converted by owners in 1973 from C17 stables

    The Rectory (Revd & Mrs L Marsh) New garden being laid out around new rectory. Visitors invited to inspect progress over next few years as owners wish to continue their support for the NGS

Grantchester Gardens ✿ 2m SW of Cambridge. A10 from S, L at Trumpington (Junction 11, M11). M11 from N, L at Junction 12. Palestrina Singers will be performing at the Old Vicarage. Craft Fair at Manor Farm, quality handmade goods; wooden toys; pottery, stained glass; glass blowing demonstration; honey and demonstrations of beekeeping. Plant stall by Cambridge City Council (John Hobson) and Art exhibition at North End House. TEAS. *(Share to Grantchester Church®). Sun June 26 (2-6)*

    43 Broadway ⅍✿ (Mr & Mrs R Hill) 2 separate footpaths from Broadway. 1-acre lawns and formal garden with trees and alpine sink gardens; rest paddock backing onto farm meadows

    Home Grove ⅍ (Dr & Mrs C B Goodhart) 1-acre mature, orchard-type garden with shrub roses. Specimen trees and lawns and carefully planned kitchen garden

    North End House ⅍✿ (Sir Martin & Lady Nourse) 1 acre, newly laid out; shrub and herbaceous borders; old-fashioned roses; water garden and rockery. Small conservatory. Art exhibition

    The Old Mill (Jeremy Pemberton Esq) ½-acre on both sides of Mill Race in attractive rural setting. The Old Mill, mentioned in Rupert Brooke's poem 'Grantchester', was burnt down in 1928

> **Regular Openers.** Too many days to include in diary. Usually there is a wide range of plants giving year-round interest. See head of county section for the name and garden description for times etc.

The Old Vicarage ⅍✿✻ (Lord & Dr Archer) 2½ acres; house dating from C17; informal garden laid out in mid C19 with C20 conservatory; lawn with fountain; ancient mulberry tree; many other interesting trees incl cut-leaf beech; beyond garden is wilderness leading to river bank bordered by large old chestnut trees immortalised by Rupert Brooke, who lodged in the house 1910-1912

Greystones, Swaynes Lane ⅍✿✻ (Dr & Mrs Lyndon Davies) Comberton. 5m W of Cambridge. From M11 take exit 12 and turn away from Cambridge on A603. Take first R B1046 through Barton to Comberton; follow signs from Xrds. Garden of approx ½ acre attractively planted with wide range of flowering plants framed by foliage and shrubs. Gravel bed and troughs give contrast; vegetable garden. TEAS. *Adm £1 Chd 50p (Share to Herbal Research). Sun June 19 (2-5.30). Private visits welcome, please* **Tel 0223 264159**

¶**Hardwicke Farm** ⅍✿ (Mr & Mrs N H M Chancellor) Gt Gransden. Situated mid way between the villages of Gt Gransden and Caxton (A1198) 12m W of Cambridge, 8m S of Huntingdon, 12m N of Royston. House on R travelling towards Gt Gransden. 4-acre garden, herbaceous border, shrubs and recently planted courtyard incorporating 1830 red brick barn. Decorative pond and conservatory. TEAS in aid of WI. *Adm £1.50 Chd 50p. Sun June 12 (2-6)*

Hardwicke House see Fen Ditton Gardens

¶**Hemingford Abbots Gardens** ⅍✿ 4m E of Huntingdon. Turn off A604 at Little Chef. Follow signs to Village, turn R into Common Lane. Car parking opp Meadow Lane. TEAS. *Combined adm £1.50 Chd free (Share to Parkinson Disease Society®). Sun July 3 (2-6)*

    ¶**Heathermead, 25 Common Lane** (Mr & Mrs N Everdell) ⅓-acre. Over 200 rose bushes of 170 varieties, specimen trees and shrubs, pond with great crested newts, small bog garden, organic vegetable garden. Pink and white mixed border

    ¶**68 Common Lane** (Mr & Mrs D Flanagan) Approx 1 acre of 6-yr-old garden, mature trees backing onto woodland. Cottage style herbaceous borders, vegetable garden, pond and wild areas.

83 High Street, Harlton ⅍✿✻ (Dr Ruth Chippindale) 7m SW of Cambridge. A603 (toward Sandy); after 6m turn L (S) for Harlton. ⅓-acre interesting design which includes many different features, colours and a wide diversity of plants. TEAS. *Adm £1 Chd free (Share to Harlton Church Restoration Fund®). Sun May 29 (2-6); also by appointment* **Tel 0223 262170**

Inglethorpe Manor ✿✻ (Mr & Mrs Roger Hartley) Emneth, near Wisbech. 2m S of Wisbech on A1101. 200yds on L beyond 40mph derestriction sign. Entrance opp Ken Rowe's Garage. Large garden with interesting mature trees incl giant wellingtonia, lawns, mixed and herbaceous borders, shrub roses, rose walk and lakeside walk. Victorian house (not open). Plants for sale and TEAS in aid of NSPCC. *Adm £1.50 Chd free. Sun June 19 (2-6)*

Island Hall &⚘ (Mr Christopher & The Hon Mrs Vane Percy) Godmanchester. In centre of Godmanchester next to car park, 1m S of Huntingdon (A1) 15m NW of Cambridge (A604). Station: Huntingdon (1m). An important mid-C18 mansion of great charm owned and being restored by an award winning Interior Designer. Tranquil riverside setting with ornamental island forming part of the grounds. The 1-acre garden has been reclaimed from neglect and from the Nissen huts put there when the house was requisitioned in World War II. Formal shaped borders planted with different box are either side of the gravel terrace. The gaps have been filled with pyramids of fastigiate yew. New shrubberies have been planted with a walk through to white and blue borders, with urns, hedges and good vistas. The Island is being cleared and wild flowers encouraged. An exact replica of the original Chinese bridge over the millstream was completed in 1988. TEAS in aid of Godmanchester Church Organ Restoration Fund. *Adm £1.50. Sat May 28 (2-5)*

King's College Fellows' Garden &⚘ Cambridge. Fine example of a Victorian garden with rare specimen trees. Colour booklet available £1.50, free leaflet describing numbered trees. TEAS. *Adm £1 Chd free. Suns April 10, July 24 (2-6)*

¶**15 Latham Road** &⚘ (Dr J F Procope) Cambridge. Latham Rd lies between Cambridge and Trumpington, running W off the Trumpington Rd 200yds S of the Botanical Gardens. The entry marked by a pink cottage on the N side with a panda crossing over the Trumpington Rd to the S. 'Whitsunden', 15 Latham Rd is at the far end on L. Enclosed Edwardian suburban garden, 1¼ acres approx, restored. Laid out in compartments around central octagonal lawn. Sunken garden. *Adm £1.50 Chd 50p. Sun Aug 28 (2-6)*

Leckhampton &⚘ (Corpus Christi College) 37 Grange Rd, Cambridge. Grange Rd is on W side of Cambridge and runs N to S between Madingley Rd (A1303) and A603; drive entrance opp Selwyn College. 10 acres; originally laid out by William Robinson as garden of Leckhampton House (built 1880); George Thomson building added 1964 (Civic Trust Award); formal lawns, rose garden, small herbaceous beds; extensive wild garden with bulbs, cowslips, prunus and fine specimen trees. TEAS. *Adm £1 Chd free. Sun June 5 (2-6)*

¶**The Lodge** &⚘⚘ (N M Buchdahl) Clayhithe Rd, Horningsea. 4m NE of Cambridge to Newmarket rd; 1½m N of A45 on Clayhithe Rd (B1047); ¾m out of Horningsea on L towards R Cam. 3 acres of well-landscaped garden framed by mature willows and old native trees; many shrubs and old roses; large water garden and many wide herbaceous borders. Unusual herbaceous plants for sale from specialist nursery on site. Car park. *Adm £1.50 Chd 50p (Share to Arthur Rank House Hospice®). Sun June 12 (2-5.30)*

Madingley Hall Cambridge ⚘ (University of Cambridge) 4m W, 1m from M11 Exit 13. C16 Hall set in 7½ acres of attractive grounds. Features include landscaped walled garden with hazel walk, borders in individual colours and rose pergola. Meadow, topiary and mature trees. TEAS. *Adm £1 Chd free (Share to Madingley Church Restoration Fund®). Sun June 12 (2.30-5.30)*

Melbourn Bury &⚘⚘ (Mr & Mrs Anthony Hopkinson) 2¼m N of Royston; 8m S of Cambridge; off the A10 on edge of village, Royston side. 5 acres; small ornamental lake and river with wildfowl; large herbaceous border; fine mature trees with wide lawns and rose garden. TEAS in aid of WI. *Combined adm with **Melbourn Lodge** £1 Chd free. Sun July 3 (2-6)*

Melbourn Lodge &⚘⚘ (J R M Keatley Esq) Melbourn 3m N of Royston, 8m S of Cambridge. House in middle of Melbourn village. 2-acre garden maintained on 9 hrs work in season. C19 grade II listed house (not open). TEAS at Melbourne Bury. *Combined adm with **Melbourn Bury** £1 Chd free. Sun July 3 (2-6)*

¶**Mill House** &⚘⚘ (Anthony & Valerie Jackson) North End. On the NW outskirts of Bassingbourn, on the rd to Shingay. Take North End at the war memorial in the centre of Bassingbourn which is just W of the A1198, 2m N of Royston. Garden created out of open countryside by garden designer owners. Clever use of walls, pergolas, water and varying land levels provide a backdrop for many very fascinating plants, giving interest and colour throughout the year. Rare plants for sale. *Adm £1.50 Chd 50p. Sun July 3 (2-5.30)*

¶**Monksilver Nursery** ⚘⚘ (J L Sharman) Cottenham. 6m N of Cambridge. Take A45 or M11 onto A604, take 1st turn to Oakington, Cambridge and Dry Drayton, go over flyover, through Oakington and Westwick. Monksilver Nursery is then 1m from Westwick on RH-side. 1 acre of formal garden in process of development. Herbaceous borders and yew hedges, rare trees, shrubs. National collections (NCCPG) of galeobdolon, lamium and vinca. Large collections of helianthus, chrysanthemum, aster, echinops, veronica, sedum, monarda, lathyrus, potentilla, pulmonaria and centaurea. *Donations. Sats April 9, May 14, June 11, July 9, Aug 13, Sept 10, Oct 8 (10-4)*

¶**Netherhall Manor** ⚘ (Timothy Clark) Soham. Enter Soham from Newmarket, Tanners Lane is 1st R 80yds after Webbs Store. Enter Soham from Ely, Tanners Lane is 2nd L after War Memorial. 1-acre walled garden incl courtyard featured on Geoffrey Smiths 'World of Flowers' and 'Gardeners World'. Florists ranunculus (picotee and bizarre), tulips (rose, bizarre, byblomen). Also during Aug formal beds of Victorian pelargonium, calceolaria, lobelia and heliotrope. *Collecting Box. May 7 to 14, month of Aug (2-5)*

Nuns Manor &⚘⚘ (Mr & Mrs J R L Brashaw) Shepreth nr Royston Herts. 8m SW of Cambridge 200yds from A10 Melbourn-Shepreth Xrds. C16 farmhouse surrounded by 2-acre garden (extended 1987); interesting plants, large pond, woodland walk, kitchen garden. Mixed and herbaceous borders. *Adm £1 Chd free. Sun July 10 (2-6); also private visits welcome May to Aug, please Tel 0763 260313*

By Appointment Gardens. These owners do not have a fixed opening day usually because they do not like crowds or have insufficient parking space. Owner will often give guided tour.

Padlock Croft &&& (Mr & Mrs P E Lewis) West Wratting. From dual carriageway on A604 between Linton and Horseheath take turning N (Balsham W Wratting); Padlock Road is at entry to village. Plantsman's organic garden of ⅔-acre, home of the National Campanula Collection; mixed borders, troughs, alpine house etc inc rare plants; rock and scree gardens; potager with raised beds. *Combined Adm £1.50 Chd 50p with* **Scarletts Farm** *and* **Weavers Cottage.** *Sats April 30, May 28, June 18, July 16, Mons April 4, May 30 (2-6). Private visits also welcome, weekdays, please* Tel 0223 290383

Pampisford Gardens &&& 8m S of Cambridge on A505. TEAS at the Old Vicarage in aid of RDA. *Combined adm £1.50 Chd free. Sun July 17 (2-5.30)*
> **The Dower House** (Dr & Mrs O M Edwards) 7 High Street. Medieval house surrounded by well designed and interesting garden
> **Glebe Crescent** A group of pensioners houses with very colourful small gardens
> No 3 (Mr & Mrs Rutter)
> No 4 (Mr & Mrs Duller)
> No 5 (Mr & Mrs Frosdick) Won the 1st prize for best kept small garden in S Cambs
> No 6 (Mr & Mrs Freestone)
> **4 Hammond Close** (Mr & Mrs Beaumont) This pretty garden has been cleverly designed to incl a water garden and conservatory
> **The Old Vicarage** (Mr & Mrs Nixon) Next to Church in village. 2½-acres; mature trees; shrub and herbaceous borders with good ground cover plants; small Victorian style conservatory planted with rare species

Peckover House &&& (The National Trust) Wisbech. In centre of Wisbech town, on N bank of R Nene (B1441). Garden only open. 2-acre Victorian garden; rare trees, inc maidenhair (Ginkgo), tulip trees etc. Many old-fashioned roses and colourful borders. Orange trees growing in well-stocked greenhouse. *Adm £1 Chd 50p.* ▲ *Thurs June 23, Aug 11 (2-5)*

¶**Quanea** &&& (Mr & Mrs John Green) Quanea Drove. SE of Ely, 2nd turning L travelling S from Ely on A142, signposted Quanea Drove. 5-acre garden. Avenue focused on Ely Cathedral. Roses in trees, clematis, shrubbery, herbaceous. TEA. *Adm £1 Chd 50p. Sun June 12 (2-5). Also open* **Ely Gardens**

Rose Cottage && (Mr & Mrs K W Goodacre) 36 Church Walk, Upton. 5m W of Peterborough. Turn off A47 between Castor and Wansford at roundabout signed Upton. Small cottage garden; pond; herbs; octagonal greenhouse; many varieties of plants and shrubs giving colour. *Adm 60p Chd 10p. June 1 to 30. Private visits welcome, please* Tel 0733 380450

Scarlett's Farm &&& (Mr & Mrs M Hicks) Padlock Rd, West Wratting. From dual carriageway on A604 between Linton and Horseheath taking turning N (W Wratting 3½); Padlock Road is at entry to village. Scarlett's Farm at end of Padlock Road. ⅓-acre mixed country garden, planted for long season of interest; small nursery attached. TEAS. *Combined adm £1.50 Chd 50p with* **Padlock Croft** *and* **Weavers Cottage.** *Sats April 30, May 28,* *June 18, July 16, Mons April 4, May 30 (2-6). Private visits welcome, please* Tel 0223 290812

¶**31 Smith Street** &&& (Drs J D & J M Twibell) Elsworth. Approx 9m from Cambridge, Huntingdon, St Ives and St Neots. From A45 (St Neots) enter village and turn L at T-junction at "Poacher" public house. 2nd house on L. 2nd house on R on entering village from Hilton end. ¾-acre cottage garden. Herbs, scented, insectivorous and other unusual plants. National collections of artemisia (featured Channel 4 Garden Club Sept 1992) and nerium oleander. TEA. *Adm £1 Chd 50p. Sun June 19 (10-6). Private visits welcome, please* Tel 0954 267 414

Stibbington Gardens && 8m W of Peterborough off the A1. 107 Elton Rd is W of A1 on B671 Elton Rd S of Wansford. Old Castle Farmhouse is in Stibbington Village E of A1. Signed Stibbington from A1. TEAS at Old Castle Farmhouse. *Combined adm £1 Chd free. Sun July 31 (2-6)*
> **107 Elton Road** (Mr & Mrs J Ferris) 1 acre, comprising lawns with many roses; mainly annuals and dahlias; enclosed with mature trees
> **Old Castle Farmhouse** & (Mr & Mrs J M Peake) Culde-sac S of church. Mainly lawn and shrubs with pond, garden borders a small backwater of R Nene and covers approx 2 acres

Stibbington House & (Mr & Mrs Michael Thompson) Wansford. 8m W of Peterborough W of A1 on B671 Elton Rd S of Wansford. Approx 3 acres of trees, shrubs, mixed borders, lawns running down to mill stream (R Nene). Site of old paper mill. River walks and longhorn cattle in field. TEAS. *Adm £1 Chd free. Sun June 26 (12-5)*

¶**Sutton Gardens** &&& 6m W of Ely on A142, turn L at roundabout into village. TEAS. *Combined adm £1.50 Chd 50p. Sun June 26 (2-6)*
> ¶**Bellamore, Station Road** (Mr & Mrs A E Thomson) Plantsman's garden with elaeagnus quicksilver, koelreuteria paniculata, geranium spinners, crambe cordifolia, euphorbias, alliums, grasses and hardy geraniums
> ¶**1 Church Lane** (Miss B M Ambrose & Miss B I Ambrose) Small garden near church filled with an unusual range of shrubs, climbers (clematis), perennials and alpines, collection of silver and gold plants. Raised beds, troughs, greenhouse. TEAS
> ¶**91 The Row** (Mr & Mrs M Cooper) Recently created garden managed on organic principles on the edge of extensive tracts of open fenland. In addition to the usual elements of an English garden the owners have created a traditional English hedgerow, an area to encourage natural flora and fauna incl a pond. The garden is home for a large population of great crested newts, collection of herbs for demonstration purposes and daily use, a secluded scented garden. TEAS in aid of Sutton Scout Group

Tetworth Hall & (Lady Crossman) 4m NE of Sandy; 6m SE of St Neots off Everton-Waresley Rd. Large woodland and bog garden; rhododendrons; azaleas, unusual shrubs and plants; fine trees. Queen Anne house (not open). TEA in aid of Waresley Church. *Adm £1.50 Chd free. Suns May 22, 29 (2-6.30). Private visits welcome April 15 to June 15, please* Tel 0767 50212

Thorpe Hall ᏻᏱ (Sue Ryder Foundation) Thorpe Rd, Longthorpe, Peterborough. 1m W of Peterborough city centre. Thorpe Hall 1665 Grade I house in Grade II listed garden with original walls; gate piers; urns and niches. Unique garden in course of replanting. Victorian stone parterre; iris collection; rose garden and 1650 herbaceous borders. TEAS. *Adm Garden only £1 Chd 50p (Share to Sue Ryder Foundation®). Sun May 15 (2-5.30)*

Trinity College, Fellows' Garden ᏻᏱ Queen's Road, Cambridge. Garden of 8-acres, originally laid out in the 1870s by W.B. Thomas; lawns with mixed borders, shrubs, specimen trees. Drifts of spring bulbs. *Adm £1 Chd free. Sun April 10 (2-6)*

Walcot Hall, Barnack – see Lincolnshire

Waterbeach Gardens Ᏹ Cambridge 7m N of Cambridge on E of A10, well signed. Flower Festival, crafts, toilets and Teas at St Johns Chruch in aid of Church funds. *Combined adm £1 Chd free. Mon May 2 (2-6)*

  90 Bannold Rd ❀ (Mr & Mrs R L Guy) Feature front garden of coloured barks (rubus bifloris) etc. Small garden to rear

  18 Cattels Lane ᏻ❀ (Mr & Mrs Vincent) Model vegetable garden with fruit trees, small pond and rockery, greenhouse, shrubs

Weaver's Cottage ᏻᏱ❀ (Miss Sylvia Norton) Streetly End, West Wickham. From dual carriageway on A604 between Linton and Horseheath take turning N (W Wratting 3½m then 1st turning R (Streetly End 1¼m). Keep L at triangle. Weaver's Cottage is 5th on the R. ½-acre garden planted for fragrance with bulbs; shrubs; herbs;

perennials; honeysuckle; old shrub and climbing roses. National Lathyrus Collection. TEA. *Combined adm £1.50 Chd 50p with* **Padlock Croft** *and* **Scarletts Farm***. Sats April 30, May 28, June 18, July 16, Mons April 4, May 30 (2-6). Visitors welcome any time by appt* Tel 0223 892399

West Wratting Park ᏻᏱ❀ (Mr & Mrs Henry d'Abo) 8m S of Newmarket. From A11, between Worsted Lodge and Six Mile Bottom, turn E to Balsham; then N along B1052 to West Wratting; Park is at E end of village. Georgian house (orangery shown), beautifully situated in rolling country, with fine trees; rose and herbaceous gardens; walled kitchen garden. TEAS. *Adm £1 Chd free. Sun June 26 (2-7)*

Wimpole Hall ᏻᏱ (National Trust) Arrington. 5m N of Royston signed off A603 to Sandy 7m from Cambridge or off A1198. Part of 350-acre park. Vivid show of many varieties of daffodils is main attraction in April; fine trees and marked walks in park. Guided tours available 11.00, 15.00 hrs given by Head Gardener. Lunches & TEA. *Adm £1.50 Chd free (Guided Tours extra).* ▲*Fri April 8 (10.30-5)*

Wytchwood Ᏹ❀ (Mr & Mrs David Cox) Gt Stukeley. 2m N of Huntingdon. Turn off B1043 into Owl End by Great Stukeley village hall. Parking at village hall and in Owl End. 1 acre yr-round interest. Lawns, shrubs, perennial plants, trees, pond, roses, area of wild plants and grasses. Vegetables and rare poultry. In 1992 this garden finished in the top ten of Gardener Of The Year competition. Sponsored by Garden News and Thompson and Morgan Seeds. TEA. *Adm £1 Chd 50p. Sun Aug 7 (2-5.30)*

Cheshire & Wirral

Hon County Organiser: Nicholas Payne Esq, The Mount, Whirley, Macclesfield, Cheshire SK11 9PB
Assistant Hon County Organisers: Mrs T R Hill, Salterswell House, Tarporley, Cheshire CW6 OED
   Mrs N Whitbread, Lower Huxley Hall, Hargrave, Chester CH3 7RJ

DATES OF OPENING

By Appointment
For telephone numbers and other details see garden descriptions. Private visits welcomed

37 Bakewell Road, Hazel Grove
Cholmondeley Castle Gardens, Malpas
The Old Hall, Willaston
Orchard Villa, Alsager
17 Poplar Grove, Sale
2 Stanley Road, Heaton Moor
85 Warmingham Road, nr Crewe
The Well House, Tilston

Wood End Cottage, Whitegate
Woodsetton, Alsager

Regular openings
For details see garden descriptions

Arley Hall & Gardens, Northwich.
  Every Tues to Sun inc & Bank
  Hols April to Oct
Capesthorne, Siddington. For dates
  see text
Cholmondeley Castle Gardens,
  Malpas. Weds, Thurs, Suns &
  Bank Hol Mons
Dunge Farm Gardens, Kettleshulme.
  Daily May 1 to Sept 30
Lyme Park, Disley. For dates see text

Norton Priory, Runcorn. For dates,
  see text
Peover Hall, Knutsford. Mons &
  Thurs, May to Oct
The Quinta, Swettenham. Daily April
  1 to Oct 31

April 3 Sunday
  The Old Hall, Willaston
April 10 Sunday
  Poulton Hall, Bebington
  The Well House, Tilston
April 17 Sunday
  Woodsetton, Alsager
April 24 Sunday
  Penn, Alderley Edge

May 1 Sunday
Penn, Alderley Edge
Tushingham Hall, Whitchurch
May 2 Monday
Orchard Villa, Alsager
Penn, Alderley Edge
May 8 Sunday
Beeston House, Bunbury
The Quinta, Swettenham
Rode Hall, Scholar Green
Willaston Grange, South Wirral
May 10 Tuesday
Orchard Villa, Alsager
May 15 Sunday
Haughton Hall, nr Bunbury
May 17 Tuesday
Orchard Villa, Alsager
May 18 Wednesday
The Quinta, Swettenham
May 21 Saturday
Peover Hall, Knutsford
May 22 Sunday
Dorfold Hall, Nantwich
Hare Hill Gardens, Over
    Alderley
Manley Knoll, Manley
Peover Hall, Knutsford
Woodsetton, Alsager
May 24 Tuesday
Orchard Villa, Alsager
May 25 Wednesday
Reaseheath, nr Nantwich
May 29 Sunday
Bolesworth Castle, Tattenhall
Henbury Hall, nr Macclesfield
Little Moreton Hall, Congleton
Penn, Alderley Edge

May 30 Monday
Ashton Hayes, Chester
Penn, Alderley Edge
May 31 Tuesday
Orchard Villa, Alsager
June 1 Wednesday
Reaseheath, nr Nantwich
June 4 Saturday
The Old Parsonage, Arley
    Green
June 5 Sunday
35 Heyes Lane, Timperley
Norton Priory, Runcorn
The Old Hall, Willaston
The Old Parsonage, Arley Green
June 7 Tuesday
Orchard Villa, Alsager
June 8 Wednesday
Cholmondeley Castle Gardens,
    Malpas
Reaseheath, nr Nantwich
June 11 Saturday
Arley Hall & Gardens, Northwich
Lyme Park, Disley
June 12 Sunday
Lyme Park, Disley
Poulton Hall, Bebington
The Stray, Neston
85 Warmingham Road, nr Crewe
June 14 Tuesday
Orchard Villa, Alsager
June 15 Wednesday
Reaseheath, nr Nantwich
June 18 Saturday
Ness Gardens, Ness
June 19 Sunday
The Old Hough, Warmingham

June 22 Wednesday
Reaseheath, nr Nantwich
June 26 Sunday
Burton Village Gardens, Burton
The Well House, Tilston
June 27 Monday
Tatton Park, Knutsford
June 29 Wednesday
Reaseheath, nr Nantwich
July 3 Sunday
Free Green Farm, Lower Peover
35 Heyes Lane, Timperley
July 6 Wednesday
Reaseheath, nr Nantwich
July 9 Saturday
Broxton Old Hall, nr Malpas
Old Fanshawe Vicarage,
    Siddington
July 10 Sunday
Old Fanshawe Vicarage,
    Siddington
Wood End Cottage, Whitegate
July 13 Wednesday
Reaseheath, nr Nantwich
July 17 Sunday
The Mount, Whirley
July 20 Wednesday
Reaseheath, nr Nantwich
July 27 Wednesday
Reaseheath, nr Nantwich
August 3 Wednesday
Capesthorne, Siddington
Ness Gardens, Ness
August 14 Sunday
Dunham Massey, Altrincham
August 29 Monday
Thornton Manor, Wirral

DESCRIPTIONS OF GARDENS

Arley Hall & Gardens &❀ (Hon M L W Flower), 6m W of Knutsford. 5m from M6 junc 19 & 20 & M56 junc 9 & 10. 12 acres; gardens have belonged to 1 family over 500 yrs; great variety of style and design; outstanding twin herbaceous borders (one of earliest in England); unusual avenue of clipped Ilex trees, walled gardens; yew hedges; shrub roses; azaleas, rhododendrons; herb garden; scented garden; woodland garden and walk. Arley Hall and Private Chapel also open. Lunches and light refreshments (in C16 converted barn adjacent to earlier 'Cruck' barn), Gift shop. Specialist plant nursery. *Adm Gardens & Chapel only £2.80, Chd under 16 £1.40. Hall £1.60 extra; Chd 80p under 5 free (Share to David Lewis Centre®). April to Oct every Tues to Sun incl & Bank Hols (12-5) last adm to gardens 4.30. For NGS Sat June 11 (12-5). Special rates and catering arrangements for pre-booked parties.* **Tel 0565 777353**

Ashton Hayes (Michael Grime Esq) Chester. Midway between Tarvin and Kelsall on A54 Chester-Sandiway rd; take B5393 N to Ashton and Mouldsworth. Approach to Ashton Hayes can be seen halfway between Ashton and Mouldsworth. The ¾m drive is beside former lodge. About 12 acres, incl arboretum and ponds. Predominantly a valley garden of mature trees and flowering shrubs. Great variety of azaleas and rhododendrons; notable embothrium. TEAS. *Adm £1.50 OAPs £1 Chd 50p (Share to Church of St John the Evangelist, Ashton Hayes®). Mon May 30 (2-6)*

¶37 Bakewell Road ⚘ (Mr & Mrs H Williams) Hazel Grove. From Manchester on A6 following signs to Buxton, bear R at Rising Sun Public House, Hazel Grove. Taking the Macclesfield Rd (A523) take 1st R (Haddon Rd) then 1st L into Bakewell Rd. Small suburban garden 17yds × 6½yds heavily planted with azaleas, rhododendrons (several rare and unusual varieties), hydrangeas; pool and waterfall. Excellent example of how much can be planted in a small area. TEAS. *Adm £1 Chd free. Private visits welcome, May & June* **Tel Mr Cofield 061 491 4952**

> **Regular Openers.** Too many days to include in diary. Usually there is a wide range of plants giving year-round interest. See head of county section for the name and garden description for times etc.

¶**Beeston House** ර.*[*]* (Mr & Mrs B S Jenkins) Bunbury. Off A49 3m S of Tarporley, 10m N of Whitchurch. Turn W at Bunbury Xrds lge brown sign for Beeston Castle 100yds from A49. 3 acres of traditional English country garden, rhododendrons, azaleas, flowering shrubs, foliage plants and herbaceous borders all designed to create all the year round interest. TEAS. *Adm £1.50 Chd 50p (Share to Tarporley War Memorial Hospital®). Sun May 8 (2-6)*

Bolesworth Castle ර.*[*]* (Mr & Mrs A G Barbour) Tattenhall. Enter by lodge on A41 1m N of Broxton roundabout. Landscape with rhododendrons, trees, shrubs and borders. TEAS. *Adm £2 Chd free (Share to Harthill & Burwardsley Churches®). Sun May 29 (2-5.30)*

¶**Broxton Old Hall** * (Mr & Mrs Malcolm Walker) Nr Malpas. 1m E of Broxton roundabout on A534. Turn R after Frog Manor Hotel, ½m to entrance on R. Lge garden imaginatively designed and planned in the last 6yrs and of great interest and beauty. Rhododendrons, formal gardens with box and yew hedges, herbaceous borders, rose and walled gardens, terraced lawns with far reaching views, lake, yew avenue, follies and woodland walks. TEAS. *Adm £2.50 Chd £1. Sat July 9 (2-5)*

Burton Village Gardens *[*]* 9m NW of Chester. Turn off A540 at Willaston-Burton Xrds (traffic lights) and follow rd for 1m to Burton. TEAS. *Combined adm £1.50 Chd free (Share to St Johns Hospice®). Sun June 26 (2-6)*
  Bank Cottage (Mr & Mrs J R Beecroft) Small, very colourful, mixed cottage garden with old roses backing on to village cricket ground
  Briarfield * (Mr & Mrs P Carter) About an acre of rare trees and shrubs in woodland setting
  Rake House (Mr & Mrs R I Cowan) In enclosed sandstone courtyard, with pond, relaid with original cobbles and York stone, old orchard with potager. TEAS in aid of St John's Hospice. Short woodland trail to and from **Lynwood**
  Lynwood * (Mr & Mrs P M Wright) On the fringe of the village on the Neston Road. ⅓-acre garden with shrub borders; rockery, pond with waterfall, pergola, arbour with climbers, heathers and alpines

Capesthorne ර. (Mr & Mrs W A Bromley-Davenport) 5m W of Macclesfield. 7m S of Wilmslow on A34. Bus stop: Capesthorne (Congleton to Manchester route). Medium-sized garden; daffodil lawn; azaleas, rhododendrons; flowering shrubs; herbaceous border; lake, pool and arboretum. Georgian chapel built 1722 on view. Hall open from 2pm until 4pm (extra charge). Illustrated book on garden/woodland walks available at £1. Historic parks and gardens. TEAS and LUNCHES. Free car park. *Adm garden £2.25 OAPs £2 Chd £1; Hall extra £2.50 Chd £1. Combined tickets £4, £3.50, £1.50. Suns April to Sept incl; Weds May to Sept incl; Tues & Thurs June to July; also Good Fri & Bank hols. For NGS Wed Aug 3 (12-6)*

Cholmondeley Castle Gardens ර.* (The Marchioness of Cholmondeley) Malpas. Situated off A41 Chester/Whitchurch rd and A49 Whitchurch/Tarporley rd. Romantically landscaped gardens full of variety. Azaleas, rhododendrons, flowering shrubs; rare trees; herbaceous borders

and water garden. Lakeside picnic area; rare breeds of farm animals, incl Llamas, gift shops. Ancient Private Chapel in the park. Tearoom offering light lunches etc. TEAS. *Adm gardens only £2.50 OAPs £1.50 Chd 75p. Weds & Thurs (12.30-5) Suns & Bank Hol Mons (12-5.30). Reduced rate for coach parties. For NGS Wed June 8 (12.30-5). Private visits also welcome, please* **Tel 0829 720383** *or* **720203**

Dorfold Hall *[*]* (Mr & Mrs Richard Roundell) Nantwich. 1m W of Nantwich on A534 between Nantwich and Acton. 18-acre garden surrounding C17 house with formal approach; lawns and recently planted herbaceous borders; spectacular spring woodland garden with rhododendrons, azaleas, magnolias and bulbs. TEAS in aid of Acton Parish Church. *Adm £1.50 Chd 75p. Sun May 22 (2-5.30)*

●**Dunge Farm Gardens** *[*]* (Mr & Mrs David Ketley) Kettleshulme. Take B5470 rd from Macclesfield. Kettleshulme is 8m from Macclesfield. Turn R in village signed Goyt Valley and in ½m at Xrds, turn R down lane to Dunge Farm. Surrounded by romantic hills and set in 5½ acres, at 1000ft, this is the highest garden in Cheshire; mature trees, woodland, stream with waterfall, bog gardens, herbaceous borders, species rhododendrons, magnolias, acers and meconopsis. Yr-round interest, an oasis in the Pennine foothills. TEAS. *Adm £2 weekdays £2.50 weekends Chd 50p (Share to NGS®). (Sat, Sun due to restricted parking max 40 cars). Open daily May 1 to Sept 30 (10.30-4.30). Groups by appt* **Tel 0663 733787**

Dunham Massey ර.*[*]* (The National Trust) Altrincham. 3m SW of Altrincham off A56. Well signed. Garden over 20 acres, on ancient site with moat lake, mount and orangery. Mature trees and fine lawns with extensive range of shrubs and herbaceous perennials suited to acid sand, many planted at waterside. Set in 350 acres of deer park. TEAS. *Adm £2 Chd £1 (car entry £2).* ▲*For NGS Sun Aug 14 (12-5)*

¶**Free Green Farm** ර.* (Sir Philip & Lady Haworth) Lower Peover. Free Green Lane connects the A50 with the B5081. From Holmes Chapel take the A50 past the Drovers Arms. L into Free Green Lane, the farm is on the R. From Knutsford take the A50, turn R into Middlewich Lane (B5081), turn L into Broom Lane, turn L into Free Green Lane, the farm is on the L. 2-acre garden with pleached limes; herbaceous borders; ponds and new parterre. Natural British woodland for conservation. TEAS. *Adm £1.50 Chd 50p. Sun July 3 (2.30-6)*

Hare Hill Gardens ර.* (The National Trust) Over Alderley. Between Alderley Edge and Prestbury, turn off N at B5087 at Greyhound Rd [118:SJ85765]. Bus: Cheshire E17 Macclesfield–Wilmslow (passing BR Wilmslow and Prestbury) to within ¾m. Stations: Alderley Edge 2½m, Prestbury 2½m. Attractive spring garden featuring a fine display of rhododendrons and azaleas. A good collection of hollies and other specimen trees and shrubs. The 10-acre garden includes a walled garden which hosts many wall shrubs including clematis and vines. The borders are planted with agapanthus (African lily) and geraniums. *Adm £2.50 Chd £1.25.* ▲*For NGS Sun May 22 (10-5.30)*

Haughton Hall ✿ (Mr & Mrs R J Posnett) nr Bunbury. 5m NW of Nantwich, 6m SE of Tarporley via Beeston Castle; N of A534 Nantwich, Wrexham Rd. Medium-sized garden; species of rhododendron, azaleas, shrubs, rock garden; lake with temple; waterfall. Collection of ornamental trees. Home-made TEAS. *Adm £1.50 Chd 50p. Sun May 15 (2-6)*

Henbury Hall &✿✿ (Mr & Mrs Sebastian de Ferranti) nr Macclesfield. 2m W of Macclesfield on A537 rd. Turn down School Lane, Henbury at Blacksmiths Arms: East Lodge on R. Lge garden with lake, beautifully landscaped and full of variety. Azaleas, rhododendrons, flowering shrubs, rare trees, herbaceous borders. *Adm £2 Chd 50p. Sun May 29 (2.30-5)*

35 Heyes Lane ✿✿ (Mr & Mrs David Eastwood) Timperley. Heyes Lane is a turning off Park Rd (B5165) 1m from the junction with the A56 Altrincham-Manchester Rd 1½m N of Altrincham. Or from A560 turn W in Timperley Village for ¼m. Newsagents shop on corner. A small suburban garden 30′ × 90′ on sandy soil maintained by a keen plantswoman member of the Organic Movement (HDRA). An all-year-round garden; trees; small pond; greenhouses; fruit and vegetables with a good collection of interesting and unusual plants. TEA. *Adm £1 Chd free (Share to Parrswood Centre for Rural Education, Didsbury®). Suns June 5, July 3 (2-5)*

Little Moreton Hall &✿✿ (The National Trust) Congleton. On A34, 4m S of Congleton. 1½-acre garden surrounded by a moat and bordered by yew hedges, next to finest example of timber-framed architecture in England. Herb and historic vegetable garden, orchard and borders. Knot garden based on design in 'The English Gardener' published by Leonard Meager in 1670, though probably Elizabethan in origin. Adm includes entry to the Hall with optional free guided tours. Wheelchairs and electric mobility vehicle available. Disabled toilet. Picnic lawns. Shop and restaurant serving coffee, lunches and afternoon teas. TEAS. *Adm £3.60 Chd 1.80.* ▲*For NGS Sun May 29 (12-5)*

●**Lyme Park** (Stockport Metropolitan Borough Council The National Trust) Disley. 6m SE of Stockport just W of Disley on A6 rd. 17-acre garden retaining many original features from Tudor and Jacobean times; high Victorian style bedding; a Dutch garden; a Gertrude Jekyll style herbaceous border; an Edwardian rose garden, a Wyatt orangery and many other features. Also rare trees, a wild flower area and lake. Guided tours June 11, 12, at 2pm, 3pm, 4pm. Donations to NGS. *Adm £3.20 per car, pedestrians free. Prices under revision. April to Sept daily (10.30-5), Oct to March Tues to Suns (10.30-4). Closed Dec 25, 26.* **Tel 0663 766492**

Manley Knoll & (Mrs D G Fildes) Manley, NE of Chester. Nr Mouldsworth. B5393. Quarry garden; azaleas and rhododendrons. TEAS. *Adm £1 Chd 25p. Sun May 22 (2-6.30)*

The Mount &✿✿ (Mr & Mrs Nicholas Payne) Whirley. The Mount is situated about 2m due W of Macclesfield along A537 rd. Opp Blacksmiths Arms at Henbury, go up Pepper St, turn L into Church Lane which becomes Anderton Lane in 100yds. The Mount is about 200yds up Anderton Lane on L. Adequate parking. The garden is approx 1½ acres and is of architectural character with hedges, terraces and walls. About ¼-acre of rhododendrons, azaleas, roses, herbaceous and some bedding plants; and also interesting trees including eucryphia nymansensis, fern leaved beech and sciadopitys. The garden is very much compartmentalized with lawns; shrubberies; herbaceous border; swimming pool and short vista of Irish Yews. TEAS. *Adm £1.50 Chd 50p. Sun July 17 (2-5.30)*

Ness Gardens &✿✿ (University of Liverpool) Neston. Between Neston and Burton, 10m NW of Chester; 4m from end of M56; signed A540 and A550. 45 acres of landscaped gardens. Notable collection of rhododendrons, azaleas, camellias, magnolias, cherries, rowans, birches, conifers, roses, primulas, lilies, etc. Large rock and alpine garden; terrace gardens; herbaceous borders; plants for autumn and winter colour; conservatory and greenhouses; woodland and water gardens; laburnum arch. Tree and nature trails; Chinese plants collected by George Forrest. Children's play and picnic area (no ball games). Parts of the gardens suitable for wheelchairs. No dogs. Free parking for over 1000 cars. Licensed refreshment rooms, gift shop. TEAS. *Adm £3 Chd (10-18)/OAP £2, Family £7. For NGS Sat June 18, Wed Aug 3 (9.30-5)*

Norton Priory &✿✿ (Norton Priory Museum Trust Ltd) Tudor Road, Manor Park, Runcorn. Runcorn New Town 1m, Warrington 5m. From M56 Junction 11 turn for Warrington and follow signs. From Warrington take A56 for Runcorn and follow signs. 16 acres well established woodland gardens; Georgian summerhouses; rock garden and stream glade; 3-acre walled garden of similar date (1760s) recently restored. Georgian and modern garden designs; fruit training; rosewalk; colour borders; herb garden, cottage garden and exhibition. Priory remains of museum also open. *Combined adm £2.40 Concessions £1.20. Daily April to October (12-5) weekends and bank hols (12-6) Nov to March (12-4) (Walled garden closed Nov-Feb). For NGS Sun June 5 (12-6)*

¶**Old Fanshawe Vicarage** &✿ (Mr & Mrs William Wrather) Siddington. 4½m S of Alderley Edge, 4m W of Macclesfield. Use drive off A34, ¼m S of entrance to Capesthorne Hall and ¾m N of B5392. Ample parking. 5 acres, attractive setting next to Redesmere Lake. Interesting natural old garden with some formality, stream, woodland walk, herb and vegetable garden. TEAS. *Adm £1.50 Chd 75p. Sat, Sun July 9, 10 (2-5.30)*

The Old Hall &✿✿ (Dr & Mrs M W W Wood) Hadlow Rd, Willaston S Wirral, 8m NW of Chester on village green. ¾-acre; mixed border; interesting plants; daffodils; winter flowering shrubs and colour. C17 house. TEAS, June 5 only. *Adm £1.50 Chd free (Share to Muscular Dystrophy Group®). Suns April 3, June 5 (2-6); also private visits welcome, please* **Tel 051 327 4779**

By Appointment Gardens. These owners do not have a fixed opening day usually because they do not like crowds or have insufficient parking space. Owner will often give guided tour.

¶The Old Hough &✗ (Mr & Mrs D S Varey) Warmingham. [OS sheet 118. Grid Ref: 699624]. 5m from either junction 17 or 18 on M6. From Middlewich take A50 to Nantwich, after approx 2m turn L to Warmingham. At T-junction turn L garden is ½m on R. From Sandbach take A533 to Middlewich, just after Elworth Village turn L to Warmingham. At T-junction turn R, garden is approx 2½m on L. Young garden in old setting. 2½ acres surrounding listed C16 to C19 house with large courtyard. Extensive use of stone and brick for paths, walls and ornaments. Enclosed formal gardens to S with quiet lawns; varied climbers; mixed borders with interesting shrubs, bulbs, roses, ferns and ivies. Central goldfish pond fed by planted rill: young yew hedges to make future divisions. Informal gardens to N & W with wildlife pond, mature oak wood, herbaceous borders, young trees with interesting bark. Garden to relax in. TEAS in aid of Warmingham Church. *Adm £1.50 Chd 50p (Share to St Leonard's Church, Warmingham®). Sun June 19 (2-6)*

The Old Parsonage &✿ (The Hon Michael & Mrs Flower) Arley Green; 5m NNE of Northwich and 3m Great Budworth; 6m W Knutsford; 5m from M6 junctions 19, 20 and M56 junctions 9, 10. Follow signposts to Arley Hall and Gardens and at central crossroad follow notices to The Old Parsonage. The Old Parsonage lies across park at Arley Green, a cluster of old buildings in a very attractive rural setting beside a lake. 2-acre garden has old established yew hedges sheltering herbaceous and mixed borders, shrub roses and climbers, a newly planted woodland garden and pond, with some unusual young trees and foliage shrubs. Waterplants, rhododendrons, azaleas, meconopsis. Plant stall. TEAS. *Adm £1.50 Chd 75p (Share to Red Cross®). Visitors will be admitted to* **Arley Hall Gardens** *(teas, plants, shop available) at concessionary rate (£1.50 Chd under 17 75p) on production of their Old Parsonage ticket. Sat, Sun June 4, 5 (2-6)*

Orchard Villa ✗✿ (Mr & Mrs J Trinder) 72 Audley Rd, Alsager. At traffic lights in Alsager town centre turn S towards Audley, house is 300yds on R beyond level Xing. Long and narrow, this ⅓-acre has been designed to grow a wide range of herbaceous plants, iris and alpines in features such as scree, peat, raised, light and shade beds. TEAS. *Adm £1 Chd Free. Bank Hol Mon May 2; TEA Tues May 10, 17, 24, 31; June 7, 14 (1.30-5); also private visits welcome, please* **Tel 0270 874833**

Penn ✗✿ (R W Baldwin Esq) Macclesfield Rd, Alderley Edge. ¾m E of Alderley Edge village, on B5087, Alderley Edge-Macclesfield rd. Turn L into Woodbrook Rd for car parking. 2½ acres. This garden, which has been built up by the present owner and his late wife for 45 years, contains an exceptional collection of flowering shrubs and trees, on a hillside looking over the Cheshire plain. The many hundreds of rhododendron species and cultivars include some Himalayans (Macabeanum, rex, eximium, montroseanum, etc, now small forest trees), yellow & blue species (wardii, augustinii etc.), many famous cultivars such as Loderi, Cornish Cross, Penjerrick, Mariloo, Naomi, Prelude, Laura Aberconway), masses of azaleas plus a wide range of camellias & magnolias including superb varieties from Cornwall, and many fairly rare trees including gingko, davidia (handerchief tree), golden elm, embothriums, plus for added interest 2 sequoia sempervirens (now 30ft high struck in 1965 from a block of

wood bought in the Muir woods across the Golden Gate in San Francisco). TEA. *Adm £2 OAPs £1.25 Chd 50p. Suns April 24, May 1, 29; Mons May 2, 30 (2-5)*

Peover Hall &✗ (Randle Brooks Esq) Over Peover. 3m S of Knutsford on A50, Lodge gates off Blackden Lane. 15-acres. 5 walled gardens: lily pond, rose, herb, white and pink gardens; C18 landscaped park, moat, C19 dell, rhododendron walks, large walled kitchen garden, Church walk, purple border, blue and white border, pleached lime avenues, fine topiary work. Dogs in park only. TEAS. *Adm £1.50 Chd 50p. Mons & Thurs (2-5) May to Oct. NOT Bank Hols. Other days by appt for parties. For NGS Sat, Sun May 21, 22 (2-6)*

17 Poplar Grove ✗✿ (Gordon Cooke Esq.) Sale. From the A6144 at Brooklands Station turn down Hope Rd. Poplar Grove 3rd on R. This small town garden has been created in 6 yrs by the owner who is a potter and landscape designer. It has a special collection of unusual plants in an artistic setting with many interesting design features and details. TEA. *Adm £1 Chd 50p (Share to North Manchester General Hospital®). Private visits welcome, May & June, please* **Tel 061 969 9816**

Poulton Hall &✗ (The Lancelyn Green Family) Poulton Lancelyn, 2m from Bebington. From M53, exit 4 towards Bebington; at traffic lights (½m) R along Poulton Rd; house 1m on R. 2½ acres; lawns, ha-ha, wild flower meadow, shrubbery, walled gardens. TEAS. *Adm £1.50 Chd 20p. Suns April 10, June 12 (2-6)*

The Quinta &✗ (Sir Bernard Lovell) Swettenham. Turn E off A535 at Twemlow (Yellow Broom Cafe) and follow signs to Swettenham. 10-acre collection of rare trees and shrubs leading to woodland walks overlooking the Dane Valley and to the thirty-nine step descent to Swettenham Brook. TEA NGS days, Bank Hols & parties by arrangement. *Adm £2 Acc chd free. Open daily April 1 to Oct 31 (2-sunset). For NGS Sun May 8, Wed May 18 (2-sunset)* **Tel 0477 571254**

Reaseheath &✗✿ (Reaseheath College) nr Nantwich. 1½m N of Nantwich on the A51. The Gardens, covering 12 acres, are based on a Victorian Garden surrounding Reaseheath Hall and contain many mature trees of horticultural interest. The gardens are used as a teaching resource. There are specialised features of particular interest including, glasshouses; model fruit garden; rose garden; woodland garden; lakeside bog garden and extensive shrub borders, lawns and sports facilities. TEA. *Collecting Boxes. Weds May 25, June 1, 8, 15, 22, 29, July 6, 13, 20, 27 (2-4.30)*

Rode Hall ✿ (Sir Richard & Lady Baker Wilbraham) Scholar Green [National Grid reference SJ8157] 5m SW of Congleton between A34 and A50. Terrace and rose garden with view over Humphrey Repton's landscape is a feature of Rode gardens, as is the Victorian wild flower garden with a grotto and the walk to the lake past the old Stew pond. Other attractions include a restored ice house and working walled kitchen garden. TEAS. *Adm £1.50 Chd 50p (House extra £2) (Share to Christie Hospital NHS Trust®). Sun May 8 (2-5.30)*

2 Stanley Road ✿✿ (Mr G Leatherbarrow) Heaton Moor. Approx 1½m N of Stockport. Follow Heaton Moor Rd off A6. Stanley Rd on L. 1st house on R. Tiny town garden with all year interest. Old species and English roses, clematis, hardy geraniums, ivies, varied evergreens, daphnes, hellebores, delphiniums, mixed herbaceous; ponds. Max no. of visitors 2 – no room for more. TEA. *Adm £1.25 Chd 60p. Private visits welcome April to Sept, please* Tel 061 442 3828

¶The Stray ✿✿✿ (Mr & Mrs Anthony Hannay) Neston. Approx 10m NW of Chester. ½m NW of Shrewsbury Arms (traffic lights). Turn off A540 into Upper Raby Rd. After ³⁄₁₀m turn R into unmade lane and The Stray is immediately on the L. 1½ acres of new shrubs, herbaceous border and espalier fruit set in an old garden. Replanting commenced in 1991. A chance to see a new garden maturing. TEAS in aid of RNLI. *Adm £1.50 Chd free. Sun June 12 (2-6)*

Tatton Park ✿✿✿ (Cheshire County Council: The National Trust) Knutsford. Well sign-posted on M56 junction 7 and from M6 junction 19. 2½m N of Knutsford. Gardens contain many unusual features and rare species of plants, shrubs and trees. Considered to be the very finest and most important of all gardens within The National Trust they rank among England's 'Top Ten'. Features include orangery by Wyatt, fernery by Paxton, Japanese, Italian and rose gardens. Greek monument and African hut. Hybrid azaleas and rhododendrons, swamp cypresses, tree ferns, tall redwoods, bamboos and pines. An exotic garden offering a new and delightful surprise round every corner, a palimpsest of 200 years development by the Egerton family. The Tatton Garden Society part of the garden will also be open. TEAS. *Adm £2.50 Group £2 Chd £1.70 Group £1.40.* ▲*For NGS Mon June 27 (10.30-5)*

Thornton Manor ✿ (The Viscount Leverhulme) Thornton Hough, Wirral. From Chester A540 to Fiveway Garage; turn R on to B5136 to Thornton Hough village. From Birkenhead B5151 then on to B5136. From M53, exit 4 to Heswall; turn L after 1m. Bus: Woodside-Parkgate; alight Thornton Hough village. Lge garden of yr-round interest. TEAS. Free car park. *Adm £1.50 OAPs/Chd 50p. Bank Hol Mon Aug 29 (2-7)*

Tushingham Hall (Mr & Mrs P Moore Dutton) 3m N of Whitchurch. Signed off A41 Chester-Whitchurch Rd; Medium-sized garden in beautiful surroundings; bluebell wood alongside pool; ancient oak, girth 26ft. TEAS. *Adm £1.50 Chd 30p (Share to St Chad's Church, Tushingham®). Sun May 1 (2-6.30)*

85 Warmingham Road ✿✿ (Mr & Mrs A Mann) Coppenhall. Approx 3m N of Crewe town centre towards Warmingham Village. Close by White Lion Inn, Coppenhall. ⅓-acre plantsman's garden, with shrubs, perennial borders, raised beds, troughs, rock garden, peat garden, pond and greenhouse with cacti and succulents. Speciality alpines. TEA. *Adm £1 Chd free. Sun June 12 (12-5). Private visits welcome May to Sept, please* Tel 0270 582030

The Well House ✿✿ (Mrs S H French-Greenslade) Tilston, nr Malpas. 12m S of Chester, follow signs to Tilston from A41 S of Broxton roundabout, taking Malpas Rd through Tilston. House and antique shop on dangerous bend. Parking if possible in a field or on roadside. Approx ¾-acre small cottage garden, divided by a natural stream. Land over the stream, only acquired autumn 1990, is reached by a bridge; all plantings still very young. Attractive summerhouse, tiny pond and pumped waterfall. Winding paths through variety of small areas; herbs; shrubs and secret garden. At its best when the many bulbs are out in the spring. TEAS. *Adm £1.50 Chd 25p (Share to Cystic Fibrosis®). Suns April 10, June 26 (2-5.30). Private visits also welcome April - July, please* Tel 0829 250332

Willaston Grange ✿ (Sir Derek and Lady Bibby) Willaston. A540 Chester to West Kirby until opposite the new Elf Garage. Proceed down B5151 Hadlow Rd, towards Willaston. Borders, rock garden, vegetable garden, orchard, about 3 acres. Special feature-woodland walk. TEA. *Adm £1.50 OAPs £1 Chd free. Sun May 8 (2-6)*

Wood End Cottage ✿✿ (Mr & Mrs M R Everett) Grange Lane, Whitegate. Turn S off A556 (Northwich/Chester) to Whitegate village, opp school follow Grange Lane for 300 yds. ½-acre sloping to a natural stream; developed as a plantsman's garden. Mature trees; herbaceous; clematis; raised beds. TEAS. Large plant stall. *Adm £1.50 Chd 50p (Share to British Epilepsy Assoc®). Sun July 10 (2-6); also private visits welcome in May, June, July, please* Tel 0606 888236

Woodsetton ✿✿ (Mr & Mrs Eric Barber) Alsager. At town centre follow B5078, take 3rd turning L into Pikemere Road and then 2nd turning on R. Approx 1-acre, interesting plants; trees; shrubs; rhododendrons; lge natural wildlife pool; scree and alpines. TEAS. *Adm £1 Chd free (Share to St. Lukes Hospice 'Grosvenor House', Winsford, Cheshire®). Suns April 17, May 22 (2-5.30) also private visits welcome May, June, July, please* Tel 0270 877623

Clwyd

See separate Welsh section beginning on page 291

Cornwall

Hon County Organiser: G J Holborow Esq, Ladock House, Ladock, Truro, Cornwall Tel 0726 882274
Assistant Hon County Organisers: Mrs W Eliot (Publicity) Tregye Cottage, Carnon Down, Truro TR3 6JH
                                    Tel 0872 864739
                                    Mrs D Morison (W Cornwall) Boskenna, St Martin, Manaccon, Helston
                                    Tel 0326 231 210
                                    Mrs S Jerram (N Cornwall) Trehane, Trevanson, Wadebridge
                                    Tel 0208 812523
                                    Mrs Michael Latham (E. Cornwall) Trebartha Lodge, North Hill, Launceston
                                    PL15 7PD Tel 0566 82373
Cornwall Leaflet   Tony Shaw Esq, Rope House, Cliff Street, Mevagissey, nr St Austell, Cornwall
                                    PL26 6QL Tel 0726 842819
Hon County Treasurer: Mrs Cynthia Bassett, 5 Athelstan Park, Bodmi, PL31 1DS
                                    Tel 0208 73247

DATES OF OPENING

By appointment
For telephone numbers and other
details see garden descriptions.
Private visits welcomed

Chyverton, Zelah
The Hollies, Grampound, nr Truro
Penpol House, Hayle
Polgwynne, Feock
Trelean, St Martin-in-Meneage
Trevegean, Manor Way, Heamoor
Woodland Garden, Garras

Regular openings
For details see garden descriptions

Carwinion, Mawnan Smith. Daily
   April to Oct
Headland, Polruan. Open every
   Thurs June, July, Aug & Sept
Heligan Gardens, Mevagissey. Daily
Ken Caro, Bicton, nr Liskeard. Every
   Sun, Mon, Tues, Wed April 10 to
   June 30, Tues & Weds July & Aug
Lanterns, Restronguet, nr Mylor.
   Daily throughout the year
Long Cross Victorian Gardens,
   Trelights. Open all year
Prideaux Place, Padstow. Open Sun
   to Thurs April 3 to Sept 29
Trebah, Mawnan Smith. Daily
   throughout the year
Tregrehan, Par. Daily Mid March to
   end June & Sept
Trewithen, Probus, nr Truro. Mon to
   Sat March 1 to Sept 30
Woodland Garden, Garras. Sats April
   2 to Oct 1

March 20 Sunday
Penwarne, nr Falmouth

April 3 Sunday
Tremeer, St Tudy
Watergate, Trelill

April 9 Saturday
Bosloe, Mawnan Smith

April 10 Sunday
Trelissick, Feock

April 16 Saturday
Porthpean House, nr St Austell

April 17 Sunday
Penjerrick, Budock, nr Falmouth

April 24 Sunday
Boconnoc, nr Lostwithiel
High Noon, Ladock
Ladock House, Ladock, Truro
Pinetum, Harewood
Polgwynne, Feock
St Michael's Mount, Marazion

May 1 Sunday
Estray Parc, Budock
Tregrehan, Par

May 4 Wednesday
Antony, Torpoint

May 8 Sunday
Cotehele House, St. Dominick,
   Saltash
Pinetum, Harewood

May 14 Saturday
Glendurgan, Mawnan Smith

May 15 Sunday
Paradise Park, Hayle
Peterdale, Millbrook
Pinetum, Harewood

May 19 Thursday
Headland, Polruan

May 22 Sunday
Carlew Gardens,
   Perran-ar-Worthal
Lanhydrock, Bodmin
Treworder Mill, Truro

May 26 Thursday
Headland, Polruan

June 5 Sunday
Jimmers, St Neot

Lamorran House, St Mawes
Newton House, Lanhydrock
Northwood Farm, St Neot
The Old Barn, St Neot
Pinetum, Harewood

June 12 Sunday
Creed House, Creed nr Truro
The Hollies, Grampound, nr Truro
Newton House, Lanhydrock
Trerice, nr Newquay

June 19 Sunday
Ferny Park, Bossiney, Tintagel
Mary Newman's Cottage, Saltash
Tregilliowe Farm, Ludgvan

June 26 Sunday
Pine Lodge Gardens, Cuddra, St
   Austell
Roseland House, Chacewater

July 3 Sunday
Penpol House, Hayle

July 10 Sunday
Roseland House, Chacewater

July 17 Sunday
Tregilliowe Farm, Ludgvan

July 20 Wednesday
Peterdale, Millbrook

August 7 Sunday
Pinetum, Harewood

August 14 Sunday
Ferny Park, Bossiney, Tintagel

August 21 Sunday
Bosvigo House, Truro
Higher Truscott, St Stephens

September 11 Sunday
The Old Mill Herbary, Helland
   Bridge, nr Bodmin

September 25 Sunday
Trebartha, nr Launceston

October 23 Sunday
Trelean, St Martin-in-Meneage

DESCRIPTIONS OF GARDENS

Antony ✕ (National Trust: Trustees of the Carew Pole Trust) 5m W of Plymouth via Torpoint car ferry; 2m NW of Torpoint, N of A374; 16m SE of Liskeard; 15m E of Looe. In a Repton landscape with fine vistas to the R Lynher. Features a formal courtyard, terraces, ornamental Japanese pond and knot garden. National collection of hemerocallis (500 varieties) **Antony Woodland Garden and Woods**: an established woodland garden and natural woods extending to 100 acres. Designed as one of natural beauty and scientific interest. Over 300 types of camellias. TEAS. *Adm £1. Wed May 4 (1.30-5.30)*

Boconnoc ♿✕❀ (Mr & Mrs J D G Fortescue) 2m S of A390. On main rd between middle Taphouse and Downend garage, follow signs. Privately owned gardens covering some 20 acres, surrounded by parkland and woods. Magnificent old trees, flowering shrubs and views. TEAS. *Adm £1.50 Chd Free (Share to Boconnoc Church Window Fund©). Sun April 24 (2-6)*

Bosloe ♿✕ (The National Trust) Mawnan Smith, 5m S of Falmouth. In Mawnan Smith, take Helford Rd and turn off for Durgan. Medium-sized garden; fine view of R Helford. *Adm £1 Chd free. Sat April 9 (2-5)*

Bosvigo House ✕❀ (Mr & Mrs M Perry) Bosvigo Lane. ¾m from Truro centre. Take Redruth Rd. At Highertown, turn R before Shell garage, down Dobbs Lane. After 400yds entrance to house is on L, after nasty L-hand bend. 3-acre garden still being developed surrounding Georgian house (not open) and Victorian conservatory. Series of enclosed and walled gardens with mainly herbaceous plants for colour and foliage effect. Woodland walk. Many rare and unusual plants. Partly suitable for wheelchairs. TEAS, served in servants' hall on charity Suns only. *Adm £1.50 Chd 50p. ▲For NGS Sun Aug 21 (2-5)*

Carclew Gardens ✕ (Mrs Chope) Perran-ar-Worthal, nr Truro. From A39 turn E at Perran-ar-Worthal. Bus: alight Perran-ar-Worthal 1m. Lge garden, rhododendron species; terraces; ornamental water. TEAS. *Adm £1.50 Chd 50p (Share to Barristers Benevolent Fund®). Sun May 22 (2-5.30)*

Carwinion ❀ (Mr H A E Rogers) Mawnan Smith via Carwinion Rd. An unmanicured or permissive valley garden of some 10 acres with many camellias, rhododendrons and azaleas flowering in the spring. Apart from an abundance of wild flowers, grasses, ferns etc, the garden holds the premier collection of temperate bamboos in the UK. TEAS April to Oct (2-5.30). *Adm £1 Chd free. Open daily throughout the year (2-5.30)*

Chyverton (Mr & Mrs N T Holman) Zelah, N of Truro. Entrance ¾m SW of Zelah on A30. Georgian landscaped garden with lake and bridge (1770); large shrub garden of great beauty; outstanding collection magnolias, acers, camellias, rhododendrons, primulas, rare and exotic trees and shrubs. Visitors personally conducted by owners. *Adm £2.50 (£2 for parties over 20 persons) Chd & Students £1. Private visits welcome weekdays March to June, please* **Tel 0872 540324**

Cotehele House ✕❀ (The National Trust) 2m E of St Dominick, 4m from Gunnislake (turn at St Ann's Chapel); 8m SW of Tavistock; 14m from Plymouth via Tamar Bridge. Terrace garden falling to sheltered valley with ponds, stream and unusual shrubs. Fine medieval house (one of the least altered in the country); armour, tapestries, furniture. Dogs in wood only and on lead. Lunches and TEAS. *Adm house, garden & mill £5 Chd £2.50; garden, grounds & mill £2.50 Chd £1.50 Sun May 8 (11-5.30)*

Creed House ♿❀ (Mr & Mrs W R Croggon) Creed. From the centre of Grampound on A390 (halfway between Truro & St Austell). Take rd sign-posted to Creed. After 1m turn L opp Creed Church and the garden is on L. Parking in lane. 5-acre landscaped Georgian Rectory garden. Tree collection; rhododendrons; sunken alpine and formal walled herbaceous gardens. Trickle stream to ponds and bog. Natural woodland walk. Restoration began 1974 – continues & incl recent planting. TEAS. *Adm £1.50 Chd free. Sun June 12 (2-5.30)*

Estray Parc (Mr & Mrs J M Williams) Penjerrick. Leave Penjerrick main entrance on R follow the rd towards Mawnan Smith until entrance to The Home Hotel on L. Directly opp turn R and follow the signs. In 1983 most of this 3-acre garden was a bramble thistle-infested field. A considerable variety of plants have been introduced and continuous grass cutting has produced passable sloping lawns interspersed by a lge collection of trees and shrubs. *Adm £1 OAPs/Chd 50p. Sun May 1 (2-6)*

¶Ferny Park ✕ (Mrs Mendoza) Bossiney. B3263 1½m N of Tintagel 3m S of Boscastle. Park in Rocky Valley Car Park at bottom of hill. ½-acre garden with natural stream creating water feature. TEAS in aid of S.S.A.F.A. *Adm £1 Chd free. Suns June 19, Aug 14 (2-5)*

Glendurgan ✕❀ (The National Trust) Mawnan Smith, take rd to Helford Passage, 5m SW of Falmouth. Follow NT signposts. Walled garden, laurel maze, giants stride, valley with specimen trees, bluebells and primulas running down to Durgan fishing village on R Helford. Lge car park. *Adm £2.60 Chd £1.30. ▲Sat May 14 (10.30-5.30)*

Headland ✕ (Jean & John Hill) Battery Lane, Polruan. On E of Fowey estuary; leave car in public park; walk down St Saviour's Hill, turn L at Coast Guard office. 1¼-acre cliff garden with sea on 3 sides; mainly plants which withstand salty gales but incl sub-tropical. Spectacular views of Coast; cove for swimming. Cream TEAS. *Adm £1 Chd 50p. Open every Thurs June, July, Aug, Sept. For NGS Thurs May 19, 26 (2-8)*

¶Heligan Manor Gardens ♿❀ (Mr Tim Smit) Pentewan. From St Austell take B3273 sign-posted Mevagissey, follow signs. Heligan Manor Gardens is the scene of the lgest garden restoration project undertaken since the war. Of special interest in this romantic Victorian garden are; the fern ravine, 4 walled gardens with peach houses, vineries, melon grounds, a splendid collection of Beeboles, crystal grotto, Italian garden with a pool, an Elizabethan beacon 'Mount' and a large tropical Japanese valley garden. All are connected by an intricate web of over 2½m of ornamental footpaths, most unseen for more than half a century. TEAS and light refreshments. *Adm £2.50 Chd £1.50 Open every day (10-4.30). Groups welcome.* **Tel 0726 844157**

¶High Noon ❀ (R E Sturdy) Ladock. 7m E of Truro on A39. 3½ acres ornamental trees, rhododendrons, camellias, and magnolias, 10yrs old; rose garden; daffodils; lawns; formal pool; S-facing slope with good views. *Combined adm with* **Ladock House** *£2 Chd free. Sun April 24 (2-5.30)*

Higher Truscott ✿❀ (Mr & Mrs J C Mann) St Stephens. 3m NW of Launceston between St Stephens & Egloskerry. Sign-posted. Year-round elevated garden of 1 acre in a natural setting. Trees, shrubs, climbers; herbaceous plants & alpines, (many unusual). Splendid views. Ornamental vegetable garden. TEAS. *Adm £1 Chd free. Sun Aug 21 (2-6)*

The Hollies ⚹✿❀ (Mr J & Mrs N B Croggon) Grampound, nr Truro. In centre of village on Truro-St Austell rd. 2-acre garden of unusual design; unusual mixed planting of trees, shrubs and alpines. TEAS. *Adm £1 Chd free. Sun June 12 (2-5.30); also private visits welcome April-Sept, please* **Tel 0726 882474**

Jimmers, St Neot (Mr & Mrs P Kent) On L up Bush Hill. ¾-acre garden laid out in rooms with surprises and changes in atmosphere; varied planting; interesting trees; shrubs incl small collection of hollies, perennials, two ponds, patio, lawns and views; tranquil setting. *Combined adm with* **The Old Barn** *and* **Northwood Farm** *£3 Chd free. Sun June 5 (2-5.30)*

● Ken Caro ✿❀ (Mr & Mrs K R Willcock) Bicton, Pensilva, 5m NE of Liskeard. From A390 to Callington turn off N at Butchers Arms, St Ive; take Pensilva Rd; at next Xrds take rd signed Bicton. 2 acres mostly planted in 1970, with a further 2-acre extension in 1993; well-designed and labelled plantsman's garden; rhododendrons, flowering shrubs, conifers and other trees; herbaceous borders. Panoramic views. Collection of waterfowl and aviary birds. Featured in NGS gardens video 2, see page 344. *Adm £2 Chd 50p. April 10 to June 30 every Sun, Mon, Tues, Wed; Tues & Weds only July & Aug (2-6). Groups by appt* **Tel 0579 62446**

¶Ladock House ⚹ (Mr G J & Lady Mary Holborow). Ladock. 7m E of Truro on A39. Car park and entrance by church. Georgian old rectory with 4 acres of lawns, rhododendrons, camellias and azaleas with woodland garden. All planted during last 15yrs. TEAS in aid of Ladock Church. *Combined adm with* **High Noon** *£2 Chd free. Sun April 24 (2-5.30)*

Lamorran House ✿❀ (Mr & Mrs Dudley-Cooke) Upper Castle Rd, St Mawes. First turning R after garage; signposted to St. Mawes Castle. House ½m on L. Parking in rd. 4-acre sub-tropical hillside garden with beautiful views to St Anthonys Head. Extensive water gardens in Mediterranean and Japanese settings. Lge collection of rhododendrons, azaleas, palm trees, cycads, agaves and many S hemisphere plants and trees. TEAS. *Adm £2 Chd free. Sun June 5 (10-5)*

Lanhydrock ⚹✿❀ (The National Trust) Bodmin, 2½m on B3268. Station: Bodmin Parkway 1¾m. Large-sized garden; formal garden laid out 1857; shrub garden with good specimens of rhododendrons and magnolias and fine views. Lunches and TEAS. Closed Mondays. *Adm house & garden £5 Chd £2.50; garden only £2.60 Chd £1.30. Sun May 22 (11-5.30; last adm to house 5)*

¶Lanterns ❀ (G D & I Chapman) Mylor. 1m NE of Mylor. From Mylor follow the Restronguet Passage/Pandora Inn rd signs, Lanterns is on the RH-side before reaching the waterfront. ½-acre mature garden in natural setting planted by owners. Wide variety of shrubs, bulbs, herbaceous perennials, climbers, conservatory/greenhouse plants. Interesting in any season; small streams and dry areas; waterside walks. Owner always pleased to advise on plants and planting. *Collecting box. Open every day throughout the year (11am-dusk)*

Long Cross Victorian Gardens ⚹❀ (Mr & Mrs Crawford) Trelights, St Endellion. 7m N of Wadebridge on B3314. Charm of this garden is mazelike effect due to protecting hedges against sea-winds; views of countryside and sea scapes (Port Isaac and Port Quinn Bays) Garden specially designed to cope with environment of Cornwall's N Coast. Cream TEAS, coffee, evening meal. *Adm £1 Chd free, paid into NGS collecting box at gate. Open all year (10.30 until dusk)*

Mary Newman's Cottage ✿❀ (Tamar Protection Society) Culver Rd, ¼m from Saltash town centre; park on waterfront. Cottage garden with herbaceous, annuals and herbs. Overlooks R Tamar and Bridges. Recently restored C15 cottage, former home of Sir Francis Drake's first wife. TEAS. *Adm £1 Chd free (Share to Tamar Protection Society©). Sun June 19 (2-6)*

¶Newton House ⚹✿ (Mrs Michael Trinick) Lanhydrock. 3½m SE of Bodmin on W bank of R. Fowey nr Respryn Bridge. Follow signs to Lanhydrock and Respryn. Surrounded by woods in the beautiful valley of the R. Fowey; 3 acres of old-fashioned walled garden, lawns, shrubs, herbaceous border and old shrub roses, fruit, vegetables and orchard. TEAS. *Adm £1.50 Chd free. (Share to Lanhydrock Church®). Suns June 5, 12 (2-6)*

Northwood Farm, St Neot ✿ (Mr & Mrs P K Cooper) take rd out of village to Wenmouth Cross. L and first R. Follow very narrow rd and NGS posters to Farm on R. House & garden on site of a China Clay Dri used 150 yrs ago. House rebuilt from barn and garden from old sunken pits still being developed. Discovery of several natural springs led to creation of ponds now with collection of water birds. TEA. *Combined adm with* **The Old Barn** *and* **Jimmers** *£3 Chd free. Sun June 5 (2-5.30)*

The Old Barn, St Neot ⚹❀ (Mr & Mrs H S Lloyd) nr Liskeard. Turn R by garage, down lane to Holy Well. Cross field. 1st on L. Park in field. Riverside garden, mature trees, shrubs; mixed perennials, roses, clematis, pelargoniums, lawns, pond with water lilies. TEAS. *Combined adm with* **Northwood Farm** *and* **Jimmers** *£3 Chd free. Sun June 5 (2-5.30)*

The Old Mill Herbary ✿✤ (Mr & Mrs R D Whurr) Helland Bridge, Bodmin. [OS Map Ref SX065717]. Approx 4 acres semi-wild garden; natural woodland walks, alongside R Camel. Many wild flowers; adjacent Camel trail. Extensive planted named display of culinary, medicinal and aromatic herbs; shrubs; climbing and herbaceous plants. Active mill leat, water garden, raised patio pond with aquatics, Koi and other fish. Statuary, small raised alpine gardens. Treneague camomile lawn. A specialist's garden of historical and botanical interest. TEAS. *Adm £1.50 Chd 50p.* ▲*For NGS Sun Sept 11 (10-5)*

¶**Paradise Park** ⅄✿✤ (Mr Michael Reynolds) Hayle. Follow the A30 to Hayle, go to St Ives/St Erth roundabout then follow official brown and white signs to Paradise Park. The 2-acre walled garden is part of the 14 acres of Paradise Park. The park opened in 1973 as 'The rare and endangered birds breeding centre'. In recent yrs much effort has been expended to make the gardens a suitable setting for what has become a bird breeding collection of international importance. The World Parrot Trust is based here. In the walled garden and elsewhere are pergolas, trellis and gazebos; climbing roses, clematis, lilies and passiflora are featured. Open throughout the yr from 10am to 5pm. Cafe in Park. *Adm £4.95 (£1 reduction for members of any garden society) Chd £2.95. Sun May 15 (10-5)*

Penjerrick Garden ✤ (Rachel Morin) Budock. 3m SW of Falmouth between Budock and Mawnan Smith. Entrance at junction of lanes opp. Penmorvah Manor Hotel. Parking on verge along drive. Room to park one coach at gate. 15-acre garden of historical and botanical interest. Home of Barclayi and Penjerrick rhododendron hybrids. The upper garden with lovely view to the sea, contains many rhododendrons, camellias, magnolias, azaleas, bamboos, tree ferns and magnificent trees. The lower luxuriant valley garden features ponds in a wild woodland setting. *Adm £1 Chd 50p (Shore to Cornwall Garden Trust®).* ▲*For NGS Sun April 17 (11-5). Guided tours* **Tel 0872 870105**

Penpol House ⅄✿✤ (Major & Mrs T F Ellis) From Foundry Sq. Hayle take rd L of White Hart Hotel (Penpol Rd) then 2nd L into Penpol Avenue; ½ way up car park on R; from car park enter garden by main gates. Old-fashioned garden surrounds C16 house on hill above town covering 3 acres, different in character from the majority of Cornwall. Delphiniums, all types of roses, iris, herbaceous borders, walled garden with pond; fuchsia, yew and box hedges with lawns and other pocket gardens; climbing and rambling roses dress walls and trellises; granite stones, troughs and staddle stones are reminders of the past. Unusual for Cornwall the garden has an alkaline soil. TEAS in aid of Hayle Committee CRMF. *Adm £1.50 Chd 50p. Sun July 3 (2-6). Private visits also welcome, May 1 to July 31, please* **Tel 0736 753146**

Penwarne ⅄✿ (Dr & Mrs H Beister) 3¼m SW of Falmouth. 1½m N of Mawnan. Garden with many varieties of flowering shrubs, rhododendrons, magnolias, New Zealand shrubs, formal and informal garden; walled garden. Ornamental ducks. *Adm £1 Chd 50p. Sun March 20 (2-5)*

Peterdale ✿✤ (Mrs Ann Mountfield) St John's Road, Millbrook. Take new rd to Southdown. 1st L at new roundabout, straight ahead up St Johns Rd. Peterdale last bungalow on L. Small garden started 1980 from field; designed and created by owner on different levels; interesting collection of shrubs, trees, herbaceous plants combined with several mini lawns. TEA. *Adm £1.50 Chd free. Sun May 15; Wed July 20 (10-4)*

Pine Lodge Gardens ⅄✿✤ (Mr & Mrs R H J Clemo) Cuddra. On A390 E of St Austell between Holmbush and Tregrehan. Follow signs. 6-acre garden set in 16 acres natural woodland. Wide range well-labelled rare plants, shrubs in herbaceous borders using original designs and colour combinations. Rhododenderons, camellias, specimen trees. Many interesting features, incl bog garden, fish pond. TEAS. *Adm £2 Chd free. Sun June 26 (1-5)*

Pinetum ⅄✿✤ (Mr & Mrs G R Craw) Harewood. 6m SW of Tavistock. From A390 Tavistock-Callington Rd proceed towards Calstock. After 1m follow sign to Harewood Parish Church. At church continue straight on. 3rd house on R. 2 acres with unusual and specimen pine trees, unusual shrubs, conifers; camellias, rhododendrons and herbaceous borders. Ongoing programme of improvements. TEAS. *Adm £1 Chd free. Suns April 24; May 8, 15; June 5; Aug 7 (2-6)*

Polgwynne ⅄✿✤ (Mrs P Davey) Feock. 5m S of Truro via A39 (Truro-Falmouth rd) and then B3289 to 1st Xrds; straight on ½m short of Feock village. 3½-acre garden and grounds. Fruit and vegetable garden, woodlands extending to shore of Carrick Roads; magnificent Ginkgo Biloba (female, 12' girth) probably the largest female ginkgo in Britain; other beautiful trees; many rare and unusual shrubs. Lovely setting and view of Carrick Roads. TEAS. *Adm £1.50 Chd free. Sun April 24 (2-5.30). Private visits welcome, please* **Tel 0872 862612**

Porthpean House ⅄✿ (Christopher Petherick Esq) 2m SE of St Austell. Take turning off A390 signed Porthpean, L after Mount Edgcumbe Hospice down Porthpean Beach Rd, lge white house at very bottom of hill. 3-acre garden adjoining seashore, panoramic views, planted 1950s; varied and outstanding collection of camellias, rhododendrons and azaleas; special feature a hillside covered with primroses and daffodils. TEAS. *Adm £1.50 Chd free.* ▲*For NGS Sat April 16 (2-5)* **Tel 0726 72888**

Prideaux Place ⅄ (Mr & Mrs Prideaux-Brune) Padstow. On the edge of Padstow follow brown signs for Prideaux Place, from ring rd (A389). Surrounding Elizabethan house the present main grounds were laid out in the early C18 by Edmund Prideaux. Ancient deer park with stunning views over Camel estuary; victorian woodland walks currently under restoration. Newly restored sunken formal garden. A garden of vistas. Cream TEAS. *Adm £1.50 Chd free. April 3 to Sept 29 Sun to Thurs (1.30-5)*

Roseland House ✤ (Mr & Mrs Pridham) Chacewater, nr Truro. Situated in Chacewater 4m W of Truro, at Truro end of main st. Parking in village car park (100yds) or surrounding rds. 1-acre garden, with a lge range of plants, some unusual, many scented, most plants in the garden propagated for sale. Garden is divided into several different areas, with pond, old orchard and Victorian conservatory (open). TEAS. *Adm £1.50 Chd free. Suns June 26, July 10 (2-5). Also groups by appt* **Tel 0872 560451**

St Michael's Mount ✿✤ (The Rt Hon Lord St Levan; The National Trust) Marazion. ½m from shore at

Marazion by Causeway; otherwise by ferry. Flowering shrubs; rock plants, castle walls; fine sea views. TEAS. *Adm Castle & gardens £3, Chd £1.50 (under 16).* ▲*Sun April 24 (10.30-4.45)*

● **Trebah** ✿ (Trebah Garden Trust) 1m SW of Mawnan Smith and 500 yards W. of Glendurgan, 4m SW of Falmouth. Excellent parking (free) and access for coaches. 25-acre S. facing breathtaking ravine garden, planted in 1850's by Charles Fox. The extensive collection of rare and mature trees and shrubs incl glades of huge tree ferns over 100 years old and sub-tropical exotics. Hydrangea collection covers 2½ acres. Water garden with waterfalls and rock pool stocked with mature Koi Carp. A magical garden of unique beauty for the plantsman, the artist and the family. Play area and trail for children. Use of private beach. Tea/Coffee and light refreshments. *Adm £2.50 Chd and disabled £1. Open every day throughout year (10.30-5 last admission). For special arrangements* **Tel 0326 250448)**

Trebartha (The Latham Family) North Hill, SW of Launceston. Nr junction of B3254 & B3257. Wooded area with lake surrounded by walks of flowering shrubs; woodland trail through fine woods with cascades and waterfalls; American glade with fine trees. TEAS. *Adm £1.50 Chd 50p (Share to North Hill Parish Church Roof Fund®). Sun Sept 25 (2-6)*

Tregilliowe Farm ঌ✿✿ (Mr & Mrs J Richards) Penzance-Hayle A30 Rd from Penzance turn R at Crowlas Xrds. After approx 1m turn sharp L on to St Erth Rd. 2nd farm lane on R. 2-acre garden still developing. Herbaceous beds with wide range of perennials and grasses. Raised Mediterranean bed. TEAS June in aid of Cancer Relief Macmillan Fund. July in aid of St Julias Hospice. *Adm £1.50 Chd free. Suns June 19, July 17 (2-6)*

Tregrehan ঌ✿✿ (T Hudson Esq) Tregrehan. Entrance on A390 opp Britannia Inn 1m W of St Blazey. Access for cars and coaches. Garden largely created since early C19. Woodland of 20 acres containing fine trees, award winning camellias raised by late owner and many interesting plants from warm temperate climes. Show greenhouses a feature containing softer species. TEA. *Adm £2 Chd 50p. Mid March to end June, and Sept daily.* ▲*For NGS Sun May 1 (10.30-5)*

Trelean ঌ✿ (Sqn-Ldr G T Witherwick) St Martin-in-Meneage. 8m E of Helston. From Helston take St Keverne rd B3293; after 4m turn L for Mawgan then follow signs. Medium-sized valley garden of 3 acres. Contained within 20 acres of natural woodland. A ¼m Helford riverside walk with a freshwater, fern-clad stream discharging onto beach. A plantsman's domain, purpose planted for autumn colour, yet of all seasons interest. Autumn colour film show. TEAS. *Adm £1.50 Chd Free. Sun Oct 23 (12-5). Also private visits welcome (owner conducted tour), please* **Tel 0326 231255** *(evenings)*

Trelissick ঌ✿✿ (The National Trust; Mr & Mrs Spencer Copeland) Feock, 4m S of Truro, nr King Harry Ferry. On B3289. Large garden; superb view over Falmouth harbour. Georgian house (not open). TEAS. *Adm £3 Chd £1.50* ▲ *For NGS Sun April 10 (1-5.30)*

Tremeer Gardens St Tudy, 8m N of Bodmin; W of B3266, all rds signed. 7-acre garden famous for camellias

and rhododendrons with water; many rare shrubs. *Adm £1 Chd 50p. Sun April 3 (2-6)*

Trerice ঌ✿✿ (The National Trust) Newlyn East 3m SE of Newquay. From Newquay via A392 and A3058; turn R at Kestle Mill (NT sign-posts). Small manor house, rebuilt in 1571, containing fine plaster ceilings and fireplaces; oak and walnut furniture and tapestries. Lunches & TEAS. *Adm house & garden £3.60 Chd £1.80.* ▲*Sun June 12 (11-5.30). Guided garden tour 2.30*

Trevegean ✿✿(Mr & Mrs E C Cousins) 9 Manor Way. Take Penzance by-pass; take first L off roundabout towards Treneere and Heamoor. Sharp R turn for Manor way. ⅓-acre divided into series of enclosed areas; planting some formal, informal, topiary garden, shrubs and perennials; connected by brick and slab paths some edged with box. TEAS. *Adm £1 Chd free (Share to St Julias Hospice Hayle®). Private visits welcome April 1 to July 31 (2-5), please* **Tel 0736 67407**

● **Trewithen** ঌ✿ (A M J Galsworthy Esq) Truro. ½m E Probus. Entrance on A390 Truro-St Austell Rd. Sign-posted. Large car park. Internationally renowned garden of 30 acres laid out by Maj G Johnson between 1912 & 1960 with much of original seed and plant material collected by Ward and Forrest. Original C18 walled garden famed for towering magnolias and rhododendrons; wide range of own hybrids. Flatish ground amidst original woodland park. Featured in NGS video 2; see page 344. TEAS. *Adm £2 Chd £1. Mon to Sat March 1 to Sept 30 (10-4.30). Special arrangements for coaches. Mrs Norman* **Tel 0726 882763**

¶**Treworder Mill** ✿✿ (Derek & Pearl Rutter) Kenwyn. 2½m W of Truro. A390 Truro to Redruth. Turn at Treliske Hospital roundabout. Pass Duchy Hospital. Turn L at T junction. Car parking at bottom of hill. R Kenwyn Valley Garden. 2¾ acres with streams and a wide range of moisture-loving plants in an informal setting. Banks of heathers and shrubs. New pond area. TEAS in aid of Save the Children Fund. *Adm £1.50 Chd free. Sun May 22 (2-5)*

Watergate Trelill ✿ (Lt Col & Mrs G B Browne) 5m SW of Camelford; N of St Kew Highway; NE of Trelill; sign-posted from A39. 3-acre garden in a delightful setting with a stream running through it. In spring there is a display of many varieties of narcissus and camellias, rhododendrons and magnolias. Water garden with variety of primulas and moisture-loving plants. Also herbaceous borders, shrubs and old-fashioned roses. TEAS. *Adm £1.50 Chd free. Easter Sun April 3 (2-5.30)*

●**Woodland Garden** ✿✿ (Mr & Mrs N Froggatt) On Helston/St Keverne Rd B3293, turn R ¼m past Garras village at Woodland Garden sign. Entrance on R after ½m. Informal 2½-acre garden in wooded valley, planted in the last 14 years with camellias, rhododendrons, magnolias, trees and shrubs, primulas and many unusual plants. Planting and development continue. Lovely spring succession of wild daffodils, primroses and then bluebells. Small pond and stream. ¼-mile walk to 9 acres on Goonhilly Downs, an impressive area of heathers (especially the Erica Vagans, best July-Sept). Dogs allowed only on Downs. *Adm £1 Chd free. Sats April 2 to Oct 1 (2-5). Also private visits welcome* **Enquiries Tel 0326 22295**

Cumbria

Hon County Organiser: (South)
Assistant Hon County Organiser: (North)

Mrs R E Tongue, Paddock Barn, Winster, Windermere LA23 3NW
Mrs E C Hicks, Scarthwaite, Grange-in-Borrowdale, Keswick CA12 5UQ

DATES OF OPENING

By appointment
For telephone numbers and other details see garden descriptions. Private visits welcomed

The Beeches, Houghton
Browfoot, Skelwith Bridge
38 English St, Longtown, Carlisle
Greystones, Embleton, Cockermouth
Matthew How, Troutbeck
Palace How, Brackenthwaite
Rydal Mount, Eskdale Green, nr Gosforth

Regular openings
For details see garden descriptions

Brockhole, Windermere. Daily Mar 24 to Nov 2
Holehird, Windermere. Daily
Holker Hall & Gardens. Suns to Fris April 1 to Oct 31
Hutton-in-the-Forest. Daily except Sats
Levens Hall, Kendal. Daily except Fris and Sats April 1 to Sept 30
Lingholm, Portinscale. Daily April 1 to Oct 31
Muncaster Castle, Ravenglass. Daily

April 3 Sunday
Rannerdale Cottage, Buttermere
April 6 Wednesday
Green Bank, Grasmere
April 17 Sunday
Copt Howe, Chapel Stile
April 18 Monday
Levens Hall, Kendal
May 1 Sunday
Copt Howe, Chapel Stile
Dallam Tower, Milnthorpe
Rydal Mount, Eskdale Green, nr Gosforth
May 4 Wednesday
Lingholm, Portinscale, nr Keswick
Rydal Mount, Eskdale Green, nr Gosforth

May 7 Saturday
Acorn Bank, Temple Sowerby
May 8 Sunday
Browfoot, Skelwith Bridge, Ambleside ‡
Green Bank, Grasmere ‡
Palace How, Brackenthwaite, Loweswater
Stagshaw, Ambleside ‡
May 11 Wednesday
Brockhole, Windermere
May 12 Thursday
Muncaster Castle, Ravenglass
May 15 Sunday
Browfoot, Skelwith Bridge, Ambleside ‡
Copt Howe, Chapel Stile, Ambleside ‡
Green Bank, Grasmere ‡
Lindeth Fell Country House Hotel
May 18 Wednesday
Brockhole, Windermere
May 21 Saturday
Galesyke, Wasdale
May 22 Sunday
Browfoot, Skelwith Bridge, Ambleside ‡
Copt Howe, Chapel Stile, Ambleside ‡
Fell Yeat, Kirkby Lonsdale
Galesyke, Wasdale
Halecat, Witherslack ‡
High Beckside Farm, nr Grange-Over-Sands ‡
St Annes, Great Langdale ‡
May 25 Wednesday
Brackenburn, Manesty, nr Keswick
May 28 Saturday
Holehird, Windermere
May 29 Sunday
Fellside, Millbeck, nr Keswick
Matson Ground, Windermere
June 5 Sunday
Hazelmount, Thwaites, Millom
Hutton-in-the-Forest, Penrith
Station House, Lamplugh, nr Workington
Stagshaw, Ambleside ‡
Yews, Middle Entrance Drive, Bowness-on-Windermere ‡

June 12 Sunday
Greystones, Embleton, Cockermouth
High Hesket School, High Hesket ‡
Marton House, Long Marton ‡
June 19 Sunday
Dallam Tower, Milnthorpe
Fell Yeat, Kirkby Lonsdale
Rannerdale Cottage, Buttermere
June 22 Wednesday
Scarthwaite, Grange-in-Borrowdale
June 25 Saturday
Acorn Bank, Temple Sowerby
June 26 Sunday
Askham Hall, Penrith ‡
Scarthwaite, Grange-in-Borrowdale
Whitbysteads, Askham ‡
July 9 Saturday
Sizergh Castle, nr Kendal
July 10 Sunday
High Cleabarrow, Windermere
July 17 Sunday
Dallam Tower, Milnthorpe ‡
38 English St, Longtown, Carlisle
Halecat, Witherslack ‡
Holehird, Windermere
July 30 Saturday
Acorn Bank, Temple Sowerby
August 3 Wednesday
Lingholm, Portinscale
August 7 Sunday
Hutton-in-the-Forest, Penrith
August 28 Sunday
Rannerdale Cottage, Buttermere
Rydal Mount, Eskdale Green, nr Gosforth
August 31 Wednesday
Rydal Mount, Eskdale Green, nr Gosforth
September 4 Sunday
Matson Ground Settlement, Windermere
September 26 Monday
Levens Hall, Kendal

DESCRIPTIONS OF GARDENS

Acorn Bank &%& (The National Trust) Temple Sowerby. 6m E of Penrith on A66; ½m N of Temple Sowerby. Bus: Penrith-Appleby or Carlisle-Darlington; alight Culgaith Rd end. Medium-sized walled garden; fine herb garden; orchard and mixed borders; wild garden with woodland/riverside walk. Dogs on leads only woodland walk. *Adm £1.60 Chd 80p. April 1 to Oct 31 daily (10-5). For NGS Suns May 7, June 25, July 30 (10-5)*

Askham Hall %& (The Earl & Countess of Lonsdale) 5m S of Penrith. Turn off A6 for Lowther and Askham. Askham Hall is a pele tower, incorporating C14, C16 and early C18 elements in courtyard plan. Formal outlines of garden with terraces of herbaceous borders and original topiary, probably from late C17. Shrub roses and recently created herb garden. Kitchen garden. TEA. *Adm £1 Chd free (Share to Askham & Lowther Churches®). Sun June 26 (2-5.30)*

The Beeches %& (Mr & Mrs J B McKay Black) 42 The Green, Houghton. 2m NE of Carlisle. Leave M6 at junction 44. Take B6264 (Brampton & Carlisle Airport). After 1m turn R over M6 into village. Parking in lay-by on R at end of village green. The Beeches is 10 yards further. Plantsman's garden approx ¾-acre. Herbaceous, mixed borders, raised beds of alpines, peat garden, troughs and pool. Many dwarf bulbs in Spring. Alpine house and frame. Good collections of hostas and dwarf rhododendrons. *Adm £1 Chd free. Private visits only, please Tel 0228 22670*

¶Brackenburn (Prof & Mrs D C Ellwood) Manesty. Take rd signed Portinscale and Grange off A66. Follow all signs for Grange. Garden is 1½ acres on the mountainside on RH-side of rd 3½m from A66. The Garden has wonderful views of Lake Derwent Water. There are several water features planted for damp acid conditions with many rhododendrons, azaleas, ferns and primulas. Brackenburn is the former home of author Sir Hugh Walpole. *Adm £1 Chd free. Wed May 25 (2-5)*

Brockhole & (Lake District National Park) Windermere. 2m NW of Windermere on A591 between Windermere and Ambleside. 10 acres formal gardens, designed by Thomas Mawson. Acid soils and mild aspect, many unusual or slightly tender plants; shrub roses, herbaceous borders, scented garden. 20 acres informal grounds, wide variety of trees and shrubs. Picnic area, adventure playground, boat trips on Lake Windermere. Garden walks. TEAS. *Adm free (Pay & display car parking £2.20 per car, season ticket for car park £14). Daily March 24 to Nov 2; for NGS Wed May 11, 18 (10-5)*

Browfoot && (Mr Trevor Woodburn) Skelwith Bridge 2½m SW of Ambleside on A593. Turn down lane at Skelwith Bridge. Woodland garden developed by owner; rhododendrons; azaleas; species trees and natural rock garden. Approx 2 acres. Parking & TEAS provided by and in aid of the Community Centre, only on May 8. *Adm £1 Chd 40p. Suns May 8, 15, 22 (11-5.30). Private visits welcome May, please Tel 05394 32248*

Copt Howe & (Professor R N Haszeldine) Chapel Stile. Great Langdale ¼m W of Chapel Stile on B5343 from Ambleside. Parking at adjacent Harry Place Farm. 2-acre plantsman's garden, new areas under development. Extensive collections of acers (especially Japanese), camellias, azaleas, rhododendrons, quercus, fagus, many rare shrubs and trees, perennials; herbaceous and bulbous species; alpines and trough gardens; dwarf and large conifers; Japanese and Himalayan plants; mountain views. Featured by the media, gardening magazines, etc. No teas or plants April 17, May 1. Cream TEAS. *Adm £1.50 Chd free (Share to Langdales Society© May 15, Friends of the Lake District® April 17, May 1, 15, 22) (10-5.30). Private visits welcome April to Sept, please Tel 05394 37685*

Dallam Tower & (Brigadier & Mrs C E Tryon-Wilson) Milnthorpe, 7m S of Kendal. 7m N of Carnforth, nr junction of A6 and B5282. Station: Arnside, 4m; Lancaster, 15m. Bus: Ribble 553, 554 Milnthorpe-Lancaster via Arnside, alight at Lodge Gates. Medium-sized garden; natural rock garden, waterfalls, rambler and polyanthus roses; wood walks, lawns, shrubs. *Adm 80p Chd free. Suns May 1, June 19, July 17 (2-5)*

¶38 English Street %& (Mr & Mrs C Thomson) Longtown, Carlisle. M6 junction 44, A7 for 6m into Longtown. 300yds on L next door to Annes Hairdressers. Entrance through open archway. Terraced house garden. Red sandstone and water features; containers and troughs, pergola and herbaceous. TEA. *Adm £1 Chd free (Share to Cat Protection League®). Sun July 17 (2-5). Private visits welcome, please Tel 0228 791364*

Fell Yeat &%& (Mr & Mrs O S Benson) Casterton, nr Kirkby Lonsdale. Approx 1m E of Casterton Village on the rd to Bull Pot. Leave A65 at Devils Bridge, follow A683 for a mile, take the R fork to High Casterton at the golf course, straight across at two sets of Xrds, the house is immediately on the L about ¼m from no through rd sign. 1-acre informal country garden with mixed borders, herbaceous, old roses, small fernery, herb garden and small pond. Extensive views of the Lune Valley from a still developing garden. TEAS (in aid of S Lakeland Cot Death Group®). *Adm £1 Chd 20p. Suns May 22, June 19 (2-5.30)*

Fellside % (Mr & Mrs C D Collins) Millbeck, 2m N of Keswick. Turn off A591 Keswick-Bassenthwaite rd opp sign to Millbeck (2m from Keswick); at T-junc in Millbeck village turn right; garden 300yds on left. 1-acre, informal, shrub garden; 300 varieties of rhododendrons, camellias, azaleas, on steep terraced site. Pretty glen with beck; magnificent views of Derwent Water and Bassenthwaite. Tea John Gregg, The Cottage, Millbeck or The Old Mill (Nat Trust) Mirehouse. *Adm 60p Chd 30p. Sun May 29 (2-5)*

¶Galesyke &% (Christine & Mike McKinley) Wasdale. From the N enter Gosforth and follow signposts to Nether Wasdale. Pass through Nether Wasdale, following signs to the Lake and Wasdale Head. After approx ¾m, entrance on R. From the S head towards Santon Bridge turn off A595 at Holmrook or app from Eskdale. Turn R at Santon Bridge following signs to Wasdale Head. Approx 3m to entrance. Secluded landscaped riverside garden on the banks of the R Irt with magnificent views of the

Screes and Wasdale Fells. Approx 1½ acres the garden contains a variety of mature trees and flowering shrubs. There is access to a riverside meadows walk and to the far bank with its secluded woodland walks. TEAS. *Adm £1.20 Chd under 12 free (Share to NSPCC®). Sat, Sun May 21, 22 (11-6)*

¶Green Bank ⚹ (Mr & Mrs Reg Gifford) Grasmere. 4m from Ambleside off the A591 Keswick Rd. Turn R between Swan Hotel and its car park. 5-acre steep hillside garden with woodland walks and mountain stream under a 5yr renovation plan. Features a unique collection of rare trees, rhododendrons, camellias and azaleas brought to England by the late Michael Black from Bhutan, Chile, Nepal, etc. Great interest to plant enthusiasts. Teas in adjacent hotels or cafes in Grasmere. *Adm £2 Chd/OAPs £1. Wed April 6, Suns May 8, 15 (10.30-5)*

¶Greystones ⚹❀ (Mr & Mrs D Cook) Embleton. Just off A66, 4m E of Cockermouth, 2m W of Bassenthwaite Lake. Take turning marked 'Wythop Mill' with watermill sign. Lane 200yds on R. 1 acre of mostly new garden being developed on various levels around mature trees, with shrubs, herbaceous beds and borders, woodland garden, pond, scree, spring bulbs. Organic fruit and vegetable beds. Teas at Wythop Mill ½m. *Adm £1 Chd free. Sun June 12 (2-5). Private visits welcome, please Tel 07687 76375*

Halecat ⅃⚹❀ (Mrs Michael Stanley) Witherslack, 10m SW of Kendal. From A590 turn into Witherslack following the Halecat brown signs. L in township at another brown sign and L again, signpost 'Cartmel Fell'; gates on L [map ref. 434834]. Medium-sized garden; mixed shrub and herbaceous borders, terrace, sunken garden; gazebo; daffodils and cherries in Spring, over 70 different varieties of hydrangea; beautiful view over Kent estuary to Arnside. Nursery garden attached. TEA. *Adm 80p Chd free (Share to Leukaemia Campaign®). Suns May 22, July 17 (2-5)*

Hazelmount ⅃⚹❀ (Mrs J Barratt) Thwaites, Millom, 2m from Broughton-in-Furness off A595 up hill after crossing Duddon River Bridge. 5-acre woodland garden, small lake with stream; spring display of species rhododendrons, azaleas and flowering shrubs. Mature trees and exceptional views of Duddon Estuary and sea. TEAS. *Adm £1 Chd free (Share to CRMF®). Sun June 5 (2-5.30)*

High Beckside Farm ⚹ (Mr & Mrs P J McCabe) Cartmel. 1¼m N of Cartmel. Take the Haverthwaite Rd, from the PO in the village. A newly created conservation area, a wild garden with ponds, waterfalls, waterfowl; flowering bushes and a number of rare trees. An arboretum in the very early stages of formation. 11 acres of wild flowers on a hillside with fine views. A small house garden. Approx ¼m from house to conservation area. Stout shoes. TEA. *Adm £1 Chd 25p. Sun May 22 (1-5)*

High Cleabarrow ⅃⚹❀ (Mr & Mrs R T Brown) 3m SE of Windermere off B5284 Crook to Kendal Rd (nr Windermere Golf Course). 1½-acre newly designed and planted garden comprising wide variety of herbaceous, old-fashioned roses, shrubs, unusual plants on different levels; woodland area. TEAS. *Adm £1.20 Chd 50p. Sun July 10 (1.30-5.30)*

¶High Hesket School ⅃⚹ (Mr P Howard) Nr Carlisle. The school is just off the A6 halfway between Penrith and Carlisle. Backs onto the A6 but visitors must turn off to High Hesket and will find the school at the top of the hill. Wildlife garden featuring a variety of habitats – pond, bog meadows, hedge and tree plantings. Cultivated garden for flowers and vegetables, specially designed maths and science area with waterfall, sundial, sand pit etc. The development was started in 1990 and occupies ½ acre of the school's playing field. It won the 1991 Cumbria County Council Environment Award for best project by a school, college or youth group. TEA. *Adm £1 Chd free (Share to High Hesketh School Association©). Sun June 12 (1-5)*

Holehird (Lakeland Horticultural Society) ⚹ Patterdale Road, Windermere. ½m N of Windermere town on A591. Turn R onto A592 to Patterdale. Garden signposted on R ¾m on A592. Car park along private drive. The garden of nearly 5 acres is set on a hillside with some of the best views in Lakeland, with a great diversity of plants that grow well in this area, incl alpine and heather beds and a collection of rhododendrons and azaleas. The walled garden is mostly herbaceous. National collections of astilbes, polystichum ferns and hydrangeas. Partially suitable wheelchairs. *Garden always open. Entrance by donation £1 Chd free. Warden available throughout summer (11-5). Coach parties by appointment, guides available Tel 05394 46008. For NGS Sat May 28, Sun July 17 (11-5)*

●Holker Hall & Gardens ⅃⚹ (Lord & Lady Cavendish) Cark-in-Cartmel. 4m W of Grange-over-Sands. 12m W of M6 (junction 36). 24 acres of magnificent formal and woodland gardens associated with Joseph Paxton & Mawson. Rare trees, shrubs, exotic flowering trees, magnolias and rose garden. Water features incl superb limestone cascade. New elliptical formal garden and rhododendron and azalea arboretum. Winners of Christies - H.H.A. Garden of the Year Award (1991). C19 Wing of Holker Hall, Motor Museum, Patchwork & Quilting Display, Kitchen Exhibition, Adventure Playground, Deer Park, Shop & Cafeteria. *Garden tours Thurs 11.30am & 2.30pm or by appt. Discounted Adm & catering to groups 20+ by prior arrangement. The Garden Festival June 3 to 5. Adm prices not available at time of going to press. Sun to Fris April 1 to Oct 31 (10.30-6 last entry 4.30)*

Hutton-in-the-Forest (Lord Inglewood) 5m NW of Penrith. 3m from exit 41 of M6. Magnificent grounds with C18 walled flower garden, terraces and lake. C19 Low garden, specimen trees and topiary; woodland walk and dovecote. Mediaeval House with C17, C18 and C19 additions. TEAS. *Adm £1.50 gardens, grounds, £3 house, gardens & grounds Chd free gardens, grounds £1 house & garden & grounds. Gardens and grounds open daily all year except Sats (11-5). House and tea room open Easter Sun, April 4–8 incl. Thurs, Fris, Sats May 1 to Oct 2. Also Weds in Aug and Bank Hol Mons (1-4). For NGS Suns June 5, Aug 7 (11-5)*

By Appointment Gardens. Avoid the crowds. Good chance of a tour by owner. See garden description for telephone number.

Levens Hall ⅃⅍❀ (C H Bagot Esq) 5m S of Kendal on Milnthorpe Rd (A6); Exit 36 from M6. 10 acres incl famous topiary garden and 1st ha-ha laid out by M Beaumont. Celebrating 300th Anniversary in 1994 by creating a new garden feature. Magnificent beech circle; formal bedding; herbaceous borders. Elizabethan mansion, added to C13 pele tower, contains superb panelling, plasterwork and furniture. Steam collection illustrating history of steam 1830-1920. Only gardens suitable for wheelchairs. *Adm House & Garden £3.90 OAPs £3.40 Chd £2.30. Garden only £2.60 OAPs £2.40 Chd £1.60. Reduction for groups. April 1 to Sept 30. House and garden, gift shop, tearoom. children's play area, picnic area. Sun, Mon, Tues, Wed, Thurs house (11-4.30), grounds (10-5), steam collection (2-5). Closed Fri & Sat. For NGS Mons April 18, Sept 26 (10-5)*

Lindeth Fell Country House Hotel ⅃ (Air Commodore & Mrs P A Kennedy) 1m S of Bowness on A5074. 6-acres of lawns and landscaped grounds on the hills above Lake Windermere, probably designed by one of the Mawson school around 1907; majestic conifers and specimen trees best in spring and early summer with a colourful display of rhododendrons, azaleas and Japanese maples; grounds offer splendid views to Coniston mountains; rose garden and herbaceous border newly developed. TEAS in hotel 50p. *Adm £1 Chd free. Sun May 15 (2-5)*

Lingholm ⅃⅍❀ (The Viscount Rochdale) Keswick. On W shore of Derwentwater; Portinscale 1m; Keswick 3m. Turn off A66 at Portinscale; drive entrance 1m on left. Ferry: Keswick to Nicol End, 10 mins walk. Bus: Keswick to Portinscale, 1m; 'Mountain Goat' minibus service from town centre passes drive end. Formal and woodland gardens; garden walk 1m; rhododendrons, azaleas, etc. Spring daffodils, autumn colour. Plant centre. Free car park. TEAS. *Adm £2.60 (incl leaflet) Chd free. April 1 to Oct 31 daily. For NGS Weds May 4, Aug 3 (10-5)*

¶**Marton House** ⅍❀ (Mr & Mrs M S Hardy-Bishop) Long Marton, Turn off A66 2m W of Applesby signposted Long Marton. Follow rd through village under bridge. House/Car park on R. A 4½ acre walled garden nestling in the foothills of the Pennines. Magnificent Cedar of lebanon, herbaceous borders, new Italian garden leading to small lake, ducks, woodland walk, parterre, views. Ongoing landscaping and refurbishment. TEAS. *Adm £1.50 Chd 25p. Sun June 12 (1-6)*

Matson Ground ⅃⅍❀ (Matson Ground Settlement) Windermere. From Kendal turn R off B5284 signposted Heathwaite, 100yds after Windermere Golf Club entrance. Lane joins another in ¼m. Continue straight on. Garden is on L after ¼m. From Bowness turn L onto B5284 from A5074. After ¾m turn L at Xrds follow sign to Heathwaite. Garden on L ¾m along lane. A watercourse flows through the ornamental garden ending at a large pond in the wild garden of meadow grassland with spring bulbs and later wild flowers. Azaleas and rhododendrons, large mixed shrub/herbaceous borders and some very imaginative topiary work. Landscape designer John Brookes has been behind much of the recent changes in the garden. There is also a ½-acre walled kitchen garden being run on organic methods with greenhouses and a dovecote. Adjacent to the ornamental garden is a 2-acre amenity woodland. TEAS. *Adm £1 Chd 50p. Suns May 29, Sept 4 (12-5)*

Matthew How ⅍ (Mr & Mrs John Griffiths) Troutbeck. 2½m equidistant from Windermere & Ambleside. From Windermere after Lakes School turn R up Bridge Lane off A591. From Ambleside L up Holbeck Lane between Townend (NT) and Post office. 1-acre typical lakeland terraced garden on steep fell site. Surrounding C17 (Yeoman Farmers House). Views overlooking Troutbeck Valley. Spring flowering bulbs; rhododendrons, camellias, azaleas, alpines, old roses, yew and box hedges, topiary. Interesting wild bird life incl. nut hatches and pied fly catchers. TEA. *Adm £1. Private visits welcome anytime April, May, June and late Autumn, please* **Tel 0539 433276**

Muncaster Castle ⅃❀ (Mrs P R Gordon-Duff-Pennington) 1m E of Ravenglass, 17m SW of Whitehaven on A595. 77 acres; famous large collection of species rhododendrons, azaleas and camellias, some unique in UK; arboretum; historic and scenic site at foot of Eskdale. Owl centre. Giftshop. Also extensive plant centre. Coach parties and schools by appt. Special arrangements for disabled at front gate. CAFE. *Castle, Garden and Owl Centre 1994 Adm price on application* **Tel 0229 717614.** *Gardens and Owl Centre open all year. Castle open daily from Mar 20 to Oct 30 except Mons (also open all Bank Hol Mons). Castle (1-4) garden and Owl Centre (11-5). For NGS Thurs May 12 (11-5)*

Palace How ⅃⅍❀ (Mr & Mrs A & K Johnson) Brackenthwaite, Loweswater, 6m SE of Cockermouth on B5292 and B5289 or from Keswick 10m over Whinlatter Pass, through Lorton village, follow signs for Loweswater. Established 10-yr-old damp garden set in lovely situation amongst mountains. Acid soil supporting unusual trees and shrubs, especially rhododendrons and acers. Pond with bog plants; iris; candelabra primulas; Himalayan poppies and hostas, roses and alpines. Lunches and Teas at Loweswater Village Hall in aid of W Cumbria Hopice at Home. *Adm £1.20 Chd free. Sun May 8 (10-5)*

Rannerdale Cottage ⅃❀ (The McElney Family) Buttermere. 8m S of Cockermouth, 10m W of Keswick. ½-acre cottage garden with beck and woodland walk overlooking Crummock Water, splendid mountain views. Herbaceous, shrubs, roses, perennial geraniums, tree peonies, pond with fish. TEAS. *Adm £1 Chd free. Suns April 3, June 19, Aug 28 (11-5)*

Rydal Mount ❀ (Don & Toni Richards) Eskdale Green, Holmrook. Turn off A595 where signed 6m to Eskdale Green. Turn sharp R opp Eskdale Stores. 2nd house on R. 1½-acre garden on natural rock facing SW. Heathers and tree heaths with shrubs and small trees favouring acid soil; eucalyptus and American blueberrys; water garden. Blueberry TEAS. *Adm 75p Chd free (Shore to West Cumbria Hospice at Home®). Suns, Weds May 1, 4; Aug 28, 31 (2-5). Also private visits welcome, please* **Tel 09467 23267**

Regular Openers. See head of county section.

St Annes ❀ (Mr & Mrs R D Furness) Great Langdale. 5m from Ambleside on B5343. Follow signs for Langdale/Old Dungeon Ghyll. At Skelwith Bridge take R hand fork and at Elterwater take R hand. Through Chapel Stile, ¾m on L hand side travelling W. 3-acre partial woodland with established variety of conifers and trees, azaleas and rhododendrons. Natural rock faces with alpines, streams and rocky paths. Magnificent views Langdales. Partially suitable for wheelchairs. TEAS. *Adm £1 Chd free. Sun May 22 (12-5). Open for groups by appt, please* **Tel 05394 37271**

Scarthwaite ❀❀ (Mr & Mrs E C Hicks) Grange-in-Borrowdale. From Keswick take B5289 to Grange; cross bridge, house ¼m on L. Ferns, cottage garden plants and many others closely packed into ⅓ acre. *Adm 80p Acc chd free. Wed June 22, Sun June 26 (2-5)*

Sizergh Castle ❀❀ (The National Trust) nr Kendal. Close to and W of the main A6 trunk road, 3m S of Kendal. An approach road leaves A6 close to and S of A6/A591 interchange. ⅔-acre Limestone Rock Garden is the largest owned by the National Trust; it has a large collection of Japanese maples, dwarf conifers, hardy ferns, primulas, gentians and many other perennials and bulbs; water garden with bog and aquatic plants; on walls around main lawn are shrubs and climbers, many half-hardy; rose garden contains specimen roses along with shrubs, climbers, ground cover and lilies; also wild flower banks, herbaceous border, crab apple orchard with spring bulbs and 'Dutch' garden. *Castle & gdn adm £3.30 Chd £1.70; Gdn adm £1.70 Chd 90p. For NGS Sat July 9 (12.30-5.30)*

Stagshaw ❀ (The National Trust) ½m S of Ambleside. Turn E off A 591, Ambleside to Windermere rd. Bus 555 Kendal-Keswick alight Waterhead. Woodland gdn incl fine collection of rhododendrons and azaleas. Ericaceous trees & shrubs incl magnolias, camellias, embothriums. Views over Windermere. *Adm £1 Chd 50p. For NGS Suns May 8, June 5 (10-5.30)*

Station House ❀❀ (Mr & Mrs G H Simons) Wright Green. Lamplugh approx 6m from Workington, Whitehaven and Cockermouth signposted off A5086 Lilyhall-Workington from Cockermouth-Egremont Rd ½m under disused railway line from Workington-Whitehaven A595 at Leyland roundabout take rd signposted Branthwaite-Loweswater. 2-acre garden created over site of disused railway line and station. Features shrubs and trees; vegetable and fruit garden. TEAS. *Adm 50p Chd 25p. Sun June 5 (10.30-4.30)*

Whitbysteads ❀ (The Hon Mrs Anthony Lowther) Askham nr Penrith 8m from Penrith. Turn R at Eamont Bridge off the A6. Turn L at Y fork after Railway Bridge signed Askham. Through village, turn R at Queen's Head. 1-acre garden on several levels surrounding farmhouse on edge of fells, featuring wide variety shrub roses, unusual herbaceous plants and geraniums. Pergola; fountain. Magnificent views over Eden Valley. TEAS. *Adm £1 Chd free (Share to St Michael & All Angels Church, Lowther®). Sun June 26 (2-5)*

Yews ❀❀ (Sir Oliver & Lady Scott) Bowness-on-Windermere. Middle Entrance Drive, 50yds. Medium-sized formal Edwardian garden; fine trees, ha-ha, herbaceous borders. TEAS. *Adm £1 Chd free (Share to Marie Curie Cancer Care®). Sun June 5 (2-5.30)*

Derbyshire

Hon County Organiser: Mr & Mrs R Brown, 210 Nottingham Rd, Woodlinkin, Langley Mill, Nottingham NG16 4HG Tel 0773 714903

Hon County Treasurer: Mrs G Nutland

DATES OF OPENING

By appointment
For telephone numbers and other details see garden descriptions. Private visits welcomed

Bath House Farm, Ashover
Birchfield, Ashford in the Water
Birchwood Farm, Coxbench
Cherry Tree Cottage, Hilton
Dam Farm House, Ednaston
Darley House, nr Matlock
Gamesley Fold Cottage, Glossop
Green Farm Cottage, Offcote
The Limes, Apperknowle
23 Mill Lane, Codnor
Oaks Lane Farm, Brockhurst

57 Portland Close, Mickleover
The Riddings Farm, Kirk Ireton
Thatched Cottage, Radbourne
Valezina Hillside, Heage

Regular openings
For details see garden descriptions

Lea Gardens, nr Matlock. Daily March 20 to July 17
Renishaw Hall, nr Sheffield. Suns June, July, Aug

March 6 Sunday
Quarndon Hall, Derbyshire
April 3 Sunday
Mount Cottage, Ticknall

Quarndon Hall, Derbyshire
Renishaw Hall, nr Sheffield

April 4 Monday
Mount Cottage, Ticknall
Renishaw Hall, nr Sheffield

April 10 Sunday
Radburne Hall, nr Derby

April 17 Sunday
Dam Farm House, Ednaston
32 Heanor Road, Codnor
Meynell Langley, Kirk Langley
57 Portland Close, Mickleover
Shottle Hall Guest House, Belper

April 20 Wednesday
57 Portland Close, Mickleover

April 24 Sunday
Fir Croft, Calver, nr Bakewell

May 1 Sunday
Mount Cottage, Ticknall
Quarndon Hall, Derbyshire
Renishaw Hall, nr Sheffield
The Riddings Farm, Kirk Ireton

May 2 Monday
Mount Cottage, Ticknall
Renishaw Hall, nr Sheffield

May 8 Sunday
Cherry Tree Cottage, Hilton
The Limes, Apperknowle

May 15 Sunday
Dam Farm House, Ednaston
Dove Cottage, Clifton, Ashbourne
Fir Croft, Calver, nr Bakewell
Gamesley Fold Cottage, Glossop
32 Heanor Road, Codnor
The Limes, Apperknowle

May 18 Wednesday
The Old Slaughterhouse, Shipley
Gate

May 22 Sunday
Broomfield College, Morley
The Limes, Apperknowle
57 Portland Close, Mickleover

May 25 Wednesday
57 Portland Close, Mickleover

May 29 Sunday
Dam Farm House, Ednaston
Darley House, nr Matlock
The Limes, Apperknowle
Mount Cottage, Ticknall
Renishaw Hall, nr Sheffield

May 30 Monday
Mount Cottage, Ticknall
Renishaw Hall, nr Sheffield

June 2 Thursday
Kedleston Hall, Derby

June 5 Sunday
Fir Croft, Calver, nr Bakewell
Quarndon Hall, Derbyshire
Thatched Farm, Radbourne

June 8 Wednesday
Quarndon Hall, Derbyshire

June 12 Sunday
Cherry Tree Cottage, Hilton
Dam Farm House, Ednaston
The Old Slaughterhouse, Shipley
Gate
The Poplars, Derby

June 15 Wednesday
Cherry Tree Cottage, Hilton

June 19 Sunday
Birchwood Farm, Coxbench
Darley House, nr Matlock
Dove Cottage, Clifton, Ashbourne
Fir Croft, Calver, nr Bakewell
Gamesley Fold Cottage, Glossop
The Poplars, Derby

June 21 Tuesday
The Poplars, Derby

June 25 Saturday
Bath House Farm, Ashover
Mount Cottage, Ticknall
Renishaw Hall, nr Sheffield

June 26 Sunday
Dam Farm House, Ednaston
Mount Cottage, Ticknall
210 Nottingham Road, Woodlinkin
Prospect House, Swanwick
Tudor House Farm, Kirk Langley

June 29 Wednesday
Oaks Lane Farm, Brockhurst

July 3 Sunday
32 Heanor Road, Codnor
The Limes, Apperknowle
Locko Park, Spondon
23 Mill Lane, Codnor
Oaks Lane Farm, Brockhurst
The Old Slaughterhouse, Shipley
Gate

July 9 Saturday
Renishaw Hall, nr Sheffield
Tissington Hall, nr Ashbourne

July 10 Sunday
Cherry Tree Cottage, Hilton
Dam Farm House, Ednaston
Darley House, nr Matlock
Lea Hurst, nr Matlock
Oaks Lane Farm, Brockhurst
Prospect House, Swanwick

July 17 Sunday
Hardwick Hall, Doe Lea
The Limes, Apperknowle
159 Longfield Lane, Ilkeston

July 24 Sunday
Dove Cottage, Clifton,
Ashbourne
Shottle Hall Farm Guest House,
Belper

July 27 Wednesday
Calke Abbey, Ticknall

August 7 Sunday
Bath House Farm, Ashover
Daisy Hill Cottage, Longford
32 Heanor Road, Codnor
23 Mill Lane, Codnor

August 14 Sunday
Dam Farm House, Ednaston
Dove Cottage, Clifton, Ashbourne

August 28 Sunday
Renishaw Hall, nr Sheffield

August 29 Monday
Renishaw Hall, nr Sheffield
Tissington Hall, nr Ashbourne

DESCRIPTIONS OF GARDENS

Bath House Farm &&& (Mr & Mrs Hetherington) Ashover. 4½m N of Matlock on A632 Chesterfield Rd. Take 1st R after leaving village of Kelstedge and next R at T-junction. Overlooking Ashover and with extensive views this recently landscaped garden has a wide variety of heathers and mixed borders and a large water feature with waterfall, pond and stream surrounded by well chosen plants and rare shrubs and trees. Home-baked TEAS. *Adm £1 Chd free (Share to West Derby Federal Self Help Group mentally ill®). Sat June 25, Sun Aug 7 (11.30-4). Also private visits welcome June to Aug, please* **Tel 0246 590562**

¶**Birchfield** &&& (Brian Parker) Dukes Drive, Ashford in the Water. 2m NW of Bakewell on A6 to Buxton. Beauti-

fully situated terraced garden of approx ¾ acre mostly constructed within last 7 yrs. Designed for all-yr-round colour, it contains a wide variety of shrubs and perennials, bulbs, roses, water and scree gardens. Areas of copse with wild flowers are being developed in adjacent field. TEA. *Adm £1 Chd free (Share to Bakewell and District Mobile Physiotherapy Assn®). Private visits welcome April to Sept, please* **Tel 0629 813800**

Birchwood Farm &&& (Mr & Mrs S Crooks) Coxbench. 5m N Derby, from A38 take B6179 by Little Chef, through Little Eaton, till 1st Xrds, turn L then R over the railway crossing and take the rd to Holbrook, drive 100yds on L. Car parking in field at top of drive. ⅓-acre garden enclosed within old brick and stone walls. This garden is for plant enthusiasts, the wide range of herbaceous plants include hardy geraniums, hostas, penstemons, silver plants, campanulas, delphiniums, English roses. The garden is surrounded by woods and includes a pond. Nursery adjacent. TEA. *Adm £1 Acc chd free. Sun June 19 (1.30-5.30). Private visits welcome July and Aug, please* **Tel 0332 880685**

Broomfield College &&& Morley on A608, 4m N of Derby and 6m S of Heanor. Landscaped garden of 10 ha; shrubs, trees, rose collection, herbaceous borders; glasshouses; display fruit and vegetable gardens. TEAS. *Adm £1 Chd 20p. Sun May 22 (12-4.30)*

Calke Abbey & (The National Trust) Ticknall. 9m S of Derby on A514 between Swadlincote and Melbourne. Extensive walled gardens constructed in 1773. Divided into flower garden, kitchen garden and physic garden. Restoration commenced in 1987. Surrounding the walled garden the pleasure ground has been re-fenced and replanting is underway. Ruined orangery is subject to recent fundraising appeal. TEAS. *Adm £2 Chd £1. Wed July 27 (11-5)*

Cherry Tree Cottage &&& (Mr & Mrs R Hamblin) Hilton. 7m W of Derby, turn off the A516 opp The Old Talbot Inn in village centre. Parking - small public car park in Main St. Additional parking Hilton Village Hall, Eggington Rd. A plant lover's C18 cottage garden, about 1/3-acre with herbaceous borders; large herb garden; small pool and scree garden. Many unusual and interesting plants; collections of snowdrops, specie aquilegias, old dianthus and hellebores. Featured in 'Small Gardens', 'Garden Answers' and 'Gardeners World' 1991. Also in Good Garden Guide. *Adm 75p Chd free. Suns May 8, June 12, July 10, Wed June 15 (2-5). Visitors and groups welcome by appt. weekdays April, May, June and July only. Visitors also welcome to see the snowdrops and hellebores, weather permitting, please* **Tel 0283 733778**

¶**Daisy Hill Cottage** & (Mr & Mrs Beales) On the edge of Longford, approx 9m due W of Derby. Cottage is situated on the lane from Longford to Sutton-on-the-Hill. 1/3-acre simple cottage garden with perennial and dried flower beds; vegetable garden; herb garden. TEAS. *Adm £1 Chd free. Sun Aug 7 (2-5.30)*

Dam Farm House &&& (Mrs J M Player) Yeldersley Lane, Ednaston, 5m SE of Ashbourne on A52, opp Ednaston Village turn, gate on right 500yds. 2-acre garden beautifully situated contains mixed borders, scree. Unusual plants have been collected many are propagated for sale. TEAS (some Suns). *Adm £2 Chd free. Suns April 17, May 15, 29, June 12, 26, July 10, Aug 14 (1.30-4). Private visits and groups welcome April 1 to Oct 31, please* **Tel 0335 360291**

Darley House &&& (Mr & Mrs G H Briscoe) Darley Dale, 2m N of Matlock. On A6 to Bakewell. 1½ acres; originally set out by Sir Joseph Paxton in 1845; being restored by present owners; many rare plants, trees; balustrade and steps separating upper and lower garden, a replica of Haddon Hall. As featured in BBC 'Gardeners World'. Picture Gallery. Plants and extensive range of seeds available. TEA. *Adm £1 Chd free. Suns May 29, June 19, July 10 (2-5). Private visits and groups welcome April 24 to Sept 25, please* **Tel 0629 733341**

Dove Cottage &&& (Mr & Mrs S G Liverman) Clifton. 1½m SW of Ashbourne. 3/4-acre garden by R Dove extensively replanted and developed since 1979. Emphasis on establishing collections of hardy plants and shrubs incl alchemillas, alliums, berberis, geraniums, euphorbias, hostas, lilies, variegated and silver foliage plants inc astrantias. Plantsmans garden featured on Channel 4 Garden Club, Good Garden Guide and Living Magazine 1991. TEA. *Adm £1 Chd free (Share to British Heart Foundation®). Suns May 15, June 19, July 24, Aug 14 (1.30-5)*

Fir Croft &&& (Dr & Mrs S B Furness) Froggatt Rd, Calver, Via Sheffield. 4m N of Bakewell; between Q8 filling station and junction of B6001 with B6054. Plantsman's garden; rockeries; water garden and nursery; extensive collection (over 2000 varieties) of alpines, conifers. New tufa and scree beds. *Collection box. Nursery opens every Sat, Sun, Mon (1-6) March to Dec. Adjacent garden for NGS Suns April 24, May 15, June 5, 19 (2-6)*

Gamesley Fold Cottage &&& (Mr & Mrs G Carr) Glossop. Off Glossop-Marple Rd nr Charlesworth, turn down the lane directly opp St Margaret's School, Gamesley. White cottage at the bottom. Old-fashioned cottage garden down a country lane with lovely views of surrounding countryside. A spring garden planted with herbaceous borders, wild flowers and herbs in profusion to attract butterflies and wildlife. Plants and seeds for sale. Featured in Good Housekeeping May 1993. Cream TEAS (Suns only). *Adm £1 Chd free. Suns May 15, June 19 (1-4). Private visits welcome Weds April, May, Weds June (1-4), please* **Tel 04578 67856**

¶**Green Farm Cottage** &&& (Mr & Mrs Peter Bussell) Offcote. 1½m NE of Ashbourne on T-junction Bradley-Kniveton-Ashbourne. Take Wirksworth Rd out of Ashbourne (B5035) and follow Offcote Rd sign (approx 1¼m). 1/3-acre garden designed, constructed and maintained from a wilderness in 1978 by the present owners. Terraces, lawns, wide variety of perennials, shrubs and trees; greenhouse, vegetable plot and small orchard. *Adm 75p Acc chd free. Private visits welcome April to Sept, please* **Tel 0335 343803**

Hardwick Hall &&& (The National Trust) Doe Lea, 8m SE of Chesterfield. S of A617. Grass walks between yew and hornbeam hedges; cedar trees; herb garden; herbaceous borders. Finest example of Elizabethan house in the country; very fine collection of Elizabethan needlework, tapestry. Restaurant in Old Kitchens. TEAS on days the Hall is open. *Adm hall and garden £5.50 Chd £2.70 garden only £2 Chd £1. Sun July 17 (12-5.30 last entry 5)*

¶**32 Heanor Road** &&& (Mr & Mrs Eyre) 300yds from Codnor Market Place on A6007 towards Heanor. Down lane at side of Hunt's shop. Parking on main rd. 3/4-acre garden with lawns, variety of trees, shrubs, herbaceous borders, rockery, scree; 2 ponds, pergola, spring and summer bedding. Winner of 1993 Amber Valley 'Best Kept Garden' competition. TEA. *Adm £1 Chd free (Share to Multiple Sclerosis Research®). Suns April 17, May 15, July 3, Aug 7 (2-6)*

Kedleston Hall &✿ (The National Trust) 3m NW of Derby. Signposted from junction of A38/A52. 12-acre garden. A broad open lawn, bounded by a ha-ha, marks the C18 informal garden. A formal layout to the W was introduced early this century when the summerhouse and orangery, both designed by George Richardson late C18, were moved to their present position. The gardens are seen at their best during May and June when the azaleas and rhododendrons are one mass of colour. The Long Walk, a woodland walk of some 3m, is bright with spring flowers. TEA. *Adm £1.50 Chd 75p. Thurs June 2 (11-5)*

● **Lea Gardens** &✿ (Mr & Mrs Tye) Lea, 5m SE of Matlock off A6. A rare collection of rhododendrons, azaleas, kalmias, alpines and conifers in a delightful woodland setting. Light lunches, TEAS, home-baking. Coaches by appt. *Adm £2 Chd 50p daily, season ticket £3.50. Daily March 20 to July 17 (10-7)*

Lea Hurst (Residential Home) ✿✿ (Royal Surgical Aid Society) Holloway. 6m SE of Matlock off A6, nr Yew Tree Inn, Holloway. Former home (not open) of Florence Nightingale. 5-acre garden consisting of rose beds, herbaceous borders, new shrubbery incl varieties, ornamental pond, all set in beautiful countryside. New wildlife garden 1994. TEAS in aid of RSAS. *Adm £1 Chd free. Sun July 10 (2-5)*

The Limes &✿ (Mr & Mrs W Belton) Crow Lane, Apperknowle, 6m N of Chesterfield; from A6l at Unstone turn E for 1m to Apperknowle; 1st house past Unstone Grange. Bus: Chesterfield or Sheffield to Apperknowle. 2½ acres with herbaceous borders, lily ponds, roses and flowering shrubs, scree beds & rockeries; hundreds of naturalised daffodils and formal bedding with massed bedding of pansies in the spring, geraniums and bedding plants in summer. Putting green and large natural pond with ducks and geese. Nature trail over 5 acres. Home-made TEAS. *Adm £1 Chd 25p. Suns May 8, 15, 22, 29; July 3, 17 (2-6). Coach, private parties and evening visits welcome. Please* Tel 0246 412338

Locko Park ✿ Spondon, 6m NE of Derby. From A52 Borrowash bypass, 2m N via B6001, turn to Spondon. Large garden; pleasure gardens; rose gardens. House by Smith of Warwick with Victorian additions. Chapel, Charles II, with original ceiling. TEA. *Adm 60p Chd 30p. Sun July 3 (2-6)*

159 Longfield Lane &✿✿ (David & Diane Bennett) Ilkeston (Stanton side) off Quarry Hill, opp Hallam Fields Junior School. A house in a garden, a large, informal over-flowing garden that works for its owners with fruit, vegetables, shrubs, flowers, two small fish ponds and a conservatory. A strong emphasis on texture, colour and lots of unexpected corners. Home-made TEAS. *Adm £1 Chd free. Sun July 17 (2-5.30)*

Meynell Langley &✿ (Godfrey Meynell Esq) Between Mackworth and Kirk Langley on A52 Derby-Ashbourne rd. Turn in at green iron gate by grey stone lodge on N side of road. Trees, lawns, daffodils, lake, views. TEAS in Regency country house. *Adm £1.50 Chd 50p. Sun April 17 (2-6)*

23 Mill Lane &✿✿ (Mrs S Jackson) Codnor. 12m NW of Nottingham. A610 Ripley 10m N of Derby, A38 Ripley. 2 car parks nearby. Lawns, herbaceous borders, small pond, waterfall; fruit trees; clematis. Amber Valley 'Best Kept Garden' competition Highly Commended 1993. TEA. *Adm £1 Chd free. Suns July 3, Aug 7 (11-6). Private visits also welcome June to Sept, please* Tel 0773 745707

Mount Cottage ✿✿ (Mr & Mrs J T Oliver) 52 Main Street, Ticknall, 9m S Derby, adjacent entrance Calke Abbey NT and Wheel Public House. Medium-sized cottage garden, herbaceous borders, shrubs, lawns, small pool area, numerous roses, surrounding C18 cottage. TEAS outdoors weather permitting. *Adm £1 Chd free. Sun, Mon April 3,4; May 1, 2; 29, 30; Sat, Sun June 25, 26 (1-5)*

210 Nottingham Rd (Mr & Mrs R Brown) Woodlinkin, nr Codnor; A610. ½-acre; collections of old, modern shrub and climbing roses; geraniums; hellebores; shrubs; small trees. TEA. *Adm £1 Chd free. Sun June 26 (2-5)*

Oaks Lane Farm &✿✿ (Mr & Mrs J R Hunter) Brockhurst, Ashover nr Chesterfield. At Kelstedge 4m from Matlock on A632 Chesterfield Rd, just above Kelstedge Inn, turn L up narrow rd, then turn R ½m, garden is 150yds on R. Partly suitable for wheelchairs. ¾-acre informal plantsman's garden in beautiful situation with herbaceous borders, natural streams and pond. Many varieties of hostas, euphorbia and old-fashioned roses. TEA. *Adm £1 Chd free. Wed June 29 (11-5), Suns July 3, 10 (1-5). Also private visits welcome May to Sept, please* Tel 0246 590324

The Old Slaughterhouse ✿✿ (Robert & Joyce Peck) Shipley Gate. 1m S of Eastwood, take Church St from Sun Inn traffic lights, and over A610, L to narrow rd to Shipley Boat Inn; parking near Shipley Lock (Erewash Canal) and Inn. ¾-acre long, narrow garden, restored from overgrown ash tip since 1984; 200-yrs-old stone aqueduct over river; over 400 trees planted; hard and soft surfaces; division into 'rooms'; wide variety of planting; hidden pond; pleasant extra walks in Erewash Valley (canal and river sides). TEAS. *Adm £1 Chd free (Share to Heanor Hospital League of Friends® May 18, Shilo North Action Group© June 12, Erewash Canal Assoc® July 3). Wed May 18; Suns June 12, July 3 (2-6)*

The Poplars &✿✿ (The Clemson Family) Derby. Off A6 N of Derby. (200yds S of The Broadway Inn and opp N end of Belper Rd) ½m N of cathedral. ¼-acre garden; design dates from 1882; many original features. Variety of herbaceous plants, shrubs, herbs, fruit. *Adm £1 Chd free. Suns June 12, 19; Tues June 21 (2-6)*

57 Portland Close ✿✿ (Mr & Mrs A L Ritchie) Mickleover. Approx 3m W of Derby, turn R off B5020 Cavendish Way then 2nd L into Portland Close. Small plantsman's garden, wide variety of unusual bulbs, alpines and herbaceous plants. Special interest in sink gardens, hostas, named varieties of primulas (single and double); auriculas (show, border, alpine and doubles), violas and hardy geraniums. Featured in 'Good Garden Guide'. *Adm 75p Chd free. Suns, Weds April 17, 20, May 22, 25 (2-6). Private visits also welcome, please* Tel 0332 515450

Prospect House &✿❀ (Mr & Mrs J W Bowyer) 18 Pentrich Rd, Swanwick; turn at traffic lights A61 to B6016 Pentrich. Park main rd. ¾-acre; conifers, shrubs, herbaceous plants, cordyline palms, carpet bedding with sedums, sempervivums, echeverias; collection cacti; succulents, shrub and leaf begonia, abutilons various; rock plants; geraniums; pelargoniums, hostas. Greenhouses; kitchen garden. TEA. *Adm 50p Chd 10p. Suns June 26, July 10 (1.30-6)*

Quarndon Hall &✿❀ (N A Bird) Off A6 between Allestree and Duffield. 7-acre garden planted and designed over 12 yrs. Lake, waterfalls, rockeries; camellia house, Italianate garden. Extensive collection of rhododendrons, camellias, magnolias, lilies, shrubs and trees with emphasis on the unusual. Parking restricted. *Adm £1.50 Chd free. Suns March 6, April 3, May 1, June 5 (11-5) Wed June 8 (11-4)*

Radburne Hall ✿ (Maj & Mrs J W Chandos-Pole) Kirk Langley, 5m W of Derby. W of A52 Derby-Ashbourne rd; off Radburne Lane. Large landscape garden; large display of daffodils; shrubs; formal rose terraces; fine trees and view. Hall (not open) is 7-bay Palladian mansion built c1734 by Smith of Warwick. Ice-house in garden. *Adm £1 Chd 50p. Sun April 10 (2.30-6)*

Renishaw Hall &❀ (Sir Reresby & Lady Sitwell) Renishaw. Renishaw Hall is situated equidistant 6m from both Sheffield and Old Chesterfield on A616 2m from its junction with M1 at exit 30. Italian style garden with terraces, old ponds, yew hedges and pyramids laid out by Sir George Sitwell c1900. Interesting collection of herbaceous plants and shrubs; nature trail; museum; lakeside walk. Musical evenings June 25, July 9. Shop provides wine, souvenirs, antiques. TEAS. *Adm £3 OAPs £2 Chd £1. Suns June, July, Aug. Suns, Mons April 3, 4, May 1, 2, 29, 30; Aug 28, 29 (12-5)*

¶The Riddings Farm ✿❀ (The Spencer Family) Kirk Ireton. 6m ENE of Ashbourne. Follow signs to Carsington Water. Turn off Hognaston bypass towards Kirk Ireton. After ¼m take L turn towards Callow. After ½m take L turn. Farm 200yds down lane. Car parking in field at top of drive. Informal hillside garden, about ¾-acre, created since 1979 with lovely views over Carsington Water. Spring bulbs, primroses, dwarf conifers, rhododendrons; unusual perennials, many propogated for sale; rockery, water feature, orchard with ducks and geese, woodland walk. TEA. *Adm £1 Chd free. Sun May 1 (2-5). Private visits also welcome, please* **Tel 0335 370331**

Shottle Hall Farm Guest House &❀ (Mr & Mrs P Matthews) Belper. Off B5023 Duffield to Wirksworth Rd. 200yds N of Xrds (Railway Inn) with A517 Ashbourne to Belper Rd. 2½ acres natural garden featuring shrubs; roses; bedding plants; bulbs; small herbaceous border and lawns. Cream TEAS. *Adm £1 Chd under 12 free. Suns April 17, July 24 (2-5)*

Thatched Farm &✿❀ (Mr & Mrs R A Pegram) Radbourne. Exit A52 Derby-Ashbourne road. 2m N of Derby Ring Road. 2-acre plantsman's garden in parkland setting. Alpines, bulbs, trees, shrubs, perennials and roses including rowans, willows and primulas; half hardy perennials; conservatory fully planted. C17 House. TEAS. *Adm £1 Chd free (Share to Relate®). Sun June 5 (2-6). Also private visits welcome, please* **Tel 0332 824507**

Tissington Hall ✿❀ (Sir Richard FitzHerbert, Bt) N of Ashbourne. E of A515. Large garden; roses, herbaceous borders. Tea available in village. Please park considerately. *Adm £1 Chd free. Sat July 9, Mon Aug 29 (2-5)*

Tudor House Farm ✿❀ (Mr & Mrs G Spencer) Kirk Langley. 4½m N of Derby on A52 Ashbourne Rd. Take turning opp Meynell Arms Hotel, garden 400yds on R. ¼-acre garden on two levels. Mixed beds of shrubs and perennials; small fish and lily pond; heathers and alpine troughs. TEAS. *Adm £1 Chd free. Sun June 26 (2-5)*

Valezina Hillside ✿❀ (Mr & Mrs P Bowler) Heage. Between Ripley and Belper, further details on arranging appt. A butterfly/wildlife garden of ½ acre adjacent to open countryside. In parts steeply sloping, can be slippery. Mini-habitats incl a buddleia wilderness and wildlife pond. A hillside meadow and woodland garden are overlooked by a cottage garden rich in butterfly nectar plants. Essentially kept wild (but controlled) in order to maintain a permanent breeding habitat for over 20 species of butterfly who have been encouraged to stay since 1985. Totally informal with a profusion of wild flowers. TEAS. *Adm £1 Chd free. Private visits welcome May to Sept. Butterflies most numerous in July and Aug but numbers vary greatly with weather trends. Please* **Tel 0773 853099**

Devon

Hon County Organiser:	Mervyn T Feesey Esq., Woodside, Higher Raleigh Rd, Barnstaple EX31 4JA Tel 0271 43095
Assistant County Organisers:	
Exeter & E Devon	Mrs Ruth Charter, Ravenhill, Long Dogs Lane, Ottery St Mary EX11 1HX Tel 0404 814798
Tiverton & N E Devon	Mrs Diane Rowe, Little Southey, Northcott, Nr Cullompton EX15 3LT Tel 0884 840545
Bovey Tracey & Central Devon	Miss Elizabeth Hebditch, Bibbery, Higher Bibbery, Bovey Tracey TQ13 9RT Tel 0626 833344

Torbay & Dartmouth	Major David Molloy, Mulbery House, Kingswear TQ6 0BY Tel 0803 752307
Kingsbridge & South Devon	Mrs Sheila Blake, Higher Homefield, Sherford, Kingsbridge TQ 72AT Tel 0548 531229
Plymouth & SW Devon	Mrs Sharin Court, Westpark, Yealmpton, Nr Plymouth PL8 2HP Tel 0752 880236

DATES OF OPENING

By appointment
For telephone numbers and other details see garden descriptions. Private visits welcomed

Andrew's Corner, nr Okehampton
Avenue Cottage, Ashprington
Barton House, Nymet Rowland, Crediton. (Garden Societies only)
Beaumont Rd, Plymouth
Bibbery, Bovey Tracy Gardens
Bickham Barton, Roborough
Bickham House, Kenn, nr Exeter
Blackpool House, Stoke Fleming
Bramble Cottage, West Hill
Broadhembury House, Broadhembury
Bundels, Sidbury
Burrow Farm Garden, Dalwood
Castle Tor, Torquay
Cleave House, Okehampton
Clovelly Court, Clovelly
Court Hall, North Molton
The Croft, Yarnscombe
Croftdene, Ham, nr Dalwood
Crosspark, Northlew
The Downes, Monkleigh
Farrants, Kilmington
1 Feebers Cottage, Westwood
Fore Stoke Farm, Holne, nr Ashburton
The Gate House, Lee, Ilfracombe
The Glebe House, Whitestones
Gratton's Field Cottage Northlew
Greenlands, Ash Thomas & Brithem Bottom Gardens
Higher Spriddlestone, Brixton, nr Plymouth
Holywell, Bratton Fleming
Kerscott House, nr Swimbridge
Little Cumbre, Exeter
Little Upcott Gardens, Marsh Green
The Lodge, Mannamead
Lower Coombe Royal, Kingsbridge
Membland Villa, Newton Ferrers
20 Monmouth Avenue, Topsham Gardens
The Moorings, nr Lyme Regis
16 Moorland View, Derriford
Mulberry House, Barbican Terrace, Barnstable
Oare Manor Cottage, Oare, Lynton
The Old Mill, Blakewell
The Old Rectory, Clayhidon
The Old Rectory, Woodleigh

The Orchard, Kenn
Orchard Cottage, Exmouth
38 Phillipps Avenue, Exmouth
The Pines, Salcombe
Priors, Abbotskerswell
Quakers, Membury Gardens
Setts, Bovey Tracey
Silver Copse, nr Marsh Green
Sowton Mill, Dunsford
Spillifords, nr Tiverton
41 Springfield Close, Plymstock
Stone Lane Gardens, Chagford
Vicar's Mead, East Budleigh
Warren Cottage, nr Ermington
Weetwood, nr Honiton
Westpark, Yealmpton
Withleigh Farm, nr Tiverton

Regular openings
For details see garden descriptions

Alleron, Loddiswell, nr Kingsbridge. Open all year except Mons
Avenue Cottage, Ashprington. Tues to Sats March 29 to Sept 24
Bicton College of Agriculture. Open all year Mon to Fri except Dec 25. Sats, Suns April to Oct
Burrow Farm Garden, Dalwood. Daily April 1 to Sept 30
Crosspark, Northlew. Fris, Suns April 1 to June 26
Doctyn Mill and Garden, nr Hartland. Daily March to Oct
The Downes, Monkleigh. Daily April 1 to June 12
Fernwood, Ottery St Mary. Daily April 1 to May 31
The Garden House, Yelverton. Daily March 1 to Oct 31
Gidleigh Park, Chagford. Mon to Fri except Bank Hols all year
Hill House, nr Ashburton. Open all year
Lukesland, Ivybridge. Suns, Weds, April 17 to June 5 incl.
Marwood Hill, nr Barnstaple. Daily except Christmas Day
Plant World, nr Newton Abbot
Purple Hayes, Ash Thomas and Brithem Bottom Gardens. Open Weds May, June, July
Rosemoor Garden, Great Torrington
Tapeley Park & British Jousting Centre, Instow. Easter to Oct except Sats

Wylmington Hayes, nr Honiton. Easter weekend, Suns and Bank Hols Mons until end of June

---

March 19 Saturday
The Pines, Salcombe
March 20 Sunday
Bickham House, Kenn, nr Exeter
1 Feebers Cottage, Westwood
Higher Knowle, nr Bovey Tracey
The Pines, Salcombe
Westpark, Yealmpton
March 23 Wednesday
Bickham House, Kenn, nr Exeter
Bicton College of Agriculture
Westpark, Yealmpton
March 27 Sunday
Higher Knowle, nr Bovey Tracey
April 1 Friday
Gratton's Field Cottage, Northlew
The Pines, Salcombe
Wylmington Hayes, nr Honiton
April 2 Saturday
The Moorings, nr Lyme Regis
The Pines, Salcombe
Wylmington Hayes, nr Honiton
April 3 Sunday
Alleron, Loddiswell, nr Kingsbridge
Bickham Barton, Roborough
Bundels, Sidbury
Fast Rabbit Farm, Ash, Dartmouth
Gratton's Field Cottage, Northlew
Higher Knowle, nr Bovey Tracey
The Moorings, nr Lyme Regis
38 Phillipps Avenue, Exmouth
The Pines, Salcombe
Silver Copse, nr Marsh Green
Vicar's Mead, East Budleigh
Wylmington Hayes, nr Honiton
April 4 Monday
Bickham Barton, Roborough
1 Feebers Cottage, Westwood
Higher Knowle, nr Bovey Tracey
The Moorings, nr Lyme Regis
The Pines, Salcombe
Silver Copse, nr Marsh Green
Wylmington Hayes, nr Honiton
April 7 Thursday
Whitmore, nr Chittlehamholt
April 10 Sunday
Bickham Barton, Roborough
Hartland Abbey, Hartland
Higher Knowle, nr Bovey Tracey
Meadowcroft, Plympton
Membury Gardens, nr Axminster

Mothecombe House, Holbeton
Penrose, Crediton
38 Phillipps Avenue, Exmouth
April 17 Sunday
Bickham Barton, Roborough
Bickham House, Kenn, nr Exeter
Higher Knowle, nr Bovey Tracey
Valley House, nr Axminster
Vicar's Mead, East Budleigh
April 20 Wednesday
Bickham House, Kenn, nr Exeter
April 23 Saturday
Garden House, Torquay
April 24 Sunday
Andrew's Corner, nr
  Okehampton
Bickham Barton, Roborough
Bicton College of Agriculture
Chevithorne Barton, nr Tiverton
Coleton Fishacre, Kingswear
Garden House, Torquay
Gorwell House, nr Barnstaple
Higher Knowle, nr Bovey Tracey
Holywell, Bratton Fleming
Killerton House, Broadclyst
Meadowcroft, Plympton
38 Phillipps Avenue, Exmouth
Vicar's Mead, East Budleigh
April 28 Thursday
Greenway Gardens, Churston
  Ferrers
Little Cumbre, Exeter
April 30 Saturday
Mothecombe House, Holbeton
May 1 Sunday
Alleron, Loddiswell, nr
  Kingsbridge
Bickham Barton, Roborough
Bramble Cottage, West Hill
Broadhembury House,
  Broadhembury
Bundels, Sidbury
Delamore, Cornwood, Ivybridge,
Dippers, Shaugh Prior, nr
  Plymouth
Fast Rabbit Farm, Ash, Dartmouth
Flete, Ermington, Ivybridge
Hamblyn's Coombe, Dittisham
Higher Knowle, nr Bovey Tracey
Higher Warcombe, nr Kingsbridge
Holywell, Bratton Fleming
Kings Gatchell, Higher Metcombe
The Lodge, Mannamead
Lukesland, Ivybridge
Membland Villa, Newton Ferrers
The Moorings, nr Lyme Regis
Mothecombe House, Holbeton
The Old Mill, Blakewell
38 Phillipps Avenue, Exmouth
Silver Copse, nr Marsh Green
Valley House, nr Axminster
Vicar's Mead, East Budleigh
May 2 Monday
Bickham Barton, Roborough

Bramble Cottage, West Hill
Hamblyn's Coombe, Dittisham
Higher Knowle, nr Bovey Tracey
Kings Gatchell, Higher Metcombe
The Moorings, nr Lyme Regis
Silver Copse, nr Marsh Green
May 4 Wednesday
Bundels, Sidbury
May 5 Thursday
Greenway Gardens, Churston
  Ferrers
May 7 Saturday
Broadhembury House,
  Broadhembury
Topsham Gardens, nr Exeter
May 8 Sunday
Andrew's Corner, nr
  Okehampton
Bickham Barton, Roborough
Broadhembury House,
  Broadhembury
Castle Drogo, Drewsteignton
Higher Knowle, nr Bovey Tracey
Holywell, Bratton Fleming
Knightshayes Gardens, nr Tiverton
The Orchard, Kenn
Penrose, Crediton
Topsham Gardens, nr Exeter
Vicar's Mead, East Budleigh
Wood Barton, Kentisbeare
Woodside, Barnstaple
May 11 Wednesday
Cleave House, Okehampton
Meadowcroft, Plympton
May 13 Friday
The Old Glebe, Eggesford
May 14 Saturday
Broadhembury House,
  Broadhembury
Monks Aish, South Brent
The Old Glebe, Eggesford
May 15 Sunday
Arlington Court, nr Barnstaple
Bickham Barton, Roborough
Bickham House, Kenn, nr Exeter
Broadhembury House,
  Broadhembury
The Cider House, Yelverton
Cleave House, Okehampton
Delamore, Cornwood, Ivybridge
1 Feebers Cottage, Westwood
Higher Knowle, nr Bovey Tracey
Holywell, Bratton Fleming
Lewdon Farm, Cheriton Bishop
The Old Glebe, Eggesford
38 Phillipps Avenue, Exmouth
Saltram House, Plymouth
Wood Barton, Kentisbeare
May 18 Wednesday
Bickham House, Kenn, nr Exeter
Lewdon Farm, Cheriton Bishop
May 21 Saturday
Broadhembury House,
  Broadhembury

Dartington Hall Gardens, nr
  Totnes
Ottery St Mary Gardens
Pleasant View, nr Newton Abbot
Setts, Bovey Tracey
Sunrise Hill, Withleigh
Withleigh Farm, nr Tiverton
May 22 Sunday
Addisford Cottage, nr Dolton
Andrew's Corner, nr Okehampton
Bickham Barton, Roborough
Broadhembury House,
  Broadhembury
Castle Drogo, Drewsteignton
Coleton Fishacre, Kingswear
Dartington Hall Gardens, nr
  Totnes
Fast Rabbit Farm, Ash, Dartmouth
Holywell, Bratton Fleming
Lukesland, Ivybridge
Mardon, Moretonhampstead
Meadow Court, Slapton
Meadowcroft, Plympton
The Orchard, Kenn
Ottery St Mary Gardens
Pleasant View, nr Newton Abbot
Scypen, Ringmore
Setts, Bovey Tracey
Starveacre, nr Axminster
Vicar's Mead, East Budleigh
Withleigh Farm, nr Tiverton
May 23 Monday
Yonder Hill, Colaton Raleigh
May 24 Tuesday
Yonder Hill, Colaton Raleigh
May 25 Wednesday
Stone Lane Gardens, nr Chagford
Yonder Hill, Colaton Raleigh
May 26 Thursday
Little Cumbre, Exeter
Yonder Hill, Colaton Raleigh
May 27 Friday
Yonder Hill, Colaton Raleigh
May 28 Saturday
Ash Thomas and Brithem Bottom
  Gardens, nr Tiverton
Broadhembury House,
  Broadhembury
Garden House, Torquay
Little Upcott Gardens, Marsh
  Green
Wolford Lodge, nr Honiton
Yonder Hill, Colaton Raleigh
May 29 Sunday
Addisford Cottage, nr Dolton
Bickham Barton, Roborough
Bicton College of Agriculture
Bramble Cottage, West Hill
Broadhembury House,
  Broadhembury
Bundels, Sidbury
Croftdene, Ham, nr Dalwood
Garden House, Torquay
The Glebe House, Whitestone

Gorwell House, Barnstaple
Kings Gatchell, Higher Metcombe
Lee Ford, Budleigh Salterton
Lewdon Farm, Cheriton Bishop
Little Upcott Gardens, Marsh
    Green
Mardon, Moretonhampstead
Meadow Court, Slapton
Membland Villa, Newton Ferrers
The Moorings, nr Lyme Regis
38 Phillipps Avenue, Exmouth
Robin Hill, Exeter
Silver Copse, nr Marsh Green
Twitchen Mill, nr South Molton
Vicar's Mead, East Budleigh
Yonder Hill, Colaton Raleigh

May 30 Monday
Bickham Barton, Roborough
Bramble Cottage, West Hill
The Glebe House, Whitestone
Holywell, Bratton Fleming
Kings Gatchell, Higher Metcombe
Little Upcott Gardens, Marsh
    Green
Mardon, Moretonhampstead
The Moorings, nr Lyme Regis
Silver Copse, nr Marsh Green
Yonder Hill, Colaton Raleigh

June 1 Wednesday
Bundels, Sidbury
Lewdon Farm, Cheriton Bishop

June 4 Saturday
Broadhembury House,
    Broadhembury
Pleasant View, nr Newton Abbot

June 5 Sunday
Addisford Cottage, nr Dolton
Alleron, Loddiswell, nr
    Kingsbridge
Andrew's Corner, nr Okehampton
Bickham Barton, Roborough
Broadhembury House,
    Broadhembury
The Cider House, Yelverton
1 Feebers Cottage, Westwood
Glebe Cottage, nr Warkleigh
The Glebe House, Whitestone
Gratton's Field Cottage, Northlew
Holywell, Bratton Fleming
Mardon, Moretonhampstead
Membury Gardens, nr Axminster
Monks Aish, South Brent
The Old Mill, Blakewell
Overbecks, Salcombe
Pleasant View, nr Newton Abbot
Sowton Mill, Dunsford
Vicar's Mead, East Budleigh

June 8 Wednesday
Little Upcott Gardens, Marsh
    Green
Scypen, Ringmore

June 11 Saturday
Bovey Tracey Gardens
Broadhembury House,
    Broadhembury

June 12 Sunday
Bovey Tracey Gardens
Broadhembury House,
    Broadhembury
Dippers, Shaugh Prior, nr
    Plymouth
The Glebe House, Whitestone
Gratton's Field Cottage, Northlew
Lewdon Farm, Cheriton Bishop
The Lodge, Mannamead
Mothecombe House, Holbeton
Riversbridge, nr Dartmouth
Vicar's Mead, East Budleigh

June 15 Wednesday
Bramble Cottage, West Hill
Lewdon Farm, Cheriton Bishop

June 16 Thursday
Ash Thomas and Brithem Bottom
    Gardens, nr Tiverton

June 18 Saturday
Bramble Cottage, West Hill
Broadhembury House,
    Broadhembury
Bundels, Sidbury
Little Upcott Gardens, Marsh
    Green

June 19 Sunday
Addisford Cottage, nr Dolton
Andrew's Corner, nr Okehampton
Bickham Barton, Roborough
Bickham House, Kenn, nr Exeter
Bramble Cottage, West Hill
Broadhembury House,
    Broadhembury
Bundels, Sidbury
The Glebe House, Whitestone
Heddon Hall, Parracombe
Little Upcott Gardens, Marsh
    Green
Little Webbery, Alverdiscott
Lower Kerse, Thurlestone
16 Moorland View, Derriford
38 Phillipps Avenue, Exmouth
Riversbridge, nr Dartmouth
Saltram House, Plymouth
Vicar's Mead, East Budleigh
Woodside, Barnstaple

June 22 Wednesday
Bickham House, Kenn, nr Exeter
Bundels, Sidbury

June 23 Thursday
Bundels, Sidbury
Little Cumbre, Exeter

June 25 Saturday
Barton House, Nymet Rowland
Broadhembury House,
    Broadhembury

June 26 Sunday
Addisford Cottage, nr Dolton
Barton House, Nymet Rowland
Broadhembury House,
    Broadhembury
Cleave House, Okehampton
The Croft, Yarnscombe
Croftdene, Ham, nr Dalwood

Feniton Old Village Gardens
1 Feebers Cottage, Westwood
Glebe Cottage, nr Warkleigh
The Glebe House, Whitestone
Gorwell House, Barnstaple
Kerscott House, nr Swimbridge
Little Southey, Culm Valley, nr
    Culmstock
Membland Villa, Newton Ferrers
The Old Parsonage, Warkleigh
Overbecks, Salcombe
Priors, Abbotskerswell
41 Springfield Close, Plymstock
Vicar's Mead, East Budleigh

June 27 Monday
Barton House, Nymet Rowland

June 29 Wednesday
Little Upcott Gardens, Marsh
    Green
Stone Lane Gardens, nr Chagford

June 30 Thursday
Whitmore, nr Chittlehamholt

July 1 Friday
Dippers, Shaugh Prior, nr
    Plymouth

July 3 Sunday
Addisford Cottage, nr Dolton
Alleron, Loddiswell, nr
    Kingsbridge
Feniton Old Village Gardens
The Glebe House, Whitestone
Knightshayes Gardens, nr Tiverton
Mulberry House, Barnstaple
The Old Parsonage, Warkleigh
Sowton Mill, Dunsford

July 9 Saturday
Little Upcott Gardens, Marsh
    Green

July 10 Sunday
Addisford Cottage, nr Dolton
Arlington Court, nr Barnstaple
Court Hall, North Molton
The Croft, Yarnscombe
The Glebe House, Whitestone
Killerton House, Broadclyst
Little Upcott Gardens, Marsh
    Green
Mothecombe House, Holbeton
Mulberry House, Barnstaple
Robin Hill, Exeter
Sampford Peverell Gardens, nr
    Tiverton
Vicar's Mead, East Budleigh

July 13 Wednesday
The Garden House, Yelverton

July 16 Saturday
Pleasant View, nr Newton Abbot
Portington, nr Lamerton
Silver Copse, nr Marsh Green

July 17 Sunday
Andrew's Corner, nr Okehampton
Bickham House, Kenn, nr Exeter
Fast Rabbit Farm, Ash, Dartmouth
1 Feebers Cottage, Westwood
Glebe Cottage, nr Warkleigh

Heddon Hall, Parracombe
Higher Warcombe, Kingsbridge
The Old Mill, Blakewell
Pleasant View, nr Newton Abbot
Sampford Peverell Gardens, nr Tiverton
Silver Copse, nr Marsh Green
Starveacre, nr Axminster
Twitchen Mill, nr South Molton
Vicar's Mead, East Budleigh
Woodside, Barnstaple

July 20 Wednesday
Bickham House, Kenn, nr Exeter
Little Upcott Gardens, Marsh Green

July 23 Saturday
Lewdon Farm, Cheriton Bishop

July 24 Sunday
Addisford Cottage, nr Dolton
Bicton College of Agriculture
Glebe Cottage, nr Warkleigh
The Lodge, Mannamead
Oare Manor Cottage, Oare, Lynton
41 Springfield Close, Plymstock
Vicar's Mead, East Budleigh

July 25 Monday
Fardel Manor, nr Ivybridge

July 27 Wednesday
Stone Lane Gardens, nr Chagford
Sunrise Hill, Withleigh

July 30 Saturday
Portington, nr Lamerton

July 31 Sunday
Ash Thomas and Brithem Bottom Gardens
Glebe Cottage, nr Warkleigh
Gorwell House, nr Barnstaple

Oare Manor Cottage, Oare, Lynton
The Old Parsonage, Warkleigh

August 3 Wednesday
Sunrise Hill, Withleigh

August 6 Saturday
Pleasant View, nr Newton Abbot

August 7 Sunday
Addisford Cottage, nr Dolton
Glebe Cottage, nr Warkleigh
Gratton's Field Cottage, Northlew
Pleasant View, nr Newton Abbot

August 14 Sunday
Glebe Cottage, nr Warkleigh
Gratton's Field Cottage, Northlew
Penrose, Crediton

August 17 Wednesday
The Garden House, Yelverton

August 21 Sunday
Bickham House, Kenn, nr Exeter

August 24 Wednesday
Bickham House, Kenn, nr Exeter

August 27 Saturday
Barton House, Nymet Rowland
Garden House, Torquay

August 28 Sunday
Barton House, Nymet Rowland, Crediton
Bicton College of Agriculture
Fast Rabbit Farm, Ash, Dartmouth
Garden House, Torquay
Glebe Cottage, nr Warkleigh
Kerscott House, nr Swimbridge
Membland Villa, Newton Ferrers
Oare Manor Cottage, Oare, Lynton
The Old Parsonage, Warkleigh
Silver Copse, nr Marsh Green
Vicar's Mead, East Budleigh

Whitmore, nr Chittlehamholt

August 29 Monday
Barton House, Nymet Rowland
Silver Copse, nr Marsh Green

September 3 Saturday
Pleasant View, nr Newton Abbot

September 4 Sunday
1 Feebers Cottage, Westwood
Glebe Cottage, nr Warkleigh
Gorwell House, Barnstaple
Pleasant View, nr Newton Abbot

September 10 Saturday
Ash Thomas and Brithem Bottom Gardens, nr Tiverton

September 11 Sunday
Vicar's Mead, East Budleigh

September 18 Sunday
Bickham House, Kenn, nr Exeter
Bicton College of Agriculture
Membland Villa, Newton Ferrers
The Old Parsonage, Warkleigh
Vicar's Mead, East Budleigh

September 21 Wednesday
Bickham House, Kenn, nr Exeter

September 25 Sunday
1 Feebers Cottage, Westwood
Glebe Cottage, nr Warkleigh

October 3 Sunday
Gorwell House, Barnstaple

October 9 Sunday
1 Feebers Cottage, Westwood

October 16 Sunday
Starveacre, nr Axminster

October 30 Sunday
Lukesland, Ivybridge

November 6 Sunday
The Moorings, nr Lyme Regis

DESCRIPTIONS OF GARDENS

Addisford Cottage ௸ (Mr & Mrs R J Taylor) West Lane, Dolton. ½m W of Dolton. From village centre past Royal Oak for ½m to bottom of valley, gate on R across ford. 1-acre garden surrounding picturesque thatched cottage in secluded wooded valley. Natural stream, large pond and water garden with hardy moisture loving and woodland plants. Extensive herbaceous borders, densely planted for sun and shade alongside many wild species. Large collection of geraniums. TEAS. *Adm £1 Chd free. Suns May 22, 29 June 5, 19, 26 July 3, 10, 24, Aug 7 (11-5)*

Alleron ௸ (Mr & Mrs Jeremy Davies) Loddiswell. Turn off Loddiswell-S Brent rd, just N of Lodd Village. Follow signed lane, across T-junction and take R fork down bumpy private drive. Drive slowly, large car park at rear. 3-acre informal garden in lovely wooded valley, streams, lakes, bog plants, spring bulbs, autumn colours, old roses and some herbaceous. Walk around lovely wood, beautiful in bluebell season. Unique circular walled garden, thatched topping to walls, possibly dating early C19, origin unknown. Picnic area, ample car parking. Stone Butter house with own spring water. TEAS April to Sept

incl. *Adm £1.50 OAP £1 Chd free (Share to Multiple Sclerosis Society®). Open all year except Mons. For NGS Suns Apr 3, May 1 June 5, July 3 (11-dusk). Parties by arrangement please* Tel 0548 550306

Andrew's Corner ௸ (H J & Mr & Mrs R J Hill) Belstone, 3m E of Okehampton signed to Belstone. Parking restricted but may be left on nearby common. Plantsman's garden 1,000ft up on Dartmoor, overlooking Taw Valley; wide range unusual trees, shrubs, herbaceous plants for year round effect inc alpines, rhododendrons, bulbs, dwarf conifers; well labelled. TEAS. *Adm £1 Chd free. Suns April 24; May 8, 22; June 5, 19; July 17; (2.30-6); also private visits welcome, please* Tel 0837 840332

Arlington Court ௸ (The National Trust) Shirwell, nr Barnstaple. 7m NE of Barnstaple on A39. Rolling parkland and woods with lake. Rhododendrons and azaleas; fine specimen trees; small terraced Victorian garden with herbaceous borders and conservatory. Regency house containing fascinating collections of objet d'art. Carriage collection in the stables. Restaurant. *Adm garden only £2.40 Chd £1.20. ▲Suns May 15, July 10 (11-5.30)*

¶Ash Thomas and Brithem Bottom Gardens ✕ 5m SE of Tiverton. A373 Tiverton to M5, 2m S of Halberton. A route map to each garden will be available on open days. TEAS at Greenlands. *Combined adm £1.50 Chd 50p. Sats May 28, Sept 10, Thurs June 16, Sun July 31 (2.30-6.30)*

¶Greenlands ঌ✿ (Dr & Mrs J P Anderson) Ash Thomas. ⅓-acre developing garden in open rural setting with far-reaching views. Alpine beds and troughs, herbaceous borders, roses and rustic screening, annuals, herbs, fruit garden, vegetable plot, pond and wild areas. Parking in surrounding lanes, except disabled. TEAS. *(Share to St Francis Hospital, Katete, Zambia©). Private visits also welcome May to Sept, please* **Tel 0884 821257**

¶Lower Beers ঌ (Mr & Mrs G Nicholls) Brithem Bottom. Listed C16 longhouse fronts a developing 3-acre hidden garden, incl ornamental herb and vegetable garden, herbaceous beds, woodland dell and large open area leading to stream. Parking in adjoining yard

¶Lower Coombe Farm (Mr & Mrs M Weekes) Brithem Bottom. Large cottage garden with an interesting selection of plants, old roses and a ditch garden situated behind C17 farmhouse. Parking in farmyard

¶Purple Hayes ✿ (Kim & Bruce Thomas) Lake Farm, Halberton. B3391 ¼m SE of Halberton. Plantaholic's garden of 1 acre, started in 1987. Bold herbaceous planting, unusual plants, ornamental grasses, ponds, bog and herb garden. Pigmy goats. Plants for sale in adjoining nursery. *(Share to Cats' Protection League®). Also open Weds May, June, July (11-5)*

Avenue Cottage ঌ (Mr R J Pitts & Mr R C H Soans) Ashprington. A381 from Totnes to Kingsbridge. 3m SE Totnes from centre of village past church for 300yds, drive on R. 11 acres of garden with woodland walks and ponds. Part of C18 landscape garden undergoing re-creation by designers/plantsmen, garden guide available. *Adm £1 Chd 25p. Collecting box. Tues to Sat March 29 to Sept 24 (11-5). Private visits welcome, please* **Tel 0803 732769.** *No coaches*

Barton House ✕✿ (Mr and Mrs A T Littlewood) Nymet Rowland. 9m NW of Crediton. Follow signs to Nymet Rowland from A377 at Lapford or B3220 at Aller Bridge. Garden opposite C15 church. 1-acre garden designed and maintained by owners. Beautiful views to Dartmoor. Individual areas developed with varied character. Herbs; pond; herbaceous; yew garden; ferns, grotto, roses and fountain pool. Cream TEAS. *Adm £1 Chd 50p (Share to St Bartholomew's Church, Nymet Rowland®). Sats, Suns, Mons June 25, 26, 27; Aug 27, 28, 29 (2-6) Garden societies by appt*

41 Beaumont Road ✕ (E M Parsons) St Judes, Plymouth. ½m from city centre, 100yds from Beaumont Park; take Ebrington St exit from Charles X roundabout in city centre. Parking in nearby side rds. Matchbox sized, walled town garden; intensive tub-culture of uncommon shrubs, small trees, climbers; compact and colourful with roses; pieris, camellias and clematis. Prize winning garden shown on TSW & Gardener's World. TEA. *Adm 75p Chd 20p. Private visits usually welcome July* **Tel 0752 668640**

Bickham Barton ✕✿ (Helen Lady Roborough) Roborough, 8m N of Plymouth. Take Maristow turn on Roborough Down, ½-way between Plymouth and Tavistock, then follow poster directions. Bus stop: Maristow sign on Roborough Down; posters at Maristow turning 1m from house. Shrub garden; camellias; rhododendrons; azaleas; cherries; bulbs; trees. Lovely views. *Adm £1. Every Sun April 3 to June 5 and June 19; Mons April 4, May 2, 30 (2-5.30); also private visits welcome until end of June, please* **Tel 0822 852478**

Bickham House ঌ✕✿ (Mr & Mrs John Tremlett) Kenn. 6m W of Exeter 1m off A38. Plymouth-Torquay rd leave dual carriage-way at Kennford Services, follow signs to Kenn. 1st R in village, follow lane for ¾m to end of no-through rd. Ample parking. No shade for dogs. 5-acre garden in peaceful wooded valley. Lawns, mature trees and shrubs; naturalised bulbs, mixed borders. Conservatory, small parterre, pond garden; 1-acre walled kitchen garden; lake. Cream TEAS. *Adm £1 Chd 50p. Suns March 20, April 17, May 15, June 19, July 17, Aug 21, Sept 18; Weds March 23, April 20, May 18, June 22, July 20, Aug 24, Sept 21 (2-6). Private visits also welcome, please* **Tel 0392 832671**

Bicton College of Agriculture ঌ✿ Entrance to the College is by Sidmouth Lodge, half-way between Budleigh Salterton and Newton Poppleford on A376. Proceed up famous monkey puzzle avenue with fine views of the parkland and trees. From the top of the drive follow signs to garden car park. The gardens are linked to the old Georgian mansion and extend via the arboretum to the old walled garden and glasshouses, being the centre of the Horticultural Dept. Rich variety of plants in beds and borders, laid out for teaching and effect; including NCCPG national collections of agapanthus & pittosporum; arboretum extends for ½m with various trees and shrubs inc magnolia, camellia and flowering cherries. Parking in gardens car park, short walk to gardens. Entrance tickets obtainable at Plant Centre. Where plant centre closed please use box by gate. Plant centre closes 4pm. Garden and arboretum guides available. *Adm £1.50 Chd free. Wed March 23, Suns April 24, May 29, July 24, Aug 28, Sept 18 (10.30-5). Gardens also open Mon to Fri throughout year, except Christmas day (10.30-5.00)*

Blackpool House ✕ (Lady A Newman) Stoke Fleming, 4½m SW of Dartmouth. Opp car park at Blackpool Sands. Shrub garden, on steep hillside, containing many rare, mature and tender shrubs. Beautiful sea views. Tea Blackpool Sands take-away on sands. *Adm £1 Chd free. Private visits welcome, spring & summer, please* **Tel 0803 770261**

Bovey Tracey Gardens Gateway to Dartmoor. A382 midway Newton Abbot to Moretonhampstead. Teas locally. *Combined adm £1.50 Chd 25p. Sat, Sun June 11, 12 (2-6)*

26 Beckett Road (Mrs D C Starling) off Coombe Close nr Church. Very small garden with interesting and choice plants

Bibbery ✿ (Misses E & A Hebditch) Higher Bibbery. B3344 to Chudleigh Knighton. Cul-de-sac behind Coombe Cross Hotel. Plantspersons small garden, sheltered corners harbouring interesting shrubs and tender plants. *Also private visits welcome, please* **Tel 0626 833344**

Church View ❀ (Mr & Mrs R Humphreys) East Street. B3344 opp St Peter & St Paul's Church. Small garden, but many unusual plants, incl secluded vegetable area. Disabled parking

Fig Tree Cottage (Kenneth & Marjorie Snook) East Street. Small unpretentious cottage garden reflecting owners interest in plants. Large free car park Mary St 200 yds

¶**Smithays Cottage** (Mr & Mrs Arthur Mann) Fore Street. Small traditional walled cottage garden

Sunnyside (Mr & Mrs Green) Hind Street. Near town centre off A382. Opp Baptist church. Well established enclosed garden; trees and shrubs; herbaceous and colourful conservatory; productive vegetable area. Parking nearby

Bramble Cottage ❀❀ (Captain & Mrs Brian Norton) Lower Broad Oak Rd, West Hill, Ottery St Mary. From A3052 Exeter-Sidmouth rd turn N at Halfway Inn on B3180 for 2m, then right at Tipton Cross, then left fork and continue down hill to turn left at bottom into Lower Broad Oak Rd to second house on right. ¾-acre semi-woodland garden, plus ½-acre woodland, ponds and bog area; interesting shrubs; troughs; primulas a special feature in late spring. Adjoining Kings Gatchell. *Adm 75p Chd 15p. Suns, Mons May 1, 2; 29, 30, Wed June 15, Sat, Sun June 18, 19 (11-5); also private visits welcome May to June, please* **Tel 0404 814642**

¶**Broadhembury House** ❀❀ (Mr & Mrs W Drewe) Broadhembury. 5m equidistant on A373 from Honiton-Cullompton signed Broadhembury. 2-acre informal garden in C16 picturesque thatched village. A spring garden with rhododendrons and azaleas, daffodils and bluebells. Ample parking in village square. *Adm £1.25 Chd 50p. Sats, Suns May, June (2-5). Larger groups welcome by appt during May and June, please* **Tel 040484 326**

Bundels ♿❀ (Mr & Mrs A Softly) Ridgway, Sidbury. From Sidmouth B3175 turn left at free Car Park in Sidbury. From Honiton A375, turn right. Garden 100yds up Ridgway on left. 1½-acre organic garden inc small wood and pond set round C16 thatched cottage (not open); over 100 varieties of old-fashioned and other shrub roses. Typical cottage garden with accent on preservation of wild life. GRBS Gift stall. Teas in village. *Adm 50p Chd 10p. Suns April 3, May 1, 29, June 19; Weds May 4, June 1, 22; Thurs June 23; Sat June 18 (2-6). Private visits also welcome May to July, please* **Tel 0395 597312**

Burrow Farm Garden ♿❀ (Mr & Mrs John Benger) Dalwood, 4m W of Axminster. A35 Axminster-Honiton rd; 3½m from Axminster turn N near Shute Garage on to Stockland Rd; ½m nr Ivy path. Secluded 5 acre garden with magnificent views has been planned for foliage effect and includes woodland garden in a dell with rhododendrons, azaleas etc; large bog garden; pergola walk with rose-herbaceous borders. Nursery adjoining. Cream TEAS (Suns, Weds & Bank Hols). *Adm £2 Chd 50p. April 1 to Sept 30 daily (2-7). Private visits also welcome in the morning, please* **Tel 0404 831285**

Castle Drogo ♿❀❀ (The National Trust) Drewsteignton. W of Exeter, S of A30. Medium-sized garden with formal beds and herbaceous borders; shrubs, woodland walk overlooking Fingle Gorge. Wheelchair available. Plant centre. Restaurant. Tea room. *Adm gardens only £2 Chd £1. For NGS Suns May 8, 22 (10.30-5.30)*

Castle Tor ❀ (Leonard Stocks) Wellswood, Torquay. From Higher Lincombe Rd turn E into Oxlea Rd. 200yds on right, entrance identified by eagles on gate pillars. Spectacular scenic listed garden superbly designed and laid out under the influence of Lutyens in the mid-30s. Stepped terraces, orangery, paved work and ornamental water. *Adm £1 Chd 25p. Private visits welcome, please* **Tel 0803 214858**

Chevithorne Barton (Michael Heathcote Amory Esq) Chevithorne. 3m NE of Tiverton. A terraced walled garden and further informal planting in woodland of trees and shrubs incl NCCPG National Oak Collection. In spring the garden features magnolias, rhododendrons and azaleas. TEA. *Adm £1 Chd 50p (Share to CPRE®). Sun April 24 (2-6)*

The Cider House ❀❀ (Mr & Mrs M J Stone) Buckland Abbey, Yelverton. From A386 Plymouth-Tavistock, 100yds S of Yelverton roundabout follow NT signs to Buckland Abbey. At Xrds before Abbey entrance turn N signed Buckland Monachorum. Drive 200yds on L, or short walk for visitors to Abbey. Peaceful and secluded garden with restrained planting complementing mediaeval house, part of a Cistercian monastery. Terrace borders and herbs, former Abbey walled kitchen garden with fruit, vegetables and flowers. Unspoilt aspect over wooded valley surrounded by NT land. Cream TEAS. *Adm £1 Chd 50p. Suns May 15, June 5 (2-6)*

Cleave House ❀ (Ann & Roger Bowden) Sticklepath, 3½m E of Okehampton on old A30 towards Exeter. Cleave House on left in village, on main road just past small right turn for Skaigh. ½-acre garden with mixed planting for all season interest. National Collection of hostas with 300 varieties, 100 of these are for sale. *Adm 50p. Suns May 15, June 26; Wed May 11 (10.30-5.30). Private visits also welcome April to Oct, please* **Tel 083784 0481**

Clovelly Court ♿❀ (The Hon Mrs Rous) Clovelly. 11m W of Bideford. A39 Bideford to Bude turn at Clovelly Cross Filling Station, 1m lodge gates and drive straight ahead; also 'Long Walk' pedestrian entrance 200yds from top of village (back rd) at large green gate shared with entrance to coastal footpath. 25 acres parkland with beautiful open views through woodlands towards sea. 1-acre walled garden with borders, fruit and vegetables. 500yds walk from village (through green gate) along path lined with ancient trees and rhododendrons. Medieval Manor adjacent C14 Church nr coastline. Free parking in drive. Directions at Garden entrance, blue doors in Church Path. *Adm £1 Chd 20p (Share to NSPCC®; Braunton Cheshire Home®). Private visits and coach parties welcome May 1 to Sept 30, please* **Tel 0237 431215**

> **Regular Openers.** Too many days to include in diary. Usually there is a wide range of plants giving year-round interest. See head of county section for the name and garden description for times etc.

Coleton Fishacre ॐ (The National Trust) 2m NE of Kingswear. 20-acre garden planted and developed according to personal taste of the D'Oyly Carte family during 1926-1947 and unaltered by subsequent owners, now under restoration; wide range of tender and uncommon trees and shrubs in spectacular coastal setting. TEAS weather permitting. Unusual plants sale. *Adm £2.60 Chd £1.30. Suns April 24, May 22 (10.30-5.30)*

Court Hall ॐ (Mr & Mrs C Worthington) North Molton. 2½m N from A361 Barnstaple-Tiverton rd. In N Molton drive up the hill into the square with church on your L take the only drive beside the old school buildings and Court Hall is just round the bend. A very small south facing walled garden; large conservatory; rose, clematis, honeysuckle arbours surround a swimming pool garden with tender plants, rock wall and table. *Adm £1 Chd 20p. Sun July 10 (2-6). Private visits also welcome June 25 to July 10, please* **Tel 059 84 224**

The Croft ॐ (Mr & Mrs Jewell) Yarnscombe. From A377, 5m S of Barnstaple turning W opposite Chapelton Railway Stn. for 3m. Drive on L at village sign. From B3232 ¼m N of Huntshaw TV mast Xrds, turn E for 2m. 1-acre garden on edge of village with unspoilt distant views to West. Alpine area and wide selection of unusual plants and shrubs. Island beds, much herbaceous material, ponds and bog area. No toilets. Cream TEAS. *Adm £1 Chd free (Share to St. Andrews Church®). Suns June 26, July 10 (2-6). Private visits also welcome, please* **Tel 0769 60535**

Croftdene ॐ (Joy and Phil Knox) Ham Dalwood. Between Axminster and Honiton. From A35 3½m W of Axminster turn N nr Shute Garage signed Dalwood and Stockland. Keep L up Stockland Hill until just past television mast. Turn R signed Ham. 1½m to Ham Cross. Park by telephone box. From A30 5m E of Honiton turn R signed Axminster and Stockland 3m to televsion mast turn L to Ham. 1½-acre garden in the making since 1988 with further 1 acre of natural woodland. Wide range of shrubs; herbaceous; ericaceous; alpines; woodland and water plants. Island beds; rock garden; peat beds; stream-side and pond. Featured on TV 'Gardens For All 1991'. TEAS at **Burrow Farm**. *Adm £1 Chd free. Suns May 29, June 26, (2-6). Private visits also welcome, please* **Tel 0404 831271**

Crosspark ॐ (Mrs G West) Northlew. From Okehampton follow A30 for 1m turn R to Holsworthy drive for 6m past Garage turn R signposted Northlew, over bridge, turn L to Kimber, we are 3m along this rd on L, or 2½m from Highampton on the Northlew Rd. 1-acre plantswoman's garden by colour theme; herbaceous borders; ponds, incl wildlife pond; bog garden; rockery heathers and conifers. Wide range of plants. Featured on BBC Gardeners World and ITV. Large variety of unusual plants for sale. TEA. *Adm 75p Chd 20p. Fris, Suns April 1 to June 26 (2-6). Private visits also welcome, coaches welcome also, please* **Tel 0409 221518**

By Appointment Gardens. Avoid the crowds. Good chance of a tour by owner. See garden description for telephone number.

Dartington Hall Gardens ॐ (Dartington Hall Trust) Approx 1½m NW of Totnes. From Totnes take A384, turn R at Dartington Parish Church. 28-acre garden surrounds C14 Hall and Tiltyard. Plant sales shop and nursery. *Adm (donation) £2.00 recommended.* ▲*Sat, Sun May 21, 22 (dawn to dusk)*

Delamore ॐ (Mrs F A V Parker) Cornwood, Ivybridge. A38; leave at turning for Lee Mill and Cornwood 6m E of Plymouth. 4-acre garden with flowering shrubs, lawns and mature trees. Swimming pool available. TEAS. *Adm £1 Chd 50p. Suns May 1, 15 (2-5)*

¶**Dippers** ॐ (Mr & Mrs R J Hubble) Shaugh Prior. 8m NE of Plymouth on edge of Dartmoor. From A38 take Ivybridge exit and follow signs to Cornwood, continue on same rd to Shaugh Prior. From A386 follow signs to Bickleigh from Roborough then signs to Shaugh. Garden approx 100yds down lane opp church near top of village. Park in village or at White Thorn public house. No parking in lane. ¾-acre informal garden with further 1 acre being developed as nature reserve with stream and small bluebell wood. Emphasis on foliage contrast with varied collection of dwarf rhododendrons, azaleas, dwarf conifers and shrubs together with herbaceous and heathers; peat-bed; wildlife pond. Extensive collection of alpines, dwarf willows, gentians in raised beds, scree and 18 troughs. Special interest in pinks; scented pink walk. NCCPG National collection of dianthus. Choice alpines and unusual herbaceous for sale. *Adm £1 Chd free (Share to St Edmunds Church®). Suns May 1, June 12 (2-6) Fri July 1 (11-5)*

Doctyn Mill and Garden ॐ (Mr & Mrs M G Bourcier) Spekes Valley nr. Hartland. Off A39: From N Devon via Clovelly Cross & Hartland to Stoke, or from N Cornwall via Kilkhampton to the West Country Inn. On either route turn L and follow Elmscott signs towards Lymebridge in Spekes Valley for 3½m. A garden for all seasons (depicted on BBC TV in Spring, Summer and Autumn) with working water mill dated 1249, situated in one of Devon's outstanding beauty spots where garden blends with natural landscape. Nearly 8 acres of sheltered wooded valley 1500yds from Spekes Mill Mouth coastal waterfalls and beach. Mill pond, leats, trout stream crossed by footbridges and smaller streams. Cultivated areas including bog garden, rockery, outcrops, woodland, and orchard. Displays in their seasons of narcissi, primulas, shrub roses, specimen trees, shrubs and herbaceous plants beside a profusion of wild primroses, bluebells, foxgloves and ferns. Lunch, tea at Hartland Quay. *Adm £1.50 Chd 50p. Daily March to Oct (10-5). Parties by prior arrangement* **Tel 0237 441369**

The Downes ॐ (Mr & Mrs R C Stanley-Baker) 4½m S of Bideford; 3m NW of Torrington. On A386 to Bideford turn left (W) up drive, ¼m beyond layby. 15 acres with landscaped lawns; fine views overlooking fields and woodlands in Torridge Valley; many unusual trees and shrubs; small arboretum; woodland walks. Featured in Homes and Gardens June 1993. TEA Sats, Suns only. *Adm £1 Chd 20p. Daily April 1 to June 12 (all day); private visits also welcome June to Sept, please* **Tel 0805 22244**

Fardel Manor &※※ (Dr A G Stevens) 1¼m NW of Ivybridge; 2m SE of Cornwood; 200yds S of railway bridge. 5-acre, all organic garden, maintained with conservation and wildlife in mind. Partly reticulated. 2½ acres developed over past 10 years with stream, pond and lake. Also, small courts and walled gardens around C14 Manor, with orangery, herbaceous borders, formal pond and shrub garden. TEAS. *Adm £1.50 Chd 50p (Share to Frame®). Mon July 25 (11-4.30)*

Farrants &※ (M Richards) Kilmington. 2m W of Axminster. A35, turn S at Kilmington Cross into Whitford Rd; garden about ¼m on left. 1-acre garden with stream planted since 1963; mostly shrubs and ground cover for colour contrast around C16 cottage. *Adm £1 Chd free. Private visits usually welcome, please Tel 0297 32396*

Fast Rabbit Farm ※※ (Mr & Mrs Mort) Ash Cross. 1½m from Dartmouth off the Dartmouth-Totnes rd pass park and ride. Turn L at Rose Cottage. Opp direction, from Totnes or Kingsbridge, pass Woodland Park on R, drive past Norton Park on L turn R at Rose Cottage. Newly created garden in sheltered valley with natural stream. Several ponds and lake; partially wooded; rockery; extensively planted; extends 8 acres with new woodland planting and walks being created through woodland at head of valley. Small specialist nursery. Car park. Some level walks. 'Invalids' please phone prior to visit. TEAS. *Adm £1 Chd 50p. Suns April 3, May 1, 22, July 17, Aug 28 (11-5).* **Tel 0803 712437**

1 Feebers Cottage &※※ (Mr & Mrs M J Squires) Westwood. 2m NE of Broadclyst from B3181 (formerly A38) Exeter-Taunton, at Dog Village (Broadclyst) bear E to Whimple, after 1½m fork left for Westwood. ⅔-acre cottage garden on level site with wide variety of trees, shrubs, rock-plants, alpines, old-fashioned roses, small pond with water plants. Nursery. Cream TEAS June 26 only, tea and biscuits on other days. *Adm £1 Chd free. Sun March 20, Mon April 4, Suns May 15, June 5, 26, July 17, Sept 4, 25 Oct 9 (2-6). Private visits also welcome, please Tel 0404 822118*

¶Feniton Old Village Gardens ※※ From Honiton 4m and Exeter 13m turn N off A30 at Fenny Bridges. From Cullompton M5 turn R off A373 after Colliton, follow priority rd to New Feniton, turn L immediately before railway crossing. TEAS. *Combined adm £2 Chd 50p. Suns June 26, July 3 (2-6)*

  ¶9 Barton Rise (Mr & Mrs J Leeming) Small garden, extensive collection of fuchsias and annual planting
  ¶1 Chestnut Mews (Mrs E Sutherland) Small cottage garden
  ¶3 Chestnut Mews (Mrs J McSkimming) Small cottage garden
  ¶Court Barton (Sir John & Lady Palmer) Recently planted small garden with formal, informal and courtyard areas
  ¶Hunters Cottage (Mr & Mrs J Arkwright) Small cottage garden

Fernwood ※※ (Mr & Mrs H Hollinrake) Toadpit Lane, 1½m W of Ottery St Mary; ¼m down Toadpit Lane (off B3174). 2-acre woodland garden; wide selection of flowering shrubs, conifers and bulbs; species and hybrid rhododendrons and azaleas special feature in spring. *Adm £1 Acc chd free. Open every day from April 1 to May 31. Private visits also welcome, please Tel 0404 812820*

¶Flete (Country Houses Association) Ermington, 2m W of Modbury on A379 Plymouth-Kingsbridge rd. Entrance adjacent to Sequers Bridge. 5 acres of gardens overlooking R Erme and valley. Landscaped in 1920's by Russell Paige and incl an Italian garden and water garden which Lawrence of Arabia helped to construct. Many fine trees and shrubs. Interesting cobbled terrace to W face of original Tudor manor. TEA. *Adm £1.50 Chd 75p. Sun May 1 (2.30-4.30)*

Fore Stoke Farm ※ (Mrs Anne Belam) Holne, nr Ashburton. ½-acre garden at 900' on Dartmoor full of hardy shrubs and flowers incl own collection of hosta. Clematis, roses, hardy geraniums and grasses. Unusual annuals in the autumn. Rabbits and ponies to look at. Dogs on leads. TEA (DIY 30p) in sun room. Good selection of homegrown plants for sale. *Adm £1 Chd 50p. Private visits usually welcome, mid May to mid July and during Sept but with notice, please Tel 0364 3394*

Garden House ※ (Mr & Mrs W Rawson) Lower Warberry Road, Torquay. From harbour, Babbacombe Road, 7th turning left. Garden ½m on L at widening of rd, opp 'Sorento'. 1-acre S sloping with sea view from upper level of garden. Terraced with water garden, featuring lily pond, fountain, waterwheel. Parking on roadway. TEAS. *Adm £1 Chd 50p. Sats, Suns April 23, 24; May 28, 29; Aug 27, 28 (2-6). Private visits also welcome, please Tel 0803 292563*

The Garden House ※※ (The Fortescue Garden Trust) Buckland Monachorum, Yelverton. W of A386, 10m N of Plymouth. 8-acre garden of interest throughout year; inc 2-acre walled garden, one of finest in the country; fine collections of herbaceous and woody plants. Coaches and parties by appt only. TEAS. *Adm £2.50 Chd 50p (Share to NGS). March 1 to Oct 31 daily. For NGS Weds July 13, Aug 17 (10.30-5)*

¶The Gate House (Mr & Mrs D Booker) Lee Coastal Village. 3m W of Ilfracombe. Park in village car park. Take lane alongside The Grampus public house. Garden is 50yds past inn buildings. Peaceful streamside garden with a range of habitats; bog garden (with a National Collection of Rodgersia), woodland, herbaceous borders, patio garden with hardy 'exotics'. 2¼ acres, where no chemicals are used, only a few minutes walk from the sea and dramatic coastal scenery. Good food at the Grampus. *Collecting box. Private visits usually welcome, please Tel 0271 862409*

Gidleigh Park (Paul & Kay Henderson) From Chagford R into Mill St. 150yds, fork R, to bottom of hill then follow sign for 1¾m. 700ft up on edge of Dartmoor, within the National Park, in beautiful surroundings. Tumbling streams with boulders and natural granite outcrops; terrace and parterre with herb garden; extensive natural water garden; woodland walks underplanted with rhododendrons and azaleas; massed bulbs in spring. Park in hotel car park, not in drive. Lunches and cream teas £4-£10. *Adm £1. Open Mon to Fri except bank hols all year round, tours and parties by prior appt Tel 0647 432367*

Glebe Cottage ⚹✿ (Mrs C Klein) Warkleigh. 5m from South Molton on B3227 to Umberleigh, L at Homedown Xrds towards Chittlehamholt, straight on at next Xrds, 200yds on L, parking at bottom of track. 1-acre cottage garden, S sloping, terraced wide collection of interesting plants in different situations; stumpery with ferns to hot dry garden with mediterranean subjects; new herbaceous plantings. Cottage garden favourites alongside rare plants. Wide variety of unusual plants available from adjoining nursery (open Wed-Sun). *Adm £1 Chd free. Suns June 5, 26; July 17, 24, 31; Aug 7, 14, 28; Sept 4, 25 (2-5), please* **Tel 0769 540 554**

The Glebe House ⚹ (Mr & Mrs John West) Whitestone. 2½-acre mature garden at 650ft S facing with outstanding views ranging from Exe estuary to Dartmoor. Garden on 3 levels; lower level with extensive lawns, mature trees and lge heather garden; middle level where house walls and buildings covered by climbing roses, clematis, honeysuckles and jasmines; upper level, given over to lawns with families of trees, acer, birch and eucalyptus underplanted with many types of rose. Over 300 varieties of rose most notable being Rosa filipes 'Kiftsgate', probably largest rose in UK, stretching over 130ft along Tithe Barn in courtyard and close to its equally vigorous double seedling 'St Catherine'. Former Rectory part C14 with Georgian frontage (not open). C14 Tithe Barn (Ancient Monument). C13/14 Church adjoins. Parking in lanes around Church. *Adm £1 Chd free (Share to Whitestone Church®). Sun, Mon May 29, 30, Suns June 5, 12, 19, 26, July 3, 10 (2-6). Private visits also welcome, please* **Tel 0392 811200**

Gorwell House ♿✿ (Dr J A Marston) 1m E of Barnstaple centre, on Bratton Fleming rd, drive entrance between two lodges on left. 4 acres of trees and shrubs, walled garden; mostly created since 1982; small temple; summer house with views across estuary to Lundy and Hartland Point. TEAS. *Adm £1 Acc chd free. Suns April 24, May 29, June 26, July 31, Sept 4, Oct 3 (2-6)*

Gratton's Field Cottage ⚹✿ (Mrs C F Luxton) Northlew. 8m W of Okehampton. Northlew Square towards Highampton. ½m from village on L. Small cottage garden; spring bulbs; shrubs; fuchsias; fish pond. Recent additional tree and shrub planting. TEA. *Adm 50p. Easter Fri, Sun April 1, 3; Suns June 5, 12, Aug 7, 14 (11-5). Private visits also welcome, please* **Tel 0409 221361**

Greenway Gardens ♿✿ (Mr & Mrs A A Hicks) Churston Ferrers, 4m W of Brixham. From B3203, Paignton-Brixham, take rd to Galmpton, thence towards Greenway Ferry. Partly suitable for wheelchairs; 30 acres; old-established garden with mature trees; shrubs; rhododendrons, magnolias and camellias. Recent plantings; commercial shrub nursery. Woodland walks by R Dart. Limited parking. TEA and biscuits. *Adm £1 Chd 50p. Thurs April 28, May 5 (2-6).* **Tel 0803 842382**

Regular Openers. Too many days to include in diary. Usually there is a wide range of plants giving year-round interest. See head of county section for the name and garden description for times etc.

Hamblyn's Coombe (Capt R S McCrum RN Ret'd & Mrs B McCrum) Dittisham. From B3207 to Dittisham, turn sharp R at Red Lion Inn, along The Level. After public car park on L fork R up steep private rd. Field car park signposted at top. 10 min very pretty walk to garden. 7 acres sloping steeply to R Dart, with dramatic view across river to Greenway House. Extensive planting of trees and shrubs; wild meadows and mature broad-leaf woods. Woodland walks, stream and ponds and long river foreshore at bottom of garden. Sculpture by Bridget McCrum around garden. Ideal for children and dogs. TEA. *Adm £1 Chd free (Share to National Hospital for Neurology & Neurosurgery®). Sun, Mon May 1, 2 (2-6)*

Hartland Abbey (Sir Hugh Stucley & the Hon Lady Stucley) Hartland. Turn off A39 W of Clovelly Cross. Follow signs to Hartland through town on rd to Stoke and Quay. Abbey 1m from town on right. 2 woodland shrubberies with camellias, rhododendrons; wildflower walk through bluebell woods to remote Atlantic cove (Private walled gardens also open for NGS). TEAS. *Adm £1 Chd 50p (Share to St Nectan's Church, Hartland®).* ▲ *Sun April 10 (2-5.30) Tel The Administrator* **0237 441264**

Heddon Hall (Mr & Mrs W H Keatley) Parracombe. 10m NE of Barnstaple off A39. 400yds N up hill from village centre. Entrance to drive on R. Ample parking 200yds. Garden of former rectory on edge of Exmoor under restoration extending to 3 acres. Walled garden with formal layout and herbaceous beds; sheltered flower garden; semi shaded S sloping shrubbery with paths leading down to natural stream and water garden. Cream TEAS. *Adm £1 Chd 50p. Suns June 19, July 17 (2-6)*

Higher Knowle (Mr & Mrs D R A Quicke) Lustleigh, 3m NW of Bovey Tracey A382 towards Moretonhampstead; in 2½m L at Kelly Cross for Lustleigh; in ¼m L/R at Brookfield along Knowle Rd; in ½m steep drive on left. 3-acre steep woodland garden; rhododendrons, camellias, magnolias on a carpet of primroses, bluebells; water garden and good Dartmoor views. Teas in village. *Adm £2 Chd free (Share to St John the Baptist Church, Lustleigh®). Suns March 20, 27 April 3, 10, 17, 24; May 1, 8, 15; Mons April 4, May 2, (2-6)* **Tel 064 77 275**

Higher Spriddlestone ♿ (Mr & Mrs David Willis) Brixton, nr Plymouth. A379 5m E from Plymouth, S at Martin's Garden Centre sign, ¾m to top of hill, R opp Spriddlestone sign, entrance 50yds on L. 1½-acre developing garden in rural setting. Level area around house, with borders, informal wildlife and kitchen gardens and ponds. Teas at Martin's Garden Centre. *Adm £1 Chd free. Private visits also welcome, please* **Tel 0752 401184**

Higher Warcombe ⚹✿ (Mr & Mrs A Treverton) Nr Kingsbridge. 2m N of Kingsbridge on the B3194 between Sorley Green Cross and Stumpy Post Cross. Take 1st turning L signposted Warcombe, house and garden approx ½m down lane. 1-acre garden on SW facing slope started in 1982 incl lawns, trees, rhododendrons, shrubs and herbaceous. Two steep banks planted for ground cover are a special feature and there is a pretty courtyard with container planting and a small walled garden. TEAS. *Adm £1 Chd 50p. Suns May 1, July 17 (2-5.30)*

Hill House Nursery & Gardens &೫ (Mr & Mrs R Hubbard) Landscove. Between Dartington & Ashburton signed A38 or A384 Buckfastleigh-Totnes. Old Vicarage beside church both designed by John Loughborough Pearson, architect of Truro Cathedral. The 3 acre garden was the subject of 'An Englishman's Garden' by Edward Hyams, a previous owner. Also featured in 'English Vicarages and Their Gardens' and several times on TV. Said by many well known horticulturists to be one of the finest collections of plants anywhere. TEAS. *Free entrance open all year, Tea Room Mar to Oct. Collection box for NGS (11-5)*

Holywell &೫೫ (Mr & Mrs R Steele) Bratton Fleming. 7m NE of Barnstaple. Turn W beside White Hart Inn (opp White Hart Garage) signed Village Hall. At 300yds fork L for Rye Park. Entrance drive ¼m at sharp L. Parking at house. Garden on edge of Exmoor in woodland setting of mature trees, in all about 25 acres. Stream, ponds and borders. Woodland walk to Lower River meadow and old Lynton Railway Track. Many unusual plants for sale. TEAS. *Adm £1 Chd free. Suns April 24; May 1, 8, 15, 22; June 5; Mon May 30 (2-5). Private visits also welcome, please* Tel 0598 710213

Kerscott House &೫ (Mrs J Duncan) Swimbridge, Barnstaple-South Molton (former A361) 1m E of Swimbridge, R at top of hill, immediate fork L, 100yds on L, 1st gate past house. Developing 6-acre garden surrounding C16 farmhouse in peaceful rural setting. Ornamental trees, wide selection of shrubs, herbaceous and tender perennials, pond and bog garden. Cream TEAS May and June only. *Adm £1 Chd free. Suns June 26, Aug 28 (2-6). Private visits also welcome during July, please* Tel 0271 830943

Killerton Garden &೫೫ (The National Trust) 8m N of Exeter. Via B3181 Cullompton Rd (formerly A38), fork left in 7m on B3185. Garden 1m follow NT signs. 15 acres of spectacular hillside gardens with naturalised bulbs sweeping down to large open lawns. Delightful walks through fine collection of rare trees and shrubs; herbaceous borders. Wheelchair and 'golf' buggy with driver available. Restaurant. Tea room, plant centre. *Adm gardens only £2.80 Chd £1.40. For NGS Suns April 24, July 10 (10.30-5.30)*

Kings Gatchell &೫೫ (Kenneth Adlam) Higher Metcombe. From Exeter, A30 to Airport, pass straight on through Aylesbeare over Tipton Cross, through beech copse (don't bear R), down hill, house on L. Neighbouring Bramble Cottage, West Hill. ⅔-acre wide variety many unusual plants, strong in daphnes, alpines, hebes, ferns (NCCPG National Collection), smaller rhododendrons, ilex. Greenhouses. *Adm £1 Chd free. Suns, Mons May 1, 2; 29, 30 (11 5)*

Knightshayes Gardens &೫೫ (The National Trust) 2m N of Tiverton. Via A396 Tiverton-Bampton; turn E in Bolham, signed Knightshayes Court; entrance ½m on left. Large 'Garden in the Wood', 50 acres of landscaped gardens with pleasant walks and views over the Exe valley. Choice collections of unusual plants, incl acers, birches, rhododendrons, azaleas, camellias, magnolias, roses, spring bulbs, alpines and herbaceous borders; formal gardens; Wheelchair available. Restaurant. *Adm garden only £2.80 Chd £1.40. Suns May 8, July 3 (10.30-5.30)*

Lee Ford &೫ (Mr & Mrs N Lindsay-Fynn) Budleigh Salterton. Bus:DG, frequent service between Exmouth railway station (3½m) and Budleigh Salterton, alight Lansdowne corner. 40 acres parkland, formal and woodland gardens with extensive display of spring bulbs, camellias, rhododendrons, azaleas and magnolias. Adam pavilion. Picnic area. Car park free. Home made cream TEAS (3-5.30) and charity stalls. *Adm £1.40 OAPs £1 Chd 60p Special rate for groups 20 or more £1 (Share to other charities). Sun May 29 (1.30-5.30); also by prior appt for parties only* Tel 0395 445894

¶Lewdon Farm &೫ (Betty Frampton) 1½m N of Cheriton Bishop. From A30 Exeter-Okehampton. L for Cheriton Bishop. 2nd R at village shop on Yeoford Rd. After 1½m take R fork. Garden in 150yds. 1-acre garden with wide variety of plants surrounding a C16 farmhouse, with lovely views. Troughs, raised beds and rockeries on W side featuring alpines, miniature shrubs and conifers linked by formal grey and white parterre to herbaceous borders on E side. Plants available from adjoining nursery. Cream TEAS weekends only. *Adm £1 Chd free. Suns May 15, 29, June 12; Weds May 18, June 1, 15; Sat July 23 (2-6)*

¶Little Cumbre ೫ (Dr & Mrs John Lloyd) Exeter. At top of Pennsylvania Rd, 50yds below telephone kiosk on same side. Extensive views of Dartmoor and the Exe Estuary. ½-acre 8-yr-old mixed shrub and herbaceous garden. Collection of hellebores, clematis and small ornamental trees chosen for bark. Ample parking in rd. *Adm £1.50 Chd 50p. Thurs April 28, May 26, June 23 (2-6). Private visits also welcome, please* Tel 0392 58315

Little Southey &೫೫ (Mr & Mrs S J Rowe) Northcott, Nr Culmstock. Uffculme to Culmstock rd, through Craddock then turn R at 6'6 restriction sign, Little Southey ½m on L. Culmstock to Uffculme turn L at restriction sign to Blackborough, right at Xrds to Northcott. House on R. Garden surrounding C17 farmhouse. Wide variety of plants grown for round the year interest. Limited parking if wet. Plant sale partly in aid of NCCPG. TEAS. *Adm £1 Chd free. Sun June 26 (2-6)*

Little Upcott Gardens &೫೫ (Mr & Mrs M Jones) Marsh Green signposted off A30 Exeter to Honiton rd 4m E of M5 junction 29. Also signposted off B3180 and then from village. Informal 2-acre garden with many features of visual interest on different levels, featured on TV in 1992. Sensitive combination of plant styles and colour and unusual varieties of conifers, shrubs, perennials and alpines, some of which are available for sale. The original cottage garden is also open and there is a newly landscaped water feature with ornamental ducks. Plenty of seats available and assistance given to disabled incl partially sighted, by prior arrangement. Parties welcomed with cream teas, available by appt. TEAS. *Adm £1 Chd 50p (Share to Cats Protection League, Ottery Branch). Sat, Sun, Mon May 28, 29, 30; Sats, Suns June 18, 19, July 9, 10; Weds June 8, 29 July 20 (1.30-5.30). Private visits also welcome, please* Tel 0404 822797

By Appointment Gardens. Avoid the crowds. Good chance of a tour by owner. See garden description for telephone number.

Little Webbery ⬥⬥ (Mr & Mrs J A Yewdall) Webbery Cross, Alverdiscott. Approx 2½m E of Bideford. Accessible either from Bideford (E The Water) along the Alverdiscott Rd or from the Barnstaple to Torrington Rd B3232 taking the rd to Bideford at Alverdiscott and passing through Stoney Cross. Parking adjacent Xrds. Approx 3-acre garden with two large borders near the house with lawns running down a valley, a pond, mature trees on either side and fields below which are separated by a Ha Ha. It has a walled garden with box hedging, which is partly used for fruit, vegetables, and incl a greenhouse; lawns; rose garden and trellises; shrubs and climbing plants. There is a tennis court below and a lake beyond. TEA 60p. *Adm £1 Chd 50p. Sun June 19 (2-6)*

The Lodge ⬥⬥ (Mr & Mrs M H Tregaskis) Hartley Ave, Mannamead, Plymouth. 1½m from City Centre via Mutley Plain. Turn right at Henders Corner into Eggbuckland Rd, 3rd right at Tel kiosk to end of cul de sac. ½-acre S sloping aspect with variety of unusual shrubs, conifers, camellias and ground cover plants. Former L.A. Nursery with range of lean-to glasshouses for fruit and tender subjects. Featured on TV 'Gardens For All'. TEA. *Adm £1 Chd 20p (Share to St. Luke's Hospice®). Suns May 1, June 12, July 24, (2-5.30). Private visits also welcome please* **Tel 0752 220849**

Lower Coombe Royal ⬥⬥ (Mr & Mrs H Sharp) Kingsbridge. ½m N of Kingsbridge on Loddiswell Rd. Sign at gate. Historic woodland garden with rhododendrons, camellias, azaleas, magnolias and rare trees; terraces with tender and unusual shrubs; lawns, herbaceous borders; eucalypts. (Commercial shrub nursery open daily.) *Adm 50p Chd 25p. Private visits welcome please* **Tel 0548 853717**

¶Lower Kerse ⬥⬥ (Mr & Mrs S O Parker-Swift) Thurlestone. Village of Thurlestone is 4m W of Kingsbridge. Garden is on fringe of village signposted Kerse at Kerse Cross before entering village. 7 acres of natural garden set in a delightful valley ½m from the coast, bounded by a stream and 2 ponds. *Adm £1 Chd 50p. Sun June 19 (2-5)*

¶Lukesland (Mr & Mrs J Howell) Ivybridge. 1½m from Ivybridge on Harford Rd, E side of Erme valley. 15 acres of flowering shrubs, wild flowers and fine and rare trees with pinetum in Dartmoor National Park. Beautiful setting of small valley around Addicombe Brook with small lakes, numerous waterfalls and pools. Extensive and unusual collection of large and small leaved rhododendrons and one of the largest Magnolia Campbellii in the country. Partially suitable for wheelchairs. TEA. *Adm £2 Chd 50p. Suns, Weds April 17 to June 5 incl. For NGS Suns May 1, 22, Charity Day May 29, also Oct 30 for autumn colour (2-6). Coaches on application only,* **Tel 0752 893390**

Mardon ⬥ (His Honour & Mrs A C Goodall) ½m from Moretonhampstead, from the Xrds in Moretonhampstead take the Chagford rd A382, then R at once (not sharp R to Church), down hill, over a stream, enter by cattle grid on R before hill. 2-acres with lawns and terrace, rhododendrons; trout pond and streams; fine view of Moretonhampstead church. Teas in Moretonhampstead. *Adm £1 Chd free. Suns May 22, 29; Mon May, 30; Sun June 5 (2-5.30)*

Marwood Hill ⬥⬥ (Dr J A Smart) Marwood, 4m N of Barnstaple signed from A361 Barnstaple-Braunton rd. In Marwood village, opp church. 20-acre garden with 3 small lakes. Extensive collection of camellias under glass and in open; daffodils, rhododendrons, rare flowering shrubs, rock and alpine scree; waterside planting; bog garden; many clematis; Australian native plants. National Collection astilbe, iris ensata, tulbaghia. Plants for sale between 11-1 and 2-5. Teas in Church Room (Suns & Bank Hols or by prior arrangement for parties). *Adm £2 OAP £1.50 Acc chd under 12 free. Daily except Christmas Day (dawn-dusk)*

Meadow Court ⬥ (Ken & Heather Davey) Slapton. Entering the village of Slapton from the A379 at the Memorial on the beach. Take 2nd R and 1st L to house and garden in middle of village. Large free parking area. Level garden of 1 acre created in the last 12 yrs and maintained by the owner. Large pond with waterfall; Gunnera and marginals, water hens nest here. Large lawned area with trees and shrubs; heathers and shrub roses. TEAS. *Adm £1 Chd 25p. Suns May 22, 29 (2-6)*

Meadowcroft ⬥⬥ (Mrs G Thompson) 1 Downfield Way, Plympton. From Plymouth left at St Mary's Church roundabout, along Glen Rd, 3rd right into Downfield Drive; garden on right. From A38, Plympton turn-off L at 1st roundabout, R at 2nd down Hillcrest Drive and Glen Rd, L at bottom of hill. Opp Dillons into Downfield Drive. Medium size; stream; rhododendrons, azaleas, trees, flowering shrub borders. TEA. *Adm 80p Chd free. Suns April 10, 24, May 22; Wed May 11 (2-5.30)*

¶Membland Villa ⬥⬥ (Mr & Mrs L J Hockaday) Newton Ferrers. 10m E of Plymouth. A374 Plymouth-Kingsbridge. At Yealmpton, S to Newton Ferrers. Sharp L at Widey Cross to Bridgend, then L to Membland. 2nd house on L from top of Membland Hill. Small 'Revelstoke' house set in country garden. Laid out and planted over 22yrs by present owner. Ornamental pond. Old roses, camellias, bulbs, trees, shrubs, climbers, herbaceous. Many unusual plants. Garden incl many acres steep bluebell woods spectacular in the season. TEA. *Adm £1 Chd free. Suns May 1, 29, June 26, Aug 28, Sept 18 (2-5). Private visits also welcome, please* **Tel 0752 872626**

Membury Gardens 3m NW of Axminster. A35 to Honiton, ½m W of Axminster turn N signed Membury. *Combined adm £1.50 Chd 50p. Suns April 10, June 5 (2-5.30)*

    Quakers ⬥⬥ (Mr & Mrs T J Wallace) At L turning about 1m S of the Church. Interesting small terraced flower garden around old Quaker Meeting House. Across lane, more a plantsman's whimsical collection than a garden. Mixed unusual tree & shrub plantings leading down to and over a wooded stream. *Private visits also welcome, please* **Tel 040 488 312**

    ¶Yarty House ⬥ (Mr & Mrs P L Bibby) 500yds S of Quakers, take the drive on R (at the lodge). Daffodil walk from lodge to herbaceous borders and shrubs around the house and walled garden. Woodland walk for bluebells, azaleas and rhododendrons. Fine views of the Yarty valley. Ample parking

¶**Monks Aish** (Capt & Mrs M J Garnett) 1m W of South Brent, near the hamlet of Aish, off B3372 W of village. Follow signposts to Aish. After going under Aish railway bridge up hill, 3rd house on L next to Great Aish. [Grid Ref 688603]. 1-acre cottage garden with small stream. Variety of shrubs, trees, flowers, fruit and vegetables. Restored over last 25yrs. TEA. *Adm £1 Chd under 12 50p (Share to The Missions to Seamen®). Sats May 14, June 5 (2-5)*

The Moorings ❀ (Mr & Mrs A Marriage) Rocombe, Uplyme, 2m NW of Lyme Regis. A3070 out of Lyme Regis, turn right 150yds beyond The Black Dog; over Xrds, fork right into Springhead Rd; top gate to garden 500yds on left. From Axminster A35; in 2m, 200yds beyond Hunters Lodge (Shell garage on Xrds), fork right twice then straight on 1m, top gate to garden on right. 3-acre peaceful woodland garden, developed since 1965, on hillside with terraced paths, overlooking unspoilt countryside. Fine trees inc many species eucalyptus, unusual pines, nothofagus; flowering shrubs inc some rare; daffodils and other spring flowers, ground cover, many ferns, autumn colour. *Adm 75p Chd free. Sat April 2; Suns, Mons April 3, 4; May 1, 2; 29, 30; Sun Nov 6 (for Autumn colour) (11-5). Private visits also welcome please Tel* **0297 443295**

16 Moorland View ⚘ (Mr & Mrs G E J Wilton) Derriford, Plymouth. From Plymouth or A38 take A386 Tavistock Rd. From Derriford roundabout 1st L into Powisland Drive, 1st R into Roborough Ave, then L at bottom. Garden is approx 4m from Plymouth City centre. Small town garden with variety of plants. A typical lady's garden. TEA. *Adm 50p. Sun June 19 (2-5). Private visits also welcome, please Tel* **0752 708800**

Mothecombe House ♿⚘❀ (Mr & Mrs A Mildmay-White) Holbeton, SE of Plymouth 4m. From A379, between Yealmpton and Modbury, turn S for Holbeton. Queen Anne house (not open). Walled gardens, herbaceous borders. Orchard with spring bulbs; camellia walk and flowering shrubs. Newly planted bog garden; streams and pond; bluebell woods leading to private beach. Walk through picturesque thatched cottages to the Old School Teahouse and along the coastal footpath to the stunning Erme Estuary. TEAS. *Adm garden £1.50 Chd free (Share to Holbeton Church®). Suns, Sats, April 10, 30, May 1, June 12, July 10 (2-5)*

Mulberry House ♿ (Dr & Mrs David Boyd) Barbican Terrace, Barnstaple. From the new rd (A361) follow signs to the Barbican Industrial Estate. This takes you L past a corner shop with Benson & Hedges sign down Summerland St. At the end fork R into Barbican Terrace, Mulberry House 2nd entrance on L. Parking at Trinity Churchyard which is also accessible from the south end. 1-acre varied planting; foliage, especially gold and variegated; climbers and shade plants. TEA. *Adm £1 Chd 50p (Share to Trinity Church®). Suns July 3, 10 (2-6). Private visits also welcome, please Tel* **0271 45387**

¶**Oare Manor Cottage** ⚘❀ (Mr & Mrs J Greenaway) Oare. 6m E of Lynton off A39. R after county gate to Oare. 50yds from Oare Church immortalized, in R D Blackmore's 'Lorna Doone'. Sheltered cottage garden in the romantic Oare Valley. Old-fashioned herbaceous borders, unusual shade plants, alpines, roses, Mediterranean pot plants. Fine views of the moor. Parking opp church or in Lower Field. TEAS. *Adm £1 Chd 50p (Share to Oare Church®). Suns July 24, 31, Aug 28 (2-6). Private visits also welcome, please Tel* **059 87 242**

The Old Glebe ♿⚘❀ (Mr & Mrs Nigel Wright) Eggesford, 4m SW of Chulmleigh. Turn S off A377 at Eggesford Station (½-way between Exeter & Barnstaple), cross railway and River Taw, drive straight uphill (signed Brushford) for ¾m; turn right into bridle path. 5-acre garden of former Georgian rectory with mature trees and several lawns, courtyard, walled herbaceous borders and a bog garden; emphasis on species and hybrid rhododendrons and azaleas 500 varieties. TEAS. *Adm £1.50 Chd 50p (Share to The Abbeyfield Chulmleigh®). Fri, Sat, Sun May 13, 14, 15 (2-6)*

The Old Mill ⚘ (Mr & Mrs Shapland) Blakewell Muddiford, nr Barnstaple. ½m N past District hospital off B3230 to Ilfracombe signed Blakewell Fisheries then L again into Fisheries car park. Follow signs to Old Mill along lane to end, parking in field, limited parking by house. 3-acre garden on S facing slope nestles at the rear of a grade 11 listed Mill, surrounded by beautiful countryside views. A variety of conifers, rhododendrons, shrubs, heathers and herbaceous plants; also newly planted lime tree avenue, water gardens and many other interesting features. *Adm £1 Chd free. Suns May 1, June 5, July 17 (2-6). Private visits also welcome, please Tel* **0271 75002**

The Old Parsonage ⚘❀ (Mr & Mrs Alex Hill) Warkleigh. 4m SW South Molton on B3226 past Clapworthy Mill (Hancocks Cider) R at stone barn signs to Warkleigh. From S through Chittlehamholt then 2nd R at War Memorial. Telephone kiosk marked on OS landranger sheet 180. 1-acre garden around former C16 Parsonage. Herbaceous border at entrance; enclosed stepped terraced garden behind house with wide range of plants and raised beds. Hillside above planted with trees and shrubs for autumn colour. Cream TEAS. *Adm £1 Chd 50p (Share to NCCPG®). Suns June 26, July 3, 31, Aug 28, Sept 18 (2-6)*

The Old Rectory, Clayhidon ⚘❀ (Mr & Mrs K J Wakeling) 4m from Wellington via South St or M5 exit 26 for Ford St. House next to Half Moon Inn and Church. 3-acres woodland garden with new plantings amid mature native trees; large numbers of naturalized bulbs mainly daffodils and snowdrops. Walled garden with mixed borders, ponds and rockery. *Adm 60p Chd 30p. Private visits usually welcome, please Tel* **0823 680534**

The Old Rectory, Woodleigh ♿⚘ (Mr & Mrs H E Morton) nr Loddiswell. 3½m N of Kingsbridge E off Kingsbridge-Wrangaton Rd at Rake Cross (1m S of Loddiswell). 1½m to Woodleigh. Garden on R in hamlet. C19 Clergyman's garden partly enclosed by stone walls; restored and added to by present owners; mature trees with collection of rhododendrons, camellias and magnolias and other shrubs; large numbers of naturalised bulbs especially crocus and daffodils in early March. *Adm £1 Chd 10p. Private visits usually welcome, please Tel* **0548 550387**

The Orchard ᕗ❀ (Mrs Hilda M Montgomery) Kenn. 5m S of Exeter off A38. ¾ acre; mostly trees; variety of conifers, azaleas, camellias, rhododendrons, many shrubs; fishponds and flowerbeds. Masses of spring bulbs. Ample parking nr Church. *Adm £1 OAPs/Chd 50p (Share to Redgate Bird Sanctuary, Exmouth©). Suns May 8, 22 (2-5.30); private visits also welcome, please* **Tel 0392 832530**

Orchard Cottage ᕗ❀ (Mr & Mrs W K Bradridge) 30, Hulham Rd, Exmouth, From Exeter A376 L into Hulham Road, just before first set of traffic lights. Entrance lane between Nos 26 and 32 Hulham Rd, opp lower end of Phillips Avenue. ¼-acre typical cottage garden. Parking in Hulham Road or Phillips Avenue. *Adm £1 Chd free. Private visits usually welcome, please* **Tel 0395 278605** *(2.30-5.30)*

Ottery St Mary Gardens Town maps available at each garden. Suggested car park in Brook St will be signposted. TEAS at Ernespie. *Combined adm £1.50 Chd 50p. Sat, Sun May 21, 22 (2-6)*

  Ernespie, Longdogs Lane ᕗ (Dr & Mrs G Ward) Next to Ravenhill, connected by garden gate. South facing hot, dry garden and badger playground, planted for easy care, cutting and continuous colour; rhododendrons, heathers, roses; level terrace. TEAS in aid of GDBA

  Little Beaumont, Ridgeway ⚹ (Mr & Mrs I A Martin) From town centre, pass church on L (Honiton Rd), take 1st R on bend into Ridgeway. Approx 200yds on R. Partly walled ¼-acre garden with shrubs, trees and herbaceous border

  Ravenhill, Longdogs Lane ᕗ⚹❀ (Ruth & Guy Charter) Take Sidmouth Rd from town square, 200yds up Tip Hill turn L up narrow Longdogs Lane, 5th house on R. Medium-sized garden with a wide variety of unusual plants. South aspect, country views; pond; keen NCCPG propagator. Unusual plants for sale (Share to NCCPG®)

  10 Slade Close ⚹❀ (Betty & Jenny Newell) From town centre take B3174 towards Seaton. Turn R into Slade Rd, then L into Slade Close and R again. Small garden, mixed shrubs, spring flowers, small pond, scree garden

Overbecks ⚹ (The National Trust) Sharpitor 1½m SW of Salcombe. From Salcombe or Malborough follow NT signs. 6-acre garden with rare plants and shrubs; spectacular views over Salcombe Estuary. *Adm garden only £2 Chd £1. Suns June 5, 26 (10-8 sunset if earlier)*

Penrose ⚹❀ (Mr & Mrs A Jewell) Crediton. A377 main Exeter to Barnstaple road, turn into Park Rd by Hillbrow Residential Home. Garden opp third turning on L. ⅓-acre town garden with small lawns, shrubs and herbaceous borders, pond with waterfall and wishing well, areas for fruit and veg and for growing produce for exhibition. Spring bulbs and summer annuals. TEA. *Adm 50p Chd free. Suns April 10; May 8; Aug 14 (2-5)*

38 Phillipps Avenue ᕗ⚹❀ (Mr & Mrs R G Stuckey) Exmouth. From Exeter, turn L into Hulham rd just before 1st set of traffic lights, 1st L into Phillipps Avenue (ample parking). Small, highly specialised alpine and rock garden containing extensive collection of rock plants and mina-ture shrubs, many rare and unusual; peat bed; scree bed; troughs; New Zealand collection. National NCCPG Helichrysum collection. Small alpine nursery. Teashops Exmouth. *Adm 50p Chd free. Suns April 3, 10, 24, May 1, 15, 29; June 19 Helichrysum Day (Share for NCCPG®) (2-6). Private visits also welcome, please* **Tel 0395 273636**

The Pines (R A Bitmead) Main Rd, Salcombe. At junction of Devon and Sandhills rds; lower entrance and parking Sandhills rd. All seasons ¾-acre S facing garden; fine coastal views to Sharpitor Headland and N Sands Valley. Informal garden of surprises; many interesting and unusual shrubs, trees; water gardens; bulbs, camellias, azaleas, heathers. *Adm £1.50 Chd free. Sat, Sun March 19, 20; Fri, Sat, Sun, Mon April 1, 2, 3, 4 (11-5). Private visits also welcome all year, please* **Tel 0548 842198**

Plant World ❀ (Ray & Lin Brown) St. Mary Church Rd Newton Abbot. Follow brown signs from A380 Penn Inn Roundabout. Car park on L past Water Gardens. 4-acre Hillside Garden, laid out as a map of the world with native plants. Alpines, especially primulas and gentians, shrubs, herbaceous. Himalayan and Japanese gardens. Comprehensive cottage garden with double primroses, auriculas etc. 3 National Primula Collections. Seen on ITV June 1987 and BBC Gardeners World June 1993. Rare and unusual plants sold in adjacent nursery. Picnic area, viewpoint over Dartmoor and Lyme Bay. Collecting box. *Adm 50p Chd free. Open daily (9-5)* **Tel 0803 872939**

Pleasant View ᕗ⚹❀ (Mr & Mrs B D Yeo) Two Mile Oak, nr Denbury. 2m from Newton Abbot on A381 to Totnes. R opp 2m Oak Garage signed Denbury. ¾m on L. Large car park. 2-acre plantsman's garden surrounded by open countryside with pleasant views. Wide variety of uncommon shrubs many tender. Began planting in field beside nursery in Autumn 1993. National Collections of Abelia and Salvia. Plants for sale in adjoining nursery (see advert). *Adm £1.20 Chd 25p. Sats, Suns May 21, 22; June 4, 5; July 16, 17; Aug 6, 7; Sept 3, 4 (2-6)*

Portington ⚹ (Mr & Mrs I A Dingle) nr Lamerton. From Tavistock B6632 to Launceston. ¼m beyond Blacksmiths Arms, Lamerton, fork L (signed Chipshop). Over Xrds (signed Horsebridge) first L then L again (signed Portington). From Launceston R at Carrs Garage and R again (signed Horsebridge), then as above. Small garden in peaceful rural setting with fine views over surrounding countryside. Mixed planting with shrubs and borders; woodland walk to small lake. TEAS. *Adm £1 Chd 25p (Share to St Luke's Hospice®). Sats July 16, 30 (2-5.30)*

Priors ᕗ⚹❀ (Mrs Hunloke) Abbotskerswell. 1½m SW of Newton Abbot on Totnes-Newton Rd, signposted Abbotskerswell. Garden at bottom of village. ⅔-acre enclosed colourful garden, long herbaceous borders, old shrub roses; unusual plants. *Adm £1 Chd 50p. Sun June 26 (2-5.30)*

Riversbridge (Mr & Mrs Sutton-Scott-Tucker) ½m inland from Blackpool sands and signed from A3122. Small walled gardens adjoining farmyard in lovely unspoilt valley with ponds and stream; herbaceous plants, roses and some unusual shrubs. TEAS. *Adm £1 Chd free. Suns June 12, 19 (2-6)*

Robin Hill ✕ (Dr G Steele-Perkins) Deepdene Park, Exeter. From Barrack Rd turn W into Wonford Rd; entry to drive on left beyond Orthopaedic Hospital. ½-acre around house on level ground with variety of ornamental trees and shrubs; wall plants, ground cover and small pond. *Adm £1 Chd free. Suns May 29, July 10 (2-6)*

Rosemoor Garden ⌂✕❀ (The Royal Horticultural Society) Great Torrington. 1m SE of Great Torrington on B3220 to Exeter. Original plantsman's garden started in 1959; rhododendrons (species and hybrid), ornamental trees and shrubs; dwarf conifer collection, species and old-fashioned roses, scree and raised beds with alpine plants, arboretum. The Society is expanding the Garden from 8 acres to 40. The new Garden already contains 2000 roses in 200 varieties, two large colour theme gardens, herb garden, potager, 200 metres of herbaceous border, a large stream and bog garden and a cottage and foliage garden. A fruit and vegetable garden open in 1994. The new Visitors Centre contains a restaurant, shop, and plant centre selling interesting and unusual plants. *Adm £2.50 Chd 50p Groups £2 per person. Open daily all year (10-6 April to Sept. 10-4 Oct to March) collecting box for NGS*

51 Salters Road ✕❀ (Mrs J Dyke) Exeter. Typical small town garden; specialising in unusual plants inc primulas, auriculas and alpines (owner has for many years been Committee member of Exeter Branch of Alpine Garden Society). *Collecting box for NGS. Private visits usually welcome, please* **Tel 0392 76619**

Saltram House ⌂✕ (The National Trust) Plympton, 3m E of Plymouth, S of A38, 2m W of Plympton. 8 acres with fine specimen trees; spring garden; rhododendrons and azaleas. C18 orangery and octagonal garden house. George II mansion with magnificent plasterwork and decorations, incl 2 rooms designed by Robert Adam. Wheelchair available. Restaurant. *Adm gardens only £2.20 Chd £1.10. For NGS Suns May 15, June 19 (10.30-5.30)*

Sampford Peverell Gardens 6m from Tiverton on A373, 1m from junction 27 on M5. Canal walks. TEAS at Challis. *Combined adm £1.50 Chd 50p. Suns July 10, 17 (2-6)*

   Challis ❀ (Mr & Mrs G Issac) Next to Globe Inn in the centre of the village. A well established garden with trees and shrubs. Large lawned area with flower beds, fish ponds and rockery. Some interesting outbuildings with many hanging baskets in the courtyard. The garden leads directly to the tow path of the Grand Western Canal. TEAS

   High Cross House ✕❀ (Mr & Mrs Bowers) Higher Town. Adjacent to Church. ¾-acre garden in sections comprising walled garden, courtyard garden, lawns with beds containing specimen shrubs and herbaceous plants. Large vegetable plot. Garden extends to the canal

   Millstream Cottage ✕❀ (Dave Regester & Chris Tully) Higher Town. 1st R after PO (from village centre); cottage at bottom of lane. ⅓-acre garden with stream. Raised herb beds, pergola, pond, wild area and vegetable plot. Cordon and fan-trained fruit trees

   Norold ✕ (Mr & Mrs Thorley) Opp Parkway Station Rd. Parking in layby opp. Small garden with lawns, bedding plants, dahlias, petunias, roses, geraniums, sweet peas, chrysanthemums, antirrhinums, shrubs etc, vegetable area

The Old Rectory ✕ (Janet & Greville Jefcoate) Higher Town. Simple garden around a C16 grade 11 listed Rectory with many different types of roses, herbaceous borders and some shrubs, with lawns, fruit and vegetables, in a beautiful setting in the village centre next to the church. The garden is on two levels, the lower level runs alongside the Grand Western Canal, which is a Country Park

Scypen ✕ (Mr & Mrs John Bracey) Ringmore. 5m S of Modbury. From A379 Plymouth-Kingsbridge S at Harraton Cross on B3392. R at Pickwick Inn (signed Ringmore). Park in Journey's End car park on L opp church. ½-acre coastal garden, integrating design, landscaping and mixed planting for year-round effect and to take advantage of lovely views of church, sea and unspoilt Nat. Trust coast and farmland. Salt and wind tolerant plants; silver wedding garden; organic kitchen garden; chamomile and thyme lawns. Featured on BBC Gardener's World. TEAS. *Adm £1 Chd 25p. Sun May 22, Wed June 8 (2-5)*

Setts ⌂ (Mrs Jack Cutler) Haytor Rd, Bovey Tracey. 1m W of Bovey Tracy. Take B3344 to Widecombe Rd, after ¼m fork L, garden ¼m on R on Haytor Rd, next door to Edgemoor Hotel. ⅔-acre garden, herbaceous borders, wood containing rhododendrons (species and hybrids), azaleas, camellias, acers etc. *Adm £1 Chd 25p. Sat, Sun May 21, 22, (2-6). Private visits also welcome (Spring, Summer, Autumn), please* **Tel 0626 833043**

Silver Copse ✕❀ (Mrs V E Osmond) nr Marsh Green. From Exeter; A30 to Jack-in-the-Green, R to Rockbeare and Marsh Green, L towards Ottery. Garden ¾m on the R. From Sidmouth; A3052 to Half-way Inn. B3180 N for 1½m L at Xrds towards Marsh Green, garden 200yds on L. 3 acres, all seasons garden, wide selection shrubs, rhododendrons, azaleas, ornamental pools and alpines, as shown T.S.W. *Adm £1 Chd free. Suns, Mons April 3, 4; May 1, 2, 29, 30, Sat, Sun July 16, 17, Sun, Mon Aug 28, 29 (10-5). Private visits also welcome, please* **Tel 0404 822438**

Sowton Mill ⌂✕❀ (A Cooke and S Newton) nr Dunsford. From Dunsford take B3193 S for ½m. Entrance straight ahead off sharp R bend by bridge. From A38 N along Teign Valley for 8m. Sharp R after humpback bridge. 4 acres laid out around former mill, leat and river. Part woodland, ornamental trees and shrubs, mixed borders and scree. Year round interest. TEA. *Adm £1 Chd 50p (Share to Cygnet Training Theatre©). Suns June 5, July 3 (2-6). Private visits also welcome, please* **Tel 0647 52347**

¶Spillifords (Dr Gavin Haig) Lower Washfield. On W bank of R Exe N of Tiverton. A396 Tiverton to Bampton. After 2m L over Iron Bridge, signposted Stoodleigh and Ravenswood. L again following signs to Washfield, after 1m from bridge, garden on L. Please note narrow lanes and limited parking opp house. 1½-acre wildlife and wild flower garden, ideal for those interested in natural history. On steeply sloping bank of R Exe (unsuitable for disabled) in which a wide range of wild flowers, butterflies, birds and other wildlife abound in an ideal arboreal and riverside environment. Frequently featured in media on various wildlife programmes. TEA. *Adm £2 Chd £1. Maxi-*

mum benefit for visitors would be derived from direct guidance from owner, hence garden open by appointment only. Weds, Sats April to Aug (2-6). Please **Tel 0884 252422**

41 Springfield Close ⚭❀ (Mr & Mrs Clem Spencer) Plymstock, 4m SE of Plymouth city centre. Leave A379 to Kingsbridge opp Elburton Hotel, follow Springfield Rd across Reservoir Rd, 1st right into Springfield Close. Medium landscaped surburban garden with country atmosphere; wide range of interesting plants, pond, waterfall, doves, exhibition of paintings and woodturnings. TEA. *Adm £1 Chd free. Suns June 26, July 24, (11.30-4.30). Private visits also welcome June to Aug, please* **Tel 0752 401052**

Starveacre ⚭❀ (Mr and Mrs Bruce Archibold) Dalwood. Leave Axminster on A35 travelling W. After 3m (Shute Xrds) turn R at staggered Xrds signposted Dalwood. Follow signs to Dalwood and go through village, over stream, round sharp L bend. Follow road, ignoring left turn, up steep hill and at top turn L. Under pylons and up hill. After crest, take L turn before white 5-bar gate. Starveacre is at end of lane. A plantsman's garden of 5 acres on a hillside facing S and W with superb views. Mixed plantings of rhododendrons, camellias, conifers, acers, magnolias and much more. TEAS. *Adm £1 Chd under 14 free. Suns May 22, July 17, Oct 16 (2-5)*

¶**Stone Lane Gardens** ⚭❀ (Kenneth & June Ashburner) Chagford. On NE edge of Dartmoor National park. A382 at Whiddon Down signed Drewsteighton for 1½m. 2nd R (Stone Lane). Parking in farmyards on L. 5-acres informally landscaped specialist arboretum with emphasis on foliage and bark and featuring collections of wild-origin birch and alder from around the northern hemisphere; natural streams and ponds. Open views of Dartmoor. Exhibition of work within garden by sculptors and designers inspired by nature, myth and folklore June-Sept. No coaches. TEA. *Adm £2 OAPs £1 Chd 50p. Gardens open daily except Mons mid-June to mid-Nov (2-6). For NGS Weds May 25, June 29, July 27 (2-6). Private visits also welcome, please* **Tel 0647 231311**

¶**Sunrise Hill** ⚭❀ (Chris & Sharon Britton) Withleigh. 3m W of Tiverton on B3137 rd to Witheridge and South Molton. Garden reached through Withleigh Nurseries, situated at E end of village. Approx 1 acre of developing colourful garden. Mixed borders, unusual plants, herbaceous, lawns and vegetables. Plants for sale in adjacent nursery (on open days 10% of plant sales for NGS). TEAS Weds only. *Adm £1 Chd 50p. Sat May 21, Weds July 27, Aug 3 (2-6)*

Tapeley Park & British Jousting Centre ⚭❀ (H T C Christie Esq) Instow. On A39 Barnstable-Bideford rd. Beautiful Italian Garden of Horticultural interest in all seasons; ice house; shell house; walled kitchen garden; woodland walk to lily pond; pets; putting; picnic area. Glyndebourne Opera Costume Display. Children play area. Tours of house for parties of minimum of 15. Jousting. Lunches & cream TEAS in Queen Anne Dairy & on lawn. *Adm £3.50 OAP £3 Chd £2. House tours £1.50 Chd £1 prices increase on jousting days. Collecting Box for NGS Easter to Oct daily except Sats (10-6)*

Topsham Gardens 4m from Exeter. Free parking in Holman Way car park. Teas at 20 Monmouth Ave. *Adm 50p each garden Chd free. Sat, Sun May 7, 8 (2-6)*

  4 Grove Hill ⚭❀ (Margaret and Arthur Boyce) Off Elm Grove Rd, opp junction with Station Rd. A small town garden with some rare plants, troughs and screes with alpine plants and unusual bulbs

  20 Monmouth Avenue ⚭❀ (Anne & Harold Lock) Access to Monmouth Ave by footpath on the L after leaving Holman Way car park. ⅓-acre level garden, wide range of unusual plants and shrubs giving year round effect, mixed curved borders, herbaceous, shrubs and bulbs ind a collection of hardy geraniums and alliums. Some old fashioned roses. Featured on TV 'Gardens For All'. TEAS. *Private visits also welcome, please* **Tel 0392 873734**

Twitchen Mill ⚭❀ (Mr & Mrs G Haydon) 6m NE of South Molton. A361 S Molton to Taunton, 400yds past caravan site on outskirts of town at top of hill, L signed Twitchen for 5m. Straight on at last fork 200yds before Mill. 1-acre level garden on the foothills of Exmoor, in beautiful wooded valley, bordered with leat and clear water stream. Parking on roadside also in field. TEAS. *Adm £1 Chd free. Suns May 29, July 17 (10-6)*

Valley House ⚭❀ (Dr & Mrs Michael Morgan) Churchill. Axminster to Chard A358 for 1m L after Weycroft Mill, traffic lights signed Smallridge. 2nd R after Ridgeway Inn to Chardstock and Churchill. 150yds down hill, 1st R into cul-de-sac, house last on L. 1-acre enthusiasts garden on sloping site overlooking open farmland, largely planted since 1980 with ornamental trees, shrubs, bulbs. Includes extensive water garden featuring hostas, astilbes and grasses. Considerate parking in nearby lanes, please. TEAS. *Adm £1 Chd 20p. Suns April 17, May 1 (2-6)*

Vicar's Mead ⚭❀ (Mr & Mrs H F J Read) Hayes Lane, East Budleigh, 2m N of Budleigh Salterton. From B3178. Newton Poppleford-Budleigh Salterton, turn off W for East Budleigh; Hayes Lane is opp 'Sir Walter Raleigh'; garden 100yds W of public car park. 3½ acres of informal plantings around a 500yr-old historic former vicarage; wide range of unusual and rare shrubs, trees, bulbs and perennials etc, displayed on a steep terraced escarpment. Hostas and 4 National Collections a feature. Tea in village. *Adm £1 Chd free. Suns April 3, 17, 24; May 1, 8, 22, 29; June 5, 12, 19, 26; July 10, 17, 24; Aug 28; Sept 11, 18 (2-6). Private visits also welcome, please* **Tel 03954 42641**

Warren Cottage ❀ (Margaret Jock & Libs Pinsent) Higher Ludbrook, Ermington, Ivybridge. 1¼m E of Ermington on A3121 turn R signed Higher Ludbrook. 1½-acres started from field 1986, with sloping lawn; mixed beds and borders. Small pond with marginals. Some unusual plants. *Collecting Box for NGS. Private visits usually welcome May to Sept, please* **Tel 0548 830698**

Weetwood ❀ (Mr & Mrs J V R Birchall) Offwell, 2m from Honiton. Turn S off A35 (signed Offwell), at E end of Offwell. 1-acre all seasons garden; rhododendrons, azaleas, shrubs, ornamental pools, rock gardens, collection of dwarf conifers. Teashops Honiton. *Adm 50p Chd 10p (Share to The Forces Help Society, Lord Roberts Workshops). Private visits usually welcome spring, summer & autumn please* **Tel 0404 831363**

Right Vann, Surrey. *Photograph by Andrew Lawson*
Below Wytchwood, Cambridgeshire. *Photograph by
Brian Chapple*

Hen Ysgoldy, Gwynedd.
Photograph by Ron Evans

Cae Hir, Dyfed.
Photograph by Sheila Orme

Right Three Chimneys, Clwyd. *Photograph by Trish Walters*
Below Cottesbrooke Hall, Northamptonshire. *Photograph by Brian Chapple*

Left The Dingle, Dyfed. *Photograph by John Glover*
Below The Dorothy Clive Garden, Staffordshire.
Photograph by Brian Chapple

Darley House, Derbyshire. *Photograph by Hugh Palmer*

Left Inglethorpe Manor, Cambridgeshire.
Photograph by Brian Chapple
Below The Old Rectory, Burghfield, Berkshire.
Photograph by Brian Chapple

Renishaw Hall, Derbyshire. *Photograph by Hugh Palmer*

Westpark ✵✿ (Mr & Mrs D Court) Yealmpton, 7m E of Plymouth; on Kingsbridge Rd (A379) Xrds centre of village, turn S on Newton Ferrers rd; park end of Torr Lane. An old fashioned rambling 2-acre garden in peaceful country setting. Year round colour and variety. Old rose, pergola, mulberry (1907), wood with cyclamen, ferns, bulbs, fruit cage, vegetable garden. Interesting C19 narcissi March/April. TEAS. *Adm £1.25 Chd 30p. Sun, Wed March 20, 23 (2-5). Private visits also welcome mid Feb to mid Oct please* Tel 0752 880236

Whitmore ✵✿ (Mr & Mrs Cyril Morgan) Chittlehamholt. 12m SE Barnstaple, house marked on O.S. Landranger 180 series. From the village take rd S past Exeter Inn and High Bullen Hotel; Whitmore is ¼m further on L down long tree-lined drive. 3-acre garden with ponds, stream and herbaceous borders. An interesting collection of trees and shrubs planted for landscape value. Further 3 acres of woodland garden mainly ferns with pleasant sylvan walks, amongst wood warblers and box breeding pied flycatchers and nuthatches. TEAS. *Adm £1 Chd 50p. Thurs April 7, June 30; Sun Aug 28 (2-5)*

Withleigh Farm ✿ (T Matheson) Withleigh village. 3m W of Tiverton on B3137, 10yds W of 'Withleigh' sign, entrance to drive at white gate. Peaceful undisturbed rural setting with valley garden, 14 years in making; stream, pond and waterside plantings; bluebell wood walk under canopy of mature oak and beech; wild flower meadow, primroses and daffodils in spring, wild orchids. TEA. *Adm £1 Chd 25p (Share to Cancer & Arthritis Research®). Sat, Sun May 21, 22 (2-5). Private visits also welcome, please* Tel 0884 253853

Wolford Lodge ♿ (The Very Rev. the Dean of Windsor and Mrs Patrick Mitchell) Dunkeswell. Take Honiton to Dunkeswell rd. L at Limer's Cross. Drive ½m on L at white entrance gate and lodge. 4 acres semi-woodland with massed rhododendrons, azaleas and camellias. Distant views to S over unspoilt Devon countryside. Woodland walks. *Adm £1 OAP/Chd 50p. Sat May 28 (2-6)*

Regular Openers. See head of county section.

¶**Wood Barton** ♿✵✿ (Mr & Mrs Richard Horton) Kentisbeare. 3m from M5 exit 28. A373 Cullompton to Honiton rd. 2m turn L signed Goodiford for 1m and turn L again at White Cottages. Farm drive, 100yds R. Bull on sign. [Landranger 192. Lat 09 Long 05/06]. 2 acres woodland garden planted 45yrs with species trees on S facing slope. Magnolias, azaleas, camellias, rhododendrons, acers; small pond. *Adm £1 Chd 50p. Suns May 8, 15 (11-5)*

Woodside ✵ (Mr & Mrs Mervyn Feesey) Higher Raleigh Rd, Barnstaple. On outskirts of Barnstaple, A39 to Lynton, turn right 300yds above fire station. 2 acres, S sloping-semi woodland; intensively planted; collection of ornamental grasses, bamboos, sedges and other monocots; raised beds, troughs; variegated, acid loving and unusual shrubs, dwarf conifers, emphasis on foliage; New Zealand collection. *Adm £1 Chd 50p. Suns May 8, June 19, July 17 (2-5.30)*

Wylmington Hayes ✵✿ (Mr and Mrs P Saunders) Wilmington. 5½m NE of Honiton on A30, turn R. Signposted Stockland 3m/Axminster 10m, after 3½m entrance gates on R (before Stockland TV Station) or from A35 3½m W of Axminster turn N nr Shute Garage on to Stockland Road for 3m, entrance on L nr TV mast. Reclaimed gardens, created in 1911. 83 acres of gardens and woodlands with spectacular hybrid rhododendrons, azaleas, magnolias, camellias, acers. Lakes, ponds, topiary, arboretum, woodland walks with abundant wildlife. Interesting collection of ornamental and domestic waterfowl including black swans. TEAS. *Adm £2.50 Chd £1. Easter Fri, Sat, Sun, Mon April 1, 2, 3, 4; Suns and Bank Hol Mons until end of June (2-5). Coaches & parties by appt please* Tel 0404 831751

¶**Yonder Hill** ♿✵✿ (Mrs M H Herbert) Colaton Raleigh. A3052 at Newton Poppleford. B3178 towards Budleigh Salterton. 1m 1st L signposted to Dotton then immediately R into small lane. ¼m 1st house on R. Approx 2-acre peaceful garden of a keen plantswoman. Extensive new areas planted since May 1992 with special features and unconventional ideas. Rare and unusual plants for sale as avilable. Good car parking. Easy access for wheelchairs. *Adm £1 Chd 50p. Daily May 23 to 30 (2-4)*

Dorset

Hon County Organiser:	Mrs Hugh Lindsay, The Old Rectory, Litton Cheney, Dorchester DT2 9AH Tel 0308 482383
Assistant Hon County Organisers:	Mrs Raymond Boileau, Rampisham Manor, Dorchester DT2 0PT Tel 0935 83612
	Stanley Cherry Esq., Highbury, Woodside Rd, West Moors, Ferndown BH22 0LY Tel 0202 874372
	Mrs John Greener, Langebride House, Long Bredy, Dorchester Tel 0308 482257
	Mrs G D Harthan, Russets, Rectory Lane, Child Okeford, Blandford DT11 8DT Tel 0258 860703
	Mr & Mrs W E Ninniss, 52 Rossmore Road, Parkstone, Poole BH12 3NL Tel 0202 740913
Hon County Treasurer:	Mrs R Patterson, 10 Herringston Road, Dorchester DT1 2BS

DATES OF OPENING

By appointment
For telephone numbers and other details see garden descriptions. Private visits welcomed

Arnmore House, Bournemouth
Bridge House Water Garden, Portesham
Broadlands, Hazelbury Bryan
Cartref, Stalbridge
Chiffchaffs, Bourton
Cox Hill, Marnhull
Domineys Yard, Buckland Newton
Edmondsham House, Cranborne
Friars Way, Upwey
Highbury, West Moors
Langebride House, Long Bredy
Little Platt, Plush
Moulin Huet, West Moors
Oakmead, nr Beaminster
The Old Mill, Spetisbury
The Old Rectory, Fifehead Magdalen
The Old Rectory, Seaborough
Orchard House, Portesham Gardens
Pumphouse Cottage, Alweston
46 Roslin Road South, Bournemouth
Star Cottage, Wimborne
Welcome Thatch, Witchampton
Wincombe Park
2 Winters Lane, Portesham Gardens

Regular openings
For details see garden descriptions

Abbotsbury Gardens, nr Weymouth. Daily March 1 to Oct 31
Aurelia Gardens, West Moors. Open Fris, Sats & Suns
Broadlands, Hazelbury Bryan. Every Wed June, July & Aug
Cartref, Stalbridge. Tues, Fri, April to Nov
Chiffchaffs, Bourton. Open various Suns, Weds, & Thurs March 27 to Sept 25
Compton Acres Gardens, Poole. Daily March 1 to Oct 31
Cranborne Manor Gardens, Cranborne. Weds March to Sept incl
Deans Court, Wimborne Minster. Open various Suns, Tues & Thurs See Text
Forde Abbey, nr Chard. Daily
Heatherwood, Ashington, Wimborne. Daily except Dec 24 to Jan 1
Horn Park, Beaminster. Tues, Weds, Suns, Bank Hol Mon April to Oct 1
Ivy Cottage, Ansty. Every Thurs April to Oct

Kingston Maurward, Dorchester. April to Sept
Mapperton Gardens, nr Beaminster. Daily March to Oct
Minterne, nr Cerne Abbas. Daily April 1 to Oct 31
The Old Mill, Spetisbury. Every Wed May 4 to Aug 17
Parnham, Beaminster. Suns, Weds & Bank Hols April 1 to Oct 30
Snape Cottage, Bourton. Every Wed April 6 to Sept 28 (closed Aug)
Stapehill Abbey, Wimborne. Open Daily April to Oct. Closed Mon & Tue Nov to March
Star Cottage, Wimborne. Open Sats & Suns all year
Sticky Wicket, Buckland Newton. Thurs June to Sept incl

March 20 Sunday
Langebride House, Long Bredy
Netherbury Court, Netherbury

March 27 Sunday
Frith House, Stalbridge
Langebride House, Long Bredy

April 1 Friday
Catnap Cottage, Hilton

April 2 Saturday
Ashley Park Farm, Damerham

April 3 Sunday
Chiffchaffs, Bourton
Frankham Farm, Ryme Intrinseca
Horn Park, Beaminster
The Old Rectory, Litton Cheney
Snape Cottage, Bourton
Stockford, East Stoke

April 4 Monday
Broadlands, Hazelbury Bryan
Edmondsham House, Cranborne

April 6 Wednesday
Edmondsham House, Cranborne

April 10 Sunday
Aller Green, Ansty
Domineys Yard, Buckland Newton
Fernhill House, Witchampton ‡
Ivy Cottage, Ansty
Langebride House, Long Bredy
Stour House, Blandford
Welcome Thatch, Witchampton ‡

April 13 Wednesday
Cranborne Manor Gardens, Cranborne ‡
Edmondsham House, Cranborne ‡

April 17 Sunday
Bexington, Lytchett Matravers
Boveridge Farm, Cranborne
Cartref, Stalbridge
Chiffchaffs, Bourton
Stratton Gardens
Thistledown, Alweston

April 20 Wednesday
Edmondsham House, Cranborne

April 24 Sunday
Broadlands, Hazelbury Bryan
Corfe Barn, Broadstone
St Nicholas Close, Wimborne
Thistledown, Alweston

April 27 Wednesday
Edmondsham House, Cranborne

April 30 Saturday
Ashley Park Farm, Damerham
Stepleton, Iwerne Stepleton

May 1 Sunday
Chiffchaffs, Bourton ‡
Eurocentre Language School, Bournemouth
Frankham Farm, Ryme Intrinseca
Pumphouse Cottage, Alweston ‡‡
St Nicholas Close, Wimborne
Snape Cottage, Bourton ‡
Stockford, East Stoke
Thistledown, Alweston ‡‡

May 2 Monday
Long Ash Cottage, Milton Abbas
Pumphouse Cottage, Alweston ‡
Thistledown, Alweston ‡

May 5 Thursday
Melbury House, nr Yeovil

May 8 Sunday
Bridge House Water Garden, Portesham
Broadlands, Hazelbury Bryan
Charlton Cottage, Tarrant Rushton
Hilltop Cottage, Woodville
North Leigh House, nr Wimborne
The Old Rectory, Seaborough
Thistledown, Alweston

May 11 Wednesday
Hilltop Cottage, Woodville

May 12 Thursday
Knitson Old Farmhouse, Corfe Castle

May 14 Saturday
Studland Bay House, nr Swanage

May 15 Sunday
Bexington, Lytchett Matravers
Boveridge Farm, Cranborne
Corfe Barn, Broadstone
2 Curlew Road, Bournemouth
Fernhill Cottage, Witchampton ‡
Fernhill House, Witchampton ‡
Kesworth, Wareham
The Old Rectory, Litton Cheney
Slape Manor, Netherbury
Smedmore, Kimmeridge
Studland Bay House, nr Swanage
Sturminster Newton Gardens
Thistledown, Alweston
Throop Mill Cottage, Throop, Bournemouth

Welcome Thatch, Witchampton ‡

May 18 Wednesday
Wincombe Park, nr Shaftesbury

May 19 Thursday
Kingston Maurward, Dorchester

May 22 Sunday
Aller Green, Ansty ‡
Broadlands, Hazelbury Bryan
Cartref, Stalbridge
Highwood Garden, Wareham
Ivy Cottage, Ansty ‡
Kesworth, Wareham
Moigne Combe, nr Dorchester
Pumphouse Cottage,
Alweston ‡‡
52 Rossmore Road, Parkstone
Star Cottage, Wimborne
Thistledown, Alweston ‡‡

May 26 Thursday
Knitson Old Farmhouse, Corfe
Castle
Melbury House, nr Yeovil

May 28 Saturday
Ashley Park Farm, Damerham
Cox Hill, Marnhull

May 29 Sunday
Chiffchaffs, Bourton ‡
Cox Hill, Marnhull
Edgeways, Poole
Friars Way, Upwey
Glebe House, East Lulworth
Highwood Garden, Wareham
Moigne Court, nr Dorchester
46 Roslin Road South,
Bournemouth
Snape Cottage, Bourton ‡
Stockford, East Stoke

May 30 Monday
Horn Park, Beaminster
46 Roslin Road South,
Bournemouth
Thistledown, Alweston

June 1 Wednesday
Glebe House, East Lulworth

June 4 Saturday
The Manor House, Abbotsbury

June 5 Sunday
7 Church St, Upwey, Weymouth ‡
Farriers, Puddletown ‡‡
Frith House, Stalbridge
2 Greenwood Avenue, Ferndown
High Hollow, Corfe Mullen
Holworth Farmhouse, Holworth
Kingston Lacy, nr Wimborne
Minster
The Manor House, Abbotsbury
Northbrook Farm, Puddleton ‡‡
Portesham Gardens
52 Rossmore Road, Parkstone
Sticky Wicket, Buckland Newton
West Manor, Upwey ‡
Wimborne Minster Model Town &
Gardens
Woodside Lodge, East Lulworth

June 8 Wednesday
Hilltop Cottage, Woodville
The Orchard, Blynfield Gate, nr
Shaftesbury

June 9 Thursday
7 Church St, Upwey, Weymouth
Red House Museum and
Gardens, Christchurch

June 11 Saturday
Cranborne Manor Gardens,
Cranborne
The Manor House, Chaldon
Herring

June 12 Sunday
Bexington, Lytchett Matravers
Boveridge Farm, Cranborne
Charlton Cottage, Tarrant Rushton
Corfe Barn, Broadstone
Deans Court, Wimborne Minster
2 Greenwood Avenue, Ferndown
High Hollow, Corfe Mullen
Hyde Farm, Frampton
Long Ash Cottage, Milton Abbas
26 Milestone Road, Poole
The Old Mill, Spetisbury
The Old Rectory, Fifehead
Magdalen
Snape Cottage, Bourton

June 15 Wednesday
Chilcombe House, nr Bridport
The Orchard, Blynfield Gate, nr
Shaftesbury

June 16 Thursday
Melbury House, nr Yeovil

June 18 Saturday
Three Bays, Beacon Hill

June 19 Sunday
Fernhill Cottage, Witchampton ‡
Fernhill House, Witchampton ‡
Frankham Farm, Ryme
Intrinseca
The Old Vicarage, Stinsford
Star Cottage, Wimborne
Three Bays, Beacon Hill
Welcome Thatch, Witchampton ‡
Weston House, Buckhorn Weston
Woodside Lodge, East Lulworth

June 22 Wednesday
The Orchard, Blynfield Gate, nr
Shaftesbury

June 26 Sunday
Chiffchaffs, Bourton ‡
The Cobbles, Shillingstone
Domineys Yard, Buckland Newton
Edgeways, Poole
Friars Way, Upwey
Higher Melcombe, Melcombe
Bingham
Priest's House, Wimborne
46 Roslin Road South,
Bournemouth
Snape Cottage, Bourton ‡
Steeple Manor, nr Wareham
Stratton Gardens

June 29 Wednesday
Chilcombe House, nr Bridport
The Orchard, Blynfield Gate, nr
Shaftesbury

June 30 Thursday
Melbury House, nr Yeovil

July 3 Sunday
7 Church St, Upwey, Weymouth ‡
The Cobbles, Shillingstone
Farriers, Puddletown
2 Greenwood Avenue, Ferndown
Pumphouse Cottage, Alweston ‡‡
Sticky Wicket, Buckland
Newton
Thistledown, Alweston ‡‡
West Manor, Upwey ‡
Wimborne Minster Model Town
& Gardens

July 6 Wednesday
The Orchard, Blynfield Gate, nr
Shaftesbury

July 7 Thursday
7 Church St, Upwey, Weymouth

July 9 Saturday
Three Bays, Beacon Hill

July 10 Sunday
Bexington, Lytchett Matravers
Corfe Barn, Broadstone
Deans Court, Wimborne Minster
2 Greenwood Avenue, Ferndown
Holworth Farmhouse, Holworth
Portland House, Weymouth
Pumphouse Cottage, Alweston ‡
Sturminster Newton Gardens
Thistledown, Alweston ‡
Three Bays, Beacon Hill

July 13 Wednesday
The Orchard, Blynfield Gate, nr
Shaftesbury

July 14 Thursday
Kingston Maurward, Dorchester
Knitson Old Farmhouse, Corfe
Castle

July 16 Saturday
Three Bays, Beacon Hill

July 17 Sunday
2 Curlew Road, Bournemouth
Edgeways, Poole
26 Milestone Road, Poole
Oakmead, nr Beaminster
The Old Mill, Spetisbury
Snape Cottage, Bourton
Stour House, Blandford
Thistledown, Alweston
Three Bays, Beacon Hill
Throop Mill Cottage, Throop,
Bournemouth
Weston House, Buckhorn
Weston

July 21 Thursday
Fernhill Cottage, Witchampton
Melbury House, nr Yeovil

July 24 Sunday
Hilltop Cottage, Woodville

Melplash Court, nr Bridport
46 Roslin Road South,
   Bournemouth
Thistledown, Alweston
July 28 Thursday
Fernhill Cottage, Witchampton
July 31 Sunday
Chiffchaffs, Bourton
High Hollow, Corfe Mullen ‡
7 Highfield Close, Corfe Mullen ‡
North Leigh House, nr Wimborne
August 4 Thursday
Fernhill Cottage, Witchampton
August 7 Sunday
7 Church St, Upwey, Weymouth ‡
Edgeways, Poole
Farriers, Puddletown ‡
High Hollow, Corfe Mullen ‡‡‡
7 Highfield Close, Corfe
   Mullen ‡‡‡
Northbrook Farm, Puddletown ‡‡
Sticky Wicket, Buckland Newton
Waterfalls, Bournemouth
West Manor, Upwey ‡
August 10 Wednesday
Hilltop Cottage, Woodville
August 11 Thursday
7 Church St, Upwey, Weymouth
Fernhill Cottage, Witchampton

Knitson Old Farmhouse, Corfe
   Castle
August 14 Sunday
Bexington, Lytchett Matravers
Frith House, Stalbridge
Higher Melcombe, Melcombe
   Bingham
26 Milestone Road, Poole
Stour House, Blandford
August 21 Sunday
Domineys Yard, Buckland Newton
Eurocentre Language School,
   Bournemouth
Hilltop Cottage, Woodville
August 27 Saturday
Three Bays, Beacon Hill
August 28 Sunday
Aller Green, Ansty ‡
Chiffchaffs, Bourton
Ivy Cottage, Ansty ‡
The Old Parsonage, Kimmeridge
Rosedene, Bournemouth
Three Bays, Beacon Hill
September 4 Sunday
7 Church St, Upwey, Weymouth
Rosedene, Bournemouth
Sticky Wicket, Buckland Newton
Wimborne Minster Model Town &
   Gardens

September 8 Thursday
Knitson Old Farmhouse, Corfe
   Castle
September 11 Sunday
Bexington, Lytchett Matravers
Rosedene, Bournemouth
Welcome Thatch, Witchampton
September 18 Sunday
Cartref, Stalbridge
Hyde Farm, Frampton
Oakmead, nr Beaminster
The Old Rectory, Litton Cheney
Thistledown, Alweston
September 25 Sunday
Aller Green, Ansty ‡
Chiffchaffs, Bourton
Ivy Cottage, Ansty ‡
Thistledown, Alweston
October 2 Sunday
Deans Court, Wimborne Minster
October 5 Wednesday
Edmondsham House, Cranborne
October 12 Wednesday
Edmondsham House, Cranborne
October 19 Wednesday
Edmondsham House, Cranborne
Wincombe Park, nr Shaftesbury
October 26 Wednesday
Edmondsham House, Cranborne

DESCRIPTIONS OF GARDENS

● **Abbotsbury Gardens** ❀ (Ilchester Estates) 9m NW of Weymouth. 9m SW of Dorchester. From B3157 Weymouth-Bridport, turn off 200yds W of Abbotsbury village, at foot of hill. 20 acres; uniquely mild Mediterranean-type climate, started in 1760 and considerably extended in C19; much replanting during past few years; very fine collection of rhododendrons, camellias, azaleas; wide variety of unusual and tender trees and shrubs. Peacocks. Children's play area, woodland trail, aviarys and plant centre. Partly suitable for wheelchairs. TEAS. *Adm £3.50 OAPs £3 Chd free, reduced rate in winter. (For party rate* Tel 0305 871387*) March 1 to Oct 31 (10-5); winter (10-3)*

Aller Green ❀ (A J Thomas Esq) Aller Lane, Ansty, 12m N of Dorchester. From Puddletown take A354 to Blandford; After public house, take 1st L down Long Lane signed Dewlish-Cheselbourne; through Cheselbourne to Ansty then 1st R before Fox Inn down Aller Lane. 1-acre typical Dorset cottage garden; unusual trees, shrubs and perennials in old orchard setting and many perennials grown for Autumn Colour. Garden featured on Channel 4 'Garden Club' 1992. TEAS at Ivy Cottage Suns only. *Combined adm with* **Ivy Cottage** *£2.25 Chd 30p. Suns April 10 (Share to RNLI®); May 22 (Share to the Samaritans®); Aug 28 (Share to Blandford Museum©); Sept 25 (Share to the Red Cross®) (2-5.30)*

Regular Openers. See head of county section.

Arnmore House ❀❀ (Mr & Mrs David Hellewell) 57 Lansdowne Rd, Bournemouth B3064. 1-acre garden combines classical formality with diversity and efficiency; beautiful modern garden, with its Victorian house, created over a period of 25yrs by its owner, well known composer David Hellewell, who has published a booklet describing the garden's evolution; topiary; specimen trees and plants; the garden has been featured in 'Homes & Garden' magazine Nov 1988. *Adm £1 Chd free. Open all year. Private visits welcome, please* Tel 0202 551440

Ashley Park Farm ❀ (David Dampney Esq). Damerham. Follow yellow signs off B3078, immediately W of village, 5m from Fordingbridge. Newly created gardens of 5 acres with farm and woodland walks. With many interesting trees, an arboretum in the making although now mature enough for visiting, Eucalyptus grove; wild flower meadow. Many exciting plants for south facing walls, borders. TEAS, also every Sun. *Adm £1 Chd free (Share to Damerham Church®).* ▲*For NGS Sats April 2, 30; May 28 (2-5.30). (See also* **Boveridge Farm***)*

¶**Aurelia Gardens** ❀❀❀ (Mr & Mrs Robert Knight) Newman's Lane, West Moors. N of the village off B3072 Bournemouth-Verwood rd. Heathers, conifers and golden foliage plants are a special interest of the owners. 5 acres are devoted to a gradually increasing garden of these plants, in island beds with wide grass walks, all in rural surroundings. Nature Conservancy Council manages adjacent heathland. Adequate off road free car parking adjacent to nursery area. *Adm 50p Acc chd free. Fris, Sats, Suns all year (9-5)*

Bexington ㅅ✿✤ (Mr & Mrs Robin Crumpler) Lytchett Matravers. In Lime Kiln Rd, opp old School at W end of village. Colourful garden of ½-acre maintained by owners, with mixed borders of many interesting and unusual plants, heathers and dwarf conifers with shrubs and trees. Planted ditch forms a bog garden of primulas and hostas etc. Part of garden recently reclaimed and planted provides an interesting contrast. TEAS & plant stall for Alzheimer Disease Society & gardening charities. *Adm 70p Chd 20p. Suns April 17, May 15, June 12, July 10, Aug 14, Sept 11 (2-6)*

Boveridge Farm ✤✿ (Mr & Mrs Michael Yarrow) Cranborne. Leave Cranborne on Martin Rd unclass, thence take 2nd R Boveridge Farm. A plantsman's garden of 2 acres on 3 levels, part chalk and part acid; with lawns around old farmhouse, formerly manor house of the Hooper family; in rural surroundings with fine views. Fountain, fern bank and many rare and interesting trees and shrubs. Specimen acer 'Brilliantissimum', prunus 'Shidare Yoshino', prunus 'Pendula Rubra', Paulownia tomentosa. Teas at Ashley Park, Damerham (next village 3m). *Adm £1 Chd free (Share to Cranborne Church®). Suns April 17, May 15, June 12 (2-5). (See also **Ashley Park Farm***)

Broadlands ㅅ✿✤ (Mr & Mrs M J Smith) Hazelbury Bryan. 4m S of Sturminster Newton. From A357 Blandford to Sherborne rd, take turning signed Hazelbury Bryan, garden ½m beyond Antelope PH. 2-acre garden in country setting with extensive views, begun in 1975, made and maintained by owners. Island beds; herbaceous borders by colour theme; ornamental woodland underplanted with hellebores, spring bulbs etc; rockery; heathers and conifers; ponds incl one for conservation. Wide range of plants incl magnolias, rhododendrons, hydrangeas and unusual perennials. TEA every Wed June, July and Aug. *Adm £1.50 Acc chd free. Open every Wed in June, July and Aug (Share to the NGS). Also May 8, 22. For NGS Mon April 4 Sun April 24 (2-5.30) (Share to Dorset Trust for Nature Conservation®). Also private visits welcome, please* Tel 0258 817374

Cartref ✤✿ (Nesta Ann Smith) Station Rd, Stalbridge. From A30, S at Henstridge for 1m. Turn L opp Stalbridge PO, House 80yds on R. Free car park nearby. A plantsman's garden approx ¼-acre, cottage garden and unusual plants. Small woodland area with choice shade-loving plants. Small potager, organically grown. Plants for sale. TEA. *Adm £1.50 Chd free. Suns April 17, May 22, Sept 18 (10-5); Tues (2-6), Fris (10-6) April to Nov. Parties welcome by appt, please ring after 6 pm* Tel 0963 63705

Catnap Cottage ㅅ✿✤ (Mrs M J Phillips) Hilton, Blandford. 1m W from Milton Abbas, 10m SW Blandford. Please park at Hilton church. 2 min walk. Disabled parking at house. 1¼ acres of individual cottage gardens, trees, shrubs, perennials and herbs. Planted for all seasons, especially spring. *Adm £1 Chd 50p. Good Friday April 1 (10-5)*

Charlton Cottage ㅅ (The Hon Penelope Piercy) Tarrant Rushton. 3m SE of Blandford Forum B3082. Fork L top of hill out of Blandford, R at T-junction, first L to Tarrant Rushton, R in village to last thatched cottage on L of st.

Garden on both sides st. Herbaceous borders, shrubs, water garden, views of Tarrant valley. *Adm £1 Chd 25p (Share to Church of England Childrens Society®). Suns May 8, June 12 (2-6)*

Chiffchaffs ✤✿ (Mr & Mrs K R Potts) Chaffeymoor. Leave A303 (Bourton by pass) at junction signposted Gillingham, Blandford and Bourton at W end of Bourton village. House signposted Chaffeymoor Lane. A garden for all seasons with many interesting plants, bulbs, shrubs, herbaceous border, shrub roses. Attractive walk to woodland garden with far-reaching views across the Blackmore Vale. Shown on TSW 'Gardens for All' October 92, also in Gardeners World magazine Sept 92. Nursery open Tues-Sat and on garden open days. TEAS last Sun and Bank Hol weekends. *Adm £1.50 Chd 50p (Share to St Michael's Church, Penselwood®). Open every Sun and Bank Holiday weekend, Weds & Thurs (except for 2nd Sun, Wed & Thurs April and May and 1st Sun, Wed & Thurs June to Sept) March 27 to Sept 25. For NGS last Sunday of each month and Suns of Bank Holiday weekends plus 10% of all receipts (2-5.30). Parties by appt at other times* Tel 0747 840841

Chilcombe House ✿ (John & Carly Hubbard) Chilcombe. Take S turning off dual carriageway on A34 4m E of Bridport. 9m W of Dorchester. 2-acre hillside garden with beautiful setting and views; wild areas; courtyards and walled garden divided into smaller sections; mixed plantings, flowers, herbs, tender perennials and old roses. TEAS on NGS days. *Adm £2 Chd free. Weds June 8, 22, July 6, 13 (2-6). For NGS Weds June 15, 29 (2-6)*

7 Church Street ㅅ✤✿ (Ann & Gordon Powell) Upwey, nr Weymouth. ½m from bottom of Ridgeway Hill on A354 Dorchester–Weymouth rd turn R B3159 (Bridport rd) L turn at bottom of hill. Limited parking for disabled only. 3 acres of mixed planting. Main trees planted 1972 with recent additions of shrubs and perennials. Woodland planted early 50's. Teas at Wishing Well. *Adm £1 Chd free. Suns June 5, July 3, Aug 7, Sept 4; Thurs June 9, July 7, Aug 11 (2-6)*

The Cobbles ✤✿ (Mr & Mrs A P Baker) Shillingstone. 5m NW of Blandford. In middle of village opp Old Ox Inn, Shillingstone. Plantsman's 1½-acre chalk garden round C17 cottage. Borders thickly planted with a mixture of shrubs, herbs, wild flowers, old roses, foliage plants & perennials incl many hardy geraniums. Small lake, stream and ditch garden. TEAS in aid of Shillingstone Parish Church. *Adm £1 Chd free. Suns June 26, July 3 (2.30-5.30)*

● **Compton Acres Gardens** ㅅ✤✿ Canford Cliffs Road, Poole, Dorset. Signposted from Bournemouth and Poole. Wilts & Dorset Buses 147, 150, 151. Yellow Buses nos 11 & 12 stop at entrance. Reputed to be the finest gardens in Europe incl Japanese, Italian, Rock and Water, Heather Dell Woodland Walk and Sub-Tropical Glen. Magnificent bronze and marble statuary. Large selection of plants and stoneware garden ornaments. Refreshments available. Large free car/coach park. *March 1 to Oct 31 daily. 10.30-6.30 last admission 5.45pm.* Tel 0202 700778

Corfe Barn ✿❀ (John & Kathleen McDavid) Corfe Lodge Rd, Broadstone. From main roundabout in Broadstone W along Clarendon Rd, ¾m N into Roman Rd, after 50yds W into Corfe Lodge Rd. ⅔ acre on three levels on site of C19 lavender farm. Informal country garden with much to interest both gardeners and flower arrangers. Parts of the original farm have been incorporated in the design. A particular feature of the garden is the use made of old walls. TEAS. *Adm 50p Chd 25p. Suns April 24, May 15, June 12, July 10 (2-5)*

Cox Hill &✿❀ (Capt & Mrs J R Prescott) 3m N of Sturminster Newton, turning L at Walton Elm; 3m E of Stalbridge via Stour River Bridge at Kings Mill. 2 acres of old-established cottage garden incorporating recently developed water garden, tree plantation and lawns; specialist roses. Colour and contrast within secluded areas a particular feature. TEA. *Adm £1.50 to incl brochure and entry to Art Exhibition Chd free. Sat, Sun May 28, 29 (2-5.30) also groups by appt June, please* **Tel 0258 820059**

Cranborne Manor Gardens &✿❀ (The Viscount & Viscountess Cranborne) Cranborne. 10m N of Wimborne on B3078. Beautiful and historic gardens laid out in C17 by John Tradescant and enlarged in C20, featuring several gardens surrounded by walls and yew hedges: white garden, herb and mount gardens, water and wild garden. Many interesting plants, with fine trees and avenues. *Adm £2.50 OAPs £2 (Share to Salisbury Hospitals Trust®). Weds March to Sept inc (9-5). For NGS Wed April 13, Sat June 11 (9-5)*

2 Curlew Road &✿❀ (Mr & Mrs Gerald Alford) Strouden Park, Bournemouth. From Castle Lane West turn S into East Way, thence E into Curlew Rd. Small town garden 200' × 30' divided into rooms and linked by arches. Conifers, acers, rhododendrons, clematis; spring and summer bedding; three water features. Winner of Bournemouth in Bloom Spring Competition 1993; Best Council Garden 1992–1993; Joint winners of Bournemouth in Bloom Summer Competition 1993. The owners are seriously disabled and their garden is thus of especial interest to other disabled people. *Adm 75p Chd 25p. Suns May 15, July 17 (2-6)*

Deans Court &✿❀ (Sir Michael & Lady Hanham) Wimborne. Just off B3073 in centre of Wimborne. 13 acres; partly wild garden; water, specimen trees, free roaming peacocks. House (open by written appt) originally the Deanery to the Minster. Herb garden with about 150 species chemical free plants for sale. Walled vegetable garden with chemical free produce for sale as available. Free car parking. TEAS. *Adm £1.50 Chd 70p. Bank Hol Mons (10-6) and preceeding Suns. Tues, Thurs April to Sept. For NGS Suns June 12, Oct 2 (2-6). Groups by written arrangement. For other days contact Wimborne TIC* **Tel 0202 886116**

Domineys Yard &✿ (Mr & Mrs W Gueterbock) Buckland Newton, 11m from Dorchester and Sherborne 2m E of A352 or take B3143 from Sturminster Newton. Take 'no through rd' between church and 'Gaggle of Geese' public house next to phone box. Entrance 200 metres on L. Park in lane. 2½-acre garden on chalk, clay and green sand surrounding C17 thatched cottage with adjacent terraced cottages and gardens, with large kitchen garden and lawn tennis court. Developed over 33 years with unusual plants, shrubs and trees incl camellias, clematis, roses, lilies and other bulbs, spring and autumn colour making it a garden for all seasons. Heated swimming pool available for summer opening. TEAS. *Adm £1.50 Chd 30p (Share to Leonard Cheshire Foundation Family Support Service®). Suns April 10, June 26, Aug 21 (2-6), also private visits welcome, please* **Tel 0300 345295**

Edgeways &✿❀ (Mr & Mrs Gerald Andrew) 4 Greenwood Ave, Poole. From Lilliput Rd nr Compton Acres turn N into Compton Ave, W into Fairway Rd, thence L into Greenwood Ave. Please do not park by roundabout of cul-de-sac. Delightful informal design of ⅓ acre in a mature treed setting, created and maintained by present owners. Emphasis is on plant associations and foliage contrasts forming vistas and yr-round living pictures. Bog, water and rock gardens, many choice herbaceous plants. *Adm 80p Acc chd free. Suns May 29, June 26, July 17, Aug 7 (11.30-5.30)*

Edmondsham House &✿❀ (Mrs Julia Smith) Edmondsham, nr Cranborne. B3081, turn at Sixpenny Handley Xrds to Ringwood and Cranborne; thereafter follow signs to Edmondsham. Large garden; spring bulbs, trees, shrubs; walled garden with herbaceous border; vegetables and fruit; grass cockpit. Early church nearby. TEAS Easter Mon, TEA Weds. *Adm £1 Chd 50p under 5 free (Share to PRAMA®). Mon April 4, Weds April 6, 13, 20, 27; Oct 5, 12, 19, 26 (2-5); also private visits welcome, please* **Tel 0725 517207**

Eurocentre Language School &✿ (Eurocentres (UK)) 22-28 Dean Park Rd, Bournemouth. Off Wimborne Rd (A347) ¼m N of Richmond Hill roundabout. Series of 4 linked gardens, now being restored to reflect the original surroundings of the late Victorian houses. Mature specimen trees and lawns; rhododendrons, small trees and flowering shrubs; spring and summer bedding, climbers, dahlia borders and small fernery. TEA. *Adm 70p Chd 30p (Share to Bournemouth General Hospital Scanner Appeal®). Suns May 1, Aug 21 (2.30-6)*

Farriers &❀ (Mr & Mrs P S Eady) 16 The Moor. On the A354 Puddletown-Blandford Rd opp the rd to Piddlehinton, close to the Blue Vinney public house, Dorchester 5m. ⅓-acre informal country garden with much to interest gardeners and flower arrangers, designed and maintained by owners; shrubs, herbaceous, dahlias, sweet peas, vegetable plot, greenhouse with collection of begonias and streptocarpus, pond. TEAS. *Combined adm with* **Northbrook Farm** *(not open July 3) £1 Chd free. Suns June 5, July 3, Aug 7 (2-5.30)*

Fernhill Cottage ✿❀ (Miss Shirley Forwood) Witchampton. Next to Fernhill House, directions as below. Small thatched cottage garden, interesting perennials, species and shrub roses. *Adm 50p Chd free (Share to Hahneman and Herbert Hospitals LoF®). Thurs evenings July 21, 28 Aug 4, 11 (6-8).* **Parking off bend.** *Combined adm £1.50 Chd free with* **Fernhill House** *((Share to Dorset Respite and Hospice Trust®). Suns May 15, June 19 (2-5)*

Fernhill House ✻✿ (Mrs Henry Hildyard) Witchampton. 3½m E of Wimborne B3078 L to Witchampton then L up Lower St. (Blandford rd,) house on R 200yds. Spring bulbs and blossom, roses and herbaceous borders, woodland walk with water garden and shrubs. Teas in village (except April 10). *Adm £1 Chd free. Sun Apr 10 (2-5). Joint opening with* **Fernhill Cottage,** *Adm £1.50 Chd free (Share to Dorset Respite and Hospice Trust®). Suns May 15, June 19 (2-5)*

● **Forde Abbey** ⅁✿ (M Roper Esq) 4m SE of Chard. 7m W of Crewkerne; well signed off A30. 'Christies Garden of the Year 1993'. 30 acres; many fine shrubs and some magnificent specimen trees incl post-war arboretum; herbaceous borders, rock and kitchen gardens; in bog garden one of larger collections Asiatic primulas in SW. Refreshments 11-4.30 during summer. *Adm £3.25 OAPs £2.75 Chd under 15 and wheelchairs free. Open daily all year (10-4.30)*

Frankham Farm ⅁✻✿ (Mr & Mrs R G Earle) Ryme Intrinseca. A37 Yeovil-Dorchester; 3m S of Yeovil turn E at Xrds with garage; drive ¼m on L. 2 acres started in 1960s; Plantsman's garden with shrubs, trees, spring bulbs, clematis, roses, vegetables & fruit; extensive wall planting. Recently planted unusual hardwoods. TEAS in aid of Ryme Church. *Adm £1 Chd free. Suns April 3, May 1, June 19 (2-5.30)*

¶**Friars Way** ✻✿ (Les & Christina Scott) Upwey. Twixt Weymouth and Dorchester. From Wishing Well, on B3159 Martinstown Rd, past church and thatched cottage is immediately opp church car park where cars may be left. ¾-acre steeply sloping, S facing site. Terraces, lawns and woodland area. Cottage garden in process of development and construction by present owners (1991). Many unusual plants. TEAS. *Adm £1 Chd free. Suns May 29, June 26 (2-6). Private visits also welcome, please* **Tel 0305 813243**

Frith House ⅁✿ (Urban Stephenson Esq) Stalbridge. Between Milborne Port & Stalbridge, 1m S of A30. Turn W nr PO in Stalbridge. 4 acres; self-contained hamlet: lawns; 2 small lakes; woodland walks. Terrace in front of Edwardian house, mature cedars; flower borders, excellent kitchen garden. TEAS. *Adm £1 Chd free. Suns March 27, June 5, Aug 14 (2-6)*

Glebe House ⅁✿ (Mr & Mrs J G Thompson) East Lulworth. 4m S of Wool 6m W of Wareham. Take Coombe Keynes Rd to East Lulworth. Glebe House just to E of Weld Arms and War Memorial. Shrub garden with lawns; walks and terrace, 2 acres with interesting and varied planting. TEAS. *Adm £1 Chd free (Share to Wool & Bovington Cancer Relief®). Sun May 29, Wed June 1 (2-6)*

¶**2 Greenwood Avenue** ✿ (Mr & Mrs P D Stogden) Ferndown. Off Woodside Rd which is between Ringwood Rd (A348) and Wimborne Rd (C50 ex-A31), E of town centre. ⅓-acre designed and maintained by owners. An interesting and informal garden, with accent on herbaceous plants; many rare and unusual. Hostas, sempervivums and plants for flower arranging are a special interest of the owners. Soft fruits and vegetable garden. Arbour and pergola. Dogs must be kept on leads. TEAS. *Adm 75p Acc chd free. Suns June 5, 12, July 3, 10 (11-5)*

Heatherwood ✻✿ (Mr & Mrs Ronald Squires) 1m S of Wimborne. Leave A349 Wimborne-Poole rd at Merley Bridge, signed Ashington, into Merley Park Rd. Thence garden is ¾m on L. ½-acre garden created by present owners from original woodland. Main theme of the garden is heathers (800 in 50 varieties), conifers (300 in 30 varieties), azaleas and acers. Large lawn with ornamental pool and rockery. Featured on TVs 'That's Gardening'. Large car park at adjacent nursery. *Collection box. Daily except Dec 24 to Jan 1 (9-5, Suns 9.30-12)*

High Hollow ✻✿ (Paul & Valerie Guppy) 15 Chapel Close, Corfe Mullen. From Wareham Rd W end of village at Naked Cross turn N into Waterloo Rd; after 1m turn E into Chapel Lane. Please park nearby and not in Chapel Close. Beautiful and colourful garden of ¼ acre surrounding bungalow, with many unusual plants and cultivars. Herbaceous border, ferns and roses. The use of water is a special feature. TEAS. *Adm 50p Chd 25p (Share to the Cats Protection League®). Suns June 5, 12, July 31, Aug 7 (2-5)*

Highbury ⅁✻✿ (Stanley Cherry Esq) West Moors, 8m N of Bournemouth. In Woodside Rd, off B3072 Bournemouth-Verwood rd; last rd at N end of West Moors village. Garden of ½ acre in mature setting surrounding interesting Edwardian house (1909 listed). Many rare and unusual plants and shrubs; herb borders; botanical & horticultural interest for gardeners & plantsmen, with everything labelled. Weather station. Seen on T,V. Featured in detail in Blue Guide Gardens of England. TEAS in orchard when fine. *House and garden, organised parties Adm £1 (incl TEA); Otherwise by appt. Garden only 75p (2-6). April to Sept* **Tel 0202 874372**

Higher Melcombe ⅁✻ (Lt Col and Mrs J M Woodhouse) Melcombe Bingham. 11m N of Dorchester. From Puddletown A354 to Blandford. After ½m take turning L (after inn). Follow signs to Cheselbourne then to Melcombe. At Xrds in Melcombe Bingham follow signpost 'Private rd to Higher Melcombe'. 1½-acre garden being redeveloped. Fine views and setting outside Elizabethan house and chapel. Parking adjoining field. *Adm £1 Chd free (Share to the Old Brewery Hall, Ansty©). TEA Sun June 26, TEAS Sun Aug 14 (2-5.30)*

7 Highfield Close ✻✿ (Mr & Mrs Malcolm Bright) Corfe Mullen. From Wareham Rd turn E in Hanham Rd, thence ahead into Highfield Close. Colourful ⅓-acre summer garden designed and made by owners over 15yrs. Bedding plants, fuchsias and pelargoniums interplanted with shrubs; fish pond and ornamental pool. Much to interest gardeners in a small area. TEAS. *Adm 50p Chd 25p. Suns July 31, Aug 7 (2-5)*

Highwood Garden ✿ (H W Drax Esq) Charborough Park, Wareham, 6m E of Bere Regis. Enter park by any lodge on A31; follow signpost to Estate Office, then Highwood Garden. Large garden with rhododendrons and azaleas in woodland setting. TEAS. *Adm £1.50 Chd 50p (7-16 yrs) (Share to Red Post Parish©). Suns May 22, 29 (2.30-6)*

Regular Openers. See head of county section.

Hilltop Cottage ✿❀ (Mr & Mrs Emerson) approx 5m N Sturminster Newton on B3092 turn R at Stour Provost Xrds, signposted Woodville. After 1¼m a thatched cottage on the RH-side. Parking in lane outside. Old cottage garden with a wealth of different and interesting perennials. Very colourful. An inspiration to those with smaller gardens. Includes a small nursery. TEAS. *Adm 50p Chd free. Suns May 8, July 24, Aug 21; Weds May 11, June 8, Aug 10 (2-6)*

¶**Holworth Farmhouse** ✿❀ (Anthony & Philippa Bush) Holworth. 7m E of Dorchester, 1m S of A352. Follow signs to Holworth up the hill, through the farmyard, past duck pond on R. After 300yds turn L to the farmhouse. 3 acres of garden surrounding C16 grade II farmhouse on side of hill with lovely views. Main planting from 1980; considerable use of hedges as protection from exposed windy conditions; partially walled garden terraced and replanted in 1990 with a wide variety of herbaceous plants, shrubs and old roses. Also small wood, orchard, vegetable garden and recently excavated pond. Home-made TEAS in aid of Joseph Weld Hospice & "Fight for Sight". *Adm £1.50 Chd free. Suns June 5, July 10 (2-7)*

Horn Park ✿❀ (Mr & Mrs John Kirkpatrick) Beaminster. On A3066 1½m N of Beaminster on L before tunnel. Ample parking, toilet. Large garden; magnificent view to sea; listed house built by pupil of Lutyens in 1910 (not open). Worth visiting at all seasons, many rare and unusual plants and shrubs in terraced, herbaceous, rock and water gardens; rhododendrons, camellias and pieris; separate woodland garden. In spring, walk in bluebell woods by ponds; wild flowers and orchids in summer. Teas at Beaminster & Craft Centre, Broadwindsor. *Adm £2.50 Chd free. Open every Tues, Weds, Suns, also Bank Hol Mons April to Oct 1st. For NGS Sun April 3, Bank Hol Mon May 30 (2-6)*

¶**Hyde Farm** ✿ (Major & Mrs K Hubbard) Frampton. 5½m NW of Dorchester on A356 to Crewkerne. 500yds W of Frampton. 1¼m E of Maiden Newton on S side of rd. ¾-acre chalk garden, sloping to R Frome; courtyard; terrace, summer house garden; conservatory, good plants, shrub roses. 250yds river walk with wild flower area leading to bird watching hide, over footbridge and water meadow to 2½-acre woodland and pond area with hide. TEAS. *Adm £1 Chd 30p. Suns June 12, Sept 18 (2-6)*

Ivy Cottage ✿❀ (Anne & Alan Stevens) Aller Lane, Ansty, 12m N of Dorchester. A354 from Puddletown to Blandford; After pub take 1st L down Long Lane signed Dewlish-Cheselbourne, through Cheselbourne to Ansty then 1st R before Fox Inn, down Aller Lane. 1½-acre excellent plantsman's garden specialising in unusual perennials, moisture-loving plants; specimen trees and shrubs; well laid out vegetable garden. Featured in the book 'The New Englishwoman's Garden' and TVS 'That's Gardening' 1990. Garden on Channel 4 'Garden Club' 1992. TEAS Suns only. *Combined adm with **Aller Green** £2.25 Chd 30p. Also every Thurs April to Oct (10-5). For NGS Sun April 10 (Share to R.N.L.I®); Sun May 22 (Share to Samaritans®); Sun Aug 28 (Share to Blandford Museum®); Sun Sept 25 (Share to Red Cross®). (2-5.30). Parties by appt only* **Tel 0258 880053**

Kesworth (H J S Clark Esq) 1½m N of Wareham. Turn off A351 almost opp school at Sandford, down Keysworth Drive to level Xing. Grounds incl 600-acre wildlife sanctuary at W end of Poole Harbour suitable for picnics, birdwatching, walks through unspoilt woods and marshes amongst fine wild scenery; herd of Galloway cattle. Elegant and colourful small garden round house. Tea Wareham. *Adm £1 Chd free (Share to Sandford Church®). Suns May 15, 22 (12.30-7). Last adm 5.30 pm*

Kingston Lacy ♿✿❀ (The National Trust) 1½m W of Wimborne Minster on the Wimborne-Blandford rd B3082. The setting landscaped in the C18, to W J Bankes's Kingston Lacy House. Magnificent trees planted over 175 years by Royal and famous visitors; avenue of limes and cedars; 9 acres of lawn; Dutch garden; sunken garden laid out to 1906 plans. TEAS and lunches. *Adm House & Garden £5.20, Gardens £2.10, Chd half price. For NGS Sun June 5 (12-6)*

Kingston Maurward ♿✿❀ A delightful Edwardian garden set in a C18 landscape. E of Dorchester turning off the roundabout at end of Dorchester by-pass A35. Bus alight Stinsford ¼m. Enter grounds through the farm animal park. Kingston Maurward house is a classical Georgian mansion set in gardens laid out in the C18 incl a 5-acre lake and overlooks the Dorchester watermeadows. An extensive restoration programme is nearing completion in the Edwardian gardens which are divided by hedges and stone balustrading. Each intimate garden contains a wealth of interesting plants and stone features, including the National Collection of salvias and penstemons. In addition an original Elizabethan walled garden is laid out as a demonstration of plants suitable for Dorset. TEAS. *Adm £2.50 Chd £1.50. Open Easter to end Sept. For NGS Thurs May 19, July 14 (1-5)*

¶**Knitson Old Farmhouse** ✿❀ (Rachel & Mark Helfer) Knitson. Signposted L off A351 Knitson is approx 1m W of Swanage 3m E of Corfe Castle. Ample parking in yard or in adjacent level field. Approx 1 acre of mature cottage garden. Herbaceous borders, rockeries, climbers, shrubs – many interesting cultivars. Large organic kitchen garden, orchard. TEAS in aid of F.A.R.M. Africa. *Adm £1 Chd 50p. Thurs May 12, 26, July 14, Aug 11, Sept 8 (2-7)*

Langebride House ✿ (Maj & Mrs John Greener) Long Bredy. ½-way between Bridport and Dorchester, S off A35, well signed. Substantial old rectory garden with many designs for easier management. 200-yr-old beech trees, bi-colour beech hedge, pleached limes and yew hedges, extensive collections of spring bulbs, bulbarium, herbaceous plants, flowering trees and shrubs. Tea in aid of Joseph Weld House. *Adm £1 Chd free. Suns March 20, 27 (2-5), April 10 (2-5.30). Private visits welcome March to end July* **Tel 0308 482 257**

By Appointment Gardens. These owners do not have a fixed opening day usually because they do not like crowds or have insufficient parking space. Owner will often give guided tour.

Little Platt ᏱᏒ᯦ (Sir Robert Williams) Plush, 9m N of Dorchester by B3143 to Piddletrenthide, then 1½m NE by rd signed Plush & Mappowder, 1st house on L entering Plush. 1-acre garden created from a wilderness since 1969; interesting collection of ornamental trees and flowering shrubs, incl several daphnes, spiraeas and viburnums; spring bulbs, hellebores, numerous hardy geraniums and unusual perennials. *Adm £1 Chd free. Private visits welcome March to Aug* Tel 0300 348320

Long Ash Cottage ᏱᏒ᯦ (Mr & Mrs A Case) Milton Abbas. 10m From Blandford-Dorchester on A354, 3m from Milbourne St Andrew on Ansty Rd not Milton Abbas Rd. Private ½-acre cottage garden adjoining The Rare Poultry, Pig and Plant Centre, with many unusual and old-fashioned flowers. Also exhibition of paintings by botanical artist Susan Goodricke. *Adm 75p Chd 25p. Mon May 2; Sun June 12 (2-5.30)*

The Manor House, Abbotsbury ᯦ (Mr D Nabarro) Abbotsbury is equidistant (9m) from Dorchester, Weymouth and Bridport. The Manor House is in Church St opp St Nicholas church. Cars can park in the public carpark by the Swan Inn. There is no parking by The Manor House. The gardens extending to 2½ acres were designed in 1988 by Ian Teh. They feature 4 inter-connecting ponds surrounded by herbaceous borders and a herb garden. The gardens lie below St Catherine's chapel and are in sight of the sea. TEAS. *Adm £1.50 Chd free. Sat, Sun June 4, 5 (2.30-6)*

The Manor House, Chaldon Herring ᯦ (Dale & Alice Fishburn) 9m E of Dorchester, mid way between Dorchester-Wareham on A352, turn S at sign to East Chaldon. 2 acres in valley in chalk hills, blends into surroundings; plantsman's garden with many perennials and climbers; small but fine kitchen garden. Home-made TEAS. *Adm £2 Chd free (Share to St Nicholas Church, Chaldon Herring®). Sat June 11 (4-8)*

● **Mapperton Gardens** ᏱᏒ᯦ (Montagu Family) nr Beaminster. 6m N of Bridport off A35. 2m SE of Beaminster off B3163. Descending valley gardens beside one of Dorset's finest manor houses (C16-C17) House and garden listed Grade I. Gardens featured in Discovering Gardens TV series (1990-91). Magnificent walks and views. Fish ponds, orangery, formal Italian-style borders and topiary; specimen trees and shrubs; car park. Upper levels only suitable for wheelchairs. House open to group tours by appt Tel 0308 862645. *Adm garden £2.50 Chd £1.50, under 5 free. March to Oct daily (2-6)*

Melbury House ᏱᏒ᯦ 6m S of Yeovil. Signed on Dorchester-Yeovil rd. 13m N of Dorchester. Large garden; very fine arboretum; shrubs and lakeside walk; beautiful deer park. Garden only. Last season saw many changes and more are planned for this year. TEAS. *Adm £2 OAPs/Chd £1 (Share to CRMF®). Thurs May 5, 26; June 16, 30; July 21 (2-5)*

Melplash Court ᏱᏒ (Mr & Mrs Timothy Lewis) Melplash. On the A3066 between Beaminster and Bridport, just N of Melplash. Turn W and enter between field gates next to big gates and long ave of chestnut trees. While the gardens as they exist today were originally designed by Lady Diana Tiarks they continue to evolve and consist of park planting, bog garden, croquet lawn and adjacent borders. Formal kitchen garden and herb garden, ponds, streams and lake; new borders and areas of interest are added and opened up each year. TEAS in aid of Melplash Church. *Adm £2 Chd free. Sun July 24 (2-6)*

¶**26 Milestone Road** ᏒᏱ (Mr & Mrs P M Fraser) Oakdale. At Oakdale Poole traffic lights on Wimborne Rd, turn S into Vicarage Rd then 1st L into Milestone Rd. ¼-acre town garden, divided into three rooms. Features include ornamental ponds and waterfall, pergola with roses and other climbing plants, natural wooded area with wild flowers and ferns and many interesting shrubs. TEAS. *Adm 50p Chd 20p. Suns June 12, July 17, Aug 14 (2-6)*

● **Minterne** (The Lord Digby) Minterne Magna. On A352 Dorchester-Sherborne rd. 2m N Cerne Abbas; woodland garden set in a valley landscaped in the C18 with small lakes, cascades and rare trees; many species and hybrid rhododendrons and magnolias tower over streams and water plants. *Adm £2 Accompanied chd and parking free. Open daily April 1 to Oct 31 (10-7)*

Moigne Combe (Maj-Gen H M G Bond) 6m E of Dorchester. 1½m N of Owermoigne turn off A352 Dorchester-Wareham Rd. Medium-sized garden; wild garden and shrubbery; heathers, azaleas, rhododendrons etc; woodland paths and lake walk. Tea Wyevale Garden Centre, Owermoigne. *Adm £1 1st chd 25p thereafter 10p. Suns May 22, 29 (2-5.30)*

Moulin Huet ᏱᏒ᯦ (Harold Judd Esq) 15 Heatherdown Rd, West Moors. 7m N of Bournemouth. Leave A31 at West Moors Garage into Pinehurst Rd, take 1st R into Uplands Rd, then 3rd L into Heatherdown Rd. thence into cul-de-sac. ⅓-acre garden made by owner from virgin heathland after retirement. Considerable botanical interest; collections of 90 dwarf conifers and bonsai; many rare plants and shrubs; alpines, sink gardens, rockeries, wood sculpture. Featured on TV 'Gardeners' World' 1982. Garden News Gardener of the Year Award 1984. *Adm 50p Chd free. Private visits and parties welcome, please* Tel 0202 875760. *Also 2 days in May locally advertised*

¶**Netherbury Court** ᯦ (Mr & Mrs Mark Culme-Seymour) Bridport. In Netherbury off A3066 2m from Beaminster 4m from Bridport. Parking in village, garden starts at gates directly past church on R. Tranquil garden of approx 4 acres; thirties lay-out incl Italian garden with canal; courtyard garden; stone paths, yew hedges and many fine mature trees; camellias and rhododendrons; splendid hellebore and spring heather. Woodland garden in process of restoration. TEAS in aid of Church Hall. *Adm £1.50 OAP £1 Chd free. Sun March 20 (2-6)*

Northbrook Farm ᏱᏒ (Shelia & Tim Cox) Take A354 Puddletown to Blandford. After Blue Vinney public house take 1st L (Long-lane) signed Dewlish-Cheselbourne turn L into farm rd marked Northbrook Farm. ½-acre garden created from a field since 1987, comprising mixed shrub/herbaceous borders in harmonising colours, conifer/heather bed. Unusual plants. TEAS. *Combined adm with* Farriers *£1 Chd free. Suns June 5, Aug 7 (2-5.30)*

North Leigh House ✿ (Mr & Mrs Stanley Walker) Colehill, 1m NE of Wimborne. Leave B3073 (formerly A31) nr Sir Winston Churchill public house into North Leigh Lane, thence ¾m. 5 acres of informal parkland with fine trees, small lake, rhododendrons; ornamental shrubs; specimen magnolia grandiflora and Green Brunswick fig; colony of orchis morio and naturalised spring bulbs in lawns; Victorian features include balustraded terrace, fountain pool, walled garden and superb conservatory, all being restored and maintained by owners. Dogs on leads welcome. Suitable wheelchairs in parts. NCCPG plant sale May. Teas in Tea Cottage. *Adm £1 Chd 20p (Share to Animal Aid®, May; Bournemouth & District Animal Ambulance Service© July). Suns May 8, July 31 (2-6)*

Oakmead &✿ (Mr & Mrs P D Priest) Mosterton. On A3066 N of Beaminster in centre of village. Roadside parking. ⅔-acre 'all seasons' garden. The skilful design incorporates traditional herbaceous border, fine heather bed, azaleas, camellias, shrub rose border, modern roses with lawns and gravel beds. Its bold sweeps of colour, interesting trees, shrubs and unusual plants make it "a model of modern gardening" (Anna Pavord in The Independent) and "should be high on anyone's visiting list" (The Dorset Garden Guide). TEAS. *Adm £1 Chd free. Suns July 17, Sept 18 (2-6). Private visits welcome, please* Tel 0308 868466

The Old Mill &✿ (The Rev & Mrs J Hamilton-Brown) Spetisbury, Spetisbury Village opposite school on A350 3m SE of Blandford. 2 acres mainly water garden by R Stour; small rockery; herbaceous plants. TEAS in aid of Spetisbury Church. *Adm £1 Chd free. Suns June 12, July 17, also every Weds May 4 to Aug 17 (2-5) also private visits welcome, please* Tel 0258 453939

The Old Parsonage & (Major & Mrs Mansel) Kimmeridge. 7m S of Wareham. Turn W off A351 Wareham-Swanage at sign to Kimmeridge. 1st house on R in Kimmeridge. ½-acre garden newly planted 1989; many unusual perennials and shrubs planned for all-yr interest; penstemon and grey foliage plants; clematis and hydrangeas; small pond; small vegetable and fruit garden; beautiful sea view; dogs on leads; Teas in village. *Adm £1 Chd under 15 free. Sun Aug 28 (2.15-5.15)*

The Old Rectory, Fifehead Magdalen &✿ (Mrs Patricia Lidsey) 5m S of Gillingham just S of the A30. Small garden with interesting shrubs and perennials; pond; plant stall. *Adm 80p Chd free. Sun June 12 (2-6) also private visits welcome, please* Tel 0258 820293

The Old Rectory, Litton Cheney ✿ (Mr & Mrs Hugh Lindsay) 1m S of A35, 10m Dorchester. 6m Bridport. Limited parking for infirm and elderly, otherwise park in centre of village and follow signs. Greatly varied garden with small walled garden recently redesigned; 4 acres beautiful natural woodland on steep slope with streams and ponds, primulas, native plants; wild flower lawn; (stout shoes recommended). TEAS in aid of Dorchester Volunteer Bureau & Red Cross. *Adm £1 Chd 20p. Easter Sun April 3; Suns May 15, Sept 18 (2-5.30)*

Old Rectory, Seaborough ✿ (Mr & Mrs C W Wright) 3m S of Crewkerne. Take B3165, after derestriction sign 2nd L, ¾m 1st R, then after 2½m 2nd L in village. 2-acre garden constructed since 1967; splendid views; rare trees, conifers, magnolias, flowering shrubs, roses, Himalayan plants, bulbs throughout the year, ferns; over 1000 species and cultivars. TEAS in aid of Church. *Adm £1 Chd 20p. Sun May 8 (2-6); also private visits welcome all year, please* Tel 0308 868426

The Old Vicarage, Stinsford ৶✿ (Mr & Mrs Antony Longland) Off roundabout at E end of Dorchester bypass A35. Follow signs for Stinsford Church 400yds. Use church car park. 1¼ acres incl an Italianate garden, herbaceous and mixed borders with unusual plants and shrubs, nearly 200 roses, lawns, terraces with exuberant pots, and fruit. Thomas Hardy, C Day Lewis and Cecil Hanbury, creator of gardens at La Mortola and Kingston Maurward, commemorated in church next door. TEAS. *Adm £1.50 Chd 50p. Sun June 19 (2-6)*

The Orchard ৶✿ (Mr & Mrs K S Ferguson) Blynfield Gate. 2m W of Shaftesbury on the rd to Stour Row rd. From Shaftesbury take the B3091 to St James's Church then onto the Stour Row rd. A 3-acre country garden, orchard and wild flower meadow on SE slope of Duncliffe Hill developed by the owners since 1981. Lawns, paths and grass walks link formal, informal and wild areas. Numerous colourful mixed borders and island beds are stocked with a wide variety of plants, several chosen for their intermingling qualities and lengthy flowering period. Hedgebanks of hardy geraniums, interesting trees and shrubs, small natural pond and plenty of seats. Homemade TEAS. *Adm £1.50 to incl descriptive guide Chd free (Share to Red Cross®). Weds June 8, 15, 22, 29; July 6, 13 (2-6)*

● **Parnham** & (Mr & Mrs John Makepeace) ½m S of Beaminster on A3066, 5m N of Bridport. 14 acres extensively reconstructed early this century; much variety of form and interest, topiary; terraces; gazebos; spring fed water rills; small lake; fine old trees; grand herbaceous borders featured in Discovering Gardens (1990/91). Old roses in formal front courtyard; riverside walk and woodland; many unusual plants. House (Grade 1 listed, dating from 1540) exhibitions of contemporary craftsmanship, also John Makepeace furniture workshops. Restaurant, coffee, lunches. TEAS. *Adm to whole site £4 Chd 10-15 £2 under 10 free. April 1 to Oct 30 every Sun, Wed & Bank Hol incl. Good Friday (10-5). Group visits by appt Tues & Thurs* Tel 0308 862204

Portesham Gardens 7m W of Weymouth on coast rd, B3157 to Bridport. From Dorchester take A35 W, turn L in Winterborne Abbas and follow signs to Portesham; parking in village. Teas at Millmead Country Hotel. *Combined adm £3. Sun June 5 (2-6)*

Regular Openers. Too many days to include in diary.
Usually there is a wide range of plants giving
year-round interest. See head of county section for
the name and garden description for times etc.

Bridge House Water Garden ✍ (Mr & Mrs G Northcote) Designed and constructed in 1987 in Japanese manner; featured on BBC2, and in 'Garden Answers!' Stone and ceramic lanterns, 'half-moon' stone and timber bridges, trout stream, borrowed scenery, pine island, waterfall, local stone-walled terraces, over 300 plantings suitable for smaller seaside garden; new rear patio with 'Isles of the Blest' feature and kare-sansui garden; garden planning exhibition in studio. *Also open Sun May 8. Adm £1 Chd free. Also private visits welcome April to Sept, please* **Tel 0305 871685**

Orchard House ♿✍❀ (Mr & Mrs F J Mentern) ⅓-acre walled cottage garden; organic and wild garden, ground cover, herbs; unusual old-fashioned perennials; rockeries and water garden; fruitful veg area, working greenhouses run as a small nursery open daily for charity. *Also private visits welcome May to July, please* **Tel 0305 871611**

Portesham House ♿✍❀ (Mrs G J Romanes) Home of Admiral Sir Thomas Masterman Hardy with 300-yr-old mulberry tree; over an acre of family garden with excellent modern dry stone walling, old walls and stream. Paeonies and unusual trees and shrubs

2 Winters Lane ✍ (Mr & Mrs K Draper) Portesham. Winters Lane is signposted in village to Coryates. ¼-acre garden with ponds and water features. Many ideas for smaller gardens such as small herb garden; container garden and dry garden. 50 varieties of clematis, wishing well and miniature village; most plants labelled. *Private visits welcome July and Aug, please* **Tel 0305 871316**

Portland House The National Trust (Mr & Mrs A Phillipson) 24 Belle Vue Rd. 1m from Weymouth town centre. Take Portland Rd from town centre; turn L from Rodwell Rd into Bincleaves Rd then into Belle Vue Rd on R. Park in Belle Vue Rd. Over 4 acres of mature trees, lawns, hydrangeas and fuchsias, avenue of palm trees; superb views over Portland harbour (weather permitting). TEAS. *Adm £1 Chd free. Sun July 10 (2-6)*

Priest's House ✍❀ (The Priest's House Museum Trust) 23 High St, Wimborne. Public car parks nearby. Old 'borough plot' garden of ½ acre, at rear of local museum, in partly C16 town house. Extending to mill stream and containing many unusual plants, trees and exhibits. Tearoom daily. *Adm £1.50 OAP £1 Chd 50p.* ▲*Sun June 26 (2-5)*

Pumphouse Cottage ❀ (Mr & Mrs R A Pugh) Mundens Lane. Alweston is 3m SE of Sherborne on A3030 to Blandford. Take L turning 50yds after PO marked Mundens Lane. 1st cottage on L. ½-acre cottage garden with erratic stream, collection of old roses, herbaceous borders, and spring bulbs. *Adm £1 Chd free. Sun, Mon May 1, 2, Suns May 22, July 3, 10 (2-6) Private visits welcome throughout the year, please* **Tel 0963 23535**

Red House Museum and Gardens ♿✍❀ (The Hampshire Museum Service) Quay Road, Christchurch. Tranquil setting in heart of town's conservation area. Gardens of ½ acre developed from early 1950's to complement Museum; plants of historic interest; herb garden with sunken lawn, south garden with lawns, herbaceous and woodland plants; old rose border. Gardens used as gallery display area for sculpture exhibitions. Admission to Museum and Art Gallery included. *Adm £1 OAP/Chd 60p (under five free) (Share to the Mayor of Christchurch's Appeal of the Year©).* ▲*For NGS Thurs June 9 (10-5)*

Rosedene ✍❀ (Mr & Mrs J M Hodges) 98 Hill View Road, East Howe, parallel with and ½m distant from A347 main Wimborne Rd in N Bournemouth. Walled town garden 120ft × 35ft, lined with mature espalier fruit trees, with 2 greenhouses and 18ft geodesic solar dome together containing 7 varieties of grape, fruit being a special interest of the owners. Other houses contain carnations, chrysanthemums and vegetables. Large pool with fish. There is much of interest contained in this small plot. Parts suitable for wheelchairs. *Adm 50p Chd 20p. Suns Aug 28, Sept 4, 11 (2-5)*

46 Roslin Road South ✍❀ (Dr & Mrs Malcolm Slade) Bournemouth. W of N end of Glenferness Ave in Talbot Woods area of Bournemouth. ⅓-acre walled town garden of yr-round interest. Features include rose pergola, 2 pools, sunken lawn, with many colourful and mature herbaceous and shrub plantings. Carefully tended fruit and vegetable garden. *Adm 50p Chd 20p. Suns May 29, June 26, July 24; Mon May 30 (1.30-5). Also private visits welcome from May to July, please* **Tel 0202 510243**

52 Rossmore Road ✍❀ (Mr & Mrs W E Ninniss) Parkstone, Poole. From A348 Poole-Ringwood rd turn SE into Rossmore Rd, thence ¼m. ⅓-acre interesting town garden designed in rooms; containing many rare and unusual plants; small knot garden; scree garden; herb garden. Featured on TVS 'That's Gardening' 1991. TEAS. *Adm 80p Chd 25p. Suns May 22, June 5 (2-6)*

St Nicholas Close ✍ (Mr & Mrs Arthur Thorne) 38 Highland Rd, Colehill, Wimborne. Leave B3073 (formerly A31) at traffic lights turn N into St John's Hill, after small roundabout into Rowlands Hill, after ¼m turn R into Highland Rd and park. The garden is approached on foot, please, by short lane. ⅓-acre created by owners, with specialist collections of unusual species: cultivars of rhododendrons, azaleas, camellias against mature trees, incl eucalyptus. *Adm 50p Chd free. Suns April 24, May 1 (2-6)*

¶**Slape Manor** ♿✍❀ (Mr & Mrs Antony Hichens) Netherbury. 1m S of Beaminster turn W off A3066 to village of Netherbury. House ⅓m S of Netherbury on back road to Bridport. River valley garden — extensive lawns and lake. Azaleas, rhododendrons; specimen trees. Cream TEAS in aid of Netherbury Village Hall. *Adm £1.50 Chd 50p under 5 free. Sun May 15 (2-6)*

Smedmore ♿✍❀ (Dr Philip Mansel) Kimmeridge, 7m S of Wareham. Turn W off A351 (Wareham-Swanage) at sign to Kimmeridge. 2 acres of colourful herbaceous borders; display of hydrangeas; interesting plants and shrubs; walled flower gardens; herb courtyard. *Adm £2 Chd £1. Sun May 15 (2.15-5.15). Enquiries to Mr T Gargett* **Tel 0929 480 719**

Snape Cottage ❀❀ (Mr & Mrs I S Whinfield) Leave A303 (Bourton bypass) at junction signposted Gillingham, Blandford and Bourton. Garden at W end of Bourton village; lane signed Chaffeymoor. Opp Chiffchaffs. ½-acre plantsman's cottage garden full of old-fashioned and uncommon plants, most labelled. Beautiful views, wildlife pond. Plants and herbs for sale. Windsor chairmaker's workshop and pole-lathe on view. *Adm £1 Chd free. Suns April 3; May 1, 29; June 12, 26; July 17, also every Weds April 6 to Sept 28 (closed Aug) (2-6). Parties welcome by appt* Tel 0747 840330

● **Stapehill Abbey** ❀❀ Wimborne Rd West, Ferndown. 2½m W of Ferndown on the old A31, towards Wimborne, ½m E of Canford Bottom roundabout. Early C19 Abbey, its gardens and estate restored and renovated to lawns, herbaceous borders; rose and water gardens; victorian cottage garden; lake and orchid house. Mature trees. Busy working Craft Centre; Countryside Museum featuring the National Tractor Collection, all under cover. Refreshments available in former refectory throughout the day. Large free car/coach park. TEAS. *Adm £4.50 OAPs £4 Chd £2.50. Open daily April to Oct (10-5); Oct to Easter (10-4); closed Mons and Tues Nov to March.* Tel 0202 861686

Star Cottage ❀❀ (Lys de Bray) 8 Roman Way, Cowgrove, Wimborne. Leave B3082 at Wimborne Hospital, along Cowgrove Rd for approx 1½m to Roman Way on R. Created in 1992 from a field, the garden is rapidly becoming another 'living library' of botanical artist and author Lys de Bray, lately of Turnpike Cottage, Wimborne. Visitors will have an opportunity of meeting Miss de Bray and seeing a specialised garden in the making. The owner is a RHS gold medallist whose botanical drawings and paintings are on permanent exhibition in her working studio which is open throughout the year at weekends and bank holidays. *Adm 75p Chd 40p. Garden and Studio open Sats and Suns all year. Easter to end Oct (2-6). End Oct to end March (2-4). For NGS Suns May 22, June 19 (2-6). Private visits also welcome, please* Tel 0202 885130

Steeple Manor ❀❀❀ (Mr Julian & the Hon Mrs Cotterell) Steeple, 5m SW of Wareham in Isle of Purbeck. Take Swanage rd from Wareham, or bypass, R in Stoborough. A beautiful garden designed by Brenda Colvin 1920's round C16/17 Purbeck stone manor house (not open); lovely setting in folds of Purbeck hills in small hamlet of Steeple next to ancient church, specially decorated for the occasion. Approx 5 acres the garden includes walls, hedges, enclosed gardens, ponds, stream, bog garden and meadow, collection old roses; many interesting and tender plants and shrubs for the plantsman. Parts garden suitable for wheelchairs. Free parking. Cream TEAS. *Adm £2.50 (to include written guide) OAPs £1.50 Chd under 16 free. Sun June 26 (2-6)*

¶**Stepleton** ❀❀ (Mr & Mrs Derek Coombs) Iwerne Stepleton. Stepleton House is situated 4m N of Blandford Forum on the A350. Approx 1m N of Stourpaine. Grade I park and garden on English Heritage register undergoing extensive restoration. 27 acres incl C18 lake, river walk and walled garden; rose pergola, interesting shrubs and

perennials; the park was replanted in 1987 under the guidance of Alan Mitchell VMH. TEAS in aid of Action Research. *Adm £1.50 Chd 50p. Sat April 30 (2-5)*

Sticky Wicket ❀❀❀ (Peter & Pam Lewis) Buckland Newton. 11m from Dorchester and Sherborne. 2m E of A352 or take B3143 from Sturminster Newton. T-junction midway Church, School and Gaggle of Geese public house. 1½-acre garden created since 1987, unusual designs, well documented showing wild life interest; fragrant cottage garden planting incl many perennials and herbs. Features include the Round Garden, a 'floral tapestry' of gently flowing colours, informal white garden. Featured on TV and in publications including 'English Private Gardens'. TEAS. *Adm £1.50 Chd 75p. Every Thurs June to Sept incl (10.30-8). Suns June 5, Sept 4 (2-6). Parties by appt* Tel 0300 345476. *For NGS Suns July 3, Aug 7 (2-6)*

Stockford ❀ (Mrs A M Radclyffe) East Stoke, 3½m W of Wareham on A352. Drive marked Stockford almost opp Stokeford Inn. 3 acres of woodland and walled gardens. Very old thatched house. *Adm £1 Chd 25p. Suns April 3, May 1, 29 (2-6)*

Stour House ❀❀❀ (T S B Card Esq) East St, Blandford. On 1-way system, 100yds short of market place. 2½-acre town garden, half on a romantic island in R Stour reached by a remarkable bridge; bulbs; borders well planted with perennials and many rare shrubs; river views. TEAS. *Adm 60p Chd 20p (Teas and share to Blandford Parish Church, July). Suns April 10, July 17, Aug 14 (2-6)*

¶**Stratton Gardens** ❀ 3m NW of Dorchester off A37 to Yeovil turn into village, gardens signed at the church. TEAS in aid of Stratton Village Hall & Church. *Combined adm £1.50 Chd free. Suns April 17, June 26 (2.30-5.30)*
    ¶**1 Manor Close** (Mr & Mrs W A Butcher) ⅕-acre with alpine garden at front and to the rear a heather garden, perennials and vegetable garden
    ¶**Manor Orchard** (Mr & Mrs G B David) 1-acre enthusiast's garden overlooking water meadows; kitchen garden with fruit arch and topiary; lawn with spring bulbs, herbaceous and shrub borders; pond, roses and vine

Studland Bay House ❀❀ (Mrs Pauline Ferguson) Studland. On B3351 5m E of Corfe Castle. Through village, entrance on R after Studland Bay House. Ample parking (no coaches). From Bournemouth, take Sandbank ferry, 2½m, garden on L after Knoll House Hotel. 6-acre spring garden overlooking Studland Bay. Planted in 1930's on heathland; magnificent rhododendrons, azalea walk, camellias, magnolias, ferns and stream; recent drainage and replanting, garden suitable for wheelchairs. TEAS in aid of Joseph Weld Hospice. *Adm £1.50 Chd free. Sat, Sun May 14, 15 (2-6)*

Sturminster Newton Gardens ❀❀ Off A357 between Blandford and Sherborne take turn opp Nat West Bank. Park in car park or behind Stourcastle Lodge. Walk down Penny St for **Ham Gate** and Goughs Close for **Stourcastle Lodge**. TEAS at **Ham Gate**. *Combined adm £1.50 Chd free. Suns May 15, July 10 (2-6)*

Ham Gate &# (Mr & Mrs H E M Barnes) Informal 2-acre garden with shrubs, trees, lawns running down to R Stour, pleasant woodland views across water meadows, over the last few years Pam Lewis has helped redesign the garden

Stourcastle Lodge # (Jill & Ken Hookham-Bassett) A S facing secluded cottage style garden, well stocked with herbaceous plants and shrubs with laid out vegetable garden

Thistledown #® (Mr & Mrs E G Gillingham) Alweston 3m SE of Sherborne. From main A3030, turn into Mundens Lane by Oxfords Bakery. Garden 100yds along lane; park in drive/lane, 1-acre plant enthusiast's garden with views to Bulbarrow Hill; garden planted for yr-round interest with spring bulbs, rhododendrons, shrubs, herbaceous borders by colour theme, conifers, old-fashioned and modern roses, clematis, ornamental trees and ponds. *Adm £1 Chd free. Suns, Mons April 17, 24, May 1, 2, 8, 15, 22, 30, July 3, 10, 17, 24, Sept 18, 25 (1.30-5)*

Three Bays #® (Mr & Mrs Christopher Garrett) 8, Old Wareham Rd, Beacon Hill, (nr Limberlost junction with A350) 1½m SW of Corfe Mullen. Garden of ½ acre made and maintained by owners. There is a Japanese flavour to the garden, with stone lanterns, dovecot and water features. Fuchsias are a special interest of the owners and there is a covered fuchsia garden. New rose garden 1993 with 150 plants in 34 varieties. Shrubs and herbaceous borders with much use of sloping site. TEA. *Adm 75p OAPs and Chd 50p (Share to Cancer Research Campaign). Sats, Suns June 18, 19; July 9, 10, 16, 17 (10-5). Illuminated garden Adm 50p Sat, Sun Aug 27, 28 (8.30-10.30). Parties by appt Tel 0202 623352*

¶**Throop Mill Cottage** (Dr & Mrs James Fisher) Throop Rd, Bournemouth. Turn N from Castle Lane (A3060) at Broadway public house. After ½m Broadway Lane turns L into Throop Rd. Car park between mill and cottage. 1-acre cottage garden separated from fields by ha-ha and river, notable for its design. Bulbs and spring flowers, water plants, interesting collection of ferns, mature trees. TEAS. *Adm £1 Chd 25p. Suns May 15, July 17 (2-6)*

Waterfalls (Jane & Roger Butler) 59 Branksome Wood Rd, Bournemouth. 1m W from Bournemouth Square, nr Coy Pond Rd. ⅓-acre redesigned garden. Made by owners over past 11 years utilising a steeply inclined site and featuring a series of waterfalls and a new koi pond. Mature trees provide a setting for ericaceous plants and ferns against a woodland background. *Adm 75p Chd 25p. Sun Aug 7 (2-6)*

Welcome Thatch #® (Mrs Diana Guy) Witchampton. 3½m E of Wimborne, B3078 L to Witchampton, thence through village past church & shop to last but one on R.

Listed thatched house with well-planted ⅔-acre cottage garden. Featured in Amateur Gardening Jan 1993. Plantsperson's borders, wild area with poultry, potager, timber decking with exotics, summerhouse, wildlife pond and bog. Not suitable for elderly, infirm or very young children. TEA. *Adm £1 Chd free. Suns April 10, May 15, June 19, Sept 11 (2-5.30). Private visits also welcome, please* **Tel 0258 840894**

West Manor &# (Mr & Mrs R Bollam) Church St, Upwey. ½m from bottom of Ridgeway Hill on A354 Dorchester-Weymouth rd. Turn R on B3159 (Bridport rd). At bottom of hill turn L, Church St. Limited parking for disabled only. ¾-acre low maintenance garden, worked on organic principles; lawns, borders, shrubs, woodland, small pond and vegetable garden. Teas at Wishing Well. *Adm £1 Chd free. Suns June 5, July 3, Aug 7 (2-6)*

Weston House &# (Mr & Mrs E A W Bullock) Buckhorn Weston. 4m W of Gillingham and 4m SE of Wincanton. From A30 turn N to Kington Magna, continue towards Buckhorn Weston and after railway bridge take L turn towards Wincanton. 2nd on L is Weston House. 1 acre; old roses; herbaceous and shrub beds; lawns; view of Blackmore Vale. TEAS in aid of Buckhorn Weston Parish Church. *Adm £1 Chd free. Suns June 19, July 17 (2-6)*

Wimborne Minster Model Town & Gardens &#® (The Wimborne Minster Model Town Trust®). King St 200yds W of Minster, opp. public car park. 1½-acre grounds with ⅒ scale models of the town in early fifties, surrounded by landscaped gardens. Herbaceous borders, alpines, herbs, heather and rose gardens, with many rare and unusual plants, with pools and fountain, making a colourful pleasure garden. Many seats and views over Stour valley. Refreshments daily. *Adm £2 OAPs £1.75 Chd £1 (3-15) under 3 free. For NGS Suns June 5, July 3, Sept 4 (10-5)*

Wincombe Park ® (The Hon M D Fortescue) 2m from Shaftesbury. Off A350 to Warminster signed to Wincombe and Donhead St Mary. Plantsman's garden surrounding house set in parkland; raised beds, shrubs, perennials; walled kitchen garden; view of valley with lake and woods. Unusual plants for sale. TEAS. *Adm £1.50 Chd free. Weds May 18, Oct 19 (2-5.30), also groups by appt Tel 0747 52161*

Woodside Lodge & (Mr & Mrs K H Lewis) E Lulworth. 5m SW of Wareham just N of B3070 nr village green and telephone box, follow signs. Extends to 1¾ acres graduating from formal to semi wild, with natural pond area; many shrub and tree species with rhododendrons, azaleas, camellias, iris and other herbaceous plants. TEAS in aid of Church. *Adm £1 Chd free (Share to Church Restoration Fund®). Suns June 5, 19 (2-6)*

Co. Durham

Hon County Organiser: Mrs Ian Bonas, Bedburn Hall, Hamsterley, Bishop Auckland DL13 3NN
Tel 0388 88231

DATES OF OPENING

By appointment
*For telephone numbers and other details see garden descriptions.
Private visits welcomed*

St Aidan's College, Durham

Regular openings
For details see garden descriptions

Raby Castle, Staindrop. See text for details

St Aidan's College, Durham. All year except Christmas and Easter
University of Durham Botanic Garden. Nov 1 to Oct 31

May 22 Sunday
Lartington Hall, Barnard Castle
May 29 Sunday
Barningham Park, nr Barnard Castle
Westholme Hall, Winston
June 12 Sunday
Eggleston Hall Gardens, nr Barnard Castle

June 19 Sunday
Lartington Hall, Barnard Castle
Low Walworth Hall, Darlington
June 26 Sunday
The Gainford Gardens
July 3 Sunday
Westholme Hall, Winston
July 10 Sunday
Bedburn Hall, Hamsterley
July 24 Sunday
Westholme Hall, Winston
August 7 Sunday
Lartington Hall, Barnard Castle
August 28 Sunday
Westholme Hall, Winston

DESCRIPTIONS OF GARDENS

Barningham Park (Sir Anthony Milbank) 6m S of Barnard Castle. Turn S off A66 at Greta Bridge or A66 Motel via Newsham. Woodland walks, trees and rock garden. House (not open) built 1650. Home-made TEAS. *Adm £1.50 Chd (under 14) 50p. Sun May 29 (1-6)*

Bedburn Hall &❀ (Ian Bonas Esq) Hamsterley, 9m NW of Bishop Auckland. From A68 at Witton-le-Wear, turn off W to Hamsterley; turn N out of Hamsterley-Bedburn and down 1m to valley. From Wolsingham on B6293 turn off SE for 3m. Medium-sized garden; terraced garden on S facing hillside with streams; lake; woodland; lawns; rhododendrons; herbaceous borders; roses. TEAS. *Adm £1.50 Chd 50p. Sun July 10 (2-6)*

Eggleston Hall Gardens &❀❀ (Sir William Gray) Eggleston, NW of Barnard Castle. Route B6278. Large garden with many unusual plants; large lawns, rhododendrons, greenhouses, mixed borders, fine trees, large extension of kitchen garden (all organically grown). Garden centre open. Homemade TEAS. *Adm £1.50 Chd 30p. Sun June 12 (2-5.30)*

The Gainford Gardens On A67, 8m W of Darlington; 8m E of Barnard Castle. One of the loveliest villages in the county, lying around a large tranquil green between A67 and R Tees. Georgian flavour predominates. TEAS. *Combined adm £1 Chd 50p (Share to St Marys Church, Westend Development®). Sun June 26 (2-6)*
   1 Academy Gardens (Dr & Mrs A G Leishman)
   38 Academy Gardens (Mrs E Sheridan)
   16 High Street (Dr & Mrs M Neville)
   24 Low Green (Mrs M R Ferens)
   Orchard House (Mrs M L Wilson)

¶**Lartington Hall** &❀ (Mrs R A Rackham) Barnard Castle. Lartington Hall is 2m W of Barnard Castle on the Cotherstone Rd. Approx 2 acres of formal gardens with long terraces and interesting statues. TEAS. *Adm £1.50 Chd 50p (Share to The After Stroke Club©). Suns May 22, June 19, Aug 7 (2-6)*

Low Walworth Hall &❀ (Mr & Mrs Peter Edwards) 3½m W of Darlington, on Staindrop Rd. B6279 (½m drive). Old walled garden; herbaceous borders, shrubs, roses; trout rearing pond. Interesting and varied shrubs and greenhouse plants for sale. Homemade cream TEAS. *Adm £1.50 Chd 50p (Share to Northumbria Historic Churches©). Sun June 19 (2-5.30)*

● **Raby Castle** &✗ (The Rt Hon The Lord Barnard) Staindrop, NW of Darlington. 1m N of Staindrop on A688 Barnard Castle-Bishop Auckland. Buses: 75, 77 Darlington-Barnard Castle; 8 Bishop Auckland-Barnard Castle; alight Staindrop, North Lodge, ¼m. Large walled garden; informal garden with ericas; old yew hedges; shrub and herbaceous borders; roses. Castle also open, principally C14 with alterations made 1765 and mid-C19; fine pictures and furniture. Collection of horse-drawn carriages and fire engines. Garden only suitable wheelchairs. TEAS at Stables. Special terms for parties on application. *Adm Castle Gardens and carriages £3.30 OAPs £3 Chd £1.50; Gardens & carriages only £1 OAPs/Chd 75p. Sat to Wed April 2 to 6, May 1 to June 30, Weds, Suns only; July 1 to Sept 30 daily (except Sats); also Bank Hol weekends, Sat to Tues (Castle 1-5); garden and park 11-5.30, last adm 4.30); also by appt for parties* Tel 0833 660202

By Appointment Gardens. These owners do not have a fixed opening day usually because they do not like crowds or have insufficient parking space. Owner will often give guided tour.

St Aidan's College & (By kind permission of the Principal) Durham. 1m from City centre. A1050 N towards Durham City; turn W at South End House, where St Aidan's College signposted. St Aidan's College was designed by Sir Basil Spence and the grounds laid out according to a plan by Prof Brian Hackett about 1966. The maturing garden (3 acres) includes shrub planting, rose beds and raised beds; several specimen trees of interest incl cedrus libani, have been planted. From the garden there are unequalled views of Durham Cathedral, Durham City and Durham University Observatory, designed by Anthony Salvin. In porter's lodge are available, booklets £1 & postcards 20p. *Gardens open all year except Christmas and Easter. Please arrange with Bursar* Tel **091 374 3269** *Donations to NGS*

University of Durham Botanic Garden & 🌿🌸 1m from centre of Druham. Turn off A167 (old A1) at Cock O'The North roundabout, direction Durham for 1m; turn R into Hollingside Lane which is between Grey and Collingwood Colleges; gardens 600yds on R. 18 acres on a beautiful SW facing hillside features 12-yr-old North American Arboretum planted 1980, woodland and ornamental bog garden, winter heather beds and tropical and desert display glasshouses. The Prince Bishop's garden contains 6 statues. TEAS in Visitor Centre. *Adm £1 Chd 50p. March 1 to Oct 31 (10-5) Nov 1 to Feb 28 every afternoon weather permitting*

Westholme Hall & 🌸 (Capt & Mrs J H McBain) Winston. 11m W of Darlington. From A67 Darlington-Barnard Castle, nr Winston turn N onto B6274. 5 acres of gardens and grounds laid out in 1892 surround the Jacobean house (not open). Rhododendrons, flowering shrubs, mixed borders, old-fashioned rose garden. The croquet lawn leads on to an orchard, stream and woodland. Home made TEAS. *Adm £1.50 Chd 50p. Suns May 29; July 3, 24; Aug 28 (2-6)*

Dyfed

See separate Welsh section beginning on page 291

Essex

Hon County Organiser: Mrs Hugh Johnson, Saling Hall, Great Saling, Braintree CM7 5DT
Assistant Hon County Organiser: Mrs Rosemary Kenrick, The Bailey House, Saffron Walden CB10 2EA
Hon County Treasurer: Eric Brown Esq, 19 Chichester Road, Saffron Walden CB11 3EW

DATES OF OPENING

By appointment
For telephone number and other details see garden description

Private visits welcomed
Feeringbury Manor, Feering
The Fens, Langham
Lower Dairy House, Nayland
Olivers, nr Colchester
Reed House, Great Chesterford
Volpaia, Hockley
Warwick House, Great Dunmow

Parties only
Beth Chatto Gardens, Elmstead Market
8 Dene Court, Chelmsford
6 Fanners Green, Great Waltham
Hyde Hall, Rettendon
The Magnolias, Brentwood
Park Farm, Great Waltham
Saling Hall, Great Saling

Regular openings
For details see garden descriptions

Beth Chatto Gardens, Elmstead Market. March 1 to Oct 31 Mons to Sats. Nov 1 to March 1 Mons to Fris. Closed all Bank Hols
Feeringbury Manor, Feering. Weekday mornings May 2 to July 29 Closed weekends & Bank Hols
The Fens, Langham. Thurs, Sats March to Aug
Hyde Hall RHS Garden, Rettendon. Sat, Sun, Wed, Thurs & Bank Hols March 27 to Oct 23
Saling Hall, Great Saling. Weds in May, June, July
Volpaia, Hockley. Thurs & Suns April 3 to June 26

March 27 Sunday
The Magnolias, Brentwood
April 2 Saturday
Lower Dairy House, Nayland, Colchester
April 3 Sunday
Lower Dairy House, Nayland, Colchester
The Magnolias, Brentwood
Warwick House, Great Dunmow
April 4 Monday
Lower Dairy House, Nayland, Colchester
Saling Hall Lodge, Great Saling
April 9 Saturday
Lower Dairy House, Nayland, Colchester

April 10 Sunday
The Fens, Langham
Lower Dairy House, Nayland, Colchester
The Magnolias, Brentwood
Saling Hall Lodge, Great Saling
April 17 Sunday
Glen Chantry, Wickham Bishops
Olivers Farm, Toppesfield
Park Farm, Great Waltham
April 18 Monday
Park Farm, Great Waltham
April 20 Wednesday
Olivers, nr Colchester
April 23 Saturday
Lower Dairy House, Nayland, Colchester
April 24 Sunday
The Fens, Langham
Lower Dairy House, Nayland, Colchester
The Magnolias, Brentwood
April 27 Wednesday
Olivers, nr Colchester
April 30 Saturday
Lower Dairy House, Nayland, Colchester
May 1 Sunday
Glen Chantry, Wickham Bishops
Lower Dairy House, Nayland, Colchester
Park Farm, Great Waltham

Warwick House, Great Dunmow
May 2 Monday
Glen Chantry, Wickham Bishops
Lower Dairy House, Nayland,
Colchester
Park Farm, Great Waltham
May 4 Wednesday
Olivers, nr Colchester
May 7 Saturday
Olivers, nr Colchester
May 8 Sunday
6 Fanners Green, Great
Waltham ‡
The Magnolias, Brentwood
Old Hill House, Aldham
Olivers, nr Colchester
Park Farm, Great Waltham ‡
Saling Hall Lodge, Great Saling
May 9 Monday
Park Farm, Great Waltham
May 11 Wednesday
Olivers, nr Colchester
May 14 Saturday
Lower Dairy House, Nayland,
Colchester
May 15 Sunday
Glen Chantry, Wickham Bishops
Lower Dairy House, Nayland,
Colchester
Olivers Farm, Toppesfield
May 18 Wednesday
Olivers, nr Colchester
May 21 Saturday
Lower Dairy House, Nayland,
Colchester
May 22 Sunday
Lower Dairy House, Nayland,
Colchester
The Magnolias, Brentwood
Park Farm, Great Waltham
Saling Hall Lodge, Great Saling
Whalebone House, Langham
May 23 Monday
Park Farm, Great Waltham
May 25 Wednesday
Olivers, nr Colchester
May 28 Saturday
Lower Dairy House, Nayland,
Colchester
May 29 Sunday
8 Dene Court, Chelmsford ‡
Glen Chantry, Wickham Bishops
Lower Dairy House, Nayland,
Colchester
Park Farm, Great Waltham ‡
Warwick House, Great Dunmow
May 30 Monday
Glen Chantry, Wickham Bishops
Lower Dairy House, Nayland,
Colchester
Park Farm, Great Waltham
June 1 Wednesday
Olivers, nr Colchester

June 4 Saturday
Lower Dairy House, Nayland,
Colchester
June 5 Sunday
The Fens, Langham
Lower Dairy House, Nayland,
Colchester
The Magnolias, Brentwood
Park Farm, Great Waltham
Saling Hall Lodge, Great Saling
June 6 Monday
Park Farm, Great Waltham
June 8 Wednesday
Olivers, nr Colchester
June 11 Saturday
Lower Dairy House, Nayland,
Colchester
Stamps & Crows, Layer Breton
Heath
June 12 Sunday
Amberden Hall, Widdington
8 Dene Court, Chelmsford ‡
Glen Chantry, Wickham Bishops
Lofts Hall, Elmdon, nr Saffron
Walden
Lower Dairy House, Nayland,
Colchester
Olivers Farm, Toppesfield
Park Farm, Great Waltham ‡
Stamps & Crows, Layer Breton
Heath
Warwick House, Great Dunmow
June 13 Monday
Park Farm, Great Waltham
June 15 Wednesday
Olivers, nr Colchester
Stamps & Crows, Layer Breton
Heath
June 18 Saturday
Lower Dairy House, Nayland,
Colchester
June 19 Sunday
Clavering Gardens, nr Saffron
Walden
Cobbs, Howe St, nr Chelmsford ‡
6 Fanners Green, Great
Waltham ‡
Fanners Farm, Great Waltham ‡
Lower Dairy House, Nayland,
Colchester
The Magnolias, Brentwood
Park Farm, Great Waltham ‡
Shore Hall, Cornish Hall End
June 20 Monday
Cobbs, Howe St. nr Chelmsford ‡
Park Farm, Great Waltham ‡
June 22 Wednesday
Fanners Farm, Great Waltham
Olivers, nr Colchester
June 25 Saturday
Lower Dairy House, Nayland,
Colchester
Tye Farm, Elmstead Market

June 26 Sunday
8 Dene Court, Chelmsford ‡
Folly Faunts House, Goldhanger
Lower Dairy House, Nayland,
Colchester
Park Farm, Great Waltham ‡
Saling Hall, Great Saling ‡‡
Saling Hall Lodge, Great
Saling ‡‡
Tye Farm, Elmstead Market
Warwick House, Great Dunmow
June 27 Monday
Park Farm, Great Waltham
June 29 Wednesday
Olivers, nr Colchester
July 2 Saturday
Lower Dairy House, Nayland,
Colchester
July 3 Sunday
Glen Chantry, Wickham Bishops
Lower Dairy House, Nayland,
Colchester
The Old Vicarage, Rickling
Park Farm, Great Waltham
July 4 Monday
Park Farm, Great Waltham
July 9 Saturday
Lower Dairy House, Nayland,
Colchester
July 10 Sunday
8 Dene Court, Chelmsford
The Fens, Langham
Lower Dairy House, Nayland,
Colchester
July 17 Sunday
6 Fanners Green, Great
Waltham ‡
Granta House, Littlebury, Saffron
Walden
The Magnolias, Brentwood
Park Farm, Great Waltham ‡
July 18 Monday
Park Farm, Great Waltham
July 24 Sunday
8 Dene Court, Chelmsford
August 7 Sunday
8 Dene Court, Chelmsford
August 14 Sunday
The Magnolias, Brentwood
August 21 Sunday
8 Dene Court, Chelmsford
August 28 Sunday
The Magnolias, Brentwood
September 4 Sunday
Glen Chantry, Wickham Bishops
September 11 Sunday
Saling Hall Lodge, Great Saling
September 18 Sunday
Glen Chantry, Wickham Bishops
The Magnolias, Brentwood
Whalebone House, Langham
October 23 Sunday
The Magnolias, Brentwood

DESCRIPTIONS OF GARDENS

Amberden Hall ᴦ✿❀ (Mr & Mrs D Lloyd) Widdington. 6m from Saffron Walden. E off B1383 nr Newport. Follow signs to Mole Hall Wildlife Park. Drive ½m beyond park on R. Medium-sized walled garden with collection of unusual hardy plants, shrubs and ivy allée. Raised vegetable garden. TEAS. *Adm £2 Chd free (Share to St Mary's Church, Widdington®). Sun June 12 (2-6)*

● **Beth Chatto Gardens** ᴦ✿❀ (Mrs Beth Chatto) On A133, ¼m E of Elmstead Market. 5 acres of attractively landscaped garden with many unusual plants, shown in wide range of conditions from hot and dry to water garden. Adjacent nursery open. *Adm £1.50 Chd free. March 1 to Oct 31, every Mon to Sat but closed Bank Hols (9-5); Nov 1 to end of Feb every Mon to Fri but closed Bank Hols (9-4). Parties by appt*

Clavering Gardens ᴦ✿❀ Clavering. On B1038 7m N of Bishops Stortford. Turn W off B1368 (old A11) at Newport. TEAS in Cricket Pavilion on village green in aid of Clavering Cricket Club. *Adm £2 Chd free. Sun June 19 (2-5.30)*

> **Clavering Court** (Mr & Mrs S R Elvidge) Approx 1½ acres fine trees, shrubs and borders. Walled garden, Edwardian greenhouse
>
> **Deers** (Mr & Mrs S Cooke) Shrub and herbaceous borders; ponds; old roses in formal garden; walled vegetable garden; flower meadow; trees. 4 acres. Parking in yard next to house
>
> **Piercewebbs** (Mr & Mrs B R William-Powlett) Includes old walled garden, shrubs, lawns, ha ha, yew and stilt hedges, pond and grass tennis court. Extensive views. New trellised rose garden (1992)
>
> **Shovellers** (Miss J & Miss E Ludgate) Stickling Green. 3-acre extended cottage garden, orchard and meadow

¶**Cobbs** ᴦ✿ (Mr & Mrs St Aubyn) Howe St, nr Chelmsford. Take old A130 6m N from Chelmsford to Gt Waltham through village approx 1m to village of Howestreet. Turn R down Parsonage Lane, over river 1st L (no through rd). House on L. Approx 1-acre garden, large herbaceous border; bog garden; kitchen garden and roses. *Adm £1 Chd free under 16. Sun, Mon June 19, 20 (2-6)*

8 Dene Court ✿❀ (Mrs Sheila Chapman) Chelmsford. W of Chelmsford (Parkway). Take A1060 Roxwell Rd for 1m. Turn R at traffic lights into Chignall Rd, Dene Court 3rd exit on R. Parking in Chignall Rd. Well maintained and designed compact garden (250 sq yds) circular lawn surrounded by many unusual plants incl wide variety of clematis, roses, ferns and grasses; ornamental well; three pergolas; rose-covered perimeter wall. *Adm £1 Chd free (Share to Audrey Appleton Trust for the Terminally Ill®). Suns May 29, June 12, 26, July 10, 24, Aug 7, 21 (2-6). Parties by appt*

Fanners Farm ᴦ✿ (Mr & Mrs P G Lee) 4m N of Chelmsford. In Great Waltham turn into South Street opp Six Bells public house. Garden 1¼m on R. Informal garden of approx 2 acres surrounding C14 house (not open). Conservatory and small collection of vintage cars. TEAS Sun only. *Adm £1 Chd free. Sun, Wed June 19, 22 (2-6)*

6 Fanners Green ✿❀ (Dr & Mrs T M Pickard) 4m N of Chelmsford. In Great Waltham turn into South Street opp Six Bells public house. Garden 1¼m on the R. A 15-year-old small country garden of ⅓ acre divided into different areas of informal planting. Herb garden and conservatory. *Adm £1 Chd free. Suns May 8, June 19, July 17, (2-6). Parties by appt Tel 0245 360035*

Feeringbury Manor ᴦ (Mr & Mrs G Coode-Adams) Coggeshall Rd, Feering, on rd between Coggeshall and Feering. 7-acre garden bordering R Blackwater. Many unusual plants including wide variety of honeysuckles, clematis, old-fashioned roses; rare bog-loving plants, border ponds and streams; small Victorian water wheel. *Adm £1.50 Chd £1. Weekday mornings May 2 to July 29 (8-1) Closed weekends and Bank Hols. Also private visits welcome, please Tel 0376 561946*

The Fens ᴦ✿❀ (Mrs Ann Lunn) Old Mill Rd, Langham. 5m N of Colchester off A12. Old Mill Rd starts at T-junction with High St and is an extension of Chapel Rd, leading to Boxted-Dedham Rd. Undulating 2-acre cottage garden maintained with pond; by owners, shade and ditch gardens recreated after 1987 storm; primulas and a wide variety of interesting plants; nursery open. TEAS for charity. *Adm £1 Chd 50p. Thurs, Sat March to Aug. Suns April 10, 24, June 5, July 10 (2-5). Also private visits welcome, please Tel 0206 272259*

Folly Faunts House ᴦ❀ (Mr & Mrs J C Jenkinson) Goldhanger. Between Maldon and Colchester on B1026; signed ½m from both directions. 5-acre garden and grounds, divided into 5 different types of garden, created from scratch since 1962. During 1989 a further 6 avenues and 12 acres of land have been planted with a wide variety of trees. A large number of unusual and rare trees, shrubs and plants. Large car park. TEAS. *Adm £1.50 Chd 50p. Sun June 26 (2-5)*

Glen Chantry ᴦ✿❀ (Mr & Mrs W G Staines) Wickham Bishops 1½m SE of Witham. Take Maldon Rd from Witham and 1st L to Wickham Bishops. Pass Benton Hall Golf Course; cross narrow bridge over R Blackwater and turn immediately L up track by side of Blue Mills. 3-acre garden with emphasis on mixed borders with unusual perennials & shrub roses. Limestone rock gardens with associated ponds form a dominant feature, formal specialist white garden and foliage beds with grasses and hostas; range of plants for sale. TEAS. *Adm £1 Chd 50p. Suns April 17; May 1, 15, 29; June 12; July 3; Sept 4, 18; Mons May 2, 30 (2-5)*

¶**Granta House** ᴦ❀ (Mr & Mrs R A Lloyd) Littlebury. 2m from Saffron Walden. Opp Littlebury Church on B1383 1m N of Audley End House, entrance in Littlebury Green Rd. Old walled garden of 1 acre, unusual shrubs; herbaceous plants and roses. TEAS. *Adm £1 Chd free. Sun July 17 (2-6)*

Hyde Hall Garden ᴦ✿❀ (Royal Horticultural Society) Rettendon. 7m SE of Chelmsford; 6m NE of Wickford. Signed from A130. Flowering trees, shrubs, perennials, roses, bulbs, ornamental greenhouses and ponds; all-year-round colour. Restaurant. *Adm £2.50 Chd 50p 6-14. Parties 20+ £2. Every Sat, Sun, Wed, Thurs and Bank Hols March 27 to Oct 23 (11-6)*

Lofts Hall &✿✿ (Maj & Mrs C R Philipson) Elmdon. 8m E of Royston. 5m W of Saffron Walden off B1039. Large garden, 6 acres; roses; herbaceous and shrub borders; kitchen garden; lake and C16 carp pond. Early C17 dovecote (reputedly 2nd largest in England), stud farm. TEAS. *Adm £1.50 Chd 50p. Sun June 12 (2-6)*

Lower Dairy House &✿✿ (Mr & Mrs D J Burnett) 7m N of Colchester off A134. Turn L at bottom of hill before Nayland village into Water Lane, signed to Little Horkesley. Garden ½m on L past farm buildings. Plantsman's garden approx 1½ acres. Natural stream with waterside plantings; rockery and raised beds; lawns; herbaceous borders; roses. Many varieties of shrubs and ground cover plants. Garden made and maintained by owners for year round colour and variety. Good spring bulbs and blossom. Tudor House (not open). TEAS. *Adm £1 Chd 50p. Sats, Suns, Mons April 2, 3, 4, 9, 10, 23, 24, 30; May 14, 15, 21, 22, 28, 29, 30; June 4, 5, 11, 12, 18, 19, 25, 26; July 2, 3, 9, 10 (2-6). Also private visits welcome, please* Tel 0206 262 220

The Magnolias ✿✿ (Mr & Mrs R A Hammond) 18 St John's Ave, Brentwood. From A1023 turn S on A128; after 300yds R at traffic lights; over railway bridge; St John's Ave 3rd on R. ½-acre well-designed informal garden with particular appeal to plantsmen; good collection spring bulbs; ground-cover; trees and shrubs incl maples, rhododendrons, camellias, magnolias and pieris. Koi ponds and other water interests. TEA. *Adm £1 Chd 50p. Suns March 27; April 3, 10, 24; May 8, 22; June 5, 19; July 17; Aug 14, 28; Sept 18; Oct 23 (10-5). Also open for parties March to Oct incl* Tel 0277 220019

Old Hill House &✿ (Mr & Mrs J S d'Angibau) Aldham. On A604, 5m W of Colchester; top of Ford Street Hill. From A12 and A120, turn off at Marks Tey; N past Marks Tey Station, R at Xrds by Aldham Church. 1-acre garden with mixed shrubs and herbaceous borders and formal herb garden, maintained by owners for year round interest. TEAS. *Adm £1 Chd free (Share to NSPCC®). Sun May 8 (2-5.30)*

¶The Old Vicarage ✿✿ (Mr & Mrs James Jowitt) Rickling. 7m from Saffron Walden: from Newport take B1038 W to Wicken Bonhunt. In village turn L to Rickling, The Old Vicarage is on the L after 1m. 2-acre garden with herbaceous and mixed borders; rose garden and shrubbery. TEAS. *Adm £1.25 Chd free. Sun July 3 (2-6)*

Olivers &✿ (Mr & Mrs D Edwards) 3m SW of Colchester, between B1022 & B1026 From Colchester via Maldon Rd, turn L into Gosbecks Rd at Leather Bottle public house; R into Olivers Lane (signposted Roman River Centre). C18 house (not open) overlooks Roman river valley, surrounded by terrace and yew backed borders; closely planted with wide variety of plants, many unusual and for varying conditions. Lawns; 3 lakes; meadow; woodland with fine trees underplanted with shrubs including rhododendrons and old roses; spring bulbs and bluebells. TEA. *Adm £1.50 Chd free. Sat, Sun May 7, 8 (2-6) Weds April 20, 27; May 4, 11, 18, 25; June 1, 8, 15, 22, 29 (2-5). Parties by appt all year, please* Tel 0206 330575

Olivers Farm &✿✿ (Mr & Mrs J G Blackie) Toppesfield. Garden is situated 1½m W of A604 between Great Yeldham and Toppesfield. Last house on L before T-junction, down drive. Nearest town, Halstead 7m. 1½-acre garden created since 1978. Woodland garden, trees, shrubs, roses and herbaceous. Lime avenue in paddock; C16 farm house (not open). Small vineyard, TEAS in aid of Riding For Disabled. *Adm £1 Chd 50p. Suns April 17, May 15, June 12 (2-6)*

Park Farm ✿✿ (Mrs J E M Cowley & Mr D Bracey) Great Waltham. Take B1008 N from Chelmsford through Broomfield Village. On Little Waltham bypass turn L into Chatham Hall Lane signposted Howe St; Park Farm ½m on L. 2 acres of garden in separate "rooms" formed by yew hedges with climber-obscured old farmhouse and dairy in centre. Many different species of bulbs; shrubs; roses and herbaceous perennials; designing still proceeding with new projects underway. TEAS. *Adm £1 Chd 50p. Suns, Mons April 17, 18: May 1, 2, 8, 9, 22, 23, 29, 30: June 5, 6, 12, 13, 19, 20, 26, 27; July 3, 4, 17, 18 (2-6). Parties by appt* Tel 0245 360871

Reed House &✿ (Mrs W H Mason) Great Chesterford. 4m N of Saffron Walden and 1m S of Stump Cross, M 11. On B184 turn into Great Chesterford High Street. Then L at Crown & Thistle public house into Manor Lane. ¾-acre garden with collection of unusual plants developed in the last 6 years. *Adm £1.50 Chd 50p. Private visits welcome, please* Tel 0799 530312

Saling Hall &✿ (Mr & Mrs H Johnson) Great Saling, 6m NW of Braintree. A120; midway between Braintree-Dunmow turn off N at the Saling Oak. 12 acres; walled garden dated 1698; small park with fine trees; extensive new collection of unusual plants with emphasis on trees; water gardens. TEAS Sun only. *Adm £1.50 Chd free (Share to St James's Church, Great Saling®). Weds in May, June, July (2-5). Sun June 26 with* **Saling Hall Lodge** *combined adm £2 (2-6). Also parties by appt*

Saling Hall Lodge &✿✿ (Mr & Mrs K Akers), Great Saling. 6m from Braintree. Turn N off A120 between Braintree and Dunmow at the Saling Oak public house. Drive at end of village on L, please park in village. Well-designed and maintained ½-acre garden with pond, limestone rock garden, small peat garden, tufa bed and sinks. TEA. *Adm 80p Chd free. Suns April 10, May 8, 22, June 5, 26 with* **Saling Hall** *combined adm £2 (2-6), July 11 (2-5)*

¶Shore Hall ✿✿ (Mr & Mrs Peter Swete) Cornish Hall End, nr Braintree. 2½m NE of Finchingfield. ½m W of Cornish Hall End on Gt Sampford Rd. Long drive with poplars. 2½-acre garden surrounding C17 house (not open) with several enclosed formal areas and interesting shrubs. 100-yr-old box hedges enclose formal beds planted with herbaceous and old roses; ornamental rose garden surrounding lily ponds; newly planted ornamental vegetable and fruit garden and many young rare trees. TEAS in aid of Cornish Hall End Church Restoration Fund. *Adm £1.50 Chd free. Sun June 19 (2-5)*

Regular Openers. See head of county section.

Stamps and Crows &❀ (Mr & Mrs E G Billington) Layer Breton Heath. 5½m S of Colchester on B1022 take L fork signposted Birch and Layer Breton. Garden on R side of Layer Breton Heath. 2½ acres of moated garden surrounding C15 farmhouse (not open). Herbaceous borders, mixed shrubs, old roses and good ground cover. Recently created formal garden. Fine views towards Layer Marney Tower. TEAS (Sun only). *Adm £1 Chd free (Share to St. Mary's Church, Layer Breton®). Sat, Sun, Wed June 11, 12, 15 (2-6)*

Tye Farm &❀ (Mr & Mrs C Gooch) On A133 ½m Elmstead Market, (opp end of village to Beth Chatto). About 1 acre incl old formal herb garden and large conservatory; roses. TEAS in aid of Friends of Elmstead Church. *Adm £1.50 Chd 50p. Sat Sun June 25, 26 (2-6)*

● **Volpaia** ❀❀ (Mr & Mrs D Fox) 54 Woodlands Rd, Hockley. 2¾m NE of Rayleigh. B1013 Rayleigh-Rochford, turn S from Spa Hotel into Woodlands Rd. On E side of Hockley Woods. 1-acre containing many exotic trees, rhododendrons, camellias besides other shrubs. Carpets of wood anemones and bluebells in spring, underplanting is very diverse esp with woodland, liliaceous plants and ferns. Home of Bullwood Nursery. TEA. *Adm £1 Chd 30p (Share to Essex Group of NCCPG®). All Thurs &* *Suns from April 3 to June 26 (2.30-6). Also private visits welcome, please* **Tel 0702 203761**

Warwick House &❀❀ (Mr & Mrs B Creasey) Easton Lodge. 1m N of Great Dunmow on B184, take rd to Lt Easton, ½m turn L to Easton Lodge, 1¼m to white gates marked Easton Lodge, through these gardens ½m on right. Originally wing of Easton Lodge, home of Countess of Warwick; old house now demolished and gardens of 6 acres created since 1972 on much of old house site. Includes recently acquired 4.5 acres of the abandoned gardens designed by Harold Peto at the turn of the century, now under restoration. Features inc C18 dovecote; conservatory; cobbled, herringbone courtyard with fountain; ponds with koi and water fowl. History of Easton Lodge and American Air Force Exhibits. TEA. *Adm £1.50 OAPs £1 Chd 50p (Share to Five Parishes®). Suns April 3; May 1, 29; June 12, 26 (2-6). Private visits welcome, please* **Tel 0371 873305**

Whalebone House &❀❀ (Mr & Mrs W Durlacher) Dedham Rd, Langham. N on A12 from Colchester, ignore sign to Langham and turn off to Stratford St Mary. 1st L into Dedham Rd, entrance ½m on L beyond thatched pink cottage. 3½-acre garden of well maintained mixed borders with wide variety of shrubs, perennials and trees. TEAS for charity. *Adm £1 Chd 50p. Suns May 22; Sept 18 (2-6)*

Glamorgan

See separate Welsh section beginning on page 291

Gloucestershire

Hon County Organisers:	Mr & Mrs Witold Wondrausch, The New Inn, Poulton, Cirencester GL7 5JE Tel 0285 850226
Assistant Hon County Organisers:	Mr Guy Acloque, Alderley Grange, Wotton-under-Edge GL12 7QT
	Mrs Wendy Dare, Old Mill Dene, Blockley, Moreton-in-Marsh GL56 9HU
	Mrs Jennie Davies, Applegarth, Alstone, nr Tewkesbury GL20 8JD
	Mrs Sally Gough, Trevi, Over Old Road, Hartpury GL19 3BJ
	Mr A V Marlow, Greenedge, 32 Dr Browns Road, Minchinhampton GL19 3BT
	Mrs Elizabeth-Anne Pile, Ampney Knowle, nr Cirencester GL7 5ED
Hon County Auditor:	Mr H J Shave, ACCA (Bradings) 31 Castle Street, Cirencester GL7 1QD

DATES OF OPENING

By appointment

For telephone numbers and other details see garden descriptions. Private visits welcomed

Ampney Knowle, Barnsley, Cirencester
Bank House, Lower Meend Gardens, St Briavels, nr Lydney
The Bell House, Westbury-on-Severn
Beverston Castle, nr Tetbury
Bhardonna, nr Newent
Boilingwell, Sudeley Hill, nr Winchcombe
Burnside, Prestbury & Southam Gardens

Camp Cottage, Highleadon, nr Newent
Casa Mia, nr Huntley
Cecily Hill House, Cirencester Gardens
The Chipping Croft, Tetbury Gardens
Cotswold Farm, nr Cirencester
Ewen Manor, nr Cirencester
Frampton Court, Frampton-on-Severn
Gentian Cottage, Stow
Grove Cottage, Lower Lydbrook, Cinderford
Hodges Barn, Shipton Moyne, nr Tetbury
Hunts Court, North Nibley, nr Dursley
8 Hyatts Way, Bishops Cleeve
Jasmine House, Bream, nr Lydney

Laurel Cottage, Brockweir Gardens
Millend House, nr Coleford
The New Inn, Poulton Gardens, nr Cirencester
The Old Manor, Twyning
Old Mill Dene, Blockley
Orchard Cottage, Gretton, Winchcombe
Osborne House, Frocester, nr Stonehouse
The Red House, Staunton, nr Gloucester
Redwood House, Halmore, Berkeley
Rodmarton Manor, nr Cirencester
St Francis, Minchinhampton Gardens
20 St Peter's Road, Cirencester Gardens
Sunningdale, Grange Court, nr Westbury

Threeways, Brockweir Gardens, nr
   Chepstow
153 Thrupp Lane, nr Stroud
Tin Penny Cottage, Whiteway, nr
   Stroud
Trevi Garden, Hartpury, nr
   Gloucester
Upton Wold, nr Moreton-in-Marsh
Westbury Court Gardens,
   Westbury-on-Severn
Willow Lodge, nr Longhope,
   Gloucester

Regular openings
For details see garden descriptions

Barnsley House, nr Cirencester.
   Mons, Weds, Thurs & Sats
Batsford Arboretum, nr
   Moreton-in-Marsh. March 1 to
   Mid Nov
Bourton House, Bourton-on-the-Hill.
   Every Thurs and Fris May 26 to
   Sept 30, Bank Hol Mons May 30,
   Aug 29
Camp Cottage, Highleadon, nr
   Newent. See text for dates
Cerney House, North Cerney
   Gardens, nr Cirencester. All year,
   Tues, Wed & Fri
Grove Cottage, Lower Lydbrook,
   Cinderford. Every Sun March 6 to
   Sept 18
Hidcote Manor Garden, nr Chipping
   Campden. Daily except Tues &
   Fri April to Oct 1
Hodges Barn, Shipton Moyne, nr
   Tetbury. Mons, Tues & Fris April
   1 to Aug 15
Hunts Court, North Nibley, nr
   Dursley. Tues-Sats all year except
   Aug, also Bank Hol Mons
Kiftsgate Court, nr Chipping
   Campden. Every Sun, Wed, Thurs
   & Bank Hols April 1 to Sept 30.
   Sats in June and July
Lydney Park, Lydney. Every Sun
   Wed & Bank Hol April 3 to June
   5. Every day May 29 to June 5
Misarden Park, Miserden, nr
   Cirencester. Tues, Wed & Thurs
   April 5 to Sept 29
The Old Manor, Twyning. Every Mon
   Mar 1 to Oct 31
Painswick Rococo Garden,
   Painswick. Every Wed to Sun &
   Bank Hol Mons Feb 2 to mid
   December
Rodmarton Manor, nr Cirencester.
   Sats, May 14 to Aug 27
Sezincote, nr Moreton-in-Marsh.
   Every Thurs, Fri & Bank Hols,
   except Dec

Stanway House, nr Winchcombe.
   Tues & Thurs June to Aug
Sudeley Castle, Winchcombe. Daily
   April 1 to Sept 30
Tin Penny Cottage, Whiteway, nr
   Stroud. See text for dates
Trevi Garden, Hartpury, nr
   Gloucester. See text for dates

February
Every Wed
   Tin Penny Cottage, Whiteway,
   nr Stroud
February 3 Thursday
   Home Farm, Huntley, nr Newent
February 17 Thursday
   Home Farm, Huntley, nr Newent
February 27 Sunday
   Green Cottage, Lydney
March
Every Sun
   Grove Cottage, Lower Lydbrook,
   Cinderford
Every Mon
   The Old Manor, Twyning
Every Wed
   Tin Penny Cottage, Whiteway, nr
   Stroud
March 3 Thursday
   Home Farm, Huntley, nr Newent
March 6 Sunday
   Green Cottage, Lydney
March 13 Sunday
   Green Cottage, Lydney
   Minchinhampton Gardens
   153 Thrupp Lane, nr Stroud
March 17 Thursday
   Home Farm, Huntley, nr Newent
   Trevi Garden, Hartpury, nr
   Gloucester
March 20 Sunday
   Green Cottage, Lydney
March 24 Thursday
   Trevi Garden, Hartpury, nr
   Gloucester
March 27 Sunday
   Boilingwell, Sudeley Hill, nr
   Winchcombe
   Brockweir Gardens, nr Chepstow
   Burnside, Prestbury & Southam
   Gardens
   Newark Park, nr
   Wotton-under-Edge
   Painswick Rococo Garden,
   Painswick
March 31 Thursday
   Home Farm, Huntley, nr Newent
   Trevi Garden, Hartpury, nr
   Gloucester
April
Every Sun
   Grove Cottage, Lower Lydbrook,
   Cinderford

Every Sun, Tues
   Camp Cottage, Highleadon, nr
   Newent
Every Mon
   The Old Manor, Twyning
Every Wed
   Tin Penny Cottage, Whiteway, nr
   Stroud
Every Thurs
   Trevi Garden, Hartpury, nr
   Gloucester
April 3 Sunday
   The Bell House,
   Westbury-on-Severn
   Bhardonna, nr Newent ‡
   Hodges Barn, Shipton Moyne, nr
   Tetbury
   Jasmine House, Bream, nr Lydney
   Newark Park, nr
   Wotton-under-Edge
   North Rye House, nr Broadwell,
   Moreton-in-Marsh
   Old Mill Dene, Blockley
   Redwood House, Halmore,
   Berkeley
   Ryelands House, Taynton, nr
   Newent ‡
   Trevi Garden, Hartpury, nr
   Gloucester ‡
April 4 Monday
   Ashley Gardens, nr Tetbury
   The Bell House,
   Westbury-on-Severn
   Bhardonna, nr Newent ‡
   Camp Cottage, Highleadon, nr
   Newent ‡
   Jasmine House, Bream, nr Lydney
   Redwood House, Halmore,
   Berkeley
   Ryelands House, Taynton, nr
   Newent ‡
   Tin Penny Cottage, Whiteway, nr
   Miserden
   Trevi Garden, Hartpury, nr
   Gloucester ‡
April 10 Sunday
   Ashley Gardens, nr Tetbury
   Bredon Manor, nr Tewkesbury
   Minchinhampton Gardens
   Misarden Park, Miserden, nr
   Cirencester
   Ryelands House, Taynton, nr
   Newent
   Westonbirt Gardens, at
   Westonbirt School
April 14 Thursday
   Home Farm, Huntley, nr Newent
   Jasmine House, Bream, nr Lydney
April 17 Sunday
   Abbotswood, nr
   Stow-on-the-Wold
   Beverston Castle, nr Tetbury
   Boilingwell, Sudeley Hill, nr
   Winchcombe

Jasmine House, Bream, nr Lydney
Osborne House, Frocester, nr
   Stonehouse
Pinbury Park, nr Cirencester
Ryelands House, Taynton, nr
   Newent
Tin Penny Cottage, Whiteway, nr
   Stroud

April 18 Monday
Beverston Castle, nr Tetbury

April 20 Wednesday
Daylesford House, nr
   Stow-on-the-Wold

April 23 Saturday
Sudeley Castle, Winchcombe

April 24 Sunday
Brockweir Gardens, nr Chepstow
Burnside, Prestbury & Southam
   Gardens ‡
The Chipping Croft, Tetbury
Lydney Park, Lydney
Pigeon House, Prestbury &
   Southam Gardens ‡
Ryelands House, Taynton, nr
   Newent
Stanway House, nr Winchcombe
Upton Wold, nr Moreton-in-Marsh

April 28 Thursday
Home Farm, Huntley, nr Newent
Jasmine House, Bream, nr Lydney

May
Every Sun
   Grove Cottage, Lower Lydbrook,
      Cinderford
Every Sun, Tues
   Camp Cottage, Highleadon, nr
      Newent
Every Mon
   The Old Manor, Twyning
Every Wed
   Tin Penny Cottage, Whiteway, nr
      Stroud
Every Thurs
   Trevi Garden, Hartpury, nr
      Gloucester

May 1 Sunday
Ampney Knowle, Barnsley,
   Cirencester
The Bell House,
   Westbury-on-Severn
Blockley Gardens,
   Moreton-in-Marsh
Eastcombe, Bussage & Brownshill
   Gardens
Green Cottage, Lydney ‡
Hodges Barn, Shipton Moyne, nr
   Tetbury
Jasmine House, Bream, nr
   Lydney ‡
Millend House, nr Coleford ‡
Nympsfield Gardens, nr
   Nailsworth
Trevi Garden, Hartpury, nr
   Gloucester

May 2 Monday
The Bell House,
   Westbury-on-Severn ‡
Camp Cottage, Highleadon, nr
   Newent
Eastcombe, Bussage & Brownshill
   Gardens
Grove Cottage, Lower Lydbrook,
   Cinderford ‡
Jasmine House, Bream, nr
   Lydney ‡
Millend House, nr Coleford ‡
Redwood House, Halmore,
   Berkeley
Tin Penny Cottage, Whiteway, nr
   Stroud ‡

May 4 Wednesday
Lydney Park, Lydney

May 7 Saturday
Barnsley House, nr Cirencester

May 8 Sunday
Abbotswood, nr Stow on the Wold
Batsford Arboretum, nr
   Moreton-in-Marsh
Green Cottage, Lydney
Hidcote Manor Garden, nr
   Chipping Campden
The Manor, Boddington, nr
   Cheltenham
Snowshill Manor, nr Broadway

May 12 Thursday
Home Farm, Huntley, nr Newent
Jasmine House, Bream, nr Lydney

May 14 Saturday
Kiftsgate Court, nr Chipping
   Campden

May 15 Sunday
Boilingwell, Sudeley Hill, nr
   Winchcombe
Ewen Manor, nr Cirencester
Green Cottage, Lydney ‡
Jasmine House, Bream, nr
   Lydney ‡
Lindors Country House,
   St Briavels, nr Lydney ‡
Millend House, nr Coleford ‡
Priors Mesne Cottage, Aylburton,
   Lydney ‡
Stowell Park, nr Northleach
Tin Penny Cottage, Whiteway, nr
   Stroud

May 16 Monday
Camp Cottage, Highleadon, nr
   Newent

May 22 Sunday
The Bell House,
   Westbury-on-Severn
Green Cottage, Lydney ‡
Lower Meend Gardens, St
   Briavels, nr Lydney ‡
Upper Cam Gardens, nr Dursley

May 23 Monday
Camp Cottage, Highleadon, nr
   Newent

May 26 Thursday
Bourton House,
   Bourton-on-the-Hill
Home Farm, Huntley, nr Newent
Jasmine House, Bream, nr Lydney

May 29 Sunday
Bourton House,
   Bourton-on-the-Hill
Bourton-on-the-Hill Gardens
Brockweir Gardens, nr
   Chepstow ‡
Eastington Gardens, nr
   Northleach
Green Cottage, Lydney ‡
Hartpury College, nr Gloucester
Icomb Place, nr
   Stow-on-the-Wold
Jasmine House, Bream, nr
   Lydney ‡
Millend House, nr Coleford ‡
Nympsfield Gardens, nr
   Nailsworth
The Red House, Staunton, nr
   Gloucester
Willow Lodge, nr Longhope,
   Gloucester ‡

May 30 Monday
Brackenbury, Wotton-under-Edge
Camp Cottage, Highleadon, nr
   Newent ‡
Eastington Gardens, nr
   Northleach
Grove Cottage, Lower Lydbrook,
   Cinderford ‡
Jasmine House, Bream, nr
   Lydney ‡
Millend House, nr Coleford ‡
The Red House, Staunton, nr
   Gloucester
Stancombe Park, Stinchcombe,
   nr Dursley
Tin Penny Cottage, Whiteway, nr
   Stroud
Willow Lodge, nr Longhope,
   Gloucester ‡

June
Every Sun
   Grove Cottage, Lower Lydbrook,
      Cinderford
Every Sun, Mon, Tues
   Camp Cottage, Highleadon, nr
      Newent
Every Mon
   The Old Manor, Twyning
Every Wed
   Tin Penny Cottage, Whiteway, nr
      Stroud
Every Thurs
   Trevi Garden, Hartpury, nr
      Gloucester

June 1 Wednesday
Green Cottage, Lydney

June 2 Thursday
Old Mill Dene, Blockley

June 4 Saturday
Barnsley House, nr Cirencester
Blundells, Broadwell,
Stow-on-the-Wold

June 5 Sunday
Blundells, Broadwell,
Stow-on-the-Wold
25 Bowling Green Road,
Cirencester Gardens
The Chestnuts, nr
Minchinhampton
Green Cottage, Lydney
Hodges Barn, Shipton Moyne, nr
Tetbury ‡
North Cerney & Marsden Manor
Gardens, nr Cirencester
Redwood House, Halmore,
Berkeley
Stanway House, nr Winchcombe
Sunningdale, Grange Court, nr
Westbury
Tetbury Gardens ‡

June 8 Wednesday
Green Cottage, Lydney

June 9 Thursday
Jasmine House, Bream, nr Lydney
Old Mill Dene, Blockey

June 11 Saturday
Rodmarton Manor, nr
Cirencester

June 12 Sunday
The Bell House,
Westbury-on-Severn ‡
Boilingwell, Sudeley Hill, nr
Winchcombe
25 Bowling Green Road,
Cirencester Gardens
Frampton-on-Severn Gardens
Green Cottage, Lydney ‡
Hunts Court, North Nibley, nr
Dursley ‡‡
Jasmine House, Bream, nr
Lydney ‡
Millend House, nr Coleford ‡
Pitt Court, North Nibley,
Dursley ‡‡
Prestbury & Southam Gardens, nr
Cheltenham
Sunningdale, Grange Court, nr
Westbury ‡
153 Thrupp Lane, nr Stroud
Willow Lodge, nr Longhope,
Gloucester ‡

June 15 Wednesday
Green Cottage, Lydney

June 16 Thursday
Old Mill Dene, Blockey

June 18 Saturday
Chalford Gardens, nr Stroud

June 19 Sunday
Adlestrop Gardens,
Stow-on-the-Wold
25 Bowling Green Road,
Cirencester Gardens

Chalford Gardens, nr Stroud
Cotswold Farm, nr Cirencester
Green Cottage, Lydney
Hunts Court, North Nibley, nr
Dursley ‡
Kemble Gardens, nr Cirencester
Pitt Court, North Nibley, Dursley ‡
Poulton Gardens, nr Cirencester
The Red House, Staunton, nr
Gloucester
Rookwoods, Waterlane, nr Bisley
Willow Lodge, nr Longhope,
Gloucester
Witcombe Gardens, nr Gloucester

June 23 Thursday
Bourton House,
Bourton-on-the-Hill
Jasmine House, Bream, nr Lydney
Old Mill Dene, Blockey

June 26 Sunday
Blockley Gardens,
Moreton-in-Marsh
Brackenbury, Wotton-under-Edge
Brockweir Gardens, nr Chepstow
Campden House, Chipping
Campden
Hunts Court, North Nibley, nr
Dursley
Jasmine House, Bream, nr Lydney
North Rye House, nr Broadwell,
Moreton-in-Marsh
Stanton Gardens, nr Broadway
Stowell Park, nr Northleach
Stratton Gardens, nr Cirencester
Sunningdale, Grange Court, nr
Westbury ‡
Tin Penny Cottage, Whiteway, nr
Stroud
Willow Lodge, nr Longhope,
Gloucester ‡

June 29 Wednesday
Daylesford House, nr
Stow-on-the-Wold

June 30 Thursday
Old Mill Dene, Blockey

July
Every Sun
Grove Cottage, Lower Lydbrook,
Cinderford
Every Sun, Tues
Camp Cottage, Highleadon, nr
Newent
Every Mon
The Old Manor, Twyning
Every Wed
Tin Penny Cottage, Whiteway, nr
Stroud
Every Thurs
Trevi Garden, Hartpury, nr
Gloucester

July 3 Sunday
Beverston Castle, nr Tetbury ‡
Combend Manor, Elkstone, nr
Cheltenham

Hodges Barn, Shipton Moyne, nr
Tetbury ‡
Hunts Court, North Nibley, nr
Dursley
Millend House, nr Coleford
Misarden Park, Miserden, nr
Cirencester
Orchard Cottage, Beverston,
Tetbury ‡
Redwood House, Halmore, Berkeley
Upton Wold, nr Moreton-in-Marsh

July 4 Monday
Beverston Castle, nr Tetbury
Camp Cottage, Highleadon, nr
Newent
Orchard Cottage, Beverston,
Tetbury

July 7 Thursday
Jasmine House, Bream, nr Lydney

July 10 Sunday
Boilingwell, Sudeley Hill, nr
Winchcombe
25 Bowling Green Road,
Cirencester Gardens ‡‡
Broad Campden Gardens, nr
Chipping Campden
Casa Mia, Clifford Manor, nr
Newent ‡
Hunts Court, North Nibley, nr
Dursley
Jasmine House, Bream, nr Lydney
Oxwold House, Barnsley
Quenington Gardens, nr Fairford
The Red House, Staunton, nr
Gloucester
Rockcliffe, nr Upper Slaughter,
Stow
20 St Peter's Road, Cirencester
Gardens ‡‡
Sezincote, nr Moreton-in-Marsh
Sunningdale, Grange Court, nr
Westbury ‡
Willow Lodge, nr Longhope,
Gloucester ‡

July 11 Monday
Camp Cottage, Highleadon, nr
Newent

July 17 Sunday
Casa Mia, Clifford Manor, nr
Newent ‡
Cirencester Gardens
Pinbury Park, nr Cirencester
Sunningdale, Grange Court, nr
Westbury ‡
Tin Penny Cottage, Whiteway, nr
Miserden
Willow Lodge, nr Longhope,
Gloucester ‡

July 18 Monday
Camp Cottage, Highleadon, nr
Newent

July 21 Thursday
Casa Mia, Clifford Manor, nr
Newent

Jasmine House, Bream, nr Lydney
July 24 Sunday
25 Bowling Green Road,
Cirencester Gardens
Casa Mia, Clifford Manor, nr
Newent ‡
Gardeners Way, Kings Stanley, nr
Stroud
Jasmine House, Bream, nr
Lydney ‡
Millend House, nr Coleford ‡
Willow Lodge, nr Longhope,
Gloucester ‡
July 28 Thursday
Bourton House,
Bourton-on-the-Hill
July 31 Sunday
Brackenbury, Wotton-under-Edge
Brockweir Gardens, nr Chepstow
Minchinhampton Gardens
Sunningdale, Grange Court, nr
Westbury
August
Every Sun
Grove Cottage, Lower Lydbrook,
Cinderford
Every Sun, Tues
Camp Cottage, Highleadon, nr
Newent
Every Mon
The Old Manor, Twyning
Every Wed
Tin Penny Cottage, Whiteway, nr
Stroud
Every Thurs
Trevi Garden, Hartpury, nr
Gloucester
August 1 Monday
Minchinhampton Gardens
August 4 Thursday
Jasmine House, Bream, nr Lydney
Sunningdale, Grange Court, nr
Westbury
August 7 Sunday
Boilingwell, Sudeley Hill, nr
Winchcombe
25 Bowling Green Road,
Cirencester Gardens
Jasmine House, Bream, nr
Lydney
Redwood House, Halmore,
Berkeley
Sunningdale, Grange Court, nr
Westbury ‡
Trevi Garden, Hartpury, nr
Gloucester
Willow Lodge, nr Longhope,
Gloucester ‡
August 11 Thursday
Sunningdale, Grange Court, nr
Westbury
August 14 Sunday
25 Bowling Green Road,
Cirencester Gardens

Millend House, nr Coleford ‡
Sunningdale, Grange Court, nr
Westbury ‡
Tin Penny Cottage, Whiteway, nr
Miserden
Willow Lodge, nr Longhope,
Gloucester ‡
August 18 Thursday
Jasmine House, Bream, nr Lydney
August 20 Saturday
Kiftsgate Court, Chipping
Campden
August 21 Sunday
Jasmine House, Bream, nr Lydney
Westonbirt Gardens, at
Westonbirt School
August 25 Thursday
Bourton House,
Bourton-on-the-Hill
Jasmine House, Bream, nr Lydney
August 28 Sunday
Bourton House,
Bourton-on-the-Hill
Bourton-on-the-Hill Gardens
Brockweir Gardens, nr
Chepstow ‡
Eastington Gardens, nr Northleach
Jasmine House, Bream, nr
Lydney ‡
Millend House, nr Coleford ‡
August 29 Monday
Brackenbury, Wotton-under-Edge
Camp Cottage, Highleadon, nr
Newent
Eastington Gardens, nr Northleach
Jasmine House, Bream, nr
Lydney ‡
Millend House, nr Coleford ‡
Tin Penny Cottage, Whiteway, nr
Stroud
September
Every Sun
Camp Cottage, Highleadon, nr
Newent
Every Mon
The Old Manor, Twyning
Every Wed
Tin Penny Cottage, Whiteway, nr
Stroud
September 1 Thursday
Trevi Garden, Hartpury, nr
Gloucester
September 4 Sunday
Boilingwell, Sudeley Hill, nr
Winchcombe
Green Cottage, Lydney
Grove Cottage, Lower Lydbrook,
Cinderford
Redwood House, Halmore,
Berkeley
Westbury Court Gardens,
Westbury-on-Severn
Westonbirt Gardens, at
Westonbirt School

September 6 Tuesday
Camp Cottage, Highleadon, nr
Newent
September 8 Thursday
Jasmine House, Bream, nr Lydney
Trevi Garden, Hartpury, nr
Gloucester
September 10 Saturday
Sudeley Castle, Winchcombe
September 11 Sunday
Green Cottage, Lydney ‡
Grove Cottage, Lower Lydbrook,
Cinderford ‡
Jasmine House, Bream, nr
Lydney ‡
September 13 Tuesday
Camp Cottage, Highleadon, nr
Newent
September 15 Thursday
Trevi Garden, Hartpury, nr
Gloucester
September 18 Sunday
Grove Cottage, Lower Lydbrook,
Cinderford
September 20 Tuesday
Camp Cottage, Highleadon, nr
Newent
September 22 Thursday
Trevi Garden, Hartpury, nr
Gloucester
September 25 Sunday
Brockweir Gardens, nr Chepstow
Tin Penny Cottage, Whiteway, nr
Stroud
September 30 Thursday
Bourton House,
Bourton-on-the-Hill
October
Every Mon
The Old Manor, Twyning
Every Wed
Tin Penny Cottage, Whiteway, nr
Stroud
October 2 Sunday
Boilingwell, Sudeley Hill, nr
Winchcombe
October 9 Sunday
Painswick Rococo Garden,
Painswick
November
Every Wed
Tin Penny Cottage, Whiteway, nr
Stroud
December
Every Wed
Tin Penny Cottage, Whiteway, nr
Stroud

By Appointment Gardens.
Avoid the crowds. Good chance
of a tour by owner. See garden
description for telephone number.

DESCRIPTIONS OF GARDENS

Abbotswood (Dikler Farming Co) 1m W of Stow-on-the-Wold, nr Lower Swell. Beautiful, extensive heather and stream gardens; massed plantings of spring bulbs and flowers; rhododendrons, flowering shrubs, specimen trees; extensive herbaceous borders, roses, formal gardens; fine example of garden landscape. Buses not allowed in grounds. TEAS. Car park free. *Adm £1.50 Chd free. Suns April 17, May 8 (1.30-6)*

Adlestrop Gardens &❀ 3m E of Stow-on-the-Wold, off A436. A delightful small village made famous by Jane Austen and the poet Edward Thomas. A variety of gardens will be on show. Produce and plant stalls in aid of Church Fabric Fund. TEAS in aid of village hall. *Adm £1.50 Chd free. Sun June 19 (2-6)*

Ampney Knowle ❀ (Mr & Mrs Richard Pile) nr Cirencester. 4m NE Cirencester B4425 ¼m S of Barnsley on Ampney Crucis road. Medium-sized garden planted since 1970 with plant packed terrace; mixed borders and old shrub roses. Woodland garden with indigenous wild flowers and 40-acre bluebell wood. Picnic site. TEAS in aid of Royal British Legion Women's Section. *Adm £1.50 Chd free. Sun May 1 (12-6). Private visits welcome, please* **Tel 0285 740230**

Ashley Gardens 3m NE of Tetbury on A433, turn R through Culkerton to Ashley. *Combined adm £1.50 Chd free (Share to Ashley Church©). Mon April 4, Sun April 10 (2-6)*
   Ashley Grange &✿ (Miss A L Pearson) Old garden of one-time Georgian/Victorian rectory with fine landscape views. Shrubs and herbaceous borders. Sensitively redesigned since 1971 for easier upkeep
   Ashley Manor ✿ (Mr & Mrs M J Hoskins) Old garden altered since 1982 with pond garden; mature yew hedges, collection of clematis, climbing and shrub roses, herbaceous border; terrace of herbs; kitchen garden. Typical Cotswold pigeon house and tithe barn. Manor house C15 and early C18 (not open)

Barnsley House &✿❀ (Mrs Rosemary Verey) Barnsley 4m. NE of Cirencester on A433. Mature garden with interesting collection of shrubs and trees; ground cover; herbaceous borders; pond garden; laburnum walk; knot and herb gardens; formal kitchen garden; C18 summer houses. C17 house (not open). *Adm £2 OAPs £1 Chd free (no charge Dec-Feb). Mons, Weds, Thurs & Sats (10-6). Parties by appt only* **Tel 0285 740281**. *For NGS (Share to Barnsley Church®). Sats May 7, June 4 (2-6)*

Batsford Arboretum ❀ (The Batsford Foundation) 2m NW of Moreton-in-Marsh, A44/A429 intersection. Arboretum & wild garden; over 1000 named trees (many rare) and shrubs; magnolias, flowering cherries, bulbs; beautiful views from Cotswold escarpment. House not open. TEAS at Garden Centre open all year round (10-5) Arboretum. *Adm £2 Chd/OAPs and parties £1.50. March 1 to mid Nov daily (10-5). For NGS Sun May 8 (2-5)*

The Bell House ✿❀ (Mr & Mrs G J Linklater) Bell Lane, Westbury-on-Severn. 9m SW of Gloucester close to A48 in village next to Westbury Court Gardens (NT). Painter's garden on dramatic, S-facing, 2 acre site next to unusual church with view to R Severn and Newnham. Fan-shaped garden designed by Jefferies of Cirencester in 1940s with terraces, sweeping lawns and mature trees, many exotic. Long mixed borders, naturalised bulbs, fritillarias, heather and azalea beds. Water gardens with enormous slabs of forest stone. Featured in TV 'Gardeners World'. No dogs. Permanent exhibition of water colours by Jan Linklater. Featured in NGS video 2, see page 344. TEAS. *Adm £1.50 Chd 50p (Share to Westbury Parish Hall fund®). Suns, Mons, April 3, 4, May 1, 2, 22, June 12 (2-6) Parties by appt in April, May and June, please* **Tel 0452 760388**

Beverston Castle &❀ (Mrs L Rook) Beverston. 2m W of Tetbury on A4135. Overlooked by romantic C12-15 castle ruin the overflowingly planted paved terrace leads from C17 house across moat to sloping lawn with spring bulbs in abundance and full herbaceous and shrub borders. Large walled kitchen garden and greenhouses. TEA (April 17) TEAS (July 3). Plants for sale July. *Adm £1 Chd under 12 yrs 50p (Share to Tetbury Hospital®). Suns, Mons, April 17, 18; July 3, 4 (2-6). Private visits by written appt all year*

Bhardonna &❀ (Mr & Mrs G W Webb) 1m N of Newent on Ledbury-Dymock road B4215. Recently created landscaped garden of 1½ acres rich in colour and plant interest. Shrubs; spring bulbs; borders; fish ponds; collection of horse ploughs. TEA. *Adm £1 Chd free. Sun, Mon April 3, 4 (2-6). Private visits welcome May 1 to Sept 30, please* **Tel 0531 822169**

Blockley Gardens ✿❀ NW of Moreton-in-Marsh. A44 Moreton-Broadway; turning E. TEAS at St George's Hall. *Combined Adm £2 or 50p per garden Chd free. Suns May 1, June 26 (2-6)*
   Broughton Cottage (Mr & Mrs R A Smeeton) Small garden on steep slope overlooking village
   Elm Barns (Sir Thomas & Lady Skyrme) Shrubs; lawns; pool; beautiful views
   The Garage (Mr & Mrs Stuart-Turner) Unusual garden making the best of a difficult slope; varied plantings
   Grange Cottage (Mrs J Moore) Small garden with unusual plants
   ¶Holly House ✿❀ (Simon Ford & Robert Ashby) Secluded garden 'rooms', lovely views, unusual trees, small formal kitchen garden.
   Laggan Cottage (Mr A Corrie) ½-acre sloping garden; mainly shrubs with herbaceous border; fruit trees and lily pond. *Open only May 1*
   Malvern Mill (Mr & Mrs J Bourne) Converted mill with pond and stream; 2-acres inc orchard
   Old Mill Dene (Mr & Mrs B S Dare) 2½-acre garden with terraced slopes and mill pool, not safe for small children. *Also open Sun April 3 (2-6). Thurs June 2, 9, 16, 23, 30. Adm £1.50 Chd 50p. Private visits welcome, please* **Tel 0386 700457**
   The Old Mill (Dr J Shackleton Bailey) Garden with millpond, stream, bulbs, flowers and shrubs. *Open only May 1*
   The Old Quarry (Mr & Mrs A T Hesmondhalgh) 1-acre landscaped garden in old quarry with grass walks & lovely views
   Paxton House (Mr & Mrs Peter Cator) Walled garden on different levels; unusual plants, spring bulbs, shrub roses

Pear Trees (Mrs J Beckwith) Small secluded, walled cottage garden with unusual plants. *Open only June 26*
Rodneys (Mr & Mrs T Q Abell) Newly designed formal walled garden. *Open only May 1*

Blundells &❀ (Mr & Mrs Joe Elliott) Broadwell 1m N of Stow-on-the-Wold off A429. Medium-sized garden with large variety of hardy plants and alpines, trees, shrubs, herbaceous borders, lilies, 25 plus old stone sinks and troughs planted with alpines. TEAS. *Adm £1.50 Chd free (Share to GRBS®). Sat, Sun June 4, 5 (2-6)*

Boilingwell ❀ (Canon & Mrs R W Miles) Sudeley 1½m SE of Winchcombe. Take Castle St. out of Winchcombe, or Rushley Lane on Broadway road (signed Guiting Power); ¼m up hill beyond Sudeley Castle North Lodge. 1½-acre garden, with no room for grass, featuring a wide variety of species intensively planted for year round colour and easy maintenance. TEAS. *Adm £1.50 Chd free (Share to Stanley Pontlarge Church®). Suns March 27, April 17, May 15, June 12, July 10, Aug 7, Sept 4, Oct 2; (2-5) Private visits welcome, please Tel 0242 603337*

Bourton House Garden ❀❀ (Mr & Mrs R Paice) Bourton-on-the-Hill 2m W of Moreton-in-Marsh on A44. This handsome C18 Cotswold village house (not open) with fine views is enhanced by a medium sized garden largely created under the present ownership. Well kept lawns, quiet fountains, a knot garden and stone walls set off a number of imaginatively planted herbaceous borders. New for 1994, long terraces on the main lawn to be planted with low growing shrubs, perennials and alpines. C16 tithe barn where you can help yourself to TEAS. *Adm £2 Chd free. Every Thurs & Fri May 26 to Sept 30 (12-5). For NGS last Thurs of every month. Also Bank Hol Mons May 30, Aug 29 (12-5) in conjunction with* **Bourton-on-the-Hill Gardens** *Suns May 29, Aug 28*

Bourton-on-the-Hill Gardens ❀❀ 2m NW Moreton-in-Marsh A44 to Broadway. Wide selection of gardens of varied character in charming hillside village. Plant stall. Cream TEAS (2-5). *Gardens adm £2.50 (including* **Bourton House** *as above) Chd free (Share to village Old School®). Suns May 29, Aug 28 (1-6)*

> **The Chantry** (Mr & Mrs J Coram-James) Large lawns with mixed borders – excellent views
> **3 Chantry Gardens** (Mr & Mrs G Glaser) Small well planned garden with pond
> **Glebe House** (Sir Peter & Lady Herbert) Ex rectory garden. Mixed borders. Views
> **Hillcrest** (Mr & Mrs M Gaden) Small garden, mixed borders
> **Porch House** (Mr & Mrs A Firth) Established terraced garden next to Churchyard
> **Springwood** (Mr & Mrs D Storey) Cottage garden. Mixed borders
> **Tawnies** (Mr & Mrs P Hayes) Raised beds with ericaceous plants. Long lawn

25 Bowling Green Road see Cirencester gardens

Brackenbury ❀ (Mr & Mrs Peter Heaton) Coombe, 1m NE of Wotton-under-Edge. From Wotton Church ½m on Stroud rd (B4058) turn right (signed Coombe); from Stroud left off B4058, 300yds past Wotton-under-Edge

sign; house 300yds on right. ⅔-acre terraced plantsman's and flower arranger's garden; foliage a special feature. Well stocked mixed borders, cottage garden, pool; 600 different hardy perennials and 200 different shrubs. Fruitcage, vegetables on deep-bed system. National Collection of Erigeron cultivars. Home-made TEAS. *Adm £1 Chd free (Share to Cotswold Care Hospice®). Mon May 30, Suns June 26, July 31, Mon Aug 29 (2-6)*

¶**Bredon Manor** ❀ (Mr & Mrs Richard George) 3m from Tewkesbury on the B4080. The house is next to the NT Tithe Barn in Bredon. 5 acres of well stocked formal gardens incl a ½ acre walled kitchen garden, a walled rose garden, sunken garden of various shrub roses and hostas, water garden with C17 monks fishpond and riverside meadows. Cream TEAS in aid of Save the Children. *Adm £2 Chd free. Sun April 10 (2-5)*

Broad Campden Gardens &❀❀ 5m E of Broadway 1m SE of Chipping Campden. TEAS at Village Hall. *Combined adm £2.50 or 60p each garden Chd free. Sun July 10 (2-6). Free car park. Coaches by appt only Tel 0386 840467*

> **The Angel House** (Mr & Mrs Bill Boddington) Garden in old damson and apple orchard, with view of church and C17 and C18 cottages
> **Cherry Orchard Cottage** (Mr & Mrs David Brook) ¾-acre orchard, shrub bank and secret garden
> **The Farthings** (Mr & Mrs John Astbury) Terraced cottage garden
> **The Malt House** (Mr & Mrs Nick Brown) Sheltered garden with small stream, being gradually replanted with shrubs from herbaceous for simplified management
> **Manor Barn** (Mr Michael Miles & Mr Christopher Gurney) 1½-acres. Formal terraces, sweeping cultivated meadow, newly planted woodland and shrubbery, boundary of wandering stream with falls
> **Oldstones** (Mr & Mrs H R Rolfe) A new ¾-acre garden, started 1989. Designed and constructed with the exception of the stone walling by the owners; terraced garden leading down to a stream with lawns, shrubs and roses
> **Pinders** (Mr & Mrs Ian Dunnett) 1-acre garden on several levels, rare shrubs and trees
> **Sharcomb Furlong** (Mr & Mrs Basil Hasberry) ¾-acre; wide range of shrubs, shrub roses and trees
> **Vine Cottage** (J M Murray) Small cottage garden in idyllic situation. Large selection of roses and herbaceous around a well and lawn
> **Withy Bank** (Mr & Mrs Jim Allen) ½-acre; acers and shrubs

Brockweir Gardens &❀❀ From A466 Chepstow to Monmouth rd, cross R Wye to Brockweir, ¾m uphill take L turning to Coldharbour, L at Xrds. 2m Tintern Abbey. TEAS at Laurel Cottage & Fernleigh. *Adm 75p each garden. Suns March 27, April 24, May 29, June 26, July 31, Aug 28, Sept 25 (2-6)*

> **Fernleigh** (Capt & Mrs J P Gould) 2½ acres of well established garden situated at an altitude of 500'. Many old trees, camellias and spring bulb collection. A peaceful garden with splendid views across the valley of the R Wye. *Suns March 27, April 24, May 29, June 26, Sept 25 only*

Laurel Cottage ⭑ (David & Jean Taylor) Informal 1-acre cottage garden with lovely views over Offas Dyke. Dry stone walling creates gardens within a garden with lawns, herbaceous flowers and spring bulbs. Interesting selection of unusual shrubs and plants. Outside the main garden are a small vegetable garden, arboretum and orchard. *Private visits welcome all year, please* Tel **0291 689565**

Threeways (Iorrie & Gwen Williams) Follow signs from A466 Brockweir Bridge or from B4228 at Hewelsfield Xrds: also on foot from Laurel Cottage. 2-acre garden developed since 1984. Former paddock planted with unusual shrubs and trees. Small woodland area, bog garden and stream. Formal area with water feature and well stocked herbaceous borders. *Private visits welcome, please* Tel **0291 689686**

Burnside see Prestbury and Southam Gardens

Camp Cottage ⭑❀❁ (Mr L R Holmes & Mr S O'Neill) Highleadon, nr Newent. 6m NW of Gloucester. From Glos take A40 Ross rd, turn R onto B4215 Newent rd, 2½m along turn R at sign for Upleadon. The cottage is about 100yds up lane on L hand side. A plant lovers C17 cottage garden. ¾-acre approx. Old roses, pergola with arches, climbing plants, many unusual plants including alpines, shrubs, perennials, herbs. Short shrubland walk and Bog garden. Widely featured incl TV 'Gardeners' World'and 1993 Channel 4 TV Garden Club. TEA on Suns and some weekdays *Adm £1 Chd 50p. Suns, Tues April 3 to Sept 25. Mons May 16 to July 18. Bank Hol Mons April 4, May 2, 30; Aug 29 (2-6). Private visits welcome all year, please* Tel **0452 790352**

Campden House ⭑❀ (Mr & Mrs Philip Smith) Chipping Campden. Drive entrance on Chipping Campden to Weston Subedge rd, about ¼m SW of Campden. 2-acre garden with mixed borders of plant and colour interest; fine parkland; Manor house with C17 tithe barn in hidden valley. TEAS and plant stall in aid of the Gloucestershire Macmillan Nurses. *Adm £1 Chd free. Sun June 26 (2-6)*

Casa Mia ⭑❀ (Mr & Mrs Bryan Jones) Clifford Manor, Judges Lane. Off B4216 Newent to Huntley rd approx 2½m from Newent turn R signposted May Hill. Garden is on L about ¾m. Enthusiast's 1½-acre garden in idyllic setting. Mixed shrub and herbaceous borders, with a variety of plants, some unusual. Plants labelled. Mature trees, stream and vegetable garden. TEAS. Parking available within grounds. *Adm £1 Chd free. Suns July 10, 17, 24; Thurs July 21 (2-6). Groups by appt July only, please* Tel **0452 830404**

Cerney House see North Cerney Gardens

Chalford Gardens ❁ 4m E of Stroud on A419 to Cirencester. Both gardens on Marle Hill high above the Chalford Vale are reached on foot by steep climb from car park on main rd. Teas at Springfield House Hotel, opp side of A419. *Combined adm £1.50 Chd free. Sat, Sun, June 18, 19 (11-5)*

   Brendan House (Anthony J Ault) Approx 1-acre garden on steep hillside, partly terraced with some sculpture and architectural features adding to the structured informality of the choice of plants and mature wooded setting with its fine views.

   The Old Chapel (F J & F Owen) Artists' 1-acre Victorian chapel garden on precipitous hillside. A tiered tapestry of herbaceous borders, formal potager, small orchard, pond and summer house, old roses. Gothic pergola and rose tunnel, many unusual plants all laid out on terraced S-facing Marle Cliff. Biennial studio Exhibition of garden paintings. Featured in Gardens Illustrated Dec '93 edition

The Chestnuts ❁❀ (Mr & Mrs E H Gwynn) Minchinhampton. From Nailsworth by Avening rd (B4014) L Weighbridge Inn ¼m up hill. From Minchinhampton 1m via New Rd or Well Hill. ⅔-acre walled garden; shrubs; bulbs; roses; clematis; rock garden; pool garden; wildflower lawn. ⅔-acre arboretum, planted since 1972 with wide variety of unusual trees and shrubs inc many sorbus species and shrub roses. Lovely views of hills, woods and fields. Featured Channel 4 TV Garden Club Oct '93. *Adm £1.50 Chd free (Share to Gloucestershire Wildlife Trust®). Sun June 5 (2-6)*

The Chipping Croft – See Tetbury Gardens

Cirencester Gardens Cecily Hill is on W side of Cirencester near gates into Park and open air swimming pool. TEAS at 42 Cecily Hill. *Combined adm £2 Chd under 16 free. Sun July 17 (2-6)*

   ¶**25 Bowling Green Road** (Fr & Mrs John Beck) From Cirencester take A417 to Gloucester just to traffic lights, cross or turn R into The Whiteway then 1st L to no 25 on R of rd bend. Please respect neighbours' driveways, no pavement parking. Fast developing new garden of owners recently moved from well-known garden in Cecily Hill. Many perennials, roses and clematis, and some plant surprises. Featured Channel 4 TV Garden Club Oct 93. *Also open Suns June 5, 12, 19; July 10, 24, Aug 7, 14 Adm £1 (2-5)*

   40 Cecily Hill. Exhibition of botanical pictures and china by Annette Firth, NDD, SBA

   42 Cecily Hill (Mr & Mrs Philip Beckerlegge) Medium-sized walled family garden. Clematis, roses, herbaceous border; shrubs, rock garden.

   Cecily Hill House (Mr & Mrs Rupert de Zoete) Walled town garden with tranquil atmosphere; herbaceous and shrub borders; small ornamental kitchen garden. *Private visits also welcome mid June to July 31, please* Tel **0285 653766**

   20 St Peter's Road ❀ (Meg and Jeff Blumsom) Off Cricklade St. turn R into Ashcroft Rd then L then R. Small town garden entirely remade without grass; herbaceous, clematis, rockery, pond. Featured in The Gardener, May 91. *Also open Sun July 10 Adm 50p (2-6). Private visits welcome, please* Tel **0285 657696**

Combend Manor ❁❀ (Mr & Mrs Noel Gibbs) Elkstone. On A417 halfway between Cirencester and Cheltenham turn R signed Elkstone immediately R through pillars 1m on R. 3-acre mature garden in beautiful setting, partly laid out by Gertrude Jekyll; a variety of gardens within the main garden incl arboretum; water garden; old-fashioned roses, heather garden. TEAS. *Adm £1.50 Chd £1.00 (Share to Elkstone Parish Church®). Sun July 3 (2-6)*

Cotswold Farm ⚹ (Major & Mrs P D Birchall) 5m N of Cirencester on A417; signed immediately W of Five Mile House Inn. Cotswold garden in lovely position on different levels with a terrace designed by Norman Jewson in 1938; shrubs, mixed borders, alpine border, spring flowers, shrub roses; walled kitchen garden. *Adm £1.50 Chd free. Sun June 19 (2-6). Private visits welcome May, June and July Adm £2, please* **Tel 0285 653856**

Daylesford House Ꮭⵕ❁ (Sir Anthony & Lady Bamford) Daylesford. Between Stow-on-the-Wold and Chipping Norton off A436. Magnificent lakeside and woodland walks amidst unusual shrubs and trees and massed plantings of spring bulbs. Large decorative formal fruit and vegetable walled garden with orchid house, peach house and working glasshouses. Trellised rose garden on raised terrace. Grounds immediately around the Grade 1 house not open *Adm £1.50 Chd free (Share to Daylesford Church and 'Church of our Lady' Stow®). Weds April 20, June 29 (2-6)*

Eastcombe, Bussage & Brownshill Gardens 3m E Stroud. 2m N of A419 Stroud to Cirencester on turning signposted to Bisley and Eastcombe. Cream TEAS at Eastcombe Village Hall. *Combined adm £2.50 Chd free (Share to Glos Macmillan Nurses Appeal®). Sun, Mon, May 1, 2 (2-6)*
Eastcombe:
　Ashcroft (Mr & Mrs H T Cornell) Dr Crouch's Rd. Small garden with many bulbs, primulas and year-round colour
　Brewers Cottage Ꮭ (Mr & Mrs T G N Carter) Easily managed hillside garden with laburnum covered pergola, shady & sunny borders and a small hidden courtyard. All year colour
　21 Farmcote Close Ꮭⵕ (Mr & Mrs R Bryant) A housing estate garden, designed with curved beds to soften appearance. Over 300 varieties of interesting perennials, bulbs, shrubs and old roses on various colour themes. Espalier fruit
　Fidges Hill House (Mr & Mrs R Lewis) From building site with knee high weeds to cottage garden in 7 years; secluded and lovely view. No car access, please park in village
　Glenview (Mr & Mrs J Carroll) Dr Crouch's Road. 5-yr-old garden; colour scheme of yellow, blue and white with two exceptions.
　Jasmine Cottage (Mr & Mrs K Hopkins) Colourful cottage garden with view of the beautiful Toadsmoor valley. *Sun May 1 only*
　Vatch Rise Ꮭⵕ (Mr & Mrs R G Abbott) Small garden with beautiful view. Extensive and interesting collection of bulbous plants, alpines and unusual perennials
Brownshill:
　¶**Beechcroft** Ꮭ (Mr & Mrs R H Salt) Garden surrounds Edwardian House bounded by meadow. Mature trees, shrubs, borders, vegetables, fruit, conservatory and wild area
　Bovey End (Sir Norman & Lady Wakefield) Brownshill. A large, informal garden sloping steeply with beautiful views across the Golden and Toadsmoor Valleys; many trees and shrubs
Bussage:
　Pine Corner (Mr & Mrs W Burns-Brown) ¾-acre terraced garden overlooking Toadsmoor Valley. Spring bulbs, shrubs, alpines; kitchen & herb garden. TEA

Redwood ❁ (Mr & Mrs D Collins) Terraced garden with informal lawns and planting; trees; shrubs; bulbs; alpines and vegetable garden with cordon fruit trees
Spindrift, The Ridge Ꮭ (Mr & Mrs B Wilson) Small garden on housing estate devoted largely to plant breeding experiments including a foxglove mutation

Eastington Gardens 1m SE of Northleach (A40). Charming Cotswold village with lovely views. TEAS at **Middle End**. *Combined adm £1.50 Chd free (Share to Northleach Church®). Suns, Mons May 29, 30, Aug 28, 29 (2-6)*
　Bank Cottage (Mr & Mrs E S Holland) Lower End. Colourful cottage garden
　Middle End ❁ (Mr & Mrs Owen Slatter) Medium-sized garden of general interest
　Yew Tree Cottage (M Bottone Esq) Cottage garden with shade-loving plants

Ewen Manor Ꮭ (Lady Gibbs) 4m S of Cirencester via A429 3m from Cirencester turn at signpost Ewen 1m. Medium-sized garden; herbaceous border, lily pool, sunken garden, cedar trees, yew hedges, Georgian Cotswold manor (not open). TEAS. *Adm £1.50 Chd free (Share to Gloucestershire Association for Mental Health®). Sun May 15 (2-6). Also private visits welcome, please* **Tel 0285 770206**

Frampton-on-Severn Gardens Ꮭ SW of Gloucester nr Stonehouse 2m from M5 junction 13. TEAS in Village Hall in aid of WI. *Adm 60p per garden Chd free (Share to Gloucestershire Wildlife Trust and International League for Protection of Horses and NCCPG, Glos®). Sun June 12 (2-6)*
　Buckholt (Brigadier & Mrs C E H Sparrow) 200yds beyond the S end of the village green on the L. Walled garden of about 1-acre, mature trees, shrubs and herbaceous borders, lavender garden with roses
　Frampton Court (Mrs P F S Clifford) L hand side of village green. Fine view of Gothic orangery, 1760, standing at the end of a formal canal with water lilies and mixed shrub border on one side. Mature trees. *Groups welcome, please* **Tel 0452 740267**
　Frampton Manor (Mr & Mrs Rollo Clifford) R hand side of village green. Fragrant walled garden with yew and lavender hedges. Mixed shrub and herbaceous borders. C15 timbered house, reputed birthplace of 'Fair Rosamund'

¶**Gardeners Way** ⵕ❁ (GRBS) Kings Stanley, 3m W of Stroud off A419, 2nd turn R after church in village. The ten bungalows provided by the Gardeners' Royal Benevolent Society for retired gardeners are a colourful showpiece of gardening skills. The gardens are all of individual design and character and contain many interesting plants and ideas. Seen on HTV May 1993 at the official opening by Rosemary Verey. Gardening questions gladly answered. TEA. *Adm £1.50 OAP's £1 Chd under 14 free (Share to the GRBS®). Sun July 24 (2-6)*

Regular Openers. Too many days to include in diary. Usually there is a wide range of plants giving year-round interest. See head of county section for the name and garden description for times etc.

Gentian Cottage ✿❀ (Mrs J D Lefeaux) Stow-on-the-Wold. From Bourton on A429 continue N over both sets of traffic lights in Stow - 100yds after second lights turn L into Fosse Lane. Small garden partly replanted during the last few years. Shrubs, bulbs, herbaceous borders – rock plants a speciality, including gentians. *Adm 50p Chd free. Private visits welcome May 2 to Aug 29, please* **Tel 0451 830322**

Green Cottage &❀ (Mr & Mrs F Baber) At far end of Lydney from Gloucester on A48 turn R into narrow lane just after derestriction sign. Garden 50 yds on R. Ample shady car park. An informal country garden of approx 1 acre with planted stream bank, hostas, hellebores, iris and cottage garden. Many herbaceous paeonies, incl the National Reference Collection of pre and early post 1900 cultivars (1824-1918). Collection featured in Homes and Gardens. Large wayward specimen of clematis montana rubens (May). Specie and officinalis paeonies (May). National Collection 60-70 cultivars (June) Hellebores (Feb and March). TEAS Suns May, June & Sept only. *Adm £1 Chd free. Suns Feb 27, March 6, 13, 20 (12.30-4.00) (Hellebores), May 1, 8, 15, 22, 29 June 5, 12, 19, Sept 4, 11, (2-6) Weds June 1, 8, 15 (11-5)*

Grove Cottage ✿❀ (Mr Graham Birkin & Mr Allan Thomas) Forge Hill, Lower Lydbrook. 5m NW of Cinderford. Leave car in public car park by river, mount facing flight of 115 steps to Forge Hill: garden 2nd L from top step. 2-acre garden on precipitous slope overlooking Wye valley. Many steps and steep paths to negotiate but a garden full of unusual plants and bulbs. Peat beds, pond, raised herbaceous beds, shrub borders and ¼-acre rockery with many little known alpines. Extensive collection of iris and shade loving plants. Not suitable for small children. TEA. *Adm £1 Chd 50p. Every Sun March 6 to Sept 18, Mons May 2, 30 (2-6). Private visits welcome, please* **Tel 0594 860544**

Hartpury College &✿❀ Hartpury House, 5m N of Gloucester. Take A417 Gloucester-Ledbury; clearly signposted. 14 acres; large lawns; trees, shrubs and terraces; glasshouses; herbaceous borders; alpine beds; late Victorian ornamental gardens designed by Thomas Mawson. TEA. *Adm £1 Chd free. Sun May 29 (2-5)*

Hidcote Manor Garden &✿❀ (The National Trust) 4m NE of Chipping Campden. Series of formal gardens, many enclosed within superb hedges, incl hornbeam on stems. Many rare trees, shrubs, plants. Coffee, lunches and teas. *Adm £4.80 Chd £2.40. Daily except Tues & Fri, April to Oct 31 (11-7); no entry after 6 or an hour before dusk if earlier). For NGS Sun May 8 (11-6)*

Hodges Barn &❀ (Mr & Mrs C N Hornby) Shipton Moyne 3m S of Tetbury on Malmesbury side of Shipton Moyne. Very unusual C15 dovecot converted into a family home. Cotswold stone walls act as host to climbing and rambling roses, clematis, vines and hydrangeas; and together with yew, rose and tapestry hedges they create the formality of the area around the house; mixed shrub and herbaceous borders, shrub roses and a water garden; woodland garden planted with cherries, magnolias and spring bulbs. Featured in Country Life & House & Garden. Also open for NGS; adjoining garden of **Hodges Farm-**

house, by kind permission of Mr & Mrs Clive Lamb. *Combined adm £2 Chd free. Mons, Tues & Fris April 1 to Aug 15 (2-5). For NGS Suns April 3, May 1, June 5 July 3 (2-6). Private visits and parties welcome, teas by arrangement, please* **Tel 0666 880202**

Home Farm (Mrs T Freeman) Huntley. On the B4216 ½m from the A40 in Huntley travelling towards Newent. The house and gardens are in an elevated position with exceptional views over the Vale of Gloucester and up to the Cotswold escarpment. Over 1m of woodchip paths winding through woods to show carpets of spring flowers. Snowdrops, wood anemones, daffodils, bluebells and orchids. Enclosed garden with heather bed and fern border. One wood recently planted with rhododendrons and azaleas. *Adm £1 Chd free. Thurs Feb 3, 17, March 3, 17, 31, April 14, 28, May 12, 26 (2-6 or dusk if earlier)*

Hunts Court &✿❀ (Mr & Mrs T K Marshall) North Nibley, Dursley. 2m NW of Wotton-under-Edge. From Wotton B4060 Dursley rd turn R in Nibley at Black Horse; fork L after ¼m. Unusual shrubs, 450 varieties old roses, large collection of penstemons in peaceful 2½-acre garden with lawns set against tree clad hills and Tyndale monument. Superb views. House (not open) probably birth place of William Tyndale. Picnic area. Home-made TEAS (Suns only). *Adm £1 Chd free. Garden and Nursery open Tues-Sat all year ex Aug; also Bank Hol Mons. For NGS Suns June 12, 19, 26; July 3, 10 (2-6); Private visits welcome, please* **Tel 0453 547440**

8 Hyatts Way ✿❀ (Mr & Mrs P M Herbert and Paul Herbert) Bishops Cleeve, 4m N of Cheltenham; take A435 towards Evesham, at roundabout take road to Bishops Cleeve; at Bishops Cleeve turn R past Esso Garage, follow road to school, turn L, then 2nd R. Small plantsman's garden, slightly untidy but featuring over 500 varieties, inc digitalis and salvia species; many other unusual plants and alpines in sinks. *Adm 70p Chd 25p. Private visits welcome April 10 to Aug 7, please* **Tel 0242 673503**

Icomb Place ✿ (Mr & Mrs T L F Royle) 4m S of Stow-on-the-Wold; after 2m on A424 Burford rd turn L to Icomb village. 100-year-old sizeable garden extensively restored. Featuring woodland walk through mature & young trees in arboretum; rhododendrons & azaleas; grotto; pools, stream and water garden; parterre; lawned garden with extensive views. C14 manor house (not open). TEAS. *Adm £2 Chd £1 (Share to Deus Laudamus Trust®). Sun May 29 (2-6)*

Jasmine House &✿❀ (Mr & Mrs V M Bond) Bream. In picturesque Royal Forest of Dean. From Lydney take B4231 Bream rd; in 3 miles turn R to village; immediately after Xrds turn R into concealed lane Blue Rock Crescent opp. school; house 200yds on L. Plantsman's garden of ¾ acre; alpines, fuchsias, bonsai, old-fashioned cottage plants, many unusual plants. Featured in Amateur Gardening Aug 93 *Adm £1 Chd free. Suns April 3, 17; May 1, 15, 29; June 12, 26; July 10, 24; Aug 7, 21, 28; Sept 11. Bank Hol Mons April 4, May 2, 30; Aug 29, Thurs April 14, 28, May 12, 26, June 9, 23; July 7, 21; Aug 4, 18, 25 Sept 8 (2-6). Private visits welcome all the year. Garden clubs especially welcome, please* **Tel 0594 563688**

Kemble Gardens 4m SW of Cirencester on A429 to Malmesbury. TEAS by WI Kemble House. *Combined adm £1.50 Chd free. Sun June 19 (2-6)*

Kemble House ᐊᐧᐡ (Mrs Donald Peachey) Large, mature, old-fashioned garden makes a lovely setting for Teas

Limes Cottage ᐊᐧᐡ (Mrs M Brazier) Small walled garden; mixed planting shrubs and herbaceous; shrub roses; troughs; small pond

Old Orchard ᐊᐧᐡ (Mr & Mrs J K Johnston) A cottage style garden with herbaceous and shrub areas; roses and clematis; pond and alpines; urns and hanging baskets; plant filled conservatory

Kiftsgate Court ᐧᐡ (Mr & Mrs J G Chambers) 3m NE of Chipping Campden, adjacent to Hidcote Nat Trust Garden. 1m E of A46 and B4081. Magnificent situation and views; many unusual plants and shrubs; tree paeonies, hydrangeas, abutilons, species and old-fashioned roses, inc largest rose in England, R.filipes Kiftsgate. TEAS (May 14, 29 to Aug 31). Buses by appt. *Adm £2.50 Chd £1. Suns, Weds, Thurs & Bank Hols April 1 to Sept 30. Also Sats in June & July (2-6). For NGS (Share to Sue Ryder Home, Leckhampton Court®) Sats May 14, Aug 20, (2-6)*

Lindors Country House (Alan & Sandra Irving) St. Briavels off A466 Bigsweir Bridge 8m S of Monmouth 10m N of Chepstow. Mature gardens laid out over 100 yrs ago; meandering streams with steps; waterfalls and ponds descend to River Wye; 9-acre tranquil grounds with many non-native trees, shrubs and fine views of Wye Valley. TEAS in marquee. *Adm £1.50 Chd free. Sun May 15 (2-6)*

Lower Meend Gardens ᐧᐡ 5m NW Lydney nr St Briavels, ½m from St Briavels Castle down B4228 to hairpin bend. Walk of 200yds from car parking. No coaches. TEA **Brook Cottage** in aid of Cobalt Unit, Cheltenham. *Combined adm £1.50 Chd free. Sun May 22 (11-5)*

Bank House (Wallace & Sylvia Neale) Terraced hillside garden intensively planted with shrubs, herbaceous and alpine plants; troughs. Approx ¼-acre. Magnificent views of Wye Valley. *Private visits welcome June to Sept, please Tel 0594 530433*

Brook Cottage (Patrick & Ann Mills) Sloping landscaped garden with small parterre and other interesting features

The Hampden (Phillip & Doreen Powell-Tuck) About 1½ acres of wild garden and shrubs, including azaleas and rhododendrons; many lesser known hardy plants to discover in the meandering terraced beds; paddock with ornamental trees

Lydney Park ᐡ (Viscount Bledisloe) Lydney. On A48 Gloucester-Chepstow rd between Lydney & Aylburton. Drive is directly off A48. 8 acres of extensive valley garden with many varieties of rhododendron, azaleas and other flowering shrubs; trees and lakes. Garden round house; magnolias and daffodils (April). Roman Temple Site and Museum. Deer park with fine trees. TEAS; also picnic area (in park). *Adm £2 Weds £1 (Acc chd & cars free). Easter Sun & Mon; Every Sun, Wed & Bank Hol from Sun April 3 to June 5, but every day Sunday May 29 to June 5 (11-6). For NGS Sun April 24, Wed May 4 (11-6). Also private parties welcome, please Tel 0594 842844*

The Manor ᐊᐧᐡ (Robert Hitchins Ltd) Boddington 3m W of Cheltenham off the A4019 Cheltenham to Tewkesbury rd. After crossing the M5 motorway take first turning L which is signed to Boddington. Old garden altered and restored since 1985 including wild flower woodland walk, mature specimen trees, extensive lawns and lakes with recently planted bog garden, and large collection of conifers. Neo-Gothic manor house (not open). Cream TEAS. *Adm £1 Chd free. Sun May 8 (2-6)*

Millend House ᐧᐡ (Mr & Mrs J D'A Tremlett) Coleford. 1½m SW out of Coleford on the Newland road, centre of Coleford clocktower signposted (Newland 2m). 2-acre hillside garden with picturesque valley views; many varied & interesting herbaceous and shade-loving plants & shrubs. Paths to secluded seating places & through well-maintained wood. Also small vegetable garden & gazebo. TEAS in aid of Gloucestershire Macmillan Nurses. *Adm £1 Chd free. Suns May 1, 15, 29; Mon May 2, 30; Suns June 12, July 3, 24; Aug 14, 28, Mon Aug 29 (2-6). Private groups welcome May 1 to Sept 30, please Tel 0594 832128*

Minchinhampton Gardens ᐊᐧᐡ Minchinhampton 4m SE Stroud. From Market Sq down High St 100yds; then right at Xrds; 300yds turn left. Free car parking. Over 8 acres of adjacent gardens. Cream TEAS. *Combined adm £2 Chd free (Share to Minchinhampton Centre for the Elderly®). Suns March 13, April 10, July 31, Mon Aug 1 (2-6)*

Derhams House (Mr & Mrs Mark Byng) Garden created since 1957; water garden; shrubs, herbaceous borders; snowdrops and crocus in March

Lammas Park (Mr & Mrs P Grover) Lawns, herbaceous borders, wild garden, restored 'hanging gardens'. Superb views

St Francis (Mr & Mrs Peter Falconer) Garden made in old park round modern Cotswold stone house. Fine beech avenue; terraced garden; trough gardens; bonsai trees; unusual plants; giant snowdrops (spring); C18 ice-house. Picnickers welcome. *Also private visits welcome, please Tel 0453 882188*

Misarden Park ᐊᐧᐡ (Maj M T N H Wills) Miserden 6m NW of Circencester. Follow the signs off the A417 or B4070 from Stroud. Spring flowers, shrubs, fine topiary (some designed by Sir Edwin Lutyens) and herbaceous borders within a walled garden; roses (recently refurbished); fine specimen trees; C17 manor house (not open) standing high overlooking Golden Valley. Garden featured in 'Country Life' 1992. Garden Nurseries open daily except Mons. TEAS. *Adm £2 Chd free. April 5 to Sept 29 every Tues, Wed & Thurs (9.30-4.30). For NGS (Share to Miserden Village Hall©) Suns April 10, July 3 (2-6)*

Newark Park (Mr Robert Parsons) Ozleworth, 1½m E of Wotton-under-Edge, 1½m S of junc A4135/B4058. Steeply terraced romantic woodland garden in 10 acres around C16 hunting lodge house (not open). Spring bulbs and cyclamen on hillside leading down to carp pond and C18 walled garden and summer house. Garden under restoration. Spectacular views. TEAS. *Adm £1 Chd 50p (Share to the Arthritis and Rheumatism Council©). Suns March 27, April 3 (2-5)*

North Cerney & Marsden Manor Gardens North Cerney, with famous C13 church, 4m N Cirencester on A435 Cheltenham road. **Cerney House** behind church: **Scrubditch Farm** on Woodmancote-Perrots Brook Lane. Woodland walk between the two gardens. **Marsden Manor** on A435 midway between Rendcomb and Colesbourne. *Combined adm £2 Chd free. Sun June 5 (2-6)*
Cerney House ♿✿❀ (Sir Michael & Lady Angus) Large mature garden with trees, shrubs, lawns, old roses, spring bulbs. Herb & rock gardens. Walled garden with herbaceous borders and vegetables. TEAS June 5 only. *Also open all year. Adm £1.50 Chd free every Tues Wed and Fris (2-6)*
Marsden Manor ❀ (Mr & Mrs Richard Worsley) A series of characterful gardens and growing areas. Mature herbaceous borders, elevated rose bed; fish pond, large variety of shrubs and trees. Dogs may be walked in scenic woodland grounds along the R. Churn
Scrubditch Farm ♿✿❀ (Mr & Mrs J Herdman) 3-acre informal garden evolved over the years from an orchard. New planting this season. Mainly trees and shrubs with old roses. Planted and maintained for wildlife. TEAS

North Rye House ♿✿❀ (Mr & Mrs Peter Stoddart) nr Broadwell, Moreton-in-Marsh. On A429 Foss Way halfway between Moreton-in-Marsh and Stow-on-the-Wold. Also signed from Broadwell village. Recently created and still developing 3-acre garden with modern ha-ha designed to blend scenically into its surrounding parkland setting with mature trees. Spring bulbs, mixed borders, shrub roses, alpines, small vegetable garden and gardener's cottage garden provide continuous colour and interest. TEAS. *Adm £1 Chd free. Suns April 3, June 26 (2-5)*

Nympsfield Gardens ✿❀ 3m NW of Nailsworth. Signed from B4066 Stroud-Dursley rd. TEAS **Coach House**. *Combined adm £1.50 Chd free (Share to St Bartholomews Church and Nympsfield Village Hall©). Suns May 1, 29 (2-6)*
Barberi Cottage ❀ (Mrs F Mack) Small garden with alpines. *May 1, 29*
Bath Road Farm (Mr & Mrs K Wright) Windswept cottage garden under construction; interesting wild plants, pond, vegetables. *May 1, 29*
Candle Cottage (Mr & Mrs A N Pearce) Small landscaped cottage garden. *May 29*
The Coach House (Mr & Mrs R Overton) Small tree-lined garden. Unusual plants all labelled. *May 1, 29*
Four Wells (Mr J Price) Small cottage garden. *May 29*
Highlands (Mr & Mrs R Easton) Garden on sloping windswept site. *May 1*
Pen-y-Banc (Mr Philip Reynolds) adjoining above garden. *May 1, 29*
The Post Office (Mr & Mrs B Westwood) Small garden featuring heathers & violas. *May 1, 29*
White Hart Court (Mr & Mrs M Reynolds) Small formal garden with pool. C 16 Coach House (part open). *May 1, 29*

By Appointment Gardens. These owners do not have a fixed opening day usually because they do not like crowds or have insufficient parking space. Owner will often give guided tour.

The Old Manor ♿✿❀ (Mrs Joan Wilder) Twyning. 3m N of Tewkesbury via A38 to Worcester; follow sign to Twyning; garden opposite T-junction at top end of village. 2 acres, walled garden full of interest. Unusual shrubs, trees, herbaceous, alpines; two areas of developing arboretum; pool; terrace plantings; troughs. Field walks for picnics. Featured in TV 'Gardeners World'. Small nursery, all stock from garden (catalogue 30p and large SAE). TEA on Bank Hol Mons only. *Adm £1.30 Chd 60p (Share to GRBS & RGOF®). Every Mon Mar 1 to Oct 31 (2-5, or dusk if earlier) Private visits welcome except Suns including winter months, please* **Tel 0684 293516** *evenings*

Old Mill Dene, Blockley ✿❀ (Mr & Mrs B S Dare) School Lane, Blockley. From A44, Bourton-on-the-Hill, take the turn to Blockley. 1m down hill turn left behind 30mph sign, labelled cul de sac. 2½-acre garden with steep lawned terraces facing south and a mill-pool in a frost pocket with stream. Vegetable garden parterre with views over the hills. Dangerous for young children. TEAS Suns only. *Adm £1.50 Chd 50p (Share to Gloucestershire Churches Preservation Trust®). Sun April 3 (2-6) Thurs June 2, 9, 16, 23, 30. Also open with* **Blockley Gardens** *Suns May 1, June 26. Private visits welcome April to July & Sept, please* **Tel 0386 700457**

¶**Orchard Cottage** ✿❀ (Mr & Mrs H L Pierce) Beverston, 2m W of Tetbury on A4135 rd to Dursley. On corner by memorial garden. ⅔-acre. Shrubs, roses, knotted weeping ash, ivies and ferns. Walled garden at back in shallow quarry with mixed borders, kitchen garden, herbs, fruit tunnel and small wooded walk. *Adm £1 Chd free. Sun, Mon July 3, 4 (2-6)*

Orchard Cottage ✿❀ (Mr Rory Stuart) Gretton. 2m N of Winchcombe. Up Duglinch Lane beside Bugatti Inn in the middle of Gretton. Approx 300yds up lane turn R after Magnolia Grandiflora and opp black railings. Approx 1½-acres. Romantically overplanted, owner-maintained garden, created largely by the late Mrs Nancy Saunders. Always some interest. Teas in Winchcombe. *Adm £1. Open all year. Private visits welcome, please* **Tel 0242 602491**

Osborne House ♿❀ (Mr & Mrs G L Atkinson-Willes) Frocester. 2m SW of Stonehouse (or 2m S of M5 junction 13) midway between Eastington and Frocester. 2 acres containing herbaceous and shrub borders, island beds; many spring bulbs; small arboretum planted since 1975 incl collection of birches; climbing plants on house and outbuilding walls. Dried flowers. TEA. *Adm £1 Chd free. Sun April 17 (2-6). Private visits welcome March to Sept, please* **Tel 0453 822579**

Oxwold House ♿ (Mr & Mrs James D'Arcy Clark) Barnsley. 4m NE of Cirencester. From A433 Cirencester-Burford rd, on the outskirts of Barnsley, turn L signposted Coln Rogers. 3-acre garden surrounded by parkland with woodland walk; shrubs; trees; herbaceous borders; mature chestnut avenue approach and fine view. Cream TEAS. *Adm £1.50 Chd free. Sun July 10 (2-6)*

Painswick Rococo Garden ✿ (Painswick Rococo Garden Trust Reg no 299792) ½m outside village on B4073. Unique C18 garden restoration from the brief Rococo period combining contemporary buildings, vistas, ponds and winding woodland walks. Coach House restaurant for coffee, lunches, TEAS. 'Present Collection' shop. *Adm £2.50 OAP £2.10 Chd £1.25. Feb 2 to mid-December. Weds to Sundays and Bank Hol Mons (11-5). Private groups welcome, please* **Tel 0452 813204.** *For NGS Suns March 27, Oct 9 (11-5)*

¶**Pigeon House** see Prestbury and Southam Gardens

Pinbury Park ⬥ (Mr & Mrs John Mullings) Cirencester 6½m. Signed off Sapperton-Winstone rd between A419 and A417. 5-acres; topiary, yew avenue, lawns, bulbs, impressive view, gazebo. Tudor Manor house (not open) former Royal residence of King Penda. *Adm £1 Chd 50p. Suns April 17, July 17 (2-5)*

Pitt Court ⬥✗✿ (Mr & Mrs M W Hall) North Nibley. Turn E off the B4060 at North Nibley past the Black Horse Inn into Barrs Lane. Continue for approx ¾m. A small garden of approx ⅓ acre, interesting use of 'hard' features; paving, dwarf walls, etc. variety of smaller trees, shrubs and herbaceous borders; conifers; lawn and alpine area. Very limited car parking. Teas at **Hunts Court** open nearby with plenty of parking (½m). *Adm 70p Chd free. Suns June 12, 19 (2-6)*

Poulton Gardens ⬥ 5m E of Cirencester on A417. Cream TEAS at **Poulton Manor**. *Combined adm £2 Chd free. Sun June 139(2-6)*
  Almas Cottage (Mr & Mrs G Lavin) Tiny garden overflowing with traditional cottage plants
  The New Inn ✿ (Mr & Mrs Witold Wondrausch) On A417 opp sign to Quenington/Bibury. An acre behind erstwhile pub transformed into idiosyncratic collection of plants; spring bulbs; cottagey flowers, climbing plants, wild garden with pond, vegetable patch. *Private visits welcome, please* **Tel 0285 850226**
  The Old School (Mr & Mrs Derek Chalk) Small walled garden with interesting shrubs, clematis, roses, herbaceous plants
  Poulton House (Mr & Mrs Tom Boyd) 1½-acre Cotswold garden; herbaceous border, rose border, pond, shrubs, kitchen garden and specimen trees
  Poulton Manor ✿ (Mrs Anthony Sanford) 2 acres reconstructed for minimal maintenance; old yew hedges, hornbeam avenue, mixed borders, herb parterre, walled kitchen garden, natural area with trees, pond and bog garden. Charles II house (not open)
  Sarnia (Mr & Mrs W M Young) ½-acre garden with shrubs and perennials to give colour and interest throughout the year

¶**Prestbury and Southam Gardens** ✗ Prestbury 1½m and Southam 3m NE of Cheltenham, both off B4632 to Winchcombe. TEAS at Capel Court, Prestbury and Pigeon House, Southam. *Combined adm £2 Chd free. Sun June 12 (2-6)*
Prestbury
¶**Burnside** ✗✿ (Mr & Mrs John Anton-Smith) Mill Lane. 1½-acre working garden specialising in plant-breeding of Hellebores, Pulsatillas, Geraniums, Erodiums and other plants, and production of unusual herbaceous plants. Stock beds, large rockery, stream. *(Share to NCCPG Glos Group®). Also open Suns March 27 (2-5), April 24 (2-6): Adm £1. Private visits welcome, please* **Tel 0242 244645**
¶**The Lower Mill** ⬥✗ (Mr & Mrs W R Marsh) Mill St. Mature ¾-acre country garden on varying levels with mill stream and waterfalls surrounded by specimen trees, big borders of shrubs and herbaceous plants, and old roses
¶**Tatchley House** ⬥✗ (Dr & Mrs R W Lyle) Tatchley Lane. Small walled family garden matured by 40 yrs of controlled but enthusiastic over planting. Shrub and perennial borders meander about the lawn, pond and bricked patio areas
Southam
¶**Pigeon House** ✗ (Mr & Mrs Julian Taylor) Southam Lane. Revitalised 2-acre garden surrounding C14 manor house. Small lake and bubbling water garden with fish and bog plants. Wide range of flowering shrubs and borders designed to create multitude of vistas and plant interest. TEAS. *Also open Sun April 24 (2-6): Adm £1*

Priors Mesne Cottage ✿ (Mr & Mrs T F Cox) Aylburton 4m S of Lydney. Take A48 towards Chepstow. In Aylburton take 1st right at The George, Church Rd. 2m up hill to junc, left at sign to Alvington and Woolaston, entrance 1st on right. Woodland walk to remains of romantic 2-acre wild garden with three pools, fine trees, azaleas, bamboos. Subject of book A Gloucestershire Wild Garden 1899 and featured in the film The Assam Garden. *Adm £1 Chd free. Sun May 15 (2-6)*

Quenington Gardens ⬥✗✿ 2m N of Fairford, E of Cirencester. Peaceful Cotswold riverside village with church renowned for Norman doorways. TEAS in aid of The Home Farm Trust at **The Old Rectory**. *Combined adm £2 Chd free. Sun July 10 (2-6)*
  Apple Tree Cottage (Mrs P Butler-Henderson) Interesting small cottage garden protected by its own 'micro-climate' conservatory with unusual plants
  Court Farm (Mr & Mrs Frank Gollins) Natural riverside landscape; part of historic grounds of Knights Hospitallers with dovecote, woodland walk and water garden
  26 The Green (Miss Sandra Lawrence) Mass of summer flowers on raised bed and patio. Large rockery and pond
  Mallards (Mrs Joyce Roebuck) Summer flowers, large well-stocked fish pond, aquatics and walled vegetable garden
  The Old Rectory (Mr & Mrs David Abel-Smith) Picturesque and varied riverside garden with herbaceous border and wilderness; extensive organic vegetable garden
  Pool Hay (Mr & Mrs A W Morris) Small is beautiful. Picturesque riverside cottage garden
  Quenington House (Mr & Mrs Geoffrey Murray) Walled gardens, pergolas, old shrub roses, wide herbaceous borders. Lots of clematis, salvias and penstemons

The Red House ⌂✿ (Mr & Mrs K Turner) Pillows Green, Staunton, 8m NW of Gloucester on A417; from Staunton Xrds ½m off B4208. Split level 2 acre organic garden and wildlife garden with herbaceous borders; rockery and terrace with containers; parterre; also flower meadow. C17 House (part open). Garden designed & maintained by owners. All plants for sale grown from garden stock. TEA. *Adm £1 Chd free (Share to Gloucestershire Wildlife Trust®). Sun, Mon May 29, 30; Suns June 19, July 10 (2-6). Private visits welcome, please* **Tel 0452 840505**

Redwood House ⌂✿✿ (Mr & Mrs Eric Sadler) Halmore. 2½m NE Berkeley and SW Slimbridge. Turn off A38 at The Prince of Wales and follow signs to Halmore. First R out of Halmore into Slimbridge Lane for ½m to garden on L handside of sharp bend. ⅓ acre. 600 different cottage garden perennials and herbs, all labelled; old roses, shrubs and trees planted for scent and wildlife. *Adm 80p Chd free. Sun, Mon, April 3, 4, Mon May 2, Suns June 5, July 3, Aug 7, Sept 4 (2-6). Private visits welcome all year, please* **Tel 0453 811421**

Rockcliffe ✿✿ (Mr & Mrs Simon Keswick) nr Lower Swell. On B4068. From Stow-on-the-Wold turn R into drive 1½m from Lower Swell. 5-acre garden incl herbaceous borders, pink and white and blue gardens, rose terrace, walled kitchen garden and orchard. TEAS in aid of St Peters Church, Upper Slaughter. *Adm £1.50 Chd free. Sun July 10 (2-6.30)*

Rodmarton Manor ⌂✿✿ (Mr & Mrs Simon Biddulph) Cirencester. Between Cirencester and Tetbury off A433. House designed by Ernest Barnsley. Gardens laid out in the 1920's and made famous by Mary Biddulph during the 1960's-1980's. Many separate areas of distinctive character and a wide range of plants, shrubs, topiary, hedging, alpines and the well known herbaceous borders. TEAS (June 11 only). *Adm £1.50 Sats, £2 any other time Chd free. Every Sat May 14 to Aug 27. (2-5) Private visits welcome please* **Tel 0285 841253**. *For NGS (Share to Rodmarton PCC®) Sat June 11 (2-6)*

Rookwoods (Mr & Mrs R Luard) Waterlane, Oakridge, 5m E of Stroud, 7m W of Cirencester just N of A419. 1¼m SE of Bisley. 3-acre well structured garden with herbaceous borders to colour themes. Pleached Whitebeam around recently designed pool area. Wide variety of old-fashioned and modern climbing and shrub roses (labelled), water gardens and outstanding views. TEAS. *Adm £1.50 Chd free. Sun June 19 (2-6). Coaches by appt*

Ryelands House ✿ (Capt & Mrs Eldred Wilson) Taynton, 8m W of Gloucester. ½-way between Huntley (A40) and Newent (B4215) on B4216. Fascinating sunken garden, great variety of plants, many rare; trees, shrubs, bulbs, herbaceous borders, species and old roses; waterside plants, pools and herbs. Also unique, very popular woodland and country walk. Outstanding views and abundance of wild flowers; famed for wild daffodils. 2-acre lake in beautiful setting. Good selection of plants always for sale. Dogs welcome on walk only. TEAS. *Adm £2 Chd free. Suns April 3, 10, 17, 24, Mon April 4, (2-6)*

20 St Peters Road see Cirencester Gardens

Sezincote ✿ (Mr & Mrs David Peake) 1½m SW of Moreton-in-Marsh. Turn W along A44 towards Evesham; after 1½m (just before Bourton-on-the-Hill) take turn left, by stone lodge and white gate. Exotic oriental water garden by Repton and Daniell with lake, pools and meandering stream, banked with massed perennial plants of interest. Large semi-circular orangery, formal Indian garden, fountain, temple and unusual trees of vast size in lawn and wooded park setting. House in Indian manner designed by Samuel Pepys Cockerell was insipiration for Brighton Pavilion. TEAS (NGS day only). *Adm £2.50 Chd £1 under 5 free. Open every Thurs Fri & Bank Hols (except Dec) (2-6). For NGS Sun July 10 (2-6)*

Snowshill Manor ✿ (The National Trust) 3m SW of Broadway. Small terraced garden in which organic and natural methods only are used. Highlights include tranquil ponds, old roses, old-fashioned flowers and herbaceous borders rich in plants of special interest. House contains collections of fine craftmanship incl musical instruments, clocks, toys, bicycles. *Adm house & gdn £4.20 Chd £2.10. Family ticket £11. House & garden are open April & Oct Sats, Suns (1-5) Easter Sat to Mon open (1-6); May to end Sept Wed to Sun and Bank Hol Mon (1-6 or sunset if earlier). For NGS Sun May 8 (1-6)*

Stancombe Park ⌂✿ (Mrs B S Barlow) Stinchcombe, nr Dursley. ½-way between Dursley and Wotton-under-Edge on B4060. Bus stop: 30yds from gates. 2 gardens; (1) around house. Herbaceous borders. Pleached limewalk. New tree and shrub planting; (2) a short walk along valley descending into the historic Folly Garden. Lake. Temple. Grotto. Tunnels. Cream TEAS. *Adm £2 Chd 50p (Share to St Cyr Church, Stinchcombe®). Mon May 30 (2-6)*

Stanton ⌂✿ Nr Broadway. One of the most picturesque and unspoilt C17 Cotswold villages with many gardens (16 open in 1993) ranging from charming cottage to large formal gardens. Plant stall. Car park £1. TEAS from 3-5.30. *Adm £2 Chd free (Share to Stanton Burland Hall©). Sun June 26 (2-6)*

Stanway House (Lord Neidpath) 1m E of B4632 Cheltenham-Broadway rd on B4077 Toddington to Stow-on-the-Wold rd. 20 acres of planted landscape in early C18 formal landscape setting. Arboretum, historic pleasure grounds with specimen trees inc pinetum; remains of ornamental canal and cascade; chestnut and oak avenue; folly; daffodils and roses in season. Striking C16 Manor with gatehouse, tithe barn and church. Tea at The Bakehouse, Stanway. *Adm gardens only £1 Chd 50p; House and Gardens £3 OAP £2.50 Chd £1. Also house open Tues & Thurs June to Aug (2-5). For NGS (Share to Gloucestershire Aids Trust®) Suns April 24, June 5 (2-5)*

Stowell Park ✿ (The Lord & Lady Vestey) 2m SW of Northleach. Off Fosseway A429. Large garden, lawned terraces with magnificent views over the Coln Valley. Fine collection of old-fashioned roses and herbaceous plants, with a pleached lime approach to the House. Two large walled gardens contain vegetables, fruit, cut flowers and ranges of greenhouses, also a long rose pergola and wide, plant-filled borders divided into colour sections. House (not open) originally C14 with later additions. TEAS. *Adm £1.50 Chd free (Share to St John's Ambulance Brigade and Royal British Legion®). Suns May 15, June 26 (2-5)*

Stratton Gardens &&※ 1m NW of Circencester on A417 to Gloucester. Three of the gardens are in a housing development started in the 1960's. Teas by WI in the Village Hall. *Combined adm £1.50 Chd free (Share to St Peter's Church, Stratton®). Sun June 26 (2-6)*

¶**Churn House** (Mrs Sheilah Michael) Town garden of ¼ acre recently redesigned and planted with trees, shrubs and old roses

St Peter's Church On Daglingworth rd. Display of flower arrangements

Straddle Stones (Mr & Mrs D P Williams) Baunton Lane. A small and informal flower arrangers garden with foliage; also alpine plants, conifers and water feature

Stratton Park (Mr & Mrs G W T Goodrich) Last house on R on A417 after leaving Stratton from Cirencester. 6-acre garden recently developed; terraced lawns with raised beds and mixed borders; established wooded area and young arboretum

15 Vale Road (Mr & Mrs W J Crook) A paved garden designed and constructed for minimal maintenance with maximum variety. Densely planted mixed herbaceous borders with shrubs, alpine troughs and rockery, heathers, roses, fruit and vegetables

Whitcroft, 19 Tinglesfield (Mr & Mrs P H Webb) ⅓-acre with herbaceous and summer bedding, water features; greenhouses; cactus collection and spinney walk

Sudeley Castle &&※ (Lord and Lady Ashcombe) Winchcombe. The gardens of historic C15 castle, home of Queen Katherine Parr. The Queen's Garden, with double yew hedges, has been replanted with old-fashioned roses, herbs and perennials. Richard III's Banqueting Hall is backdrop for romantic 'ruined' garden while the Tithe Barn displays an impressive collection of species roses. Also formal pools, extensive lawns with fine trees and spring bulbs; magnificent views. 'Sudeley Castle Roses'. Specialist plant centre, with old roses, topiary, herbs and other unusual plants. Restaurant. TEAS. *Garden adm £3.30 OAPs £2.90 Chd £1.60. Open daily April 1 to Oct 31. For NGS Sats April 23, Sept 10 (11-5.30)*

Sunningdale &&※ (Mr J Mann Taylor) Grange Court. 8m W of Gloucester, 2m NE of Westbury-on-Severn. Turn off A48 at Hunt Hill near Chaxhill or turn off A40 in middle of Huntley. ¾ acre. A peaceful paradise of plants, in particular Phlomis, promising a positive plethora of pulchritude. A poetic pageant of panchromatic profusion. Pastoral, panoramas and pond. A perennial pleasure to participate in – or possibly past it and pathetically pitiful. (The National Collection of Phlomis should be at its best in June/July) Teas in Westbury. *Adm £1 Chd 50p. Suns June 5, 12, 26; July 10, 17, 31; Aug 7, 14; Thurs Aug 4, 11 (2-5). Private visits welcome, please* **Tel 0452 760268**

Tetbury Gardens, Tetbury. *Combined adm £2 Chd free. Sun June 5 (2-6)*

The Chipping Croft ※ (Dr & Mrs P W Taylor) At bottom of Chipping Hill approached from market place. 2-acre, secluded, walled town garden on three levels, with mature trees, shrubs, herbaceous borders, rose beds and unusual plants; spring blossom and bulbs. A series of formal gardens, incl fruit and vegetable/flower potager all informally planted; also a water garden. C17 Cotswold house (not open). TEAS

in aid of Action Research for the Crippled Child and Leighterton Church. *Also open Sun April 24 (2-6) Adm £1.50. Private visits welcome, please* **Tel 0666 503178**

The Old Stables ※ (Brigadier and Mrs J M Neilson) Enter New Church St B3124 from Long St at Xroads signed to Stroud and Dursley. Turn L at Fire station into Close Gardens. Small walled garden on two levels in old stable yard of a town house. Flowering shrubs; clematis; bonsai; water garden; paved area with alpines in troughs

153 Thrupp Lane ※※ (Mr & Mrs D Davies) 1½m E of Stroud. Take A419, Thrupp Lane is on L 1m from Stroud, then ½m along Thrupp Lane. ⅓-acre on sloping site, full of interesting and unusual plants, rockeries, shrubs and ponds - all planted to encourage wild life. Good winter interest. TEAS. *Adm 75p Chd free. Suns March 13, June 12 (2-6). Private visits welcome, please* **Tel 0453 883580**

Tin Penny Cottage ※※ (E S Horton) Whiteway, near Miserden, 6m NE Stroud between Birdlip & Stroud on B4070. At Fostons Ash Public House take rd signed Bisley then immediately L to Whiteway ½m; 300yd walk to garden. Enthusiast's medium-sized garden on cold clay. Designed to be visually attractive and grow a wide variety of hardy plants, many unusual and rarely seen, and incl a collection of Sempervivum. TEAS in Village Hall Bank Hol Mons April 4, May 2, 30; Aug 29. *Adm £1. Chd free. Weds all year. Bank Hol Mons April 4, May 2, 30, Aug 29. Suns April 17, May 15, June 26, July 17, Aug 14, Sept 25 (2-6) Private visits welcome all year, please* **Tel 0285 821482**

Trevi Garden &※ (Gilbert & Sally Gough) Hartpury 5m NW of Gloucester via A417. In village sharp back right into Over Old Road before War Memorial. 1 acre of gardens within a garden; winding water garden; laburnum/clematis walk, shrubberies, herbaceous borders, collection of hardy geraniums; all year round interest. Garden completely designed and maintained by owners. Featured in NGS video 1, see page 344. TEAS (except April 3 & 4). *Adm £1 Chd free. Sun, Mon April 3, 4; Suns May 1; Aug 7 (2-6); also open Thurs March 17, 24, 31; April 7, 14, 21, 28; May 5, 12, 19, 26; June 2, 9, 16, 23, 30; July 7, 14, 21, 28; Aug 4, 11, 18, 25; Sept 1, 8, 15, 22 (2-6); coaches/groups by appt on other dates* **Tel 0452 700370**

Upper Cam Gardens ※※ 1m W of Dursley. Grouped around St George's Church. Upper Cam signposted from B4066. TEAS. *Combined adm £1.50 Chd free. Sun May 22 (2-6)*

Bell Courts (Mr & Mrs E W V Acton) ¾-acre; shrubs, herbaceous plants and kitchen garden

Cleveland (Mr & Mrs R Wilkinson) Plant enthusiast's small garden on windy site. Shrubs, herbaceous and unusual plants. Vegetable plot

17 Everlands (T Edwards) Small new garden, bowl's green; ducks; R Cam flows through the garden

---

Regular Openers. Too many days to include in diary. Usually there is a wide range of plants giving year-round interest. See head of county section for the name and garden description for times etc.

20a Everlands (Mr & Mrs A A Pearce) Shrubs, herbaceous plants, rockery, kitchen garden

Homefield House (Mr & Mrs J Grove) Little garden with shrubs, colourful flowers, pond and kitchen garden

Lynwood, 20 Everlands (Mr & Mrs D G Atkin) ½-acre garden, trees, shrubs, walled vegetable garden. Scree garden with alpines and conifers. Miniature railway for children

Noggins Hollow (Mr & Mrs K Hall) Stream-side garden with new herbaceous beds, shrubs & vegetable garden

16 Springhill (Old Court) (Mr & Mrs J E Beebee) Mature garden with open aspect. Shrubs, herbaceous and rock plants, pond. Display of complementary stained glass

The Vicarage (Rev Chris & Mrs Gill Malkinson) Small walled garden recently replanted; trees; shrubs and spring/summer rockery with labelled plants

Upton Wold ❀ (Mr & Mrs I R S Bond) 5m W of Moreton-in-Marsh, on A44 1m past A424 junction at Troopers Lodge Garage. Recently created garden architecturally and imaginatively laid out around C17 house with commanding views. Yew hedges; old shrub roses; herbaceous walk; some unusual plants and trees; vegetable garden; pond garden and woodland garden. *Adm £1.50 Chd free (Share to Chipping Norton Theatre Trust®). Suns April 24, July 3 (10-6). Private visits welcome May to July, please* **Tel 0386 700667**

Westbury Court Garden ⅼ (The National Trust) Westbury-on-Severn 9m SW of Gloucester on A48. Formal Dutch style water garden, earliest remaining in England; canals, summer house, walled garden; over 100 species of plants grown in England before 1700. *Adm £2.20 Chd £1.10. April to end Oct. Wed to Sun & Bank Hol Mon (11-6) Closed Good Fri. Other months by appt only. For NGS Sun Sept 4 (11-6)*

Westonbirt Gardens at Westonbirt School ⅼ 3m S of Tetbury. A433 Tetbury-Bristol. 22 acres. Formal Victorian Italian garden now Grade 1 listed, terraced pleasure garden, rustic walks, lake redredged & stocked with carp. Rare, exotic trees and shrubs. Tea at Hare & Hounds Hotel, Westonbirt ½m, (to book for parties **Tel 0666 880233**). *Adm £1.50 Chd 25p. Suns April 10, Aug 21, Sept 4 (2-5.30)*

Willow Lodge ⅼ⌀❀ (Mr & Mrs John H Wood) on A40 between May Hill & Longhope 10m W of Gloucester, 6m E of Ross-on-Wye. 1½-acre plantsman's garden with great variety of unusual plants many rare incl shrubs, herbaceous borders, an alpine walk, stream and pool with water features, several greenhouses, vegetable garden; plants labelled, ample parking. Grounds extend to 4 acres with many wild flowers. TEAS. *Adm £1 Chd free. Sun & Mon May 29, 30, Suns June 12, 19, 26 July 10, 17, 24, Aug 7, 14 (2-6). Groups and private visits welcome, please* **Tel 0452 831211**

Witcombe Gardens ⅼ 4m E of Gloucester on A417 turn R at 12 Bells Inn for Church Cottage and Witcombe Park; ½m up A417 from Inn turn L signed **Court Farm House**. TEAS **Witcombe Park**. *Combined adm £1.50 Chd free. Sun June 19 (2-6)*

    Church Cottage ⅼ⌀❀ (Sir Christopher & Lady Lawson) Great Witcombe. 2 acres; typical cottage flowers; shrubs; stream and ponds. Soft drinks

    Court Farm House ⅼ⌀❀ (Mr & Mrs Andrew Hope) Little Witcombe. An informal family garden of 1 acre. Shrubs, roses, herbaceous perennials and self-seeding annuals; pond, pergola; wild garden, rock garden, herb garden, scree bed, play area; children welcome

    Witcombe Park ⅼ⌀ (Mrs W W Hicks Beach) Great Witcombe. A plant connoisseur's medium-sized garden set in beautiful Cotswold scenery. Richly planted borders, flowering shrubs, roses; walled garden, cottage garden area and hidden sunken water garden; C17 gazebo. *(Share to Gloucestershire Wildlife Trust®)*

Gwent & Gwynedd

See separate Welsh section beginning on page 291

Hampshire

Hon County Organiser:	Mrs A R Elkington, Little Court, Crawley nr Winchester SO21 2PU
Assistant Hon County Organisers:	Mrs G E Coke, Jenkyn Place, Bentley, nr Farnham GU10 5LU
	Mrs R J Gould, Ewell House, 44 Belmore Lane, Lymington SO41 9NN
	Mrs D Hart Dyke, Hambledon House, Hambledon PO7 4RU
	JJ Morris Esq, The Ricks, Rotherwick, Nr Basingstoke RG27 9BL
	Mrs Miles Rivett-Carnac, Martyr Worthy Manor, nr Winchester SO21 1DY
	C K Thornton Esq, Merrie Cottage, Woodgreen, Nr Fordingbridge SP6 2AT
	M H Walford Esq, Little Acre, Down Farm Lane, Headbourne Worthy, Winchester SO23 7LA
Hon County Treasurer:	M S Hoole Esq, c/o Lloyds Bank plc, 63 London Rd, Southampton SO9 3LE

DATES OF OPENING

By appointment

For telephone numbers and other details see garden descriptions. Private visits welcomed

Abbey Cottage, Itchen Abbas
Beechenwood Farm, nr Odiham
Bramdean House, nr Alresford
Brandy Mount House, Alresford
Broadhatch House, Bentley
Croylands, nr Romsey
Court Lodge, West Meon
Durmast House, Burley
Fairfield House, Hambledon
Greatham Mill, Greatham, nr Liss
Hambledon House, Hambledon
The Hedges, East Wellow
53 Ladywood, Eastleigh
Little Barn Garden and Barnhawk
   Nursery, Woodgreen, nr
   Fordingbridge
Little Court, Crawley
Long Thatch, Warnford
The Manor House, Upton Grey
Marycourt, Odiham
Merdon Manor, Hursley
Merrie Cottage, Woodgreen
Rotherfield Park, East Tisted
Rowans Wood, Ampfield
Sowley House, Sowley, Lymington
Spinners, Boldre
Springfield, Hayling Island
Vernon Hill House, Bishop's Waltham
White Windows, Longparish

Regular openings

For details see garden descriptions

Exbury Gardens, nr Southampton.
   Open daily Feb 12 to Oct 23
Furzey Gardens, Minstead. Daily
   except Dec 25 & 26
Highclere Castle, nr Newbury Open
   Wed to Suns, July, Aug, Sept,
   Easter & Bank Hols
Sir Harold Hillier Arboretum, Nr
   Romsey Daily
Jenkyn Place, Bentley Thurs to Suns
   & Bank Hols, April 7 to Sept 11
The Little Cottage, Lymington, Tues
   June 1 to Sept 30
Long Thatch, Warnford Weds March
   2 to Sept 14
Lymore Valley Herbs, Milford-on-Sea
   Daily except Dec 25 to Mar 1
Macpenny Woodland Garden &
   Nurseries, Bransgore Daily except
   Dec 25, 26 & Jan 1
The Manor House, Upton Grey,
   Every Weds May, June & July
Petersfield Physic Garden, Daily
   except Dec 25

Rotherfield Park, East Tisted for
   details see text
Southview Nurseries, Eversley
   Cross. For details see text
Spinners, Boldre for details see text
Stratfield Saye House, Reading
   Open daily (except Fri) May 1 to
   last Sun in Sept

March 6 Sunday
Longthatch, Warnford
March 12 Saturday
Long Thatch, Warnford
March 13 Sunday
Long Thatch, Warnford
March 20 Sunday
Bramdean House, Bramdean, nr
   Alresford ‡
Brandy Mount House, Alresford ‡
Pennington Chase, Lymington ‡‡
Sadlers Gardens, Lymington ‡‡
March 27 Sunday
Durmast House, Burley
Eversley Gardens, Eversley
Little Court, Crawley
March 28 Monday
Little Court, Crawley
April 3 Sunday
Bramdean House, Bramdean, nr
   Alresford ‡
Woodcote Manor, Alresford ‡
April 4 Monday
Bramdean House, Bramdean, nr
   Alresford
Sadlers Gardens, Lymington
April 10 Sunday
Crawley Gardens, Nr Winchester
East Lane, Ovington
Mylor Cottage, Swanmore Rd,
   Droxford
The Old House, Silchester
April 11 Monday
Crawley Gardens, nr Winchester
April 17 Sunday
Appleshaw Manor, nr Andover
Ashford Gardens, Steep
Beechenwood Farm, nr Odiham
Bramdean House, Bramdean, nr
   Alresford ‡
60 Lealand Road, Drayton
Rowans Wood, Ampfield
Tichborne Park, Alresford ‡
April 24 Sunday
Belmore Lane Gardens, Lymington
Brandy Mount House, Alresford
Hall Place, West Meon
The Old House, Silchester
Rowans Wood, Ampfield
May 1 Sunday
Abbey Cottage, Itchen Abbas
The Cottage, Chandlers Ford
Vernon Hill House, Bishop's
   Waltham

May 2 Monday
Abbey Cottage, Itchen Abbas
The Cottage, Chandlers Ford
House-in-the-Wood, Beaulieu
Rookley Manor, Up Somborne
Vernon Hill House, Bishop's
   Waltham
May 8 Sunday
Brandy Mount House, Alresford
Burkham House, nr Alton
Cold Hayes, Steep Marsh
The Dower House, Dogmersfield
Eversley Gardens, Eversley
Lithend, Crawley Gardens, nr
   Winchester ‡
Little Court, Crawley ‡
North Ecchinswell Farm, nr
   Newbury
The Old House, Silchester
Rowans Wood, Ampfield
May 9 Monday
Lithend, Crawley ‡
Little Court, Crawley ‡
May 11 Wednesday
Exbury Gardens, nr Southampton
May 14 Saturday
3 St Helens Road, Hayling Island
May 15 Sunday
Ashford Gardens, Steep ‡‡
Bramdean House, Bramdean, nr
   Alresford
The Dower House, Dogmersfield
Greatham Mill, Greatham, nr Liss
Hackwood Park (The Spring
   Wood), Basingstoke
Pennington Chase, Lymington ‡
Petersfield Physic Garden ‡‡
Pylewell Park, Lymington ‡
3 St Helens Road, Hayling Island
South End House, Lymington ‡
Tylney Hall Hotel, Rotherwick
May 18 Wednesday
The Hedges, East Wellow
May 19 Thursday
The Hedges, East Wellow
Maurys Mount, West Wellow
May 21 Saturday
Coles, Privett, nr Alton
May 22 Sunday
Cobwood House, nr Newbury
Coles, Privett, nr Alton
The Cottage, Chandlers Ford
Fiddlers Cottage, Woodgreen ‡
Heatherland, Woodgreen ‡
Heathlands, 47 Locks Rd, Locks
   Heath
The Hedges, East Wellow
53 Ladywood, Eastleigh
Little Barn Garden and Barnhawk
   Nursery, Woodgreen, nr
   Fordingbridge ‡
The Old House, Silchester
Pylewell Park, Lymington
Rowans Wood, Ampfield
Walhampton, Lymington

The Wylds, Liss Forest
May 23 Monday
Rowans Wood, Ampfield
May 25 Wednesday
The Hedges, East Wellow
May 26 Thursday
The Hedges, East Wellow
May 28 Saturday
Fernlea, Chilworth, Southampton
Verona Cottage, 6 Webb Lane,
Hayling Island
May 29 Sunday
Bury Farm, Marchwood,
Southampton
The Clock House, Northwood
Park, Sparsholt
Croylands, nr Romsey
Eversley Gardens, Eversley
The Hedges, East Wellow
60 Lealand Road, Drayton ‡
Littlewood, Hayling Island
Long Thatch, Warnford
Monxton Gardens, nr Andover
Rumsey Gardens, Clanfield
Sadlers Gardens, Lymington
Verona Cottage, 6, Webb Lane,
Hayling Island ‡
May 30 Monday
The Clock House, Northwood
Park, Sparsholt
Long Thatch, Warnford
Monxton Gardens, nr Andover
June 1 Wednesday
The Clock House, Northwood
Park, Sparsholt
Croylands, Nr Romsey
The Manor House, Upton Grey
June 2 Thursday
Littlewood, Hayling Island
June 5 Sunday
Croylands, nr Romsey
Durmast House, Burley
Jenkyn Place, Bentley
Landford Lodge, Salisbury
Maurys Mount, West Wellow
Sowley House, Sowley, Lymington
June 8 Wednesday
The Clock House, Northwood
Park, Sparsholt
Croylands, nr Romsey
The Hedges, East Wellow
June 9 Thursday
The Hedges, East Wellow
June 12 Sunday
Applecroft, Woodgreen ‡
Beechenwood Farm, nr Odiham
Cranbury Park, Otterbourne
Croft Mews, Botley ‡‡
Croylands, nr Romsey
Harfield Farm House,
Curdridge ‡‡
The Hedges, East Wellow
Merrie Cottage, Woodgreen ‡
The Old Vicarage, Appleshaw

Robins Return, Tiptoe
Southview Nurseries, Eversley
Cross
Vernon Hill House, Bishop's
Waltham
June 13 Monday
Applecroft, Woodgreen
Merrie Cottage, Woodgreen
June 15 Wednesday
Croylands, nr Romsey
The Hedges, East Wellow
June 16 Thursday
The Hedges, East Wellow
June 18 Saturday
34 Avenue Road, Lymington
Nine Springs Nursery, Whitchurch
June 19 Sunday
34 Avenue Road, Lymington ‡‡
Bramdean House, Bramdean, nr
Alresford ‡
Bramdean Lodge, Alresford ‡
Brandy Mount House, Alresford ‡
Broadhatch House, Bentley
Crookley Pool, Horndean ‡‡‡
Croylands, Nr Romsey
Droxford Gardens, Droxford
The Garden House, Lymington ‡‡
Glevins, Lymington ‡‡
The Hedges, East Wellow
John Hine's Studio, Aldershot
53 Ladywood, Eastleigh
Longstock Park Gardens, nr
Stockbridge
Mylor Cottage, Swanmore Rd,
Droxford
Nine Springs Nursery, Whitchurch
Petersfield Physic Garden ‡‡‡
Tichborne Park, Alresford ‡
West Silchester Hall, Silchester
June 20 Monday
Broadhatch House, Bentley
June 22 Wednesday
Crookley Pool, Horndean
Croylands, nr Romsey
June 25 Saturday
Hinton Ampner, nr Alresford
June 26 Sunday
Apple Court & Apple Court
Cottage, nr Lymington
Brocas Farm, Lower Froyle, nr
Alton
Crossways, Woodgreen Common
Fairfield House, Hambledon ‡‡
Fritham Lodge, nr Lyndhurst ‡
Hambledon House, Hambledon ‡‡
Headbourne Worthy Gardens,
Winchester
Hinton Ampner, nr Alresford
Holt End House, Newbury
Ivalls Farm Cottage, Bentworth
Lake House, Northington,
Alresford
60 Lealand Road, Drayton
Long Thatch, Warnford

Marycourt, Odiham
Mottisfont Abbey, nr Romsey
Old Meadows, Silchester
Pullens, West Worldham, nr Alton
Southview Nurseries, Eversley
Cross
Waldrons, Brook, Lyndhurst ‡
June 27 Monday
Fairfield House, Hambledon
June 29 Wednesday
Pullens, West Worldham, nr Alton
July 3 Sunday
Jenkyn Place, Bentley
Marycourt, Odiham
Moundsmere Manor, Preston
Candover
Tunworth Old Rectory, nr
Basingstoke
Vernon Hill House, Bishop's
Waltham
July 6 Wednesday
Marycourt, Odiham
July 9 Saturday
Manor Lodge, Crawley
July 10 Sunday
Broadhatch House, Bentley
Cold Hayes, Steep Marsh
Court Lodge, West Meon
Manor Lodge, Crawley ‡
Paige Cottage, Crawley ‡
July 11 Monday
Broadhatch House, Bentley
Paige Cottage, Crawley
July 16 Saturday
Fernlea, Chilworth,
Southampton
July 17 Sunday
Apple Court & Apple Court
Cottage, nr Lymington
Bramdean House, Bramdean, nr
Alresford ‡
Bramdean Lodge, Alresford ‡
Heathlands, 47 Locks Rd, Locks
Heath
Highclere Castle, nr Newbury
Merdon Manor, Hursley
Sadlers Gardens, Lymington
Tylney Hall Hotel, Rotherwick
July 18 Monday
Merdon Manor, Hursley
July 23 Saturday
Longmead House, Longparish
July 24 Sunday
Highclere Castle, nr Newbury
53 Ladywood, Eastleigh
Littleton House, nr Winchester
Longmead House, Longparish
The Vyne, Sherborne St John
July 27 Wednesday
The Hedges, East Wellow
July 28 Thursday
The Hedges, East Wellow
July 30 Saturday
12 Rozelle Close, Littleton

July 31 Sunday
The Hedges, East Wellow
Hill House, Old Alresford
John Hines Studio, Aldershot
Little Court, Crawley ‡
Long Thatch, Warnford
12 Rozelle Close, Littleton ‡
Veronica Cottage, Lymington

August 1 Monday
Little Court, Crawley

August 7 Sunday
The Barn House, Rectory Rd,
Oakley
Martyr Worthy Gardens, nr
Winchester
Oakley Manor, Church Oakley
West Silchester Hall, Silchester

August 14 Sunday
Highclere Castle, nr Newbury

Little Court, Crawley
White Windows, Longparish

August 15 Monday
Little Court, Crawley
White Windows, Longparish

August 20 Saturday
Empshott Grange, nr Selborne
Somerley, nr Ringwood

August 21 Sunday
Bramdean House, Bramdean, nr
Alresford ‡
Bramdean Lodge, Alresford ‡
Empshott Grange, nr Selborne
Fernlea, Chilworth, Southampton
Highclere Castle, nr Newbury

August 28 Sunday
Abbey Cottage, Itchen Abbas

August 29 Monday
Abbey Cottage, Itchen Abbas

John Hine's Studio, Aldershot

September 3 Saturday
Wonston Lodge, Wonston

September 4 Sunday
Wonston Lodge, Wonston

September 10 Saturday
Hinton Ampner, nr Alresford

September 11 Sunday
Greatham Mill, Greatham, nr Liss
Hambledon House, Hambledon ‡
Hinton Ampner, nr Alresford
White Cottage, Hambledon ‡

October 16 Sunday
Abbey Cottage, Itchen Abbas ‡
Chilland, Martyr Worthy, nr
Winchester ‡

DESCRIPTIONS OF GARDENS

Abbey Cottage &✿❀ (Colonel P J Daniell) Rectory Lane, Itchen Abbas. Turn off B3047 Alresford-Kingsworthy Rd, 1m E of Itchen Abbas. Interesting walled garden and meadow with trees, designed and maintained by owner. Featured on BBC TV "The Great British Gardening Show". *Adm £1 Chd free (Share to Winchester Cathedral®). Suns Mons, May 1, 2, Aug 28, 29 Sun Oct 16 (12-5.30) private visits welcome. please Tel 0962 779575*

Apple Court & Apple Court Cottage &✿❀ (Mrs D Grenfell, Mr R Grounds & Mrs M Roberts) Lymington. From the A337 between Lymington and New Milton turn N into Hordle Lane at the Royal Oak at Downton Xrds. Formal 1½-acre garden being created by designer-owners within the walls of former Victorian kitchen garden. Four National Reference Collections incl small leafed hosta. White garden, daylily display borders, collection of ferns and grasses. Small specialist nursery. Adjoining small cottage garden with variegated catalpa. TEAS at Royal Oak, Downton. Cold drinks available. *Adm £1 Chd 25p (Share to All Saints Church, Hordle®). Suns June 26, July 17 (2-5.30)*

¶Applecroft ✿ (Mr & Mrs G T Creber) Brook Lane, Woodgreen. 3m N of Fordingbridge on A338 turn E to Woodgreen. Turn R at Horse and Groom and R again along the edge of the common. Park on common and walk down through 5-barred gate. ⅓-acre garden facing SW with outlook over the Avon valley. Pond, mixed herbaceous borders with shrubs, some annuals and vegetables. TEA (Mon). *Adm 50p Chd free Sun, Mon June 12, 13 (2-5.30)*

Appleshaw Manor &✿ (The Hon Mrs Green) Nr Andover. Take A342 Andover-Marlborough Rd. Turn to Appleshaw 1m W of Weyhill. Fork L at playing field. Entrance on R after ½m next to white Church. 7-acre garden and grounds surrounded by wall. Shrubs, herbaceous, roses, wood garden, arboretum. Notable beech and yew hedges. Spring bulbs. TEAS. *Adm £1.50 Chd free (Share to The Countess of Brecknock Hospice®). Sun April 17 (2-5)*

Ashford Gardens ✿ Steep, nr Petersfield. 2m N of Petersfield, off Alresford Rd (no. C18); fork right ½m past Cricketers Inn at Steep. 12 acres set in valley of the Ash under steep wooded hangers of Stoner and Wheatham, described by poet Edward Thomas (who lived for a time at Berryfield before killed in France in 1917). Landscaped pools; waterfalls, beautiful trees; interesting shrubs, banks of azaleas and rhododendrons add colour and variety to this naturally lovely setting. *Combined adm £1.50 Chd 25p. Suns April 17, May 15 (2-6)*
    Ashford Chace (Ashford Chace Management)
    Old Ashford Manor (J Abrahams Esq)

Ashley Park Farm. See Dorset

¶34 Avenue Road ✿ (Jan & Sheila Page) Lymington. Immediately adjacent Town Hall visitors car park. Four small themed gardens redesigned since 1990 around town centre bungalow. Incl Mediterranean garden, shade alley, mixed borders, interesting use of paving, gravel, garden ornaments, arbour and pergola, some unusual tender plants in acid soil. *Adm £1 Chd free. Sat, Sun June 18, 19 (2-6)*

The Barn House ✿❀ (Brigadier & Mrs H R W Vernon) Rectory Rd, Oakley. 5m W of Basingstoke. From Basingstoke towards Whitchurch on B3400. Turn L at Station Rd ½m W of Newfound and follow signs. Bus No 55 Basingstoke to Oakley. Small garden, mixed borders, alpines, clematis and unusual plants, maintained by owner. Tea at **Oakley Manor**. *Combined adm with Oakley Manor £2 Chd free. Free parking at Manor. Sun Aug 7 (2-5.30)*

Beechenwood Farm &✿❀ (Mr & Mrs M Heber-Percy) Hillside; turn S into King St. from Odiham High St. Turn L after cricket ground for Hillside and follow signs. 2-acre woodland garden with spring bulbs, walled herb garden, rock garden, pergola, orchard and vegetable garden, conservatory and fruit cage. Views over Odiham, newly planted 8 acre wood. Open from 1pm for picnics. WI TEAS. *Adm £1 Chd free. Sun April 17 (2-5); Sun June 12 (2-6) also private visits welcome April to July, please Tel 0256 702300*

Belmore Lane Gardens ✿❀ Lymington. Go to the Public Car Park behind Waitrose Supermarket. From here exit on foot W entering Belmore Lane and turn L for 44 & 48. *Combined Adm £1.50 Chd 50p. Sun April 24 (2-5.30)*

Auburn ✿✿❀ (Mr & Mrs R K Pooley) 100 yds down the hill on the R immediately S of Ewell House. This ¼-acre garden was, until 1970, part of Ewell House and is now separated by a Sussex brick wall. There are island beds of azaleas, rhododendrons and other shrubs; a pond, terrace, rockeries and a small shrubbery

Ewell House ✿✿ (Mr & Mrs R J Gould) 100 yds down on your R. This is a town garden of ⅓ acre and was completely replanned and replanted in 1986. It is acquiring some maturity but new planting is still taking place. There is a variety of shrubs incl camellias and small rhododendrons. Cream TEAS

Bramdean House ✿❀ (Mr & Mrs H Wakefield) In Bramdean village on A272. Carpets of spring bulbs. Walled garden with famous herbaceous borders, working kitchen garden, large collection of unusual plants. TEAS. *Adm £1.50 Chd free (Share to Bramdean Parish Church®). Mon April 4, Suns March 20 April 3, 17 May 15, June 19, July 17, Aug 21, (2-5); also private visits welcome, please* **Tel 0962 771214**

Bramdean Lodge ✿ (Hon Peter & Mrs Dickinson) Bramdean village nr Alresford, on A272 (car park and TEAS as for Bramdean House). 1¾ acres, walled garden, freely planted, including more than 80 varieties of clematis and 150 of roses. *Adm £1 Chd free. Suns June 19, July 17, Aug 21 (2-5)*

Brandy Mount House ✿❀ (Mr & Mrs M Baron) Alresford centre, first R in East St before Sun Lane. Please leave cars in Broad St. 1-acre informal plantsman's garden, spring bulbs, hellebores, species geraniums, snowdrop collection, daphne collection, clematis, herbaceous and woodland plants. Featured in Gardeners World Feb 1993. *Adm £1 Chd free. Suns March 20, April 24, May 8, June 19 (2-5). Also private visits welcome on Sats, please* **Tel 0962 732189**

Broadhatch House ✿✿❀ (Bruce & Lizzie Powell) Bentley; 4m NE of Alton; on A31 between Farnham/Alton; Bus AV452; go up School Lane. 3½ acres formal garden, double herbaceous borders; rose gardens, old-fashioned roses; unusual flowering shrubs. Included and illustrated in 'Rose Gardens of England'. *Adm £1.50 Chd free (Share to Red Cross®). Suns June 19, July 10, (2-6); Mons June 20, July 11 (11-6). Also private visits welcome, please* **Tel 0420 23185**

Brocas Farm ✿✿❀ (Mrs A A Robertson) Lower Froyle. ½m up road to Lower Froyle from A31 turning just W of Bentley; medium-sized garden with herbaceous; rose and shrub borders; vegetables and arboretum of small trees. TEAS. *Adm £1.50 Chd 75p (Share to CRMF®). Sun June 26 (2-6)*

> **By Appointment Gardens.** Avoid the crowds. Good chance of a tour by owner. See garden description for telephone number.

Burkham House ✿ (Mr & Mrs D Norman) nr Alton. 5m NW of Alton from A339 between Basingstoke and Alton. On Alton side of Herriard, turn off W for Burkham. 10 acres of beautiful mature trees, azaleas, acers, spring flowers, lake, and new arboretum, cottage garden and herbaceous borders. TEAS. *Adm £1.50 Chd 25p. Sun May 8 (2-5.30)*

¶**Bury Farm** ✿✿ (Adam & Carolyn Barker-Mill) Marchwood, situated on Bury Rd, midway between Totton and Marchwood, map ref: [SU 378115]. 2 acres started in 1983. A spiral yew labyrinth within a shrubbery. Three brick towers, a woodland walk by a crinkle-crankle wall leading to a wisteria pergola; an octagonal pool reached by a mysterious tunnel; a circular, walled brick paved organic kitchen garden; coloured borders surround a well at its centre. Featured in Country Life. Cream TEAS in aid of Solent Subfertility Trust. *Adm £1.50 Chd free. Sun May 29 (2-6)*

Chilland ✿✿ (Mrs L A Impey) Martyr Worthy. Midway between Winchester and Alresford on B3047. Mature garden. Fine situation. Shrub borders designed for foliage colour. Many interesting plants. *Adm £1.50 Chd free. Sun Oct 16 (2-5.30). Also Sun Aug 7 with* **Martyr Worthy Gardens**

The Clock House ✿✿ (Mr & Mrs David Gibbs) Northwood Park, Sparsholt, 3m W of Winchester. Turn off A272 Winchester-Stockbridge Rd opp railings and sign for Sparsholt College. Converted stables in a courtyard, with a walled garden (11ft high). Created on clay and chalk over the past 10 years with many unusual shrubs and varied climbers on the walls; Paul's Himalayan musk rose envelops a fallen apple tree. Some specimen trees; (catalpa, robinia decaisneana, cornus controversa, koelreuteria paniculata). Laburnum and wisteria arcade, far reaching views, large Victorian greenhouse. TEAS Sun & Mon only. *Adm £1.50 Chd free. Sun, Mon May 29, 30; Weds June 1, 8 (2-6)*

Cobwood House ✿✿❀ (Mr & Mrs R F Kershaw) Woolton Hill. Off Newbury-Andover A343. 1st R after Newbury derestriction sign to Ball Hill and East Woodhay. Take next L, after ½m L again, white gate 20yds on L. 2-acre spring garden originally planted by the late Sir Kenneth Swan QC in 1940; rhododendrons, azaleas, camellias, magnolias and other specimen trees and shrubs, vegetable garden. TEAS. *Adm £1.50 Chd (under 14) free. Sun May 22 (2-5.30)*

Cold Hayes (Mr & Mrs Brian Blacker) Steep Marsh. Turn off A3 (Petersfield bypass) to Steep Marsh. Turn off Petersfield-Alresford Rd 3m from Petersfield. From Steep village observe direction signs. Medium-sized garden; flowering shrubs, trees, beautiful views. TEA. *Adm £1 Chd 25p. Suns May 8, July 10 (2-6)*

¶**Coles** ✿ (W B S Walker) Privett, Nr Alton. From Alton take A32 S to Fareham. After approx 6m after Farringdon and East Tisted turn L at small Xrds on brow of gentle hill. Just past the Xrds on R is the Lawns/Pig and Whistle public house. Turn L at sign for Froxfield continue for just under ½m. At T-junction turn L to Froxfield and continue just under 1m turn L at small Xrds by bungalow and continue along lane. Turn R after 350yds at entrance marked car park. If approaching from S turn R off A32 just after Pig and Whistle/Lawns public house. 26 acres of spectacular secluded gardens set out over undulating grounds. Extensive lawns with paths and clearings opening onto diverse views. Beech and other woodland; a wide variety of acid loving plants including unusual varieties of azaleas and rhododendrons, acers, 2 ponds one in a secret garden *Adm £3 Chd £1.50. Sat, Sun May 21, 22 (2-5.30)*

The Cottage ⚘✤ (Mr & Mrs H Sykes) 16 Lakewood Rd, Chandler's Ford. 6m S of Winchester. Leave M3 at junction 12, follow signs to Chandler's Ford. At Hanrahans public house on Winchester Rd, turn W into Merdon Ave, then 3rd rd on L. ¾-acre garden planted for yr-round interest with spring colour from bulbs, camellias, rhododendrons, azaleas and magnolias. Woodland, conifers, herbaceous borders, bog garden, ponds, fruit and vegetable garden; bantams. TEAS. *Adm £1 Chd 10p (Share to British Heart Foundation®). Sun, Mon May 1, 2; Sun May 22 (2-6)*

Court Lodge ⚘✤ (Patricia Dale) West Meon. 8m W of Petersfield, S on A32. ¼-acre specialist cottage garden, home of botanical artist Patricia Dale and her husband. Many unusual and old-fashioned summer plants, mixed up in the old style, incl a few vegetables. Miniature gardens in sinks, small pond, old roses, and gravel paths with interesting edge plants. Regret not very suitable for small children. Studio also open with collection of paintings, cards etc. Teas in village. *Adm £1 Chd 50p. Sun July 10 (2-7). Private visits also welcome, please* **Tel 0730 829473**

Cranbury Park ⚘ (Mr & Mrs Chamberlayne-Macdonald) Otterbourne, 5m S of Winchester. 2m N of Eastleigh; main entrance on old A33 between Winchester-Southampton, by bus stop at top of Otterbourne Hill. Entrances also in Hocombe Rd, Chandlers Ford and Poles Lane, Otterbourne. Extensive pleasure grounds laid out in late C18 and early C19; fountains; rose garden; specimen trees; lakeside walk. Family carriages will be on view. TEAS. *Adm £1.50 Chd 50p. Sun June 12 (2-5)*

Crawley Gardens 5m NW of Winchester, off A272 Winchester-Stockbridge Rd. Gardens signed from centre of village. Please park nr church. TEA Sun only. *Combined adm £2 Chd free (Share to Wessex Childrens Hospice.®). Sun, Mon April 10, 11 (2-5.30)*

  Glebe House ⚘ (Lt-Col & Mrs John Andrews) 1½-acres; mainly lawn, bulbs, shrubs and herbaceous borders. TEA in conservatory
  Lithend ⚘✤✤ (Mrs F L Gunner) Small cottage garden. *Also open Suns, Mons May 8, 9 (Share to RSPB®) (2-5.30). Combined adm £1.50 Chd free with* **Little Court**
  Little Court ⚘✤✤ (Professor & Mrs A R Elkington) *Also open on Suns, Mons, March 27, 28, July 31, Aug 1, 14, 15. See entry under* **Little Court**
  Manor Lodge ⚘✤✤ (Mr & Mrs K Wren) See separate entry. *Also open July 9, 10*

¶**Croft Mews** ⚘✤ (Captain & Mrs W T T Pakenham) Botley. 2m N of Botley on B3354, on L under trees (M27 exit

7). A recently created garden of about 2 acres, in the grounds of an old farm. Brick walls, lawns and mixed borders, new ha ha with view over meadows, pond, kitchen garden and woodland area. TEAS. *Adm £1 Chd free. Sun June 12 (2-6)*

¶**Crookley Pool** ⚘✤✤ (Mr & Mrs F S K Privett) Horndean. Turn up Blendworth Lane by the main bakery form the centre of Horndean. House 200yds before church on L. Off the A3 5m S of Petersfield. Medium sized garden with mixed borders; unusual plants, walled kitchen garden. *Adm £1 Chd 25p. Sun, June 19 (2-6); Wed June 22 (2-5)*

Crossways ⚘✤ (J Egerton-Warburton) Woodgreen Common. 3m N of Fordingbridge on A338 turn E to Woodgreen, bear L in village and R immediately after the Horse and Groom, on to the common turn R. Parking on the common. Garden now 6 yrs old gravelly soil, a wide variety of herbaceous plants and shrubs; rose garden with emphasis on colour. A garden for everybody. TEAS *Adm £1 Chd free. Sun June 26 (2-6)*

Croylands ⚘✤✤ (The Hon Mrs Charles Kitchener) Old Salisbury Lane, Romsey. From Romsey take A3057 Stockbridge Rd, L after 1m at Dukes Head, fork L after bridge, 1m on R. Wheelwright's cottage on Florence Nightingale's Family Estate, surrounded by 2 acres unusual, interesting trees, shrubs and plants. Peony garden. TV appearances on TV South and features on Granada TV in Spring 1994 before opening. TEAS. *Adm £1.50 Chd free. Sun May 29, June 5, 12, 19; Weds, June 1, 8, 15, 22 (2-6). Also private visits welcome all June, please* **Tel 0794 513056**

The Dower House ⚘ (Mr & Mrs Michael Hoare) Dogmersfield. Turn N off A287. 6-acre garden including bluebell wood with large and spectacular collection of rhododendrons, azaleas, magnolias and other flowering trees and shrubs; set in parkland with fine views over 20-acre lake. TEAS. *Adm £1.50 Chd free (Share to Dogmersfield Church Organ Fund®). Suns May 8, 15 (2-6)*

Droxford Gardens 4½m N of Wickham on A32 approx mid-way between Alton-Portsmouth. *Combined adm £2.50 Chd 50p 1 garden £1. Sun June 19 (2-6)*
  Fir Hill ✤ (Mrs Derek Schreiber) 4½ acres; roses, shrubs, herbaceous and shrub borders. Home-made TEAS. Car park
  The Mill House ⚘ (Mrs C MacPherson) Garden of 2 acres; shrubs, flower beds, orchard, mill stream, roses, pond. Garden featured in 'Trainers' on BBC 1 3 yrs ago. Car park
  Mylor Cottage ⚘✤ (Dr & Mrs Martin ffrench Constant) ½m S of Droxford on the Swanmore Rd. Car park. Trees, shrubs and herbaceous border. *Also open Sun April 10 (2-5) see under* **Mylor Cottage**
  ¶**Park View** ⚘✤ (Mrs F V D Aubert) Small town garden, flowers, shrubs, very small wooded walk at end

---

Regular Openers. Too many days to include in diary. Usually there is a wide range of plants giving year-round interest. See head of county section for the name and garden description for times etc.

Durmast House &%❀ (Mr & Mrs P E G Daubeney). 1m SE of Burley, nr White Buck Hotel. 4-acre garden designed by Gertrude Jekyll in 1907 in the process of being restored from the original plans. Formal rose garden edged with lavender, 130-yr-old Monterey pine, 100-yr-old cut leaf beech and large choisya. Victorian rockery, lily pond, coach-house, large wisteria and herbaceous border. *Adm £1 Chd 50p (Share to Hampshire Garden Trust and Delhi Women's Assoc Clinic®). Suns March 27, June 5 (2.30-5.30). Private visits welcome, please* Tel 0425 403527

East Lane % (Sir Peter & Lady Ramsbotham) Ovington A31 from Winchester towards Alresford. Immediately after roundabout 1m west of Alresford, small sign to Ovington turn sharp L up incline, down small country rd to Ovington. East Lane is the only house on left, 500yds before Bush Inn. 4 acres, spring bulbs, mixed herbaceous and shrubs; woodland plantings; walled rose garden. Terraced water garden ample parking. *Adm £1.50 OAPs £1 Chd free. Sun April 10 (2-6)*

Empshott Grange % (Sir James & Lady Scott) Nr Selborne. Take B3006 from Alton. Turn R 2m out of Selborne towards Empshott Green entrance 600m on L. Or from A3 head N from roundabout at West Liss towards Farnham. L onto B3006. 2m L as above. Close to Greatham Mill. Restored Victorian garden on upper greensand laid out by owner's family from 1860. next to C12 church. 3 acre garden surrounded by 30 acres magnificent hanger of mixed woodland and park with large pond fed by stream from Noar Hill. (Open) Good trees and shrubs - magnolia grandiflora, liquidamber, judas, myrtle, loquat, medlar and acers. Formal yew hedges. The walled garden contains a traditionally managed kitchen garden, mature fig, espalier apples backing a double mixed border, fruit and vegetables interspersed with flowers and the original greenhouse with large vine and wall trained fruit. Gates open noon for picnicing. TEAS in aid of Empshott Church. *Adm £1 Chd free. Sat, Sun Aug 20, 21 (2-5)*

Eversley Gardens ❀ On B3016. Signposted from A30 (just west of Blackbush Airport) and from B3272 (Formerly A327). E of the cricket ground at Eversley Cross. *Combined adm £1.50 Chd free. Suns March 27 (2-5); May 8, 29 (2-6)*

    Kiln Copse & (A Jervis O'Donohoe Trust) 8 acres; daffodil and bluebell wood; foxgloves; good collection of rhododendrons; roses; natural lake; bogside plants. New curving mixed borders; shrub roses; round garden with gazebo and roses into trees. Small kitchen garden; greenhouses

    Kiln Copse Cottage Small cottage garden in the grounds of Kiln Copse

    Little Coopers (Mr & Mrs J K Oldale) 10-acre garden. Drifts of daffodils in March. A woodland walk meanders through bluebells, rhododendrons, azaleas and unusual shrubs most of which are labelled. Shaded by mature trees, walk leads to water & bog garden with ponds and stream, then onto extensive lawn in front of house surrounded by Mediterranean and rose gardens. Small Japanese garden by the house. Featured on TV Channel 4 Garden Club 1993. TEA (March 27) TEAS (May) in aid of Arthritis and Rheumatism Research

● **Exbury Gardens** &❀ (Exbury Gardens Trust) Exbury, 2½m SE of Beaulieu; 15m SW of Southampton. Via B3054 SE of Beaulieu; after 1m turn sharp R for Exbury. 200 acres of woodland garden incorporating the Rothschild Collection of azaleas, rhododendrons, magnolias, maples and camellias. Luncheons and teas. Plant Centre and Gift Shop. *Spring Season: Sat Feb 12 to mid April Adm £3 OAPs £2.50. Parties of 15 or more £2.50 Chd 10-16 £2. Adm mid April-early June £4 OAPs & groups £3.50 (OAPs reduced 50p Weds and Thurs) Chd 10-16 £3. (All main season prices except OAPs increase by 50p weekends and Bank Hols). Mid June to July 10 Adm £3 OAPs £2.50. Parties £2.50 Chd £2. Gardens N of Gilbury Lane Bridge open Summer July 11 to Sept 16 Adm adults & parties £2.50 OAPs & Chd 10-16 £1.50. Autumn Sept 17 to Oct 24. Adm £2.50 OAPs & groups £2 Chd 10-16 £1.50. Open daily 10-5.30/dusk. For NGS Wed May 11*

Fairfield House &%❀ (Mrs Peter Wake) Hambledon. 10m SW of Petersfield. Hambledon village. 5-acre informal garden on chalk, with extensive walls, fine mature trees; large collection of shrubs and climbing roses mixed with wide variety of small trees and interesting perennials. Adjacent car park and wild flower meadow. Featured in 'A Heritage of Roses' by Hazel Le Rougetel, 'The Rose Gardens of England' by Michael Gibson, 'The Latest Country Gardens' by George Plumptre. TEAS. *Adm £1.50 Chd free. Sun, Mon June 26, 27 (2-6). Also private visits welcome anytime by appt; suitable for groups, please* Tel 0705 632431

Fernlea %❀ (Mr & Mrs P G Philip) Chilworth. N of Southampton on A27 at junction of M3 and M27, take A27 towards Romsey. After 1m turn L at Clump Inn (Lunches available). Proceed along Manor Rd into Chilworth Drove for about ½m. Under restoration from rhododendron ponticum. Habitat gardening to encourage native flora and fauna. Bulbs, azaleas, rhododendrons, heathers and mediterranean plants. Specimen trees dating back to mid C19. Set on high ground with views to Isle of Wight. Garden merges into woodland. 15 acres in all. Picnics welcome. TEA. *Adm £1.50 Chd free. Sats May 28, (12-4) July 16, Sun Aug 21 (12-5).*

Fiddlers Cottage ❀ (Group Capt & Mrs Musgrave) Woodgreen. 3m E of Fordingbridge on A338. Turn E to Woodgreen. Turn R at Horse and Groom, continue for 1¼m; enter through Little Barn Garden. Relaxed 3-acre woodland garden started in 1965. Lawns of wild heather mown once a year. Featured in "Creating a wild life garden". Mature eucalyptus and collection of shrubs for acid soil. TEAS. *Adm £1 Chd free. Sun May 22 (2-6)*

¶**Fritham Lodge** &%❀ (Christopher and Rosie Powell) Fritham, nr Lyndhurst. 3m NW of Cadnam junction 1 on M27. Follow signs to Fritham, after approx 3m, turn into Fritham village, turn down gravel track low sign Fritham Lodge only; parking in field. Set in heart of New Forest. Approx 1-acre garden surrounding grade II listed house (not open) originally one of Charles II's hunting lodges. Parterre of old roses, potager, pergola, herbaceous, blue and white mixed borders, ponds. TEAS *Adm £1 Chd free. Sun June 26 (2-5)*

● **Furzey Gardens** &※※ (Furzey Gardens Charitable Trust) Minstead, 8m SW of Southampton. 1m S of A31; 2m W of Cadnam and end of M27; 3½m NW of Lyndhurst. 8 acres of informal shrub garden; comprehensive collections of azaleas and heathers; water garden; fernery; summer and winter flowering shrubs. Botanical interest at all seasons. Also open (limited in winter) Will Selwood Gallery and ancient cottage (AD 1560). High-class arts and crafts by 150 local craftsmen. Tea Honey Pot ¼m. *Adm £2.50 OAPs £2 Chd £1.50 March to Oct. £1.50 OAPs £1 Chd 75p winter. Daily except Dec 25 & 26 (10-5; dusk in winter)*

The Garden House ※※ (Mr & Mrs C Kirkman) Lymington. Off Lymington High St opp Woolworths. An explosion of unusual herbaceous, roses, grasses, house leeks agaves and shrubs, interspersed with a riot of annuals, punctuated by 2 ponds and an ornamental kitchen garden full of fruit and vegetables. Prime example of close boscage. All in ¾-acre surrounded by walls of Napoleonic brick; ample parking. Home-made cream TEAS. *Adm £1 Chd free (Share to Oakhaven Hospice®). Sun June 19 (2-6)*

Glevins &※※ (Mrs Clarke) Lymington. Situated off Lymington High St. between Lloyds Bank and Nat West Bank. ½-acre small walled garden with wide view of the Solent and Yarmouth I.O.W. Mixed borders, small rockery, conservatory. *Adm £1 Chd free. Sun June 19 (2-6)*

Greatham Mill &※※ (Capt E N Pumphrey) Greatham, nr Liss. 5m N of Petersfield. From A325, at Greatham turn onto B3006 towards Alton; after 600yds L into 'No Through Rd' lane to garden. Interesting garden with large variety of plants surrounding mill house, with mill stream and nursery garden. Featured in NGS video 1, see page 344. *Adm £1 Chd free (Share to Greatham PCC). April 11 to end of Sept every Sun & Bank Hol. For NGS Suns May 15, Sept 11 (2-6). Private visits welcome, please Tel 0420 538219*

Hackwood Park (The Spring Wood) ※※ (The Viscount and Viscountess Camrose) 1m S of Basingstoke. Entrance off Tunworth Rd. Signed from A339 Alton--Basingstoke. 80 acres delightful C17-C18 semi-formal wood with pavilions, walks, glades; magnificent ornamental pools, amphitheatre, interesting trees and bulbs. Home-made TEAS and produce. *Adm £1.50 OAPs £1 (Share to St Leonard's Church, Cliddesden and St Mary's Church, Herriard®). Sun April 10, (2-6) Oct 9 (1.30-5.30) For NGS Sun May 15 (2-6)*

Hall Place & (Mr & Mrs Dru Montagu) West Meon. 7m W of Petersfield. From A32 in West Meon, take rd to East Meon, garden on R. Parking in drive. Large collection of rare and unusual daffodils in 8 acres of garden designed by Lanning Roper 30 years ago. Grass walks, spring bulbs, many varieties of trees and shrubs; walled kitchen garden. *Collecting box. Sun April 24 (2-6)*

Hambledon House ※※ (Capt & Mrs David Hart Dyke) Hambledon. 8m SW of Petersfield. In village centre behind George Hotel. Approx 2 acres partly walled garden with unusual plants, shrubs suited to chalk soil. Centred

around 150 yr-old copper beech. Special interest in grasses, salvias, penstemons. Constant new development. Featured on TV 1992. TEAS. *Adm £1.50 Chd free. Suns June 26, Sept 11 (2-6) also private visits welcome, please Tel 0705 632380*

¶**Harfield Farm House** ※ (Mr & Mrs P Cartwright) Curdridge. On B3035 from Bishops Waltham to Botley 1st entrance on L after the signpost Curdridge at bottom of hill. Park in field at brow of hill. Walk to house next door. 1½ acres surrounding C17 farm house and C18 barns; walled garden with mixed shrub and herbaceous border espalier apple walk. Courtyard, old fashioned roses, herb and white garden. The whole comprising of several small gardens in different compartments and levels. TEAS. *Adm £1 Chd 50p. Sun June 12 (2-6)*

Headbourne Worthy Gardens 2m N Winchester B3420 to Three Maids Hill roundabout, take rd signed The Worthys. Follow 1½m, under railway bridge. *Combined adm £3 Chd free. Sun June 26 (2-5)*

¶**Little Acre** &※ (Mr M Walford) Formerly open as The White Cottage. Little Acre is a Swedish bungalow built in the garden of White Cottage. 1½ acres of grass, shrubs and trees. Foliage a speciality, new plantings incl a Mediterranean scree garden and a shade border

The Manor House &※ (Mr & Mrs P Anker) C17 house, 2 acres spring bulbs and shrubs, recently restored 300-yr-old cob wall. Mature trees and borders

Upper Farm &※ (Mr & Mrs S Browne) Garden comprises 2 parts, an older formal area terraced with mixed borders, and hedged vegetable garden approx 1½ acres. Young woodland garden with wide variety bulbs approx 2½ acres. TEA

Heatherland & (Col & Mrs W F Cubitt) Woodgreen. 3m NE of Fordingbridge via A338, turn to Woodgreen; bear L in village and turn R at Horse and Groom to Common; Heatherland is ¼m on L for other gardens continue on same rd. 2-acre mature garden in a woodland setting, with lawns and a wide variety of shrubs, incl rhododendrons, camellias, azaleas and pieris. Heather beds, rockery and a chain of pools. Vegetables and soft fruit. *Adm £1 Chd free. Sun May 22 (2-6)*

Heathlands & (Dr John Burwell) 47 Locks Rd, Locks Heath. Locks Rd runs due S from Park Gate into Locks Heath. No 47 is 1m down on the R hand side [Grid Ref 513 069]. 1-acre garden designed & developed by the owner since 1967. An attempt has been made to give yr-round interest against a background of evergreens & mature trees. Spring bulbs, rhododendrons, paulownias, cyclamen, ferns and some less usual plants. Topiary, small herbaceous border. National Collection of Japanese anemones. 'A treat for garden visitors' Stefan Buczacki TVS. TEAS. *Adm £1 Chd free. Suns May 22, July 17 (2-5.30)*

By Appointment Gardens. These owners do not have a fixed opening day usually because they do not like crowds or have insufficient parking space. Owner will often give guided tour.

The Hedges ⭑✿❀ (Mr & Mrs F J Vinnicombe) E Wellow, 3m from Romsey. At M27 junction 2, take A36 N 2m, turn R into Whinwhistle Rd. Hamdown Cres is 3rd turning on L. ¼ acre densely planted mixture of bulbs; hardy perennials; shrubs and trees including two small ponds. Small collections of ferns, erysimum, hedera, cistus and pulmonaria. TEA. *Adm £1 Chd free. Weds May 18, 25 June 8, 15, July 27 Thurs May 19, 26 June 9, 16, July 28 (11-5) Suns May 22, 29, June 12, 19, July 31 (2-5.30) Also private visits welcome, please* **Tel 0794 322539**

Highclere Castle ⭑✿❀ (The Earl of Carnarvon) Nr Newbury. Entrance on A34 4½m S of Newbury. Spectacular Charles Barry Mansion set in Capability Brown parkland with extensive lawns; specimen trees, orangery; C18 walled garden with yew walks, large areas of herbaceous beds, ornamental trees and shrubs. Gift shop & plant centre, picnic area. TEAS. *Adm £2 (garden only). Open Weds to Suns July, Aug, Sept. Suns & Mons Easter, May & Aug Bank Hols. For NGS Suns July 17, 24; Aug 14, 21 (2-6) last entry 5pm*

Hill House, Old Alresford ⭑ (Maj & Mrs W F Richardson) From Alresford 1m along B3046 towards Basingstoke, then R by church. 2 acres with large old-fashioned herbaceous border and shrub beds, set around large lawn; kitchen garden. TEA. *Adm £1.20 Chd free. Sun July 31 (2-6)*

¶●Sir Harold Hillier Arboretum ⭑✿❀ Jermyns Lane, Ampfield. Situated between Ampfield and Braishfield, 3m NE of Romsey. Signposted from A31 and A3057. From M27 junction 3, follow signs to Romsey. Parking at the gardens. 160-acres of landscaped gardens containing the finest collection of hardy trees and shrubs in the UK. Home to 9 national collections quercus, carpinus, cornus, cotoneaster, ligustrum, lithocarpus, corylus, photinia, pinus. Pond, scree beds, heather garden, peat garden, centenary border and acer valley. Wonderful spring and autumn colour with guided tours at 2pm every Suns and Weds in May and Oct. Fine collections of magnolias, azaleas and rhododendrons. TEAS. *Adm £3 OAP £2.50 Chd £1. Daily April 1 to Oct 31 (10.30-6) Nov 1 to March 31 (10.30-5 or dusk)*

Hinton Ampner ⭑✿ (The National Trust) S of Alresford. On Petersfield-Winchester Rd A272. 1m W of Bramdean village. 12-acre C20th shrub garden designed by Ralph Dutton. Strong architectural elements using yew and box topiary, with spectacular views. Bold effects using simple plants, restrained and dramatic bedding. Orchard with spring wild flowers and bulbs within formal box hedges; magnolia and philadephus walks. Dell garden made from chalk pit, now restored and maturing. Shrub rose border dating from 1950s. Special interest viburnum, buddleia, cotinus, foxgloves. TEAS. *Adm £2.30 Chd £1.15. Sats, Suns June 25, 26; Sept 10, 11 (1.30-5)*

¶Holt End House ✿❀ (Maj & Mrs J B B Cockcroft) Ashford Hill, Newbury. Ashford Hill is on B3051 between Kingsclere and Tadley. The garden is in the village on the R going E. Medium-sized garden with extensive collection of old-fashioned, shrubs and climbing roses, mixed borders, mature shrubs and trees incl large ginkgo biloba. TEAS *Adm £1.25 Chd free. Sun June 26 (2-6)*

House-in-the-Wood (Countess Michalowska) 1½m from Beaulieu; signed from Motor Car Museum, Beaulieu. R turn to Southampton off B3056 Beaulieu-Lyndhurst Rd. 13-acre woodland garden; rhododendrons and azaleas. Coach parties by appt. **Tel Beaulieu 612346.** *Adm £2 Chd 50p. Mon May 2 (2.30-6.30)*

Ivalls Farm Cottage ✿❀ (Major & Mrs Ward) Bentworth. Alton 4½m. Take A339 W from Alton. 4m on turn sharp L to Bentworth. Approx 1 acre, essentially a cottage garden owner maintained. Over 200 roses, small herbaceous borders; pool and wild pond; kitchen garden. TEAS. *Adm £1 Chd free. Sun June 26 (2.30-6.30)*

Jenkyn Place ⭑✿❀ (Mrs G E Coke) Bentley. 400yds N of Xrds in Bentley. Heritage sign on A31. Bus: Guildford-Winchester, alight Bentley village, 400yds. Well designed plantsman's garden, many interesting shrubs and perennials, double herbaceous borders. Featured in NGS video 1, see page 344. Car park free. Disabled may set down at gates (Coaches only by prior appt). *Adm £2 Chd 75p. Thurs, Fris, Sats, Suns & Bank Hol Mons April 7 to Sept 11 (2-6). For NGS Suns June 5, July 3 plus 5 per cent of other receipts*

John Hines Studios ✿ (Mr John Hine) 2 Hillside Rd, Aldershot. From A31 take 3rd exit off large roundabout on E side of Farnham. Signed Farnborough A325 and Basingstoke A30, at next roundabout take 3rd exit signed Aldershot B3007. After 1m, with railway bridge ahead, rd bends sharply L and becomes Eggars Hill. Hillside Rd is 400yds on L. Garden is 2nd entrance on R. A small newly created courtyard garden (approx 50' x 60') surrounded by a restored C17 barn (open). Garden is planted with a wide range of climbers & herbaceous plants to give maximum colour and interest over a long season. Garden also includes hanging baskets, window boxes, containers and a dovecote. TEAS in traditional English tea room. *Adm £1 Chd 50p. Suns June 19, July 31; Mon Aug 29 (10.30-4.30)*

¶53 Ladywood ✿❀ (Mr & Mrs D Ward) Eastleigh. Leave A33/M3 at junction 12, signed A335 Eastleigh N and follow A335 towards Eastleigh. R at roundabout into Woodside Ave, 2nd R into Bosville. Ladywood is 5th R off Bosville please park in Bosville. A plant lover's very small garden, 45' x 45', developed by the owners over the last 5 yrs, giving many ideas for the small garden. Over 1000 plants labelled. Rustic fences have been built to give vertical space for clematis and climbing roses. A secluded shade garden, a pond garden and a tiny lawn; collections of hardy geraniums, pulmonarias, asters for the small garden and many foliage plants. TEAS (2-5). *Adm £1 Chd 50p. Suns May 22, June 19, July 24, (10-5). Private visits welcome May to Sept, except Weds, please* **Tel 0703 615389**

¶Lake House ⭑❀ (Lord & Lady Ashburton) Northington, Alresford. 4m N of Alresford off B3046. Follow English heritage signs to The Grange. From Winchester take A33 N turning R at Lunway Inn follow signs to Northington and The Grange. Large garden in Candover Valley. 2 lakes set off by mature woodland with waterfalls formed by streams, abundant bird life and long landscape vistas.

Sizeable walled garden with rose pergola leading to moon gate, formal flower garden, borders and kitchen garden also numerous flowering pots. Visit can conveniently be continued with seeing The Grange, an English Heritage property in the Greek revival style. TEAS *Adm £2 Chd free. Sun June 26 (2-6)*

Landford Lodge Landford see Wiltshire

60 Lealand Road &✿❀ (Mr F G Jacob) Drayton. 2m from Cosham E side of Portsmouth. Old A27 (Havant Rd) between Cosham and Bedhampton. Small garden created and designed by owner since 1969. Featured in National Gardening Magazines. A first prize winner in 'The News' Gardening Competitions 1992. Exotic plants (including cacti) with rockery, ponds and dwarf conifers etc. TEA. *Adm 60p Chd 25p. Suns April 17, May 29, June 26 (11-5). Also private visits welcome, please* **Tel 0705 370030**

Lithend &✿❀ (Mrs F L Gunner) For directions see under Crawley Gardens open April 18. Also open with **Little Court, Crawley** *Combined adm £1.50 Chd free. Sun, Mon May 8, 9 (2-5.30)*

Little Barn Garden & Barnhawk Nursery &❀ (Drs R & V A Crawford) Woodgreen. 3m NE of Fordingbridge via A338. Turn E to Woodgreen; bear L in village; R immediately past Horse and Groom, continue for 1¼m; 2½ acres of mature informal garden with all year interest in form, colour and texture; rhododendron; azalea; camellia; magnolia; acer and collector's plants with peat, scree, rock, woodland, bog and water area. *Adm £1 Chd 25p. For NGS Sun May 22 (2-6). Also private visits welcome, please* **Tel 0725 512213**

The Little Cottage ✿ (Wing Commander & Mrs Peter Prior) In Lymington on A337; opp Toll House Inn. ¼ acre garden divided into small formal gardens with intricate paving, box and topiary, each with a precise colour scheme - blue/yellow, blue/white, pink/lime, mauve/silver, apricot/copper, red/purple and white courtyard garden with tender white climbers on S-facing cottage wall. Hard landscaping is now complete, but planting continues. Featured RHS "The Garden" Sept 1993. *Adm £1 Open most Tues June 1 to Sept 30 (10-dusk). Private visits welcome, please* **Tel 0590 679395**

Little Court &✿❀ (Prof & Mrs A R Elkington) Crawley 5m NW of Winchester off A272 in Crawley village; 300yds from either village pond or church. Please park near church. Sheltered walled chalk garden Drifts of bulbs; informal planting for peaceful effect incl silver border. Special interests incl euphorbia, geraniums, eryngiums and honeysuckles. Traditional walled kitchen garden; greenhouse vines. Beautiful views to Farley Mount. Bantams and geese. TEA Suns only. *Adm £1. Suns, Mons March 27, 28; July 31, Aug 1, 14, 15 (2-5.30) Also open Suns, Mons, April 10, 11 May 8, 9 with* **Crawley Gardens** *(Share to RSPB). Also private visits welcome, please* **Tel 0962 776365**

> **By Appointment Gardens.** See head of county section

Littleton House &✿ (Mr & Mrs James Butler) Crawley 5m NW of Winchester, off A272 Winchester-Stockbridge Rd. 1m from Littleton Church towards Crawley. 4 acres lawns; borders; vegetable garden ; 2 new island shrub beds; conservatory. TEA. *Adm £1 Chd free. Sun July 24 (2-5)*

¶Littlewood &✿❀ (Steven and Sheila Schrier) 163 West Lane, Hayling Island. From A27 Havant/Hayling Island roundabout, travel S 2m, turn R into West Lane. Travel 1m and Littlewood is on R in a wood. 2½-acre garden. Combines shrub sections featuring azaleas, rhododendrons, camellias and many other interesting shrubs and perennials. Pond, bog garden and an oak woodland walk. Patio and family conservatory with many pot plants. Picnickers welcome. Easy for the elderly and wheelchair bound. TEAS. *Donations. Sun May 29, Thurs June 2 (11-6)*

¶Longmead House &✿ (Mr & Mrs J H Ellicock) Longparish. Off B3048 in Longparish next to The Cricketers Inn. 2½-acre organic garden, mainly trees and shrubs. Large hedged vegetable garden with deep beds, poly tunnel, fruit cage and composting display. A fishpond and wildlife pond, wildflower meadow, Shetland pony, angora goats and chickens. TEAS *Adm £1 Chd free. Sat, Sun July 23, 24 (2-5.30)*

Longstock Park Gardens &✿❀ (Leckford Estate Ltd; Part of John Lewis Partnership) 3m N of Stockbridge. From A30 turn N on to A3057; follow signs to Longstock. A water garden of repute with extensive collection of aquatic and bog plants set in 7 acres of woodland with rhododendrons and azaleas. A walk through the park leads to an arboretum, herbaceous border and nursery. The water garden has featured in several TV programmes and gardening books. *Adm £2 Chd 50p. Sun June 19 (2-5)*

Long Thatch &✿❀ (Mr & Mrs P Short) Warnford. 1m S of West Meon on A32 turn R at George & Falcon, 100 yds turn R at T-junction, continue for ¼m; thatched C17th house on R, parking opp house. Interesting 2-acre garden rolling down to the R. Meon. Plantsmans garden continually being enhanced with fine selection of specimen trees and shrubs; 4 new hellebore beds; alpine and bog gardens rejuvenated. Fine lawns with herbaceous borders to give maximum colour and interest through the season. *Adm £1 Chd free. Weds March 2 to Sept 14 (10-5), Sat March 12 (2-5). Suns March 6, 13, May 29, June 26, July 31 (2-6) Mon May 30 (2-6). Also private visits by Societies welcome, please* **Tel 0730 829285**

Lymore Valley Herbs &✿❀ (N M Aldridge) Braxton Farm 3m W of Lymington. From A337 at Everton take turning to Milford-on-Sea, 70 yds on L is Lymore Lane. Turn into Lane and gardens are at Braxton courtyard on L. Attractive courtyard with raised lily pool and dovecote. Restored C19th barn leading into formal walled garden. Spring bulbs incl galanthus, narcissi and fritillaria. Extensive summer and autumn borders; knot garden and lawns. Horticultural societies welcome. Special evening visits. TEAS. Shop, plants nursery, no dogs in courtyard or walled garden (dog rings & water provided). *Adm 75p Chd free. Open 9-5 all year round except Dec 25 to March 1st*

Macpenny Woodland Garden & Nurseries ৬ৠ (Mr & Mrs T M Lowndes) Burley Road, Bransgore. Midway between Christchurch and Burley. From Christchurch via A35, at Cat and Fiddle turn left; at Xrds by The Crown, Bransgore turn R and on ¼m. From A31 (travelling towards Bournemouth) L at Picket Post, signed Burley; through Burley to Green Triangle then R for Bransgore and on 1m beyond Thorney Hill Xrds. 12 acres; gravel pit converted into woodland garden; many choice, rare plants incl camellias, rhododendrons, azaleas, heathers. Large selection shrubs and herbaceous plants available. Tea Burley (Forest Tearooms) or Holmsley (Old Station Tea Rooms). *Collecting box. Daily except Dec 25 & 26 and Jan 1. (Mons-Sats 9-5; Suns 2-5)*

The Manor House ⚘ৠ (Mr & Mrs J Wallinger) 6m SE of Basingstoke in Upton Grey village on hill immediately above the church. 5-acre garden designed by Gertude Jekyll in 1908: meticulously restored over last 10 yrs to original plans, which will be on display, and with few exceptions plants are as she specified: Nuttery, tennis lawn, bowling green, rose garden, formal garden with herbaceous borders and dry stone walling; wild garden with pond. Garden has yet to mature but overall shape and colour are perfectly evident. Parking in field nearby. TEA. *Adm £2 Chd free (Share to Hampshire Gardens Trust). Weds May, June & July (2-5); also groups by appt May to July, please* **Tel 0256 862827**

Manor Lodge ৬⚘ৠ (Mr & Mrs K Wren) Crawley. Signposted from A272 and near the village pond. Drive with many specie roses growing through yew trees; shrub borders. Walled garden with low maintenance, mixed border; over 50 varieties old and new roses incl 3 chinenis mutabilis. Considered colour combinations; thatched summer house; small courtyard. Converted barn with small garden; ancient walnut tree. Cream TEAS in garden room in aid of WWF. Parking outside House only. *Adm £1 Sat, Sun July 9, 10 (2-5.30). Also open with* **Crawley Gardens** *April 10, 11*

Martyr Worthy Gardens Midway between Winchester and Alresford on B3047. Gardens joined by Pilgrims Way through Itchen Valley, approx ½m. TEAS in Village Hall (Aug 7 only). *Adm £1.50 per garden Chd free. Sun Aug 7 (2-5.30)*
    Chilland ৬ (Mrs L A Impey) Mature garden. Fine situation. Shrub borders designed for foliage colour. Many interesting plants. *Also open Oct 16*
    Manor House ৬ৠ (Cdr & Mrs M J Rivett-Carnac) Large garden, roses, mixed borders, lawns, shrubs & fine trees, next to C12 church

Marycourt ৬⚘ৠ (Mr & Mrs M Conville) Odiham 2m S of Hartley Wintney on A30 or Exit 5 on M3; In Odiham High St. 1-acre garden and paddocks. Old garden roses; shrubs; ramblers dripping from trees. Silver/pink border, long shrubaceous and colourful herbaceous borders; hosta beds and new delphinium planting. Dry Stone Wall/alpines thriving. Grade II starred house. *Adm £1.50 Chd free (Share to Jonathan Conville Memorial Trust®). Suns June 26, July 3 (2-6); Wed July 6 (all day) also private visits welcome, please* **Tel 0256 702100**

Maurys Mount ৬⚘ৠ (Dr & Mrs P Burrows) Slab Lane, West Wellow. On A36 midway between Salisbury and Southampton, Slab Lane is a turning between the roundabout and Red Rover Inn on A36 in West Wellow. An Edwardian style garden created over three generations of family. 10 acres of woodland, garden and paddocks incl young arboretum, conservatory, formal herb and vegetable gardens and mature trees incl judas tree and 300-old-oak; woodland walk with natural pond and orchard with wild flower meadow. Jacob sheep, ducks, geese, hens and horses. TEAS. *Adm £1.50 Chd 50p. Thurs May 19, Sun June 5 (2-5)*

Meadow House, nr Newbury See Berkshire

Merdon Manor ⚘ৠ (Mr & Mrs J C Smith) Hursley, SW of Winchester. From A3090 Winchester-Romsey, at Standon turn on to rd to Slackstead; on 2m. 5 acres with panoramic views; herbaceous and rose borders; small secret walled water garden (as seen on TV). Ha-ha and sheep. TEAS. *Adm £1 Chd 25p. Sun, Mon July 17, 18 (2-6); also private visits welcome, please* **Tel 0962 775215** *or* **775281**

Merrie Cottage ৬⚘ৠ (Mr & Mrs C K Thornton) Woodgreen 3m N of Fordingbridge on A338 turn E to Woodgreen. Fork R at PO towards Godshill. Entrance 200 yds on L. Limited parking for disabled or park on common and walk down footpath. 60ft gingko and huge pollarded beech dominate part of garden. There is no longer a Merrie. The irregular sloping shape offers vistas with a profusion of iris and primulas May & June, followed by seed-grown lilies and wide variety of moisture lovers. There is no hard landscape or colour theme but interest is held throughout year. TEAS (Sun). *Adm £1 Chd free. Sun, Mon, June 12, 13 (2-6). Private visits welcome, please* **Tel 0725 512273**

Monxton Gardens ⚘ 3m W of Andover, between A303 and A343; in Monxton TEAS in village hall in aid of Church. *Combined adm £2 Chd free. Sun, Mon May 29, 30 (2-5.30)*
    ¶**Bec House** (Mr & Mrs A J Rushworth Lund) Large spring garden designed to compliment Old Rectory. Rose garden, orchard with paddock leading to stream
    Hutchens Cottage (Mr & Mrs R A Crick) ¾-acre cottage garden with old roses, clematis, shrubs, mature trees, small orchard; mixed thyme patch and kitchen garden
    Mill Pound Cottage ⚘ (Mr & Mrs P R Coldicott) ⅓ acre cottage garden by Pill Hill Brook. Herbaceous borders, flowering trees, kitchen garden, waterside plants. Demonstration of the use of coir. Woodland views

Mottisfont Abbey & Garden ৬⚘ৠ (The National Trust) Mottisfont, 4½m NW of Romsey. From A3057 Romsey-Stockbridge turn W at sign to Mottisfont. 4 wheelchairs and battery car service available at garden. 30 acres; originally a C12 Priory; landscaped grounds with spacious lawns bordering R Test; magnificent trees; remarkable ancient spring pre-dating the Priory; walled garden contains NT's large collection of old-fashioned roses. Tea Mottisfont PO. *Adm £2.50 Chd £1.25 (June £3.50 Chd £1.75) April 2 to Oct 31 Sat to Wed (12-6) June only (12-8.30). For NGS Sun June 26 (12-8.30). Last admission 7.30 pm*

Moundsmere Manor (Mr & Mrs Andreae) 6m S of Basingstoke on B3046. Drive gates on L just after Preston Candover sign. 20 acres, incl formal rose gardens; herbaceous borders, large greenhouses, unusual trees and shrubs. Coaches by appt. *Adm £1.50 Chd £1. Sun July 3 (2-6)*

Mylor Cottage ふ器 (Dr & Mrs Martin ffrench Constant) Droxford. ½m S of Droxford on the Swanmore Rd. Car park. Gardener's garden; April: anemone blanda, cyclamen, spring bulbs and cherries; June: interesting foliage beds and specimen trees, colourful herbaceous borders. *Adm £1 Chd 50p. (Share to Multiple Sclerosis®). Sun April 10 (2-5) Sun June 19 open with* **Droxford Gardens** *(2-6) (Combined adm £2.50 Chd 50p)*

¶**Nine Springs Nursery** 器器 (Graham Burgess Esq) Whitchurch. Follow Whitchurch signs off A34. At 30mph sign turn sharp L and look for Mill Stones on L. Alternatively park in Silk Mill car park, a short walk away. 2-acre aquatic nursery, fish, peacocks and chicks, maze and garden, fed by 9 natural springs which feed the Test. Tea at famed Whitchurch Silk Mill which is also open. *Adm £1.50 Chd free. Sat, Sun June 18, 19 (2-5)*

North Ecchinswell Farm ふ器 (Mr & Mrs Robert Henderson) Nr Newbury. Turn S off A339 Newbury-Basingstoke rd. House 1m from turning (sign-posted Ecchinswell and Bishops Green) on L-hand side. Approx 6-acre garden. Shrub borders, woodland garden, fine trees incl an exceptional lime, small arboretum. *Adm £1 Chd free. Sun May 0 (£.30-5.30)*

Oakley Manor ふ器器 (Mr & Mrs R H Priestley) Oakley. 5m W of Basingstoke. From Basingstoke towards Whitchurch on B3400 turn L at Station Rd ½m W of Newfound and follow signs. Bus no. 55 Basingstoke to Oakley. Large garden, lawn, trees, water garden, borders, rose garden, greenhouses, herb garden, wild conservation area. TEA. Free parking at the Manor. *Combined adm with* **The Barn House** *£2 Chd free. Sun Aug 7 (2-5.30)*

The Old House ふ器 (Mr & Mrs M Jurgens) Bramley Road, Silchester; entrance next to Silchester (Calleva) Roman Museum. Queen Anne rectory with large garden. Fine specimen and unusual trees and shrubs. Well labelled collections of specie and hybrid rhododendrons, azaleas, camellias and shrub roses. Very colourful spring garden dating from 1920's incl dell and pergola walk, bluebell woodland, ponds and paddock. Spring bulbs. Roman town walls and Amphitheatre ¼m; medieval Church. TEAS in aid of church. *Adm £1 Chd 50p (Share to St Mary The Virgin Church, Silchester®). Suns April 10, 24 May 8, 22 (2-6). Private parties welcome March to May, please* Tel 0734 700240

Old Meadows ふ器器 (Dr & Mrs J M Fowler) Silchester. Off A340 between Reading and Basingstoke. 1m S of Silchester on rd to Bramley, signposted at Xrds. 5 acres including walled potager. Herbaceous borders, meadow walk. TEAS. *Adm £1.50 Chd free (Share to North Hampshire Medical Fund®). Sun June 26 (2-6)*

Regular Openers. See head of county section.

The Old Vicarage ふ器 (Sir Dermot & Lady De Trafford) Appleshaw. Take A342 Andover to Marlborough Rd, turn to Appleshaw 1m W of Weyhill, fork L at playing field, on L in village by clock. 2-acre walled garden mature trees, bush and rambler roses, shrub borders, shrubs and trees in grass; fruit and herb garden with box hedges. *Adm £1.50 Chd free (Share to Appleshaw Church®). Sun June 12 (2-5)*

Paige Cottage ふ器器 (Mr & Mrs T W Parker) Next to Crawley village pond. Signposted from A272. 1 acre of traditional English country garden with large shrub and herbaceous borders and including grass tennis court and walled Italian style swimming pool; roses climbing into apple trees. *Adm £1 Chd free. Sun, Mon July 10, 11 (2-5.30)*

Pennington Chase ふ器 (Mrs V E Coates) 2m SW Lymington L off A337, at Pennington Cross roundabout. 4 acres, flowering shrubs, azaleas and rhododendrons with some unusual trees in fine state of maturity. TEAS 50p. *Adm £1 Chd 50p. Suns March 20, May 15 (2-7)*

Petersfield Physic Garden ふ器器 (Hampshire Gardens Trust) 16 High St, Petersfield. Centre of town. Recreation of C17 garden in ⅔ acre planted in 1989. As featured on BBC Gardener's World in March 1993. Features include knot garden; topiary; orchard; shrubs; florist borders and physic beds. *Collecting box. Open daily (not Christmas Day) (9-5). For NGS Suns May 15, June 19 (9-5). Enquiries please* Tel 0730 268331

Pullens ふ器器 (Mr & Mrs R N Baird) W Worldham. From Alton take B3006 SE on the Selborne Rd. After 2½m turn L to W Worldham. By church turn R. Pullen 100yds on R behind wall. Approx 1-acre plantsmans garden on greensand surrounded by hedges and walls. Particular emphasis on colour and yr-round interest. Tranquil atmosphere. TEAS. *Adm £1 Chd free. Sun June 26, Wed June 29 (2-6)*

Pylewell Park ふ器 (The Lord Teynham) 2½ m E of Lymington beyond IOW car ferry. Large garden of botanical interest; good trees, flowering shrubs, rhododendrons, lake, woodland garden. *Adm £2 Chd 50p (Share to Wessex Regional Medical Oncology Unit®). Suns May 15, 22 (2-6)*

Robins Return ふ器器 (Mr & Mrs J Ingrem) Tiptoe. 2m NE of New Milton. Take B3055, at Xrds by Tiptoe Church. Turn into Wootton Rd (signposted to Wootton). Garden 400yds on L. ⅔-acre garden. Shrubs, roses and herbaceous plants; ornamental pool and rock garden; greenhouses; organic kitchen garden; recently constructed fern garden. *Adm £1 Chd free. Sun June 12 (2-5)*

Rookley Manor 器 (Lord & Lady Inchyra) Up Somborne. 6m W of Winchester. From A272 Winchester-Stockbridge Rd. At Rack and Manger turn L towards Kings Somborne. 2m on R. 2 acres; spring bulbs, flowers and blossom; herbaceous, shrub roses, kitchen garden. TEAS. *Adm £1 Chd 20p. Mon May 2 (2-6)*

Rotherfield Park &❀ (Lady Scott) East Tisted, 4m S of Alton on A32. Large garden; walled and rose garden, herbaceous borders; lovely grounds with beautiful trees; pond; greenhouses. Picnickers welcome. TEAS (only when house is open). *Adm House & garden £2.50 Chd free. Garden only £1 Chd free (Share to Rainbow Trust®) House and Garden open (2-5) every Bank Hol Sun & Mon from Easter & the first 7 days of June, July, Aug. Garden only Easter to Sept 30 every Thurs, Sun (2-5) (honesty box). Also private visits welcome, please* **Tel 042058 204**

Rowans Wood &❀❀ (Mrs D C Rowan) Straight Mile, Ampfield, on A31 (S side); 2m E of Romsey. 2m W of Potters Heron Hotel. Parking on service Rd. 2-acre woodland garden made and maintained by owners; acers and acid-loving plants, spring bulbs. Over 50 varieties of hosta; fine trees. Considerable new planting. Views. TEAS Sun only. *Adm £1 Chd 25p (Share to Winchester & Romsey Branch RSPCA®). Suns April 17, 24 (2-5) May 8, 22, Mon May, 23 (2-6). Also private visits welcome, please* **Tel 0794 513072**

12 Rozelle Close ❀ (Margaret & Tom Hyatt) Littleton. Turn E off A272 Winchester to Stockbridge Rd. Just inside Winchester 40 mph zone. 1m Hookers Nursery on R. Rozelle Close 150yds on L just short of Running Horse public house. ⅓-acre spectacular display of herbaceous and 10,000 bedding plants; tubs; troughs; hanging baskets; 2 ponds; 3 greenhouses; vegetables. *Donations. Sat, Sun July 30, 31 (9.30-5.30)*

Rumsey Gardens &❀❀ (Mr & Mrs N R Giles) 117 Drift Rd, Clanfield, 6m S of Petersfield. Turn off A3 N of Horndean, signed Clanfield. 2 acres; alpine, herbaceous; heather, rhododendrons and wild gardens. Celebrity opening May only. *Adm £1 Chd 50p. Sun May 29 (11-5)*

Sadlers Gardens &❀ (Nicholas Lock) Lymington. Take A337, S out of Lymington. Turn L at Pennington Cross roundabout. ½m down lane on R. Quantities of rare and half hardy shrubs and trees; herbaceous beds; densely planted in 3 acres. Plantsman's garden created in 1976 by the owner; rhododendrons, camellias, magnolias and acers; spring and summer bulbs. Nursery open. *Adm £1.50 Chd free. Sun March 20; Mon April 4; Suns May 29, July 17 (2-6)*

3 St Helens Road &❀ (Mr & Mrs Norman Vaughan) Hayling Island. From Beachlands on seafront, turn R 3rd turning on R into Staunton Avenue, then 1st L. Parking in drive. ⅓-acre ornamental garden with conifers in variety. Interesting trees and shrubs; water garden; old roses. Prizewinning garden featured in 'Amateur Gardening' 1992. TEAS. *Adm by donation. Sat, Sun May 14, 15 (11-6)*

Somerley ❀ (The Earl & Countess of Normanton) 2m N of Ringwood off A338 between Ringwood & Ibsley. Turn to Ellingham Church and follow sign to Somerley House. From bus alight Ellingham Cross. Country house garden with herbaceous and rose borders, pergola and herb gardens and ornamental kitchen garden and gift shop. Views over R Avon Valley and fine specimen trees in parkland. *Adm £1. Sat Aug 20 (2-6)*

South End House &❀ (Mr & Mrs Peter Watson) Lymington. At town centre, turn S opp St Thomas Church 70yds, or park free behind Waitrose and use walkway. Walled town garden to Queen Anne house, home of garden lecturer and writer Elizabeth Watson. ¼-acre, architecturally designed as philosophers' garden. Pergolas, trellises and colonnade attractively planted with vines, clematis, wisteria and roses, combine with sculpted awnings to form 'outdoor rooms', enhanced by fountains, music and lights. Wide pavings, easy access, extensive seating. Featured on TV "That's Gardening' and NGS video 2, see page 344. TEAS. *Adm £1 Chd free. Sun, May 15 (2.30-5.30)*

¶Southview Nurseries ❀❀ (Mr & Mrs Mark Trenear) Chequers Lane, Eversley Cross. On B3016 signposted from A30 W of Blackbush airport and from B3272 2m W of Yatley. Turn up Chequers Lane alongside The Chequers public house. Car park signposted. A ½-acre plantsmans garden with well designed herbaceous areas. Old pinks garden, "Roman garden", white garden; formal herbaceous border, old roses, all featuring many unusual and well known plants with bold colour schemes in mind as shown on channel 4 Gardening Club 1993. Pinks featured on Gardeners World July 1993. Teas at The Chequers Inn % to NGS. *Nursery and garden open Thurs, Fri, Sat, Feb to Nov. For NGS Adm £1 Chd 50p. Suns June 12, 26 (2-6)*

Sowley House &❀❀ (Mr & Mrs O Van Der Vorm) Sowley. At Lymington follow signs to I.O.W. ferry. Continue E on this rd past the ferry nearest to the Solent for 3m until Sowley pond on L. Sowley House is opp the pond. Old garden in country setting approx 4-5 acre with far reaching views over the Solent to the I.O.W. Walled herb garden, with many old roses, clematis, herbaceous and shrub borders, cottage, gardens. Orchard, woodland and bog garden still in the making. Famous for its drifts of daffodils mixed with wild primroses and violets. Stream walk down to the Solent where you might spot kingfishers. TEA. *Adm £1.50 Chd free (Share to Oakhaven Hospice Lymington®). Sun June 5 (2-5). Private visits also welcome, please* **Tel 0590 65231**

Spinners ❀❀ (Mr & Mrs P G G Chappell) Boldre. Signed off the A337 Brockenhurst Lymington Rd. Garden made by owners. Azaleas, rhododendrons, magnolias, hydrangeas, maples etc interplanted with a wide range of choice herbaceous plants and bulbs. Nursery contains a wide selection of less common and rare hardy plants, trees and shrubs subject of TV programme in last 7 yrs. *Adm £1.50 Chd under six free. April 20 to Sept 1 daily (10-5) but closed Mons & Tues from July 1. Nursery open all the year and part of garden daily but closed Mons, Tues (except private visits welcome, please* **Tel 0590 673347***) July 1 to April 1*

Springfield ❀❀ (Vice-Adm Sir John & Lady Lea) 27 Brights Lane, Hayling Island. From Havant take main rd over Hayling bridge, 3m fork R at roundabout into Manor Rd, Brights Lane ¼m on R. Bus: from Havant, ask for Manor Rd, Hayling Island, alight at Manor Rd PO. ⅓-acre walled cottage garden; mainly mixed borders containing wide variety of labelled plants; vegetables, greenhouses. Partially suited for wheelchairs. *Adm by donation. Private visits welcome, please* **Tel 0705 463801**

● **Stratfield Saye House** ⅋ (Home of the Dukes of Wellington) Off A33, equidistant between Reading and Basingstoke. House built 1630; presented to the Great Duke in 1817; unique collection of paintings, prints, furniture, china, silver and personal mementoes of the Great Duke. Special Wellington Exhibition; Great Duke's funeral carriage. American, rose and walled gardens and grounds. Refreshments. Also, nearby, Wellington Country Park with woodlands, meadowlands and lake. TEAS. *Adm £4 Chd £2 special rates for 20 or more.* **Tel 0256 882882.** *Open daily (except Fri) 1st May until the last Sun in Sept. House (12-4), grounds (11.30-6)*

Swallowfield Park, nr Reading see Berkshire

Tichborne Park ⅋❀ (Mrs J Loudon) Alresford. 1m S off A31 New Alresford on B 3046. 2m N of the A272 New Cheriton on B 3046. Approx 10-acres. Lake, River Itchen, large lawns, trees, shrubs, daffodils, kitchen gardens, glasshouse. Large collection of fuchsias. TEAS. *Adm £1.50 Chd £1. Suns April 17, June 19 (2-5)*

Tunworth Old Rectory ⅋❀❀ (The Hon Mrs Julian Berry) 5m SE of Basingstoke. 3m from Basingstoke turn S off A30 at sign to Tunworth. Garden laid out with yew hedges, enclosing different aspects of the garden i.e. swimming pool, double rose and mixed border; ruby wedding garden; pleached hornbeam walk; lime avenue, ornamental pond, interesting trees incl beech lined walk to church. TEAS. *Adm £2 OAP £1 Chd free (Share to Church Roof Fund All Saints Church Tunworth®). Sun July 3 (2-5.30)*

Tylney Hall Hotel ⅋❀ From M3 Exit 5 Via A287 and Newnham, M4 Exit 11 via B3349 and Rotherwick. Large garden. 67 acres surrounding Tylney Hall Hotel with extensive Woodlands and fine vistas now being fully restored with new plantings; fine avenues of Wellingtonias; rhododendron and azaleas; Italian Garden; lakes; large water and rock garden and dry stone walls originally designed with assistance of Gertrude Jekyll. TEA. *Adm £1.50 Chd free. Suns May 15, July 17 (2-6)*

Vernon Hill House ❀ (Lady Newton) 1m from Bishop's Waltham. Turn off Beeches Hill. Attractive 6-acre spring and summer garden; wild garden with bulbs growing informally; fine trees, roses, unusual shrubs; kitchen garden. Picnickers welcome. TEA. *Adm £1 Chd 25p. Suns May 1, Mon May 2, Sun June 12, July 3 (2-7) also private visits welcome May to early July, please* **Tel 0489 892301**

Verona Cottage ⅋❀❀ (David J Dickinson Esq) 6 Webb Lane, Mengham, Hayling Island. 4m S of Havant. From A3023 fork L to Mengham shops with car parking facilities. Entrance to garden opp Rose in June public house. Three separate gardens making a medium-sized L-shaped garden featuring a wide variety of early summer shrubs and flowers incl a new rose garden; replanting in style of Gertrude Jekyll. Also small display of old gardening books. TEA. *Adm 80p Chd free. Sat, Sun, May 28, 29 (11-6)*

By Appointment Gardens. See head of county section

Veronica Cottage ⅋❀ (Mr & Mrs E J Hartwell) East End. At Lymington follow signs to I.O.W. ferry. Continue E on this rd past the ferry for 2½m. Veronica Cottage is on the R just beyond the East End Arms. [O.S. ref 363969] Work began on this ⅓-acre garden in 1985. The cottage well supplies several ponds and waterfalls which are surrounded by marginal plants, grasses and shrubs. Meandering borders contain many unusual and labelled shrubs and trees. Cream teas at East End Arms. *Adm £1 Chd free (Share to South Baddesley Church®). Sun July 31 (2-6)*

The Vyne ⅋❀ (The National Trust) Sherborne St John, 4m N of Basingstoke. Between Sherborne St John and Bramley. From A340 turn E at NT signs. 17 acres with extensive lawns, lake, fine trees, herbaceous border, display of tools and machinery. Gardener available to answer questions. TEAS. *Adm house & garden £4 Chd £2; garden only £2 Chd £1. Sun July 24 (12.30-5.30)*

¶**Waldrons** ❀❀ (Major & Mrs J Robinson) Brook, Lyndhurst. 1m W from exit 1 M27 (on A3079). 1st house L passed the Green Dragon public house and directly opp the Bell Inn. A C18 listed cottage with a conservatory, in a garden of 1 acre, containing lawns; a herbaceous border, shrubs and flower beds created around old orchard trees. Small duck pond (free roaming call ducks); fruit cage, herb garden, arbour, rose trellis and a small stable yard. TEAS. *Adm £1 Chd free (Share to Sight Savers®). Sun June 26 (11.30-5)*

Walhampton ⅋❀ (Walhampton School Trust) Lymington. 1m along B3054 to Beaulieu. 90 acres with azaleas; rhododendrons; lakes; shell grotto. TEAS. *Adm £1 Chd 50p. Sun May 22 (2-6)*

West Silchester Hall ⅋❀ (Mrs Jenny Jowett) Bramley Rd, Silchester. Off A340 between Reading and Basingstoke. 1½ acres; Herbaceous and perennial borders, rhododendrons, azaleas, many unusual spring and summer plants; good collection of half hardy plants, small pond and water garden; kitchen garden all owner maintained. Exhibition of Jenny Jowett's botanical paintings. TEAS. *Adm £1.50 Chd 50p. Suns June 19, Aug 7 (2-6). Parties by appt March-Sept* **Tel 0734 700278**

White Cottage ❀ (Mr & Mrs A W Ferdinando) Speltham Hill, Hambledon. Speltham Hill is the lane between The George Inn and village grocer's shop. Parking in village or in layby atop Speltham Hill. Small ornamental garden. Of hillside this garden, of vista and view. Of pools and of bridges, of steps quite a few. See dragons, see tombstone climb heights, crossings dare. Enjoy all you see here, have fun and take care. *Donations. Sun Sept 11 (2-6)*

White Windows ❀❀ (Mr & Mrs B Sterndale-Bennett) Longparish. 5m E of Andover off A303 to village centre on B3048. ⅔ acre with unusual range of hardy perennials, trees and shrubs planted for year round foliage interest and colour blendings in garden rooms. Garden featured on TV, in 'Hortus' and 'English Private Gardens'. TEAS, Sun. *Adm £1 Chd free. Sun, Mon Aug 14, 15 (2-6). Also private visits welcome Weds April to Sept, please* **Tel 0264 720222**

Wonston Lodge ⅋ (Mr & Mrs N J A Wood) Wonston. A34 or A30 to Sutton Scotney. At War Memorial turn to Wonston-Stoke Charity; ¾m in Wonston centre. 3 acres, owner maintained. Pond with aquatic plants and ornamental ducks; shrub roses; clematis; topiary. TEAS in barn (with pigeon loft). *Adm £1.50 Chd free. (Share to Wessex Medical Trust®) Sat, Sun Sept 3, 4 (2-6)*

Woodcote Manor ⅋ (Mrs J S Morton) Bramdean, SE of Alresford. On A272 Winchester-Petersfield Rd, ½m E of

Bramdean. Woodland garden; bulbs, shrubs. C17 manor house (not open). *Adm £1.50 OAPs £1 Chd free. Easter Sun April 3 (2-5)*

The Wylds ⅋ (Gulf International) Warren Rd, Liss Forest. 6m N of Petersfield; follow signs from Greatham on A325 and Rake on A3. 40 acres; 10-acre lake; 100 acres of woodland; rhododendrons, azaleas, heathers; many other shrubs and trees. TEA. *Adm £1.50 Chd 50p. Sun May 22 (2-6)*

Hereford & Worcester

Hon County Organisers:

(Hereford) Lady Curtis, Tarrington Court, nr Hereford
(Worcester) Mrs Graeme Anton, Summerway, Torton, nr Kidderminster Tel 0299 250388

Assistant County Organisers

(Worcester) Jeremy Hughes Esq. Hillwood Farm, Eastham, Tenbury Wells, Worcs WR15 8PA Tel 058479 366
(Worcester) Mrs William Carr, Conderton Manor, nr Tewkesbury, Glos GL20 7PR
(Hereford) Mr & Mrs Roger Norman, Marley Bank, Whitbourne, Worcester WR6 5RU Tel 0886 821576

DATES OF OPENING

By appointment
For telephone numbers and other details see garden descriptions. Private visits welcomed

Arrow Cottage, nr Weobley
Barnard's Green House, Malvern
Bredon Pound, Ashton under Hill
Brilley Court, Whitney-on-Wye
Brookside, Bringsty
Chennels Gate, Eardisley
Churchfield Cottage, Whitbourne
Conderton Manor, nr Tewksbury
6 Elm Grove, nr Stourport-on-Severn
Frogmore, nr Ross-on-Wye
Grantsfield, nr Leominster
28 Hillgrove Crescent, Kidderminster
Ivytree House, Clent
Keepers Cottage, Alvechurch
Lower Hope, Ullingswick
Marley Bank, Whitbourne
Nerine Nursery, Welland
St Egwins Cottage, Norton, Evesham
Stone House, Scotland, Wellington
Stone House Cottage Gardens, Stone
Strawberry Cottage, Hamnish
21 Swinton, Lane Worcester
Torwood, Whitchurch
Well Cottage, Blakemere
Westwood Farm, Hatfield
White Cottage, Stock Green, nr Inkberrow

Regular openings
For details see garden descriptions

Abbey Dore Court, nr Hereford. Daily March 5 to Oct 16 except Weds
Arrow Cottage, nr Weobley. Every Sun April 3 to July 31 incl
Barnard's Green House, Malvern. Every Thurs April to Sept incl
Chennels Gate, Eardisley. Various dates see text
Churchfield Cottage, Whitbourne, 1st & 3rd Suns, April to Sept incl ⧺
The Cottage Herbery, Boraston, Tenbury Wells. Every Sun April 17 to Sept 18, Bank Hol Mons May 2, 30
Dinmore Manor, Wellington. Open all year
Eastgrove Cottage Garden Nursery, nr Shrawley. For dates see text
Hergest Croft Gardens, Kington. Daily April 1 to Oct 30
How Caple Court, Ross-on-Wye. Mon to Sat, April 1 to Oct 31. Suns May to Sept 25
Lingen Nursery, Lingen. Daily Feb to Oct
The Manor House, Birlingham. Thurs March 31 to July 21 incl, Sept 1 to Sept 29 ‡
Marley Bank, Whitbourne. 1st & 3rd Suns, April to Sept ‡⧺
The Picton Garden, Colwall. Weds to Suns, April to Oct

The Priory, Kemerton. Every Thurs May 26 to Sept 29 ‡
Staunton Park, Staunton-on-Arrow. Weds & Suns, Easter and Bank Hols, April to end Sept
Stone House Cottage Gardens, Stone. Wed, Thurs, Fri and Sats, March to Oct
Strawberry Cottage, Hamnish. 1st & 3rd Sun, 2nd & 4th Thurs, Bank Hol Mons, May 1 to Sept 22
White Cottage, Stock Green, nr Inkberrow April 1 to Oct 9 closed Thurs and alternative Suns (closed Aug). Nursery open daily April 1 to Oct 9 (closed Thurs)
Whitlenge House Cottage, Hartlebury. Thurs, Fris, Sats and some Suns March to Sept

---

March 20 Sunday
Robins End, Eastham
March 27 Sunday
Holland House, Cropthorne
Little Malvern Court, nr Malvern
Overbury Court, nr Tewkesbury
Whitlenge House Cottage, Hartlebury
April 1 Friday
Spetchley Park, nr Worcester
April 3 Sunday
White Cottage, Stock Green, nr Inkberrow

April 4 Monday
Stone House Cottage Gardens,
Stone
Whitlenge House Cottage,
Hartlebury
April 7 Thursday
Conderton Manor, nr Tewkesbury
April 10 Sunday
Garnons, nr Hereford
Ripple Hall, nr Tewkesbury
Staunton Park, Staunton-on-Arrow
Whitlenge House Cottage,
Hartlebury
Wormington Grange, nr Broadway
April 17 Sunday
Astley Horticultural Society
Brookside, Bringsty
Lower Hope, Ullingswick
Newcote, Moccas
Stone House, Scotland,
Wellington
White Cottage, Stock Green, nr
Inkberrow
Wichenford Court, Wichenford
Wind's Point, Malvern
April 24 Sunday
Barbers, Martley, nr Worcester
Dinmore Manor, Wellington
Whitlenge House Cottage,
Hartlebury
May 1 Sunday
Arley House, Upper Arley, nr
Bewdley
Barnard's Green House, Malvern
Brilley Court, nr Whitney-on-Wye
Brookside, Bringsty ‡
Lakeside, Whitbourne ‡
Stone House Cottage Gardens,
Stone
White Cottage, Stock Green, nr
Inkberrow
Whitlenge House Cottage,
Hartlebury
Windyridge, Kidderminster
May 2 Monday
Stone House Cottage Gardens,
Stone ‡
Whitlenge House Cottage,
Hartlebury ‡
May 5 Thursday
Conderton Manor, nr Tewkesbury
May 8 Sunday
Spetchley Park, nr Worcester
Stone House Cottage Gardens,
Stone ‡
Windyridge, Kidderminster ‡
May 15 Sunday
Brookside, Bringsty
Lingen Nursery, Lingen
Stone House Cottage Gardens,
Stone
White Cottage, Stock Green, nr
Inkberrow

May 16 Monday
Ivytree House, Clent
May 22 Sunday
Bodenham Arboretum, Wolverley
Caves Folly Nursery & Gardens,
Colwall Green
28 Hillgrove Crescent,
Kidderminster ‡
Lingen Nursery, Lingen
Pershore Gardens, Pershore
Priors Court, Long Green
The Priory, Kemerton
Red House Farm, Bradley Green
Stone House, Scotland,
Wellington
Stone House Cottage Gardens,
Stone ‡
May 29 Sunday
Hartlebury Castle, nr
Kidderminster ‡
St Egwins Cottage, Norton,
Evesham
Stone House Cottage Gardens,
Stone ‡
Tedstone Court, nr Bromyard
White Cottage, Stock Green, nr
Inkberrow
Whitlenge House Cottage,
Hartlebury ‡
May 30 Monday
Stone House Cottage Gardens,
Stone ‡
Whitlenge House Cottage,
Hartlebury ‡
June 2 Thursday
Conderton Manor, nr Tewkesbury
21 Swinton Lane, Worcester
June 5 Sunday
Frogmore, nr Ross-on-Wye
Madresfield Court, nr Malvern
Stone House Cottage Gardens,
Stone
Torwood, Whitchurch
Whitfield, Wormbridge
June 8 Wednesday
St Egwins Cottage, Norton,
Evesham
June 12 Sunday
Ash Farm, Much Birch
Brookside, Bringsty ‡
Cedar Lodge, Blakeshall, nr
Wolverley
Holland House, Cropthorne
How Caple Court, Ross-on-Wye
Lakeside, Whitbourne ‡
The Marsh Country Hotel, Eyton
Moccas Court, nr Hereford
Pershore College of Horticulture
The Priory, Kemerton ‡‡
Staunton Park, Staunton-on-Arrow
Stone House Cottage Gardens,
Stone
Upper Court, Kemerton ‡‡

White Cottage, Stock Green, nr
Inkberrow
June 15 Wednesday
Torwood, Whitchurch
June 19 Sunday
Bell's Castle, Kemerton ‡
Birtsmorton Court, nr Malvern
Charlton House, Lulsley,
Knightwick
St Egwins Cottage, Norton,
Evesham
St Michael's Cottage, Broadway
Stone House Cottage Gardens,
Stone
Tedstone Court, nr Bromyard
Torwood, Whitchurch
Upper Court, Kemerton ‡
June 20 Monday
Ivytree House, Clent
June 22 Wednesday
St Egwins Cottage, Norton,
Evesham
June 23 Thursday
Grantsfield, nr Leominster
June 25 Saturday
Hergest Croft Gardens, Kington
June 26 Sunday
Berrington Hall, Leominster ‡
Brilley Court, nr Whitney-on-Wye
Colwall Green & Evending
Gardens
Croft Castle, Kingsland ‡
Grantsfield, nr Leominster ‡
28 Hillgrove Crescent,
Kidderminster ‡‡
Linton Hall, Gorsley
Red House Farm, Bradley
Green
Shucknall Court, Hereford
Stone House, Scotland,
Wellington
Stone House Cottage Gardens,
Stone ‡‡
Westwood Farm, Hatfield
White Cottage, Stock Green, nr
Inkberrow
Whitlenge House Cottage,
Hartlebury ‡‡
Yew Tree House, Ombersley
June 27 Monday
Linton Hall, Gorsley
Westwood Farm, Hatfield
June 29 Wednesday
Shucknall Court, Hereford
Torwood, Whitchurch
June 30 Thursday
Conderton Manor, nr
Tewkesbury
21 Swinton Lane, Worcester
July 3 Sunday
Broadway Gardens, Broadway
Hanbury Hall, nr Droitwich
The Marsh Country Hotel, Eyton

St Egwins Cottage, Norton,
Evesham
Spetchley Park, nr Worcester
Torwood, Whitchurch
July 6 Wednesday
Torwood, Whitchurch
July 9 Saturday
28 Cornmeadow Lane, Claines,
Worcester
July 10 Sunday
Bredenbury Court (St Richards),
Bredenbury
6 Elm Grove, nr
Stourport-on-Severn
Lower Hope, Ullingswick
The Orchard Farm, Broadway ‡
The Priory, Kemerton
White Cottage, Stock Green, nr
Inkberrow
Wormington Grange, nr
Broadway ‡
July 13 Wednesday
St Egwins Cottage, Norton,
Evesham
July 17 Sunday
Arley Cottage, Upper Arley, nr
Bewdley
The Bannut, Bringsty, Bromyard
Stone House, Scotland,
Wellington
Torwood, Whitchurch
July 18 Monday
Ivytree House, Clent
July 24 Sunday
Caves Folly Nursery & Gardens,
Colwall Green

Red House Farm, Bradley Green
White Cottage, Stock Green, nr
Inkberrow
July 27 Wednesday
Torwood, Whitchurch
July 28 Thursday
21 Swinton Lane, Worcester
July 31 Sunday
Torwood, Whitchurch
Whitlenge House Cottage,
Hartlebury
August 7 Sunday
28 Hillgrove Crescent,
Kidderminster
The Priory, Kemerton
Tedstone Court, nr Bromyard
August 10 Wednesday
Torwood, Whitchurch
August 13 Saturday
Wych & Colwall Horticultural
Society Show, The Elms School
August 14 Sunday
Brookside, Bringsty
St Egwins Cottage, Norton,
Evesham
August 21 Sunday
The Bannut, Bringsty, Bromyard
Torwood, Whitchurch
August 25 Thursday
21 Swinton Lane, Worcester
August 27 Saturday
Monnington Court, Hereford
August 28 Sunday
Caves Folly Nursery & Gardens,
Colwall Green
Monnington Court, Hereford

The Priory, Kemerton
Stone House Cottage Gardens,
Stone ‡
White Cottage, Stock Green, nr
Inkberrow
Whitlenge House Cottage,
Hartlebury ‡
August 29 Monday
Monnington Court, Hereford
Stone House Cottage Gardens,
Stone ‡
Whitlenge House Cottage,
Hartlebury ‡
September 4 Sunday
Barnard's Green House, Malvern
September 7 Wednesday
Torwood, Whitchurch
September 11 Sunday
Brookside, Bringsty
The Priory, Kemerton
White Cottage, Stock Green, nr
Inkberrow
September 25 Sunday
The Marsh Country Hotel, Eyton
White Cottage, Stock Green, nr
Inkberrow
Whitlenge House Cottage,
Hartlebury
October 2 Sunday
Dinmore Manor, Wellington
October 9 Sunday
White Cottage, Stock Green, nr
Inkberrow
October 16 Sunday
Nerine Nursery, Welland

DESCRIPTIONS OF GARDENS

● **Abbey Dore Court** ♿✿❀ (Mrs C L Ward) 11m SW of Hereford. From A465 midway between Hereford-Abergavenny turn W, signed Abbey Dore; then 2½m. 4 acres bordered by R. Dore of rambling and semi formal garden with unusual shrubs, perennials and many clematis in large borders. Pond and rock garden made in a field. River walk with ferns and hellebores leading to a fairly new area, on the site of an old barn and roadway, planted for foliage colour. Large collection of late summer anemones. NCCPG Euphorbia collection. Featured in NGS video 1, see page 344. Many unusual plants for sale. Out of the ordinary gift gallery. Lunch and TEAS. Food from 11. *Adm £1.50 Chd 50p (Share to Mother Theresa®). Sat March 5 to Sun Oct 16 daily except Weds (11-6). Earlier private visits welcome, please Tel 0981 240419*

By Appointment Gardens. These owners do not have a fixed opening day usually because they do not like crowds or have insufficient parking space. Owner will often give guided tour.

Arley Cottage ♿ (Woodward family) Upper Arley, nr Bewdley. 5m N of Kidderminster off A442. Small country garden with lawns bordered by interesting shrubs and collection of rare trees. TEAS. *Adm £1 Chd free (Share to SOS©). Sun July 17 (2-5)*

Arley House ✿ (R D Turner Esq) Upper Arley, 5m N of Kidderminster. A442. Arboretum containing specimen conifers and hardwoods, rhododendrons, camellias, magnolias, heathers; Italianate garden; greenhouses with orchids, alpines. Aviary with ornamental pheasants, budgerigars. TEA. *Adm £1.50 Chd free (Share to St Peter's, Upper Arley®). Sun May 1 (2-7)*

Arrow Cottage ✿❀ (Mr & Mrs L Hattatt) 10m NW Hereford via Burghill and Tillington towards Weobley. Take Ledgmoor turning then R (No through Rd) 1st Hse on Left. A plantsman's garden of nearly 2 acres, arranged as a series of immaculately maintained garden rooms. White garden, red border, 19th century shrub roses, kitchen garden, rockery, pool and stream. Featured on Channel 4 television 1991 and Central Television 1993. The garden is unsuitable for children. TEAS if fine. *Adm £1.50. (Sun April 3 and every Sun thereafter until July 31 (2-5). Private visits welcome, please Tel 0544 318468*

¶**Ash Farm** ✻ (David & Alison Lewis) Much Birch. From Hereford take A49 S to Much Birch (approx 7m). After the Pilgrim Hotel take 1st turning R at Xrds into Tump Lane. Garden is on L. Ample parking. Small walled farmhouse garden and ½-acre new garden created from old fold yard for all year interest over past 5 yrs. Small trees, old roses, herbaceous borders, blue and white borders. TEA. *Adm £1 Chd free. Sun June 12 (10-6)*

Astley Horticultural Society ✻✿ 3m W of Stourport on Severn on B4196 Worcester to Bewdley rd. A selection of mature and new country gardens at their best in April. Start from the Astley Parish Room and drive around the Parish of Astley and Dunley. Several exceptional gardens. TEAS. *Adm £2 Chd free (Share to St Peters Church, Astley©). Sun April 17 (1-6)*
   6 Elm Grove Plantsman's garden
   Koi Cottage Bonsai, bulbs and koi for the connoisseur
   Little Yarhampton Spring garden
   Mill House Primroses, daffodils and heliebores.
   Pool House Languid pools, primroses and daffodils
   Woodland Farm A lovely mixed garden
   The Woodlands Early rhododendron & bulbs

The Bannut ✻✿ (Mr Maurice & Mrs Daphne Everett) Bringsty. 3m E of Bromyard on A44 Worcester Rd. (½m E of entrance to National Trust, Brockhampton). A 1-acre garden, planted with all year colour in mind; mainly established by the present owners since 1984. Mixed borders and island beds of trees, shrubs and herbaceous plants and a small 'damp' garden. Walls, pergola, and terraces around the house are used to display unusual climbers and colourful pots and urns. The Sept 1993 issue of 'Practical Gardening' contained photographs of the heather garden designed around a Herefordshire cider mill and an unusual heather knot garden with water feature. Plants for sale. TEAS. *Adm £1 Chd free. Suns July 17, August 21 (2-5). Also groups by appt, please* **Tel 0885 482206**

Barbers ✻✻✿ (Mr & the Hon Mrs Richard Webb) Martley 7m NW of Worcester on B4204. Medium-sized garden with lawns, trees, shrubs, pools and wild garden. Home-made TEAS. *Adm £1 Chd free (Share to Martley Church). Sun April 24 (2-6)*

Barnard's Green House ✻✻✿ (Mr & Mrs Philip Nicholls) 10 Poolbrook Rd, Malvern. On E side of Malvern at junction of B4211 and B4208. 3-acre cultivated garden; herbaceous, rockeries, heather beds, woodland/water garden, vegetable plot; several unusual plants and shrubs; 2 fine cedars, lawns. Mrs Nicholls is a specialist on dried flowers, on which she has written a book. Half timbered house (not open) dates from 1635; home of Sir Charles Hastings, founder of BMA. Coach parties by appt. TEAS. *Adm £1.50 Acc chd free (Share to Save the Children Fund®). Suns May 1, Sept 4 and every Thursday April to Sept incl. (2-6). Also private visits welcome, please* **Tel 0684 574446**

Bell's Castle ✿ (Lady Holland-Martin) Kemerton, NE of Tewkesbury. 3 small terraces with battlements; wild garden outside wall. The small Gothic castellated folly was built by Edmund Bell (Smuggler) c1820; very fine views. TEAS. *Adm £1 Chd free. Sun June 19 (2-6)*

Berrington Hall ✻✻ (The National Trust) 3m N of Leominster on A49. Signposted. Bus Midland Red (W) x 92, 292 alight Luston, 2m. Extensive views over Capability Brown Park; formal garden with personal favourites; wall plants, unusual trees, camellia collection, herbaceous plants, wisteria. Woodland walk, recent rhododendron planting. Light lunches and TEAS. *Adm house & garden £3.50 Chd £1.75. Grounds only £1.60 Chd 80p.* ▲*For NGS Sun June 26 (12.30-5.30)*

Birtsmorton Court ✻✻ (Mr & Mrs N G K Dawes) nr Malvern. 7m E of Ledbury on A438. Fortified manor house (not open) dating from C12; moat; Westminster pool, laid down in Henry V11's reign at time of consecration of Westminster Abbey; large tree under which Cardinal Wolsey reputedly slept in shadow of ragged stone. Topiary. Motor Museum extra. Featured in NGS video 1, see page 344. TEAS. *Adm £1.50 Chd 25p. Sun June 19 (2-6)*

Bodenham Arboretum (Mr & Mrs J D Binnian) 2m N of Wolverley; 5m N of Kidderminster. From Wolverley Church follow signs. 134 acres landscaped & planted during the past 20 years; 2 chains of lakes & pools; woods and glades with over 1600 species & shrubs; Laburnum tunnel; Grove & Swamp Cypress in shallows of 3-acre lake. Bring wellingtons or strong boots. TEA. NO COACHES. *Adm £1.50 Chd free (Share to The Kemp House Trust, Home Care Hospice®). Sun May 22 (2-6) parties by appt at other times of the year* **Tel 0562 850382**

Bredenbury Court (St Richards) ✻ (Headmaster: R E H Coghlan Esq) Bredenbury, 3m W of Bromyard. On A44 Bromyard-Leominster; entrance on right (N) side of rd. 5-acre garden; 15 acres parkland with fine views. Simple rose garden and herbaceous borders. Picnics allowed. Use of swimming pool 30p extra. TEAS. *Adm £1 Chd 50p (Share to St Richards Hospice®). Sun July 10 (12-6)*

Bredon Pound ✻✿ (Mr & Mrs David King) Ashton under Hill. 6m down the Cheltenham Rd from Evesham. A recently landscaped garden at the foot of Bredon Hill with fine views over the Vale of Evesham to the Cotswold Hills. Shrub roses, heathers and an interesting collection of trees and shrubs. TEAS. *Adm £1 Chd free (Share to Spastics Society®). Private visits welcome May to Sept, please* **Tel 0386 881209**

Brilley Court ✻✻ (Mr & Mrs D Bulmer) nr Whitney-on-Wye 6m E Hay-on-Wye. 1½m off main A438 Hereford to Brecon Rd signposted to Brilley. Medium-sized walled garden spring and herbaceous. Valley stream garden; spring colour. New ornamental kitchen garden. Excellent views to Black Mountains. TEAS. *Adm £1.50 OAPs £1 Chd 50p (Share to CRMF®). Suns May 1, June 26 (2-6). Also private visits welcome April to July, please* **Tel 0497 831467**

Broadfield Court ✻✿ (Mr & Mrs Keith James) Bodenham 7m SE Leominster A49 from Leominster or Hereford & A417 to Bodenham; turn left to Risbury signposted at Bodenham. 4 acres of old English gardens; yew hedges; spacious lawn; rose garden; herbaceous. Picnic area. 17 acres of vineyard; wine tasting included in entrance charge. TEAS. *Adm £2 OAP £1.50 Chd 50p. Sun June 26 (11-4.30)*

Broadway Gardens &&&& All three gardens are on Snowshill Rd out of Broadway. *Combined adm £1 Chd free (Share to Lifford Hall, Broadway©). Sun July 3 (2-6)*

¶**Far Bunchers** (Mrs A Pallant) A recently developed mixed garden of about 1 acre with an emphasis on shrub roses and organic vegetable growing

The Mill (Mr & Mrs Hugh Verney) 2½-acre paddock, bounded by 2 streams, transformed since 1975 into an attractive garden which will support a variety of wild life. Informal planting of trees, shrub roses and other shrubs, moisture loving plants and bulbs. Minimal annual maintenance required

Mill Hay Cottage (Dr & Mrs W J A Payne) The garden approx 2 acres is of relatively recent origin and is still being developed. Informally planted terraces, orchard areas and wild garden. A special feature is the number of rare fruiting plants and an attempt is being made to accommodate these with the demands of wild life

Brookside &&& (Mr & Mrs John Dodd) Bringsty; 3m E of Bromyard via A44 10m W of Worcester; Bringsty Common turn down track to 'Live & Let Live'; at PH carpark bear left to Brookside. C16 cottage with 1½-acre garden designed by Denis Hoddy; specimen trees and shrubs in grass sloping to lake; mixed beds with all year interest. Unusual plants. Small alpine collection. Parties by arrangement only. TEAS on terrace. *Adm £1 Chd 20p (Share to Save the Children Fund®). Suns April 17, May 1, 15, June 12, Aug 14, Sept 11 (2-5.30). Private visits welcome, please Tel 0886 821835*

Cedar Lodge &&& (Mr & Mrs Vivian Andrews) Blakeshall. 4m N of Kidderminster off B4189. 1½m from Wolverley Village. ¾-acre plantsman's garden with extensive range of trees, shrubs and plants (some rare), in country setting adjoining Kinver Edge. The garden was the 1991/92 overall winner of Practical Gardening magazine's 'My Garden' competition. TEAS. *Adm £1 Chd free. Sun June 12 (2-5.30)*

Charlton House && (Mr & Mrs S Driver-White) Lulsley, Knightwick. 9m W of Worcester via A44, turn 1st L after Knightsford Bridge towards Alfrick, 1st L after Fox & Hounds signed Hill Rd, Lulsley; 1m at end of lane. ⅔-acre intimate garden of shrubs, shrub roses and flowers created by owner since 1970. Fine barns. *Adm £1 Sun June 19 (1-5) Coach parties by appt*

Chennels Gate &&& (Mr & Mrs Kenneth Dawson) Eardisley. 5m S of Kington. ½m from Tram Inn on Woodseave Lane. Signposted. A 2-acre plantsman's cottage garden, set in 15 acres with newly planted woodland and orchards. Rose and herb gardens; herbaceous borders; water gardens, one with water fowl; conservatory with planted beds. Interesting selection of plants for sale (Share to St Mary Magdalene Church, Eardisley). TEAS. *Adm £1.20 Chd free. Suns April 17, May 1, 15, 29, June 12, 26, July 3, 10, 24, 31, Aug 7, 14, 21, Sept 4, Mons April 18, May 2, 16, 30, June 13, 27, July 4, 11, 25 Aug 1, 8, 15, 22, Sept 5 (2-6). Private visits welcome, please Tel 0544 327288*

¶**Churchfield Cottage** &&& (Peter & Barbara Larner) Turn off A44 at Wheatsheaf public house. 5m E of Bromyard. Through village, down hill, turn R at bottom. 200 yds past Church on L. 1-acre garden extended and re-planted since 1985 around some mature shrubs and trees. Large mixed borders, all-yr interest, many unusual plants. Ponds, bog garden, conservatory. TEA. *Adm £1 Chd 50p. 1st & 3rd Suns April to Sept incl. (2-5.30). Private visits welcome, please Tel 0886 821495*

Colwall Green & Evendine Gardens &&& 3m SW Malvern and 3m E of Ledbury on B2048. TEAS at Caves Folly Nurseries and Gardens. *Combined adm £1.50 Chd free. Maps available showing parking. Sun June 26 (2-6)*

Caves Folly Nursery & Gardens &&& (Mrs S Evans) Evendine Lane, Off Colwall Green. Medium-sized garden of old converted stables; started from meadowland 1977. Nursery established 10 years. Specialising in herbaceous and alpine plants, some unusual. All plants are grown organically in peat-free compost. Also a selection of Guernsey goats, ducks, chickens, plus recently planted herbaceous borders and a wildflower meadow. *Also open Suns May 22 (Share to Greenpeace®), July 24, Aug 28 (2-6)*

The Picton Garden at Old Court Nursery (Mr & Mrs Paul Picton) for details see **Picton Garden**

Tustins (Mrs D Singleton) Medium-size garden containing large numbers of unusual plants

Conderton Manor & (Mr & Mrs William Carr) 5½m NE of Tewkesbury. Between A435 & B4079. 7-acre garden with magnificent views of Cotswolds; many trees and shrubs of botanical interest. 100yd long mixed borders, rose walks and formal terrace. Teas available at the Silk Shop in the village. *Adm £2 Chd 25p. Thurs April 7, May 5, June 2, 30 (2-6). Also private visits welcome, please Tel 0386 725389*

28 Cornmeadow Lane &&& (Rev P J Wedgwood) Claines is a northern suburb of Worcester; follow signpost Claines at roundabout junction of A449 and M/way link rd; R at church. House beside 3rd hall on L about ½m down Cornmeadow Lane. Parking in Church Hall grounds. Small town garden packed with rare and tropical plants with plenty of colour. TEAS. *Adm £1 Chd free. Sat July 9 (2-6)*

The Cottage Herbery &&& (Mr & Mrs R E Hurst) 1m E of Tenbury Wells on A456, turn for Boraston at Peacock Inn, turn R in village, signposted to garden. Half timbered C16 farmhouse with fast-flowing Cornbrook running close to its side and over ford at the bottom of garden. ½-acre of garden specializing in a wide range of herbs, aromatic and scented foliage plants, planted on a cottage garden theme; also unusual hardy perennial and variegated plants; early interest bulbs, pulmonarias, euphorbias, symphytums. Nursery sells large selection of herbs. Organic garden. Chelsea Medallists 1992 & 93. Featured in Central TV My Secret Garden. No toilets. TEAS (served in garden). *Adm £1 Chd free. Every Sun April 17 to Sept 18, also Bank Hol Mons May 2, 30 (10-6)*

Regular Openers. Too many days to include in diary. Usually there is a wide range of plants giving year-round interest. See head of county section for the name and garden description for times etc.

Croft Castle ೬ # (The National Trust) 5m NW of Leominster. On B4362 (off B4361, Leominster-Ludlow). Large garden; borders; walled garden; landscaped park and walks in Fishpool Valley; fine old avenues. Light lunches and Teas Berrington Hall. *Adm £3 Family £8.25 Chd £1.50. For NGS Sun June 26 (2-6)*

Dinmore Manor ೬ # # (R G Murray Esq) Hereford, 6m N of Hereford. Route A49. Bus: Midland Red Hereford-Leominster, alight Manor turning 1m. Spectacular hillside location. A range of impressive architecture dating from C14-20; chapel; cloisters; Great hall (Music Room) and extensive roof walk giving panoramic views of countryside and beautiful gardens below; stained glass. TEAS for NGS Sun April 24, Oct 2, unusual plants for sale. *Adm £2 Acc chd free (Share to NSPCC®). For NGS Suns April 24, Oct 2 (10-5.30). Open throughout the year (10.30-5.30)*

●**Eastgrove Cottage Garden Nursery** # # (Mr & Mrs J Malcolm Skinner) Sankyns Green, Shrawley. 8m NW of Worcester on rd between Shrawley (on B4196) and Great Witley (on A443). Set in 5 acres unspoilt meadow and woodland, this unique 1-acre garden and nursery is of particular interest to the plantsman. Expanding collection of hardy and tender perennial plants in old world country flower garden with much thought given to planting combinations both of colour and form. C17 half-timbered yeoman farmhouse (not open). Garden and nursery maintained by owners since 1970. Featured in Country Life and Daily Telegraph. Wide range of well grown less usual plants for sale, all grown at Nursery. Help and advice always available from owners. *Adm £1.50 Chd 20p. April 1 to July 31 Thurs, Fri, Sat, Sun, Mon. Closed Tues & Weds.* **Closed throughout August.** *Sept 1 to Oct 15; Thurs, Fri, Sat only (2-5)*

The Elms School see Wych & Colwall Horticultural Society Show

6 Elm Grove ೬ # # (Michael Ecob) Astley Cross. W of Stourport on Severn. Turn S on B4196 towards Worcester-Bewdley. ⅓-acre garden with mature trees, borders, patio area, pool and small conservatory. By July the borders take on a cottage garden appearance with many unusual plants amongst old favourites: small vegetable area used for show produce. Several neighbouring gardens in The Grove will also be open in conjunction with No 6. TEAS. *Adm £1 Chd free. Sun July 10 (1-6). Also private visits welcome, please* **Tel 0299 822167**

Frogmore ೬ # # (Sir Jonathan & Lady North) Pontshill. 4m SE of Ross-on-Wye. 1m S of A40 through Pontshill. 2-acre garden with fine mature trees and many unusual young trees and shrubs. Mixed borders with nut walk and ha ha. Mown walk along stream and to spinney. TEAS (in aid of Hope Mansel Church). Hardy geranium nursery, open Mons only 10-6 April to Sept or private visits welcome, please **Tel 0989 750214.** *Adm £1.50 Chd free. Sun June 5 (2-6)*

Garnons ೬ # (Sir John & Lady Cotterell) 7m W of Hereford on A438; lodge gates on right; then fork left over cattle grid. Large park landscaped by Repton; attractive spring garden. House is remaining wing (1860) of house pulled down in 1957. TEA. *Adm part of house & garden*

£2 Chd free; garden only £1 Chd free (Share to Byford Church®). Sun April 10 (2-5.30)

Grantsfield ೬ # # (Col & Mrs J G T Polley) nr Kimbolton, 3m NE of Leominster. A49 N from Leominster, turn right to Grantsfield. Car parking in field; not coaches which must drop and collect visitors at gate. Contrasting styles in gardens of old stone farmhouse; wide variety of unusual plants and shrubs, old roses, climbers; herbaceous borders; superb views. 4-acre orchard and kitchen garden with flowering and specimen trees. Spring bulbs. TEAS Sun June 26, TEA Thurs 23. *Combined adm with* **Strawberry Cottage** *£1.80 Chd free. Adm £1.20 Chd free (Share to Hamnish Church®). Thurs, Sun June 23, 26 (2-5.30). Private visits welcome April to end Sept, please* **Tel 0568 613338**

Hanbury Hall ೬ # (The National Trust) Hanbury, 3m NE of Droitwich, 6m S of Bromsgrove. Signed off B4090. Recreation of C18 formal garden by George London. Victorian forecourt with detailed planting. William & Mary style brick house of 1701 with murals by Thornhill; contemporary Orangery and Ice House. TEAS. *Adm house & garden £3.50 Chd £1.80. Sun July 3 (2-6)*

Hartlebury Castle ೬ # (The Rt Revd The Lord Bishop of Worcester) Medieval moated castle reconstructed 1675, restored 1964. Many Tudor and Hanoverian Royal connections. Rose garden in forecourt. Wheelchairs ground floor. *Adm gardens & state rooms 75p Chd 25p. Sun May 29 (2-5)*

● **Hergest Croft Gardens** ೬ # (W L Banks Esq & R A Banks Esq) ½m off A44 on Welsh side of Kington, 20m NW of Hereford: Turn left at Rhayader end of bypass; then 1st right; gardens ¼m on left. 50 acres of garden owned by Banks' family for 4 generations. Edwardian garden surrounding house (not open); Park wood with rhododendrons up to 30ft tall; old fashioned kitchen garden with spring and herbaceous borders. One of finest private collections of trees and shrubs; now selected to hold National Collections Maples and Birches. TEAS for NGS day **Tel Kington 230160.** *Adm £2.30 Chd under 15 free (Share to NCCPG®). Fri April 1 to Sun Oct 30 daily. For NGS Sat June 25 (1.30-6.30)*

28 Hillgrove Crescent # # (Mr & Mrs D Terry) Kidderminster. Crescent linking Chester Rd (A449) & Bromsgrove Rd (A448). A town garden designed to maximize the planting areas without losing a feeling of space. Many unusual plants including alpines, herbaceous, shrubs, ferns and clematis planted with skilful use of colour. *Adm £1 Chd free (Share to CRMF®). Suns May 22, June 26, Aug 7 (2-6). Also private visits welcome, please* **Tel 0562 751957**

Holland House # (Warden: Mr Peter Middlemiss) Main St, Cropthorne, Pershore. Between Pershore and Evesham, off A44. Car park at rear of house. Gardens laid out by Lutyens in 1904; thatched house dating back to 1636 (not open). TEAS. *Adm £1 Chd 30p (Share to USPG®). Suns March 27, June 12 (2.30-5)*

How Caple Court ✿ (Mr & Mrs Peter Lee) How Caple, 5m N of Ross on Wye 10m S of Hereford on B4224; turn right at How Caple Xrds, garden 400 yds on left. 11 acres; mainly Edwardian gardens in process of replanting, set high above R. Wye in park and woodland; formal terraces: yew hedges, statues and pools; sunken florentine water garden under restoration; woodland walks; herbaceous and shrub borders, shrub roses, mature trees: Mediaeval Church with newly restored C16 Diptych. Nursery specialising in old rose varieties and apple varieties, unusual herbaceous plants. Fabric and menswear shop. *Adm £2.50 Chd £1.25. Open Mon to Sat, April 1 to Oct 31. Also Suns May to Sept 26 (10-5). For NGS Sun June 12 (10-5)*

¶**Ivytree House** ✿ (Dr & Mrs H Eggins) OS139 91.79 Bromsgrove Rd, Clent. 3m SE of Stourbridge and 5m NW of Bromsgrove, off A491 Stourbridge to Bromsgrove dual carriageway. Car parking next door at Woodman Hotel. Over 1,000 varieties of small trees, shrubs and herbaceous plants in approx ½-acre plantsman's cottage garden; tree ivies and ivytrees, collection of aucubus, small conservatory with fuchsia trees, pond garden, fruit and vegetables, bantams and bees. *Adm £1 Chd free. Mons May 16, June 20, July 18 (2-5). Also private visits welcome, please* **Tel 0562 884171**

Keepers Cottage ✿✿ (Mrs Diana Scott) Alvechurch. Take main A441 rd through Alvechurch towards Redditch. Turn opp sign to Cobley Hill and Bromsgrove for 1m over 2 humpback bridges. 3-acre garden at 600ft with fine views towards the Cotswolds; rhododendrons, camellias; old fashioned roses; unusual trees and shrubs; rock garden; 2 alpine houses; paddock with donkeys. Show jumping as seen on TV 1m away at Wharf Meadow. TEAS. *Adm £1 Chd 50p (Share to St Mary's Hospice®). Private visits welcome in May and June, please* **Tel 0214 455885**

Lakeside ✿✿ (Mr D Gueroult & Mr C Philip) Gaines Rd, Whitbourne. 9m W of Worcester off A44 at County boundary sign (ignore sign to Whitbourne Village). 6-acres, large walled garden with many mixed beds and borders; spring bulbs, climbers, unusual shrubs and plants, heather garden, bog garden, newly extended lake walk, medieval carp lake with fountain. Uncommon plants for sale. Steep steps and slopes. TEAS in aid of Red Cross. *Adm £1.50 Chd free. Suns May 1, June 12 (2-6)*

Lingen Nursery and Garden ✿✿ (Mr Kim Davis) Lingen. 5m NE of Presteigne take B4362 E from Presteigne, 2m turn L for Lingen, 3m opposite Chapel in village. 2 acres of specialist alpine and herbaceous nursery and general garden intensively planted giving a long period of interest having large areas of rock garden and herbaceous borders, a peat bed, raised screes and an Alpine House and stock beds, together with 2 acres of developing garden where picnics are welcome. Many unusual plants with comprehensive labelling. Wide range of plants for sale from the nursery frames. Catalogue available. TEAS (NGS days only). *Adm £1 Chd free. Suns May 15, 22 (2-6) for NGS. Also open Feb-Oct everyday (10-6). Coach parties by appt* **Tel 0544 267720**

¶**Linton Hall** ✿✿ (Mr & Mrs Sanders & Mr & Mrs Berrington) Gorsley. 5m E of Ross-on-Wye, junction 3 off M50 toward Newent. Entrance ½m on RH-side on county boundary. 8½ acres of woodland and gardens undergoing construction. Mature trees including wellingtonias; orchard; croquet lawn; old-fashioned roses. TEAS. *Adm £1.50 Chd 50p. Sun, Mon June 26, 27 (2-6)*

Little Malvern Court ✿✿ (Mr & Mrs T M Berington) 4m S of Malvern on A4104 S of junc with A449. 10 acres attached to former Benedictine Priory, magnificent views over Severn valley. An intriguing layout of garden rooms, and terrace round house. Newly made and planted water garden below, feeding into chain of lakes. Wide variety of spring bulbs, flowering trees and shrubs. Notable collection of old-fashioned roses. TEAS. *Adm £2.20 Chd 50p (Share to SSAFA). Sun March 27 (2-6)*

Lower Hope ⚹✿ (Mr & Mrs Clive Richards) Ullingswick. From Hereford take the A465 N to Bromyard. After 6m this road meets the A417 at Burley Gate roundabout. Turn L on the A417 signposted Leominster. After approx. 2m take the 3rd turning on the R signposted Lower Hope and Pencombe. Lower Hope is 0.6m on the LH-side. 5-acre garden facing S and W constitutes principally herbaceous borders, rose borders, water gardens, woodland walks; in addition other features include a Laburnum Walk, conservatories and greenhouses, a fruit and vegetable garden. Surrounding the gardens are paddocks in which the prize-winning Herd of Pedigree Poll Hereford cattle and flock of Pedigree Suffolk sheep are grazed. TEAS. *Adm £2 Chd £1. Sun April 17, July 10 (2-6). Also private visits welcome, please* **Tel 0432 820557**

Madresfield Court ⚹ (The Hon Lady Morrison) Nr Malvern. 60 acres formal and parkland garden incl rare species of mature trees, Pulhamite rock garden, maze, majestic avenues and a mass of wild flowers. TEAS. *Adm £2 Chd 50p. Sun June 5 (2-5.30)*

The Manor House ✿✿ (Mr & Mrs David Williams-Thomas) Birlingham, nr Pershore. Very fine views of Bredon Hill, frontaging on the River Avon. Walled white and silver garden and gazebo as featured in 'The White Garden' by Diana Grenfell and Roger Grounds and in 'Practical Gardening' Aug 1993. Visitors are invited to picnic by the river. TEAS. *Adm £1 Chd free. Every Thurs March 31 to July 21 incl (11-5.30) and Sept 1 to Sept 29 incl (11-5)*

Marley Bank ✿✿ (Mr & Mrs Roger Norman) From A44 (5m E Bromyard) follow Whitbourne & Clifton-on-Teme signs for 1.2m. 1½-acre garden with a wide range of plants to give all-yr interest, set in 3.5 acres old orchard; good views. Steep paths and steps. Trees, shrubs, mixed borders, alpine terraces, troughs, peat beds, naturalised snowdrops & daffodils. TEA. *Adm £1.50 Chd free. First and third Sun April to Sept inc (2-5.30). Closed Sun July 3, Sept 4* **Tel 0886 821576**

By Appointment Gardens. These owners do not have a fixed opening day usually because they do not like crowds or have insufficient parking space. Owner will often give guided tour.

The Marsh Country Hotel ⚹ (Mr & Mrs Martin Gilleland) Eyton. 2m NW of Leominster. Signed Eyton and Lucton off B4361 Richard Castle Rd. A 1½-acre garden created over the past 6 years. Herbaceous borders, small orchard, lily pond, herb garden and stream with planted banks and walk. Landscaped reed bed sewage treatment system. C14 timbered Great Hall listed grade II* (not open). TEAS. *Adm £1 Chd 50p. Suns June 12, July 3, Sept 25 (1.30-5)*

Moccas Court ⚹ (Richard Chester-Master Esq) 10m W of Hereford. 1m off B4352. 7-acres; Capability Brown parkland on S bank of R. Wye. House designed by Adam and built by Keck in 1775. TEAS in village hall. *Adm house & garden £1.80 Chd £1 (Share to Moccas Church®). Sun June 12 (2-6)*

Monnington Court (Mr & Mrs John Bulmer) Monnington. The ¾m lane to Monnington on Wye to Monnington Court is on the A438 between Hereford and Hay 9m from either. Approx 5 acres. Lake, pond and river walk. Sculpture garden (Mrs Bulmer is the sculptor Angela Conner); various tree lined avenues including Monnington Walk, one of Britain's oldest, still complete mile long avenues of Scots pines and yews, made famous by Kilvert's Diary; collection of swans and ducks; foundation farm of the British Morgan Horse – a living replica of ancient horses seen in statues in Trafalgar Square, etc; working cider press; FREE horse and carriage display at 3.30 each of open days. The C13, C15, C17 house including Mediaeval Moot Hall is also open. Barbecue on fine days. TEA 10.30-6.30. Indoor horse display and films on rainy days. *Adm house and garden £3.50 Chd £2.50, garden only £2.50 Chd £1.50 (Share to British Morgan Horse Society®). Sat, Sun, Mon Aug 27, 28, 29 (10.30-7)*

Nerine Nursery ⚹✿ (Mr & Mrs I L Carmichael) Brookend House, Welland, ½m towards Upton-on-Severn from Welland Xrds (A4104 × B4208). Internationally famous reference collection of Nerines, 30 species and some 800 named varieties in 5 greenhouses and traditional walled garden with raised beds, hardy nerines. Coaches by appt only. TEAS. *Adm £1.50 Chd free. Sun Oct 16 (2-5). Private visits welcome, please* Tel 0684 594005

Newcote ⚹ (Mr John & Lady Patricia Phipps). Moccas. From Moccas village, ⅓m on rd to Preston-on-Wye. 2½ acres including woodland garden. Speciality shrubs and exotic trees. Water garden and pond area. *Adm £1.20 Chd 50p. Sun April 17 (2-6)*

The Orchard Farm ⚹✿ (Miss S Barrie) Broadway. On A44. At bottom of Fish Hill; 7-acres incl interesting trees, shrubs, mixed borders, topiary, yew hedges, kitchen garden, lake and paddock. House (not open) c1650. Free Car Park. Home-made TEAS. *Adm £1 Chd free. Sun July 10 (1-6)*

Overbury Court ⚹✿ (Mr & Mrs Bruce Bossom) 5m NE of Tewkesbury, 2½m N of Teddington Hands Roundabout, where A438 crosses A435. Georgian house 1740 (not open); landscape gardening of same date with stream and pools. Daffodil bank and grotto. Plane trees, yew hedges. Shrub, cut flower, coloured foliage, gold and sil-

ver, shrub rose borders. Norman church adjoins garden. Cream TEAS in aid of Village Hall. *Adm £1.50 Chd free. Sun March 27 (2-6). By appt for groups of 15 or more*

Pershore College of Horticulture ⚹✿ 1m S of Pershore on A44, 7m from M5 junction 7. 180-acre estate; ornamental grounds; arboretum; fruit, vegetables; amenity glasshouses; wholesale hardy stock nursery. Plant Centre open for sales. West Midlands Regional Centre for RHS. Plant Centre open for gardening advice. TEA. *Adm £1 Chd 50p. Sun June 12 (2-5.30)*

Pershore Gardens ⚹ Defford Rd and Bridge St. Variety of gardens, incl riverside, all within easy walking distance. Park in Broad St in town centre. TEAS. *Combined adm £2 Chd free. Sun May 22 (2-6)*

The Picton Garden ⚹✿ (Mr & Mrs Paul Picton) Walwyn Rd, Colwall. 3m W of Malvern on B4218. 1½-acres W of Malvern Hills. A plantsman's garden extensively renovated in recent years. Rock garden using Tufa. Moist garden. Rose garden with scented old and modern varieties. Mature interesting shrubs. Large herbaceous borders full of colour from early summer. NCCPG National Reference collection of asters, michaelmas daisies, occupies its own vast borders and gives a tapestry of colour from late Aug through Sept and Oct. If wet there will be a small display of Asters under cover. *Adm £1.50 Chd free. Open Wed to Sun April to Oct inc (10-1; 2.15-5.30). Also in conjuction with* **Colwall Green and Evendine Gardens**

¶**Priors Court** ✿✿ (Robert Philipson-Stow) Long Green. From Tewkesbury take A438 to Ledbury. Exactly 5m pass under M50. Garden on hill on L of A438. From Ledbury, Worcester or Gloucester aim for Rye Cross (A438 and B4208) then take A438 for Tewkesbury. Priors Court is approx 3m from Rye Cross on R. 3-acre garden established in 1920s by owner's parents surrounding C15 house (not open). Rock, herb and vegetable gardens, also mature trees and shrubs, herbaceous and rose borders; stunning views. Norman church 250yds over field will be open. TEAS. *Adm £1 Chd 20p (Share to Berrow & Pendock Parish Church®). Sun May 22 (2-6)*

The Priory ⚹✿ (The Hon Mrs Peter Healing) Kemerton, NE of Tewkesbury B4080. Main features of this 4-acre garden are long herbaceous borders planned in colour groups; stream, fern and sunken gardens. Many unusual plants, shrubs and trees. Featured in BBC2 Gardeners' World and 'The Garden magazine'. Small nursery. TEAS Suns only *Adm £1.50 Chd over 7 yrs 50p (Share to Leonard Cheshire Foundation®). Aug 7, St Mary's Hospice® Aug 28, SSAFA® Sept 11). May 26 to Sept 29 every Thurs; also Suns May 22, June 12, July 10, Aug 7, 28, Sept 11 (2-7)*

Red House Farm ✿✿ (Mrs M M Weaver) Flying Horse Lane, Bradley Green. 7m W of Redditch on B4090 Alcester to Droitwich. Turn opp The Red Lion. Approx ½-acre plant enthusiast's cottage garden containing wide range of interesting herbaceous perennials; roses; shrubs; alpines. Garden and small nursery open daily offering wide variety of plants mainly propogated from garden. *Adm £1 Chd free. Sun May 22, June 26, July 24 (11-5)*

Ripple Hall &✿ (Sir Hugo Huntington-Whiteley) 4m N of Tewkesbury. Off A38 Worcester-Tewkesbury (nr junction with motorway); Ripple village well signed. 6 acres; lawns and paddocks with donkeys; walled vegetable garden; cork tree and orangery. TEAS. *Adm £1.50 Acc chd free (Share to St. Richard's Hospice, Worcester®). Sun April 10 (2-6)*

Robins End ✿✿ (Mr & Mrs A Worsley) Eastham. 15m W of Worcester, turn L off A443 2m after Eardiston to Eastham. ½m turn R to Highwood, 1st gate on L. Queen Ann Rectory garden in peaceful surroundings. Splendid display of snowdrops and daffodils. TEAS. *Adm £1.25 Chd free (Share to Eastham Parish Church®). Sun March 20 (2.30-5.30)*

¶St Egwins Cottage ✿✿ (Mr & Mrs Brian Dudley) Norton. 2m N of Evesham on A435. 300 yds past 'Little Chef'. Park in St Egwins Church car park. Walk through churchyard to Church Lane (50yds). Please do not park in Church Lane. ⅕-acre plantsman's garden, many unusual plants; mainly perennials including hardy geraniums, campanulas and salvias. Small thatched cottage next to C12 church (open). TEA. *Adm £1 Chd free. Suns, May 29, June 19, July 3, August 14; Weds June 8, 22, July 13 (2-6). Also private visits welcome April to September, please* Tel 0386 870486

St Michael's Cottage ✿ (Mr & Mrs K R Barling) Broadway. 5m SE of Evesham. Thatched cottage opp St Michael's Parish Church, 200yds along rd from The Green to Snowshill. (Public car park nearby, via Church Close.) Approx ⅓-acre of intensively planted cottage style and herbaceous garden planned in colour groups, including a small white sunken garden. Modest informal fishpond; views to Cotswold Way. Cream TEAS and home-made cakes. *Adm £1 Acc chd free. Sun June 19 (2-5.30)*

¶Shucknall Court ✿ (Mr & Mrs Henry Moore) 5½m E of Hereford off A4103, sign-posted Weston Beggard. Garden 100 yds from main rd. Large collection of specie, old-fashioned and shrub roses. Mixed borders in the old walled farmhouse garden. Wild garden, small stream garden, vegetables and fruit. Partly suitable for wheelchairs. TEAS. *Adm £1.50 Chd free (Share to St. John's Ambulance®). Sun, Wed June 26, 29 (2-6)*

Spetchley Park &✿✿ (R J Berkeley Esq) 2m E of Worcester on A422. 30-acre garden containing large collection of trees, shrubs and plants. Red and fallow deer in nearby park. TEAS. *Adm £2.10 Chd £1. Good Fri April 1 (11-5) & Suns May 8, July 3 (2-5)*

Staunton Park &✿ (Mr E J L & Miss A Savage) Staunton-on-Arrow. 3m from Pembridge; 6m from Kington on the Titley road. 18m from Hereford; 11m from Leominster; 16m from Ludlow. Signposted. 14-acres of garden, specimen trees, herbaceous borders, herb garden, rock garden, hosta border, lake, lakeside garden, woodland walk, spring bulbs. New scented border for enjoyment of the blind. Wild flower area. Ice-house. TEAS. *Adm £1.50 Chd free. Weds, Suns April to end Sept. Easter and Bank Holidays. For NGS Suns April 10, June 12 (2-5.30)*

¶Stone House ✿ (Peter & Sheila Smellie) Wellington. A49 6m N of Hereford, end of dual carriageway, turn L for Westhope. ¾m turn R up narrow track. Parking ¼m Parking difficult in wet conditions. 1-acre S sloping garden with views over countryside. Garden is terraced, subdivided by hedging and contains a wide selection of plants, many unusual. Small wild garden and childrens play area. *Adm £1.50 Chd 50p. Suns April 17, May 22, June 26, July 17 (10-6). Private visits welcome, please* Tel 0432 830470

● **Stone House Cottage Gardens** &✿✿ (Maj & the Hon Mrs Arbuthnott) Stone, 2m SE of Kidderminster via A448 towards Bromsgrove next to church, turn up drive. 1-acre sheltered walled plantsman's garden with towers; rare wall shrubs, climbers and interesting herbaceous plants. In adjacent nursery large selection of unusual shrubs and climbers for sale. Featured in The Garden, Country Life and Hortus. Coaches by appt only. *Adm £1.50 Chd free. Suns May 1, 8, 15, 22, 29; June 5, 12, 19, 26; Aug 28; Mons April 4, May 2, 30; Aug 29 (10-6); also open March to Oct every Wed, Thurs, Fri, Sat (10-6). Private visits welcome Nov* Tel 0562 69902

¶Strawberry Cottage ✿✿ (Mr & Mrs M R Philpott) Hamnish. 3m E of Leominster. A44 E from Leominster, turn L at 1st Xrds to Hamnish. A 2-acre cottage garden created over the past 5 yrs. Part of garden on steep slope with large rockeries. Wide variety of plants and shrubs, over 200 roses, mixed and herbaceous borders. Beds with single colour themes. Pond and wild garden area, herb and large kitchen garden. Spring bulbs. Superb position with spectacular views. TEAS. *Adm £1.20 Chd free (Share to Hamnish Church® & Leominster Community Hospital®). Combined adm with* Grantsfield *June 23 & 26 £1.80 Chd free. 1st & 3rd Suns, 2nd & 4th Thurs May 1 to Sept 22 (2-5.30). Private visits welcome, please* Tel 056 882 319

¶21 Swinton Lane ✿✿ (Mr A Poulton & Mr B Stenlake) Worcester. 1½m W of City Centre off A4103 Hereford Rd turning into Swinton Lane between Portabello public house and Boughton Golf Course. ⅓-acre town garden featuring a wide variety of plants. Herbaceous borders, silver garden and red border. Many interesting tender plants are used both in the garden and in containers for the summer. *Adm £1 Chd free. Thurs June 2, 30, July 28, Aug 25 (11-6). Also private visits welcome, please* Tel 0905 422265

Tedstone Court ✿✿ (Mrs N C Bellville) Approx 17m from Hereford. From Bromyard take road for Stourport B4203 for 3m. Turn R signed Whitbourne, Tedstone Delamere. Spring garden, daffodils, rhododendrons; rockery; kitchen garden; fine views. Plants for sale. In June tour of deer farm. Calves arriving (separate charge). TEAS. *Adm £2 Chd 25p. Suns May 29, June 19, Aug 7 (2-6)*

Regular Openers. Too many days to include in diary. Usually there is a wide range of plants giving year-round interest. See head of county section for the name and garden description for times etc.

Torwood &✿✿ (Mr & Mrs S G Woodward) Whitchurch. Ross-on-Wye to Monmouth A40 turn to Symonds Yat West. Garden 50yds from Main Rd next to school. Interesting garden of conifers, shrubs, herbaceous plants and water features. Featured by Central Television 'My Secret Garden' shown earlier this year. TEA. *Adm £1 Chd free. Suns June 5, 19, July 3, 17, 31, Aug 21 (2-6). Weds June 15, 29 July 6, 27, Aug 10, Sept 7 (2-6). Any other times April to Oct private visits welcome, please* **Tel 0600 890306**

Upper Court & (Mr & Mrs W Herford) Kemerton, NE of Tewkesbury B4080. Take turning to Parish Church from War Memorial; Manor behind church. Approx 13 acres of garden and grounds inc a 2-acre lake where visitors would be welcome to bring picnics. The garden was mostly landscaped and planted in 1930s. TEAS. *Adm £1.50 Chd free. Suns June 12, 19 (2-6)*

Well Cottage &✿ (R S Edwards Esq) Blakemere. 10m due W of Hereford. Leave Hereford on A465 (Abergavenny) rd. After 3m turn R towards Hay B4349 (B4348). At Clehonger keep straight on the B4352 towards Bredwardine. Well Cottage is on L by phone box. ¾-acre garden of mixed planting plus ½ acre of wild flower meadow suitable for picnics. There is a natural pool with gunnera and primulae. Good views over local hills and fields. Featured in Diana Saville's book 'Gardens for Small Country Houses'. *Adm £1 Chd free. Private visits welcome May to Aug, please* **Tel 0981 500475**

Westwood Farm (Mr & Mrs Caspar Tremlett). From Bromyard take A44 towards Leominster. R turn to Hatfield and Bockleton 2m R turn down Westwood Lane. First Farm. From Leominster, take A44 toward Worcester 6m L to Hatfield and Bockleton. Map ref OS sheet 149 60.59. ¾ acre of cottage type garden with unusual plants and trees, small conservatory and pond with waterside plants. Dogs can be exercised in car park field. *Adm £1 Chd free. Sun, Mon June 26, 27 (2-6). Also private visits welcome May to June, please* **Tel 0885 410212**

White Cottage &✿✿ (Mr & Mrs S M Bates) Earls Common Rd, Stock Green. A422 Worcester-Alcester; turn L at Red Hart PH (Dormston) 1½m to T junc in Stock Green. Turn L. 2-acre garden, developed since 1981; large herbaceous and shrub borders, many unusual varieties; specialist collection of hardy geraniums; stream and natural garden carpeted with primroses, cowslips and other wild flowers; nursery; featuring plants propagated from the garden. Teas at Jinny Ring Craft Centre at Hanbury. *Adm £1 OAPs 75p Chd free. April 1, to Oct 9 Daily (10-5).* **Closed Thurs and alternate Suns except** *Suns April 3, 17; May 1, 15, 29; June 12, 26; July 10, 24; Aug 28; Sept 11, 25; Oct 9. Nursery open daily April 1 to Oct 9 and all Bank Hol Mons Aug by prior appt only* **Tel 0386 792414**

Whitfield & (G M Clive Esq) Wormbridge, 8m SW of Hereford on A465 Hereford-Abergavenny Rd. Parkland, large garden, ponds, walled kitchen garden, 1780 gingko tree, 1½m woodland walk with 1851 Redwood grove. Picnic parties welcome. TEAS. *Adm £1.50 Chd 50p. Sun June 5 (2-6)*

Whitlenge House Cottage &✿✿ (Mr & Mrs K J Southall) Whitlenge Lane, Hartlebury. S of Kidderminster on A449. Take A442 (signposted Droitwich) over small island, ¼m, 1st R into Whitlenge Lane. Follow signs. Professional landscaper's own demonstration garden with over 400 varieties of trees, shrubs, conifers, herbaceous, heathers and alpines, giving year-round interest. Small water features, rustic work, gravel gardens surrounded by rockeries and stone walls. Evolved over 9 years into 2 acres of informal plantsman's garden and incorporating an adjacent nursery specialising in large specimen shrubs. *Adm £1.50 Chd free. Suns March 27, April 10, 24 May 1, 29 June 26 July 31 Aug 28 Sept 25. Every Thurs, Fri, Sat March to Sept (10-5) Bank Hol Mons April 4, May 2, 30, Aug 29 (10-6)*

Wichenford Court &✿✿ (Lt Col & Mrs P C Britten) Wichenford. 7m NW of Worcester; turn right off B4204 at Masons Arms pub; 1m on right. Medium-sized garden dating from 1975; interesting young trees; daffodils and spring bulbs; flowering cherries; clematis; flowering shrubs and shrub roses. House dating back to C11 (not open), parts of original moat still in existence. C17 dovecote (NT). Picnic area open at noon. TEA. *Adm £1.50 Chd 30p (Share to Worcestershire Royal Infirmary, Newtown®). Sun April 17 (2-6)*

Wind's Point ✿ (Cadbury Trustees) British Camp. 3m SW of Malvern on Ledbury Rd. Medium-sized garden; unusual setting, lovely views. Last home of great Swedish singer Jenny Lind and where she died 1887. *Adm £1 Chd free. Sun April 17 (12-5)*

Windyridge ✿✿ (Mr P Brazier) Kidderminster. Turn off Chester Rd N (A449) into Hurcott Rd, then into Imperial Avenue. 1-acre spring garden containing azaleas, magnolias, camellias, rhododendrons, mature flowering cherries and davidia. Please wear sensible shoes. *Adm £1 Chd free. Suns May 1, 8 (2-6)*

Wormington Grange & (Mr & Mrs John Evetts) 4m W of Broadway. A46 from Broadway-Cheltenham, take 2nd turning for Wormington. Large natural garden; herb garden, old-fashioned roses. Lovely trees. Large lake with wildfowl. Interesting arts and crafts gates. Croquet lawn, very good views. Visitors may play croquet if they wish. *Adm £1 Chd free (Share to St Catherine's Church®). Suns April 10, July 10 (2-6)*

●**Wych & Colwall Horticultural Society Show**. The Elms School &✿ (L A C Ashley, Headmaster) Colwall Green. Medium-sized garden, herbaceous borders, fine views of Malvern Hills. Interesting exhibits of perennials, shrubs and crafts. Classes for flowers, vegetables, art & handicrafts. TEAS. *Adm to show and garden 80p. Share to NGS Sat Aug 13 (2-6)*

Yew Tree House & (Mr & Mrs W D Moyle) Ombersley. Turn off A449 up Woodfield Lane R at T-junction. 2½-acre garden with many rare herbaceous plants and shrubs. Pretty walled garden with alpines and lily pond, numerous old-fashioned roses. Mature plantings of blue, pink and white borders around tennis court and other yellow and white beds. Orchard, copse and lawns with lovely views set around c1640 timber framed house. TEA. *Adm £1 Chd 50p. Sun June 26 (2-6)*

Hertfordshire

Hon County Organiser: Mrs Antony Woodall, The Old Rectory, Wyddial, Buntingford SG9 0EN
Assistant Hon County Organisers: Mrs Edward Harvey, Wickham Hall, Bishop's Stortford CM23 1JQ
Mrs Hedley Newton, Moat Farm House Much Hadham SG10 6AE
Mrs Leone Ayres, Patmore Corner, Albury, Ware, Herts SG11 2LY
Hon County Treasurer: Mrs John Lancaster, Manor Cottage, Aspenden, Nr Buntingford SG9 9PB

DATES OF OPENING

By appointment
For telephone numbers and other details see garden descriptions.
Private visits welcomed

Abbots House, Abbots Langley
Deansmere, West Hyde, Rickmansworth
Garden Cottage, Abbots Langley
1 Gernon Walk, Letchworth
St Paul's Walden Bury, Hitchin
Waterdell House, Croxley Green
West Lodge Park, Hadley Wood

Regular openings
For details see garden descriptions

Benington Lordship, nr Stevenage. For dates see text
Capel Manor Gardens, Enfield. For dates see text
Hopleys (Gardens & Nursery) nr Bishop's Stortford. See text
The Manor House, Ayot St Lawrence. Suns May 1 to Sept 30
West Lodge Park, Hadley Wood. Every Wed

April 4 Monday
Holwell Manor, nr Hatfield
April 10 Sunday
Hanbury Manor Hotel, nr Ware
Pelham House, Brent Pelham
April 17 Sunday
St Paul's Walden Bury, Hitchin

April 24 Sunday
Great Munden House, nr Ware
Odsey Park, Ashwell
Old Brickfields, Guilden Morden
May 15 Sunday
The Abbot's House, Abbots Langley
Hipkins, Broxbourne
Pelham House, Brent Pelham
May 21 Saturday
Cockhamsted, Braughing
May 22 Sunday
Cockhampstead, Braughing
St Paul's Walden Bury, Hitchin
Wrotham Park, Barnet
May 29 Sunday
Great Sarratt Hall, Rickmansworth
Moor Place, Much Hadham
Queenswood School, Hatfield
Street Farm, Bovingdon
May 30 Monday
Queenswood School, Hatfield
June 1 Wednesday
Street Farm, Bovingdon
June 4 Saturday
Cockhamsted, Braughing
June 5 Sunday
Cockhamsted, Braughing
Odsey Park, Ashwell
Old Brickfields, Guilden Morden
St Paul's Walden Bury, Hitchin
West Lodge Park, Hadley Wood
June 12 Sunday
Hill House, Stanstead Abbotts
Wheathampstead Gardens, Wheathampstead
June 19 Sunday
Hanbury Manor Hotel, nr Ware
Mackerye End House, Harpenden

June 21 Tuesday
The Abbot's House, Abbots Langley
June 25 Saturday
Benington Lordship, nr Stevenage
June 26 Sunday
Benington Lordship, nr Stevenage
Waterdell House, Croxley Green
July 2 Saturday
The Barn, Serge Hill, Abbots Langley ‡
Rushmead, Abbotts Langley ‡
Serge Hill, Abbots Langley ‡
July 3 Sunday
St Paul's Walden Bury, Hitchin
Street Farm, Bovingdon
July 10 Sunday
Deansmere, West Hyde, Rickmansworth
The Mill House, Tewin, nr Welwyn
July 13 Wednesday
Deansmere, West Hyde, Rickmansworth
July 31 Sunday
The Manor House, Ayot St Lawrence
August 28 Sunday
The Abbot's House, Abbots Langley
September 25 Sunday
Hopleys (Garden & Nursery), nr Bishop's Stortford
October 2 Sunday
Knebworth House, Stevenage
October 16 Sunday
Capel Manor Gardens, Enfield
October 23 Sunday
West Lodge Park, Hadley Wood

DESCRIPTIONS OF GARDENS

The Abbots House 閪閪閪 (Dr & Mrs Peter Tomson) 10, High Street, Abbots Langley NW of Watford (5m from Watford). Junction 20 M25, junction 6 M1. Parking in free village car park. 1¾-acre garden with interesting trees; shrubs; mixed borders; sunken garden; ponds; conservatory. Nursery featuring plants propagated from the garden. TEAS. *Adm £1.50 Chd free (Share to The Hospice of St Francis, Berkhamsted®). Suns, Tues, May 15, June 21, Aug 28 (2-5). Also at other times by appt Tel 0923 264946*

The Barn 閪閪 (Tom Stuart-Smith and family) Abbots Langley. ½m E of Bedmond in Serge Hill Lane. 1-acre plantsman's garden. Small sheltered courtyard planted with unusual shrubs and perennials, contrasts with more open formal garden with views over wild flower meadow. Tea at Serge Hill. *Combined adm £3 with Serge Hill (Share to Tibet Relief Fund UK®). Sat July 2 (2-5.30)*

By Appointment Gardens. Avoid the crowds. Good chance of a tour by owner. See garden description for telephone number.

Benington Lordship &&& (Mr & Mrs C H A Bott) 5m E of Stevenage, in Benington village. Terraced plantsman's garden overlooking lakes, formal rose garden; Victorian folly, Norman keep and moat; spring rock and water garden; spectacular double herbaceous borders. Small nursery. Snowdrops. *Adm £2.20 Chd free. Easter, Spring and Summer Bank Holiday Mons (12-5) Weds. April to Sept 28 (12-5). Suns April to Aug 28 (2-5) (Share to St Peters Church©). For NGS TEAS and Floral Festival in Church adjoining garden. Sat, Sun June 25, 26 (12-6)*

Capel Manor Gardens &&& (Horticultural & Environmental Centre) Bullsmoor Lane, Enfield, Middx. 3 mins from M25 junction M25/A10. W at traffic lights. Nearest station Turkey Street - Liverpool Street line (not Suns). 30 acres of historical and modern theme gardens, Japanese garden, large Italian style maze, rock and water features. 5 acre demonstration garden run by Gardening Which? Walled garden with rose collection, display glasshouses and woodland walks. TEAS. *Adm £3 OAP £2 Chd £1.50. Open daily April to Oct, weekdays only Nov to March (10-4.30) (5.30 weekends). For NGS (Share to Horticultural Therapy©) Sun Oct 16 (10-6). For other details* **Tel 0992 763849**

Cockhamsted &&& (Mr & Mrs David Marques) Braughing. 2m E of village towards Braughing Friars (7m N of Ware). 2 acres; informal garden; shrub roses surrounded by open country. Island with trees surrounded by water-filled C14 moat. TEAS in aid of Leukaemia Research. *Adm £1.50 Chd free. Sat, Sun May 21, 22; June 4, 5 (2-6)*

Deansmere &&& (Mr & Mrs Derek Austen) Old Uxbridge Rd, West Hyde. 3m SW of Rickmansworth, off A412. Leaving M25 junction 17, follow the sign 'Maple Cross'. In 200 yds at roundabout take 2nd exit; across traffic lights at Maple Cross (A412), at mini roundabout turn L (signposted 'Harefield'), in 100yds at T junction turn L, 100yds. Deansmere is opposite St. Thomas's Church. 2-acre garden old, new and in the making, full of variety and interest. Perennials, bedding plants, containers, bulbs, heather, shrubs, trees: summerhouses; aviary; rhododendron bed; pergola; vegetables, fruit trees; two small ponds; dell; viola and penstemon collections; greenhouses and view of the lake. TEAS. *Adm £1.25 Chd 50p (Share to Harrow Ciné & Video Society®). Sun, Wed July 10, 13 (2-6). Private parties welcome with tea, please* **Tel 0923 778817**

Garden Cottage & (Anthony House) 85 Furtherfield, Abbots Langley. NW of Watford 5m from Watford junction 20 M25 junction 6 M1. A small plantsman's garden in total 100' long by 20' wide; planted in 1991, filled with unusual perennials and interesting features all year. TEAS. *Adm £1 Chd 50p. Private visits welcome, please* **Tel 0923 260571**

1 Gernon Walk & (Miss Rachel Crawshay) Letchworth (First Garden City). Tiny town garden (100ft long but only 8ft wide in middle) planned and planted since 1984 for year-round and horticultural interest. *Collecting box. Private visits only, please* **Tel 0462 686399**

Great Munden House && (Mr & Mrs D Wentworth-Stanley) 7m N of Ware. Off A10 on Puckeridge by-pass turn W; or turning off A602 via Dane End. 3½-acre informal garden with lawns, mixed shrub and herbaceous borders; variety shrub roses, trees; kitchen and herb garden. Plant stall. TEAS. *Adm £1.50 Chd 50p. Sun April 24 (2.30-5.30)*

Great Sarratt Hall &&& (H M Neal Esq) Sarratt, N of Rickmansworth. From Watford N via A41 (or M1 Exit 5) to Kings Langley; and left (W) to Sarratt; garden is 1st on R after village sign. 4 acres; herbaceous and mixed shrub borders; pond, moisture-loving plants and trees; walled kitchen garden; rhododendrons, magnolias, camellias; new planting of specialist conifers and rare trees. TEAS. *Adm £1.50 Chd free (Share to Courtauld Institute of Art Fund©). Sun May 29 (2-6)*

Hanbury Manor Hotel & (Poles Ltd) Thundridge. 2m N of Ware on A10, turn L 100 yds past end of dual carriageway from London or turn R past 'Sow & Pigs' travelling S. Garden well known in Victorian times, now part of hotel grounds. Restoration work commenced 1989, now well under way. Walled garden with listed 'moongate', extensive herbaceous borders, herb garden and fruit houses; yew hedged walks with spring bulbs planted orchard and period rose garden; secret garden in woodland setting; pinetum. TEAS. *Adm £1.50 Chd 75p. Suns April 10, June 19 (2-6)*

Hill House && (Mr & Mrs R Pilkington) Stanstead Abbotts, near Ware. From A10 turn E on to A414; then B181 for Stanstead Abbotts; left at end of High St, garden 1st R past Church. Ample car parking. 6 acres incl wood; species roses, herbaceous border, water garden, conservatory, aviary, woodland walk. Lovely view over Lea Valley. Modern Art Exhibition in loft gallery (20p extra). Unusual plants for sale. Home-made TEAS. *Adm £2 OAPs £1.50 Chd 50p (Share to St Andrews Parish Church of Stanstead Abbotts®). Sun June 12 (2-5.30)*

Hipkins && (Michael Goulding Esq) Broxbourne. From A10 to Broxbourne turn up Bell or Park Lane into Baas Lane, opposite Graham Avenue. 3-acre informal garden with spring fed ponds; azaleas and rhododendrons; shrub and herbaceous borders specialising in plants for flower arrangers; many unusual plants; fine trees and well kept kitchen garden. TEAS. *Adm £1.50 Chd 50p. Sun May 15 (2-6)*

Holwell Manor && (Mr & Mrs J Gillum) Nr Hatfield. On W side of B1455, short lane linking A414 with B158 between Hatfield (3m) and Hertford (4m). B1455 joins the A414 roundabout and is signposted Essendon. Holwell is 500yds from this roundabout. Natural garden with large pond, mature trees, river walks; approx 2-3 acres. Island in pond covered with daffodils and narcissi in spring. TEAS. *Adm £1 Chd 50p. Mon April 4 (2-5)*

Hopleys (Garden and Nursery) &✿✿ (Mr Aubrey Barker) 5m from Bishop's Stortford on B1004. M11 (exit 8) 7m or A10 (Puckeridge) 5m via A120. 50yds N of Bull public house in centre of Much Hadham. 3½ acres of constantly developing garden; trees, shrubs, herbaceous and alpines; island beds with mixed planting in parkland setting; pond and many unusual and rare (incl variegated) plants. *Open every Mon, Wed, Thurs, Fri, Sat (9-5) and Sun (2-5) excl Jan. For NGS TEAS. Adm £1.50 Chd 50p. Sun Sept 25 (11-6)*

Knebworth House &✿ (The Lord Cobbold) Knebworth. 28m N of London; direct access from A1(M) at Stevenage. Station and Bus stop: Stevenage 3m. Historic house, home of Bulwer Lytton; Victorian novelist and statesman. Lutyens garden designed for his brother-in-law, the Earl of Lytton, comprising pleached lime avenues, rose beds, herbaceous borders, yew hedges and various small gardens in process of restoration; Gertrude Jekyll herb garden. Restaurant and TEAS. *Adm £1.50 Chd £1.* ▲*For NGS Sun Oct 2 (12-5)*

Mackerye End House ✿✿ (Mr & Mrs David Laing) Harpenden. A1 junc 4 follow signs for Wheathampstead then Luton. Garden ½m from Wheathampstead on R. M1 junct to follow Lower Luton Rd to Cherry Tree Inn. Turn L to Wheathampstead. A 1550 Grade 1 manor house set in 11 acres of gardens and park. Front garden set in framework of formal yew hedges with a long border (best in early summer) and a fine C17 tulip tree. Victorian walled garden now divided into smaller sections; path maze; cutting garden; quiet garden; vegetables. Newly created W garden enclosed by pergola walk of old English roses and vines. Lunches and TEAS. *Adm £1.50 Chd 50p (Share to Spinal Injuries®). Sun June 19 (12-5)*

The Manor House Ayot St Lawrence &✿ (Mrs Peter Thwaites) Bear R into village from Bride Hall Lane, ruined Church on L and the Brocket Arms on R. On bend there is a pair of brick piers leading to drive - go through white iron gates. The Manor house is on your L. New garden, with formal garden, mixed borders and nut grove, large walled garden and orchard. TEA NGS days only. *Adm £2 OAP/Chd £1 (under ten free). Open every Sun May 1 to Sept 30. Also by appt for parties, please Tel 0438 820943. For NGS Sun July 31 (2-6)*

¶The Mill House &✿✿ (Dr and Mrs R V Knight) Tewin, nr Archers Green. 3½m W of Hertford and 3½m E of Welwyn on B1000. Parking at Archers Green which is signposted on B1000. On the banks of the R Mimram. Approx 20 acres; mature gardens incl fine hedges, woodlands, many rare trees labelled, shrub and herbaceous borders, spring fed water gardens, with an abundance of wildlife in a lovely valley setting. Plants and TEAS in aid of Hospice Care, E Herts. *Adm £2 Chd under 10 free. Sun July 10 (2-6)*

Moor Place &✿ (Mr & Mrs Bryan Norman) Much Hadham. Entrance either at war memorial or at Hadham Cross. 2 C18 walled gardens. Herbaceous borders. Large area of shrubbery, lawns, hedges and trees. 2 ponds. Approx 10 acres. TEAS. *Adm £1.50 Chd 50p. Sun May 29 (2-5.30)*

Myddelton House see London

Odsey Park &✿ (Mr & The Hon Mrs Jeremy Fordham) Ashwell. Situated equidistant between Royston and Baldock 4½m each way. On N carriageway of A505 enter by Lodge and drive into park as signposted. Recently remade medium-sized garden originally dating from 1860 with walled garden, set in park with mature trees, spring bulbs, tulips; small colourful herbaceous border, roses, shrubs and small herb garden. Car parking free. TEAS June 5 only. *Adm £1.50 Chd free (Share to Ashwell Church Restoration Fund®). Suns April 24 (1-5); June 5 (2-6)*

¶Old Brickfields &✿✿ (Mr & Mrs Robert Rosier) Guilden Morden. Approx. 4m N of the A505 Baldock to Royston rd. Old Brickfields is ¼m out of the village on the L on the Wendy-Shingay rd. 1-acre informal gardens of lawns, 'shrubaceous' borders with interesting labelled plants and vegetable garden. 1½ acres of wild area of meadow and lge pond. Area for picnics overlooking pond. *Adm £1 Chd free. Suns April 24, June 5 (11-5)*

¶Pelham House &✿✿ (Mr David Haselgrove & Dr Sylvia Matfinelli) Brent Pelham. On E side of Brent Pelham on B1038. When travelling from Clavering immed after the village sign. 3½-acre informal garden on alkaline clay started by present owners in 1986. Plenty of interest to the plantsman. Wide variety of trees and shrubs especially birches and oaks. Bulb frames, raised beds with alpines and acid-loving plants and small formal area with ponds. Many daffodils and tulips. *Adm £1 Chd free (Share to Brent Pelham Church®). Suns April 10, May 15 (2-6)*

Queenswood School ✿✿ Shepherds Way. From S. M25 Junction 24 signposted Potters Bar. In ½m at lights turn R onto A1000 signposted Hatfield. In 2m turn R onto B157. School is ½m on the R. From N. A1000 from Hatfield 5m turn L on B157. 120 acres informal gardens and woodlands. Rhododendrons, fine specimen trees, shrubs and herbaceous borders. Glasshouses; fine views to Chiltern Hills. Picnic areas. Lunches & TEAS. *Adm £1.50 OAPs/Chd 75p. Sun, Mon May 29, 30 (11-6)*

¶Rushmead ✿✿ (Mr & Mrs Brian Munnery) Abbots Langley. Garden sited midway between Abbots Langley and Bedmond on main Watford-Leverstock Green Rd. M25 junction 20 or M1 junction 6. A ¼-acre garden with variety of shrubs, trees and perennials; a lge, deep pond (care needed with children) with ornamental lilies and fish. Plants propagated from the garden. *Adm £1.50 Chd free (Share to Ovingdean Hall School®). Sat July 2 (2-5)*

St Paul's Walden Bury ✿ (Simon Bowes Lyon and family) Whitwell, on B651 5m S of Hitchin; ½m N of Whitwell. Formal woodland garden listed Grade 1. Laid out about 1730, influenced by French tastes. Long rides and avenues span about 40 acres, leading to temples, statues, lake and ponds. Also more recent flower gardens and woodland garden with rhododendrons, azaleas and magnolias. Dogs on leads. TEAS. *Adm £1.50 Chd 75p (Share to St Pauls Walden Church®). Suns April 17, May 22, June 5 (2-7), July 3 (2-6) followed by lakeside concert 7pm. Also other times by appt Tel 0438 871218 or 871229*

Serge Hill ⚭❀ (Murray & Joan Stuart-Smith) Abbots Langley. ½m E of Bedmond. The house is marked on the OS map. Regency house in parkland setting with fine kitchen garden of ½ acre. A range of unusual wall plants, mixed border of 100yds. New small courtyard garden and wall garden planted with hot coloured flowers. TEAS. *Combined adm £3 with* **The Barn** *(Share to Herts Garden Trust©). Sat July 2 (2-5)*

Street Farm ⚭❀ (Mrs Penelope Shand) Bovingdon. Marked on ordnance survey map; on rd between Bovingdon and Chipperfield exactly 1m from the Chesham Rd entrance to Bovingdon High St. Approx 3 acres comprising extensive lawns, long herbaceous borders. A large pond with an island surrounded by decorative shrubs and boasting beautiful water lilies and various miscanthas. Also raised beds, island beds and shrubberies with unusual plants in an attractive sylvan setting. A miniature paved garden enclosed by a yew hedge with tiny clipped box hedges surrounding several beds containing herbs, auricula and alpine strawberries. *Adm £1.50 OAP's £1 Chd free (Share to RSPB®). Suns May 29, July 3, Wed June 1 (2-6)*

Tarn, Oxhey Drive South, Norwood *see* London.

Waterdell House ⚭❀⚭ (Mr & Mrs Peter Ward) Croxley Green. 1½m from Rickmansworth. Exit 18 from M25. Direction R'worth to join A412 towards Watford. From A412 turn left signed Sarratt, along Croxley Green, fork right past Coach & Horses, cross Baldwins Lane into Little Green Lane, then left at top. 1½-acre walled garden developed and maintained over many years to accommodate growing family; mature and young trees, topiary holly hedge, herbaceous borders; modern island beds of shrubs, old-fashioned roses; vegetable and fruit garden. New pond garden. TEAS 80p. *Adm £1.50 OAPs/Chd £1. Sun June 26 (2-6) and private visits welcome May-mid July (2-6), please* **Tel 0923 772775**

West Lodge Park ⚭ (T Edward Beale Esq) Cockfosters Rd, Hadley Wood. On A111 between Potters Bar and Southgate. Exit 24 from M25 signed Cockfosters. Station: Cockfosters underground (Piccadilly Line); then bus 298 to Beech Hill. Beale Arboretum, set in 10-acre section of West Lodge Park, consists of splendid collection of trees, some 500 varieties, all labelled; many original and interesting specimens, some old-established as well as scores planted since 1965; magnificent leaf colour. TEA (or lunch if booked in advance in adjoining hotel). *Adm £1.50 Chd 30p (Share to GRBS®). Suns June 5 (2-5.30); Oct 23 (12-4), Weds every week (2-5). Organised parties anytime by appt. Collecting box.* **Tel 081 440 8311**

Wheathampstead Gardens 6m N of St Albans on B651 or 3m from junction 4 of A1 on B653. Car parking free. Not within walking distance of each other. *Combined adm £2 Chd free (Share to Tradescant Trust). Sun June 12 (11-5)*

Lamer Hill ⚭❀ (Mr & Mrs Peter Flory) Lower Gustard Wood. Proceed N from Wheathampstead Village on B651 towards Kimpton for 1m then with entrance to Mid-Herts Golf Club on L and cottages by triangle of grass on R, turn R (private road). Proceed for 200yds. Lamer Hill is on the R just before wood. Old garden of 4 acres which was re-designed 8yrs ago. Incl mature and young trees; pleached hornbeams, borders, shrub roses, cottage garden, woodland paths. Light refreshments all day

Lamer Lodge ⚭⚭ (Mr & Mrs J Wilson) Lamer Lane. From roundabout N of Wheathampstead continue N towards Kimpton on Lamer Lane (B651) for ½m; 1st (Lodge) house on R on blind L bend. 2½ acres of informal garden, woodland paths, lawns, varied trees, shrubs and old roses; paved pond area with summer display in tubs; countryside surroundings. Picnicers welcome

Wrotham Park ⚭❀ (Mr Robert Byng) M25 Junction 23, take A1081 towards Barnet, first left to Bentley Heath into Dancers Hill Rd. Lodge in village 1½m on R opp church. 30 acres in Parkland setting. Woodland, rhododendrons, azaleas, herbaceous. Picnic area. TEA. *Adm £2 OAPs/Chd 50p. Sun May 22 (2-6)*

Humberside

Hon County Organiser: Peter Carver Esq., The Croft, North Cave, East Yorkshire HU15 2NG
Tel 0430 422203

DATES OF OPENING

By appointment
For telephone numbers and other details see garden descriptions. Private visits welcomed

The Cottages, Barrow-Haven, nr Barton
Grange Cottage, Cadney
Lanhydrock Cottage, Skerne
8 Welton Old Rd, Welton

Regular opening
For details see garden descriptions

Burton Agnes Hall, Nr Driffield April to Oct

April 3 Sunday
The Croft, North Cave
April 10 Sunday
Croft House, Ulceby
April 24 Sunday
Lanhydrock Cottage, Skerne

May 1 Sunday
Evergreens, 119 Main Rd‡
il Giardino, Bllton‡
May 2 Monday
The White Cottage, Halsham
May 22 Sunday
Lanhydrock Cottage, Skerne
8 Welton Old Rd, Welton
May 29 Sunday
Castle Farm Nurseries, Barmby Moor
The Cottages, Barrow-Haven, nr Barton

Evergreens, 119 Main Rd‡
il Giardino, Bilton‡

May 30 Monday
The Cottages, Barrow-Haven, nr
Barton

June 5 Sunday
Castle Farm Nurseries, Barmby
Moor
Croft House, Ulceby

June 11 Saturday
Burton Agnes Hall "Gardeners
Fair"

June 12 Sunday
Burton Agnes Hall "Gardeners
Fair"
The Old Rectory, Nunburnholme
Saltmarshe Hall, Saltmarshe

June 15 Wednesday
23 Parthian Rd, Bilton Grange

June 19 Sunday
The Croft, North Cave
Lanhydrock Cottage, Skerne
23 Parthian Rd, Bilton Grange
Parkview, South Cave

June 25 Saturday
Houlton Lodge, Goxhill

June 26 Sunday
Grange Cottage, Cadney‡
The Green, Lund‡‡
Houlton Lodge, Goxhill
Laburnum Cottage, Cadney‡
5 Lockington Rd, Lund‡‡

July 3 Sunday
Evergreens, 119 Main Rd‡
il Giardino, Bilton‡

July 10 Sunday
Boynton Hall, Bridlington
Chatt House, Burton Pidsea‡

Houghton Hall, Market Weighton
The White Cottage, Halsham‡

July 17 Sunday
Lanhydrock Cottage, Skerne

August 14 Sunday
Lanhydrock Cottage, Skerne

August 28 Sunday
The Cottages, Barrow-Haven, nr
Barton

August 29 Monday
The Cottages, Barrow-Haven, nr
Barton
The White Cottage, Halsham

September 11 Sunday
Evergreens, 119 Main Rd
Lanhydrock Cottage, Skerne

DESCRIPTIONS OF GARDENS

Boynton Hall &❀ (Mr & Mrs R Marriott) Bridlington. On B1253 2m W of Bridlington S from Boynton Xroads. Lawn and yew hedge around Elizabethan house and lovely old walled garden with shrubs and roses; also gate house and knot garden (recently created). House Tour (extra). TEAS in aid of church. *Adm £1.50 Chd £1. Sun July 10 (1.30-5)*

Burton Agnes Hall &❀ (Mr & Mrs N Cunliffe-Lister) nr Driffield. Burton Agnes is on A166 between Driffield & Bridlington. 8 acres of gardens incl lawns with clipped yew and fountains, woodland gardens and a walled garden which has been recently redeveloped, it contains a potager, herbaceous and mixed borders; maze with a thyme garden; jungle garden; campanula collection garden and coloured gardens containing giant games boards. 'Gardeners Fair' Sat, Sun June 11, 12; specialist nurseries; gardening advice; dried flower & herb craft; machinery & garden construction demonstrations. TEAS. *Adm £2 Chd £1. April 1 to Oct 31 (11-5)*

Castle Farm Nurseries &❀❀ (Mr & Mrs K Wilson) Barmby Moor. Turn off A1079 Hull/York rd, ¾m from Barmby Moor at Hewson & Robinson's Garage, towards Thornton; ½m on R is sign for nursery. 13yr-old garden of 1¼ acres created and maintained by owners; incl trees, mixed borders, herbaceous border, rock garden, rhododendrons and water garden; emphasis on heather and conifer beds. Nursery open. Cream TEAS in aid of local Methodist Church. *Adm £1 Chd free. Suns May 29, June 5 (2-5.30)*

Chatt House &❀ (Mrs Harrison) Burton Pidsea. In mid-Holderness, approx 10m Hull via Hedon and Burstwick. Old-established garden with much re-organisation taking place in the pond area. Walled garden, lawns, arboretum, herbaceous, kitchen garden and greenhouse. TEAS. *Adm £1.50 Chd 50p. Sun July 10 (2-5)*

The Cottages ❀❀ (Mr & Mrs E C Walsh) 4m due E of Barton-on-Humber, adjacent to Barrow-Haven Railway Station. Turn L 3m E of Barton. Variable shrub-lined walks adjacent to reed bed hides. Large range of trees,

shrubs, perennials, insects, birds and butterflies abound. Organic vegetable garden, photographic hides. An all-the-year-round garden created in 11yrs on 1¼ acres, of a once derelict tile yard. Runner up in 'Birdwatching' Large Garden Competition in 1989. Large selection of plants for sale, hostas, lobelia etc. Partly suitable for wheelchairs. TEAS. *Adm £1 OAPs £1 Chd free. Suns, Mons May 29, 30; Aug 28, 29 (11-5). Also private visits welcome, please Tel 0469 31614*

The Croft &❀❀ (Mr & Mrs Peter Carver) North Cave. On B1230 (1½m from exit 38, M62). Entrance 100yds S War Memorial in village centre (towards South Cave). Stewardship by same family since Queen Victoria's reign pervades this large garden of much pleasure and permanence. Recent additions include jardin potager, yew hedging (1985) and 'Tapis Vert' statue garden (1991). Included in garden books; subject of press articles and featured on BBC TV with Geoffrey Smith 3 times and ITV with Susan Hampshire. Featured in NGS video 2, see page 344. Private car parking. TEAS in aid of St John Ambulance. *Adm £1.50 Chd free. Weds May 25, June 29, July 13. Also for NGS Suns April 3 (Easter), June 19 (2-5)*

Croft House &❀ (Mr & Mrs Peter Sandberg) Ulceby. Immingham exit off A180 L to Ulceby. At War Memorial L into Front Street follow sign to Pitmoor Lane. 2 acres plantswoman's garden largely created and solely maintained by present owners. Mixed borders; bulbs; lawns; fine trees; hedging. Victorian greenhouse. TEAS. *Adm £1.50 Chd free. Suns April 10, June 5 (2-5)*

¶**Evergreens** &❀❀ (Phil & Brenda Brock) Bilton. 5m E of Hull. Leave city by A165. Exit B1238. Bungalow ¼m on L nearly opposite the Asda Store. Over 1 acre developed since 1984. Features incl mosaics and sundials; raised beds; rockeries and landscaped pond; Japanese garden; conifer, heather and mixed beds. Collection of potentillas and approx 150 dwarf conifers, many labelled. Photographs showing development of garden; small conifer/heather nursery open. Yorkshire recipe TEAS in aid of Spastics Society. *Adm £1 Chd free. Suns May 1, 29; July 3; Sept 11 (1-6)*

Grange Cottage ⋇❀ (Mr & Mrs D Hoy) Cadney. 3m S of Brigg. In Brigg turn L into Elwes St; follow rd to Cadney. From Market Rasen to Brigg Rd, turn L in Howsham on to Cadney Rd. ⅓-acre cottage garden; many unusual and old-fashioned plants; old roses; pond; orchard; conservatory with interesting tender plants. *Adm £1 Chd free. Sun June 26 (2-5). Private visits also welcome May to July, please* Tel 0652 678771

The Green ⅋⋇❀ (Mr & Mrs Hugh Helm) Lund. 7m N of Beverley. Off B1248 Beverley Malton Rd. ¼-acre cottage garden; pool, rockery; climbing roses; shrubs; herbaceous plants, natural gravel garden. Established 9 years in this delightful award winning "Britain in Bloom" village. Also open **5 Lockington Road**. *Adm 75p Chd free. Sun June 26 (2-5)*

Houghton Hall ⅋ (Lord & Lady Manton) Market Weighton. 1m (on N Cave Rd) from Market Weighton (due S). 4m N from N Cave. Drive entrance on R. Roses; shrubs; lawns and lake. Approx 2 acres, set in attractive parkland around Georgian Mansion (not open). High hedges and some topiary. TEA. *Adm £1 Chd free. Sun July 10 (2-5)*

¶Houlton Lodge ⅋⋇❀ (Mr & Mrs M Dearden) Goxhill. 6m E of Barton-on-Humber. Follow signs to Goxhill, do not go into village centre but straight on over railway bridge and take 5th turning on R. Houlton Lodge is about 100yds from junction on LH-side. Park cars outside property. A well established very neat garden approx ¾ acre. Shrub rose and mixed borders; large island bed and rockery and conifer bed. TEAS in aid of Goxhill Methodist Church. *Adm £1 Chd free. Sat, Sun June 25, 26 (2-6)*

Il Giardino ⅋⋇❀ (Peter & Marian Fowler) Bilton. 5m E of Hull City Centre. Take A165 Hull to Bridlington Rd. Turn off; take B1238 to Bilton Village. Turn L opp. St Peter's Church. "Il Giardino" is at bottom of Limetree Lane on L. No. 63. Once neglected garden approx ⅓ acre redesigned and revived over last 6yrs by present owners. Features incl mixed borders and island beds stocked with many unusual plants, shrubs and trees. Attractive beech hedge, small allotment, herb garden, orchard of old apple trees; pear; plum; cherries; medlar and filberts; cedarwood greenhouse with many pelargoniums; fuchsias; grapevine; fig tree; meyer lemon and other less common plants. TEAS. *Adm 75p Chd free. Suns May 1, 29, July 3 (1-5)*

¶Laburnum Cottage ⅋⋇ (Colin & Jessie Lynn) Cadney. 3m S of Brigg. In Brigg turn L into Elwes St, follow rd to Cadney. from Market Rasen to Brigg Rd turn L in Howsham on to Cadney Rd. 1-acre, herbaceous and mature shrub borders; island beds; smaller separate gardens within the garden; rose covered walk leading to shrub roses; wild flowers and small orchard; wildlife and formal pond. TEAS in aid of Blue Cross Animal Hospital. *Adm £1 Chd free. Sun June 26 (12-6)*

Lanhydrock Cottage ⋇❀ (Mrs Jan Joyce) Skerne. 3m SE Driffield; follow signs to Skerne. Delightful small cottage garden of much interest, started by present owner, containing old-fashioned roses, herbs and many fragrant perennials and wild flowers grown together naturally to

provide a habitat for butterflies and wild life. TEAS. *Adm 75p Chd free. Suns April 24, May 22, June 19, July 17, Aug 14, Sept 11 (11-5). Also private visits welcome, please* Tel 0377 253727

5 Lockington Road ⅋⋇ (Miss E Stephenson) Lund. Lund is off B1248 Beverley-Malton Rd. Small walled garden converted from old fold yard on edge of village with old-fashioned roses and cottage garden plants. "Charmingly English". *Adm 75p Chd free. Sun June 26 (2-5)*

The Old Rectory ⅋⋇ (Martin & Jean Stringer) Nunburnholme. A1079 Hull-York rd, turn to Nunburnholme in Hayton and follow signposts. Owner maintained, large garden for chalk loving plants, with streams and herbaceous borders blending into surrounding countryside. TEAS. *Sun June 12 (1.30-5.30)*

Parkview ⅋⋇❀ 45 Church Street (Mr & Mrs Christopher Powell) South Cave. 12m W of Hull on A63 turn N to S Cave on A1034. In centre of village turn L by chemists. 250yds on L black gates under arch. Plantsman's sheltered garden of approx ⅓-acre. Island beds packed with perennials & shrubs, spring garden area. Yorkstone terrace with sinks, pots and urns. Organic fruit & vegetable plot. Greenhouse & compost bins, pond & bog garden. TEAS 65p. *Adm 70p Chd 25p. (Share to PCC Church Yard Plant Fund®). Sun June 19 (2-5)*

¶23 Parthian Road ⋇❀ (Mrs Paddy Forsberg) Bilton Grange. In E Hull take Holderness Rd, R into Marfleet Lane, Staveley Rd, L into Griffin Rd. Parthian Rd immed on R. A small secluded (hedged all round) 30yr old established garden, designed by a keen flower arranger with the welfare of birds, butterflies and fish in mind. Several Victorian chimney pots act as containers for alpine and other non invasive plants. Situated in the heart of an urban housing estate it demonstrates what can be achieved in a very restricted area. Delightful. *Adm 75p Chd free. Wed June 15 (1.30-4.30) Sun June 19 (2.30-5)*

Saltmarshe Hall ⅋⋇ (Mr & Mrs Philip Bean) Howden. N bank of R Ouse. Approx 3½m E of Howden. Follow signs to Laxton through Howdendyke and then signs to Saltmarshe. House in park west of Saltmarshe village. Approx 10 acres beautifully situated on the banks of the R Ouse. Fine old trees, woodland, walled garden and courtyards. Recent planting includes herbaceous borders and old roses. TEAS in aid of Laxton Church. *Adm £1.50 Chd free. Sun June 12 (2-5.30)*

8 Welton Old Road ❀ (Dr & Mrs O G Jones) Welton. In village of Welton 10m W of Hull off A63. Coming E turn L to village past church, turn R along Parliament St. and up hill. House 50yds on R opp Temple Close. From E take A63 and turn off at flyover to Brough; turn R for Welton and follow above instructions. Roadside parking in village. Informal 1-acre garden developed by owners over 30yrs. Imaginative planting with unusual shrubs, plants and less common trees; natural pond and lily pond. TEA in aid of Leukaemia Research. *Adm £1 Chd 20p. Sun May 22 (2-5). Private visits welcome May to July* Tel 0482 667488

The White Cottage ✻❀ (Mr & Mrs John Oldham) Halsham. 1m E of Halsham Arms on B1362, Concealed wooded entrance on R. Parking available in grounds. The garden was created by its owners 20yrs ago and is surrounded by open countryside. Delightful specialised and unusual planting in island beds. Natural pond; vegetable and herb garden; architect designed sunken conservatory. Featured with Geoffrey Smith on BBC2 in 1992. TEAS. *Adm £1.50 Chd free (Share to Veterinary Benevolent Fund®). Mons May 2, Sun July 10, Mon Aug 29 (1-5)*

Isle of Wight

Hon County Organiser: Mrs John Harrison, North Court, Shorwell I.O.W. PO30 3JG
Hon County Treasurer: Mrs S Robak, Little Mead, Everard Close, Freshwater Bay, I.O.W. PO40 9PT

DATES OF OPENING

By appointment
For telephone numbers and other details see garden descriptions.
Private visits welcomed

Fountain Cottage, Bonchurch, nr
   Ventnor
Highwood, The Five Gardens of
   Cranmore
Owl Cottage, Mottistone
Westport Cottage, Yarmouth
Yaffles, Bonchurch

April 10 Sunday
   Woolverton House,
   St Lawrence
April 17 Sunday
   Blackwater Mill, Newport ‡
   Rock Cottage, Blackwater ‡
April 24 Sunday
   Gatcombe House, Gatcombe
May 15 Sunday
   The Watch House, Bembridge
May 22 Sunday
   Brook Edge, Binstead
May 29 Sunday
   North Court Gardens, Shorwell
June 5 Sunday
   Pitts Cottage, Calbourne

June 8 Wednesday
   Mottistone Manor Garden,
   Mottistone
June 19 Sunday
   Pitt House, Bembridge
June 22 Wednesday
   The Five Gardens of Cranmore,
   Cranmore
June 26 Sunday
   The Pippins, Brighstone ‡
   Waldeck, Brighstone ‡
July 3 Sunday
   Nunwell House, Brading
July 24 Sunday
   Conifers, 23 Witbank Gardens,
   Shanklin

DESCRIPTIONS OF GARDENS

¶**Blackwater Mill** &✻❀ (Mrs Jacqueline Humphreys) Newport. Take the main Sandown rd from Newport, turn R at the junction to Blackwater. Pass the garage on your L and the garden open is approx 200yds on the R by the bus stop. Look for the Blackwater Mill Retirement Home sign. Garden set in 6 acres incl 2-acre lake with waterfowl; river walk and bridges; lge selection of shrubs; herbaceous, grasses, trees, conifers and heathers; scree bed, spring bulbs and many unusual plants. Easy walks around. TEA *Combined adm with* **Rock Cottage** *£1.50 Chd free. Sun April 17 (2.30-5)*

Brook Edge &❀ (Dr & Mrs Philip Goodwin) Binstead, at the bottom of Binstead Hill to Ryde rd. Parking available at factory car-park. 2½ acres of undulating garden on edge of old quarry with two streams flowing through. Fine woodland trees, waterside plants and shrubs. TEAS. *Adm £1 Chd 20p. Sun May 22 (2.30-5)*

Conifers ✻❀ (Mr & Mrs J Horrocks) 23 Witbank Gardens. From Shanklin centre take the Languard rd. to Languard Manor rd, turn R at Green Lane, turn R at Spar shop to Witbank Gardens. 1-acre semi-formal ornamental garden with varied and colourful selection of trees, shrubs, perennials and bedding plants; small aviary with exotic birds. Sale of plants by Haylands Farm. *Adm £1 Chd free. Sun July 24 (2-5)*

The Five Gardens of Cranmore &✻❀ Cranmore Ave is approx halfway between the town of Yarmouth and the village of Shalfleet on the A3054. From Yarmouth the turning is on the L hand side, opp a bus shelter approx 3m out of Yarmouth on an unmade rd. TEAS at Freshfields. *Combined adm £1.50 Chd 50p. Wed June 22 (2-7)*
   Cranmore Lodge (Mr & Mrs W Dicken). This is a garden in the making. Approx 1 acre with perennials, shrub roses and climbers. A small pond and woodland area
   Freshfields (Mr & Mrs O Butchers) Approx 1-acre garden, patio, pond with marginal planting, raised bed and an interesting display of fuschias and a wild garden
   Funakoshi (Mr & Mrs D Self) A 1-acre garden divided by an aviary, patio, greenhouses, tunnels and vegetable plot into areas with shrubs, perennials, climbers and conifers
   Halcyon A smaller garden consisting of a conservatory of unusual plants and colourful shrubs and perennials
   Highwood ❀ (Mr & Mrs Cooper) 10-acre site with approx 4 acres under cultivation; woodland area, pond with marginal planting with many unusual trees, shrubs and perennials. *Private visits welcome March to Oct, please Tel 0983 760 550*

Regular Openers. See head of county section.

Fountain Cottage (Mr & Mrs P T Dodds) Bonchurch. Approx ½m E from central Ventnor at junction of Bonchurch Village Rd, Trinity Rd and St Boniface Rd. Reasonable parking in these rds and on forecourt of garage/ stable opposite. Originally a gardener's cottage with approx 2 acres formerly part of a country estate landscaped in the 1830's with ponds, stream, waterfalls and fountains being a feature. South facing slope, partly wooded and terraced. Really a spring garden but with hydrangea and roses providing colour later in the year. Light refreshments if required. *Adm £1 Chd free. Private visits welcome April to end Aug, please* **Tel 0983 852 435**

Gatcombe House ⚹ (Mr & Mrs C Scott) Gatcombe. 3m SW of Newport. Large park and woodland with ornamental trees, shrubs and lake. Listed C18 house (not open). Norman church. TEAS. *Adm £1.50 Chd free. Sun April 24 (2-5)*

Mottistone Manor Garden ✿ (The National Trust) Mottistone. 8m SW Newport on B3399 between Brighstone and Brook. Medium-sized formal terraced garden, backing onto mediaeval and Elizabethan manor house, set in wooded valley with fine views of English Channel and coast between Needles and St. Catherine's Point. TEAS. *Adm £1.80 Chd 90p. Wed June 8 (2-5.30)*

North Court Gardens ⚹✿✿ (Mrs C D Harrison, Mr & Mrs J Harrison, Mr & Mrs L Harrison) Shorwell 4m S of Newport on B3323, entrance on right after rustic bridge, opp thatched cottage. 14 acres, 3 varied gardens consisting of landscaped terraces, stream and water garden, woodland, walled rose garden, herbaceous borders, shrubs surrounding Jacobean Manor House (part open). TEAS. *Combined adm £1.50 Chd 20p. Sun May 29 (2.30-5.30)*

Nunwell House ✿✿ (Col & Mrs J A Aylmer) Brading. 3m S of Ryde; signed off A3055 in Brading into Coach Lane. 5 acres beautifully set formal and shrub gardens with fountains. Exceptional view of Solent. House developed over 5 centuries, full of architectural interest. Coaches by appt only. TEAS. *Adm £1 Chd 10p; House £1.30 Chd 50p extra. Sun July 3 (2-5)*

Owl Cottage ⚹✿ (Mrs A L Hutchinson) Hoxall Lane, Mottistone. 9m SW of Newport, from B3399 at Mottistone turn down Hoxall Lane for 200yds. Interesting cottage garden, view of sea. Home-made TEAS. Plant sale. *Adm £1.50 Chd 20p. Visits by appointment only May, June, July, Aug, parties of 10 or more (2.30-5.30)* **Tel after 6pm 0983 740433**

¶**The Pippins** ⚹✿ (Mr & Mrs R H Buckett) Brighstone. In short cul-de-sac on RH-side of the main rd through Brighstone, almost opp Moortown Lane Road to Calbourne. Approx ½ acre; 300 rose bushes; cordon, dwarf, pyramid and bush apple trees, numerous shrubs and flower beds. *Combined adm with* **Waldeck** *£1.50 Sun June 26 (2.30-5)*

¶**Pitt House** ⚹✿✿ (L J Martin Esq) Bembridge. NE of Bembridge Harbour. Enter Bembridge Village, pass museum and take 1st L into Love Lane. Continue down lane (5 min walk) as far as the bend; Pitt House is on L. Enter tall wrought iron gates. If coming by car enter Ducie Ave 1st L before museum. Pitt House at bottom of ave, on the R. Parking in lane. Approx 4 acres with varied aspects and points of interest. A number of sculptures dotted around the garden; also victorian greenhouse, mini waterfall and 4 ponds. TEA *Adm £1 Chd 10p. Sun June 19 (10.30-5)*

¶**Pitts Cottage** ⚹ (Mr & Mrs R Henderson) Lynch Lane, Calbourne. On reaching Calbourne take the Brighstone rd opp garage and public house. Continue past church; 570 metres further on LH-side. Ltd parking along rd, or park in village. Attractive thatched cottage surrounded by 2 acres of hillside cottage garden with mixed planting. TEA *Adm £1 Chd 10p. Sun June 5 (10-6)*

¶**Rock Cottage** ✿ (Mary & Cliff Pain) Blackwater. From Newport take main rd to Ventnor. Park in Blackwater on/off main rd **but not** in Sandy Lane. Short walk, approx 200yds, up Sandy Lane to Rock Cottage. ⅓-acre. Cottage garden. Some flowering shrubs, spring bulbs, numerous clematis and hardy perennials; fruit and vegetables. Lawn and numerous small plots divided by grass paths. Tea at Blackwater Mill. *Combined adm with* **Blackwater Mill** *£1.50 Chd free. Sun April 17 (2.30-5)*

¶**Waldeck** ✿ (Mr & Mrs G R Williams) Brighstone. 8m SW of Newport. Take Carisbrooke-Shorwell rd, then B3399 to Brighstone. Through village centre, turn R off main rd into Moor Lane. Limited parking in lane. ¾-acre garden informally planted to provide some colour and interest from trees, shrubs and perennial plants throughout the year. Special emphasis placed on foliage and shade tolerant plants such as acers, ferns, hostas, etc. Teas available in village. *Combined adm with* **Pippins** *£1.50 (Share to Society for the Blind®). Sun June 26 (2.30-5.30)*

The Watch House ✿✿ (Sir William Mallinson) Bembridge. Most easterly part of I of W. St Helens-Bembridge. Before ascending hill by Pilot Inn turn L to Silver Beach Cafe. Last house on R. ¾-acre garden best known for its garden architecture and sea views (house built for the Admiralty). Formal garden at rear of house with fruit trees, rose arches and box hedges. *Adm £1 Chd 10p. Sun May 15 (2-5)*

Westport Cottage ✿✿ (Kitty Fisher & K R Sharp) Cottage is 100 yds SE up Tennyson Close off Tennyson Rd, Yarmouth. This is the main rd through the town. Entrance is to the R of the metal gate and footpath into the walled yard with parking. Victorian walled working garden. Small collections of semi-hardy shrubs, aquatics, fruits, hederas; vegetables and flowers for the house; culinary herbs; swimming pool for visitors use, bordered by ground geraniums, penstemons, roses etc. *Adm £1 Chd 20p. Private visits welcome, please* **Tel 0983 760751**

By Appointment Gardens. These owners do not have a fixed opening day usually because they do not like crowds or have insufficient parking space. Owner will often give guided tour.

Woolverton House (Mr & Mrs S H G Twining) St Lawrence. 3m W of Ventnor; Bus 16 from Ryde, Sandown, Shanklin. Flowering shrubs, bulbs, fine position. Home-made TEAS. *Adm £1.50 Chd 20p (Share to St Lawrence Village Hall®). Sun April 10 (2-5)*

Yaffles ❀ (Mrs Wolfenden) The Pitts. The garden may be approached through Bonchurch Village, up the hill past the parish church 1st on L or from the top rd (Shanklin 2m to the E) turn L down the Bonchurch Shute, garden is immediately above St Boniface Church and next to the cul de sac The Pitts. Park in the rd. A 60′ flowering cliff sculptured into glades; it is full of interesting plants and commands excellent views of the Channel. Only suitable for wheelchairs on the top level where the teas and toilet are situated. Joan Wolfenden's book the Year from Yaffles is sold in aid of the NGS. Coffee and TEAS in aid of church. *Adm £1 Chd free. Open all year, private visits welcome. Parties of 10 or more preferred. Please,* **Tel 0983 852193** *after 12 noon*

Kent

Hon County Organiser: Mrs Valentine Fleming, Stonewall Park, Edenbridge TN8 7DG
Assistant Hon County Organisers: Mrs Jeremy Gibbs, Upper Kennards, Leigh, Tonbridge TN11 8RE
Mrs Nicolas Irwin, Hoo Farmhouse, Minster, Ramsgate CT12 4JB
Mrs Richard Latham, Stowting Hill House, nr Ashford TN25 6BE
Miss E Napier, 447 Wateringbury Road, East Malling ME19 6JQ
The Hon Mrs Oldfield, Doddington Place, nr Sittingbourne ME9 OBB
Mrs M R Streatfeild, Hoath House, Chiddingstone Hoath, Edenbridge TN8 7DB
Mrs Simon Toynbee, Old Tong Farm, Brenchley TN12 7HT
Hon County Treasurer: Valentine Fleming Esq, Stonewall Park, Edenbridge TN8 7DG

DATES OF OPENING

By appointment only
For telephone number and other details see garden descriptions. Private visits welcomed

Beech Court, Challock
Bog Farm, Brabourne Lees
Brewhouse, Boughton Aluph
Close Farm, Crockham Hill
The Coach House, Eastling
Flint Cottage, Bishopsbourne
Greenways, Berry's Green, nr Downe
115 Hadlow Road, Tonbridge
Kypp Cottage, Biddenden
43 Layhams Road, West Wickham
Little Trafalgar, Selling
Long Acre, Selling
Oswalds, Bishopsbourne
Pevington Farm, Pluckley
The Pear House, Sellindge
Saltwood Castle, nr Hythe
Stoneacre, Otham, Maidstone
2 Thorndale Close, Chatham
39 Warwick Crescent, Borstal
Westview, Hempstead, Gillingham
Woodpeckers, Hythe

Regular openings
For details see garden descriptions

Cobham Hall, Cobham
Doddington Place, nr Sittingbourne

Finchcocks, Goudhurst
Goodnestone Park, nr Wingham, Canterbury
Great Comp Charitable Trust, Borough Green
Groombridge Place, Groombridge
Hever Castle, nr Edenbridge
Marle Place, Brenchley
Mount Ephraim, Hernhill, Canterbury
Penshurst Place, Penshurst
The Pines Garden & The Bay Museum, St Margaret's Bay
Riverhill House, Sevenoaks
Squerryes Court, Westerham
Woodlands Manor, Adisham

February 13 Sunday
Goodnestone Park, nr Wingham, Canterbury
Woodlands Manor, Adisham
March 6 Sunday
Great Comp, Borough Green
March 13 Sunday
Great Comp, Borough Green
Weeks Farm, Egerton
March 20 Sunday
Copton Ash, Faversham
March 23 Wednesday
Great Maytham Hall, Rolvenden
March 27 Sunday
Church Hill Cottage, Charing Heath
Crittenden House, Matfield
2 Thorndale Close, Chatham ‡

39 Warwick Crescent, Borstal ‡
Woodlands Manor, Adisham
April 3 Easter Sunday
Church Hill Cottage, Charing Heath
Copton Ash, Faversham
Crittenden House, Matfield
Godinton Park, nr Ashford
Jessups, Mark Beech, nr Edenbridge
Longacre, Selling
Mere House, Mereworth
The Pines Garden & The Bay Museum, St Margaret's Bay
Street End Place, nr Canterbury
Yalding Gardens
April 4 Easter Monday
Brewhouse, Boughton Aluph
Church Hill Cottage, Charing Heath
Copton Ash, Faversham
Crittenden House, Matfield
Longacre, Selling
Street End Place, nr Canterbury
April 9 Saturday
Glassenbury Park, nr Cranbrook
April 10 Sunday
Church Hill Cottage, Charing Heath
Cobham Hall, Cobham
Finchcocks, Goudhurst
Glassenbury Park, nr Cranbrook
Godmersham Park, nr Ashford
Hole Park, Rolvenden
New Barns House, West Malling
Spilsill Court, Staplehurst

2 Thorndale Close, Chatham ‡
39 Warwick Crescent, Borstal ‡

April 17 Sunday
The Beehive, Lydd ‡
Church Hill Cottage, Charing
   Heath
Coldham, Little Chart Forstal
Crittenden House, Matfield
Edenbridge House, Edenbridge
Hole Park, Rolvenden
Lodge House, Smeeth
The Vine House, Lydd ‡
Whitehurst, Chainhurst, Marden

April 20 Wednesday
Bog Farm, Brabourne Lees ‡
Brewhouse, Boughton Aluph
Great Maytham Hall, Rolvenden
Lodge House, Smeeth ‡
Westview, Hempstead, Gillingham

April 23 Saturday
Pett Place, Charing
Westview, Hempstead, Gillingham

April 24 Sunday
Collingwood Grange, Benenden
Longacre, Selling ‡
Luton House, Selling ‡
Maurice House, Broadstairs
Mount Ephraim, Hernhill,
   Faversham
Pett Place, Charing
2 Thorndale Close, Chatham
Torry Hill, nr Sittingbourne
Withersdane Hall, Wye

April 27 Wednesday
Brewhouse, Boughton Aluph
Hault Farm, Waltham, nr
   Canterbury
Hole Park, Rolvenden
Sissinghurst Garden, Sissinghurst

April 30 Saturday
Riverhill House, Sevenoaks

May 1 Sunday
Beech Court, Challock
Bradbourne House, East Malling
Church Hill Cottage, Charing
   Heath
Coldharbour Oast, Tenterden
Copton Ash, Faversham
Crittenden House, Matfield
Doddington Place, nr
   Sittingbourne
Hole Park, Rolvenden
Ladham House, Goudhurst
Longacre, Selling
Northbourne Court, nr Deal
The Oast, Stilebridge, Marden
Oswalds, Bishopsbourne
Petham House, Petham
Updown Farm, Betteshanger

May 2 Monday
Brewhouse, Boughton Aluph
Church Hill Cottage, Charing
   Heath
Copton Ash, Faversham

Crittenden House, Matfield
Longacre, Selling
Oswalds, Bishopsbourne
Stoneacre, Otham

May 4 Wednesday
Penshurst Place, Penshurst
Rock Farm, Nettlestead

May 5 Thursday
Geddesden, Rolvenden Layne

May 7 Saturday
Peddars Wood, St Michaels,
   Tenterden
Rock Farm, Nettlestead

May 8 Sunday
Beech Court, Challock
Charts Edge, Westerham
Church Hill Cottage, Charing
   Heath ‡
Doddington Place, nr
   Sittingbourne
Edenbridge House, Edenbridge
Hole Park, Rolvenden
Horseshoe Cottage, Charing
   Heath ‡
Meadow Wood, Penshurst
The Oast, Stilebridge, Marden
Stonewall Park, nr Edenbridge
2 Thorndale Close, Chatham ‡‡
Thornham Friars, Thurnham
39 Warwick Crescent, Borstal ‡‡

May 11 Wednesday
Rock Farm, Nettlestead

May 12 Thursday
Geddesden, Rolvenden Layne

May 14 Saturday
Emmetts Garden, Ide Hill
Glassenbury Park, nr Cranbrook
Rock Farm, Nettlestead

May 15 Sunday
Beech Court, Challock
Bilting House, nr Ashford
Brenchley Gardens
Brewhouse, Boughton Aluph
Charts Edge, Westerham
Crittenden House, Matfield
Doddington Place, nr
   Sittingbourne
Glassenbury Park, nr
   Cranbrook
Larksfield, Crockham Hill ‡
Larksfield Cottage, Crockham
   Hill ‡
Little Trafalgar, Selling ‡‡
Longacre, Selling ‡‡
Oxley House, nr Lenham
Ramhurst Manor, Leigh,
   Tonbridge
The Red House, Crockham
   Hill ‡
St Michael's House, Roydon,
   Peckham Bush
Torry Hill, nr Sittingbourne
Turkey Court, Maidstone
Upper Mill Cottage, Loose

May 17 Tuesday
Ightham Mote, nr Sevenoaks

May 18 Wednesday
Great Maytham Hall,
   Rolvenden ‡
Hole Park, Rolvenden ‡
Rock Farm, Nettlestead
Upper Mill Cottage, Loose
Westview, Hempstead, Gillingham

May 19 Thursday
Geddesden, Rolvenden Layne

May 21 Saturday
Rock Farm, Nettlestead
Sissinghurst Place Gardens
Westview, Hempstead, Gillingham

May 22 Sunday
The Anchorage, West Wickham
Beech Court, Challock
Church Hill Cottage, Charing
   Heath
Doddington Place, nr
   Sittingbourne
Goudhurst Gardens
Hault Farm, Waltham, nr
   Canterbury
Hole Park, Rolvenden
Larksfield, Crockham Hill ‡
Larksfield Cottage, Crockham
   Hill ‡
Long Barn, Weald, Sevenoaks
Nettlestead Place, Nettlestead
Pevington Farm, Pluckley
The Red House, Crockham Hill ‡
St Michaels House, Roydon,
   Peckham Bush
Sea Close, Hythe
Sissinghurst Place Gardens,
   Sissinghurst
Squerryes Lodge, Westerham ‡‡
Tanners, Brasted ‡‡
2 Thorndale Close, Chatham
Town Hill Cottage, West Malling
Waystrode Manor, Cowden

May 25 Wednesday
Edenbridge House, Edenbridge
Rock Farm, Nettlestead
Waystrode Manor, Cowden

May 26 Thursday
Geddesden, Rolvenden Layne

May 27 Friday
Kypp Cottage, Biddenden

May 28 Saturday
Kypp Cottage, Biddenden
Riverhill House, Sevenoaks
Rock Farm, Nettlestead

May 29 Sunday
Beech Court, Challock
Church Hill Cottage, Charing
   Heath
Copton Ash, Faversham
Crittenden House, Matfield
Hartlip Gardens
Hole Park, Rolvenden
Kypp Cottage, Biddenden

Ladham House, Goudhurst
Little Trafalgar, Selling ‡
Longacre, Selling ‡
Marle Place, Brenchley
Northbourne Court, nr Deal
Olantigh, Wye
Oxon Hoath, nr Hadlow
The Pines Garden & The Bay
    Museum, St Margaret's Bay
Ringfield, Knockholt
Updown Farm, Betteshanger
Walnut Tree Gardens, Little Chart

May 30 Monday
Brewhouse, Boughton Aluph
Church Hill Cottage, Charing
    Heath
Copton Ash, Faversham
Forest Gate, Pluckley
Kypp Cottage, Biddenden
Little Trafalgar, Selling ‡
Longacre, Selling ‡
Mere House, Mereworth
Scotney Castle, Lamberhurst
Stoneacre, Otham
Walnut Tree Gardens, Little Chart
Whitehurst, Chainhurst, Marden

May 31 Tuesday
Kypp Cottage, Biddenden

June 1 Wednesday
Knole, Sevenoaks
Kypp Cottage, Biddenden
Penshurst Place, Penshurst
Rock Farm, Nettlestead
Rosefarm, Chilham

June 2 Thursday
Geddesden, Rolvenden Layne

June 3 Friday
Rosefarm, Chilham

June 4 Saturday
Horseshoe Cottage, Charing
    Heath
29 The Precincts, Canterbury
Peddars Wood, St Michaels,
    Tenterden
Rock Farm, Nettlestead
Rosefarm, Chilham

June 5 Sunday
Amber Green Farmhouse, Chart
    Sutton
Brewhouse, Boughton Aluph
Congelow House, Yalding
Horseshoe Cottage, Charing
    Heath
Kypp Cottage, Biddenden
Petham House, Petham
29 The Precincts, Canterbury
2 Thorndale Close, Chatham
Walnut Tree Gardens, Little Chart
Whitehill, Wrotham

June 6 Monday
Kypp Cottage, Biddenden

June 7 Tuesday
Kypp Cottage, Biddenden

June 8 Wednesday
Belmont, Throwley, nr Faversham

Hole Park, Rolvenden
Kypp Cottage, Biddenden
29 The Precincts, Canterbury
Rock Farm, Nettlestead
Rosefarm, Chilham
Sissinghurst Garden,
    Sissinghurst
Upper Pryors, Cowden

June 9 Thursday
Geddesden, Rolvenden Layne
Nonington & Woodnesborough
    Gardens

June 11 Saturday
29 The Precincts, Canterbury
Rock Farm, Nettlestead

June 12 Sunday
Amber Green Farmhouse, Chart
    Sutton
Brenchley Manor, Brenchley ‡
Church Hill Cottage, Charing
    Heath
Copton Ash, Faversham
Forest Gate, Pluckley ‡‡
Horton Priory, Sellindge
Kypp Cottage, Biddenden
Little Trafalgar, Selling ‡‡‡
Longacre, Selling ‡‡‡
Lullingstone Castle, Eynsford
Mere House, Mereworth
Mill House, Hildenborough
Northbourne Court, Nr Deal
Pevington Farm, Pluckley ‡‡
Portobello, Brenchley ‡
29 The Precincts, Canterbury
Shipbourne Gardens
Slip Mill, Hawkhurst
Waystrode Manor, Cowden
Weeks Farm, Egerton
Woodlands Manor, Adisham

June 13 Monday
Kypp Cottage, Biddenden

June 14 Tuesday
Kypp Cottage, Biddenden

June 15 Wednesday
The Coach House, Mereworth
    Lawn
Hole Farm, Rolvenden
Kypp Cottage, Biddenden
Rock Farm, Nettlestead
Slip Mill, Hawkhurst
Waystrode Manor, Cowden

June 16 Thursday
Geddesden, Rolvenden Layne

June 18 Saturday
Downs Court, Boughton Aluph
Pett Place, Charing
Rock Farm, Nettlestead
The Silver Spray, Sellindge
Sissinghurst Place Gardens,
    Sissinghurst

June 19 Sunday
The Anchorage, West Wickham
Battel Hall, Leeds, nr Maidstone
Downs Court, Boughton Aluph
Edenbridge House, Edenbridge

Goudhurst Gardens
Kypp Cottage, Biddenden
Lodge House, Smeeth
Long Barn, Weald, Sevenoaks
The Old Parsonage, Sutton
    Valence
Old Place Farm, High Halden
Pett Place, Charing
Sissinghurst Place Gardens,
    Sissinghurst
2 Thorndale Close, Chatham ‡
Town Hill Cottage,
    West Malling ‡‡
Walnut Tree Gardens, Little
    Chart
39 Warwick Crescent, Borstal ‡
Went House, West Malling ‡‡

June 20 Monday
Kypp Cottage, Biddenden

June 21 Tuesday
Kypp Cottage, Biddenden
The Old Parsonage, Sutton
    Valence

June 22 Wednesday
Brewhouse, Boughton Aluph
The Coach House, Mereworth
    Lawn
Kypp Cottage, Biddenden
Lodge House, Smeeth
Rock Farm, Nettlestead
Wyckhurst, Mill Rd, Aldington

June 23 Thursday
Geddesden, Rolvenden Layne
The Old Parsonage, Sutton
    Valence

June 25 Saturday
Horseshoe Cottage, Charing
    Heath
The Old Parsonage, Sutton
    Valence
Rock Farm, Nettlestead
Sibton Park, Lyminge, nr
    Folkestone
The Silver Spray, Sellindge

June 26 Sunday
Brome House, West Malling
Groome Farm, Egerton
Horseshoe Cottage, Charing
    Heath
Kypp Cottage, Biddenden
Little Trafalgar, Selling ‡
Longacre, Selling ‡
Manor House, Upper Hardres
Northbourne Court, nr Deal
Olantigh, Wye
Otham Gardens
Oxley House, nr Lenham
Placketts Hole, Bicknor, nr
    Sittingbourne
Plaxtol Gardens
Ringfield, Knockholt
St Clere, Kemsing
Torry Hill, nr Sittingbourne
Waystrode Manor, Cowden
Wyckhurst, Mill Rd, Aldington

June 27 Monday
Kypp Cottage, Biddenden
June 28 Tuesday
Kypp Cottage, Biddenden
June 29 Wednesday
Great Maytham Hall, Rolvenden
Kypp Cottage, Biddenden
Rock Farm, Nettlestead
June 30 Thursday
Geddesden, Rolvenden Layne
July 2 Saturday
Rock Farm, Nettlestead
July 3 Sunday
Coldham, Little Chart Forstal
Field House, Staplehurst
Kypp Cottage, Biddenden
The Oast, Stilebridge, Marden
South Hill Farm, Hastingleigh
2 Thorndale Close, Chatham
Upper Mill Cottage, Loose
Walnut Tree Gardens, Little Chart
Went House, West Malling
Worth Gardens
July 4 Monday
Kypp Cottage, Biddenden
July 5 Tuesday
Kypp Cottage, Biddenden
July 6 Wednesday
Cares Cross, Chiddingstone Hoath
Chartwell, Westerham
Chiddingstone Gardens
Kypp Cottage, Biddenden
Rock Farm, Nettlestead
The Silver Spray, Sellindge
July 7 Thursday
Geddesden, Rolvenden Layne
July 9 Saturday
Luton House, Selling
Peddars Wood, St Michaels,
    Tenterden
Rock Farm, Nettlestead
The Silver Spray, Sellindge
July 10 Sunday
Bilting House, nr Ashford
Brewhouse, Boughton Aluph
Godinton Park, nr Ashford
Kypp Cottage, Biddenden
Ladham House, Goudhurst
Little Trafalgar, Selling ‡
Longacre, Selling ‡
Northbourne Court, nr Deal
Squerryes Court, Westerham
Walnut Tree Gardens, Little Chart
West Farleigh Hall, nr Maidstone
Withersdane Hall, Wye
July 11 Monday
Kypp Cottage, Biddenden
July 12 Tuesday
Kypp Cottage, Biddenden
July 13 Wednesday
185 Borden Lane, Sittingbourne
Kypp Cottage, Biddenden
Rock Farm, Nettlestead
Sissinghurst Garden, Sissinghurst

July 14 Thursday
Geddesden, Rolvenden Layne
July 16 Saturday
Elham Gardens
Rock Farm, Nettlestead
July 17 Sunday
The Beehive, Lydd ‡
Church Hill Cottage, Charing
    Heath
Edenbridge House, Edenbridge
Goodnestone Park, nr Wingham,
    Canterbury
115 Hadlow Road, Tonbridge
Kypp Cottage, Biddenden
Long Barn, Weald, Sevenoaks
The Oast, Stilebridge, Marden
Sea Close, Hythe
2 Thorndale Close, Chatham
Turkey Court, Maidstone
Vine House, Lydd ‡
Walnut Tree Gardens, Little Chart
July 18 Monday
The Beehive, Lydd ‡
Kypp Cottage, Biddenden
Vine House, Lydd ‡
July 19 Tuesday
Kypp Cottage, Biddenden
July 20 Wednesday
Kypp Cottage, Biddenden
Rock Farm, Nettlestead
The Silver Spray, Sellindge
July 21 Thursday
Geddesden, Rolvenden Layne
July 23 Saturday
Rock Farm, Nettlestead
The Silver Spray, Sellindge
July 24 Sunday
Brewhouse, Boughton Aluph
Copton Ash, Faversham
Little Trafalgar, Selling ‡
Longacre, Selling ‡
Northbourne Court, nr Deal
July 27 Wednesday
Groombridge Place, Groombridge
Rock Farm, Nettlestead
July 28 Thursday
Geddesden, Rolvenden Layne
July 30 Saturday
Rock Farm, Nettlestead
July 31 Sunday
185 Borden Lane, Sittingbourne
Cobham Hall, Cobham
Groome Farm, Egerton
The Oast, Stilebridge, Marden
Spilsill Court, Staplehurst
2 Thorndale Close, Chatham
Walnut Tree Gardens, Little Chart
Woodpeckers, Hythe
August 3 Wednesday
185 Borden Lane, Sittingbourne
Knole, Sevenoaks
Rock Farm, Nettlestead
August 4 Thursday
Geddesden, Rolvenden Layne

August 6 Saturday
Peddars Wood, St Michaels,
    Tenterden
Rock Farm, Nettlestead
August 7 Sunday
Field House, Staplehurst
Little Trafalgar, Selling
Marle Place, Brenchley
Orchard Cottage, Bickley, Bromley
Walnut Tree Gardens, Little Chart
Withersdane Hall, Wye
August 11 Thursday
Geddesden, Rolvenden Layne
August 14 Sunday
Chevening, Sevenoaks
Church Hill Cottage, Charing
    Heath
Finchcocks, Goudhurst
Northbourne Court, nr Deal
Walnut Tree Gardens, Little Chart
August 18 Thursday
Geddesden, Rolvenden Layne
August 21 Sunday
Goodnestone Park, nr Wingham,
    Canterbury
Squerryes Court, Westerham
West Studdal Farm, nr Dover
August 24 Wednesday
The Silver Spray, Sellindge
August 25 Thursday
Geddesden, Rolvenden Layne
August 28 Sunday
Church Hill Cottage, Charing
    Heath
Copton Ash, Faversham
115 Hadlow Road, Tonbridge
Little Trafalgar, Selling ‡
Longacre, Selling ‡
Northbourne Court, nr Deal
The Pines Garden & The Bay
    Museum, St Margaret's Bay
Sea Close, Hythe
Walnut Tree Gardens, Little Chart
Whitehurst, Chainhurst, Marden
August 29 Monday
Church Hill Cottage, Charing
    Heath
Copton Ash, Faversham
Little Trafalgar, Selling ‡
Longacre, Selling ‡
The Silver Spray, Sellindge
Walnut Tree Gardens, Little Chart
September 1 Thursday
Geddesden, Rolvenden Layne
September 4 Sunday
185 Borden Lane, Sittingbourne
Coldharbour Oast, Tenterden
Horton Priory, Sellindge
Whitehurst, Chainhurst, Marden
Withersdane Hall, Wye
September 7 Wednesday
Bog Farm, Brabourne Lees
September 8 Thursday
Geddesden, Rolvenden Layne

September 11 Sunday
Copton Ash, Faversham
Little Trafalgar, Selling ‡
Longacre, Selling ‡
Nettlestead Place,
   Nettlestead
Northbourne Court, nr Deal
September 15 Thursday
Geddesden, Rolvenden Layne
September 18 Sunday
Oxley House, nr Lenham
September 21 Wednesday
Great Maytham Hall, Rolvenden

September 22 Thursday
Geddesden, Rolvenden Layne
September 25 Sunday
Little Trafalgar, Selling
Mount Ephraim, Hernhill,
   Canterbury
Northbourne Court, nr Deal
September 29 Thursday
Geddesden, Rolvenden
   Layne
October 2 Sunday
Marle Place, Brenchley
Sea Close, Hythe

October 8 Saturday
Emmetts Garden, Ide Hill
October 9 Sunday
Hole Park, Rolvenden
Whitehurst, Chainhurst, Marden
October 16 Sunday
Hole Park, Rolvenden
October 22 Saturday
Copton Ash, Faversham
October 23 Sunday
Copton Ash, Faversham
November 6 Sunday
Great Comp, Borough Green

DESCRIPTIONS OF GARDENS

¶**Amber Green Farmhouse** ✗ (Mr & Mrs J Groves) Chart Sutton, 7m SE of Maidstone. Turn W off A274 onto B2163, in 1m turn L at Chart Corner, next R is Amber Lane, house ½m W. C17 listed weatherboarded farmhouse (not open) in 1-acre garden. Cottage garden theme, set by predecessors, continued by owners, with hardy perennials and old-fashioned roses. Trees and a shrub bed have been added and two natural ponds brought into greater prominence. *Adm £1 Acc chd free. Suns June 5, 12 (2-5.30)*

The Anchorage ✗❀ (Mr & Mrs G Francis) 8 Croydon Road, W Wickham. 4m SW of Bromley. 100yds from A232 and A2022 roundabout; enter from A232 opp Manor House public house, as rd is one way. ⅓-acre garden, lovingly created since 1988, inspired by Sissinghurst, comprising small compartments individually designed for colour within recently-planted hedges; old-fashioned roses, irises & large collection of unusual perennials; herb garden, walled garden, vegetables, trained fruit trees; conservation & wild-life area incl pond, woodland & meadow flowers. Featured on BBC Gardeners World 1993. TEAS. *Adm £1 Chd 25p (Share to Coney Hill School Appeal; Shaftesbury Society®). Suns May 22, June 19 (2-5.30)*

Battel Hall ᯤ✗ (John D Money Esq) Leeds, Maidstone. From A20 Hollingbourne roundabouts take B2163 S (signed Leeds Castle), at top of hill take Burberry Lane, house 100yds on R. Garden of approx 1 acre created since 1954 around medieval house; roses, herbaceous plants, shrubs and ancient wisteria. TEAS. *Adm £1.50 Chd £1 (Share to Macmillan Fund for Cancer Relief®). Sun June 19 (2-6)*

Beech Court ᯤ✗❀ (Mr & Mrs Vyvyan Harmsworth) Challock, 7m N of Ashford; entrance on A252, Challock being midway between Charing and Chilham, informal garden inspired by Inverewe garden Wester Ross. Fine collection of acers, rhododendrons, azaleas, conifers and shrubs set in 4 acres of lawns. TEAS on NGS days. *Adm £1.50 Chd 50p. Open May 2, 30. For NGS Suns May 1, 8, 15, 22, 29 (2-5.30); also private visits welcome, please Tel 0233 740641*

The Beehive ✗ (C G Brown Esq) 10 High Street, Lydd. S of New Romney on B2075, in centre of Lydd opp Church. Small walled garden, tucked behind village street house dating from 1550, with over 200 varieties of plants. There are paths and cosy corners in this cottage garden with pond and pergola; a pool of seclusion; the busy world outside unnoticed passes by. Teas usually available in the church. *Adm £1 Chd 50p (Share to Horder Centre for Arthritis, Crowborough®). Suns April 17, July 17; Mon July 18 (2.30-5.30)*

Belmont ᯤ❀ (The Harris (Belmont) Charity) Throwley 4m SW of Faversham. Take A251 (Faversham-Ashford Rd), from Badlesmere follow brown tourist signs. Walled pleasure garden and orangery; small pinetum; long yew walk and folly; Victorian grotto; pets' cemetery. House by Samuel Wyatt c.1792. TEAS. ▲*Adm £1.50 Chd 50p (Share to St Michaels Church, Throwley©). Wed June 8 (2-5)*

Bilting House ᯤ✗ (John Erle-Drax Esq) A28, 5m NE of Ashford, 9m from Canterbury. Wye 1½m. Old-fashioned garden with ha-ha; rhododendrons, azaleas; shrubs. In beautiful part of Stour Valley. TEAS £1. *Adm £1.50 Chd 50p (Share to BRCS®). Suns May 15, July 10 (1.30-5.30)*

Bog Farm ᯤ✗❀ (Mr & Mrs K J Hewett) Brabourne Lees, 4m E of Ashford; via M20 junction 10 (Ashford), 3m S of Ashford on A20 turn E in Smeeth, proceed ½m to Woolpack Inn; bear R, continue 700yds following sign to garden on R down single track lane. 1-acre garden, planned and planted by owners since 1959 around small Kentish farmhouse (not open); good collection of shrubs, trees, species plants, ferns, bulbs arranged to give interest to each season; mixed borders; moisture plants; old roses; herb garden. *Adm £1 Chd 20p. Weds April 20, Sept 7 (2-7). Private visits welcome, please Tel 030 381 3101*

185 Borden Lane ᯤ✗❀ (Mr & Mrs P A Boyce) ½m S of Sittingbourne. 1m from Sittingbourne side of A2/A249 junction. Small informal garden with many varieties of fuchsia; hardy perennials; shrubs; pond; fruit, vegetable and herb garden. Home-made TEAS. *Adm £1 Acc chd free. Suns July 31, Sept 4; Weds July 13, Aug 3 (2-6)*

Bradbourne House Gardens ᯤ (East Malling Trust for Horticultural Research & Horticulture Research International) East Malling, 4m W of Maidstone. Entrance is E of New Road, which runs from Larkfield on A20S to E Malling. The Hatton Fruit Garden consists of demonstration fruit gardens of particular interest to amateurs, in a walled former kitchen garden and incl intensive forms of apples and pears. Members of staff available for questions. TEAS. *Adm £1.50 Acc chd free. Sun May 1 (2-5)*

Brenchley Gardens 6m SE of Tonbridge. From A21 1m S of Pembury turn N on to B2160, turn R at Xrds in Matfield signed Brenchley. *Combined adm £2 Acc chd free. Sun May 15 (2-6)*

Holmbush &✗ (Brian & Cathy Worden Hodge) 1½-acre informal garden, mainly lawns, trees and shrub borders, planted since 1960

Portobello (Barry M Williams Esq) 1½ acres, lawn, trees, shrubs incl azaleas and shrub roses; walled garden. C17 barn containing 1936 Dennis fire engine in running order. House (not open) built by Monckton family 1739

Puxted House &❀ (P J Oliver-Smith Esq) 1½ acres with rare and coloured foliage shrubs, water and woodland plants. Alpine and rose garden all labelled. Present owner cleared 20yrs of brambles in 1981 before replanting. TEA

Brenchley Manor &✗ (Mr & Mrs Barry Bruckmann) Brenchley, 6m SE of Tonbridge; from A21 at 1m S of Pembury turn N onto B2160; at Matfield Xrds turn R, signed Brenchley. Medium- sized garden, currently being restored; ornamental yew hedge; knot garden; herbaceous borders; Domesday oak; pond & woodland. Early timber-framed house with fine renaissance arch. *Adm £1.50 Acc chd free. Sun June 12 (2-6)*

Brewhouse &✗❀ (Mr & Mrs J A H Nicholson) Malthouse Lane, Boughton Aluph, 3m N of Ashford. Garden off Pilgrims Way. ¼m N and signed from Boughton Lees village green, on A251 Ashford-Faversham. 1-acre plantsman's garden with new features this year. C16 farmhouse (not open) with fine views of open chalkland. Collections of old roses, other old-fashioned flowers, herbaceous and foliage plants. TEAS (in aid of All Saints Church; not April & June). *Adm £1 Chd 25p. Suns May 15, June 5, July 10, 24; Mons April 4, May 2, 30; Weds April 20, 27; June 22 (2-6); also private visits welcome throughout season, please* Tel 0233 623748

¶Brome House &✗ (Mr & Mrs Graeme Odgers) High Street, West Malling. Next to church at S end of High Street. 2-acre walled garden of mixed planting carefully designed to create different colour effects, with church as backdrop; planted terrace with pond and small vegetable garden. TEAS. *Adm £1 Chd 50p. Sun June 26 (2-6)*

Cares Cross &❀ (Mr & Mrs R L Wadsworth) Chiddingstone Hoath. [Ordnance Survey Grid ref. TQ 496 431.] Landscaped garden around C16 house (not open). Dramatic views to N Downs over fields with old oaks, restored hedgerows, wildfowl lake and vineyard. Garden features old roses; water garden; innovative ground cover; rare shrubs and trees; speciality American plants. Featured on BBC Gardeners World 1990. TEAS. *Adm £2 OAPs £1.50 Acc chd free. By appt to groups of 5-20, weekdays only May 15 to July 30; and under* Chiddingstone Hoath Gardens *on Wed July 6 (2-6)*

Charts Edge & (Mr & Mrs John Bigwood) Westerham, ½m S of Westerham on B2026 towards Chartwell. 7-acre hillside garden being restored by present owners; large collection of rhododendrons, azaleas, acers & magnolias; specimen trees & newly-planted mixed borders; Victorian folly; walled vegetable garden; rock garden. Fine views over N Downs. Dressage display at 3.30pm. TEAS. *Adm £1.50 Chd 25p (Share to BHS Dressage Group©). Suns May 8, 15 (2-5)*

Chartwell (The National Trust) 2m S of Westerham, fork L off B2026 after 1½m, well signed. 12-acre informal gardens on a hillside with glorious views over Weald of Kent. Fishpools and lakes together with red-brick wall built by Sir Winston Churchill, the former owner of Chartwell. The avenue of golden roses given by the family on Sir Winston's golden wedding anniversary will be at its best. Self-service restaurant serving coffee, lunches and teas. *Adm £2 Chd £1.* ▲*Wed July 6 (12-5)*

Chevening & (By permission of the Board of Trustees of Chevening Estate and the Rt Hon Douglas Hurd) 4m NW of Sevenoaks. Turn N off A25 at Sundridge traffic lights on to B2211; at Chevening Xrds 1½m turn L. 27 acres with lawns and woodland garden, lake, maze, formal rides, parterre. Garden being restored. TEAS in aid of Kent Church Social Work and overseas charities. *Adm £1.50 OAPs £1 Chd 50p. Sun Aug 14 (2-6)*

Chiddingstone Hoath Gardens 4m E of Edenbridge, via B2026, at Cowden Pound turn E to Mark Beech. Old Buckhurst is 1st house on R after leaving Mark Beech on Penshurst Rd. Maps will be provided. Teas in Chiddingstone village. *Combined adm £2.50 OAPs £2 Acc chd free (Share to St Mary's Church®). Wed July 6 (2-5.30)*

Cares Cross &❀ (Mr & Mrs R L Wadsworth) For garden description, see individual entry

Old Buckhurst (Mr & Mrs J Gladstone) Chiddingstone Hoath Rd, Mark Beech. 1-acre garden surrounding C15 farmhouse (not open). Part walled ornamental & kitchen gardens designed & planted 1988 onwards. 'New English' shrub roses; range of clematis, shrubs & herbaceous plants. Parking in 1-acre paddock

Church Hill Cottage &✗❀ (Mr & Mrs Michael Metianu) Charing Heath, 10m NW of Ashford. Leave M20 at junction 8 (Lenham) if Folkestone-bound or junction 9 (Ashford West) if London-bound: then leave A20 dual carriageway ½m W of Charing signed Charing Heath and Egerton. After 1m fork R at Red Lion, then R again; cottage 250yds on R. C16 cottage surrounded by garden of 1½ acres, developed & planted by present owners since 1981. Several separate connected areas each containing island beds & borders planted with extensive range of perennials, shrubs, spring bulbs & foliage plants. Picnic area. Lunches/snacks at Red Lion. *Adm £1.50 Chd 50p (Share to Canterbury Pilgrims Hospice®). Suns March 27, April 3, 10, 17, May 1, 8, 22, 29, June 12, July 17, Aug 14, 28; Mons April 4, May 2, 30, Aug 29 (11-5); also private visits welcome, please* Tel 0233 712522

Close Farm &✗❀ (Joan & Geoffrey Williams) Crockham Hill, 2½ N of Edenbridge on B2026. Turn into narrow private lane immediately adjacent to PO/antique shop. Close Farm is first house ½m along lane by grass triangle. Garden approx 1 acre; natural springs, watercourses and pond. Early flowering naturalised bulbs, hellebores, many perennials, shrub roses. Autumn colour. High path walk with good views. *Adm £1.50 Chd 50p. Private visits welcome Feb to Nov incl, please* Tel 0732 866228

The Coach House, Eastling &✿ (Mr & Mrs Roger Turner) Faversham. From A2 in Faversham take Brogdale Rd, continue S to Eastling, house on right after Meesons Close. Informally planted ⅓-acre garden on chalk; mixed borders incl climbing and shrub roses; sheltered paved courtyard with formal fishpond; moisture loving plants contrast with sun loving species. *Adm £1 Chd 20p. Private visits welcome April 25 to July 8, please* **Tel 0795 890304**

The Coach House, Mereworth Lawn ✿✿ (Mr & Mrs J Frisby) 3m E of Borough Green. On E side of B2016 (Seven Mile Lane) 2½m from both A20 at Wrotham Heath & A26 at Mereworth roundabout. ½-acre converted Victorian walled kitchen garden, redesigned after 1987 hurricane; many specialist plants. Limited parking. TEAS. *Adm £1.50 Acc chd free (Share to St Christopher's Hospice®). Weds June 15, 22 (2-6)*

Cobham Hall & (Westwood Educational Trust), Cobham. next to A2/M2 8m E of junction 2 of M25, midway between Gravesend and Rochester on B2009. Beautiful Elizabethan mansion in 150 acres landscaped by Humphry Repton at end of C18. Acres of daffodils and flowering trees planted in 1930s; grounds now being restored by Cobham Hall Heritage Trust. TEAS. *Adm House £2.50 Chd £2 Garden £1 (Share to Cobham Hall Heritage Trust®).* ▲*For NGS Suns April 10; July 31 (2-5). For details of other open days, please* **Tel 0474 823371/824319**

Coldham &✿✿ (Dr & Mrs J G Elliott) Little Chart Forstal, 5m NW of Ashford. Leave M20 at junction 8 (Lenham) if Folkestone-bound or junction 9 (Ashford West) if London-bound: then leave A20 at Charing by road signposted to Little Chart, turn E in village, ¼m. 2-acre garden developed since 1970 in setting of old walls; good collection of rare plants, bulbs, alpines, mixed borders. C16 Kent farmhouse (not open). TEA on July 3. *Adm £2 Chd 50p. Suns April 17, July 3 (2-5.30)*

Coldharbour Oast &✿✿ (Mr & Mrs A J A Pearson) Tenterden. 300yds SW of Tenterden High St (A28), take lane signed West View Hospital, after 200yds bear R on to concrete lane signed Coldharbour, proceed for 600yds. Garden started in late 1987 from ¾-acre field in exposed position. Pond; dry stream; unusual shrubs and perennials maintained by owners. TEA in aid of Steam Locomotive Restoration. *Adm £1 Acc chd free. Suns May 1, Sept 4 (12.30-5.30)*

Collingwood Grange &✿✿ (Mrs Linda Fennell), Benenden, SE of Cranbrook 100yds on E of rd to Iden Green from village centre. Bus: Cranbrook-Tenterden. Flowering cherries; rhododendrons, incl large collection of dwarf kinds; autumn colour. Former home of the late Capt Collingwood 'Cherry' Ingram. Special botanical interest. TEAS. *Adm £1.50 Acc chd free. Sun April 24 (2-6)*

Congelow House & (Mrs D J Cooper) Yalding, 8m SW of Maidstone. Approx mid-way between Tonbridge and Maidstone, and S of Yalding. 4-acre garden created from an orchard since 1973; backbone of interesting ornamental trees planted about 1850, with recent plantings; walled vegetable garden; pleasure gardens incl rhododendrons, azaleas, irises, roses, shrub roses. Vegetables, organically grown, on sale. TEAS. *Adm £1.50 Chd 50p (Share to Henry Doubleday Research Assoc®). Sun June 5 (2-5.30). Also April 3 with* **Yalding Gardens**

Copton Ash &✿✿ (Mr & Mrs John Ingram & Drs Tim & Gillian Ingram) 105 Ashford Rd, Faversham, 1m. On A251 Faversham-Ashford rd opp E-bound junction with M2. 1½-acre plantsman's garden developed since 1978 on site of old cherry orchard. Wide range of plants in mixed borders and informal island beds; incl spring bulbs, alpine and herbaceous plants, shrubs, young trees and collection of fruit varieties. Good autumn colour. Special display of apple and pear fruits Oct 22 & 23. TEAS. *Adm £1 Acc chd free (Share to National Schizophrenia Fellowship, East Kent Group®). Suns March 20, April 3, May 1, 29, June 12, July 24, Aug 28, Sept 11, Oct 23; Mons April 4, May 2, 30, Aug 29; Sat Oct 22 (2-6)*

Crittenden House ✿ (B P Tompsett Esq) Matfield, 6m SE of Tonbridge. Bus: MD 6 or 297, alight Standings Cross, Matfield, 1m. Garden around early C17 house completely planned and planted since 1956 on labour-saving lines. Featuring spring shrubs (rhododendrons, magnolias), roses, lilies, foliage, waterside planting of ponds in old iron workings, of interest from early spring bulbs to autumn colour. Rare young trees mentioned in Collins Guide to Trees in UK and Europe, by Alan Mitchell. Subject of article in *R.H.S. Journal*, 1990. Tea Cherry-trees, Matfield Green. *Adm £1.50 Chd (under 12) 25p. Suns March 27, April 3, 17, May 1, 15, 29; Mons April 4, May 2 (2-6)*

Doddington Place &✿ (Mr Richard & the Hon Mrs Oldfield) 6m SE of Sittingbourne. From A20 turn N opp Lenham or from A2 turn S at Teynham or Ospringe (Faversham) (all 4m). Large garden, landscaped with wide views; trees and yew hedges; woodland garden with azaleas and rhododendrons, Edwardian rock garden; formal garden planted for late summer interest. Featured in NGS video 2, see page 344. TEAS, restaurant, shop. *Adm £2 Chd 25p (Share to Kent Assoc for the Blind and Doddington Church®). Every Wed and Bank Holiday Mon from Easter to end Sept; Suns in May only. For NGS, Suns May 1, 8, 15, 22 (11-6)*

Downs Court &✿✿ (Mr & Mrs M J B Green) Boughton Aluph, 4m NE of Ashford off A28. Take lane on L signed Boughton Aluph church, fork R at pillar box, garden is next drive on R. Approx 3 acres with fine downland views, sweeping lawns and some mature trees and yew hedges. Mixed borders largely replanted by owners in last 10 years; shrub roses. TEAS Sunday only in aid of Multiple Sclerosis Research. *Adm £1.50 Chd 50p. Sat, Sun June 18, 19 (2-6)*

Edenbridge House &✿ (Mrs M T Lloyd) Crockham Hill Rd, 1½m N of Edenbridge, nr Marlpit Hill, on B2026. 5-acre garden of bulbs, spring shrubs, herbaceous borders, alpines, roses and water garden. House part C16 (not open). TEAS. *Adm £1.50 OAPs £1 Chd 25p. Suns April 17, May 8, June 19, July 17; Wed May 25 (2-6); also private visits welcome for groups, please* **Tel 0732 862122**

Elham Gardens *&&* 7m from Hythe, 11m from Canterbury. Enter Elham on B2065 from Lyminge or Barham (Hythe/Canterbury road). Start at The Old School House, entrance on E side of High Street between Brown's (estate agent) & St Mary's Road. A collection of at least four small gardens full of colour and all very different, within easy walking distance (maps available). Flower Festival in church. TEAS for the church. *Combined adm £2 Chd 25p. Sat July 16 (2-6)*

Emmetts Garden *&* (The National Trust) Ide Hill, 5m SW of Sevenoaks. 1½m S of A25 on Sundridge-Ide Hill Rd. 1½m N of Ide Hill off B2042. 5-acre hillside garden. One of the highest gardens in Kent, noted for its fine collection of rare trees and shrubs; lovely spring and autumn colour. TEAS. *Adm £2.50 Chd £1.30. April to end Oct every Wed, Thur, Fri, Sat & Sun. Open Bank Hol Mons. For NGS Sats May 14, Oct 8 (1-6) last adm 5, or sunset if earlier*

Field House *&&&* (Mr & Mrs N J Hori) Clapper Lane, Staplehurst. W of A229, 9m S of Maidstone and 1½m N of Staplehurst village centre. Garden approx 1½ acres on Wealden clay developed by owners over 30 yrs. Interesting mixed borders and island beds; water gardens; secret garden and one acre of wild-life meadow with pond. TEAS. *Adm £1 Chd 50p. Suns July 3, Aug 7 (2-5.30)*

¶**Finchcocks** *&&* (Mr & Mrs Richard Burnett) Goudhurst. 2m W of Goudhurst, off A262. 4-acre garden surrounding early C18 manor, well-known for its collection of historical keyboard instruments. Spring bulbs; mixed border; autumn garden with unusual trees; walled garden recently replanted to complement 1994 Music Festival celebrating C18 pleasure gardens. TEAS. *Adm £4.50 House & garden, £1 Garden, Chd £3 & 50p. Suns April 3 to Sept 25; Bank Hol Mons April 4, May 2; Aug every Wed to Sun (2-6). ▲For NGS Suns April 10, Aug 14 (2-6)*

Flint Cottage *&&* (Mr & Mrs P J Sinnock) Bourne Park, Bishopsbourne, 4m S of Canterbury turn off A2 to Bridge, through village turn W at church, follow garden signs. Small garden; alpines in gravel beds, sink gardens; water feature; mixed borders and small heather beds; herb garden. *Adm £1 Chd 40p (Share to Foundation for the Study of Infant Death®). Private visits welcome, please Tel 0227 830691*

Forest Gate *&&* (Sir Robert & Lady Johnson) Pluckley, 8m W of Ashford. From A20 at Charing take B2077 to Pluckley village; turn L signed Bethersden, follow 1m to garden 100yds SW of Pluckley station. 2-acre garden on heavy clay; well stocked mixed borders, laburnum tunnel, ponds and interesting herb collection. Many plants labelled. C17 house (not open). Picnics allowed in meadow. TEAS. *Adm £1.20 Acc chd free (Share to Cystic Fibrosis Trust®). Mon May 30, Sun June 12 (2-6)*

¶**Geddesden** *&&* (Mr & Mrs J R Hunt) Friezingham Lane, Rolvenden Layne: At junction 4m S of Tenterden, follow sign Rolvenden Layne, in village turn L 30 yds on from Wooden Tops shop into Friezingham Lane; garden 1st drive L. Garden started in 1985 on sloping N-facing site on clay with rose, heather, bog and pond gardens; flowers for all seasons, azaleas, rhododendrons, cherries,

Jekyll-style summer borders, autumn colour. *Adm £1.50 Chd 75p. Every Thurs from May 5 to Sept 29 (1.30-4.30)*

Glassenbury Park *&&&* (Mr & Mrs C J de Jong) Between Goudhurst and Cranbrook. A21 from Tunbridge Wells direction Hastings. Turn L A262 signed Goudhurst-Cranbrook. 1m after Goudhurst turn R B2085 at Peacock Inn. Entrance gate ½m on R. 50 acres rolling parkland. Daffodils and tulips. Specimen trees, rhododendrons, azaleas. Wide variety newly planted trees. Ponds and lakes. TEAS. *Adm £2 Chd 50p. Sats, Suns April 9, 10, May 14, 15 (2-6)*

Godinton Park *&* (Alan Wyndham Green Esq) Entrance 1½m W of Ashford at Potter's Corner on A20. Bus: MD/EK 10, 10A, 10B Folkestone-Ashford-Maidstone, alight Hare & Hounds, Potter's Corner. Formal and wild gardens. Topiary. Jacobean mansion with elaborate woodwork. Unique frieze in drawing room depicting arms drill of Kent Halbardiers 1630. *Adm garden only 70p, house & garden £2, Chd under 16 70p. ▲Suns April 3, July 10 (2-5)*

Godmersham Park *&&* (John B Sunley Esq) off A28 midway between Canterbury and Ashford; garden signed from either end of Park loop rd. Early Georgian mansion (not shown) in beautiful downland setting. 24 acres formal and landscape gardens, superb daffodils, restored wilderness; topiary; rose beds; herbaceous borders. Associations with Jane Austen. TEA. *Adm £1.50 Chd 75p (Share to Godmersham Church®). Sun April 10 (11-6)*

Goodnestone Park *&&&* (The Lady FitzWalter) nr Wingham, Canterbury. Village lies S of B2046 rd from A2 to Wingham. Sign off B2046 says Goodnestone. Village St is 'No Through Rd', but house and garden at the terminus. Bus: EK13, 14 Canterbury-Deal; bus stop: Wingham, 2m. 5 to 6 acres; good trees; woodland garden, walled garden with old-fashioned roses. Connections with Jane Austen who stayed here. Picnics allowed. TEAS Weds & Suns from May 23 to Aug 29. *Adm £2 OAP £1.60 Chd under 12 20p (Disabled people in wheelchair £1). Suns April 3 to Oct 2 (12-6); Mons, Weds to Fris March 28 to Oct 28 (11-5) For NGS Suns Feb 13 (snowdrops), July 17, Aug 21 (12-6)*

Goudhurst Gardens 4m W of Cranbrook on A262. TEAS. *Combined adm £2 Acc chd free. Suns May 22, June 19 (1-6)*

Crowbourne Farm House *&&&* (Mrs Stephanie Coleman) 2-acre farmhouse garden in which replanting started in 1989. Established cottage garden; shrub roses; vegetable garden; and areas newly planted with trees and shrubs. Former horse pond now stocked with ornamental fish

¶**Hyland** *&&* (Mr & Mrs K Bronwin) Village garden, the front paved, with an interesting variety of topiary. Rear garden with borders; rock and water feature. Extensive views

Tara *&&&* (Mr & Mrs Peter Coombs) 1¼ acres redesigned in 1982 into a number of linked garden areas, including a formal herb garden, each providing a different atmosphere, using an interesting range of plants and shrubs

Tulip Tree Cottage &.&& (Mr & Mrs K A Owen) 1½ acres with sweeping lawn, established trees in herbaceous and shrub borders; 90ft Liriodendron tulipifera, said to be one of finest in country, also fine Cedrus atlantica glauca. In May azalea garden of ½-acre, established 1902

Great Comp Charitable Trust &.&& (R Cameron Esq) 2m E of Borough Green. A20 at Wrotham Heath, take Seven Mile Lane, B2016; at 1st Xrds turn R; garden on L ½m. Delightful 7-acre garden skilfully designed by the Camerons since 1957 for low maintenance and year round interest. Spacious setting of well-maintained lawns and paths lead visitors through a plantsman's collection of trees, shrubs, heathers and herbaceous plants. From woodland planting to more formal terraces good use is made of views to plants, ornaments and ruins. Good autumn colour. Early C17 house (not shown). TEAS on Suns, Bank Hols and NGS days (2-5). *Adm £2.50 Chd £1. Open Suns in March and every day April 1 to Oct 31 (11-6). Opening for NGS (Share to Tradescant Trust®). Suns Mar 6, 13 (for hellebores, heathers and snowflakes); Nov 6 (for autumn colour) (11-6)*

¶**Great Maytham Hall** &&& (Country Houses Association) Rolvenden, 4m SW of Tenterden. On A28 in Rolvenden turn L at church towards Rolvenden Layne; Hall ½m on R. Lutyens house (not open) and garden, 18 acres of parkland with bluebells, daffodils and flowering trees in spring; formal gardens incl blue and silver border, roses, hydrangeas and autumn colour. Walled garden inspired Frances Hodgson Burnett to write her novel 'The Secret Garden'. TEAS. *Adm £1.50 Chd 75p (Share to Country Houses Association©). Weds March 23, April 20, May 18, June 29, Sept 21 (2-5)*

Greenways &.&& (Mr & Mrs S Lord) Single Street, Berry's Green, nr Downe. Gardener's garden; interesting design ideas; willows, jasmines, honeysuckles and alpines; large collection of bonsai; collection of miniature gardens; gardens combining fruit and vegetables, trees, shrubs and flowers; small pool, conservatory and pottery. *Adm £1 Chd 50p (Share to Save the Children Fund®). Private visits welcome, anytime, please* **Tel 0959 574691**

Groombridge Place &&& (Andrew de Candole Esq) 4m SW of Tunbridge Wells. Take A264 towards E. Grinstead, after 2m take B2110: Groombridge Place entrance on L, past the church. Surrounded by parkland this medieval site includes the famous C17 walled gardens set against a backdrop of C17 moated mansion. Walks through ancient 'Enchanted Forest' with spring-fed pools and waterfalls overlooking dramatic views of the Weald. TEAS. *Adm £3 Concessions/Chd £2 Groups by arrangement. Open April & May weekends and Bank Hols: June 1 to Sept 30 daily except Thurs & Fris 2-6; in Oct first and second weekends only. For NGS Wed July 27 (2-6)*

Groome Farm &&& (Mr & Mrs Michael Swatland) Egerton, 10m W of Ashford. From A20 at Charing Xrds take B2077 Biddenden Rd. Past Pluckley turn R at Blacksmiths Arms; R again, until Newland Green sign on L, house 1st on L. 1½ acres; still being developed around C15 farm-house and oast (not open). Interesting collection trees, shrubs, roses and herbaceous plants; also water, heather and rock gardens. Picnics welcome in field. TEAS. *Adm £1 Acc chd free. Suns June 26, July 31 (1-6)*

115 Hadlow Road &&& (Mr & Mrs Richard Esdale) in Tonbridge. Take A26 from N end of High St signed Maidstone, house 1m on L in service rd. ¼-acre unusual terraced garden with roses, herbaceous borders, clematis, hardy fuchsias, shrubs, alpines, kitchen garden and pond; well labelled. TEA. *Adm £1 Acc chd free. Suns July 17, Aug 28 (2-6); also private visits welcome, please* **Tel 0732 353738**

Hartlip Gardens 6m W of Sittingbourne, 1m S of A2 midway between Rainham and Newington. Parking for Craiglea in village hall car park and The Street. TEAS at Hartlip Place for Kent Gardens Trust. *Combined adm £2 Acc chd free. Sun May 29 (2-6)*
> **Craiglea** &.&& (Mrs Ruth Bellord) The Street. Small cottage garden crammed with interesting shrubs and plants; vegetable garden; tiny pond
> **Hartlip Place** && (Lt-Col & Mrs J R Yerburgh) Secret garden concealed by rhododendrons, planted with old roses; shrub borders; wilderness walk; sloping lawns; pond

¶**Hault Farm** &.& (Mr & Mrs T D Willet) Waltham, 7m S of Canterbury, between Petham and Waltham. From B2068 turn R signed Petham/Waltham; after Petham, 1m on L. Approx 4 acres, woodland and bog garden; herbaceous and mixed borders, rose garden and sunken scree garden. TEAS. *Adm £2 Chd £1. Suns May 1, June 19; Weds May 18, July 3. For NGS Wed April 27; Sun May 22 (2-5)*

● **Hever Castle** &.& (Broadland Properties Ltd) 3m SE of Edenbridge, between Sevenoaks and East Grinstead. Signed from junctions 5 and 6 of M25, from A21 and from A264. Formal Italian gardens with statuary, sculpture and fountains; large lake; rose garden and Tudor style gardens with topiary and maze. Romantic moated castle, the childhood home of Anne Boleyn, also open. No dogs in castle, on lead only in gardens. Refreshments available. *Open every day from March 15 to Nov 6 (11-6 last adm 5 Castle opens 12 noon) Adm Castle and gardens £5.20 OAPs £4.70 Chd £2.60 Family (2 adults 2 chds) £13; Gdns only £3.80 OAPs £3.30 Chd £2.20 Family £9.80*

Hole Park &.& (D G W Barham Esq) Rolvenden-Cranbrook on B2086. Beautiful parkland; formal garden with mixed borders, roses, yew hedges and topiary a feature, many fine trees. Natural garden with daffodils, rhododendrons, azaleas, conifers, dell and water gardens; bluebell wood in spring. Autumn colour. *Adm £2 Chd under £2 50p (Share to St Mary's Church, Rolvenden© and Romney Marsh Churches®). Suns April 10, 17, May 1, 8, 22, 29; Oct 9, 16; Weds April 27, May 18, June 8, 15 (2-6)*

> **Regular Openers.** Too many days to include in diary. Usually there is a wide range of plants giving year-round interest. See head of county section for the name and garden description for times etc.

Horseshoe Cottage ✿❀ (Mr & Mrs P Robinson) Charing Heath, 10m NW of Ashford, to W of A20. Proceed to Charing Heath, at Red Lion take Egerton rd, after crossing M20, garden ¼m on L. Main garden of about 1 acre has island beds; mature shrubs and conifers; terraced lower garden with variety of unusual plants. Extensive views. TEAS in aid of Lord Whisky Animal Sanctuary Fund. *Adm £1 Acc chd free. Suns May 8, June 5, 26; Sats June 4, 25 (2-5); also private visits welcome, please* **Tel 0233 712204**

Horton Priory よ (Mrs A C Gore) Sellindge, 6m SE of Ashford. From A20 Ashford-Folkestone, 1m from Sellindge, turn E along Moorstock Lane, signed Horton Priory. Bus: EK/MD 10, 10A, 10B Maidstone-Ashford-Folkestone; alight Sellindge, 1m. Herbaceous and rose border, lawn, pond and rock garden. Priory dates back to C12; church destroyed in reign of Henry VIII, but remains of W doorway and staircase to S aisle of nave can be seen by front door. Along W front Norman buttresses (all genuine) and C14 windows (some restored); one genuine small Norman window. Outer hall only open to visitors. *Adm £1 Chd 50p. Suns June 12, Sept 4 (2-6)*

¶Ightham Mote よ✿❀ (The National Trust) Ivy Hatch. 6m E of Sevenoaks, off A25 and 2½m S of Ightham [188: TQ584535] Buses: Maidstone & District 222/3 from BR Borough Green: NU-Venture 67/8 Sevenoaks to Plaxtol passing BR Sevenoaks: alight Ivy Hatch ½m walk to Ightham Mote. 14-acre garden and moated medieval manor c.1340. Mixed borders with many unusual plants; lawns; courtyard; newly-planted orchard; water features incl small lake, leading to woodland walk with rhododendrons and shrubs. TEAS. ▲*Adm £2 Chd £1. Tues May 17 (11.30-5). Special opening of garden, house not open; NT members to pay*

Jessups よ❀ (The Hon Robin Denison-Pender) Mark Beech. 3m S of Edenbridge. From B2026 Edenbridge-Hartfield rd turn L opp Queens Arms signed Mark Beech, 100yds on L. Small established garden, spring bulbs and shrubs, fine views to Sevenoaks Weald. Small wood. Wildfowl pond (25 different breeds). TEAS. *Adm £1.50 Acc chd free. Sun April 3 (2-5)*

Knole よ✿ (The Lord Sackville; The National Trust) Sevenoaks. Station: Sevenoaks. Pleasance, deer park, landscape garden, herb garden. TEAS. *Adm Car park £2.50: garden 50p Chd 30p; house £4 Chd £2.* ▲*Weds June 1, Aug 3 (11-4.30 last adm 4)*

Kypp Cottage ✿❀ (Mrs Zena Grant) Woolpack Corner, Biddenden. At Tenterden Rd A262 junction with Benenden Rd. Cottage garden (planted and maintained by owner) started about 1964 from rough ground; extensive collection of interesting plants; enjoy perfumed, shady nooks provided by over 200 climbing and shrub roses, intertwined with clematis; variety of geraniums and other ground cover plants. Good examples of trees suitable for small gardens. Morning coffee & home-made TEAS. *Adm £1 Chd 30p (Share to NSPCC®). Suns May 29, June 5, 12, 19, 26; July 3, 10, 17; Mons May 30, June 6, 13, 20, 27; July 4, 11, 18; Tues May 31, June 7, 14, 21, 28; July 5, 12, 19; Weds June 1, 8, 15, 22, 29; July 6, 13, 20; Fri*

May 27; Sat May 28 (Suns 2-6, weekdays 10.30-6); also private visits welcome all summer, please **Tel 0580 291480**

Ladham House ✿❀ (Betty, Lady Jessel) Goudhurst. On NE of village, off A262. 10 acres with rolling lawns, fine specimen trees, rhododendrons, camellias, azaleas, shrubs and magnolias. Arboretum. Spectacular twin mixed borders; fountain and bog gardens. Fine view. Subject of many magazine articles. TEAS. *Adm £2 Chd under 12 50p. Suns May 1, 29, July 10 (11-6); open other times for private visits and for coaches*

Larksfield よ✿ (Mr & Mrs P Dickinson) Crockham Hill, 3m N of Edenbridge, on B269 (Limpsfield-Oxted). Octavia Hill, a founder of the NT, lived here and helped create the original garden; fine collection of azaleas, shrubs, herbaceous plants, rose beds and woodlands; views over Weald and Ashdown Forest. **The Red House** and **Larksfield Cottage** gardens open same days. TEAS at The Red House. *Combined adm £2 OAPs £1.50 Chd 50p. Suns May 15, 22 (2-6)*

Larksfield Cottage よ✿❀ (Mr & Mrs J Mainwaring) Crockham Hill, 3m N of Edenbridge, on B269. An enchanting garden redesigned in 1981 with attractive lawns and shrubs. Views over the Weald and Ashdown Forest. **Larksfield** and **The Red House** gardens also open same days. *Combined adm £2 OAPs £1.50 Chd 50p. Suns May 15, 22 (2-6)*

43 Layhams Road よ✿ (Mrs Dolly Robertson) West Wickham. Semi-detached house recognisable by small sunken flower garden in the front. Opp Wickham Court Farm. A raised vegetable garden, purpose-built for the disabled owner with easy access to wide terraced walkways. The owner, who maintains the entire 24ft × 70ft area herself, would be pleased to pass on her experiences as a disabled gardener so that others may share her joy and interest. *Collecting box. Private visits welcome all year, please* **Tel 081-462 4196**

Little Trafalgar よ✿❀ (Mr & Mrs R J Dunnett) Selling, 4m SE of Faversham. From A2 (M2) or A251 make for Selling Church, then follow signs to garden. ¾-acre garden of great interest both for its wealth of attractive and unusual plants, and its intimate, restful design. Emphasis is placed on the creative and artistic use of plants. TEAS. *Adm £1 Acc chd free. Suns May 15, 29; June 12, 26, July 10, 24, Aug 7, 28, Sept 11, 25; Mons May 30, Aug 29 (2-6); also private visits welcome, please* **Tel 0227 752219**

Lodge House よ (Mr & Mrs J Talbot) Smeeth, 4m E of Ashford. Turn N off A20, then R at Woolpack, follow road ½m to entrance. 2-acre garden in lovely setting, with sloping lawns, daffodils, shrubs and herbaceous flower beds. Field walk. Musicians on June 19. **Bog Farm** also open on April 20. TEAS. *Adm £1 Acc chd free (Share to Brabourne Church®). Suns April 17, June 19, Weds April 20, June 22 (2-6)*

By Appointment Gardens. Avoid the crowds. Good chance of a tour by owner. See garden description for telephone number.

Longacre ௵ (Dr & Mrs G Thomas) Perry Wood, Selling, 5m SE of Faversham. From A2 (M2) or A251 follow signs for Selling, passing White Lion on L, 2nd R and immediately L, continue for ¼m. From A252 at Chilham, take turning signed Selling at Badgers Hill Fruit Farm. L at 2nd Xrds, next R, L and then R. Small plantsman's garden with wide variety of interesting plants, created and maintained entirely by owners. Lovely walks in Perry Woods adjacent to garden. TEAS in aid of local charities. *Adm £1 Acc chd free (Share to Canterbury Pilgrims Hospice®). Suns April 3, 24, May 1, 15, 29, June 12, 26, July 10, 24, Aug 28, Sept 11; Mons April 4, May 2, 30, Aug 29 (2-5); also private visits welcome, please* **Tel 0227 752254**

Long Barn ௸ (Brandon & Sarah Gough) Weald, 3m S of Sevenoaks. Signed to Weald at junction of A21 & B245. Garden at W end of village. 1st garden of Harold Nicolson and Vita Sackville-West. 3 acres with terraces and slopes, giving considerable variety. Dutch garden designed by Lutyens, features mixed planting in raised beds. Teas in village. *Adm £2 OAPs £1 Chd 50p under 5 free (Share to Hospice at Home®). Suns May 22, June 19, July 17 (2-5)*

Lullingstone Castle ௵ (Mr & Mrs Guy Hart Dyke) In the Darenth Valley via Eynsford on A225. Eynsford Station ½m. All cars and coaches via Roman Villa. Lawns, woodland and lake, mixed border, small herb garden. Henry VII gateway; Church on the lawn open. TEAS. *Adm garden £1.50 OAPs/Chd £1; house 50p extra. Sun June 12 (2-6)*

Luton House ௸ (Sir John & Lady Swire) Selling, 4m SE of Faversham. From A2 (M2) or A251 make for White Lion, entrance 30yds E on same side of rd. 4 acres; C19 landscaped garden; ornamental ponds; trees underplanted with azaleas, camellias, woodland plants. *Adm £1.50 Acc chd free. Sun April 24; Sat July 9 (2-6)*

The Manor House ❀ (Mr & Mrs John Shipton) Upper Hardres, 7m S of Canterbury. Take B2068, turn L at Street End (Granville public house), after 2m Upper Hardres Church on R, S-bend in rd, ½m on are white gates with yellow house set back. From A2 at Bridge turn W to Petts Bottom, past Duck Inn, 1m on turn R at stables, house on L at top of steep hill behind white gates. 8 acres of fine old trees; walled garden; rose, laburnum and wisteria walks; woodland bulb walk in spring; vegetables and small orchard. TEAS. *Adm £1.50 Chd 50p. Sun June 26 (2-6)*

Marle Place ௵ (Mr & Mrs Gerald Williams) Brenchley, 8m SE of Tonbridge, signed from Brenchley, on B2162, 1m S of Horsmonden and 1½m NW of Lamberhurst. Turn W on Marle Place Rd. Victorian gazebo; plantsman's shrub borders; walled scented garden, large herb rockery and herb nursery. Woodland walk; collection of bantams. C17 listed house (not open). TEAS. *Adm £2 OAP/Chd £1.50. Every day April 1 to Oct 31 (10-5.30). For NGS Suns May 29, Aug 7, Oct 2 (10-6)*

Maurice House ௵ (The Royal British Legion Residential Home) Callis Court Rd, Broadstairs. From Broadstairs Broadway take St Peter's Park Rd; turn R under railway arch into Baird's Hill; join Callis Court Rd entrance on R, 100yds beyond Lanthorne Rd turning. Well-maintained 8-acre garden; lawns, flowering trees, shrubs; formal flower beds; rose and water gardens; orchard. Spring bedding displays of wallflowers, tulips, polyanthus; wide variety of herbaceous plants and shrubs especially suited to coastal conditions. TEA. *Adm £1 Chd 25p (Share to the Royal British Legion®). Sun April 24 (2-5.30)*

Meadow Wood ௵ (Mr & Mrs James Lee) Penshurst. 1¼m SE of Penshurst on B2176 in direction of Bidborough. 1920s garden, on edge of wood with long southerly views over the Weald, and with interesting trees and shrubs; azaleas, rhododendrons and naturalised bulbs in woods with mown walks. TEAS. *Adm £2 Chd £1 (Share to Relate®). Sun May 8 (2-6)*

Mere House ௵ (Mr & Mrs Andrew Wells) Mereworth, midway between Tonbridge & Maidstone. From A26 turn N on to B2016 and then into Mereworth village. 6-acre garden with C18 lake; ornamental shrubs and trees with foliage contrast; lawns, daffodils; Kentish cobnut plat. TEAS. *Adm £1 Chd 25p. Suns April 3, June 12; Mon May 30 (2.30-6)*

Mill House ௵ (Dr & Mrs Brian Glaisher) Mill Lane, ½m N of Hildenborough, 5m S of Sevenoaks. From B245 turn into Mill Lane at Mill garage. 3-acre garden laid out in 1906; herbaceous and mixed borders; new secluded herb garden; old shrub roses and climbers; clematis and many fine trees. Formal garden with topiary; ruins of windmill and conservatory with exotics. TEAS. *Adm £1.50 Chd 25p. Sun June 12 (2-6)*

Mount Ephraim (Mrs M N Dawes and Mr & Mrs E S Dawes) Hernhill, Faversham. From M2 and A299 take Hernhill turning at Duke of Kent. Herbaceous border; topiary; daffodils and rhododendrons; rose terraces leading to a small lake; Japanese rock garden with pools; water garden; small vineyard. TEAS daily; lunches only Bank Hol Suns & Mons. *Adm £2 Chd 25p. Open April to Sept (1-6). For NGS Suns April 24, Sept 25 (1-6)*

Nettlestead Place ௵ (Mr & Mrs Roy Tucker) Nettlestead, 6m W/SW of Maidstone. Turn S off A26 onto B2015 then 1m on L (next to Nettlestead Church). C13 manor house set in 7-acre garden; garden on different levels, defined by ragstone walls and yew hedges with fine views of open countryside; garden in course of further development, including pond garden, new terraces and plant collections. TEAS. *Adm £1.50 Acc chd free (Share to St Mary's Church, Nettlestead®). Suns May 22, Sept 11 (2-6)*

New Barns House ௵ (Mr & Mrs P H Byam-Cook) West Malling. Leave M20 at Exit 4 to West Malling. In High Street turn E down Waters Lane, at T-junction turn R, take bridge over by-pass, follow lane 400yds to New Barns House. 1-acre garden with fine trees and flowering cherries. Walled garden, mixed borders and shrubs. TEAS. *Adm £1 Acc chd free. Sun April 10 (2-6)*

Regular Openers. See head of county section.

¶**Nonington & Woodnesborough Gardens** &✿ 6m & 3m from Sandwich respectively on Sandwich-Woodnesborough-Nonington Road. *Combined adm £2.50 Chd £1 (Share to Macmillan Fund for Cancer Relief.®). Thurs June 9 (12-6)*

Birnam (Mr & Mrs Douglas Miller) Hamill Road, ½m SW of Woodnesborough. ¾-acre garden on clay, designed in 1963 by Anthony du Gard Pasley for a windswept site. Interesting trees, shrubs, roses. TEA

Gooseberry Hall Cottage (Mr & Dr Edward Carey) Nonington. From A2 take B2046 at Barham, after 300yds turn R for Nonington, proceed for 3m, passing disused Snowdon Colliery through Nonington village to mini-roundabout, turn R, house further ¾m on L. Cottage garden, with special-interest hedges and croquet lawn

Gooseberry Hall Farm (Mr & Mrs F McL Hayward) Nonington. 400yds from **Gooseberry Hall Cottage** down Gooseberry Lane on R. ½-acre garden surrounding Grade II thatched hall house. Herbaceous borders, lawns, climbing and hybrid roses, mature elms and small vegetable garden aimed at self sufficiency

Northbourne Court ✿✿ (The Hon Charles James) W of Deal. Signs in village. Great brick terraces, belonging to an earlier Elizabethan mansion, provide a picturesque setting for a wide range of shrubs and plants on chalk soil; geraniums, fuchsias and grey-leaved plants. *Adm £2.50 OAPs/Chd £1.50 (Share to National Art Collections Fund®). Suns May 1, 29, June 12, 26, July 10, 24, Aug 14, 28, Sept 11, 25 (2-5)*

¶**The Oast, Hurst Green Farm** &✿ (Mr & Mrs Bedford) Stilebridge, Marden, 6m S of Maidstone. On A229 (Maidstone-Hastings) ½m S of Stilebridge inn, 2m N of Staplehurst. 20-year-old 1¾-acre garden, incl ¼ acre of water, landscaped with shrubberies, rockeries, with dwarf conifers and heathers, raised beds of seasonal bedding, kitchen garden; also ornamental fish and small collection of waterfowl. TEA. *Adm £1.50 Chd 50p (Share to The Mike Colinwood Trust®). Suns May 1, 8, July 3, 17, 31 (2-6)*

Olantigh &✿ (J R H Loudon Esq) Wye, 6m NE of Ashford. Turn off A28 either to Wye or at Godmersham; ¾m from Wye on rd to Godmersham. Edwardian garden in beautiful setting; water garden; rockery; shrubbery; herbaceous border; extensive lawns. *Adm £1.50 Chd 30p. Suns May 29, June 26 (2-5)*

The Old Parsonage &✿✿ (Dr & Mrs Richard Perks) Sutton Valence, 6m SE of Maidstone. A274 from Maidstone or Headcorn, turn E into village at King's Head Inn and proceed on upper rd through village; climb Tumblers Hill and entrance at top on R. 4-acre labour-saving garden planted since 1959 with emphasis on ground cover; trees, shrubs and mixed borders; cranesbills and shrub roses. Ancient nut plat now developed as a wild garden. Fine views over Low Weald. In grounds is Sutton castle, C12 ruined keep, permanently open to the public. *Adm £1.50 Chd 50p. Sun June 19, Tue June 21, Thur June 23, Sat June 25 (2-6)*

Old Place Farm &✿ (Mr & Mrs Jeffrey Eker) High Halden, 3m NE of Tenterden. From A28 take Woodchurch Rd (opp Chequers public house) in High Halden, and follow for ½m. 3½-acre garden, mainly designed by Anthony du Gard Pasley, surrounding period farmhouse & buildings with paved herb garden & parterres, small lake, ponds, lawns, mixed borders, cutting garden, old shrub roses, lilies & foliage plants; all created since 1969 & still developing. Featured in *Country Life*, & *House & Garden* in 1990. TEAS in aid of St Mary's Church, High Halden. *Adm £1.50 Chd 50p. Sun June 19 (2-6)*

¶**Orchard Cottage** &✿✿ (Professor & Mrs C G Wall) 3 Woodlands Road, Bickley, 1½m E of Bromley, about 400 yds from the A222. From Bickley Park Road turn into Pines Road, then 1st R into Woodlands Road, no 3 is 1st house on L. Attractive ⅓-acre garden in course of development; mixed borders with many interesting herbaceous plants and shrubs; scree beds and troughs with alpines and other small plants. TEA. *Adm £1 Chd 25p. Sun Aug 7 (2-5.30)*

Oswalds &✿✿ (Mr & Mrs J C Davidson) Bishopsbourne, 4m S of Canterbury. Turn off A2 at B2065, follow signs to Bishopsbourne, house next to church. 3-acre plantsman's garden created since 1972 by present owners. Year-round interest includes bulbs, spring garden; mixed borders; rockeries; pools; bog garden; potager; pergola; old roses; and many fruit varieties. NCCPG National Collections of *Photinia* and *Zantedeschia*. House (not open) has interesting literary connections. Teas at village hall nearby. *Adm £1.50 Chd 50p (Share to Kent Gardens Trust®). Sun May 1; Mon May 2 (2-5.30); also private visits welcome, please* **Tel 0227 830340**

Otham Gardens 4m SE of Maidstone. From A2020 or A274 follow signs for Otham 1m. Parking restricted to official car parks except for disabled people. TEAS. *Combined adm £2.50 Acc chd free (Share to Maidstone Mencap®). Sun June 26 (2-6)*

Bramley (Miss Ware) Interesting old garden on different levels; new water garden

Greenhill House (Dr & Mrs Hugh Vaux) Established herbaceous and shrub borders; wild garden; new herb garden

Little Squerryes & (Mr & Mrs Gerald Coomb) Established garden; herbaceous borders; interesting trees

The Limes & (Mr & Mrs John Stephens) Well established garden with herbaceous borders and wisteria pergola

¶**The Old School** (Mr & Mrs David Marchant) Converted school playground with many interesting plants

Stoneacre Special opening; *NT members to pay.* For garden description see individual entry

Swallows & (Mr & Mrs Eric Maidment) Cottage garden with colourful terrace

Tulip Cottage & (Mrs Gloria Adams) Shows what can be done in a small space

¶**Oxley House** &✿✿ (Dr & Mrs I D H McMullen) Boughton Road, Sandway, 8m from Ashford or Maidstone. From Lenham Square take Headcorn Road, 1st L after Lenham BR station, house 300yds on L, before 'White Horse'. About 1½ acres on heavy clay and sand, largely developed since 1987 storm, surrounding Queen Anne & Victorian house; wide variety of perennials, shrubs and old roses; small woodland garden with bulbs and hellebores. *Adm £1.50 Chd 50p (Share to Heart of Kent Hospice®). Suns May 15, June 26, Sept 18 (2-5)*

Oxon Hoath &✿ (Mr & Mrs Henry Bayne-Powell) nr Hadlow, 5m NE of Tonbridge. *Car essential.* Via A20, turn off S at Wrotham Heath onto Seven Mile Lane (B2016); at Mereworth Xrds turn W, through West Peckham. Or via A26, in Hadlow turn off N along Carpenters Lane. 10 acres, landscaped with fine trees, rhododendrons and azaleas; woodland walk; replanted cedar avenue; formal parterre rose garden by Nesfield; peacocks. Large Kentish ragstone house (not shown) principally Georgian but dating back to C14; Victorian additions by Salvin. Once owned by Culpeppers, grandparents of Catherine Howard. View over C18 lake to Hadlow Folly. TEAS in picnic area if fine. *Adm £1.50 Chd 50p (Share to W. Peckham Church©). Sun May 29 (2-7)*

The Pear House &✿✿ (Mrs Nicholas Snowden) Sellindge, 6m E of Ashford. Turn L off A20 at Sellindge Church towards Brabourne into Stone Hill. ⅔ acre developed by present owner; still evolving. Contains smaller gardens with informal planting; bulbs, roses (mostly old-fashioned), shrubs, small orchard with climbing roses, pond garden, shady areas. *Adm £1 Chd 40p. Private visits welcome only May 1 to July 10* Tel 0303 812147

Peddars Wood &✿✿ (Mr & Mrs B J Honeysett) 14 Orchard Rd, St Michaels, Tenterden. From A28, 1m N of Tenterden, turn W into Grange Rd at Crown Hotel, take 2nd R into Orchard Rd. Small plantsman's garden created by present owner since 1984. One of the best collections of rare and interesting plants in the area, incl over 100 clematis, 50 climbing roses, lilies and ferns. TEAS. *Adm £1 Chd 20p (Share to Baptist Minister's Help Society). Sats May 7, June 4, July 9, Aug 6 (2-6); also private visits welcome, please* Tel 05806 3994

Penshurst Place ✿ (Viscount De L'Isle), S of Tonbridge on B2176, N of Tunbridge Wells on A26. 10 acres of garden dating back to C14; garden divided into series of 'rooms' by over a mile of clipped yew hedge; profusion of spring bulbs: herbaceous borders; formal rose garden; famous peony border. All year interest. TEAS and light refreshments. *Adm House & Gardens £4.95 OAPs £4.50 Chd £2.75: Gardens £3.50 OAPs £3 Chd £2.25. Open daily March 26 to Oct 2. For NGS Weds May 4, June 1 (11-6)*

Petham House &✿✿ (Mr & Mrs Nicholas Graham) Petham, 6m S of Canterbury. From B2068 turn R, signposted Petham village at Chequers public house, down steep hill past church to T-junction in centre of Petham, turn L; continue up slight incline & fork L into Duckpit, a minor rd, entrance on R. Garden mainly lawns with recently planted trees and shrubs for foliage effect; woodland strip; walled garden undergoing extensive restoration; vine house. House (not open) in Italianate style c. 1848 by Robert Palmer Browne. *Adm £1.50 Chd 50p. Suns May 1, June 5 (1.30-6)*

Pett Place ✿✿ (Mrs I Mills, Mr C I Richmond-Watson & Mr A Rolla) Charing, 6m NW of Ashford. From A20 turn N into Charing High St. At end turn R into Pett Lane towards Westwell. Four walled gardens covering nearly 4 acres. Within formal framework of old walls, much planting has been carried out since 1981 to make a garden of different, pleasing vistas and secret places. A ruined C13 chapel is a romantic feature beside the manor house (not open), which was re-fronted about 1700 and which Pevsner describes as 'presenting grandiloquently towards the road.' TEAS. *Adm £1.50 Chd 50p (Share to Kent Gardens Trust®). Sats, Suns April 23, 24, June 18, 19 (2.30-5)*

Pevington Farm &✿ (Mr & Mrs David Mure) Pluckley, 3m SW of Charing. From Charing take B2077 towards Pluckley, before Pluckley turn R towards Egerton. Pevington Farm ½m on. From SW go through Pluckley, turn L for Egerton. ¾-acre garden with wonderful views over the Weald. Mixed borders with many interesting plants. Ploughman's lunch. TEA in aid of St Nicholas Church, Pluckley. *Adm £1.50 Chd 50p. Suns May 22, June 12 (11-5); also private visits welcome, please* Tel 0233 840317

The Pines Garden & The Bay Museum &✿ (The St Margaret's Bay Trust) Beach Rd, St Margaret's Bay, 4½m NE of Dover. Beautiful 6-acre seaside garden. Water garden. Statue of Sir Winston Churchill complemented by the Bay Museum opposite. Fascinating maritime and local interest. TEAS. *Adm £1 Chd 50p. Gardens open daily except Christmas Day. Museum open May to end Aug (closed Mon and Fri). For NGS Suns April 3, May 29, Aug 28 (10-5)*

Placketts Hole &✿✿ (Mr & Mrs D P Wainman) Bicknor 5m S of Sittingbourne, and W of B2163. Owners have designed and planted 2-acre garden around charming old house (C16 with Georgian additions); interesting mix of shrubs, large borders, rose garden, a formal herb garden and sweet-smelling plants. TEAS. *Adm £1.50 Acc chd free (Share to Bicknor Church®). Sun June 26 (2-6.30)*

Plaxtol Gardens 5m N of Tonbridge, 6m E of Sevenoaks, turn E off A227 to Plaxtol village. TEAS. Tickets and maps available at all gardens. Parking at Spoute Cottage. *Combined adm £2.50 Acc chd free (Share to Friends of Plaxtol Church©). Sun June 26 (2-6)*

  Malling Well House (Mr & Mrs Cedric Harris) The Street, Plaxtol; next to Papermakers Arms. An open garden of about 1¼ acres, created over last 16 years by present owners; herbaceous border, pond, marsh garden and large vegetable plot

  Schoolfield (Mr & Mrs Colin Creed) Turn L at the church, entrance 300 yds on L. 2½-acre garden created in the last 8 years, with ponds, a variety of borders and vegetable garden. Lovely views

  Spoute Cottage ✿✿ (Mr & Mrs Donald Forbes) situated at the bottom of Plaxtol St on L side opp Hyders Wrought Iron Works. ¾ acre of mixed borders of contrasting flowering and foliage plants, especially for flower arranging; small pond & stream. New Japanese garden. Plant nursery attached

  ¶**Wendings** ✿ (E E Peckham) The Street. ¼-acre garden created and maintained by present owner. Contrasting shrubs, ground cover and climbers

  ¶**Wickenden Farm** ✿ (Mr & Mrs S Furness) The Street. ¾-acre sloping garden leading to small paddock with views over the Bourne valley; newly created herb garden; pergola, pond and cottage garden borders

---

By Appointment Gardens. See head of county section

Portobello (Barry M Williams Esq) Brenchley, 6m SE of Tonbridge. From A21, 1m S of Pembury turn onto B2160, turn R at Xrds in Matfield sign-posted Brenchley. For garden description see under **Brenchley Gardens** May 15, when this garden is open again. *Adm £1 Acc chd free. Sun June 12 (2-6)*

29 The Precincts ✿❀ (The Archdeacon of Canterbury & Mrs T Till) Canterbury. Enter Cathedral Precincts by main (Christ Church) gate, follow path round W end of Cathedral into cloister, entry through gate N side of cloister. **No access for cars; please use public car parks.** ¾-acre of medieval walled garden with perpetual presence of the Cathedral soaring above. Enter Cellarer's Hall beneath earliest known carving of Thomas Becket, past a noble descendant of the mulberry tree in whose shade (allegedly) Becket's murderers washed their hands. TEAS. *Adm £1 Chd 50p (Share to L'Arche Overseas®). Sats, Suns June 4, 5, 11, 12; Wed June 8 (2-5.30)*

Ramhurst Manor ✿ (The Lady Rosie Kindersley) Powder Mill Lane, Leigh, Tonbridge. Historic property once belonged to the Black Prince and Culpepper family. Formal gardens; roses, azaleas, rhododendrons, wild flowers. TEAS. *Adm £1 Acc chd free. Sun May 15 (2.30-6)*

The Red House ✿✿❀ (K C L Webb Esq) Crockham Hill, 3m N of Edenbridge. On Limpsfield-Oxted Rd, B269. Formal features of this large garden are kept to a minimum; rose walk leads on to 3 acres of rolling lawns flanked by fine trees and shrubs incl rhododendrons, azaleas and magnolias. Views over the Weald and Ashdown Forest. TEAS. **Larksfield** and **Larksfield Cottage** gardens also open same days. *Combined adm £2 OAPs £1.50 Chd 50p (Share to The Schizophrenia Association of Great Britain®). Suns May 15, 22 (2-6)*

Ringfield ✿ (Professor Sir David Smithers) Knockholt. Via A21 London-Sevenoaks; from London turn at Pratts Bottom roundabout, also reached from Orpington-Bromley turn off from M25 or from Sevenoaks at Dunton Green (Rose & Crown). Rhododendrons, over 4,000 rose trees, incl recent varieties, and wide vistas. TEAS. *Adm £1 Chd 40p. Suns May 29, June 26 (2-6)*

Riverhill House ✿❀ (The Rogers family) 2m S of Sevenoaks on A225. Mature hillside garden with extensive views; specimen trees, sheltered terraces with roses and choice shrubs; bluebell wood with rhododendrons and azaleas; picnics allowed. TEAS. *Adm £2 Chd 50p (Share to Mental Health Foundation®). Every Sunday from April 1 to June 30 and Bank Hol Weekends in this period (12-6). For NGS Sats April 30, May 28 (12-6)*

Rock Farm ✿✿❀ (Mrs P A Corfe) Nettlestead. 6m W of Maidstone. Turn S off A26 onto B2015 then 1m S at Wateringbury turn R. 1½-acre garden, skilfully set out around old farm buildings; planted since 1968 and maintained by owner; plantsman's collection of shrubs, herbaceous plants, ornamental pond. Plant nursery adjoining garden. *Adm £1.50 Chd 50p (Share to St Mary's Church, Nettlestead®). Weds May 4, 11, 18, 25, June 1, 8, 15, 22, 29, July 6, 13, 20, 27, Aug 3; Sats May 7, 14, 21, 28, June 4, 11, 18, 25, July 2, 9, 16, 23, 30, Aug 6 (11-5)*

Rosefarm ✿✿❀ (Dr D J Polton) 1m NW of Chilham. 6m equidistant Canterbury and Faversham. ¼m along narrow lane. Signed 'Denne Manor' at Shottenden Xrds. ½-acre garden with interesting and unusual plants. *Adm £1 Acc chd free. Weds June 1, 8; Fri June 3; Sat June 4 (2-6)*

St Clere ✿✿ (Mr & Mrs Ronnie Norman) Kemsing, 6m NE of Sevenoaks. Take A25 from Sevenoaks toward Ightham; 1m past Seal turn L signed Heaverham and Kemsing; in Heaverham take rd to R signed Wrotham and West Kingsdown; in 75yds straight ahead marked Private rd; 1st L and follow rd to house. 4-acre garden with herbaceous borders, shrubs, rare trees. C17 mansion (not open). TEAS. *Adm £1.50 Chd 50p. Sun June 26 (2-6)*

St Michael's House ✿✿❀ (Brig & Mrs W Magan) Roydon, Peckham Bush. 5m NE Tonbridge, 5m SW Maidstone. On A26 at Mereworth roundabout take S exit (A228) signed Paddock Wood, after 1m turn L at top of rise (signed Roydon). Gardens ¼m up hill on L. Old vicarage garden of ¾ acre round house & enclosed by shaped yew hedge; roses, climbing roses, iris border, rock roses, herbaceous; courtyard and 6-acre meadow with extensive views. Original oil paintings and watercolours for sale. TEAS. *Adm £2 OAPs £1 Chd 50p. Suns May 15, 22 (2-6)*

● **Saltwood Castle** (The Hon Mrs Clark) 2m NW of Hythe, 4m W of Folkestone; from A20 turn S at sign to Saltwood. Medieval castle, subject of quarrel between Thomas à Becket and Henry II. C13 crypt and dungeons; armoury; battlement walks and watch towers. Lovely views; spacious lawns and borders; courtyard walls covered with roses. Picnics allowed. Saltwood Castle closed to the general public in 1994. *Private parties of 20 or more by appt weekdays only, please* **Tel 0303 267190**

Scotney Castle ✿✿ (Mrs Christopher Hussey; The National Trust) On A21 London-Hastings, 1¼m S of Lamberhurst. Bus: (Mon to Sat) M & D 246 & 256, Tunbridge Wells-Hawkhurst; alight Spray Hill. Famous picturesque landscape garden, created by the Hussey family in the 1840s surrounding moated C14 Castle. House (not open) by Salvin, 1837. Old Castle open May – mid-Sept (same times as garden). Gift Shop. Picnic area in car park. Tea Goudhurst. *Adm £3.20 Chd £1.60; Pre-booked parties of 15 or more (Wed-Fri) £2 Chd £1; April 2-end Oct, daily except Mons & Tues, but open Bank Hol Mons (closed Good Fri). Wed-Fri 11-6, Sats & Suns 2-6 or sunset if earlier; Bank Hol Mons & Suns preceeding 12-6. For NGS (Share to Trinity Hospice, Clapham Common®) Bank Hol Mon May 30 (12-6)*

Sea Close ✿❀ (Maj & Mrs R H Blizard) Cannongate Rd, Hythe. A259 Hythe-Folkestone; ½m from Hythe, signed. A plantsman's garden; 1¼ acres on steep slope overlooking the sea; designed, laid out & maintained by present owners since 1966. Approx 1000 named plants & shrubs, planted for visual effect in many varied style beds of individual character. Cold refreshments. Teas Hythe. *Adm £1 Acc chd free (Share to Royal Signals Benevolent Fund®). Suns May 22, July 17, Aug 28 (2-5.30), Oct 2 (2-4.30)*

Regular Openers. See head of county section.

¶**Shipbourne Gardens** 3m N of Tonbridge, 5m E of Sevenoaks on A227. TEAS in village hall. Maps available at gardens and village hall. Parking on village green. *Combined adm £2.50 Acc chd free. Sun June 12 (2-6)*

1 Batey's Cottage &✿ (Mr & Mrs E Martin) Stumble Hill. Small cottage garden with vegetable patch, herbaceous borders, shrubs

Brookers Cottage &✿✿ (Ann & Peter Johnson) Back Lane. ²⁄₃-acre garden with natural pond, herbaceous borders and island beds; large collection of hardy geraniums (cranesbills); small fruit and vegetable patch

The Coach House ✿✿ (Mrs Ann Buckett) The Grange. Small informal garden, ⅓ acre, in former orchard; herbaceous and shrub borders with roses growing through apple trees; small pond; vegetable garden

Waylands & (Pat & Michael Bustard) Back Lane. 1-acre garden, with island beds, shrubberies, rockery; small vegetable patch; planted containers; paddock with sheep and two donkeys

Yew Tree Cottage ✿ (Susan & Ian Bowles) The Green. Small cottage garden, partially walled, with herbaceous border, small gravel garden and old roses. Studio of wild life artist Ian Bowles will be open

¶**Sibton Park** &✿ (Mrs Ridley-Day & Mr & Mrs C Blackwell) Lyminge, 8m NW of Folkestone. Off Elham Valley road, N of Lyminge, turn L for Rhodes Minnis, ¼m on L. Landscaped garden with spacious lawns (6 acres), 20 feet high yew hedges and topiary; old walled garden; children's adventure playground (own risk). TEAS. *Adm £1.50 OAP £1 Chd 50p. Sat June 25 (2-6)*

The Silver Spray &✿✿ (Mr & Mrs C T Orsbourne) Sellindge. 7m SE of Ashford on A20 opposite school. 1-acre garden developed and planted since 1983 and maintained by owners. Attractively laid out gardens and wild area combine a keen interest in conservation (especially butterflies) with a love of unusual hardy and tender plants. TEAS. *Adm £1 Acc chd free (Share to St Mary's Church, Sellindge®). Weds July 6, 20, Aug 24; Sats June 18, 25, July 9, 23; Mon Aug 29 (2-5)*

Sissinghurst Garden &✿✿ (Nigel Nicolson Esq; The National Trust) Cranbrook. Station: Staplehurst. Bus: MD5 from Maidstone 14m; 297 Tunbridge Wells (not Suns) 15m. Garden created by the late V. Sackville-West and Sir Harold Nicolson. Spring garden, herb garden. Tudor building and tower, partly open to public. Moat. **Because of the limited capacity of the garden, visitors may often have to wait before entry. The Property is liable to be closed once it has reached its visitor capacity for the day.** Lunches and TEAS. *Adm £5 Chd £2.50 (Share to Charleston Farmhouse Trust®). Garden open April 1 to Oct 15. (Closed Mons incl Bank Hols). Tues to Fri 1-6.30 (last adm 6pm); Sats and Suns 10-5.30 (last adm 5pm). For NGS Weds April 27, June 8, July 13 (1-6.30)*

Sissinghurst Place Gardens &✿✿ Sissinghurst, 2m N of Cranbrook, E of village on A262. TEAS. *Combined adm £1.50 Chd 25p (Share to Cranbrook CAB®). Sats, Suns May 21, 22, June 18, 19 (2-6)*

Sissinghurst Place (Mr & Mrs Simon macLachlan) Large garden of herbaceous beds, lawns, rhododendrons, fine trees, shrubs and roses; herbs and climbers in ruin of original house, wild garden and pond

The Coach House (Mr & Mrs Michael Sykes) House and garden adjacent and originally part of Sissinghurst Place. In 1983, the owners designed and planted a new garden within established yew hedges. Many unusual trees, shrubs and plants

Slip Mill &✿ (Mrs Sheila Doyle) Hawkhurst, 3½m S of Cranbrook. From A21 at Flimwell take A268 signed Hawkhurst; turn 1st L after hospital, garden ½m on. 1½ acres with lawns; herbaceous plants; roses and established trees bounded on two sides by streams. TEAS. *Adm £1 Acc chd free. Sun June 12; Wed June 15 (10-6)*

South Hill Farm &✿ (Sir Charles Jessel Bt) Hastingleigh, E of Ashford. Turn off A28 to Wye, go through village and ascend Wye Downs, in 2m turn R at Xrds marked Brabourne and South Hill, then first L. Or from Stone Street (B2068) turn W opp Stelling Minnis, follow signs to Hastingleigh, continue towards Wye and turn L at Xrds marked Brabourne and South Hill, then first L. 2 acres high up on N Downs, C18 house (not open); old walls; ha-ha; formal water garden; old and new roses; unusual shrubs, perennials and foliage plants. TEAS. *Adm £1.50 Chd 25p. Sun July 3 (2-6)*

Spilsill Court &✿✿ (Mr & Mrs C G Marshall) Frittenden Road, Staplehurst. Proceed to Staplehurst on A229 (Maidstone-Hastings). From S enter village, turn R immediately after Elf garage on R & just before 30mph sign, into Frittenden Rd; garden ½m on, on L. From N go through village to 40mph sign, immediately turn L into Frittenden Rd. Approx 4 acres of garden, orchard and paddock; series of gardens including those in blue, white and silver; roses; lawns; shrubs, trees and ponds. Small private chapel. Jacob sheep & unusual poultry. TEA. *Adm £1.50 Chd under 16 50p (Share to Gardening for the Disabled Trust®). Suns April 10, July 31 (11-5)*

Squerryes Court & (Mr & Mrs John Warde) ½m W of Westerham signed from A25 Edenbridge Rd. 15 acres incl lake & woodland; well documented historic garden laid out in 1689; owners restoring the formal garden in William & Mary style; parterres, borders, 300-yr-old lime trees, dovecote, gazebo, cenotaph commemorating Gen Wolfe. TEAS. *Adm £2 Chd £1 (House & garden £3.50 Chd £1.60). Weds, Sats, Suns from April 1 to Sept 30 (2-6). For NGS (Share to St Mary's Church, Westerham©). Suns July 10, Aug 21 (2-6)*

¶**Squerryes Lodge** &✿ (Mr & Mrs W S Churchill) Westerham: in Lodge Lane, which is opp junction of A25 and B2026 to Croydon. R. Darenth flows through 4-acre garden; with rhododendrons and azaleas; lake and fine yew hedge. No parking, please park in town. TEAS. *Adm £1.50 Chd 50p (Share to St Catherine's Hospice, Crawley®). Sun May 22 (2-6)*

By Appointment Gardens. These owners do not have a fixed opening day usually because they do not like crowds or have insufficient parking space. Owner will often give guided tour.

Regular Openers. See head of county section.

Stoneacre &❀ (Mrs Rosemary Alexander; The National Trust) Otham, 4m SE of Maidstone, between A2020 and A274. Old world garden recently replanted. Yew hedges; herbaceous borders; ginkgo tree. Timber-framed Hall House dated 1480. Subject of newspaper and magazine articles. (National Trust members please note that this opening in aid of the NGS is on a day when the property would not normally be open, therefore adm charges apply). TEAS. *Adm £1.50 Chd 50p. Mons May 2, 30 (2-5); also open with Otham Gardens on June 26; and private visits welcome, please* Tel 0622 862871

Stonewall Park (Mr & Mrs V P Fleming) Chiddingstone Hoath, 5m SE of Edenbridge. ½-way between Mark Beech and Penshurst. Large walled garden with herbaceous borders. Extensive woodland garden, featuring species and hybrid rhododendrons and azaleas; wandering paths, lake. Also open at no extra charge **North Lodge** (Mrs Dorothy Michie) traditional cottage garden full of interest. TEA. *Adm £2 Acc chd free (Share to Kent Gardens Trust®). Sun May 8 (2-5.30)*

Street End Place &❀❀ (Mr & Mrs R Baker White) Street End. 3m S of Canterbury-Hythe rd (Stone St). Drive gates at Granville Inn. Long established garden incl walled garden, in pleasant setting; large area of naturalised daffodils with lawns of flowering shrubs; fine trees. *Adm £1 Chd 50p. Sun April 3, Mon April 4 (2-4.30)*

Tanners ❀❀ (Lord & Lady Nolan) Brasted, 2m E of Westerham. A25 to Brasted; in Brasted turn off alongside the Green & up the hill to the top; 1st drive on R opp Coles Lane. Bus stop Brasted Green & White Hart 200yds. 5 acres; mature trees & shrubs; maples, magnolias, rhododendrons & foliage trees; water garden; interesting new planting. Teas in Village Tearoom, High Street, Brasted. *Adm £1.50 Chd 25p. Sun May 22 (2-6)*

2 Thorndale Close &❀❀ (Mr & Mrs L O Miles) Chatham. From A229 Chatham-Maidstone rd turn E opp Forte Posthouse into Watson Ave, next R to Thorndale Close. Minute front and rear gardens of 11 × 18ft and 20 × 22ft. Plantsman's garden with alpines, pool, bog garden, rockery, peat and herbaceous beds. *Adm £1 Chd 25p. Suns March 27, April 10, 24, May 8, 22, June 5, 19, July 3, 17, 31 (2-6); also private visits welcome, please* Tel 0634 863329

Thornham Friars &❀ (Geoffrey Fletcher Esq) Pilgrims Way, Thurnham, 4m NE of Maidstone. From M20 or M2 take A249, at bottom of Detling Hill turn into Dutling and 1m along Pilgrims Way to garden. 2-acre garden on chalk. Distant views across parkland. Many unusual shrubs; trees; lawns with special beds for ericaceous shrubs. Tudor house. *Adm £1 Chd 25p. Sun May 8 (2-5.30)*

Torry Hill &❀❀ (Lord & Lady Kingsdown) 5m S of Sittingbourne. Situated in triangle formed by Frinsted, Milstead and Doddington. Leave M 20 at junction 8 for A20, at Lenham turn N for Doddington; at Great Danes N for Hollingbourne and Frinsted (B2163). From M2 Intersection 5 via Bredgar and Milstead. From A2 and E turn S at Ospringe via Newnham and Doddington. 8 acres; large lawns, specimen trees, flowering cherries, rhododendrons, azaleas and naturalised daffodils; walled gardens with lawns, shrubs, roses, herbaceous borders, wild flower areas and vegetables. Extensive views to Medway and Thames estuaries. TEA. *Adm £1.50 Chd over 12 50p (Share to St Dunstan's Church, Frinsted©). Suns April 24, May 15, June 26 (2-5)*

Town Hill Cottage ❀❀ (Mr & Mrs P Cosier) 58 Town Hill, West Malling. From A20 6m W of Maidstone, turn S onto A228. Top of Town Hill at N end of High St. Part walled small village garden of C16-C18 house, with many interesting plants. Hardy ferns for sale. TEAS. *Adm £1 Chd 50p. Suns May 22, June 19 (2-5)*

Turkey Court &❀❀ (Mr & Mrs Peter Young) Ashford Road, Maidstone. Leave M20 at exit 7 to town centre, then A20 E for ½m. Large garden 1st established in early C17, now with lawns, lake, river and waterfall. Walled garden, beautiful trees, herbaceous borders and shrubs; yr-round interest. TEAS. *Adm £1.25 Chd 30p. Suns May 15, July 17 (2-6)*

Updown Farm &❀ (Mr & the Hon Mrs Willis-Fleming) Betteshanger, 3m S of Sandwich. From A256 Sandwich-Dover, turn L off Eastry by-pass SE of Eastry, signed Northbourne, Finglesham. Again 1st L; house 1st on R. 3-acre garden begun in 1975 and still in the making, round Tudor and C18 farmhouse. One of the most extensive figgeries in East Kent; cherry and plum orchards with old roses and climbers; terrace garden; herbaceous borders, unusual trees and shrubs. TEAS in aid of Save the Children Fund & The Spastics Society. *Adm £1.50 OAPs 80p Chd 30p. Suns May 1, 29 (2-6)*

Upper Mill Cottage ❀❀ (Mr & Mrs D Seeney) Salts Lane, Loose, 3½m S of Maidstone. Turn W off A229 to Loose. Parking in village; proceed 300yds on foot up Salts Lane. 1½-acre cottage garden created and maintained by owners, on site of old water mill with natural stream. Plantsman's garden with many unusual varieties. *Adm £1.50 Chd 50p. Suns May 15, July 3; Wed May 18 (2-5.30)*

Upper Pryors &❀ (Mr & Mrs S G Smith) Cowden, 4½m SE of Edenbridge. From B2026 Edenbridge-Hartfield, turn R at Cowden Xrds and take 1st drive on R. 10 acres recently redesigned to incorporate parkland and a water garden. The terrace, with courtyard and wisteria walkway leads out onto large lawns, borders and open views. TEAS. *Adm £1.50 Chd 50p. Wed June 8 (2-6)*

Vine House ❀❀ (Dr & Mrs Peter Huxley-Williams) 62 High St, Lydd. S of New Romney on B2075, past the church in High St on R-side. Informal gardens of about 1 acre surrounding C16 farmhouse; many unusual small trees & shrubs; ponds with waterfall; vineyard; new planting of old roses. Teas usually available in the church. *Adm £1 Acc chd free (Share to All Saints Church, Lydd®). Suns April 17, July 17; Mon July 18 (2.30-5.30)*

By Appointment Gardens. See head of county section

Walnut Tree Gardens ৬৯৯ (Mr & Mrs M Oldaker) Swan Lane, Little Chart. 6m NW of Ashford. Leave A20 at Charing signed to Little Chart. At Swan public house turn W for Pluckley, gardens 500yds on L. Romantic 4-acre garden set in and around walls dating from early C18. Large collection of old roses; extensive range of unusual and interesting plants, shrubs and young trees. TEAS subject to weather. *Adm £1.50 Acc chd free (Share to German Shepherd Dog Rescue©). Suns May 29, June 5, 19, July 3, 10, 17, 31, Aug 7, 14, 28; Mons May 30, Aug 29 (2-5) Coaches by appt, please* **Tel 0233 840214**

39 Warwick Crescent ৯৯ (Mr & Mrs J G Sastre) Borstal, Rochester. From A229 Maidstone-Chatham at 2nd roundabout turn W into B2097 Borstal-Rochester rd; turn L at Priestfields, follow Borstal St to Wouldham Way, 3rd turning on R is Warwick Cres. Small front & rear plantsperson's gardens; most plants labelled; alpine terraces, peat & herbaceous beds; rockery with cascade & pool, bog garden, borders. Featured in NGS video 2, see page 344. *Adm £1 Acc chd free. Suns March 27, April 10, May 8, June 19 (2-6); also private visits welcome, please* **Tel 0634 401636**

Waystrode Manor ৬৯৯ (Mr & Mrs Peter Wright) Cowden, 4½m S of Edenbridge. From B2026 Edenbridge-Hartfield, turn off at Cowden Pound. Station: Weekdays Cowden; Suns Oxted or East Grinstead. 8 acres; large lawns, small grey garden, borders, ponds, bulbs, shrub roses and clematis. Subject of many magazine articles. All plants and shrubs labelled. House C15 (not open). Last entry ½-hour before closing time. TEAS. Gift shop. *Adm £2 Chd 50p. Suns May 22, June 12, 26 (2-6), Weds May 25, June 15 (1.30-5.30); also private visits welcome for groups*

¶**Weeks Farm** ৬৯ (Robin & Monica de Garston) Bedlam Lane, Egerton, 3½m E of Headcorn. Take Smarden Road out of Headcorn, Bedlam Lane is 3rd turning on L, Weeks Farm approx 1½m on R. 1½-acre garden on Wealden clay, showing varied use of badly drained site; double herbaceous borders flanking gateway, vista a feature; orchard with spring bulbs. Pond with abundance of wild life. TEAS. *Adm £1 Acc chd free. Suns March 13, June 12 (2-6)*

Went House ৬৯ (Mr & Mrs Robin Baring) Swan Street, West Malling. From A20, 6m W of Maidstone turn S onto A228. Turn E off High Street in village towards station. Queen Anne house with secret garden surrounded by high wall. Interesting plants, water gardens, woodland and parterre. TEAS. *Adm £1.50 Acc chd free (Share to Lane-Fox Respiratory Patients Assoc, St Thomas's Hospital®). Suns June 19, July 3 (2-6)*

West Farleigh Hall ৬ (Mr and Mrs Stephen Norman) 4½m W of Maidstone, turn S off A26 Maidstone-Tonbridge rd at Teston Bridge turn W at T-junction, garden on L. Roses, herbaceous borders, woodland walk. TEA. *Adm £1.50 Acc chd free. Sun July 10 (2-5)*

Regular Openers. Too many days to include in diary. Usually there is a wide range of plants giving year-round interest. See head of county section for the name and garden description for times etc.

West Studdal Farm ৬৯ (Mr & Mrs Peter Lumsden) West Studdal, N of Dover half-way between Eastry and Whitfield. From Eastry take A256, after 2½m pass Plough & Harrow, then 2nd L and 1st R, entrance ¼m on L. From Whitfield roundabout take A256, after 2½m pass High & Dry public house, ¼m fork R at 3-way junction, entrance ½m on R. Medium-sized garden around old farmhouse set by itself in small valley; herbaceous borders, roses and fine lawns protected by old walls and beech hedges. TEAS in Duodecagonal folly. *Adm £1.25 Chd 50p. Sun Aug 21 (2-6)*

Westview ৯ (Mr & Mrs J G Jackson) Spekes Rd, Hempstead. From M2 take A278 to Gillingham; at 1st roundabout follow sign to Wigmore, proceed to junction with Fairview Av, turn L & park on motorway link rd bridge, walk into Spekes Rd, Westview 3rd on L. ¼-acre town garden on very sloping site with many steps; good collection of plants & shrubs suitable for a chalk soil; designed by owners for all-year interest and low maintenance. Good autumn colour. TEAS. *Adm £1 Acc chd free. Weds April 20, May 18; Sats April 23, May 21 (2-5); also private visits welcome, please* **Tel 0634 230987**

¶**Whitehill** ৯ (Mrs Henderson) Wrotham. On A20 at Wrotham, between junctions 2A (M26) and 2 (M20). 3-acre garden, incl 1½ acres with design by Gertrude Jekyll in 1919, now carefully restored from original plans. *Adm £1.50 Chd 50p (Share to Kent Air Ambulance©). Sun June 5 (2-5.30)*

Whitehurst ৬৯ (Mr & Mrs John Mercy) Chainhurst, 3m N of Marden. From Marden station turn R into Pattenden Lane and under railway bridge; at T-junction turn L; at next fork bear R to Chainhurst, then second turning on L. 1½ acres of trees, roses & water garden. Tree walk. Exhibition of root dwellings. *Adm £1 Chd 50p (Share to Stroke Assoc®). Suns April 17, Aug 28, Sept 4, Oct 9; Mon May 30 (2-5.30)*

Withersdane Hall ৬৯ (University of London) Wye College, Wye, NE of Ashford. A28 take fork signed Wye. Bus EK 601 Ashford-Canterbury via Wye. Well-labelled garden of educational and botanical interest, containing several small carefully designed gardens; flower and shrub borders; spring bulbs; herb garden. Rain-fed garden. Free guide book with map available. TEAS. *Adm £1.50 Chd 50p. Suns April 24, July 10, Aug 7, Sept 4 (2-5)*

Woodlands Manor ৯৯ (Mr & Mrs Colin B George) Adisham, 5m SE of Canterbury. On A2 Canterbury-Dover, leave at sign to **Barham** ⅔m; at bottom of exit rd turn sharp L, follow signs marking rd to house, 1m. Approaching from E, from Adisham village turn R at end of The Street; at Woodlands Farm, ¾m on, follow signs. Station: Adisham. Small Georgian house of architectural interest (not open) set in old walled gardens. Spring garden a speciality; pleached lime and woodland walks; sunny corners; rose garden; gazebo. Good vistas; park. Picnics allowed. TEAS. *Adm £1.50 Acc chd under 12 free. Suns Feb 6, 20 (snowdrops, 2-5), March 20 to May 22 (2-5), June 12 to 30 (2-6); Weds March 24 to May 18 (2-5), June 15, 22, 29 (2-6). For NGS Suns Feb 13 (2-5), March 27, June 12 (2-6)*

Woodpeckers ⚘❀ (Mrs J Cronk & Mr D Dyer) Cannongate Road, Hythe. A259 Hythe-Folkestone rd ½m from Hythe, N end of Cannongate Road. ⅓-acre cliff top garden with views over Hythe Bay, well stocked with collection of plants specially suited to coastal conditions. Refreshments. *Adm £1 Chd 25p. Sun July 31 (2-5). Private visits welcome by appt, please* Tel 0303 266735

Worth Gardens ♿⚘❀ 2m SE of Sandwich and 5m NW of Deal, from A258 signed Worth. A group of cottage gardens in wide variety in peaceful village setting. Maps and tickets available at each garden. TEAS. *Combined adm £1.50 Chd 25p. Sun July 3 (2-5)*

¶**Wyckhurst** ♿⚘ (Mr & Mrs C D Older) Mill Road, Aldington, 4m SE of Ashford. Leave M20 at junction 10, on A20 travel S to Aldington turning; proceed 1½m to Aldington village hall, 'Walnut Tree' take rd signed to Dymchurch, after ¼m turn R into Mill Road is on R. C16 cottage (not open) surrounded by 1-acre cottage garden; old roses; herbaceous borders; unusual perennials. Extensive views across Romney Marsh. TEAS in aid of Bonnington Church. *Adm £1.50 Chd 50p. Wed June 22; Sun June 26 (11-6)*

Yalding Gardens ⚘❀ 6m SW of Maidstone, three gardens S & W of village. *Combined adm £2 Chd £1. Sun April 3 (2-5.30)*

    Congelow House ❀ (Mrs D J Cooper) S of village on B2162. For garden description see individual entry

    Long Acre (Mr & Mrs G P Fyson) is on L in Cheveney Farm Lane, just off Yalding-Hunton rd (Vicarage Road) ⅓m from Yalding War Memorial. Long, narrow garden comprising shrubberies, lawns, a vegetable and fruit garden and a paddock with young specimen trees. Shrubberies have been recently developed to eliminate the work in maintaining flower beds. TEAS in aid of RNLI

    Parsonage Oasts ⚘❀ (Mr & the Hon Mrs Raikes) Between Yalding village and station turn off at Anchor public house over bridge over canal, continue 100yds up the lane. ¾-acre riverside garden with walls, shrubs, daffodils

Lancashire, Merseyside & Greater Manchester

Hon County Organisers: Mr & Mrs R Doldon, Old Barn Cottage, Greens Arms Road, Torton Nr Bolton BL7 0ND Tel 0204 852139

Assistant Hon County Organiser: J Bowker Esq, Swiss Cottage, 8 Hammond Drive, Read, Burnley

DATES OF OPENING

By appointment
For telephone numbers and other details see garden descriptions. Private visits welcomed

Cross Gaits Cottage, Blacko
Lindeth Dene, Silverdale
Stonestack, nr Turton

Regular openings
For details see garden descriptions

Sellet Hall Gardens, Whittington
    daily March to Sept 30

April 10 Sunday
    Lindeth Dene, Silverdale
May 1 Sunday
    Bank House, Borwick
May 8 Sunday
    Spring Bank House, Cow Ark
May 22 Sunday
    191 Liverpool Road South, Maghull
    Loxley, Wrightington, nr Wigan
    Swiss Cottage, Read

May 29 Sunday
    Catforth Gardens, Catforth
    Cross Gaits Cottage, Blacko
    Lindeth Dene, Silverdale
    191 Liverpool Road South, Maghull
    Montford Cottage, Fence, nr Burnley
    Old Barn Cottage, Turton
May 30 Monday
    Cross Gaits Cottage, Blacko
    Montford Cottage, Fence, nr Burnley
    Old Barn Cottage, Turton
June 5 Sunday
    Bank House, Borwick
    Rufford Old Hall, Rufford, nr Ormskirk
    Skeke Hall, The Walk, Liverpool
June 12 Sunday
    Loxley, Wrightington, nr Wigan
    Mill Barn, Salmesbury Bottoms
    Swiss Cottage, Read
June 25 Saturday
    Clearbeck House, Tatham Green
June 26 Sunday
    Catforth Gardens, Catforth
    Clearbeck House, Tatham Green
    Mill Barn, Salmesbury Bottoms
    Windle Hall, St Helens

July 3 Sunday
    Bank House, Borwick
    Lindeth Dene, Silverdale
    Spring Bank House, Cow Ark
July 10 Sunday
    Weeping Ash, Glazebury
July 17 Sunday
    Cross Gaits Cottage, Blacko
July 24 Sunday
    Greyfriars, Walker Lane, Fulwood, Preston
July 31 Sunday
    Catforth Gardens, Catforth
August 7 Sunday
    Bank House, Borwick
August 21 Sunday
    Old Barn Cottage, Turton
August 27 Saturday
    Stonestack, Turton
August 28 Sunday
    Stonestack, Turton
August 29 Monday
    Stonestack, Turton
September 4 Sunday
    Bank House, Borwick
    Windle Hall, St Helens
September 11 Sunday
    Weeping Ash, Glazebury
October 2 Sunday
    Bank House, Borwick

DESCRIPTIONS OF GARDENS

Bank House ⚹❀ (Mr & Mrs R G McBurnie) Borwick. 2m NE of Carnforth off A6. Leave M6 at junction 35. Plantsman's garden of 2 acres designed to provide all year round shape, colour and form. Divided into different areas of interest including shady borders, sunny gravel area with old-fashioned roses, arboretum, fruit and vegetables. Island beds, silver and gold borders. Collection of carnivorous plants. Featured in 'English Private Gardens'. TEAS. *Adm £1 Chd 25p. Suns May 1, June 5, July 3, Aug 7, Sept 4, Oct 2 (2-6)*

Catforth Gardens ⭐❀ Leave M6 at junction 32 turning N on A6. Turn L at 1st set of traffic lights; 2m to T-junction, turn R. Turn L at sign for Catforth, L at next T-junction, 1st R into Benson Lane. Bear L at church into Roots Lane. Includes adjoining garden of Willowbridge Farm with access through Catforth Gardens Nursery. TEAS NGS days only. *Combined adm £1 Chd 10p. Suns May 29, June 26, July 31 (12-5) adjacent nursery open March 19 to Sept 18 (10.30-5). Parties by appt, please* **Tel 0772 690561/690269**

> **Catforth Gardens Nursery** (Mr & Mrs T A Bradshaw) 1-acre informal country garden, planted for year round interest and colour. Wide variety of unusual shrubs; trees; rhododendrons, azaleas; unusual and rare herbaceous plants including euphorbias, dicentras, pulmonarias; ground cover plants; national collection of hardy geraniums; 2 ponds with bog gardens, large rockery and woodland garden
>
> **Willow Bridge Farm** (Mr & Mrs W Moore) ¼-acre garden planted with a wide variety of herbaceous perennials (many rare & unusual). Planted with particular attention to colour from spring to autumn, giving a cottage garden effect

Clearbeck House ❀ (Peter & Bronwen Osborne) Higher Tatham about 12m E of Lancaster. Follow A683 then B6480 to Wray, turn R on by-road up the pretty Hindburn Valley through Millhouses. Turn R again and follow signs. From terraces and borders near the house, vistas lead into surrounding meadows and hills. Varied planting in the still developing garden includes bog, rose and herbaceous areas. A pyramid grotto within a symbolic garden and wildlife lakes are recent additions. This is essentially a garden to walk in and has its surprises. Partially suitable for wheelchairs. TEAS in aid of Save the Children Fund. *Adm £1 Chd 50p. Sat, Sun, June 25, 26 (11-5)*

Cross Gaits Cottage ⚹❀ (Mr & Mrs S J Gude) Take M65 exit junction 13. Follow Barrowford signs then Barnoldswick signs. Garden 1½m on Barnoldswick Road opp Cross Gaits Inn. ⅔-acre walled cottage garden, shrub and herbaceous borders. 2 ornamental ponds. 700ft above sea level; fine view of Pennines. TEA/coffee. *Adm £1 Chd 50p. Sun, Mon May 29, 30, Sun July 17 (12-5). Private visits welcome, please* **Tel 0282 617163**

By Appointment Gardens. These owners do not have a fixed opening day usually because they do not like crowds or have insufficient parking space. Owner will often give guided tour.

Greyfriars ⭐⚹ (Mr & Mrs William Harrison) Walker Lane, Fulwood, 2m N of Preston. junction 32 off M6 (M55); S to Preston; at Black Bull Xrds right to Boys Lane Xrds ½m entrance on R. 8 acres; lawns, rose beds, fuchsias; 5 greenhouses with hybrid begonias, geraniums and carnations; fountains and water display. TEAS. *Adm £1.50 Chd 50p. Sun July 24 (2-5.30)*

Lindeth Dene ⭐❀ (Mrs B M Kershaw) 38 Lindeth Rd, Silverdale. 13m N of Lancaster. Take M6 to junction 35, turn L (S) on A6 to Carnforth traffic lights. Turn R follow signs Silverdale. After level crossing ¼m uphill turn L down Hollins Lane. At T junction turn R into Lindeth Rd. Garden is 4th gateway on L, park in rd. Approx 1¼ acres overlooking Morecombe Bay on W facing slope. Large limestone rock garden, trees, shrubs, hardy perennials, troughs, pools, heather garden, veganic kitchen garden with raised beds. Collections of saxifrages, geraniums, New Zealand plants. Teas and toilets available in village. *Adm £1 Acc chd free. Suns April 10, May 29, July 3 (2-5). Private visits welcome, please* **Tel 0524 701314**

191 Liverpool Rd South ⭐❀ (Mr & Mrs D Cheetham) Maghull. From A59 take turning for Maghull Town Centre. Turn L at traffic lights and veer R over canal bridge. Garden ¼m on R. ½-acre suburban garden; rhododendrons, azaleas, camellias, rockery, pool, sink gardens, primulas, a variety of trees (some unusual), shrubs, bulbs and herbaceous plants for all year colour in the smaller garden. TEA or coffee. *Adm £1 Acc chd free. Suns May 22, 29 (1.30-5.30)*

Loxley ⭐❀ (Mr & Mrs D Robinson) Robin Hood Lane, Wrightington, nr Wigan. Situated 1m from junction 27 of the M6. Continue past Wrightington Hospital to Xrds, turn R by the garage ½m up the rd situated on the L. ¼-acre garden designed on two levels with water feature & ornamental fish pond. Variety of shrubs, conifers, rhododendrons, azaleas and perennials. TEA. *Adm £1 Acc chd free. Suns May 22, June 12 (12-5)*

Mill Barn ⭐⚹❀ (Dr C J Mortimer) Goose Foot Close, Samlesbury Bottoms, Preston. 6m E of Preston. From M6 junction 31 2½m on A59/A677 B/burn. Turn S. Nabs Head Lane, then Goose Foot Lane 1m. 1-acre tranquil, terraced garden on banks of R Darwen. Mixed planting with many uncommon perennial plants on the site of C18 corn and cotton mills. A garden which is still developing. TEAS. *Adm £1 Chd free. Suns June 12, 26 (2-6)*

Montford Cottage ⭐❀ (C Bullock & A P Morris) Fence, nr Burnley. Situated on the B6248 between Brierfield and Fence. From the M65 junction 13, take the A6068 (signs for Fence) and in 2m turn L onto the B6248 (signs for Brierfield). Proceed down the hill for ½m, entrance to garden is on L (near dangerous bend-drivers please take care). Comparatively young walled garden ⅔-acre developed over last 9 yrs and now maturing, with many unusual plants of particular interest to flower arrangers and plantsmen. Particular emphasis on variety of foliage, with varied shrubs, trees, herbaceous plants and pools and featuring new oriental garden. No coaches. TEAS. *Adm £1 Chd 50p. Sun, Mon, May 29, 30 (2-6)*

Old Barn Cottage &❀ (Mr & Mrs R Doldon) Greens Arms Rd, Turton. Midway between Bolton and Darwen on B6391 off A666, or through Chapeltown Village High St (B6391). 1-acre developing garden on moorland site. Spring flowering trees; shrubs; azaleas, rhododendrons; water garden; heathers; conifers, herbaceous beds; moorland views. TEAS in aid of Birtenshaw Hall Special School for Handicapped (May), Beacon Counselling Service (Aug). *Adm £1 Chd free. Sun, Mon, May 29, 30, Sun Aug 21 (1-5)*

¶**Rufford Old Hall** & (The National Trust) Rufford. On A59 Liverpool to Preston rd in village of Rufford, 7m N of Ormskirk. Set in 14 acres of garden and woodland. Informal garden and walks. Spectacular in May and June for spring flowering rhododendrons and azaleas. TEAS. *Adm £1.60 Chd 80p (Garden only). Sun June 5 (12-4.30)*

● **Sellet Hall Gardens** &❀❀ (Mr & Mrs Gray) 1m SW of Kirkby Lonsdale. From A65 take turning signed Burton & Hutton Roof follow rd up until brown tourist signs indicate the garden. Garden approx 3½ acres including a herb garden formally laid out. Wild garden, bog area, parterre, shrub and herbaceous borders. The garden has a nursery open all year. TEA. *Adm £1 Acc chd free. The garden is open daily from March to end Sept*

Speke Hall &❀ (The National Trust) Liverpool. 8m SE of Liverpool adjacent to Liverpool Airport. Follow signs for Liverpool Airport. A formal garden with herbaceous border, rose garden; moated area with formal lawns. A stream garden now open this yr. A wild wood is included. Approx size of estate 35 acres. TEAS. *Adm £1 Chd 50p. (Garden only). Sun June 5 (12-5.30)*

Spring Bank House ❀❀ (Joan & Philip Lord) Cow Ark. Situated 6m NW of Clitheroe between Bashall Eaves and Whitewell within ½m of Browsholme Hall, which is well signposted. From Clitherow take Longridge Rd (B6243) then take 1st R after Edisford Bridge Hotel. A country garden of 6½-acres, made and maintained by the owners since 1975. Stretching away from the house, 2 acres of informal garden are planted with a large variety of trees, shrubs and herbaceous plants, many of them unusual, to provide yr-round interest; while the remaining 4½ acres make up the woodland garden. This steeply wooded valley planted with species rhododendrons, acers, magnolias and other woodland plants, together with many native wild flowers. TEA in aid of St Michael's Church, Whitewell. *Adm £1 Chd 50p. Suns May 8, July 3 (1-5.30)*

Stonestack &❀❀ (Frank Smith Esq) 283 Chapeltown Rd, Turton; 4½m N of Bolton, via A666 leading to B6391 nr Turton Tower. 2½-acre garden; shrubs, rhododendrons, azaleas; herbaceous borders; rockeries, waterfall, ornamental fishpond, fountain, rose garden, bog garden, fuchsias and abutilons a special feature; sweet peas, soft fruit area; orchard, greenhouses and plant houses. As seen on BBC Gardener's World 1985 and BBC Look North TV Aug 88. TEA (Tea/plant sales to Bleakholt Animal Sanctuary). *Adm £1 Acc chd free. Sat, Sun, Mon Aug 27, 28, 29 (2-6). Private visits welcome July & August, please* Tel 0204 852460

Swiss Cottage ❀ (James & Doreen Bowker) 8 Hammond Drive, Read. 3m SE of Whalley on A671 Whalley to Burnley Road, turn by Pollards Garage, up George Lane to T junction, L into Private Rd. 1½-acre Hillside Garden designed on two levels in mature woodland setting, outstanding views. Variety of shrubs, trees, rhododendrons, azaleas, perennials and alpines. Stream and bog garden feature. Featured in Lancashire Life. TEAS. *Adm £1 Chd free. Suns May 22, June 12 (1-5)*

Weeping Ash ❀ (John Bent Esq) Glazebury. ¼m S A580 (East Lancs Rd Greyhound roundabout, Leigh) on A574 Glazebury/Leigh Boundary. 1-acre garden of year long interest on heavy soil. A broad sweep of lawn surrounded by deep mixed borders of shrubs and herbaceous perennials gives way to secret areas with a wide range of planting. A pool with candelabra primulas; a rose bed with gazebo; island beds of penstemons, conifers and heathers. Rhododendrons and sorbus are just a few of the features of this garden undergoing continuous review and development. Teas 100yds N at Garden Centre. *Adm £1 Chd 50p (Shore to Macmillan Leigh Home Care Unit®). Suns July 10, Sept 11 (2-6)*

Windle Hall &❀ (The Lady Pilkington) N of E Lancs Rd, St Helens. 5m W of M6 via E Lancs Rd, nr Southport junction. Entrance by bridge over E Lancs Rd. 200yr-old walled garden surrounded by 5-acres of lawns and woodland full of spring flowers; rock and water garden; Victorian thatched cottage. Tufa stone grotto; herbaceous borders, pergola and rose gardens containing exhibition blooms, miniature ornamental ponies, pheasants; greenhouses. TEAS. *Adm £1 Chd 50p. Suns June 26, Sept 4 (2-5)*

Regular Openers. See head of county section.

Leicestershire & Rutland

Hon County Organisers: (Leicestershire) Mr John Oakland, Old School Cottage, Oaks-in-Charnwood, nr Loughborough LE12 9YD Tel 0509 502676
(Rutland) Mrs R Wheatley, Clipsham House, Oakham LE15 7SE
Tel 0780 410238

Hon County Treasurer (Rutland):   A Whitamore Esq., The Stockyard, West Street, Easton-on-the-Hill, Stamford, Lincs PE9 3LS

DATES OF OPENING

By appointment
For telephone number and other details see garden descriptions. Private visits welcomed

15 Creaton Court, Wigston
7 Hall Road, Burbage Gardens, Burbage
Long Close, Woodhouse Eaves
Orchards, Walton nr Lutterworth
Paddocks, Shelbrook, Ashby-de-la-Zouch
Stepping Stones Old Farm, Little Beeby
Stoke Albany House, Market Harborough
Vine Cottage, Sheepy Magna Gardens, Atherstone
Whatton House, Loughborough

Regular openings
For details see garden descriptions

Arthingworth Manor, Market Harborough Every Weds May, June, July
Whatton House, nr Loughborough Suns, Weds, Easter to end Aug, Bank Hol Mons

March 17 Thursday
Burbage Gardens, Burbage
March 27 Sunday
Long Close, Woodhouse Eaves
April 4 Monday
Gunthorpe, Oakham
April 5 Tuesday
Whatton House, Loughborough
April 11 Sunday
Exton Park, Oakham
April 17 Sunday
Paddocks, Shelbrook, Ashby-de-la-Zouch
Rose Cottage, Owston, nr Oakham
April 20 Wednesday
Paddocks, Shelbrook, Ashby-de-la-Zouch
April 21 Thursday
Burbage Gardens, Burbage
April 24 Sunday
Ashwell Lodge, Oakham

May 1 Sunday
Belvoir Lodge, nr Grantham ‡
Hoby Gardens, Hoby, nr Melton Mowbray
Reservoir Cottage, Knipton ‡
May 8 Sunday
Wakerley Manor, Uppingham
May 12 Thursday
Burbage Gardens, Burbage
May 15 Sunday
Burrough House, Melton Mowbray
Derwen, Coalville
Long Close, Woodhouse Eaves
May 22 Sunday
Ashwell House, Oakham
Paddocks, Shelbrook, Ashby-de-la-Zouch
May 25 Wednesday
Paddocks, Shelbrook, Ashby-de-la-Zouch
May 29 Sunday
Long Close, Woodhouse Eaves
May 31 Tuesday
Whatton House, Loughborough
June 5 Sunday
The Bell House, Lyddington, Oakham
Park Farm, Normanton, Bottesford (see Nottinghamshire)
Woodyton Farmhouse, Coalville
June 12 Sunday
Burbage Gardens, Burbage
Prebendal House, Empingham
June 18 Saturday
Sheepy Magna Gardens, Atherstone
June 19 Sunday
Arthingworth Manor, Market Harborough
Beeby Manor, Beeby ‡
The Old Rectory, Teigh
Queniborough Gardens, Leicester ‡
Sheepy Magna Gardens, Atherstone
June 22 Wednesday
Beeby Manor, Beeby
Orchards, Walton, nr Lutterworth
June 26 Sunday
Barkby Hall, nr Syston
Clipsham Gardens, Oakham
Derwen, Coalville ‡
The Gables, Thringstone ‡
Hoby Gardens, Hoby, nr Melton Mowbray

Orchards, Walton, nr Lutterworth
Sutton Bonington Hall, Sutton Bonington
July 3 Sunday
Paddocks, Shelbrook, Ashby-de-la-Zouch
Preston Gardens, Uppingham
South Luffenham Hall, nr Stamford
July 5 Tuesday
Stoke Albany House, Market Harborough
July 6 Wednesday
Paddocks, Shelbrook, Ashby-de-la-Zouch
Stoke Albany House, Market Harborough
July 10 Sunday
Stoke Albany House, Market Harborough
July 12 Tuesday
Stoke Albany House, Market Harborough
July 13 Wednesday
Stoke Albany House, Market Harborough
July 16 Saturday
The Gardens of Plungar, Leicester
July 17 Sunday
The Gardens of Plungar, Leicester
Woodyton Farmhouse, Coalville
July 24 Sunday
Aylestone Gardens, Leicester ‡
Market Bosworth Gardens, Nuneaton
University of Leicester Botanic Garden, Oadby ‡
August 14 Sunday
Paddocks, Shelbrook, Ashby-de-la-Zouch
August 17 Wednesday
Paddocks, Shelbrook, Ashby-de-la-Zouch
September 18 Sunday
Brooksby College, nr Melton Mowbray
Whatton House, Loughborough
October 2 Sunday
1700 Melton Road, Rearsby
October 9 Sunday
Whatton House, Loughborough

DESCRIPTIONS OF GARDENS

Arthingworth Manor ❀ (Mr & Mrs W Guinness) 5m S of Market Harborough. From Market Harborough via A508 at 4m L to Arthingworth; from Northampton via A508. At Kelmarsh turn R at bottom of hill for Arthingworth. In village turn R at church 1st L. 6 to 7-acre beautiful garden; collection shrub roses; white garden; delphiniums, herbaceous and mixed borders; greenhouses. Newly planted 3-acre arboretum. Original house now restored. TEA. Limited wheelchair access. *Adm £1.20 Chd 50p (Share to St John Ambulance, Northants®). Weds, May, June, July; Sun June 19 (2-5)*

Ashwell House &.& (Mr & Mrs S D Pettifer) 3m N of Oakham, via B668 towards Cottesmore, turn L for Ashwell. 1½-acre vicarage garden, 1812; vegetable garden; almost original format partly given over to specialist flowers for drying. Pleasure garden with summer pavilion in classical style and architectural features by George Carter. TEAS. Home-made produce stall. *Adm £1 Chd 50p (Share to St Mary's Church®). Sun May 22 (2-6)*

Ashwell Lodge &.&.& (Mrs B V Eve) Ashwell, 3m N of Oakham. From Al, 10m N of Stamford, turn W through Greetham and Cottesmore; then turn R for Ashwell. Park in village st. Medium-sized garden redesigned by Percy Cane c.1973; spring bulbs; herbaceous borders, paved rose garden, shrubs, greenhouse. As featured in 'Country Life' Nov 1990. TEAS. *Adm £1 Chd free (Share to Forces Help Soc & Lord Roberts Workshops®). Sun April 24 (2-6)*

¶Aylestone Gardens On A426 out of Leicester, through Aylestone, ½m onwards on Lutterworth Rd just before the Soar Valley Way. Unrestricted parking on main rd. TEAS. *Combined adm £1.25 Chd 50p (Share to St. Andrew's Parish Church®) Sun July 24 (2-6)*
  ¶48 Lutterworth Rd &.& (Mr & Mrs J R Schofield) ½-acre garden with lawns and mixed borders. Incl shrubbery and vegetable garden. Features Italian garden with pool
  ¶52 Lutterworth Rd &.& (Mr & Mrs N D Cooper) ½-acre formal garden with lawns and borders. Large formal ornamental pools
  ¶65 Lutterworth Rd &.& (Mr & Mrs A Dickson) ⅓-acre garden containing mixed beds and borders, conifer bed and shrubbery. Incl large variety of shrubs and herbaceous perennials

Barkby Hall &.& (Mr & Mrs A J Pochin) Barkby, nr Syston. 5m NE of Leicester. Woodland garden; azaleas, rhododendrons, ericas, conifers, roses, herbaceous, shrubs; mature trees; scented garden; interesting church nearby. TEAS. *Adm £1 Chd 25p (Share to Barkby Church Fabric Fund®). Sun June 26 (3-6)*

Beeby Manor &.&.& (Mr & Mrs Philip Bland) Beeby. 8m E of Leicester. Turn off A47 in Thurnby and follow signs through Scraptoft. 3-acre mature garden with venerable yew hedges, walled herbaceous border, lily ponds, rose towers and box parterre. Plus the start of a 1-acre arboretum. C16 and C18 house (not open). TEAS. *Adm £1.60 Chd 30p (Share to Village Tree Project©). Sun, Wed June 19, 22 (2-6)*

The Bell House &.& (Mrs F Borgerhoff Mulder) Lyddington. 1½m S of Uppingham between A6003 and B672. Small old-world walled garden, roses, other good plants. Close to C12 Bede House. TEA. *Adm £1 Chd 50p. Sun June 5 (2-6)*

Belvoir Lodge &.& (Mr & Mrs J S Wood) 7m W of Grantham. Between A52 and A607, nr Belvoir Castle opp Estate Office gates. Medium-sized garden; roses and delphiniums. TEAS. *Adm £1 Chd free. Sun May 1 (2-6)*

Brooksby College &.&.& 6m SW of Melton Mowbray. From A607 (9m from Leicester or 6m from Melton Mowbray) turn at Brooksby; entrance 100yds. Bus: Leicester-Melton Mowbray-Grantham; alight Brooksby turn, 100yds. Grounds inc extensive lawns, lake, ornamental brook, flowering shrub borders, heather bed, large collection young trees; other ornamental features; glasshouses, nursery. Church built 1220 open. TEA. *Adm £1 Chd free. Sun Sept 18 (1-5)*

Burbage Gardens ❀ From M69 junction 1, take B4109 signed Hinckley. *Combined adm £1.50 Chd 20p (Share to LOROS®). Sun June 12 (11-5)*
  6 Denis Road &.❀ (Mr & Mrs D A Dawkins) Sketchley Manor Estate. 1st L after roundabout. Small garden planted for scent with alpine house, scree area, alpines in troughs, herbaceous borders with old roses; collection of clematis and spring bulbs. *Also open Thurs March 17, April 21 & May 12 (2-5). Combined adm with 7 Hall Rd, 80p on Thurs. TEA Thurs only. Also private visits welcome, please Tel 0455 230509*
  7 Hall Road Burbage (Mr & Mrs D R Baker) Sketchley Manor Estate. From Hinckley; 1st roundabout 1st L to Sketchley Lane; 1st R; 1st R; 1st R again; 1st L to Hall Rd. Medium-sized garden; mixed borders; alpines; sink gardens; scree area; collection of hellebores and hosta; unusual plants; foliage plants. Also open March 17, April 21, May 12 (2-5). *Combined adm with 6, Denis Rd 80p on Thurs. Also private visits welcome, please Tel 0455 635616*
  The Long Close &. (Mr & Mrs A J Hopewell) Bullfurlong Lane, Burbage. From Hinckley, 1st R onto Coventry Road 2nd R onto Bullfurlong Lane, garden on L. Limited parking, park if poss on Coventry Rd. ½-acre family garden. Mixed borders; 'natural' ponds; vegetable plot; greenhouse and cool orchid house. Local orchid society in attendance. Cream TEAS, ploughman's lunches; toilets
  11 Primrose Drive (Mr & Mrs D Leach) Take 2nd turning on R into Sketchley Rd. 1st L into Azalea Drive, 1st R into Marigold Drive, 1st L Begonia Drive, 1st R into Primrose Drive. No 11 is on L on bend. Small cottage garden, large collection of clematis and paeonies. Plants and pressed flower work for sale

¶Burrough House &.&.& (Mrs Barbara Keene) Burrough on the Hill. 6m W of Oakham, 5m S of Melton Mowbray. From A606 at Langham, take rd signposted to Cold Overton and Somerby, continue through Somerby to Burrough on the Hill. Approx 5½ acres of garden with an interesting small collection of rhododendrons and azaleas in late May; spring bulbs highlighted in 2 woodland walks; a timber, thatch-roofed Bower House used by the Prince of Wales and Mrs Simpson; cascading water pools and rose garden. The garden was created by an enthusiastic plantsman, Sir Raymond Greene in the early 1920's and retains much of his original structural concepts. TEAS. *Adm £1.50 Chd free (St Mary's Church Roof Appeal®). Sun May 15 (2.30-6)*

By Appointment Gardens. These owners do not have a fixed opening day usually because they do not like crowds or have insufficient parking space. Owner will often give guided tour.

Clipsham Gardens &. On B 668 2m E of A1 NE of Oakham. TEAS Clipsham House. *Combined adm £1.50 Chd 25p (Share to St Mary's Church©). Sun June 26 (2-6)*

Clipsham Hall (Sir David & Lady Davenport Handley) 5-acres; shrubs, roses; yew avenue (access from road only). House c1780

Clipsham House ✿ (Mr & Mrs Robert Wheatley) 2-acres around early C19 former Rectory; lawns, good trees, walled garden with summer house; herbaceous borders, roses, variety of shrubs, folly in small park featured in 'The Gardener' magazine. Featured in NGS video 1, see page 344

¶15 Creaton Court ⚘✿ (Mrs P Thornett) Leicester. 4m SE of Leicester via A50. Opp police/fire station, turn up Kelmarsh Ave., go up hill, just past shops/public house turn R into Creaton Rd, Creaton Court at end on L. Very small established garden, alpines in troughs, scree, raised bed. Herbaceous borders with penstemons, campanulas, unusual climbers and shrubs; tree paeonies and clematis; small pond and bog area with arum lilies, lobelia etc. Front garden, conifers, heathers, bulbs etc plus summer bedding and baskets. *Adm 50p. Private visits welcome during May to Aug, please* Tel 0533 880538

Derwen ⚘✿ (Dr & Mrs Martin Wenham) 68a Greenhill Rd, Coalville. From A50 (Coalville by-pass) take the turning to Shepshed, then fork R at St David's Church, ½m on R. From B587 turn into top of Greenhill Road near Bull's Head, 1m on L. Town garden, largely redesigned and reconstructed during 1988-9 to give a wide variety of shape and texture using simple local materials. Planting is of perennials and shrubs with an emphasis on form and foliage. TEA. *Adm 75p Chd 20p (Share to Army Benevolent Fund®). Suns May 15, June 26 (2-6)*

Exton Park &.⚘ (Viscount & Viscountess Campden) 5m E of Oakham. 8m from Stamford off A1 (A606 turning). Extensive park, lawns, specimen trees and shrubs, lakes, private chapel and C19 house (not open). Good show of daffodils. TEAS. *Adm £1.50 Chd 50p (Share to Rutland House Community Trust©). Sun April 11 (2-6)*

The Gables &.⚘✿ (Mr & Mrs P J Baker) Main Street, Thringstone. Leave A512 Loughborough to Ashby de la Zouch rd at Bull's Head, sign-posted Thringstone. Main St is off the village green. ⅓-acre country garden. Herbaceous borders, many unusual plants, containers, clematis and old roses. Grade II listed cottage not open. TEAS. *Adm £1 Chd 25p. Sun June 26 (2-6)*

Gunthorpe &. (A T C Haywood Esq) 2m S of Oakham. On Uppingham Rd; entrance by 3 cottages, on R going S. Medium-sized garden; springs flowers and flowering trees in good setting. TEAS. *Adm £1.50 Chd 50p (Share to C.R.M.F.®). Easter Mon Apr 4 (2-5.30)*

Hoby Gardens ⚘ 8m NE of Leicester, 1m NW of A607 Leicester-Melton rd. Turn at Brooksby Agricultural College. *Combined adm £1.25 Chd free (Share to St John's Ambulance® and Riding for the Disabled®). Suns May 1, June 26 (2-6)*

Glebe House &.✿ (Mr & Mrs J M Peck) Church Lane. 1 acre of shrubs and herbaceous mixed borders, created since 1977, mainly within lovely C18 wall; paddock, vegetable garden. Pleasing views over glebe land. TEAS

Rooftree Cottage (D Headly Esq) Main Street. Small garden to a medieval cruck cottage. The site slopes down towards the R Wreake and the garden is planned to lead to pastoral views across the valley. Traditional and indigenous plantings

Long Close ✿ (Mrs George Johnson) 60 Main St, Woodhouse Eaves, S of Loughborough. From A6, W in Quorn B591. 5 acres rhododendrons (many varieties), azaleas, flowering shrubs, old shrub roses, many rare shrubs, trees, heathers, conifers, forest trees; lily pools; fountain; terraced lawns. Featured in *Country Life* TEA March 27, May 15. TEAS May 29. Specialist plant sale March 27, May 29. *Adm £1.50 Chd free. Sun March 27, (2-5) May 15, 29 (2-6). Also private visits welcome March to June, please* Tel 0509 890616 *business hrs*

Market Bosworth Gardens &. 1m off A447 Coalville to Hinckley Rd, 3m off A444. Pay on Market Bosworth Market Place. Village plan available. Other gardens will also open. TEAS. *Combined adm £1.50 Chd 50p. Sun July 24 (2-6)*

16 Northumberland Avenue ⚘ (Mr & Mrs K McCarthy) Newly landscaped garden

24 Northumberland Avenue ⚘ (Mr & Mrs E G Watkins) Flowers, shrubs and lawns

11 Stanley Road ⚘✿ (Mrs O Caldwell) Garden with flowers and shrubs

273 Station Road ⚘ (Mrs R J Baker) Flower garden and model village

8 Weston Drive ⚘ (Mr & Mrs J Earl-Davies) Flower garden, fuchsias a speciality

Witherstitch Farm (Ann Carter) Farm garden with rockery

1700 Melton Road ⚘✿ (Mr & Mrs J Kaye) Rearsby, N of Leicester on A607. In Rearsby, on L.H. side from Leicester. 1-acre developing garden with wide range of interesting herbaceous plants; some shrubs and trees. Nursery. *Adm 25p Chd 10p. Daily March to Oct (Wed to Sat 10-5.30, Sun 10-12). Also SPECIAL OPEN DAY Sun Oct 2 (2-5.30). Adm £1 Chd 30p (Share to Samaritans®). TEAS Oct 2 only*

The Old Rectory &.⚘✿ (Mr & Mrs D B Owen) Teigh. 5m N of Oakham. Between Wymondham and Ashwell; or from A1 via Thistleton and Market Overton. Medium-sized walled garden; mixed borders; good variety shrubs, herbaceous and climbing plants. Unusual C18 church next door. TEAS. *Adm £1 Chd free (Share to Holy Trinity Church, Teigh®). Sun June 19 (2-6)*

Orchards ⚘✿ (Mr & Mrs G Cousins) Hall Lane, Walton, nr Lutterworth. 8m S of Leicester via the A50 take a R turn just after Shearsby (sign-posted Bruntingthorpe); thereafter follow signs for Walton. 1-acre garden; courtyard with many unusual plants on the walls; orchard, rose, pool and wild gardens with a wide range of trees and shrubs. View over countryside. Featured on TV's Garden Club. TEAS. *Adm £1.20 Chd free. Wed June 22, Sun June 26 (2-5.30). Also private visits welcome June to Sept, please* Tel Lutterworth 556958

Paddocks &✗❀ (Mrs Ailsa Jackson) Shelbrook. 1½m W of Ashby-de-la-Zouch on B5003 towards Moira. A planta-holic's garden with over 2000 varieties in 1 acre incl snowdrops, hellebores, astrantias and many less common herbaceous plants & shrubs. Plants propagated from gar-den for sale. NCCPG collection of old named double and single primulas. Silver medallist at Chelsea and Vincent Square. TEA. *Adm £1 Chd free. Suns and Weds April 17, 20; May 22, 25, July 3, 6; Aug 14, 17 (2-5). Also private visits welcome, please* **Tel 0530 412606**

¶**Plungar Gardens** &❀ 16m E of Nottingham take A52, turn R 1m after Bingham. 12m N of Melton Mowbray via Scalford, Eastwell and Stathern. Art exhibition in church. Lunches and TEAS. *Combined adm £1.50 Chd free (Share to St Helen's Church®) Sat, Sun July 16, 17 (11-6)*

¶**Church House** (Mr & Mrs M S B Cross) Newly land-scaped garden, shrubs, flowers, trees (converted barn)
¶**Cordwainer's Cottage** (Mr & Mrs D A Wells) Shrubs, lawn, mixed borders, stream, vegetables
¶**Elsian Deane** (Mr & Mrs D Marriott) Cottage garden, mixed borders, annuals, vegetables
The Old Barn Gardens (G W Miller Esq & Mr & Mrs A E Pear) Trees, shrubs, lawns, view of lake

Other gardens open

Prebendal House & (Mr & Mrs J Partridge) Empingham. Between Stamford & Oakham on A606. House built in 1688; summer palace for the Bishop of Lincoln Recently improved old-fashioned gardens incl water garden, topi-ary and kitchen gardens. TEAS. *Adm £1.50 Chd 50p. Sun June 12 (2-6)*

Preston Gardens 2m N of Uppingham on A6003 be-tween Uppingham & Oakham. Teas in Village Hall. *Com-bined adm £2 Chd free (Share to Preston Village Hall©). Sun July 3 (2-6)*

Corner Cottage ✗ (Dr & Mrs T D Brentall). Small cot-tage garden
The Dower House &✗❀ (Mrs F G Norton-Fagge) Small garden; herbaceous, flowering shrubs and species roses; collection of clematis
14 Main Street &✗ (Mr & Mrs J B Goldring) ¾-acre village garden; several small borders of differing as-pect; tender wall shrubs; variety of climbers incl cle-matis, herbaceous plants, seasonal shrubs (particularly old roses), and bulbs
Preston Hall &❀ (Captain & Mrs Micklethwait) Magnificent views on 3 sides and the garden is planned to frame and complement these. Formal rose garden and a collection of shrub roses with many other shrubs and herbaceous plants

¶**Queniborough Gardens** ✗❀ A607 N out of Leicester. 6m from Leicester. 9m from Melton Mowbray. *Combined adm £1 Chd free. Sun June 19 (11-5).*

¶**21 Barkby Road** (Mr & Mrs P Hemingray) Small, to-tally organic plantswoman's garden, planned for wild-life. 2 ponds, greenhouse. Extensive plant collection
¶**40 The Ringway** (Mr & Mrs W D Hall) Small garden with alpine scree, tufa bed, alpine house. Large pond and bog, herbaceous plants and greenhouse. Parking can be difficult; if possible, please leave cars on main rd and walk 100 yds

¶**8 Syston Road** (Mrs R A Smith) Plant enthusiasts cottage style garden; old English roses, small pond with frogs and newts; mature grape vine, organic veg-etable garden

Reservoir Cottage & (Lord & Lady John Manners) Knipton, 7m W of Grantham. W of A1; between A52 and A607; nr Belvoir Castle. Medium-sized country garden with lovely views over the lake. TEA. *Adm £1 Chd free. Sun May 1 (2-6)*

Rose Cottage & (Mr & Mrs J D Buchanan) Owston. 6m W of Oakham via Knossington, 2m S of Somerby. From Leicester turn L 2m E of Tilton. Undulating 1¾-acres; shrub and flower borders; spring bulbs, roses, alpines; ponds, waterfall; fine views. Plants and sundries stalls. TEAS. *Adm £1.50 Chd free (Share to Owston Church®). Sun April 17 (2-6)*

Sheepy Magna Gardens &✗ B4116 2 ½m N of Ather-stone on Atherstone to Twycross Rd. Teas in aid of Shee-py Magna Church. *Combined adm £2 Chd 30p (Share to Sheepy Church®). Sat, Sun June 18, 19 (2-6)*

Gate Cottage ❀ (Mr & Mrs O P Hall) Church Lane. Opp church. Approx ½-acre cottage garden; mixed herbaceous borders; greenhouse; vegetable garden; several specimen trees; lawns and patio
The Grange (Mr & Mrs V Wetton) Main Rd. ¼m from shop towards Twycross opp entrance to trout ponds farm. Spacious Edwardian garden redeveloped since 1989. Extensive lawns; mature specimen trees; ponds; massed roses; heather beds; mixed borders
Vine Cottage ❀ (Mr & Mrs T Clark) 26 Main Rd. Opp shop. Approx ¾-acre cottage garden; mixed herba-ceous borders; alpine gardens; ponds; vegetable plot with greenhouse. TEAS. *Also private visits welcome Adm £1. May to Sept, please* **Tel 0827 880529**

South Luffenham Hall &✗❀ (Mr & Mrs R A Butterfield) South Luffenham on A6121 between Stamford and Up-pingham. Turn off A47 at Morcot. 3-acre garden around 1630 house (not open), featured in 'The Perfect English Country House'. Shrubs, roses, herbaceous borders, lawns, pleached lime hedge and terrace with alpines and lilies. TEAS. *Adm £1.50 Chd 50p (Share to St Marys Church, S Luffenham®). Sun July 3 (2-6)*

Stepping Stones Old Farm ✗ (Mr Clem Adkin) Little Beeby. 8m E of Leicester. Off A47 at Thurnby, through Scraptoft. R at Beeby Xrds. 1st R on Hungarton Lane. 1-acre garden on site of medieval deserted village, part ex-cavated. Stream, small arboretum, shrub roses, spring bulbs in variety, spring blossom. Surprise features. Lovely countryside. TEA. *Adm £1.50 Chd 50p. Private visits wel-come March to July, please* **Tel 053 750 677**

Stoke Albany House &❀ (Mr & Mrs A M Vinton) 4m E of Market Harborough via A427 to Corby; turn to Stoke Albany; right at the White Horse (B669); garden ½m on L. Large garden with fine trees; shrubs; herbaceous borders and grey garden. TEAS on Sun only. *Adm £1.50 Chd free. Sun July 10 (2-6); Tues, Weds July 5, 6, 12, 13 (2-5)*

Sutton Bonington Hall ᏻ᳜ (Anne, Lady Elton) Sutton Bonington, 5m NW of Loughborough; take A6 to Hathern; turn R (E) onto A6006; 1st L (N) for Sutton Bonington. Conservatory, formal white garden, variegated leaf borders. Queen Anne house (not open). Picnics. TEA. *Adm £1.20 Chd 50p (Share to St Michael's and St Ann's Church, Sutton Bonington®). Sun June 26 (12-5.30)*

University of Leicester Botanic Garden ᏻ᳜᳜ Stoughton Drive South, Oadby, Leicester. On SE outskirts of Leicester, opp Oadby race course. Bus, Midland Red. Garden incorporates grounds of Beaumont Hall, Southmeade, Hastings House and The Knoll. 16 acres; trees; rose, rock, water and sunken gardens; botanical greenhouses; herbaceous borders; heather garden. Open July 4 (2-5) TEA. *Adm £1 Chd free. For NGS Sun July 24 (2-5)*

Wakerley Manor ᏻ᳜ (A D A W Forbes Esq) 6m Uppingham, right off A47 Uppingham-Peterborough through Barrowden, or from A43 Stamford to Corby rd between Duddington and Bulwick. 4 acres lawns, shrubs, herbaceous; kitchen garden; three greenhouses. TEAS. *Adm £1 Chd 10p. Sun May 8 (2-6)*

Whatton House ᏻ᳜ (Lord Crawshaw) 4m NE of Loughborough on A6 between Hathern and Kegworth; 2½m SE of junc 24 on M1. 15 acres; shrub and herbaceous borders, lawns, rose and wild gardens, pools; arboretum. Nursery open. TEAS. Teas in Old Dining Room. Catering arrangements for pre-booked parties any day or evening. *Adm £1.50 OAP/Chd 75p. Open Suns and Weds from Easter to end August. Also Bank Hol Mons. For NGS Tues April 5, May 31 (2-6). Special plant sales Suns Sept 18, Oct 9. Also private visits welcome, please* **Tel 0509 842268**

¶**Woodyton Farmhouse** ᏻ᳜᳜ (Mr & Mrs F A Slater) Coalville. On A512, 6m E of Ashby de la Zouch, 6m W of Loughborough, 3m W of M1 junction 23. ¼-acre garden, herbaceous borders, shrub roses, hydrangeas, scree and shade. TEA. *Adm £1 Chd free. Suns June 5, July 17 (2-6)*

> **Regular Openers.** Too many days to include in diary. Usually there is a wide range of plants giving year-round interest. See head of county section for the name and garden description for times etc.

Lincolnshire

Hon County Organiser: Mrs Patrick Dean, East Mere House, Lincoln LN4 2JB Tel 0522 791371
Assistant Hon County Organisers: Lady Bruce-Gardyne, The Old Rectory, Aswardby, Spilsby, Lincs PE23 4JS Tel 0790 52652
Mrs Julian Gorst, Oxcombe Manor, Horncastle, Lincs LN9 6LU Tel 0507 533227

DATES OF OPENING

By appointment
For telephone numbers and other details see garden descriptions. Private visits welcomed

21 Chapel Street, Hacconby
Luskentyre, Roman Bank, Saracens Head, nr Spalding
The Manor House, Bitchfield
Park House Farm, Walcott

Regular openings
For details see garden descriptions

Harlaxton Manor Gardens, Grantham. April 1 to Oct. Closed Mons except Bank Hol Mons

February 19 Saturday
21 Chapel Street, Hacconby
February 20 Sunday
21 Chapel Street, Hacconby

February 26 Saturday
Manor Farm, Keisby, Bourne
February 27 Sunday
Manor Farm, Keisby, Bourne
March 3 Thursday
21 Chapel Street, Hacconby
March 27 Sunday
Fulbeck Hall, nr Grantham ‡
The Old Rectory, Fulbeck, nr Grantham ‡
April 3 Sunday
21 Chapel Street, Hacconby
May 1 Sunday
83 Halton Road, Spilsby
58 Watery Lane, Butterwick
May 2 Monday
58 Watery Lane, Butterwick
May 5 Thursday
21 Chapel Street, Hacconby
May 8 Sunday
Doddington Hall, nr Lincoln
Grimsthorpe Castle Gardens, Bourne
May 12 Thursday
Grimsthorpe Castle Gardens, Bourne

May 15 Sunday
Grantham House, Grantham
May 22 Sunday
Aubourn Hall, Aubourn
Belton House, Grantham
Crowmarsh Cottage, Holbeach St Matthews ‡
Luskentyre, Roman Bank, Saracens Head, nr Spalding ‡
May 29 Sunday
Stenigot House, nr Louth
58 Watery Lane, Butterwick
May 30 Monday
58 Watery Lane, Butterwick
June 2 Thursday
21 Chapel Street, Hacconby
June 5 Sunday
Park Farm, Normanton (see Nottinghamshire)
Walcot Hall, Barnack
June 11 Saturday
Bishop's House, Lincoln
June 12 Sunday
Haconby Hall, Haconby
June 18 Saturday
Hall Farm, Harpswell

June 19 Sunday
East Mere House, nr Lincoln
June 26 Sunday
Careby Village Gardens
Gunby Hall, Burgh-le-Marsh
Marston Hall, nr Grantham
The Villa, South Somercotes,
Louth
July 7 Thursday
21 Chapel Street, Hacconby
July 10 Sunday
Harrington Hall, Spilsby

July 17 Sunday
83 Halton Road, Spilsby
July 24 Sunday
4 Butts Lane, Tattershall
July 31 Sunday
Harlaxton Manor Gardens,
Grantham
August 4 Thursday
21 Chapel Street, Hacconby
August 21 Sunday
Crowmarsh Cottage, Holbeach St
Matthews

Luskentyre, Roman Bank,
Saracens Head, nr Spalding
September 1 Thursday
21 Chapel Street, Hacconby
September 3 Saturday
Belton House, Grantham
September 4 Sunday
Hall Farm, Harpswell
September 25 Sunday
Harlaxton Manor Gardens, Grantham
October 6 Thursday
21 Chapel Street, Hacconby

DESCRIPTIONS OF GARDENS

Aubourn Hall ✍ (Sir Henry Nevile) Aubourn. 7m SW of Lincoln. Signposted off A606 at Harmston. Approx 3-acres. Lawns, mature trees, shrubs, roses, mixed borders. C11 church adjoining. Wheelchairs in dry weather only. TEAS. *Adm £1 Chd 50p. (Share to St. Peters Church Aubourn-repairs®). Sun May 22 (2-6)*

Belton House &✍ (The National Trust) 3m NE of Grantham on the A607 Grantham to Lincoln road. Easily reached and signed from the A1 (Grantham north junction). 32 acres of garden incl formal Italian and Dutch gardens, and orangery by Sir Jeffrey Wyatville. TEAS. *Adm house & garden £4.30 Chd £2.10. ▲Sun May 22, Sat Sept 3 (11-5.30)*

¶Bishop's House & (Bishop of Lincoln) Lincoln. Approaching Lincoln from N take A15 towards Cathedral. Enter Bailgate via Newport Arch, turn L into Eastgate. Bishop's House last on L before Eastgate Hotel. Various car parks in city. Approx 1½ acres walled town garden of lawns, trees, shrubs and herbaceous borders. *Adm £1 Chd 50p. Sat June 11 (2-5)*

Burghley House see Cambridgeshire

¶4 Butts Lane ✍✿ (Mr & Mrs Newstead) Tattershall. 8m S of Horncastle on A153 Sleaford to Horncastle rd. Situated opp the main entrance to Gartree Secondary Modern School, Tattershall. Approx ¾-acre garden, landscaped and developed by owners during the past 10 years. Extensively planted with a wide variety of trees, shrubs and herbaceous plants, incorporating rockery, scree and water feature. TEAS. *Adm £1 Chd 50p. Sun July 24 (2-6)*

¶Careby Village Gardens ✍ 6m N of Stamford on B1176. 5m E of A1 at Stretton. Free central parking. TEAS in aid of Lincolnshire Air Ambulance. *Combined adm £3 Chd £1. Sun June 26 (11-5)*
    Careby Manor Garden (Nigel & Ros Colborn) A large, plantsman's garden full of interesting perennials and featuring varieties of old roses together with unusual trees and shrubs
    ¶Glen Lodge (Martyn & Marjorie Bradshaw) ¾-acre garden created in the last 6 yrs, with sweeping lawn to R Glen; herbaceous beds and young trees. A small pedigree flock of Southdown sheep can also be seen

¶Old Glen Cottage (Jeff & Judy Midwood) ⅓-acre walled cottage garden redesigned in 1987 with shrubs and herbaceous plants; features incl north facing bank and former stable-yard
¶Walnut Cottage & (Roy & Sue Grundy) Another young garden with a small woodland feature and ponds; the ½ acre garden has interesting herbaceous plantings and a small herb garden and greenhouse

21 Chapel Street ✍✿ (Cliff & Joan Curtis) A15 3m N of Bourne, turn E at Xrds into Hacconby. Small village garden with alpine house, rockeries, scree bed, old stone troughs planted as miniature gardens. Herbaceous borders with climbing roses and numerous clematis, collections of snowdrops, primula allionii, lewisia, rhodohypoxis. Featured on TV. TEAS. *Adm £1 Chd free (Share to Marie Curie Memorial Foundation®). Sat, Sun Feb 19, 20 (11-4) Sun April 3 (11-6) Thurs March 3, May 5, June 2, July 7, Aug 4, Sept 1, Oct 6 (2-6). Private visits and parties welcome, please Tel 0778 570314*

¶Crowmarsh Cottage ✿ (Les & Janet Doy) Holbeach St Matthews. 9m E of Spalding. From A17 at Holbeach take Pennyhill turning and follow Holbeach St Matthews signs (approx 3m). A cottage garden recently redeveloped with natural pond. Large selection of foliage plants and shrubs; also wide selection of perennials. TEAS. *Adm 80p Chd 20p. Suns May 22, Aug 21 (1-6)*

Doddington Hall &✍ (Antony Jarvis Esq) 5m SW of Lincoln. From Lincoln via A46, turn W on to B1190 for Doddington. Superb walled gardens; thousands of spring bulbs; wild gardens; mature trees; Elizabethan mansion. Free Car Park. Lunches and TEAS available from 12 noon in fully licensed garden restaurant. *Adm house & garden £3.50 Chd £1.75. Garden only £1.75 Chd 85p (Share to Lincolnshire Old Churches Trust©). ▲Sun May 8 (2-6)*

East Mere House &✍✿ (Mr & Mrs Patrick Dean) Lincoln. 3m S of Lincoln on A15. 1m E on B1178. Mixed shrubs, roses and herbaceous borders vegetable and herb gardens. TEAS. *Adm £1 Chd 50p. Sun June 19 (2-6)*

Regular Openers. Too many days to include in diary. Usually there is a wide range of plants giving year-round interest. See head of county section for the name and garden description for times etc.

Fulbeck Hall &✿ (Mrs M Fry) Grantham. On A607 14m S of Lincoln, 11m N of Grantham. 1m S of X-roads of A17 at Leadenham. 11-acres incl formal Edwardian garden with yew hedges, tulip tree, cedars and venetian well head; spring bulbs. There has been much recent planting of unusual trees, shrubs and herbaceous plants. TEAS. *Combined adm with* **The Old Rectory** *£2.50 Chd £1. Sun March 27 (2-5)*

Grantham House &✿ (Lady Wyldbore-Smith) Castlegate, opp St Wulframs Church, Grantham. An old English garden of approx 5 acres of bulbs, many unusual shrubs and trees; river walk and water garden. TEAS. *Adm £1 Chd 50p. Sun May 15 (2-6)*

Grimsthorpe Castle Gardens & (Grimsthorpe and Drummond Castle Trust) 8m E of A1 on the A151 from the Colsterworth junction, 4m W of Bourne. 15 acres of formal and woodland gardens which incl bulbs and wild flowers. The formal gardens encompass fine topiary, roses, herbaceous borders and an unusual ornamental kitchen garden. TEAS. *Adm £1 Chd 50p. ▲Sun, Thurs May 8, 12 (2-6) Last entry 5*

Gunby Hall &✿ (Mr & Mrs J D Wrisdale; The National Trust) 2½m NW of Burgh-le-Marsh; S of A158. 7 acres of formal and walled gardens; old roses, herbaceous borders; herb garden; kitchen garden with fruit trees and vegetables. Tennyson's 'Haunt of Ancient Peace'. House built by Sir William Massingberd 1700. Plant centre, games. TEAS. *Adm garden only £1.50 Chd 70p (Share to St Barnabas Hospice (Lincoln)®). ▲Sun June 26 (2-6)*

¶**Haconby Hall** ✿✿ (Mr & Mrs J F Atkinson) Haconby. 3m N of Bourne, ¾m E of A15 in Haconby village. A large established plantsman's garden comprising a wide variation of herbaceous borders, trees, shrubs, lawns and troughs; knot garden, alpine house and ha-ha. TEA. *Adm £1.50 Chd £1. Sun June 12 (2-6)*

Hall Farm &✿ (Pam & Mark Tatam) Harpswell. 7m E of Gainsborough on A631. 1½m W of Caenby Corner. ¾-acre garden with mixed borders of trees, shrubs, roses and perennials (many of the plants are unusual). Over 80 varieties of rose - mainly old varieties. Recently constructed sunken garden and pond. Short walk to old moat and woodland. Free seed collecting in garden Sept 4. TEAS. *Adm £1 Chd 25p. Sat June 18, Sun Sept 4 (2-6)*

¶**83 Halton Road** ✿✿ (Jack & Joan Gunson) Spilsby. In Spilsby take B1195 towards Wainfleet; garden on L. Limited parking on Halton Rd, free car park Post Office Lane, Spilsby. ¼-acre town garden and hardy plant nursery, divided into a series of smaller gardens featuring densely planted mixed borders, incl many unusual plants and hardy geraniums, collection of over 100 varieties spring bulbs a feature. TEAS. *Adm £1 Chd free. Suns May 1, July 17 (2-6)*

> **By Appointment Gardens.** These owners do not have a fixed opening day usually because they do not like crowds or have insufficient parking space. Owner will often give guided tour.

¶**Harlaxton Manor Gardens** (University of Evansville) Grantham. 1m W of Grantham off A607 Melton Mowbray rd. Historically important 110-acre formal gardens and woodland currently undergoing restoration. 6½ acre walled gardens, extremely ornate walls; plantsman's and theme gardens. Harlaxton Manor was built by Gregory Gregory and the house and garden built to rival anything in Europe. The restoration project is being monitored for a television series. Formal gardens built as a walk around European styles, Dutch canal, Italian gardens, French terracing, views. Partially suitable for wheelchairs. TEAS. *Adm £2.50 Chd £1.25. April 1 to Oct closed Mons except Bank Hol Mons. For NGS Suns July 31, Sept 25 (11-5)*

¶**Harrington Hall** ✿✿ (Mr & Mrs David Price) Spilsby. 6m NW of Spilsby. Turn off A158 (Lincoln-Skegness) at Hagworthingham, 2m from Harrington. Approx 5-acre tudor & C18 walled gardens, incl recently designed kitchen garden with herbaceous borders, roses and other flowering shrubs. High terrace mentioned in Tennyson's 'Maud'. *Adm £1 Chd 25p. Sun July 10 (2-6)*

Luskentyre ✿ (Mr & Mrs C Harris) 7m E of Spalding signed from A17 at Saracen's Head. Attractive small garden extensively planted with a wide range of interesting plants mainly chosen for their ability to withstand dry conditions and give year-round interest. *Adm 80p Chd 20p. Suns May 22, Aug 21 (1-5). Private visits welcome, please* **Tel 0406 23987**

Manor Farm ✿✿ (Mr & Mrs C A Richardson) Keisby. 9m NW of Bourne, 10m E of Grantham, signed to Keisby from Lenton and Hawthorpe. ½-acre plantsman's garden. Snowdrop collection and hellebores. *Adm £1 Chd free (Share to Stamford and Bourne CRMF®). Sat, Sun Feb 26, 27 (1-4)*

The Manor House ✿ (John Richardson Esq) Bitchfield; 6m SE of Grantham, close to Irnham and Rippingale. A52 out of Grantham to Spital Gate Hill roundabout; take B1176 to Bitchfield; House on right after public house. 1½-acres entirely re-created in 1972; essentially a shrub rose garden (96 varieties) with shrubs and other perennials; 50 by 40ft pond planted spring 1985; small box hedged formal garden; ha-ha, new large garden room with fountain and over 100 plants. *Adm £2. Parties of 20 or more welcome by appointment only after June 1 to mid-July. Please* **Tel Ingoldsby 261**

Marston Hall &✿ (The Rev Henry Thorold) 6m N of Grantham. Turn off A1, 4½m N of Grantham; on 1½m to Marston. Station: Grantham. Notable trees; wych elm and laburnum of exceptional size. House C16 continuously owned by the Thorold family. Interesting pictures and furniture. TEAS *Adm house & garden £2 Chd £1 (Share to Hougham Church Restoration Fund®). ▲Sun June 26 (2-6)*

The Old Rectory ✿ (Mr & Mrs N D S Brown) Fulbeck. On A607 11m N of Grantham and 15m S of Lincoln. Adjoining the church with views across the Trent Valley. Spring bulbs, shrubs and roses are planted within the last 10 years. Signposted from Fulbeck Hall through the churchyard. Teas at the hall. *Combined adm with* **Fulbeck Hall** *£2.50 Chd £1. Sun March 27 (2-5)*

Park House Farm &💥❀ (Mr & Mrs Geoffrey Grantham) Walcott. 16m S of Lincoln on B1189 between Billinghay and Metheringham. Traditional farm buildings have been adapted to enclose 1 acre of informal gardens with mixed borders; white garden, alpine and scree beds; climbers a speciality. Wild garden with pond; old orchard and mini nature reserve. *Adm £1 Chd 50p. Private visits welcome May to Sept, please* **Tel 0526 860409**

Stenigot House 💥❀ (Mr & Mrs Peter Dennis) nr Louth. 6m S of Louth. Turn W off A153 at sign to Stenigot, 2m. Spacious lawns with lovely view over Wolds. Water garden; shrub roses and borders; kitchen garden. TEAS. *Adm £1.50 Chd 30p (Share to St Nicholas Church repairs®). Sun May 29 (2-6)*

The Villa 💥❀ (Michael & Judy Harry) South Somercotes. 8m E of Louth. Leave Louth by Eastfield Rd. Follow signs to S Cockerington. Take rd signposted to North & South Somercotes. House on L 100 yds before church. ¼-acre densely planted in the cottage style; large collection of herbs, old-fashioned and unusual perennials; orchard with interesting old varieties ot fruit trees. Livestock incl flock of Lincoln Longwool Sheep. TEAS. *Adm £1 Chd free. Sun June 26 (2-6)*

¶**Walcot Hall** &💥❀ (Mr & Mrs Darby Dennis) Barnack. 3m S of Stamford. Take Walcot Rd out of Barnack, entrance is 400 yds beyond Cricket Club. An arboretum of 20 acres with lake and follies, around a Carolean house. Visit the Secret Garden and have tea in the lovely old Courtyard. Garden featured in BBC TV major drama production of George Eliot's Middlemarch. TEAS in aid of Barnack Play Group. *Adm £2 OAP 50p. Sun June 5 (2-6)*

58 Watery Lane &💥❀ (Mr & Mrs F Jervis) Butterwick. Take the A52 Skegness Rd out of Boston. Butterwick turn about 5m on the R. Carry on into the village keeping the Five Bells Inn on your R. Watery Lane 2nd turning L. We are the 2nd bungalow on the R. The garden is approx ¼-acre consisting of mainly alpines, over 300 grown. Rockery and raised beds, also containers; alpine house; 2 ponds. *Adm 80p Chd free. Suns, Mons May 1, 2, 29, 30, (10.30-6.30)*

London (Greater London Area)

Hon County Organiser: Mrs Maurice Snell, Moleshill House, Fairmile, Cobham, Surrey KT11 1BG
Tel 0932 864532

Assistant Hon County Organisers: Mrs Stuart Pollard, 17 St Alban's Rd, Kingston-upon-Thames, Surrey
Tel 081 546 6657
Miss Alanna Wilson, 38 Ornan Road, London NW3 4QB Tel 071 794 4071
Mrs V West 11 Charlwood Terrace, Putney, SW15 Tel 071 584 1274

DATES OF OPENING

By appointment
For telephone numbers and other details see garden descriptions. Private visits welcomed

43 Brodrick Road SW17
15 Langbourne Avenue N6
13 Mercers Road N19
33 Mundania Road SE22
Flat 1, 1F Oval Road NW1
43 Penerley Road SE6
St Michael's Convent, Richmond
Southwood Lodge N6
Tarn, Oxhey Drive South, Northwood
15 Upper Grotto Road, Strawberry Hill, Twickenham TW1
42 Woodville Gardens, Ealing W5

Regular openings
For details see garden descriptions

Barbican Conservatory EC2. Sats, Suns, Bank Hols all year

Chelsea Physic Garden SW3. Suns April 3 to Oct 30, Weds April 6 to Oct 26, Mon to Fri May 23 to May 27, Mon to Fri June 6 to June 10
Myddelton House, Enfield. Weekdays except Aug 29, Dec 26 to 30 and last Sun in the month

March 19 Saturday
The Elms, Kingston-on-Thames
March 20 Sunday
The Elms, Kingston-on-Thames
April 3 Sunday
Chelsea Physic Garden SW3
April 4 Monday
Myddelton House Enfield
Tarn, Oxhey Drive South, Northwood
April 9 Saturday
Lambeth Palace SE1
April 16 Saturday
The Elms, Kingston-on-Thames
April 17 Sunday
The Elms, Kingston-on-Thames

Fenton House NW3
7 The Grove N6
3 Radnor Gardens, Twickenham
April 23 Saturday
Trinity Hospice SW4
April 24 Sunday
Chiswick Mall W4
29 Deodar Road SW15
Edwardes Square W8
St Mary's Convent & Nursing Home W4
Trinity Hospice SW4
7 Woodstock Road W4
May 1 Sunday
39 Boundary Road NW8
20 Eatonville Road SW17
Eccleston Square SW1
30 Hercies Road, Hillingdon
1 Hocroft Avenue NW2
7 Upper Phillimore Gardens W8
47 Winn Road SE12
May 2 Monday
26 Nassau Road, Barnes Gardens
1 Hocroft Avenue NW2
May 8 Sunday
32 Atney Road SW15

46 Canonbury Square N1,
51 Cholmeley Crescent N6
17 Fulham Park Gardens SW6
37 Heath Drive NW3
Malvern Terrace N1
2 Millfield Place N6
Southwood Lodge N6
The Water Gardens,
   Kingston-on-Thames
May 14 Saturday
The Elms, Kingston-on-Thames
May 15 Sunday
The Elms, Kingston-on-Thames
49 & 51 Etchingham Park Road
   N3
5 Greenaway Gardens NW3
Hall Grange, Croydon
Hornbeams, Stanmore
33 Mundania Road SE22
Museum of Garden History,
   Tradescant Trust
3 Radnor Gardens, Twickenham
131 Upland Road SE22
May 18 Wednesday
12 Lansdowne Road W11
May 19 Thursday
12a Selwood Place SW7
May 21 Saturday
Highwood Ash NW7
May 22 Sunday
Chiswick Mall W4
117 Hamilton Terrace NW8
Highwood Ash NW7
22 Loudoun Road NW8
15 Norcott Road N16
95 North Road, Kew
43 Ormeley Road SW12
43 Penerley Road SE6
Wimbledon Gardens SW19
May 29 Sunday
Regents College NW1
May 30 Monday
Myddelton House Enfield
66 Wallingford Avenue W10
June 3 Friday
Flat 1, 1F Oval Road NW1
June 4 Saturday
Lambeth Community Care Centre
   SE11
Flat 1, 1F Oval Road NW1
June 5 Sunday
Barbican Conservatory EC2
43 Brodrick Road SW17
7 The Grove N6
Lambeth Community Care Centre
   SE11
North Ruislip Gardens

Flat 1, 1F Oval Road NW1
7 St George's Road, Twickenham
South London Botanical Institute
   SE24
June 11 Saturday
15 Lawrence Street SW3
Muswell Hill Gardens N10
Trinity Hospice SW4
June 12 Sunday
Barbican Conservatory EC2
Barnes Gardens SW13
28 Barnsbury Square N1
Canonbury Gardens N1
52 Mount Park Road W5
2 Northbourne Road SW4
Southwood Lodge N6
Trinity Hospice SW4
June 18 Saturday
29 Mostyn Road SW19
June 19 Sunday
54 Burnfoot Avenue SW6
101 Cheyne Walk SW10
The Coach House, Landridge
   Road SW6
Eccleston Square SW1
17 Fulham Park Gardens SW6
5 Greenaway Gardens NW3
11 Hampstead Way NW11
Highgate Village N6
Kensington Gardens W8
10 Lawn Road NW3
Leyborne Park Gardens TW9
Little Lodge, Thames Ditton
29 Mostyn Road SW19
78 Palace Road SW2
43 Penerley Road SE6
7 St George's Road, Twickenham
131 Upland Road, SE22
3 Wellgarth Road, NW11
June 25 Saturday
19 St Gabriel's Road NW2
June 26 Sunday
133 Haverstock Hill NW3
5 Hillcrest Avenue NW11
125 Honor Oak Park SE23
21a The Little Boltons SW10
95 North Road, Kew
Ormeley Lodge, Richmond
47 Winn Road SE12
23 Woodville Road, Ealing W5
July 3 Sunday
65 Castelnau, Barnes SW13
Goldsborough, Blackheath SE3
10a The Pavement, Chapel Road
   SE27
3 Radnor Gardens, Twickenham
15 Upper Grotto Road,

Twickenham
July 10 Sunday
46 Canonbury Square N1
17 Fulham Park Gardens SW6
36 Marryat Road SW19
35 Perrymead Street SW6
3 Radnor Gardens, Twickenham
9 Ranelagh Avenue SW6
14 Sebright Road, High Barnet
13 Trecastle Way N7
15 Upper Grotto Road,
   Twickenham
10 Wildwood Road NW11
July 17 Sunday
15a Buckland Crescent NW3
5 Greenaway Gardens NW3
12 Greenheys Close,
   Northwood
117 Hamilton Terrace NW8
15 Norcott Road N16
Ranulf Road Gardens NW2
July 23 Saturday
Trinity Hospice SW4
27 Wood Vale N10
July 24 Sunday
29 Addison Avenue W11
108 Camden Mews NW1
4 Cliff Road NW1
37 Heath Drive NW3
Trinity Hospice SW4
27 Wood Vale N10
July 31 Sunday
20 Eatonville Road SW17
2 Millfield Place N6
Myddelton House Enfield
12 Peterborough Villas SW6
57 St Quintin Avenue W10
66 Wallingford Avenue W10
August 21 Sunday
73 Forest Drive East E11
1 Lister Road E11
August 28 Sunday
47 Winn Road SE12
September 10 Saturday
Trinity Hospice SW4
September 11 Sunday
43 Penerley Road SE6
Trinity Hospice SW4
September 18 Sunday
17 Fulham Park Gardens SW6
October 2 Sunday
The Water Gardens,
   Kingston-on-Thames
October 30 Sunday
Chelsea Physic Garden SW3

DESCRIPTIONS OF GARDENS

29 Addison Avenue, W11 ⛱ (Mr & Mrs D B Nicholson)
No entry for cars from Holland Park Avenue; approach via
Norland Square and Queensdale Rd. Station: Holland

Park. Bus 12, 94. Small prizewinning town garden with
country feel. Lawn, fruit trees, unusual wall shrubs and
perennials. Phlox paniculata a speciality: over 25 varieties
in shades of pink, mauve, purple and red. *Adm £1 Chd
50p (Share to the Tradescant Trust®). Sun July 24 (2-6)*

The Anchorage see Kent

32 Atney Road, SW15 ✗ (Sally Tamplin) Off Putney Bridge Rd. Tubes, Putney Bridge or East Putney. Bus 14, 22, 37, 74, 80, 85, 93, 220. Mixed borders, terrace with pots, lawn, woodland area all compressed into 90' L-shaped garden perpetually changing to accommodate needs of obsessive gardener with too little time for gardening, TEAS. *Adm £1 (Share to All Saints' Church®). Sun May 8 (2-6)*

Barbican Conservatory, EC2 ♿✗❀ Silk Street, nearest tube station Barbican and Moorgate. City of London's largest conservatory, part of the Barbican Centre; collection of temperate plants incl palms, orchids and climbers. Large collection of cactus and succulents with many rare varieties. Time allowed approx 1½ hours, but many other gardens with interesting plants to be seen in the locality. TEAS in restaurant. *Adm £1 OAP/Chd 60p Family (2 adults, up to 4 chd) £2.40. Sats, Suns, Bank Hols all year. Telephone Operational Services Department 071 638 4141 for opening times. For NGS Suns June 5, 12 (12-5.30)*

Barnes Gardens Barnes, SW13. TEAS at 25 Castelnau. *Adm £4 for 5 gardens or £1 each garden, OAP £2 for 5 gardens or 50p each garden, Chd free. Sun June 12 (2-6)*
25 Castelnau ✗ (Dr & Mrs P W Adams) Castelnau is on the main route from Hammersmith Bridge. The garden is approx 120' X 40' designed in 1978 by Malcolm Hillier and the late Colin Hilton, well known for their books on flowers and garden design. The garden was planned for ease of maintenance and family living. There is a good variety of herbaceous plants, some attractive roses and a compact working vegetable area and screened swimming pool. Cornish cream TEAS
29 Lonsdale Road ✗ (Mr & Mrs R Morris) Over Hammersmith Bridge first R or Underground Hammersmith. Bus 9, 33, 72. ⅓-acre S facing walled garden with York terrace. Designed to give all year interest. A plantsman's garden with herbaceous borders. Old English roses, clematis, peonies, iris, lilies and flowering shrubs, lavender walk with spring bulbs and hostas
26 Nassau Road ♿❀ (Captain & Mrs Anthony Hallett) 26 Nassau Road lies midway between the Thames and Barnes Pond and is approached via Lonsdale Road or Church Road in Barnes. Long, slim, terraced garden with tallest wisteria in Barnes, shrouded on all sides by weigela, philadelphus, pittosporum, chaemomeles, ceanothus with borders of hebe, cistus, rose, delphiniums, potentilla and spiraea. New borders with blue and yellow, red hot lilies, cool white phlox and campanula. 200ft of dense green and gold but freaks of misplanted colour add to the confusion. Plants for sale. *Also on Mon May 2*
8 Queen's Ride ♿✗ (His Honour Judge White & Mrs White) Train: Barnes Station, turn R down Rocks Lane, then L along Queen's Ride. Bus, 22 terminus at Putney Hospital; 3 minutes walk W along Queen's Ride. House is at the junction of Queen's Ride and St Mary's Grove. ⅔-acre garden facing Barnes Common. Croquet lawn with herbaceous and mixed borders and a small history of the rose garden. TEA

12 Westmoreland Road ✗❀ (Mr & Mrs Norman Moore) From Hammersmith take Bus 9, 33, or 72 to the Red Lion. Briefly retrace steps along Castelnau turn L into Ferry Rd then L at Xrds. Small garden with raised stone terrace planted with choisya, convolvulus, euonymus, honeysuckle and decorative herbs, leading to lower lawn. Borders densely planted with wide variety of flowering shrubs. *(Share to St Mary's Church-yard®)*

28 Barnsbury Square, N1 ✗ (F T Gardner Esq) Islington N. 1¾m N of King's Cross off Thornhill Rd. Bus stop: Islington Town Hall, Upper St or Offord Rd, Caledonian Rd, Tube Highbury and Islington. Small prize-winning Victorian garden; gazebo; pond; grotto; roses, shrubs, plants of interest throughout year. *Adm £1 Chd free (Share to CRMF®). Sun June 12 (2-6)*

39 Boundary Road, NW8 ✗ (Hermoine Berton) St John's Wood. Between Finchley Rd and Abbey Rd. Buses 13, 113, 82, 46, 159; ask for Boundary Rd or 6 min walk between Swiss Cottage and St John's Wood station. Unusual walled garden closely planted to provide wild life sanctuary for birds, frogs, newts, toads, squirrels; accent on foliage, texture, fern and perfume; includes ponds, waterfall and rocks. As seen on Gardeners World 1992 and filmed for 'Inside Britain' 1993. *Adm £1 Chd 20p (Share to London Lighthouse Aids Centre®). Sun May 1 (2-6)*

43 Brodrick Road SW17 ✗ (Helen Yemm) Wandsworth Common. Approx 1m S of Wandsworth Bridge, off Trinity Rd. A long (110'), tranquil garden of a typical Victorian terrace house, surrounded by mature trees. Its length is broken by a bank of shrubs and a pond - frogs, newts etc, overhung by an ancient rose-clad apple tree. Elsewhere the garden is stuffed with flowering shrubs, herbaceous planting for semi-shade, clematis and roses - distinctly un-urban. Open for the first time 93. New this yr: a deeper north-facing border and shingle area. *Adm £1 Chd 50p. Sun June 5 (2-6). Private visits welcome May to Sept please Tel 081 672 1473*

15a Buckland Crescent, NW3 ♿✗❀ (Lady Barbirolli) Swiss Cottage Tube. Bus: 46, 13 (6 mins) or Hampstead Hoppa (request stop nearby). ⅓-acre; interesting collection of shrubs and trees in well-designed garden featured in Country Life Nov 88, also in books 'Private Gardens of London' by Arabella Lennox Boyd and 'Town Gardens' by Caroline Boisset. *Adm £1 Chd over 12 50p (Share to Befrienders International, the Samaritans Worldwide®). Sun July 17 (2.30-6.30)*

54 Burnfoot Avenue, SW6 ✗ (Lady Jocelyn) nearest tube Parson's Green, then walk W on Fulham Rd, R up Munster Rd, 3rd street on L of Munster Rd. 14 bus along Fulham Rd. directions as above; 11 bus along Dawes Rd and walk down through Filmer Rd. 74 bus along Fulham Palace Rd walk through to Burnfoot Ave. Small walled paved garden 20' × 30' with raised beds, the emphasis on leaf shapes and colours; fruit trees; climbing plants; frequently changing due to deaths and new ideas; the garden is used as an extra room of the house. *Adm £1 Chd free (Share to St Joseph's Hospice Hackney®). Sun June 19 (2-6)*

108 Camden Mews, NW1 &&& (A Dougall) Located off York Way but beware of one way system. Distant tube stations; Camden and Caledonian Rd. Buses C12 10 29 253. Rivulets of helxine soften the brick and york stone of this miniature garden. Alpines, thymes and other small flowers drift past on a sea of green, waving not drowning. TEAS (incl waffles). *Combined odm with* **4 Cliff Rd** *£1.50 Chd free. Sun July 24 (2.30-6)*

Canonbury Gardens &&& Station: Highbury & Islington. Bus: 4, 19, 30, 43, 104, 279 to Highbury Corner or Islington Town Hall, 30 to New Crown public house stops outside 60 St Paul's Rd. A1 runs through Canonbury Sq. *Combined odm £2.50 or £1 each garden Chd £1.25 or 50p each garden. Sun June 12 (2-6)*

37 Alwyne Road &&&& (Mr & Mrs J Lambert) Bordering the new river walk. Open and surprisingly rural views; enclosed and urban hidden garden of clipped formality. Old-fashioned roses if it hasn't been too hot. Lilies if it hasn't been too cold. A garden writer's garden. TEAS. (Share to SOS Childrens villages®)

Canonbury House & (John Addey Esq) Canonbury Place. Replanted over the last five years the garden is maturing well; mulberry tree planted in 1619 by Sir Francis Bacon; most historic setting in Islington

60 St Paul's Road &&& (John & Pat Wardroper) Typical back-of-terrace walled garden, planted chiefly for shade, and to create a quiet, green enclosed atmosphere just off a busy street; designed on 3 levels with paved patios, border of flowering shrubs

46 Canonbury Square, NI &&& (Miss Peggy Carter) Station: Highbury & Islington Bus: 4, 19, 30, 43, 104, 279 to Highbury Corner or Islington Town Hall. A1 runs through Canonbury Sq. Walled garden lying behind 2 end-of-terrace Georgian houses with statuary; pool; waterfall; sping blossom. *Adm £1 Chd 50p. Suns May 8, July 10 (2.30-6)*

Capel Manor Farm and Gardens see Hertfordshire

65 Castelnau SW13 && (Prof & Mrs G Teeling Smith) Barnes. From Hammersmith, buses 9A, 33, 72 to Castelnau library. No 65 is 50yds S of library. Two Londoners' idea of a country garden. Herbaceous border, roses, shrubs, grass and behind a high clipped hedge, a small kitchen garden with narrow box edged beds where vegetables and flowers for cutting are grown. *Adm odult & chd £1. Sun July 3 (2-6)*

Chelsea Physic Garden, SW3 &&& (Trustees of the Garden) 66 Royal Hospital Rd, Chelsea. Bus 239 (Mon-Sat) alight outside garden (Cheyne Court). Station: Sloane Square (10 mins). Cars: restricted parking nr garden weekdays; free Sundays, or in Battersea Park (across river) weekdays. Entrance in Swan Walk (except wheelchairs). Second oldest Botanic Garden in UK; 3.8 acres; medicinal and herb garden, incl an ethnobotanical 'Garden of World Medicine' perfumery border; family order beds; historical walk, glasshouses and over 5,000 trees, shrubs and herbaceous plants, many rare or unusual. TEAS. *Adm £2.50 Students/Chd £1.30. Suns April 3 to Oct 30 (2-6); Weds April 6 to Oct 26 (2-5); also in Chelsea Flower Show week Mon-Fri May 23-27 and in Chelsea Festival Week Mon-Fri June 6-10 (12-5). For NGS Suns April 3, Oct 30 (2-6)*

101 Cheyne Walk, SW10 &&& (Malcolm Hillier Esq) The garden is situated just to the W of Battersea Bridge on Cheyne Walk. Parking on Sunday is possible in Millman St, Beaufort St and in the wider parts of Cheyne Walk with a single yellow line or on residents spaces. The garden, in three sections, is long and narrow 115ft × 18ft with a terrace leading up through ferns and topiary to a winding path and then onto a raised pillared arbour. There is a mixture of old roses, shrubs and hardy perennials with many interesting container plantings. TEAS. *Adm £1 Chd free. Sun June 19 (1-6)*

Chiswick Mall, W4 &&& Station: Stamford Brook (District Line). Bus: 290 to Young's Corner from Hammersmith. By car A4 Westbound turn off at Eyot Gdns S, then R into Chiswick Mall. *Suns April 24 (2-6), May 22 (2-7)*

16 Eyot Gardens && (Dianne Farris) Between Great West Road and river, at junction of Chiswick Mall and Hammersmith Terrace. If coming from outside London go down to river at Hogarth roundabout. Very small town garden at end of terrace of houses. Front has mostly yellow, blue and white flowers, a lot of pink in the back garden with raised beds and a little terrace, wisteria and camellias. Many unusual plants. TEAS. *Adm £1 Chd free*

Walpole House &&& (Mr & Mrs Jeremy Benson) Plantsman's garden; specie and tree peonies; water garden; spring flowers. Features in 'The Englishmans Garden'. Mid C16 to early C18 house, once home of Barbara Villiers, Duchess of Cleveland. Seeds and some plants for sale. *Adm £1 OAP/Chd 20p (Share to Bishop Creighton House Settlement and West London Committee for the Protection of Children®)*

¶**51 Cholmeley Crescent, N6** && (Ernst & Janet Sondheimer) Highgate. Between Highgate Hill and Archway Rd, off Cholmeley Park. Nearest tube Highgate. Approx ⅓-acre garden with many alpines in screes, peat beds, tufa and greenhouse; shrubs, rhododendrons, camellias, magnolias, pieris, ceanothus etc. Clematis, bog plants, roses, primulas. TEA. *Adm £1 Chd 50p. Sun May 8 (2-6)*

4 Cliff Road, NW1 && (Ewen Henderson Esq) Cliff Road is between Camden Park Rd and York Way. A 60′ × 20′ garden of tone, texture and ambiguity; containing owner's sculpture and found objects. *Combined odm £1.50 with* **108 Camden Mews**. *Sun July 24 (2.30-6)*

The Coach House, SW6 &&& (Dr John Newton) Landridge Rd. Nearest underground station Putney Bridge. Across New Kings Rd into Burlington Rd, R into Rigault Rd. The garden is at the end of Rigualt Rd behind the white wall. Small 34′ × 36′ walled garden with pond, fountain; herbaceous borders, surrounding small lawn designed to have a year round flowering. *Adm 80p Chd 40p. Sun June 19 (2-5.30)*

By Appointment Gardens. These owners do not have a fixed opening day usually because they do not like crowds or have insufficient parking space. Owner will often give guided tour.

29 Deodar Road, SW15 &&&& (Peter & Marigold Assinder) Putney. Off Putney Bridge Rd Bus: 14, 22, 37, 74, 80, 85, 93, 220. Tubes: Putney Bridge and East Putney. Small garden 130ft × 25ft running down to Thames with lovely view. Camellias, wide range of variegated shrubs, hardy geraniums. Featured in Private Gardens of London by Arabella Lennox Boyd 1990. Cuttings and visits at other times by arrangement **Tel 081 788 7976**. TEA. *Adm £1 Chd 50p (Share to Royal Hospital & Home Putney SW15®). Suns April 24 (2-5)*

20 Eatonville Road, SW17 (Pamela Johnson & Gethyn Davies) Tooting. 400yds from Tooting Bec tube (Northern Line). Off Trinity Rd and Upper Tooting Park. Bus stop on Trinity Rd at top of Eatonville Rd Nos. 249, 219, 349 or on Balham High Rd outside tube Nos. 155, 355. 42′ × 23′ S facing garden. Filled with an imaginative variety of plants to give yr-round colour and form. Mixed borders, climbing plants, containers and small pond. Also tiny front garden. TEAS. *Adm 50p Chd 20p. Suns May 1, July 31 (2-6)*

Eccleston Square, SW1 &&&& (Garden Manager Roger Phillips) Central London; just off Belgrave Road near Victoria Station, parking allowed on Suns. 3-acre square was planned by Cubitt in 1828. The present Garden Committee have worked intensively over the last 12 years to see what can be created despite the inner city problems of drought, dust, fumes, shade and developers. Within the formal structure the garden is sub-divided into mini-gardens incl camellia, iris, rose, fern, and container garden. A national collection of ceanothus incl more than 50 species and culitvers is held in the square. TEAS. *Adm £1 Chd 50p. Suns May 1, June 19 (2-5)*

Edwardes Sq, W8 &&& (Edwardes Sq Garden Committee) Edwardes Sq is off Kensington High Street. Accessible by bus and underground. Car parking is allowed on Sundays. 3-acres laid out circa 1815. Spring flowering trees, shrubs and bulbs. *Adm £1 Chd 50p. Sun April 24 (2-6)*

The Elms &&& (Dr & Mrs R Rawlings) Kingston-on-Thames entry via Manorgate Rd. 1m E Kingston on A308. Buses to Kingston Hospital: LT 213, 85, 57, 71; G line 714, 715, 718. BR Norbiton Station 100yds. Enter via garages in Manorgate Rd which is off A308 at foot of Kingston Hill. Wheelchairs limited to parts of the garden and tea area. Small (55′ × 25′) compact town-house rear garden, of special interest to horticulturists and plant lovers. Truly a collector's garden with numerous rare and unusual plants, particularly featuring rhododendrons, magnolias, camellias, dwarf conifers and a wide range of evergreen and deciduous shrubs. Small trees, herbaceous, ground cover plants, a two-level pool with geyser and well planted margins, roses, clematis and other choice and tender climbers, alpine trays are also featured. This small garden even bears some fruit namely, plum, pear, and soft fruits. Seeds and plants available. The garden has been featured on the radio and in various publications. TEAS in aid of Home Farm Trust and Princess Alice Hospice. *Adm £1 Chd 50p. Sats, Suns March 19, 20; April 16, 17; May 14, 15 (2-5)*

49 & 51 Etchingham Park Rd, N3 &&& (Robert Double, Gilbert Cook and Diane & Alan Langleben) Finchley. Off Ballards Lane overlooking Victoria Park. Station: Finchley Central. 2 rear gardens. ⅝-acre; lawn, small orchard, shrubs, large selection of hostas. Sculpture by Wm Mitchell. Exhibition and sale of water colour paintings by Robert Double. TEAS. *Adm £1 Chd free. Sun May 15 (2-6)*

Fenton House, NW3 & (The National Trust) 300yds NNW of Hampstead Underground Station. 600yds S of Heath by Jack Straw's Castle. 1½-acre walled garden in its first decade of development. It is on three levels with compartments concealed by yew hedges and containing different plantings, some still in the experimental stage. The herbaceous borders are being planned to give yr-round interest while the recently brick paved sunken rose garden is already donning the patina of age. The formal lawn area contrasts agreeably with the rustic charm of the orchard and kitchen garden. *Adm £1.50 Chd 50p. Sun April 17 (11-6)*

Frogmore Gardens see Berkshire

¶**73 Forest Drive East**, E11 &&& (A J Wyllie) Leytonstone. Into Whipps Cross Rd, then SW into James Lane. 1st L into Clare Rd, 1st R into Forest Drive East. By bus to Whipps Cross Hospital or tube to Leytonstone and bus to James Lane. 20′ × 65′ country garden in miniature, but with full-sized plants, behind a terraced house. Small lawn with mixed borders leading to a shrub and woodland area. Two fountains and various unusual plants. Also 20′ front garden informally planted round formal paths and centre piece. TEA. *Adm £1 Chd 50p (Share to Army Benevolent Fund®). Sun Aug 21 (11-5)*

17 Fulham Park Gardens, SW6 & (A Noel Esq) Putney Bridge Tube. Refer to A-Z. Up Kings Road L at Threshers Off-licence, (Elysium St.) into Fulham Park Gardens. Turn R, on R hand side. 40ft × 17ft romantic silver and white garden, with interesting variety of plants in harmoniously designed form. An oasis of peace in a hostile environment. Featured in Sunday Times and on ITV. *Adm £2, OAPs £1. Suns May 8, June 19, July 10, Sept 18 (2.30-6)*

Goldsborough, SE3 &&& 112 Westcombe Park Rd, Blackheath. Located between Greenwich Village Centre and The Standard Blackheath. N of Blackheath Heath and E of Greenwich Park. Nearest BR Westcombe Park (10 mins walk) or Maze Hill (15 mins walk). Buses to the Standard from Central London and surrounding areas. Hoppa buses stop directly outside. Westcombe Park Rd situated in A-Z of London. Car parking available. Community garden for close care and nursing home residents. Approx ½ acre of landscaped gardens, incl walkways of rose-covered pergolas; fish ponds; herbaceous borders and colourful annuals. A very sheltered and peaceful garden. TEAS. *Adm £1 Chd 50p. Sun July 3 (1.30-5)*

Regular Openers. See head of county section.

By Appointment Gardens. Avoid the crowds. Good chance of a tour by owner. See garden description for telephone number.

5 Greenaway Gardens, NW3 &* (Mrs Marcus) Tube equidistant (½ mile) Hampstead or Finchley Road Stations. Buses: Finchley Road, West End Lane stop, nos. 13, 82, 113. From Finchley Road, turn up Frognal Lane, 2nd on L. Unusually large and varied London garden landscaped on three levels with year-round interest. Terrace with variety of climbing plants; water feature and swimming pool; steps to large lawn surrounded by borders with wide variety of trees, shrubs and herbaceous perennials, decorative urns and furniture. Partially suitable for wheelchairs. TEAS July 17 only. *Adm 80p Chd 30p. Suns May 15, June 19, July 17 (2-6)*

¶12 Greenheys Close &* (Mrs Joan G Moody) Northwood. 10min walk from Northwood Met Line. L into Green Lane, L at Maxwell Rd, L again at Murray Rd (Police St on corner). Greenheys Close on L past pillar box. From M25 at junction 18, take 404 Rickmansworth direction, after Mount Vernon Hospital, go over lights at Green Lane, Northwood, take 2nd on L into Murray Rd, Greenheys Close on R. A well-maintained town garden - plus! Accent on colour through the yr. Extensive collection of healthy roses flowering over a long period, unusual bulbs, climbers and shrubs, many herbaceous and annual plants. Open plan garden in a Neo-Georgian Close. *Adm £1 Chd 50p. Sun July 17 (2-5)*

7 The Grove, N6 * (Thomas Lyttelton Esq) The Grove is between Highgate West Hill & Hampstead Lane. Stations: Archway or Highgate (Northern Line, Barnet trains) Bus: 210, 271 to Highgate Village. ½-acre designed for maximum all-yr-round interest with minimum upkeep. TEAS June 5 only. *Adm £1 OAPs/Chd 50p. Suns April 17, June 5 (2-5)*

Hall Grange &* (Methodist Home for the Aged) Croydon. Situated in Shirley Church Rd near to junction with Upper Shirley Rd. From N leave A232 at junction of Shirley Rd and Wickham Rd. From S leave A212 at junction of Gravell Hill and Shirley Hills Rd. The garden was laid out circa 1913 by Rev William Wilkes secretary to the RHS and breeder of the Shirley Poppy. Approx 5 acres of natural heathland is planted with azaleas, rhododendrons, heathers and shrubs and remains unchanged. A grassy area contains many wild flowers and is mown only once a year to permit natural reproduction. No parking at garden. TEAS. *Adm £1 Chd free. Sun May 15 (2-5.30)*

117 Hamilton Terrace, NW8 &* (Mrs K Herbert and the Tenants Association). Hamilton Terrace is parallel with Maida Vale to the E. Buses from Marble Arch 16, 16a, 8, go up Edgeware Road to Maida Vale. Alight at Elgin Avenue, cross Maida Vale and go up Abercorn Place. 117 is to the L. There is room in Hamilton Terrace to park cars. 117 is the opp end of Hamilton Terrace from Lords nearly opp St Mark's Church. This is a large garden for London. The lawn at the back is kept partly wild with different grasses and wild flowers. There is a tiny garden in memory of Dame Anna Neagle who lived in the house. There is a standard rose near the house given in her memory. TEA. *Adm £1 Chd 20p (Share to the Spastics Society®). Sun May 22, July 17 (2-6)*

11 Hampstead Way, NW11, *& (Mr & Mrs R L Bristow). Nearest tube station Golders Green, 10 minute walk up North End Road, L into Wellgarth Road, R up Hampstead Way. 1/4-acre prize winning garden, water features. unusual plants around lawns in the front and patio at the back. TEAS. *Adm £1 Chd 50p. Sun June 19 (2-6). Opening together with* **3 Wellgarth Road**

133 Haverstock Hill, NW3 *& (Mrs Catherine Horwood). Belsize Park Tube Station turn L out of station. Buses C11, C12, 168 (Haverstock Arms stop). Prizewinning 120ft long narrow garden divided into rooms. New design features incl paved terrace and newly established bed of old and English roses with clematis and cottage garden companion planting. Many unusual tender perennial and scented plants; wildlife pond. Featured in Country Life and Wonderful Window-boxes. Highly Commended in The Gardener Magazine Gardener of the Year competition. *Adm £1 Chd free. Sun June 26 (2-6)*

37 Heath Drive, NW3 &*& (Mr & Mrs C Caplin) Station: Finchley Rd; buses: 82, 13 & 113 Heath Drive. Many uncommon plants; lawn; pond; rockery; ferns. Unusual treatment of fruit trees, greenhouse and conservatory. 1982, 1983, 1987, 1988, 1989, 1991 winner of Frankland Moore Trophy. Featured in Arabella Lennox-Boyd's Private Gardens of London. TEA. *Adm £1 Chd 50p. Suns May 8, July 24 (2.30-6)*

30 Hercies Road &*& (Mr & Mrs J Gates) Hillingdon. From London West on A40 to Master Brewer Motel, N Hillingdon 1st L after traffic lights No 30 is on the R.h.s. From Oxford E on A40 to Uxbridge, roundabout past junction 1 Swakeleys turn R onto B483 Park Rd. 1st L Honeycroft Hill continue into Hercies Rd. By tube Hillingdon (Swakeleys) turn R over bridge. Front garden: Parterre and screed garden, leading to a long narrow mature cottage style back garden, patio with tubs and vine; herbaceous planting, wild garden with trees, shrubs and rhododendrons. TEAS. *Adm £1 Chd 10p. Sun May 1, (10.30-5)*

Highgate Village, N6 * The Grove is between Highgate West Hill & Hampstead Lane Stations: Archway or Highgate (Northern Line, Barnet trains). Bus: 210, 271 to Highgate Village. Tea Lauderdale House & Kenwood. *Adm £1 each garden Chd 50p. Sun June 19 (2-5)*
    4 The Grove (Cob Stenham Esq) 2-tiered with formal upper garden; view across Heath; orchard in lower garden
    5 The Grove (Mr & Mrs A J Hines) Newly-designed garden on 2 levels

Highwood Ash, NW7 * (Mr & Mrs R Gluckstein) Highwood Hill, Mill Hill. From London via A41 (Watford Way) to Mill Hill Circus; turn right up Lawrence St; at top bear left up Highwood Hill; house at top on right. Station: Edgware (Northern Line) Bus 251 (Sat only). 3¼-acre incl rose garden, shrub and herbaceous borders, rhododendrons, azaleas, lake with waterfall, a mixture of formal and informal. TEAS. *Adm £1 Chd 50p. Sat, Sun, May 21, 22 (2-6)*

¶**5 Hillcrest Avenue NW11** ✿ (Mrs R M Rees) Hillcrest Ave is off Bridge Lane. By bus to Temple Fortune, Buses 13, 82, 102, 260. Nearest Tube Golders Green or Finchley Central. Walk down Bridge Lane. Small labour saving colourful garden with many interesting features; rockery, fish pond, conservatory, tree fern. Low maintenance, all-round interest, acid bed. TEAS. *Adm 80p Chd 40p (Share to ADS®). Sun June 26 (2-6)*

1 Hocroft Avenue NW2 ✿✿✿ (Dr & Mrs Derek Bunn) 113 bus (stop at Cricklewood Lane). Travelling N from the Finchley Rd on the Hendon Way (A41), take 3rd turn on L into Hocroft Ave. Easy parking. Prize-winning garden with yr-round interest, especially in the spring. Front garden shown on BBC Gardeners' World, in their Front Garden series. Black and white feature in The Independent and The Evening Standard. Mixed borders in the back garden with a wide variety of plants against a background of trees. Subject of an article by Tony Venison in Country Life focusing on plant sales in the NGS. Homemade TEAS. *Adm £1 Chd free. (Share to Special Trustee Fund for Bart's Hospital®) Sun, Mon May 1, 2 (2-6)*

¶**125 Honor Oak Park** SE23 ✿✿ (Mrs Heather West) BR station: Honor Oak Park turn R. Off South Circular (A205) via Honor Oak Rd. Small 75′ × 45′ multifarious froth on two levels: the lower shady with small beds, the upper sunny with grass, verandah and pots. TEAS in aid of BHHI. *Adm £1 Chd 50p. Sun June 26 (2-6)*

Hornbeams ✿✿✿ (Dr & Mrs R B Stalbow) Priory Drive, Stanmore. 5m SE of Watford; underground: Stanmore; Priory Drive private rd off Stanmore Hill (A4140 Stanmore-Bushey Heath Rd). ½ acre; flowering shrubs, al pines, hardy cyclamen, species tulips; unusual plants; vegetable garden; vine; pool; greenhouse, conservatory. Lemonade & biscuits. *Adm £1 Chd free (Plant proceeds to Jerusalem Botanic Garden). Sun May 15 (2.30-6)*

Kensington Gardens W8 ✿ Stations: Kensington High St or Gloucester Rd. Bus Milestone for 9, 46, 52, 72; Gloucester Rd for 49, 74. From Gloucester Rd turn into Victoria Grove then into St Alban's Grove or R for Cottesmore Gdns. *Combined adm £3 Chd 50p. Sun June 19 (2-6)*

11 Cottesmore Gardens (Hon Mrs Adrian Berry) Informal, N facing, densely planted walled garden, with a large collection of pots of all sizes
6 St Albans Grove (Mr & Mrs S Keswick) Small London garden planted in the last 3yrs specialising in tender shrubs
7 St Albans Grove (Mrs E Norman-Butler) A country garden designed for all seasons and one pair of hands, which won the Brighter Kensington Back Garden prize in 1993

Lambeth Community Care Centre, SE11 ✿✿✿ Monkton Street. Lambeth North tube, turn onto Kennington Rd until Brook Drive, then R between bakery and office and through passage to Monkton St or drive through St Mary's Gardens. Elephant & Castle tube, cut through behind swimming baths to opposite end of Brook Drive, L into passage through Sullivan Rd. Buses: 3, 159, 109 Kennington Rd; 176, 12, 63, 68 Elephant & Castle. ⅔-acre

garden ideal for people in wheelchairs to see all aspects of garden. Mixed shrubs, trees, small rose garden, herbs, interesting walkways and mixed borders. Part of award winning hospital designed by Edward Cullinan Architects. Indoor planted area also open. Prize winner in London Hospital Gardens Competition. TEAS. *Adm 75p OAP/Chd 25p (Share to St. Thomas's Trustees for the garden®). Sat, Sun June 4, 5 (2-5)*

Lambeth Palace, SE1 ✿✿ (The Archbishop of Canterbury & Mrs Carey) Waterloo main line and underground, Westminster, Lambeth and Vauxhall tubes all about 10 mins walk. 3, 10, 44, 76, 77, 159, 170, 507 buses go near garden. Entry to garden on Lambeth Palace Rd (not at gatehouse) 2nd largest private garden in London. Land in hand of Archbishops of Canterbury since end C12. Work on garden carried out over last 100 years but significant renewal has taken place during last 6 years; restored rose walk, new border beneath wall by Beth Chatto, herb garden, shrub border, wild garden, rhododendrons, spring bulbs and camellias. *Adm £2 OAP/Chd 10-16 £1 (Share to Lambeth Fund®). Sat April 9 (2-5)*

15 Langbourne Avenue, N6 ✿ (R P St J Partridge) Holly Lodge Estate. Off Highgate West Hill. Entrance by car via Swains Lane. A steeply rising garden behind a semi-detached house, full of dramatic foliage interspersed with flowers; large leaved plants such as bergenia, ciliata, melianthus, hydrangea aspera, gunnera and many others, create an impression of seclusion and mystery in a small garden. *Adm £1. Private visits welcome* Tel 081 340 5806

12 Lansdowne Rd, W11 ✿ (The Lady Amabel Lindsay) Holland Park. Turn N off Holland Park Ave nr Holland Park Station; or W off Ladbroke Grove ½-way along. Bus: 12, 88, GL 711, 715. Bus stop & station: Holland Park, 4 mins. Medium-sized fairly wild garden; border, climbing roses, shrubs; mulberry tree 200 yrs old. *Adm £1 Chd 50p. Wed May 18 (2-6)*

10 Lawn Road, NW3 ✿✿✿ (Mrs P Findlay) Tube to Belsize Park or go up Haverstock Hill. Turn R at Haverstock Arms then L. House 200yds on R, with blue door. ⅒-acre approx; uniquely curvaceous design of intersecting circles, set in rectangular format. Organically cultured garden, very heavily stocked; many unusual and native species plants. *Adm £1 Chd 50p. Sun June 19 (2.30-6)*

15 Lawrence Street, SW3 ✿ (John Casson Esq) Between King's Road and the river down Old Church Street S from King's Road to the river, turn L round the statue of Sir Thomas More then L (behind garden) into Lawrence Street. Garden at top of street on L. Nearest tubes: Sloane Square and South Kensington. Prize winning small Chelsea cottage type garden, old-fashioned flowers, clematis, roses and some unusual plants. Plants to cover each season. House built c1790, not open except for access to garden. *Adm £1 Chd 50p (Share to Chelsea Physic Garden®). Sat June 11 (2-6)*

By Appointment Gardens. See head of county section

Leyborne Park Gardens ⚘⚘ Two minute walk from Kew Gardens station. Take exit signposted Kew Gardens. On leaving station forecourt bear R past shops. Leyborne Park is 1st rd on R. Bus 391, R68 to Kew Gdns station. Bus 65 to Kew Gdns, Victoria Gate. Access by car is from Sandycombe Rd. TEAS. *Combined adm £1.50 Chd free (Share to Arthritis and Rheumatism Council for Research®). Sun June 19 (2-5.30)*
> **36 Leyborne Park** (David & Frances Hopwood) 120ft long mature, family garden; architect designed for minimum upkeep with maximum foliage effects; patio; imaginative children's play area; huge eucalyptus. TEAS
> **38 Leyborne Park** ⚘ (Mr & Mrs A Sandall) 120ft long organic family garden; lawn with mixed borders; containers; long established vine; alliums, lavenders, eryngiums, scented pelargoniums, bamboos, plants for the dry garden
> **40 Leyborne Park** (Debbie Pointon-Taylor) 120ft long garden; heather and conifer garden; lawn and mixed borders; mature shrubs; patio with containers

1 Lister Road, E11 ⚘⚘ (Myles Challis Esq) Leytonstone underground station (central line). 5mins to High Rd Leytonstone. Hills garage marks cnr of Lister Rd which is directly off High Rd. Garden designer's unexpected, densely planted sub-tropical garden containing a mixture of tender plants such as daturas, gingers, cannas, tree ferns, bananas and hardy exotics including gunneras, bamboos, cordylines, phormiums and large leaved perennials in a space unbelievably only 40' × 20'. TEAS. *Adm £1 Chd 50p. Sun Aug 21 (11-5)*

21a The Little Boltons, SW10 ⚘ (Mrs D Capron) Between Fulham and Old Brompton Rd off Tregunter Rd, next to The Boltons. Nearest tube Earls Court, buses 30, 14, 74. 70ft prize winning herbaceous plant collection. Portrayed in the book 'Private Gardens of London' by Arabella Lennox-Boyd. *Adm £1 Chd 25p. Sun June 26 (12-6)*

Little Lodge &⚘⚘ (Mr & Mrs P Hickman) Watts Rd, Thames Ditton (Station 5 mins). A3 from London; after Hook underpass turn left to Esher; at Scilly Isles turn R towards Kingston; after 2nd railway bridge turn L to Thames Ditton village; house opp library after Giggs Hill Green. A cottage style informal garden within 15m of central London. Many British native plants. Garden has an atmosphere of tranquillity, featuring plants with subtle colours and fragrance; small brick-pathed vegetable plot. TEAS. *Adm £1 Chd free (Share to Cancer Research®). Sun June 19 (11.30-6)*

22 Loudoun Road, NW8 (Ruth Barclay) 3 to 4 min walk to St. John's Wood tube station. Lies between Abbey Road and Finchley Rd serviced by buses, minutes from bus stop. Small front garden, well matured, started from scratch 9 years ago. A strong emphasis on design with leaf and flowers subtle colour combination, water, arbour garden within a garden. Back Italianate courtyard, romantic and mysterious. Prizewinner for 4 consecutive years. Featured in a number of gardening books. Most recently 'Town Gardens'. TEAS. *Adm £1 Chd 25p. Sun May 22 (2-6.30)*

Malvern Terrace, Barnsbury, N1 & Approach from S via Pentonville Rd into Penton St, Barnsbury Rd; from N via Thornhill Rd opp Albion pub. Tube: Highbury & Islington. Bus: 19, 30 to Upper St Town Hall. Unique London terrace of 1830s houses built on site of Thos Oldfield's dairy and cricket field. Cottage-style gardens in cobbled cul-de-sac; music. Victorian plant stall. Home-made TEAS. *Combined adm £1.50 Chd free. Sun May 8 (2-5.30)*
> **1 Malvern Terrace** (Mr & Mrs Martin Leman)
> **2 Malvern Terrace** (Mr & Mrs K McDowall)
> **3 Malvern Terrace** (Mr & Mrs A Robertson)
> **4 Malvern Terrace** (Mr & Mrs P Dacre)
> **5 Malvern Terrace**
> **6 Malvern Terrace** (Dr B A Lynch)
> **7 Malvern Terrace** (Joanna Smith & Mark Vanhegan)
> **8 Malvern Terrace** (Mr & Mrs R Le Fanu)
> **10 Malvern Terrace** (Dr & Mrs P Sherwood)

¶**36 Marryat Road SW19** ⚘⚘ (Mrs Annie Finch) 1m from Wimbledon Station. Up the hill turn R from village and green. Access for wheelchairs ltd to terrace. 1-acre garden with large area of mixed borders for yr-round interest. Unusual plants, special feature of containers on terrace. TEAS. *Adm £1 Chd free. Sun July 10 (2-5)*

¶**13 Mercers Road N19** ⚘ (Dr & Mrs N Millward) off Holloway Rd (A1) N of Odeon Cinema. 30' × 15' front garden featuring cool whites, greys and greens. 30' × 20' rear garden on two levels. Profusion of pastel shades from April to Sept. Many small-flowered clematis, pink schizophragma, rosa soulieana and other interesting climbers and perennials. *Adm £1 Chd 50p. Private visits welcome for small groups and individuals please* Tel 071 281 2674

2 Millfield Place, N6 &⚘ Garden is off Highgate West Hill, E side of Hampstead Heath. Buses 210, 271 to Highgate Village or C2, C12, 214 to Parliament Hill Fields terminus. Nearest train stations Kentish Town, Tufnell Park and North London BR line to Gospel Oak. 1½-acre spring and woodland garden with camellias and rhododendrons. Long mixed herbaceous border with some formal bedding schemes; small orchard. TEAS only May 8. *Adm £1 Chd 50p. Suns May 8, July 31 (2-6)*

29 Mostyn Road SW19 ⚘⚘ (Chris & Sue Spencer) Merton Park is 1m N of Wimbledon. From London cross Wimbledon Common, through Wimbledon Village, down Wimbledon Hill into The Broadway. Follow one-way system after Wimbledon Station following it round to the L before turning L into Hartfield Rd. Turn R at the end of Hartfield Rd cross level crossing. Mostyn Rd is 3rd on L. Greystones is 200 metres on R. ⅕-acre small garden laid out by Gertrude Jekyll in 1913 with further plantings added by her between 1913 and 1922. The garden has been restored by the present owners. Re-planting was carried out in 1992 using Jekyll's original plant lists. The garden is far from mature and the owners are still in the process of trying to arrange plantings to Jekyllian principles. The garden has been featured in Traditional Homes and Period House and Its Garden. Also BBC Television's Gardeners' World. TEAS. *Adm £1 Chd 50p (Share to St Mary's The Virgin®). Sat, Sun June 18, 19 (2-6)*

52 Mount Park Road, W5 ✿✿ (Mr & Mrs Paddy O'Hagan) Ealing. 7min walk N from Ealing Broadway station. No 52 is opposite No 71. 100ft × 50ft triangular garden on 2 levels. Designed for wildlife in 1989 by Chris Baines; woodland, pond and bog area. Terrace with interesting pots and architectural plants; decorative vegetable garden and glass fountain; classical music; conservatory. TEAS in aid of SATFA. *Adm 80p Chd 30p. Sun June 12 (2-6)*

33 Mundania Road SE 22 ✿✿ (Ms Helen Penn) 63 bus to Honor Oak. Nearest BR station Peckham Rye. Plantswoman's garden; 15' × 40' shaded N facing front garden, small woodland plants some unusual; 100' × 40' S facing back garden with variety of bulbs, herbaceous plants and shrubs. Small pond with native grasses. Conservatory with tender plants. 50' × 20' organic vegetable and herb garden adjoining. TEAS. *Adm £1 Chd free. Sun May 15 (2-6). Private visits welcome May to June please* **Tel 081 693 4741**

Museum of Garden History, The Tradescant Trust ✿✿✿ St Mary-at-Lambeth, Lambeth Palace Road, SE1. Bus: 507 Red Arrow from Victoria or Waterloo, alight Lambeth Palace. 7,450 sq ft. replica of C17 garden planted in churchyard with flowers known and grown by John Tradescant. Tombs of the Tradescants and Admiral Bligh of the 'Bounty' in the garden. Opened by HM the Queen Mother in 1983. Museum being established in restored church of St Mary-at-Lambeth saved from demolition by The Trust. TEAS. *Adm £1 OAPs/Chd 50p (Share to Museum of Garden History®).* ▲*Sun May 15 (10.30-5)*

Muswell Hill Gardens N10 ✿ Just off Alexandra Park Rd between Muswell Hill and the North Circular Rd. Teas in aid of St Andrew's Church, vicarage garden or church hall if wet. *Combined odm £1.50, 80p per garden Chd free. Sun June 11 (2-5)*
   5 Cecil Road (Ben Loftus Esq) 70' × 20' garden designer's peaceful garden; old apple trees, roses, species foxgloves, masses of lilies, paeonies, unusual hellebores, ferns, bulbs and evergreens; many scented plants, rich and varied foliage
   52 Cecil Road (Mr & Mrs A Pask) Family garden with 2 long raised beds. Many climbing plants, clematis, jasmines, akebia, passiflora etc, variegated foliage for flower arranging; flowering shrubs and perennials. Also very small pond
   ¶**37 Creighton Avenue** ✿ (Tim Elkins & Margaret Weaver) Buses 43, 134, 243 from Highgate tube to Muswell Hill Broadway-Fortis Green Rd, along Tetherdown, turn R into Creighton Avenue at mini-roundabout. 120' × 30' well stocked rear garden S facing, patio with pots, alpines, mixed borders and ornamental trees

Myddelton House ✿✿✿ (Lee Valley Regional Authority) Enfield. A short distance from A10 Great Cambridge Rd and Bullsmore Lane junction which is 100yds S of junction 25 of M25. Station: Turkey St on Liverpool St Line. The 4-acres of garden were created by Edward A Bowles, author of gardening trilogy 'My Garden in Spring, Summer, Autumn and Winter'. The gardens feature a diverse and unusual plant collection including a large selection of many species and varieties of naturalised bulbs, as well as the national collection of award winning bearded

irises. The grounds have a large pond with terrace, two conservatories and interesting historical artefacts. TEA and plants for sale on NGS days and Suns only. *Adm £1.20 Concessions 60p. Open every weekday except Aug 29, Dec 26 to 30 (10-3.30) and last Sunday in the month (2-5) Feb to Oct. NGS days Mons April 4, May 30, Sun July 31 (2-5). No concessions on NGS days and Suns*

15 Norcott Road, N16 ✿✿ (Amanda & John Welch) Buses 73, 149, 76, 67, 243 (see bus map and A to Z) Clapton or Stoke Newington Stations (Rectory Rd closed Suns). Largish (for Hackney) walled back garden. Pond (enlarged since 93), fruit trees, herbs, tubs, herbaceous plants especially irises, geraniums and campanulas. TEAS. *Adm 70p Chd 50p (Share to St Joseph's Hospice®). Suns May 22, July 17 (2-6)*

95 North Road ✿✿ (Michael Le Fleming Esq) Kew. 500yds S of Kew Gardens Station (District Line & North London Link) on its eastern, down-line side. Exit in North Rd. Buses 391, R68. 100ft garden on a flowing plan with a high wall and interesting mixed planting to disguise the basic plot. Old roses and wisteria; irises; good foliage; a small pond and paved area with urns, pots and conservatory. TEA. *Adm £1 Chd 50p. Suns May 22, June 26 (11-6)*

North Ruislip Gardens Ruislip, Middlesex. *Combined odm £1.50 Chd free. Sun June 5 (2-5)*
   235 Eastcote Road ✿✿ (Messrs T & J Hall) From Ruislip High Street take the B466 (Eastcote Road) nearest tube Ruislip Manor. Parking off Eastcote Rd in Evelyn Ave please. Medium sized suburban garden. 115ft × 80ft. Contains a wide variety of herbaceous perennials and shrubs, shady patio area and ponds. TEA
   82 Evelyn Avenue ✿ (Mr & Mrs K Morgan) Refer to A-Z. Nearest Underground Station – Ruislip Manor. Turn R out of Station. Continue up and over the hill; cross the Eastcote Rd and turn 1st R into Evelyn Ave. Suburban garden 40ft × 170ft. Curving borders and island beds planted with shrubs and herbaceous plants to give yr-round interests. Lawns and mature trees
   ¶**86 Evelyn Avenue** (Isabel & Frank Thornton) Med-sized working garden approx 180' × 40'. Pond, productive vegetable plot, soft fruit, shrubs and herbaceous plants to give continuing interest. Mature fruit trees

¶**2 Northbourne Road** SW4 ✿✿ (Mr & Mrs Edward A Holmes) Clapham Common tube. Buses 137, 137A, 37. W facing, walled garden 36' × 56' with good architectural planting and rose pergola. Designed with a young family in mind and planted In Feb 1991. TEAS. *Adm £1 OAPs/Chd 50p (Share to the Foundation for the Study of Infant Deaths®). Sun June 12 (2-6)*

Orchard Cottage see Kent

By Appointment Gardens. These owners do not have a fixed opening day usually because they do not like crowds or have insufficient parking space. Owner will often give guided tour.

Ormeley Lodge ✍ (Lady Annabel Goldsmith) Ham Gate Avenue, Richmond. From Richmond Park, exit at Ham Gate into Ham Gate Avenue. First house on R. From Richmond A307, 1½m past New Inn on R, first turning on L. House is last on L. Bus: 65. Large walled garden in delightful rural setting on Ham Common. Newly designed formal garden, wide herbaceous borders, box hedges. Walk through to newly planted orchard with wild flowers. Vegetable garden. Secluded swimming pool area, trellised tennis court with roses and climbers. TEA. *Adm £1 Chd 20p. Sun June 26 (3-6)*

¶**43 Ormeley Road** SW12 ✍❀ (Richard Glassborow & Susan Venner) Nearest tube and BR station Balham, 5 mins walk, off Balham High Rd. Small gardens within a small garden 30′ X 18′ approx, SW facing, full of unusual plants. *Adm £1 Chd free (Share to Friends of the Earth®). Sun May 22 (2-6)*

Flat 1, 1F Oval Road, NW1 ✍ (Sheila Jackson) Tube station Camden Town. Buses: any bus to Camden Town, C2 and 274 stop very near. Parking difficult near centre on Sunday. A small side garden approaches an illustrator's very small hidden back garden approx 24ft × 20ft which abuts the Euston railway line. The garden is stuffed with a great variety of plants, many in pots banked to create interesting shapes and compositions, making use of a variety of levels. Featured in 'Blooming Small, A City Dwellers Garden' *Adm £1 Chd 50p. Fri June 3 (6-9) Sat, Sun June 4, 5 (2-5). Also private visits welcome, please Tel 071 267 0655*

¶**78 Palace Road** SW2 ✍❀ (Mr & Mrs D S Senior) BR station Streatham Hill 15min walk (NB Tulse Hill BR closed Sundays). Buses 2, 68, 196 to Tulse Hill station. By car S Circular Rd, just W of Tulse Hill one-way system. Located corner Palace Rd and Northstead Rd. 90′ × 60′ garden planted mainly for foliage effect and yr-round interest. Shrubs, bamboos, grasses, some interesting small trees. Part planted with Mediterranean plants to suit hot dry conditions, areas left wild to encourage wildlife, pond. *Adm £1 Chd free. Sun June 19 (2-6)*

¶**10A The Pavement** SE27 ❀ (Brendan Byrne) Chapel Rd. Located off Ladas Rd down alleyway behind All Seasons Fish Bar. Buses 68 to Knights Hill alight at S London College or W Norwood Bus Garage. No. 2 to bus garage or Gypsy Rd. BR W Norwood. Come out Knights Hill, turn L. Chapel Rd is 10 mins walk on L after passing bus garage. Possibly the smallest garden in London (entry restricted to 5 people at any one time). A hidden oasis behind houses and shops. Collection of plants and shrubs incl roses, blackberries, raspberries, wild flowers, herbaceous and bedding plants, daturas. Plants and shrubs in containers, hanging baskets, window boxes. *Adm 80p Chd free (Share to Horses & Ponies Protection Assoc®). Sun July 3 (10-12, 2-6)*

¶**43 Penerley Rd** SE6 ⅍✍❀ (Mr & Mrs E Thorp) BR stations Catford, Catford Bridge (15 mins walk). Buses 36, 36B, 47, 54, 75, 124, 160, 172, 180, 181, 185, 202, 208, 284, 306, (5mins walk). Off A21 just S of S Circular Rd. Plant lover's shady garden 33′ × 100′, full of interesting and unusual plants. Formal lawns, informal planting,

paved areas with ferns, hostas and other foliage plants in pots. TEA. *Adm £1 Acc chd free. Suns May 22, June 19, Sept 11, (2-6). Private visits welcome June to Sept, please Tel 081 698 1741*

35 Perrymead St, SW6 ✍ (Mr & Mrs Richard Chilton) Fulham. New King's Rd W from Chelsea; 1st on left after Wandsworth Bridge Rd. Stations: Fulham Broadway or Parsons Green; bus 22 from Chelsea; 28 from Kensington. Small paved garden with ornamental feature; surrounded by mature trees. Shrubs, climbers (especially clematis) interspersed with summer planting suitable for shade. *Adm £1 Chd 50p. Sun July 10 (2-6)*

¶**12 Peterborough Villas** SW6 ⅍✍❀ (Mr & Mrs Richard Bullock) From Fulham Broadway station (underground Wimbledon line; 14 bus) take Harwood Rd (opp station) S to New Kings Rd (11 and 22 buses); turn R, then immediately L into Bagley's Lane, Peterborough Villas is cul-de-sac on West L side of Bagley's Lane 25yds from New Kings Rd, No. 12 at far end. Parking in neighbouring streets but not in Peterborough Villas. Walled garden approx 40′ × 40′. Herbaceous borders with shrubs and ornamental trees to give yr-round interest. Lawn, mature apple and pear trees. Clematis, solanum and other climbers. TEAS. *Adm £1 OAPs/Chd 50p. Sun July 31 (2-5.30)*

3 Radnor Gardens ✍❀ (Ms Jill Payne) Twickenham. Turn off Heath Rd into Radnor Rd by Tamplins garage and R into Radnor gardens. Small garden of an 11′ 6″ wide terraced house owned by a compulsive plant collector. Front garden – raised bed and terracotta pots. Back garden – 45′ long, 6′ × 6′ patio, winding brick path and two tiny ponds. Garden crammed with a motley collection ranging from native wild flowers to tender plants. Small conservatory. *Adm 50p Chd 20p. Suns April 17, May 15, July 3, 10 (10-5)*

¶**9 Ranelagh Avenue** SW6 ❀ (Mrs P Tham) Nearest tube Putney Bridge. Approx 60′ × 40′. A semi-formal two level garden featuring shade tolerant plants, incl many hostas and trees; arbutus, Judas, magnolia, crab apple. Small patio with container grown plants; datura, hostas, vegetables. A resident but crowd-shy-toad! *Adm £1 Chd 50p. Sun July 10 (2-5.30)*

Ranulf Road Gardens NW2 ✍❀ At junction of Finchley Rd with Platts Lane and Fortune Green Rd enter Ardwick Rd and bear L into Ranulf Rd, nos. 9 and 11 are on L at brow of hill. Junction is 150yds S of junction of Finchley Rd and Hendon Way. Buses 13, 113, 82 from Finchley Rd station, 13, 82, 28 from Golders Green, 28 from West Hampstead station. TEAS. *Combined adm £1.50 Chd 20p. Sun July 17 (2-6)*

9 Ranulf Road (Sir Patrick Garland) S facing terraced garden with open view; varied interest with vines, fruit, vegetables, conservatory and cactus collection; pots and troughs on terraces; lawn

11 Ranulf Road (Mr & Mrs Jonathan Bates) Medium-sized garden, surrounded by trees, full of colour; herbaceous borders, roses, lilies, fuchsias, bedding plants and many geranium filled pots

Regents College, NW1 ❀ Regents Park. Regents College is located at the junction of York Bridge and the Inner Circle opp Queen Mary's Rose Garden in Regents Park. Baker Street tube is on the Bakerloo, Jubilee, Metropolitan, Hammersmith & City and Circle lines and is 5 mins walk. Buses: 1, 2, 2B, 13, 27, 30, 74, 159. Enter via gate on York Bridge Rd or the Garden Gate which is reached via the footbridge at Clarence Gate. The college and grounds occupy a site of approx 10 acres. The large lawns and mature trees echo the surrounding parkland. This landscape gives way to more ornamental planting near the buildings; special features incl a quadrangle garden, a gold border; folly garden on lake edge, herb area with bees. The focus will be on the more intimate former Botany Garden, a quiet and fairly secluded place, landscaped in a more traditional decorative style with pond, pergola, arbour and herbaceous plants. TEA. *Adm £1 Concessions/Chd 50p. Sun May 29 (12-5)*

¶19 St Gabriel's Road NW2 ⅋ (Mrs Penelope Mortimer) St Gabriel's Rd is a short walk from Willesden Green Tube (Jubilee Line). When Penelope Mortimer moved here in 1991 she brought two van-loads of plants from her Cotswold garden. With the help of a splendid balsam poplar, a great deal of muck and hard work, what was 150ft of exhausted grass and rubbish is now a miniature country garden brimming with old roses and rare herbaceous plants. "A sanctuary!" *Adm £1 Chd under 14 free. Sat June 25 (2.30-6.30)*

7 St George's Rd ⅋❀ (Mr & Mrs Richard Raworth) St Margaret's, Twickenham. Off A316 between Twickenham Bridge and St Margarets roundabout. ½-acre maturing town garden backing onto private parkland. Garden divided into 'rooms' by yew, thuja and hornbeam hedges. Unusual shrubs, clematis and old English roses. Large conservatory with rare plants and climbers. Knot garden with herbs. Sink garden. Pergola covered in solanum jas. alba, roses and honeysuckle. New sunken paved garden with Pithari pot and planting. Small gravel garden. Mist propagation. Propagated specimens and unusual plants for sale. Featured in several books including Penelope Hobhouse's 'Garden Style' and 'Private Gardens of London' by Arabella Lennox Boyd, and Homes & Garden. TEA. *Adm £1 Chd 50p. Suns June 5, 19 (2-6) or private visits welcome, please* Tel 081 892 3713

St Mary's Convent & Nursing Home, W4 ⅋❀ (Sister Jennifer Anne) Chiswick. Exit W from London on A4 to Hogarth roundabout. Take A316 signposted Richmond. St Mary's is 500yds down on L. Parking in Corney Rd, 1st turning L after Convent. 2½-acre walled garden with fine specimen trees; herbaceous borders and shrub borders being planted for all-year-round interest, incl spring flowering shrubs and bulbs. TEAS. *Adm £1 Chd 50p. Sun April 24 (2-5)*

¶St Michael's Convent, Ham ⅋❀ (Community of The Sisters of The Church) 56 Ham Common. From Richmond or Kingston, A307, turn onto the common at traffic lights nr the New Inn, 100 yds on the R adjacent to Martingales Close. 4-acre walled organic garden. Bible garden and circle garden of meditation. Extensive herbaceous borders, two orchards, wild life areas, working kitchen garden, vinehouse and ancient mulberry tree. Collection Box. *Private visits welcome please* Tel 081 940 8711

57 St Quintin Avenue, W10 ⅋❀ (H Groffman Esq) 1m from Ladbroke Grove/White City Underground. Turn into North Pole Rd from Wood Lane (White City, Shepherds Bush or Harrow Road approaches) or L into Cambridge Gdns, R into St Marks Rd from Ladbroke Grove station. Bus; 7, 220 to North Pole Road, or 72, 283 to Du Cane Road. 30ft × 40ft walled garden; year-round selection of shrubs, perennials, summer bedding schemes. Patio; small pond; hanging baskets. 11 times winner Brighter Kensington & Chelsea Gardens competition. 3 gold medals and Banksian Medal from London Gardens Society in 1993. Featured in Channel 4's Flowering Passions and LWT's Gardening Roadshow. To be incl in forthcoming 'Learn How to Create Your Perfect Garden' video in May 1994 edition of Ideal Home magazine. TEAS. *Adm £1.30 Chd 70p. Sun July 31 (2-6.30)*

¶14 Sebright Road ⅋❀ (Julian Bishop & Rhian Morgan) High Barnet. Short walk W of Barnet High St. From M25 junction 23, follow A1081 to Barnet. Take 3rd R, into Alston Rd, 2nd R into Puller Rd and follow one way system to Sebright Rd. From S follow the A1000 at bottom of High St, take A411 to Elstree. Go along Wood St, 2nd exit at roundabout, continue along The Avenue and Alston Rd, pass Sebright Rd and take L into Puller Rd, following one way system. Parking possibly difficult - public car park at junction of Stafford Rd and Staplyton Rd, 3 min walk. Nearest tube High Barnet, 20 mins; buses 34, 84, 84A, 107, 234, 263, 326, 384, 385, 399, N1, N13, N92 - mostly to High St. Small 120' × 20' newly designed town garden, with traditional herbaceous borders, vegetable patch, fruit trees and little wildlife pond. Many old-fashioned roses, honeysuckles, unusual foxgloves and geraniums. TEAS. *Adm £1 Chd 25p (Share to Pet Protection League®). Sun July 10 (11-6)*

12a Selwood Place, SW7 ⅋ (Mrs Anthony Crossley) South Kensington, adjacent to 92 Onslow Gardens (cul-de-sac). South Kensington tube 8 mins walk, no. 14 bus down Fulham Rd (Elm Place request stop). Long green and white border; pink border in L-shaped walled garden; collection of roses, peonies, camellias, iris, lilies, poppies, vegetables; terraced herb garden. Suitable for wheelchairs only if dry. *Adm 70p Chd 35p. Thurs May 19 (2.30-6)*

South London Botanical Institute, SE24 ⅋❀ 323 Norwood Rd. From South Circular Rd (A205) at Tulse Hill, turn N into Norwood Rd; Institute is 100yds on R. Small botanic garden, formally laid out; many rare and interesting species; over 200 labelled plants. TEA. *Adm £1 Chd 50p (Share to South London Botanical Institute®). Suns June 5(2-5)*

Southwood Lodge, N6 ⅋❀ (Mr & Mrs C Whittington) 33 Kingsley Place. Off Southwood Lane. Buses 210, 271. Tube Highgate. A romantic, hidden garden laid out last century on a steeply sloping site, now densely planted with a wide variety of shrubs, bulbs, roses and perennials. Pond waterfall, frogs. Many unusual plants are grown and propagated for sale. Featured in several recent books. *Adm £1 Chd 40p. Suns May 8, June 12 (2-6). Private visit welcome* Tel 081 348 2785

Tarn ✿✿ (Mr & Mrs R Solley) Oxhey Drive South, Northwood. From Northwood Station turn R into Green Lane. At mini roundabout (signposted NATO Headquarters) follow sign turning L into Watford Rd, take 3rd R into Sandy Lane; at top U-turn into Oxhey Drive South, 2nd house on L. Approx ⅓-acre garden of special interest to horticulturists and plant lovers. Featured by Francesca Greenoak in 'The Times' Saturday Gardening Page April 1993, entitled 'Harmony in Variety'. Visited by the International Camellia Society, and the Garden Club of Milan. Many unusual shrubs, trees and plants; large collection of rhododendrons; camellias; magnolias and allied species. Spring blossom, drifts of bulbs including wild cyclamen, anemones, erythronium; bluebells; primroses etc. Greenhouses with camellias and many rare plants. Large collection of clematis and climbing roses growing informally through trees. Old world terrace with pond. Very old standard wisteria. Much of the garden was 'tree lifted' by present owner from Hampstead in 1970 where it had a mention by the late Lanning Roper in the 'Sunday Times'. *Adm £1 Chd 50p. Mon April 4 (2-5.30). Also private visits welcome Feb to June, please* **Tel 0923 828373**

¶13 Trecastle Way N7 ✿✿ (Mrs Vera Quick) Carleton Rd. Camden Rd buses 29, 253 to Dalmeny Ave. 1st R from Dalmeny Ave into Trecastle Way (nr Holloway Prison). A very pretty garden. Small in size approx 0′ × 30′. Full of colour, lots of interesting plants, ornamental pond and waterfall. Bedding plants grown from seeds and cuttings. TEAS. *Adm 80p Chd free. Sun July 10 (2-6)*

Trinity Hospice ♿✿✿ 30 Clapham Common North Side, SW4. Tube: Clapham Common. Bus: 37, 137 stop outside. 2-acre park-like garden restored by Lanning Roper's friends as a memorial to him and designed by John Medhurst. Ricky's sculpture a feature. TEAS. *Adm 50p Chd free. Sats, Suns April 23, 24; June 11, 12; July 23, 24; Sept 10, 11 (2-5)*

¶131 Upland Road ♿✿✿ (Ms G Payne & Ms P Harvey) East Dulwich. Nearest BR Peckham Rye. Buses 78, 12, 63. 78, 12 to Barry Rd. Get off 1st stop opp Peckham Rye Common. Upland Rd 50yds on L. House ¼m on L. 63 to Peckham Rye Common. Get off Forest Hill Rd. Cross over to Piermont Green leading to Upland Rd. Turn L house 50yds on L. Small garden full of surprises. Unusual, semi-oriental-style rear garden with pond and waterfall plus 2 'dinosaur eggs'! Informal planted areas incl varieties of clematis, acers, rhododendrons and NZ natives. 20′ × 40′ designed for effect and low maintenance. Front and side areas incl shade loving plants, bamboos, camellias, magnolias and viticellas. TEAS. *Adm 50p Chd 25p. Suns May 15, June 19 (2-6)*

15 Upper Grotto Road ✿✿ (Jean Rankin) Strawberry Hill, Twickenham. Stations Strawberry Hill or Twickenham. Buses R68, 33 to Pope's Grotto, then Pope's Grove 1st R into Radnor Rd, 1st L Upper Grotto Rd or 90B, 267, 281, 290 to Heath Rd, into Radnor Rd, 2nd L into Upper Grotto Rd. Small sunken suntrap courtyard garden designed and constructed with advancing age and arthritis in mind; raised borders with small shrubs, herbaceous perennials, self sown annuals and some half-hardy annuals for infill; wall shrubs, clematis and other climbers; plants in pots and tiny fountain over pebbles. TEA. *Adm 50p Chd 25p.*

Suns July 3, 10 (2-6). Private visits welcome please, **Tel 081 891 4454**

7 Upper Phillimore Gardens W8 ✿✿ (Mr & Mrs B Ritchie). From Kensington High St take either Phillimore Gdns or Camden Hill Rd; entrance Duchess of Bedford Walk. 100′ × 35′ garden; rockery, sunken garden; Italian wall fountain, ground cover planting, pergola. TEA. *Adm 75p Chd 35p. Sun May 1 (2.30-6)*

66 Wallingford Avenue (off Oxford Gdns), W10 ✿ (Mrs R Andrups). Nearest underground station: Latimer Rd and Ladbroke Grove. Nearest bus stop Oxford Gdns (7) or Ladbroke Grove (7, 52, 70, 295, 302). Small garden 20′ × 40′. Raised beds, mixed borders, ponds, conservatory. All-year-round garden. 7 times winner Brighter Kensington & Chelsea Gardens Competition. Refreshments 30p. *Adm £1 Chd 50p. Mon May 30, Sun July 31 (2-6)*

The Water Gardens ✿ Warren Road, Kingston (Residents' Association). From Kingston take the A308 (Kingston Hill) towards London about ½m on R turn R into Warren Road. Japanese landscaped garden originally part of the Coombe Wood Nursery, approx 9 acres with water cascade features. *Adm £1 Chd 50p. Suns May 8, Oct 2 (2-5)*

3 Wellgarth Road, NW11 ✿✿ (Mr & Mrs A M Gear) Hampstead Garden Suburb. Approx 4m N of London centre. Turning off the North End Road which runs between Hampstead and Golders Green, (buses 268, 210 stop quite near). Golders Green tube station (Northern Line) is the nearest, 7 mins walk and is also a terminal for buses from many parts of London. Medium-size garden. A walk all round the house, swathe of grass with long borders of bushes, trees and climbers now established and not too difficult to maintain. Close planting, herbaceous beds, roses, heathers and lavenders: herbs and mints, some uncommon plants. Paving, pots, tubs and old oak tree, and now newly added a small pond with bubbling water. Hampstead Gardens Competition Winner in 1989, 90, 91 & 92, and 1st in class in the London Gardens Society '92. Home-made TEAS. *Adm £1 (Share to Friends of Queen Mary's©). Sun June 19 (2-6)*

10 Wildwood Rd NW11 ♿✿ (Dr J W McLean) Hampstead. Wildwood Rd is between Hampstead Golf Course and N end of Hampstead Heath. From North End Rd turn by Manor House Hospital into Hampstead Way, then fork R. Garden planned and maintained by owner; one of finest herbaceous borders in North London, pond, HT roses; owner-grown prize winning delphiniums and seedlings. TEA. *Adm £1 Chd free. Sun July 10 (2-7)*

Wimbledon Gardens ✿ SW19 Train: Wimbledon station, turn R, then 2nd L (Worple Rd), 4th on R (Spencer Hill). Turn L at Church, then R into Denmark Rd. Car: A219 (Wimbledon Hill Rd). turn into B235 (Worple Rd). 4th on R (Spencer Hill); turn L past church into St John's Rd and park. Walk up Denmark Rd (1st on R) which is a one-way st coming down. TEAS. *Combined adm £2.50 Chd 50p. Sun May 22 (2-6)*

Regular Openers. See head of county section.

86 Copse Hill &✿ (Mrs John Fox) Sunny cottage garden with a good mix of bulbs, herbaceous and shrubs
8 Denmark Road (Mrs Peggy Pyke-Lees) Tiny front garden plus rear patio garden 22ft square. Shrubs, bulbs, ground-cover. 1820 artisan cottage set in a very pretty small st of similar cottages
¶3 Murray Road SW19 & (Mr & Mrs Michael Waugh) Wimbledon. 10 mins walk from Wimbledon BR and Tube Station, on the corner of St Johns Rd (opp entrance to church) and the lower end of Murray Rd which leads into Spencer Hill. Access from Worple Rd on The Ridgeway. Small suburban garden attempting informality of a cottage garden. A continuous narrow plot around 3 sides of the house. Fruit trees, small pond, climbers roses; approx 308 sq.yds. TEAS
11 Spencer Hill (Mr & Mrs Brian Willott) Walled garden 100′ × 50′. Unusual shrubs, climbers, shrub roses, pergola. Laid out 12 yrs ago to accommodate 4 chd, 4 pets, 4 adults plus owners' uncontrollable desire to keep buying new plants. Vegetable and fruit plot

¶47 Winn Road SE12 &✿ (Mr & Mrs G Smith) Lee. 8m SE central London. 15mins walk from either BR Lee station (Sidcup Line to Dartford) or Grove Park (Orpington Line) from Charing Cross. By car, ½m from A20 Sidcup bypass or A205 S Circular. ⅓-acre mature garden maintained by owners. Mixed borders, alpine beds, fruit and vegetables, 3 greenhouses featuring colourful displays of pelargoniums, fuchsias, begonias, cacti and succulents and other interesting plants. TEA. Adm £1 Chd 50p (Share to The Fifth Trust©). Suns May 1, June 26, Aug 28 (2-5)

27 Wood Vale, N10 ✿✿ (Mr & Mrs A W Dallman) Muswell Hill 1m. A1 to Woodman public house; signed Muswell Hill; Muswell Hill Rd sharp R Wood Lane leading to Wood Vale; Highgate tube station. ¾-acre garden with herbaceous borders; ponds; orchard and kitchen garden. Unusual layout full of surprises. Numerous shrubs, roses, trees and conifers; greenhouses. Visitors may also wander in neighbouring gardens, all of which are of high

standard. TEAS. Adm £1 Chd under 14 free (Share to British Legion and Meeting Point For St Georges Church®). Sat, Sun July 23, 24 (2-6)

7 Woodstock Road, W4 ✿ (Mr & Mrs L A Darke) Buses 94, 27. Underground district line to Turnham Green. (Piccadilly line stops Sunday). Turn R from station and over zebra crossing into Woodstock Rd. No. 7 is on L side beyond Sydney House flats and Bedford Rd. Victorian garden with large original rockery behind Norman Shaw house in Bedford Park, the earliest garden suburb. Wide selection of fine flowering trees; shrubs; herbaceous plants, roses and bulbs made over 40 years by present owners. Featured in 'London's Pride', the 1990 exhibition of the history of the capital's gardens in the Museum of London. Adm 80p Chd free. Sun April 24 (2-5)

42 Woodville Gardens, Ealing W5 ✿ (J Welfare) Off Hanger Lane (A406) approx half way between junctions with A40 and A4020. Large town garden with alpine area and herbaceous borders, paving plants, beds of shade and sun-loving plants, bog garden, shrubs, many euphorbias, pulmonarias, geums, eryngiums, hellebores, etc. Plantsman's garden with many unusual plants. Seedlings and cuttings for sale. Collection box. Private visits welcome April to Sept **Tel 081 998 4134**

¶23 Woodville Road W5 ✿✿ (Jill & Taki Argyropoulos) Ealing. 5min walk N of Ealing Broadway Station. (Central and District Line tubes, and BR from Paddington).By car, Woodville Gardens which becomes Woodville Rd, is directly off Hanger Lane (N Circular Rd) about halfway between the gyratory system and the junction with Uxbridge Rd. 65 bus from Kingston also terminates by Ealing Broadway station. Mediterranean style paved front garden with lots of tubs and pots. Secluded walled garden at rear, approx 100′ × 40′, well stocked with flowering shrubs, climbers and many herbaceous plants. Small fish pond with waterfall and bog garden, vegetable, fruit and herb area. TEAS. Adm 50p Chd free. Sun June 26 (11-6)

Norfolk

Hon County Organisers: Lady Blofeld, Hoveton House, Nr Wroxham, Norwich NR12 8JE
Tel 0603 782202
Mrs Neil Foster, Lexham Hall, King's Lynn PE32 2QJ
Assistant County Organisers: Mrs David Mcleod, Park House, Old Hunstanton, King's Lynn PE36 6JS
Mrs David McCosh, Baconsthorpe Old Rectory, Holt NR25 6LU
Hon Treasurer: Denzil Newton Esq, Briar House, Gt Dunham, King's Lynn PE32 2LX

DATES OF OPENING

By appointment
For telephone numbers and other details see garden descriptions. Private visits welcomed

Besthorpe Hall, Attleborough
Cubitt Cottage, Sloley

Dell Farm, Aylsham Gardens, Aylsham
4 Green Lane, Mundford
Lanehead, Garboldisham
10 St Michael's Close, Aylsham Gardens, Aylsham
Wretham Lodge, East Wretham

Regular openings
For details see garden descriptions

Hoveton Hall Gardens, nr Wroxham
For dates see text
Norfolk Lavender Ltd, Heacham Daily
(closed 3 weeks over Christmas)
The Plantation Garden, Norwich,
Suns April to Oct

Raveningham Hall, nr Beccles Suns.
Weds & Bank Hols March 21 to
Sept 11
Sandringham Grounds. Daily April 1
to Oct 2 but see text for
exceptions

April 3 Sunday
Lake House, Brundall
April 4 Monday
Lake House, Brundall
April 10 Sunday
The Old House, Ranworth
April 24 Sunday
The Birches, Wreningham
May 1 Sunday
Minns Cottage, Chapel Rd, Potter
Heigham
The Plantation Garden, Norwich
May 8 Sunday
Hoveton House, nr Wroxham
Raveningham Hall, nr Beccles
Ryston Hall, Downham Market
Wretham Lodge, East Wretham
May 15 Sunday
Breccles Hall, Attleborough
Burgh House, Aylsham
Elmham House Gardens, North
Elmham
How Hill Farm, Ludham
Rippon Hall, Hevingham, nr
Norwich
May 20 Friday
Hoveton Hall Gardens, nr
Wroxham
May 22 Sunday
Barwick House, Stanhoe
Sheringham Park, Upper
Sheringham
May 29 Sunday
Aylsham Gardens, Aylsham
Cubitt Cottage, Sloley
Lexham Hall, nr Swaffham
June 5 Sunday
Besthorpe Hall, Attleborough
4 Green Lane, Mundford

Grove House, By Alby Crafts,
Erpingham
Letheringsett Gardens,
Letheringsett
Sheringham Park, Upper
Sheringham
June 12 Sunday
Conifer Hill, Starston
The Garden in an Orchard, Bergh
Apton
Gillingham Hall, nr Beccles ‡
Minns Cottage, Chapel Rd, Potter
Heigham
Raveningham Hall, nr Beccles ‡
Southgate House, South Creake
June 18 Saturday
Ellingham Hall, nr Bungay for
details see Suffolk
June 19 Sunday
72 Branthill
Cottages,Wells-next-the-Sea ‡
Elsing Hall, nr Dereham
Ludham Gardens
Old Catton Gardens, The Firs,
Spixworth Rd
Southgate Barn, South Creake ‡
Wootton Road Gardens, King's
Lynn
June 26 Sunday
Bayfield Hall, nr Holt
Cubitt Cottage, Sloley
Felbrigg Hall, nr Cromer
4 Green Lane, Mundford
Heggatt Hall, Horstead, nr
Norwich ‡
Horstead House, nr Norwich ‡
Intwood Hall, nr Norwich
Lanehead, Garboldisham ‡‡
Oak Tree House, 6 Cotman Rd,
Thorpe
Wicken House, Castle Acre, nr
King's Lynn
Wretham Lodge, East
Wretham ‡‡
July 10 Sunday
Blickling Hall, Aylsham ‡
Gayton Hall, King's Lynn

Wolterton Park, nr Aylsham ‡
July 17 Sunday
Easton Lodge, Easton
The Plantation Garden, Norwich
July 24 Sunday
Felbrigg Hall, nr Cromer
Hoveton Hall Gardens, nr
Wroxham
The Lodge, Old Lakenham,
Norwich
Oxburgh Hall Gardens, nr
Swaffham
July 28 Thursday
Holkham Hall, Wells-next-the-Sea
July 29 Friday
Park House, Old Hunstanton
July 30 Saturday
Park House, Old Hunstanton
July 31 Sunday
The Garden in an Orchard, Bergh
Apton
Oak Tree House, 6 Cotman Rd,
Thorpe, Norwich
Park House, Old Hunstanton
Wickmere House, Wickmere
August 1 Monday
Park House, Old Hunstanton
August 7 Sunday
Blickling Hall, Aylsham
Minns Cottage, Chapel Rd, Potter
Heigham
Oxburgh Hall Gardens, nr
Swaffham
August 21 Sunday
The Birches, Wreningham
August 28 Sunday
Barningham Hall, Matlaske
Oak Tree House, 6 Cotman Rd,
Thorpe, Norwich
September 18 Sunday
Minns Cottage, Chapel Rd, Potter
Heigham
October 9 Sunday
Mannington Hall, nr Aylsham and
Holt

DESCRIPTIONS OF GARDENS

Aylsham Gardens *Combined adm £2.25 Chd 50p*
5 Cromer Road よ⚹ (Dr & Mrs James) Aylsham.
100yds N of Aylsham Parish Church down old Cromer
Rd on LH-side. Approx 1 acre of semi-wild garden nr
town centre with large willow trees and grass. Shrubs
and small natural pond. Mixed borders, heathers and
vegetable garden. *Sun May 29 (2-6)*
Dell Farm よ⚹ (Mrs M J Monk) Aylsham. Approx ¼m
W of centre of Aylsham turn L off Blickling Rd on to
Heydon Rd (signposted Oulton). 400yds on to copper
beech arching rd. Turn R through gate onto gravelled
yard. 4-acre garden, Magnificent mature trees and
shrubs. Various rose collections, rhododendrons, aza-

leas, heathers. Spring bulbs, primroses etc in old orchard and wild flower garden. TEA. *(Also private visits
welcome especially for spring bulbs, please* Tel 0263
732 277 *Adm £1 Chd 50p). Sun May 29 (2-6)*
10 St Michael's Close ⚹❀ (M I Davies Esq)
Aylsham NW on B1354 towards Blickling Hall; 500yds
from market place, turn R, Rawlinsons Lane, then R
again. Front gravelled area with mixed shrub and herbaceous border; small rockery. Back garden with large
variety of shrubs, herbaceous plants, bulbs, small
lawn, roses, azaleas. Plant, pond. Aviary, guinea pigs.
TEA. *Sun May 29 (11-6). Private visits welcome, please*
Tel 0263 732174

Regular Openers. See head of county section.

West Lodge ও (Mr & Mrs Jonathan Hirst) Aylsham. ¼m NW of market square on N side of B1354 (entrance in Rawlinsons Lane) Large 9-acre garden with lawns, mature trees, rose garden, herbaceous borders, ornamental pond and walled kitchen garden; Georgian House (not open) and outbuildings incl a well-stocked toolshed (open) and greenhouses. TEAS. *Adm £1.50 Chd free (Share to Aylsham Church Restoration Fund®). Sun May 29 (2-5)*

Barningham Hall ও ❀ (Lady Mott-Radclyffe) Matlaske, NW of Aylsham. Medium-sized garden, vistas, lake. TEAS. *Adm £2 Chd free. Sun Aug 28 (2-6.30)*

Barwick House ও ❀ (Mrs R Ralli) Stanhoe. 10m NW of Fakenham off B1155. Large garden surrounded by park with many mature trees; mixed borders; woodland walk; azaleas and rhododendrons. TEAS. *Adm £1.50 Chd free (Share to St John Ambulance®). Sun May 22 (2-5)*

Bayfield Hall ও ❀ (Mr & Mrs R H Combe) 1m N of Holt, off A148. Formal but simple pleasure gardens with medieval church ruin. Old-fashioned roses, herbaceous and shrub borders; magnificent view over lake and park. Wildflower centre adjacent to garden. Church Fete stalls in aid of St Martins Church, Glandford. TEA. *Adm £1.50 Chd 50p. Sun June 26 (2-5)*

Besthorpe Hall ও ❀❀ (John Alston Esq) 1m E of Attleborough. On Attleborough-Bunwell Rd; adjacent to Besthorpe Church. Garden with shrubs, trees and herbaceous borders within Tudor enclosures; walled kitchen garden; tilting ground. Coach parties by appt. TEAS. *Adm £2 Chd free (Share to Besthorpe Church®). Sun June 5 (2-5). Also private visits welcome, please* **Tel 0953 452138**

The Birches ও ❀❀ (Mr & Mrs J McCarthy) Top Row. 8m S of Norwich on B1113 Norwich-New Buckenham Rd. Take 1st turning L ¼m after Bird in Hand Restaurant. 1¼-acre garden landscaped with lawns, herbaceous, shrub and rose beds. Rockery, pond and alpine scree garden, orchard with naturlized bulbs. Vegetable garden, greenhouses and conservatory. TEAS. *Adm £1.50 Chd free. Suns April 24, Aug 21 (2-6)*

Blickling Hall ও ❀❀ (The National Trust) 1¼ miles NW of Aylsham on N side of B1354. 15m N of Norwich (A140). Large garden, orangery, crescent lake, azaleas, rhododendrons, herbaceous borders. Historic Jacobean house. Wheelchairs available. TEAS and lunches. *Adm £2.50 Chd £1.25. Suns July 10, Aug 7 (12-5)*

72 Branthill Cottages ❀ (Timothy Leese Esq.) Wells-next-the-Sea. 2m from Wells. Off Fakenham-Wells rd. At Xrds unmarked by signpost, turn L, opp yellow sign to Branthill Farm ¼m down lane, cottage on LH-side. NGS posters and signposts on open day. Around a farm cottage, a ¼ acre of rather impractical garden, rigidly laid out and informally planted over the last 9 yrs. Not uncommon flowers, old roses and shrubs, closely planted to make garden appear larger, and to cut down on weeding. Very light alkaline soil. TEAS at Southgate Barn. *Adm £1 Chd free (Share to Wells Cottage Hospital®). Sun June 19 (2-6)*

¶Breccles Hall (Major & Mrs R J Archdale) Attleborough. On the B1111 midway between East Harling and Watton. Leave the A11 just S of Attleborough and take the Shropham Rd to the B1111. Turn R. Breccles Hall is 1m from this corner on the R just before Breccles Church. Approx 10-acre garden, fine Elizabethan house (not open) surrounded by walled gardens incl rose garden and herbaceous borders. Wild garden with rhododendrons and bulbs and mature trees. The gardens were originally laid out by Gertrude Jekyll. TEAS. *Adm £1.50 Chd free (Share to Quidenham Children's Hospice®). Sun May 15 (2-5)*

¶Burgh House ❀ (Mr & Mrs Richard Burr) Aylsham. Off A140 between Norwich and Cromer. 300yds E of Aylsham town square. Free public car park in Burgh Rd. Very old 4-acre mixed deciduous woodland with ponds. 1st yr of a slow project to uncover its history and reclaim paths, areas of bulbs etc. Haven for small birds. TEAS. *Adm £1 Chd free. Sun May 15 (12-6)*

Conifer Hill ও ❀ (Mr & Mrs Richard Lombe Taylor) Starston, Harleston. 18m S of Norwich. A140 to Pulham Xrds. Turn L to B1134. 1m NW of Harleston, off B1134. Take Redenhall Rd out of Starston. Conifer Hill on L ½m out of village. Steep bend and white gates. 4-acre Victorian garden. Lawns, shrubs, roses, herbaceous and kitchen garden. ½-acre pinetum, in steep escarpment of old quarry. TEAS. *Adm £1.50 Chd free. Sun June 12 (2-6)*

Cubitt Cottage ও ❀❀ (Mrs Jane Foulkes) Sloley. 11m N of Norwich just off B1150 Coltishall to North Walsham Rd. 2nd R after Three Horseshoes public house at Scottow. Into village, then Low Street, R at next signpost. 1-acre garden with lawns, herbaceous and shrub border, over 100 varieties of old roses, clematis and unusual plants; wildflower meadow; wild life pond and bog garden; vegetable garden and greenhouses. TEAS. *Adm £1.50 Chd free. Suns May 29, June 26 (2-6). Plus some other Sundays in June, July, Aug. Also private visits welcome, please* **Tel 0692 69295**

Easton Lodge ❀❀ (J M Rampton Esq) Easton, 6m W Norwich. Cross the new Southern Norwich Bypass at the Easton Roundabout and take the Ringland Rd. Entrance at the W gate approx 1m from EC bus stop 'The Dog' on the old A47. Large garden in magnificent setting above river surrounded by fine trees; walks amongst interesting shrubs, roses, plants; herbaceous border; walled kitchen garden. Late Georgian house with Jacobean centre portion (not open). TEAS. *Adm £1.50 Chd free. Sun July 17 (2.30-5.30)*

Ellingham Hall nr Bungay. See Suffolk for details

Elmham House ও ❀❀ (Mr & Mrs R S Don) North Elmham, 5m N of East Dereham, on B1110. Entrance opp Church. Medium-sized garden; wild garden; C18 walled garden; view of park and lake; vineyard, tours of winery. TEAS. *Adm £1.50 Chd free (Share to St Mary's Church N Elmham®). Sun May 15 (2-6)*

> **By Appointment Gardens.** See head of county section

Elsing Hall ◈❀ (Mrs D Cargill) Dereham. 2m E of Dereham off A47; sign to Elsing. Medieval house surrounded by moat. Over 200 varieties of old-fashioned roses; wild flower lawn, walled kitchen garden with roses, fruit trees & clematis. Many water plants by moat and fish stew. Rare and interesting trees in arboretum; newly planted formal garden with clipped box, lavender, sage, santolina and thyme. Suitable wheelchairs in places. TEAS. *Adm £1.50 Chd free (Share to Elsing Church restoration fund®). Sun June 19 (2-6)*

Felbrigg Hall ◈❀ (The National Trust) Roughton, 2½m SW of Cromer, S of A148; main entrance from B1436; signed from Felbrigg village. Large pleasure gardens; mainly lawns and shrubs; orangery with camellias; large walled garden restored and restocked as fruit, vegetable and flower garden; vine house; dovecote; dahlias; superb colchichum; wooded parks. 2 Electric wheelchairs available. Lunches, pre booking essential. TEAS. *Adm £1.80 Chd 80p. For NGS Suns June 26, July 24 (11-5)*

The Garden in an Orchard ◈❀ (Mr & Mrs R W Boardman) Bergh Apton, Norwich. 6m SE of Norwich off A146 at Hellington Corner signed to Bergh Apton. Down Mill Rd 300 yds. 3½-acre garden set in an old orchard. Many rare and unusual plants set out in an informal pattern of wandering paths. ½-acre of wild flower meadows, many bamboos, specie roses, 9 species of eucalyptus. In all a plantsman's garden. TEAS. *Adm £1.50 Chd free. Sun June 12, July 31 (11-6)*

Gayton Hall ◈❀ (Mr & Mrs Julian Marsham) 6m E of King's Lynn off B1145; signs in Gayton village. 20 acres; wild woodland, water garden. Fete stalls in aid of Gayton Church. TEAS. *Adm 50p Chd free & Collecting Box (Share to St Nicholas Church, Gayton®). Sun July 10 (2-5)*

¶Gillingham Hall ◈❀ (Mr & Mrs Robin Bramley) Beccles. 16m SE of Norwich, 1½m from Beccles off A146. 14-acre garden with lake, lawns, borders, rose garden, specimen plane trees, wild flower areas, bulbs; Mansion house (not open) c1600. TEAS. *Adm £1.50 Chd 50p (Share to Church Restoration Fund®). Sun June 12 (2-5)*

4 Green Lane ◈❀(Mr & Mrs Dennis Cooper) Mundford. From main Mundford roundabout take A1065 to Swaffham. After ¼m turn L down Green Lane. Divided into 'rooms' giving a cottage garden effect, a 1-acre garden filled with island beds, intensively planted with unusual perennials and cottage garden plants. Ponds and planted gravel areas. Wide variety of unusual plants avail-bale from adjoining nursery. *Adm £1 Chd free. Suns June 5, 26 (2-6). Private visits welcome, please Tel 0842 878496*

Grove House ◈❀ (Mr & Mrs John Alston) Erpingham. On A140 4m N Aylsham by Alby Crafts, parking by Alby Crafts car park. 4-acre garden. Primroses, spring bulbs, irises, old-fashioned roses, mixed borders, 4 ponds (1 with wild flower and conservation area). Plantsman's garden. TEAS. *Adm £1.50 Chd free. Sun June 5 (10-5)*

¶Heggatt Hall ◈❀ (Mr & Mrs Richard Gurney) Horstead. From Norwich take B1150 signposted North Walsham

continue 5m. Turn R 1m before Horstead signposted Heggatt Hall. Turn L at T junction, house set in park on L. 3-acre early Victorian garden (c1830). Rose garden, mixed borders, kitchen garden, interesting collection of sweet chestnuts in park; many lovely old trees and some recently planted. TEAS *Adm £1.50 Chd free. Sun June 26 (2-6)*

Holkham Hall ◈❀ (The Viscount Coke) Wells-next-the-Sea. 2m W of Wells off A149. Arboretum with many rare specimens of trees and shrubs; shell house. TEAS. *Adm 50p Chd 20p.* ▲*For NGS Thurs July 28 (1.30-4.40)*

Horstead House (Dr & Mrs David Nolan) Horstead. 7m from Norwich. Off B1150 N Walsham Rd opp 'Recruiting Sergeant'; drive gate by Horstead Mill Pool; bus 736 from Norwich. Landscaped garden on riverbank; walled garden; exceptionally good toolhouse. Home-made TEAS. *Adm £1.50 Chd free. Sun June 26 (2-5)*

Hoveton Hall Gardens ◈❀ (Mr & Mrs Andrew Buxton) nr Wroxham. 8m N of Norwich; 1m N of Wroxham Bridge on A1151 Stalham Rd. Approx 10-acre gardens and grounds featuring principally daffodils, azaleas, rhododendrons and hydrangeas in a woodland setting and a large, mature, walled herbaceous garden. Water plants, a lakeside walk and walled kitchen garden provide additional interest. Early C19 house (not open). TEAS. *Adm £2 Chd 50p. Gardens open, every Wed, Fri, Sun and Bank Hols and Thurs in May, Easter Sun to Sept 18 incl (2-5.30). For NGS Fri May 20, Sun July 24 (2-5.30)*

Hoveton House ◈❀ (Sir John & Lady Blofeld) 9m N Norwich, ½m Wroxham on B1062, Horning-Ludham Rd. Interesting old-fashioned walled garden; herbaceous and other borders; rock garden; many unusual plants and bulbs. Established rhododendron grove. Kitchen garden. Lawns, walks etc. William & Mary House (not open.) TEAS. *Adm £2 Chd free. Sun May 8 (2-6)*

How Hill Farm ◈ (P D S Boardman Esq) 2m W of Ludham on A1062; then follow signs to How Hill; Farm Garden – S of How Hill. Very pretty garden started in 1968 in water garden setting with three ponds; recent 3-acre broad (dug as conservation project) with variety of water lilies and view over the R. Ant; fine old mill. Winding paths through rare conifers (mainly dwarf); unusual and rare rhododendrons with massed azaleas; other ornamental trees and shrubs; a few herbaceous plants and lilies; collection of English holly, ilex aquifolium (over 50 varieties). Partly suitable for wheelchairs. TEA. *Adm £1.50 Chd free (Share to How Hill Trust©). Sun May 15 (2-5)*

Intwood Hall ◈ (The Hon Julian & Mrs Darling) 3½m SW of Norwich. Via A11 to Cringleford; fork L (avoid dual carriageway); over Cringleford Bridge, turn L; over Xrds and level Xing for ½m. 2 walled flower gardens (one Tudor); walled vegetable garden, greenhouses, roses; lovely trees. Saxon Church in grounds. TEAS. *Adm £1.50 Chd free. Sun June 26 (2-6)*

By Appointment Gardens. Avoid the crowds. Good chance of a tour by owner. See garden description for telephone number.

Lake House ❀ (Mr & Mrs Garry Muter) Brundall. Approx 5m E of Norwich on A47; take Brundall turn at Roundabout. Turn R into Postwick Lane at T-junction. An acre of water gardens set among magnificent trees in a steep cleft in the river escarpment. Informal flower beds with interesting plants; a naturalist's paradise; unsuitable for young children or the infirm. Wellingtons advisable. 'Unusual plants for sale.' TEAS. *Adm £2 Chd free (Share to Water Aid©). Easter Sun & Mon (11-5)*

Lanehead ⅋ (Mrs N A Laurie) Garboldisham, 8m W of Diss off A1066 at village Xrds take the A1118 for ½m to 1st R. Signs on roadside on open day. Medium-sized garden created by owner; featured in a television programme, visited by many horticultural groups; well designed natural walks with shrubs and specimen trees; colour co-ordinated borders for all-year interest; water and bog garden; roses and woodland. Coffee, TEAS. *Adm £1.50 Chd free (Share to Garboldisham Church Fabric Fund®). Sun June 26 (10.30-5.30). Also private visits welcome, please* Tel 0953 81380

Letheringsett Gardens ⅋ 1m W of Holt on A148. Car park King's Head, Letheringsett for disabled near church. TEAS at The Glebe. *Combined adm £1.50 Chd free. Easter Sun June 5 (2-5.30)*
> **The Glebe** ⅋❀ (Hon Beryl Cozens-Hardy) Medium-sized riverside garden, with island, wild flowers, water garden, shrub borders, clematis
> **Letheringsett Hall** (Mrs English) Home for the Elderly; medium-sized garden
> **Letheringsett Estate Garden** (Mr & Mrs Robert Carter) Large garden; wooded walks, fountain, lake, water plants, wild flowers. Hydraulic rams 1852 and 1905
> **The Old Foundry House** (Peter Miller Esq) Small unusual garden. Roses

Lexham Hall ⅋❀❀ (Mr & Mrs Neil Foster) 2m W of Litcham off B1145. 3-acre woodland garden with azaleas and rhododendrons; walled garden, shrubs, roses; lake and parkland. TEAS. *Adm £2 Chd free (Share to St Andrews Church, E. Lexham®). Sun May 29 (2-6)*

¶**The Lodge** ❀ (Mr & Mrs P J E Smith) Old Lakenham. SE of Norwich just off ring rd (Barrett Rd). Turn out of city at Mansfield Lane traffic lights. 200yds on L opp St John's Church (also open). 1½-acres of contoured garden in beautiful setting leading down to R Yare. Herbaceous and shrub borders, enclosed croquet lawn, 1920's sunken garden, muscovy and other ducks. TEAS. *Adm £1.50 Chd free (Share to St John's Church®). Sun July 24 (2-6)*

Ludham Gardens B1062 Wroxham to Ludham 7m. Turn R by Ludham village church into Staithe Road. Gardens ¼m from village. *Sun June 19 (2-6)*
> **The Dutch House** ❀ (Mrs Peter Seymour) Long narrow garden designed and planted by the painter Edward Seago, leading through marsh to Womack Water. Approx 2½ acres. TEA. *Adm £1.50 Chd free*
> **The Mowle** ❀❀ (Mrs N N Green) Approx 2½ acres running down to marshes. Interesting shrub borders, unusual trees etc including tulip trees and a golden catalpa. TEAS. *Adm £1.50 Chd free*

Mannington Hall ⅋❀❀ (The Lord & Lady Walpole) 2m N of Saxthorpe; 18m NW of Norwich via B1149 towards Holt. At Saxthorpe (B1149 & B1354) turn NE signed Mannington. 20 acres feature roses, shrubs, lake and trees. Heritage rose, scented and walled gardens, autumn colour and rose hips. Extensive countryside walks and trails. C15 moated manor house (not open). Saxon church with C19 follies. TEAS and lunches. *Adm £2.50 OAPs/students £2 Chd free (Share to Itteringham Village Hall©). Sun Oct 9 (12-5)*

¶**Minns Cottage** ⅋❀ (Mr & Mrs Derek Brown) Chapel Rd, Potter Heigham. From Norwich take A1151 then A149 to Potter Heigham Xrds. Turn L into Station Rd on to T junction, turn L into School Rd. Turning into Green Lane. At telephone box turn R into Chapel Rd. Approx 1¼-acres winding lawns leading through pergola's to rose garden with old English roses and other small gardens with mixed borders, recently planted woodland area with rhododendrons and bulbs. A garden to walk round peacefully at all seasons. TEAS. *Adm £1.50 Chd free. Suns May 1 (2-5), June 12, Aug 7, (2-6), Sept 18 (2-5)*

Norfolk Lavender Ltd ⅋❀ Caley Mill, Heacham. On A149 13m N of Kings Lynn. National collection of lavenders set in 2 acres (lavender harvest July-Aug); herb garden with many varieties of native herbs; rose garden. TEAS. *Adm free. Collecting box (Share to Heacham Parish Church). Daily to Christmas (10-5). Closed for three weeks Christmas holiday*

Oak Tree House ❀ (W R S Giles Esq) 6 Cotman Rd, Thorpe. E of Norwich off A47 Thorpe Rd. ¼m from Norwich Thorpe Station. From Yarmouth direction follow one way system towards City Centre, turn R at traffic lights opposite Min. of Fisheries & Agric. Approx 300yds on, turn L opposite Barclays Bank. Botanical illustrators interesting plantsmans garden, of approx ½-acre on a hillside. Containing a mixture of hardy and tender plants giving a strong subtropical Mediterranean influence, containing tree ferns, bamboos, palms, bananas, cannas, agaves and many more. Also tradtional herbaceous borders and a woodland garden with fernery. This garden has appeared in various TV programmes, magazines and books. TEAS. *Adm £1.60, Chd 30p. Suns, June 26, July 31, Aug 28 (1.30-5.30)*

¶**Old Catton Gardens, The Firs** ⅋❀ ⅓m N of Norwich ring rd. Take ring road to N Walsham roundabout, take B1150 away from city centre, turn L at traffic lights; continue down George Hill and then turn R at T-junction on to Spixworth Rd. Entrance 100yds on L. TEA. *Combined Adm £1.50 Chd 25p (Share to The Disablement Income Group®). Sun June 19 (2-5)*
> ¶**69 Spixworth Rd** (Mr & Mrs Robert Simpson) Informal walled garden leading into 1-acre woodland
> ¶**71 Spixworth Rd** ⅋ (Mrs Constance Campion) Exceptional collection of old shrub roses inspired by a visit to the garden of the Empress Josephine at Malmaison. Interesting groups of shrubs and perennials are used for contrast, all set against an outstanding example of Georgian domestic architecture
> ¶**73 Spixworth Rd** ⅋ (Mr & Mrs John Scott) Semi-formal walled garden merging into 2 acres light woodland with mature and recently planted trees and shrubs; wild flowers; perennials; fruit and vegetables

The Old House, Ranworth ✗ (Mr Francis & The Hon Mrs Cator) 9m NE of Norwich off B1140. Turn L in S Walsham to Ranworth on inner broad below church. Attractive linked and walled gardens alongside beautiful, peaceful Ranworth inner broad. Bulbs, shrubs, potager, pond with many species of ducks and geese. ½m of woodland walk adjacent to Norfolk Naturalist Trust Conservation Centre and Nature Trail (entrance extra). Historic church nearby; mown rides through recently established arboretum where dogs may be walked on leads. TEA. *Adm £2.00 Chd free. Sun April 10 (2-5.30)*

Oxburgh Hall Garden ৬✗ (The National Trust) 7m SW of Swaffham, at Oxburgh on Stoke Ferry rd. Hall and moat surrounded by lawns, fine trees, colourful borders; charming parterre garden of French design. Lunches, cream TEAS. *Adm £1 Chd 50p. Suns July 24, Aug 7 (12-5)*

Park House ৬✗ (Mr & Mrs D McLeod) 1m E of Hunstanton off A149. Drive opp St Mary's Church, Old Hunstanton. 3-acre garden with walled rose garden, herbaceous and shrub borders, flowering trees; model railway. *Adm £1 Chd free (Share to St Mary's Church, Old Hunstanton®). Fri, Sat, Sun, July 29, 30, 31, Mon, Aug 1 (10-5)*

The Plantation Garden ৬✗❀ (Plantation Garden Preservation Trust) 4 Earlham Rd, Norwich. Entrance between Crofters and Beeches Hotels, nr St John's R C Cathedral. 3-acre Victorian town garden created 1856-96 in former medieval chalk quarry. Still undergoing restoration by volunteers, remarkable architectural features include 60ft Italianate terrace and unique 30ft Gothic fountain. Surrounded by mature trees. 10 min walk city centre, beautifully tranquil atmosphere. *Adm £1.50 Chd free (Share to Plantation Garden Preservation Trust©). Suns April to Oct (2-5.30). For NGS TEAS Suns May 1, July 17 (2-5.30)*

Raveningham Hall ৬❀ (Sir Nicholas Bacon) 14m SE of Norwich, 4m from Beccles off B1136. Large garden specialising in rare shrubs, herbaceous plants, especially euphorbia, agapanthus and shrub roses. Victorian conservatory and walled vegetable garden, newly planted Arboretum. Adm £2 Chd free (Share to Priscilla Bacon Lodge©). *Nursery open 9-4 every day except weekends in November, December, January, February. Garden open every Sunday, Bank Hols and Weds March 21 to September 11 (2-5.30) Weds (1-4). For NGS TEAS Suns May 8, June 12 (2-5.30)*

Rippon Hall ৬❀ (Miss Diana Birkbeck) Hevingham, 8m N of Norwich. From A140 Norwich-Aylsham rd, turn R (E) at Xrds just N of Hevingham Church. Rhododendrons and azalea borders. Large herd of rare breed of British White Cattle. TEAS. *Adm £1.50 Chd 25p. Sun May 15 (2-5.30)*

¶**Ryston Hall** ৬❀ (Mr & Mrs Piers Pratt) Downham Market. 1m S of Downham Market off A10. 6-acre garden with azaleas and rhododendrons; orangery; walled kitchen garden being restored and woodland walk. TEAS. *Adm £1.50 OAPs/Chd £1.* ▲ *Sun May 8 (2-6)*

Regular Openers. See head of county section.

Sandringham Grounds ৬✗❀ By gracious permission of H.M. The Queen, the House, Museum and Grounds at Sandringham will be open. 60 acres of informal gardens, woodland and lakes, with rare plants and trees. Donations are given from the Estate to various charities. For further information see p 13. TEAS. *Adm House and Grounds £3.50 OAPs £2.50 Chd £2; Grounds only £2.50 OAPs £2 Chd £1.50. April 1 to Oct 2 daily. House closed July 19 to Aug 4 incl & Grounds closed July 23 to Aug 3 incl. Hours House 10.30 (Sun 12 noon) to 4.45; Grounds 10.30 (Sun 11.30) and Good Friday to 5*

Sheringham Park ৬ (The National Trust) 2m SW of Sheringham. Access for cars off A148 Cromer to Holt Road, 5m W of Cromer, 6m E of Holt (signs in Sheringham Town). 50-acres of species rhododendron, azalea and magnolia. Also numerous specimen trees incl handkerchief tree. Viewing towers, waymarked walks, sea and parkland views. Special walk way and WCs for disabled. Teas at Felbrigg Hall nearby. *Adm £2.30 per car. Suns May 22, June 5 (10-5)*

Southgate Barn ✗❀ (Mrs Philip Anley) South Creake. 5m N of Fakenham off B1355 to Burnham Market. 100yds past turning to R signed Waterden turn L down lane. Entrance 100yds on L. Small garden of approx 2 acres made 10 yrs ago around a converted barn. Shrubs and trees in front. At back large terrace, roses, pergola, herbaceous border. Cream TEAS. *Adm £1.50 Chd free (Share to Rumanian Relief for Children in Orphanages®). Sun June 19 (2-6)*

¶**Southgate House** ৬✗❀ (Mr & Mrs Harry Schulman) South Creake. 5m NW of Fakenham. Follow B1355 towards Burnham Market. Just after sign to Waterden on R, turn L at signs. Entrance approx 200yds. A challenging garden of approx 1½ acres developed from 3 paddocks 5 yrs ago. Many interesting trees and unusual shrubs, plants and bulbs. A must for anyone discouraged by wind and lack of shelter. TEAS. *Adm £1 Chd free (Share to St Mary's Church, North Creake®). Sun June 12 (2-6)*

Wicken House ৬✗❀ (Lord & Lady Keith) Castle Acre, 5m N of Swaffham off A1065; W at Newton to Castle Acre; then 2m N off the rd to Massingham. Large walled garden planted in sections with many roses and unusual herbaceous plants; gravel paths and greenhouses; swimming pool garden; spring and wild gardens. Fine views. Approx 6 acres. Rare plants for sale. Cream TEAS. *Adm £1.50 Chd free. Sun June 26 (2-6)*

Wickmere House ৬❀ (Mr & Mrs Noel Bolingbroke-Kent) 6m N of Aylsham, 5m S of Cromer. Take A140 to Matlaske turning, on 3m, turn L to Wickmere and Round Church Tower. 3 acres of gardens. 2 Italianate walled gardens featuring many unusual plants, 1 designed by Lanning Roper; small Japaneses garden; lawns and shrubs; peacocks; mediaeval church with interesting monuments at entrance (open). TEAS. *Adm £1.50 Chd 50p (Share to St Andrews Church, Wickmere®). Sun Jul 31 (2-6)*

Wolterton Park ৬✗❀ (The Lord & Lady Walpole) Wolterton is signposted W from Norwich to Cromer Road

(A410) via Erpingham. Approx 8m from Cromer, 6m from Aylsham. Historic park of 340-acres with lake. Gardens at present being redeveloped. Shrubs, borders, large kitchen garden. TEAS. *Adm £2 Students/OAPs £1.50 Chd free (Share to Wolterton Church Tower Appeal®). Sun July 10 (2-5)*

¶Wootton Road Gardens ⚘ E side King's Lynn between Gaywood (clock) and The New Inn traffic lights. All 3 gardens are together opp Mobil Garage. TEA. *Combined adm £1.50 Chd free (Share to St Foith's Church Funds, King's Lynn®). Sun June 19 (2-6)*

¶258 Wootton Road (Mr & Mrs Eric Dent) Long narrow garden, as featured on HTV Garden Club programme, with fuchsias, herbaceous and alpine plants and over 200 flowering shrubs, trees and conifers. Borders contain large collection of roses

¶260 Wootton Road (Miss Janet Dent) Delightfully landscaped garden, with wide number of species of shrubs, conifers and heathers. Impressive lawns and water features, incl informal rockery

262 Wootton Road ও⚘ (Mr & Mrs L Dyer) Average size suburban/town garden comprising wide range of established trees/shrubs and conifers all informally landscaped for colour, shape and easy maintenance

Wretham Lodge ও⚘⚘ (Mrs Anne Hoellering) East Wretham. A11 E from Thetford; L up A1075; L by village sign; R at Xrds then bear L. In May masses of spring flowers and apple blossom; specie tulips, bluebell walk. In June hundreds of old, specie and climbing roses, walled garden, trained fruit trees, interesting mixed borders extensive lawns. Fine old trees. TEAS. *Adm £1.50 Chd free (Share to Norfolk Churches Trust in May, and to Wretham Church in June®). Suns May 8, June 26 (2.30-5.30). Also private visits welcome, please Tel 0953 498 366*

Northamptonshire

Hon County Organiser: Mrs John Boughey, Butts Close, Farthinghoe, Brackley NN13 5NY Tel 0295 710411

Asst Hon County Organisers: Mrs John Bussens, Glebe Cottage, Titchmarsh, Kettering NN14 3DB Tel 0832 732510
Mrs R H N Dashwood, Farthinghoe Lodge, Nr Brackley, Northants NN13 5NX
Mrs R Blake, Lodge Lawn, Fotheringhay, Peterborough PE8 5HZ

Hon County Treasurer: R H N Dashwood, Esq Farthinghoe Lodge, nr Brackley, Northants NN13 5NX Tel 0295 710377

DATES OF OPENING

By appointment
For telephone numbers and other details see garden descriptions. Private visits welcomed

72 Larkhall Lane, Harpole Gardens, Northampton
Maidwell Hall, Northampton
19 Manor Close, Harpole Gardens, Northampton
The Spring House, nr Banbury
Sudborough, The Old Rectory

Regular openings
For details see garden descriptions

Coton Manor, Guilsborough. Open Weds, Suns & Bank Hols Easter to end Sept. Thurs July & Aug
Cottesbrooke Hall, nr Creaton. Open Bank Hols Mons & Thurs April 7 to Sept 29

March 20 Sunday
Sudborough, The Old Rectory

April 3 Sunday
Evenley Wood Garden, Brackley
April 4 Monday
Evenley Wood Garden, Brackley
Titchmarsh Gardens nr Thrapston
April 10 Sunday
Charlton, nr Banbury
April 17 Sunday
Finedon Gardens, nr Wellingborough
April 24 Sunday
Great Brington Gardens, nr Northampton
Maidwell Hall, Northampton
May 1 Sunday
The Haddonstone Show Garden, nr Northampton
May 2 Monday
The Haddonstone Show Garden, nr Northampton
Titchmarsh Gardens nr Thrapston
May 8 Sunday
Aldwincle Gardens, nr Thrapston ‡
Barnwell Manor, nr Peterborough ‡
Chacombe Gardens, nr Banbury
Edgcote, Banbury
Holdenby House, Northampton

May 15 Sunday
Deene Park, nr Corby
May 22 Sunday
Barnwell Manor, nr Peterborough
Bulwick Rectory, Bulwick
Guilsborough and Hollowell Gardens
May 26 Thursday
Coton Manor, Guilsborough
May 29 Sunday
Sholebroke Lodge, Towcester
Slapton Gardens, nr Towcester
Sudborough, The Old Rectory
June 5 Sunday
Benefield, Lower Benefield, nr Oundle
Cottesbrooke Hall, nr Creaton
Gamekeepers Cottage, nr Creaton
Lois Weedon House, nr Towcester
Preston Capes Gardens
Stoke Park, Stoke Bruerne, Towcester
Versions Farm, nr Brackley
June 11 Saturday
Canons Ashby House, Daventry
June 12 Sunday
Evenley Gardens, Brackley
Great and Little Harrowden Gardens, nr Wellingborough

Litchborough Gardens, nr Towcester
Pilton & Stoke Doyle Gardens, nr Oundle

June 13 Monday
Evenley Gardens, Brackley

June 15 Wednesday
Great and Little Harrowden Gardens, nr Wellingborough

June 18 Saturday
Flore Gardens, nr Northampton

June 19 Sunday
Creaton Gardens, nr Northampton
Flore Gardens, nr Northampton
Fotheringhay Gardens, nr Oundle
Sudborough, The Old Rectory
Weedon Lois Gardens, nr Towcester

June 26 Sunday
Aynho Gardens, nr Banbury
Easton Neston, Towcester
Fulford Farm, Culworth, Banbury
Harpole Gardens, Northampton
Irthlingborough Gardens, nr Wellingborough ‡
Wilby Gardens, nr Wellingborough ‡

July 2 Saturday
The Old Vicarage, Gt Cransley, nr Kettering

July 3 Sunday
The Old Vicarage, Gt Cransley, nr Kettering
West Haddon Gardens, nr Northampton

July 10 Sunday
Cranford Gardens, nr Kettering ‡
Pytchley House, nr Kettering ‡

July 17 Sunday
Castle Ashby House, nr Northampton
Guilsborough Court, Guilsborough
Ravensthorpe Gardens

July 20 Wednesday
Ravensthorpe Nursery

July 24 Sunday
Guilsborough Court, Guilsborough

August 7 Sunday
Bulwick Gardens, nr Corby

August 16 Tuesday
Coton Manor, Guilsborough

September 4 Sunday
Cottesbrooke Hall, nr Creaton
Gamekeepers Cottage, nr Creaton
The Haddonstone Show Garden, nr Northampton

September 11 Sunday
Canons Ashby House, Daventry
The Menagerie, Horton nr Northampton

October 2 Sunday
Bulwick Rectory, Bulwick

DESCRIPTIONS OF GARDENS

Aldwincle Gardens ✄ 4m S of Oundle; 3m N of Thrapston on A605. Turn at The Fox at Thorpe Waterville. Aldwincle village 1½m. TEAS at The Maltings. *Combined adm £1.50 Chd free. Sun May 8 (2-6)*

¶**4 Lowick Lane** ✄ (Mr & Mrs Ian Macleod) Small garden surrounding Edwardian house, gravel planted area and hidden courtyard with interesting use of containers

The Maltings ♿✄ (Mr & Mrs N Faulkner) ¾-acre old farm house garden incl farm yard; walled garden, lawns, mixed borders, scree bed, tender wall shrubs; many plants in containers; spring bulbs, small tree plantation

The Manor House ♿✄ (Mr & Mrs G Anderson) 3 acres of garden in process of being replanned and replanted; orchard with bulbs and wild spring flowers, herbaceous beds, wooded area, sweeping lawns overlooking nature reserve and Nene Valley

Old School House ♿ (Mr & Mrs R Raymond-Anderson) Small secluded mainly walled garden. Previously a rough lawn and vegetable patch; present design started in 1989, care being taken to preserve old box hedge and trees

Aynho Gardens ❀ 6m SE of Banbury on B4100. Teas in Village Hall. *Combined adm £2 Chd free (Share to Aynho Village Hall®). Sun June 26 (2.30-6)*

2 The Butts ♿✄ (Mrs Betty Thoenes) ⅓-acre garden with conifers, shrubs, herbaceous borders, roses, bulbs, alpines and scree garden

9 The Butts (Mr & Mrs R G Cheney) ⅓-acre garden with good variety of trees and shrubs accent on attractive foliage; many roses of all types; new rockeries mainly for alpines; fish and lily pond and herbaceous borders

Catton House (Mr & Mrs C H Harmer) Well-established small walled garden with mature trees, various shrubs and specialising in roses & clematis; sunken walled rose garden

Friar's Well (Mr & Mrs T R Sermon) 3-acre garden on top of hill with magnificent view; divided into sections with mixed hedges and stone walls, pleached limes and hornbeams, unusual shrubs and roses

Puente Sierra (Mr & Mrs R Sawbridge) 1 Cartwright Gardens. A ½-acre walled garden with interesting mature evergreens, shrubberies and deciduous trees, bulbs, lilies, palms and hibiscus. Also a fruit and vegetable area

16 Roundtown (Mrs E A Bazin) Old-fashioned cottage garden with inner walled section, herbaceous borders, roses, shrubs and fruit trees

Barnwell Manor ♿ (HRH Princess Alice Duchess of Gloucester & The Duke & Duchess of Gloucester) nr Peterborough. 2m S of Oundle; 4½m NE of Thrapston on A605. Pleasant grounds, spring flowers. C13 castle ruins. Car park free. TEAS. *Adm £1 Chd Free. Suns May 8, 22 (2.30-6)*

Benefield House ♿✄ ❀ (Mr & Mrs John Nicholson) Lower Benefield. 3m W Oundle off A427. Oundle-Corby Rd. 2½-acre garden with large herbaceous border with interesting plants. Shrubbery laid out in 1992. Old walled kitchen gardens containing vegetables and flowers. TEA. *Adm £1.50 Chd free (Share to St Mary's Church®). Sun June 5 (2-6)*

Bulwick Gardens Bulwick village 7m NE of Corby, 10m SW of Stanford, ½m off A43. *Combined adm £2 Chd free (Share to Multiple Sclerosis Research®). Sun Aug 7 (2-5.30)*

Bulwick Park ♿ (Mr & Mrs G T G Conant) In Bulwick Village turn in Red Lodge Rd, enter park over cattle grid. Formal terraced 8-acre walled garden leading to river and island. 50 metre double herbaceous borders. 100 metre holly walk ending at attractive C18 wrought iron gates. C19 orangery and colonnade; large newly planned kitchen garden; fine mature trees; peacocks. TEAS

¶**The Shambles** ✗ (Roger Glithero Esq) Approx ⅓-acre garden, mixed herbaceous borders, vegetable garden with fruit and an original village well; variety of flowering plants in pots and tubs

Bulwick Rectory ৬✗❀ (Revd & Mrs Mervyn Wilson) Bulwick. 8m NE of Corby; 13m NE of Kettering; next to Bulwick Church. 1½-acre old rectory garden largely re-made and replanted since 1978 as a number of gardens with vistas and surprises. Dovecote; folly; stonewalls. Shrubs, old roses, mixed borders with wide variety of plants. Fruit trees 30 varieties of apple, 15 of pear and 12 of plum in various forms of training and quince medlar and vegetables cultivated on organic principles. TEAS May only. *Adm £1 Chd 50p (Share to St Nicholas Church®). Suns May 22, Oct 2 (2-5)*

Canons Ashby House ৬✗ (The National Trust) nr Daventry. Formal gardens enclosed by walls being developed. Gate piers from 1710; fine topiary; axial arrangement of paths and terraces; wild flowers, old varieties of fruit trees, newly planted gardens. Home of the Dryden family since C16, Manor House 1550 with contemporary wall paintings and Jacobean plastering. TEAS. *Adm £3.20 Chd £1.60 (includes house). Reduced party rate. For NGS Sat June 11, Sun Sept 11 (12-5.30)*

Castle Ashby House ৬ (The Marquis of Northampton) 6m E of Northampton. 1½m N of A428 Northampton-Bedford; turn off between Denton and Yardley Hastings. Parkland incl avenue planted at suggestion of William III in 1695; lakes etc by Capability Brown; Italian gardens with orangery; extensive lawns and trees. Nature trail. Elizabethan house (not open). TEA. *Adm £2 Chd & OAPs £1. For NGS Sun July 17 (11-6)*

Chacombe Gardens 4m NE of Banbury. On A361 from Banbury centre turn R signed to Chacombe. TEAS **17 Silver St**. *Combined adm £1.50 Chd free (Share to St Peter & St Paul Church®). Sun May 8 (2-6)*
   Cartmel ✗ (Mr & Mrs John Willis) Small informal elevated garden with herbaceous plants, spring bulbs, roses, shrubs and small trees; pond and rockery with wide variety of plants. Greenhouse with tender plants for summer planting. Surrounded on three sides by hedges and old stone walls
   Pear Tree House (Capt & Mrs Peter Northey) A 1-acre garden leading up to church with spring bulbs, mature trees and shrubs surrounding an extended C17 cottage
   Poplars Farm ❀ (Mr & Mrs Geoff Jones) 4 acres mixed borders; streamside with ferns, species primulas and bog plants; kitchen garden; dry garden with alpines; wild areas with some growing willow for fuel, spring and summer meadow areas being developed, greenhouse with cacti and carnivorous plants. Thatched 1654 farmhouse (not open); stone barns, interesting cacti, carnivorous and herbaceous plants raised in the gardens for sale
   17 Silver St (Dr & Mrs Stephen Large) 2-acres under development; paddocks with shetland ponies; wild stream-side; mixed borders; rose garden with wall plantings; small court; some sculpture on display in garden

Charlton 7m SE of Banbury, 5m W of Brackley. From A41 turn off N at Aynho; or from A422 turn off S at Farthinghoe. Home-made TEAS **the Cottage**. *Combined adm £1.50 Chd 75p (Share to Charlton Playing Fields©). Sun April 10 (2-6)*
   The Cottage ✗ (Lady Juliet Townsend) Flowering shrubs, spring bulbs, roses, lawns, woodland walk, stream and lakes. House in village street
   Holly House (The Hon Nicholas Berry) Walled garden with beautiful views. C18 house (not open)

Coton Manor ৬❀ (Mr & Mrs Ian Pasley-Tyler) 10m N of Northampton. 11m SE of Rugby nr Ravensthorpe Reservoir. From A428 & A50 follow Tourist signs. C17 stone manor house with water gardens, herbaceous borders, rose garden, old holly and yew hedges; interesting variety of foliage plants; collection of ornamental waterfowl, cranes and flamingoes. Home-made TEAS. *Adm £2.70 OAPs £2.10 Chd £1. Open Weds, Suns & Bank Hols. Easter to end Sept; also Thurs July & Aug. For NGS Thurs May 26, Tues Aug 16 (2-6)*

Cottesbrooke Hall ৬✗❀ (Capt & Mrs J Macdonald-Buchanan) 10m N of Northampton. Nr Creaton on A50; nr Brixworth on A508. Car park free. Large formal and wild gardens; herbaceous borders, fine old cedars. (Brixworth Church, 2½m, dates back to C7, is well worth a visit). TEAS. *Adm £3.50. Gardens only £1.50. House and Gardens, but not greenhouses, open Bank Hol Mons and Thurs April 7 to Sept 29 (2-5.30) For NGS Suns June 5, Sept 4 (2-6) Adm £1.50 Chd 50p (Share to All Saints Church®)*

Cranford Gardens 4½m E of Kettering. A14 Kettering-Thrapston. TEAS, Station House, Oakrise. Car parking available. *Combined adm £1.50 Chd 50p (Share to Cranford Churches Restoration Fund®). Sun July 10 (2-6)*
   16 Duck End (Miss Margaret Thomson) Very small cottage garden overlooking the church. Borders of perennials and shrubs
   The Manor House ❀ (Mr & Mrs J M Bentley) Very interesting large stone walled traditional Manor House garden
   Oakrise ৬ (Mr & Mrs G T Oakes) 5 The Green. ½ acre with variety of shrubs, perennials, dwarf conifers; Japanese water garden with Koi Carp and water plants; lovely view
   Station House ৬ (Mr & Mrs A Bates) Garden created from the original railway station. Old platform now a walled patio with fish pond and rockery. Many varieties of trees, new planting of shrubs, herbaceous perennials. Natural wildlife pond

Creaton Gardens 8m N of Northampton on A50. Turn R into village onto village green. Teas at Creaton House in aid of St Michael & All Angels Church. *Combined adm £1.25 Acc chd free. Sun June 19 (2-6)*
   Creaton Lodge ৬ (Mrs R T Gibbs) 2-acres well established garden with lawns, fine mature trees, shrubs, herbaceous borders and conifer banks. New water garden
   11 Home Farm Close ❀ (Daphne & Patrick Clark) ¼ acre, newly designed garden for all seasons, surrounding modern house. Vegetable plot; herb garden; greenhouse; ponds; informal patios

Stoneacre ✿ (Mr & Mrs R J E Hopewell) ⅓-acre, slightly sloping, mainly walled garden but with open views. A cottage garden with lawns, ponds, summerhouse, greenhouse, vegetable and fruit plots and containing some less usual trees, flowering shrubs and herbaceous plants in the mixed borders. Plant stall in aid of St. Michael & All Angels Church

Deene Park ᏼ✿ (Edmund Brudenell Esq) 5m N of Corby on A43 Stamford-Kettering Rd. Large garden; long mixed borders, old-fashioned roses, rare mature trees, shrubs, natural garden, large lake and waterside walks. Parterre designed by David Hicks echoing the C16 decoration on the porch stonework. Interesting Church and Brudenell Chapel with fine tombs and brasses. TEAS. *Adm £1.50 Chd 50p. Sun May 15 (2-5)*

Easton Neston ᏼ✿✿ (The Lord & Lady Hesketh) Towcester. Entrance on Northampton Rd (old A43). Hawkesmoor's only Private house. Large formal garden; ornamental water, topiary; walled garden; woodland walk with C14 church (not open) in grounds. TEA. *Adm £2 Chd 50p. Sun June 26 (2-6)*

Edgcote ᏼ✿ (Mr & Mrs C J Courage) 6m NE of Banbury. On E of A361; from Banbury turn R in Wardington Village. Unspoilt Georgian house (not open) set in grounds of mature trees and lawns with 8 acres of lake. TEA. *Adm £1 Chd 50p. Sun May 8 (2-6)*

Evenley Gardens ᏼ✿✿ From Brackley 1m S on A43. Teas at Evenley Hall. *Combined adm £1.40 Chd 40p. Sun, Mon June 12, 13 (2-6)*

15 Church Lane (Mr & Mrs K O'Regan) ⅓-acre garden, newly built terrace pond, mixed borders and vegetable garden

Five Gables ✿✿ (Mr & Mrs M Bosher) SE facing sloping garden of 1½ acres. Designed in 'compartments' and still being developed

Hill Grounds ᏼ✿ (Mr & Mrs C F Cropley) 2-acres S facing sheltered garden re-developed since 1982; mature trees, 200 yds of yew hedge; terrace; old roses, winter garden; wide range of unusual plants

The Manor House (Mr & Mrs H Bentley) Church Lane, just off NW corner of village green. Established garden on ½-acre sloping site; topiary and an ambience in harmony with fine Elizabethan Manor House (not open)

¶Evenley Wood Garden (R T Whiteley) Brackley. A43 ¾m S turn L to Evenley straight through village towards Mixbury 1st turning L. A woodland garden spread over a 60-acre mature wood. Acid and alkaline soil. Magnolias, rhododendrons, azaleas, malus, quercus, acers, euonymus collection and many other species. A large collection of bulbous plants. *Adm £2 Chd £1. Suns, Mons May 1, 2; 29, 30 (2-7). For NGS Sun, Mon April 3, 4 (2-7)*

> **Regular Openers.** Too many days to include in diary. Usually there is a wide range of plants giving year-round interest. See head of county section for the name and garden description for times etc.

Finedon Gardens ᏼ Wellingborough. 2m NE of Wellingborough on the A510, 6m SE Kettering on the A6. TEA. *Combined adm £1.50 Chd free. Sun April 17 (2-6)*

4 Harrowden Lane (Mr & Mrs D J West) ½-acre garden on a steep slope, created in last 10 years from waste land; lawns, rose and flower beds; ornamental fish pond with cascade fountain, aviary and greenhouses

Thingdon Cottage (Mrs M A Leach) 4½ acres of garden, originally Finedon Hall grounds. Lawns, ancient trees, shrubs, spring flowers, brook, hillside pasture with unique view of Finedon Hall and Church

Flore Gardens 7m W of Northampton, 5m E of Daventry on A45. Flower Festival at All Saints Church and U.R Chapel inc light lunches, Teas, plants, etc. *Combined adm £2 Chd free (Share to Flower Festival®). Sat, Sun June 18, 19 (11-6)*

Beech Hill ✿ (Dr & Mrs R B White) The garden of approx 1 acre is on a hillside facing S over the Nene Valley. It is laid out to lawns, herbaceous and shrub borders with mature trees. There is a vegetable garden and an orchard, an alpine house and cool greenhouse. The terrace has hanging baskets and tubs

The Croft (John & Dorothy Boast) ⅓-acre garden of C17 cottage with mature trees, shrubs, lawns and interesting perennials

¶The Grange ✿ (Mr & Mrs C R Buswell) Mature 2½-acre garden with lawns, trees, herbaceous beds, shrubs and pond. Partly suitable for wheelchairs

The Manor House ✿ (Richard & Wendy Amos) 1-acre garden with established lawns and herbaceous border surrounded by mature trees. Formal pond and walled kitchen garden. Partly suitable for wheelchairs

The Old Manor ✿ (Mr & Mrs Keith Boyd) Early C18 house (not shown) with medium-sized garden, comprising lawn, herbaceous border, rose garden, vegetables and fruit. Pleasant views over the Nene valley. Also paddock with pond and shrubs

6 Thornton Close (Mr & Mrs D L Lobb) Medium-sized garden; trees, shrubs, herbaceous plants, conifers and alpines. 2 small ponds with fish

The White Cottage ᏼ✿ (Mr & Mrs G Menzies) Large cottage garden. Approx 1 acre; lawns, shrubs, perennial beds; fruit trees and vegetable garden

Fotheringhay Gardens 4m NE of Oundle signposted from A605 3m S of Wansford from A47 and A1. Teas available in village hall. *Combined adm £2 Chd free (Share to St Mary & All Saints Church®). Sun June 19 (11-6)*

The Blacksmith's Cottage ✿✿ (Mr & Mrs G M B Wilson) ⅓-acre with recently constructed raised terrace; many trees and shrubs planted since 1986; 'Compost heaps a speciality'

Chestnut Tree Cottage ✿✿ (Mr & Mrs John Ingram) ¼ acre country cottage garden; roses, flowering shrubs, large vegetable garden and greenhouse

Lodge Lawn ᏼ✿ (Mrs R Blake) Medium-sized informal cottage garden. Developed since 1984

The Old Vicarage ᏼ✿✿ (Mr & Mrs Peter Fryer) 1-acre of well established gardens, herbaceous borders shrubs, old roses and mature trees, unusual plants

Willow House ය (Mr & Mrs C M Saunders) A 15yr-old-house and garden of ⅔-acre; mixed fruit and vegetables, herbaceous plants, shrubs and family play areas

Fulford Farm ✿ (Mr & Mrs M Moerman) Culworth, nr Banbury. Follow rd Banbury to Northampton turn L at sign Sulgrave. After approx 2m turn L at sign Culworth. Unusual continental garden with beautiful views approx 3 acres. Most of the garden is only 10yrs-old, young herbaceous borders with unusual plants; pond; little birds wood; lawns, terraced garden. TEAS. *Adm £1 Chd free (Share to St Michael's Church, Culworth® 0. Sun June 26 (2-6)*

Gamekeepers Cottage Garden ය✿ (Mr & Mrs D Daw) Cottesbrooke. 10m W of Northampton, nr Creaton on A50; nr Brixworth on A508. Cottage garden featuring unusual herbaceous plants, flowers for drying, fruit, vegetables. *Combined adm £1.50 Chd 50p with* **Cottesbrooke Hall**. *Suns June 5, Sept 4 (2-6)*

Great Brington Gardens ✿ 7m NW of Northampton off A428 Rugby rd. 1st L turn past main gates of Althorp. Tickets/maps at church. Gardens signed in village. Parking facilities. Ploughman's lunches, TEAS. Exhibition and plant stall at various village venues in aid of St Mary's Church. *Combined adm £1.50 Chd free. Sun April 24 (11-5)*

    Brington Lodge ය✿ (Mr & Mrs P J Cooch) An old garden on the edge of the village, approx ¾ acre, partially walled with a number of spring flowering trees and shrubs

    ¶**Dairy Farm** ය✿ (Ian & Alex Ward) ½-acre garden comprising lawn with mixed borders, cottage garden, rose garden, secret garden; orchards, vegetables and pond; also farmyard animals

    Folly House ✿ ✿ (Capt & Mrs L G Bellamy) Early C18 house (not shown) 1-acre garden, lawns, herbaceous, shrubs and vegetable garden. Interesting setting using different levels with the church as background

    30 Great Brington ය✿ (Mr & Mrs John Kimbell) Interesting small garden attached to old stone cottage, well-stocked with shrubs, climbers and perennials. Small pond with bog area, secret garden

    The Last Straw ය✿ (Mr & Mrs A Johnson) C15 thatched cottage with cottage garden. Pleasent views of Althorp. Many spring-flowering bulbs, summer hut

    ¶**New Cross** ය✿ (R J Kimbell) ½-acre old country garden surrounding a mellow Northamptonshire stone house. Mature trees and shrubs with many spring flowering bulbs

    The Old Rectory ය✿ (Mr & Mrs R Thomas) 3-acre garden, with mature trees, yew hedging, formal rose garden, vegetable and small herb gardens. ½ acre of orchard

    Ridgway House ✿ (Mr & Mrs John Gale) 1½ acres with lawns, herbaceous borders and many spring-flowering shrubs and bulbs

Great & Little Harrowden Gardens On A509 2m N of Wellingborough on the L. 5m S of Kettering on the R. TEAS in aid of ARC. *Combined adm £2 Chd free. Sun, Wed June 12, 15 (2-6)*

Dolphins ය✿✿ (Mr & Mrs R C Handley) Gt Harrowden. 2-acre country garden surrounding old stone house. Many old roses grown among interesting trees, shrubs and a wide range of hardy perennials

Great Harrowden Lodge ය✿✿ (Mrs J & Mr R M Green) 1¼-acre garden on a dry exposed site, recently extended. Wide variety of herbaceous perennials. *Sun June 12 only*

¶**South View** ය✿ (Mr & Mrs D W Osborne) Little Harrowden. Small lane off Main St near to church. Recently constructed terraced garden, with S facing rural aspect. Herbaceous and shrub borders, interesting kitchen garden encl by different varieties of trained fruit trees, wild flower area

Guilsborough Court ය✿ (Mr & Mrs John Lowther) Guilsborough. 10m N of Northampton off A50. 10m NE of Daventry; 10m E of Rugby; ¼m outside Guilsborough on Cold Ashby rd. 4-acre garden, many fine mature trees, beautiful views, interesting shrubs, large lawn and herbaceous border. Good plant sales area. TEAS. *Adm £1 Chd free. Suns July 17, 24 (2-6)*

Guilsborough and Hollowell Gardens 10m NW of Northampton between A50 - A428. 10m E of Rugby. Cream Teas at **Dripwell House** by Guilsborough WI. TEAS at Hollowell Village Hall. *Combined adm £1.50 Chd 50p. Sun May 22 (2-6)*

    Dripwell House ✿✿ Guilsborough (Mr & Mrs J W Langfield, Dr C Moss, Mr & Mrs P G Moss) 2¼-acre mature garden; many fine trees and shrubs on partly terraced slope. Rock garden, herbaceous border, herb garden. Some unusual shrubs and many rhododendrons and azaleas in woodland garden. Cream teas in garden

    ¶**Gower House** (Peter & Anne Moss) Small garden evolving since 1991 on part of Dripwell vegetable garden. A plantsman's garden with herbaceous alpine, climbing plants and shrubs

    Rosemount, Hollowell ✿✿ (Mr & Mrs J Leatherland) In centre of village, up hill behind bus shelter towards Church, entrance 100yds on R. ½-acre plantsman's garden reconstructed in 1982, unusual plants and shrubs, alpine garden, fish pond, small collections of clematis, conifers, camellias, daphne and abutilons. Partly suitable for wheelchairs. Car parking and teas at village hall behind Church

The Haddonstone Show Garden, East Haddon Manor ය✿✿ (Mr & Mrs R Barrow) 10m N of Northampton, 12m S of Rugby, from A50. Walled garden on different levels, old shrub roses, ground cover plants, conifers, clematis and climbers; swimming pool surrounded by Haddonstone Colonnade, over 30 planted pots and containers. Refreshments. TEAS. *Adm £2.50 Chd free (Share to NSPCC®) Garden Festival Weekend Sun, Mon May 1, 2, (10-5). Adm £2 Chd free. Sun Sept 4 (2-5).* Special autumn plant sale

---

Regular Openers. Too many days to include in diary. Usually there is a wide range of plants giving year-round interest. See head of county section for the name and garden description for times etc.

Harpole Gardens 4m W Northampton on A45 towards Weedon; turn right at 'The Turnpike' into Harpole. TEAS at **The Grange**. *Combined adm £1.50 Chd free. Sun June 26 (2-6)*

The Close ✿❀ (Mr & Mrs Orton Jones) 68 High Street. Old-fashioned English country garden with large lawns, herbaceous borders and mature trees; stone house, various plant stalls

¶**Darnley** ✿ (Mr & Mrs Peter Rixon)47b High St. An enclosed garden of ⅛th acre, consisting of cottage garden borders, a rockery, pond, rose and herb areas; a Japanese style feature and a large collection of cacti and succulents

The Grange ✿✿ 55 Upper High St; 2-acre garden with interesting shrubberies, walks, borders, fruit trees, kitchen garden; C18 family home (not open)

72 Larkhall Lane ✿ (Mr & Mrs R G Murton) ⅙-acre well designed garden for all seasons; a flower to bloom everyday of the year; shrubs; variety of conifers and alpines. *Private visits welcome, please* **Tel 0604 830680**

19 Manor Close ✿ (Mr & Mrs E Kemshed) 40yd × 10yd flower arranger's garden on new estate; cultivated by present owners since 1975. *Private visits welcome, please* **Tel 0604 830512**

32 School Lane ✿ (Mr & Mrs A C Digby) Small 40' × 25' sun-lovers walled garden featuring potted and wall trained fruit; sunken garden with rockeries; herbs; tubs and alpine sinks. Lovely views over open countryside

Holdenby House ✿✿ (Mr & Mrs James Lowther) 7m W of Northampton. Signposted from A50 and A428. Impressive remains of terrace gardens of Holdenby Palace, where Charles I was imprisoned; Elizabethan garden; fragrant and silver borders. Rare breeds farm animals; museum, falconry centre. TEAS. *Adm £2.50 (groups of 25 or more £2) OAP £2 Chd £1.50.* ▲*For NGS Sun May 8 (2-6). House open by appt for groups of 25 or more Adm £3.50*

Irthlingborough Gardens ✿✿❀ 5m E of Wellingborough, off the A6. TEAS in aid of Barnardo's. *Combined adm £1 Chd free. Sun June 26 (2-6)*

45 Finedon Road (Mr & Mrs G Brown) A garden of formal design with informal planting of trees, shrubs, bulbs, climbers and perennials. Pond and courtyard

49 Finedon Road (Mr & Mrs D Ingall) A garden of approx 1 acre full of interest and unusual plants, incl herbaceous border, shrubs, pools, gravel bed and rock, wild and scented areas. Also fruit and vegetables

Litchborough Gardens ✿ Nr Towcester, Litchborough village is mid-way between Northampton and Banbury. Teas in WI Hall, Farthingstone Rd. *Combined adm £2 Chd free (Share to St Martins Church®). Sun June 12 (2-6)*

Bruyere Court, Farthingstone Rd ✿ (Mr & Mrs R Martin) 4 acres of landscaped garden featuring lawns; 2 ornamental lakes with rock streams and fountain; shrub borders; rhododendron and azalea borders; herbaceous border; old-fashioned rose hedge; ornamental trees and conifers

The Hall ✿ (A R Heygate Esq) Large garden with open views of parkland; laid to lawns and borders with clipped hedges around the house; the extensive wild garden has large numbers of specimen trees and shrubs; walks wind through this area and round the lakes

The Old Rectory (Mr & Mrs T R Sykes) Partly walled garden adjoining churchyard; mostly laid to lawn with mixed shrubs and herbaceous borders recently planted heather and conifer bank and small pond. Kitchen garden area and hazel walk

Orchard House ❀ (Mr & Mrs B Smith) Banbury Rd, Landscape architects country garden designed for low maintenance; orchard, pools, conservatory and working pump

Stone End (Mr & Mrs F Smith) Chapel Close. A recently developed garden of 1 acre with central rockery incorporating waterfall and pool planted with alpines; many flowering shrubs and views of surrounding country

Lois Weedon House ❀ (Mr & Mrs John Greenaway) Weedon Lois. 7m from Towcester on the edge of Weedon Lois village. Pass through village going E towards Wappenham; as you leave village Lois Weedon House next entrance on R, further on is second entrance which has a lodge. Medium-sized garden with terraces and fine views; lawns; pergola; water garden; mature yew hedges; new large pond. TEAS. *Adm £1.50 Chd free (Share to Lois Weedon PCC®). Sun June 5 (2-6)*

Maidwell Hall ✿❀ (Mr & Mrs J H Paul, of Maidwell Hall School) A508 N from Northampton, 6m S of Market Harborough, entrance via cattle grid on S fringe of Maidwell village. 45 acres of lawns, playing fields, woodland. Colourful display of spring bulbs, magnolias and early flowering shrubs; mature rose garden; lake and arboretum. TEA. *Adm £1.50 Chd free (Share to St Mary's Church, Maidwell®). Sun April 24 (2-6) Private visits welcome April to July, Sept to Oct, please* **Tel 060128 234**

The Menagerie ✿ (Mr G Jackson-Stop & Mr I Kirby). 6m S of Northampton. On B526 turn L 1m S of Horton. An C18 folly with Rococo plasterwork room (open). A garden in the making. Designed as an architectural journey, with formal water gardens, informal wetlands. Rose garden and a spiral mound. 4.5 acres. TEAS. *Adm £2 Chd 50p. Thurs April to Sept (10-4). For NGS Sun Sept 11 (2-6)*

The Old Rectory, Sudborough ✿❀ (Mr & Mrs Huntington) Corby exit off A14. Village just off A6116 between Thrapston & Brigstock. Classic English country garden re-opening following a year of further improvements, many rare and unusual plants cram this 3-acre plantsman's garden surrounding a fine Georgian Rectory (not open). Features incl colour themed mixed and herbaceous borders; formal rose garden; shrubberies and pond; woodland walk; intricate potager designed by Rosemary Verey and developed by the owners with Rupert Golby. Many well planted containers; in March a comprehensive display of helleborus x orientalis (Lenten Rose) can be seen massed with spring bulbs. Featured in House & Garden, June 93. TEAS. *Adm £2 Chd free (Share to All Saints Church, Sudborough®). Suns March 20, May 29, June 19 (2-6)*

By Appointment Gardens. See head of county section

¶The Old Vicarage ⚹ (Mr & Mrs M J Percival) Great Cransley. 3m SW of Kettering off A43 signposted to Broughton and 1m to Great Cransley. 1½ acres of English country garden with lawns, mature trees and hedges; mixed herbaceous and shrub borders. TEAS. *Adm £1.50 Chd free (Share to St Andrews Church®). Sat, Sun July 2, 3 (2-6)*

Pilton & Stoke Doyle Nr Oundle. Take A605 and midway between Oundle and Thrapston turn W at cross roads to go past Lilford Park to Pilton. For Stoke Doyle continue to next crossroads and turn R. Teas available at Wadenhoe Village Hall. *Combined adm £1.20 Chd free. Sun June 12 (2-6)*

Elmes House ⚹ (Mr and Mrs J H Otter) Pilton. Two walled gardens with various perennial and shrub borders. Grass tennis court leading to over 2-acres of rough ground with woodland walk. Trees planted in 1973
Mill House ⚹✿ (Mr & Mrs H Faure Walker) Stoke Doyle. Medium-sized walled garden, mixed borders; gravel garden; vegetable garden; area from field leading to stream recently planted with trees, yews and shrub roses. Plant stall

Preston Capes Gardens ⚹ Approx 7m S of Daventry, 3m N of Canon's Ashby. TEAS and plants in aid of St Peter's & St Paul's Church. *Combined adm £2 Chd 50p. Sun June 5 (2-6)*

Archway Cottage (Mr & Mrs King) Approx ½-acre garden, with outstanding views over Northants countryside. Lawns with specimen shrubs, herbaceous borders and ornamental fish pond. Sloping plot being converted to nature garden, with natural pond, marginal plants and berry-bearing trees and shrubs
City Cottage ⚹✿ (Mr & Mrs Gavin Cowen) A mature garden in the middle of an attractive village, with a walled herbaceous border, rose beds, flowering shrubs, wisteria and magnificent magnolia tree
Old West Farm ⚹✿ (Mr & Mrs Gerard Hoare) Little Preston. Between Charwelton (A361) and Maidford. 2-acre garden re-designed since 1980. Small woodland area with bulbs, borders, roses and flowering shrubs for year round interest

Pytchley House ⚹✿ (Lady Glover) Pytchley, 3m S of Kettering. Between A43 & A509. Rose garden, lawns, fine trees and topiary; Temple of Zeus. House 1633. **Essential** dogs kept on leads. Produce stall. TEAS. *Adm 75p Chd 25p (Share to NSPCC®). Sun July 10 (2.30-6)*

¶Ravensthorpe Gardens Halfway between Rugby and Northampton. Signposted Ravensthorpe 1½m from the A428. TEAS by Ravensthorpe WI in aid of Gordon Robinson Memorial Trust at Ravensthorpe Nursery. *Combined adm £1.50 Chd free. Sun July 17 (2-6)*

¶32 The High St (Mr & Mrs J Patrick) Moderate size garden planted over the last 5yrs. Mostly perennials but some shrubs and roses; also greenhouse and vegetables
¶Lingles Farm ⚹ (Mr & Mrs A Mold) Large garden with mixed island beds

---

Regular Openers. See head of county section.

¶Ravensthorpe Nursery ⚹✿ (Mr & Mrs Richard Wiseman) Approx 1-acre new show garden being developed to display plants; wide range of shrubs, trees and hardy perennials, incl shrub rose and mixed borders with fine views; also private ¼-acre owners' plantsman's garden. *Also open Wed July 20 (6.30-9)*

Sholebroke Lodge ⚹✿ (A B X Fenwick Esq) Whittlebury, 3m S of Towcester. Turn off A413 Towcester end of Whittlebury village. 5-acres informal garden; large new planting of shrubs, bulbs, wild flowers and interesting plants in established setting. Garden shop. Home-made TEAS. *Adm £1 Chd 50p. Sun May 29 (2-6)*

¶Slapton Gardens ⚹✿ Slapton, a tiny village 4m W of Towcester ¼m on the Towcester to Wappenham Rd. Superb small 13/14th century church. TEAS & car park at Slapton Lodge. *Combined adm £2 Chd free. Sun May 29 (2-6)*

¶The Old Mill (Mr & Mrs R Post) At N end of village a lane, signposted leads down from Slapton Mill, footpaths lead back from The Mill to Slapton Lodge and village rd. 'A garden in the making'. 2 acres of grass bordered by a brook, R Tove and small Mill race with ancient pollarded willows. Most of the garden is liable to flood and so planting is limited to varieties that tolerate being underwater for short periods in winter and baked dry in summer; a long term project started 1yr ago.
¶The Old Royal Oak (Mr & Mrs D Mumford) A garden for the gardener and plantsman, approx ⅓-acre, started from bare site 1989. Imaginative use of layout to take in different levels and difficult soil conditions. Trees, flowering shrubs, (many unusual) herbaceous, alpines and lawn; large cottage borders
¶Slapton Lodge (Mr & Mrs Webster) In beautiful grounds and parkland

The Spring House (Mr & Mrs C Shepley-Cuthbert) Mill Lane Chipping Warden on A361 between Banbury and Daventry. Garden originally laid out by Miss Kitty Lloyd Jones in the thirties and now mature. Approx 3 acres app through a 16' tapestry hedge. April-May spring flowers, bulbs and blossom. June-Sept bog and water garden at its most colourful. Other times unconventional borders, shrub roses and specimen trees with many new plantings. Ploughmans lunches and Teas available for groups & clubs by arrangement. *Private visits welcome, please* Tel 0295 86261

Stoke Park ⚹ (A S Chancellor Esq) Stoke Bruerne Towcester. Stoke Bruerne village lies 1m off A508 between Northampton and Stony Stratford. Stoke Park is down a private road ¾m, first turning left, ¼m beyond village. Approx 3-acres. Terraced lawn with ornamental basin, orchard, herb garden, shrub and other borders, as setting to two C17 pavillions and colonnade. TEA. *Adm £1 Chd 50p. ▲Sun June 5 (2-6)*

Titchmarsh Gardens 2m N of Thrapston, 6m S of Oundle on A605, Titchmarsh signposted as turning to E. TEAS. *Combined adm £2 Chd free (Share to St Marys Church, Titchmarsh©). Mons April 4, May 2 (2-6)*

Glebe Cottage ⚹⚹ (Mr & Mrs J Bussens) ⅓ acre; NE aspect; informal herbaceous and shrub borders and beds. Clematis in a variety of situations

The Manor House &⚘ (Mr Leonard Harper) A one-acre garden comprising a wide range of well-matured flowering shrubs and rose beds. Paddock with spring flowers and good views of countryside

16 Polopit ⚘ (Mr & Mrs C Millard) ½ acre. Developed since 1984; rockeries, ornamental and herbaceous borders; fruit decorative shrubs

Titchmarsh House &⚘ (Mr & Mrs Ewan Harper) 4 acres extended and laid out since 1972; cherries, magnolias, herbaceous irises; shrub roses, clematis, range of shrubs, walled borders

Versions Farm &⚘⚘ (Mrs E T Smyth-Osbourne) Brackley 2m N of Brackley on the Turweston Rd. 3-acres plantsmans garden; old stone walls; terraces; old-fashioned rose garden; shrubs and trees some unusual; pond and knot garden. Conservatory. TEAS. *Adm £1.20 Chd free (Share to Whitfield Church®). Sun June 5 (2-6)*

Weedon Lois Gardens ⚘ Nr Towcester. 8m W of Towcester. TEAS. *Combined adm £1.50 Chd free. Sun June 19 (2-6)*

    Elizabeth House ⚘⚘ (Mr & Mrs A Cartwright) A C17 vicarage garden of 1½ acres. Herbaceous beds, a walled vegetable garden and wild wooded area

    The Leys ⚘ (Mr & Mrs Peter French) A garden of 1-acre sloping away from the house; designed to incl attractive vistas; separate areas and styles formed to suit, water, alpine screes, Japanese gravel gardens and mixed borders

    The Old Barn ⚘⚘ (Mr & Mrs John Gregóry) Small ⅓-acre plantsman's garden designed by the owners to compliment converted C18 barn; with interesting selection of herbaceous perennials, climbing plants, shrub roses and gravel gardens. Many unusual plants for sale, incl white varieties

West Haddon Gardens As seen on BBC TV in 1992. The village is on the A428 between Rugby and Northampton and lies 4m E of M1 exit 18. Teas in village hall. *Combined adm £1.50 Chd free (Share to West Haddon Parish Church and West Haddon Baptist Church©). Sun July 3 (2-6)*

    The Bungalow ⚘ West Haddon Hall (John and Jean Terry) Small secluded informal garden surrounded by mature trees with rockery; lawns; mixed borders; two aviaries and pond

    Crystal House &⚘ (Pat and Dick Hughes) ¼-acre of landscaped garden, mostly walled, informal terrace areas, lawn and mixed borders, many containers and hanging baskets, new summerhouse and vegetable garden

    Lime House ⚘ (Leslie and David Roberts) ½-acre of walled garden with rockeries, herbaceous borders, walk-through shrubbery, rose beds; croquet lawn. Summerhouse and patio with greenhouse

    The Mews ⚘ (Rob and Jane Dadley) ½-acre of secluded walled garden including lawns, secret garden, herbaceous border, formal and informal ponds, statuary and pergolas

    Well Cottage ⚘ (Rosemary Wright) Very small walled garden on various levels displaying many containers, pond and a variety of plants

    West Cottages & (Geoff and Rosemary Sage) ⅔-acre of mixed borders and lawns; informal pond; lawn tennis court and kitchen garden. Newly acquired additional land; garden under construction. Open views

Wilby Gardens. 3m SW of Wellingborough on the A4500 to Northampton signposted Wilby. TEAS at **Glebe Farmhouse.** *Combined adm £1.50 Chd free. Sun June 26 (2-6)*

    Glebe Farmhouse &⚘ (Mr & Mrs K B Shipp) Medium-sized garden with shrub and herbaceous borders

    7 Mears Ashby Road ⚘ (Mr & Mrs K H Coleman) Small garden containing shrubs and herbaceous borders. Variety of plants in containers, plenty of colour

    Wilby Cottage ⚘ (Mrs B K Gale) Well established cottage garden, surrounded by walls and hedge, shrubs, herbaceous border, rockery and tubs, a plantsman's garden

Northumberland & Tyne and Wear

Hon County Organiser:	Mrs G Baker Cresswell, Preston Tower, Chathill, Northumberland NE67 5DH Tel 0665 89210
Assistant Hon County Organiser:	Mrs T Sale, Ilderton Glebe, Ilderton, Alnwick, Northumberland NE66 4YD Tel 06687 293

DATES OF OPENING

By Appointment
For telephone numbers and other details see garden descriptions. Private visits welcomed

Bide-A-Wee Cottage, Netherwitton, Morpeth

Regular openings
For details see garden descriptions

Castle Gardens, Berwick-Upon-Tweed

April 24 Sunday
  Preston Tower, Chathill

May 15 Sunday
  Wallington, Cambo, Morpeth

May 22 Sunday
  Belsay Hall, Castle & Gardens, Belsay

Berryburn, Ancroft, Berwick-on-Tweed

May 29 Sunday
  Chillingham Castle, Chillingham, Alnwick

June 5 Sunday
  Lilburn Tower, Powburn, Alnwick
  Meldon Park, Morpeth

June 19 Sunday
  Castle Gardens, Etal, Berwick-upon-Tweed

June 23 Thursday
Herterton House, Cambo, Morpeth
June 25 Saturday
Kirkley Hall College, Ponteland
June 26 Sunday
Chesters, Humshaugh, Hexham ‡
Hexham Herbs, Chester Walled Garden, Humshaugh nr Hexham ‡
Kirkley Hall College, Ponteland
Loughbrow House, Hexham
Mindrum, Cornhill on Tweed
July 3 Sunday
Bradley Gardens, Wylam
Hartford Bridge House, nr Bedlington

Kirkwhelpington Village Gardens, Otteburn
July 6 Wednesday
Bridge House, Fox Covert Lane, Ponteland
July 13 Wednesday
Bridge House, Fox Covert Lane, Ponteland
July 17 Sunday
Cragside, Rothbury
July 20 Wednesday
Bridge House, Fox Covert Lane, Ponteland
July 21 Thursday
Herterton House, Cambo, Morpeth

July 27 Wednesday
Bridge House, Fox Covert Lane, Ponteland
July 28 Thursday
Beck 'n' Call, Warkworth
Birling Manor, Warkworth
July 31 Sunday
Kiwi Cottage, Scremerston, Berwick-on-Tweed
August 7 Sunday
Blenkinsopp Hall, Haltwhistle
August 11 Thursday
Herterton House, Cambo, Morpeth
September 11 Sunday
Belsay Hall, Castle & Gardens, Belsay

DESCRIPTIONS OF GARDENS

¶**Beck 'n Call** ⚭❀ (Mr & Mrs B Halliday) ¼m N of Warkworth on B1068. Adjacent to Birling Manor (open). ½-acre terraced country cottage garden with stream, waterside plants, herbaceous borders, mixed borders, rose garden, etc. *Adm £1.50 Chd 25p. Thurs July 28 (11-4)*

Belsay Hall, Castle & Gardens ⚭❀ (English Heritage) Ponteland. Belsay village lies 14m NW of Newcastle-upon-Tyne, on the A696 OS map 88. Ref NZ 082785. 30-acres newly restored C19 garden incl formal terraces; large heather garden; rhododendrons, rare trees & shrubs. Quarry garden covering several acres. Belsay Hall & Castle within the grounds. TEAS and refreshments. *Adm (incl Hall and Castle) £2.40 Concessions £1.80 Chd £1.20. Suns May 22, Sept 11 (10-6)*

Berryburn ❀❀ (Mr & Mrs W J Rogers-Coltman) Ancroft. 5m S of Berwick. Take Ancroft Mill Rd off A1 for 1m; drive entrance 2nd turn on R beside council bridge. 4 acres created from wilderness since 1981. Mixed borders; shrubs; shrub roses; woodland walk alongside burn with progressive tree planting. TEA & stalls in aid of Cancer Relief Macmillan Fund. *Adm £1.50 Chd free. Sun May 22 (2-5)*

¶**Bide-a-Wee Cottage** ❀❀ (M Robson) Netherwitton. 7m NNW of Morpeth. Turn L off A192 out of Morpeth at Fairmoor. Stanton is 6m along this road. Both a formal and informal garden developed out of a small stone quarry as well as some surrounding higher land. Natural rock is featured as are water and marsh areas. Garden contains mixed planting with a large number of perennial species. *Adm £1.50. Private visits welcome, please* **Tel 067072 262**

¶**Birling Manor** ❀ (M D Leighton) Warkworth. Take Aln-mouth Rd out of Warkworth over bridge. 2nd house on L. Waterfall at gate. 3 acres with 100yds waterfront onto waterfall at gate. Informal setting with rose garden, herbaceous border, lawns, fruit garden and kitchen garden. *Adm £1.50 Chd 25p. Thurs July 28 (11-4)*

Blenkinsopp Hall ⚭ (Mrs J E Joicey) Haltwhistle. Entrance off A69, ½m W of Haltwhistle. Herbaceous borders, rockery, kitchen garden. Grounds with lake and woodland walk. *Adm £1 Chd free. Sun Aug 7 (2-5)*

Bradley Gardens ⚭❀❀ (Mr & Mrs J Hick) Sled Lane, Wylam. Along A695 between Crawcrook and Prudhoe. Approx ½m W from Crawcrook, R.A.C. signposted. A69 through Wylam, over bridge S of R Tyne, 3rd turning R, ¼m up lane. Signposted from Wylam. Approx 2 acres walled garden formerly kitchen garden to Bradley Hall. We specialise in herbs, both pot grown and fresh cut. Display beds of herbs, herbaceous border, childrens play area and greenhouse to view. Cottage garden plants and a selection of shrubs and bedding also available. Scented garden and shop. TEA. *Adm £1.50 Chd free. Sun July 3 (9-5)*

Bridge House ⚭❀❀ (Dr & Mrs J C White) Fox Covert Lane, Ponteland. 8m NW of Newcastle. Just off A696, last L turn before leaving Ponteland village (travelling W). ¼m down Fox Covert Lane. 1¼-acre garden, only 8 yrs old. Incl riverside planting, vegetable garden, herbs, mixed borders and summer meadow. Winner of 'North-umbria in Bloom' 1993 – Best Garden open to the public. TEAS. *Adm £1.25 Chd free. Weds July 6, 13, 20, 27 (2-5)*

¶**Castle Gardens** ⚭❀ (Northumbria Nurseries) Ford. Follow the flower signs on the brown Ford Etal Heritage signs to Ford village, 10m N of Wooler, off A697. 1¾-acre walled garden incl display beds and growing areas. Teas available in village. Open all year Mon to Fri (9-6, or dark), March to Dec Sat, Sun (10-6, or dark). *Adm £1.50 Chd 50p For NGS Sun June 19 (10-6)*

Chesters ❀❀ (Major & Mrs J E Benson) Humshaugh. 5m N of Hexham. ½m W of Chollerford on B6318. Curved terraced border in front of C18 house with 1891 wings designed by Norman Shaw. Herbaceous borders, rock garden, lawns overlooking ha-ha and parkland with fine views over the North Tyne. TEA. *Combined adm with* **Hexham Herbs, Chesters Walled Garden** *£1.50 Chd under 10 free. Sun June 26 (2-6)*

Regular Openers. See head of county section.

Chillingham Castle ✍ (Sir Humphry Wakefield) Chillingham. N from Alnwick, S from Berwick-upon-Tweed. Parkland landscaped with avenues and lodges by Sir Geoffrey de Wyattville fresh from his Royal triumph at Windsor in 1828. Lake and woodland walks with finest specimen trees in the region. Moats removed and gardens brought up to castle 1752. Italian and French topiary garden with largest herbaceous border in Northern England all restored with urns and fountains. TEAS. *Adm £3 OAPs £2.50 Chd £2.* ▲*For NGS Sun May 29 (1.30-5)*

Cragside ✍ (The National Trust) Rothbury, 13m SW of Alnwick (B6341); 15m NW of Morpeth (B6344). Open for the first time in 1992 Lord Armstrong's original formal garden, incl orchard house, fernery, terraces and rose loggia. Extensive grounds of over 1000 acres on S edge of Alnwick Moor; famous for magnificent trees; rhododendrons and beautiful lakes. House designed by Richard Norman Shaw, famous Victorian architect; built 1864-1895; contains much original furniture designed by Shaw; also pictures and experimental scientific apparatus (it was 1st house in the world to be lit by electricity generated by water power). Restaurant. Shop. Grounds, Power Circuit and Armstrong Energy Centre. TEAS. *Adm House, Garden & Grounds £5.50; Garden & Grounds £3.40 Chd half price. Family ticket House, Garden & Grounds (2 adults & 2 chd) £14. For NGS Sun July 17 (10.30-7)*

¶**Hartford Bridge House** ✍✿ (Dr & Mrs F J B Taylor) Bedlington. On A1068/A192 where it crosses R Blyth, opposite Plessey Woods. 2m S of Bedlington. Parking at Hartford Hall 300 yds above house, entrance via Hall gates 500 yds towards Bedlington or Plessey Woods Country Park (car park 5mins walk). 1¼-acre garden on river. Interesting shrubs and trees, small woodland walk, old-fashioned roses, rock garden and herbaceous. TEAS. *Adm £1.50 Chd free. Sun July 3 (2-5)*

Herterton House ✍✿ (Frank Lawley Esq) Hartington. Cambo, Morpeth. 2m N of Cambo on the B6342 signposted to Hartington. (23m NW of Newcastle-on-Tyne). 1 acre of formal garden in stone walls around a C16 farmhouse. Incl a small topiary garden, physic garden, flower garden and a nursery garden. Planted since 1976. *Adm £1.20 Chd free.* ▲*For NGS Thurs June 23, July 21, Aug 11 (1.30-5.30)*

Hexham Herbs, Chesters Walled Garden ✍✿✿ Chollerford. 6m N of Hexham, just off the B6318. ½m W of Chollerford roundabout, past the entrance to Chesters Roman Fort, take L turning signposted Fourstones and immediately L through stone gateposts. 2-acre walled garden containing a very extensive collection of herbs. Raised thyme bank, home to the National Thyme Collection, Roman garden; National Collection of Marjoram. Elizabethan-style knot garden, gold and silver garden and collection of dye plants. Herbaceous borders contain many unusual plants and old-fashioned roses. Outside the walled garden is a newly-planted wildflower meadow and woodland walk. Hexham Herbs won a large gold medal at National Garden Festival, Gateshead 1990 and featured on BBC2's 'Gardener's World'. Shop. *Combined adm with* **Chesters** *£1.50 Chd under 10 free. Sun June 26 (1-5)*

Kirkley Hall College ✿✍✿ (Dr R McParlin) Ponteland. 2½m NW of Ponteland on C151 to Morpeth. Turn L at main college entrance. Turn R ¼m further on at the Horticultural centre signboard. Car park. These beautiful gardens and Victorian Walled Garden form a showcase for the gardening enthusiast. Inside the Walled Garden are climbers, salad potager garden, wall-trained fruit trees, borders and unusual and colourful herbaceous plants all grouped and labelled. Grounds contain skilfully shaped island beds following the contours of the land each composed for variety of profile and continuity of colour. The terrace garden with its outstanding array of beautifully planted containers leads down to the front lawn and then to a most attractive sunken garden planted with a wide range of dwarf conifers. TEAS. *Adm £1.50 OAPs 70p Chd under 8 free. Sat, Sun June 25, 26 (10-5)*

¶**Kirkwhelpington Village Gardens** ✍✿ On A696 approx 10m N of Belsay. Turn R into village. A number of small gardens in an attractive village. Each garden entirely different with something of interest for everyone. Teas in village hall. *Combined adm £1.50 Chd 50p (Share to local church®). Sun July 3 (2-5)*
 ¶**Cliff House** (Mr & Mrs I Elliot)
 ¶**3 The Green** (Mrs K Buchanan)
 ¶**The School House** (Mr & Mrs F Young)
 ¶**Sike View** (Prof & Mrs D Kinniment)
 ¶**Welburn** (Prof D Wise)
 ¶**Whitridge House** (Mr & Dr C Keating)

Kiwi Cottage ✿✍✿ (Col J I M Smail) Scremerston. Kiwi Cottage is in the village of Scremerston, about 2½m due S of Berwick-upon-Tweed. It is the 1st house on the R hand side of the village, off the A1 rd coming from the S and the last house on the L hand side of the village when travelling S from Berwick-upon-Tweed. Entrance through gateway next to War Memorial. Please drive in and do not park on the rd. 3-acre garden with lawns, annuals, herbaceous plants, providing colour and interest throughout the year. Shrubs, orchard and large vegetable garden TEA. *Adm £1.50 Chd 50p. Sun July 31 (2.30-5.30)*

Lilburn Tower ✍ (Mr & Mrs D Davidson) Alnwick. 3m S of Wooler on A697. 10 acres of walled and formal gardens including conservatory and large glass house. About 30 acres of woodland with walks and pond garden. Also ruins of Pele Tower and C15 Chapel. Rhododendrons and azaleas. TEAS. *Adm £1 Chd 25p under 5 free. Sun June 5 (2-6)*

Loughbrow House ✿✍✿ (Mrs K A Clark) Hexham. Take B6306 from Hexham fork R, lodge gates in intersection of 2nd fork, ½m up drive. 5 acres; woodland garden; herbaceous borders, roses, wide lawns; kitchen garden. Homemade TEAS. *Adm £1.50 Chd 50p. Sun June 26 (2-6)*

Meldon Park ✿✍ (M J B Cookson Esq) Morpeth. Situated 6m W of Morpeth on B6343. Victorian and Edwardian laid out garden, with walled kitchen garden, herbaceous borders, roses and woodland walk with azaleas and rhododendrons. TEA. *Adm £2 Chd 50p. Sun June 5 (2-5)*

Mindrum ぷ❀ (Hon P J Fairfax) Cornhill on Tweed. On B6352, 4m from Yetholm, 5m from Cornhill on Tweed. Old-fashioned roses; rock and water garden; shrub borders. Wonderful views along Bowmont Valley. Approx 2 acres. TEAS. *Adm £1.50 Chd 50p. Sun June 26 (2-6)*

Preston Tower ᖴぷ (Maj & Mrs T Baker Cresswell) Chathill. 7m N of Alnwick, take the turn to the R ¼m beyond Esso garage and Little Chef, signed to Preston and Chathill. Preston Tower is at the top of a hill, in 1¼m. Mostly shrubs and woodland; daffodils and azaleas. C14 Pele Tower with great views from the top. TEAS. *Adm £1.50 Chd 50p. Sun April 24 (2.30-5)*

Wallington ᖴ❀ (The National Trust) Cambo. From N 12m W of Morpeth (B6343); from S via A696 from Newcastle, 6m W of Belsay, B6342 to Cambo. Walled, terraced garden with fine shrubs and species roses; conservatory with magnificent fuchsias; 100 acres woodland and lakes. House dates from 1688 but altered and interior greatly changed c.1740; exceptional rococo plasterwork by Francini brothers; fine porcelain, furniture, pictures, needlework, dolls' houses, museum, display of coaches. Restaurant. Shop. *Adm to House and Garden £4.40; Walled garden, garden and grounds £2.20 Chd half price. Last admission (5). For NGS Sun May 15 (10-7)*

Nottinghamshire

Hon County Organisers:	Mr & Mrs A R Hill, The White House, Nicker Hill, Keyworth, Nottinghamshire NG12 5EA Tel 0602 372049
Assistant Hon County Organisers:	Mr & Mrs J Nicholson, 38 Green Lane, Lambley, Nottingham NG4 4QE Tel 0602 312998
Hon County Treasurer:	Mr J Gray, 43 Cliffway, Radcliffe-on-Trent, Nottinghamshire NG12 1AQ Tel 0602 334272

DATES OF OPENING

By appointment
For telephone number and other details see garden descriptions. Private visits welcomed

17 Bridle Rd, Burton Joyce Gardens
Holmes Villa, Walkeringham
Mill Hill House, East Stoke
Oakland House, Oxton Rd, Southwell
Springwell House, Brinkley
The White House, Keyworth

Regular openings
For details see garden descriptions

Felley Priory, Underwood. For dates see text
Hodsock Priory, Blyth. For dates see text
St Helens Croft, Halam. For dates see text

April 3 Sunday
Gateford Hill Nursing Home, Gateford
April 6 Wednesday
The Willows, Radcliffe-on-Trent
April 10 Sunday
Felley Priory, Underwood
April 13 Wednesday
37 Loughborough Road, Ruddington

Springwell House, Brinkley
April 17 Sunday
Hodsock Priory, Blyth
St Helens Croft, Halam
April 20 Wednesday
38 Green Lane, Lambley
April 24 Sunday
Morton Hall, Ranby
The Rookery, East Markham
Trent Farm House, Fiskerton
April 27 Wednesday
Rose Cottage, 82 Main Rd, Underwood
May 2 Monday
Mill Hill House, East Stoke
Thurlby Farm, Stanton-on-the-Wolds ‡
The White House, Keyworth ‡
May 4 Wednesday
The Willows, Radcliffe-on-Trent
May 8 Sunday
Colley Hill Cottage, Gringley on the Hill Gardens
Gringley Hall, Gringley on the Hill Gardens
Morton Hall, Ranby
Oakland House, Oxton Rd, Southwell
May 11 Wednesday
Springwell House, Brinkley
May 14 Saturday
7 Barratt Lane, Attenborough
May 15 Sunday
7 Barratt Lane, Attenborough
May 18 Wednesday
38 Green Lane, Lambley

May 21 Saturday
Epperstone Gardens
May 22 Sunday
Epperstone Gardens
Gringley on the Hill Gardens:
Gringley Hall, Honeysuckle Cottage, South Beeches
144 Lambley Lane, Burton Joyce
Morton Hall, Ranby
May 25 Wednesday
The Chaff Barn, Post Office Lane, Redmile
May 29 Sunday
Mill Hill House, East Stoke
Papplewick Gardens, Papplewick
June 1 Wednesday
The Willows, Radcliffe-on-Trent
June 5 Sunday
Hodsock Priory, Blyth
Park Farm, Normanton
Rose Cottage, 82 Main Rd, Underwood
Woodborough Manor, Woodborough
June 8 Wednesday
16 Prince Edward Crescent, Radcliffe-on-Trent
June 9 Thursday
Holmes Villa, Walkeringham
June 12 Sunday
Gardeners Cottage, Papplewick
Hazel Cottage, Treswell
Mill Hill House, East Stoke ‡
Skreton Cottage, Screveton ‡
Springwell House, Brinkley
June 15 Wednesday
Gardeners Cottage, Papplewick

38 Green Lane, Lambley
June 19 Sunday
The Chaff Barn, Post Office Lane, Redmile
1 Hilltop Cottage, Thurgarton
Felley Priory, Underwood
Flintham Hall, Flintham
37 Loughborough Road, Ruddington
14 Temple Drive, Nuthall
June 26 Sunday
Beauchamp Barn, Kneesall
Burton Joyce Gardens
6 Cherwell Court, Bulwell
Holmes Villa, Walkeringham
Mattersey House, Mattersey
Morton Grange, Babworth, Nr Retford
Southwell Gardens
June 29 Wednesday
Oakland House, Oxton Rd, Southwell
July 3 Sunday
Gardeners Cottage, Papplewick
Sutton Bonington Hall, Sutton Bonington ‡

Thrumpton Hall, Nottingham ‡
Upton Gardens
July 6 Wednesday
The Willows, Radcliffe-on-Trent
July 10 Sunday
Mill Hill House, East Stoke
The Old Rectory, Kirkby in Ashfield
July 13 Wednesday
Springwell House, Brinkley
July 17 Sunday
Thurlby Farm, Stanton-on-the-Wolds ‡
The White House, Keyworth ‡
July 24 Sunday
Colwick Gardens
July 31 Sunday
Greenways, Bathley
August 3 Wednesday
Meadowbrook, Bleasby
The Willows, Radcliffe-on-Trent
August 7 Sunday
14 Temple Drive, Nuthall
August 14 Sunday
1 Hilltop Cottage, Thurgarton
Mill Hill House, East Stoke

Oakland House, Oxton Rd, Southwell
Rose Cottage, 82 Main Rd, Underwood
August 17 Wednesday
Springwell House, Brinkley
September 7 Wednesday
The Willows, Radcliffe-on-Trent
September 11 Sunday
Mill Hill House, East Stoke
Rose Cottage, 82 Main Rd, Underwood
St Helens Croft, Halam
September 15 Thursday
The Willows, Radcliffe-on-Trent
September 18 Sunday
The White House, Keyworth
September 25 Wednesday
Springwell House, Brinkley
October 9 Sunday
Morton Hall, Ranby
October 16 Sunday
Springwell House, Brinkley
October 23 Sunday
St Helens Croft, Halam

DESCRIPTIONS OF GARDENS

7 Barratt Lane &✿ (Mrs D Lucking & Mr & Mrs S J Hodkinson) Attenborough. Beeston, 6m SW of Nottingham. Off A6005 nr Attenborough Station. ¾-acre established plantsman's garden featured in Garden Answers 1992 & 1993. Mature trees, unusual flowering shrubs, bulbs, hostas and dwarf bearded irises. *Adm £1 Chd 40p (Share to St Mary's Church®). Sat, Sun May 14, 15 (11-1 & 2-6)*

Beauchamp Barn (Mr & Mrs I D P Thorne) Kneesall. On A616 between Kneesall and Ompton. 3m from Ollerton roundabout, 10m from Newark. Maturing parkland garden, approx 1 acre around converted farmstead, roses, woodland walk and beautiful views. Band of South Notts Hussars playing. TEA. *Adm £1 Chd 25p (Share to CRMF Notts®). Sun June 26 (2-6)*

Burton Joyce Gardens Situated about 6m NE of Nottingham off A612 to Southwell. In Burton Joyce turn L onto Main St at 1st Xrds. L again within 100yds onto Lambley Lane. Bridle Rd is ½m on R and is an impassable-looking rd. *Combined adm £1.50 Chd 50p. Sun June 26 (2-6)*
    17 Bridle Road &✿ (Mr & Mrs C P Bates) Burton Joyce, Nottingham. 1-acre mixed borders, woodland slopes, stream and water garden with naturalised ferns, primulas, hostas and moisture loving plants. Terrace and orchard with spring and summer bulbs in grass. TEAS. *Also private visits welcome at weekends, please* Tel 0602 313725
    61 Lambley Lane ✿ (Mr & Mrs R B Powell) Approx ⅔-acre of spring flowering plants; shrubs; azaleas; bulbs and trees

¶**The Chaff Barn** ✕ (Mr & Mrs C F Everson) Redmile. 1m N of Belvoir Castle. From A52 turn S by Haven Hotel signed Belvoir Castle and Redmile. Post Office Lane is past Peacock and Windmill Inns on LH-side. Park in main street. ⅓-acre created from stackyard since 1987. Features native plants encouraged to self seed with birds and wildlife in mind. Pond, herbs, old roses, herbaceous, spring bulbs, trees and shrubs. Enclosed garden with terrace, green courtyard and conservatories. *Adm £1 Chd 25p. Wed May 25, Sun June 19 (2-6)*

6 Cherwell Court ✕✿ (Louise & Roger Whittle) Meadow Rise. Leave M1 junction 26 E towards Nottingham on A610. At 1st roundabout take 2nd L A611 towards Hucknall. 2nd R and down Hempshill Lane, 2nd L into Meadow Rise, 2nd R into Cherwell Court. Small organically managed garden; two ponds, sunken garden, old roses, many ferns; wildlife haven with mixture of native & unusual plants. Restricted parking. TEAS. *Adm 90p Chd free (Share to Nottinghamshire Wildlife Trust®). Sun June 26 (2-6)*

Colwick Gardens From Nottingham take B686 to Colwick. Bear L at 1st traffic lights after Midland Caravans. St John's Church 50yds on R, corner of Rectory Rd. Admission tickets and map to gardens at St John's Church. Tea at Church. *Combined adm £2 Chd 50p (Share to St John's Church, Colwick®). Sun July 24 (2-6)*
    1 First Avenue ✕ (Mr & Mrs H A G Roberts) Small garden incl flower beds; tubs; patio; conifers; trellis. Ivy covered arches; small vegetable patch
    10, New Vale Road ✕ (The Rev Basil Hobbs) Interestingly designed long, narrow garden incl formal and wild life ponds, many interesting plants and features. Climbing plants and secret areas

The Old Rectory &✿ (Mr & Mrs R A Northern) A walled garden with variety of shrubs; pergola; summerhouse; gravelled areas

20 Ramblers Close ✕ (Mr & Mrs L A Ashurst) Garden developed over last 5 yrs incl interesting shrubs; perennials; heathers; large pond, many fish; extensive fruit and vegetables

8 Vale Gardens ✕ (Mr & Mrs B Thompson) Garden approx 500 sq yds, open plan. Lawn; pond with wishing well. Patio and herbaceous borders; colourful containers

Epperstone Gardens 8m NE Nottingham off A6097 between Lowdham and Oxton. Parking opp Cross Keys and opp White Gates. TEAS. *Combined adm £1.50 Chd free (Share to Epperstone Village Hall Fund®). Sat, Sun May 21, 22 (2-6)*

¶**Field House** (Mr & Mrs G H Gisborne) ⅓-acre attractively laid out garden incl foliage, alpines, bulbs, water; lovely view of surrounding countryside

Hazelwych (Mr & Mrs P J Clark) ½-acre, trees, shrubbery, pond and alpine terrace

White Gates ✿ (Mrs V Pilsworth) 2 acres rhododendrons, azaleas, heathers, shrubbery, herbs and orchard

Felley Priory &✿ (The Hon Mrs Chaworth Musters) Underwood. 8m SW Mansfield. leave M1 junction 27, take A608, entrance is ½m W of M1. Old-fashioned garden round Elizabethan House. Orchard of daffodils, herbaceous borders, pond, topiary, unusual plants for sale. TEAS. *Adm £1 Chd 25p. Weds Feb 9, 23, March 9, 23, April 13, 27, May 11, 25, June 8, 22, July 13, 27, Aug 10, 24, Sept 14, 28, Oct 12, 26 (9-4). For NGS Suns April 10, June 19 (11-4.30)*

Flintham Hall ✕✿ (Myles Thoroton Hildyard Esq) 6m SW of Newark on A46. Fine trees, park and lake, wilderness, aviary, unique conservatory, herbaceous borders, woodland walk. Featured 'Country Life' Sept 89. Picnics allowed. TEAS. *Adm £1.50 Chd 50p (Share to St Augustines Church Flintham PCC®). Sun June 19 (2-6)*

Gardeners Cottage &✕✿ (Mr & Mrs J Hildyard) Papplewick; nr Papplewick Hall. 6m N of Nottingham off A60. Interesting old-fashioned garden of ½ acre with 150yd long border, shrub and rhododendrons; garden shrub roses. Large rockery and water feature; scree beds. Many unusual plants for sale. TEAS *Adm £1 Chd 25p (Share to St. James Church Window Fund®). Sun, Wed June 12, 15 Sun July 3 (2-6)*

The Gardens of Plungar – see Leicestershire & Rutland

Gateford Hill Nursing Home &✿ 1m N of Worksop on the A57. Nursing home is well signed from main rd. Impressive house built 1860. Large walled garden, putting green and extensive grounds. Spectacular display of daffodils of many varieties. Display of various dancing styles. TEAS. *Adm £1.20 Chd 75p. Sun April 3 (1.30-5)*

By Appointment Gardens. These owners do not have a fixed opening day usually because they do not like crowds or have insufficient parking space. Owner will often give guided tour.

---

38 Green Lane ✕✿ (Mr & Mrs J E Nicholson) Lambley. 6m N of Nottingham. Take B684 Woodborough Rd turn R to Lambley. Main St turn L into Church St, R into Green Lane. Small cottage garden densely planted, spring bulbs, herbaceous beds, shrub roses, varied climbers, secret corners and surprises. Separate formal vegetable garden. Beautiful views across open countryside. Exhibition and sale of paintings by Nottinghamshire artists in April. TEA. *Adm £1 Chd free. Weds April 20, May 18, June 15 (1-5). Private group visits welcome, please* **Tel 0602 312998**

Greenways &✕ (Mr & Mrs D Smith) Bathley. 1m A1. B6325 North Newark. 1½-acre, mixed trees; shrubs; enclosed rose garden; formal beds; orchard and vegetables. Newly planted pergola; alpine troughs. TEAS. *Adm £1 Chd free (Share to Arthritis Care, Newark Branch®). Sun July 31 (2-6)*

Gringley On The Hill Gardens 6m E of Bawtry, 5m W of Gainsborough on A631. TEAS May 8 in aid of Basselaw Hospice, May 22 in aid of Gringley Village Hall Fund. *Combined adm £2 Chd 50p. May 22; Adm £1.50 Chd 50p May 8*

Colley Hill Cottage ✕✿ (Mrs Sue Tallents) A densely planted, small cottage garden, created by the owner with flower arranging and nature in mind; raised beds; small pond and herbaceous area; some unusual plants and shrubs. Also alpines, spring bulbs and ferns. *Sun May 8 (2-6)*

Gringley Hall &✕✿ (Mr & Mrs I Threlfall) 2-acre English country garden with several mixed borders with different colour themes; old roses; water garden and a newly created potager. *Suns May 8, 22 (2-6)*

Honeysuckle Cottage ✕✿ (Miss J E Towler) Approx ¼-acre traditional small terraced cottage garden with rose bed and mixed borders. Interesting loose laid chevron brick wall; paths of river boulders and brick. *Sun May 22 (2-6)*

South Beeches &✕ (Dr & Mrs G R Fenton) ½-acre part of an old garden with interesting mature and young trees. Unusual plants and old stone troughs are a feature of the garden; keen vegetable gardener. *Sun May 22 (2-6)*

Hazel Cottage &✕✿ (Mr & Mrs M J Rush) Treswell. Treswell is approx 6m E of Retford; 4½m NW of A57 at Dunham-on-Trent. Parking in village st and at Church Hall. ½-acre packed plantsman's garden developed and designed since 1986 to give pleasure in every season. The garden contains many unusual trees, shrubs and herbaceous plants; also collection of old roses, clematis and climbing plants on pergolas; small pond and gravelled areas. Featured on Yorkshire TV 'Great Little Gardens' 1993. Teas and plants sales in aid of village hall at village hall 400yds from Hazel Cottage. *Adm £1 Chd free. Sun June 12 (2-6)*

¶**1 Hilltop Cottage** ✕✿ (Zoe Richmond & Gary Dixon) Thurgarton. Situated approx 3m S of Southwell on the main A612 Nottingham-Southwell Rd. Long narrow cottage-style garden designed and developed since 1990. Mixed herbaceous borders, some unusual plants, container garden area, rose arch and walk way through different garden 'rooms', small vegetable garden. TEAS & plant sales in aid of Dr Hadwin Trust. *Adm £1 Chd free. Suns June 19, Aug 14 (2-6)*

Hodsock Priory &&& (Sir Andrew & Lady Buchanan) Blyth. Off B6045, Blyth-Worksop rd approx 2m from A1. 5 acres bounded by dry moat. Grade 1 listed gatehouse circa 1500. Victorian Mansion (not open). Mature cornus, indian bean, tulip tree, swamp cypress; small lake; bog garden; snowdrops and spring bulbs; mixed borders; roses old and new. Established ilex, beech and holly hedges; featured in 'Shell Garden Guide', 'Country Life, 'Good Garden Guide' (starred) and other magazines. TEAS. *Adm £1.80 Wheelchairs/Acc Chd free. Suns Easter up to and incl second Sun in July but excluding both May Bank Hol weekends. Open 2 weekends in Feb. For NGS Sun April 17, June 5 (2-5)*

Holmes Villa &&& (Sheila & Peter Clark) Holmes Lane, Walkeringham; NE Retford and within 4m Gainsborough. Take A620 from Retford or A631 from Bawtry/Gainsborough and A161 to Walkeringham and then towards Misterton. Turn at sign R. Trent and follow signs for last mile. Interesting plantsman's and flower arrangers garden created and maintained by owners incl collections of ivies, alliums and many unusual herbaceous plants; New wild life pond and rhododendron bank. TEAS Sun only in aid of Notts Wildlife Trust. Specialist plant and craft stalls. *Adm £1 Chd free. Thurs June 9, Sun June 26 (1.30-5.30). Also private visits welcome, please Tel 0427 890233*

¶144 Lambley Lane (Mr & Mrs B P Collyer) Burton Joyce. In Burton Joyce turn N off A612 Nottingham to Southwell Rd, up Lambley Lane to top. Sloping ½-acre garden with mature trees, spring flowering shrubs, conifers, rockeries, troughs, containers and wild garden. TEA. *Adm £1 Chd free (Share to St Helens Church Centre®). Sun May 22 (2-6)*

¶37 Loughborough Road & (Mr & Mrs B H C Theobald) Ruddington. 4m S of Nottingham. From Nottingham take A60 Loughborough Rd, cross A52 ring road at Nottingham Knight. Take 1st L 400 yds beyond roundabout and immed L again up old Loughborough Rd. 1-acre garden with broad lawns and long borders, extensively developed in last 6 yrs. Shady walk with ferns, hostas etc, island beds, specimen trees and walled patio garden. Planting based on mixture of bulbs, perennials, shrubs and small trees with emphasis on unusual varieties and yr round colour. *Adm £1 Chd free. Wed April 13, Sun June 19 (2-6)*

Mattersey House &&& (Mr & Mrs T P O'Connor-Fenton) Mattersey, 6m N of Retford, 4m SE of Bawtry; from A636 at Ranskill turn E on to B6045 for Mattersey; Buses from Retford and Bawtry. Medium-sized; walled garden; shrub roses, herbaceous borders. TEA. *Adm £1 Chd 20p. Sun June 26 (2-6)*

¶Meadowbrook & (Mr & Mrs H R Gibson) Bleasby. In Thurgarton, 3m S of Southwell, take rd off A612 signed Bleasby, turn R at Goverton, cross railway to middle of village. ⅓-acre featuring gravel area, small water layouts, conifers, heathers, small ornamental trees, climbers and a variety of containers and hanging baskets. *Adm £1 Chd free. Wed Aug 3 (2-5.30)*

Mill Hill House & (Mr & Mrs R J Gregory) Elston Lane, East Stoke. 5m S of Newark on A46 turn E to Elston. Garden ½m on R. Entrance through nursery car park. ½-acre

plantsmans garden for all seasons, wide selection of unusual hardy plants; mixed borders, alpines, shade plants. *Adm £1 (Share to NCCPG®). Bank Hol Mon May 2, Suns, May 29; June 12; July 10; Aug 14, Sept 11 (2-6). Also private visits welcome daily April 1 to Oct 31, please Tel 0636 525 460*

Morton Grange &&& (Mr & Mrs F Morrell) Babworth. 4m W of Retford. From A1 take B6240; after one field turn R 2½m down private rd. 2-acre garden created since 1975; large mixed herbaceous and shrub borders, roses, lily pond, rockery and sunken garden. TEAS partly in aid of Babworth Church. *Adm £1 Chd free. Sun June 26 (2-6)*

Morton Hall & (Lady Mason) Ranby, 4m W of Retford. Entrance on Link Rd from A620 to S bound A1. Medium-sized woodland garden, flowering shrubs, rhododendrons, azaleas, specimen trees; pinetum in park, cedars and cypresses. Bulbs, autumn colour. Picnics. Partly suitable for wheelchairs. TEAS. *Adm £2 per car or £1.25p per person whichever is the least (Share to Ranby Church®). Suns April 24, May 8, 22, (2-6) Oct 9 (2-5)*

¶Oakland House && (Dr & Mrs D Skelton) Southwell. 12m NE Nottingham, 12m E Newark. From Southwell E on B6386 to Oxton. 3m on from Southwell on the R. 2½-acre garden created from paddock since 1986 inc large water feature and bog plants, ornamental garden for all yr round interest; alpine and cottage gardens together with extensive fruit and vegetable areas mainly organically managed, many unusual plants trees and shrubs. *Adm £1 Chd free. Suns May 8, Aug 14 (2-5), Wed June 29 (6-9). Also private visits welcome, please Tel 0602 652030*

¶The Old Rectory && (Mr & Mrs M F Brown) Kirkby in Ashfield. Adjacent to St Wilfrids Church on the B6018, Sutton in Ashfield to Selston Rd, 1½m W of Kirkby town centre. Park in church car park. 2½-acre garden attached to Georgian House (not open). Originally planned nearly 300yrs ago (mature trees still remaining). Recently restored by present owners after a period of neglect, incl herbaceous borders, shrubs, grasses, hostas, stone walls and steps. Several gardens in one. TEAS. *Adm £1 Chd free (Share to St Wilfrid's Church®). Sun July 10 (2-6)*

Papplewick Gardens && North end of Papplewick Village on B683, 7m N of Nottingham off the A60. Parking at Hall only. *Combined adm £2 Chd free (Share to St James Church, Papplewick®). Sun May 29 (2-6)*
    Altham Lodge (C G Hill Esq) Lovely garden of rhododendrons; azaleas and spring flowers
    Papplewick Hall (Dr & Mrs R B Godwin-Austen) Woodland garden of approx 8 acres underplanted with rhododendrons; spring bulbs and hostas

Park Farm &&& (Mr & Mrs John E Rose) Normanton, Bottesford. Park Farm is half way between Bottesford and Long Bennington on A1 side of Normanton village and sited on the old Normanton Airfield. 2½-acre garden, developed since 1987 comprising formal and mixed borders; natural and formal ponds; scree gardens and small woodland area. Mature trees moved by JCB to flat open field prior to the creation of this garden. Large enclosed scented herb garden under construction. TEA. *Adm £1.50 Chd free. Sun June 5 (11-6)*

16 Prince Edward Crescent ⚸ (Mr Geoff Denman) Radcliffe-on-Trent. From RSPCA shelter, take 2nd R (St Lawrence Boulevard) and 1st L. Very small garden with accent on foliage plants. Featured on Yorkshire TV 'Great Little Gardens'. TEA. *Adm 80p Chd free (Share to PDSA Nottingham®). Weds June 8 (2-7.30)*

The Rookery ⚸ (Mrs Judy J Banks) Low St, East Markham. 5m S of Retford on the A638. Take A57 to Lincoln for 1m. House circa 1670. Standing in 1-acre late spring garden with flowering trees and shrubs, early bulbs. Beds of roses, herbaceous border, small wooded area and paddock. TEA. *Adm £1 Chd free. Sun April 24 (2-6)*

Rose Cottage ⚸✿ (Mr & Mrs Allan Lowe) 82 Main Rd, Underwood. 1½m from junction 27 M1. Take B608 to Heanor. Join B600; after about 200-300 yds turn R into Main Rd by large sign for 'the Hole in the Wall' Inn. Flower arrangers cottage garden with ponds; shrubs; small secret garden. Rear garden of approx 1,000 sq yds with surprise features, partly developed from a field very recently; goat and other animals. Bed of show spray chrysanthemums; greenhouses. TEAS. *Adm £1 Chd free. Wed April 27, Suns June 5, Aug 14, Sept 11 (2-6)*

St Helen's Croft ⚸✿ (Mrs E Ninnis) Halam. A614 Nottingham-Doncaster, turn off at White Post roundabout to Southwell and Halam. 3m from Southwell Minster. ¾-acre plantsmans garden; trees, shrubs, herbaceous. Also 6½acres meadow, ½-acre woodland; unusual trees (handkerchief tree, catalpa bignonioides aurea etc). Meadow planted by septuagenarian for present & future generations. Thousands of cowslips, primroses, 20,000 fritillarias (which now grow wild in only 3 or 4 places in country). Mown roadway within meadow for disabled sticker cars. Featured on BBC Gardeners World. *Adm £1 Chd free. Open every day in April except Mons, Suns & Tues in June, Suns July 10, 24, Aug 21; Mon 29; Sun Sept 25; (2-5) For NGS Suns April 17, Sept 11, Oct 23 (2-5) Also private visits welcome, please* **Tel 0636 813219**

Skreton Cottage ⚸✿ (Mr & Mrs J S Taylor) Screveton, 8m SW of Newark, 12m E of Nottingham. From A46 Fosse Rd turn E to Car Colston; left at green and on for 1m. Bus: Nottingham-Newark, alight Red Lodge Inn (1m walk). 1¾-acre garden, now mature, designed to be of interest throughout year. Landscaped to create separate gardens each with its own character, containing unusual & interesting trees, plants and shrubs. Set in delightful unspoilt country village. TEAS. *Adm £1 Chd free (Share to St. Wilfrid's Church, Screveton®). Sun June 12 (2-6)*

Southwell, Bishops Manor ⚸✿ (The Rt Rev the Lord Bishop of Southwell & Mrs Harris) End of Bishops Drive on S side of Minster. Turn right for free parking on recreation ground. The house is built into a part of the old medieval Summer Palace of the Archbishops of York. The ruins form a delightful enclosed garden, lawns, 4 seasons tree garden, orchard and vegetable garden. Rockery and attractive borders in an unusual setting. TEAS (Share to Mirasol Charitable Trust). *Adm £1.50 Chd 50p. Sun June 26 (2-6)*

Springwell House ⚸✿ (Mrs Celia Steven) Brinkley. In Southwell turn off A612 by The White Lion towards Fis-

kerton. Springwell House ¾m on RH-side. Approx 2 acres, many unusual trees and shrubs; perennials in informal beds. Lovely country setting. Part of garden incl pond and waterfall being redeveloped throughout year by disabled students from Portland Training College. Collection of daffodils featuring local names supplied by world famous specialist. Autumn foliage colour; selection of plants; climbers and trees available from adjoining nursery. *Adm £1 Chd 25p. Weds April 13, May 11, Sun June 12, Wed July 13, Aug 17, Sun Sept 25, Oct 16 (2-5). Private visits welcome, please* **Tel 0636 814501**

Sutton Bonington Hall ⚸ (Anne, Lady Elton) 5m NW of Loughborough, take A6 to Kegworth, turn R (E) onto A6006. 1st left (N) for Sutton Bonington into Main St. Conservatory, formal white garden, variegated leaf borders. Queen Anne house (not open). Plant stall consisting shrubby herbaceous and some alpine plants. Picnics. TEA. *Adm £1.20 Chd 25p (Share to St Michael's & St Ann's Church, Sutton Bonington®). Sun July 3 (12-5.30). Also open for Leicestershire, Sun June 26 (12-5.30)*

14 Temple Drive ⚸⚸✿ (Mr & Mrs T Leafe) Nuthall. 4m N W of Nottingham. From M1 leave at junction 26 and take A610 towards Nottingham. Circle 1st roundabout in A6002 lane and leave on minor rd marked 'Cedarlands and Horsendale'. From Nottingham take A610, turning off at the Broxtowe Inn, Cinderhill. Parking restricted, use Nottingham rd. ⅓-acre garden with herbaceous borders; informal island beds, ornamental trees and shrubs; troughs; old-fashioned roses; clematis. Mostly labelled. Fruit and vegetable gardens. TEAS and cake stall. *Adm £1 Chd 50p (Share to Cats Protection League®). Suns June 19, Aug 7 (2-5.30)*

Thrumpton Hall ⚸ (George Seymour Esq) 8m SW of Nottingham. W of A453; 3m from M1 at Exit 24. Large lawns; massive yew hedges; rare shrubs; C17 larches, cedars, planted to commemorate historic events since George III. Lake. Early Jacobean house shown. NO DOGS in house. TEA. *Adm to Garden £1 Chd 50p; House £2 extra Chd £1 (Share to The Tradescant Trust, London®). Sun July 3 (2.30-6)*

Thurlby Farm ⚸ (Mr & Mrs M J Hemphrey) Stanton on the Wolds. 9m S of Nottingham. On A606 turn R by Shell garage, along Browns Lane, Thurlby Lane L at junction after 1m. Ample parking on site. 1 acre created in a field since 1976; varied shrubs; trees; herbaceous borders; woodland walk, spring flowers and bulbs. 5-acre rose field to be seen in season. TEA. *Adm £1 Chd free. Bank Hol Mon May 2, Sun July 17 (2-6)*

Trent Farm House ⚸✿ (Mr & Mrs G Hubbard) Fiskerton. Fiskerton village, approx 6m W of Newark and 2m from Southwell. The house is situated on Main St adjacent to village shop and Bromley Arms Inn. ⅓-acre cottage type garden fronting River Trent with heather beds; numerous conifers; herbaceous beds; mature and specimen trees, shrubs and hostas. Small woodland area. 60yd walk along riverbank to Bromley Arms who serve afternoon teas. *Adm £1 Chd 25p. Sun April 24 (2-6). Also groups by appt, please* **Tel 0636 830134**

Upton Gardens ❀ South Retford on A638 or in Eaton village, turn L to Upton. TEAS at **Willowholme Herb Farm**. *Combined adm £1.25 Chd 20p (Share to Headon Church PCC®). Sun July 3 (2-6)*
> **Manor House** ᾨ ✿ (Mr & Mrs Walker) Cottage garden with mixed borders, old orchard and vegetables
> **Willowholme Herb Farm** ✿ (Mr & Mrs Farr) Cottage garden, with established herb garden containing culinary, aromatic and medicinal herbs

The White House ✿❀ (Mr & Mrs A R Hill) Nicker Hill, Keyworth. Approx 8 miles SE Nottingham. From A606 at Stanton-on-the-Wolds, by Shell Garage, turn into Browns Lane. Follow Keyworth signs into Stanton Lane, and continue into Nicker Hill. ¾-acre garden, designed and largely developed since 1987. Extensive water & bog garden, pergola; mixed borders with many unusual trees; shrubs and perennials especially bulbs, primulas, euphorbias, grasses, penstemon, asters and tender perennials. Many of the unusual plants seen in garden available on plant stall. Featured on NGS video 2, see page 344. *Adm £1 Chd free. Bank Hol Mon May 2, Sun July 17 (2-6), Sun Sept 18 (2-5). Also private visits welcome, please* **Tel 0602 372049**

The Willows ✿❀ (Mr & Mrs R A Grout) 5 Rockley Ave, Radcliffe-on-Trent. 6m E of Nottingham; Radcliffe-on-Trent is N of A52; from High St PO turn into Shelford Rd; over railway bridge, 300yds opp green seat turn left into Cliff Way, then 2nd right. Restricted parking. Designed 1982 62yds × 12yds garden; a quart in a pint plot; featured 'Gardeners World' TV 1986 and Yorks TV 'Great Little Gardens' 1992. Many rare and unusual plants; collections of hostas, hellebores, pulmonarias, paeonias, clematis, snowdrops. Holders of National Collection of Crocus Chrysanthus Cultivars. Colour planned island beds throughout the year. Coaches strictly by appt **Tel 0602 333621.** TEAS. *Adm £1 Chd free (Share to National Council for Conservation of Plants & Gardens®). Wed April 6, May 4, June 1, July 6, Aug 3, Sept 7, Thurs Sept 15 (2-5.30)*

¶**Woodborough Manor** (Mr & Mrs C R Hanson) Woodborough. 7m NE of Nottingham. Turn R off the B684 down Bank Hill, turn R at bottom. Approx 1.6 acres. A woodland frontage features mature trees incl giant wellingtonias, azaleas, rhododendrons, hostas, herbaceous borders, large kitchen garden. *Adm £1 Chd free. Sun June 5 (2-6)*

Oxfordshire (including Vale of the White Horse)

Hon County Organisers:	Col & Mrs J C M Baker, Hartford Greys, Sandy Lane, Boars Hill Oxford, OX1 5HN Tel 0865 739360
Hon County Treasurer:	Col J C M Baker
Assistant Hon County Organisers:	
Vale of the White Horse (Abingdon, Wantage & Faringdon areas)	Mrs D J Faulkner, Haugh House, Longworth, Abingdon, Oxon OX13 5DX Tel 0865 820286
N Oxon (Chipping Norton & Banbury areas)	Mrs A D Loehnis, Haughton House, Churchill, nr Chipping Norton, Oxon OX7 6NU Tel 0608 658212
S Oxon (Henley, Wallingford & Thame areas)	Mrs J Kimberley, Madhuban, Hinksey Hill, Oxford OX1 5BE Tel 0865 735521
E Oxon (Oxford & Bicester areas)	Mrs P F Naccache, 376 Woodstock Road, Oxford OX2 8AF Tel 0865 513736
W Oxon (Bampton, Burford & Steeple Aston areas)	Mrs H H Atkinson, Ampney Lodge, High Street, Bampton OX18 2JN Tel 0993 850120

DATES OF OPENING

By appointment
For telephone numbers and other details see garden descriptions. Private visits welcomed

23 Beech Croft Road, Summertown
7 Bells Cottage, Garsington Gardens
Broadwell House, Lechlade
Brook Cottage, Alkerton, nr Banbury
The Clock House, Coleshill
Carinya, Goring Road, Woodcote
Greystone Cottage, Kingwood Common, nr Henley
Hearns House, Gallows Tree Common

Heron's Reach, Whitchurch, nr Pangbourne
Holywell Manor, Oxford
Home Farm, Balscote, nr Banbury
Home Farm House, Steeple Aston & Middle Aston Gardens
Little Place, Clifton Hampden
Mount Skippet, Ramsden ‡
4 Northfield Cottages, Oxford
Nutford Lodge, nr Farringdon
Shucklets, Ramsden ‡
Stansfield, Stanford-in-the-Vale
Town Farm Cottage, Kingston Blount
Wardington Manor, Wardington
Wilcote House, Finstock ‡
Yeomans, Tadmarton

Regular openings
For details see garden descriptions

Brook Cottage, Alkerton, nr Banbury. Mon to Fri April 1 to Oct 31
Kingston Bagpuize House. Suns, Bank Hol Mons April 1 to Sept 30
Salford Gardens, nr Chipping Norton 1st Tues of every month April - Sept
Stansfield, Stanford-in-the-Vale. Every Tues April 5 to Sept 20
Stanton Harcourt Manor, for various days see text

March 6 Sunday
Greystone Cottage, Kingwood
Common, nr Henley
March 27 Sunday
Ashbrook House, Blewbury
Magdalen College, Oxford ‡
Taynton House, nr Burford
Wadham College, Oxford ‡
April 3 Sunday
Clifton Hampden Manor
Faringdon House
Little Place, Clifton Hampden
The Mill House, Sutton Courtenay
Souldern Gardens
April 4 Monday
Epwell Mill, nr Banbury ‡
Home Farm, Balscote, nr
Banbury ‡
April 10 Sunday
Bignell House, Chesterton
Broadwell Gardens, nr Lechlade ‡
Buckland, nr Faringdon
Haseley Court & Coach House, nr
SE Oxford
Kencot Gardens, nr Lechlade ‡
Quarry Bank House, Gibraltar Hill,
nr Tackley
Swyncombe House, nr Nettlebed
Wootton Place, nr Woodstock
April 17 Sunday
Bampton & Weald Gardens
Broughton Poggs & Filkins
Gardens
Lime Close, Drayton
The Mill House, Stadhampton
The Old Rectory, Coleshill
Shotover House, nr Wheatley
Stanton Harcourt Manor
April 24 Sunday
Barton Abbey, Steeple Barton
Kingston Bagpuize House
Loreto, Ewelme
Wick Hall, Radley, nr Abingdon
May 1 Sunday
Adderbury Gardens
The Grange, Bampton
The Old Rectory, Albury, nr
Tiddington
Westwell Gardens, nr Burford
May 2 Monday
Garsington Manor, nr S Oxford
Sparsholt Manor, nr Wantage
May 8 Sunday
Checkendon Court, nr Reading
Epwell Mill, nr Banbury
Greystone Cottage, Kingwood
Common, nr Henley
The Manor House, Sutton
Courtenay
40 Osler Road, Headington
Gardens, Oxford
May 13 Friday
Hearns House, Gallows Tree
Common

May 14 Saturday
Greys Court, nr Henley
Hearns House, Gallows Tree
Common
May 15 Sunday
Clock House, Coleshill
Chivel Farm, Heythrop, nr
Chipping Norton
Garsington Gardens, nr S Oxford
Hearns House, Gallows Tree
Common
Wilcote House, nr Finstock
Woodperry House, nr Beckley
May 22 Sunday
Foxcombe End, Boars Hill ‡
Headington Gardens, Oxford
Sibford Ferris Gardens
Wardington Gardens
Wood Croft, Boars Hill ‡
May 25 Wednesday
Sibford Ferris Gardens, nr Banbury
May 29 Sunday
Adwell House, nr Tetsworth
Dundon House, Minster Lovell
Hornton Gardens, nr Banbury
The Malt House, Henley
Nutford Lodge, nr Faringdon
The Yews, Swerford, nr Chipping
Norton
May 30 Monday
Longworth Gardens
Lower Chilworth Farm, Milton
Common
Nutford Lodge, nr Faringdon
The Old Vicarage,
Weston-on-the-Green
Swerford Park, nr Chipping
Norton ‡
Wroxton Gardens
The Yews, Swerford, nr Chipping
Norton ‡
June 5 Sunday
Balscote Gardens, nr Banbury ‡
Charlbury Gardens
Middle Aston House, nr Bicester
South Newington Gardens, nr
Banbury ‡
Stansfield, Stanford-in-the-Vale
Steeple Aston and Middle Aston
Gardens
Stratton Audley Gardens
University Arboretum, Nuneham
Courtenay
Waterperry Gardens, nr Wheatley
June 8 Wednesday
Stratton Audley Gardens
June 12 Sunday
Bloxham Gardens, nr Banbury
The Grange, Bampton
Haseley Court & Coach House, nr
SE Oxford
Hill Farm, Elsfield, nr Oxford
Kiddington Hall, nr Woodstock
Lime Close, Drayton

Pettifers, Wardington, nr
Banbury
June 18 Saturday
Hill Court, Tackley
June 19 Sunday
The Clock House, Coleshill
Hill Court, Tackley
Langford Gardens
Sibford Gower Gardens, nr
Banbury
Towersey Manor, nr Thame
Town Farm Cottage, Kingston
Blount
White's Farm House, Letcombe
Bassett
June 22 Wednesday
Sibford Gower Gardens, nr
Banbury
Towersey Manor, nr Thame
June 25 Saturday
Lower Chilworth Farm, Milton
Common
Salford Gardens, nr Chipping
Norton
June 26 Sunday
Broadwell House, Broadwell
Gardens, nr Lechlade ‡
Broughton Castle, nr Banbury
East Hagbourne Gardens, nr
Didcot
Greys Green Gardens, nr
Henley-on-Thames
Iffley Gardens, S Oxford
Kencot House, Kencot Gardens,
nr Lechlade ‡
Manor Farm, Kencot Gardens, nr
Lechlade ‡
Manor Farm, Old Minster Lovell
The Manor House, Wheatley
The Mill House, Sutton
Courtenay
Querns, Goring Heath
Stanton Harcourt Manor
June 29 Wednesday
New College, Oxford
July 3 Sunday
Exeter & New Colleges, Oxford
Great Rollright Gardens, nr
Chipping Norton ‡
Heron's Reach, Whitchurch, nr
Pangbourne
Stonewalls, Hempton, nr
Deddington ‡
Westwell Gardens, nr Burford
July 10 Sunday
Adwell House, nr Tetsworth
Brightwell-cum-Sotwell Gardens,
nr Wallingford
Garsington Gardens, nr S Oxford
Manor Barn House, Wendlebury,
nr Bicester
Sibford Gower Gardens, nr
Banbury
Swinbrook Gardens, nr Burford

July 15 Friday
Hearns House, Gallows Tree
Common
July 16 Saturday
Hearns House, Gallows Tree
Common
July 17 Sunday
Chivel Farm, Heythrop, nr
Chipping Norton
Headington Gardens, Oxford
Hearns House, Gallows Tree
Common
Rewley House, Oxford
Tusmore Park, between Bicester
& Brackley
White's Farm House, Letcombe
Bassett
July 24 Sunday
Chastleton Gardens, nr
Moreton-in-Marsh
Queens & Wadham Colleges,
Oxford
Shutford Gardens
Stansfield, Stanford-in-the-Vale
Wolfson College, Oxford
Worcester College, Oxford
July 31 Sunday
Ashbrook House, Blewbury
Churchill Gardens
Home Farm, Balscote, nr
Banbury ‡

Pettifers, Wardington, nr
Banbury ‡
Wroxton Gardens ‡
August 7 Sunday
Broughton Castle, nr Banbury
East Oxford Gardens
The Old Rectory, Brightwell
Baldwin
Waterperry Gardens, nr Wheatley
August 14 Sunday
Christ Church, Corpus Christi &
Trinity Colleges, Oxford
Colegrave Seeds Ltd
Headington Gardens, Oxford
Thames-Side Court, Shiplake
August 20 Saturday
Alkerton House, Alkerton
Brook Cottage, Alkerton
August 21 Sunday
Alkerton House, Alkerton
Brook Cottage, Alkerton
Woodperry House, nr Beckley
August 28 Sunday
Blenheim Palace, Woodstock
Loreto, Ewelme
Nutford Lodge, nr Faringdon
Tadmarton Gardens
August 29 Monday
Blenheim Palace, Woodstock
Broadwell House, Broadwell
Gardens, nr Lechlade ‡

Kencot Gardens, nr Lechlade ‡
Loreto, Ewelme
Nutford Lodge, nr Faringdon
The Old Vicarage,
Weston-on-the-Green
Tadmarton Gardens
September 4 Sunday
Benson Gardens
Faringdon House
September 11 Sunday
The Clock House, Coleshill ‡
The Old Rectory, Coleshill ‡
Rofford Manor, Little Milton
September 18 Sunday
Bottom House, Bix, nr Henley
Epwell Mill, nr Banbury
Evelegh's, Long Wittenham, nr
Abingdon
Little Place, Clifton Hampden
September 25 Sunday
Templeton College, Kennington,
Oxford
October 2 Sunday
Garsington Manor, nr S Oxford
Hook Norton Manor, nr Banbury
The Mill House, Sutton Courtenay
October 9 Sunday
Wilcote House, nr Finstock

DESCRIPTIONS OF GARDENS

Adderbury Gardens On A4260, 3m S of Banbury. A
large village with many quaint lanes and a beautiful
church. TEAS. *Combined adm £1.50 Chd free. Sun May 1
(2-6)*
West of A423
Berry Hill House &.≪ (Mr & Mrs J P Pollard) Berry
Hill Rd, off A4260 signed Milton, Bloxham, W Adderbury. 2-acre garden reclaimed since 1982. Mature
trees; shrubbery; mixed herbaceous and shrub
borders. Kitchen garden
Crosshill House (Mr & Mrs Gurth Hoyer Millar) Manor
Rd. 4-acre classic Victorian walled gardens around
stone Georgian House
Ivy House &.❀ (Miss E Suter) Church Lane. 3 acres
with old walled garden, shrub roses, paddocks and
lake. House dates from early C17

Adwell House &.≪ (Mr & Mrs W R A Birch-Reynardson)
Nr Tetsworth, 4m SW of Thame. From London leave M40
at exit 6, turn L in Lewknor. From Oxford A40, turn R in
Tetsworth. Roses, formal and water gardens, ornamental
lakes, fine trees, lawns; new tree and shrub planting.
Commemorative garden with monument. Recently designed potager. TEAS. Plant sale (subject to availability).
*Adm £2 Chd free (Share to Adwell Church PCC). Suns May
29, July 10 (2.30-5.30)*

> **By Appointment Gardens.** See head of county
> section

Alkerton House (Mr & Mrs H Ewer) Alkerton (For direction see **Brook Cottage**). 2½ acres of trees, shrubs and
conifers. *Combined adm with **Brook Cottage** at extra
charge of 50p. Sat, Sun Aug 20, 21 (2-7)*

Arboretum see Oxford University Gardens

Ashbrook House &.≪❀ (Mr & Mrs S A Barrett) Blewbury. 4m SE of Didcot on A417; 3½-acre chalk garden
with small lake, stream, spring bulbs. Teas Lantern Cafe
March, Ashbrook House July. *Adm £1 Chd free. Suns
March 27, July 31 (2-6)*

Balscote Gardens &.❀ Pretty hill village ½m off A422
5m W of Banbury. TEAS May only at a nearby garden in
aid of Church (C14 St Mary Magdalene). *Combined adm
£2 Chd free. Sun June 5 (2-6)*
Home Farm (Mr & Mrs G C Royle) C17 house and
barn with attractive views from ½-acre closely planted
elevated garden designed for year-round interest with
contrasting foliage, flowering shrubs, bulbs, heathers,
alpines, herbaceous, roses, young trees. Featured in
Maison et Jardin, No 19 Spring 1992 and R.H.S. The
Garden July 1992. *Also open Mon April 4, Sun July 31.
Adm £1.50. Private visits also welcome April 1 to Oct
31, please Tel 0295 738194*
Homeland (Dr & Mrs J S Rivers) ¾-acre, developed
since 1982 with shrubs, roses, perennials and rock
garden, includes field adjacent to church, planted with
trees. *Open only June 5*

Bampton & Weald Gardens On A4095 Witney-Faringdon rd. TEAS at **Weald Manor**. *Combined adm £1.50 Chd free. Sun April 17 (2-5.30)*
    Bampton Manor &.& (Earl & Countess of Donoughmore) Interesting wild spring garden with beautiful views of church. Masses of varied spring flowers. *(Share to Dr Clark Memorial Fund)*
    Weald Manor &. (Maj & Mrs R A Colvile) Medium-sized old garden; woodland area with many daffodils; topiary and shrub borders; fine trees; small lake *(Share to Lord Roberts Workshops)*

Barton Abbey &.&& (Mrs R Fleming) On B4030; 1m Middle Barton; ½m from junction of A4260 and B4030. 4 acres lawns; 3 acres of lake; fine trees; kitchen garden and glasshouses; prize rosette display. Plants and home produce stall. TEAS. *Adm £1.50 Chd free. Sun April 24 (2-6)*

23 Beech Croft Road && (Mrs A Dexter) Summertown, Oxford. A 23yd by 7yd, south-facing, plant lover's paved garden of a terraced house has been made secluded by planting evergreen shrubs, roses and clematis all round the brick walls; the 2 herbaceous, 2 alpine, 2 shady beds all contain many unusual plants, shrubs, ferns; troughs filled with small alpines. NO push-chairs. *Adm £2.50. Private visits welcome April to Sept 30* **Tel 0865 56020**

Benson Gardens && Off High St Benson off A423 Oxford-Henley, 2m from Wallingford. TEAS at **Mill Lane House**. *Combined adm £1.50. Sun Sept 4 (2-6)*
    Hethersett (Dr Anne Millar) ½-acre garden on natural chalk stream; climbing plants and bog area; colour coordination and plant-form a feature of mixed beds
    Mill Lane House (Marion & Geoff Heywood) ¼-acre garden with alpine rockeries and banks sloping to stream, pond, bog garden, small island and spring. Dried flower crafts display

Bignell House && (Mr & Mrs P J Gordon, Lord & Lady of Bignell) Chesterton. On A4095 2m SW Bicester. 16-acre traditional English country house garden; lawns leading to lake system with rock pool; stone arches; bridge to daffodil island; fine mature trees inc wellingtonia and spruce; aconites; primroses; variety of wild species; woodland plants. House designed by Wm Wilkinson mid C19 (one wing only remains). Stall and TEAS in aid of Bicester Friends of the Earth. *Adm £1 Chd free. Sun April 10 (2-6)*

Blenheim Palace && (His Grace the Duke of Marlborough) Woodstock, 8m N of Oxford. Bus: 44 Oxford-Chipping Norton-Stratford, alight Woodstock. Original grounds and garden plan by Henry Wise. Park landscaped and lake created by 'Capability' Brown in late C18. Maze; butterfly house; cafeteria; adventure play area; *Adm charge not available on going to press.* ▲*For NGS Sun, Mon Aug 28, 29 (11-5)*

Bloxham Gardens &&& A large village near Banbury on A361 to Chipping Norton. Has a fine church with a 198ft spire. TEAS in aid of WI. *Combined adm £1.50 Chd free. Sun June 12 (2-6)*
    25 The Avenue (Miss E Bell-Walker) A small informal garden with emphasis on small shrubs; sub shrubs and herbaceous plants

71 Courtington Lane && (Mr P Sheasby) About ⅓ acre with herbaceous borders, shrubs, rockeries and small peat beds; there is a small pond and a series of alpine troughs; the greenhouse contains cacti and a large succulent collection especially Lithops, Haworthia and Echeveria; a wide range of herbaceous species are grown
    Rose Cottage && (Mr & Mrs David Willmott) Small cottage garden developed in recent yrs. Concentration of alpines; shrubs and roses on elevated site

Bottom House &.&& (Mrs G Scouller) Bix, 1½m NW of Henley-on-Thames on A423 (dual carriageway) 2-acre family garden with good mixed autumn borders, many unusual plants. Small formal garden with topiary; silver and yellow garden. Highly recommended by Eluned Price, Radio Oxford 1993. TEAS. *Adm £1 Chd free. Sun Sept 18 (2-6)*

Brightwell-cum-Sotwell Gardens && Off A4130 between Didcot (4m) and Wallingford (2m). The road through this ancient village is long and narrow, winding between many timber-framed cottages. Parking in village centre. TEAS at **Sotwell House**. *Combined adm £1.50 Chd free. Sun July 10 (2-6)*
    Mackney Lane Three neighbouring cottage gardens of different character
    Lucksall Cottage && (Miss P Grierson) Informal ⅓-acre garden with mixed borders, old roses; unusual plants
    Mead Cottage (Dr & Mrs C Newnham) Rockery, patio roses and pinks
    Workman Cottage (Mrs V Mold) Varied borders and containers

    The Priory &.&& (Mr & Mrs C Scroggs) Walled garden, designed for yr-round use, to S of C16 small farmhouse with gravelled courtyard on E side. Some 2,000 plantings in small shrubbery, rose bed and broad herbaceous border, also brick-paved vegetable/herb garden with interesting climbing plants on walls concealing swimming pool
    Sotwell House (Mr & Mrs D Dobbin) 3 acres with moat surrounding property; informal garden with roses, shrubs and annuals

Broadwell Gardens 5m NE Lechlade, E of A361 to Burford. Delightful Cotswold village with interesting church. TEAS (not June). *Combined adm with* **Kencot** *£2 Chd free. Sun April 10, Mon Aug 29.* **Broadwell House** *only £1.50 Chd free. Sun June 26 (2-6)*
    Broadwell House &.& (Brigadier & Mrs C F Cox) Mature 2-acre garden planted for colour throughout the year. Many interesting trees and shrubs including wellingtonia, ginkgo, acers, aralias, salix, cornus, clematis. Topiary, rare plants, many golden, silver and variegated; unusual grasses, penstemons and osteospermums, also many hardy geraniums. Featured in 'Over the Hills from Broadway'. Listed house and old barn. Gardening clubs welcome. *Suns April 10, June 26, Mon Aug 29 (2-6). Private visits welcome, please* **Tel 0367 860230**

Regular Openers. See head of county section.

Broadwell Old Manor ✤ (Mr & Mrs M Chinnery) 1-acre garden with listed house. Shrub borders, courtyard and topiary garden. Pleached lime hedge, old mulberry tree, young tulip and sorbus trees. *April 10 only*

Brook Cottage ✤ (Mr & Mrs D Hodges) Alkerton, 6m W of Banbury. From A422, Banbury-Stratford, turn W at sign to Alkerton, L opp Alkerton War Memorial, into Well Lane, R at fork. 4-acre hillside garden, formed since 1964, surrounding C17 house. Wide variety of trees, shrubs and plants of all kinds in areas of differing character; water garden; alpine scree; one-colour borders; over 200 shrub and climbing roses; many clematis. Interesting throughout season. DIY Tea & Coffee on all open weekdays. TEAS in aid of Shenington Nursery Aug 20, 21 and refreshments for groups on other dates by arrangement. *Adm £2 OAPs £1.50 Chd free. Mon to Fri April 1 to Oct 31 (9-6). Sat, Sun Aug 20, 21 (2-7). Evenings, other weekends and all group visits by appt* Tel 0295 670303 or 670590

Broughton Castle &✤ (Lord Saye & Sele) 2½m W of Banbury on Shipston-on-Stour rd (B4035). 1-acre shrub, herbaceous borders, walled garden, roses, climbers seen against background of C13-C16 castle surrounded by moat in open parkland. House also open, extra charge. TEAS. *Adm Garden only £1.50 Chd 75p.* ▲*For NGS Suns June 26, Aug 7 (2-5)*

Broughton Poggs & Filkins Gardens & Enchanting limestone villages between Burford and Lechlade, just E of A361. A number of gardens varying in size from traditional cottage garden to over 2 acres, growing wide variety of plants. Mill in process of restoration. TEAS. *Combined adm £2 Chd free. Tickets from* **The Court House, Broughton Hall** *or* **Little Peacocks** *(Share to Broughton & Filkins Church Funds®). Sun April 17 (2-5.30)*
Broughton Poggs:
  Broughton Hall (Mr & Mrs C B S Dobson)
  Broughton Mill (J Huggins Esq)
  Corner Cottage (Mr & Mrs E Stephenson)
  The Court House (Richard Burls Esq)
  ¶**The Garden Cottage** (Mr & Mrs R Chennells)
  The Old Rectory (Mrs E Wansbrough)
  Rose Cottage (Mr & Mrs R Groves)
Filkins:
  Fox House (Lady Ann Cripps)
  Little Peacocks (Colvin & Moggridge, Landscape Consultants)
  The Old Smithy (Mrs Frances Fynn)
  St Peter's House (J Cambridge Esq)

Buckland ✤ (Mrs Richard Wellesley) Signposted to Buckland off A420, lane between two churches. Beautiful lakeside walk; fine trees; daffodils; shrubs. Norman church adjoins garden. TEAS. *Adm £1 Chd free. Sun April 10 (2-7)*

Carinya ✿✤ (Mrs S J Parsons) Goring Rd, Woodcote. 8m NW of Reading; 5m SE of Wallingford on SW edge of Village on B471. ⅓-acre plant lover's cottage style garden, densely planted with a wide variety of plants, many rare or unusual with interest at all times of the year. *Adm £1 Chd free. Private visits welcome April 1 to Sept 30, please* Tel 0491 680663

Charlbury Gardens ✿✤ Large historic village on B4022 Witney-Enstone. TEAS. *Combined adm £1.50 Chd 50p (Share to Wytham Hall Sick Bay for Medical Care of Homeless®). Sun June 5 (2-6)*
  Gothic House (Mr & Mrs Andrew Lawson) Near Bell Hotel. ⅓-acre walled garden, planted for sculpture display and colour association. False perspective, pleached lime walk with bulbs, trellis, alpine pyramid, terrace pots
  The Priory & (Dr D El Kabir and others) Adjacent church. A collector's garden in the making. Over 1 acre planted with many fine specimens of trees and shrubs in a formal topiary garden with terraced beds incorporating colour scheme foliage

Chastleton Gardens 3m SE of Moreton-in-Marsh and W of Chipping Norton off A44. TEAS in aid of Chastleton Church. *Combined adm £2 Chd free. Sun July 24 (2-6)*
  Chastleton Glebe &✤ (Prue Leith) 1m from village on lane to Moreton-in-Marsh. 5 acres; old trees; terraces (one all red); small lake, island; Chinese-style bridge, pagoda; formal vegetable garden; Cotswold house; views; new rose tunnel
  Kitebrook End Farm & (Mr & Mrs W G Bamford) Directions as for Chastleton Glebe. ½-acre garden created in 1988 from derelict farm yard. Designed to be labour-saving; walls; paving and shaped borders around a lawn. Massed shrubs and herbaceous planting for ground cover and colour, southerly aspect, opened up with raised ha-ha wall
  The Old Post Office ✤ (Prof & Mrs Griffith Edwards) in Chastleton. ⅔-acre roses, shrubs and perennials in attractive sheltered setting below historic Chastleton House

Checkendon Court &✿ (Sir Nigel Broackes) Checkendon, NW of Reading. 2m NE of Woodcote on B479 nr Checkendon church. 15 acres, attractively laid out with yew hedges, herbaceous borders, roses, kitchen garden; work continues to woodland areas. New rhododendrons and azalea planting and new laburnum pergola walk now complete. TEAS at **Greystone Cottage**. *Adm £2 Chd free. Sun May 8 (2-5)*

Chivel Farm &✿✤ (Mr & Mrs J D Sword) Heythrop, 4m E of Chipping Norton, off A44 or A361. High and open to extensive view, medium-sized garden designed for continuous interest. Old-fashioned and modern shrub roses, unusual shrubs and herbaceous plants; small formal white garden. TEAS. *Adm £1 Chd free. Suns May 15, July 17 (2-6)*

Christ Church See Oxford University Gardens

Churchill Gardens Churchill 3m SW of Chipping Norton on B4450. From Burford, W for Churchill via A361. TEAS in aid of village church. *Combined adm £1.50 Chd free. Sun July 31 (2-6)*
  Haughton House &✤ (Mr & Mrs A D Loehnis) Medium-sized garden recently reclaimed. Terrace with fine views, borders, formal white garden, meadow. All season interest. Also fine kneelers in nearby church
  ¶**Rynehill Farm** &✿ (Mr & Mrs M D Bell) On B4450 1m S of Churchill. 1-acre farmhouse garden. Well-stocked kitchen garden, walled area, mixed borders, annuals, roses

Clifton Hampden Manor &※※ (Mr C Gibbs) 4m E of Abingdon on A415. 4-acre romantic C19 garden above R. Thames with statuary and far-reaching views; long pergola, new lime tunnel, herbaceous borders, bulbs, wild riverside walks, much new planting in progress. TEAS in aid of St Michael's and All Angels Church. *Combined adm with* **Little Place** *£2 Chd free. Sun April 3 (2.30-5.30)*

Clock House &※※ (Michael & Denny Wickham & Peter Fox) Coleshill, 3½m SW of Faringdon on B4019. Garden at top of village. Planted around site of Coleshill House, which was burnt down in the 50's, the main floor plan has been laid out and is being planted as a memorial to this famous house. Walled garden in old laundry drying ground; with big greenhouse, unusual plants, vegetables and herbs; good views across Vale of the White Horse and parkland. Toilets not suitable disabled. TEAS. *Adm £1 Chd free. Suns May 15, June 19, Sept 11 (2-6). Private visits welcome, please* Tel 0793 762476

Colegrave Seeds Ltd &※ Milton Rd, West Adderbury off A423 Banbury-Oxford Rd. From M40 travelling S leave at junction 11: travelling N leave at junction 10. In Adderbury head for Milton and Bloxham. Trial grounds ½m on right. Seed trials grounds and new display gardens containing thousands of summer flowering annuals and perennials. Many new items in trial prior to introduction. A festival of colour unique in Oxfordshire. Covered display area of hanging baskets and containers, (Note strictly wholesale; no retail sales). Parking. Light lunches and TEAS. *Adm £1.50 Chd free (Share to RNLI®). Sun Aug 14 (11-5)*

Corpus Christi College (see Oxford University Gardens)

Dundon House &※※ (Mr & Mrs W Pack) In Old Minster Lovell, charming Cotswold village on R Windrush. Off B4047 Witney-Burford Rd opp White Hart, signed to Minster Lovell Hall, 1st drive on R, parking in field to L. Disabled parking at house. Mainly C16 house, (not open), owned in C18 by the Dundons, a notorious family of highwaymen; moved in 1930s to old quarry. Beautiful views across Windrush valley. 4-acre terraced garden built over last 11yrs. Yew hedges and stone walls enclose flower, shrub rose and wild gardens. Planted pool and new woodland gardens. TEAS by WI. *Adm £1.50 Chd free. Sun May 29 (2-6)*

East Hagbourne Gardens &※※ 1½m SE of Didcot. 5 gardens in exceptionally pretty village. A brook flows through village and several gardens. Mediaeval cross. Flower festival in C11-12 church with C14 stained glass. Renowned bell-ringers viewable 3-5. Art galleries. TEAS at **Buckels** and **Manor Farm**. *Combined adm £2 Chd free. Sun June 26 (2-6)*

Buckels (Rear Adm & Mrs Jamieson) ⅓-acre of colourful partially walled garden on several levels. House (1605) once village bakery

1 Church Close (Mr & Mrs N V Linklater) ¼-acre, very much a cottage garden; small greenhouse. Elizabethan house once 3 cottages. Plant sale in aid of BBONT

Kingsholm (Mr & Mrs J Lawson) Partly Elizabethan, partly C17 house (with mediaeval origins). ¾-acre with fine English and Irish yews and topiary in box and yew. Herbaceous and shrub borders

Manor Farm (Mr & Mrs R W Harries) Water surrounds the main house in the form of a moat and full use has been made of this feature. 2 acres incl swimming pool with pergola

Parsonage Farm & (Sir John & Lady Lucus Tooth) 2½ acres mixed borders of unusual shrubs and plants. Old rose garden with yew topiary. Large established orchard. Pot garden in brick and gravel yard. Early C18 house

East Oxford Gardens & Off Cowley Rd, Oxford 1m E from the Plain. Parking at **Restore** TEAS at **Restore** and **St John's Home**. *Combined adm £1 Chd free (Share to Restore and St John's Home®). Sun Aug 7 (2-5)*

Restore ※ Manzil Way N off Cowley Rd leading to E Oxford Health Centre. A town garden and plant nursery run as a mental health rehabilitation project. Sample beds of shrubs, perennials, herbs, alpines and annuals. Large range of plants for sale, also handmade crafts and cards

St John's Home St Mary's Rd, off Leopold St S of Cowley Rd. 3-acre grounds of All Saints Convent and St John's Home for the Elderly. Mature trees, lawns, secluded prayer garden; cherry orchard and vegetable garden

Epwell Mill ※ (Mr R A Withers) Epwell, 7m W of Banbury, between Shutford and Epwell. Medium-sized garden, interestingly landscaped in open country, based on former water-mill, terraced pools; bulbs; azaleas. TEAS. *Adm £1 Chd free (Share to Epwell Church®). Mon April 1, Suns May 8, Sept 18 (2-6). Please apply in writing for groups outside opening dates*

Evelegh's &※※ (Mr & Mrs J H Rose) High St, Long Wittenham. 4m NE of Didcot. From A415 turn S at Clifton Hampden or N from B4016 to Long Wittenham. Long narrow 1-acre garden leading to backwater of R. Thames. Character changes from borders to informal woodland by river. Interesting plantings; herbaceous, shrubs, roses, small herb garden, alpines in scree, annuals to give long season of colour. *Combined adm with* **Little Place, Clifton Hampden** *£2 Chd free. Sun Sept 18 (2-6)*

Exeter College see Oxford University Gardens

Faringdon House & (Dr S Zinovieff) Faringdon. Large garden; spring bulbs; autumn borders; orangery; park; lakeside walk; fine trees; Norman church adjoining. TEAS in aid of All Saints Church. *Adm £1 Chd free. Suns April 3, Sept 4 (2-5)*

Foxcombe End &※ (Mr & Mrs R Stevens) Foxcombe Lane, Boars Hill, 3 m S of Oxford. From roundabout at junction of ring rd with A34 S of Oxford follow signs to Wootton and Boars Hill. Foxcombe Lane is 1st on L after entering Boars Hill. Parking at Foxcombe End reserved for disabled **only**. 11 acres of natural garden, incl a nature trail, a pasture with two donkeys and an abundance of wild flowers, particularly orchids. Extensive oak woodlands, within which are magnolia and azalea gardens and rhododendrons. Yew walk and ornamental yew hedges around the house. TEAS in aid of Sobell House Hospice. *Adm £1 Chd free. Sun May 22 (2-6)*

Garsington Gardens SE of Oxford, N of B480. TEAS in aid of St Mary's Church. *Combined adm £1. Suns May 15, July 10 (2-6)*

Home Close ✿❀ (Mrs M Baker) Southend. 2-acre garden, being redeveloped, surrounding C17 listed bailiff's house and granary. Mixed borders; walled garden with water feature; herb garden; pergola; kitchen garden; orchard; woodland areas

Seven Bells Cottage ⚫✿❀ (Dr Michael & Mrs Lesley Pusey) Southend. 1-acre garden of surprises, developed since 1986, with views to Berkshire Downs and the Chilterns. A diversity of interesting trees, shrubs, plants, vegetables and herbs. Herbaceous border, island beds, wildlife areas, ponds and bog garden. Garden sculptures. Small C16 thatched farmhouse. *Adm 70p. Private visits welcome April 1 to Sept 30, please* **Tel 086736 488**

Garsington Manor ❀ (Mr & Mrs L V Ingrams) SE of Oxford N of B480. House C16 of architectural interest (not open). Monastic fish ponds, water garden, dovecot c.1700; flower parterre and Italian garden laid out by Philip and Lady Ottoline Morrell; fine trees and yew hedges. Free car park. TEAS. *Adm £2 Chd free. Mon May 2, Sun Oct 2 (2-6)*

The Grange ⚫❀ (Mrs R Johnston & Mr & Mrs P Taylor) Bampton. Entrance in High St. Large garden: lovely specimen trees, interesting shrubs and borders, pond, walled ornamental kitchen garden. Homemade TEAS in beautiful courtyard. *Adm £1.50 Chd free. Suns May 1, June 12 (2-6)*

Great Rollright Gardens 3m N of Chipping Norton, off A34 or A361. TEAS at **Old Rectory** in aid of St Andrews Church Restoration Fund. *Adm £1.50 Chd free. Sun July 3 (2-6)*

Barston House ⚫✿ (Miss E L Jackson) 1-acre, formal garden with herbaceous borders, shrubs; kitchen garden; views

Duck End ✿ (Mr & Mrs J Lively) Informal ½-acre cottage garden, surrounding listed C17 farmhouse with dovecote; streams; yew hedges, shrub roses; parking available in adjoining paddock only

The Old Beer House (Mr & Mrs B A Tucker) ½-acre village garden with small knot garden and conservatory; orchard

The Old Rectory ⚫✿ (Mr Michael & Lady Joanna Stourton) 3 acres with beautiful views to south. Herbaceous border, lawns, knot garden; tree walk; water garden with brook, small lake; many specimen trees

Rectory Cottage (Mrs J Lawrence) ¼-acre of C17 cottage. Sheltered, S facing, divided by trellis. Small woodland garden; pond

Greys Court ✿❀ (Lady Brunner; The National Trust) Rotherfield Greys, 3m W of Henley-on-Thames on rd to Peppard. 8 acres amongst which are the ruined walls and buildings of original fortified manor. Rose, cherry, wisteria and white gardens; lawns; kitchen garden; ice house; Archbishop's maze. Jacobean house open with C18 alterations on site of original C13 house fortified by Lord Grey in C14. Donkey wheel and tower. Large sale of

unusual plants. TEAS. *Adm garden £2.80 Chd £1.40 House £1 extra, Chd 50p extra. For NGS Sat May 14 (2-5.30)*

Greys Green Gardens ⚫✿❀ Rotherfield Greys, 3m W of Henley-on-Thames. Two secluded gardens close to Greys Green War memorial. *Combined adm £1. Sun June 26 (2-6)*

Greys House (Mr & Mrs K S Barker) Informal garden in 1¼ acres designed by Robin Williams. Interesting flowering shrubs, roses, and herbaceous borders, large lawn, pond with Koi, apple walk, open views, parking

Green Place (Mr & Mrs R P Tatman) 1-acre garden with extensive views towards the East. Roses, fuchsias and herbaceous borders

Greystone Cottage ⚫✿❀ (Mr & Mrs W Roxburgh) Colmore Lane, Kingwood Common. Between B481 Nettlebed-Reading rd and Sonning Common-Stoke Row rd; turn N at 'Unicorn'. 2-acre garden in woodland setting. Many unusual shrubs and plants, including varied collection of hostas, geraniums, grasses, fritillary species, ferns and old fashioned roses. Woodland walk with azaleas, narcissus, hellebores, bilberries and cistus. 80-year-old arched pear tree walk, wildlife ponds, sink gardens, small Mediterranean garden, golden garden. Planted for year round interest. Featured in 'Practical Gardening'. Small nursery. TEAS. *Adm £1 Chd free. Suns March 6, May 8 (2-6). Private visits welcome March 1 to Sept 1, please* **Tel 0491 628559**

Haseley Court & Coach House ⚫✿❀ SE of Oxford. From London M40 exit 7, L to A329, 1st L to Great Haseley then to Little Haseley. From Oxford A40, L on A418 to Aylesbury, 1st R onto A329 and over M40. TEAS. *Combined adm £1.50 Chd free. Suns April 10, June 12 (2-6)*

The Coach House (Mrs C G Lancaster) Hornbeam and laburnum tunnels, orchard, spring bulbs; courtyard borders; walled garden with box hedges; summer-house; large collection of old roses and herbaceous plants; Rosa mundi hedge; potager; white garden

Haseley Court (Mr & Mrs D Heyward) Topiary chess set in box and yew; mixed borders planted in 1990; woodlands with many spring flowers; ornamental canal

Headington Gardens ✿❀ East Oxford, off London Road, ¾m W of ring road. TEAS in parish hall, Dunstan Rd. TEAS (May 8 TEAS in garden). *Adm £1. Sun May 8, 40 Osler Rd only. Combined adm £1.80 OAPs £1.50 Chd free. Suns May 22, July 17, Aug 14 (2-6)*

2 Fortnam Close (Mr & Mrs D Holt) Off Headley Way. Winner best back garden, Oxford in Bloom 1991 and 1993. Featured on TV. ¼-acre garden on 3 levels, trees, shrubs including heathers, azaleas and a large wisteria. Roses, bearded iris and other herbaceous plants in a planned layout which includes a pond and pergola. There are watercolour paintings and pressed flower arrangements to view if you wish. *May 22, July 17, Aug 14*

Mary Marlborough Lodge & (Nuffield Orthopaedic Centre) Windmill Rd. 2 easy-to-manage gardens with raised beds featuring herbaceous plants and vegetables; roses; raised cold frames; array of hanging baskets; display of lightweight tools. A splendid source of ideas for less able gardeners and those wishing to simplify garden work. Ample parking. *July 17 only (Share to MML©)*

40 Osler Road (Mr & Mrs N Coote) 2/3-acre 'secret garden' in built-up area on the edge of old Headington. Semi-formal design with statuary and extensive use of decorative pots with tender shrubs and plants supporting Mediterranean atmosphere of house. Plants for dry soil (neutral sand), some rare or unusual, many chosen for foliage effect. Luxuriant spring display. Featured in 'English Private Gardens'; 'Practical Gardening' and 'Garden Source Book'. *May 8, 22, July 17, Aug 14. No plant stall May 8, Aug 14*

Pumpkin Cottage & (Mr & Mrs M Davis) 6 St Andrew's Lane, Old Headington, off St Andrew's Rd, nr to Church. Small garden, 20m × 16m, enclosed within stone walls situated at rear of Grade II listed cottage. Small pool and rockery; mixed planting; paved areas with some container grown plants. Small cobble paved front garden. Wheelchair access possible by arrangement. *May 22, July 17, Aug 14*

Hearns House && (Mr & Mrs J Pumfrey) Gallows Tree Common, 5m N of Reading, 5m W of Henley. From A4074 turn E at The Fox, Cane End. Limited car parking in the garden so additional Friday and Saturday openings. Architects house in 2-acre expanding garden in woodland setting. Featured in Amateur Gardening. Emphasis on design, good foliage and single colour areas with paved courtyard and shady walks. New small garden. Unusual plants for sale. TEAS or coffee in aid of Water Aid. *Adm £1 Chd free. Fris, Sats, Suns May 13, 14, 15; July 15, 16, 17 (10-12; 2-5); private visits also welcome in Sept, please* Tel 0734 722848

Heron's Reach ❀ (Mr & Mrs B Vorhaus) Eastfield Lane, Whitchurch. From Pangbourne take tollbridge rd over Thames to Whitchurch; at The Greyhound turn R into Eastfield Lane. 1 acre in beautiful Thames-side setting with views of the Chiltern hills; woodland garden with pond, stream and waterfall; shrubs, and herbaceous borders. TEA. *Adm £1 Chd free. Sun July 3 (2-6). Private visits also welcome in July, please* Tel 0734 843140

Hill Court &❀❀ (Mr & Mrs Andrew Peake) Tackley. 9m N of Oxford. Turn off A4260 at Sturdy's Castle. Walled garden of 2 acres with clipped yew cones at the top of the terrace as a design feature by Russell Page in the 1960s. Terraces incl silver, pink and blue plantings, white garden, herbaceous borders, shrubberies, replanted orangery. Many rare and unusual plants. Entry incl History Trail (not suitable for wheelchairs) with illustrated leaflet giving notes on unique geometric fishponds (1620), C17 stables and pigeon house, C18 lakes, icehouse etc (stroll of at least 1hr). TEAS. *Adm £1.50 Chd free (Share to Tackley Local History Group and Church Tower Appeal®). Sat, Sun June 18, 19 (2-6)*

Regular Openers. See head of county section.

Hill Farm ❀❀ (Mr & Mrs J Garson) Elsfield. 5m N of Oxford. A40 flyover signed Marston and Elsfield. Mixed borders, shrubs, trees; good view of Oxford. TEAS. *Adm £1 Chd free (Share to Elsfield Church®). Sun June 12 (2-6)*

Hook Norton Manor ❀ (Mr & Mrs N Holmes) SW of Banbury. From A361, 1m from Chipping Norton turn N and follow signs. 2½-acres terraced lawns leading down to streams; trees, shrubs and bog garden. TEAS in aid of St Peter's Church. *Adm 80p Chd free. Sun Oct 2 (2-5.30)*

Hornton Gardens 6m NW of Banbury. Between A422 and B4100. An attractive village known for its quarry which produced Hornton stone for the neighbourhood. Fine old buildings around the village green. TEAS in aid of Hornton School. *Combined adm £1.50 Chd free. Sun May 29 (2-6)*

Bellevue ❀❀ (Mr & Mrs E W Turner) Bell St. Approx 1½-acre hillside garden of many aspects. Bordered walks; a 'surprise' garden leading to water falling to pools, flower beds and the finest views of Hornton Village. Added attraction miniature windmill 1/3 scale of original at Hornton

Sunnyside &❀❀ (Philip Williams Esq) A cottage garden of approx ½-acre with attractive borders of mixed perennials; shrub planting and pond area. Created from rough ground over 6 years and still adding

West End House &❀ (The Hon William & Mrs Buchan) Small, well stocked garden with interesting layout. Herb garden

Iffley Gardens ❀❀ S Oxford. Secluded old village within Oxford's ring road, off A4158 from Magdalen Bridge to Littlemore roundabout. Renowned Norman church, featured on cover of Pevsner's Oxon guide. Short footpath from Mill Lane leads to scenic Iffley Lock and Sandford-Oxford towpath. TEAS from 3-5 at thatched village hall, Church Way. Plant stall in aid of the White House Nursery. *Combined adm £1.50 Chd free. Sun June 26 (2-6)*

8 Abberbury Road (F S Tordoff Esq) Off Church Way. ½-acre plantsman's garden developed since 1971. Mature trees, shrubs, coloured and variegated foliage, many old and modern shrub roses and climbers

24 Abberbury Road (Mr & Mrs E Townsend-Coles) ½-acre family garden with fruit, flowers and vegetables

¶**65 Church Way** ❀ (Mrs J Woodfill) Small cottage garden planted with shrubs, perennials and herbs, many of them grown for their historical associations

71 Church Way (Mr & Mrs R D Harrison) A small, low maintenance front garden with mixed shrubs and herbaceous plantings

¶**122 Church Way** (Prof & Mrs J H Elliott) Small secluded cottage style garden with trees, shrubs, roses and herbaceous plants behind listed house with view of church tower

¶**The Mill House** (Mrs P A Lawrence) 30 Mill Lane. A terraced garden dropping westwards to the river at the old mill-race

Rosedale ❀ (Mrs T Bennett) Mill Lane, off Church Way. ½-acre garden on different levels, hidden behind walls. A mixture of trees, shrubs, roses and herbaceous plants with a large rockery and tiny woodland garden

Kencot Gardens &✕& 5m NE of Lechlade, E of A361 to Burford. A most charming Cotswold village with interesting church. TEAS (not June). *Combined adm with* **Broadwell** *£2 Chd free. Sun April 10, Mon Aug 29 (2-6)*
Kencot House & Manor Farm *(with Broadwell. £1.50 Chd free. Sun June 26*

De Rougemont (Mr & Mrs D Portergill) ½-acre garden with very varied planting: over 350 named plants; beds for perennials, conifers, fuchsias, herbs and roses; spring bulbs; vegetables and fruit trees; soft fruit cage; greenhouse with vine; well. *Sun April 10, Mon Aug 29*

The Gardens (Lt-Col & Mrs J Barstow) ¼-acre cottage garden featuring spring bulbs, iris, roses, herbaceous, rock plants, old apple trees and a well. *Sun April 10, Mon Aug 29*

Ivy Nook (Mr & Mrs W Gasson) Cottage garden; rockeries, lawns, mixed borders. *Sun April 10, Mon Aug 29*

Kencott Cottage (Mrs M Foster) Very small garden with spring bulbs and bedding, also bonsai trees. *Sun April 10, Mon Aug 29*

Kencot House (Mr & Mrs A Patrick) 2-acre garden with lawns, trees, borders; quantities of daffodils and other spring bulbs; roses and over 50 different clematis; notable ginkgo tree. Interesting carved C13 archway. *Suns April 10, June 26, Mon Aug 29. (Share to RSPB®) £1.50*

Kencot Manor (Mrs A Davies) 2-acre family garden with some mature plants and trees, incl grape vines, yew hedge, glaucous cedar. Much replanting in the last 3yrs to give all round colour. *Mon Aug 29 only*

Manor Farm (Mr & Mrs J R Fyson) 2-acre garden with lawns and herbaceous borders; naturalised spring bulbs; incl long-established fritillaries; clipped yew, pleached lime walk, pergola with rambling and gallica roses. Mature orchards. C17 listed farmhouse. *Sun April 10, June 26*

The Old Rectory (Mr & Mrs A Lamburn) 1-acre family garden with lawns, trees and bulbs. *Sun April 10, Mon Aug 29*

Kiddington Hall ✕ (Hon Maurice & Mrs Robson) 4m NW of Woodstock. From A44 Oxford-Stratford, R at Xrds in Kiddington and down hill; entrance on L. Partly suitable for wheelchairs. Large grounds with lake, parkland designed by Capability Brown; terraced rose garden and orangery beside house designed by Sir Charles Barry; C12 church, C16 dovecote and large walled kitchen garden. TEAS in aid of St Nicholas Church, Kiddington. *Adm £1.50 Chd free. Sun June 12 (2-6)*

Kingston Bagpuize House &✕ (Lady Tweedsmuir) Kingston Bagpuize, A415/A420, 5½m W of Abingdon. Flowering shrubs, bulbs; woodland garden; herbaceous plants; hydrangeas. Charles II Manor house. House not suitable wheelchairs. TEAS. *Adm house & garden adults £2.50, OAPs £2, Chd £1.50 (under 5 not admitted to house). Garden only 50p, under 5's free (Share to British Red Cross and Lucy Faithful House). Suns, Bank Hols Mons April 1 to Sept 30 (2.30-5.30). For NGS Sun April 24 (2.30-5.30). Last adm 5pm*

By Appointment Gardens. See head of county section

Langford Gardens &❀ E of A361 Burford-Lechlade: W of A4095 Witney-Faringdon. Mixture of cottage and formal gardens in old limestone village which makes a feature of roses. Saxon church decorated with flowers. Large free car park. TEAS in aid of St. Matthew's Church. Chamber ensemble playing. *Combined adm £2 Chd free. Sun June 19 (2-6)*

Bakery Cottage (Miss R Amies)
The Barn (Mr & Mrs D E Range)
Bridgewater House (Mrs P M C Scott)
¶**Lime Tree Cottage** (Mr & Mrs M G Schultz)
Lockey House (Mr & Mrs A S H Kemp)
The Old School and Barn (Sir Hardy Amies)
The Old Vicarage (Dr & Mrs E B Raftery)
Pember House (Mr & Mrs H K Hughes)
Rectory Farm (Mr & Mrs R J Kirby)
Threeways (Mrs M M Wilson)
Wellbank (Mrs A Hudson-Davies)
Wellbank House (Mr & Mrs P G Booth)

Lime Close &❀ (Miss de Laubarede) 35 Henleys Lane, Drayton. 2m S of Abingdon. 3-acre mature garden with very rare and unusual trees, shrubs, perennials and bulbs. Raised beds, rock garden and troughs with alpines. Creation of new borders and much new planting in progress. New ornamental kitchen garden with pergola under construction. Herb garden designed by Rosemary Verey. Listed C16 house (not open). Unusual plants for sale from Green Farm Plants. TEAS. *Adm £1.50 Chd free. Suns April 17, June 12 (2-6.30)*

Little Place ✕ (His Honour Judge & Mrs Medd) Clifton Hampden. 5m E of Abingdon. Leaving Abingdon on A415, At Clifton Hampden turn R at traffic lights and take 1st turning R. Garden 200yds on R. 1½-acre terraced garden originally made at turn of century (part possibly designed by Gertrude Jekyll) but replanned by present owners; with small woodland garden. TEAS. *Adm £2 Chd free (Share to Barristers Benevolent Association®). Combined adm with **Clifton Hampden Manor** Sun April 3 (2.30-5.30). Combined adm with **Evelegh's, Long Wittenham** Sun Sept 18 (2-6). Private visits welcome March to Sept, please Tel 086 730 7702*

Longworth Gardens &❀ nr Kingston Bagpuize 7m W of Abingdon N off A420 Oxford Faringdon Rd. TEAS (at **Longworth Manor**) in aid of St Mary's Church. *Combined adm £2 Chd free. Mon May 30 (2-6)*

Haugh House (Mrs D Faulkner) 2 acres old shrub roses, mixed borders; unusual plants

Longworth Manor (Lt-Col & Mrs J Walton) Medium-size garden with tulips and borders; shrubs and ornamental ponds. C17 Cotswold stone house with good views over R. Thames. A wild flower meadow is now established

Loreto &✕❀ (Mr & Mrs R J Styles) Between Ewelme and Benson off B4009 NE of Wallingford. 5 acres; extensively replanted and developed since 1974. Emphasis on water gardens, shrubs and conifers, herbaceous and bedding plants. TEAS. *Adm £2 Chd free. Suns April 24, Aug 28, Mon Aug 29 (2-6)*

Lower Chilworth Farm &❀ (Mr & Mrs Michael Hedges) Milton Common is on A329 Thame to Wallingford Rd by junction 7 and 8 off M40 and signposted off A418 Thame to Oxford Rd. The farm is ½m NW of village on old A40 (line of poplar trees down drive). 1-acre informal garden in a lovely setting, incl walled, sunken and courtyard gardens, scree, herbaceous and shrub borders; water feature. Nature trail incl a 2-acre lake and old railway track. Dogs welcome on trail only. TEAS. *Adm £1 Chd free. Mon May 30, Sat June 25 (2-6)*

Magdalen College. See Oxford University Gardens

The Malt House ✄ (Mr & Mrs D F K Welsh) 59 Market Place, Henley-on-Thames, nr Town Hall. ½-acre unusual, imaginatively-designed town garden, featuring C16 malthouse, round lawn, beds of less common plants and shrubs. (Unsuitable for pushchairs or young children). TEAS in aid of Samaritans. *Adm £1 Chd free. Sun May 29 (2-6)*

Manor Barn House &❀ (Mr & Mrs Charles Swallow) Wendlebury. 12m NE of Oxford off A421 to Bicester. Small barn converted in 1979. Garden and field 3½ acres developed over last 15 years from neglected farmyard and adjoining land. Large pond, dug in 1985 and fed from roofs and high water table. Variety of rushes and aquatic plants, trout, crayfish. Rose walk, specimen trees and shrubs. Homemade TEAS, ice cream and plants for sale in aid of Wendlebury Church. *Adm £1 Chd 50p. Sun July 10 (2-6)*

Manor Farm &❀ (Sir Peter & Lady Parker), Old Minster Lovell, beautiful Cotswold village in Windrush valley. Off B4047 Witney-Burford rd; turn R at sign to Old Minster Lovell and Leafield; in ¼m cross Windrush bridge, turn R at Old Swan; no parking in village, follow signs to large free car park. 5-acre garden around small Cotswold farmhouse adjoining churchyard and ruins of Minster (open); mediaeval barns divide garden into sections; pools, informal herbaceous areas; shrubs and specie roses. C14 dovecote. Owner is author of book about her garden: 'Purest of Pleasures'. TEAS by WI. *Adm £1.50 Chd free. Sun June 26 (2-5)*

The Manor House &✄❀ (The Hon David Astor) Sutton Courtenay. 4m S of Abingdon. Out of Abingdon on the A415. Turn off to Culham – Sutton Courtenay. From A34 going N come into Milton Village take last rd on R to Sutton Courtenay. 10 acres of garden approx 100 acres of land. ½m R Thames Bank. TEAS. *Adm £1.50 Chd 50p. Sun May 8 (2-6)*

The Manor House ✄❀ (Mr & Mrs T G Hassall) 26 High St, Wheatley. Off A40 E of Oxford. 1½-acre garden of Elizabethan manor house; formal box walk, established fruit trees, incl espalier apples; herb garden, cottage garden with rose arches and a shrubbery with old roses. TEAS in aid of Wheatley Windmill Restoration Society. *Adm £1 Chd free. Sun June 26 (2-6)*

The Mill House, Stadhampton &❀ (Mr & Mrs F A Peet) A329/B480, 8m SE of Oxford. 1-acre family garden with old mill and stream. Mill not working but machinery largely intact and wheel turning with pumped water.

Parking on green; parking for disabled only at house. TEAS. *Adm £1 Chd free (Share to Stadhampton Church Restoration Fund®). Adm £1. Sun April 17 (2-5.30)*

The Mill House, Sutton Courtenay &✄❀ (Mrs J Stevens) S of Abingdon. Approx 8½ acres; R Thames runs through garden which is on several islands with mill pond and old paper mill. TEAS. *Adm £2 Chd £1; under 4's free. Suns April 3, June 26, Oct 2 (2-6)*

Mount Skippet &❀ (Dr & Mrs M A T Rogers) Ramsden, 4m N of Witney. At Xrds turn E towards Finstock; after 30yds, turn R (sign-post Mount Skippet). After 400yds turn L (No Through Way sign) for 75yds. 2 acres; 2 rock gardens; alpine house; stone troughs; shrubs; herbaceous beds; primulas; conservatory; many rare plants. Fine views. Cotswold stone house largely CI7. Teas for groups by prior arrangement. *Adm £1 Chd free. Private visits welcome April 1 to Sept 30, please* Tel 0993 868253

New College. See Oxford University Gardens

4 Northfield Cottages &❀ (Miss S E Bedwell) Water Eaton, nr Kidlington. A cottage garden of approx ¼-acre designed and planted over the last 6 years. Mainly herbaceous with some unusual plants and large greenhouse. *Adm £1 Chd free. Private visits welcome all year round, please* Tel 0865 378910

Nuffield Place &✄❀ (By kind permission of the Warden & Fellows of Nuffield College) Huntercombe. Signposted off A423 midway between Henley-on-Thames & Wallingford. Former home of Lord Nuffield, the founder of Morris Motors. 4-acre garden with mature trees, yew hedges, rose pergola and rockery. Laid out during and just after the First World War. Adjoining bluebell woods. Morris and Wolseley cars on display. TEAS. *Adm £1.50 Chd free. Sun May 16 (2-5)*

Nutford Lodge &❀ (Mrs P Elmore) In Longcot Village next to The King & Queen public house. 1m S of A420 between Faringdon and Shrivenham. 1½ acres with ornamental vegetable plot, herb and alpine rockeries, colour schemed borders, sculpture trail with many interesting features. An indoor gallery. *Adm 75p Chd free (Share to Headway in Oxford). Suns, Mons May 29, 30; Aug 28, 29 (2-6). Also private visits welcome, please* Tel 0793 782258

The Old Rectory, Albury &✄❀ (Mr & Mrs J Nowell-Smith). Nr Tiddington. 4m W of Thame, at end of cul-de-sac off A418 Wheatley-Thame rd. Approx 5 acres incl lawns and borders wooded walk around lake. TEAS and plants in aid of St Helens Church. *Adm £1 Chd free. Sun May 1 (2-6)*

¶**The Old Rectory, Brightwell Baldwin** &✄❀ (Mr & Mrs Donald Chilvers) 2m W of Watlington via Cuxham (B480) or 1½m E of Benson on B4009 and then signposted to Brightwell Baldwin; on R side, E of church 100yds. 1½-acre garden and parkland surrounding beautiful Georgian rectory. Open views to S over ha-ha. Formal garden layout with herb, rose and herbaceous beds, terracing and walls. Designed by owners and planted 1990, yet mature; rare breed sheep. Teas at village hall by C14 church. *Adm £1.50 Chd free. Sun Aug 7 (2-5.30)*

The Old Rectory, Coleshill & (Mr & Mrs Martin) 3m W of Faringdon. Coleshill (a Nat Trust village) is on B4019, midway between Faringdon and Highworth. Medium-sized garden; lawns and informal shrub beds; wide variety shrubs, inc old-fashioned roses; 40-yr-old standard wisteria. Distant views of Berkshire and Wiltshire Downs. House dates from late C14. TEAS. *Adm £1 Chd free. Suns April 17 (2-6), Sept 11 (2-5)*

The Old Rectory, Farnborough nr Wantage. See Berkshire

The Old Vicarage &❀ (Mrs T A Laurie) Weston-on-the-Green 4½m SW of Bicester, take Bletchingdon turn into village centre. 2½-acre old-fashioned vicarage garden imaginatively restored keeping its tranquil secluded atmosphere. Many unusual plants and colour combinations. Stream in a woodland walk and lily ponds. Something of interest for everyone. TEAS in aid of St Mary's Church. *Adm £1 Chd free. Mons May 30, Aug 29 (2-6)*

Oxford see also 23 Beech Croft Road, East Oxford, Headington, Iffley

Oxford University Gardens

Christ Church ✗ **Masters' Garden** Entrance on Christ Church Meadow (through War Memorial garden on St Aldates). Created in 1926, has herbaceous borders and a new border with some unusual shrubs. A walk past Pocock's Plane, an oriental plane planted 1636, leads through Cathedral garden to Deanery garden where Lewis Carroll's Alice played; Cheshire Cat's chestnut tree. *Adm 75p Chd free. Sun Aug 14 (2-5)*

Corpus Christi &✗ Entrance from Merton St or Christ Church **Fellows' garden**. Several small gardens and courtyards overlooking Christchurch meadows. Fellows private garden not normally open to the public. *Adm 75p. Sun Aug 14 (2-5)*

Exeter College ✗ **Rector's Lodgings** The Turl, between High & Broad Sts, Oxford. Small enclosed garden, recently replanted, herbaceous and shrubs, especially clematis. *Combined adm with* **New College** *£1.50 Chd free. Sun July 3 (2-5)*

Holywell Manor ✗ (Balliol College) Central Oxford at corner of Manor Rd and St Cross Rd on L of St Cross Church opp law library. College garden of about 1 acre, not normally open to the public. Imaginatively laid out 50 yrs ago around horse chestnut to give formal and informal areas. Mature ginkgo avenue, spinney with spring flowers and bulbs. *Adm 75p Chd free. Please tel or call at Porters lodge any time of the year.* Tel 0865 271501

Magdalen College and Fellows' Garden (and President's Garden not normally open to the public) &✗ High Street Oxford. Entrance in High St. 60 acres including deer park, college lawns, numerous trees 150-200 yrs old, notable herbaceous and shrub plantings; Magdalen Meadows containing the deer herd is surrounded by Addison's Walk, a tree lined circuit by the R Cherwell developed since the late C18. TEAS. *Adm £1.50 Child £1. Sun March 27 (11-5)*

New College ✗ **Warden's Garden** Entered from New College Lane, off Catte St. Secret walled garden, replanted 1988 with interesting mix of herbaceous and shrubs. *Adm £1 Chd free. Wed June 29. Combined adm with* **Exeter College** *£1.50. Sun July 3 (2-5)*

Queen's College ✗ **Fellows' Garden** High St. ½-acre with splendid herbaceous borders seen against high old stone walls; large ilex tree. Teas 43 St Giles (in their garden if fine). *Combined adm with* **Wadham College** *£1.50 Chd free. Sun July 24 (2-5)*

Rewley House &✗ (Oxford University Dept for Continuing Education) Wellington Sq., St John Street. Roof Garden, 60ft × 26ft, and courtyard gardens, planted by townscaper, Jeanne Bliss, with variegated shrubs, climbers, trailing plants in mobile boxes on wheels. Maintained by Oxford Gardeners under the direction of Christopher Herdman. TEA. *Adm 75p Chd free. Sun July 17 (2-5)*

¶**Templeton College** &❀ Kennington. The College is signposted off the A423 S ring rd and Abingdon Rd out of Oxford. It is situated in the triangle between A34 and A423. Landscaped for ease of maintenance by Alan Mitchell, well known author of Collins 'A Field Guide to the Trees of Britain & Northern Europe', the College's 37 acres have been planted with more than 20,000 trees during the past 24yrs. Alan's mastery of colour and shape should be shown at its best in the Autumn and the entire site is ringed by footpaths. Informal pond and cottage garden plantings designed by Stephanie Carter to harmonise with the uncompromised modern main buildings and the more traditional graduate residences at Egrove Farmhouse. TEA. *Adm £1.50 OAPs £1 Chd free. Sun Sept 25 (2-5.30)*

Trinity College &✗❀ **President's Garden** Entrance in Broad St. Surrounded by high old stone walls, recently re-designed, has mixed borders of herbaceous and shrubs, and statuary. Historic main college gardens with specimen trees inc 200-yr-old forked catalpa and splendid fraxinus, fine long herbaceous border and handsome garden quad originally designed by Wren. TEAS in aid of Flexicare. *Adm 75p Chd free. Sun Aug 14 (2-5)*

University Arboretum ✗❀ 6m S of Oxford on A423, 400yds S of Nuneham Courtenay. 55 acres incl informal rhododendron walks, camellia, bamboo and acer collections, natural woodland and oak woodland, meadow with pond and associated aquatics and marginals; fine collection of mature conifers; many 150 yrs old. Staff available to answer queries. Large sale of unusual plants. Plant stall in aid of Oxford University Botanic Garden. *Adm £1 Chd free. Sun June 5 (2-6)*

Wadham College: **&✗ **Fellows' Private Garden & Warden's Garden Parks Rd. 5 acres, best known for trees and herbaceous borders. In the Fellows' main garden superb purple beech, fine ginkgo and Magnolia acuminata, etc; in the Back Quadrangle very large Tilia tomentosa 'Petiolaris'; in the Warden's garden an ancient tulip tree; in the Fellows' private garden Civil War embankment with period fruit tree cultivars, recently established shrubbery with unusual trees and ground cover amongst older plantings. Teas 43 St Giles (July 24 only). *Adm £1 Chd free. Sun March 27. Combined adm with* **Queen's College** *£1.50, Sun July 24 (2-5)*

Regular Openers. See head of county section.

Wolfson College &❀ End of Linton Rd, off Banbury Rd, between city centre and Summertown shops. 9 acres by R Cherwell; garden developed in recent years with comprehensive plant collection tolerant of alkaline soils, grown in interesting and varied habitats both formal and informal, around a framework of fine mature trees; award winning building designed by Powell & Moya; President's garden. TEAS. *Adm 75p Chd free. Sun July 24 (2-6)*

Worcester College ❀ **Provost's Garden** Entrance through lodge at junction of Beaumont St and Walton St. The college has 26 acres of grounds, landscaped in early C19 with a large naturalised lake. The garden is not normally open to the public and comprises a rose garden, wooded lakeside walk and orchards. *Adm £1 Chd free. Sun July 24 2-6)*

Quarry Bank House &❀ (Mr & Mrs D J Smith) nr Tackley. 2m E of Woodstock. From A423 take A4095 to Bicester; entrance at bottom of Gibraltar Hill on sharp bend of river bridge. 4¾ acres with abundance of early spring flowers in sheltered situation on R. Cherwell; lawns, fine cedar, orchard and banks of trees and shrubs; attractive walks in natural quarry setting. TEAS in aid of Bletchingdon Church. *Adm £1 Chd free. Sun April 10 (2-6)*

Queen's College see Oxford University Gardens

Querns &❀❀ (Mr M & the Hon Mrs Whitfeld) Goring Heath. 3m NE of Pangbourne. Take B4526 from A4074 Reading-Oxford Rd. After ½m follow signs. 2-acre garden: shrub and herbaceous borders, rose garden, shrub rose garden, courtyard and new formal pond. Listed house dating from early C16 with large thatched C17 barn. TEAS. *Adm £1 Chd free. Sun June 26 (2-6)*

Rewley House see Oxford University Gardens

Rofford Manor &❀❀ (Mr & Mrs J L Mogford) Little Milton. 10m SE of Oxford. 1m from Little Milton on Chalgrove Rd. Signposted Rofford only. 2 acres of gardens, within old walls laid out since 1985. Vegetable, herb, rose and swimming pool gardens. Box garden with raised pool. Yew hedges and pleached limes. Twin herbaceous borders planted Autumn 1989 flanking lawn leading to recently constructed ha-ha. TEAS. *Adm £1.50 Chd free. Sun Sept 11 (2-6)*

Salford Gardens ❀ 2m W of Chipping Norton. Off A44 Oxford-Worcester. TEAS. *Combined adm £1.50 Chd free. Sat June 25 (2-6). Also open 1st Tuesday of month April to Sept (10-4)*

  Old Rectory &❀ (Mr & Mrs N M Chambers) Shrub roses, herbaceous and foliage plants; shrubs; ground cover. Kitchen garden.

  Willow Tree Cottage ❀ (Mr & Mrs J Shapley) Small walled twin gardens; one created by owners since 1979 with shrub and herbaceous borders, many clematis; other created 1985 from old farmyard with heathers and large alpine garden. Featured in 'Successful Gardening'

Shotover House &❀ (Lt-Col Sir John Miller) Wheatley, 6m E of Oxford on A40. Bus: Oxford-Thame or Oxford-High Wycombe-London; alight Islip turn. Large unaltered landscape garden with ornamental temples, lawns and specimen trees. Also small collection of rare cattle, sheep and birds. TEAS (in arcade with view of lake). *Adm £1 Chd free. Sun April 17 (2-6)*

Shucklets ❀❀ (Dr & Mrs G Garton) High Street Ramsden. 3m N of Witney off B4022, near centre of village. Plantsman's garden of 2 acres, with a variety of different areas: rock garden, raised beds, troughs; foliage plants, shrubs, old-fashioned roses; ornamental vegetable garden, small vineyard. *Adm £1 Chd free. Private visits welcome April 1 to Sept 30, please Tel 0993 868659*

Shutford Gardens ❀❀ An unspoilt village 5m W of Banbury, between A422 to Stratford and B4035 to Shipston. TEAS. *Combined adm £2 Chd free. Sun July 24 (2-6)*

  ¶**Beggars Barn** ❀ (Mr & Mrs James Perry) Out of village at bottom of hill on rd to Wroxton. Over 6 acres comprising a mixture of formal gardens and parkland incl a lake, pond and brook

  Fiveways Cottage (Dr & Mrs M R Aldous) Just over ½ acre in present form started 1986. Essentially cottage garden style, with shrubs, roses and many herbaceous plants, small fish pond edged by alpine bed and troughs, many trees still immature

  Shutford Manor ❀ (Mr & Mrs N D Cadbury) 1½-acre walled garden of dramatic C16 house with pastoral view. Yellow and white border; formal beds with modern shrubs roses; avenue of poplars

Sibford Ferris Gardens ❀ Near the Warwickshire border, S of B4035 (Banbury 6½m, Shipston-on-Stour 7½m). TEAS in aid of Sibford Primary School PTA. *Combined adm £1 Chd free. Sun, Wed May 22, 25 (2-6)*

  Back Acre ❀ (Mr & Mrs F A Lamb) Almost an acre, much of which is wild woodland and rough grass with wild flowers; rockery and pond, constructed about 100 years ago and restored over the last few years

  Home Close (Mr & Mrs P A Randall) Cotswold stone house fronting formal 1¼-acre garden designed by Baillie-Scott in 1911, under restoration. Courtyard with ornamental fountain and Roman-style stone recesses. Terraced garden, large variety of shrubs including rare species

  The Old Court House (Mr & Mrs R Springate) A small garden of unusual design and sub-divisions. Hidden courtyard, many pot plants and other decorative features

Sibford Gower Gardens Near the Warwickshire border, S of B4035 (Banbury 7m, Shipston-on-Stour 7m) Superlative views and numerous intriguing tucked away lanes are features of this village. TEAS **Sun, Wed June 19, 22** (2-6) *Combined adm £1 Chd free*

  Handywater Farm ❀❀ (Mr & Mrs W B Colquhoun) ½m N of Sibford Gower on rd to Epwell; 1½ acre family garden in process of creation since 1980. Lovely setting in open rolling countryside. Westerly sloping lawns, stream and ponds, shrub and herbaceous beds

Meadow Cottage &&& (Mr & Mrs Roger Powell) 6 The Colony. At S end of village. A 1.3-acre garden started from a field in 1988. Large 'shrubaceous' borders; over 1300 different plants; many unusual. Conifers; shrub roses and alpines in raised beds; budding arboretum and series of waterfalls leading to stream. Views

Sun July 10 *(2-6) Combined adm £1.50 Chd free*

Carters Yard (Mr & Mrs W J S Clutterbuck) Next to Wykeham Arms. ⅓-acre very private cottage garden. Various beds and rockeries in soft colours

The Manor House & (Mr & Mrs M Edwards) Opp Wykeham Arms. Completely reconstructed May 1989, the gardens (under 1 acre) are already well established and complement the romantic atmosphere of this recently renovated rambling thatched manor house

Meadow Cottage (as described for earlier date)

Temple Close &&& (Mr & Mrs E Jones) E of Wykeham Arms. 1¼ acres with rockery, various beds of shrubs, roses, perennials and herbs; paved stream-side walk running through extensive water garden between two ponds with fountains; pets paddock; good view

Souldern Gardens & Between Banbury (8m) and Bicester (7m) off B4100. 5 gardens in picturesque 'Best Kept' prizewinning village. TEAS. *Combined adm £2 Chd free (Share to Souldern Trust). Sun April 3 (2-6)*

The Barn &&& (Mr J Talbot) Sheltered garden with pond; wide mixed borders

Great House Close &&& (Mrs C E Thornton) Long, varied gardens and orchard framed by old farm buildings

The Old Forge (Mr & Mrs D Duthie) Resourceful, densely planted cottage garden with stone walling

Souldern House & (Maj & Mrs A H Gray) Walled garden round C17 house; gazebo dated 1706, ancient yew hedge; bantams

Souldern Manor & (Mr & Dr C Sanders) 25 acres of C17 house with much fresh development. Linked ponds, rock garden, waterfall, fountains, temple, pavilions and view of Cherwell valley are enhanced by many newly planted mature trees. Children's play area and pony rides

South Newington Gardens A small village 1½m from Bloxham, nr Banbury on A361 to Chipping Norton. It has a fine church, with superb mediaeval wall paintings. TEA at the village hall with stalls. 3 gardens within easy walking distance. *Combined adm £1.50. Sun June 5 (2-6)*

Applegarth &&& (Mr & Mrs Kenneth Butcher) ¾-acre cottage garden with a rose walk featuring old-fashioned roses and lavenders; herbaceous borders and mixed borders with some unusual shrubs and young trees; small water garden and pond

The Barn &&& (Mrs Rosemary Clark) Green Lane. 1 acre of lawns and mixed borders with outdoor chess game, croquet lawn, vine walk and vegetable patch

The Little Forge & (Mr M B Pritchard) Small garden with shrubs; trees and vegetable patch

Sparsholt Manor (Sir Adrian & Lady Judith Swire) Off B4507 Ashbury Rd 3½m W of Wantage. Spring garden, lakes and wilderness. *Adm £1 Chd free (Share to St John Ambulance, Wantage Division®). Mon May 2 (2-6)*

Stansfield &&& (Mr & Mrs D Keeble) 49 High St, Stanford-in-the-Vale. 3½m SE of Faringdon. Turn off A417 opp Vale Garage into High St 300yds. Park in street. Plantsman's 1¼-acre garden on alkaline soil. Wide range of plants, many uncommon. Scree bed, sinks and troughs, damp garden, herbaceous borders, ornamental grasses. Copse underplanted with hellebores and shade loving plants. Aromatic plants. Unusual trees and shrubs. Yr-round interest. Wide range of plants for sale. TEAS. *Adm £1 Chd free. Every Tues April 5 to Sept 20 (10-4) Suns June 5, July 24 (2-6). Private visits also welcome, please* Tel 0367 710340

Stanton Harcourt Manor &&& (Mr Crispin & The Hon Mrs Gascoigne) W of Oxford on B4449. Picturesque stone manor house with unique C15 Great Kitchen, Chapel and Pope's Tower. Formal gardens leading to woodland area with remains of moat and medieval stew ponds. *Adm House and garden £3 Chd/OAP's £2. Garden only £1.50 Chd/OAP's £1. Thurs April 14, 28, May 12, 26, June 9, 23, July 7, 21, Aug 4, 18, 25, Sept 8, 22, Suns April 3, 24, May 1, 15, 29, June 12, 26, July 10, 24, Aug 7, 21, 28, Sept 11, 25, Bank hol Mons April 4, May 2, 30, Aug 29. For NGS Suns April 17, June 26 (2-6)*

Steeple & Middle Aston Gardens. Beautiful stone villages midway between Oxford & Banbury, ½m off A4260. Villages bordering Cherwell valley; interesting church and winding lanes with a variety of charming stone houses and cottages. Map available at all gardens. TEAS at Canterbury House. *Combined adm £2 Chd free. Sun June 5 (1-6)*

Canterbury House (Mr & Mrs M G Norris) Former rectory in 2-acre garden intersected by walls. Mature trees, herbaceous borders, lavender, herb garden, newly planted rose garden

Home Farm House &&& (Mr & Mrs T J G Parsons) Opp Middle Aston House, ¾m N of Steeple Aston, opp Middle Aston House. 1-acre informal garden surrounding C17 farmhouse, fine view. Mixed planting, incl unusual perennials, shrubs and roses. Vegetables and Jacob sheep. Interesting small nursery. *Private visits welcome May to Sept, please* Tel 0869 40666

Kralingen (Mr & Mrs Roderick Nicholson) 2-acre informal garden designed for low maintenance. Great variety of interesting trees and shrubs; water garden and wild flower area

Middle Aston House && (Mr & Mrs B C Box) ¾m N of Steeple Aston. 20 acres of grounds landscaped in C18 by William Kent, incl 2 lakes, granary and icehouse

Rowans &&&& (Mr & Mrs M J Clist) The Dickredge, opp White Lion. An acre of orchard and mixed garden, incl shrubs, herbaceous borders, alpines, vegetables and small streamside area

Willow Cottage & (Mr & Mrs M Vivian) The Dickredge, opp White Lion. Hornton stone cottage with ½-acre garden. Old-fashioned shrub roses, many unusual plants in garden and conservatory. Fish pond with Koi

Stonewalls &&& (Mr & Mrs B Shafighian) Hempton. 1½m W of Deddington on B4031. A plantsman's garden of 1½ acres divided into many interesting areas, incl shrubbery, herbaceous border, conifer and heather bed, nearly 200 clematis and climbers. Sunken pool. TEA. *Adm £1 Chd free. Sun July 3 (2-6)*

Stratton Audley Gardens &✿✿ 3m NE of Bicester, off A421 to Buckingham. Village dates from Roman times. Church is largely mediaeval with spectacular late C17 tomb. *Combined adm £1 Chd free (Share to Helen House Hospice®). Sun June 5, Wed June 8 (2-6)*
  1 Church Cottages (Mr & Mrs L Sweetman) About ½-acre. A proper country cottage garden with rockery pools and stonework, vegetables, seasonal bedding, orchids
  Mallories (Mr P Boyd) Mainly walled garden of ¾ acre behind row of C17 cottages converted to house. Sunny and shady herbaceous borders, old roses and other shrubs, wall plants and climbers, small conservatory. A new border is being planted this year

Swalcliffe Gardens W of Banbury on B4035 halfway between Banbury and Shipston-on-Stour. TEAS. *Adm £1 Chd free. Sun June 27 (2-6)*
  The Manor House ✿ (Mr & Mrs F Hitching) Swalcliffe next to church. Large garden around C13 Manor house (not open). Mixed borders, interesting plants, sunken garden with shrub roses, walled herb garden. Fine church, all pre C15, early tithe barn housing farm implement collection adjacent. Parking at Tithe Barn
  Sparrow Hall &✿ (Mrs J Panks) ½-acre walled garden, planted for easy care with wide collection miniature conifers, heathers and alpines; English/Japanese effect. Large Patio with stone troughs, etc planted for seasonal display. *Private visits welcome all year round, please* Tel 0295 78433

Swerford Park (Mr & Mrs J W Law) 4m NE of Chipping Norton, just off A361 to Banbury, ½m W of Swerford Church. In extensive parkland setting with lakeside walks, garden of Georgian house overlooks spectacular wooded valley with series of lakes linked by waterfalls. Approach along front drive where signed; parking at rear only, may not be very close. TEAS at **The Yews**, ½m E of Church. *Adm £1 Chd free. Mon May 30 (2-6)*

Swinbrook Gardens &✿ 2½m E of Burford, off A40. Unspoilt Cotswold village in Windrush Valley with interesting church. TEAS. *Combined adm £1.50 or £1 each garden Chd free (Share to Swinbrook PCC®). Sun July 10 (2-6)*
  Swinbrook House (Mr & Mrs J D Mackinnon) 1½m N of Swinbrook on Shipton-under-Wychwood Rd. Large garden; herbaceous border; shrubs; shrub roses; large kitchen garden; fine views. Picnics allowed
  Swinbrook Manor Farm (Mrs S Freund) Medium-sized garden in exceptionally pretty surroundings next to church

Swyncombe House &✿ (Mr W J Christie-Miller) Cookley Green on B481 Nettlebed-Watlington. Tranquil setting in a large park; rare trees; many mature flowering shrubs and spring bulbs in woodland. C11 church in grounds. TEA (in aid of St Botolph's Church). *Adm £1 Chd free. Sun April 10 (2-7)*

Tadmarton Gardens 5m SW of Banbury on B4035. Ploughmans lunches and teas at village hall in aid of St Nicholas Church, Tadmarton. *Combined adm £1.50. Sun, Mon Aug 28, 29 (12-5)*

Tadmarton Manor &✿ (Mr & Mrs R K Asser) Old established 2½-acre garden; beautiful views of unspoilt countryside; great variety of perennial plants and shrubs; tunnel arbour; C15 barn and C18 dovecote
Yeomans (Mrs A E Pedder) For description and other dates see **Yeomans** in main text

Taynton House &✿✿ (Mr & Mrs David Mackenzie) Taynton, off A424 Burford to Stow-on-the-Wold. Medium-sized garden behind listed stone house in delightful Cotswold village with interesting church. Stream and copse with thousands of daffodils and spring flowers. TEAS. *Adm £1 Chd free (Share to St John's Church, Taynton®). Sun March 27 (2-6)*

Templeton College see Oxford University Gardens

Thames-Side Court &✿ (Mr U E Schwarzenbach) Shiplake. Take A4155 (Reading Rd) out of Henley-on-Thames to Shiplake memorial (approx 2 mls). Turn into Station Rd go over level Xing. Turn immed L into Bolney Rd, and continue to the end of this rd. Spend hrs in these 8 acres of outstanding riverside gardens; sunken, Japanese and water gardens, dramatic tropical glasshouse, greenhouses. Children and adults are invited to ride on superb steam trains along a magnificently landscaped track and to have the chance to play croquet and boule. TEAS. *Adm £5 Chd £2.50. Sun Aug 14 (11-5)*

Towersey Manor &✿ (Mr & Mrs U D Barnett) Towersey, 1¼m SE of Thame, 300 yds down Manor Rd from Xrds in middle of village. Main 2-acre garden lying behind house, has all been laid out and planted within last 18 years. Formal hornbeam hedges frame smaller informal areas incorporating many shrubs, trees and old-fashioned and modern shrub roses. TEAS Sun, TEA Wed in fine old timbered barn. *Adm £1 Chd free. Sun, Weds June 19, 22 (2-6)*

Town Farm Cottage &✿✿ (Mr & Mrs J Clark) 4m S of Thame. 4m NE of Watlington. 1½m NE of junction 6, M40 on B4009. 1-acre colourful garden developed over 6 yrs by present owners. Herbaceous borders, rockeries, scree beds and shrubs, rare English native black poplar trees by small lake. Many unusual plants. TEAS. *Adm £1 Chd free. Sun June 19 (2-6). Private visits also welcome April to Aug, please* Tel 0844 352152

Trinity College see Oxford University Gardens

Tusmore Park &✿ (Tusmore Park Holdings) On A43, Baynards Green 2m, Brackley 3½m. About 20-acres of lawns, herbaceous borders, woodland garden and terraces; 6-acre lake, 3 greenhouses. TEAS. *Adm £1 Chd free. Sun July 17 (2-6)*

University Arboretum see Oxford University Gardens

Wadham College see Oxford University Gardens

Wardington Gardens 5m NE of Banbury. TEAS May only. *Combined adm £2.50 Chd free. Sun May 22*
  Pettifers &✿✿ (Mr J & the Hon Mrs Price) Lower Wardington C17 village house. 1-acre garden frames an exceptional view of sheep pastures and wooded hills. A lot of new planting, with some areas reaching maturity. Unusual plants for sale (2-6). *Also Suns June 12, July 31. Adm £1 Chd free*

Wardington Manor &❀ (The Lord Wardington) 5-acre garden with topiary, rock garden, flowering shrub walk to pond. Carolean manor house 1665 (2-5.30). *Private visits by groups also welcome adm £1.50, please* Tel 0295 750202

Waterperry Gardens &❀❀ 2½m from Wheatley M40 Junction 8. 50m from London, 62m from Birmingham, 9m E of Oxford. Gardens well signed locally with Tourist Board 'rose' symbol. 20-acres; ornamental gardens, nurseries, parkland; many interesting plants; shrub, herbaceous and alpine nurseries; glasshouses and comprehensive fruit section. High quality plant centre, garden shop **(Tel 0844 339226)**. TEA SHOP. Saxon church with famous glasses and brasses in grounds. *Adm Gardens & Nurseries £2.20 OAPs £1.70 Chd £1 under 10 free. Open daily. Coach parties by appt only* Tel 0844 339254. ▲*For NGS (Share to NCCPG). Suns June 5, Aug 7 (10-6)*

Weald Manor see Bampton & Weald Gardens

Westwell Gardens 2m SW of Burford; from A40 Burford-Cheltenham, turn L after ½m on narrow rd signposted Westwell. Unspoilt hamlet with delightful church. TEAS. *Combined adm £2 Chd 50p (Share to St Mary's Church Westwell®). Suns May 1, July 3 (2-6.30)*
> **The Dower House** ❀❀ (Mr & Mrs Paul Moore) Incl box garden; orchard; young arboretum of specialist trees; river bed; tubs; hanging baskets and herbaceous borders
> **Westwell Manor** ❀❀ (Mr & Mrs T H Gibson) 6 acres surrounding old Cotswold manor house; knot and water gardens; potager; shrub roses; herbaceous borders; topiary; moonlight garden

White's Farm House &❀ (Dr & Mrs M Shone) Letcombe Bassett 3m SW of Wantage. Take B4507 signed Ashbury, then through Letcombe Regis. 2½ acres; mixed borders; wild garden with 30 yrs growth of chalk-tolerant trees, shrubs, unusual herbaceous plants, summer bulbs. Gravel scree bed, plants in pots and tubs, pond, playground and monster adventure walk. TEAS in C18 barn. *Adm £1.50 Chd free. Suns June 19, July 17 (2-6)*

Wick Hall & Nurseries &❀❀ (Mr & Mrs P Drysdale) Between Abingdon & Radley on Audlett Drive. Parking for disabled at house, some off-street parking. Approx 10 acres lawns and wild garden; topiary; ericaceous bed; pond garden; rockeries; walled garden enclosing knot garden. Young arboretum. Early C18 house, barn and greenhouses garden restored and developed since 1982. TEAS. *Adm £1 Chd free. Sun April 24 (2-5)*

Wilcote House &❀ (The Hon C E & Mrs Cecil) Finstock. Between Finstock & North Leigh. East of B4022 Witney-Charlbury Road. 4 acres set in parkland surrounding an early C17-C19 Cotswold stone house. Shrub and herbaceous borders, old-fashioned rose garden and 40yd laburnum walk (planted 1984). Old orchard being replanted as an arboretum. Spring bulbs, flowering trees, sheep and lovely views. TEAS. *Adm £1 Chd free (Share to Homelife DGAA & British Legion®). Sun June 26. For NGS Suns*

May 15, Oct 9 (2-5.30). Private visits also welcome, please contact Mr Pollard on Tel 0993 868 606

Wolfson College see Oxford University Gardens

Wood Croft ❀❀ (St Cross College) Foxcombe Lane, Boars Hill, S of Oxford. From ring rd follow signs to Wootton and Boars Hill. From junction at top Hinksey Hill, house first on L. 1½ acres designed and planted by the late Prof G E Blackman FRS. Rhododendrons, camellias, azaleas, many varieties primula in woodland and surrounding natural pond; fine trees. TEA. *Adm £1 Chd free (Share to Royal Marsden Hospital Development Appeal®). Sun May 22 (2-6)*

Woodperry House ❀❀ (Mr & Mrs Robert Lush) nr Stanton St John. 4m E of Oxford off B4027 on road from Headington to Horton-cum-Studley. C18th house of architectural interest (not open). Approx 5 acres including lime tree avenue, formal garden, 1 acre of walled vegetable garden. Large herbaceous and shrub borders. Water gardens under construction. Good views and country walks (Aug). TEAS in aid of Stanton St John Village Fund (May) in aid of Cancer Research Campaign (Aug). *Adm £1.50 Chd free. Suns May 15, Aug 21 (2-5)*

Wootton Place &❀❀ (Mr & Mrs H Dyer) 3m N of Woodstock off A34, next to Church. Laid out by Capability Brown; 150 varieties of daffodil, very fine trees incl huge ancient walnut; walled garden. TEAS. *Adm £1.50 Chd free (Share to Sir Michael Sobell House Hospice®). Sun April 10 (2-5.30)*

Worcester College see Oxford University Gardens

Wroxton Gardens 3m NW of Banbury off A422. Grounds of Wroxton Abbey open free. Teas at village fete May. TEAS **Laurels Farm** July. *Combined adm £1. Mon May 30, Sun July 31 (1-6)*
> **6 The Firs Stratford Rd** &❀ (Mr & Mrs D J Allen) Approx ⅓-acre family garden with island beds, shrubs, herbaceous perennials and rockery incl collection of 120 cranesbill geraniums
> **Laurels Farm** ❀ (Mr & Mrs R Fox) ½-acre with island beds, shrubs, old roses and herbaceous perennials. TEAS. *Adm 80p. Also open Sun Aug 1*

Yeomans ❀❀ (Mrs A E Pedder) Tadmarton 5m SW of Banbury on B4035. Small garden on 4 levels, featured in 'Easy Plants for Difficult Places' by Geoffrey Smith; C16 thatched cottage. Colourful from spring to autumn; wide variety annuals, perennials, shrubs; many climbers inc roses, clematis; shrub roses with hips. *Adm 70p Chd free (Share to Katharine House Hospice Trust®). April to Sept by appointment only* Tel 0295 78285. *Also open with* **Tadmarton Gardens**. *Sun, Mon Aug 28, 29*

The Yews &❀❀ (Mr & Mrs F W Timms) Swerford, a pretty village 5m NE of Chipping Norton, just off A361 to Banbury. 2-acre walled garden with mature trees and many flowering shrubs; water gardens, waterfall, fountains; swimming pool. TEAS from 2pm in aid of British Diabetic Association. *Adm £1.50 Chd free under 12yrs. Sun, Mon May 29 (2-6), 30 (12-6)*

Powys

See separate Welsh section beginning on page 291

Rutland
See Leicestershire

Shropshire

Hon County Organisers:	Mrs J H M Stafford, The Old Rectory, Fitz, Shrewsbury SY4 3AS Tel 0743 850555 Mr & Mrs James Goodall, Rectory Cottage, Chetton, Bridgnorth, Shropshire WV16 6UF
Hon County Treasurer:	Mrs P Trevor-Jones, Preen Manor, Church Preen, nr Church Stretton SY6 7LG

DATES OF OPENING

By appointment
For telephone numbers and other details see garden descriptions. Private visits welcomed

Acton Round, Morville, nr Bridgnorth
Adcote School, Little Ness
Ashford Manor, nr Ludlow
Badger Farmhouse, Badger, nr Shifnal
Bakers House, Bromley, nr Bridgnorth
Brownhill House, Ruyton XI Towns
Church Bank Westbury
Cricklewood Cottage, Minsterley
Farley House, Much Wenlock
Field House, Clee St Margaret, nr Ludlow
Hatton Grange, Shifnal
Haye House, nr Bridgnorth
Herbert Lewis Garden, Merton Nurseries, Bicton
Limeburners, Ironbridge
Lower Hall, Worfield
The Patch, Acton Pigot
Preen Manor, nr Church Stretton
Radnor Cottage, Clunton
Ruthall Manor, Ditton Priors
Swallow Hayes, Albrighton

Regular openings
For details see garden descriptions

Nordybank Nurseries, nr Ludlow. Open every Sun, Mon & Wed June 5 to Aug 28
Weston Park, Shifnal. Open Easter to Sept
Wollerton Old Hall, Market Drayton. Every Fri June 3 to Aug 26

February 27 Sunday
Erway Farm House, Dudleston Heath
March 27 Sunday
Erway Farm House, Dudleston Heath

April 2 Saturday
Erway Farm House, Dudleston Heath
April 3 Sunday
Erway Farm House, Dudleston Heath
April 4 Monday
Badger Farmhouse, Badger, nr Shifnal
Erway Farm House, Dudleston Heath
The Patch, Acton Pigot
April 10 Sunday
New Hall, Eaton-under-Heywood
April 17 Sunday
New Hall, Eaton-under-Heywood
April 24 Sunday
Erway Farm House, Dudleston Heath
Swallow Hayes, Albrighton
May 1 Sunday
Morville Hall Gardens, nr Bridgnorth
May 2 Monday
Millichope Park, Munslow
May 8 Sunday
Adcote School, Little Ness
Gatacre Park, nr Bridgnorth
Swallow Hayes, Albrighton
May 11 Wednesday
Cricklewood Cottage, Minsterley
May 15 Sunday
Astley Abbotts House, Bridgnorth
Brownhill House, Ruyton XI Towns
Gatacre Park, nr Bridgnorth
May 16 Monday
Mawley Hall, Cleobury Mortimer
May 21 Saturday
Peplow Hall, Hodnet
May 22 Sunday
Adcote School, Little Ness
Bitterley Court, Ludlow
Hatton Grange, Shifnal
The Lyth, Ellesmere
Peplow Hall, Hodnet
Willey Park, Broseley
May 28 Saturday
Brownhill House, Ruyton XI Towns
May 29 Sunday
Brownhill House, Ruyton XI Towns

Erway Farm House, Dudleston Heath
Longnor Hall, nr Dorrington
Walcot Hall, Lydbury North
May 30 Monday
Dudmaston, nr Bridgnorth
Longnor Hall, nr Dorrington
Oteley, Ellesmere
Walcot Hall, Lydbury North
June 2 Thursday
Preen Manor, nr Church Stretton
June 5 Sunday
Adcote School, Little Ness
Limeburners, Ironbridge
The Old Vicarage, Cardington
June 8 Wednesday
Cricklewood Cottage, Minsterley
June 12 Sunday
The Old Rectory, Fitz
The Old Vicarage, Cardington
June 14 Tuesday
The Patch, Acton Pigot
Weston Park, Shifnal
June 18 Saturday
Acton Round, Morville, nr Bridgnorth
Fairfield, Oldbury
June 19 Sunday
Acton Round, Morville, nr Bridgnorth ‡
Adcote School, Little Ness
2 Beacon Hill, Monkhopton ‡
Bitterley Court, Ludlow
Brownhill House, Ruyton XI Towns
Fairfield, Oldbury
Herbert Lewis Garden, Merton Nurseries, Bicton
The Old Vicarage, Cardington
June 20 Monday
Mawley Hall, Cleobury Mortimer
June 22 Wednesday
Morville Hall Gardens, nr Bridgnorth
June 23 Thursday
Preen Manor, nr Church Stretton
June 25 Saturday
Ruthall Manor, Ditton Priors
Whittington Village Gardens, nr Oswestry
June 26 Sunday
Benthall Hall, Broseley

David Austin Roses Ltd, nr
Wolverhampton
Erway Farm House, Dudleston
Heath
Field House, Clee St Margaret, nr
Ludlow
Millichope Park, Munslow
The Old Vicarage, Cardington
Whittington Village Gardens, nr
Oswestry
Wollerton Old Hall, Market Drayton

July 1 Friday
Moortown, nr Wellington

July 2 Saturday
Moortown, nr Wellington

July 3 Sunday
Herbert Lewis Garden, Merton
Nurseries, Bicton
Moortown, nr Wellington
The Old Vicarage, Cardington

July 6 Wednesday
Herbert Lewis Garden, Merton
Nurseries, Bicton

July 7 Thursday
Preen Manor, nr Church Stretton

July 10 Sunday
Harnage Farm, Cound,
Shrewsbury ‡
The Mill Cottage, Cound,
Shrewsbury ‡
The Old Vicarage, Cardington

July 13 Wednesday
Burford House Gardens, nr

Tenbury Wells
Cricklewood Cottage, Minsterley

July 16 Saturday
Brownhill House, Ruyton XI Towns

July 17 Sunday
Brownhill House, Ruyton XI Towns
The Old Vicarage, Cardington

July 18 Monday
Mawley Hall, Cleobury Mortimer

July 19 Tuesday
Weston Park, Shifnal

July 21 Thursday
Preen Manor, nr Church Stretton

July 24 Sunday
Astley Abbotts House, Bridgnorth
Herbert Lewis Garden, Merton
Nurseries, Bicton
Linley Hall, nr Bishop's Castle

July 30 Saturday
Church Bank, Westbury

July 31 Sunday
Church Bank, Westbury
Erway Farm House, Dudleston
Heath

August 6 Saturday
Hodnet Hall Gardens, nr Market
Drayton

August 7 Sunday
Herbert Lewis Garden, Merton
Nurseries, Bicton
Wollerton Old Hall, Market
Drayton

August 8 Monday
Hawkstone Hall, Shrewsbury

August 9 Tuesday
Hawkstone Hall, Shrewsbury

August 10 Wednesday
Cricklewood Cottage, Minsterley

August 13 Saturday
Hodnet Hall Gardens, nr Market
Drayton

August 17 Wednesday
Burford House Gardens, nr
Tenbury Wells

August 28 Sunday
Erway Farm House, Dudleston
Heath
Herbert Lewis Garden, Merton
Nurseries, Bicton
Stottesdon Village Gardens

August 29 Monday
Stottesdon Village Gardens

September 11 Sunday
Brownhill House, Ruyton XI Towns

September 14 Wednesday
Burford House Gardens, nr
Tenbury Wells
Cricklewood Cottage, Minsterley

September 25 Sunday
Erway Farm House, Dudleston
Heath
Oteley, Ellesmere

October 2 Sunday
Preen Manor, nr Church Stretton

DESCRIPTIONS OF GARDENS

Acton Round ⚭❀ (Mr & Mrs Hew Kennedy) 6m W of Bridgnorth. A458 Morville-Shrewsbury, 2m after Morville turn L (W). 1½-acre garden with yew hedges; rose, herbaceous and newly planted borders; various follies; attractive church and beautiful early Georgian house (not open). TEAS. *Adm £1.50 Chd £1 (Share to Acton Round Church®). Sat, Sun June 18, 19 (2-6.30). Garden also open by appt Tel 0746 31203*

Adcote School ⚭ (Adcote School Educational Trust Ltd) Little Ness, 8m NW of Shrewsbury via A5 to Montford Bridge, turn off NE follow signs to Little Ness. 20-acres; fine trees inc beeches, tulip trees, oaks (American and Evergreen); atlas cedars, Wellingtonia etc; rhododendrons, azaleas; small lake; landscaped garden. House (part shown) designed by Norman Shaw RA; Grade 1 listed building; William Morris windows; De Morgan tiles. TEAS. *Adm £1 Acc chd free. Suns May 8, 22 June 5, 19 (2-5). Other times strictly by appt only Tel 0939 260202*

Ashford Manor ⚭❀ (Kit Hall Esq) Ashford Carbonel, 2¾m S of Ludlow. E of A49 Ludlow-Leominster. Garden of 2-acres, herbaceous foliage and shrubs grown in the hope of maintaining interest through the entire year, hence very few flowers. Worked entirely by owner. Picnic area – Dogs welcomed. Reasonably level ground. *Adm 50p. Private visits welcome all year, please Tel 0584 872100*

Astley Abbotts House ❀ (Mrs H E Hodgson) 3m NW of Bridgnorth. B4373 from Bridgnorth turn R at Cross Lane Head. Bus: Bridgnorth-Broseley or the Smithies; alight Cross Lane Head ½m. 10 acres, 5 acres lavender, PYO at July opening; bee village; herbs; wild woodland garden; fine trees; lawns; rhododendrons. Only partly suitable for wheelchairs. TEAS. *Adm £1 Chd free (Share to Wolverhampton Eye Infirmary®, July only). Suns May 15 (2-6) July 24 (10-6)*

Badger Farmhouse (Mr & Mrs N J D Foster) Badger. From A464 Shifnal to Wolverhampton Rd turn S to Burnhill Green. In Burnhill Green turn W to Beckbury. At T junction in Beckbury turn S, ¾m on R. 3-acre garden. Over 100 varieties of daffodils and narcissi in a mature setting. Mainly in three orchards, one of apple one pear and plum and one of cherry. Also fine trees, shrubs and roses. TEAS. *Adm £1.20 Chd free (Share to St Mary's Church, Shifnal®). Easter Mon April 4 (2-6). Private visits welcome, please Tel 074 65 222*

Bakers House ⚭❀ (Miss L M North) Bromley. 2m from Bridgnorth. From Bridgnorth to Wolverhampton Rd (A454) signposted Bromley approx 1m from B'th or Bridgnorth to Telford Rd (A442) signposted Bromley approx 2m from Bridgnorth, Timbered cottage opp phone box. Approx ½-acre cottage garden with unusual and interesting perennials, shrubs and old roses. Scree garden for alpines, alpine house; peat bed and stone troughs; informal planting in cottage garden style in a very pretty rural setting. Best months May & June. *Adm £1 Chd 25p. Parties welcome. Private visits welcome April to July please* **Tel 0746 763296**

2 Beacon Hill ✿ (Mr & Mrs J Link) Monkhopton. 5¾m W of Bridgnorth on Bridgnorth-Craven Arms rd. From Bridgnorth take A458 (Shrewsbury); turn L at Morville B4386 situated on L at 1st Xrds 2¾m. Small garden with fish pools; small conifers; shrubs; perennials. Winner of the 'Roy Lancaster Special Award' for 'The Plantsmans Garden'. (Shropshire Star) 1993. TEA. *Adm £1 Chd 50p. Sun June 19 (2-6)*

Benthall Hall ✿ (Mr & Mrs James Benthall; The National Trust) 1m NW of Broseley, 4m NE of Much Wenlock (B4375); turning up lane marked with brown sign. Garden 3-acres; shrub roses; rockery banks; lawns; former kitchen garden; wild garden. Interesting plants and fine trees. C16 house also open. *Adm £2 Chd £1 (House & Garden £3 Chd £1). Sun June 26 (1.30-5.30)*

Bitterley Court ♿✿❀ (Mr & Mrs J V T Wheeler) Ludlow. Next to Bitterley Church. Follow A4117 E from Ludlow and turn off to Bitterley after about 2m. 5m from Ludlow altogether. A 6-acre garden comprising mainly lawns, specimen trees and shrubs, shrub roses and some borders. TEAS. *Adm £1 Chd 50p. Suns May 22, June 19 (2-6)*

Brownhill House ✿❀ (Roger & Yoland Brown) Ruyton XI Towns. 10m NW of Shrewsbury on B4397, in village. Park at Bridge Inn. Unusual and distinctive hillside garden bordering River Perry; which has been shown on BBC2 'Gardeners World'. Great variety of features and style including laburnum walk; parterre; formal terraces; extensive shrub planting; woodland paths; glasshouses; fruit and large kitchen garden. New developments every year. TEAS. *Adm £1.20 Chd free. Sun May 15; Sat, Sun May 28, 29 Sun June 19, Sat, Sun July 16, 17, Sun Sept 11 (2-6). Private visits welcome May to Aug, please* **Tel 0939 260626**

Burford House Gardens ♿✿❀ (Treasures of Tenbury) 1m W of Tenbury Wells. 400yds S of A456. Bus: CM Ludlow-Tenbury Wells. 4-acre garden designed in 1954 by owner in beautiful surroundings on R Teme. Flowering shrubs, herbaceous plants, extensive lawns. National Clematis Collection (held on behalf of NCCPG). Nursery specializing in clematis, herbaceous, many unusual shrubs and climbers. Fine church adjacent containing Cornwall monuments. Gift shop. DOGS on lead, nursery only. TEAS; light lunches. *Adm £1.95 Chd 80p. Season ticket £7.50, Family Season £15. Parties (by appt); 25 or more £1.60 each.* ▲Wed July 13, Aug 17, Sept 14 (10-5)

Church Bank ✿❀ (Mr & Mrs B P Kavanagh) Rowley 12m SW of Shrewsbury on B4386 Montgomery Rd continuing through Westbury. After ⅓m turn R for Rowley. After 3½m turn L at Xrds for Brockton. Church Bank is on L after 120yds. A plant enthusiast's, S facing garden set in a beautiful and little known part of the county, begun 5 years ago and continuing to develop and change. *Adm £1 Chd free. Sat, Sun July 30, 31 (2-6); also private visits welcome May to Sept, please* **Tel 0743 891661**

¶Cricklewood Cottage ✿❀ (Paul & Debbie Costello) Plox Green. On A488 1m SW of Minsterley. Pretty ⅓-acre cottage garden, bordered by trout stream with waterfalls and natural bog garden; colour-schemed borders of shrubs and perennials, all packed with plants, particularly shrub roses, day lilies and hardy geraniums. TEAS. *Adm £1 Chd free (Share to League of Friends of Shrewsbury Hospitals®). Weds May 11, June 8, July 13, Aug 10, Sept 14 (1.30-5.30). Private visits also welcome, please* **Tel 0743 791229**

David Austin Roses ♿❀ (Mr & Mrs David Austin) Bowling Green Lane, Albrighton, 8m NW of Wolverhampton. 4m from Shifnal (A464) left into Bowling Green Lane; or junc 3, M54 to Albrighton, right at sign 'Roses & Shrubs', Bowling Green Lane 2nd R. Famous nursery and gardens; 700 varieties old roses, shrub, species and climbing roses; rose breeding trials; rose fields; small herbaceous display garden. Private garden recently redesigned with many plants. Sculpture. TEAS. *Adm £1.20 Chd free. Sun June 26 (2-6)*

Dudmaston ✿❀ (Sir George & Lady Labouchere; The National Trust) 4m SE of Bridgnorth on A442. Bus stop at gates ½m. 8 acres with fine trees, shrubs; lovely views over Dudmaston Pool and surrounding country. Dingle walk. TEAS. *Adm £2 Chd 50p. Mon May 30 (2-6)*

Erway Farm House ✿❀ (Mr & Mrs A A Palmer) 3m N of Ellesmere, 2m S of Overton on Dee. Signposted from B5068 Ellesmere-St Martins Road and B5069 Overton-Uswestry Road. 1-acre Plantswoman's garden in light woodland, packed with rare and interesting plants. (Featured on TV, 'Gardeners World'). Hellebores in profusion, many varieties of snowdrop. Later, daphnes, hardy geranium, peaonia, and other shade loving plants. Unusual plants from garden for sale. *Adm £1 Chd 50p. Sat, Sun, Mon, April 2, 3, 4 (2-6), also last Sun in every month Feb to Sept (2-6)*

Fairfield ♿✿ (Mr & Mrs G P Beardsley) Oldbury. On B4363 Bridgnorth to Cleobury Mortimer Rd. 100yds from SVR railway bridge. Informal landscaped garden extending to over 3 acres containing sweeping lawns, many interesting trees and shrubs; water garden and arboretum. TEAS. *Adm £1 Chd free (Share to St Mary's Church Restoration Fund®). Sat, Sun June 18, 19 (2-6)*

Farley House ✿ (Mr & Mrs R W Collingwood) From A458 at Much Wenlock turn N on to A4169 signed Ironbridge; house 1m on L. 1-acre garden made since 1980 by owners; alpines, herbaceous island beds, shrubs and trees. Gardening clubs and WI welcome. *Adm £1 Chd free. Private visits welcome April to Oct, please* **Tel 0952 727017**

Field House ❀ (Dr & Mrs John Bell) Clee St Margaret. 8m NE of Ludlow. Turning to Stoke St Milborough and Clee St Margaret. 5m from Ludlow, 10m from Bridgnorth along B4364. Through Stoke St Milborough to Clee St Margaret. Ignore R turn to Clee Village. Carry on to Field House on L. Parking. 1-acre garden created since 1982 for yr-round interest. Mixed borders; rose walk; pool garden; herbaceous borders; organic vegetable garden; spring bulbs and autumn colours. TEAS. *Adm £1.50 Chd 50p. Sun June 26 (12-6). Private visits welcome, please* **Tel 0584 75242**

Gatacre Park &✿ (Lady Thompson) Six Ashes, 6m SE of Bridgnorth on A458. Stourbridge-Bridgnorth Rd. 8 acres. Originally a Victorian garden partly redeveloped over the last 56 years by present owner. Flowering shrubs, fine trees, inc 100ft tulip tree and manna ash; topiary walk; large woodland garden with pieris, azaleas, rhododendrons inc many interesting species now fully grown. Lovely views over Park. TEA. *Adm £1.50 Chd free (Share to Tuck Hill Church, Six Ashes®). Suns May 8, 15 (2-6)*

Harnage Farm &✿ (Mr & Mrs Ken Cooke) Cound. 8m SE of Shrewsbury on A458. Turn to Cound 1m S of Cross Houses. Harnage Farm 1m, bearing L past church. ½-acre farmhouse garden; well stocked with unusual herbaceous plants, shrubs and climbers. Extensive views over beautiful Severn Valley. TEAS. *Combined adm with* **The Mill Cottage** *£1.50 Chd 50p (Share to MRI Appeal, Oswestry®). Sun July 10 (2-6)*

Hatton Grange &✿ (Mrs Peter Afia) Shifnal. Lodge gate entrance on A464, 2m S of Shifnal. 1m up drive. Large dingle with pools, rhododendrons, azaleas, fine old trees; shrubbery; rose-garden; lily pond garden. TEAS. *Adm £1.20 Chd 50p (Share to CRMF®). Sun May 22 (2-7). Parties by appt, please* **Tel 0952 460415**

Hawkstone Hall (Redemptorist Study Centre) 13m NE of Shrewsbury. 6m SW of Market Drayton on A442. Entrance from Marchamley. Large formally laid out garden. Features include ornamental flower beds; herbaceous border; rockery; pools and magnificent trees. Georgian mansion (open) with courtyard garden and winter garden. TEAS. *Adm garden only £1 Chd 50p reduced rates for pre-booked parties of 20 or more.* ▲*Mon, Tues, Aug 8, 9 (2-5)* **Tel 063084 242**

Haye House ✿✿ (Mrs Paradise) Eardington. 2m S of Bridgnorth, sign Highley B4555. 1m through village Eardington. 1-acre garden especially planted by the owner, for her work as a National & International flower demonstrator. Grade 2 listed house (not open). TEAS. *Adm £1.20. Private visits welcome, April to Oct, please* **Tel 0746 764884**

Herbert Lewis Garden, Merton Nurseries &✿✿ (Herbert Lewis & Family) Bicton. 3m NW of Shrewsbury on B4380 (old A5) towards Oswestry. The Herbert Lewis is attached to Merton Nurseries. The acre of garden is a plantsman's collection of widely available and unusual plants. It is a garden for all seasons containing over 200 varieties of conifers and heathers for autumn and winter interest. However the outstanding feature is the vast collection of herbaceous perennials growing in borders and island beds. A woodland garden contains rhododendrons and azaleas as well as a selection of moisture and shade loving plants incl magnificent specimens of gunnera manicata. Open for hospice rest of the year. Guided tours if required; coach parties. TEAS in aid of Shropshire Hospice. *Adm £1.50 Chd 50p. Weds, July 6, Sun June 19, July 3, 24; Aug 7, 28; (11-6). Private evening visits welcome, please* **Tel 0743 850773**

By Appointment Gardens. See head of county section

Hodnet Hall Gardens &✿ (Mr & the Hon Mrs A Heber-Percy) 5½m SW of Market Drayton; 12m NE Shrewsbury; at junc of A53 and A442. 60-acre landscaped garden with series of lakes and pools; magnificent forest trees, great variety of flowers, shrubs providing colour throughout season; featured on TV and Radio. Unique collection of big-game trophies in C17 tearooms. Gift shop and kitchen garden. TEAS; parties to pre-book. Free car-coach park. *Adm £2.60 OAP £2.10 Chd £1. April 1 to end of Sept (Mon to Sat 2-5; Suns & Bank Hols 12-5.30). Reduced rates for organised parties of 25 or over* **Tel 0630 685 202**. *For NGS Sats Aug 6, 13 (2-5)*

Limeburners &✿ (Mr & Mrs J E Derry) Lincoln Hill. On outskirts of Ironbridge, Telford. From Traffic Island in Ironbridge take Church Hill and proceed up hill for ½m, garden on L 300yds below The Beeches Hospital. Prize Winning garden formerly site of a rubbish tip developed by owners as a Nature garden to attract wildlife. Many unusual shrubs giving year round interest. TEAS in aid of Arthritis & Rheumatism Council for Research. *Adm £1.25 Chd 25p. Sun June 5 (2-6). Private visits also welcome April to Sept, please* **Tel 0952 433715**

Linley Hall &✿ (Lady More) 3m NE of Bishop's Castle. Turn E off A488 nr Lydham. Parkland; lawns, rose garden, herbaceous border; lake; temple. Teas nearby. *Adm £1.50 Chd Free. Sun July 24 (2-6)*

Longnor Hall &✿✿ (Mr & Mrs A V Nicholson) Longnor. Take A49 road S of Shrewsbury to Longnor. Entry to Longnor Hall garden through grounds of Longnor Church. 70-acre garden and parkland. Interesting varieties of trees; herbaceous borders, yew and beech hedges; walled kitchen garden; stable yard and C17 house (not open); sheep and deer; Cound Brook; views of The Lawley and Caer Caradoc hills. Adjacent C13 Longnor Church. TEAS. *Adm £1.50 Chd 50p (Share to St. Mary's Church, Longnor®). Sun, Mon May 29, 30 (2-6)*

Lower Hall &✿ (Mr & Mrs C F Dumbell) Worfield, E of Bridgnorth, ½m N of A454 in village centre. 4 acres on R Worfe; stream; pool; shrub and woodland garden. Tudor half-timbered house (not open). Plant sales to local charity. TEAS. *Adm £2 OAPs £1.50 Chd free. Private visits welcome. By appt — Coach parties May to Aug and evening parties with local catering.* **Tel 074 64607**

The Lyth &✿✿ (Mr & Mrs L R Jebb) 1m SE of Ellesmere; entrance between Whitemere and junc of A528/A495. 2-acre garden; rhododendrons, azaleas; good outlook on park-land; heath bed, shrub borders. Regency colonial house (not open), birthplace of founder of Save The Children, Eglantyne Jebb. Meres nearby worth a visit. TEAS by local Save the Children Fund. *Adm £1.50 Chd 50p. Sun May 22 (2-6)*

Mawley Hall &✿ (Mr & Mrs R A Galliers-Pratt) 2m NE of Cleobury Mortimer. On A4117 Bewdley-Ludlow Rd. Bus: X92, alight at gate. A natural garden in beautiful country with magnificent views; designed for wandering amongst roses, herbs, flowering shrubs; fine old trees. TEAS. *Adm £1.50 OAPs £1 Chd under 15, 50p. Mons May 16, June 20, July 18 (2-6)*

The Mill Cottage ♿☕☺ (Mrs A J Wisden & Miss J M Hawkes) Cound. 8m SE of Shrewsbury on A458. Turn to Cound 1m S of Cross Houses. Mill Cottage 300yds on L. ¼-acre cottage garden. Many unusual & lovely herbaceous & alpine plants. Large collection of clematis. Good & varied collection of hostas. *Combined adm with* **Harnage Farm** *£1.50 Chd 50p. (Share to MRI Appeal, Oswestry®) Sun July 10 (2-6)*

Millichope Park (Mr & Mrs L Bury) Munslow, 8m NE of Craven Arms. From Ludlow (11m) turn L off B4368, ¾m out of Munslow. 13-acre garden with lakes; woodland walks; fine specimen trees, wild flowers; herbaceous borders. TEAS. *Adm £1.50 Chd 50p. Mon May 2, Sun June 26 (2-6)*

Moortown ♿☕☺ (David Bromley Esq) 5m N of Wellington. Take B5062 signed Moortown 1m between High Ercall and Crudgington. Approx 1-acre plantsman's garden. Here may be found the old-fashioned, the unusual and even the oddities of plant life, in mixed borders of 'controlled' confusion. *Adm £2 Chd 50p. Fri, Sat, Sun July 1, 2, 3 (2-5.30)*

Morville Hall Gardens ♿ nr Bridgnorth. 3m NW of Bridgnorth on A458 at junction with B4368. TEA. *Combined adm £2 Chd 50p. (Share to Morville Church®). Sun May 1, Wed June 22 (2-6)*
   The Dower House (Dr K Swift) 1½-acre formal garden begun 1989; ornamental kitchen garden
   The Gate House (Mr & Mrs A Rowe) Cottage garden with small vineyard
   Morville Hall (Mr & Mrs John Norbury & The National Trust) Recently restored 2-acre garden with newly planted parterre and vineyard; C12 Church, Elizabethan House (not open) in fine setting

New Hall (Mrs R H Treasure) Eaton-under-Heywood, 4m SE of Church Stretton. Between B4368 and B4371. 10 acres of woodland with grass walks, pools, wild flowers, streams. Garden suitable for wheelchairs only in dry weather. *Adm £1 Chd 10p. Suns April 10, 17 (2-5)*

Nordybank Nurseries ☕ (Polly Bolton) Clee St. Margaret. 7½m NE of Ludlow. Turning to Stoke St Milborough and Clee St Margaret 5m from Ludlow, 10m from Bridgnorth along B4364, through Stoke St Milborough on the Lane to Clee St Margaret. 1-acre hillside cottage garden; trees, shrubs & unusual herbaceous plants with cottage garden favourites. Also 'field garden' displaying approx 500 varieties of herbaceous plants; daffodil & narcissi bulbs in May. Also small rose garden displaying old shrub rose varieties June/July; buddleias July/Aug. TEAS. *Adm £1 OAP 50p Chd 20p. Open every Sun, Mon, & Wed June 5 until Aug 28 (11-6)*

The Old Rectory ☕☺ (Mrs J H M Stafford) Fitz; A5 NW of Shrewsbury; turn off at Montford Bridge, follow signs; from B5067 turn off at Leaton, follow signs. 1¼-acre botanists garden; shrub roses, vegetables; water garden. TEAS. *Adm £1.20 Chd 20p. Sun June 12 (12-6)*

The Old Vicarage ♿ (W B Hutchinson Esq) Cardington, 3m N of B4371 Church Stretton-Much Wenlock Rd, signed, or turn off A49 Shrewsbury-Ludlow Rd at Leebot-wood, 2½-acre scenic garden; trees, shrubs, roses, primulas, alpines, water garden. Lunch and tea picnics allowed; on site parking. *Adm £1 Chd free. Suns June 5, 12, 19, 26; July 3, 10, 17 (12-5.30)*

Oteley ☕ (Mr & Mrs R K Mainwaring) Ellesmere 1m. Entrance out of Ellesmere past Mere, opp Convent nr to A528/495 junc. 10 acres running down to Mere, inc walled kitchen garden; architectural features many interesting trees, rhododendrons and azaleas, views across Mere to Ellesmere Church. Wheelchairs only if dry. TEAS (For NSPCC). *Adm £1.50 Chd 50p. Mon May 30 (2-6) Sun Sept 25 (1-5)*

¶The Patch ♿☕☺ (Mrs J G Owen) Acton Pigot. 8m SE of Shrewsbury between A49 and A458. Take Cressage Rd from Acton Burnell. Turn L after ½m, signpost Acton Pigot. A newly established plantsman's garden. Early spring bulbs, hellebores, primulas, National Collection of Epimediums. June early herbaceous, shrubs and trees. TEAS and plants in aid of St. Anthony's Cheshire Home. *Adm £1.50. Mon April 4, Tues June 14 (2-6), Sun Feb 12 1995 (11-5). Private visits also welcome, please* **Tel 0743 718846**

Peplow Hall ♿☕ (The Hon & Mrs R V Wynn) 3m S of Hodnet via A442; turn off E. 10-acre garden with lawns, azaleas, rhododendrons, etc; roses, herbaceous borders; walled kitchen garden; 7-acre lake. TEAS. *Adm £2 Chd 50p. Sat, Sun May 21, 22 (1.30-5)*

Preen Manor ☕☺ (Mr & Mrs P Trevor-Jones) Church Preen, nr Church Stretton; 5m SW of Much Wenlock. On B4371 3m turn R for Church Preen and Hughley; after 1½m turn L for Church Preen; over Xrds, 1¼m drive on R. 6 acres on site of C12 Cluniac monastery, later Norman Shaw mansion (now demolished); garden restored and replanned now contains a variety of different gardens: walled, terraced, wild, water, kitchen and chess gardens; fine trees in park; woodland walks. C12 monastic church with oldest yew tree in Europe. Featured in NGS video 1, see page 344. TEAS. *Adm £1.75 Chd 50p. Thurs June 2, 23, July 7, 21 (2-6); Sun Oct 2 (2-5). Coach parties by appt June & July only* **Tel 0694 771207**

¶Radnor Cottage ☕☺ (Pam and David Pittwood) Clunton. 8m W of Craven Arms, 1m E of Clun on B4368 midway between Clunton and Clun. 2 acres S-facing slope, overlooking Clun Valley. Recently developed for all-year-round interest. Daffodils; cottage garden borders; dry stone wall and terracing with herbs and alpines; stream and bog garden with willow collection; native trees, orchard, wild flower meadow. TEAS. *Adm £1 Chd 50p. Private visits welcome, please* **Tel 0588 640451**

Ruthall Manor ♿☕ (Mr & Mrs G T Clarke) Ditton Priors, Bridgnorth. Weston rd from village church 2nd L, garden ¾m. 1-acre garden with pool and specimen trees. Designed for easy maintenance with lots of ground-covering and unusual plants. Old Shires Tea Room in village open (10-5) daily except Weds. *Adm £1.50 Chd free. Sat June 25 (3-7.30). Private visits welcome April to Sept, please* **Tel 0746 34608**

Stottesdon Village Gardens &&& (Stottesdon Garden Committee). 7m from Bridgnorth on B4363 turn R 3m. From Kidderminster 11m on A4117 turn R 4m. A village community in unspoilt countryside. A variety of gardens, new and old; cottage flowers; unusual plants; vegetables; bedding displays. TEAS in aid of St Mary's Church. *Combined adm £1.50 Chd 50p. Sun, Mon Aug 28, 29 (2-6)*

Swallow Hayes && (Mrs P Edwards) Rectory Rd, Albrighton WV7, 7m NW of Wolverhampton. M54 exit 3 Rectory Rd 1m towards Wolverhampton off A41 just past Roses and Shrubs Garden Centre. 2-acres; planted since 1968 with emphasis on all-the-year interest and ease of maintenance; National collection of Hamamellis and Russell Lupins. Nearly 3000 different plants, most labelled. TEAS. *Adm £1 Chd 10p (Share to Compton Hospice®). Suns April 24; May 8 (2-6); also by appt for parties, please* **Tel 0902 372624**

Walcot Hall && (The Hon Mrs E C Parish) Bishops Castle 3m. B4385 Craven Arms to Bishops Castle, turn L by Powis Arms, in Lydbury N. Arboretum planted by Lord Clive of India's son, now undergoing restoration. Cascades of rhododendrons, azaleas amongst specimen trees and pools. Fine views of Sir William Chambers Clock Towers, with lake and hills beyond. TEAS. *Adm £1.50 Chd 15 and under free. Sun, Mon May 29, 30, (2-6)*

Weston Park & (The Weston Park Foundation) Shifnal. 7m E of Telford on the A5 in the village of Weston-under-Lizard. Easy access junction 12 M6 and junction 3 M54. Free car/coach park. 28 acres Capability Brown landscaped gardens and arboretum, incl fine collection of nothofagus, rhododendrons and azaleas. Formal gardens of SW terrace recently restored to orginal C18 design, together with colourful adjacent Broderie Garden. Wide variety of trees, shrubs and flowers provides colour throughout the season. C17 house (open adm £1.50). TEAS and light meals available in The Old Stables restaurant. *Adm £3 OAPs £2.50 Chd £2 reduced rates for parties of 20 or more. Open Easter to September (enquiries for dates & times* **Tel 095276 207**). *For NGS Tues June 14, July 19 (11-5)*

Whittington Village Gardens && Daisy Lane Whittington. 2½m NE of Oswestry. Turn off B5009 150yds NW of church into Top St then into Daisy Lane. Car parking at Whittington Castle and Top St. Group of adjoining gardens from small to ⅔ acre. Range of garden pools, kitchen gardens, gravel garden and bubble fountain. Collection of hardy geraniums. TEAS at Cedarville, Daisy Lane. *Combined adm £1.50 Chd free. Sat, Sun June 25, 26 (1-5.30)*

Willey Park && (The Lord & Lady Forester) Broseley 5m NW of Bridgnorth. Turn W off B4373. Much Wenlock 4m. Formal garden with ½m woodland-rhododendron walk; spectacular azalea bed near house. TEAS. *Adm £1.50 Chd 75p (Share to The Lady Forester Hospital Trust, Broseley®)). Sun May 22 (2-6)*

Wollerton Old Hall && (John & Lesley Jenkins) Wollerton. From Shrewsbury take A53 to Hodnet 13m. Follow same road out towards Market Drayton. Turn R just after 'Wollerton' sign. Go 300 yards over a bridge to a brick pound. Garden ahead on L. 2-acre garden created around a C16 house (not open). A combination of formal design, plant associations, and intensive cultivation of perennials; a number of separate gardens with different atmospheres. Wide range of plants, some unusual and rare. Continuing expansion of garden. Featured in NGS video 1, see page 344. Partly suitable wheelchairs. Light lunches, TEAS. *Adm £1.50 Chd 50p. Suns June 26, Aug 7, open every Fri June 3 to Aug 26 (1-5)*

Somerset

Hon County Organiser:	Mrs K Spencer-Mills, Hooper's Holding, Hinton St George, Somerset TA17 8SE Tel 0460 76389
Assistant Hon County Organisers:	Mrs M R Cooper, 21 Lower St, Merriott, Somerset
	Miss P Davies-Gilbert, Coombe Quarry, West Monkton, Taunton
Somerset Leaflet:	Mrs B Hudspith, Rookwood, West St, Hinton St George, Somerset TA17 8SA Tel 0460 73450
Hon County Treasurer:	John A Spurrier Esq, Tudor Cottage, 19 Comeytrowe Lane, Taunton, Somerset TA1 5PA Tel 0823 333827

DATES OF OPENING

By appointment

For telephone numbers and other details see garden descriptions. Private visits welcomed

Broadview, Crewkerne
Cobbleside, Milverton Gardens, Taunton

Elworthy Cottage, Elworthy
Fig Tree Cottage, Hinton St George
    Gardens, Crewkerne
Garden Cottage, Milverton Gardens, Taunton
Greencombe, Porlock
Hadspen Garden, nr Castle Cary
Hooper's Holding, Hinton St George
    Gardens, Crewkerne

Landacre Farm, Withypool
Leaside, Bruton
Littlecourt, West Bagborough
Lovibonds Farm, Burrowbridge
Manor Farm, Stone Allerton
    Gardens, nr Wedmore
The Mill, Henley Lane, Wookey
Mill House, Stone Allerton Gardens,
    nr Wedmore
The Mount, West Hill, Wincanton

Shepton Nursery Garden, Shepton Mallet
Withey Lane Farmhouse, Barton St David

Regular openings
For details see garden descriptions

Clapton Court Gardens, Crewkerne. March to Oct daily except Sats. Other dates see text
East Lambrook Manor Garden, South Petherton. Daily Mon to Sat. Closed Nov to Feb 28
Elworthy Cottage, Elworthy. Every Tues and Thurs March 17 to Oct 11 (except Aug)
Greencombe, Porlock. Sats to Tues, April to July
Hadspen Garden, nr Castle Cary. Thurs to Suns & Bank Hol Mons, March 1 to Oct 1
Hatch Court, Hatch Beauchamp Gardens. See text
Lower Severalls, Crewkerne. Open April 1 to Sept 30
Watermeadows, Clapton. Open Mon to Sat, April to Sept

March 27 Sunday
Elworthy Cottage, Elworthy
Peart Hall, Spaxton

April Sat, Sun, Mon, Tues, Wed, Thurs, & Fri 2 to 8 & Sat 30
Broadview, Crewkerne

April 3 Sunday
Fairfield, Stogursey

April 10 Sunday
Smocombe House, Enmore
Wayford Manor, Crewkerne
Wootton House, Butleigh Wootton

April 16 Saturday
Greencombe, Porlock

April 17 Sunday
Barrington Court, Ilminster
Hangeridge Farm, Wellington Gardens

April 23 Saturday
The Mount, West Hill, Wincanton
Pear Tree Cottage, Stapley

April 24 Sunday
The Mount, West Hill, Wincanton
Pear Tree Cottage, Stapley

May Sun, Mon, Tues, Wed, & Thurs, 1 to 5 & 28 to 31
Broadview, Crewkerne

May 1 Sunday
The Mount, West Hill, Wincanton
Spaxton Gardens, Spaxton
Stowell Hill, Templecombe
Wayford Manor, Crewkerne

May 3 Tuesday
Shepton Nursery Garden, Shepton Mallet

May 4 Wednesday
Shepton Nursery Garden, Shepton Mallet
Withey Lane Farmhouse, Barton St David

May 7 Saturday
Higher Luxton Farm, Churchingford
Kingsdon, Somerton
Pear Tree Cottage, Stapley

May 8 Sunday
Higher Luxton Farm, Churchingford
Kingsdon, Somerton
Pear Tree Cottage, Stapley
Stowell Hill, Templecombe
West Bradley House, Glastonbury

May 11 Wednesday
Withey Lane Farmhouse, Barton St David

May 15 Sunday
Court House, East Quantoxhead
Elworthy Cottage, Elworthy
Lovibonds Farm, Burrowbridge
Milton Lodge, Wells
Smocombe House, Enmore
Stowell Hill, Templecombe
Wayford Manor, Crewkerne
37 Whitmore Road, Taunton

May 18 Wednesday
37 Whitmore Road, Taunton
Withey Lane Farmhouse, Barton St David

May 22 Sunday
Bruton Gardens
Cannington College Gardens
Stowell Hill, Templecombe

May 25 Wednesday
Withey Lane Farmhouse, Barton St David

May 29 Sunday
Chinnock House, Middle Chinnock
East Lambrook Manor Garden, South Petherton
Greencombe, Porlock
Hinton St George Gardens, Crewkerne
The Mill House, Castle Cary
Milton Lodge, Wells
Stone Allerton Gardens, nr Wedmore
Wayford Manor, Crewkerne
Westhay, Kingston St Mary

May 30 Monday
Beryl, Wells
Chinnock House, Middle Chinnock
Dodington Hall, Nether Stowey
Hinton St George Gardens, Crewkerne
The Mill House, Castle Cary

Stone Allerton Gardens, nr Wedmore

June 1 Wednesday
Broadview, Crewkerne
The Mount, West Hill, Wincanton
Withey Lane Farmhouse, Barton St David

June 2 Thursday
Broadview, Crewkerne

June 4 Saturday
Kingsdon, Somerton

June 5 Sunday
Bicknells Farm, Drayton, Langport ‡
Drayton Gardens, Langport ‡
Kingsdon, Somerton
Landacre Farm, Withypool
The Mill, Cannington
Montacute House, Montacute

June 7 Tuesday
Shepton Nursery Garden, Shepton Mallet

June 8 Wednesday
The Mill, Cannington
The Mount, West Hill, Wincanton
Shepton Nursery Garden, Shepton Mallet
Withey Lane Farmhouse, Barton St David

June 12 Sunday
Lovibonds Farm, Burrowbridge
Lower Severalls, Crewkerne
Milton Lodge, Wells
North Curry Village Gardens

June 15 Wednesday
Withey Lane Farmhouse, Barton St David

June 18 Saturday
The Old Rectory, Swell

June 19 Sunday
Hassage House, Faulkland
Hatch Beauchamp Gardens ‡
Montacute Gardens, nr Yeovil
The Old Rectory, Swell
Stogumber Gardens, Taunton ‡

June 22 Wednesday
Withey Lane Farmhouse, Barton St David

June 25 Saturday
Bruton Gardens
Greencombe, Porlock.

June 26 Sunday
Bruton Gardens
Cherry Bolberry Farm, Henstride
Elworthy Cottage, Elworthy ‡
Gaulden Manor, Tolland ‡
Milverton Gardens, Taunton
Wambrook Gardens, Chard

June 29 Wednesday
Withey Lane Farmhouse, Barton St David

July Sat, Sun, Mon, Tues, Wed & Thurs 2 to 7
Broadview, Crewkerne

SOMERSET **227**

July 2 Saturday
Kingsdon, Somerton
Leaside, Bruton
Stapleton Manor, Martlock
Wellington Gardens

July 3 Sunday
Kingsdon, Somerton
Landacre Farm, Withypool
Leaside, Bruton
Wellington Gardens

July 5 Tuesday
Shepton Nursery Garden,
Shepton Mallet

July 6 Wednesday
Shepton Nursery Garden,
Shepton Mallet

July 10 Sunday
Barford Park, Spaxton
Elworthy Cottage, Elworthy
Field Farm, Shepton Mallet
Lower Severalls, Crewkerne
Milton Lodge, Wells
Sutton Hosey Manor, Long Sutton

July 16 Saturday
The Red House, Cannington

July 17 Sunday
Brent Knoll Gardens, Highbridge
Forge House, Oake
Greencombe, Porlock
Hadspen Garden, nr Castle Cary
Kites Croft, Westbury-sub-Mendip
The Red House, Cannington

July 20 Wednesday
Kites Croft, Westbury-sub-Mendip

July 24 Sunday
Barrington Court, Ilminster
Thurloxton Gardens, nr Taunton

July 31 Sunday
Stapleton Manor, Martlock
Tintinhull House, nr Yeovil

August Sat, Sun, Mon, Tues & Wed 27 to 31
Broadview, Crewkerne

August 2 Tuesday
Shepton Nursery Garden,
Shepton Mallet

August 3 Wednesday
Shepton Nursery Garden,
Shepton Mallet

August 4 Thursday
Dunster Castle, nr Minehead

August 7 Sunday
Landacre Farm, Withypool
The Mill, Cannington

August 10 Wednesday
The Mill, Cannington

August 13 Saturday
Birdwood, Wells

August 14 Sunday
Birdwood, Wells
Lower Severalls, Crewkerne

August 21 Sunday
Coombe House, Bove Town,
Glastonbury

August 29 Monday
Beryl, Wells

September 1 Thursday
Broadview, Crewkerne

September 11 Sunday
Kites Croft, Westbury-sub-Mendip

September 14 Wednesday
Kites Croft, Westbury-sub-Mendip

September 25 Sunday
Elworthy Cottage, Elworthy

DESCRIPTIONS OF GARDENS

Barford Park &❀ (Mr M Stancomb) Spaxton. 4½m W of Bridgwater, midway between Enmore and Spaxton. 10 acres including woodland walk. Formal garden, wild garden and water garden, surrounding a Queen Anne house with park and ha ha. TEA. *Adm £1.50 Chd free. Sun July 10 (2-6)*

Barrington Court &❀❀ (The National Trust) Ilminster. NE of Ilminster. Well known garden constructed in 1920 by Col Arthur Lyle from derelict farmland (the C19 cattle stalls still exist). Gertrude Jekyll approved of the design and layout; paved paths with walled iris, white and lily gardens, large kitchen garden. Licensed restaurant, plant sales and garden shop. Lunches and TEAS. *Adm £3.10 Chd £1.50. Suns April 17, July 24 (11-5.30)*

Beryl &❀ (Mr & Mrs E Nowell) ½m N of Wells off B3139 to Bath. Left at Hawkers Lane. Victorian park created in 1842. Walled vegetable garden broken into quadrangles with box hedging and double flower picking borders. More recent planting of trees and shrubs and creation of walks and vistas. Morning coffee and TEAS. *Adm £1 OAP/Chd 50p. Bank Hol Mons May 30, Aug 29 (11-5.30).* Tel 0749 678738

¶**Birdwood** ❀❀ (Mr & Mrs R A Crane) 1½m NE Wells on B3139. Last house in Wells on edge of Mendip Hills nr double bend sign. House has long stone garden wall close to rd. Traditional Victorian garden with stone walls, lawns, herbaceous border, organic vegetable garden, small wood and wild area with conservation in mind. Special features incl many stone walls and terraces at different levels and interesting trees. TEAS. *Adm £1 Chd free. Sat, Sun Aug 13, 14 (10-7)*

Brent Knoll Gardens ❀ off A38 2m N of Highbridge and M5 exit 22. A mixture of 3 colourful country gardens. TEAS at Copse Hall in aid of Parish Hall. *Combined adm £2 Chd free. Sun July 17 (2-6)*
¶**Anvil Cottage** (Mr W & Miss J Owen) How to make use of a small space
Copse Hall ❀ (Mrs S Boss & Mrs N Hill) Terraced gardens, crinkle crankle kitchen garden wall, kiwi fruit. Display and sale of fuchsias by Brent Knoll Friendly Fuchsia Society
¶**Pippins** (Mrs S Allen) Collection of medicinal plants used in therapy

Broadview ❀❀ (Mr & Mrs R Swann) East Street, Crewkerne. Take the A30 Yeovil Rd out of Crewkerne approx 200 yds on the left hand side. Please enter drive by turning R from the E Yeovil side. 1-acre terraced garden on elevated site with panoramic views over Crewkerne. Interesting plants and shrubs, many for sale. TEA. *Adm £1 Chd free. Sat to Sat April 2 to 8 & Sat 30; Sun to Thurs May 1 to 5; Sat to Tues May 28 to 31; Wed, Thurs June 1, 2. Sat to Thurs July 2 to 7; Sat to Wed Aug 27 to 31; Thurs Sept 1 (11-6). Also private visits welcome, please* Tel 0460 73424

Bruton Gardens TEAS. *Combined adm £1.50 Chd free. Sat, Sun June 25, 26 (2-6)*
14 Burowfield ❀ (Mr & Mrs D Atkins) N of Bruton on the A359 to Frome. Semi-detached house with small front garden and beautifully maintained back garden with aviary and flowers
Tolbury Farm ❀❀ (Mr & Mrs M King) In Bruton turn N at Blue Bell Inn. 200 yds to public car park on L. Follow signs thereafter on foot. 1 acre of well-designed hillside garden with imaginative planting, good herbaceous borders, trees and rockery

Cannington College Gardens ⚭✿❀ Cannington, 3m NW of Bridgwater. On A39 Bridgwater-Minehead Rd. Old College: Benedictine Priory 1138; fine Elizabethan W front; 7 old sandstone walled gardens protect wide range of plants, inc many less hardy subjects, ceanothus, Fremontias, Wistarias etc; 10 very large greenhouses contain exceptionally wide range of ornamental plants. New College (built 1970); magnificent views to Quantocks; tree and shrub collections; ground cover plantings; lawn grass collection and trials; horticultural science garden; one of the largest collections of ornamental plants in SW England including 8 national plant collections. TEAS. *Adm for both College grounds £1.50 Chd (& organised parties of OAPs) 75p. Special rates for party bookings. For NGS Sun May 22 (2-5)*

Cherry Bolberry Farm ⚭ (Mr & Mrs C Raymond) Henstridge. From Henstridge traffic lights continue on A357 through Henstridge towards Stalbridge. In centre of Henstridge turn R at small Xrd signed Furge Lane. Farm at end of lane. 5m E of Sherborne, 7m S of Wincanton. ¾-acre owner-designed young garden planted for year round interest. Nature ponds, small fish pond, extensive views. TEAS. *Adm £1. Sun June 26 (2.30-5.30)*

Chinnock House ⚭✿❀ (Guy & Charmian Smith) Middle Chinnock. Off A30 between Crewkerne and Yeovil. 1½-acre walled gardens, silver, white and herbaceous; recently redesigned. TEAS. *Adm £1.50 Chd free. Sun, Mon May 29, 30 (2-6)*

● **Clapton Court** ✿❀ (Capt S J Loder) 3m S of Crewkerne on B3165 to Lyme Regis. 10 acres; worth visiting at all seasons; many rare and unusual plants, shrubs and trees of botanical interest in lovely formal and woodland settings; largest and oldest ash in Great Britain; newly designed rose garden. Plant Centre selling choice, rare clematis, herbaceous, shrubs and trees. LUNCHES (licensed) and TEAS April to Sept. *Adm £3 Chd (4-14) £1. Pre-booked groups special tariff. March to Oct daily ex Sats. (Weekdays 10.30-5; Suns 2-5); also Sats April 2 (2-5), April 23 (11-5)* Tel 0460 73220/72200

¶**Coombe House** ⚭✿❀ (Colin Wells-Brown & Alan Gloak) Glastonbury. Bove Town top of Glastonbury High St. Coombe House approx ¼m up on R. A very new garden (established 1993) for an old house on very old site. Lawns, shrubs, herbaceous, kitchen garden, orchard/wild garden in approx 1 acre. Variety of features incl pools; mediaeval walls, and charming views, unusual plants for sale. TEAS in aid of Godney Village Hall. *Adm £1 Chd 75p (London Lighthouse Aids Hospice®). Sun Aug 21 (2-6)*

Court House ❀ (Sir Walter & Lady Luttrell) East Quantoxhead 12m W of Bridgwater off A39; house at end of village past duck pond. Lovely 5-acre garden; trees, shrubs, roses and herbaceous. Views to sea and Quantocks. Partly suitable for wheelchairs. Teas in Village Hall. *Adm £2 Chd free. Sun May 15 (2-5.30)*

Regular Openers. Too many days to include in diary. Usually there is a wide range of plants giving year-round interest. See head of county section for the name and garden description for times etc.

Dodington Hall ✿❀ (Grania & Paul Quinn) A39 Bridgwater-Minehead. 2m W of Nether Stowey turn at signpost opp Castle of Comfort. ¼m turn R. Entrance through churchyard. Reclaimed 1½-acre terrace garden; clematis, shrub roses, bulbs; Tudor house (part open). TEAS in aid of Meningitis Research. *Adm £1.50 Chd 50p. Mon May 30 (2-5.30)*

¶**Drayton Gardens** ½m S of A378 between Curry Rivel and Langport. TEAS at Podgers Orchard. *Combined adm £1.50. Sun June 5 (2-6)*

¶**Bicknells Farm** (Mrs Beryl Phillips) Garden on L going towards Muchelney, 100yds past PO on opp side of rd. ¾-acre garden. Lawns and shrubs either side of drive; wild flower garden in old orchard behind outbuildings; wild life pond next to small wood, with wild bank covered in foxgloves, etc; also rose bank; walled cottage garden behind house; contemporary outdoor sculptures, not usually associated with country gardens; stable now gallery for contemporary artwork

¶**Podgers Orchard** ⚭ (Kate Selbourne) 1-acre cottage garden with part wild orchard; some rare herbaceous plants and shrubs featured in Homes and Gardens 1992

Dunster Castle ✿ (The National Trust) On A396 3m SE of Minehead. Terraces of sub-tropical plants, shrubs and camellias surrounding the fortified house of the Luttrells for 600 years; fine views. Self-drive battery operated car available. Teas in village. *Adm Garden Only £2.60 Chd £1.20. Family ticket £6.50. For NGS Thurs Aug 4 (11-5)*

East Lambrook Manor Garden ✿❀ (Mr & Mrs A Norton) 2m NE of South Petherton. Off A303 to S Petherton; Martock Rd, then left to E Lambrook at bottom of hill. Traditional 'cottage style' garden created by the late Margery Fish and made famous by her many gardening books. Many unusual and now rare plants, trees and shrubs. The Margery Fish Nursery sells plants from the garden. TEAS (May 29 only). *Adm £2 OAPs £1.80 Chd 50p. Open Mon-Sat (10-5). Closed Nov 1 to Feb 28. For NGS Sun May 29 (10-5); private parties welcome, but please* Tel 0460 40328 Fax 0460 42344

Elworthy Cottage ✿❀ (Mike & Jenny Spiller) Elworthy, 12m NW of Taunton on B3188 5m N of Wiveliscombe. 1-acre informal garden, yr-round, cottage-style plantings, island beds, mixed planting. Bulbs, alpines, unusual herbaceous plants. Large collection of hardy geraniums (over 150 varieties); campanulas, penstemons, michaelmas daisies, grasses and plants for foliage effect. Teas in next village. *Adm £1 Chd free (Share to Cancer & Leukaemia in Childhood Trust®). Collecting box for NGS. Garden and nursery open March 17 to Oct 11 (1.30-4.30). Suns March 27, May 15, June 26, July 10, Sept 25 (1.30-5.30) closed Aug except private visits. Private visits welcome, please* Tel Stogumber 56427

Fairfield ⚭ (Lady Gass) Stogursey, 11m NW of Bridgwater 7m E of Williton. From A39 Bridgwater-Minehead turn N; garden 1½m W of Stogursey. Woodland garden with bulbs and shrubs; paved maze. Views of Quantocks. Dogs in park and field only. TEA. *Adm £1.50 Chd free (Share to Stogursey Church®). Easter Sun April 3 (2-5.30)*

Field Farm ☙ (Mr & Mrs D R Vagg) ½m S Shepton Mallet on A371 Cannards Grave Rd. Large farmhouse garden with lovely mixed planting; old and climbing roses, variegated plants, water garden, large rockery; many old stone features. TEAS. *Adm £1.50 Chd free (Share to Doulting Church©). Sun July 10 (2-6)*

¶**Forge House** &☙☙ (Peter & Eloise McGregor) Oake. East of Taunton midway between Taunton & Wellington. On A38 take signpost for Bradford-on-Tone, Oake. 1st house on R entering village. ¾-acre informal country garden with some interest in all seasons incl pond and wildlife area. Emphasis on colour borders and fragrance; fancy poultry. TEAS. *Adm £1 Chd 50p. Sun July 17 (2-6). Disabled & parties especially welcome by appt May to Sept, please* **Tel 0823 461 500**

Gaulden Manor ☙☙ (Mr & Mrs J Le G Starkie) Tolland. Nr Lydeard St Lawrence. 9m NW Taunton off A358. Medium-sized garden made by owners. Herb; bog; scent and butterfly gardens. Bog plants, primulas and scented geraniums. Partly suitable for wheelchairs. Cream TEAS. *Adm house & garden £2.80, garden only £1.25, Chd £1.25. Sun June 26 (2-5.30)*

Greencombe &☙☙ (Miss Joan Loraine, Greencombe Garden Trust) ½m W of Porlock, left off road to Porlock Weir. 47 year old garden on edge of ancient woodland, overlooking Porlock Bay. Choice rhododendrons, azaleas, camellias, maples, roses, hydrangeas, ferns, small woodland plants and clematis. National collection of Polystichum the 'thumbs up' fern, and of Erythronium, Vaccinium and Gaultheria. Completely organic, with compost heaps on show. Featured in NGS video 1, see page 344. *Adm £2.50 Chd 50p. Sats, Suns, Mons, Tues April, May, June & July (2-6); private visits welcome, please* **Tel 0643 862363**. *For NGS Sats April 16, June 25, Suns May 29, July 17 (2-6)*

Hadspen Garden &☙☙ (N & S Pope) 2m SE of Castle Cary on A371 to Wincanton. 5-acre Edwardian garden featuring a 2-acre curved walled garden with extensive colourist borders of shrub roses and choice herbaceous plants; woodland of fine mature specimen trees; meadow of naturalised native flowers and grasses. National Rodgersia Collection. Lunches, TEAS Thurs, Fri, Sat, TEAS only Sun & Bank Hol Mon. *Adm £2 Chd 50p. Garden and Nursery open Thurs, Fri, Sat, Sun & Bank Hol Mon (9-6); private visits welcome, March 1 to October 1, please* **Tel 0749 813707** *(after 6pm). For NGS Sun July 17 (2-6)*

Hassage House ☙☙ (Mr & Mrs J Donnithorne) Faulkland. 8m S of Bath on Trowbridge-Radstock Rd A 366, 1½m West Norton St Philip, 1m E Faulkland. Turn off at Tuckers Grave Inn. 300yds turn R, house at end of lane. 1½-acres of informal garden; shrubs, herbaceous, roses; lily pond; small bog garden; conservatory. Cream TEAS. *Adm £1 Chd free. Sun June 19 (1.30-6)*

Hatch Beauchamp Gardens 5m SE of Taunton (M5 junction 25) off A358 to Ilminster. Turn L in village of Hatch Beauchamp at Hatch Inn. Parking at Hatch Court. TEAS. *Combined adm £2 Chd £1 under 12 free. Sun June 19 (2.30-5.30)*

Hatch Court &☙ (Dr & Mrs Robin Odgers) Turn L in village at Hatch Inn. 5-acre garden with 30 acres of parkland and deer park surrounding a perfect 1750 Palladian mansion. Extensive, recent and continuing restoration, redesign and replanting. Breathtaking walled kitchen garden, fine display of roses, shrubs, clematis and many young trees. Glorious views and a lovely setting. TEAS. *Adm Garden only £1.50, Chd £1.00 under 12 free, house and garden £3. Thurs June 2 to Sept 29 (garden) Thurs June 16 to Sept 15 and Aug Bank Hol Mon (house) (2.30-5.30). For NGS Sun June 19*
Hatch Court Farm &☙ (John Townson Esq) ⅓-acre walled garden created over the past 5 years from derelict farm buildings. Mixed borders and wild area with large pond surrounded by wood and parkland

¶**Higher Luxton Farm** ☙ (Mr & Mrs Peter Hopcraft) 1½m out of Churchingford on Honiton Rd. Over county boundary into Devon past thatched farmhouse on R; next turning on L before Xrds. 9m S of Taunton, 9m N of Honiton. Approx 1 acre with species trees and bulbs; walls with clematis; ponds with primula; lovely views. Pony stud. Partially suitable for wheelchairs. TEAS. *Adm £1 Chd free. Sat, Sun May 7, 8 (2-6)*

Hinton St George Gardens 2m NW of Crewkerne. N of A30 Crewkerne-Chard; S of A303 Ilminster Town Rd, at roundabout signed Lopen & Merriott, then R to one of Somerset's prettiest villages. TEAS & dog park provided at Hooper's Holding. *Combined adm £2 Chd free. Sun, Mon May 29, 30 (2-6)*
> **Fig Tree Cottage** &☙ (Mr & Mrs Whitworth) Old walled cottage garden and courtyard of stables made from kitchen garden of neighbouring rectory, over the past 15 years by owners inspired by Margery Fish. Ground cover, shrubs, old-fashioned roses. Three giant fig trees, all perennials. *Private visits welcome, please* **Tel 0460 73548**
> **Holly Oak House** (Mr & Mrs Michael O'Loughlin) Gas Lane. ½-acre garden with terraced lawns and south facing views. A mixture of flower beds, shrubs and herbaceous borders
> **Hooper's Holding** &☙ (Ken & Lyn Spencer-Mills) High St. ⅓-acre garden, in a formal design; lily pool; dwarf conifers, rare herbaceous and shrubby plants; NCCPG National Collection of Hedychiums; fancy poultry. TEAS in aid of Cats Protection League. (Hedychiums flowering Sept and Oct). *Private visits welcome, please,* **Tel 0460 76389**
> ¶**Rookwood** (Ian & Betty Hudspith). ¼-acre, modern garden, herbaceous borders, pond, greenhouse, vegetable garden and fruit cage
> **Springfield House** &☙ (Capt & Mrs T Hardy) 1½-acres; semi-wild wooded dell, mature trees framing view to Mendips, shrubs, herbaceous plants, bulbs

Iford Manor see Wiltshire

Kingsdon &☙☙ (Mr & Mrs Charles Marrow) 2m SE of Somerton off B3151 Ilchester Rd. From Ilchester roundabout on A303 follow NT signs to Lytes Cary; left opp gates ½m to Kingsdon. 2-acre plantsman's garden and nursery garden. Over 500 varieties of unusual plants for sale. Teas in Village Hall. *Adm £2 Chd free. Sats, Suns May 7, 8; June 4, 5; July 2, 3 (2-7)*

Kites Croft ✿❀ (Dr & Mrs W I Stanton) Westbury-sub-Mendip 5m NW of Wells. At Westbury Cross on A371 turn uphill, right to square and left up Free Hill to Kites Croft 2-acre garden with fine views to Glastonbury Tor. Winding paths lead from the terrace to different levels; lawn, pond, rockery, herbaceous borders, shrubs and wood. Many unusual plants of interest to the flower arranger and cottage gardener. As featured on Channel 4 Garden Club. *Adm £1 Chd 30p. Sun July 17, Wed July 20, Sun Sept 11, Wed Sept 14 (2-5); also private groups welcome, please* **Tel 0749 870328.** *No coaches*

Landacre Farm ✿❀❀ (Mr & Mrs Peter Hudson) Withypool, nr Minehead. On the B3223 Exford/S. Molton Rd 3m W of Exford not in Withypool village. 9m NW of Dulverton ¼m above Landacre Bridge. ½-acre terraced garden 1000ft up on Exmoor. Developed from a field over past 18yrs by present owners; rockery, stream and bog garden, octagonal pergola, rhododendrons and shrub roses. Exposed position with fantastic views of Barle Valley and open moorland; specializing in climbers and hardy perennials. TEAS. *Adm £1. Chd free. Suns June 5, July 3, Aug 7 (2-.5.30). Private visits welcome, please* **Tel 064 383 223**

Leaside ❀❀ (Mr & Mrs M Hedderwick) Bruton. 1m SE of Bruton on B3081 (signposted Wincanton) turn E to Stourton 1st cottage on R. 1-acre field transformed into a nature garden with nearly 1000 fragrant shrubs and trees. Informal pond and old-fashioned roses. TEAS. *Adm £1 Chd free (Share to Bristol Area Kidney Patients Association®). Private visits welcome, please* **Tel 0749 813759**

Littlecourt ❀❀❀ (Jane Kimber & John Clothier) West Bagborough. 7m N of Taunton signed from A358. 6-acre garden in fine setting with woodland and water; spectacular new borders, interesting and extensive planting; wonderful views. *Private visits only, please* **Tel 0823 432281**

Lovibonds Farm ❀❀❀ (Mr & Mrs J A Griffiths) Burrowbridge. A361 from Taunton to Glastonbury, in village of Burrowbridge turn L immediately over bridge ½m on. 3-acre garden reclaimed 6yrs ago from derelict farmyard; herbaceous; shrub; bog garden; ponds and woodland walk; small lake with ornamental duck and geese. TEAS in aid of Burrowbridge WI. *Adm £1.50 Chd free. Suns May 15, June 12, 26 (2-5.30). Private visits welcome, please* **Tel 0823 698173**

Lower Severalls ❀❀❀ (Howard & Audrey Pring) 1½m NE of Crewkerne. Turning for Merriott off A30; or Haselbury Rd from B3165. Recently enlarged 1½-acre plantsman's garden beside early Ham stone farmhouse. Herbaceous borders incl collection of salvias and herbaceous geraniums. Herb garden. Shrubbery nursery (*open daily March 1 to Oct 31 10-5, Suns 2-5). Closed all day Thurs.* Sells herbs, unusual herbaceous plants and half-hardy conservatory plants. *Garden open April 1 to Sept 30.* TEAS. *Adm £1 Chd free. For NGS Suns June 12, July 10, Aug 14 (2-5)*

Regular Openers. See head of county section.

¶The Mill ❀❀❀ (Peter & Sally Gregson) Wookley. 2m W of Wells off A371. Turn L into Henley Lane, driveway 100 yds on L. 2½ acres beside R Axe. Traditional and unusual cottage plants informally planted in formal beds with roses, pergola, lawns and 'hot red border'. As seen on TV. Ornamental kitchen garden adjoining Nursery. Wide selection of plants from garden for sale. TEA. *Adm 75p Chd free. Private visits welcome, please* **Tel 0749 676966**

The Mill ❀❀ (Mr & Mrs J E Hudson) 21 Mill Lane, Cannington. 4m W of Bridgwater on A39. Turn opposite Rose & Crown. ¼-acre cottage type plantsman's garden with waterfall and pond, over 70 clematis and National Caltha Collection. Featured in NGS video 1, see page 344. TEA in aid of Cannington W.I. *Adm £1.50 Chd free (Share to NCCPG®). Suns June 5, Aug 7 (11-5). Weds June 8, Aug 10 (2-5). Private visits welcome, please* **Tel 0278 652304**

The Mill House ❀❀❀ (Mr & Mrs P J Davies) Castle Cary. Do not go into Castle Cary Town Centre, but follow signs to Torbay Rd Industrial Estate (W). Entrances to Trading Estate on L proceed E along Torbay Rd about 200yds. Garden on the R. Approx 1-acre terraced sloping garden, with stream and waterfalls. Emphasis on Natural look. Many interesting plants mingled with native flora. Bog garden; small orchard and vegetable plot. TEAS and plants in aid of Oncology Centre BRI Bristol. *Adm £1.50 Chd free. Sun, Mon May 29, 30 (2-6)*

Milton Lodge ❀❀ (D C Tudway Quilter Esq) ½m N of Wells. From A39 Bristol-Wells, turn N up Old Bristol Rd; car park first gate on L. Mature terraced garden with outstanding views of Wells Cathedral and Vale of Avalon. Mixed borders; roses; fine trees. Separate 7-acre arboretum. TEAS: Suns & Bank Hol Mons April to Sept. *Adm £2 Chd under 14 free (Share to National Eye Research Centre®). Open daily (2-6) ex Sats, Easter to end Oct; parties by arrangement. For NGS Suns May 15, 29, June 12, July 10 (2-6)*

Milverton Gardens 9m W of Taunton on the new B3227 (old A361) L at roundabout to Milverton. *Combined adm £1.50 Chd free. Sun June 26 (2-6)*

> **Barn Elms** ❀❀❀ (Mrs Pauline Dodd). L at Glebe Inn down Roebank Rd R at Houndsmoor Lane. 1-acre wild garden and ponds. Small formal garden; many interesting plants; imaginative design. TEAS (Share to Milverton Surgery Defibrillator Fund)
>
> **Cobbleside** ❀❀❀ (Mr & Mrs C Pine) ¾-acre walled garden incl newly laid out herb garden and potagere. Completely redesigned, with photographs illustrating the old layout. *Private visits welcome May to Sept please* **Tel 0823 400404**
>
> **3 The College** ❀ (Mr Eric Thresher) Small interesting garden, featuring fireplaces amongst shrubs and borders
>
> **Garden Cottage** ❀❀❀ (Mr & Mrs R Masters) Interesting plantsman's garden with many unusual plants for sale. TEAS in aid of Milverton Surgery Defibrillator Fund. Primroses in variety and other spring flowers for visitors by appt. *Private visits welcome May to Sept, please* **Tel 0823 400601**

Montacute Gardens 4m from Yeovil follow A3088, take slip road to Montacute, turn L at T-junction into village. TEAS. *Combined adm £2 Chd free. Sun June 19 (2-5.30)*

    Abbey Farm ❀ (Mr & Mrs G Jenkins) Turn R between Church and Kings Arms (no through Rd). 2½-acre of mainly walled gardens on sloping site provide setting for mediaeval Priory gatehouse. Garden laid out in 1966 and now being improved and extended. About half the garden suitable for wheelchairs. Parking available. TEAS in aid of St Catherine's Church Fund

    Park House ❀ (Mr & Mrs Ian McNab) Turn L (signposted Tintinhull) after red brick Council Houses and immediately R. Approx. 2-acres, spacious lawns; shrubs; walled garden with herbaceous borders and vegetable garden at present being redesigned. The literary Powys family lived here during their father's lifetime. Cream TEAS in aid of St Catherines Church Fund

Montacute House ᕀ✿❀ (The National Trust) Montacute. NT signs off A3088 4m W of Yeovil and A303 nr Ilchester. Magnificent Tudor House with contemporary garden layout. Fine stonework provides setting for informally planted mixed borders and old roses; range of garden features illustrates its long history. TEAS. *Adm Garden only £2.60 Chd £1.20. For NGS Sun June 5 (11.30-5.30)*

The Mount ✿❀ (Alison & Peter Kelly) Wincanton. Follow one-way system round lower half of town, bear L at signposted Castle Cary, on up hill, house on L. 1¼-acre. Plantswomans garden with hidden surprises. Alpine lawn and garden, half terraced shrub borders, gravel bed, rockery and pond. TEAS Suns. *Adm £1.50 Chd free. Sats April 23, Suns April 24, May 1; Weds June 1, 8 (2-5.30). Private visits welcome at weekends April to end June, please Tel 0963 32487 after sundown*

North Curry Village Gardens. North Curry 7m E of Taunton. Come to North Curry Village Centre. Gardens that open will be signed from there and there will be a map in the Post Office. TEAS. *Combined adm £2.50 Chd under 12 free. Sun June 12 (2-6)*

    2 Church Road ✿ (Mrs B D Barkham). A small cottage garden, long and narrow with herbaceous border, fruit trees and 3 small lawns.

    Fosse Cottage ᕀ (Mrs M Stone). ½-acre mixed shrubs, pond, rockery and small bog area; lawns, herbaceous and rose beds, cottage style

    Monksleigh ᕀ (Maj & Mrs Ian McDowall). ½-acre garden of mixed lawns, shrubs and herbaceous flower beds. Some old shrub roses

    ¶**Scallard House** ᕀ (Dr & Mrs Philip Hickman) ½-acre garden with lawns, climbers of interest; trees; shrubbery and herbaceous dingle; small organic vegetable plot, manicured field hedge; paving and brickwork

    1 Stoke Road ᕀ✿ (Mr & Mrs D Evans) ½-acre garden laid to lawn with colourful shrubs and perennial borders. Patio garden, tubs and hanging baskets

    Tanners ✿ (John Treble Esq) W side of Church Rd 100yds down from Queen Square. Approx ¼ acre small enclosed garden

    Thatchers ✿ (Maj & Mrs G W Lamb) Approx 1½ acres of garden with a large listed barn; lily pond; fine herbaceous border; many different roses and varied trees, shrubs. TEAS

¶**The Old Rectory** ᕀ❀ (Cdr & Mrs J R Hoover) Swell. 4m W of Langport on A378; signposted Swell, ½m S of A378. Mature informal garden of approx 1½ acres. Good trees; pool/bog plants; old-fashioned roses; a stone belfry from nearby ancient Church of St Catherine. TEAS. *Adm £1 Chd 50p. Sat, Sun June 18, 19 (2-6)*

Pear Tree Cottage ᕀ❀ (Mr & Mrs C R Parry) Stapley. 9m S of Taunton nr Churchingford. Charming cottage garden leading to 2½-acre newly made park; well planted with interesting trees and shrubs leading to old leat and mill pond. TEAS. *Adm £1 Chd 50p. Sat, Sun April 23, 24; May 7, 8 (2-6)*

Peart Hall ᕀ✿❀ (Mr & Mrs J Lawrence-Mills) Spaxton. Bridgwater 6m. Take West Street (signposted Spaxton) off dual carriageway Broadway (A39) in Bridgwater. In village, take Splatt Lane opp school, then L to church and garden. Extensive gardens include rockeries sloping to trout stream, riverside walk with weirs, waterfalls; Victorian herb garden; daffodils; many rare trees. TEAS in aid of Spastics. *Adm £1.50 Chd free. Sun March 27 (2-5)*

The Red House ᕀ✿❀ (Mr & Mrs James Lloyd) High Street, Cannington, Bridgwater. M5 exits 23 or 24. Take A38 to Bridgwater. From Bridgwater take the Minehead Rd. Cannington is 3m. The Red House is 300yds past War Memorial on the R. 3-acre garden on level site, created from a field since 1976. Walled garden (1710); good cross section of trees and shrubs; interesting herbaceous, perennials and bedding. TEAS in aid of St Mary the Virgin Church, Cannington. *Adm £1.50 Chd 50p. Sat, Sun July 16, 17 (2.30-5). Private visits welcome June and July (2.30-5), please Tel 0278 652239*

Shepton Nursery Garden ᕀ✿❀ (Mr & Mrs P W Boughton) Shepton Mallet. From SW of Shepton Mallet take Glastonbury Rd, turn R at Island Road sign to Community Hospital. On L 300yds. Yr-round informal cottage garden built over small concrete farmyard. Interesting and unusual plants and shrubs; numerous container plantings and interesting pelargoniums; climbers (mostly roses). *Adm £1. Tues, Weds May 3, 4; June 7, 8; July 5, 6; Aug 2,3 (all day). Private visits welcome at other times, please Tel Shepton Mallet 343630*

Smocombe House ✿❀ (Mr & Mrs Dermot Wellesley Wesley) Enmore. 4m W of Bridgwater take Enmore Rd, 3rd L after Tynte Arms. 5-acres S facing in Quantock Hills. Lovely woodland garden rising up hill behind the house; views down to stream and pool below; rhododendron woodland and waterside stocked with wide variety of interesting plants for spring display; 100 tree arboretum designed by Roy Lancaster; charming old kitchen garden. TEAS in aid of Enmore Parish Church. *Adm £1.50 Chd free. Suns April 10, May 15 (2-6)*

Spaxton Gardens ❀ Take A39 and Spaxton Rd W from Bridgwater. In village take Splatt Lane opp school. TEAS in aid of Spaxton Church. *Combined adm £1.50 Chd free. Sun May 1 (2.30-5.30)*

    Old Mill House ✿❀ (Mr & Mrs W Bryant) 2-acre beautiful, peaceful plantsman's garden beside a weir and trout stream. Many interesting plants. *(Plant stall in aid of RAF Benevolent Fund)*

Tuckers ⚘⚘ (Mrs John Denton) ½-acre delightful cottage garden with orchard leading over leat to Old Mill House. One way system to Old Mill House from Tuckers

Stapleton Manor ⚘⚘⚘ (Mr & Mrs G E L Sant) 1m N of Martock on B3165 Long Sutton Rd. 2½-acres of roses, shrubs; herbaceous and mixed borders; pool/bog garden; dahlia walk; grass area with small trees and shrubs; fine mature trees. Scheduled Georgian Hamstone house (not open). *Adm £1.50 Chd free. Sat July 2, Sun July 31(12-6)*

Stogumber Gardens ⚘⚘ A358 NW from Taunton for 11m. Sign to Stogumber W near Crowcombe. Seven delightful gardens of interest to plantsmen in lovely village at edge of Quantocks. TEAS. *Combined adm £2 Chd free. Sun June 19 (2-6)*

    Brook Cottage ⚘⚘ (Mrs M Field) Stogumber. Good plants incl. lilies in a lovely setting; small pond for added interest

    Butts Cottage (Mr & Mrs J A Morrison) Cottage garden with old roses, old-fashioned perennials, alpines, pond, small vine house and vegetable garden

    ¶**Cridlands Steep** (Mrs A M Leitch) Large and interesting garden with young collection of trees

    ¶**Manor House** (Mr & Mrs R W Lawrence) Large garden with borders and beds planted to give yr-round interest and colour

    ¶**Manor Linney** (Dr F R Wallace) A medium-sized garden full of colour and interest

    Orchard Deane ⚘⚘ (Mr & Mrs P H Wilson) Medium-sized garden, beds and borders with wide variety of hardy plants, bulbs and alpines

    Wynes ⚘ (Mr & Mrs L Simms) Large garden with orchard; shrubs; ponds; perennials; alpines and vegetable garden

Stone Allerton Gardens 11m NW of Wells, 2m from A38, signposted from Lower Weare. TEAS. *Combined adm £1.50 Chd free. Sun May 29, Mon May 30 (2-6)*

    Berries Brook ⚘ (Mr & Mrs D J Searle) ½-acre cottage garden. Roses, shrubs, pond

    Fallowdene ⚘ (Prof. & Mrs G H Arthur) ½-acre of walled gardens surrounding C18 house (not open). Rose and honeysuckle pergola, mixed shrub and herbaceous borders, lawns, kitchen garden and splendid view to the Quantocks

    Greenfield House ⚘ (Mr & Mrs D K Bull) Walled garden with climbers and mixed planting. House listed 1741 (not open). TEAS on Monday in aid of Guide Dogs for the Blind

    Manor Farm ⚘⚘⚘ (Mr & Mrs P Coate) 1-acre of mixed herbaceous and shrub beds, foliage bed, wall borders, water garden. Old orchard and many climbing plants, a painter's garden. Listed C18 House (not open). TEAS on Sunday in aid of Calcutta Rescue Fund. *Private visits welcome, please* Tel 0934 713015

    Mill House ⚘⚘⚘ (Mr & Mrs B W Metcalf) ¼-acre cottage style, plantsman's garden with unusual and a great variety of plants. Extensive views over levels to Quantocks. *Private visits welcome, please* Tel 0934 712459

Stowell Hill ⚘⚘ (Mr & Mrs Robert McCreery) NE of Sherborne. Turn at Stowell, ½m N of Templecombe on A357. Spring bulbs; collection of flowering shrubs; inc rhododendrons, azaleas, magnolias, Japanese cherries. TEAS. *Adm £1 Chd 50p. Suns May 1, 8, 15, 22 (2-5.30)*

Sutton Hosey Manor ⚘⚘ (Roger Bramble Esq) On A372 just E of Long Sutton. 2-acres; ornamental kitchen garden, lily pond, pleached limes leading to amelanchier walk past duck pond; rose and juniper walk from Italian terrace; Judas tree avenue. TEA. *Adm £1.50 Chd over 3 yrs 50p (Share to Marie Curie Cancer Research®). Sun July 10 (2.30-6)*

Thurloxton Gardens 4 m N of Taunton on A38, turn off at Maypole Inn and follow signs. TEAS. *Combined adm £1.50 Chd under 10 free (Share to Thurloxton Church Fabric Fund®). Sun July 24 (2-6)*

    ¶**Adsborough Farm** ⚘⚘ (Mr & Mrs Roger Stoakley) 14-yr-old garden constructed in the original farm yard with fine views over the Levels to the Mendip Hills. No parking, park nr Maypole Inn (200 yds)

    Coombe Quarry ⚘ (Miss Patricia Davies-Gilbert) Enchanting cottage garden; interesting plants and shrubs

    Magnolias ⚘⚘ (Margaret & Peter Brown) 1½ acres of informal mixed borders planted since 1986. Very wide range of plants incl many rare varieties

    The Old Rectory ⚘⚘ (Ann & Peter Comer) 2½ acres, mixed borders; shrubs; conservatory plants; tubs; hanging baskets; new pergola; beautiful views over Somerset Levels

    Porter's Cottage ⚘⚘ (Mrs Joyce Mason) 1 acre of established village garden with rose beds; pond and herbaceous borders

Tintinhull House ⚘⚘ (The National Trust) NW of Yeovil. NT signs on A303, W of Ilchester. Famous 2-acre garden in compartments, developed 1900-1960, influenced by Gertrude Jekyll and Hidcote; many good and uncommon plants. C17 & C18 house (not open). TEAS in aid of St Andrews Church. *Adm £3.30 Chd £1.60. (Party rate £2.60 Chd £1.20). For NGS Sun July 31 (2-6)*

Wambrook Gardens 2m SW Chard. Turn off A30 Honiton rd 1m W of Chard at top of hill. 6 gardens in beautiful wooded countryside; romantic views. TEAS/ Plants in aid of Wambrook Church Fabric Fund. *Combined adm £2 or 50p per garden Chd free. Sun June 26 (2-6)*

    The Cotley Inn ⚘ (Mr & Mrs D R Livingstone) Pub garden approx 1-acre created in the last 2 years comprising large lawn area with fishpond, shrubs, young trees and long flower border. TEAS

    Dennetts Farm ⚘⚘ (Mr & Mrs F J Stubbings) Working cottage garden with many herbs and vegetables grown for sale. Emphasis on ease of working and use of salvaged materials

    The Old Rectory ⚘⚘ (Mr & Mrs T P Jackson) Hillside garden in beautiful setting. Rose terrace; young rhododendrons, camellias, azaleas and heathers; water garden and ponds. Vegetable garden

    Wambrook House ⚘⚘ (Brig & Mrs Guy Wheeler) 2-acre organically run garden surrounding Regency rectory (not open); mature trees, mixed borders, roses; rockery, small water garden, walled vegetable garden with small vineyard

---

Regular Openers. See head of county section.

Yew Tree Cottage ✿✿ (Ron & Joan White) A picture book Thatched Cottage surrounded by lawns; herbaceous borders; shrubbery and productive organic vegetable garden

Watermeadows �&✿ (Mr & Mrs R Gawen) 200yds down the road from Clapton Court. A sophisticated cottage garden made from a field over 16yrs. There is something of everything including one hundred and twenty of the old-fashioned roses. Car park. TEA on request. *Adm £1 Chd free. Open Mon to Sat April to Sept (9-5). Private parties welcome, please* Tel 0460 74421

Wayford Manor ✿ (Mr & Mrs Robin L Goffe) SW of Crewkerne. Turning on B3165 at Clapton; or on A30 Chard-Crewkerne. 3 acres, noted for magnolias and acers. Bulbs; flowering trees, shrubs; rhododendrons. Garden redesigned by Harold Peto in 1902. Fine Elizabethan manor house (not open). TEAS. *Adm £1.50 Chd 50p. Suns April 10, May 1, 15, 29 (2-6); also private parties welcome, but please* Tel 0460 73253

Wellington Gardens ✿ W of Wellington 1m off A38 by-pass signposted Wrangway. 1st L towards Wellington Monument over motorway bridge 1st R. TEAS *Combined adm £1.50. Sat, Sun July 2, 3 (2-6)*
   Hangeridge Farm �&✿ (Mr & Mrs J M Chave) Wrangway. 1-acre garden, large lawns, herbaceous borders, flowering shrubs and heathers, raised rockeries, spring bulbs. Lovely setting under Blackdown Hills. *Also April 17 (2-6) Adm £1*
   Marlpit Cottage ✿ (Mr & Mrs John Manning) Wrangway. 200 yds above **Hangridge Farm**. An 8yr-old ½-acre garden. Informal mixed herbaceous borders, many interesting plants
   The Mount �&✿ (Jim & Gilly Tilden) Chelston. Off M5 1m NW of junction 26. At A38 Chelston roundabout take Wellington rd. After 200yds turn R to Chelston. 1st house on R. Enclosed garden with herbaceous borders and shrubs; trees, old roses, more shrubs and pond outside. 1 acre altogether. TEAS in aid of Wellington Stroke Club

West Bradley House �&✿ (Mr & Mrs E Clifton-Brown) Glastonbury. 2½m due E of Glastonbury. Turn S off A361 (Shepton Mallet/Glastonbury Rd) at W Pennard. House is next to church in scattered village of W Bradley. 3-acre open garden lying alongside 3 old carp ponds. 70 acres of apple orchards around house, hopefully in full blossom when garden open. Visitors welcome to walk (or even drive) through orchards. Parking available. TEAS in aid of W Bradley Church. *Adm garden & orchards £1.50 Chd 50p (Share to National Listening Library®). Sun May 8 (2-6)*

Westhay ✿ (Mr & Mrs T Thompson) Kingston St Mary Taunton. 1st house on the R up the hill after the White Swan Inn, Kingston St Mary. Landscaped walled garden, bog garden, small lake; wood walk; spring daffodil lawn; streams and informal shrubberies. Suitable for wheelchairs in parts. Cream TEAS. *Adm £1.50 Chd free. Sun May 29 (2-6)*

37 Whitmore Rd ✿✿ (Mr & Mrs E Goldsmith) Taunton. Leave Taunton following signs to Kingston; turn 1st left past Bishop Fox School; turn 2nd right into Whitmore rd. ⅓-acre flower garden with herbaceous and perennial plants laid out to make maximum use of space for pleasure garden, fruit and vegetable garden. Tea Taunton. *Adm 50p Chd 20p. Sun May 15, Wed May 18 (2-5)*

Withey Lane Farmhouse �& ✿✿ (Sqn Ldr & Mrs H C Tomblin) Barton St David. 4m E of Somerton, turn off B3153 in Keinton Manderville. Turn R in Barton opp Old Chapel Restaurant. 200yds turn L at Manor House. 300yds turn R into small lane; farmhouse 300yds on right. ½-acre plantsman's garden with many unusual and interesting plants; herbaceous beds with shrubs; raised alpine beds; old roses; climbing plants; vegetables grown organically in deep beds 1½-acre old cider orchard. *Adm £1 Chd 50p. Weds May and June (2-5.30); private visits welcome, please* Tel 0458 50875

Wootton House �&✿ (The Hon Mrs John Acland-Hood) Butleigh Wootton, 3m S of Glastonbury. Herbaceous borders; rose garden; shrubs, trees, bulbs; rock garden; woodland garden. C17 house (not open). TEA. *Adm £1.50 Chd under 5 free (Share to British Red Cross Society®). Sun April 10 (2-5.30)*

Staffordshire & part of West Midlands

Hon County Organisers: Mr & Mrs D K Hewitt, Arbour Cottage, Napley, Market Drayton, Shropshire TF9 4AJ Tel 0630 672852

DATES OF OPENING

By appointment
For telephone numbers and other details see garden descriptions. Private visits welcomed

The Covert, nr Market Drayton
12 Darges Lane, Great Wyrley

26 Fold Lane, Biddulph
Heath House, nr Eccleshall
Lower House, Sugnall Parva, Eccleshall
Manor Cottage, Chapel Chorlton
Park Farm, High Offley
Wedgwood Memorial College, Barlaston

The Wombourne Wodehouse, Wolverhampton

Regular openings
For details see garden descriptions

Dorothy Clive Garden, Willoughbridge. April 1 to Oct 31

Manor Cottage, Chapel Chorlton.
Every Mon May 2 to Sept 26

April 23 Saturday
Dorothy Clive Garden,
Willoughbridge
May 7 Saturday
Lower House, Sugnall Parva,
Eccleshall
May 8 Sunday
Lower House, Sugnall Parva,
Eccleshall
May 15 Sunday
The Bradshaws, Codsall
Hales Hall, Hales, nr Market
Drayton
May 22 Sunday
The Bradshaws, Codsall
Heath House, nr Eccleshall
Little Onn Hall, Church Eaton, nr
Stafford
Wedgwood Memorial College,
Barlaston
Wightwick Manor, Compton
May 29 Sunday
The Hollies Farm,
Pattingham ‡
Moor Croft, Pattingham ‡

The Wombourne Wodehouse,
Wolverhampton
June 5 Sunday
The Garth, Milford, Stafford
June 12 Sunday
12 Darges Lane, Walsall
26 Fold Lane, Biddulph
Little Onn Hall, Church Eaton, nr
Stafford
June 19 Sunday
Arbour Cottage, Napley
Moseley Old Hall, Fordhouses,
Wolverhampton
Park Avenue Gardens, Stafford
The Willows, Trysull
June 24 Friday
Farley Hall, Oakamoor
June 25 Saturday
Grafton Cottage,
Burton-under-Needwood
June 26 Sunday
The Garth, Milford, Stafford
July 3 Sunday
Biddulph Grange Garden, Biddulph
12 Darges Lane, Walsall
Eccleshall Castle Gardens,
Eccleshall
41 Fallowfield Drive,
Burton-under-Needwood

Grafton Cottage,
Burton-under-Needwood
July 10 Sunday
The Covert, nr Market Drayton
July 17 Sunday
Heath House, nr Eccleshall
August 7 Sunday
41 Fallowfield Drive,
Burton-under-Needwood
Grafton Cottage,
Burton-under-Needwood
The Willows, Trysull
August 28 Sunday
41 Fallowfield Drive,
Burton-under-Needwood
Grafton Cottage,
Burton-under-Needwood
September 3 Saturday
Dorothy Clive Garden,
Willoughbridge
September 18 Sunday
Biddulph Grange Garden,
Biddulph
October 9 Sunday
Wightwick Manor, Compton
October 16 Sunday
Wedgwood Memorial College,
Barlaston

DESCRIPTIONS OF GARDENS

Arbour Cottage ♿⚹❀ (Mr & Mrs D K Hewitt) Napley. 4m N of Market Drayton. Take A53 then B5415 signed Woore, turn L 1¾m at telephone box. Cottage garden 2 acres of alpine gardens, grasses, shrub roses and many paeonias, bamboos etc. Colour all the year round from shrubs and trees of many species. TEAS. *£1.50 Chd 50p (Share to St Mary's Church, Mucklestone®). Sun June 19 (2-5.30)*

Biddulph Grange Garden ⚹ (The National Trust) Biddulph. 5m SE of Congleton, 7m N of Stoke-on-Trent on A527. An exciting and rare survival of a high Victorian garden extensively restored since 1988. Conceived by James Bateman, the 15 acres are divided into a number of smaller gardens designed to house specimens from his extensive plant collection. An Egyptian Court; Chinese Pagoda, Willow Pattern Bridge; Pinetum and Arboretum together with many other settings all combine to make the garden a miniature tour of the world. TEAS. *Adm £3.90 Chd £1.95 Family £9.75. March 30 to Oct 30 Wed to Fri (12-6); Sat to Sun (11-6). For NGS Suns July 3, Sept 18 (11-6)* **Tel 0782 517999**

¶The Bradshaws ♿⚹❀ (Mrs R Smith & Miss S Smith) Oaken. 5m NW of Wolverhampton on A41 Wolverhampton-Newport Rd, 5m S off junction 3, M54. 15-acre landscaped garden, rhododendrons and azaleas planted 35yrs ago. Pools with wildfowl; specimen trees. **Dower Cottage** nearby with conservatory and cottage garden. TEAS. *Combined adm £1.50 Chd free (Share to Leonard Cheshire Foundation®). Suns May 15, 22 (2-6)*

The Covert ♿⚹❀ (Mr & Mrs Leslie Standeven) Burntwood Loggerheads. On Staffordshire/Shropshire borders. Turn off A53 Newcastle-Market Drayton Rd onto Burntwood at Loggerheads Xrds. A plantsman's cottage garden of approx ¾ acre, pool; bog garden, yucca bank; mixed borders and scree beds. Featuring many architectural, rare and unusual plants, shrubs and trees. TEAS. *Adm £1.50 Chd 50p. Sun July 10 (2-6). Private visits welcome, please* **Tel 0630 672677**

12 Darges Lane ⚹❀ (Ann and Ken Hackett) 12 Darges Lane, Great Wyrley. From A5 take A34 towards Walsall. Darges Lane is 1st turning on R (over brow of hill). House on R on corner of Cherrington Drive. ¼-acre well stocked plantsmans and flower arrangers garden. Foliage plants a special feature. Mixed borders including trees, shrubs and rare plants giving year round interest. As featured in Channel 4 Garden Club Sep 93. TEAS *Adm £1 Chd 50p. Suns June 12, July 3 (2-6). Also private visits welcome, please* **Tel 0922 415064**

Dorothy Clive Garden ♿ Willoughbridge. On A51 between Stone and Nantwich. 8-acre garden: woodland with rhododendrons and azaleas, spring bulbs, shrub roses; water garden and large scree in fine landscaped setting. Colourful flower borders in late summer and autumn are a feature. Car park. TEAS. *Adm £2 Chd 50p. April 1 to Oct 31. For NGS Sats April 23, Sept 3 (10-5.30)*

Eccleshall Castle Gardens ♿ (Mr & Mrs Mark Carter) ½m N of Eccleshall on A519; 6m from M6, junction 14 (Stafford); 10m from junction 15 (Stoke-on-Trent). 20 acres incl wooded garden with moat lawns around William and Mary mansion house; herbaceous, rose garden, wide variety of trees and shrubs; also recently renovated C14 tower. Home-made cream TEAS. Free car/coach parking. *Adm £1.50 Chd 50p.* ▲*For NGS Sun July 3 (2-5.30)*

41 Fallowfield Drive ♿✂❀ (Mrs S Webster) Barton-under-Needwood. Take B5016 from Barton-under-Needwood to Yoxall. Turn L before leaving Barton onto Park Drive, leading to Fallowfield Drive. ¼-acre colourful garden of summer flowers and shrubs with pool. TEAS. *Adm £1.50 Chd 25p. Suns July 3, Aug 7, 28 (1-6)*

Farley Hall ✂❀ (Lady Bamford) Oakamoor. From Uttoxeter follow signs to Alton Towers. On R 200 yds past Alton Towers entrance. Walled vegetable, fruit and perennial gardens; formal lawn containing pleached limes and yew hedges. *Adm £1.50 Chd free. Fri June 24 (2-5.30)*

26 Fold Lane ✂❀ (Mr & Mrs D Machin) Biddulph. 5m SE Congleton off the A527. Follow the signs for Biddulph Grange Gardens, turn into Grange Rd pass the entrance for Grange Gardens. 2nd L into Fold Lane, parking in garden & lane. 2-acre garden with herbaceous border. Informal cottage garden. Wild life pond area and old herb garden. TEAS. *Adm £1.50 Chd 50p (Share to Leek Memorial Hospital Gardens®). Sun June 12 (2-6). Also private visits welcome Mons June 13 to July 25 (2-6), please* **Tel 0782 513028**

The Garth ❀ (Mr & Mrs David Wright) 2 Broc Hill Way, Milford, 4½m SE of Stafford. A513 Stafford-Rugeley Rd; at Barley Mow turn R (S) to Brocton; L after 1m. ½-acre; shrubs, rhododendrons, azaleas, mixed herbaceous borders, naturalized bulbs; plants of interest to flower arrangers. Rock hewn caves. Fine landscape setting. Coach parties by appt. TEAS. *Adm £1 Chd 50p. Suns June 5, 26 (2-6)*

Grafton Cottage ✂ (Margaret & Peter Hargreaves) Bar Lane, Barton-under-Needwood. 5m N of Lichfield. Take B5016 between Barton-under-Needwood and Yoxall. Bar Lane is ½m W of Top Bell public house. ¾m along lane. A plant lovers cottage garden. ¼-acre. Designed and maintained by owners. Old roses; trelises with arches; mixed borders. Wide range of perennials with all-summer interest, stream. TEAS. *Adm £1.50 Chd 25p (Share to RNIB, Midland Region®). Sat, Suns June 25, July 3, Aug 7, 28 (1-6)*

¶Hales Hall ♿✂ (Mr & Mrs R Hall) Hales. Signposted to Hales due S from A53 between Market Drayton & Loggerheads. C18 house (not open) in beautiful setting. 15 acres of mixed garden particularly rhododendrons, azaleas, woodland and wild garden. Partially suitable for wheelchairs by prior arrangement. TEAS. *Adm £2 Chd 50p. Sun May 15 (2-5.30)*

Heath House ✂❀ (Dr & Mrs D W Eyre-Walker) Nr Eccleshall. 3m W of Eccleshall. Take B5026 towards Woore. At Sugnall turn L, after 1½m turn R immediately by stone garden wall. After 1m straight across crossroads. 1½-acre garden. Borders, bog garden, woodland garden. Many unusual plants. Car parking limited and difficult if wet. TEAS. *Adm £1.50 Chd free (Share to Parish Church®). Suns May 22, July 17 (2-6). Also private visits welcome, please* **Tel 0785 280318**

¶The Hollies Farm ✂❀ (Mr & Mrs J Shanks) Pattingham. From Wolverhampton A454 W, follow signs to Pattingham. Cross traffic lights at Perton, 1½m R for Hollies Lane. From Pattingham take Wolverhampton Rd 1m turn L to Hollies Lane. 2-acre plantsman's landscaped garden with very interesting trees and shrubs. TEAS. *Adm £1 Chd free. Sun May 29 (2-6)*

Little Onn Hall ♿ (Mr & Mrs I H Kidson) Church Eaton, 6m SW of Stafford. A449 Wolverhampton-Stafford; at Gailey roundabout turn W on to A5 for 1¼m; turn R to Stretton; 200yds turn L for Church Eaton; or Bradford Arms - Wheaton Aston & Marston 1¼m. 6-acre garden; herbaceous lined drive; abundance of rhododendrons; formal paved rose garden with pavilions at front; large lawns with lily pond around house; old moat garden with fish tanks and small ruin; fine trees; walkways. Paddock open for picnics. TEAS. *Adm £1.50 Chd 50p. Suns May 22, June 12 (2-6)*

Lower House ♿❀ (Mrs J M Treanor) Sugnall Parva, Eccleshall. 2m W of Eccleshall. On B5026 Loggerheads Rd turn R at sharp double bend. House ½m on L. Approx 1 acre in open countryside of mixed borders; pond; shrubs and rockery gradually being shaped from originally flat lawn areas. TEAS. *Adm £1.50 Chd free. Sat, Sun May 7, 8 (1-6). Also private visits welcome, please* **Tel 0785 851 378**

Manor Cottage ♿✂❀ (Mrs Joyce Heywood) Chapel Chorlton. 6m S of Newcastle-U-Lyme. On A51 Nantwich to Stone Rd turn behind Cock Inn at Stableford; white house on village green. ⅔-acre unusual plants in flower arrangers cottage garden, of special interest, ferns and grasses. TEAS. *Adm £1.50 Chd 50p. Mons May 2 to Sept 26 (2-5) also private visits welcome, please* **Tel 0782 680206**

¶Moor Croft ✂ (Mr & Mrs Peter Hollingsworth) Pattingham. Take the A454 signed to Bridgnorth. Follow signs to Pattingham. Cross traffic lights at Perton, 1m turn L Gt Moor Rd. Coming from Pattingham follow main rd to Wolverhampton for 1½m. Turn R at top of small rise for Great Moor. An interesting landscaped garden of mixed beds and trees leading to an old water meadow with stream. Fine old willows and alders together with more recent plantings. *Adm £1 Chd 50p. Sun May 29 (2-6)*

Moseley Old Hall ♿✂❀ (The National Trust) Fordhouses, 4m N of Wolverhampton, between A460 & A449 south of M54 motorway; follow signs. Small modern reconstruction of C17 garden with formal box parterre; mainly includes plants grown in England before 1700; old roses, herbaceous plants, small herb garden, arbour. Late Elizabethan house. TEAS. *Adm House & Garden £3.20 Chd £1.60; Garden £1.60 Chd 80p. Sun June 19 (2-5.30)*

¶**Park Avenue Gardens** ⚹ Rising Brook. Leave M6 at Junction 13, A449 towards Stafford, approx 2m, past Royal Oak on R, past Westway on L, next turn L. From Stafford A449 over railway bridge, 4th turn on R. *Combined adm £1 Chd free (Share to St Mary's Church®). Sun June 19 (2-5.30)*

36 Park Avenue (Mr & Mrs W Harper) ⅛-acre, roses, shrubs and mixed borders

38 Park Avenue (Mr & Mrs E V Aspin) Small suburban mixed garden from nearly formal to nearly wild. Old roses, shrubs, clematis, fruit trees. TEA

¶**Park Farm** ᏻ⚹❀ (Mr & Mrs Peter Celecia) High Offley. 4m W of Eccleshall. Take A519 towards Newport. At Woodseaves sign turn R into Back Lane, at T-junction turn R Park Lane 1m on R. A developing informal country cottage garden of 1 acre. Interesting trees, shrubs, mixed borders; pool and vegetable garden. *Adm £1.50 Chd free (Share to Multiple Sclerosis®). Private visits welcome, Suns April 10 to July 31, Weds June 8 to July 27* **Tel 0785 284248** *before 9-30 am*

Wedgwood Memorial College ❀ Station Rd, Barlaston. In centre of Barlaston Village 5m S of Stoke on Trent. Leave M6 at junctions 14 or 15 take A34. Extensive grounds and gardens, the main feature being the aboretum with nearly 400 species of tree incl cherry, sorbus, and maple. Contemporary sculpture garden incorporated in the grounds and arboretum. TEAS. *Adm £1.50 Chd 50p. Suns May 22 (2-5.30), Oct 16 (2-4.30) also private visits welcome May to Oct, please* Tel 0782 372105

Weston Park see Shropshire

Wightwick Manor ᏻ (The National Trust) Compton, 3m W of Wolverhampton A454, Wolverhampton-Bridgnorth, just to N of rd, up Wightwick Bank, beside Mermaid Inn. Partly suitable for wheelchairs. 17-acre, Victorian-style garden laid out by Thomas Mawson; yew hedges; topiary; terraces; 2 pools; rhododendrons; azaleas. House closed. Coffee & biscuits. *Adm £2 Chd £1. For NGS Suns May 22, Oct 9 (2-6)*

The Willows ᏻ⚹❀ (Mr & Mrs Nigel Hanson) Trysull. 7m SW of Wolverhampton. From A449 at Himley B4176 towards Bridgnorth, 2¼m turn R to Trysull. ¾m on L. 2-acre garden created and maintained by present owners since 1981. Designed for all-year-round interest. Natural pool, hostas, rhododendrons, old fashioned roses, colour theme borders with a wide range of unusual shrub and perennials. Teas in village hall. *Adm £1.50 chd free. Suns June 19, Aug 7 (2-6)*

The Wombourne Wodehouse ᏻ⚹❀ (Mr & Mrs J Phillips) 4m S of Wolverhampton just off A449 on A463 to Sedgley. 18-acre garden laid out in 1750. Mainly rhododendrons, herbaceous and iris border, woodland walk, water garden. TEAS. *Adm £1.50 Chd free (Share to Cancer Research®). Sun May 29 (2-6); also private visits welcome, please* **Tel 0902 892202**

> **Regular Openers**. See head of county section

Suffolk

Hon County Organisers:

(East) Mrs Robert Stone, Washbrook Grange, Washbrook, Nr Ipswich Tel 0473 730244

(West) Lady Mowbray, Hill House, Glemsford, Nr Sudbury Tel 0787 281 930

Asst Hon County Organiser: (East) Mrs B R Jenkins, SRN, SCM, Paigles, 6 The Street, Holton-St-Peter, Halesworth 1P19 8PH Tel 0986 873731

Mrs R I Johnson, The Old Farmhouse, Flixton Road, Bungay NR35 1PD

(West) Mrs M Pampanini, The Old Rectory, Hawstead, Bury St Edmunds IP29 5NT Tel 0284 386 613

Hon County Treasurer (West): Sir John Mowbray

DATES OF OPENING

By appointment

For telephone numbers and other details see garden descriptions. Private visits welcomed

Bucklesham Hall, Bucklesham
4 Church Street, Hadleigh
13 Drapers Lane, Ditchingham
Gable House, Redisham
Grundisburgh Hall, Woodbridge
Pippin Cottage, nr Newmarket
2 Pound Cottages, Long Melford Gardens

Rosemary, East Bergholt
Rumah Kita, Bedfield
St Stephens Cottage, Spexhall
Thrift Farm, Cowlinge, nr Newmarket
Thumbit, Walsham-le-Willows
25 Westbury Ave, Bury St Edmunds

Regular openings

For details see garden descriptions

Blakenham Woodland Garden, Daily except Sat March 1 to June 30

Euston Hall, nr Thetford June 2 to Sept 29

April 3 Sunday

Barham Hall, Barham Ipswich
Darsham House, nr Saxmundham
Warwick House, Bury St Edmunds
25 Westbury Avenue, Bury St Edmunds

April 10 Sunday

Great Thurlow Hall, Haverhill
Nedging Hall, nr Hadleigh
St Stephens Cottage, Spexhall

April 24 Sunday
The Abbey, Eye
Blakenham Woodland Garden
Magnolia House, Yoxford
The Rookery, Eyke

May 1 Sunday
Blakenham Woodland Garden
13 Drapers Lane, Ditchingham
Felsham House, Bury St Edmunds

May 2 Monday
13 Drapers Lane, Ditchingham

May 14 Saturday
Warwick House, Bury St Edmunds

May 15 Sunday
Catkins, Lawshall, nr Bury St
Edmunds ‡
Keepers Cottage, Lawshall ‡
Warwick House, Bury St Edmunds

May 22 Sunday
The Abbey, Eye
Battlies House, Rougham
The Priory, Stoke by Nayland
Ruggs Cottage, Raydon
Woottens, Wenhaston

May 29 Sunday
Chequers, Boxford
Grundisburgh Hall, Woodbridge
Riverside House, Stoke Rd, Clare

June 5 Sunday
The Lawn, Walsham-le-Willows
The Old Rectory, Brinkley, nr
Newmarket ‡
The Rookery, Eyke
Thrift Farm, Cowlinge, nr
Newmarket ‡

June 12 Sunday
Hengrave Hall, Hengrave
Moat Cottage, Great Green,
Cockfield
The Old Rectory, Cockfield

Pippin Cottage, nr Newmarket
Rosemary, East Bergholt
Somerleyton Hall, Lowestoft
Stour Cottage, East Bergholt
The Spong, Groton

June 18 Saturday
Ellingham Hall, Nr Bungay

June 19 Sunday
Gable House, Redisham
Little Thurlow Hall, Haverhill
Long Melford Gardens, Long
Melford
Playford Hall, Ipswich
Rumah Kita, Bedfield
Warwick House, Bury St Edmunds
Woottens, Wenhaston

June 26 Sunday
The Abbey, Eye
Euston Hall, nr Thetford
Gifford's Hall, Wickhambrook
Grundisburgh Hall, Woodbridge
Hillside, Freston
North Cove Hall, Beccles
Pippin Cottage, nr Newmarket
Ruggs Cottage, Raydon
Thumbit, Walsham-le-Willows
Tollemache Hall, Offton
Wyken Hall, Stanton

June 27 Monday
Ruggs Cottage, Raydon

June 28 Tuesday
Ruggs Cottage, Raydon

July 3 Sunday
21 Bederic Close, Bury St
Edmunds
Garden House, 5 Brookside,
Moulton
South View, Hawstead Green

July 10 Sunday
Holbecks, Hadleigh

Redisham Hall, Beccles
Woottens, Wenhaston

July 17 Sunday
Catkins, Lawshall, Nr Bury St
Edmunds
Fort Henry, Martlesham Heath

July 23 Saturday
Orchard End, Rishangles

July 24 Sunday
Orchard End, Rishangles

August 7 Sunday
Akenfield, 1 Park Lane, Charsfield
The Beeches,
Walsham-Le-Willows
Ruggs Cottage, Raydon
Woottens, Wenhaston

August 8 Monday
Akenfield, 1 Park Lane,
Charsfield
Ruggs Cottage, Raydon

August 9 Tuesday
Akenfield, 1 Park Lane, Charsfield

August 10 Wednesday
Akenfield, 1 Park Lane, Charsfield

August 11 Thursday
Akenfield, 1 Park Lane, Charsfield

August 12 Friday
Akenfield, 1 Park Lane, Charsfield

August 13 Saturday
Akenfield, 1 Park Lane, Charsfield

August 14 Sunday
Akenfield, 1 Park Lane, Charsfield

August 21 Sunday
21 Bederic Close, Bury St Edmunds

September 4 Sunday
Euston Hall, nr Thetford
Ickworth House, Park & Gardens,
Bury St Edmunds

September 25 Sunday
St Stephens Cottage, Spexhall

DESCRIPTIONS OF GARDENS

The Abbey &✿❀ (Mrs K Campbell) Eye. 6m S of Diss, Norfolk. Leaving Eye on B1117 passing Eye Church on L cross River Dove and The Abbey is immediately on the L with ample parking. Marked remains of Benedictine Priory on some maps. The garden is approx. 3 acres and surrounds a red brick and flint timber framed house incorporating a Benedictine Abbey founded in the 11th century. The remains of the church such as are above ground make for interesting gardening with walls and courtyards. Raised beds and sink gardens and 2 large glasshouses. Unusual plants, many double primroses and auriculas, iris and roses and a large herbaceous collection. Minature geraniums and succulents are in the glasshouses. Ample parking. TEAS. *Adm £1.50 OAP & Chd 75p. Suns April 24, May 22, June 26 (2-5.30)*

Akenfield, 1 Park Lane ✿❀ (Mrs E E Cole) Charsfield, 6m N of Woodbridge. On B1078, 3m W of Wickham Market. ½-acre council house garden; vegetables, flowers for

drying, 2 greenhouses; small fishponds with water wheel; many pot plants etc. In village of Charsfield (known to many readers and viewers as Akenfield). TEAS Sunday only. *Adm £1 OAPs 75p Chd free. ▲For NGS Sun Aug 7 daily to Sun Aug 14 (10.30-7)*

Barham Hall &✿❀ (Mr & Mrs Richard Burrows) Barham. Ipswich to A45 going W. 4m sign Great Blakenham to roundabout beneath motorway. Leave by 3rd turning to Claydon. Through Claydon, after decontrolled signs turn R up Church Lane to Barham Green. ½m up Church Lane. Barham church on L.h.s Barham Hall behind long brick wall. 7 acres of undulating gardens mainly recreated during the last 5yrs. 3 herbaceous borders, a lake surrounded by azaleas and bog plants, a woodland shrub garden full of spring flowers; a very considerable collection of victorian roses set in well kept lawns with mature trees; a water garden and many other interesting features. St Peter's Church open with famous Henry Moore sculpture. TEAS. *Adm £1.50 OAPs £1 Chd 25p (Shore to St Mary's & St Peters Church Barham®). Sun April 3 (2-5)*

Rattlies House ఈ * (Mr & Mrs John Darrell) Bury St Edmunds. Turn N off the A45 at the GT Barton and Rougham industrial estate turning, 3m E of Bury St Edmunds. In ½m turn R by the lodge. 8-acre garden laid out to lawns; shrubberies; woodland walk with a variety of old trees; rhododendrons; elms and conifers. TEAS. *Adm £1.50 Chd free (Share to St Nicholas' Hospice®). Sun May 22 (2-5.30)*

21 Bederic Close *&&* (Mrs S Robinson) Bury St Edmunds. Leave A45 at exit for Bury St Edmunds (E) and Sudbury. Proceed N and at 1st roundabout (Sainsbury's entrance) turn L into Symonds Rd. After R angled turn at end take 1st R into Bederic Close. ⅙ acre surbuban garden enthusiastically developed over 10yrs with rockery and water garden. Over 500 old-fashioned, unusual rare plants and shrubs. Emphases on conservation to encourage wildlife. Finalist in Gardener of the Year Competition. *Adm £1.50 Chd free.* ▲*For NGS Suns July 3, Aug 21 (2.30-6)* Tel 0284 764310

¶The Beeches ఈ (Dr & Mrs A J Russell) Walsham-le-Willows. 10m NE of Bury St Edmunds; signed Walsham-le-Willows off A143. At Xrds in village pass Church on L, after 50yds turn L along Grove Rd. Pink house behind Church. 3 acres; lawns, herbaceous border, mature and newly-planted trees. Potager, thatched summer house with ornamental pond, gazebo and wild garden by stream. TEAS. *Adm £1.50 Chd free (Share to St Mary's Church, Walsham-le-Willows©). Sun Aug 7 (2-6)*

Blakenham Woodland Garden *&* Little Blakenham. 4m NW of Ipswich. Follow signs from 'The Beeches' at Lt Blakenham, 1m off the old A1100, now called B1113. 5-acre bluebell wood densely planted with fine collection of trees and shrubs; camellias, magnolias, cornus, azaleas, rhododendrons, roses, hydrangeas. *Adm £1 Chd £1. Open daily (1-5) except Sats, March 1 to June 30. For NGS Suns Apr 24, May 1 (1-5)*

Bucklesham Hall *&&* (Mr & Mrs P A Ravenshear) Bucklesham 6m SE of Ipswich, 1m E of village opp to Bucklesham Village School. 7 acres; created and maintained by owners since 1973; unusual plants, shrubs, trees; shrub/rose garden; water and woodland gardens. Partly suitable for wheelchairs. *Adm £2 Chd free. Reduction for large parties. Private visits welcome, please* Tel 0473 659263

¶Catkins * (Mr & Mrs K W Lorking) Lawshall. 6m S of Bury St Edmunds. From A134 Bury to Sudbury turn R at Lawshall signpost. Approx 2m through village past church. Turn L at Village Hall into Lambs Lane. Last bungalow on R before Xrds. Medium-sized plantsman's garden full of interesting plants; specialities incl hostas, day lilies, hellebores, aroids, iris, clematis, grasses and ferns; herbaceous borders shaded areas; ponds, patio featuring many container subjects. Tranquil setting with hidden treasures. TEA. *Adm £1 Chd 50p. Suns May 15, July 17 (10-6)*

Chequers ఈ (Miss J Robinson) Boxford, 5m W of Hadleigh via A1071. From Sudbury A134 then A1071. From Ipswich A1071, from Colchester A134. 2-3-acre plantsman's walled and stream gardens full of rare plants. TEA. *Adm £1.25 Chd free. Sun May 29 (2-6)*

4 Church Street *&&* (Lewis Hart) Hadleigh. Approx 6m W of Ipswich on the A1071. 25yds from St Mary's Church. ⅓-acre old walled garden. Wide range of lesser known plants. Many clematis, penstemon, iris, euphorbia, alpines; trees and shrubs incl. sorbus, skimmia, indigofera. Collection of plants in sinks and tubs. *Donation box. Private visits welcome, please* Tel 0473 822418

¶Darsham House ఈ*&&* (Mr & Mrs Peter Low) About 6m N of Saxmundham on A12. Take 1st R after level crossing, through village to Church, signed from there. About 4 acres of relatively newly designed garden. Lime avenue, daffodils, woodland, good trees, pergola, shrubs. *Adm £1.50 Chd 50p. Sun April 3 (2-5)*

13 Drapers Lane *&&* (Mr & Mrs Borrett) Ditchingham. 1¼m Bungay off the B1332 towards Norwich. ⅓-acre containing many interesting, unusual plants including 80 plus varieties of hardy geraniums, climbers and shrubs. Herbaceous perennials a speciality. Owner maintained. TEAS. *Adm £1 Chd free. Sun, Mon May 1, 2 (10-4). Private visits also welcome, please* Tel 0986 893366

¶Ellingham Hall ఈ*&&* (Col & Mrs H M L Smith) On A143 between Beccles 3m and Bungay 2m. Georgian house set in parkland. An enormous amount of tree planting and conservation work has been carried out since 1984. The 2-acre garden has been restored and laid out. Designed by Sue Gill (see Great Campston, Gwent). It is now planted in deep borders with a wide and unusual variety of plants and trees. Walled garden with fan trained fruit trees. TEAS. *Adm £1.50 Chd 50p. Sat June 18 (2-5.30)*

●Euston Hall *&* (The Duke & Duchess of Grafton) on the A1088 12m N of Bury St Edmunds. 3m S of Thetford. Terraced lawns; herbaceous borders, rose garden, C17 pleasure grounds, lake. C18 house open; famous collection of paintings. C17 church; temple by William Kent. Craft shop. Wheelchair access to gardens, tea-room and shop only. TEAS in Old Kitchen. *Adm house & garden £2.50 OAPs £2, Chd 50p Parties of 12 or more £2 per head (Share to NGS®). Thurs June 2 to Sept 29; Suns June 26 & Sept 4 (2.30-5)*

Felsham House ఈ*&* (The Hon David & Mrs Erskine) Felsham 7m SE of Bury St Edmunds off A134, 8m W of Stowmarket via Rattlesden. 5 acres incl meadow with wild flowers, established trees, shrubs, roses; herb garden. TEAS. *Adm £1.20 Chd 50p. Sun May 1 (2-6)*

Fort Henry ఈ*&* (Gerald Ashton Esq) 17 York Rd. Martlesham Heath. Turn L at Telecom roundabout into Eagle Way, approx ¼m turn 2nd L into Lancaster Rd which leads into York Rd. Small interesting garden planted with box parterres, roses and bedding. Deep pond and fountains. Medusa's Grotto. (Unsuitable for small children). *Adm £1 (Share to Ipswich Diabetic Centre©). Sun July 17 (2-6)*

By Appointment Gardens. These owners do not have a fixed opening day usually because they do not like crowds or have insufficient parking space. Owner will often give guided tour.

Gable House &%✿ (Mr & Mrs John Foster) Redisham. 3½m S of Beccles. Mid-way between Beccles and Halesworth on Ringsfield-Ilketshall St Lawrence Rd. Garden of 1 acre, mixed borders, alpines, fruit and vegetables. Home-made TEAS. *Adm £1 (Share to St Peters Church Redisham, Beccles, Suffolk®). Sun June 19 (2-5.30). Private visits welcome Suns from May to Sept* Tel 0502 79298

Garden House &%✿ (Mr & Mrs J F Maskelyne) Moulton. 3m E of Newmarket. Follow signs for Gazeley. In Moulton village turn R down Brookside bordering the village green. 9m from Bury St Edmunds. Interesting ¾-acre plantsmans garden; roses, small woodland area, alpines and mixed borders. Lge collection of clematis; committee member of British Clematis Society; maintained by owners. TEAS. *Adm £1 Chd 50p. Sun July 3 (2-6)*

Gifford's Hall &% (Mrs J M Gardner) Wickhambrook; 10m SW of Bury St Edmunds, 10m NE of Haverhill, ¾m from Plumbers' Arms, Wickhambrook in direction of Bury St Edmunds on A143, garden ¾m up lane. Medium-sized garden; roses; herbaceous borders. C15 moated manor house (not open). TEA. *Adm £1.25 Chd (under 14) 25p. Sun June 26 (2-5.30)*

Great Thurlow Hall & (Mr & Mrs George Vestey) Haverhill. N of Haverhill. Great Thurlow village on B1061 from Newmarket; 3½m N of junction with A143 Haverhill-Bury St Edmunds rd. 20 acres. Walled kitchen garden, herbaceous borders, shrubs, roses, spacious lawns, river walk, trout lake. Daffodils and blossom. TEA. *Adm £1.50 Chd free. Sun April 10 (2-5)*

Grundisburgh Hall &%✿ (Lady Cranworth) 3m W of Woodbridge on B1079, ¼m S of Grundisburgh on Grundisburgh to Ipswich Rd. Approx 5 acres walled garden with yew hedges; wisteria walk and mixed borders. Old rose garden; lawns and ponds. TEAS. *Adm £2 Chd free (Share to St Marys Grundisburgh, St Botolphs Culpho®). Suns May 29, June 26 (2-6). Private visits also welcome, please* Tel 0473 735 485

¶**Hengrave Hall** &%✿ Hengrave. 3½m NW Bury St Edmunds on A1101. Tudor mansion (tours available). Lake and woodland path. 5-acre formal garden with spacious lawns. Mixed borders with some unusual plants. Kitchen garden. TEAS in aid of Hengrave Bursary Fund. *Adm £2 OAPs £1 Chd free. Sun June 12 (2-6)*

¶**Hillside** %✿ (Mr & Mrs J M Paul) Freston. 3m S of Ipswich on the S bank of the R Orwell on the B1456 to Shotley just before the Freston Boot public house on the R. Approx 3 acres of gently sloping garden on well-drained light land. A wide variety of trees, shrubs and herbaceous plants, incl some more tender species due to the proximity to the R Orwell and lack of hard frosts. Vegetable garden, greenhouses and newly developed swimming pool garden. TEAS. *Adm £1.50 Chd free. Sun June 26 (2-6)*

Holbecks ✿ (Sir Joshua & Lady Rowley) Hadleigh. From Hadleigh High St turn into Duke St signed to Lower Layham; immediately over bridge go right up concrete rd to top of hill. 3 acres; early C19 landscape terraced and walled gardens, flowerbeds, roses and ornamental shrubs. TEA. *Adm £1 Chd 25p (Share to Suffolk Historic Churches Trust®). Sun July 10 (2-5.30)*

Ickworth House, Park & Gardens &% (The National Trust) Horringer. 3m SW of Bury St. Edmunds on W side of A143 (155:TL8161) 70 acres of garden. South gardens restored to stylized Italian landscape to reflect extraordinary design of the house. Fine orangery, agapanthus, geraniums and fatsias. North gardens informal wild flower lawns with wooded walk; the Buxus collection, great variety of evergreens and Victorian stumpery. New planting of cedars. The Albana Wood, an C18th feature, initially laid out by Capability Brown, incorporates a fine circular walk. Restaurant. *Adm £1.50 (park and garden) Chd 50p. Sun Sept 4 (10-4.30)*

Keepers Cottage &% (Mr & Mrs P Coy) Bury Rd Lawshall. 6m S of Bury St Edmunds; from A134 Bury St Edmunds to Sudbury turn R at Lawshall signpost; proceed for 2½m through village to T junction turn R on Bury Road and proceed for ½m. ½-acre garden surrounding a C15 thatched cottage; many mixed borders of shrubs; perennials; roses and bulbs; backing on to woodland. TEAS. *Adm £1.50 Chd free. Sun May 15 (2-6)*

The Lawn & (Mr & Mrs R Martineau) Walsham-le-Willows. 10m NE of Bury St Edmunds. Leave A143 on Ixworth by-pass at sign Walsham-le-Willows. House on R ½m short of village. 3-acres, herbaceous borders, lawns, small walled garden. The main garden overlooks parkland. Woodland walk, short circuit 5-10 mins. Large circuit 10-15 mins. TEAS. *Adm £1 Chd free. Sun June 5 (2.30-6)*

Little Thurlow Hall &✿ (Mr & Mrs E Vestey) Thurlow. On B1061 between Newmarket and Haverhill, in the middle of village. A re-made garden started in 1987; herbaceous and lily borders; sunken garden; rose garden, ancient canals; orchard, formal box edged herb and kitchen gardens, greenhouses and conservatory, shrubberies, many unusual plants; woodland and lakeside walks. Approx 20 acres in all. Paddocks with horses. TEA. *Adm £1.50 Chd 50p. Sun June 19 (2-6)*

Long Melford Gardens Gardens on Long Melford Village Green. Ely House, Church Walk. 2 Pound Cottages S of Ely House. Sun House in centre at village opp the Cock and Bell. TEAS at Sun House. Long Melford is 3½m N of Sudbury on A134. *Combined adm £2 Chd free (Share to Friends of Holy Trinty Church, Long Melford®). Sun June 19 (2-6)*

  Ely House & (Miss Jean M Clark) Small walled garden; mixed borders; ponds and fountains
  2 Pound Cottages %✿ (Dr Jack Litchfield) A small front garden and a long narrow back garden of approx ¼-acre; informally planted with a wide variety of shrub and herbaceous plants including many lilies and unusual plants. *Private visits also welcome, please* Tel 0787 312730
  Sun House &% (Mr & Mrs John Thompson) Two attractive adjacent walled gardens with roses, shrubs and herbaceous borders. Interesting collection of clematis. Water and architectural features

Magnolia House ⚘ (Mr Mark Rumary) On A1120 in centre of Yoxford. Small, completely walled village garden. Mixed borders with flowering trees, shrubs, climbers, bulbs, hardy and tender plants. *Adm £1 Chd free. Sun April 24 (2.30-6)*

Moat Cottage ⚘ (Stephen & Lesley Ingerson) Great Green. Cockfield. Take A134 S from Bury St Edmunds. After Sicklesmere village turn sharp L for Cockfield Green and R at 1st Xrds. Follow winding rd through Bradfield St Clare. At Great Green fork L Moat Cottage is opp garage at far end. 1 acre of enchanting cottage garden created over the last 6yrs and forever changing. The garden is divided into smaller areas incl white, herb and rose gardens, herbaceous borders, with a kitchen garden that provides the owners with all year round vegetables. Teas at Old Rectory (½m). *Combined adm with The Old Rectory £1.50 OAPs £1 Chd free. Sun June 12 (2-6)*

Nedging Hall ⚘ (Mr & Mrs Brian Buckle) Nedging. 4m N of Hadleigh via A1141 and B1115 towards Bildeston. Keep R for Nedging on B1078. House on R-side of rd. 15 acres of park-like garden, especially good in spring with bulbs. Lake and many fine trees; baby lambs. TEAS. *Adm £1 Chd 50p. Sun April 10 (2-5)*

North Cove Hall ⚘ (Mr & Mrs B Blower) Beecles. Just off A146 3½m E of Beecles on Lowestoft Rd. Take sign to North Cove. 5 acres of garden; large pond; mature and interesting young trees. Walled kitchen garden; shrub roses; herbaceous borders; woodland walks. TEAS. *Adm £1.50 Chd free. Sun June 26 (2.30-6)*

The Old Rectory, Brinkley ⚘ (Mr & Mrs Mark Coley) 6m S of Newmarket B1061, then B1052. After Brinkley post office, 1st left down Hall Lane, Old Rectory at bottom on R with white gates. 2-acre garden created over last 15yrs; mixed borders and some interesting trees. TEA. *Adm £1 Chd 50p. Sun June 5 (2-6)*

The Old Rectory, Parsonage Green ⚘ (Mr & Mrs David Marshall) Cockfield. Take A134 S from Bury St Edmunds. After 5 ½m turn SE onto A1141, signposted Lavenham. 1 ¼m turn L (E) signposted Cockfield and Stowmarket. Old Rectory 1m on R by small green. ½m to Moat Cottage. Approx 8 acres with moat, lawns, mature trees and walled garden with herbaceous beds. TEAS. *Combined adm with Moat Cottage £1.50 OAPS £1 Chd free. Sun June 12 (2-6)*

Orchard End ⚘ (Mr & Mrs N C Cass) Rishangles. 3m S of Eye on rd between Occold and Bedingfield. ½-acre recently created garden with island beds and water feature. Mostly perennials and shrubs but also extensive and interesting geranium collection. 2 acres being developed for wildlife. TEA. *Adm £1.50 OAPs £1 Chd free. Sats, Suns July 23, 24 (2-6)*

Pippin Cottage ⚘ (Mr & Mrs Sanders) Woodditton. Leave E end of Newmarket on B1061 for Haverhill, almost immediately fork L (signpost Woodditton) continue approx 3m and at 2nd Xroads turn R. Garden is 2nd thatched cottage on L nearly opposite Three Blackbirds public house. 1½-acre garden designed and planted by owners, surrounding a C17 cottage; large collection of

trees, shrubs, hardy perennials, shrub roses etc; natural pond and paved areas covered with alpines, paddock and small wooded area; TEA. *Adm £1 Chd 30p. Suns June 12, 26 (2-6). Also open by appointment* **Tel 0638 730857**

Playford Hall ⚘ (Mr & Mrs R D Innes). Edge of Playford Village, situated between Ipswich and Woodbridge. Moated Elizabethan house surrounded by 10-acre garden with lake, lawns, fine trees, herbaceous borders enclosed by yew hedges, shrub borders with many rare shrubs and interesting selection of shrub and climbing roses. TEAS. *Adm £1.50 Chd free. Sun June 19 (2-6)*

The Priory ⚘ (Mr & Mrs H F A Engleheart) Stoke-by-Nayland (1m); 8m N of Colchester, entrance on B1068 rd to Sudbury. Interesting 9-acre garden with fine views over Constable countryside, with lawns sloping down to small lakes & water garden; fine trees, rhododendrons & azaleas; walled garden; mixed borders & ornamental greenhouse. Wide variety of plants; peafowl. TEAS. *Adm £1.50 Chd free. Sun May 22 (2-6)*

Redisham Hall ⚘ (Mr Palgrave Brown) SW of Beccles. From A145 1½m S of Beccles, turn W on to Ringsfield-Bungay Rd. Beccles, Halesworth or Bungay, all within 6m. 5 acres; parkland and woods 400 acres. Georgian house C18 (not shown). Safari rides. TEAS (3.30-5 only). *Adm £1.50 Chd free (Share to East Suffolk Macmillan Nurses®). Sun July 10 (2-6)*

Riverside House ⚘ (Mr & Mrs A C W Bone) Stoke Rd, Clare. On the A1092 leading out of Clare towards Haverhill. Approx 1 acre riverside garden, mainly walled, laid out with lawns, trees, shrubs, bulbs and herbaceous borders. Teas at 'Kate's Kitchen' in Clare. *Adm £1.50 Chd free. Sun May 29 (2-6)*

The Rookery ⚘ (Captain & Mrs Sheepshanks) Eyke. 5m E of Woodbridge turn N off B1084 Woodbridge-Orford Rd when sign says Rendlesham. 10-acre garden; planted as an arboretum with many rare specimen trees and shrubs; landscaped on differing levels, providing views and vistas; the visitor's curiosity is constantly aroused by what is round the next corner; ponds, bog garden, shrubbery, alpines, garden stream, bulbs, herbaceous borders and a 1-acre vineyard. TEAS. *Adm £1.50 Chd 50p. Suns April 24, June 5 (2-5.30)*

Rosemary ⚘ (Mrs N E M Finch) Rectory Hill. Turn off the A12 at East Bergholt and follow rd round to church. Rosemary is 100yds down from the church on L. Mature 1-acre garden adapted over 20yrs from an old orchard loosely divided into several smaller gardens; mixed borders; herb garden; over 70 old roses, unusual plants. TEAS. *Adm £1 Chd free. Sun June 12 (2-6) and private visits welcome May & June, please* **Tel 0206 298241**

Ruggs Cottage ⚘ (Mrs Patricia Short) Raydon. 12m NE of Colchester and 11m S of Ipswich, off A12 between Colchester and Ipswich. Turn N on B1070 towards Hadleigh. Raydon is 2m from A12. Car park available at Chequers Inn. Ruggs Cottage is on R just before Chequers Inn. ¾-acre designer plantsman's garden with wide selection of flowering shrubs and trees, herbaceous and unusual plants, small herb garden, grassy walks, roses and bulbs, small greenhouse with mimosa. TEAS by PCC Suns only. No plants Aug 8. *Adm £1.50 Chd free. Suns May 22, June 26, Aug 7, (2-6) Mons June 27, Aug 8, Tue June 28 (11-3)*

Rumah Kita & (Mr & Mrs I R Dickings) (O/S map ref TM223665) Bedfield is situated 2½m NW of the A1120 on secondary rd turning between Earl Soham and Saxted Green. 1½-acre garden designed and planted by owners since 1978. Contains many rare and interesting plants; mixed borders, formal and informal; parterre for spring and summer effect; blue white and silver pond garden. Extensive collection of half hardy perennials. TEAS. *Adm £1.25 Chd free. Sun June 19 (2-6) and private visits welcome until end Oct, please* **Tel 0728 628401**

St Stephens Cottage & ✿ (Mr & Mrs D Gibbs) Spexhall, 2m N of Halesworth. Approx 1-acre garden. Features inc natural pond leading to bog, herb and white garden. Many established deciduous and coniferous trees and shrubs; rockeries; herbaceous borders and island beds containing interesting and unusual plants, many for sale. Newly acquired 3-acre field being developed; plans for formal Elizabethan garden, tree lined avenue & rosary leading to arboretum & wild flower meadow. Members of the Cottage Garden Society and Hardy Plant Society. Conservatory featured on Gardeners World. TEAS if dry. *Adm £1 Chd free. Suns April 10, Sept 25 (10-5), also private visits welcome all year, please* **Tel 0986 873394**

Somerleyton Hall & ✿ (The Lord & Lady Somerleyton) 5m NW of Lowestoft. Off B1074. Large garden; famous maze, beautiful trees and avenue. House C16 remodelled in 1840's. Grinling Gibbons' carving, library, tapestries. Mentioned in Domesday Book. Miniature railway. Light lunches & TEAS. *Adm £3.50 Chd £1.60. House open 2-5 Gardens 12.30-5.30: Easter Sun to end Sept, Thurs, Suns, Bank Hol Mons; Tues, Weds, July and Aug; in addition miniature railway will be running on most days. For NGS (Share to Samaritans) Sun June 12 (12.30-5.30)*

South View ✿✿ (Glyn David Hammond) Hawstead Green. 4m S of Bury St Edmunds. signposted from 2nd roundabout at Southgate Green. in Hawstead turn L by telephone box onto village green. Garden on L. 11 acres, comprising garden with perennial borders, shrubs, water garden, kitchen garden and orchard. Walk through pastured field and brookside wood, mainly native trees and shrubs, wildlife pond, all maintained with emphasis on wildlife conservation. TEA. *Adm £1 Chd 50p Sun July 3 (2-6)*

The Spong ✿ (Joseph Barrett Esq & John Kirby Esq) Groton, Boxford. 5m W of Hadleigh on A1071. Leave Boxford via Swan Street, bear R at Fox and Hounds follow main road past Groton Church, take next R. The Spong is the pink house at the bottom of the hill. 8-yr-old garden of ⅔-acre; approached over stream; planned as a series of small gardens due to irregular shape; mixed herbaceous/shrubs; ponds; pergola. TEAS. *Adm £1 Chd 50p. Sun June 12 (2-6)*

By Appointment Gardens. See head of county section

Stour Cottage ✿ (Mr J H Gill) East Bergholt. Halfway between Ipswich and Colchester on the A12, turn at the sign for E Bergholt, follow rd around to the R towards the village centre. Car parking in the centre of the village. Take the lane to the R by the post office and Stour Cottage Garden entrance is the first large gate on the L side of lane. Formal walled garden of about ⅓-acre, Italianate in feeling. Many unusual half hardy shrubs and climbers. Features incl fountain and water garden. Comprehensive collection of herbaceous perennials. *Adm £1 Chd free. Sun June 12 (2-6)*

Thrift Farm & ✿✿ (Mrs H A Oddy) Cowlinge. 7m SE of Newmarket, centrally between Cowlinge, Kirtling and Gt Bradley. On the Gt Bradley rd from Kirtling. Picturesque thatched house set in a cottage style garden extending to approx 1½ acres. After the 1987 storm the garden took on its new mantle of island beds filled with herbaceous plants amongst shrubs and ornamental trees in great variety. It is a garden which encourages you to walk round but many will just sit and enjoy the vistas. TEAS. *Adm £1 Chd 50p. Sun June 5 (2-6). Also private visits welcome, please* **Tel 0440 83274**

¶**Thumbit** (Mrs Ann James) Walsham-le-Willows. 10m NE of Bury St Edmunds. Leave A143 at Walsham-le-Willows sign and continue to Xrds by church at centre of village. Take Badwell Rd to outskirts of village (½m). House is part of thatched C16 one-time inn. Shared driveway - (please do not drive in). Small informal cottage-style garden with strong emphasis on structural design and plant association for subtlety of form and colour. Pergola, pool, topiary. 500 choice herbaceous plants and shrubs, roses and climbers. Featured in Independent on Sunday and Weekend Telegraph. TEA. *Combined adm with Wyken Hall £3 Chd free. Sun June 26 (2-6). Private visits also welcome adm £1.50 OAPs £1 Chd free. Please* **Tel 0359 259 414**

¶**Tollemache Hall** & ✿ (Mr & Mrs M Tollemache) Offton, nr Ipswich. 4 acres of recently renovated garden in a lovely rural setting. Shrubs, rose and knot gardens. A large walled garden with interesting herbaceous borders. Also woodland walk planted with many conifer species. TEAS. *Adm £1.50 Chd free. Sun June 26 (2-6)*

¶**Warwick House** & ✿ (Dr & Mrs H Parris) Bury St Edmunds. Entrance in Westgate St opp R C Church; this st runs E from double roundabout at junction of A134 and A143 in Bury St Edmunds. ⅓-acre walled hidden garden in centre of Bury St Edmunds behind C17 house, but redesigned to given several vistas and different places to sit and relax. Wall fountain, conservatory and some unusual herbs, plants and specimen trees, chosen whenever possible for scent. *Adm £1 (Share to International Council of Women®). Sat May 14, Suns April 3, May 15, June 19, (11-6)*

25 Westbury Avenue ✿✿ (Mr & Mrs D J Payne) Bury St Edmunds. 1m West of town centre. Parkway roundabout (Kings Rd)-Queens Rd-Westbury Ave. ½-acre to lawns, shrubs and trees, many spring flowers and bulbs. Heathers, conifers, fuschias, roses. Patio and sunken garden; Mediterranean area. Water features, seasonal beds and borders, greenhouse. TEAS. *Adm £1 Chd under 14 free. Sun April 3 (11-6) also private visits welcome, please* **Tel 0284 755 374**

Woottens &%※ (M Loftus) Blackheath Rd. Woottens is situated between A12 and B1123 follow signposts to Wenhaston. Woottens is a small romantic garden with attached plantsman nursery, in all about ¾-acre; scented leafed pelargoniums, violas, cranesbills, lilies, salvias, penstemons primulas, etc. TEAS. *Adm £1 OAPs 50p Chd 20p. Suns May 22, June 19, July 10, Aug 7 (2-6)*

Wyken Hall &※ (Mr & Mrs K Carlisle) Stanton, 9m NE from Bury St Edmunds along A143; leave A143 between Ixworth and Stanton. 4-acre garden much developed recently; with knot and herb gardens; old-fashioned rose garden; wild garden; lawns and gazebo; shrubs and trees. Woodland walk, vineyard. TEAS. *Adm £2 OAPs £1.50 Chd free. Combined adm with* **Thumbit** *£3. Sun June 26 (2-6)*

Surrey

Hon County Organiser: Lady Heald, Chilworth Manor, Guildford GU4 8NL Tel 0483 61414
Assistant Hon County Organisers: Mrs J Foulsham, Vale End, Albury, Guildford GU5 9BE Tel 0483 202594
Mrs D Hargreaves, The Old Rectory, Albury, Guildford GU5 9AX
Tel 0483 203463
Mrs P Karslake, Oakfield Cottage, Guildford Road, Cranleigh GU6 8PF
Tel 0483 273010
Mrs D E Norman, Spring Cottage, Mannings Hill, Cranleigh GU6 8QN
Tel 0483 272620
Mrs J Pearcy, Far End, Pilgrims Way, Guildford GU4 8AD Tel 0483 63093
Hon County Treasurer: Mr Ray Young, Paddock View, 144 Dorking Road, Chilworth, Guildford GU4 8RJ
Tel 0483 69597

DATES OF OPENING

By appointment
For telephone number and other details see garden descriptions. Private visits welcomed

Brookwell, Bramley
Chauffeur's Flat, Tandridge
Chilworth Manor, Guildford
The Coppice, Reigate
2 Court Avenue, Old Coulsdon
Coverwood Lakes, Ewhurst
Four Aces, Pirbright
High Meadow, Churt
The Homestead, Old Lodge Lane, Kenley
Hookwood Farm House
Knightsmead, Chipstead
Lansdowne House, West Ewell, nr Epsom
Pinewood House, Heath House Rd, Woking
Postford House, Chilworth
Pyrford Court, nr Woking
Ridings, 56 Cross Rd, Tadworth
Rise Top Cottage, Mayford
South Park Farm, South Godstone
Spring Cottage, Cranleigh
Stonywood, Haslemere
Unicorns, Farnham
Vann, Hambledon
Walton Poor, Ranmore
Woodside, Send
Yew Tree Cottage, Haslemere
67 York Rd, Cheam

Regular openers
For details see garden descriptions

Coverwood Lakes, Ewhurst. For dates see text
Crosswater Farm,Churt. Daily May 1 to June 12
25 Little Woodcote Estate, Wallington
Painshill, Cobham. Suns Apt 10 to Oct 16
Weds & Sats April 2 to Sat 24 Sept
Ramster, Chiddingfold. For dates see text

February 6 Sunday
Wintershall, Bramley
March 6 Sunday
Wintershall, Bramley
March 13 Sunday
Maryland, Worplesdon
March 20 Sunday
27 Foley Rd, Claygate
90 Foley Rd, Claygate
April 3 Sunday
High Meadow, Churt
Whinfold, Hascombe
April 4 Monday
High Meadow, Churt
Wintershall, Bramley
April 5 Tuesday to April 10 Sunday
Vann, Hambledon
April 9 Saturday to April 13 Wednesday
Chilworth Manor, Guildford

April 17 Sunday
27 Foley Rd, Claygate
90 Foley Rd, Claygate
Hascombe Court, Godalming
Lodkin, Hascombe
April 20 Wednesday
The Coppice, Reigate
April 24 Sunday
Coverwood Lakes, Ewhurst
Highlands, Leatherhead
Street House, Thursley
Woodside, Send
May 1 Sunday
Compton Lodge, Moor Park, Farnham
Coverwood Lakes, Ewhurst.
Fairfield, Dorking
Feathercombe, nr Hambledon
Snowdenham House, Bramley
Wintershall, Bramley
May 2 Monday
Feathercombe, nr Hambledon
Walton Poor, Ranmore
May 3 Tuesday to May 8 Sunday
Vann, Hambledon
May 4 Wednesday
Fairfield, Dorking
May 7 Saturday to May 11 Wednesday
Chilworth Manor, Guildford
May 7 Saturday
The Old Croft, South Holmwood
May 8 Sunday
Highlands, Leatherhead
The Old Croft, South Holmwood
Westbourn, Virginia Water

May 11 Wednesday
Westland Farm, Ewhurst
May 14 Saturday
Pyrford Court, nr Woking
May 15 Sunday
Brook Lodge Farm Cottage,
    Blackbrook
Claremont Landscape Garden,
    Esher
Compton Lodge, Moor Park,
    Farnham
Hascombe Court, Godalming
Montfleury, Virginia Water
Polesden Lacey, Bookham
Postford House, Chilworth
Pyrford Court, nr Woking
87 Upland Rd, Sutton
Westland Farm, Ewhurst
Whinfold, Hascombe ‡
Windlesham Park, nr Bagshot
Winkworth Arboretum,
    Hascombe ‡
May 18 Wednesday
Brook Lodge Farm Cottage,
    Blackbrook
Broom House, Headley, nr
    Leatherhead
Postford House, Chilworth
May 22 Sunday
Bradstone Brook, Shalford
Copt Hill Shaw, Kingswood,
    Tadworth
Hookwood Farm House, West
    Horsley
Munstead Wood, Nr Godalming
Postford House, Chilworth
41 Shelvers Way, Tadworth
Street House, Thursley
May 28 Saturday
Crosswater Farm, Churt
Merrist Wood College,
    Worplesdon
May 29 Sunday
Crosswater Farm, Churt ‡
Feathercombe, nr Hambledon
High Meadow, Churt ‡
15 Highview Rd, Lightwater
Merrist Wood College, Worplesdon
Munstead Wood, Nr Godalming
Olivers, Church Rd, Hascombe
Postford House, Chilworth
Snowdenham House, Bramley
May 30 Monday
Crosswater Farm, Churt ‡
Feathercombe, nr Hambledon
High Meadow, Churt ‡
May 31 Tuesday to June 5
    Wednesday
Vann, Hambledon
June 1 Wednesday
Rise Top Cottage, Mayford
June 4 Saturday
Dovecote, Cobham
June 5 Sunday

2 Chinthurst Lodge, Wonersh
Cutt Mill House, Puttenham
Dovecote, Cobham
Mitchen Hall, Shackleford
Walton Poor, Ranmore
Wintershall, Bramley
June 6 Monday
Rise Top Cottage, Mayford
June 8 Wednesday
Hookwood Farm House
Spring Cottage, Cranleigh
Walton Poor, Ranmore
June 11 Saturday to June 15
    Wednesday
Chilworth Manor, Guildford
June 12 Sunday
37 Hare Lane, Claygate
Haslehurst, Haslemere ‡
Spring Cottage, Cranleigh
Yew Tree Cottage, Haslemere ‡
June 15 Wednesday
The Coppice, Reigate
37 Hare Lane, Claygate
June 18 Saturday
Knightsmead, Chipstead
South Park Farm, South Godstone
June 19 Sunday
Brook Lodge Farm Cottage,
    Blackbrook
27 Foley Rd, Claygate ‡
90 Foley Rd, Claygate ‡
Four Aces, Pirbright
Hascombe Court, Godalming
High Hazard, Blackheath ‡‡
Knightsmead, Chipstead
Merrist Wood College, Worplesdon
South Park Farm, South Godstone
Street House, Thursley
Thanescroft, Shamley Green ‡‡
June 20 Monday
Four Aces, Pirbright
South Park Farm, South Godstone
June 25 Saturday
The Moorings, Horley
June 26 Sunday
High Meadow, Churt
Moleshill House, Cobham
The Moorings, Horley
Ridings, 56 Cross Rd. Tadworth ‡
41 Shelvers Way, Tadworth ‡
Vale End, Albury
June 27 Monday
High Meadow, Churt
July 3 Sunday
Maryland, Worplesdon ‡
White House, nr Guildford ‡
Wintershall, Bramley
July 9 Saturday
Little Mynthurst Farm, Norwood
    Hill
July 10 Sunday
Little Mynthurst Farm, Norwood
    Hill
Lodkin, Hascombe

July 13 Wednesday
Broom House, Headley, nr
    Leatherhead
July 16 Saturday to July 20
    Wednesday
Chilworth Manor, Guildford
July 16 Saturday
The Old Croft, South Holmwood
July 17 Sunday
The Old Croft, South Holmwood
Polesden Lacey, Bookham
41 Shelvers Way, Tadworth
67 York Rd, Cheam
July 23 Saturday
East Clandon Gardens, Clandon
The Homestead, Old Lodge Lane,
    Kenley
July 24 Sunday
Brook Lodge Farm Cottage,
    Blackbrook
East Clandon Gardens, Clandon
The Homestead, Old Lodge Lane,
    Kenley
July 27 Wednesday
The Coppice, Reigate
July 31 Sunday
Vale End, Albury
August 6 Saturday to August
    10 Wednesday
Chilworth Manor, Guildford
August 7 Sunday
Chiddingfold House, Chiddingfold
The Coppice, Reigate
Odstock, Bletchingley
August 10 Wednesday
Brook Lodge Farm Cottage,
    Blackbrook
August 21 Sunday
Brook Lodge Farm Cottage,
    Blackbrook
August 28 Sunday
Annesley, Haslemere
High Meadow, Churt
August 29 Monday
High Meadow, Churt
September 18 Sunday
Haslehurst, Haslemere
September 25 Sunday
Claremont Landscape Garden, Esher
Maryland, Worplesdon
Painshill Park, Cobham
October 2 Sunday
Albury Park, Albury
White House, nr Guildford
October 9 Sunday
Walton Poor, Ranmore
October 16 Sunday
Pyrford Court, nr Woking
Winkworth Arboretum, Hascombe
October 19 Wednesday
Brook Lodge Farm Cottage,
    Blackbrook
October 30 Sunday
Lodkin, Hascombe

DESCRIPTIONS OF GARDENS

¶**Albury Park Garden** &✿ (Trustees of Albury Estate) Albury 5m SE of Guildford. From A25 take A248 towards Albury for ¼m, then L up new rd, entrance to Albury Park immediately on L. 14-acre pleasure grounds laid out in 1670's by John Evelyn for Henry Howard, later 6th Duke of Norfolk. ¼m terraces, fine collection of trees, lake and river. TEAS. *Adm £1.50 Chd 50p. Sun Oct 2 (2-5)*

Annesley &✿ (Capt & Mrs Trechman) Three Gates Lane, Haslemere. 1st R from Haslemere High St (A286), ¼m down lane on R. 3 acres; shrubs, roses, annuals and items of interest to flower arrangers. TEAS. *Adm £1 Chd 20p. Sun Aug 28 (2-6)*

Bradstone Brook ✿ (Scott Brownrigg & Turner) Shalford. 3m S of Guildford on A281 towards Horsham; in Shalford take A248 to Dorking and Wonersh; past Shalford Common look for sign on L for Bradstone Brook. 20 acres. The layout for the present garden was advised by Gertrude Jekyll; known for its water gardens, rockeries, herbaceous borders; naturalized bulbs of which there are over 150,000; trees some of which are under a preservation order; Betula nigra (black birch) is the largest in the country. TEAS. *Adm £1.25 Chd and OAPs 50p. Sun May 22 (2-6)*

Brook Lodge Farm Cottage &✿✿ (Mrs Basil Kingham) Blackbrook, 3m S of Dorking. Take L-hand turning for Blackbrook off A24, 1m S of Dorking 500yds past Plough Inn. 3½-acre 45 year old plantsman's garden made by present owner. Entrance provides vista of spacious lawns, curving borders of shrubs, flowering trees and shrub roses; hosts of unusual plants frame main house. Fine collection of conifers cradles summer-house. Swimming pool, hidden by Hoathly stone wall leads to waterfall and rockery with woodland walk beyond. On leaving garden, pass herbaceous borders, roses, herb and kitchen gardens, greenhouses and 2 cottage gardens full of interest. Light lunches Weds, TEAS on Suns. *Adm £1.50 Chd free (Share to St Catherine's Hospice, Crawley®). Weds May 18, Aug 10, Oct 19 (11-3). Suns May 15, June 19, July 24, Aug 21 (2-6)*

Brookwell &✿✿ (Mr & Mrs P R Styles) 1½m S of Bramley on A281; turn R into private road-bridleway in Birtley Green. 2-acre garden with lake and woodland. Mixed borders, sunken garden, and knot garden planted with scented flowers and herbs. Collection of old roses, fruit tunnel and vegetable garden; greenhouses and conservatory. *Groups and individual visitors welcome by appt only, please* Tel 0483 893423 *(evenings)*

Broom House ✿✿ (Mr & Mrs G A Cannon) Headley. From Leatherhead by-pass (A24) take B2033 to Headley. Travel 1.6m. At bottom of Tot Hill turn R into lay-by next to Hyde Farm. Park in lay-by. Short walk along Crabtree Lane (a bridle path) to house. Situated on edge of Headley Heath. 2 acres of sloping lawns; mature trees and conifers, shrubs, rhododendrons and azaleas, herbaceous borders; sandstone rockery; alpine sinks. Japanese water garden. Developed and maintained by owners since 1984. TEAS. *Adm £1 Chd free. Weds May 18, July 13 (2-5)*

Chauffeur's Flat ✿ (Mr & Mrs Richins) Tandridge. Tandridge Lane lies 1m W of Oxted off the A25. Drive adjacent to church ½m from A25. Pass Lodge to your R. Fork R. Continue through to Courtyard. This fascinating and romantic garden set in just under 1 acre of land with superb views. Uses an abundant variety of trees and shrubs intermingled with wild and cultivated plants. Mainly set on two levels as a series of mini gardens the upper having a more natural woodland feel, the lower using informal planting within a formal framework. Use has been made of old building materials. Only for the surefooted. *Adm £1 Chd 25p (Share to Waylands Special Needs Unit®). Private visits welcome May 16-22, June 20-26 (10-5), please* Tel 0883 715937 *between 7-9.30am or 7-9.30pm*

Chiddingfold House ✿ (Mr & Mrs J R Morrison) Chiddingfold. In Chiddingfold turn E at top of village green on rd marked to Dunsfold. Chiddingfold House about 500 yds from green on N side of rd. A large and interesting garden divided into many smaller ones incl a beautifully underplanted Pergola; rose garden; fish pond. Very fine lawns. *Adm £1.50 Chd free. Sun Aug 7 (2-5)*

Chilworth Manor &✿ (Lady Heald) 3½m SE of Guildford. From A248, in centre of Chilworth village, turn up Blacksmith Lane. Bus: LC 425 Guildford-Dorking; alight Blacksmith Lane. Station: Chilworth. Garden laid out in C17; C18 walled garden added by Sarah, Duchess of Marlborough; spring flowers; flowering shrubs; herbaceous border. House C17 with C18 wing on site of C11 monastery recorded in Domesday Book; stewponds in garden date from monastic period. Featured in NGS video 1, see page 344. Flower decorations in house (Sats, Suns): April 9-13 Farncombe & Godalming Flower Club, May 7-11 Dorking Flower Arrangement Group, June 11-15 Bookham Flower Arrangement Group, July 16-20 Walton & Weybridge Flower Club, Aug 6-10 Guildford Floral Decoration Society. Free car park in attractive surroundings open from 12.30 for picnicking. TEAS (Sat, Sun, only). *Adm to garden £1.50 Chd free. Adm to house £1 Sat & Sun only (Share to Marie Curie Foundation Guildford Branch®); Open Sats to Weds April 9 to 13, May 7 to 11, June 11 to 15, July 16 to 20, Aug 6 to 10 (2-6); also private visits welcome, please* Tel 0483 61414

2 Chinthurst Lodge &✿✿ (Mr & Mrs M R Goodridge) Wonersh. 4m S Guildford. A281 Guildford-Horsham. At Shalford turn E onto B2128 towards Wonersh. Just after Wonersh rd sign, before village, garden on R. 1-acre year-round garden, herbaceous borders, large variety specimen trees and shrubs incl Parrotia Persica; kitchen garden; fruit cage; two wells; ornamental pond and conservatory. TEAS. *Adm £1 Chd free (Share to Guildford Branch Arthritis & Rheumatism Council®). Sun June 5 (2-6)*

Regular Openers. Too many days to include in diary. Usually there is a wide range of plants giving year-round interest. See head of county section for the name and garden description for times etc.

Claremont Landscape Garden ⚹⚹ (The National Trust) 1m SE of Esher; on E side of A307 (No access from A3 by-pass). Station: Esher. Bus GL 415, alight at entrance gates. One of the earliest surviving English landscape gardens; begun by Vanbrugh and Bridgeman before 1720; extended and naturalized by Kent; lake; island with pavilion; grotto and turf amphitheatre; viewpoints and avenues. TEAS 11-5.30. *Adm £2.60 Chd £1.30.* ▲*For NGS Suns May 15, Sun Sept 25 (10-7)*

Compton Lodge ⚹⚹ (Mr & Mrs K J Kent) Farnham. 2m E of Farnham along A31 Hogs Back turn S down Crooksbury Rd at Barfield School signposted Milford & Elstead. 1m on R Compton Way, Compton Lodge 2nd house on R. 1 ¼-acre S-facing sloping garden. Extensively renovated over the last 8 yrs by owners. Mature rhododendrons and azaleas; mature trees; raised herbaceous border with rose and clematis trellis; rose border. 2 ponds; heather bed and mixed beds; conservatory. TEAS. *Adm £1.50 Chd 50p (Share to Waverley Victim Support®). Suns May 1, 15 (11-5)*

Cooksbridge, Fernhurst (See Sussex)

The Coppice ⚹ (Mr & Mrs Bob Bushby) Reigate. M25 to junction 8. A217 (direction Reigate) down Reigate Hill immediately before level Xing turn R into Somers Rd cont as Manor Rd. At very end turn R into Coppice Lane 'The Coppice' approx 200yds on L. Partly suitable wheelchairs. 6½ acres redeveloped in last 6yrs. Mixed borders with interesting and unusual plants giving yr-round interest. Pergola and conservatory, 2 large ornamental ponds. Fritillarias and spring bulbs, April to May. Cream TEAS. *Adm £1.50 Chd 50p (Share to Winged Fellowship®). Weds April 20, June 15, July 27, Sun Aug 7 (2-5); also private visits welcome April to May, please* Tel 0737 243158

¶**Copt Hill Shaw** ⚹⚹ (Mr & Mrs M Barlow) Alcocks Lane, Kingswood. 6m S of Sutton off the A217. 1st turn on L after Burgh Heath traffic lights, Waterhouse Lane, signposted Kingswood Station and Coulsdon. Alcocks Lane 1st on L. 1½ acres of formal garden laid out in 1906. Yew hedges and topiary, azaleas, rhododendrons and mature trees. TEAS. *Adm £1 Chd 30p. Sun May 22 (2-5.30)*

2 The Cottage see **Rise Top Cottage**.

2 Court Avenue ⚹⚹⚹ (Dr K Heber) Old Coulsdon. Approach from London-Brighton Rd. A23 from S or M23/25, turn R B276 Old Coulsdon; from N after leaving Purley turn L B2030 Old Coulsdon. Follow rd to top of hill, immediately past parade of shops. Garden opposite Tudor Rose public house (food available). Flat compact garden approx ⅓-acre filled with herbaceous plants and shrubs in cottage garden layout; small ponds; good selection of unusual plants. Gives ideas for small gardens and use of foliage. *Adm £1 Chd 50p (Share to Coulsdon Rotary International Charities®). Private visits welcome, please* Tel 07375 54721

By Appointment Gardens. See head of county section

Coverwood Lakes ⚹⚹⚹ (Mr & Mrs C G Metson) Peaslake Rd, Ewhurst. 7m SW of Dorking. From A25 follow signs for Peaslake; garden ½m beyond Peaslake. Landscaped water and cottage gardens in lovely setting between Holmbury Hill and Pitch Hill; rhododendrons, azaleas, primulas, fine trees, both mature and young. 3½-acre Arboretum planted March 1990. Herd of pedigree Poll Hereford cattle and flock of sheep. Featured in NGS video 1, see page 344. (Mr & Mrs Nigel Metson). TEAS. *Adm (Gardens only) £1.50 Chd £1. (Farm and Gardens) £2 Chd £1 car park and Chd under 5 free. Gardens Suns April 24, May 1; Farm & gardens Suns May 8, 15, 22, 29 (2-6.30); Wed June 1; Sun Oct 23 hot soup and sandwiches (11-4.30). For NGS Suns April 24, May 1 (2-6.30). Also private visits welcome, please* Tel 0306 731103

Crosswater Farm ⚹⚹⚹ (Mr & Mrs E G Millais) Churt. Farnham and Haslemere 6m, from A287 turn E into Jumps Road ½m N of Churt village centre. After ¼m turn acute L into Crosswater Lane and follow signs for Millais Nurseries. 6-acre woodland garden surrounded by NT Property. Plantsmans collection of rhododendrons and azaleas including many rare species collected in the Himalayas, and hybrids raised by the owners. Ponds, stream and companion plantings. Plants for sale from specialist Rhododendron nursery. TEAS in aid of Frensham Church Restoration on NGS days only. *Adm £1.50 Chd free. Daily May 1 to June 12. For NGS Sat, Sun, Mon May 28, 29, 30 (10-5)* Tel 0252 792698

Cutt Mill House ⚹ (R A Skinner Esq) Puttenham, 4m W of Guildford. From Guildford via A31, after 2m take B3000; turn into Putenham village; turn 1st L signed Cutt Mill and Elstead; 2m on L sign to house. 12 acres incl 6-acre lake; many varieties of azaleas and rhododendrons, specimen trees. Home-made TEAS. Car Park Lower Puttenham Common. Disabled at house. *Adm £1 Chd 25p (Share to St Edward's Church, Sutton Park®). Sun June 5 (2-6)*

¶**Dovecote** ⚹ (Mr & Mrs R Stanley) Cobham. Off A307 Esher to Cobham rd near A3 bridge. Turn R from Cobham, L from Esher into Fairmile Lane. Then 4th L into Green Lane. ⅓-acre plot surrounding extended bothy. Secluded plant lovers year-round garden with natural boundaries of mature trees, shrubs and hedges developed by present owners to incl many hardy plants on light sandy soil. TEA. *Adm £1 Chd 50p. Sat, Sun June 4, 5 (11-5)*

East Clandon Gardens ⚹⚹ Situated 4m E of Guildford on A246. This C16 hamlet, public house and C12 church is well worth a visit. From M25 turn S on A3, 1m L to Ripley. Turn L in Ripley, Rose Lane, then 2nd R. East Clandon is 4m. Home-made TEAS. *Combined adm £1 Chd free (Share to Cherry Trees, respite care for handicapped children®). Sat & Sun July 23, 24 (2-6)*

Stuart Cottage (Mr & Mrs J M Leader). ½-acre garden comprising rose walk, herbaceous beds, some unusual planting; small fountain and paved garden area. Old apple trees and a collection of chimney pots providing raised planting blend with the charm of the C16 flint and brick cottage

3 The Tithe Barn (Mr & Mrs L Wharrad). As a contrast to the Stuart Cottage garden, No 3 The Tithe Barn in Ripley Rd provides a fine example of a small walled courtyard garden. The clever use of setts in circular patterns which lead to a small fountain and the many containers of plants are particularly worth noting

The Elms Kingston-on-Thames (see London)

¶**Fairfield** ✿✿✿ (Mr & Mrs D C Drummond) Dorking. S part of Dorking. From one way system after May's Garage turn L up the Horsham rd (A2003 which runs to N Holmwood roundabout A24). Knoll Road is the fourth turning R just beyond The Bush Inn. ⅓-acre town garden with many interesting and unusual plants labelled and with notes available. Mixed borders, raised beds, sinks, mini-meadow and peat bed, fern alley and some fruit and vegetables. A surprising front garden and well stocked conservatory. A comprehensive collection of Arum species for pollination research. (Suitable for wheelchairs if driven to front door). TEAS. *Adm £1 Chd free. Sun, Wed May 1, 4 (10.30-5.30)*

Feathercombe ✿ (Miss Parker) nr Hambledon, S of Godalming. 2m from Milford Station on Hambledon Rd, turn to Feathercombe off rd between Hydestile Xrds and Merry Harriers. Fine view; flowering shrubs, trees, heathers. Garden designed and made by Eric Parker. Picnic area at garden. Tea Winkworth Arboretum. *Adm £1.50 Chd 10p (Share to Order of St John, Surrey®). Suns, Mons May 1, 2, 29, 30 (2-6)*

27 Foley Road (Mr & Mrs D Love). Drive into Claygate from Esher, Hook or Hinchley Wood and follow signs. Small, informal garden with some unusual plants and ornamental grasses of particular interest to the flower arranger. TEAS. *Adm £1.50 Chd Free. Suns March 20, April 17, June 19 (2-5)*

90 Foley Road (Mr & Mrs B Mathew). Drive into Claygate from Esher, Hinchley Wood, Hook or Chessington and follow signs from Foley Arms. A plantsman's garden specialising in bulbs. The owner is the author of 13 books. Collection of species irises. *Adm £1.50 Chd free. Suns March 20, April 17, June 19 (2-5)*

¶**Four Aces** ✿✿ (Mr & Mrs R V St John Wright) 5m NW of Guildford on A322 Bagshot Road. Just before Brookwood arch, directly opp West Hill Golf Club, turn L into Cemetery Pales. After ⁹⁄₁₀m turn sharp L after village sign into Chapel Lane. Four Aces is 5th house on R. Overflow parking in village green car park, 250yds. Approx ⅔-acre 8yr-old garden with 2 ponds, terraces with pergolas, loggias and pots; mixed borders with shrubs, perennials and old roses planted in informal garden style. TEAS. *Adm £1 Chd 50p (Share to Princess Alice Hospice®). Sun June 19 (12-6) Mon June 20 (11-3) Private visits welcome May to Aug, please* **Tel 0483 476226**

Hall Grange, Croydon (see London)

37 Hare Lane ✿✿✿ (Mr & Mrs C Ingram). Claygate; 100yds on Esher side of railway bridge, 3 mins walk from Claygate Station. Entrance and parking in Loseberry Rd. Originally a narrow garden, and designed by the owner to

overcome this, more land was acquired in 1991 and has been incorporated for fruit and vegetables; hardy geraniums, cistus, roses; some interesting green ideas; designed to be labour saving. TEAS. *Adm 80p (Share to Schizophrenia Fellowship®). Sun , Wed June 12, 15 (11-5)*

Hascombe Court ✿ (Mr & Mrs O Poulsen) 2½m SE of Godalming. Off B2130 between Hascombe and Godalming. 25-acre garden with may distinct areas; Jekyll influences, mostly designed by Percy Cane in 1922. Rhododendrons, daffodils, roses and long herbaceous border. Superb specimens of some notable trees. Panoramic views over Hascombe Village and surrounding countryside. Large well-designed rock garden being replanted. TEAS. *Adm £1.50 Chd free. Suns April 17, May 15, June 19 (2-5)*

Haslehurst ✿✿ (Mrs W H Whitbread) Bunch Lane, Haslemere. Turn off High St into Church Lane, leave church on L, carry on to T-junction, turn R, Hazelhurst, 2nd on L. 2½ acres; lawns, superb trees, rhododendrons, azaleas; various shrubs; paved rose garden, double herbaceous border; woodland rockery & waterfall. C15 Barn. See **Yew Tree Cottage**. TEA. *Adm £1 Chd 50p (Share to Queen Mary's Clothing Guild®). Suns June 12, Sept 18 (2.15-6)*

High Hazard ✿✿ (Mr & Mrs P C Venning) Blackheath, Guildford. 3½m SE of Guildford from B2128 at entry to Wonersh, turn L into Blackheath Lane, straight on at Xrds in village. Rear access to garden is 300 yds on R. Park in Heath car park a further 150 yds up lane. (No access to front of house which faces the cricket ground in use). ½-acre garden designed and laid out by the present owners 10 yrs ago. Herbaceous and mixed borders containing interesting and some unusual herbaceous perennial plants, a large number of which are for sale on the premises. TEAS. *Adm £1 Chd free (Share to St Joseph's Centre for Addiction, Holy Cross Hospital, Haslemere®). Sun June 19 (2-6)*

Highlands ✿✿✿ (Mr & Mrs R B McDaniel) Givons Grove, Leatherhead. From Leatherhead By-pass (A24) at roundabout by Texaco garage 1m S of Leatherhead turn into Givons Grove and proceed up hill (The Downs) for ¾m, ignoring side turnings. Highlands is on the R. Chalk garden of 1 acre on a steep slope. Large rock garden, alpine house and sinks; mixed borders; orchard; pond; fruit and vegetable garden. Fine views over Mole Valley. TEAS in aid of Cystic Fibrosis. *Adm £1 Chd free. Suns April 24, May 8 (2-6)*

High Meadow ✿✿✿ (Mr & Mrs J Humphries) Tilford Rd, Churt. From Hindhead A3 Xrds take A287 signposted Farnham. After ½m take R fork signposted Tilford. 1.9m to Avalon PYO farm. Park here, short walk to garden. Disabled visitors park on grass verge in drive. Approx 1 acre maintained by owners. Large collection of rare and unusual plants attractively planted to provide all-year interest; large collection of old and modern shrub roses and David Austin English Roses; pergola walk, sunken garden with pond, colour co-ordinated borders, alpines in troughs; featured in Daily Mail. TEAS. *Adm £1 Chd free (Share to G.U.T.S. at Royal Surrey County Hospital). Suns, Mons April 3, 4; May 29, 30; June 26, 27; Aug 28, 29 (2-6). Private visits welcome, please* **Tel 0428 606129**

15 Highview Road ✿❀(Mr & Mrs J Pearce) Lightwater. Camberley 4m Chobham 4m 1½m S of junction (3) M3 off Macdonald Road Lightwater. ½-acre garden on hillside including rock; water; heather and Japanese garden. A good example of a steeply terraced layout. (Many steps). As seen on Channel 4 Garden Club Aug 1993. TEAS. *Adm £1 Chd free. Sun May 29 (2-6)*

¶The Homestead ঙ✿❀ (Mr & Mrs P Wallace) Kenley. 3rd dwelling down Old Lodge Lane from Wattendon Arms at junction on Old Lodge Lane. (SE off A23 Brighton Road at Reedham Station) and Hayes Lane. (SSW from A22 Godstone Road at Kenley Station). Arrangements made for parking & catering to be available for garden visitors throughout day at Wattendon Arms. Nearest bus 412. (Sat only) Old Lodge Lane Terminus (end of Old Lodge Lane Purley), ½m walk up hill (Old Lodge Lane Kenley). Designed, developed and maintained by present (amateur) owners. ½-acre prize-winning suburban garden on edge of Green Belt, close to Kenley Airfield (Battle of Britain fame). Lawns with water feature, colourful beds and borders, well stocked with shrubs and flowers, vegetable garden and greenhouses; patio and conservatory with outstanding display of hanging baskets, tubs, troughs etc. TEA. *Adm £1 Chd free. Sat, Sun July 23, 24. (10-4). Private visits welcome July, Aug, please* **Tel 081 660 9816**

Hookwood Farm House ঙ✿❀ (Mr & Mrs E W Mason) West Horsley. Approx 7m E of Guildford off A246 Guildford-Leatherhead Rd. From Guildford turn R into Staple Lane (sign-posted Shere) at end of dual carriageway. At top of Staple Lane turn L and then take 1st L into Shere Rd. (sign-posted West Horsley) then L into Fullers Farm Rd. From Leatherhead turn L into Greendene (signposted Shere) follow this for approx 2½m then R into Shere Rd. The garden made and maintained by the owners over the last 18yrs approx 1½ acres in size, is situated on a south facing slope of the North Downs. Large variety of interesting and unusual plants including alpines; herbaceous plants particularly geraniums; trees and shrubs. The garden also features a new garden in walled farmyard; a wild area with pond, a small kitchen garden and a Victorian style conservatory. Home-made TEAS in aid of Cystic Fibrosis Research Trust. Plant sales to Spastics Society. *Adm £1.50 Chd free. Sun May 22, Wed June 8 (2-6); also private visits welcome May to July, please* **Tel 0483 284760**

Knightsmead ✿❀ (Mrs Jones & Miss Collins) Rickman Hill Rd, Chipstead. 1m SW of Coulsdon. 3m SE of Banstead. From A23 in Coulsdon turn W onto B2032. Through traffic lights, L fork into Portnalls Rd. Top of hill at Xroads, turn R into Holymead Rd. R into Lissoms Rd. R into Bouverie Rd. ½-acre plantsman's garden, designed and maintained entirely by owners. Wide variety of shrubs and perennials for year round interest; pond; scented roses; raised alpine and peat beds, clematis, hostas, hardy geraniums etc. New vertical garden. Small craft exhibition. Home-made TEAS. *Adm £1 Chd 50p (Share to Surrey Wildlife Trust®). Sat, Sun June 18, 19 (2-5.30). Private visits welcome, please* **Tel 0737 551694**

¶Lansdowne House ✿❀ (Mr & Mrs J Lucas) West Ewell. Between Chessington and Ewell on the B2200 opposite Hook Rd Arena. Parking and entrance in Lansdowne Rd. Lansdowne House is on corner of Chessington Rd and Lansdowne Rd; Small garden (0.18 acre) developed over past 10yrs by garden designer, lecturer and author John Lucas. Planted mainly with shrubs and small trees, the garden is divided into rooms of varous styles and atmospheres. A garden of texture with interesting focal points, for the 'green' garden lover. TEA. *Adm £1 Chd 50p. Private visits welcome during June, please* **Tel 081 393 9946**

Little Lodge, Thames Ditton (see London)

Little Mynthurst Farm ঙ✿❀ (Mr & Mrs G Chilton) Norwood Hill. Between Leigh (2m) and Charlwood (3m); from Reigate take A217 to Horley; after 2m turn R just after river bridge at Sidlowbridge; 1st R signed Leigh; then L at T junction. 12-acre garden; walled old-fashioned roses, herbaceous borders and shrubs around old farm house (not open). Kitchen garden with greenhouses and secret garden. TEAS. *Adm £1.50 Chd free. Sat, Sun July 9, 10, (10-5.30) Coach parties welcome by prior arrangement please contact Head Gardener Mark Dobell* **Tel 0293 862181**

25 Little Woodcote Estate ঙ✿❀ (Mr & Mrs Brian Hiley) Wallington. Private Rd off Woodmansterne Lane. Signed SCC Smallholdings. Woodmansterne Lane joins B278 and A237. An exciting 1-acre plantsmans garden full of many rare unusual, tender and interesting plants; several large herbaceous borders; annual border; extensive collection of stone sinks; washing line garden and bog garden. A good collection of plant containers, garden and farm bygones. Suitable in parts for wheelchairs. *Adm £1.20 Chd free (Share to Motor Neurone Disease Association®). Every Wed & Sat April 2 to Sept 24 (9-5). Private visits welcome for parties, please* **Tel 081 647 9679**

Lodkin ❀ (Mr & Mrs W N Bolt) Lodkin Hill, Hascombe, 3m S of Godalming. Just off B2130 Godalming-Cranleigh, on outskirts of Hascombe; take narrow lane off signposted Thorncombe Street. About 5½ acres incl woodland, stream and prolific daffodils and cherries. 4 old Victorian greenhouses have been completely rebuilt and are in full use to produce fruit, flowers and vegetables. Chrysanthemums in October. Much of the old cast staging etc has been retained. In parts suitable for wheel chairs. TEAS. *Adm £1 Chd 30p. Suns April 17, July 10 (2-6), Oct 30 Adm 75p that day Chd free (2-4)*

Maryland ঙ✿❀ (Mrs J Woodroffe) Worplesdon. From Guildford (A3) take A322 Bagshot Road. 4-acre mixed garden incl woodland area; large herbaceous border, lawns; mature specimen trees; climbing and wall shrubs and many less common plants. Snowdrops in March, NCCPG National Collection of Veratrum. TEA. *Adm £1 Chd free. Suns, Mar 13 (2-5), July 3, Sept 25 (2-6)*

By Appointment Gardens. These owners do not have a fixed opening day usually because they do not like crowds or have insufficient parking space. Owner will often give guided tour.

Regular Openers. See head of county section.

Merrist Wood College ৬✿❀ Worplesdon 4m NW of Guildford. 40 acres of amenity areas, landscape demonstration gardens, 16 acres nursery stock, house a listed building (Norman Shaw 1877). Only reception hall open. One of the largest colleges of agriculture and horticulture in the UK with students from many countries. Information available for courses in Nursery, Landscape, Agriculture, Arboriculture, Countryside, Equestrian and Golf Studies. TEAS. *Adm no charge. Rare plants for sale. Percentage of Plant Shop takings to NGS. For NGS Sat, Sun, May 28, 29, June 19 (10-6) with Surrey Horticultural Federation Summer Flower Show June 19 only*

¶**Mitchen Hall** ✿❀ (Mr & Mrs Holland-Bosworth) Shackleford. 7m SW of Guildford on the A3. Take the Hurtmore, Elstead and Shackleford exit. In Shackleford take the road to Cutmill. House is ¾m outside village. Mitchen Hall is a Queen Anne house surrounded by interesting old barns set in unspoilt countryside. There are herbaceous and mixed borders; lake and woodland walks (some under construction); vegetable garden and greenhouse. Mostly suitable for wheelchairs. TEAS. *Adm £1 Chd free. Sun June 5 (2-6)*

Moleshill House ৬✿❀ (Mr & Mrs Maurice Snell) Cobham. House is on A307 Esher to Cobham Road nr A3 bridge. Parking in free car park. 1-acre flower arranger's garden. Informal planting around circular lawn; wild garden with bog; dovecote. Silver and green garden. Paving and pots. TEAS. *Adm £1.50 Chd free. Sun June 26 (2-6)*

Montfleury ✿❀ (Cdr & Mrs Innes Hamilton) Christchurch Rd, Virginia Water. From A30 at Virginia Water, opp Wheatsheaf Restaurant, turn down B389. Over roundabout. Last house on R before village. Former National Award Winners' new small garden. Propagation. Substantial, interesting plant sales. Also nursery stock for immediate effect. Unlimited parking. TEA. *Adm £1 Chd 10p. Sun May 15 (2-6)*

The Moorings ৬✿ (Dr & Mrs C J F L Williamson) 14 Russells Cres., Horley. Nr town centre between A23 and B2036; 400 yds from the railway station. 1-acre secluded country garden in centre of small town; contains all sorts of rare plants, interesting trees, many roses, pleasant vistas. An escapist's garden! See Collins Book of British Gardens. TEA. *Adm £1.25 Chd 25p. Sat, Sun June 25, 26 (2-6)*

29 Mostyn Road, Merton Park (see London)

Munstead Wood ৬✿❀ (Sir Robert & Lady Clark) nr Godalming. Take B2130 Brighton Rd out of Godalming towards Horsham. After 1m church on R, Heath Lane just thereafter on L. 400yds on R is entrance to Munstead Wood. Limited parking. 10 acres of rhododendrons, azaleas, woods and shrub and flower beds. Home until 1931 of Gertrude Jekyll; parts of garden recently refurbished. The architect for the house (not open) was Edwin Lutyens. TEAS. *Adm £2 OAP/Chd £1 (Share to Home Farm Trust®). Suns May 22, 29 (2-6)*

Odstock ✿❀ (Mr & Mrs J F H Trott) Bletchingley. Between Godstone 2m and Redhill 3m on A25. Junction 6 off M25 to Godstone. A25 towards Redhill. In Bletching-

ley from Whyte Harte up hill - Castle Square on L at top of hill. Just off A25. Parking in village. No parking in Castle Square. Bus 409 from Redhill Station alight at Red Lion public house. ⅔ of an acre maintained by owners and continually being developed for all-year interest. Covered walk created by training old apple trees plus other climbers. Interesting variety of plants and shrubs with imaginative complementary and contrasting groupings of form and colour. Japanese features; dahlias. No dig, low maintenance vegetable garden. TEAS. *Adm £1.50 Chd free (Share to NSPCC®). Sun Aug 7 (2-6). Disabled welcome — please telephone first* Tel 0883 743100

¶**The Old Croft** ✿❀ (Mrs David Lardner-Burke) South Holmwood. 3m S of Dorking. From Dorking take A24 S for 3m. Turn L at sign to Leigh-Brockham into Mill Road. ¾m on L, 2 free car parks in NT Holmwood Common. Follow directional signs for 400dyds along country walk through woodland to The Old Croft. 4 to 5 acres completely surrounded by NT property; parkland garden with lake, woodland, wild areas, herb garden, wide variety of specimen young trees, mature native trees, rhododendrons, azaleas and shrubs. Garden redeveloped and designed over last 6yrs by Virginia Lardner-Burke. TEAS. *Adm £1.50 Chd free (Share to St Catherine's Hospice, Crawley®). Sats, Suns, May 7, 8, July 16, 17 (2-6)*

¶**Olivers** ✿❀ (Mr & Mrs Charles Watson) Church Road, Hascombe. On B2130, Godalming to Cranleigh Road (Godalming 3m). Park by White Horse in Hascombe village. Olivers is 50yds up Church Rd, between public house and pond. 2½-acre informal country garden; wide variety, herbaceous borders, interesting trees, shrubs and perennials, some new development areas. All this maintained on 1 day a week. Beautiful village location by historic church. TEAS. *Adm £1 Chd 20p (Share to Church Fabric Fund®). Sun May 29 (2-6)*

Painshill ৬✿ (Painshill Park Trust) 1m W Cobham on A245. Entrance on R, 200yds E of A3/A245 roundabout. Painshill is one of Europe's finest C18 landscape gardens, contemporary with Stourhead & Stowe. Created by the Hon Charles Hamilton between 1738-1773. Ornamental pleasure grounds dominated by 14-acre lake fed from river by immense waterwheel; grotto, ruined Abbey, Temple, Chinese Bridge, castellated Tower, Mausoleum. Turkish tent and newly planted vineyard. In 1981 the Painshill Park Trust was formed and following meticulous restoration the beautiful gardens are now emerging from the wilderness. Suitable for wheelchairs with exceptions. TEA. *Adm £3, disabled, students and OAPs £2.50 Acc chd under 14 free (Share to Painshill Park Trust®). Suns only April 10 to Oct 16 (11-6). Private groups on other days. For NGS Sun Sept 25 (11-5)*

Pinewood House ৬✿ (Mr & Mrs J Van Zwanenberg) Heath House Rd, Worplesdon Hill. 3m Woking, 5m Guildford off A322 opp Brookwood Cemetery Wall. 4 acres. Newly planted Victorian clematis border. Walled garden and arboretum; water garden; bulbs in April. Interesting new house finished in Dec '86 with indoor plants. Homemade TEAS £2. *Adm house & gardens £1.50 (Share to Action Research®). Private visits welcome for parties of 2-20 April to Oct, please* Tel 0483 473241

Polesden Lacey &# (The National Trust) Bookham, nr Dorking. 1½m S of Great Bookham off A246 Leatherhead-Guildford rd. 60 acres formal gardens; extensive grounds, walled rose garden, winter garden, lavender garden, iris garden, lawns; good views. House originally a Regency villa dating early 1820's, remodelled after 1906 by the Hon Mrs Ronald Greville, well-known Edwardian hostess; fine paintings, furniture, porcelain and silver, also many photographs from Mrs Greville's albums on display. King George VI and Queen Elizabeth (now the Queen Mother) spent part of their honeymoon here. For wheelchair details contact Administrator **Tel 0372 458203.** Gift shop. Lunch and TEAS in licensed restaurant in grounds (11-6). *Adm garden £2.50, Chd £1.25; house £3 extra; Chd £1.75. For NGS garden only Suns May 15, July 17 (11-6)*

Postford House &# (Mrs R Litler-Jones) Chilworth. 4m SE Guildford Route A248 Bus LC 425 Guildford-Dorking alight nr entrance. 25 acres woodland; water garden; stream; rose garden; vegetable garden; rhododendrons, azaleas and shrubs; swimming pool open. Home-made TEAS. *Adm £1.50 Chd free (Share to Cruse Bereavement Care® May 29). Suns May 15, 22, 29, Wed May 18 (2-6). Private visits welcome, please* **Tel 0483 765880**

Pyrford Court & Pyrford Common Rd, 2m E of Woking. B367 junction with Upshott Lane; M25 exit 10 onto A3 towards Guildford off into Ripley signed Pyrford. 20 acres; wild gardens; extensive lawns; azaleas, rhododendrons, wisterias, autumn colour. TEAS. *Adm £2, Chd 70p (Share to Musicians Benevolent Fund®). Sat, Suns May 14, 15, (2-6), Oct 16 (12-4). Private visits welcome, please* **Tel 0483 765880**

●**Ramster** &# (Mr & Mrs Paul Gunn) Chiddingfold. On A283, 1½m S of Chiddingfold; large iron gates on R. Mature 20-acre woodland garden of exceptional interest with lakes, ponds and woodland walks. Laid out by Gauntlett Nurseries of Chiddingfold in early 1900s. Fine rhododendrons, azaleas, camellias, magnolias, trees and shrubs. Picnic area. TEAS (Sats, Suns, Bank Hols April to June 5). *Adm £1 Chd under 16 free (Share to NGS). Sats, Suns, Easter Mon April, June 11 to July 31; £1.50 Daily for April 30 to June 5 (2-6). Special early morning opening for photographers from 7am May 14, 15. Parties by appt.* **Tel 0428 644422**

¶**Ridings** &## (Mr & Mrs K Dutton) Tadworth. 6m S of Sutton off the A217. On 1st roundabout after Burgh Heath traffic lights take B2220 sign-posted Tadworth. Take 2nd R into Tadorne Rd; L into Cross Rd. House on corner of Epsom Lane S. ¾-acre informal garden containing interesting trees, shrubs and herbaceous plants with emphasis on colour, texture and foliage; vegetable plot. *Adm £1 Chd 30p. Sun June 26 (10.30-5). Private visits also welcome June, please* **Tel 0737 813962**

Rise Top Cottage ## (Trevor Bath Esq) Off Maybourne Rise, Mayford, Woking. Maybourne Rise is approached by a turning off the A320 3m N of Guildford. Look for yellow 'Garden Open' posters. On entering Maybourne Rise, take immediate L turn. At the top of the rise, the garden is situated along a rough track (about 100yds). Please park tactfully in Maybourne Rise. Trevor Bath is a garden

writer and lecturer who began his delightful garden 25 yrs ago; profusion of planting; many unfamiliar varieties of cottage plants and some surprises; special interests incl. aquilegias, pulmonarias, herbs, old roses and white flowers; mainly a wide range of hardy geraniums which are the subject of his new book. Included in Good Housekeeping feature on Cottage Gardens. Home-made TEAS all day. *Adm £1 Chd free (Share to Alzheimer's Disease Soc®). Wed June 1; Mon June 6 (10-5); also private visits welcome May and June, please* **Tel 0483 764958**

41 Shelvers Way ## (Mr & Mrs K G Lewis) Tadworth. 6m S of Sutton off the A217. !st turning on R after Burgh Heath traffic lights heading S. 400 yds down Shelvers Way on L. ⅓-acre suburban style with a difference. Cobbled area with bubble fountain and shingle scree leading to colourful herbaceous plantings, azaleas and Rhododendrons in spring. Designed and developed entirely by owners for year round interest. TEA June, July only in aid of Tadworth and Walton Horticultural Society *Adm £1 Chd 30p. Suns May 22 (2-5.30); June 26, July 17 (10.30-5)*

Snowdenham House &# (The Hon Lady Hamilton) Snowdenham Lane, Bramley, S of Guildford. 7 acres water, woodland and formal gardens. Georgian house. TEA. *Adm £1.50 Chd free. Suns May 1, 29 (2-6)*

South Park Farm &# (Mrs E B Stewart-Smith) South Godstone, 1m S of railway bridge over A22 at South Godstone; turn R into Carlton Rd opp. Walker's Garden Centre; follow signs for 1m. Medium-sized garden; wide variety of roses; herbaceous border; fine trees and landscape; small lake. C17 (listed) farm house (not open). Peacocks. Home-made TEAS till 6 in large C17 barn. *Adm £1.50 Chd free. Sat, Sun Mon June 18, 19, 20 (2-6). Also private visits welcome please* **Tel 0342 892141**

Spring Cottage &## (Mr & Mrs D E Norman) Cranleigh. A281 from Guildford turn L 1m out of Bramley. Turn R at roundabout then immediately L, signposted Cranleigh School & Smithwood Common; garden 1m on R. 1-acre garden with lovely view; cottage garden; small woodland garden, old roses and new pond. TEA. *Adm £1.25 Chd free. Wed June 8, Sun June 12 (2-6); private visits welcome, please* **Tel 0483 272620**

Spur Point, nr Fernhurst (See Sussex)

¶**Stonywood** ## (Mr & Mrs Noble) Chase Lane, Haslemere. From centre of town take B2131 E towards Petworth. Take 2nd turning R for Blackdown. At junction of 5 lanes go straight on towards Tennyson's Lane. At next junction (150yds) go straight on. House on L, ⅓m down lane. Please park in lane. ⅓-acre steeply sloping garden, surefooted gardeners will benefit most. Many rhododendrons, azaleas, shrubs, spring bulbs; pleasant views across Chase Valley and NT woods. TEAS. *Adm £1 Chd free (Share to Foundation for the study of Infant Deaths®). Private visits welcome Tues & Fris May & June, please* **Tel 0428 658583**

By Appointment Gardens. Avoid the crowds. Good chance of a tour by owner. See garden description for telephone number.

Street House &# (Mr & Mrs B M Francis) Thursley village ½m off A3 between Milford and Hindhead. From A3 100yds past Three Horse Shoes public house. House is on L. Car park is on recreation ground past PO in centre of village. Please park carefully in wet weather. Street House, a listed Regency building and childhood home of Sir Edwin Lutyens where he first met Gertrude Jekyll (not open). Garden of 1¼ acres divided into three separate and individual gardens. Beautiful views towards Devils Punch Bowl. Ancient wall; special features include magnificent specimen cornus kousa; Japanese snowball tree; rare old roses; special rhododendrons and camellias; rubus tridel and many surprises. Special feature Astrological Garden now completed. Home-made TEAS. *Adm £1.50 Chd 50p (Share to Thursley Horticultural Soc®). Suns April 24, May 22, June 19 (11-5)*

Thanescroft &# (Mr & Mrs Peter Talbot-Willcox) Shamley Green. 5m S of Guildford, A281 Guildford-Horsham rd, at Shalford turn E onto B2128 to Wonersh and Shamley Green. At Shamley Green Village sign turn R to Lord's Hill, ¾m on L. 4-acres mixed formal and informal garden, incl vegetables; lawns; roses; herbaceous; shrubs and specialist trees. Interesting icehouse; swimming pool. TEAS. *Adm £1 Chd 25p. Sun June 19 (2-6)*

Unicorns # (Mr & Mrs Eric Roberts) Long Hill The Sands, Farnham. Approx 4½m E of Farnham take A31 towards Guildford. After ¾m turn R into Crooksbury Rd through 's' bend then L turn to The Sands through village past Barley Mow public house on R. Long Hill 1st turning on R. Mainly woodland garden on a sloping site, rhododendrons, azaleas, ferns, plants for ground cover and many other interesting and unusual plants and shrubs. Teas at Manor Farm Seale. *Adm £1 (Share to Hydestile Wildlife Hospital®). Private visits welcome from end of April to end of August please Tel 0252 782778. Due to terrain 2 to 15 adults only*

87 Upland Road &# (Mr & Mrs David Nunn) 50yds S Carshalton Beeches station into Waverley Way, at shops into Downside Rd, then 1st on L. 0.4-acre secluded suburban plantsman's garden overlaying chalk. Shrubs; herbaceous; orchard; fruit and vegetable garden. Developed and maintained by owners. Exhibition of botanical watercolour paintings. TEAS. *Adm £1 Chd free. Sun May 15 (2-6)*

Vale End # (Mr & Mrs John Foulsham) Albury, 4½m SE of Guildford. From Albury take A248 W for ¼m. 1-acre walled garden on many levels in beautiful setting; featured in Gardeners World 1992; views from terrace across sloping lawns to mill pond and woodland; wide variety herbaceous plants and old roses; attractive courtyard. Ornamental fruit and vegetable garden. Featured in NGS video 2, see page 344. Morning coffee and home-made TEAS in aid of Albury Parish Church Fabric Fund. *Adm £1.50 Chd free. Suns June 26, July 31 (10-5)*

Vann #& (Mr & Mrs M B Caroe) Hambledon, 6m S of Godalming. A283 to Wormley. Turn L at Hambledon Xrds signed 'Vann Lane'. Follow yellow 'Vann' signs for 2m. House on left. GPO box on gate. 4½ acres surrounding Tudor, William & Mary house with later additions and alterations incorporating old farm buildings by W D Caröe 1907-1909. Formal yew walk, recently replanted ¼-acre pond, Gertrude Jekyll water garden 1911, pergola, old cottage garden. Spring bulbs, woodland, azaleas, roses. Featured in *Country Life, Field, Surrey Magazine, Mon Jardin Ma Maison, BBC Time Watch 1989, Practical Gardening 1990, Architectural Digest 1991, Homes & Gardens* and *World of Interiors 1993.* Maintained by family with 14 hours assistance per week. Part of garden suitable for wheelchairs. Party bookings, guided tours, morning coffee, lunches, home-made teas in house from Easter-July by prior arrangement. *Adm £2.50 Chd 50p. Tues-Sun April 5-10 (10-6). Tues-Sun May 3-8 (10-6), Tues-Sun May 31-June 5 (10-6). Private visits welcome, please* **Tel 0428 683413**

Walton Poor &#& (Mr & Mrs Nicholas Calvert) 4m W of Ranmore. From N and W off A246 on outskirts of East Horsley take Greendene 1st fork L Crocknorth Rd. From E take A2003 to Ranmore Rd from Dorking to E Horsley. Approx 3 acres; tranquil, rather secret garden; paths winding between areas of ornamental shrubs; landscaped sunken garden; pond; herb garden. Autumn colour. Extensive range of foliage, scented plants and herbs for sale; garden next to miles of forest paths leading to North Downs with fine views over Tillingbourne valley. TEAS (May and June) (from 3pm) *Adm £1.50 Chd 50p (Share to Leukaemia Research®). Mon May 2, Sun, Wed June 5, 8 (11-6) Sun Oct 9 (11-5) Herb garden open daily Wed to Sun Easter to Sept 30. Private visits welcome to the main garden, please* **Tel 0483 282273**

Westbourn # (Mr & Mrs John Camden) Virginia Water. From Egham 3m S on A30. Turn L into Christchurch Rd opp the Wheatsheaf Hotel. After 200 yds turn R into Pinewood Rd; Westbourn is 50 yds on the R. 4 acres landscaped woodland on two levels extensively planted with unusual trees and shrubs. Rhododendrons and azaleas predominate with over 80 different species and as many hybrids. Other notable collections well represented include acer, prunus, sorbus, hydrangea, ferns, ornamental cherries and hosta. The River Bourne, a narrow winding rivulet, forms the southern boundary of the garden. Soft drinks & biscuits. *Adm £1 Chd free. Sun May 8 (2-6)*

¶Westland Farm &# (Mrs E J Burnet) Ewhurst. 11m SE of Guildford. Join Ockley Rd (B2127) at Bull's Head N of village. Go E for ¾m. See sign on RH-side. 2½ acres plus 14 acres bluebell woodland; rhododendrons, azaleas, other acid-loving plants, lake with woodland walk, spring bulbs; Australian plants and trees around house and cottages. Interesting use of horticultural plastic for low maintenance and growth promotion; established trees and shrubs in garden extension (designer present May 11 to answer questions). Australian TEAS and pavlova ice-cream; dried flower arrangements. *Adm £1.50 Chd free. Wed May 11 (2-5.30), Sun May 15 (11-5.30)*

Whinfold &#& (Mr & Mrs A Gash) Hascombe. 3½m SE of Godalming. Turn off B2130 at top of Winkworth Hill between Godalming and Hascombe. Woodland garden about 15 acres originally planned by Gertrude Jekyll in 1897. The garden is maintained by the owners with weekend help and includes a pond, herb garden, specimen trees, magnolias, rhododendrons, azaleas and camellias with spring bulbs followed by masses of bluebells. TEA. *Adm £1 Chd free (Share to Hydon Hill Cheshire Home®). Suns April 3, May 15 (2-5)*

White House &❀ (Lt Cdr & Mrs Michael Lethbridge) Stringers Common Guildford. On A 320 Guildford to Woking Rd 2m N of Guildford centre just beyond junction with Jacob's Well Rd. 3 acres, shrubs and herbaceous borders in setting of stone walls, roses, old orchard and pond. Emphasis given to ecological improvement and maintenance of natural surroundings. TEA. *Adm £1 Chd free. (Share to Jacobs Well Ecological Society®) Suns July 3 (2-6), Oct 2 (2-5.30)*

Windlesham Park &❀ (Mr & Mrs Peter Dimmock) Woodlands Lane. 2m E of Bagshot. S of Sunningdale, NW of Chobham; from Windlesham Church S to T-junction, turn L into Thorndown Lane becoming Woodlands Lane over M3; entrance 100yds on R, white pillars. 9-acre parkland setting with many and varied well established azaleas and rhododendrons. Fine cedars and mature trees; wet areas. TEAS. *Adm £1 Chd 25p (Share to St John the Baptist Church®). Sun May 15 (2-6)*

Winkworth Arboretum (The National Trust) Hascombe, Godalming. Entrances with car parks; Upper 3m SE of Godalming on E side of B2130; Lower 2¼m S of Bramley on Bramley-Hascombe rd, turn R off A281 from Guildford by Bramley Grange Hotel, up Snowdenham Lane. Coaches (by strict arrangement) should use Upper car park on B2130. Station: Godalming 3m. 95 acres of hillside planted with rare trees and shrubs; 2 lakes; many wild birds; view over N Downs. Limited suitability for wheelchairs. Disabled visitors use lower car park. No disabled facilities. TEAS 11-6. *Adm £2 Chd 5-15 £1.* ▲*Suns May 15, Oct 16 (dawn-dusk)*

Wintershall Manor ❀ (Mr & Mrs Peter Hutley) 3m S of Bramley village on A281 turn R, then next R. Wintershall drive next on L. Bus: AV 33 Guildford-Horsham; alight Palmers Cross, 1m. 2-acre garden and 200 acres of park and woodland; snowdrop walk, acres of bluebell walks in spring; banks of wild daffodils; rhododendrons; specimen trees; several acres of lakes and flight ponds; Domesday yew tree. St Francis Chapel by Chapel Lake. Path commences The Stations of the Cross by contemporary young sculptors leading up the hill to Hollybarn and The Chapel of St Mary, Queen of Peace, with superb views. TEA from 3.30 pm, soup in winter. Picnic area. *Adm £2 OAPs £1.50 Chd 4-14 50p. Suns Feb 6, March 6, May 1, June 5, July 3 (2-5.15). Easter Mon April 4, Passion Play from 11 am performed throughout day*

Woodside ❀❀ (Mr & Mrs J A Colmer) Send Barns Lane, Send, nr Ripley, 4m NE of Guildford; on A247 (Woking/Dorking Rd) 200 yds west (Send side) at junction with B2215 (Old A3). If travelling via M25 leave at junction 10. ⅓-acre garden; main feature rock garden and alpine house; many shrubs incl rhododendrons, ericaceous species etc; herbaceous planting; specialist collection of alpines. *Adm £1 Chd free. Sun April 24 (2-6). Private visits welcome during May , please* **Tel 0483 223073**

Yew Tree Cottage ❀❀ (Mr & Mrs E E Bowyer) Bunch Lane, Haslemere. Turn off High St into Church Lane, leave church on L, carry on to T junction, turn L, 1st house on L. 2-acre garden created by owners since 1976 on hillside. Large variety of trees and shrubs, water garden, kitchen garden, Jacob and Shetland sheep, Chinese geese, Shetland pony in paddock beyond garden. See **Haslehurst**. Tea at Haslehurst. *Adm £1 Chd 50p (Share to Haslemere Educational Museum®). Sun June 12 (2.30-6). Private visits welcome, please* **Tel 0428 644130**

67 York Rd &❀❀ (F A Wood Esq) Cheam. York Rd is situated in the Sutton Cheam area and runs between Cheam Rd and Dorset Rd. 67 is located at the S end of York Rd, towards the junction with Dorset Rd, which is a turning off Belmont Rise A217. Mainly walled suburban garden just under 0.2 acres, laid out and developed by the present owner over the past 5-6yrs. The layout comprises two lawned terraces with interesting hard landscaping and footpath patterns, incl raised shrub, heather and flower beds. Good range of plants, incl viburnums, hollies, ferns, ivies and conifers, plus 75′ herbaceous border with wide range of hardy plants. Two raised ponds, one comprising an open roofed water pavilion. Good selection of wall climbers. Dried flowers for sale. *Adm £1 Chd free. Sun July 17 (10-4); also private visits welcome, please* **Tel 081 642 4260**

Sussex

Hon County Organisers:

(East & Mid-Sussex)	Mrs Michael Toynbee, Westerleigh, Mayfield Lane, Wadhurst TN5 6JE Tel 0892 783238
(West Sussex)	Mrs Nigel Azis, Coke's Barn, West Burton, Pulborough RH20 1HD Tel 0798 831636

Assistant Hon County Organisers:

(East & Mid-Sussex)	Mrs J Charlesworth, Snape Cottage, Snape Lane, Wadhurst
(West Sussex)	Mrs Jane Burton, Church Farmhouse, Lavant, nr Chichester
(West Sussex)	Mrs Mark Dunn, Windham, Stoughton, Chichester
(West Sussex)	Mrs Jane Newdick, Dale House, West Burton, Pulborough
((West Sussex)	Mrs Juliet Tuck, New Barn, Egdean, Pulborough

Hon County Treasurers:

(East & Mid-Sussex)	A C W Hunter Esq, Cottenden Oast, Stonegate, Wadhurst
(West Sussex)	W M Caldwell Esq, The Grange, Fittleworth, Pulborough

DATES OF OPENING

By appointment

For telephone number and other details see garden descriptions.
Private visits welcomed

Ardingly Gardens
Bates Green Farm, Arlington
Casters Brook, Cocking, nr Midhurst
Chidmere House, Chidham
Coates Manor, Fittleworth
Cobblers, Crowborough
Coke's Barn, West Burton
Combehurst, Frant
Cooke's House, West Burton
Coombland, Coneyhurst,
  Billingshurst
Crawley Down Gardens
Cowbeech Farm, Hailsham
Dale House, West Burton
Duckyls, Sharpthorne
116 Findon Road, Worthing
Ghyll Farm, Sweethaws
High Beeches Gardens, Handcross
Home Farm House, Buckham Hill,
  nr Uckfield
Ketches, Newick
King John's Lodge, Etchingham
Malt House, Chithurst, Rogate
Mill House, Nutbourne
Moorlands, nr Crowborough
Neptune House, Cutmill, Bosham
North Springs, Fittleworth
64 Old Shoreham Road, Hove
Orchards, Rowfant
Priesthawes, Stone Cross, Polegate
Spur Point, nr Fernhurst
Telegraph House, North Marden, nr
  Chichester

Regular openings

For details see garden descriptions

Borde Hill Garden, nr Haywards
  Heath. See text for dates
Denmans, Fontwell, nr Arundel.
  Daily except Dec 25, 26
The Garden in Mind, Stansted Park.
  Sun, Mon, Tues May to Sept
Great Dixter, Northiam. Daily April 1
  to Oct 9, for exceptions see text
High Beeches Gardens, Handcross.
  For details see text
Moorlands, nr Crowborough. Weds
  April to Oct
Parham House and Gardens, nr
  Pulborough. See text for dates
Pashley Manor, Ticehurst. For
  details see text
West Dean Gardens, nr Chichester.
  Daily March 1 to Oct 31

March 7 Monday
  Denmans, Fontwell, nr Arundel
March 13 Sunday
  Champs Hill, Coldwaltham, nr
  Pulborough
March 20 Sunday
  Champs Hill, Coldwaltham, nr
  Pulborough
March 26 Saturday
  The Manor of Dean, Tillington,
  Petworth ‡
  Petworth House, Petworth ‡
March 27 Sunday
  Champs Hill, Coldwaltham, nr
  Pulborough
  The Manor of Dean, Tillington,
  Petworth
March 28 Monday
  The Manor of Dean, Tillington,
  Petworth
March 30 Wednesday
  West Dean Gardens, nr Chichester
April 1 Friday
  Houghton Farm, nr Arundel
April 3 Sunday
  Berri Court, Yapton
  Chidmere House, Chidham
April 4 Monday
  Berri Court, Yapton
  Chidmere House, Chidham
  Highdown Gardens, Goring-by-Sea
  The Old Rectory, Fittleworth
  Penns in the Rocks, Groombridge
  Stonehurst, Ardingly
April 6 Wednesday
  Little Thakeham, Storrington
April 9 Saturday
  Northwood Farmhouse,
  Pulborough
April 10 Sunday
  Fitzhall, Iping, nr Midhurst
  Rymans, Apuldram, nr Chichester
April 11 Monday
  Northwood Farmhouse,
  Pulborough
April 16 Saturday
  The Manor of Dean, Tillington,
  Petworth
April 17 Sunday
  Cooke's House, West Burton ‡
  Hurst Mill, Petersfield
  The Manor of Dean, Tillington,
  Petworth ‡
April 18 Monday
  Cooke's House, West Burton ‡
  The Manor of Dean, Tillington,
  Petworth ‡
April 19 Tuesday
  Cooke's House, West Burton
April 24 Sunday
  Coke's Barn, West Burton ‡
  Cooke's House, West Burton ‡
  Frith Hill, Northchapel
  Merriments Gardens, Hurst Green

Malt House, Chithurst, nr Rogate
  Newtimber Place, Newtimber
  Rymans, Apuldram, nr Chichester
April 25 Monday
  Cooke's House, West Burton
April 26 Tuesday
  Cooke's House, West Burton
April 30 Saturday
  Bignor Park, nr Pulborough ‡
  Cedar Tree Cottage, Washington
  Champs Hill, Coldwaltham, nr
  Pulborough ‡
  Cooksbridge, Fernhurst
  Orchards, Rowfant
May 1 Sunday
  Bignor Park, nr Pulborough
  Bumble Cottage, Monkmead
  Lane, W Chiltington
  Champs Hill, Coldwaltham, nr
  Pulborough
  Cooksbridge, Fernhurst
  Malt House, Chithurst, nr Rogate
  Offham House, Offham
  Orchards, Rowfant
  Wadhurst Park, Wadhurst
May 2 Monday
  Bignor Park, nr Pulborough ‡
  Bumble Cottage, Monkmead
  Lane, W Chiltington
  Highdown Gardens,
  Goring-by-Sea
  Houghton Farm, nr Arundel ‡
  Malt House, Chithurst, nr Rogate
  Orchards, Rowfant
  Stonehurst, Ardingly
May 3 Tuesday
  Houghton Farm, nr Arundel
May 4 Wednesday
  Bates Green Farm, Arlington
  Cedar Tree Cottage, Washington
May 7 Saturday
  Cedar Tree Cottage, Washington
  High Beeches Gardens, Handcross
May 8 Sunday
  Berri Court, Yapton
  Ghyll Farm, Sweethaws
  Hammerwood House, Iping ‡
  Malt House, Chithurst, nr
  Rogate ‡
  Nymans, Handcross
  Puddle House, Cross in Hand
  Standen, East Grinstead
May 9 Monday
  Berri Court, Yapton
May 11 Wednesday
  Bates Green Farm, Arlington
May 14 Saturday
  Champs Hill, Coldwaltham, nr
  Pulborough ‡
  116 Findon Road, Worthing
  The Manor of Dean, Tillington,
  Petworth ‡
May 15 Sunday
  Cowdray Park, Midhurst ‡

Champs Hill, Coldwaltham, nr
   Pulborough
Chidmere House, Chidham
116 Findon Road, Worthing
Hammerwood House, Iping ‡‡
The Manor of Dean, Tillington,
   Petworth ‡
Malt House, Chithurst, nr
   Rogate ‡‡
Moorlands, nr Crowborough ‡‡‡‡
Mountfield Court, nr
   Robertsbridge
New Grove, Petworth ‡
Selehurst, Lower Beeding, nr
   Horsham
Stonehurst, Ardingly
Trotton Place, nr Rogate ‡‡‡
Trotton Old Rectory, nr
   Rogate ‡‡‡
Warren House,
   Crowborough ‡‡‡‡

May 16 Monday
Chidmere House, Chidham
The Manor of Dean, Tillington,
   Petworth
Mountfield Court, nr
   Robertsbridge

May 18 Wednesday
Bates Green Farm, Arlington
Nyewood House, Nyewood, nr
   Rogate
Sheffield Park Gardens, nr
   Uckfield

May 21 Saturday
Ardingly Gardens
Champs Hill, Coldwaltham, nr
   Pulborough ‡
Fittleworth Gardens, Pulborough ‡
Hurst House, Sedlescombe
Lane End, Midhurst

May 22 Sunday
Ardingly Gardens
Champs Hill, Coldwaltham, nr
   Pulborough ‡
Cobblers, Crowborough ‡‡‡
Cowbeech Farm, Hailsham
Fittleworth Gardens, Pulborough ‡
Ghyll Farm, Sweethaws
Greenhurst, Thakeham ‡
Lane End, Midhurst ‡‡
Legsheath Farm, nr Forest Row
Merriments Gardens, Hurst Green
Malt House, Chithurst, nr
   Rogate ‡‡
Warren House, Crowborough ‡‡‡

May 23 Monday
Lane End, Midhurst

May 25 Wednesday
Bates Green Farm, Arlington

May 28 Saturday
Gaywood Farm, Pulborough
Lane End, Midhurst

May 29 Sunday
Baker's Farm, Shipley, nr Horsham

Fitzhall, Iping, nr Midhurst ‡‡
Gaywood Farm, Pulborough ‡
Lane End, Midhurst ‡‡
Manvilles Field, Fittleworth ‡
Malt House, Chithurst, nr
   Rogate ‡‡
Moorlands, nr Crowborough

May 30 Monday
Cobblers, Crowborough ‡
Greenacres, Crowborough ‡
Highdown Gardens, Goring-by-Sea
Lane End, Midhurst ‡‡
Manvilles Field, Fittleworth
Malt House, Chithurst, nr
   Rogate ‡‡

June 1 Wednesday
Greenacres, Crowborough

June 4 Saturday
Middle Coombe, East Grinstead
North Springs, Fittleworth

June 5 Sunday
Buckhurst Park, Withyham
The Garden in Mind, Stansted
   Park
Hailsham Grange, Hailsham
Merriments Gardens, Hurst Green
Middle Coombe, East Grinstead
Neptune House, Cutmill,
   Bosham ‡
North Springs, Fittleworth
Nymans, Handcross
Offham House, Offham
Old Barklye, Heathfield
Pembury, Clayton, nr Brighton
Pondfield, Cutmill, Bosham ‡
The White House, Burpham, nr
   Arundel

June 6 Monday
Old Barklye, Heathfield
The Garden in Mind, Stansted
   Park
Little Thakeham, Storrington

June 7 Tuesday
Little Thakeham, Storrington

June 8 Wednesday
Bateman's, Burwash
Lilac Cottage, Duncton ‡
Parham House and Gardens, nr
   Pulborough
Somerset Lodge, North Street,
   Petworth ‡

June 9 Thursday
Houghton Farm, nr Arundel ‡
Parham House and Gardens, nr
   Pulborough ‡

June 10 Friday
Houghton Farm, nr Arundel

June 11 Saturday
Chantry Green House, Steyning
Coombland, Coneyhurst,
   Billingshurst
Frith Hill, Northchapel ‡
Frith Lodge, Northchapel ‡
Lilac Cottage, Duncton ‡‡

Northwood Farmhouse,
   Pulborough
Somerset Lodge, North Street,
   Petworth ‡‡
Telegraph House, North Marden,
   nr Chichester

June 12 Sunday
Chantry Green House, Steyning
Clinton Lodge, Fletching, nr
   Uckfield
Coates Manor, Fittleworth ‡‡‡
Cobblers, Crowborough ‡‡‡‡
Ebbsworth, Nutbourne, nr
   Pulborough ‡‡
Forest Lodge, West Broyle, nr
   Chichester ‡‡‡‡
Frith Hill, Northchapel ‡
Frith Lodge, Northchapel ‡
Greenacres, Crowborough ‡‡‡‡
Hurst Mill, Petersfield
Ketches, Newick
Kingston Gardens, nr Lewes
Knabbs Farmhouse, Fletching
Lilac Cottage, Duncton ‡‡‡
Lye Green House,
   Crowborough ‡‡‡‡
Mill House, Nutbourne ‡‡
Nyewood House, Nyewood, nr
   Rogate
Nutbourne Vineyards, nr
   Pulborough ‡‡
The Old Rectory, Fittleworth ‡‡‡
Priesthawes, Stone Cross,
   Polegate
Sennicotts, nr Chichester ‡‡‡
Somerset Lodge, North Street,
   Petworth ‡‡‡
Telegraph House, North Marden,
   nr Chichester
Three Oaks, West Broyle,
   Chichester ‡‡‡‡
The White House, Burpham, nr
   Arundel
Woodstock, West Broyle,
   Chichester ‡‡‡‡

June 13 Monday
Clinton Lodge, Fletching, nr
   Uckfield
Coates Manor, Fittleworth ‡
Ebbsworth, Nutbourne, nr
   Pulborough ‡
Mill House, Nutbourne ‡
Northwood Farmhouse,
   Pulborough
Nutbourne Vineyards, nr
   Pulborough ‡
Sennicotts, nr Chichester

June 14 Tuesday
Coates Farm, Fittleworth

June 15 Wednesday
Great Allfields, Balls Cross nr
   Petworth
Nyewood House, Nyewood, nr
   Rogate

June 18 Saturday
King John's Lodge, Etchingham ‡
Little Hutchings, Etchingham ‡
Winchelsea Gardens
June 19 Sunday
Baker's Farm, Shipley, nr Horsham
Casters Brook, Cocking, nr
Midhurst
King John's Lodge, Etchingham ‡
Little Hutchings, Etchingham ‡
Mayfield Cottage Gardens,
Mayfield ‡‡
Merriments Gardens, Hurst Green
Moat Mill Farm, Mayfield ‡‡
Old Barkfold, Plaistow, nr
Billingshurst
Sherburne House, Eartham
June 20 Monday
Clinton Lodge, Fletching, nr
Uckfield
June 24 Friday
Down Place, South Harting
June 25 Saturday
Chilsham House, nr Hailsham
Coombland, Coneyhurst,
Billingshurst
Crawley Down Gardens ‡
Down Place, South Harting
Orchards, Rowfant ‡
June 26 Sunday
Ambrose Place Back Gardens,
Worthing
Bates Green Farm, Arlington
Berri Court, Yapton
Casters Brook, Cocking, nr
Midhurst
Chidmere House, Chidham ‡
Chilsham House, nr Hailsham
Cobblers, Crowborough
Crawley Down Gardens ‡‡
Down Place, South Harting
Home Farm House, Buckham Hill,
nr Uckfield ‡‡‡
The Old Vicarage, Firle
Orchards, Rowfant ‡‡
Pashley Manor, Ticehurst
Pheasants Hatch, Newick ‡‡‡
Rymans, Apuldram, nr
Chichester ‡
Trotton Place, nr Rogate ‡‡‡‡
Trotton Old Rectory, nr
Rogate ‡‡‡‡
Udimore Gardens, nr Rye
Wilderness Farm, Hadlow Down
June 27 Monday
Berri Court, Yapton
Chidmere House, Chidham
Clinton Lodge, Fletching, nr
Uckfield ‡
Home Farm House, Buckham Hill,
nr Uckfield ‡
Pheasants Hatch, Newick ‡
July 2 Saturday
Gaywood Farm, Pulborough

July 3 Sunday
Coke's Barn, West Burton
Combehurst, Frant
Gaywood Farm, Pulborough
Merriments Gardens, Hurst Green
The Old Rectory, Newtimber
July 4 Monday
Little Thakeham, Storrington
July 5 Tuesday
Little Thakeham, Storrington
July 6 Wednesday
Merriments Gardens, Hurst
Green
July 9 Saturday
Crown House, Eridge
North Springs, Fittleworth
Palmer's Lodge, West Chiltington
Village
July 10 Sunday
Cobblers, Crowborough
Crown House, Eridge
Fitzhall, Iping, nr Midhurst
Greenhurst, Thakeham ‡
North Springs, Fittleworth
Palmer's Lodge, West Chiltington
Village ‡
Rustington Convalescent Home,
Rustington
July 15 Friday
St Marys House, Bramber
Wakehurst Place, Ardingly
July 16 Saturday
Ardingly Gardens
The Manor of Dean, Tillington,
Petworth
Middle Coombe, East Grinstead
Palmer's Lodge, West Chiltington
Village
Telegraph House, North Marden,
nr Chichester
July 17 Sunday
Chilsham House, nr Hailsham
Cobblers, Crowborough ‡
Frewen College, Brickwall,
Northiam
Kingston Gardens, nr Lewes
The Manor of Dean, Tillington,
Petworth
Merriments Gardens, Hurst Green
Middle Coombe, East Grinstead
Nyewood House, Nyewood, nr
Rogate
Palmer's Lodge, West Chiltington
Village
Telegraph House, North Marden,
nr Chichester
Wadhurst Gardens ‡
July 18 Monday
Chilsham House, nr Hailsham
The Manor of Dean, Tillington,
Petworth
Wadhurst Gardens
July 20 Wednesday
Merriments Gardens, Hurst Green

Nyewood House, Nyewood, nr
Rogate
July 21 Thursday
Houghton Farm, nr Arundel
July 22 Friday
Houghton Farm, nr Arundel
St Marys House, Bramber
July 23 Saturday
116 Findon Road, Worthing
July 24 Sunday
116 Findon Road, Worthing
July 30 Saturday
Bumble Cottage, Monkmead
Lane, W Chiltington
July 31 Sunday
Bates Green Farm, Arlington
Bumble Cottage, Monkmead
Lane, W Chiltington ‡
Champs Hill, Coldwaltham, nr
Pulborough ‡
Cobblers, Crowborough ‡‡
Merriments Gardens, Hurst Green
Moorlands, nr Crowborough ‡‡
August 3 Wednesday
Merriments Gardens, Hurst Green
August 6 Saturday
Bumble Cottage, Monkmead
Lane, W Chiltington ‡
Champs Hill, Coldwaltham, nr
Pulborough †
Cooksbridge, Fernhurst
August 7 Sunday
Champs Hill, Coldwaltham, nr
Pulborough ‡
Bumble Cottage, Monkmead
Lane, W Chiltington ‡
Cooksbridge, Fernhurst
Hailsham Grange, Hailsham
Wilderness Farm, Hadlow Down
August 14 Sunday
Cobblers, Crowborough
Merriments Gardens, Hurst Green
August 17 Wednesday
Merriments Gardens, Hurst Green
August 20 Saturday
Champs Hill, Coldwaltham, nr
Pulborough ‡
The Manor of Dean, Tillington,
Petworth ‡
August 21 Sunday
Champs Hill, Coldwaltham, nr
Pulborough ‡
Danny, Hurstpierpoint
The Manor of Dean, Tillington,
Petworth ‡
August 22 Monday
The Manor of Dean, Tillington,
Petworth
August 28 Sunday
Chidmere House, Chidham ‡
Cobblers, Crowborough
Merriments Gardens, Hurst
Green
Newtimber Place, Newtimber

Rymans, Apuldram, nr
Chichester ‡
August 29 Monday
Chidmere House, Chidham
Houghton Farm, nr Arundel
Penns in the Rocks, Groombridge
August 30 Tuesday
Houghton Farm, nr Arundel
August 31 Wednesday
Merriments Gardens, Hurst Green
September 3 Saturday
High Beeches Gardens, Handcross
September 4 Sunday
Fitzhall, Iping, nr Midhurst
Wilderness Farm, Hadlow Down
September 7 Wednesday
West Dean Gardens, nr Chichester
September 11 Sunday
Merriments Gardens, Hurst Green
Standen, East Grinstead
September 14 Wednesday
Merriments Gardens, Hurst Green

September 17 Saturday
The Manor of Dean, Tillington,
Petworth
September 18 Sunday
Cowbeech Farm, Hailsham
The Manor of Dean, Tillington,
Petworth
September 19 Monday
The Manor of Dean, Tillington,
Petworth
September 25 Sunday
The Garden in Mind, Stansted
Park
Houghton Farm, nr Arundel
Merriments Gardens, Hurst Green
September 26 Monday
The Garden in Mind, Stansted
Park
Houghton Farm, nr Arundel
September 28 Wednesday
Merriments Gardens, Hurst
Green

October 1 Saturday
The Manor of Dean, Tillington,
Petworth
October 2 Sunday
The Manor of Dean, Tillington,
Petworth
Merriments Gardens, Hurst Green
Warren House, Crowborough
October 3 Sunday
The Manor of Dean, Tillington,
Petworth
October 9 Sunday
Warren House, Crowborough
October 16 Sunday
Long House, Cowfold
October 19 Wednesday
Sheffield Park Garden, nr Uckfield
October 23 Sunday
Berri Court, Yapton
October 24 Monday
Berri Court, Yapton ‡
Denmans, Fontwell, nr Arundel ‡

DESCRIPTIONS OF GARDENS

Ambrose Place Back Gardens, Richmond Rd ♿✿❀
Worthing 10m E of Bognor, 7m W of Brighton. Take
Broadwater Rd into town centre, turn R at traffic lights
into Richmond Rd opp Library; small town gardens with
entrances on left; parking in rds. TEAS. *Combined adm £1
Chd 25p (Share to Christ Church and St Paul's Wor-
thing®). Sun June 26 (11-1, 2-5)*

No 1 (Mrs M M Rosenberg) Walled garden; shrubs,
pond, climbing plants
No 3 (Mr & Mrs M Smyth) Paved garden with climbing
plants and lawn
No 4 (Mr & Mrs T J Worley) Paved garden with raised
herbaceous borders, lawn and flowering summer
plants
No 6 (Mrs Leslie Roberts) Attractive garden with conservatory
No 7 (Mr M Frost) Patio garden, with conservatory
No 8 (Mr & Mrs P McMonagle) Summer flowering
plants and lawn
No 10 (Mrs C F Demuth) Paved garden with roses and
interesting trees
No 11 (Mrs M Stewart) Roses, summerhouse, flowering plants
No 12 (Mr & Mrs P Bennett) Original paved small garden with trees
No 14 (Mr & Mrs A H P Humphrey) Roses, flowering
plants, greenhouse and bonsai collection
Ambrose Villa (Mr & Mrs Frank Leocadi) Italian style
small town garden
68 Richmond Road (Mr & Mrs Denis Hayden) Worthing. ¼m W down Richmond Road (10m walk). Small
walled town garden, perennials, shrubs and containers

Ardingly Gardens ♿✿❀ 1m West of Ardingly on Street
Lane (Balcombe Road) Entrance through Knowles. Gardens are interconnecting. Teas at Church Rooms nearby.
*Combined Adm £1.50 Chd free (Share to Chailey Herit-
age®). Sat, Sun, May 21, 22, Sat July 16 (2-5.30) Private
visits welcome for each garden Adm £1*

Jordans (Mr & Mrs K Waistell) 2 acres of gardens,
some large mature trees (Gingko, Tulip, Wellington).
Herbaceous and shrub borders. **Tel 0444 892681**
Knowles ❀ (The Michell Family) 7-acre garden reconstructed after storm; water garden; wood. Acid loving
trees and shrubs; some unusual plants. Fine views;
formal and informal areas. **Tel 0444 892723**

Baker's Farm ✿❀ (Mr & Mrs Mark Burrell) Shipley, 5m
S of Horsham. Take A24 then A272 W, 2nd turn to Dra-
gon's Green, L at George and Dragon then 300 yds on L.
Large Wealden garden; lake; laburnum tunnel; shrubs,
trees, rose walks of old-fashioned roses; scented knot
garden and bog gardens. TEAS. *Adm £1.30 Chd 30p
(Share to St Mary the Virgin, Shipley®). Suns May 29,
June 19 (2-6)*

Bateman's ♿✿ (The National Trust) Burwash ½m S
(A265). From rd leading S from W end of village. Home
of Rudyard Kipling from 1902-1936. Garden laid out before he lived in house and planted yew hedges, rose garden, laid paths and made pond. Bridge to mill which
grinds local wheat into flour. LUNCHES & TEAS. *Adm
£3.50 Groups 15 or more £3 Chd £1.80. Wed June 8
(11-5)*

Bates Green Farm ♿✿❀ (Mr & Mrs J R McCutchan) Arlington. 2½m SW of A22 at Hailsham and 2m S Michel-
ham Priory, Upper Dicker. Approach Arlington passing the
'Old Oak Inn' on R continue for 350yds then turn R along
a small lane. [TQ5507]. In May follow bluebell walk rd
signs. Plantsman's tranquil garden of over 1 acre gives
year-round interest; rockery; water; mixed borders with
colour themes, and shaded foliage garden. B & B accommodation. TEAS. *Adm £1.50 Chd free. Weds May 4, 11,
18, 25, Suns June 26, July 31 (2.30-5). Private visits welcome, please* **Tel 0323 482039**

Regular Openers. See head of county section.

Berri Court ♿♣ (Mr & Mrs J C Turner) Yapton, 5m SW of Arundel. In centre of village between PO & Black Dog public house. A2024 Littlehampton-Chichester rd passes. Intensely planted 3-acre garden of wide interest; trees, flowering shrubs, heathers, eucalyptus, daffodils, shrub roses, hydrangeas and lily ponds. *Adm £1 Chd 30p. Suns, Mons April 3, 4; May 8, 9; June 26, 27, (2-5) Oct 23, 24 (12-4)*

Bignor Park ✿ (The Viscount & Viscountess Mersey) Pulborough, 5m from Petworth on West Burton rd. Nearest village Sutton (Sussex). 11 acres of trees, shrubs and magnificent views of the South Downs, from Chanctonbury Ring to Bignor Hill. Music in the temple. TEAS in aid of Sutton Village Hall. *Adm £1.50 Chd 25p. Sat, Sun, Mon April 30, May 1, 2 (2-6)*

● **Borde Hill Garden** ♿♣ (The Borde Hill Garden Co. Ltd.) 1½m. N of Haywards Heath on Balcombe Rd. Large informal garden of great botanical interest and beauty; rare trees and shrubs; extensive views; woodland walks, rhododendrons, azaleas, camellias, magnolias, at its best in the spring. Picnic area. Tea rooms, bar and restaurant. *Adm £3 Chd £1 parties of 20+ and OAPs £2.50. Open Suns, March in good weather. Daily from April 1 to Oct 16 (10-6)*

Buckhurst Park ♣✿ (Earl & Countess De La Warr) Withyham. On B2110 between Hartfield and Groombridge. Drive adjacent to Dorset Arms public house. Historic garden undergoing complete restoration. Repton park, large lake with woodland walk and ornamental waterfall and rocks created by James Pulham. Terraces, ornamental ponds and Pergolas designed by Lutyens and originally planted by Jekyll. TEAS. *Adm £1.50 Chd 50p (Share to Withyham Recreation Association©). Sun June 5 (2-5.30)*

Bumble Cottage ♣ (Mr & Mrs D Salisbury-Jones) West Chiltington. 2m E of Pulborough, 2m N of Storrington. From Pulborough turn off A283 E of Pulborough into W Chiltington Rd then R into Monkmead Lane (signed Roundabout Hotel) follow yellow signs. From Storrington take B2139 W into Greenhurst Lane, R at T Junc. 100yds fork L into Monkmead Lane then 2nd entrance after Hotel. Charming 'all seasons' garden of 1 acre created from a sandy slope. Wide variety of interesting trees, shrubs and plants combined with ponds all set off by very fine lawn. *Adm £1 Chd 25p. Sun, Mon May 1, 2, Sats, Suns July 30, 31; Aug 6, 7 (2-6)*

Cabbages & Kings see Wilderness Farm

Casters Brook ♿♣ (Mr & Mrs John Whitehorn) Cocking; 3m S of Midhurst at Cocking PO on A286 take sharp turn E; garden is 100 yds to right. Interesting 2-acre chalk garden full of surprises; slopes to old mill pond; good collection of trees; fine downland setting. TEAS. *Adm £1 Chd free (Share to Cocking Church®). Suns June 19, 26 (2-6). Private visits welcome, please Tel 0730 813537*

Cedar Tree Cottage ♿✿✿ (Mr & Mrs G Goatcher) Rock Rd, Washington. Turn W off A24 ¼m N. of Washington Roundabout. Park in 'Old Nursery' Car Park. Mixed borders with plants for the connoisseur; mature and rare

specimens in adjoining old Nursery re-developed as 5-acre garden/arboretum. Fine views of S Downs. Picnics welcome. *Adm £1 Chd 25p. Sat April 30, Wed May 4, Sat May 7 (2-6)*

Champs Hill ♿✿✿ (Mr & Mrs David Bowerman) Coldwaltham, S of Pulborough. From Pulborough on A29, in Coldwaltham turn R to Fittleworth Rd; garden 300yds on R. From Petworth turn off B2138 just S of Fittleworth to Coldwaltham, garden approx ½m on L. 27 acres of formal garden and woodland walks around old sand pit. Conifers and acid-loving plants, many specie heathers labelled. Superb views across Arun valley. Special features. March - Winter heathers and spring flowers. May - rhododendrons, azaleas, wild flowers. August - heathers and other specialities. TEAS (not March). *Adm £1.50 Chd free. Suns March 13, 20, 27; Sats April 30, May 14, 21; Suns May 1, 15, 22, July 31, Aug 7, 21; Sats Aug 6, 20 (1-6)*

¶**Chantry Green House** ✿✿ (Mr R S Forrow & Mrs J B McNeil) Steyning. 5m N of Worthing, 10m NW of Brighton off A283. Turn into Church St from High St opp White Horse Inn. Garden 150yds down on LH-side. Parking on Fletchers Croft car park, entrance opp church. An interesting 1-acre garden, redesigned over the past 5yrs by Jack Grant White. Features incl a wall fountain, herbaceous borders and extensive shrub borders with a predominance of colourful evergreens providing interest throughout the year. There is also a small arboretum and rock and water garden. TEAS and plants in aid of NSPCC. *Adm £1.30 Chd 50p. Sat, Sun June 11, 12 (2-5)*

Chidmere House ♿ (Thomas Baxendale Esq) Chidham, 6m W of Chichester. A259 1m Bus: SD276/200 Chichester-Emsworth. Interesting garden; with subject of article in 'Country Life'; yew and hornbeam hedges; bulbs, and flowering shrubs bounded by large mere, now a private nature reserve. C15 house (not open). *Adm £1.20 Chd 40p. Suns, Mons April 3, 4; May 15, 16; (2-6) June 26, 27; Aug 28, 29 (2-7). Private visits welcome for parties only, please Tel 0243 572287 or 573096*

Chilsham House ♿✿✿ (Mr & Mrs P E B Cutler) Herstmonceux. 5m NE of Hailsham. From A271 in Herstmonceux take turning by Woolpack Inn towards Cowbeech after approx ¾m turn R into Chilsham Lane, ¾m on the left. 1½ acre garden, herbaceous border, water garden, old fashioned roses. Small gardens in colour harmony, many unusual plants. Victorian garden. TEAS. *Adm £1.30 Chd 20p. Sat, Sun June 25, 26; Sun, Mon July 17, 18 (2-5.30)*

Clinton Lodge ✿✿ (Mr & Mrs H Collum) Fletching, 4m NW of Uckfield; from A272 turn N at Piltdown for Fletching, 1½m. 6-acre formal and romantic garden overlooking parkland with old roses, double herbaceous borders, yew hedges, pleached lime walks, copy of C17 scented herb garden, medieval-style potager, vine and rose allée, wild flower garden. Carolean and Georgian house (not open). TEAS. *Adm £2 Chd 50p (Share to Fletching Church Fabric Fund®). Sun June 12; Mons June 13, 20, 27 (2-6)*

By Appointment Gardens. See head of county section

Coates Manor ᴦᴬᴪ (Mrs G H Thorp) nr Fittleworth. ½m S of Fittleworth; turn off B2138 at signpost marked 'Coates'. 1 acre, mainly shrubs and foliage of special interest. Small walled garden with tender and scented plants. Often featured in UK and foreign gardening magazines. Elizabethan house (not open) scheduled of historic interest. TEAS organised by Church of England Children's Society Committee. *Adm £1.30 Chd 20p. Sun, Mon, Tues June 12, 13, 14 (11-6). Private visits welcome, please* Tel 993 82 356

Cobblers ᴦᴬᴪ (Mr & Mrs Martin Furniss) Mount Pleasant, Jarvis Brook, Crowborough. A26, at Crowborough Cross take B2100 towards Crowborough Station. At 2nd Xrds turn into Tollwood Rd for ¼m. 2-acre sloping site designed by present owners since 1968 to display outstanding range of herbaceous and shrub species and water garden, giving all season colour. Subject of numerous articles and TVS 'That's Gardening' programme June 1991. TEAS. *Adm £3 Chd £1 (incl home-made Teas). Sun, Mon May 22, 30; Suns June 12, 26, July 10, 17, 31, Aug 14, 28 (2.30-5.30). Private visits welcome, please* Tel 0892 655969

Cokes Barn ᴬᴪ (Mr & Mrs Nigel Azis) West Burton. 5m SW of Pulborough-Petworth. At foot of Bury Hill turn W off A29 to West Burton for 1m then follow signs. Just under ½ ha garden around converted barn (1670 not open) which divides into 2 natural spaces: the yard a sheltered enclosure with gravelled areas, mixed shrubs and roses and other traditional cottage perennials. Walls covered in decorative ivies, vines, roses and clematii. 2nd part of garden subdivided by hedges. Planting follows gentle contours; at far end 2 small pools surrounded by damp loving plants. Conservatory on S side of barn. *Adm £1 Chd 40p. Suns April 24, July 3 (2-5). Private visits welcome, please* Tel 0798 831636

Combehurst ᴦᴪ (Mrs E E Roberts) 3m S of Tunbridge Wells off A267, 400 yds S of B2099. 2½-acre beautifully laid out garden; shrubs, trees, plants. TEAS. *Adm £1 Chd free. Sun July 3 (2-6). Private visits welcome, please* Tel Frant 750367

Cooke's House ᴦᴬ (Miss J B Courtauld) West Burton, 5m SW of Pulborough. Turn off A29 at White Horse, Bury, ¾m. Old garden with views of the Downs, round Elizabethan house (not open); varied interest incl spring flowers, topiary, herbaceous borders, herbs. Free car park. *Adm £1 Chd free under 14. Suns, Mons, Tues April 17, 18, 19; 24, 25, 26 (2-6). Private visits welcome*

Cooksbridge ᴬ (Mr & Mrs N Tonkin) Fernhurst. On A286 between Haslemere and Midhurst, ¾m S of Fernhurst X-rds. 6 acres, landscaped garden with glade and woodland walk through adjoining bluebell wood. Pictured in the GRBS 1993 Gardens to remember calendar this plantsman's garden is situated in a fold of the downs beside the river Lodd. Features include the herbaceous border, vine and ornamental plant houses, lily pond and well stocked shrubberies. The main lawn sweeps down from the terrace to the lake which has an island with weeping willow and several species of waterfowl. TEAS. *Adm £1.50 Chd 50p 5 and under free (Share to Sussex Wildlife Trust®). Sats, Suns April 30, May 1; Aug 6, 7 (2-6)*

Coombland ᴬᴪ (Mr & Mrs Neville Lee) Coneyhurst. In Billingshurst turn off A29 onto A272 to Haywards Heath; approx 2m, in Coneyhurst, turn S for further ¾m. Large garden of 5 acres developed since 1981 with the help and advice of Graham Stuart Thomas. Undulating site on heavy clay. Old shrub-rose beds, rose species and ramblers scrambling up ageing fruit trees; extensive planting of hardy geraniums; herbaceous border with interesting planting. Oak woodland; orchard dell with hybrid rhododendrons; hostas; primulas and meconopsis. Nightingale wood with water area under development, water wheel recently added leading to 1-acre arboretum. National collection of hardy geraniums held here. TEAS. *Adm £1.50 Chd 50p. Sats June 11, 25 (10-5). Nursery open by appt only Mon to Fri (2-4)* Tel 0403 741549

Cowbeech Farm ᴬᴪ (Mrs M Huiskamp) Cowbeech. 4m NE of Hailsham. A271 to Amberstone turn off N for Cowbeech. 5-acre garden, herb garden, Japanese garden. Beautiful shrubs and trees gorgeous autumn colours. Farmhouse TEAS, plants, cakes. *Adm £2 Chd £1 (Share to Riding for the Disabled®). Suns May 22, Sept 18 (2-5.30). Private visits welcome, please* Tel 0323 832134

Cowdray Park Gardens ᴦᴬ (The Viscount Cowdray). S of A272. 1m E of Midhurst. Entrance by East Front. Avenue of Wellingtonias; rhododendrons, azaleas; sunken garden with large variety trees and shrubs, Lebanon cedar 300 yrs old; pleasure garden surrounded by ha-ha. *Adm £1. Sun May 15 (2-7)*

Crawley Down Gardens ᴬ B2028 8m N of Haywards Heath, 4m W of E Grinstead. 2½m E of M23 (junction 10). TEAS at **Bankton Cottage**. *Combined adm £1.50 Chd free. Sat, Sun June 25, 26 (2-6)*

    Bankton Cottage ᴦᴪ (Mr & Mrs Robin Lloyd) 3½-acre garden, herbaceous borders, shrub and climbing roses. Large 1-acre pond, many terracotta pots planted up round house. Large range on sale. Featured 'Country Living' 1990. *Private parties welcome, please* Tel 0342 718907

    Yew Tree Cottage ᴪ (Mrs K Hudson) ¼-acre garden planted for all year round interest and easy management. Featured in RHS 1989 and book 'Cottage Garden'. *Private visits welcome, please* Tel 0342 714633

Crown House ᴦᴬᴪ (Maj L Cave) Eridge, 3m SW of Tunbridge Wells. A26 Tunbridge Wells-Crowborough rd; in Eridge take Rotherfield turn S; house 1st on right. 1½ acres with pools; alpine garden; herbaceous border; herb garden; aviary. Full size croquet lawn. Prize winner in Sunday Express garden of the year competition. Plant and produce stalls. TEAS. *Adm £1.25 Chd free (Share to Multiple Sclerosis®). Sat, Sun July 9, 10 (2-6)*

Dale House ᴬ (Mr & Mrs Jonathan Newdick) West Burton. 5m SW of Pulborough. At foot of Bury Hill turn W off A29 to West Burton for 1m then follow signs. Small cottage garden has mixed informal borders with herbaceous perennials, old roses, orchard with spring wild flowers, paved area with containers, large decorative vegetable garden. Scented leaved pelargoniums and many other fragrant flowers. *Private visits welcomed April to Sept, please* Tel 0798 831236

¶**Danny** ✕✿ (Country Houses Association Ltd) Hurstpierpoint. Off B2116 between Hurstpierpoint and Hassocks. 9m N of Brighton. Turn into New Way Lane. 6 acres of parkland. Features incl 'Burma Road' leading to old ice house, rose garden, old English walled garden, ha-ha. 200-yr-old tulip tree. Elizabethan manor (not open). TEAS. *Adm £1.50 Chd Free. Sun Aug 21 (2.30-5.30)*

Denmans ✕✿✿ (Mrs J H Robinson) Denmans Lane, Fontwell. Chichester and Arundel 5m. Turn S on A27 at Denmans Lane, W of Fontwell Racecourse. Renowned gardens extravagantly planted for overall, all-year interest in form, colour and texture; areas of glass for tender species. Plant Centre. Garden Cafe for lunches, teas, coffees, refreshments to suit served from 10am. *Adm £2.25 OAPs £1.95 Chd £1.25. Groups over 15 persons £1.75. Open daily all year excl Christmas and Boxing Day. Coaches by appt. For NGS Mons March 7, Oct 24 (9-5)*

Down Place ✕✿ (Mr & Mrs D M Thistleton-Smith) South Harting. ¼m E down unmarked lane below top of hill. 1m SE of South Harting on B2141 towards Chichester. From Petersfield E via B2146 to South Harting. From Chichester via A286 for 4m, N of Lavant turn NW on to B2141. 7-acre hillside chalk garden on N slope of South Downs. Terraced herbaceous and shrub borders, walks through woodland and natural wild flower meadow. Fine views over South Harting. TEAS. *Adm £1.20 Chd 50p (Share to National Asthma Campaign®). Fri, Sat, Sun June 24, 25, 26 (2-6)*

Duckyls ✿ (Lady Taylor) Sharpthorne. 4m SW of E Grinstead. 6m E of Crawley. At Turners Hill take B2028 S 1m fork left to W Hoathly, turn L signed Gravetye Manor. 12-acre woodland garden. TEAS. *Adm £2 Chd £1. Private visits welcome Tues, Thurs April and May (2-6) please Tel 0342 810352*

Ebbsworth ✕ (Mrs F Lambert) nr Pulborough. Take A283 E from junction with A29 (Swan Corner) 2m with 2 L forks signposted Nutbourne. Pass Rising Sun and follow signs to garden. Charming, well-planted, owner maintained cottage garden, surrounding old cottage. Roses and lilies, together with herbaceous borders. Man-made stream and ponds planted with water plants. Teas at Old School House. *Combined adm with Mill House and Nutbourne Vineyards £1.50 Chd free. Sun, Mon June 12, 13 (2-6)*

116 Findon Road ✕✿ (Mr Charles R Noble) Worthing. Do not park on the A24, but use side roads. 500 yds N of A24/A27 junc (Offfington Corner) on E side of Findon Rd. ¼-acre garden, containing many plants of a less common nature incl lime haters growing on chalky subsoil, unusual in this area. A plantsman's garden of considerable charm. TEAS. *Adm 70p Chd 30p. Sats, Suns May 14, 15; July 23, 24 (2-6). Private visits welcome May to Oct, please Tel 09032 63282*

Fittleworth Gardens ✿✕✿ Fittleworth A282 midway Petworth-Pulborough; in Fittleworth turn onto B2138 then turn W at Swan. Park near Swan as parking is limited. TEAS. Plants in aid of NSPCC and St Mary's Church, Fittleworth. *Combined Adm £1.50 Chd free. Sat, Sun May 21, 22 (2-6)*

The Grange ✿ (Mr & Mrs W M Caldwell) 3-acre garden with island beds of azaleas, rhododendrons and other shrubs, sloping to river Rother
The Hermitage (Mr & Mrs P F Dutton) Charming informal garden; azaleas, rhododendrons, flowering shrubs; with lovely views to the river and S Downs
Lowerstreet House (L J Holloway Esq) Small garden with shrubs, bulbs, herbaceous

Fitzhall ✕✿ (Mr & Mrs G F Bridger) Iping, 3m W of Midhurst. 1m off A272, signposted Harting Elsted. 9 acres; herb garden; herbaceous and shrub borders; vegetable garden. Farm adjoining. House (not open) originally built 1550. Garden and teas all year round. *Adm £1.50p OAPs £1.25 Chd 75p. For NGS Suns April 10, May 29, July 10, Sept 4 (2-6)*

Forest Lodge ✕ (Mr & Mrs A J Seabrook) West Broyle. From roundabout N of Chichester take B2178 (Funtingdon) rd NW for 1⅓m. Turn L into Pine Grove and after 100yds R into West Way. Medium-sized garden attractively laid out with mature trees and shrubs incl rhododendrons and azaleas. Teas in aid of Save the Children at The Spinney. *Combined adm with Three Oaks and Woodstock £1.50. Sun June 12 (1.30-5.30)*

Frewen College (Brickwall) ✿ (Frewen Charitable Trust) Northiam. 8m NW of Rye on B2088. Tudor home of Frewen family since 1666. Gardens and walls built and laid out by Jane Frewen c1680; chess and lavender gardens; arboretum. *Adm £1.50 Chd under 12 free. Sun July 17 (2-5)*

Frith Hill ✕✿ (Mr & Mrs Peter Warne) Northchapel 7m N of Petworth on A283 turn E in centre of Northchapel into Pipers Lane (by Deep Well Inn) after ¾m turn L into bridleway immed past Peacocks Farm. 1-acre garden, comprising walled gardens with herbaceous border; shrubbery; pond; old-fashioned rose garden and arbour. Herb garden leading to white garden with gazebo. TEAS in June. *Adm £1.50 Chd free (Share to Cystic Fibrosis Research Fund®). Sat, Suns April 24, June 11, 12 (2-6)*

Frith Lodge ✕✿ (Mr & Mrs Geoffrey Cridland) Northchapel. 7m N of Petworth on A283 turn E in centre of Northchapel into Pipers Lane (by Deep Well Inn) after ¾m turn L into bridleway immediately past Peacocks Farm. 1-acre cottage style garden recently created around pair of Victorian game-keepers cottages. Undulating ground with roses, informal planting with paved and hedged areas; outstanding views of Sussex Weald. *Adm £1 Chd 50p. Sat, Sun June 11, 12 (2-6)*

The Garden in Mind ✿✕✿ (Mr & Mrs Ivan Hicks - Stansted Park Foundation) Stansted Park, Rowlands Castle. From A3 at Horndean follow brown signs for Stansted House. From A27M at Havant follow Stansted House brown signs. Stansted House is 3m NE of Havant. A surreal symbolic dream garden created within a ½-acre walled garden at Stansted House. Began in 1991 as a concept for BBC2 dream garden series. Extravagant planting combined with sculpture, assemblage, found objects, mirrors and chance encounters. Wide range of plants; sequioa to sempervivum, marigolds to melianthus, grasses, foliage plants, topiary and tree sculpture. Featured in numerous publications and TV – come with an open mind. TEAS. *Adm £1.01 Chd donation. Suns, Mons June, 5, 6, Sept 25, 26 (2-6)*

Gaywood Farm &✿ (Mrs Anthony Charles) nr Pulborough. 3m S of Billingshurst turn L off A29 into Gay Street Lane. After railway bridge at 2nd junction fork L and at T junction turn L signed 'no through rd'. 2-acre garden, surrounding ancient farm house, built between C14 and C18. Fine weeping Ash, black Mulberry, Irish yews and extravagantly planted borders with interesting plant assoc. Large pond surrounded by good planting. TEAS. *Adm £1 Chd free. Sat, Sun May 28, 29; July 2, 3 (2-6)*

Ghyll Farm Sweethaws ✿ (Mr & Mrs I Ball) Crowborough. 1m S of Crowborough centre on A26. L into Sheep Plain Lane immed R Sweethaws ½m. 'The Permissive Garden' planted by the late Lady Pearce. 1-acre, azaleas, camellias, woodland bluebell walk; spectacular views. TEAS. *Adm £1 Chd 50p. Suns May 8, 22 (2-5.30). Private visits welcome April to end July please* Tel **0892 655505**

Great Allfields ✿✿ (Lord & Lady Birkett) Balls Cross. 3m N of Petworth. Take 283 out of Petworth, turn 2nd R signed Balls Cross, Kirdford. At Balls Cross take L turn after Stag Inn to Ebernoe, Northchapel (Pipers Lane) 250yds entrance on R. 1 acre of garden, 2 acres of woodland, plus old walls and barns covered with many interesting climbers. TEAS. *Adm £1 Chd free (Share to Fairbridge®). Wed June 15 (10-6)*

● **Great Dixter** ✿✿ (Quentin Lloyd) Northiam, ½m N of Northiam, off A28 8m NW of Rye. Buses infrequent 340, 342, 348. Hastings & District. Alight Northiam P. Office 500 yds. Topiary; wide variety of plants. Historical house open (2-5). *Adm house & garden £3.50 Chd 50p OAPs & NT members (Fris only) £3; garden only £2.50 Chd 25p. April 1 to Oct 9 daily except Mons but open on Bank Hols (2-5); garden open May 28, 29, 30; also Suns in July, Aug; Mon Aug 29 (11-5)*

¶**Greenacres** ✿✿ (Mr & Mrs John Hindley) Crowborough. From A26 at Crowborough Cross take B2100 S. At 1st Xrd R into Montagis Way, then 2nd into Luxford Rd for 300yds. 2-acre sloping woodland garden maintained wholly by present owners. Developed over the years with interesting water features fed by natural springs: ponds, bog area, naturalised area, raised island beds. Many trees, shrubs and foliage plants. A tranquil garden with views over countryside. TEA. *Adm £1 Chd free. Mon May 30 Sun June 12 (11-5.30) Wed June 1 (2-5.30)*

Greenhurst &✿✿ (Mrs G Hopton) Thakeham. 2m N of Storrington on B2139. L into Greenhurst Lane 4th house on the L. ¾-acre S facing garden in tranquil position. Mixed garden of herbaceous borders, island beds; pathways; specimen trees; shrubs and pond. TEAS. *Adm £1.50 Chd free. Suns May 22, July 10 (2-6)*

Hailsham Grange &✿✿ (John Macdonald Esq) Hailsham. Turn off Hailsham High St into Vicarage Rd, park in public car park. Formal garden designed and planted since 1988 in grounds of former C17 Vicarage (not open). A series of garden areas representing a modern interpretation of C18 formality; Gothic summerhouse; pleached hedges; herbaceous borders, romantic planting in separate garden compartments. Teas in adjacent church in aid of The Children's Society. *Adm £1.50. Suns June 5, Aug 7 (2-5.30)*

Hammerwood House & (The Hon Mrs J Lakin) Iping, 1m N of A272 Midhurst to Petersfield Rd. Approx 3m W of Midhurst. Well signposted. Large informal garden; fine trees, rhododendrons, azaleas, acers, cornus, magnolias; wild garden (¼m away), bluebells, stream. TEAS. *Adm £1.50 Chd free. Suns May 8, 15 (1.30-6)*

● **High Beeches Gardens** ✿ (High Beeches Gardens Conservation Trust) Situated on B2110 1m E of A23 at Handcross. 20-acres of enchanting landscaped woodland and water gardens; spring daffodils; bluebell and azalea walks; many rare and beautiful plants; wild flower meadows, glorious autumn colours. Picnic area. Car park. Lunches and TEAS only on special events days April 4, May 1, 29, Oct 16 (10-5). *Daily April 12 to Oct 30 (1-5) closed June 26 to Sept 3 and on Weds. Adm £2.50 Acc chd free (Share to St Mary's Church, Slaugham®). For NGS Sats May 7, Sept 3 (1-5). Also by appt for organised groups at any time, please* Tel **0444 400589**

Highdown, Goring-by-Sea ✿ (Worthing Borough Council) Littlehampton Rd (A259), 3m W of Worthing. Station: Goring-by-Sea, 1m. Famous garden created by Sir F Stern situated in chalk pit and downland area containing a wide collection of plants. Spring bulbs, paeonies, shrubs and trees. Many plants were raised from seed brought from China by great collectors like Wilson, Farrer and Kingdon-Ward. *Collecting box.* ▲*Mons April 4, May 2, 30 (10-8)*

Home Farm House ✿✿ (Mrs P Cooper) Buckham Hill. Uckfield-Isfield back rd. Small attractive cottage garden; interesting shrubs. *Adm £1 Chd free. Sun, Mon June 26, 27 (2-5.30). Private visits also welcome Feb to see 20ft mimosa, please* Tel **0825 763960**

Houghton Farm ✿✿ (Mr & Mrs Michael Lock) Arundel. Turn E off A29 at top of Bury Hill onto B2139 or W from Storrington onto B2139 to Houghton. 1-acre garden with wide variety of shrubs and plants, interesting corners and beautiful views. Tea Houghton Bridge Tea Gardens. *Adm £1 Chd free. Fri April 1; Mon, Tues May 2, 3; Thurs, Fris June 9, 10 July 21, 22 Mon, Tues Aug 29, 30 Sun, Mon, Sept 25, 26 (2-5)*

Hurst House &✿ (Mr & Mrs J Keeling) Hurst Lane. From Sedlescombe take lane towards Brede; take 1st lane on left, 600 yds, garden on R. 6 acres; rhododendrons, azaleas, camellias, bulbs; herbaceous borders; rose garden; greenhouses. TEAS. *Adm £1.20 Chd 20p (Share to Arthritis Care Hastings Branch). Sat May 21 (2-5.30)*

By Appointment Gardens. See head of county section

Hurst Mill ☪ Hurst. 2m SE of Petersfield on B2146 midway between Petersfield and S Harting 8-acre garden on many levels in lovely position overlooking 4-acre lake in wooded valley with wildfowl. Waterfall and Japanese water garden beside historic mill. Bog garden; large rock garden with orientally inspired plantings; acers, camellias, rhododendrons, azaleas, magnolias, hydrangeas and ferns; shrubs and climbing roses; forest and ornamental trees. TEA. *Adm £1.50 Chd 50p. Suns April 17, June 12 (2-6)*

Ketches ☖☪❀ (David Manwaring Robertson Esq) Newick, 5m W of Uckfield on A272. Take Barcombe Rd S out of Newick, house is on right opp turning to Newick Church. 3 acres; old-fashioned roses; specimen trees; shrub and herbaceous borders. TEAS. *Adm £1 Chd free. Sun June 12 (2-6). Also private visits welcome mid May to mid July, please* **Tel 0825 722679**

King John's Lodge ☖☪❀ (Mr & Mrs R A Cunningham) Etchingham. Burwash to Etchingham on the A265 turn L before Etchingham Church into Church Lane which leads into Sheepstreet Lane after ½m. L after 1m. A romantic garden of over 3 acres surrounding a listed house. Formal garden with fountain and lily pond leading to a wild garden and rose walk. Large herbaceous borders with old shrub roses; secret garden and shaded white garden. B & B accommodation. Garden Statuary for sale. TEAS. *Adm £1.20 Chd free. Sat, Sun June 18, 19 (2-5.30). Also private visits welcome, please* **Tel 0500 819 232**

Kingston Gardens ❀ 2½m SW of Lewes. Turn off A27 signposted Kingston at roundabout; at 30 mph sign turn R. Home-made TEAS **Nightingales**. *Combined adm (payable at* **Nightingales** *only) £2 Chd free. Suns June 12, July 17 (2-6)*
  Nightingales (Geoff & Jean Hudson) The Avenue. Informal sloping ½-acre garden for all-year interest; wide range of plants incl shrub roses, hardy geraniums, perennials, ground cover. Mediterranean plants. Childrens play area. Short steep rough walk or drive, parking limited, to:-
  The White House ☖ (John & Sheila Maynard Smith) The Ridge. ½-acre garden on a chalk ridge. Shrubs, herbaceous border, alpines; greenhouse with unusual plants

Knabbs Farmhouse ❀ (Mr & Mrs W G Graham) 4m NW of Uckfield; from A272 turn N at Piltdown for Fletching, (TQ430/240) 1½m. Garden at N-end of village and farm. ½-acre informal garden; mixed beds and borders; shrubs, roses, perennials, foliage plants. Good views over ha-ha. TEAS at **Clinton Lodge**. *Adm £1 Chd 20p. Sun June 12 (2-6)*

Lane End ☪ (Mrs C J Epril) Sheep Lane, Midhurst. In North St turn L at Knock-hundred Row, L into Sheep lane, L to garden. Park at church or in lane. 2 acres incl wild garden; alpine rockery with pools; rhododendrons, azaleas, heath border. Below ramparts of original castle with fine views over water meadows to ruins of Cowdray House. Tea Midhurst. *Adm £1 Chd free. Sats, Suns, Mons May 21, 22, 23, 28, 29, 30 (11-6)*

Legsheath Farm ☖❀ (Mr & Mrs Michael Neal) Legsheath Lane. 2m W of Forest Row, 1m S of Weirwood Reservoir. Panoramic views over reservoir. Exciting 10 acre garden with woodland walks, water gardens and formal borders. Of particular interest, clumps of wild orchids, a fine davidia, acers, encryphia and rhododendrons. TEAS. *Adm £1.50 Chd free. Sun May 22 (2-6)*

Lilac Cottage ☪ (Mrs G A Hawkins) Willet Close, Duncton. 3m S of Petworth on the W side of A285 opp St Michaels School. Park in Close where signed. ¼-acre village garden on several levels with shrubs, small trees and approx 90 varieties of shrub and climbing roses and herb garden. *Adm 75p. TEAS. Wed, Sat, Sun, June 8, 11, 12 (2-6)*

Little Hutchings ☪❀ (Mr & Mrs P Hayes) Fontridge Lane, Etchingham. (TQ 708248). Take A265 to Etchingham from A21 at Hurst Green. 1st turning after level crossing. R after ½m. Colourful 1½-acre old-fashioned cottage garden surrounding listed house. At least 300 different roses, over 100 metres of tightly packed herbaceous borders. Large collection of clematis. Specimen trees and shrubs. Kitchen garden. TEAS. *Adm £1.50 Chd free. Sat, Sun June 18, 19 (11-6)*

Little Thakeham ☪❀ (Mr & Mrs T Ratcliff) Storrington. Take A24 S to Worthing and at roundabout 2m S of Ashington return N up A24 for 200yds. Turn L into Rock Rd for 1m. At staggered Xrds turn R into Merrywood Lane and garden is 300yds on R. From Storrington take B2139 to Thakeham. After 1m turn R into Merrywood Lane and garden is 400yds on L. 4-acre garden with paved walks, rose pergola, flowering shrubs, specimen trees, herbaceous borders and carpets of daffodils in spring. The garden laid out to the basic design of Sir Edward Lutyens in 1902 is entering its 3rd and final year of restoration. All surrounding one of the finest examples of a Sir Edward Lutyens manor house now a luxurious country house hotel. *Adm £1 Chd 50p. Wed, April 6 (2-5) Mons, Tues, June 6, 7, July 4, 5 (2-6)*

Long House ❀ (Mr & Mrs V A Gordon Tregear) Cowfold. 1m N of A272, Cowfold-Bolney Rd; 1st turning L after Cowfold. A unique opportunity to view a garden in the process of being restored after a period of decline. Comprising 2½ acres within walls surrounding house dating from early C16 (house not open). TEA. *Donation on entry. Sun Oct 16 (12-4)*

Lye Green House ☪ (Mr & Mrs Hynes) Lye Green. Lye Green is situated on the B2188 between Groombridge and Crowborough, 7m SW of Tunbridge Wells. 6-acre garden restored over 3 yrs after long neglect. 4 large ponds, woodland and rockeries; 7 enclosed gardens, herbaceous borders, rose garden, kitchen garden and lime walk. TEA. *Adm £1.50 Chd free. Sun June 12 (2-6)*

Regular Openers. Too many days to include in diary. Usually there is a wide range of plants giving year-round interest. See head of county section for the name and garden description for times etc.

Malt House ✿ (Mr & Mrs Graham Ferguson) Chithurst, Rogate. From A272, 3½m W of Midhurst turn N signposted Chithurst then 1½m; or at Liphook turn off A3 onto old A3 for 2m before turning L to Milland, then follow signs to Chithurst for 1½m. 5 acres; flowering shrubs incl exceptional rhododendrons and azaleas, leading to 50 acres of lovely woodland walks. TEA. *Adm £1.50 Chd 50p. (Share to King Edwards VII Hospital Midhurst). Suns April 24, May 1, 8, 15, 22, 29; Mons May 2, 30 (2-6); also private visits welcome for parties or plant sales, please* **Tel 0730 821433**

The Manor of Dean ৬✿ (Miss S M Mitford) Tillington, 2m W of Petworth. Turn off A272 N at NGS sign. Flowers, shrubs, specimen trees, bulbs in all seasons. A miniature pony, 2 pigmy goats, Vietnamese pigs, tame lambs. House (not open) 1400-1613. TEA 50p. *Adm £1 Chd over 5 50p. Sats, Suns, Mons March 26, 27, 28; April 16, 17, 18; May 14, 15, 16; July 16, 17, 18; Aug 20, 21, 22; Sept 17, 18, 19; Oct 1, 2, 3, (2-6)*

Manvilles Field ৬✿✿ (Mrs P J Aschan & Mrs J M Wilson) 2m W of Pulborough take A283 to Fittleworth, turn R on double bend. 2 acres of garden with orchard, many interesting shrubs, clematis, roses, other herbaceous plants. Beautiful views surrounding garden. TEAS. *Adm £1 Chd 40p. Sun, Mon May 29, 30 (2-6)*

Mayfield Cottage Gardens ✿ 8m S of Tunbridge Wells on A267. Flower festival at St Dunstan's Church. *Combined adm £1 Chd 20p. Sun June 19 (2-5.30)* **Moat Mill Farm, Mayfield** *also open*

Courtney Cottage (Mr & Mrs D Clark) ⅕-acre steeply sloping garden

Hopton (E Stuart Ogg Esq) Fletching St. ½-acre, Delphinium Specialist

Knowle Way (J Freeman Esq) West St. S of High St by Barclays Bank. ¼-acre plantsman's garden

The Oast ✿ (Mr & Mrs R G F Henderson) Fletching St. Turn off A267 by garage towards Witherenden ¼m. Charming ½-acre sloping garden, fine views. TEAS

Merriments Gardens ৬✿✿ (Mark & Mandy Buchele) Hawkhurst Rd, Hurst Green. Situated between Hawkhurst and Hurst Green. 2m SW Hawkhurst. Young 4 acre garden with richly planted mixed borders in country setting. Ponds, stream and rare plants give beautiful display all season. TEA. *Adm £1 Chd free. Suns April 24, May 22, June 5, 19, July 3, 17, 31 Aug 14, 28, Sept 11, 25, Oct 2, Weds July 6, 20 (12-7.30) Aug 3, 17, 31, Sept 14, 28 (12-5)*

Middle Coombe ৬✿✿ (Andrew & Ann Kennedy) East Grinstead. From E Grinstead 1½m SW on B2110. Turn L into Coombe Hill Rd. ¼m on L. 7½-acre garden and woodland walk with small lake. The garden was created in 16 weeks in 1990. Designed in Victorian rooms using Agriframes. Formal and informal planting to give all year colour. Light lunches and TEAS. *Adm £2 Chd free. Sats, Suns June 4, 5, July 16, 17 (12-5)*

Mill House ✿ (Sir Francis & Lady Avery Jones) Nutbourne, nr Pulborough. Take A283 E from junction with A29 (Swan Corner) 2m with 2 L forks signposted Nutbourne. Pass Rising Sun and follow signs to garden. ¾-acre surrounding old miller's house; and wild flower banks; cottage frontage with interesting walled herb garden; sloping down to water garden with stream, springfed pools and nearby mill pond. Teas at Old School House. *Combined adm with* **Ebbsworth** *and* **Nutbourne Vineyards** *£1.50 Chd free. Sun, Mon June 12, 13 (1-6) Private visits also welcome, please Tel 0798 813314*

Moat Mill Farm ✿ (Mr & Mrs C Marshall) Newick Lane, Mayfield. 1m S on Mayfield-Broadoak Rd. 8 acres, formal rose garden, herbaceous border and wild gardens. TEAS and ice creams. *Adm £1 Chd 20p. Sun June 19 (2-5.30). Also open* **Mayfield Cottage Gardens**

Moorlands ✿ (Dr & Mrs Steven Smith) Friar's Gate, 2m N of Crowborough. St Johns Rd to Friar's Gate. Or turn L off B2188 at Friar's Gate. 3 acres set in lush valley adjoining Ashdown Forest; water garden with ponds and streams; primulas, rhododendrons, azaleas, many unusual trees and shrubs. New river walk. TEAS. *Adm £2 OAPs £1.50 Chd free. Suns May 15, 29 July 31 (2-6). Private visits welcome, Weds April to Oct (11-5) please* **Tel 0892 652474**

Mountfield Court ৬✿ (T Egerton Esq) 2m S of Robertsbridge. On A21 London-Hastings; ½m from Johns Cross. 2-3-acre wild garden; flowering shrubs, rhododendrons, azaleas and camellias; fine trees. Homemade TEAS. *Adm £1 Chd 50p (Share to All Saints Church Mountfield®). Sun, Mon May 15, 16 (2-6)*

¶**Neptune House** ✿✿ (The Hon & Mrs Robin Borwick) Cutmill. E from Chichester take A259 to Fishbourne and Bosham, over roundabout at Bosham and after ½m move into reservation in rd and turn R into Newells Lane. 150yds turn L and park. From W take A259 to Emsworth. Turn L after the Bosham Inn at Chidham into Newells Lane. A 2-acre garden recently acquired with the R Cut forming the NW boundary and a canal from it taking water to the largest of 3 ponds. Planting is being increased by owners in this coastal garden. Parents are warned that water can be dangerous and children must be kept under control near river and canals. **Pondfield** is reached over small bridge. TEAS. *Combined adm with* **Pondfield** *£1.50 Chd 50p. Sun June 5 (2-6). Private visits welcome June 6 to Sept 30, please* **Tel 0243 576900**

New Grove ৬✿ (Mr & Mrs Robert de Pass) Petworth. 1m S of Petworth turn L off A285 and take next L. Follow signs. From the N at Xrds in Petworth straight across into Middle Street then L into High Street follow signs. A mature garden of about 3 acres. Mainly composed of shrubs with all year interest incl magnolias, camellias, azaleas, cornuses, roses etc. lovely views to the South Downs. TEAS in aid of King Edward VII Hospital, Midhurst, or Church of England Childrens Society. *Adm £1 Chd free. Sun May 15 (2-6)*

Newtimber Place ৬✿ (His Honour & Mrs John Clay) Newtimber. 7m N of Brighton off A281 between Poynings and Pyecombe. Beautiful C17 moated house. Wild garden, roses, mixed borders and water plants. TEAS in aid of Newtimber Church. *Adm £1.50 Chd 50p. Suns April 24, Aug 28 (2-6)*

North Springs ✿❀ (Mr & Mrs Michael Waring) Fittleworth. Garden situated between Fittleworth and Wisborough Green. Approach either from A272 outside Wisborough Green or A283 at Fittleworth and follow signs. Steep hillside garden of approx 2½ acres with spectacular views set in 40 acres woodland. Rhododendrons, camellias and other acid-loving shrubs, large mixed borders, clematis, old and modern roses, spring-fed pools and pond stocked with golden carp. *Adm £1.50 Chd 75p. Sat, Sun June 4, 5, July 9, 10 (2-6). Private visits welcome March to Aug please, Tel 079882 731*

Northwood Farmhouse ࢪ✿ (Mrs P Hill) Pulborough. 1m N of Pulborough on A29. Turn NW into Blackgate Lane and follow lane for 2m then follow the signs. Cottage Garden with bulbs, roses, pasture with wild flowers and pond all on Wealded clay surrounding Sussex farmhouse dating from 1420. TEA. *Adm £1 Chd 50p. Sats, Mons April 9, 11; June 11, 13 (2-5)*

Nutbourne Vineyards ✿ (Mr & Mrs Peter Gladwin) Gay Street, nr Pulborough. From Pulborough take A283 E, turn L to W Chiltington and Nutbourne; follow signs. These vineyards were first planted in 1980 and now total 18 acres of vines in production. 5 different types are grown; Bacchus, Schonburger, Huxelrebe, Reichensteiner and Muller Thurgan. An opportunity of learning about English wine as well as visiting historic windmill tower to taste and buy wines. Also a walk around trout lakes. Teas at Old School House. *Combined adm with **Ebbsworth** and* **Mill House** *£1.50 Chd free.* ▲ *Sun, Mon June 12, 13 (1-6)*

Nyewood House ࢪ✿❀ (Mr & Mrs Timothy Woodall) Nyewood. From A272 at Rogate take rd signposted Nyewood, S for approx 1¼m. At 40 mph sign on outskirts of Nyewood, turn L signposted Trotton. Garden approx 500 yds on R. 3-acre S facing garden recently renovated, with colour planted herbaceous borders, newly planted knot garden, pleaching, rose walk, water feature, and new potager. TEAS. *Adm £1 Chd 25p. Weds May 18, June 15, July 20 Suns June 12, July 17 (2-5.30)*

Nymans ࢪ✿❀ (The National Trust) Handcross. On B2114 at Handcross signposted off M23/A23 London-Brighton rd, SE of Handcross. Bus: 137 from Crawley & Haywards Heath (TQ265294). Rare trees and shrubs. Botanical interest. New rose garden. Wheelchairs available at the garden. TEAS. *Adm £3.50 Chd £1.75. Suns May 8, June 5 (11-7)*

Offham House ࢪ❀ (Mr & Mrs H N A Goodman; Mrs H S Taylor) Offham, 2m N of Lewes on A275. Cooksbridge station ½m. Fountains; flowering trees; double herbaceous border; long paeony bed. Queen Anne house (not open) 1676 with well-knapped flint facade. Featured in George Plumptre's Guide to 200 Gardens in Britain. Home-made TEAS. *Adm £1 Chd over 14 25p. Suns May 1, June 5 (2-6)*

¶Old Barkford ✿❀ (Mr & Mrs Michael Cave) Plaistow. Take A283 1½m S from Chiddingfold. Turn L signed Plaistow. 4m. Adjacent to church. 1-acre owner-maintained cottage garden recently created around part C17 house. Informal planting; herbaceous border, climbing roses, herb garden, with old-fashioned rose garden under construction. TEAS. *Adm £1 Chd 25p (Share to Village Church®). Sun June 19 (2-6)*

Old Barklye ✿❀ (Mr & Mrs G C Atkinson) Heathfield. [TQ 619230] 3½m W of Burwash on A265, N into Swiffe Lane, 100yds on L. 2-acre garden created by owners over past 25 yrs. Planned to be romantic and interesting, situated on hillside with magnificent views. Mixed borders, trees, shrubs, water features, wild flower meadow and new area developed in 1992 on semi-formal lines linking gravel garden to lily pond. TEAS in C18 barn in aid of Friends of Burwash Surgery. *Adm £1.50 Chd 50p. Sun, Mon June 5, 6 (2-5.30)*

The Old Rectory, Fittleworth ✿❀ (Mr & Mrs G Salmon) 2m W of Pulborough on A283 and next to Fittleworth church (parking in Church Lane and Bedham Rd). 2 acres of varied garden informally divided with interesting corners and walks. Spring bulbs; herbaceous borders; good variety of shrub roses. TEAS in aid of Fittleworth Parish Church. *Adm £1 Chd 50p. Mon April 4, Sun June 12 (2-5.30)*

¶The Old Rectory, Newtimber ࢪ❀ (Lambert & Rosalyn Coles) 7m N of Brighton off A281 between Poynings and Pyecombe. 2 acres with views of South Downs and Newtimber Church. Pond garden, fine tulip tree, perennial borders; combined kitchen and flower garden. TEAS. *Adm £1 Chd 30p. Sun July 3 (2-6)*

¶64 Old Shoreham Road ✿❀ (Mr & Mrs B M Bailey) Hove. On S side of A270 Brighton to Worthing rd between The Drive and the Upper Drive. Easy parking in The Drive or Shirley Drive. Small beautifully designed mainly walled garden of ⅛ acre on chalk and flint with yr-round interest. Pond, conservatory, arches, pergola, rose arbour, alpine bed, vegetable garden and lots of pots for the acid lovers. TEA. *Adm 80p Chd 40p. Private visits welcome at weekends (2-6), please Tel 0273 889247*

¶The Old Vicarage ࢪ✿❀ (Arabella & Charlie Bridge) Firle. 5m outside Lewes on A27 towards Eastbourne. Sign to Firle. At the top of the village on RH-side. 3½acre garden with downland views. Walled garden with mixed vegetable and flower borders. TEA. *Adm £1.30 Chd 20p. Sun June 26 (2-6).*

¶Orchards ✿❀ (Penelope S Hellyer) Rowfant. Wallace Lane off B2028. 8½m N of Haywards Heath, 4½m W of East Grinstead. Garden created by Arthur and Grace (Gay) Hellyer after 2nd World War. 6 acres with mixed herbaceous borders, orchard, woodland, natural pond planted for year-round interest. Recent and continuing restoration, redesign and replanting is being done by their daughter Penelope Hellyer. Small nursery growing plants propagated from the garden. TEA. *Adm £1.50 Acc chd free. Sats, Suns April 30, May 1, June 25, 26 Mon May 2 (2-6). Private vists welcome, please Tel 0342 718280*

By Appointment Gardens. Avoid the crowds. Good chance of a tour by owner. See garden description for telephone number.

Palmer's Lodge ✗ (R Hodgson Esq) West Chiltington Village. At Xroads in centre of West Chiltington Village opp Queens Head. 2m E of Pulborough 3m N Storrington. A charming plantsman's ½-acre garden with herbaceous and shrub borders. *Adm £1 Chd free. Sats, Suns, July 9, 10, 16, 17 (2-6)*

Parham House and Gardens ⅋ (gdns) ✗ (Hse) ✿ 4m SE of Pulborough on A283 Pulborough-Storrington Rd. Beautiful Elizabethan House with fine collection of portraits, furniture, rare needlework. 4 acres of walled garden; 7 acres pleasure grounds with lake. 'Veronica's Maze' a brick and turf maze designed with the young visitor in mind. Picnic area. Also plant sales in converted old mower shed. Light refreshments in Big Kitchen. Shop. St Peter's Church nearby. *Open Easter Sun to first Sun in Oct; Weds, Thurs, Suns & Bank Hols. Adm House & garden (1992 rates) £3.50 OAPs £3 Chd £2. Garden £2.50 Chd £1. For NGS. Wed, Thurs June 8, 9. (Garden & picnic area (1-5), House (2-5) last adm 4.30)*

Pashley Manor ✗✿ (J Sellick Esq) Ticehurst. 10m S of Tunbridge Wells. 1½m SE Ticehurst on B2099. Pashley Manor is a grade 1 Tudor timber-framed ironmaster's house. Standing in a well timbered park with magnificent views across to Brightling Beacon. The 8 acres of formal garden, dating from the C18, were created in true English romantic style and are planted with many ancient trees and fine shrubs, new plantings over the past decade give additional interest and subtle colouring throughout the year. Waterfalls, ponds and a moat which encircled the original house built 1262. TEAS on fine days. *Adm £3 OAPs £2.50 Chd £3 14 and over, £1 6 to 14 years, under 6 free (Share to St Michael's Hospice, Hastings®). Tues, Wed, Thurs, Sat and Bank Hols April 2 to Oct 15. For NGS Sun June 26 (11-5)*

Pembury ⅋✿ (Nick & Jane Baker) Clayton. 6m N of Brighton. On B2112, 100yds from junction with A273. Disabled parking at garden, otherwise follow signs along footpath. 2-acre garden on clay at foot of South Downs. Fine views; young and mature trees, shrubs, old-fashioned roses and herbaceous planting. Owner maintained; Jack and Jill windmills. Saxon Church with restored wall paintings. Childrens' play area nearby. Teas in village hall in aid of Clayton Church Fund. *Adm £1.25 Chd free. Sun June 5 (11-6)*

Penns in the Rocks ⅋ (Lord & Lady Gibson) Groombridge. 7m SW of Tunbridge Wells on Groombridge-Crowborough Rd just S of Plumeyfeather corner. Bus: MD 291 Tunbridge Wells-East Grinstead, alight Plumeyfeather corner, ¾m. Large wild garden with rocks; lake; C18 temple; old walled garden. House (not shown) part C18. Dogs allowed in park. TEAS. *Adm £2 – Up to two chd 50p each, further chd free. Bank Hol Mons April 4, Aug 29 (2.30-5.30)*

Regular Openers. Too many days to include in diary. Usually there is a wide range of plants giving year-round interest. See head of county section for the name and garden description for times etc.

¶Petworth House ✗ (The National Trust) Petworth. In centre of Petworth A272/A283. Car park on A283 Northchapel Rd. For the 1st time, the NT's pleasure grounds at Petworth House will be on show in March. 30-acre woodland garden of Elizabethan origin and redesigned by Capability Brown in 1751. Millions of daffodils and early wild flowers in March, plus new wild walks through 10,000 trees and shrubs planted since Great Storm. Park also open. 2 guided walks with NT head gardener at 1.30pm and 3.30pm (about 1hr) starting from car park kiosk. (House closed). *Adm £1.50 Chd free. Sat March 26 (1-5)*

Pheasants Hatch ⅋ (Mrs G E Thubron) Piltdown. 3m NW of Uckfield on A272. 2 acres, rose gardens with ponds and fountains; herbaceous borders; foliage; wild garden; peacocks. TEAS. *Adm £1 Chd free. Sun, Mon June 26, 27 (2-6). Also open* Home Farm, Buckham Hill

¶Pondfield ✗✿ (Dr & Mrs Peter Sainsbury) Cutmill. E from Chichester, take A259 to Fishbourne and Bosham: over roundabout at Bosham and after ½m move into reservation in rd and turn R into Newells Lane, 150yds turn L and park. From W take A259 to Emsworth. Turn L after the Bosham Inn at Chidham, into Newells Lane. Approx 2 acres laid out by owners with specific emphasis on specimen trees. This garden is very informal with interesting vistas. Neptune House is reached over small bridge. TEAS. *Combined adm with* Neptune House *£1.50 Chd 50p. Sun June 5 (2-6)*

¶Priesthawes ⅋✗✿ (Mr & Mrs Andrew Wadman) Polegate. On B2104 Eastbourne 4m and Hailsham 2½m. 1m N of Stone Cross. C15 listed house of historical interest (not open) surrounded by 2½ acres. Walls used to full advantage with large clematis collection, climbers, old roses, herbaceous borders and pergola. Mainly replanted in the last 10 yrs. Lovely views over farmland. Cream TEAS. *Adm £1.50 Chd free (Share to St Wilfreds Hospice®) Sun June 12 (2-6). Private visits also welcome mid-May to July, please* Tel 0323 763228

¶Puddle House ✗✿ (Mr & Mrs John Harwood) Cross-in-Hand. Pass through Cross-in-Hand towards Heathfield; before entering Heathfield take the R-hand fork signposted A267 to Eastbourne. About ¼m after that fork, turn R immed before Q8 garage on LH-side into New Pond Hill. 5-acre garden, with lovely views of South Downs. Extensive lawns with interesting trees, shrubs and mixed borders and 2 natural ponds. Planting, begun in 1986, incl many unusual varieties, particularly eucalyptus spp, pinus spp, rhododendron spp and old-fashioned roses. TEAS. *Adm £2 (Share to St Thomas of Canterbury Roman Catholic Church, Mayfield®). Sun May 8 (2-5.30)*

¶Rustington Convalescent Home ✗ (Worshipful Company of Carpenters). On seafront 1m E of Littlehampton and ½m S of Rustington on B2140. A Grade II listed convalescent home built and endowed by Sir Henry Harben, founder of the Prudential Assurance Company in 1897. 6 acres with grass frontage to the seafront, with a variety of herbaceous borders and roses largely within the shelter of hedges from the sea winds. Extensive vegetable gardens beautifully maintained which serve the Home. TEAS in aid of Rustington Convalescent Home Charitable Trust. *Adm £1 Chd 50p. Sun July 10 (2-6)*

Rymans &✿ (Lord & Lady Claud Phillimore) Apuldram, 1½m SW of Chichester. Witterings Rd out of Chichester; at 1½m SW turn R signposted Apuldram; garden down rd on L. Walled and other gardens surrounding lovely C15 stone house (not open); bulbs, flowering shrubs, roses. Tea shops in Chichester. *Adm £1 Chd 30p. Suns April 10, 24, (2-5); June 26, Aug 28 (2-6)*

St Marys House &✿ (Mr Peter Thorogood) Bramber. 10m NW of Brighton in Bramber Village off A283 or 1m E of Steyning. Medium-sized formal gardens with amusing topiary, large example of living-fossil Gingko tree and Magnolia Grandiflora; pools, waterfalls and fountains, ancient ivy-clad 'Monk's Walk', all surrounding listed Grade I C15th timber-framed medieval house, once a monastic inn. TEAS. *(House open but not in aid of NGS) Easter to Sept 30, Suns and Thurs (2-6) Bank Hol Mons (2-6) also Mons in July, Aug, Sept (2-6). For NGS garden only Adm £1 Chd 50p. Fris July 15, 22 (2-6)*

Selehurst &✿✿ (Mr & Mrs M Prideaux) Lower Beeding, 4½m S of Horsham on A281 opp Leonardslee. Large woodland garden recently extended with a chain of five ponds and a romantic bridge. Fine collection of camellia, azaleas, rhododendrons; walled garden, 60′ laburnum tunnel underplanted with cream and silver, fine views. TEAS. *Adm £1.50 Chd free (Share to St. John's Church, Coolhurst®). Sun May 15 (1-5)*

Sennicotts &✿✿ (John Rank Esq) Chichester. From Chichester take B2178 signposted to Funtington for 2m NW. Blind entrance at beginning of open stretch. Long drive ample parking near house. From Portsmouth A27, Havant roundabout take A259 to Emsworth, in Fishborne turn N marked Roman Palace then straight on until a T junction. Entrance opposite. 6-acre mature garden with intriguing spaces, lawns, shrubs, roses and peonies. Large walled kitchen and cutting garden; greenhouses and orchard. Teas available nearby. *Adm £1.20 Chd free. Sun, Mon June 12, 13 (2-6)*

Sheffield Park Garden &✿ (The National Trust) Midway between E Grinstead and Lewes, 5m NW of Uckfield; E of A275. The garden, with 5 lakes, was laid out by Capability Brown in C18, greatly modified early in the C20. Many rare trees, shrubs and fine waterlilies; the garden is beautiful at all times of the year. Teas Oak Hall (not NT). *Adm £4 Chd £2. For NGS Weds May 18, Oct 19 (11-6)*

Sherburne House &✿ (Mr & Mrs Angus Hewat) Eartham, 6m NE of Chichester, approach from A27 Chichester-Arundel Rd or A285 Chichester-Petworth Rd nr centre of village, 200yds S of church. Chalk garden of about 2 acres facing SW. Shrub and climbing roses; lime-tolerant shrubs; herbaceous, grey-leaved and foliage plants, pots, small herb garden, kitchen garden potager and conservatory. TEAS. *Adm £1 Chd 50p. Sun June 19 (2-6)*

Somerset Lodge (Mr & Mrs R Harris) North St, Petworth. 7m S of Northchapel on A283. 15m N of Chichester on A285 garden on A283 100 yds N of church. Parking in town car park. Charming ½-acre new garden with ponds and walled kitchen garden, small collections of old and English roses and wildflower garden. Cleverly landscaped on slope with beautiful views. *Adm 80p Chd 20p. Wed, Sat, Sun June 8, 11, 12 (2-6)*

Spur Point ✿ (Mr & Mrs T D Bishop) nr Fernhurst. 3 acres of S facing terraced gardens, created by owners since 1970. Well planted with rhododendrons, azaleas, shrubs and mixed borders. Outstanding views to South Downs. *Adm £2 Chd 50p. Private visits welcome during May, please* Tel 0483 211535

Standen ✿ (The National Trust) 1½m from East Grinstead. Signed from B2110 and A22 at Felbridge. Hillside garden of 10½-acres with beautiful views over the Medway Valley. TEAS. *Adm £3 Chd £1.50.* ▲*Suns May 8, Sept 11 (12.30-5.30. Last adm 5pm)*

Stonehurst ✿ (Mr D R Strauss) Ardingly. 1m N of Ardingly. Entrance 800yds N of S of England showground, on B2028. 30-acre garden set in secluded woodland valley. Many interesting and unusual landscape features; chain of man made lakes and waterfalls; natural sandstone rock outcrops and a fine collection of trees and shrubs. TEAS. *Adm £2.50 Chd £1 (Share to Homelife®). Mons April 4, May 2, Sun May 15 (11-5)*

Telegraph House ✿ (Mr & Mrs David Gault) North Marden, 9 m. NW of Chichester. Entrance on B2141. From Petersfield to South Harting for 2m. From Chichester via A286 for 4m N of Lavant turn W on to B2l4l. 1-acre enclosed chalk garden 700 ft asl; chalk-tolerant shrubs, shrub roses, herbaceous plants; 1m avenue of copper beeches; walks through 150-acre yew wood; lovely views. House (not shown) in small park, built on site of camphore keeper's cottage. TEAS. *Adm £1.50 Chd 75p. Sats, Suns June 11, 12; July 16, 17 (2-6). Also private visits welcome May to Aug (2-5), please* Tel 0730 825206

Three Oaks &✿✿ (Mr & Mrs J C A Mudford) West Broyle. From roundabout N of Chichester take B2178 (Funtingdon) Rd NW for about 1⅓m. Turn L into Pine Grove and after a 100yds R into West Way. Small cottage garden. TEAS in aid of Save the Children Fund. *Combined adm £1.50 with* **Woodstock**. *Sun June 12 (1.30-5.30)*

Trotton Old Rectory ✿✿ (Mr & Mrs John Pilley) 3½m W of Midhurst on A272. Medium-sized garden, old-fashioned roses, interesting shrubs, herbaceous borders, lake, water and vegetable gardens. *Adm £1.50 Chd 50p. Suns May 15, June 26 (2-6)*

Trotton Place &✿ (Mr & Mrs N J F Cartwright) 3½m W of Midhurst on A272. Entrance next to church. Large garden extending to over 4 acres surrounding C18 house (not open). Walled fruit and vegetable garden; C17 dovecote with small knot garden. Fine trees; mature borders with shrub roses; lake and woodland walk. TEAS. *Adm £1 Chd 50p. Suns May 15, June 26 (2-6)*

¶**Udimore Gardens** ✿✿ 4m from Broad Oak Xrds and 2½m from Rye on B2089. Three contrasting gardens with views of the beautiful unspoilt Tillingbourne Valley. TEAS and swimming. *Adm £2 Chd 50p. Sun June 26 (2-6)*

¶**The Hammonds** (Prince & Princess Romanov) Georgian walled rose garden, large Victorian walled kitchen garden

¶**Wick Farm** (Mr & Mrs R Mair) Long established terraced farm garden with old-fashioned roses, herbaceous borders, 200-yr-old weeping ash tree

¶**White Fox Lodge** (Mrs J Horniblow) Recently planned garden designed by Sylvia Crowe, large shrub planting and old-fashioned roses. TEAS & swimming

¶**Wadhurst Gardens** ⚏🌢 6m SE of Tunbridge Wells. Take Mayfield Lane (B2100), car park Wadhurst College. *Combined adm £2 Chd free. Sun, Mon July 17, 18 (2-6).*
  Millstones (Mr & Mrs H W Johnson) ½-acre plantsman's garden featuring an exceptionally wide range of shrubs and perennial plants
  ¶**Sunnymead** (Mr & Mrs D Goldsmith) 1¼-acre landscaped garden imaginatively for the sporting family, with newly designed kitchen garden
  Westerleigh (Mr & Mrs M R Toynbee) Well planned 5 acres of large mixed borders; kitchen garden; newly planted trees; beautiful views. TEAS

Wadhurst Park ⚏⚏ (Dr & Mrs H Rausing) Wadhurst. 6m SE of Tunbridge Wells. Turn R along Mayfield Lane off B2099 at NW end of Wadhurst. L by Best Beech public house, L at Riseden Rd. 800-acres park with 7 different species of deer. Re-created garden on C19 site; restored C19 conservatories. Trailer rides into park. TEAS. *Adm £1.50 Chd 50p. Sun May 1 (2-5.30)*

Wakehurst Place ⚏⚏ (National Trust & Royal Botanic Gardens, Kew) Ardingly, 5m N of Haywards Heath on B2028. National botanic garden noted for one of the finest collections of rare trees and flowering shrubs amidst exceptional natural beauty. Walled gardens, heath garden, Pinetum, scenic walks through steep wooded valley with lakes, attractive water courses and large bog garden. Guided tours 11.30 & 2.30 most weekends, also prebooked tours. The ranger **Tel 0444 892701**. TEAS. *Adm £3.30 OAPs/Students £1.70 Chd £1.10. Fri July 15 (10-7)*

¶**Warren House** ⚏🌢 (Mr & Mrs T Hands) Warren Rd, Crowborough. From Crowborough Cross take A26 towards Uckfield. 4th turning. 1m down Warren Rd. Beware speed ramps. 9-acre garden with views over Ashdown Forest. Series of gardens old and new, displaying a wealth of azaleas, rhododendrons, impressive trees and shrubs. Sweeping lawns framed by delightful walls and terraces, woodlands and ponds. Planted and maintained solely by owner. TEAS. *Adm £2 OAPs £1.50. Chd free. Suns May 15, 22 Oct 2, 9 (1-6)*

West Dean Gardens ⚏⚏🌢 (Edward James Foundation) On A286, 5m. N of Chichester. Extensive garden in downland setting with specimen trees; 300' pergola; gazebo; summer-houses; borders, old roses and wild garden, large working walled kitchen garden. Circuit walk (2¼m) through park and 45-acre St Roche's Arboretum. TEA. *Adm £2.50 OAPs £2.25 Chd £1 parties over 20 £2 per person. March 1 to Oct 31 daily (11-5) last adm 4. For NGS Weds March 30, Sept 7 (11-5)*

The White House ⚏ (Elizabeth Woodhouse) Burpham. Turn off A27 Arundel-Worthing Rd ½ S of Arundel. Proceed through Wepham to Burpham for 2m. Charming garden planned and planted by practicing garden designer artist. Great attention to plant forms and colour arrangements. New wild garden with pool. TEAS. *Adm £1 Chd 50p (Share to Burpham Church Restoration Fund). Suns June 5, 12 (2.30-6)*

Wilderness Farm, ⚏🌢 Cabbages & Kings Garden (Mr & Mrs Andrew Nowell) Hadlow Down, ½m S of A272 from village. A contemporary ¾ acre courtyard garden, designed and planted by Ryl Nowell to demonstrate design ideas; renovated farm buildings against the backdrop of the High Weald, the garden contains interesting construction details and a wealth of plants. Featured in 'Gardeners World' July 1991. TEAS. *Adm £1 Chd 50p. Sun June 26, Aug 7, Sept 4 (2-6)*

Winchelsea Gardens ⚏ S of Rye. *Combined adm £1.50 Chd 75p. Sat June 18 (2-6)*
  Cleveland House (Mr & Mrs S Jempson) 1½-acre semi-formal walled garden; many varied plants, ornamental trees, water feature, beautiful views, swimming in heated pool
  Cooks Green (Roger & Tina Neaves) Cottage garden with views to Rye Bay
  Nesbit (Mr & Mrs G Botterell) Formal enclosed ¼-acre garden; many and varied plants
  The Old Rectory (June & Denis Hyson) ½ acre of open lawn garden with views overlooking the Brede Valley
  ¶**The Roundal** (Lord & Lady Ritchie) Wild garden with views to Rye
  Three Chimneys (Mr & Mrs Dominic Leahy) Formal town garden. TEAS
  Three Wishes (Mrs M Fuller) Higham Green. Cottage garden old wall and gazebo
  No. 1 Trojans Plat (Mr & Mrs Norman Turner) C13 Grade II listed archway providing access to small garden of great variety

Woodstock ⚏ (Group Captain A R Gordon-Cumming) West Broyle. From roundabout N of Chichester take B2178 (Funtingdon) rd NW for 1⅓m. Turn L into Pine Grove and after 100yds R into West Way. Woodstock is at far end. ⅔-acre garden mainly woodland garden specialising in ground cover plants especially asiatic primulas and hostas (over 20 varieties of each). TEAS at The Spinney in aid of Save the Children Fund. *Combined adm with* **Forest Lodge, Three Oaks**. *£1.50 Chd free. Sun June 12 (1.30-5.30)*

Regular Openers. Too many days to include in diary. Usually there is a wide range of plants giving year-round interest. See head of county section for the name and garden description for times etc.

By Appointment Gardens. These owners do not have a fixed opening day usually because they do not like crowds or have insufficient parking space. Owner will often give guided tour.

Warwickshire & West Midlands

Hon County Organiser: Mrs D L Burbidge, Cedar House, Wasperton, Warwick CV35 8EB
Assistant Hon County Organiser: Mrs C R King-Farlow, 8 Vicarage Road, Edgbaston, Birmingham B15 3EF
Mrs Michael Perry, Sherbourne Manor, Sherbourne, Warwick CV35 8AP
Hon County Treasurer: Michael Pitts, Hickecroft, Mill Lane, Rowington, Warwickshire CV35 7DQ

DATES OF OPENING

By appointment
For telephone numbers and other details see garden descriptions. Private visits welcomed

Brook Farm, Abbots Salford
18 Grove Avenue, Moseley, Birmingham
59 Hazelwood Road, Acocks Green
Ilmington Manor, Shipston-on-Stour
Ivy Lodge, Radway
The Mill Garden, Warwick
16 Prospect Road, Moseley Gardens
Sherbourne Park, nr Warwick
8 Vicarage Road, Edgbaston
Vine Cottage, Sheepy Magna Gardens (see Leicestershire & Rutland for details)
50 Wellington Road, Edgbaston. April to July
Woodpeckers, Bidford-on-Avon

Regular openings
For details see garden descriptions

Birmingham Botanical Gardens & Glasshouses. Open daily

March 6 Sunday
Birmingham Botanical Gardens & Glasshouses
March 27 Sunday
Sherbourne Manor, nr Warwick
April 3 Sunday
59 Hazelwood Road, Acocks Green
April 4 Monday
59 Hazelwood Road, Acocks Green
April 5 Tuesday
Woodpeckers, Bidford-on-Avon
April 10 Sunday
Elm Close, Binton Rd, Welford
Ilmington Gardens
The Mill Garden, Warwick
April 16 Saturday
Castle Bromwich Hall Garden Trust
April 17 Sunday
Greenlands, Wellesbourne
Ivy Lodge, Radway

Moseley Gardens
April 24 Sunday
Hall Green Gardens, Birmingham
May 1 Sunday
Alveston Gardens, Stratford-upon-Avon
May 2 Monday
55 Elizabeth Road, Moseley, Birmingham
May 3 Tuesday
Woodpeckers, Bidford-on-Avon
May 4 Wednesday
Alveston Gardens, Stratford-upon-Avon
May 8 Sunday
Ryton Organic Gardens, nr Coventry
May 15 Sunday
Bodymoor Green Farm, Kingsbury
Brook Farm, Abbots Salford
The Mill Garden, Warwick
Wroxall Abbey School, nr Warwick
May 22 Sunday
Dorsington Gardens, Stratford-upon-Avon
Idlicote Gardens, nr Shipston-on-Stour
Ilmington Manor, Shipston-on-Stour ‡
Maxstoke Castle, nr Coleshill
Pear Tree Cottage, Ilmington ‡
May 29 Sunday
55 Elizabeth Road, Moseley, Birmingham
Greenlands, Wellesborough
Loxley Hall, nr Stratford-on-Avon
21 Poppy Lane, Erdington, Birmingham
26 Sunnybank Road, Wylde Green
May 31 Tuesday
Woodpeckers, Bidford-on-Avon
June 4 Saturday
Baddesley Clinton Gardens
June 5 Sunday
Lord Leycester Hospital, Warwick
The Mill Garden, Warwick
June 10 Friday
Admington Hall, Shipston-on-Stour
June 11 Saturday
Admington Hall, Shipston-on-Stour
June 12 Sunday
Admington Hall, Shipston-on-Stour

Bodymoor Green Farm, Kingsbury
Brook Farm, Abbots Salford
Cedar House, Wasperton, nr Warwick
Crossways, Shrewley, nr Warwick ‡
Holywell Gardens, nr Claverdon
Shrewley Pools Farm, Haseley, Warwick ‡
Wroxall Abbey School, nr Warwick ‡
June 14 Tuesday
Woodpeckers, Bidford-on-Avon
June 18 Saturday
17 Gerrard Street, Warwick
June 19 Sunday
Alscot Park, nr Stratford-on-Avon
17 Gerrard Street, Warwick
Greenlands, Wellesbourne
50 Wellington Road, Edgbaston
Whichford & Ascott Gardens
June 25 Saturday
Rowington Gardens
June 26 Sunday
Compton Scorpion Farm, nr Ilmington
Honington Village Gardens
Ilmington Manor, Shipston-on-Stour
Loxley Hall, nr Stratford-on-Avon
Pereira Road Gardens
Roseberry Cottage, Fillongley
Rowington Gardens
Russell Road, Hall Green Gardens, Birmingham
8 Vicarage Road, Edgbaston
June 29 Wednesday
Paxford, Leamington Rd, Princethorpe, Rugby
July 3 Sunday
Bodymoor Green Farm, Kingsbury
Packwood House, nr Hockley Heath
July 10 Sunday
Avon Dassett Gardens
11 Hillwood Common Road, Four Oaks
16 Hillwood Common Road, Four Oaks
Ilmington Manor, Shipston-on-Stour
Moseley Gardens
Upton House, nr Banbury
July 17 Sunday
Brook Farm, Abbots Salford

18 Grove Avenue, Moseley, Birmingham
Martineau Centre Gardens, Edgbaston
The Mill Garden, Warwick
21 Poppy Lane, Erdington, Birmingham
Warmington Village Gardens
July 21 Thursday
Charlecote Park, Warwick
July 24 Sunday
59 Hazelwood Road, Acocks Green
26 Sunnybank Road, Wylde Green
July 26 Tuesday
Woodpeckers, Bidford-on-Avon
July 31 Sunday
Hunningham Village Gardens
Paxford, Leamington Rd, Princethorpe, Rugby
August 7 Sunday
55 Elizabeth Road, Moseley, Birmingham
The Mill Garden, Warwick
August 23 Tuesday
Woodpeckers, Bidford-on-Avon

August 24 Wednesday
Paxford, Leamington Rd, Princethorpe, Rugby
August 28 Sunday
Greenlands, Wellesbourne
September 11 Sunday
Tysoe Manor, nr Warwick
September 13 Tuesday
Woodpeckers, Bidford-on-Avon
September 17 Saturday
Castle Bromwich Hall Garden Trust
September 18 Sunday
The Mill Garden, Warwick
September 25 Sunday
Birmingham Botanical Gardens & Glasshouses
Ryton Organic Gardens, nr Coventry
October 2 Sunday
The Mill Garden, Warwick

DESCRIPTIONS OF GARDENS

Admington Hall &♿& (Mr & Mrs J P Wilkerson) 6½m S of Stratford-on-Avon. Between A3400 and B4632 nr Quinton. Large garden, interesting water garden, mixed borders extensive kitchen garden, greenhouses. TEAS. *Adm £2 Chd free. Fri, Sat, Sun June 10, 11, 12 (2-6)*

Alscot Park &♿& (Mrs James West) 2½m S of Stratford-on-Avon A34. Fairly large garden; extensive lawns, shrub roses, fine trees, orangery, with C18 Gothic house (not open), river, deer park, lakes. Coach parties by appt. Home-made TEAS. *Adm £1 Chd free (Share to Warwickshire Assoc. of Boys' Clubs©). Sun June 19 (2-6)*

Alveston Gardens &♿& 2m NE of Stratford-upon-Avon. Turn left at War Memorial off B4086 Stratford-Wellesbourne rd; Alveston ¼m. TEAS at The Malt House in aid of Alveston WI. *Combined adm £1.50 Chd 20p. Sun May 1. Also open Wed May 4 (Combined adm £1), except* **Long Acre** *(2-6)*

　The Bower House & (Mr & Mrs P S Hart) 1 acre, owner-designed, unusual trees, water garden and rockeries. Pergolas, alpine sinks, choice shrubs
　Court Leys (Mr & Mrs E Barnard) 1 acre; shrubs, trees and herbaceous borders, circular raised brick planters, conservatory
　Long Acre (Dr & Mrs N A Woodward) Owner designed, 1 acre; interesting trees, shrubs and roses; rockery, barbecue area, pergola, terraces and ponds
　Parham Lodge &♿& (Mr & Mrs K C Edwards) 1 acre; designed and maintained by owners. Choice trees, shrubs; plants, bulbs; island beds with heathers, large pond, patios, tubs, rose garden

Avon Dassett Gardens &♿& 7m N of Banbury off B4100 (use Exit 12 of M40). Car parking in the village and in car park at top of hill. TEAS at **Old Mill Cottage**. *Combined adm £2 Chd free (Share to Myton Hamlet Hospice®). Sun July 10 (2-6)*

　¶**Church Cottage** (Mr R & Mrs J Mandle) Pretty cottage garden with colourful beds. Shrubs and herbaceous plants

Hill Top Farm (Mrs N & Mr D Hicks) 1-acre garden. Dramatic display of bedding plants, perennials and roses. Extensive kitchen garden. Greenhouses
The Limes (Mr & Mrs C J Baylis) Large garden with mature trees, herbaceous borders, shrubs and lawns. Collection of herbs
Old Mill Cottage (Mr & Mrs M Lewis) Conservation garden of ½ acre with shrub, perennial borders and rockeries. Collection alpines and herbs. Two ponds and kitchen garden
The Old New House (Mr & Mrs M G Potts) Established garden with specimen trees and shrubs; lawns and rose garden
The Old Pumphouse (Mr & Mrs W Wormell) Cottage garden with mixed borders featuring varieties of pinks and shrub roses and clematis. Kitchen garden and greenhouse
The Old Rectory (Mrs L Hope-Frost) 2-acre garden surrounding listed building mentioned in Doomsday Book (not open). Large variety of fine trees and shrubs. Small wood
The Old Schoolhouse (Mr & Mrs P Fletcher) Small garden with interesting plants and shrubs; pond; views over parkland
¶**Post Box Cottage** Large garden with many fine plants, trees and shrubs. Vegetable garden and pond with waterfowl; hanging baskets

Baddesley Clinton &♿ (The National Trust) ¾m W off A4141 Warwick-Birmingham road near Chadwick End. 7½m NW of Warwick. Mediaeval moated manor house little changed since 1633; walled garden and herbaceous borders; natural areas; lakeside walk. Lunches and TEAS. *Adm Grounds only £2 chd £1. Shop and restaurant open from 12.30. For NGS Sat June 4 (12.30-6)*

By Appointment Gardens. These owners do not have a fixed opening day usually because they do not like crowds or have insufficient parking space. Owner will often give guided tour.

Birmingham Botanical Gardens & Glasshouses &&& 2m SW of Birmingham City Centre, signposted from Hagley Rd (A456). 15 acres; Tropical House with large lily pond and many economic plants. Palm House; Orangery; Cactus House. Outside bedding displays; rhododendrons and azaleas; rose garden; rock garden; 200 trees. Theme, herb and cottage gardens. Fun area for children. Plant centre. Bands play every Sun afternoon. TEAS in the Pavilion. *Adm £3.20 Chd, Students & OAPs £1.60. Open daily. For NGS Suns March 6, Sept 25 (10-6)*

¶Bodymoor Green Farm &&& (Mr & Mrs P J Maiden) ¾m S of Kingsbury on B4098 to Coventry. Easy approach from junction 9, M42; take A4097 signposted Kingsbury, Nether Whitacre. Traditional C18 farmhouse with courtyard and outbuildings. 1-acre country garden with old roses and herbaceous borders. Formal secret garden with pergola and white roses, silver scheme; ornamental pools, orchard with collection of spring bulbs; large kitchen garden, many interesting features including treillage; ducks, hens, geese, sheep and lambs. TEAS. *Adm £1.50. Suns May 15, June 12, July 3 (2-6)*

Brook Farm &&& (Mr & Mrs R B Hughes) Abbots Salford, Salford Priors 5m N of Evesham on B439. 1½ acres; large mixed borders, island beds, pond; bog, scree and peat gardens. TEA. *Adm £1 Chd Free. Suns May 15, June 12, July 17 (2-6). Also private visits welcome all year, please* **Tel 0386 871122**

Castle Bromwich Hall Garden Trust Chester Rd. &&& 4m E of Birmingham. 1m from junction 5 of the M6 (exit Northbound). An example of the Formal English Garden of the C18. The ongoing restoration, started 6yrs ago now provides visitors, academics and horticulturalists opportunity of seeing a unique collection of historic plants, shrubs, medicinal and culinary herbs and a fascinating vegetable collection. Guided tours Weds, Sats & Suns. Shop. Refreshments available; meals by arrangement. TEA. *Adm £3 OAPs £1.50 Chd £1. Mons to Thur April to Sept (1.30-4.30) Sats & Suns Bank Hols (2-6). For NGS Sats April 16, Sept 17 (2-6)*

Cedar House &&& (Mr & Mrs D L Burbidge) Wasperton. 4m S of Warwick on A429, turn right between Barford and Wellesbourne, Cedar House at end of village. 3-acre mixed garden; shrubs, herbaceous borders, ornamental trees, woodland walk. TEAS. *Adm £1.50 Chd free (Share to St John's Church, Wasperton®). Sun June 12 (2-6)*

¶Charlecote Park &&& (The National Trust) Warwick. 1m W of Wellesbourne signed off A429. 6m S of Warwick, 5m E of Stratford upon Avon. Landscaped park by Capability Brown with Victorian balustraded formal gardens featuring clipped yews and terraces with urns planted with geraniums and lobelia. A C19 orangery (open for teas) and a rustic thatched summer house stand by the cedar lawn. Shakespeare is said to have poached deer in Charlecote Park, and the border close to the orangery has been planted with species mentioned in his plays. The Ladies' Walk on a raised promontory with fine park views and vistas to two churches was created in the C19 by the Lucy family. A park walk (1m) follows a route round the park along the banks of the R. Avon. TEAS. *Special opening for NGS. Adm £2 (incl NT members). Thurs July 21 (2-6)*

Compton Scorpion Farm && (Mrs T M Karlsen) nr Ilmington. As for Ilmington Manor then fork L at village hall; after 1½m L down steep narrow lane, house on L. Garden designed and created by owners in 1989 from meadow hillside, aiming at Jekyll single colour schemes. *Adm £1 Chd free. Sun June 26 (2-6)*

Crossways &&& (Mr & Mrs M P Andrews) Shrewley. 5m NW of Warwick. 16m SE of Birmingham on B4439 between Hockley Heath and Hatton at Shrewley Xrds. ¾-acre traditional flower garden; cottage garden; flowers, old roses, orchard. Organically managed and designed to encourage wildlife. TEA. *Adm £1 Chd free. (Share to Brooke Donkey Hospital, Cairo®). Sun June 12 (2-5)*

Dorsington Gardens &&& 7m SW of Stratford-on-Avon. On A439 from Stratford turn L to Welford-on-Avon, then R to Dorsington. TEAS. *Combined adm £2 Chd free (Share to St Peter's Church, Dorsington®). Sun May 22 (2-5.30)*
    Knowle Thatch (Mr & Mrs P W Turner)
    Milfield (Mr & Mrs P Carey)
    The Moat House (Mr & Mrs I Kolodotschko)
    New House Farm (Mr & Mrs G Wood-Hill)
    The Old Manor (Mr F Dennis) TEAS
    The Old Rectory (Mr & Mrs N Phillips)
    White Gates (Mrs A G Turner)
    Windrush (Mrs M B Mills)

55 Elizabeth Rd &&& (Rob & Diane Cole) Moseley. 4m S of Birmingham City centre, halfway between Kings Heath Centre & Edgbaston Cricket Ground. Off Moor Green Lane. Plantsman's garden 100′ × 30′ on 3 levels, with scree area and mixed borders of alpines, rhododendrons, primulas and many unusual plants. Alpine House & troughs. TEAS. Wide range of plants for sale. *Adm 80p Chd 20p. Mon May 2, Suns 29, Aug 7 (2-6)*

Elm Close &&& (Mr & Mrs E W Dyer) Binton Rd, Welford-on-Avon. From Stratford-on-Avon, take A4390 towards Evesham; turn L after approx 5m (signed Welford and Long Marston). Elm Close is between Welford Garage and The Bell Inn. ⅔-acre plantsman's garden designed and maintained by owners and stocked for yr-round effect. Herbaceous beds, bulbs and shrubs, alpines in troughs, pool and bog garden, clematis and hellebores a particular speciality. Listed in The Good Gardens Guide. TEAS. *Adm £1 Chd free. Sun April 10 (2-6). Parties other days by appointment, please* **Tel 0789 750793**

17 Gerrard Street && (Miss P M & Mr T K Meredith) Warwick. 100yds from castle main gate. Car park at St Nicholas. Small town garden with interesting plants. *Adm 40p Chd free. Sat, Sun June 18, 19 (11-1 & 2-6)*

Greenlands && (Mr Eric T Bartlett) Wellesbourne. Leave Stratford-upon-Avon due E on the B4086. Garden on Xrds at Loxley/Charlecote by airfield. An acre of mature trees; shrubs; shrub roses and herbaceous borders. TEAS. *Adm 80p Chd 20p. Suns April 17, May 29, June 19, Aug 28 (11-5)*

Regular Openers. See head of county section.

¶18 Grove Avenue &&& (Richard & Judy Green) Moseley. 3m S of Birmingham city centre, ½m E of Moseley village. From Moseley centre along B4217, Wake Green Rd, turn 3rd R into Grove Avenue. Garden 100yds on R. Roadside parking. Small suburban garden stocked with wide variety of unusual trees, shrubs and herbaceous, planted for continuous colour and interest. Access also arranged to garden of 16 Grove Avenue. TEAS. *Adm £1 Chd free (Share to British Diabetic Association®) Sun July 17 (11-5) Private visits also welcome, please Tel* 021 449 2477

Hall Green Gardens &&& *Adm £1 Chd free (Share to Acorns Children's Hospice, St Mary's Hospice®). Sun April 24 (2-5)*

63 Green Rd (Mrs M Wilkes) Green Rd is W off A34 Hall Green Parade. (Nr Hall Green Station). Narrow suburban garden; 4 pools, bedding plants, herbaceous, shrubs, several distinctive features made by owner

120 Russell Rd &&& (Mr D Worthington) Turn off A34 E at Swithland Motors, Hall Green, down York Rd then L into Russell Rd. Small suburban garden designed by owner; shrubs, herbaceous, climbers, old roses and fountain; tubs, hanging baskets and window boxes. TEAS in aid of REAP. *Also open Sun June 26 (2-5) TEA*

59 Hazelwood Rd &&& (Mrs J M Dudley) Acocks Green. 4m SE of Birmingham just off A41 at Acocks Green. 1st R up Shirley Rd opp Methodist Church. ⅓-acre colourful garden with spring bulbs, shrubs, trees, bedding plants, fuchsias, geraniums and chrysanthemums. Large well stocked greenhouse. See the owls. TEAS. *Adm £1 Chd 20p. Easter Sun April 3, Mon April 4 Sun July 24 (11-5) Private visits also welcome, please Tel* 021 706 3511

11 Hillwood Common Road &&& (Mr & Mrs C T Smith) Four Oaks, Sutton Coldfield. From A5127 at Mere Green traffic island take Hill Village Rd. 2nd R into Sherifoot Lane and follow L bend. Straight on into Hill Wood Common Rd. AZ ref 27.4H. ½-acre Japanese style garden with tea house; stone and water feature; Japanese courtyard. Low heeled shoes, please. Ceramics by Janet Cottrell for sale. Tea at No 27 Hillwood Common Rd. *Adm £1 Chd 50p. Sun July 10 (2-6)*

¶16 Hillwood Common Road & (Mr & Mrs John Harrison) Four Oaks, Sutton Coldfield. From A5127 at Mere Green traffic island take Hill Village Rd. 2nd R into Sherifoot Lane and follow L bend. Straight on into Hill Wood Common Rd. AZ ref 27.4H. A ½-acre garden with interesting trees and shrubs, shrub roses; herbaceous underplanting; borders; kitchen garden. Tea at No 27. *Adm £1 Chd 50p. Sun July 10 (2-6)*

Holywell Gardens &&& 5m E of Henley-in-Arden, nearest village Claverdon. TEAS in aid of Myton Hospice. *Combined adm £1.50 Chd free. Sun June 12 (11-6)*

Holywell Farm (Mr & Mrs Ian Harper) 2½-acre natural garden; lawn, trees, shrubs. Laid out in 1963 for easy maintenance, surrounding C16 half timbered house

Holywell Manor Farm (Mr & Mrs Donald Hanson) Cottage type garden round C16 half timbered farmhouse, all within moated outer boundary incl natural duck pond

Honington Village Gardens && 1½m N of Shipston-on-Stour. Take A34 towards Stratford then R signed Honington. TEAS **Honington Hall**. *Combined adm £2 Chd free (Share to All Saints Church, Honington Restoration Fund®). Sun June 26 (2.15-6)*

Holts Cottage (Mr & Mrs Whitticase)

Honington Glebe (Mr & Mrs John Orchard) Over 2 acres of informal garden interesting ornamental trees; shrubs and foliage. Parterre and raised lily pool recently laid out in old walled garden

Honington Hall (Lady Wiggin) Extensive lawns; fine trees. Carolean house (not open); Parish Church adjoining house

Honington Lodge (Lord & Lady Tombs)

The Old Cottage (Mrs Wigington)

Old Mullions (Mr & Mrs R Lawton)

Hunningham Village Gardens &&& Hunningham. From Leamington Spa B4453 to Rugby. Signposted Hunningham R after Weston-under-Wetherley. Or A425 to Southam at Fosseway (B4455) turn L. At Hunningham Hill turn L then follow signs to church. Village gardens. Plants and produce stall, TEAS. *Combined adm £1.50 Chd free (Share to St Margarets Church®). Sun July 31 (2-5.30)*

The Bungalow (Mr & Miss Rouse) A cottage garden with large vegetable plot

Highcross (Mr & Mrs T Chalk) A secluded garden, with alpines. Also 1 or 2 other gardens in village

The Olde School House (Mr & Mrs G Longstaff) A 6-yr old owner-designed and maintained 1-acre garden. Borders, shrubs, pond/wildlife area

Idlicote Gardens && 3m E of Shipston-on-Stour. TEAS. *Combined adm £2 OAPs £1 Chd free (Share to Parish Church of St James the Great®). Sun May 22 (2-6)*

Idlicote House (Mrs R P G Dill) About 4 acres. Fine views. Small Norman church in grounds also statuary and follies. Garden being improved each year. House C18 (not open) listed Grade II partly attributed to Sir John Soane. Exterior recently restored

Badgers Cottage (Dr & Mrs D R N Custance)

Badgers Farm (Sir Derek & Lady Hornby)

1 Bickerstaff Cottages (Mr & Mrs C Balchin)

Bickerstaff Farm (Sir John & Lady Owen)

¶Home Farm (Mr & Mrs G Menzies-Kitchen)

Mews Cottage (Mr & Mrs D Colton)

The Old Rectory (Mr & Mrs D Higgs)

¶Stone Cottage (Mr & Mrs M Batsford)

Woodlands (Capt & Mrs P R Doyne)

Ilmington Gardens & 8m S of Stratford-on-Avon, 4m NW of Shipston-on-Stour. Ilmington Morris dancers. Teas in the Village Hall. *Combined adm £2.50 OAPs £2 Chd free (Share to Ilmington Childrens Playground Equipment Fund©). Sun April 10 (2-6)*

Crab Mill (Prof D C Hodgkin)

Crab Mill Cottage (Mrs M Greathead)

Foxcote Hill (Mr & Mrs M Dingley)

Foxcote Hill Cottage (Miss A Terry)

Frog Orchard (Mrs C Naish)

The Manor (Mr D & Lady Flower)

Pear Tree Cottage (Dr & Mrs A Hobson)

Puddocks (Miss H Syme)

The Rectory (The Rev. Story)

Ilmington Manor &※ (Mr D & Lady Flower). 4m NW of Shipston-on-Stour, 8m S of Stratford-on-Avon. Daffodils in profusion (April). Hundreds of old and new roses, ornamental trees, shrub and herbaceous borders, rock garden, pond garden, topiary, fish ponds with geese and ducks. House (not open) built 1600. TEAS (June 26, July 10) TEA (May 22). *Adm £2 OAPs £1 Chd free. Suns May 22, June 26, July 10 (2-6). Also private visits welcome, please* Tel 060882 230

Ivy Lodge & (Mrs M A Willis) Radway 7m NW of Banbury via A41 and B4086, turn right down Edgehill; 14m SE of Stratford via A422. Left below Edgehill. 4-acres; spring bulbs and blossom; wildflower area; climbing roses; site Battle of Edgehill. TEAS. *Adm £1 Chd free. Sun April 17 (2-6). Also private visits welcome in Oct, please* Tel 0295 87371

¶**Lord Leicester Hospital** &※※ High Street, Warwick. Town centre beside West Gate. Garden adjoins historic C14 Guildhall, Chapel, courtyard, Great Hall and Museum of the Queen's Own Hussars also open to public. 1-acre walled garden, partly under reconstruction, including Norman arch and ancient finial of Nilometer. TEAS. *Adm £1 Chd free. Sun June 5 (2-5)*

Loxley Hall (Col A Gregory-Hood) 4m SE of Stratford-on-Avon. Turn N off A422 or W off A429 1½m SW of Wellesbourne. Modern sculpture, iris, shrubs, roses, trees. Small Japanese Garden. Old church adjacent can be visited. TEAS. *Adm £1 Chd 20p. Suns May 29, June 26 (2-7)*

Martineau Centre Gardens &※※ (City of Birmingham Education Dept) Priory Rd, Edgbaston. From Birmingham S via A38; R at Priory Rd (lights and box junction); entrance 100yds on right opp Priory Hospital. 2-acre demonstration gardens; hardy ornamentals, vegetables, small orchard; glasshouses; nature reserve/wild garden. Mown field for picnics. TEAS. *Adm £1 Chd 50p. Sun July 17 (10-6)*

Maxstoke Castle &※ (Mr & Mrs M C Fetherston-Dilke) nr Coleshill, E of Birmingham, 2½m E of Coleshill on B4114 take R turn down Castle Lane; Castle Dr 1¼m on R. 4 to 5 acres of garden and pleasure grounds with flowers, shrubs and trees in the immediate surroundings of the castle and inside courtyard; water-filled moat round castle. *Adm £2 OAP/Chd £1 under 6 free. Sun May 22 (2-5)*

The Mill Garden &※※ (Mr A B Measures) 55 Mill St, Warwick off A425 beside castle gate. 1 acre; series of informal, partially enclosed areas, on river next to castle. Superb setting; herb garden; raised beds; small trees, shrubs, cottage plants and some unusual plants. Use St Nicholas Car Park. Tea in Warwick. *Collecting box. Sun & Bank Hols April 2 to Oct 16 (2-6). Open for NGS Suns April 10, May 15, June 5, July 17, Aug 7, Sept 18, Oct 2. Private visits welcome, please* Tel 0926 492877

Moseley Gardens ※※ Approx 3m from Birmingham City Centre halfway between Kings Heath Centre & Moseley Village TEA April 17. TEAS July 10. *Combined adm £1.50 Chd free. Suns April 17, July 10 (2-6)*

No 14A Clarence Rd (Ms C Fahy) Small suburban garden with a difference

No 16 Prospect Rd ※ (Mrs S M & Mr R J Londesborough) Small garden with wide range of plants. Registered wildlife garden. *Also private visits welcome all year, please* Tel 021 449 8457

No 17 Prospect Rd (Mr & Mrs A Packer) Small family garden, fruit and vegetables, greenhouse, mixed borders

No 19 Prospect Rd (Mr A White) Well planted spring suburban garden. *April 17 only*

¶**No 20 Prospect Rd** (Martin Page & Annie Sofiano). Large town garden on 3 levels. July 10 only

No 30 Prospect Rd (Mrs J Taylor) South-facing terraced garden incorporating rockery-covered air-raid shelter.

No 33 School Rd (Ms J Warr-Arnold) Mixed garden containing plants with interesting histories. *Sun July 10 only*

No 65 School Rd (Mrs W Weston) Small shady garden with patio and pergola. *Sun July 10 only*

Packwood House &※ (The National Trust) 11m SE of Birmingham. 2m E of Hockley Heath. Carolean yew garden representing the Sermon on the Mount. Tudor house with tapestries, needlework and furniture of the period. Teas at Baddesley Clinton (NT) Henley in Arden or Knowle. *Adm garden only £2 Chd £1.* ▲*For NGS Sun July 3 (2-6)*

¶**Paxford** (Mr & Mrs A M Parsons) Princethorpe. 7m SE of Coventry, on B4453 approx 200yds from junction with A423. A flower arranger's garden in ¾-acre, also with heathers, fuchsias and pelargoniums which has been designed and maintained by the owners as a series of rooms. Parking on road on one side only please. TEA. *Adm £1 Chd 20p (Share to Stretton-on-Dunsmore Parish Church®). Weds June 29, Aug 24 (12-6) Sun July 31 (2-6)*

Pear Tree Cottage &※ (Dr & Mrs A F Hobson) Ilmington 8m S of Stratford-on-Avon, 4m NW of Shipston-on-Stour. Cottage garden with many interesting plants and bulbs. Designed and maintained by owners; rock garden and terrace. TEA at **Ilmington Manor**. *Adm 50p Chd 20p. Sun May 22 (2-6)*

Pereira Road Gardens ※※ Birmingham A-Z 5c p.72 between Gillhurst Rd and Margaret Grove, ¼m from Hagley Rd or ½m Harborne High St. TEAS at **No. 84** in aid of FACE IT Unit QEH. *Combined adm £1.50 Chd 30p. Sun June 26 (2-5)*

　No. 45 (Wyn & Alfred White) Harborne. ⅕ acre on four levels. Spring bulbs, rhododendrons, roses, shrubs, herbaceous borders, ornamental and fruit trees in formal and informal areas. Sale of gifts in aid of Break Through Trust for the Deaf

　No. 50 ※ (Prof M Peil) About ⅕ acre, with a wide range of shrubs and perennials for all seasons; fruit and vegetables. Large bed of plants with African connections, pond. (Plants sold in aid of Catholic Fund for Overseas Development.)

By Appointment Gardens. See head of county section

No. 84 & (Mr R E Barnett) 1/5 acre with 30 degree sloping concreted bank, now extensive rockery, interesting shrubs, herbaceous borders

¶21 Poppy Lane & (Mr & Mrs Scott) Erdington. 1/2m S of (Yenton) junction of Chester Rd and Sutton New Rd. A-Z:1A62. Approx 1/3-acre garden with variety of shrubs and trees, some tender. Spring, summer, flower, bulb displays; herbaceous borders, rose pergola in a walled area. Organic vegetable plot, herbs, fruit trees and bushes. Tropical conservatory, pond, mature rhododendrons. Teas at No 15 in aid of Taylor Memorial Home. *Adm £1 Chd free. Suns May 29, July 17 (2-6)*

Roseberry Cottage & (Mr & Mrs Richard G. Bastow) Fillongley. 6m N of Coventry on B4098 Tamworth Road. Go under motorway bridge to top of hill, take Woodend Lane, sign on R. Turn L into Sandy Lane, opp triangle of beech trees. 1st house on right in Sandy Lane. Please use one way system due to restricted parking. Garden of 1¾ acres including herbaceous border, rock garden, pool, peat and bog area, scree and small herb garden. Stone troughs, orchard with wild flowers, organically grown fruit and vegetables. Herbs for sale, thymes a speciality. TEA. *Adm £1 Chd 30p (Share to NCCPG®). Sun June 26 (2-6)*

Rowington Gardens & 6m NW of Warwick. 15m SE of Birmingham on B4439 between Hockley Heath and Hatton. Turn into Finwood Rd (signed Lowsonford); at Rowington Xrds 1st L into Mill Lane. TEA. *Combined adm £1.50 Chd 50p (Share to Myton Hospice®). Sat, Sun June 25, 26 (2-5.30)*
> **Hickecroft** (Mr J M Pitts) 2-acre garden re designed and replanted; some interesting plants, mixed borders. Home to part of the NCCPG Digitalis collection
> **Woodlands** (Mr & Mrs M J O Morley) A medium-sized English country garden surrounding C16 farmhouse. Recent tree planting on large scale. Interesting use of former swimming pool

Ryton Organic Gardens & 5m SE of Coventry (off A45 to Wolston). 8-acre site demonstrating organic gardening methods as seen on Channel 4's 'All Muck and Magic' series: composting display, herb, rose and bee garden; shrub borders; vegetable plots and fruit; garden for the blind and partially sighted; conservation area with pond and wild flowers meadow. Shop; childrens play area; award winning cafe serving organically grown food. Guide dogs allowed. TEAS. *Adm £2.50 Concessions £1.75, Chd £1.25 Family £6.50. Open daily except Christmas period. For NGS Suns May 8, Sept 25 (10-5.30)*

Sherbourne Manor & (Mr & Mrs M Perry) 2m S of Warwick just off A429 Barford Rd. Large garden contains herbaceous borders; lawns; stream; fishpond and large variety of established trees. Paddocks with rare breed sheep. TEAS in aid of All Saints Church, Sherbourne. *Adm £2.50 OAPs £1 Chd free. Sun March 27 (2-6)*

Sherbourne Park & (The Hon Lady Smith-Ryland) 3m S of Warwick off A429; 1/2m N of Barford. Medium-sized garden; lawns, shrubs, borders, roses, lilies; lake; temple; church by Gilbert Scott 1863 adjacent to early Georgian House (not open) 1730. Featured in 'New Englishwoman's Garden' (R Verey) and 'English Gardens' (P Coats). Featured in 1991 & 1992 Gardeners Royal Benevolent Society Calendar. Lunches, teas or coffee for private tours by arrangement. Free car park. *Adm £2.50 OAPs and Chd (13-16) £2, under 12 free (Share to All Saints Church, Sherbourne®). Open for private tours and by appt only, please* Tel 0926 624255 624506

¶Shrewley Pools Farm & (Mrs C W Dodd) Haseley. 4m NW of Warwick through Hatton. At roundabout turn L along Five Ways Rd, after approx ¾m farm entrance on L opp Audholi poultry farm. ¾m off A4177 from Falcon Inn (Warwick). 1-acre garden, herbaceous borders, rhododendrons, roses, irises, peonies etc. Many interesting shrubs and trees, terrace and garden pool. Farm animals and C17 farmhouse and barn. TEA. *Adm £1 Chd 30p. Sun June 12 (2-6)*

26 Sunnybank Road & (Chris & Margaret Jones) Wylde Green. ¾m S of Sutton Coldfield. Turn off A5127 towards Wylde Green Station then; 2nd L. Medium-sized town garden on sandy soil, redesigned in mid-80's by present owners as a series of 'rooms'. Yr-long interest achieved by use of bulbs, shrubs and herbaceous plants. Featured on TV's 'Garden Club'. TEAS in aid of Save the Children Fund. *Adm £1 OAPs 50p Chd free. Suns May 29, July 24 (2-6)*

Tysoe Manor & (Mr & Mrs W A C Wield) Tysoe. 5m NE of Shipston-on-Stour. Take the 4035 to Banbury. In Brailes turn L to Tysoe. The Manor is the first house on the L after reaching Upper Tysoe. 4-acre garden, large lawns with stone walls, herbaceous and flower borders; rose beds and mature ornamental and fruit trees. TEAS in aid of Tysoe Church. *Adm £1.50 Chd free. Sun Sept 11 (2-6)*

Upton House & (The National Trust) 7m NW of Banbury on A422; 2m S of Edgehill. Terraced garden, rockeries, herbaceous borders, roses, water gardens, lawns. House contains a connoisseur's collection of porcelain, tapestries and paintings. Coaches by appt. TEAS. *Adm garden only £2.15 Chd 1/2 price. For NGS Sun July 10 (2-6)*

8 Vicarage Rd & (Charles & Tessa King-Farlow) Edgbaston, 1½m W of City Centre off A456 (Hagley Rd). ¾-acre retaining in part its Victorian layout but informally planted with mixed borders of interesting and unusual plants; shrub rose border; walled potager and conservatory. TEAS. *Adm £1 Chd free (Share to St George's Church®). Sun June 26 (2-6). Also private visits welcome, please* Tel 021 455 0902

Warmington Village Gardens & 5m NW of Banbury on B4100. TEAS at **The Glebe House**. *Combined adm £1.50 Chd free (Share to Warmington PCC Restoration Fund®). Sun July 17 (2-6) Car park; coaches welcome, please* Tel 0295 89 318
> **Berka** (Mr & Mrs B J Castle) Chapel Street
> **The Glebe House** (Mr & Mrs G Thornton) Village Road

By Appointment Gardens. These owners do not have a fixed opening day usually because they do not like crowds or have insufficient parking space. Owner will often give guided tour.

Right South Luffenham Hall,
Leicestershire. *Photograph by
Brian Chapple*
Below Preen Manor, Shropshire.
Photograph by Brian Chapple

Hadspen House, Somerset. *Photograph by Andrew Lawson*

Weston Park, Shropshire. *Photograph by Sheila Orme*

Right Hawkstone Hall,
Shropshire. *Photograph by
Jackie Newey*
Below Furzey Gardens, Hampshire.
Photograph by Sheila Orme

Left Clare College, Cambridge.
Photograph by Andrew Lawson
Below Heale Gardens, Wiltshire.
Photograph by John Glover

East Lambrook Manor, Somerset. *Photograph by John Glover*

Holly Cottage (Dr & Mrs T W Martin) The Green
Mews Cottage (Mr & Mrs E J Squire) The Green
Poynters (Mrs F Ingram) School Lane
Rotherwood (Miss M R Goodison) Soot Lane
¶Sunnyside (Yvonne Farley & Michael Borlenghi)
Underedge (Mr & Mrs J Dixon) 1 Church Hill

50 Wellington Rd ᕕᕗ (Mrs Anne Lee) Edgbaston. 200yds NE of Edgbaston Old Church on the corner of Ampton Rd & Wellington Rd. 1-acre walled town garden, partly replanted in 1985. Terrace, paving, brick paths & some architectural features. 100-yr-old rhododendrons & large trees. Two long mixed borders round large lawn, fountain. TEAS. *Adm £1 50 Chd free. Sun June 19 (2-6) Private visits also welcome April to July, please* **Tel 021 440 1744**

Whichford & Ascott Gardens ᕗᕕ 6m SE of Shipston-on-Stour. Turn E off A34 at Long Compton for Whichford. Cream TEAS Sun at **Whichford House**. *Combined adm £2 Chd free (Share to Whichford Church Lighting Fund®). Sun June 19, (2-6)*

  Brook Hollow (Mr & Mrs J A Round) Garden on a bank, stream and water garden
  Combe House (Mr & Mrs D C Seel) Hidden garden surrounding house; mature fine trees
  The Old House (Mr & Mrs T A Maher) Undulating garden. Natural ponds and wildflower meadow
  Rightons Cottage (Col & Mrs C R Bourne) Medium sized garden planted for quiet enjoyment with minimal upkeep in retirement
  ¶7 Roman Row (Mr & Mrs S C Langdon) Beautiful well kept cottage garden

Stone Walls (Mrs J Scott-Cockburn) Walled garden; paved garden in foundations of old stable
Whichford House (Mr & Mrs J W Oakes) Large undulating garden with extensive views. Mainly shrubs and trees
The Whichford Pottery (Mr & Mrs J B M Keeling) Secret walled garden, unusual plants, large vegetable garden and rambling cottage garden. Adjoining pottery

Woodpeckers ᕕᕗ (Dr & Mrs A J Cox) The Bank, Marlcliff, nr Bidford-on-Avon 7m SW of Stratford-on-Avon. Off the B4085 Between Bidford-on-Avon and Cleeve Prior. 2½-acre plantsman's garden designed and maintained by owners; colour-schemed herbaceous and mixed borders, old roses, meadow garden, alpines in troughs and gravel, pool, knot garden, ornamental kitchen garden. Featured on BBC2 'Gardener's World' and in 'Practical Gardening'. *Adm £1.50 Chd free. Tues April 5, May 3, 31 June 14, July 26, Aug 23, Sept 13 (2-5). Also private visits welcome all year, please* **Tel 0789 773416**

Wroxall Abbey School ᕕᕗ (Mrs J M Gowen, Headmistress) Wroxall 6m NW of Warwick. Nr Fiveways junction on A4141. 27 acres; spring flowers, shrubs, rhododendrons, small enclosed flower garden. 'Nature trail' incl comments on plants, flowers, etc. Work in progress on surveying and re-instatement of historical pleasure grounds, by Warwickshire Garden Trust. Evensong in Chapel 5pm. TEA. *Adm £1.30 Chd 50p (Share to St Leonard's Church, Wroxall®). Suns May 15, June 12 (2-5)*

Wiltshire

Hon County Organiser: Brigadier Arthur Gooch, Manor Farmhouse, Chitterne, Warminster BA12 OLG
Assistant Hon County Organisers: Mrs David Armytage, Sharcott Manor, Pewsey
Mrs Anthony Heywood, Monkton House, Monkton Deverell
Mrs Colin Shand, Ashton House, Worton, Devizes
(& PR) Mrs John Nicolls, The Gate House, Chitterne, Warminster BA12 OLG
Tel 0985 50209

DATES OF OPENING

By appointment
For telephone numbers and other details see garden descriptions. Private visits welcomed

Ashtree Cottage, Kilmington Common
Bolehyde Manor, nr Chippenham
Bryher, Bromham
Home Covert, Devizes
Long Hall, Stockton, nr Warminster
Lower Farm House, Milton Lilbourn
Normanton Down, Wilsford-Cum-Lake
7 Norton Bavant, nr Warminster
Sharcott Manor, nr Pewsey
Thompson's Hill, Sherston

Regular openings
For details see garden descriptions

Barters Farm Nurseries, Chapmanslade, Daily
Bowood Rhododendron Walk, and Bowood Gardens see text
Broadleas, nr Devizes. Every Sun, Wed and Thurs April 1 to Oct 30
The Courts, nr Bradford-on-Avon. Open every day except Sat April to Oct
Hazelbury Manor Gardens, Box, nr Chippenham May 28 to Sept 29, weekends, Bank Hols & Thurs
Heale Gardens & Plant Centre, Middle Woodford. Open all year
Iford Manor, nr Bradford-on-Avon. Daily May to Sept except Mons & Fris. April to Oct Suns only

Lackham Gardens, nr Chippenham.
Open daily Mar 26 to Nov 6
Long Hall, Stockton, nr Warminster.
Open 1st Sat of every month,
May 7 to Aug 6
Mannington Gardens and Nursery,
nr Pewsey. Open daily except
Dec 25 to Jan 2
The Mead Nursery, nr Rudge. Wed
to Sun Feb 2 to Oct 30
Pound Hill House, West Kington.
Open Wed to Sun and Bank Hols
April 6 to Sept 25
Sheldon Manor, nr Chippenham.
Open Easter Sun & Mon. Every
Sun, Thurs & Bank Hols April 3 to
Oct 2
Stourhead Garden, Stourton, nr
Mere. Daily
Waterdale House, East Knoyle. Open
Suns April 3 to June 5

February 20 Sunday
Lacock Abbey Gardens, nr
Chippenham
February 27 Sunday
Lacock Abbey Gardens, nr
Chippenham
March 6 Sunday
Lacock Abbey Gardnens, nr
Chippenham
March 27 Sunday
Crudwell Court Hotel, nr
Malmesbury
April 3 Sunday
Lockeridge House, nr
Marlborough
April 4 Monday
Long Hall, Stockton, nr
Warminster
April 6 Wednesday
Sharcott Manor, nr Pewsey
April 10 Sunday
Easton Grey House, nr
Malmesbury
Fonthill House, nr Tisbury
Kingfisher Mill, Great Durnford
Manor House Farm, Hanging
Langford
April 17 Sunday
Broadleas, nr Devizes
Corsham Court, nr Chippenham
Lower Farm House, Milton
Lilbourne
April 24 Sunday
Iford Manor, Bradford-on-Avon
Luckington Manor, nr
Chippenham
Oare House, nr Pewsey
May 1 Sunday
Inwoods, nr Bradford-on-Avon
Lackham Gardens, nr
Chippenham ‡

Little Durnford Manor, nr
Salisbury
Spye Park, nr Chippenham ‡
May 4 Wednesday
Sharcott Manor, nr Pewsey
May 8 Sunday
Bowood Rhododendron Walks, nr
Chippenham
Conock Manor, nr Devizes
Pythouse, Semley
Ridleys Cheer, Mountain Bower
Waterdale House, East Knoyle
May 11 Wednesday
Bryher, Bromham
May 15 Sunday
Ashtree Cottage, Kilmington
Common ‡
Luckington Court, nr Chippenham
Stourhead Garden, Stourton, nr
Mere ‡
May 18 Wednesday
Bryher, Bromham
May 22 Sunday
Bowden Park, Lacock,
Chippenham
Fonthill House, nr Tisbury
7 Norton Bavant, nr Warminster
May 25 Wednesday
Bryher, Bromham
May 29 Sunday
Hyde's House, Dinton, nr
Salisbury
June 1 Wednesday
Bryher, Bromham
Sharcott Manor, nr Pewsey
June 4 Saturday
Ark Farm, Old Wardour, nr
Tisbury
June 5 Sunday
Ark Farm, Old Wardour, nr
Tisbury
Foscote Gardens, Grittleton
The Hall, Bradford-on-Avon
Landford Lodge, nr Salisbury
Maiden Bradley House, nr
Warminster
Manningford Gardens and
Nursery, nr Pewsey
The Old Rectory, Stockton
June 8 Wednesday
Bryher, Bromham
June 12 Sunday
Avebury Manor, Avebury
Bolehyde Manor, nr Chippenham
Edington and Coulston Gardens
Langley House, Chippenham
Little Durnford Manor, nr
Salisbury
Sherston Gardens ‡
Thompson's Hill, Sherston ‡
June 15 Wednesday
Bryher, Bromham
June 17 Friday
Salisbury Close Gardens

Sheldon Manor, nr Chippenham
June 19 Sunday
Ashtree Cottage, Kilmington
Common
Corsham Court, nr Chippenham
Goulters Mill Farm, Nettleton
Hillbarn House, Great Bedwyn
Job's Mill, Crockerton, nr
Warminster
Wedhampton Gardens, nr Devizes
June 25 Saturday
Barters Farm Nurseries,
Champmanslade
Hazelbury Manor Gardens, Box,
nr Chippenham
June 26 Sunday
Avon Farm House,
Stratford-sub-Castle, Salisbury ‡
Barters Farm Nurseries,
Chapmanslade
Hazelbury Manor Gardens, Box,
nr Chippenham
Kingfisher Mill, Great Durnford ‡
Long Hall, Stockton, nr
Warminster
Luckington Manor, nr Chippenham
Mannington Bruce House, nr Pewsey
Normanton Down,
Wilsford-cum-Lake, nr
Amesbury ‡
Parks Court, Upton Scudamore ‡‡
Pound Hill House, West
Kington ‡‡‡
Ridleys Cheer, Mountain
Bower ‡‡‡
Sharcott Manor, nr Pewsey
Swaynes Mead, Great
Durnford ‡‡
West House, 12 West St,
Warminster ‡‡
July 2 Saturday
Castle Combe Gardens, nr
Chippenham
The Courts, nr Bradford-on-Avon
Westwood Manor, nr Bradford on
Avon
July 3 Sunday
Biddestone Manor, nr Corsham
Castle Combe Gardens, nr
Chippenham
Hoddinotts House, Tisbury
Lower Burytown, Blunsdon
July 6 Wednesday
Sharcott Manor, nr Pewsey
July 10 Sunday
Ashtree Cottage, Kilmington
Common
Courtlands, nr Chippenham
Crudwell Court Hotel, nr
Malmesbury
Hannington Hall, Highworth, nr
Swindon
Manningford Gardens and
Nursery, nr Pewsey

Worton Gardens, nr Devizes
July 16 Saturday
The Mead Nursery, nr Rudge
July 17 Sunday
Lackham Gardens, nr Chippenham
Waterdale House, East Knoyle
July 24 Sunday
Home Covert, Devizes
Luckington Manor, nr Chippenham
Oare House, nr Pewsey
August 3 Wednesday
Sharcott Manor, nr Pewsey
August 7 Sunday
Heale Gardens & Plant Centre,
Middle Woodford
Lower Farm House, Milton
Lilbourne ‡
The Old Bakery, Milton
Lilbourne ‡
August 14 Sunday
Broadleas, nr Devizes
August 17 Wednesday
Home Covert, Devizes
August 21 Sunday
Ashtree Cottage, Kilmington
Common

August 28 Sunday
Hyde's House, Dinton, nr
Salisbury
August 29 Monday
11 Beechfield, Newton Tony
September 3 Saturday
The Courts, nr
Bradford-on-Avon ‡
Westwood Manor, nr
Bradford-on-Avon ‡
September 4 Sunday
Pound Hill House, West Kington
September 7 Wednesday
Sharcott Manor, nr Pewsey
September 11 Sunday
Ashtree Cottage, Kilmington
Common
September 17 Saturday
The Mead Nursery, nr Rudge
September 18 Sunday
Hillbarn House, Great Bedwyn
Manningford Gardens and
Nursery, nr Pewsey
The Mead Nursery, nr Rudge
September 25 Sunday
Avebury Manor, Avebury

October 2 Sunday
Ashtree Cottage, Kilmington
Common
Great Chalfield Manor, nr
Melksham
Lackham Gardens, nr Chippenham
October 5 Wednesday
Sharcott Manor, nr Pewsey

1995

February 12 Sunday
Great Chalfield Manor, nr
Melksham
February 19 Sunday
Lacock Abbey Gardens, nr
Chippenham
February 26 Sunday
Lacock Abbey Gardens, nr
Chippenham
March 5 Sunday
Lacock Abbey Gardens, nr
Chippenham

DESCRIPTIONS OF GARDENS

¶**Ark Farm** ✎ (Mr & Mrs Edward Neville-Rolfe) Tisbury. 9m from Shaftesbury. 2½m from Tisbury. From Tisbury follow English Heritage signs to Old Wardour Castle. Private rd from Castle car park to Ark Farm (400yds). 1¼ acres includes water and woodland gardens. TEAS. *Adm £2 Chd free. Sat, Sun June 4, 5 (2-6)*

Ashtree Cottage ✎❀ (Mr & Mrs L J Lauderdale) Kilmington Common. 3½m NW of Mere (A303) on B3092, ½m N of Stourhead Garden. turn W at sign for Alfred's Tower and follow NGS signs. 1 acre garden created since 1984 by owners, a series of gardens surrounding thatched cottage, with densely planted mixed borders of shrubs, roses and perennials and unusual plants, many of which are available for sale in the garden nursery. TEAS except Oct 2. *Adm £1.50 Chd 50p (Share to St Margaret's Somerset Hospice & Woodgreen Animal Shelter®). Suns May 15, June 19, July 10, Aug 21, Sept 11, Oct 2 (2-6). Also private visits welcome daily, please* **Tel 0985 844740**

Avebury Manor Garden &✎❀ (The National Trust) Avebury. On A361 9m N of Devizes 2m from Beckhampton roundabout on A4. Entrance to Manor and car park N of the village. This 4-acre garden is undergoing restoration to planting, hedges and walls. Ancient walled garden on site of former priory, divided by stone walls and topiary hedges, incl a rose garden; topiary garden, herb garden. Italian walk and half moon garden. Late mediaeval manor house under restoration (not open). *Adm £2.10 Chd £1.30.* ▲*Suns June 12, Sept 25 (11-5)*

¶**Avon Farm House** &✎❀ (Mr & Mrs Ian Wilson) Stratford sub Castle. 2m NW of Salisbury in Avon Valley. Follow rd to Stratford sub Castle out of Salisbury; through village; turn L over R Avon bridges; garden is 1st on L. Chalk garden of 2 acres looking up to Old Sarum. Being created under supervision of Coombe Bissett garden designer Mrs Sol Jordans. Pleached limes, double herbaceous borders. TEAS. *Adm £1 Chd free. Sun June 26 (2-6)*

¶**Barters Farm Nurseries** &✎❀ (Mr & Mrs C L C Walker) Chapmanslade. On A3098, 3m E of Frome, 3m W of Westbury. 3m N of Warminster, turn off A36 towards Frome. Potters garden, featuring groundcover plants, trees and half hardy perennials. 14-acre wholesale nursery, including 2 acres of stock beds, retail plant centre. TEAS in aid of Chapmanslade Church. *Adm £1 Chd free. Open daily (9-5) Suns (10-5). For NGS Sat June 25 (9-5) Sun June 26 (10-5)*

¶**11 Beechfield** ✎❀ (J Hindle) Newton Tony. 2m S of A303, off A338; turn SE off A338 into the village to 2nd thatched cottage on R. Limited parking on L further down Beechfield or on Memorial Hall playing field in village. Professionally designed village garden, approx 75' × 50' encompassing paved terrace carpeted with alpines, small wildlife pond, clematis bower and rose tunnel, knot garden, herb and vegetable beds, cordon apples and mixed borders of shrubs, old roses and herbaceous perennials. An illusion of size is created by adept use of screening, changes of direction and mood, carefully placed seating and dense planting. Open to coincide with village fete. TEAS in the marquee on the Memorial Hall playing field. *Adm £1 Chd free. Mon Aug 29 (2-6)*

Regular Openers. Too many days to include in diary. Usually there is a wide range of plants giving year-round interest. See head of county section for the name and garden description for times etc.

Biddestone Manor &✿❀ (Mr N Astrup) Biddestone, nr Corsham, 5m W of Chippenham, 3m N of Corsham. On A4 between Chippenham and Corsham turn N; or from A420, 5m W of Chippenham, turn S. Lge garden with extensive lawns; small lake; topiary; swimming pool set in attractive rose garden; newly planted orchard and herb garden. Fine C17 manor house (not open) with interesting older outbuildings. TEAS. *Adm £1 Chd 50p. Sun July 3 (2-6)*

Bolehyde Manor &✿❀ (Earl and Countess Cairns) Allington. 1½m W of Chippenham on Bristol Rd (A420). Turn N at Allington crossroads. ½m on R. Parking in field. A series of gardens around C16 Manor House; enclosed by walls and Topiary, densely planted with many interesting shrubs and climbers, mixed rose and herbaceous beds; inner courtyard with troughs full of tender plants; wild flower orchard, vegetable, fruit garden and greenhouse yard. TEAS. *Adm £1.50 Chd 50p (Share to Kingston St Michael Church©). Sun June 12 (2.30-6). Also private visits welcome, please* Tel 0249 652105

Bowden Park &✿❀ (Bowden Park Estate) Lacock, 5m S of Chippenham. From Lacock village take rd to Bowden Hill, Sandy Lane and Devizes; proceed up hill; (entrance and parking top lodge opp Spye Arch). 12 acres incl horticultural areas, shrubberies; borders; fountains; follies; woodland and water gardens. *Adm £1.50 Chd 50p. Sun May 22 (2-6)*

¶**Bowood Rhododendron Walks** ✿❀ (The Earl of Shelburne) nr Chippenham. Entrance off A342 between Sandy Lane and Derry Hill villages. A breath-taking display of rhododendrons and azaleas from the minute detail of the individual flower to the grand sweep of colour formed by hundreds of shrubs, surrounded by a carpet of bluebells. Open May & June. *For NGS Adm £2 Sun May 8(11-6). Also open* **Bowood House & Gardens** *Luncheon, TEAS. Garden centre. Adm £4.50 OPA £4 Chd 2.30. March 26 to Oct 30 (11-6)*

Broadleas ❀ (Lady Anne Cowdray) S of Devizes. Bus: Devizes-Salisbury, alight Potterne Rd. Medium-sized garden; attractive dell planted with unusual trees, shrubs, azaleas and rhododendrons; many rare plants in secret and winter gardens. Home-made TEAS (on Sundays). *Adm £2 Chd £1. April 3 to Oct 30 every Sun, Wed & Thurs. For NGS (Share to Animal Health Trust®). Suns April 17, Aug 14 (2-6)*

Bryher &✿❀ (Mr & Mrs Richard Packham) Yard Lane Bromham. 4m N of Devizes on A342 to Chippenham turn R into Yard Lane at Xrds. A compact level garden, approx ⅔ acre created around a bungalow home. Borders planted mainly for foliage effect using a wide range of red, gold, silver and variegated plants, with many unusual varieties; short wildlife walk; display greenhouses with small nursery beds. *Adm £1 Chd free. Weds May 11, 18, 25, June 1, 8, 15 (11-5). Also private visits welcome, please* Tel 0380 850455

Castle Combe Gardens Chippenham 5m M4 exit 17 S B4039 Chippenham Burton. Large car park clearly signed at top of hill. Originally Norman, now mostly C15, one of England's prettiest villages. Map of gardens available.

TEAS in village. *Combined adm £1.50 Chd free. Sat, Sun July 2, 3 (2-6)*

> **Dower House** (Margaret, Viscountess Long of Wraxall). The house is an architectural feature in the centre of the village, with 4½ acres of terrace garden largely in the course of restoration; trees, herbaceous borders; shrub roses. Good view from top
> **Preedy's Cottage** & (Mr & Mrs J A L Timpson) Roses, herbaceous border, summer bedding, lawns, swimming pool (not open)
> **61 Whitegate** & (Mr & Mrs C J Pratt) Small garden with all-year-round planting. An example of care and initiative in achieving variety in a small garden.

Conock Manor &✿❀ (Mr & Mrs Bonar Sykes) 5m SE of Devizes off A342. Mixed borders, flowering shrubs; extensive replanting including new arboretum and woodland walk. C18 house in Bath stone (not shown). TEA. *Adm £1 Chd 20p free under 5 (Share to Chirton Church, Chirton, nr Devizes®). Sun May 8 (2-6)*

Corsham Court &❀ (The Lord Methuen) 4m W of Chippenham. S of A4. Park and gardens laid out by Capability Brown and Repton. Lge lawns with fine specimens of ornamental trees; rose garden; lily pond with Indian bean trees; spring bulbs; young arboretum; C18 bath house; Elizabethan mansion with alterations. *Adm gardens £2 OAP £1.50 Chd £1 (Share to RNLI®);* ▲*For NGS Suns Apr 17, June 19 (2-6)*

Courtlands &✿ (Mr Julius Silman) 4m S of Chippenham on Corsham-Lacock Road, 2m E of Corsham. 4-acre formal garden divided by splendid yew hedges into three connecting lawned gardens. Features include 2 gazebos; sunken lily pond with fountain, large fish pond with waterfall; walled kitchen garden; greenhouse with vines. Use of heated swimming pool available £1. TEAS. *Adm £1.50 Chd under 10 free. Sun July 10 (2-6)*

The Courts &✿ (National Trust) Holt, 2m E of Bradford-on-Avon, S of B3107 to Melksham. In Holt follow National Trust signs, park at Village Hall. 3½-acres different formal gardens divided by yew hedges, raised terraces and shrubberies. Features incl conservatory, lily pond, herbaceous borders, pleached limes with interesting stone pillars, venetian gates and stone ornaments. 3½-acres wildflower and arboretum; many fine trees. NT C15 House (not shown) open every day except Sat April to Oct. Plant sales in aid of Bath Cancer Research Unit. Teas (on NGS days only) in village hall in aid of Village Hall Fund. *Adm £2.50 Chd £1.50. For NGS Sats July 2, Sept 3 (2-5)*

Crudwell Court Hotel &❀ (Nicholas Bristow Esq) Crudwell. On the A429 between Cirencester and Malmesbury. E of the rd, beside the church. 2½-acre garden surrounding C17 Rectory (now a hotel). Fine specimen 'rivers' beech, blue atlas cedar, magnolias, C12 dovecote surrounded by ancient yew hedges; Victorian sunken pond with wrought iron surround and lavender hedging. Newly planted rose garden and spring colour border outside conservatory. Herbaceous; shrub and herb borders; climbing roses; espaliered fruit trees and an Edwardian wooded walk in process of restoration. Swimming pool available in July. Coffee, lunch TEAS. *Adm £1 Chd free. Suns March 27, July 10 (11-5)*

Easton Grey House &❀ (Mr & Mrs Sheldon Gordon) 3½m W of Malmesbury on B4040. Intensively cultivated 9-acre garden of beautiful C18 house. Also contains Easton Grey Church with its interesting Norman tower, font etc. Superb situation overlooking R. Avon and surrounding countryside; lime-tolerant shrubs; tremendous display of spring bulbs, clematis, many roses; large walled garden containing traditional kitchen garden, large green-houses, rose garden and borders. Home-made TEAS in garden; produce, cake, and other stalls (in aid of Easton Grey Parish Church). *Adm £1.50 Chd free. Sun April 10 (2-6)*

Edington and Coulston Gardens 4m Westbury on B3098 halfway between Westbury and West Lavington. Follow signs and park outside Monastery garden or in Church car park for the Old Vicarage and walk up to B3098. TEAS at Monastery Garden. *Combined adm £2 Chd free (Share to Wiltshire Garden Trust®). Sun June 12 (2-6)*

Bonshommes Cottage (Michael Jones Esq). Through Old Vicarage Garden. ¼-acre garden, formerly part of the Vicarage garden with mixed herbaceous, roses, shrubs. An interesting feature is the control of Japanese knotweed, which divides the garden into different areas

Font House ✗ (Mr & Mrs R S Hicks) Coulston. 1½m E of Edington on B3090 take 1st L to Coulston, 1st house on L. 1-acre garden in rural surroundings which has been restored from a wilderness over past 30yrs and is still evolving; on two levels with courtyard, herbaceous borders, shrubs, herb and small specimen trees

The Monastery Garden & (The Hon Mrs Douglas Vivian) 2½-acre garden with many varieties of spring bulbs; orchard and shrub roses; mediaeval walls of national importance

The Old Vicarage &✗❀ (J N d'Arcy Esq) A 2-acre garden on greensand situated on hillside with fine views; Intensively planted with herbaceous borders; shrubs; a small arboretum with a growing range of trees; woodland plants; bulbs; lilies and recently introduced species from abroad. NCCPG National Collection of Evening primroses, over 20 species

Fonthill House ✗❀ (The Lord Margadale) 3m N of Tisbury. W of Salisbury via B3089 in Fonthill Bishop. Large woodland garden; daffodils, rhododendrons, azaleas, shrubs, bulbs; magnificent views; formal garden, limited for wheelchairs. TEAS. *Adm £1.50 Chd 30p (Share to Community Mediqui© - May 22 only). Suns April 10, May 22 (2-6)*

Foscote Gardens ✗❀ Grittleton, 5m NW of Chippenham. A420 Chippenham-Bristol; after 2m turn right on B4039 to Yatton Keynell, fork right for Grittleton; in village for 2m, just over motorway turn right at Xrds; house on right. Home-made TEAS. *Combined adm £1.50 Chd 30p. Sun June 5 (2-6)*

Foscote Stables ✗❀ (Mr & Mrs Barry Ratcliffe) 2½-acres; many clematis; shrub roses; unusual shrubs, trees; small collection ornamental ducks

Foscote Stables Cottage ❀ (Mrs Beresford Worswick) This adjoining garden has been re-designed and replanted but still retains its cottage character

¶Goulters Mill Farm ✗❀ (Mr & Mrs Michael Harvey) Nettleton. On B4039 5m W of Chippenham; 2m N of Castle Combe, through the Gibb. Park at top of 300 metre drive and walk down to garden. Approx ¾-acre cottage garden; mixed perennials, eremurus, old-fashioned roses; water garden and woodland walk. Home-made cream TEAS and plant stall in aid of Russian Immigrants to Israel. *Adm £1 Chd 20p. Sun June 19 (2-6)*

Great Chalfield Manor ✗❀ (The National Trust; Mr & Mrs Robert Floyd) 4m from Melksham. Take B3107 from Melksham then 1st R to Broughton Gifford signed Atworth, turn L for 1m to Manor. Park on grass outside. Garden and grounds of 7 acres laid out 1905-12 by Robert Fuller and his wife; given to NT in 1943, it remains the home of his family. Garden paths, steps, dry walls relaid and rebuilt in 1985 and roses replanted; daffodils, spring flowers; topiary houses, borders, terraces, gazebo, orchard, autumn border. C15 moated manor (not open) and adjoining Church. Harvest Festival Service 6pm Oct 2. TEA. *Adm £1 Chd free (Share to All Saints Church®).* ▲*For NGS Sun Oct 2 (2-6) Sun Feb 12, 1995 (2-4)*

The Hall ✗ (Dr A E Moulton) Bradford-on-Avon. Nr town centre on B3107. Lge garden beside R Avon with lawns, fine trees incl row of Irish yews; interesting acoustic baffle fence. Fine example of Jacobean house set on high terrace. TEAS. *Adm £1.50 Chd 50p (Share to Holy Trinity Church Roof Fund®). Sun June 5 (2-6)*

Hannington Hall & (Mrs A F Hussey Freke) Hannington. 5m N of Swindon. 2m NW of Highworth; from B4019 Highworth-Blunsdon, at Freke Arms, turn N for Hannington. 3 acres. Interesting trees and shrubs. Walled kitchen gardden. Well preserved ice house. Very interesting house built 1653. TEAS. *Adm £1 Chd free. Sun July 10 (2-6)*

Hazelbury Manor Gardens &✗❀ nr Box. 5m SW of Chippenham; 5m NE of Bath; 3m N of Bradford-on-Avon. From A4 at Box, take A365 to Melksham, L onto B3109; L again at Chapel Plaister; drive immediately on R. 8 acres of Grade II landscaped formal gardens surrounding a charming C15 fortified manor house. An impressive yew topiary and clipped beeches surround the large lawn; herbaceous and mixed borders blaze in summer; laburnums and limes form splendid walkways. Other features include rose garden, stone ring ponds, an enchanting fountain and rockery. Beyond the house is a new plantation of specimen trees. TEAS. *Adm Gardens only £2.80 OAPs £2 Chd £1. Open weekends, Bank Hols, Thurs from May 28 to Sept 29. For NGS Sats, Suns June 25, 26 (2-6)*

Heale Gardens & Plant Centre &❀ (Mr Guy Rasch & Lady Anne Rasch) Middle Woodford, 4m N of Salisbury on Woodford Valley Rd between A360 and A345. 8-acres beside R Avon; interesting and varied collection of plants, shrubs; and roses in formal setting of clipped hedges and mellow stonework surrounding C17 manorhouse where Charles II hid after the battle of Worcester. Water garden with magnolia and acer frames, an authentic Japanese Tea House and Nikki bridge. Well stocked plant centre. Gift shop. Open all year. TEAS in the house on NGS Sunday only. *Adm £2.50 Accompanied chd under 14 free. For NGS Sun Aug 7 (10-5)*

Hillbarn House ✗ (Mr & Mrs A J Buchanan) Great Bedwyn, SW of Hungerford. S of A4 Hungerford-Marlborough. Medium-sized garden on chalk with hornbeam tunnel, pleached limes, herb garden; some planting by Lanning Roper; a series of gardens within a garden. Swimming pool may be used (under 12) Topiary. TEA. *Adm £2 Chd 50p. Suns June 19, Sept 18 (2-6)*

Hoddinotts House ⌂✗🐕 (Mr & Mrs George Medley) Tisbury. 1m N of Tisbury on the rd to Hindon. Signposted from B3089 at Fonthill Bishop. 3m from the A303. 1-acre garden developed from a field since 1974 by two horticulturists. Ornamental borders with shrubs and trees; fruit garden, vegetable garden, greenhouses and frames in an attractive rural setting. Ample parking. TEAS. *Adm £1.50 Chd 50p (Share to WWF UK®). Sun July 3 (2-6)*

Hodges Barn Shipton Moyne, See Gloucestershire

Home Covert ⌂🐕 (Mr & Mrs John F Phillips) Roundway Devizes. 1m N of Devizes on minor rd signed Roundway linking A361 to A342. 1m from each main road, house signed. An extensive garden developed since 1960 by present owners, with many unusual trees, shrubs, and hardy plants. Formal herbaceous borders and water gardens 80ft below with waterfall, streams and a small lake planted with bog primulas and various waterside plants. Also many varieties hydrangeas and late-flowering clematis. Featured in NGS video 2, see page 344. TEAS on July 24 in aid of St James Church Repair Fund. *Adm £1.50 Chd free (Share to Dorothy House Foundation®). Sun July 24, Wed Aug 17 (2-6). Private visits welcome please* **Tel 0380 723407**

Hyde's House 🐕 (George Cruddas Esq) Dinton. 5m W of Wilton, off B3089, next to church. 2 acres of wild and formal garden in beautiful situation with series of hedged garden rooms and numerous shrub and herbaceous borders. Much interest in layout, old and new planting especially shrub roses. Lge walled kitchen garden, herb garden and C11 dovecote (open). Charming C16/18 Grade 1 listed house (not open), with lovely courtyard; short walk to lake; TEAS in adjacent thatched 'old school room'. *Adm £1.50 Chd free. Suns May 29, Aug 28 (2-5)*

Iford Manor (Mrs J J Cartwright-Hignett) Off A36 7 miles south of Bath – sign to Iford 1 mile or from Bradford-on-Avon/Trowbridge via Lower Westwood village (Brown Signs). Entrance & free parking at Iford Bridge. Very romantic Italian-style terraced garden, listed Grade 1, home of Harold Peto between 1898 and 1933. House not shown. *Adm £2 OAPs/Student/Chd 10+ £1.50. Open daily May to Sept (except Mons & Fris), April & Oct Suns only. For NGS Sun April 24 (2-5)*

Inwoods ⌂✗🐕 (Mr & Mrs D S Whitehead) Farleigh Wick, 3m NW of Bradford-on-Avon. From Bath via A363 towards Bradford-on-Avon; at Farleigh Wick, 100yds past Fox & Hounds, right into drive. 5 acres with lawns, borders, flowering shrubs, wild garden, bluebell wood. TEAS in aid of Home Farm Trust. *Adm £1.50 Chd 50p. Sun May 1 (2-6)*

Job's Mill 🐕 (Virginia, Marchioness of Bath) Crockerton, 1½m S of Warminster. Bus: Salisbury-Bath, alight War-

minster. Medium-sized garden; small terraced garden, through which R. Wylye flows; swimming pool; kitchen garden. TEAS. *Adm £1.50 Chd 50p (Share to WWF®). Sun June 19 (2-6)*

Kingfisher Mill (The Hon Aylmer Tryon) Gt Durnford. 2m Amesbury. From A345 turn W at High Post. Or 1m from Bridge Inn at Upper Woodford. Park in Village Road. Down short avenue of poplars. 3-acres very watery garden on R. Avon with primulas and wild garden to encourage butterflies and show beauty of wild flowers. Good daffodils from Lionel Richardson's nursery in Waterford. Spring bulbs and variety of magnolias. In June many athletic roses up willows. Garden begun 1962 from old water meadow by enthusiastic amateur. Tea at Black Horse in village. *Adm £1.50 Chd free (Share to Wiltshire Wildlife Trust®). Sun April 10, June 26 (2-5.30)*

Lackham Gardens ⌂✗🐕 (Lackham College Principal Peter Morris) Lacock, 2m S of Chippenham. Signposted N of Notton on A350. Few mins S of junction 17 on M4. Station: Chippenham. Bus: Chippenham-Trowbridge, alight drive entrance, 1m. Large gardens; walled garden with greenhouses, carnations, alstroemeria, pot plants, warm greenhouse plants, giant fruited Citron tree, propagating house, fuchsias, begonias; lawn paths separating plots well laid out, labelled with great variety of interesting shrubs, usual and unusual vegetables, herbaceous plants, fruit. Modern style Bradstone paved garden and gazebo. Willow pattern bridge and pool. Sculpture exhibition in the gardens. Pleasure gardens featuring a major historical collection of roses depicting the development of the modern rose; mixed borders, herbs, shrubs, lawns; woodland walks down to river; large bird viewing hide. Raffle drawn shortly after demonstrations at 3.30pm; in walled garden (May 1) Patio Planters for summer. (July 17), summer shrub cuttings. (Oct 2), splitting herbaceous perennials. Particulars of Lackham full and part-time courses available. Museum of Agricultural Equipment, RARE breeds. Adventure playground. Coffee shop; TEAS Bookable menu etc on request within coach party organiser pack (11-4). *Adm £3 Chd £1 (Share to Horticultural Therapy of Frome, Somerset®). Open daily Mar 26 to Nov 6. For NGS Suns May 1, July 17, Oct 2 (2-5)*

Lacock Abbey Gardens ⌂✗ (National Trust) Chippenham. A350 midway between Melksham-Chippenham Road. Follow National Trust signs. Use public car park just outside the Abbey. 9 acres of parkland surrounding the Abbey with a pond and exotic tree specimens. Display of early spring flowers with carpets of aconites; snowdrops; crocuses and daffodils. C13 Abbey with C18 gothic additions (not open till April). Teas available in village. *Adm £1 Chd free. Suns Feb 20, 27, Mar 6 (2-5). 1995 Suns Feb 19, 26, Mar 5 (2-5)*

Landford Lodge ⌂🐕 (Mr & Mrs Christopher Pilkington) 9m SE of Salisbury turn W off A36; garden ½m N of Landford. C18 House (not open) in lovely parkland overlooking lake; many fine trees. Special feature 3-acre wood with rhododendrons and azaleas. Herbaceous; ornamental terrace and swimming pool (open). Tree nursery. 500 varieties of trees planted in alphabetical order in walled garden. TEAS. *Adm £1.50 Chd 50p. Sun June 5 (2-5)*

Langley House &&& (Mrs A L Scott-Ashe) Langley Burrell. 2m NE of Chippenham on A420; 300yds from Langley Burrell rd junction. 5-acre formal garden and parkland; magnificent old trees; mainly herbaceous with shrubs, old-fashioned roses and lily pool. Lovely old coach house and stabling. C18 Georgian Manor (not open); C12 Saxon Church with Kilvert the diarist connections (open). TEAS. *Adm £1 Chd free (Share to ARMS®). Sun June 12 (2-6)*

Little Durnford Manor (Earl & Countess of Chichester) 3m N of Salisbury, just beyond Stratford-sub-Castle. Extensive lawns with cedars; walled gardens, fruit trees, large vegetable garden; small knot and herb gardens, terraces, borders, gravel garden, water garden, lake with islands, river walks. Cottage Garden also on view. Home-made TEAS. *Adm £1.50 Chd 50p (Share to Wessex Medical School Trust®). Suns May 1, June 12 (2-6)*

Lockeridge House &&& (Mr & Mrs P Lowsley-Williams) Lockeridge. 2m W of Marlborough via A4 turn S, ¼m on R. 2 acres with R Kennet running through; herbaceous rose garden, shrub roses. Ornamental vegetable, herb garden and spring bulbs. TEAS. *Adm £1.50 Chd free. Sun April 3 (2-5)*

Long Hall &&& (Mr & Mrs N H Yeatman-Biggs) Stockton 7m SE of Warminster; S of A36, W of A303 Wylye interchange. Follow signs to church in Stockton. 4-acre mainly formal garden; a series of gardens within a garden; clipped yews; flowering shrubs, fine old trees; masses of spring bulbs; fine hellebore walk. C13 Hall with later additions (not open). TEAS on NGS days. *Adm £2 Chd free. 1st Sat of every month from May 7 to August 6 (2-6) or by appt, please* **Tel 0985 50424** *Adjacent nursery specialising in organically grown plants and bulbs Wed to Sun March 23 to Oct 2 (9.30-6) For NGS Mon April 4, Sun June 26 (2-6)*

¶**Lower Burytown** &&& (Capt Francis Burne) Blunsdon. 1m off B4019 half-way between Blunsdon and Highworth. 1¼m from A419; 8m from M4 exit 15. Approached by 1m drive off B4019. 3-acre garden has been entirely made in last 3 yrs; contains herbaceous borders, shrubs and a water garden. TEA. *Adm £1 Chd 50p (Share to St Leonards Parish Church®). Sun July 3 (2-6)*

Lower Farm House &&& (Mrs John Agate) Milton Lilbourne. E of Pewsey on B3087. Turn down village street by garage at Xrds. Leave shop on R and Lower Farm House is 75yds beyond on L opposite farm yard. An enlarged and developing 7-acre landscaped garden designed by Tim Rees and planted over the last 5 years with recent new planting. The garden faces south with views to the N edge of Salisbury Plain over two ponds with a connecting stream. Winter garden; extensive spring bulbs; water garden; shrubs and herbaceous borders; extensive lawns; young trees chosen for their bark; mature trees; gazebo; kitchen garden. Conservatory; exhibition of plans and photographs showing garden development. Teas at The Old Bakery, Milton Lilbourne on Aug 7 only, entrance £1. *Adm £1.50 Chd free (Share to The Life-Anew Trust, East Knoyle®). Sun April 17, Aug 7 (2-6). Also private visits welcome March to Sept, please* **Tel 0672 62911** *or* **62096 (answer phone)**

Luckington Court &&& (The Hon Mrs Trevor Horn) Luckington village, 10m NW of Chippenham; 6m W of Malmesbury. Turn S off B4040 Malmesbury-Bristol. Bus: Bristol-Swindon, alight Luckington. Medium-sized garden, mainly formal, well-designed, amid exquisite group of ancient buildings; fine collection of ornamental cherries; other flowering shrubs. House much altered in Queen Anne times but ancient origins evident; Queen Anne hall and drawing-room shown. TEAS in aid of Luckington Parish Church. *Collecting box. Sun May 15 (2.30-6)*

Luckington Manor &&& (Mr & Mrs K Stanbridge) N.W. of Chippenham 7½ S.W. of Malmesbury on the B4040 Malmesbury-Bristol. 3½ acres, walled flower gardens; with many additions of unusual and special plants, shrubberies; arboretum. Sunken rose garden, well garden, herbs and healing plants. New extensive spring bulb feature. C17 Manor House (not open) Home-made TEAS, cake and other stalls in aid of St Mary & St Ethelbert Luckington Parish Church Roof Fund June 26 only. *Adm £2 Senior Citizens £1 Chd free. Suns April 24, June 26, July 24 (2-6)*

Maiden Bradley House &&& (The Duke & Duchess of Somerset) Maiden Bradley; 7m SW of Warminster, 1m Longleat, 3m Stourhead. Large garden; lawn; trees; herbaceous borders; woodland walk & extensive views. Early C18 house (not open). Church C11 (open). TEAS. Games and Stalls. *Adm £2 Chd 50p. (Share to Maiden Bradley Church®). Sun June 5 (2.30 5)*

Manningford Bruce House &&& (Maj & Mrs Robert Ferguson) Manningford Bruce 2m SW of Pewsey on A345 on right after Manningford Bruce sign. From Upavon to Devizes 1m after Woodbridge Inn on L. 1½ acres; lawns, shrubbery and walled garden of C17/C18 Rectory (not open). Herbaceous borders with many unusual plants, shrubs and a folly. Small kitchen garden. Owner maintained. Tea in aid of Church. *Adm £1 Chd free. Sun June 26 (2-6)*

Manningford Gardens and Nursery &&& 2m SW of Pewsey on A345. Turn right at Nursery sign to Manningford Bruce; through village and over railway, nursery on right. Display gardens, featuring exciting colour combinations of white/yellow, pink/red, blue/orange. An astrological garden and patchwork quilt garden are under construction. There is a box maze planted to celebrate the International Year of the Maze in 1991. The nursery specialises in cottage garden plants. *The gardens are open daily except Dec 25 to Jan 2. Adm free but donations welcome, these are divided equally between the NGS and maintenance of the gardens. For the NGS when the private garden is open.* TEAS. *Adm £1 Chd free. Suns June 5, July 10, Sept 18 (10.30-5)*

By Appointment Gardens. These owners do not have a fixed opening day usually because they do not like crowds or have insufficient parking space. Owner will often give guided tour.

Manor House Farm &✗ (Miss Anne Dixon) Hanging Langford. 9m NW of Salisbury S of A36 Salisbury-Warminster. 3m SE of A303 Wylye interchange. Follow signs from Steeple Langford. Series of walled gardens with masses of bulbs; herbaceous plants; many shrubs; old-fashioned roses; collection of clematis; paeonies and delphiniums. Ornamental pond; secret garden in walls of old shearing barn, superb walnut, C14/16 Wiltshire manor house (not open). Opening coincides with exhibition of Langford pedigree lambs and sheep ¼m down the road. Teas Hanging Langford Village Hall in aid of Village Hall Fund. *Adm £1.50 Chd free. Sun April 10 (2-6)*

¶**The Mead Nursery** ✗❀ (Mr & Mrs S Lewis-Dale) E of Rudge, N of railway, equidistant Frome and Westbury, between Rudge and Brokerswood. Follow signs to Woodland Park. 1-acre nursery and garden specialising in unusual herbaceous perennials and alpines; herbaceous display beds giving ideas on colour and design; raised beds and sink garden with planted tufa for alpines. Production part of nursery open on NGS days only when over 500 different varieties of plants in stock. Tufa rock and hypertufa sinks available. TEA. *Adm 50p Chd free. Feb 2 to Oct 30 Wed to Sat (9-5) Sun (2-5). For NGS Sats, Suns July 16, 17, Sept 17, 18 (2-6)*

Normanton Down ❀ (Mr & Mrs Brian Carr) Wilsford-cum-Lake. Old Stonehenge Rd from Amesbury turn L to Lake and Woodford. Follow signs for 2m. 2-acre garden recently planted and still being developed by owner from downland. Yew hedges bordering rose and shrub garden; surrounded by trees, shrubs and shrub roses in informal setting. *Adm £1.50 Chd free (Share to Cancer Research Campaign®). Sun June 26 (2-6) Private visits welcome, please* **Tel 0980 623270**

7 Norton Bavant &✗❀ (Mr & Mrs J M Royds) nr Warminster. 2m E of Warminster turn S to Sutton Veny at Heytesbury roundabout, then R to Norton Bavant. Turn R in village 1st house on R after tall conifer hedge. Unusual alpine plant collector's garden with over 300 varieties of a 30 year collection. Alpine house, several troughs and specialised collection of daphnes. Members of AGS especially welcome. *Adm 75p Chd free. Sun May 22 (2-6). Private parties also welcome April to July, please* **Tel 0985 40491**

Oare House & (Henry Keswick Esq) 2m N of Pewsey on Marlborough Rd (A345). Fine house (not open) in lge garden with fine trees, hedges, spring flowers, woodlands; extensive lawns and kitchen garden. TEA. *Adm £1 Chd 20p (Share to The Order of St John®). Suns April 24, July 24 (2-6)*

The Old Bakery &✗❀ (Joyce, Lady Crossley) Milton Lilbourne E of Pewsey on B3087. Turn down village street by garage at X-rds. The Old Bakery is opp churchyard. Fairly intensive 1-acre garden. Mixed shrub and herbaceous plantings. 3 small glasshouses; small rock garden; some rare plants. Home-made TEAS. *Adm £1 Chd free. Sun Aug 7 (2-6)*

The Old Rectory &✗❀ (Mr & Mrs David Harrison) Stockton. 7m SE of Warminster, S of A36 W of A303 Wylye interchange. The Old Rectory is just beyond the church. The 2-acre garden surrounds an attractive C18 house, with lawns and some fine old trees incl a cedar and a magnificent beech, in the front. To the S it splits into several smaller gardens; an entirely walled herb garden with a variety of herbs, leavened with climbers and some fine roses and vines; and the orchard, dominated by a stunning walnut tree, leads to three separate smaller walled gardens with a great variety of plants incl roses and peonies. TEAS. *Adm £1 Chd free. Sun June 5 (2-6)*

¶**Parks Court** ❀ (Michael Upsall Esq) 2m N of Warminster, approach from Warminster bypass or from A36 taking Upton Scudamore signs. Parks Court is 350yds E of church. 1-acre garden established a few years ago in an old setting. Different levels, some formality and compartments. TEAS and plants in aid of St Mary's Church. *Adm £1.50. Sun June 26 (2-6)*

Pound Hill House &✗❀ (Mr & Mrs P Stockitt) West Kington. 8m NNW of Chippenham, 2m NE of Marshfield exit 18 on M4 take A420 Chippenham-Bristol road N signed West Kington. At village take NO Through Road at Xrds. Around C15 Cotswold Stone House 2-acre garden in charming setting. The garden is made up of small gardens, an old-fashioned rose garden with clipped box, a small Victorian vegetable garden, pergola with wisteria, roses, clematis; a grass walk with large shrub roses, herbaceous borders backed by clipped yew hedges, re-designed shade and water garden. Courtyard garden with clipped yews and box, paved area with interesting plants in tubs, raised alpine beds. Very extensive retail plant area with plants drawn from adjacent nursery with 2000 varieties. *Open Wed to Sun and bank hols April 6 to Sept 25. TEAS in aid of Orchard Vale Trust - June 26, West Kington Church -Sept 4, June 26, Sept 4 (2-6)*

¶**Pythouse** ✗❀ (Country Houses Association) Semley. 4m NNE of Shaftesbury. Semley is E of A350. Turn N by public house on Semley Green, over railway bridge, entrance straight ahead. A parkland garden, sweeping lawns, panoramic views, woodland walk with rhododendrons, daffodils and bluebells, ice-house and orangery, magnificent house built in 1725 with Palladian elevation added in 1805 (not open). TEAS. *Adm £1 Chd free. Sun May 8 (2.30-5)*

Ridleys Cheer &✗❀ (Mr & Mrs A J Young) Mountain Bower, N Wraxall. 8m NW of Chppenham. At 'The Shoe' on A420 8m W of Chippenham turn N then take 2nd L and 1st R. 1½-acre informal garden containing interesting and unusual trees and shrubs; many shrub roses including hybrid musks and spring flowers; planted progressively over past 20 yrs; also 2 acres woodland planted 1989 including a number of less common oaks; Cream TEAS in aid of N Wraxall Church and Orchard Vale Trust. *Adm £1 Chd free. Suns May 8, June 26 (2-6.30)*

Salisbury Close Gardens & 2 gardens in Salisbury Cathedral Close. TEAS. *Adm £1 each garden Chd free. Fri June 17 (11-5)*

¶**Braybrooke House** (Mrs Kate Christopherson) ¾-acre garden in the Close, leading down to R Avon, made by present owner in 5 yrs. Herbaceous border, roses, lilies, clematis and shrubs; young orchard; summer house

Mompesson House ఈ⚘⚘ (The National Trust) The Close. The appeal of this comparatively small but attractive garden is the lovely setting in Salisbury Cathedral Close and with a well-known Queen Anne House. Planting as for an old English garden with raised rose and herbaceous beds around the lawn. Climbers on pergola and walls; shrubs and small lavender walk

Sharcott Manor ఈ⚘⚘ (Capt & Mrs David Armytage) 1m SW of Pewsey via A345. 5 acre garden with water planted for yr-round interest. Many young trees, bulbs, climbers & densely planted mixed borders of shrubs, roses, perennials and unusual plants, some of which are for sale in the small garden nursery. TEAS. *Adm £2 Chd free (Share to IFAW©). Sun June 26 (2-6) First Weds in every month from April to Oct (11-5) all for NGS. Also private visits welcome, please* **Tel 0672 63485**

Sheldon Manor ఈ⚘ (Maj M A Gibbs) 1½m W of Chippenham turn S off A420 at Allington Xrds. Eastbound traffic signed also from A4. Formal garden around C13 house (700-yrs-old); collection of old-fashioned roses in profusion; very old yew trees; many rare, interesting trees and shrubs. Maze of edible plants (in late summer). Homemade BUFFET LUNCHES (licensed) and cream TEAS. *Adm house & garden £3 OAPs £2.75p; Chd over 11 £1. Garden only £2, OAPs £1.75. Easter Sunday & Mon then every Sun, Thur & Bank Hol to Oct 2. For NGS wine and refreshments Sun June 17 (6pm-10pm)*

Sherston Gardens ⚘⚘ High Street, Sherston. 5m from Malmesbury. *Combined adm £1.50 Chd free. Sun June 12 (2-6)*
  Balcony House (Mrs E M J Byrne) Oldest house in Sherston. Small garden with old-fashioned roses, some topiary, small white garden with yew hedge separating it from coloured garden. Acid bed with azaleas, rhododendrons, acers etc. Conservatory *(Share to Multiple Sclerosis®)*
  Foresters House ఈ⚘ (R Creed Esq) Cotswold stone walled garden. Professionally designed for enthusiastic owner, planted 1984. Many interesting plants, particularly herbaceous; pond; pergola. TEAS in aid of Sherston Parish Church

Spye Park ⚘⚘ (Mr & Mrs Simon Spicer) Take A342 Chippenham and Devizes rd, turn E at Sandy Lane opp 'The George' public house. Turn S after ½m at White Lodge. Follow signs to car park. Exit only through the village of Chittoe. 25-acre woodland walk through carpets of bluebells with paths cut through the wood. Some fine old trees mostly oak and beech, survivors of the 1989 hurricane, incl the remnants of 1000 yr old King Oak with the 900-yr-old Queen still alive. *Adm £1 Chd free. Sun May 1 (11-5)*

Stourhead Garden ఈ⚘ (The National Trust) Stourton, 3m NW of Mere on B3092. One of earliest and greatest landscape gardens in the world; creation of banker Henry Hoare in 1740s on his return from the Grand Tour, inspired by paintings of Claude and Poussin; planted with rare trees, rhododendrons and azaleas over last 240yrs. Open every day of year. Lunch, tea and supper Spread Eagle Inn at entrance. NT shop. Teas (Buffet service Village Hall). *Adm March to October £4.10 Chd £2.10 parties of 15 or over £3.20. Nov to Feb Adult £2.60 Chd 1.30. For NGS Sun May 15 (8-7)*

¶**Swaynes Mead** ఈ (Lady Poett) Great Durnford. 2m SW of Amesbury, W of A345 Salisbury Rd. In Great Durnford village between Black Horse Inn and Kingfisher Mill. Park in village. Nearly 2 acres mature village garden made by present owner over 25 yrs. Shrubs, roses, clematis, apple trees and many unusual plants. Teas at Black Horse Inn. *Adm £1 Chd free. Sun June 26 (2-6)*

Thompson's Hill ⚘⚘ (Mr & Mrs J C Cooper) Sherston. 5m Malmesbury-Tetbury. In Sherston village turn left at Church down hill, bear right up Thompson's Hill. ½-acre fully planted, interestingly designed garden made since 1980. Pretty conservatory added to house 1992. Illustrated in 'House & Garden' Magazine, new issue 'The Englishwoman's Garden', 'The English Garden' by Peter Coates and the 'Good Gardens Guide'. *Adm £1.50 Chd 50p (Share to Cancer Research®). Sun June 12 (2-6.30). Private visits welcome please* **Tel 0666 840 766**

Waterdale House ⚘ (Mr & Mrs Julian Seymour) Milton, East Knoyle. North of East Knoyle on A350 turn westwards signed Milton, garden signed from village. 4-acre mature woodland garden with rhododendrons, azaleas, camellias, maples, magnolias, ornamental water and bog garden; herbaceous borders and hydrangeas. New gravelled pot garden. TEAS if fine. *Adm £1.50 Chd free. Suns April 3 to June 5. For NGS Suns May 8, July 17 (2-5.30)*

Wedhampton Gardens ఈ⚘ 5m SE of Devizes. Off N side of A342 (nr junction with B3098). TEAS. *Combined Adm £2.50 chd free. Sun June 19 (2-6)*
  ¶**Wedhampton Cottage** (Hon K & Mrs Fraser) Large cottage garden, lawns, shrubs, trees, herbaceous beds around unusual "cottage ornée" (not open)
  Wedhampton Manor (C V C Harris Esq) 2½ acres informal gardens with new and developing borders amongst the long-established. Many fine old and new trees incl remarkable rare cut leaf lime. Herbaceous border, interesting variety of shrubs, herb, vegetable and fruit gardens incl medlar, mulberry, quince and espaliered apple and pear. Greenhouses and fine William and Mary house (not open)

¶**West House** ఈ⚘⚘ (Col & Mrs Charles Lane) 12 West St, Warminster. On outskirts of Warminster on A362 Frome rd. Well-established 2-acre walled garden with ancient tulip tree. Fine collection of old roses, herbaceous borders, herb and kitchen garden. Teas at **Parks Court, Upton Scudamore**. *Adm £1.50 Chd free. Sun June 26 (2-6)*

¶**Westwood Manor** (The National Trust: Mr & Mrs Jonathan Azis) 1½m SW of Bradford on Avon, in Westwood village beside church (open). Village signposted off Bradford on Avon-Rode rd (B3109). Turning to garden opp The New Inn at E side of village. C20 topiary garden, including topiary cottage. 2 small lily ponds; box walk; NT C15 stone manor house (not open) and tythe barn (open). TEAS in aid of WI in Parish Room by church. House open every Tues, Wed, Sun April 1 to end Sept. *Adm £1 Chd 50p. For NGS Sats July 2, Sept 3 (2-6)*

Worton Gardens ᕽ᙮᙮ Devizes 3m. Devizes-Salisbury A360 turn W in Potterne or just N of West Lavington. From Seend turn S at Bell Inn, follow signs to Worton. TEAS at Ivy House. *Combined adm £2 Chd free. Sun July 10 (2-6)*

Ashton House (Mrs Colin Shand) ½-acre garden in 3 sections with herbaceous borders, many shrubs and birch grove; walled courtyard and raised vegetable garden; lovely views across Avon Vale

Ivy House (Lt Gen Sir Maurice and Lady Johnston) 2-acre series of gardens separated by yew hedges and walls; herbaceous borders; shrubs; pond garden with maples; courtyard garden and many fine trees incl swamp cypress, holm and pin oak, medlar and mulberry; interesting vegetable garden interplanted with fruit trees and large greenhouse

Oakley House ᙮ (Mr & Mrs Michael Brierley) ½-acre village garden with herbaceous borders, roses, many shrubs; small pond and bog garden within a rockery; planted by owners since 1974

Springfield Cottage (Group Captain & Mrs D N Corbyn) Cottage garden redesigned since 1983 with small pond, herbaceous plants and shrubs

Worcestershire

See Hereford

Yorkshire & Cleveland

Hon County Organisers:
(N Yorks - Districts of Hambleton, Richmond, Ryedale, Scarborough & Cleveland)

Mrs William Baldwin, Riverside Farm, Sinnington, York YO6 6RY
Tel 0751 431764

(West & South Yorks & North Yorks Districts of Craven, Harrogate, Selby & York)

Mrs Roger Marshall, The Old Vicarage, Whixley, York YO5 8AR
Tel 0423 330474

DATES OF OPENING

By appointment
For telephone numbers and other details see garden descriptions. Private visits welcomed

Beacon Hill House, nr Ilkley
Brookfield, Oxenhope
Deanswood, Littlethorpe, nr Ripon
The Dower House, Great Thirkleby
Fairview, Smelthouses
Hemble Hill Farm, Guisborough
Hillbark, Bardsey
50 Hollins Lane, Hampsthwaite
Holly Cottage, Scholes
Kelberdale, Knaresborough
78 Leeds Road, Selby
Ling Beeches, Scarcroft, nr Leeds
The Mews Cottage, Harrogate
Nawton Tower, Nawton
Old Sleningford, Mickley
Otterington Hall, Northallerton
Plum Tree Cottage, Bramham
55 Rawcliffe Drive, York
Ryedale House, Helmsley
Silver Birches. Scarcroft
Sleightholme Dale Lodge, Fadmoor
Stonegate Cottage, nr Keighley
Tan Cottage, Cononley, nr Skipton
106 Vaughan Road, Barnsley
Victoria Cottage, Stainland
5 Wharfe Close, Leeds 16
Windy Ridge, Bolton Percy
York Gate, Adel, Leeds 16

York House, Claxton

Regular openings
For details see garden descriptions

Castle Howard, nr York. Every day March 18 to Oct 31
Constable Burton Hall Gardens. Daily April 1 to Oct 1
Gilling Castle, Gilling East. Daily July & Aug
Land Farm, nr Hebden Bridge. May to end of Aug Sats, Suns, Bank Hol Mons
Newby Hall, Ripon. Daily April to Sept except Mons
Shandy Hall, Coxwold. Open every afternoon except Sats
Stockeld Park, Wetherby. Thurs only April 7 to Oct 6

March 13 Sunday
Fairview, Smelthouses
April 3 Sunday
Netherwood House, Ilkley
Otterington Hall, Northallerton
April 4 Monday
St Nicholas, Richmond
April 9 Saturday
Victoria Cottage, Stainland
April 10 Sunday
Harlsey Manor, East Harlsey
Ling Beeches, Scarcroft, nr Leeds

Shandy Hall, Coxwold
Victoria Cottage, Stainland
April 17 Sunday
Betula & Bolton Percy Cemetery ‡
Boston Spa Gardens ‡
Parcevall Hall, nr Skipton
Plum Tree Cottage, Bramham ‡
Windy Ridge, Bolton Percy ‡
April 24 Sunday
Wytherstone House, nr Helmsley
May 8 Sunday
Silver Birches, Scarcroft
York House, Claxton
May 11 Wednesday
Beacon Hill House, nr Ilkley
May 15 Sunday
Coniston Hall, Coniston Cold
Stillingfleet Lodge, Stillingfleet
May 21 Saturday
Victoria Cottage, Stainland
May 22 Sunday
Fieldhead, Boston Spa ‡
Harlsey Manor, East Harlsey
Hemble Hill Farm, Guisborough
Hillbark, Bardsey ‡
Silver Birches, Scarcroft ‡
Victoria Cottage, Stainland
Wytherstone House, nr Helmsley
May 28 Saturday
Nawton Tower, Nawton
Old Sleningford, Mickley
May 29 Sunday
Betula & Bolton Percy Cemetery
Brookfield, Oxenhope

Hunmanby Grange, nr
Scarborough
Old Sleningford, Mickley
Nawton Tower, Nawton
Woodcock, Thirsk
May 30 Monday
Nawton Tower, Nawton
Old Sleningford, Mickley
Shandy Hall, Coxwold
June 4 Saturday
Pennyholme, Fadmoor
York Gate, Adel, Leeds 16
June 5 Sunday
Creskeld Hall, Arthington ‡
Elvington Gardens, nr York
Pennyholme, Fadmoor
The Riddings, Long Preston
Shadwell Grange, Leeds ‡
Sleightholme Dale Lodge,
Fadmoor
Snilesworth, Northallerton
York Gate, Adel, Leeds 16 ‡
June 6 Monday
St Nicholas, Richmond
June 10 Friday
Nunnington Hall, Helmsley
June 11 Saturday
Kelberdale, Knaresborough
Pennyholme, Fadmoor
Ryedale House, Helmsley
June 12 Sunday
Derwent House, Osbaldwick
Holly Cottage, Scholes
Kelberdale, Knaresborough
Littlethorpe Gardens, nr Ripon
Pennyholme, Fadmoor
Victoria Cottage, Stainland ‡
The Willows, nr Brighouse ‡
June 15 Wednesday
The Old Vicarage, Whixley

June 19 Sunday
Blackbird Cottage, Scampston
Fieldhead, Boston Spa
32 Hollybank Road, York ‡
Kelberdale, Knaresborough
78 Leeds Road, Selby ‡
55 Rawcliffe Drive, York ‡
Shandy Hall, Coxwold
Windsong, Osgodby ‡
Wytherstone House, nr Helmsley
June 22 Wednesday
Shandy Hall, Coxwold
June 26 Sunday
Bossall Hall, Bossall
Hillbark, Bardsey ‡
Low Askew, Cropton, Pickering
Ness Hall, Nunnington
Parcevall Hall, nr Skipton
Skipwith Hall, nr Selby ‡
Stillingfleet Lodge, Stillingfleet ‡
Stockeld Park, Wetherby ‡
Thornton Stud Gardens, Thirsk
June 29 Wednesday
Ness Hall, Nunnington
July 2 Saturday
Kelberdale, Knaresborough
July 3 Sunday
8 Dunstarn Lane, Adel
Hunmanby Grange, nr
Scarborough
Kelberdale, Knaresborough
Millgate House, Richmond
The Old Rectory, Mirfield
York House, Claxton
July 10 Sunday
Goddards, York
Grimston Gardens, Gilling East
Hovingham Hall, Hovingham
30 Latchmere Road, Leeds 16
78 Leeds Road, Selby

Otterington Hall, Northallerton
Shandy Hall, Coxwold
July 14 Thursday
Grimston Gardens, Gilling East
July 16 Saturday
Sleightholme Dale Lodge,
Fadmoor
July 17 Sunday
Beamsley Hall, nr Skipton
Bishopscroft, Sheffield
8 Dunstarn Lane, Adel ‡
30 Latchmere Road, Leeds 16 ‡
Sedbury Hall, nr Richmond
Sleightholme Dale Lodge,
Fadmoor
5 Wharfe Close, Leeds 16 ‡
Wytherstone House, nr Helmsley
July 24 Sunday
Bennet Grange, nr Sheffield ‡
61 Carsick Hill Crescent,
Sheffield ‡
30 Latchmere Road, Leeds 16
Springfield House, Tockwith
July 31 Sunday
30 Latchmere Road, Leeds 16
August 7 Sunday
Parcevall, Hall, nr Skipton
August 17 Wednesday
The Mews Cottage, Harrogate
August 28 Sunday
The White House, Husthwaite
September 18 Sunday
The Dower House, Great
Thirkleby
Maspin House, Hillam, nr Selby
September 25 Sunday
Fairview, Smelthouses
October 2 Sunday
Betula & Bolton Percy Cemetery

DESCRIPTIONS OF GARDENS

Beacon Hill House ✻✿ (Mr & Mrs D H Boyle) Langbar. 4m NW of Ilkley. 1¼m E of A59 at Bolton Bridge. Fairly large garden sheltered by woodland, situated at 900' on the southern slope of Beamsley Beacon. Several features of interest to garden historians remain from the original Victorian garden. Interesting new plantings of borders and hardy and half-hardy shrubs and climbers making use of south facing walls. March for winter-flowering rhododendrons and snowdrops in the woodland, late summer for eucryphias. TEAS. *Adm £1.50. Wed May 11 (2-6.30). Private visits welcome, adm £2.50 incl tea, please* Tel 0943 607544

Beamsley Hall ✿✻ (Marquess & Marchioness of Hartington) Beamsley. 5m E of Skipton. 6-acre traditional English garden with new plantings; including extensive herbaceous border and kitchen garden. Minor restrictions for wheelchairs. TEAS. Also at Bolton Abbey or at Devonshire Arms. *Adm £1.50 OAPs £1 Chd under 15 free. Sun July 17 (1.30-5.30)*

Bennet Grange (Mr & Mrs Milton-Davis) Fulwood. From Sheffield centre take A57 Glossop and Manchester, through Broomhill and Crosspool. After ½m turn L (Coldwell Lane) R at Xrds (Sandygate Rd). Pass Hallamshire Golf Club. L at Xrds (Blackbrook Rd) turn R at the top (Harrison Lane). House on L in wood. A large established sheltered garden, set in lovely location with beautiful views to Derbyshire Peaks. Long herbaceous border, shrubs, and natural woodland. TEAS in aid of WI. *Adm £1 Chd 50p. Sun July 24 (1.30-5)*

Betula & Bolton Percy Cemetery ✻✿ (Roger Brook Esq) Tadcaster. 10m SW of York. Turn S off A64 immediately next to Q8 garage. Please adhere to any car park signs. An acre of old village churchyard gardened by Roger Brook, in which garden plants are naturalised and grow wild. Featured BBC Gardeners' World 1992. The National Dicentra Collection will be on view in Roger Brook's garden and allotment. Light lunches and TEAS in aid of church. *Combined adm with* **Windy Ridge** *£1.50 Sun April 17. Adm £1 Sun May 29, Oct 2 (1-5)*

Bishopscroft ❀ (Bishop of Sheffield) Sheffield. 3m W of centre of Sheffield. Follow A57 (signposted Glossop) to Broomhill then along Fulwood Road to traffic lights past Ranmoor Church. Turn Right up Gladstone Rd and then L into Snaithing Lane. Bishopscroft on R at top of hill. 1¼-acres of well-established suburban woodland garden. Small lake and stream; the aim is to present something of the feeling of countryside in the nearby Rivelin Valley; a good variety of elders, brambles and hollies; herbaceous, shrub and rose borders. TEAS. *Adm £1 Chd free (Share to the Church Urban Fund©). Sun July 17 (2-6)*

Blackbird Cottage ⬥❀ (Mrs Hazel Hoad) Scampston. 5m from Malton off A64 to Scarborough through Rillington turn L signposted Scampston only, follow signs. ⅓-acre plantswoman's garden made from scratch since 1986. A great wealth of interesting plants, with shrub, herbaceous border. Alpines are a speciality. Please visit throughout the day to ease pressure on a small but inspirational garden. Unusual plants for sale. Morning coffee and TEAS in aid of Scampston Village Hall & Church. *Adm £1 Chd free. Sun June 19 (10-5)*

Bossall Hall ⬥❀ (Brig I D & Lady Susan Watson) From York proceed in NE direction on A64 (York to Malton & Scarborough) for 7m and turn R at signpost marked Claxton & Bossall. Go straight across the Xrds in Claxton and you come to Bossall (2m). C12 church will be open. 6-acre garden with moat surrounding C17 hall. Many old trees, lawns, orchard, walled kitchen garden, shrub and rose borders. TEA. *Adm £1 Chd 20p . Sun June 26 (2-5)*

¶**Boston Spa Gardens** A659 1m S of Wetherby. Church St immed opp Central Garage. *Combined adm £2.50 incl coffee/tea Chd free (Share to Northern Horticultural Society®). Sun April 17 (11-4)*

¶**Acorn Cottage** ❀ (Mr & Mrs C M Froggatt) Garden adjacent to **Four Oaks**. A small walled Alpine rock garden with the plant collection spanning 70 yrs - 2 generations

¶**Four Oaks** ❀❀ (Richard Bothamley & Glenn Hamilton) A medium-sized established flower and foliage garden of particular interest to flower arrangers. Pergolas and a series of garden 'rooms' on differing levels create a sense of intimacy. A wide selection of the genera - acer. Terrace with pots and a pool with good waterside plantings.

Brookfield ❀❀ (Dr & Mrs R L Belsey) Oxenhope. 5m SW of Keighley, take A629 towards Halifax. Fork R onto A6033 towards Haworth. Follow signs to Oxenhope. Turn L at Xrds in village. 200yds after P O fork R, Jew Lane. A little over 1 acre, intimate garden, including large pond with island and mallards. Many varieties of candelabra primulas and florindaes, azaleas, rhododendrons. Unusual trees and shrubs; screes; greenhouse and conservatory. TEA. *Adm £1.50 Chd free. Sun May 29 (2-6). Private visits welcome, please* Tel 0535 643070

61 Carsick Hill Crescent ❀❀ (Mrs J Atkinson) Sheffield. From Sheffield centre take A57 Glossop and Manchester through Broomhill and Crosspool. After ½m turn L up Coldwell Lane to Xrds. Straight over Sandygate Rd, down Carsick Hill Rd. Carsick Hill Crescent, third turning on L. An established ¾-acre garden with interesting plantings. Good use of a sloping site incorporating; two small ponds, rockery, mixed shrub and herbaceous borders. Coffee and biscuits. *Adm £1 Chd 50p. Sun July 24 (10.30-1.30)*

● **Castle Howard** ❀ (The Hon. Simon Howard & Castle Howard Estate Ltd) York. 15m NE of York off the A64. 6m W of Malton. Partially suitable for wheelchairs. 300 acres of formal and woodland gardens laid out from the C18 to present day, including fountains, lakes, cascades and waterfalls. Ray Wood covers 50 acres and has a large and increasing collection of rhododendron species and hybrids amounting to 600 varieties. There is also a notable collection of acers, nothofagus, arbutus, styrax, magnolia and a number of conifers. There are walks covering spring, summer and autumn. Two formal rose gardens planted in the mid 1970's include a large assembly of old roses, china roses, bourbon roses, hybrid teas and floribunda. Refreshments are available in the House Restaurant and also in the Lakeside Cafe. During the summer months there are boat trips on the lake in an electric launch. There is a gift shop in the House and a plant centre by the car park. TEAS. *Adm £4 Chd £2. Every day March 18 to Oct 31 (10-4.30)*

¶**Coniston Hall** ❀ (Mr & Mrs M J R Bannister) Coniston Cold. 5m NW of Skipton on A65. Landscaped park with magnificent views over 24 acre lake and the Yorkshire Dales. Woodland walks, with new plantings; rhododendrons; cherry blossom; wild flowers. Estate Shop and Tea Room. Lunches & TEAS. *Adm £1.50 Chd 50p (Share to Yorkshire Children's Hospital Trust®). Sun May 15 (11-5)*

● **Constable Burton Hall Gardens** ⬥ (Charles Wyvill Esq) 3m E of Leyburn on A684, 6m W of A1. Bus: United No. 72 from Northallerton alight at gate. Large garden, woodland walks; something of interest all spring and summer; splendid display of daffodils; rockery with fine selection of alpines (some rare); extensive shrubs and roses. Beautiful John Carr house (not open) in C18 park. Beautiful countryside at entrance to Wensleydale. *Adm £1 Chd 50p; reduction for large parties* Tel Bedale 50428. *April 1 to Oct 1 daily (9-5.30)*

Creskeld Hall ⬥❀❀ (The Exors of Lady Stoddart-Scott) Arthington. 5m E of Otley on A659. Well established 3-4-acre large garden with woodland plantings; rhododendrons, azaleas, attractive water garden with canals, walled kitchen and flower garden. TEAS. *Adm £1.50 Chd free. Sun June 5 (12-5)*

Derwent House ⬥❀❀ (Dr & Mrs D G Lethem) Osbaldwick. On village green at Osbaldwick. 2m E of York city centre off A1079. Approx ¾ acre, a village garden extended in 1984 to provide a new walled garden with yew hedges and box parterres. Conservatories, terraces and herbaceous borders. TEAS. *Adm £1 Chd free. Sun June 12 (1.30-5)*

Regular Openers. Too many days to include in diary. Usually there is a wide range of plants giving year-round interest. See head of county section for the name and garden description for times etc.

The Dower House &♠ (Mrs M J Coupe) Great Thirkleby. 4m from Thirsk on A19 on alternative route avoiding Sutton Bank. Smallholding run as a nature reserve bounded by a stream with ponds, wildflowers, birds, fish, donkeys. Rare trees with autumn colour, fruit and rose hips. TEAS. *Adm £1 Chd free (Share to Ripon Choral Soc© and St Leonards Hospice®). Sun Sept 18 (2-6). Private visits welcome, please* **Tel 0845 501375**

8 Dunstarn Lane &♠ (Mr & Mrs R Wainwright) Adel. Leeds 16. From Leeds ring rd A6120 exit Adel, up Long Causeway. 4th junction R into Dunstarn Lane, entrance 1st R. 28 bus from Leeds centre stops near gate. Entire garden formerly known as The Heath. Featured on YTV and BBC TV. 2 acres of long herbaceous and rose borders incl 60 varieties of delphiniums. Large lawns for picnics. *Adm £1 Chd free. Suns July 3, 17 (2-6)*

Elvington Gardens ♠♠ 8m SE of York. From A1079, immed. after leaving York's outer ring road turn S onto B1228 for Elvington. Light lunches and Teas in Village Hall in aid of village hall. Large free car park. *Combined adm £2.50 Chd free. Sun June 5 (11-5)*

>   **Brook House** (Mr & Mrs Christopher Bundy) Old established garden with fine trees; herb garden with rustic summer house; kitchen garden

>   **Elvington Hall** (Mr & Mrs Pontefract) 3-4-acre garden; terrace overlooking lawns with fine trees and views; sanctuary with fish pond

>   **Eversfield** (David & Helga Hopkinson) Modest sized garden with a wide variety of unusual perennials; grasses and ferns divided by curved lawns and gravel beds. Small nursery

>   **Red House Farm** (Dr & Mrs Euan Macphail) Entirely new garden created from a field 10 years ago. Courtyard with interesting plantings and half-acre young wood

¶**Fairview** ♠♠ (Michael D Myers) Smelthouses. From B6165 12m NW of Harrogate turn R in Wilsill Village to Smelthouses. Fairview is immed after the bridge on the R. A ⅛-acre small plantsman's garden on a steep slope, packed with unusual bulbs, alpines and woodland plants. 3 NCCPG National Collections; anemone nemorosa, hepatica and primula marginata; alpine house, fernery and tiny pond; small nursery. Due to the situation of the garden there may be some necessary restrictions to entry if busy. TEAS. *Adm £1.50 Chd free. Suns March 13, Sept 25 (12-5) Private visits welcome, please* **Tel 0423 780291**

¶**Fieldhead** ♠♠ (Fiona Harrison & Chris Royffe) Boston Spa. Take A659 towards Boston Spa off A1 1m S of Wetherby. Chestnut Avenue on the R after ¾m. Please park on the main rd and walk up the avenue. A ⅓-acre garden recently created around an imposing Victorian house. Interestingly designed with a wide range of spaces, colours and textures; pools, terraces, a rose walk, shade and stone gardens. A large selection of plants; herbaceous, shrubs, ground cover and bamboos. Photographic exhibition showing development. Coffee/TEA. *Adm £1 Chd free. Suns May 22, June 19 (11-5)*

Gilling Castle ♠ (The Rt Revd the Abbot of Ampleforth) Gilling East, 18m N of York. Medium-sized terraced garden with steep steps overlooking golf course. Unsuitable

for handicapped or elderly. *Adm 80p Chd free. For NGS July & Aug daily (10-4.30)*

Goddards &♠♠ (The National Trust Yorkshire Regional Office) 27 Tadcaster Rd, Dringhouses. 2m from York centre on A64, next to Swallow Chase Hotel. 1920s garden designed by George Dillistone, herbaceous borders, yew hedges, terraces with aromatic plants, rock gardens, pond. Guided tours, TEAS. *Adm £1.50 incl NT members. Sun July 10 (12-5) No coaches please*

Grimston Gardens ♠♠ Gilling East: 17m N of York; 7m S of Helmsley on B1363. Follow sign 1m S of Gilling East. TEA. *Adm £1.50 Chd free. Sun July 10, Thurs July 14 (2-6)*

>   ¶**Bankside House** (Clive & Jean Sheridan) ½-acre garden with sloping lawn, mature trees and shrubs with shaded walk, mixed herbaceous plants, semi-formal beds, small Japanese area

>   **Grimston Chase** (Mr & Mrs R Clarke) A wooded hillside incorporating a 3-acre woodland garden, flower beds surrounding mature trees and lawns with a stream dividing up the woodland. Variety of flowers with rhododendrons along a woodland path. Magnificent views

>   **Grimston Manor Farm** (Richard & Heather Kelsey) ½-acre garden (originally our field) offering all year interest. An intricate design profusely planted with a wide collection of herbaceous plants; trees and shrubs of particular interest to the flower arranger

¶**Harlsey Manor** &♠ (Mr & Mrs Brian Holey) East Harlsey. Travelling N on the A19 drive past the Cleveland Tontine (A172 turn-off) and take next turn to the L marked East Harlsey. The driveway to Harlsey Manor is about ½m along this rd on the LH-side before the village. 6 acres of garden and woodland walks with wide variety of mature trees and shrubs. Herbaceous borders, long terrace with formal rose beds and views of Cleveland Hills; extensive replanting of rhododendrons and daffodils carried out in 1993. TEAS in aid of Guide Dogs for the Blind. *Adm £1.25 Chd 25p. Suns April 10, May 22 (1.30-5.30)*

Hemble Hill Farm &♠ (Miss S K Edwards) Guisborough, on A171 between Nunthorpe and Guisborough opp the Cross Keys Inn. Dogs welcome, 7-acre garden facing the Cleveland Hills with formal and informal areas inc lake; young arboretum; heather, rhododendrons, large conservatory. TEAS. *Adm £1 Chd free. Sun May 22 (2-6). Private visits welcome June to Sept, please* **Tel 0287 632511**

Hillbark ♠♠ (M D Simm & T P Gittins) Bardsey. 4m SW of Wetherby, turn W off A58 into Church Lane. The garden is 150yds on L just before Church. Please use village hall car park (turn R opp Church into Woodacre Lane). A young country garden of almost 1 acre, initially planted in 1987 and still evolving. Interesting design on 3 levels to take advantage of sloping S facing site. Mixed planting of shrubs, herbaceous and foliage plants; some English roses; paved and gravel terraces; water features stream with bridges to small woodland garden planted amongst mature trees; large horseshoe pond with ducks and marginal planting. Sunday Express 'Large Garden of the Year' 1990. TEA. *Adm £1 Chd 50p (Share to Cookridge Hospital Cancer Research®). Suns May 22, June 26 (11-5). Private visits welcome May to July, please* **Tel 0937 572065**

50 Hollins Lane ⚔ (Mr & Mrs G Ellison) Hampsthwaite. 2m W of Harrogate, turn R off A59 Harrogate-Skipton rd. Small ¼-acre garden with limestone rockeries; rhododendrons; azaleas and climbers. Pergolas and pool. Many unusual plants and alpines. TEA. *Adm £1.50. Private visits welcome, please* **Tel 0423 770503**

Holly Cottage ⚔❀ (Mr & Mrs John Dixon) Leas Gardens, Scholes. 8m S of Huddersfield on A616. Turn W at signpost to Scholes. ½-acre sloping garden of interest created from a field in 1988 with raised alpine bed and paved area with troughs; pond with small bog garden, rockery and herbaceous borders with good selection of plants. TEA. *Adm £1 Chd free. Sun June 12 (2-6). Private visits welcome, please* **Tel 0484 684 083**

32 Hollybank Road ⚔ (Mr & Mrs D Matthews) Holgate. A59 (Harrogate Rd) from York centre. Cross iron bridge, turn L after Kilima hotel (Hamilton Drive East). Fork slightly L (Hollybank Rd) after 400yds. A small town garden 7yds × 28yds planted for year-round interest. Shrubs, small trees, climbing plants, roses, clematis and plants in containers. Cobbled fountain feature, 4 separate patio areas, 2 small ponds, wooden bridge leading to pergola. TEA. *Adm £1 Chd free. Sun June 19 (11-5)*

Hovingham Hall ⚓ (Sir Marcus & Lady Worsley) 8m W of Malton. House in Hovingham village, 20m N of York; on B1257 midway between Malton and Helmsley. Medium-sized garden; yew hedges, shrubs and herbaceous borders. C18 dovecote; riding school; cricket ground. TEAS in aid of Hovingham Church. *Adm £1.50 Chd 50p. Sun July 10 (2-6)*

¶Hunmanby Grange ⚓⚔❀ (Mr & Mrs T Mellor) Wold Newton. Hunmanby Grange is a farm 12½m SE of Scarborough, situated between Burton Fleming and Fordon. From Hunmanby take rd to Wold Newton 4m out of village turn R at Xrds towards Fordon Farm (garden 200yds on R). From A64 take B1039 towards Filey turn R before Flixton signed Fordon. In Fordon turn L at Xrds to Burton Fleming. Farm/garden 1¼m on L. The garden has been created from exposed open fields over 10 yrs, on top of the Yorkshire Wolds near the coast, hopefully satisfying both a plantswoman's and a young family's needs. Foliage colour, shape and texture have been most important in forming mixed borders, a gravel garden, a rose hedge, orchard and laburnum tunnel. TEAS in aid of Burton Fleming Playground. *Adm £1 Chd free. Suns May 29, July 3 (11-5)*

Kelberdale ⚔❀ (Stan & Chris Abbott) Knaresborough. 1m from Knaresborough on B6164 Wetherby Rd. House on L immed after new ring rd roundabout. An attractive, owner made and maintained, medium-sized garden with river views. Planted for year-round interest with large herbaceous border, conifer and colour beds. Alpines and pond. TEA. *Adm £1 Chd free (Share to St Michael's Hospice®). Sats, Suns June 11, 12; July 2, 3; Sun June 19 (10-6). Private visits welcome, please* **Tel 0423 862140**

Land Farm ❀ (J Williams Esq) Colden, nr Hebden Bridge. From Halifax at Hebden Bridge go through 2 sets traffic lights; take turning circle to Heptonstall. Follow signs to Colden. After 2¾m turn R at 'no thru' road, follow signs to garden. 4 acres incl alpine; herbaceous, heather, formal and newly developing woodland garden. Elevation 1000ft N facing. Has featured on 'Gardeners' World'. C17 house (not open). *Adm £1.50. May to end Aug; Sats, Suns, Bank Hol Mons (10-5)*

30 Latchmere Rd ⚔❀ (Mr & Mrs Joe Brown) Leeds 16. A660 from City Centre to Lawnswood Ring Rd roundabout; turn sharp left on to ring rd A6120 for ⅓m to 3rd opening on left Fillingfir Drive; right to top of hill, turn right at top by pillar box, then left almost opposite into Latchmere Road, 3rd house on left. Bus stop at gate (Bus every 15 mins); 74 & 76 from City Centre; 54 from Brigate; 73 from Greenthorpe. Coaches to park in Latchmere Drive please. A small garden full of interest; fern garden; herbaceous borders; alpine garden; glade; camomile walk; 2 pools; patio built of local York stone; sink gardens; collection of 80 clematis. Featured Sunday Telegraph Magazine & TV with Yehudi Menuhin in *'Fiddling with Nature'* 1985. Gardeners' World, screened 1989. *Adm £1 Chd 50p (Share to GRBS®). Suns July 10, 17, 24, 31 (2.30-5.30)*

78 Leeds Rd ⚔❀ (Mrs E Marshall) Selby. 1m from Selby on A63 Leeds rd (approachable from M62 or A1; Selby turn off). ½-acre suburban garden, of particular interest to plant lovers; mature clematis, conifers, roses, small shrubs, herbaceous border, several alpine troughs, small pool and rockery. *Adm 60p Chd free. Suns June 19, July 10 (2-5); Private visits also welcome, please* **Tel 0757 708645**

Ling Beeches ⚓⚔❀ (Mrs Arnold Rakusen) Ling Lane, Scarcroft 7m NE of Leeds. A58 mid-way between Leeds and Wetherby; at Scarcroft turn W into Ling Lane, signed to Wike on brow of hill; garden ⅓m on right. 2-acre woodland garden designed by owner emphasis on labour-saving planting; unusual trees and shrubs; ericaceous plants, but some species roses, conifers, ferns and interesting climbers. Featured in The English Woman's Garden other publications and TV. TEA. *Adm £1.50. Sun April 10 (2-5); Private visits also welcome, please* **Tel Leeds (0532) 892450**

Littlethorpe Gardens ⚓⚔❀ nr Ripon. Littlethorpe lies 1½m SE of Ripon indicated by signpost close to Ripon Racecourse on the B6265 twixt Ripon and the A1. TEAS at **Littlethorpe Hall**. *Combined adm £2.50 Chd free. Sun June 12 (1.30-5.30)*

  Deanswood (Mrs J Barber) Garden of approx 1½ acres created during the last 9 years. Herbaceous borders; shrubs; special features streamside garden; 3 ponds with many unusual bog/marginal plants. Adjacent nursery open. *Private visits also welcome, please* **Tel 0765 603441**

  Littlethorpe Hall (Mr & Mrs D I'Anson) Mature garden (Victorian). 2 acres of lawns with specimen trees, azaleas; heathers and herbaceous beds. Small lake stocked with fish and a number of interesting waterside plants

  Littlethorpe House (Mr & Mrs James Hare) 2 acres with old-fashioned roses; established mixed herbaceous and shrub borders

Low Askew ✿✿ (Mr & Mrs Martin Dawson-Brown) Cropton. 5m NW of Pickering between the villages of Cropton and Lastingham. Plantsman's garden full of interest incl scree, borders, roses & shrubs. Situated in beautiful countryside with stream and walk to River Seven. Troughs & pots are a speciality, filled with rare & species pelargoniums. Plant stalls by local nurserymen. Picnic area by river. Morning coffee & TEAS. *Adm £1.50 Chd free (Share to NSPCC®). Sun June 26 (11-5)*

Maspin House ✿✿✿ (Mr & Mrs H Ferguson) Hillam Common Lane. 4m E of A1 on A63 direction Selby. Turn R in Monk Fryston after Texaco Garage. L at T junction. Maspin House 1m on L. Ample off road parking. Garden of 1½ acres started in 1985 and still evolving. Owner made and maintained. Many unusual and beautiful plants giving good late colour. Lots of features made by handy husband incl paths, patios, ponds and waterfall, raised beds and separate gardens. TEAS in aid of Monk Fryston School. *Adm £1 Chd free. Sun Sept 18 (1-5)*

The Mews Cottage ✿✿ (Mrs Pat Clarke) 1 Brunswick Dr, Harrogate. W of town centre. From Cornwall Rd, N side of Valley Gardens, 1st R (Clarence Dr), 1st L (York Rd), first L (Brunswick Dr). A small garden on a sloping site of particular interest to hardy planters. Full of unusual and familiar plants but retaining a feeling of restfulness. A courtyard with trompe l'oeil and a gravelled area enclosed by trellising, provide sites for part of a large collection of clematis. TEAS. *Adm £1 Chd 50p. Wed Aug 17 (2-5.30). Private visits for groups, societies and parties also welcome, please* **Tel 0423 566292**

Millgate House ✿✿ (Austin Lynch & Tim Culkin) Richmond Market Place. House is located at bottom of Market Place opp Barclays Bank. SE walled town garden overlooking the R Swale. Although small the garden is full of character, enchantingly secluded with plants and shrubs. Foliage plants incl ferns, hostas; old roses and interesting selection of clematis, small trees and shrubs. Featured in 'Homes & Gardens', 'Dalesman' and 'The Sunday Times'. Full of ideas for small gardens. *Adm £1 Chd 50p. Sun July 3 (8am-8pm)*

Nawton Tower ✿✿ (Mr & Mrs D Ward) Nawton, 5m NE of Helmsley. From A170, between Helmsley and Nawton village, at Beadlam turn N 2½m to Nawton Tower. Large garden; heathers, rhododendrons, azaleas, shrubs. Tea Helmsley and Kirbymoorside. *Adm £1 Chd 50p. Sat, Sun, Mon May 28, 29, 30 (2-6); private visits welcome, please* **Tel 0439 71218**

Ness Hall (Hugh Murray Wells Esq) Nunnington, 6m E of Helmsley, 22m N of York. From B1257 Helmsley-Malton rd turn L at Slingsby signed Kirbymoorside, 3m to Ness. Lge walled garden, mixed and herbaceous borders, emphasis on colour and design; orchard with shrubs and climbing roses. *Adm £1 Chd free. Sun, Wed June 26, 29 (2-6)*

Netherwood House ✿✿ (Mr & Mrs Peter Marshall) 1m W of Ilkley on A65 towards Skipton; drive on L, clearly marked Netherwood House. Daffodils, spring flowering shrubs, duck pond; new rockery, bulb and stream plantings. TEAS. *Adm £1.50 Chd free. Sun April 3 (2-5.30)*

● **Newby Hall & Gardens** ✿✿✿ (R E J Compton Esq) Ripon. 40-acres extensive gardens laid out in 1920s; full of rare and beautiful plants. Winner of HHA/Christie's Garden of the Year Award 1987. Formal seasonal gardens, reputed longest double herbaceous borders to R. Ure and National Collection holder Genus Cornus. C19 statue walk; woodland discovery walk. Miniature railway and adventure gardens for children. Lunches & TEAS in licensed Garden Restaurant. The Newby shop and plant stall. *Adm House & garden £5.20 OAPs £4 Disabled/Chd £3, Garden only £3.30, OAPs £2.60, Disabled/Chd £2.20. April to Sept daily ex Mons (Open Bank Hols) (Gardens 11-5.30; House 12-5). Group bookings and further details from Administrator* **Tel 0423 322583**

Nunnington Hall ✿✿✿ (The National Trust) 4½m SE Helmsley, signed ½m from Helmsley on A170 Thirsk rd (Sproxton turn off). Signed at Welburn on A170 Scarborough to Helmsley rd. 8-acre garden and grounds in 5 distinct areas. Mature sycamores, under-planted with shrubs and bulbs in car park; woodland of ash and sycamore with riverside hybrid rhododendrons and blossom trees. West garden with lawns, beech hedge, specimen trees and shrub borders. Main walled garden with formal lawns, rose beds, mixed borders, apple/pear orchards, clematis collection, cherry avenue, specimen trees and terraced shrubberies. TEAS. Tea garden offers light refreshments by river amongst clematis and aromatic plants. *Adm £1 Chd 50p. Fri June 10 (5-8)*

The Old Rectory, Mirfield ✿✿ (G Bottomley Esq) Exit 25 of M62; take A62 then A644 thru Mirfield Village; after approx ½m turn L up Blake Hall Drive, then 1st L, Rectory at top of hill. 1-acre garden surrounding Elizabethan Rectory. Mixed borders, Mulberry tree dating from C16; well, pergola and small ornamental pond. TEAS. *Adm £1 Chd free. Sun July 3 (2-5)*

Old Sleningford ✿✿ (Mr & Mrs James Ramsden) 5m W of Ripon, off B6108. After North Stainley take 1st or 2nd left; follow sign to Mickley for 1m from main rd. Unusual, interesting 3-acre garden with extensive lawns, interesting trees; woodland walk; exceptionally lovely lake and islands and recently planted stream-side walk; mediaeval mill; walled kitchen garden; herbaceous border, yew hedges, huge beech hedge, Victorian fernery; flowers and grasses grown for drying. Home-made TEAS. *Adm £1.50 Chd 50p (Share to N of England Christian Healing Trust©). Sat, Sun, Mon May 28, 29, 30 (1-5). Groups catered for, also private visits welcome, please* **Tel Ripon 635229**

¶**The Old Vicarage** ✿✿ (Mr & Mrs R Marshall) Whixley, between York and Harrogate. ½m from A59 3m E of A1. A ½-acre walled flower garden with mixed borders, unusual shrubs, climbers and roses. Courtyard with herb garden. Gazebo. Light lunches & TEAS. *Adm £1.50. Wed June 15 (11-6)*

By Appointment Gardens. These owners do not have a fixed opening day usually because they do not like crowds or have insufficient parking space. Owner will often give guided tour.

Otterington Hall &❀ (Sir Stephen & Lady Furness) Northallerton. 4m S of Northallerton. On A167 just N of South Otterington village. 7 acres of garden and woodland which originally opened for the NGS in 1935; outstanding topiary and yew hedges, woodland walks, shrubs. TEAS. *Adm £1 Chd 20p. Suns April 3 (2-5), July 10 (2-6). Private visits welcome on other dates April to Sept, please* **Tel 0609 772061**

Parcevall Hall Gardens ❀ (Walsingham College (Yorkshire Properties) Ltd) Skyreholme, 12m N of Skipton. From Grassington on B6265 turn S at Hebden Xrds, follow signs to Burnsall, Appletreewick to Parcevall Hall. 20-acres in Wharfedale; shelter belts of mixed woodland, fine trees; terraces; fishponds; rock garden; tender shrubs inc Desfontainea; Crinodendron; camellia; bulbs; rhododendrons; orchard for picnics, old varieties of apples; autumn colour; birds in woodland; splendid views. TEAS. *Adm £2 Chd 50p.* ▲*for NGS Suns April 17, June 26, Aug 7 (10-5)*

Pennyholme (Mr C J Wills) Fadmoor, 5m NW of Kirbymoorside. From A170 between Kirbymoorside and Nawton, turn N, ½m before Fadmoor turn left, signed 'Sleightholmedale only' continue N up dale, across 3 cattlegrids, to garden. No Buses. Large, wild garden on edge of moor with rhododendrons, azaleas, primulas, shrubs. TEAS. *Adm £1 Chd 50p (Share to St Nicholas, Bransdale®). Sats, Suns June 4, 5, 11, 12 (11.30-5)*

¶Plum Tree Cottage ❀❀ (Mr & Mrs G J Rogers) Bramham. 5m S of Wetherby off A1 take 1st L past the Red Lion towards the church. A sloping garden of about ½ acre with particular winter and spring interest. A range of shade-loving plants, epimediums, hellebores, primulas; varieties of spring bulbs; erythroniums and dodecatheons, also magnolia, trees with interesting bark and a small bog garden struggling against wild garlic! TEAS. *Adm £1 Chd free. Sun April 17 (2-5). Also private visits welcome, please* **Tel 0937 843330**

¶55 Rawcliffe Drive ❀❀ (Mr & Mrs J Goodyer) Clifton. A19 from York centre, turn R at Clifton Green traffic lights (Water Lane). Rawcliffe Drive is 1st L after Clifton Hotel. A 30yd by 10yd suburban garden on 2 levels, which has developed as the family has grown older. Planted for yr-round interest with excellent use of foliage and colour. Many unusual shrubs, herbaceous plants and bulbs; around 90 clematis some varieties of which are in flower March to Nov. TEA. *Adm £1.20 Chd free. Sun June 19 (11-4). Also private visits welcome April to July, please* **Tel 0904 638489**

The Riddings ❀❀ (Mr & Mrs T Hague) Long Preston. ¼m W of Long Preston on A65. Turn R over cattle grid up private rd. Parking adjacent to house. Designated wildlife gardens. 10 acres of grounds with mature trees, hollies and conifers. A small formal garden with heathers, alpines and some topiary; a traditional walled kitchen garden with ornamental pond; a delightful walk through rhododendron wood with beck, small waterfalls and bog garden undergoing restoration. TEA. *Adm £1.50 Chd 75p. Sun June 5 (10-5)*

Ryedale House & (Dr & Mrs J A Storrow) 41 Bridge Street, Helmsley. On A170, 3rd house on R after bridge into Helmsley from Thirsk and York. ¼-acre walled garden; varieties of flowers, shrubs, trees, herbs. Teashops in Helmsley. *Adm £1 Chd free. Sat June 11 (2-6) also private visits welcome May to July, please* **Tel 0439 70231**

St Nicholas (The Lady Serena James) 1m S of Richmond. On Brompton Catterick Bridge rd, ½ way down hill after leaving Maison Dieu. Bus: Darlington-Richmond; alight The Avenue, 500yds. Medium-large garden of horticultural interest; shrubs, topiary work. *Adm 50p Chd 25p. Mons April 4, June 6 (all day), also by appt parties only*

Sedbury Hall &❀ (Mr & Mrs W G Baker Baker) Richmond. A66 ½m W of Scotch Corner. Turn L immed after Sedbury Layby. Large established garden in approx 10 acres of grounds and parkland. Herbaceous border and roses leading to a secret garden. Wall shrubs & many varieties of climbing roses. Walled kitchen garden. Woodland walk with magnificent view over Swaledale. *Adm £1.50 Chd free. Sun July 17 (2.30-5.30)*

¶Shadwell Grange &❀❀ (Mr & Mrs Peter Hartley) Shadwell Lane, Leeds 17. Turn L at traffic lights (signed Shadwell) ¼m from Moortown on A6120 (Leeds ring-rd) travelling E. A large 4-acre Victorian garden with established woodlands. Rhododendrons, azaleas, mixed borders and new plantings. Water garden, orchard, wild garden and open views to the S. Parking in paddock. Plant stall, coffee, light lunches and TEA in aid of Yorkshire Macmillan Nurse Appeal. *Adm £1.50 Chd (over 5) 50p. Sun June 5 (11-4.30)*

Shandy Hall ❀❀ (The Laurence Sterne Trust) Coxwold, N of York. From A19. 7m from both Easingwold and Thirsk turn E signed Coxwold. C18 walled garden, unusual plants; old roses. 1-acre, with low-walled beds. Newly opened 1-acre wild garden in Quarry adjoining garden. Home of C18 author, Laurence Sterne, who made the house famous. Craft shop in grounds. Unusual plants for sale. Wheelchairs with help. Tea Coxwold (Schoolhouse Tea Room; home baking). *Adm £1 Chd 50p (Share to Laurence Sterne Trust®). House open Wed & Sun (2.30-4.30). Garden also open every afternoon except Sat (12-4.30) groups by appt. on other days or evenings during the same period. For NGS Suns April 10, June 19, July 10, Mon May 30, Wed June 22 (2-5)*

Silver Birches &❀ (Stanley Thomson Esq) Ling Lane, Scarcroft, 7m NE of Leeds. A58 mid-way between Leeds-Wetherby; at Scarcroft turn W into Ling Lane, signed Wike; garden ½m. 2½-acre woodland garden; foliage trees and shrubs; many conifers, rhododendrons, azaleas; good collection of heaths and heathers; attractive water feature, climbers and roses. TEA. *Adm £1.50 Chd free (Share to Northern Horticultural Society®). Suns May 8, 22 (2-6) also private visits welcome June to Oct for parties, please* **Tel Leeds 0532 892335**

Sinnington Gardens ❀ 4m W of Pickering on A170. A group of gardens which featured in Channel 4 series 'Nature Perfected', will be open in picturesque village. Tickets and parking on village green. TEAS. *Combined adm £2 Chd free. Sun May 8 (11-5)*

Skipwith Hall ᭤᭤ (Mr & Mrs Nigel Forbes Adam) Selby. From York take A19 to Selby (fork L at Escrick, 4m to Skipwith). From Selby take A19 to York turn R onto A163 to Market Weighton, turn L to Skipwith after approx 2m. An interesting 3-acre garden with well established shrub roses, trees, mixed borders and wall shrubs, large traditional walled kitchen garden. TEAS. *Adm £1.50 Chd 50p. Sun June 26 (2-5.30)*

Sleightholme Dale Lodge ᭤ (Mrs Gordon Foster; Dr & Mrs O James) Fadmoor, 3m N of Kirkbymoorside. 1m from Fadmoor. Hillside garden; walled rose garden; herbaceous borders. *Not* suitable for wheelchairs. No coaches. TEAS (Teas and plants not available June 5). *Adm £1.25 Chd 40p. Sun June 5 (11.30-5) Sat, Sun July 16, 17 (2-7); also private visits welcome*

Snilesworth ᭤ (Viscount & Viscountess Ingleby) Halfway between Osmotherley and Hawnby. From Osmotherley bear L sign posted Snilesworth, continue for 4½m across the moor. 4½m from Hawnby on Osmotherley Rd. Turn R at top of hill. Garden created from moorland in 1957 by present owners father; rhododendrons and azaleas in a 30 acre woodland setting with magnificent views of the Hambleton and Cleveland hills; snowgums grown from seed flourish in a sheltered corner. TEAS. *Adm £1 Chd 20p. Sun June 5 (2-5)*

Springfield House ᭤᭤᭤ (Mr & Mrs S B Milner) Tockwith. 5m E of Wetherby; 1m off B1224. Garden at west end of village. 1½ acres. Well established walled garden with herbaceous borders, water and rock gardens. Rose and conifer garden; shrub walk. Wide variety of plants. TEA. *Adm £1 Chd free. Sun July 24 (2-6)*

Stillingfleet Lodge ᭤᭤᭤ (Mr & Mrs J Cook) Stillingfleet 6m S of York, from A19 York-Selby take B1222 signed Sherburn in Elmet. ½-acre plantsman's garden subdivided into smaller gardens, each one based on a colour theme with emphasis on the use of foliage plants. Wild flower meadow and newly constructed pond, holders of National Collection of Pulmonaria. Adjacent nursery will be open. Homemade Teas in village hall in aid of local church. *Adm £1 Chd free. Suns May 15, June 26 (1.30-5.30)*

Stockeld Park ᭤᭤ (Mr & Mrs P G F Grant) 2m NW of Wetherby. On A661 Wetherby-Harrogate Rd; from Wetherby after 2m entrance 2nd lodge on left. Bus: Wetherby-Harrogate, alight Stockeld lodge gates (¼m drive). Listed grade 1 house and garden. 4-acres with lawns, grove and flowers, fine trees and roses. House built 1758 for Col Middleton by James Paine (listed Grade 1). C18 pigeon cote. Chapel 1890. *Open Thurs only April 7 to Oct 6 (2-5). For NGS Sun June 26. Gardens only TEAS Adm £1.50 Chd 75p (2-5)*

Stonegate Cottage ᭤᭤ (Mrs B Smith) Farnhill. 2m W Silsden. From Silsden or A629, follow directions to Farnhill. Stonegate Cottage is situated 100yds from Kildwick Hall towards Skipton. Cottage garden of approx 1 acre, on sloping site. Small pool and rockery. Unusual trees & shrubs. Wide variety of plants incl spring bulbs, herbaceous and roses. *Adm £1.50. Private visits welcome, please Tel 0535 632388*

Tan Cottage ᭤᭤ (Mr & Mrs D L Shaw) West Lane, Cononley. Take A629; turn off to Cononley 2¾m out of Skipton; top of village turn right onto Skipton rd. ¾-acre plantsmans garden adjoining C17 house (not open). Interesting plants, many old varieties; national collection of primroses. *Adm £1. Private visits welcome, please* **Tel 0535 32030**

Thornton Stud Gardens ᭤ (Lord Howard De Walden) 2½m N of Thirsk on the Thirsk to Northallerton rd, A168. Turn L in Thornton le Street. 8 acres of lawns with herbaceous borders, rose beds, many fine trees, lakeside walk, with unusual thatched summer house. TEA. *Adm £1 Chd 25p. Sun June 26 (2-5.30)*

¶106 Vaughan Road ᭤᭤ (Richard Darlow & Christine Hopkins) Barnsley. 2m NW Barnsley Town centre. From M1 junction 37 take A628 towards Barnsley. After ½m turn L at major Xrds to hospital. Turn L at hospital Xrds into Gawber Rd, after ½m turn L into Vernon Way. Vaughan Rd is 1st cul-de-sac on R. Mediterranean garden to rear 60ft by 30ft. Planted entirely with 'warm climate' trees, shrubs, perennials, incl many tender subjects permanently planted eg palms, cordylines, yuccas, cacti and eucalyptus; spectacular flowering shrubs and exotic plants in pots. Mainly evergreen but most colourful April to Oct. Featured in BBC 2 Gardeners World, Amateur Gardening magazine. *Adm £1.50 OAP £1. Private visits only welcome, weekends all yr, also evenings mid summer* **Tel 0226 291474**. *Not suitable for young children due to many spiky plums!*

Victoria Cottage ᭤ (John Bearder Esq) Beestonley Lane, Stainland. 6m SW of Halifax. Take the A629 (Huddersfield) from Halifax and fork R on the B6112 to Stainland. From Huddersfield take A640 Outlane, Sowood and Stainland. Turn at Black Horse Garage in Stainland (Beestonley Lane). ¾-acre plantsman garden, created by the owner from a NE sloping field since 1950. Daffodils; roses, flowering shrubs, some unusual for a hilly and wild part of the Pennines. Scenic setting. *Adm £1 Chd 30p. Sats, Suns April 9, 10; May 21, 22; Sun June 12 (10-5). Private visits welcome, please* **Tel 0422 365215/374280**

5 Wharfe Close ᭤᭤ (Mr & Mrs C V Lightman) Adel. Adel signposted off Leeds ring rd A6120 ¼m E of A660 Leeds-Otley Rd. Follow Long Causeway into Sir George Martin Drive. Wharfe Close adjacent to bus terminus. Please park on main rd. A medium-sized well stocked garden created from a sloping site incorporating pools, rock gardens, trellis work and small woodland walk using a wide variety of plantings; some unusual plants grown on a predominately acid soil. TEAS. *Adm £1 Chd free. Sun July 17 (2-5). Private visits also welcome June, July and August, please* **Tel 0532 611 363**

By Appointment Gardens. These owners do not have a fixed opening day usually because they do not like crowds or have insufficient parking space. Owner will often give guided tour.

Regular Openers. See head of county section.

The White House ৬৶෯ (Dr & Mrs A H Raper) Husthwaite. 3m N of Easingwold. Turn R off A19 signposted Husthwaite 1½m to centre of village opposite parish church. 1-acre garden created from scratch in 6 years now maturing and of particular interest to the plantswoman, containing herb garden, conservatory, gardens within the garden, herbaceous particularly a late summer 'hot' border; shrubs; borders and many fascinating unusual plants; do visit throughout the day please to ease pressure. Morning coffee & TEAS. Groups by prior arrangement. *Adm £1.50 Chd 25p (Share to Husthwaite Village Institute©). Sun Aug 28 (11-5)*

The Willows ৬৶෯ (Mr & Mrs Fleetwood) 172 Towngate, Clifton. From M62 exit 25, take A644 towards Brighouse. 1st R to Clifton. L at T junction; house approx 250 yds on L. ¾ acre owner created and maintained garden. Oriental features with pools and waterfalls. Herbaceous border, rockeries, containers and sink gardens. A wide variety of plantings in old orchard surrounding modern house. TEAS. *Adm £1 Chd 50p under 12 free. Sun June 12 (1-6)*

¶**Windsong** ෯ (Mr & Mrs Alan Gladwin) Osgodby. Take A63 2m N of Selby off A19, turn L into Sand Lane (signed Osgodby Village). A ½-acre garden created and maintained by the owners over the past 5 yrs. Many unusual features incl a moon gate; hardy plants and tender perennials packed into mixed borders. Ponds and stream-side plantings; orchard area. TEAS. *Adm £1 Chd free. Sun June 19 (2-5.30)*

Windy Ridge ৶෯ (Mr & Mrs J S Giles) Marsh Lane, Bolton Percy. 10m SW of York. Turn S off A64 immediately next to Q8 garage. Features a large collection of Barnhaven and Elizabethan primroses; Hose-in-Hose, Jack-in-the-Green, etc. Also wild and unusual hardy plants, grown in a natural cottage garden style sloping down to the Ings, greatly influenced by Margery Fish. Light lunches and teas available in village hall in aid of All Saints Church. *Combined adm with **Betula and Bolton Percy Cemetery** £1.50. Sun April 17 (1-5). Private visits welcome, please Tel 0904 744264*

¶**Woodcock** ৬৶ (Mr & Mrs David Price) ¾m E of Thirsk off A170 (Sutton Bank Rd). Turn R up bridle track. Proceed for 1m. 1½-acre garden laid out with some mature areas, always of interest. Plantings of shrubs, herbaceous, old-fashioned roses, spring bulbs, scree bed and developing camellia walk. Small woodland garden under construction. TEAS. *Adm £1 Chd 50p. Sun May 29 (2-5.30)*

Wytherstone House ෯ (Maj N & Lady Clarissa Collin) Pockley, 3m NE of Helmsley from A170 signpost. Large garden, tremendously improved recently, consisting of shrubs (some choice and hard to find) shrub roses, perennials, terracotta pots, herb garden, mediterranean garden, beech hedges and magnificent views. The arboretum consisting of rare interesting trees has recently been landscaped with pond and small water garden. TEAS. *Adm £1.50 Chd under 6 free over 6 50p (Share to York Area Appeals Committee for Mental Health®). Specialist nursery open Easter to Oct Wed to Sun incl (10-5). Sun April 24, May 22, June 19, July 17 (1.30-5.30)*

York Gate ৶෯ (Mrs Sybil B Spencer) Back Church Lane, Adel, Leeds 16. Behind Adel Church on Otley Rd out of Leeds (A660). Bus: WY 34 Leeds-Ilkley; alight Lawnswood Arms, ½m. A family garden created by father, son and mother, now maintained by Mrs Spencer and her 2 days a week gardener. 1 acre of particular interest to the plantsman and containing orchard with pool, an arbour, miniature pinetum, dell with stream and newly constructed root house, folly, nutwalk, peony bed, iris borders, fern border, herb garden, summerhouse, alley, white and silver garden, vegetable garden, pavement maze, Sybil's garden, all within 1-acre! NO COACHES. TEA. *Adm £2.50 Chd free. Sat, Sun June 4, 5 (2-6). Private visits welcome, please Tel 0532 678240*

York House ৶෯ (Mr & Mrs W H Pridmore) Claxton, 8m E of York, off A64. 1-acre plantsmans garden, created by owners since 1975; old roses, herbaceous, shrubs, fruit. Loose gravel drive could be difficult for wheelchairs. TEAS. *Adm £1 Chd 20p (Share to Northern Horticultural Society©). Suns May 8, July 3 (2-6); private visits welcome, please Tel 090 468 360*

STOP PRESS

Witley Park House ৬ (Mr & Mrs W A M Edwards) Great Witley. 9m NW of Worcester. On A443 1m W of Little Witley. Garage on L coming from Worcester and Droitwich. 18 acres inc pool; lakeside and woodland walk, water fowl; many varieties young trees, shrubs and roses. TEAS. *Adm £1 Chd 25p (Share to Worcestershire Swan Rescue Service®). Sun June 26 (2-6)*

WALES
Clwyd

Hon County Organisers:
North:

South:
Hon County Treasurer:

Mrs Richard Heaton, Plas Heaton, Trefnant, Denbigh LL16 5AF
Tel 0745-730229
Mrs Sebastian Rathbone, Bryn Celyn, Ruthin LL15 1TT Tel 0824 702077
Mrs J R Forbes, Pen-y-Wern, Pontblyddyn, nr Mold CH7 4HN Tel 0978-760531
A Challoner Esq., 13 The Village, Bodelwyddan LL18 5UR

DATES OF OPENING

By appointment
For telephone numbers and other
details see garden descriptions.
Private visits welcomed

Bryn Celyn, Llanbedr
Bryn Derwen, Mold
Byrgoed, Llandderfel
Donadea Lodge, Babell
15 Faenol Avenue, Abergele
Gardeners Lodge,Trevor Hall,
  Llangollen
Hartsheath, Pontblyddyn
Merlyn, Moelfre, Abergele
The Mount, Higher Kinnerton,
  Chester
Tir-y-Fron, Ruabon
Trem-Ar-For, Dyserth

Regular openings
For details see garden descriptions

Bryn Meifod, Glan Conwy see
  Gwynedd
Gardeners Lodge,Trevor Hall,
  Llangollen. Every Fri & Sat July &
  Aug

March 27 Sunday
  Erddig Hall Garden, Wrexham
April 2 Saturday
  Gardeners Lodge,Trevor Hall,
  Llangollen

April 3 Sunday
  Gardeners Lodge,Trevor Hall,
  Llangollen
April 4 Monday
  Gardeners Lodge,Trevor Hall,
  Llangollen
April 10 Sunday
  Pontruffydd Hall, Bodfari
  Hawarden Castle, Hawarden
April 17 Sunday
  New Abbey Bungalow, Gwespyr
April 20 Wednesday
  Hartsheath, Pontblyddyn
April 24 Sunday
  Hartsheath, Pontblyddyn
  Three Chimneys, Rhostyllen
May 7 Saturday
  Chirk Castle, nr Wrexham
May 14 Saturday
  Dibleys Nurseries, Llanelidan
May 15 Sunday
  Branas Lodge, Llandrillo ‡
  Hawarden Castle, Hawarden
  Trem-Ar-For, Dyserth
  Tyn-Y-Craig, Llandrillo ‡
May 21 Saturday
  Cerrigllwydion Hall, Llandyrnog
May 22 Sunday
  Maesmor Hall, Maerdy ‡
  Rhagatt Hall, Carrog ‡
May 29 Sunday
  Bryn Derwen, Mold
  2 Woodside Cottages, Halton,
  Chirk
June 5 Sunday
  Castanwydden, Llandyrnog

June 12 Sunday
  Abercregan, Langollen
  Byrgoed, Llandderfel
  River House, Erbistock
June 15 Wednesday
  Byrgoed, Llandderfel
June 19 Sunday
  Argoed Cottage, Overton-on-Dee
  Plas Ashpool & Coach House,
  Llandyrnog
June 26 Sunday
  Dolwen, Cefn Coch ‡
  Gwaenynog, Denbigh
  Llangedwyn Hall, Llangedwyn ‡
  New Abbey Bungalow, Gwesdyr
  Pen-y-Wern, Pontblyddyn
  Plas yn Rhos, Gellifor
July 2 Saturday
  Welsh College of Horticulture,
  Northop
July 10 Sunday
  Merlyn, Moelfre, Abergele
July 16 Saturday
  Llanasa Village Gardens, Llanasa
July 24 Sunday
  Plas-yn-Cefn, St Asaph
July 31 Sunday
  Tyn-y-Pwll, Llandegla, Nr
  Wrexham
August 7 Sunday
  Llanfair T.H.Village Gardens
September 4 Sunday
  Plas Newydd, Llanfair DC
October 23 Sunday
  Three Chimneys, Rhostyllen

DESCRIPTIONS OF GARDENS

Abercregan ఉ✿ (Mr & Mrs V Whitworth) Llangollen. A5 150yds Chirk side Llangollen Golf Club. 2½-acre water garden designed by Douglas Knight in 1985. Roses; herbaceous garden; rhododendrons. Magnificent views of Vale of Llangollen. TEAS and plant stall in aid of Clwyd Special Riding Trust. *Adm £1 Chd 50p. Sun June 12 (2-6)*

Argoed Cottage ఉ✿ (Mr & Mrs C J Billington) Overton-on-Dee. App Overton-on-Dee from Wrexham on A528 cross over Overton Bridge and in about ¾m on brow of hill turn L into Argoed Lane. 1¾-acre garden, with new features this year. Interesting trees and shrubs. Herbaceous beds; roses and vegetable garden. TEAS in aid of Wrexham Hospice Project. *Adm £1 Chd free. Sun June 19 (2-5.30)*

¶**Branas Lodge** (Mr & Mrs S C Lloyd) Llandrillo. [Nat Grid Ref: SJ018378] 1m W of Llandrillo. On leaving Llandrillo on B4401 Corwen to Bala rd take the 2nd turning R, by post box and cross R Dee. At T-junction turn L, gardens approx 150yds on R. Hillside garden of about 2 acres, developed from scrub, gorse and bracken since 1975 with rhododendrons, azaleas and other shrubs. There is a waterfall of approx 100ft falling into the garden. Good views of the Dee Valley and over the Berwyns. *Adm £1 Chd 50p (Share to Llandrillo Parish Church®). Sun May 15 (2-5.30)*

Bryn Celyn &&& (Mr & Mrs S Rathbone) Llanbedr. [OS Ref SJ 133 603]. From Ruthin take A494 towards Mold. After 1½m at the Griffin Inn turn L onto B5429. 1¼m house and garden on R. 1-acre garden; mixed borders; walled garden; old-fashioned roses. *Adm £1 Chd 50p. Private visits welcome, please* **Tel 0824 702077**

Bryn Derwen &&& (Roger & Janet Williams) Wrexham Road, Mold. ½m from Mold Cross on Mold-Wrexham rd B5444; opp Alun School and Sports Centre (large car park). ½-acre old walled garden with large sunken area. Plantsmans garden with wide variety of plants for sun and shade, giving interest from spring to autumn; allium, cistus, euphorbia, ferns, hostas, grasses, etc. Japanese garden. Featured on BBC Radio Wales Garddio and in The Good Garden Guide. TEA. *Adm £1 Chd 25p. Sun May 29 (2-5.30). Private visits welcome, please* **Tel Mold 756662**

Bryn Meifod, see Gwynedd gardens

Byrgoed & (Alan & Joy Byrne) Llandderfel. 4½m NE Bala. Off B4401 Bala-Corwen rd. L into village 1st R over stream and up hill. Fork R at old chapel, Byrgoed is ⅝m on L [OS 125 990 372]. Small well stocked terraced cottage garden. Thyme lawn, rockery and spring bulbs. TEA. *Adm £1 Chd 50p (Share to Llandderfel Parish Church®). Sun June 12, Wed June 15 (2-6). Private visits welcome any time, please* **Tel 06783 270**

Castanwydden &&& (A M Burrows Esq) Fforddlas, Llandyrnog. Take rd from Denbigh due E to Llandyrnog approx 4m. From Ruthin take B5429 due N to Llandyrnog. [OS ref 1264 (sheet 116)]. Approx 1-acre cottage garden with a considerable variety of plants and bulbs. TEAS. *Adm £1 Chd 50p (Share to Arthritis & Rheumatism Council, Ruthin Branch®). Sun June 5 (2-6)*

Cerrigllwydion Hall &&& (Mr & Mrs D Howard) Llandyrnog. E of Denbigh. B5429 ½m from Llandyrnog village on Ruthin Road. Extensive grounds with mature trees; herbaceous borders; vegetables and greenhouses. TEAS. *Adm £1.50 Chd free (Share to Llanynys Church®). Sat May 21 (2-6)*

Chirk Castle & (The National Trust) Chirk 7m SE of Llangollen. Off A5 in Chirk by War Memorial. 4½ acres trees and flowering shrubs, rhododendrons, azaleas, rockery, yew topiary. TEA. *Adm to garden £2 OAPs/Chd £1. Sat May 7 (12-5)*

¶**Dibleys Nurseries** &&& (Mr & Mrs R Dibley) Llanelidan. Take A525 to Xrds by Llysfasi Agricultural College (4m from Ruthin, 14m from Wrexham). Turn along B5429 towards Llanelidan. After 1½m turn L at Xrds with houses on the corner. Continue up lane for 1m. Nursery and gardens on the L. 8 acres of mainly young trees and shrubs planted during last 5 yrs. Spectacular views across to the Clwydian range. ¾ acre of glasshouses containing mostly streptocarpus, incl specimen plants ready for Chelsea show. TEAS. *Adm £1 Chd 50p (Share to Action Aid®). Sat May 14 (11-5)*

Dolwen &&& (Mrs F Denby) Cefn Coch Llanrhaedr-ym-Mochnant. From Oswestry take the B4580 going W to Llanrhaedr. Turn R in village and up narrow lane for 1m. Garden on R. 14m from Oswestry. 4 acres of hillside garden with pools, stream, small wood and many different types of plant and unusual annuals all backed by a stupendous mountain view. TEAS. *Adm £1 Chd free (Share to Oswestry Orthopaedic Hospital®). Every Fri and last Sun in month from May to Sept in aid of local charities. For NGS Sun June 26 (2-5)*

Donadea Lodge &&& (Mr & Mrs Patrick Beaumont) Babell. Turn off A541 Mold to Denbigh at Afonwen, signposted Babell; T-junction turn L. A55 Chester to St Asaph take B5122 to Caerwys, 3rd turn on L. Mature shady garden with unusual plants, shrubs, shrub roses and climbers; over 50 different clematis; pink, yellow and white beds. Featured on BBC Radio Wales & recommended by The Good Gardens Guide 1994. *Adm £1 Chd 50p. Private visits welcome from June 12 to Aug 12, please* **Tel 0352 720204**

Erddig Hall &&& (The National Trust) 2m S of Wrexham. Signed from A483/A5125 Oswestry Road; also from A525 Whitchurch Road. Garden restored to its C18 formal design incl varieties of fruit known to have been grown there during that period and now includes the National Ivy Collection. TEAS. Tours of the garden by Head Gardener at 1pm, 2.30pm & 4pm. *Adm £2 Chd £1. Shop & plant sales. For NGS Sun March 27 (1-5) Garden only*

15 Faenol Avenue && (Mr & Mrs A Carr) Abergele. A55 W take slip rd Abergele, Rhuddlan. Turn L at Roundabout, 150yds turn R into Faenol Ave. A55 E slip rd Prestatyn, Rhuddlan R at roundabout towards Abergele. 150yds R into Faenol Ave. Small but delightful garden, town gardeners wishing to create a cottage garden will find lots of ideas here. Alpine plants in stone sinks. *Adm 50p Chd 25p. Private visits welcome April to Sept, please* **Tel 0745 832059**

¶**Gardeners Lodge** & (Mrs M Tomlinson) Trevor Hall, Llangollen. On N side of A539 Rhuabon-Llangollen rd ¼m W of Trevor Village. Yellow direction signs from main rd. Delightful well-stocked ¾-acre cottage garden; herbaceous borders, rockery, shrubs, roses, herbs and spring bulbs. Interesting C18 church with box pews, hatchments etc nearby. TEAS. *Adm £1 Chd 50p (Share to Trevor Church®). Every Fri, Sat July and Aug, Sat, Sun, Mon April 2, 3, 4 (10-5). Private visits also welcome, please* **Tel 0978 822109**

By Appointment Gardens. Avoid the crowds. Good chance of a tour by owner. See garden description for telephone number.

Gwaenynog &&& (Maj & Mrs Tom Smith & Mrs Richard Williams) Denbigh. 1m W of Denbigh on A543, Lodge on left. 2-acre garden incl the restored kitchen garden where Beatrix Potter wrote the Tale of the Flopsy Bunnies. Small exhibition of some of her work. C16 house visited by Samuel Johnson during his Tour of Wales. Coffee and biscuits 11-12.30pm. TEAS. *Adm £1.50 OAPs £1 Chd 25p (Share to St James's Church, Nantglyn®). Sun June 26 (11-12.30) (2-6)*

Hartsheath & (Dr M C Jones-Mortimer) Pontblyddyn. ½m S of intersection with A5104. Red brick lodge on E side of A541. Large woodland garden; many varieties of flowering cherries and crab apples. Tidy picnic lunchers welcomed. Lunch & Tea at Bridge Inn, Pontblyddyn. *Adm £1 Chd £1 (Share to Pontblyddyn Church®). Wed April 20 (2-5) Sun April 24 (12-5). Also private visits welcome weekdays Feb-May, Sept-Oct, please* **Tel 0352 770 204**

Hawarden Castle && (Sir William & Lady Gladstone) On B5125 just E of Hawarden village. Large garden and picturesque ruined castle. *Adm £1.50 Chd/OAPs 50p. Suns April 10, May 15 (2-6)*

¶**Llanasa Village Gardens, Llanasa**. 3m SW of Prestatyn. Turn off A548 at Gwespyr or from A55 take A5151 turn off in Trelawnyd. TEAS. *Combined adm £4 Chd 50p. Sat July 16 (11-5)*

  ¶**Cae Mawr** &&& (Mrs N A Leicester) New garden professionally landscaped still under development; beautiful pond with carp. Future planning for small orchard and vegetable garden. Attractive shrubbery and flower beds; large patio

  Glanaber &&& (Mrs J M P Spiller) 1-acre garden created from pastureland dominated by rare maltese oak; large duck pond, bridges, arches, footpaths create pleasant walks; spring bulbs; herbaceous and bedding plants. C18 house. Old tools, machinery display

  ¶**Henblas** && (David & Bridget Lawton) Garden almost 1 acre with many mature trees, rhododendrons and clipped beech hedges; small formal rose garden with a pond; the whole area a sanctuary for many birds

  ¶**The Old Coach House** & (Mr & Mrs R Edwards) Approx ⅓-acre cottage garden, surrounded by 4-6ft high random stone walls. Front garden has stream running through it; gravel driveway and raised herbaceous beds. Back garden is lawned with borders of herbacous plants and shrubs. Patio area has many tubs and baskets of annual plants. Owners in process of extending garden, so part is under construction

  ¶**Plas yn Llan** &&& (S Jones) Garden to C18 farmhouse extending to approx 1½ acres. Lawns and mixed borders with feature conifers and heathers; small orchard and vegetable area. Rear garden remains uncultivated for wild life

  ¶**Tan y Fron** & (Mr Meirion Ellis) Typical country cottage garden with outstanding splashes of brilliant colour and a superb comprehensive vegetable garden

¶**Llangedwyn Hall** &&& (Mr & Mrs T M Bell) Llangedwyn; on the B4396 road to Llanrhaedr about 5m W of the Llynclys Xrds. Approx 4 acres; formal terraced garden on 3 levels designed and laid out in late C17 and early C18. Sunken rose garden and small water garden. TEAS. *Adm £1 OAP's & Chd 50p (Share to Llangedwyn Church®). Sun June 26 (2-6)*

¶**Llanfair T H Village Gardens, Abergele**. 5m from Abergele A548 to Llanfairtalhaiarn Village, then follow signs in village. TEA. *Combined adm £2 OAP's £1 Chd free. Sun Aug 7 (2-6)*

  ¶**Bronydd** && (Mr & Mrs Vernon Davies) 2 Lon Elwy. Small front flower garden with tubs and hanging baskets. To the side of house, raised bed with shrubs and climbers; patio area with tubs and alpine plants. Rear garden prize winning dahlias, chrysanthemums and sweet peas

  ¶**Bryn Ffynnon** & (Mr & Mrs Gwylym Williams) Landscape hillside garden; trees, hedgerows and shrubs. Beautiful views over the village and towards Snowdonia

  ¶**8 Cae Glas** & (Mrs K G Jones) Small cottage garden at front containing annuals, perennials and tubs. Small garden at back containing shrubs and various flowers

  ¶**15 Glan Elwy** &&& (Mr & Mrs T O Willliams) Flower borders at front containing a variety of bedding plants (annuals). Rear of house has 2 greenhouses and 4 flower borders containing various flowers

  ¶**16 Glan Elwy** && (Mr & Mrs D O Davies) Lge densely planted garden; mainly annuals; tubs and hanging baskets; greenhouses and tunnel at back of house. 1st prize winner

  ¶**17 Glan Elwy** && (Peter & Nanna Davies) Small flower garden at front; annuals and perennials with tubs and hanging baskets. Greenhouses at back and tunnel containing chrysanthemums

Maesmor Hall &&& (Mr & Mrs G M Jackson) Maerdy. 4m from Corwen on A5 towards Betws-y-Coed. Go through 2 sets of traffic lights, opp Goat Inn, turn L over bridge. 11 acres incl woodlands, mature trees, extensive rhododendrons, river walk and tumulus. TEAS. *Adm £1 Chd 50p. Sun May 22 (2-6)*

Merlyn && (Drs J E & B E J Riding) Moelfre, Abergele. Leave A55 (Conwy or Chester direction) at Bodelwyddan Castle, proceed uphill by castle wall 1m to Xrds. 0.1m to T-junction. (white bungalow) R B5381 towards Betws yn Rhos for 2m, then fork L (signed Llanfair TH) garden 0.4m on R. 2-acre garden developed from a field since 1987. Long mixed border; damp and gravel garden; many shrubs and old roses; rhododendrons and azaleas; spring garden. Views of sea. Teas and lunches available at Wheatsheaf, Betws yn Rhos. *Adm £1 Chd 50p. Sun July 10 (2-6). Private visits welcome Feb to Nov incl, please* **Tel 0745 824435**

The Mount &&& (Mr & Mrs J Major) Higher Kinnerton. 6m W of Chester, L off A5104 just after it crosses A55. Approx 2-acre garden with mature trees; shrubs and lawns; kitchen garden, variety of perennial plants some interesting and unusual. *Adm £1 Chd 50p. Private visits welcome, please* **Tel 0244 660 275**. *Best months June and July*

¶**New Abbey Bungalow** && (Mrs M Smyth) Gwespyr. Approx 2½m from Prestatyn on A548. Bungalow on L next to Jet Filling Station. Many spring bulbs. Intensively planted ½-acre garden with ponds, conservatory and greenhouses; over 50 containers with lilies, dwarf conifers etc. *Adm £1 Chd free (Share to Muscular Dystrophy®). Suns April 17, June 26 (2-4.30)*

Pen-y-Wern &&& (Dr & Mrs Forbes) Pontblyddyn, 5m SE of Mold, 7m NW of Wrexham. On E side of A541, ½ way between Pontblyddyn and Caergwrle. 2½-acre terraced country-house garden incl interesting small gardens. Shrubs and herbaceous borders; many varieties of roses. Magnificent copper beech with canopy circumference of 250ft. TEAS. *Adm £1 Chd 50p (Share to Hope Parish Church®). Sun June 26 (2-6)*

¶**Plas Ashpool and Coach House** &&& (Mrs G Shaw & Mrs F Bell) Llandyrnog. Nearest town Denbigh. Take Mold rd out of Denbigh to village of Bodfari. Turn R towards Llandyrnog on to B5429. House about 1½m on LH-side. 1½-acre garden to C17 house, developed from farm land by present owner. Consisting mainly of flowering shrubs and interesting trees; beautiful vistas of Clwydian Range and Vale. In conjunction with **Coach House**. Garden created by present owners over the last 5yrs, consisting of many rare and unusual herbaceous plants used in the cottage garden style within a semi-walled garden. Recent projects incl a sunken garden and summer house. TEAS. *Adm £2 Chd 25p. Sun June 19 (2-6)*

Plas Newydd &&& (Mr & Mrs Geoffrey Jackson) Llanfair DC. [Grid Ref SJ 138 562] Take A525 from Ruthin for 1½m to Llanfair DC. Turn L at signpost to Graigfechan, ½m turn sharp L where rd bears R down lane, house and garden on L. 3½ acres of restored garden; shrubs, herbaceous, roses; walled garden and orchard. TEA. *Adm £1 Chd 50p. Sun Sept 4 (2-6)*

Plas yn Cefn && (Sir Watkin & Lady Williams-Wynn) St Asaph. From St Asaph take B5381 signed Glascoed and Betws yn Rhos. 1st L after EGA Factory; continue for 1½m. House on L. C15 house situated in informal 2-acre garden. Established rose garden, fruit cages and vegetables. New areas re-designed over last 2yrs; access to woodland walk with views across to Snowdonia. TEAS. *Adm £1 Chd 50p (Share to Cefn Church Fund®). Sun July 24 (2-4.30)*

Pontruffydd Hall &&& (Mr & Mrs W F Glazebrook) nr Bodfari. On A541, 1m W of Bodfari before Pontruffydd Bridge. Landscaped garden, magnificent views; approx 8 acres of mature trees; shrubs, bulbs and water garden; ornamental waterfowl on lake. Plant bring & buy stall. TEA. *Adm £1 Chd 50p (Share to Cruse Bereavement Care®). Sun April 10 (2-5)*

Plas-Yn-Rhos &&& (Miss M E Graham) Gellifor. 3m N of Ruthin A494. L at Llanbedr DC on B5429 2¼m house on R. ¾-acre garden with wide views of the Clwydian range, surrounds old Welsh Farmhouse dated 1594. Herbaceous borders; lawns with croquet; new young wood. (Gift stall and cream TEAS in aid of Clwyd Special Riding Centre) Large car park. *Adm £1 Chd 25p. Sun June 26 (2-6)*

Rhagatt Hall &&& (Cdr & Mrs F J C Bradshaw) Carrog. 1m NE of Corwen. A5 from Llangollen, 3m short of Corwen, turn R (N) for Carrog at garage, cross ˙R Dee and keep bearing L. 1st opening on R after Carrog and seeing river again. 5-acre garden with azaleas, rhododendrons, trees, rare magnolia, bluebell wood; extensive views. Pony rides. Georgian house. TEAS. *Adm £1 Chd 50p. Sun May 22 (2-6)*

River House &&& (Mrs Gwydyr-Jones) Erbistock. 5m S of Wrexham. On A528 Wrexham-Shrewsbury rd, ¼m before Overton Bridge (opp turning A539 to Ruabon). Small garden with unusual shrubs and plants. *Adm £1 Chd 50p. Sun June 12 (2-6)*

Three Chimneys && (Mr & Mrs Hollington) 3m SW of Wrexham via Rhostyllen. From Wrexham A5152 fork R at Black Lion onto B5097. From Ruabon B5605 turn L onto B5426 signed Minera. Turn R ½m over bridge, L at Water Tower. Garden ¼m on L opp post box. Forester's garden of 1 acre; maples, conifers, cornus and sorbus species and varieties. Many small trees used in the manner of a herbaceous border. Very unusual and interesting. *Adm £1 Chd 25p. Suns Apr 24 (2-6), Oct 23 (1-5)*

Tir-y-Fron &&& (Mr & Mrs P R Manuel) Llangollen Road, Ruabon. 5m from Wrexham, take A539 from Ruabon By-Pass, signed Llangollen, turn R on brow of hill after 200yds. 1¾-acre garden with shrubs and herbaceous plants surrounded by mature trees with quarry. Offa's Dyke separates garden from drive. TEAS. *Adm £1 Chd free (Share to Llangollen Canal Boat Trust©). Private visits welcome April 1 to Sept 1, please* **Tel 0978 821633**

Trem-Ar-For & (Mr & Mrs L Whittaker) 125 Cwm Rd, Dyserth. From Dyserth to Rhuddlan rd A5151. Turn L at Xrds signed Cwm, fork L and at traffic de-restriction sign house on L. ¾-acre limestone terraced hillside garden with dramatic views towards Snowdon and Anglesey. A highly specialised garden with many rare and interesting plants with special emphasis on alpines, daphnes and specie paeonies. TEA. *Adm £1.25 OAPs £1 Chd 50p (Share to North Wales Wildlife Trust©). Sun May 15 (2-5.30). Private visits welcome April to Sept, please* **Tel 0745 570349**

Tyn-Y-Craig &&& (Maj & Mrs Harry Robertson) Llandrillo. [Grid ref: SJ008377] 1½m from Llandrillo towards Bala off the B4401 Corwen to Bala Rd. Developed over 20 yrs, a hillside garden approx 1½ acres, incorporating 6 descending landscaped pools. TEA. *Adm £1 Chd 50p (Share to Royal Marsden Hospital Cancer Appeal®). Sun May 15 (2-5.30)*

¶**Tyn-y-Pwll** &&& (Mr & Mrs Roger Percival) Llandegla. On A525 Wrexham to Ruthin. 7m SE of Ruthin, 12m W of Wrexham, 6m N of Llangollen. 500yds NE from top of Nant-y-Garth. 200yds W of junction of A525 and A542 to Llangollen. ¾-acre 18yr-old organic garden, at 900ft on limestone. Old-fashioned plants, wild flowers, varied trees and shrubs; vegetables and soft fruits; sheltered areas; field parking. TEAS. *Adm £1 Chd free (Share to Llandegla Church®). Sun July 31 (2-6)*

Welsh College of Horticulture && Northop. Village of Northop is 3m from Mold and close to the A55 expressway. Mature gardens incorporating many national award winning features. Commercial sections. Garden Centre and retail sections where produce and garden sundries can be purchased. A Golf Course is being constructed for the teaching of Greenkeeping Skills. Many local trade and craft skills are on display, vintage machinery set out by proud owners and a model railway. Student demonstrations showing various horticultural, floristry and engineering skills. TEAS. Car parking. *Adm £1.50 OAP's & Chd 50p families £3.50. Sat July 2 (10-5)*

¶2 **Woodside Cottages** &✿ (Mrs J L Wilson) Halton. 7m N of Oswestry. Follow A5-A483. R off roundabout signed Halton. R at next roundabout ¼m under bridge

and down hill. Garden on L. Alternatively N through Chirk (towards Llangollen) ¾m turn R. (signed Black Park) ½m on R. A small but interesting cottage garden with a variety of different features incl alpine, heather, shrubbery, pond and bog areas. Over 100 hardy geraniums can be seen amongst the many unusual herbaceous plants and shrubs. TEAS. *Adm £1 Chd 25p (Share to Clwyd Special Riding Trust©). Sun May 29 (12-5)*

Dyfed

Hon County Organisers:
  North (Ceredigion District)   Mrs P A Latham, Garreg Farm, Glandyfi, Machynlleth SY20 8SS
  South (Carmarthen, Dinefwr,   The Lady Jean Philipps, Slebech Hall, Haverfordwest SA 62 4AX
  Pembroke & Preseli Districts)

DATES OF OPENING

By appointment
For telephone numbers and other details see garden descriptions. Private visits welcomed

Blaengwrfach Isaf, nr Llandyssul
The Forge, Narberth
Great Griggs, Narberth
Hean Castle, Saundersfoot
Living Garden, Bryn
Llanllyr, Talsarn
The Mill House, Glandyfi
Old Cilgwyn Gardens, Newcastle
  Emlyn
Penrallt Ffynnon, Newcastle Emlyn
Winllan, nr Lampeter

Regular openings
For details see garden descriptions

Cae Hir, Cribyn. Daily, see text
The Dingle, Crundale. Daily except
  Tues March 13 to Oct 16
Hilton Court Nurseries, Roch. Daily
  March to Oct 1

Saundersfoot Bay Leisure Park. Daily
  March 30 to Sept 28
Stammers Gardens, Saundersfoot.
  Daily April to Oct
Winllan, nr Lampeter

April 24 Sunday
  Pant-yr-Holiad, Rhydlewis
May 1 Sunday
  Stammers Gardens, Saundersfoot
May 2 Sunday
  Stammers Gardens, Saundersfoot
May 8 Sunday
  Post House, nr Whitland
May 15 Sunday
  Colby Woodland Garden, Narberth
  Ffynone, Boncath
  Pant-yr-Holiad, Rhydlewis
May 22 Sunday
  Cae Hir, Cribyn
  Great Griggs, Narbeth
  Post House, nr Whitland
May 29 Sunday
  Hean Castle, Saundersfoot
  Slebech Hall, Haverfordwest
June 12 Sunday
  Cae Hir, Cribyn

Living Garden, Bryn
June 19 Sunday
  Carrog, nr Llanrhystyd
  Danhiraeth, Drefach-Felindre
  Pant-yr-Holiad, Rhydlewis
June 26 Sunday
  Llanllyr, Talsarn
July 10 Sunday
  Cae Hir, Cribyn
  Danhiraeth, Drefach-Felindre
July 17 Sunday
  Bryngoleu, Llannon
  Pant-yr-Holiad, Rhydlewis
July 23 Saturday
  Millinford, nr Haverfordwest
July 24 Sunday
  Millinford, nr Haverfordwest
July 27 Wednesday
  7 Maes yr Awel, Ponterwyd
August 7 Sunday
  Blaencilgoed House, Ludchurch
August 14 Sunday
  Great Griggs, Narberth
  Pant-yr-Holiad, Rhydlewis
September 4 Sunday
  Pant-yr-Holiad, Rhydlewis

DESCRIPTIONS OF GARDENS

Blaencilgoed House &✿ (Mr & Mrs Wyn Jones) Ludchurch. 4m SE of Narberth taking the B4314 to Princes Gate. 1-acre garden created over 25yrs. Herbaceous borders, shrubs, vegetables, conservatory. TEAS. *Adm £1 Chd free (Share to CRMF Narberth Branch®). Sun Aug 7 (11-5)*

Blaengwrfach Isaf &✿ (Mrs Gail M Farmer) Bancyffordd, 2m W of Llandysul. Leaving Llandysul on Cardigan rd, by Half Moon pub fork left; continue on this road;

approx 1½m, after village sign Bancyffordd farm track on right. ¾-acre garden incorporating woodland, wild and cottage garden aspects within a secluded and sheltered area. Created by present owners over the past 20 years. Many specie and shrub roses; old-fashioned and scented plants grown in variety of ways amongst unusual trees planted for all year interest. Areas specially created with bees, butterflies and birds in mind; new pathway bordered by wild-flower meadow open 1991. Adjacent craft workshops. Teas in village 1m. *Adm 75p Chd free. Private visits welcome April, May, June, Oct (10-4), please* **Tel 0559 362604**

¶**Bryngoleu** ✿✿ (Mr & Mrs Ivor Russell) Llannon. 13m from Swansea, 7m from Llanelli. From junction 49 (Pont Abraham) on M4 take A48(T) in the direction of Cross Hands. Turn L after approx 3kms towards Village of Llwyn Teg. At [map ref SN 56 E on OS 159.] ½-acre garden with converted stable block Visitor Centre, leading to extensive choice of walks each about ½m long in mature and newly developing woodlands and alongside natural streams. 15 acres overall incl a large lake; fine views of the surrounding countryside. Ample seating. TEAS. *Adm £1.50 Chd 50p. Sun July 17 (2-6)*

Cae Hir ✿✿ (Mr Wil Akkermans) Cribyn. W on A482 from Lampeter. After 5m turn S on B4337. Cae Hir is 2m on L. Beautiful and peaceful 6-acre garden on exposed W facing slope. Entirely created and maintained by owner from 4 overgrown fields of rough grazing. Started in 1985. Many unusual features found unexpectedly around each corner including red, yellow and blue sub-gardens, bonsai 'room', stonework, ponds, lovely views. Water garden being developed. As featured on radio and TV. TEA. *Adm £1.50 Chd 50p. Open daily except Mons April to Oct (1-6). Also open Bank Hols. For NGS Suns May 22, June 12, July 10 (1-6)*

Carrog ✿✿ (Mr & Mrs Geoffrey Williams) Llanddeiniol, NE of Llanrhystyd. From A487 Aberystwyth-Aberaeron rd, 6m S of Aberystwyth, 1m beyond Blaenplwyf TV mast. Bus stop (Aberystwyth Aberaeron) ¼m from house. 5-acres in setting of mature trees, reclaimed, replanted and maintained entirely by owners; walled garden; lawns; shrubs; young ornamental trees; pond with bog and water plants; shrub roses; conservatory with orchids. TEAS. *Adm £1 Chd 30p. Sun June 19 (2-6)*

¶**Colby Woodland Garden** ✿✿ (The National Trust) ½m inland from Amroth and 2m E of Saundersfoot. Signposted by Brown Tourist Signs on the coast rd and the A477. A 2-acre wooland garden in a secluded wooded valley with a large and impressive collection of rhododendrons and other shrubs. Tea rooms and gallery. Walled garden open by kind permission of Mr & Mrs A Scourfield Lewis. TEAS. *Adm £2.50 Chd £1. Sun May 15 (10-5)*

¶**Danhiraeth** ✿✿ (Mrs Hewitt) Velindre. Take A484 from Carmarthen (18m), or Newcastle Emlyn (4m). From Carmarthen follow sign-posts for Drefach-Felindre 2m N of Cwm-Duad. From Newcastle Emlyn follow sign-post for Drefach-Felindre, 2m E of Newcastle Emlyn. In Drefach-Felindre take turning up hill by church for approx ½m. Turn R down un-gated farm track for about ½m. Entrance via green door, ring bell, parking ltd. 1-acre woodland garden; informal terraces, ponds, statues, fountain and waterfall, ornamental trees and shrub roses. TEA. *Adm £1 No children due to water hazard. Suns June 19, July 10 (11-6)*

The Dingle ✿✿ (Mrs A J Jones) Crundale. On approaching Haverfordwest from Carmarthen on A40, take R turn at 1st roundabout signed Fishguard & Cardigan. At next roundabout take R turn on to B4329. ½m on fork R opp General Picton; then 1st right into Dingle Lane. 3-acres plantsman's garden; rose garden; formal beds; scree; herbaceous border; unusual shrubs; water garden; woodland walk. Picturesque and secluded; free roaming peacocks.

Nursery adjoining. Tearoom. *Adm £1 Chd 50p (Share to Cancer Relief Macmillan Nurses Fund®). Daily (except Tues) March 13 to Oct 16 (10-6)*

Ffynone ✿ (Earl & Countess Lloyd George of Dwyfor) Boncath. From Newcastle Emlyn take A487 to Cenarth, turn left on B4332, turn left again at crossroads just before Newchapel. Large woodland garden in process of restoration. Lovely views, fine specimen trees, rhododendrons, azaleas. Ask for descriptive leaflet. House by John Nash (1793), not shown. Later additions and garden terraces by F. Inigo Thomas c1904. TEA. *Adm £1 Chd free. Sun May 15 (2-6)*

The Forge ✿✿✿ (I & S Mcleod-Baikie) Landshipping. Nearest town Narbeth. Landshipping well sign posted. Pass New Park with pillar box; 200yds further on, gate on R. Approx 9 acres recently planted woodland garden with many varieties of bulbs, trees and shrub roses. Small, pretty very charming. Featured in NGS video 2, see page 344. *Private visits welcome mid-March to mid-April and also in June, please* **Tel 0834 891279**

¶**Great Griggs** ✿✿✿ (M A & W A Owen) Llanteg. A477 from St Clears, past Red Roses, next village Llanteg. Signposted on LH-side Colby Woodland Garden, turn L immed, 2nd entrance on R. ½-acre garden made from part of field in the last 10yrs. Mainly shrub and alpines; stonework incl seating; fish and duck ponds with ornamental water fowl. Unusual pets. TEAS. *Adm £1 Chd 50p. Suns May 22, Aug 14 (2-6). Private visits also welcome, please* **Tel 0834 83414**

Hean Castle ✿✿✿ (Mr & Mrs T Lewis) Saundersfoot. 1m N of Saundersfoot. 1½m SE of Kilgetty. Take Amroth road from Saundersfoot or the Sardis road from Kilgetty. 2-acres; mixed borders with some unusual plants and shrubs; rose garden; walled garden and greenhouse; conifers; pot plants and troughs. Good view. TEAS. *Adm £1.50 Chd free. Suns May 29 (11-5). Also private visits welcome, please* **Tel 0834 812222**

Hilton Court Nurseries ✿✿✿ (Mrs Cheryl Lynch) Roch. From Haverfordwest take the A487 to St Davids. 6m from Haverfordwest signs L to Hilton Court Nurseries. 4 acres of garden with superb setting overlooking ponds and woodlands. Spectacular lily ponds in July and August; wild flower walks; unusual trees and shrubs giving colour throughout the year. Nursery adjoining. TEAS. *Collecting box. Daily March to October 1 (9.30-5.30), October (10.30-4)*

Living Garden ✿✿ (Alan C Clarke Esq) 4a Brynmorlais Bryn, Llanelli, 2½m NE of town on B4297. Parking 'Royal Oak' Bryn. Garden near by (signed). Long, slim plantsman's garden subdivided for interest. Wide range of plants; terracotta ware, pools and water features. TEAS in aid of Hall St. Church. *Adm £1 Chd 25p. Sun June 12 (2-5.30); also private visits welcome, please* **Tel 0554 821274** *April to Oct*

Regular Openers. See head of county section.

Llanllyr &&& (Mr & Mrs Robert Gee) Talsarn 6m NW of Lampeter in B4337 to Llanrhystud. Garden of about 4 acres, originally laid out in 1830s, renovated, replanted and extended since 1986. Mixed borders; lawns; bulbs; large fish pond with bog and water plants. Formal water garden. Shrub rose borders; foliage, species and old-fashioned plants. TEAS *Adm £1 Chd 50p. Sun June 26 (2-6). Private visits welcome April to Oct. Please write*

7 Maes yr Awel && (Mrs Beryl Birch) Ponterwyd. From Aberystwyth take A44 towards Llangurig. At Ponterwyd Village, turn R on to A4120 Devil's Bridge rd, then turn 1st L almost immed. Small hillside garden in mountainous surroundings. 16yrs challenging gardening on steep acid meadowland at an altitude of approx 800ft have resulted in sheltered 'hidden' gardens with pools and fountain, herbaceous plantings, flowering shrubs and specimen trees. Ample seating; large conservatory for refreshments in inclement weather. TEA. *Adm 70p Acc chd free. Wed July 27 (10-4)*

¶The Mill House && (Prof & Mrs J M Pollock) Glandyfi. On main A487 rd from Aberystwyth to Machynlleth, 5½m from Machynlleth. Coming from Aberystwyth direction, pass through Eglwys Fach village; turn R up lane which is almost directly opposite roadside sign for Glandyfi (on L) Mill House is 2nd house up this lane (approx 150yds). [OS 691963] Approx 1-acre garden of a former water mill. Mainly woodland in character with azaleas, rhododendrons, mill pond, stream and waterfalls. *Collecting Box. Private visits welcome Suns, Weds May to June, please* **Tel 0654 781342**

Millinford && (Drs B W & A D Barton) Millin, The Rhos, 3m E of Haverfordwest; on A40 to Carmarthen turn R signed The Rhos, take turn to Millin, R at Millin Chapel then immediate L over river bridge. 4 acres on bank of Millin Creek. Plantsman's garden, large collection of trees and shrubs with alpine area, herbaceous borders and small lake. TEA. *Adm £1.50 Chd 50p (Share to NSPCC®). Sat, Sun July 23, 24 (11-6)*

Old Cilgwyn Gardens & (Mr & Mrs E Fitzwilliams) Newcastle Emlyn. Situated 1m N of Newcastle Emlyn on the B4571, turn R into entrance gates in dip in rd. 12-acre woodland garden set in parkland, 53 acres of which are Sites of Special Scientific Interest; snowdrops, daffodils, bluebells, azaleas, rhododendrons etc; ponds and Chinese bridge. For those prepared to walk, a 100yr-old tulip tree can be seen on the S.S.S.I. land. *Adm £1. Private visits welcome all year, please* **Tel 0239 710244**

Pant-yr-Holiad && (Mr & Mrs G H Taylor) Rhydlewis, 12m NW Llandysul. NE Cardigan. From coast rd take B4334 at Brynhoffnant S towards Rhydlewis; after 1m turn left; driveway 2nd L. 5-acres embracing distinctive herb garden, alpine beds, water features, rare trees and shrubs in woodland setting; extensive collection rhododendron species; fancy water-fowl. Recently completed area with collections of birch and unusual herbaceous plants. TEA. *Adm £1.50 Chd 50p (Share to Rhydlewis Village Hall®). Only open Sun April 24, May 15, June 19, July 17, Aug 14, Sept 4 (2-5)*

Penrallt Ffynnon & (Mr R D Lord & Ms Jane Lord) Cwm-cou, 3m NW of Newcastle Emlyn. Follow Cwm-cou to Cardigan rd (B4570) up long hill for 1¼m; turn right for 150yds; ignore sharp left bend, bear right along narrow lane for 400yds. Maturing collection of trees and shrubs in 4½ acres; crammed with some stunning plantings; eucalyptus species, maples, cherries, shrub roses, conifers, camellia hedge; rhododendrons, flowering Christmas to June; many varieties of daffodil. All year interest but especially Feb to early summer & autumn colour. Seeds for sale. *Collecting box. Private visits welcome all year, please* **Tel 0239 710654**

Post House && (Mrs Jo Kenaghan) Cwmbach 6m N of St Clears. From Carmarthen W on A40. Take B4298 through Meidrim; leave by centre lane signed Llanboidy. Turn right at Xrds signed Blaenwaun; right at Xrds to Cwmbach; garden bottom of hill. From Whitland E on A40, left at Ivydean nurseries, right at 3rd Xrds signed Cwmbach. 4-acre valley garden in the making; rhododendrons, azaleas, camellias, unusual trees and shrubs underplanted with hardy orchids, anemonies, trilliums, wild snowdrops, bluebells, etc. Large pool, newly developed bog garden. Old roses, herbaceous plants. Greenhouses and conservatory. Plants for sale. TEAS. *Adm £1.50 OAP's & Chd £1. ▲Suns May 8, 22 (2pm onwards)* **Tel 0994 484213**

Saundersfoot Bay Leisure Park && (Ian Shuttleworth Esq) Broadfield, Saundersfoot. On B4316, ¾m S from centre of Saundersfoot. Interesting layout of lawns, shrubs and herbaceous borders with many plants of botanical interest in 20-acre modern holiday leisure park. Large rock garden and water feature; laburnum walk. Holders of a National collection of Pontentilla fruticosa. Tea Saundersfoot. *Adm free. March 30 to Sept 28 daily (10-5)*

Slebech Hall & (The Lady Jean Philipps) 6m E of Haverfordwest. From Carmarthen via A40, take 1st turn left after Canaston Bridge, signed The Rhos; drive on left, about ½m with 1 white lodge. Bus: Haverfordwest-Tenby or Haverfordwest-Carmarthen; bus stop 3m. Large garden; fine position on bank of the Cleddau; picturesque ruins of Church of St. John of Jerusalem in garden. TEAS. *Adm £1 Chd free (Share to Uzmaston Church Restoration Fund®). Sun May 29 (2-7)*

¶Stammers Gardens && (Mr & Mrs B W Sly) Saundersfoot. ¼m W of Stammers Rock Village on Stammers Rd. 4½ acres of garden on sloping site with magnificent views over Carmarthen Bay. Restoration still in progress with collection of conifers, azaleas, rhododendrons, flowering cherries and interesting and rare shrubs. ½ acre carp ponds; further 2 acres being developed in woodland. Challenging and interesting grass walks. TEA. *Adm £1.50 OAP's and Chd 50p. Open April to Oct (10-6). For NGS Sun, Mon May 1, 2 (10-6)*

Winllan (Mr & Mrs Ian Callan) Talsarn. 8m NNW of Lampeter on B4342, Talsarn-Llangeitho rd. 6-acres wildlife garden with large pond, herb-rich meadow, small woodland and 600 yds of river bank walk. Over 200 species of wildflowers with attendant butterflies, dragonflies and birds. Limited suitability for wheelchairs. *Adm £1 Chd 50p (under 12 free). Open May & June daily (12-6). Also private visits welcome July & Aug, please* **Tel 0570-470612**

The Glamorgans

Hon County Organiser: Mrs Christopher Cory, Penllyn Castle, Cowbridge, South Glamorgan
Tel 0446 772780

DATES OF OPENING

By appointment
For telephone numbers and other details see garden descriptions. Private visits welcomed

11 Arno Road, Little Coldbrook
11 Eastcliff, Southgate, Swansea
24 Elm Grove Place, Dinas Powis
Ffynnon Deilo, Pendoylan
Newcastle House Gardens, Bridgend
19 Westfield Road, Glyncoch, Pontypridd
Silver Birches, Ty Gwyn Ave, Cardiff
9 Willowbrook Gardens, Mayals, Swansea

March 27 Sunday
Penllyn Castle, Cowbridge
April 24 Sunday
Dumgoyne, Radyr
May 8 Sunday
Dumgoyne, Radyr
Ewenny Priory, nr Bridgend
May 15 Sunday
Llanvithyn House, Llancarfan
9 Willowbrook Gardens, Mayals, Swansea
May 22 Sunday
Coedarhydyglyn, nr Cardiff
May 29 Sunday
Springside, Pen-y-Turnpike, Dinas Powys
June 5 Sunday
Ty Gwyn Gardens, Penylan, Cardiff

June 11 Saturday
Cwmpennar Gardens
June 12 Sunday
Cwmpennar Gardens
Merthyr Mawr House, Bridgend
June 19 Sunday
The Clock House, Llandaff
Gelly Farm, Cymmer
June 26 Sunday
11 Eastcliff, Southgate, Swansea
July 3 Sunday
Pontygwaith Farm, Edwardsville
July 17 Sunday
29 Min-y-Coed, Radyr
August 7 Sunday
29 Min-y-Coed, Radyr
Pontygwaith Farm, Edwardsville

DESCRIPTIONS OF GARDENS

11 Arno Road ⌗❀ (Mrs D Palmer) Little Coldbrook. From A4050 Cardiff to Barry, take roundabout marked Barry Docks and Sully. Then 2nd R into Coldbrook Rd, 2nd L into Langlands Rd, then 6th R into Norwood Cresc; 1st L into Arno Rd. 40ft × 30ft informal plantsman's garden with ponds, herbaceous plants, gravelled area planted with low growing plants. Hardy geraniums; penstemons specialities. TEAS. *Adm £1. Private visits welcome Suns March to Oct, please* **Tel 0446 743642**

The Clock House &⌗❀ (Prof & Mrs Bryan Hibbard) Cathedral Close, Llandaff, 2m W of Cardiff. Follow signs to Cathedral via A4119. Bus: Cardiff alight Maltsters Arms. Small walled garden; fine old trees; wide variety of shrubs and plants; important collection of shrub, species and old roses. NT stall. TEA. *Adm £1.50 Acc chd free. Sun June 19 (2-6)*

Coedarhydyglyn (Sir Cennydd Traherne) 5m W of Cardiff. Bus: Western Welsh, Cardiff-Cowbridge, alight gates. Natural terrain, pleasant situation; lawns, flowering shrubs, good collection of conifers; Japanese garden, fine trees. TEA. *Adm £1 Chd 20p (Share to Cardiff and District Samaritans®). Sun May 22 (2.30-6)*

Cwmpennar Gardens ⌗❀ Mountain Ash 1m. From A4059 turn R 100yds past the traffic lights; follow sign to Cefnpennar, follow rd uphill through woods for ¾m, bear right sharply uphill before bus shelter, gardens 200yds. Car park 100yds past bus shelter. Mixture of formal and informal gardens with some natural woodland in all three of conservation interest. Variety of shrubs, rhododendrons and azaleas, rockeries, shrub roses; new plantings of shrubs and roses, small ponds. Rich in bird life, with nest boxes usually occupied. Gardens high on mountain side in secluded rural surroundings of coal mining valley. Gardens filmed for BBC WALES 'Down to Earth', shown 1993. TEAS. Glamorgan Wildlife Trust Sales stall. *Combined adm £1 Chd 50p (Share to St Margarets Church Restoration Fund©). Sat, Sun June 11, 12 (2-6)*

    The Cottage (Judge & Mrs Hugh Jones)
    Ivy Cottage (Mr & Mrs D H Phillips)
    Woodview (Mrs V Bebb)

Dumgoyne ⌗❀ (Mr & Mrs Hubert Jackson) 90 Heol Isaf, Radyr. A4119 Cardiff-Llantrisant rd; 2m W of Llandaff Rd turn R on to B4262 for Radyr. Rhondda buses: alight at Radyr turning. Cardiff bus service 33 stops near house. Small, immaculate, Chelsea-inspired garden; large glasshouse with superb collection of pelargoniums. *Adm 50p Acc chd free (Share to Radyr Chain Voluntary Orgn.©). For NGS, special plant sale days Suns April 24, May 8 (2.30-5)*

11 Eastcliff &⌗❀ (Mrs Gill James) Southgate. Take the Swansea to Gower road and travel 6m to Pennard. Go through the village of Southgate and take the 2nd exit off the roundabout. Garden 200yds on the L. Seaside garden approx ⅓ acre and developed in a series of island and bordered beds for spring and summer interest. A large number of white and silver plants. Unusual plants and shrubs. TEA. *Adm £1 Chd free. Sun June 26 (2-5). Also private visits welcome, please* **Tel 0792 233310**

24 Elm Grove Place &⌗❀ (Mr & Mrs J Brockhurst) Dinas Powis. Elm Grove Place is a cul-de-sac 200yds E of Dinas Powis Railway Station on the Cardiff to Barry rd (A4055) under railway bridge, 4m from Cardiff, 3m from Barry. Plantsman's garden 60m × 30m, herbaceous, shrubs, greenhouse and several alpine and scree beds; patio area with some unusual container plants; pergola with clematis, wistaria and jasmine. TEA. *Adm £1 Chd free. Private visits welcome anytime between April to end Sept, please* **Tel 0222 513681**

Ewenny Priory &≪✤ (R C Q Picton Turbervill Esq) Ewenny, 2m S of Bridgend. Bus: Bridgend-Ogmore, alight Ewenny Bridge, ½m. Medium-sized garden; plants of interest. Old walled priory dating from 1137 and Church (house not open). NT, plant/produce stalls. NO DOGS. TEAS. *Adm £1.50 Chd 50p. Sun May 8 (2-6)*

Ffynnon Deilo ≪ (Mr & Mrs John Lloyd) Pendoylan Cowbridge 4½m. A48 Cardiff to Cowbridge. From Cardiff turn R at Sycamore Cross (½-way between St Nicholas and Bonvilston) to Peterston-Super-Ely; take 2nd L garden ¾m on R. Small cottage garden with fish pond & Holy Well; interesting plants. Difficult for wheelchairs. *Private visits welcome April to Aug, please* **Tel 0446 760292**

Gelly Farm ≪✤ (Mrs A Appleton, Mrs L Howells, Mrs S Howells) Cymmer. 10m N E of Port Talbot, on A4107, ½m beyond Cymmer, towards Treorchy, turning off rd on R. 4 small varied gardens and 1 vegetable garden grouped around the farmyard of a historically listed working hill farmstead on the slopes of a steep valley 'as much a cultural experience as a horticultural one'. TEA 50p. *Adm £1.50 Chd free (Share to The Royal Agricultural Benevolent Institution®). Sun June 19 (2-6)*

Llanvithyn House ≪ (Mr & Mrs L H W Williams) Llancarfan 1.8m S of A48 at Bonvilston, sign for Llancarfan 100yds W of Bonvilston Garage, 1m N of Llancarfan. Medium-size garden on site of C6 monastery. C17 gate house. Lawns, interesting trees, shrubs, borders. TEAS if fine. *Adm £1.50 Chd 25p. Sun May 15 (2-6)*

Merthyr Mawr House ≪✤ (Mr & Mrs Murray McLaggan) Merthyr Mawr. 2m SW of Bridgend. Large garden with flowering borders, shrubs, scree garden; wood garden with chapel ruin C14 on site of Iron Age fort. TEA. *Adm £1.50 Chd £1 (Share Mid-Glamorgan Red Cross®). Sun June 12 (2-6)*

29 Min-y-Coed ≪✤ (Mr & Mrs J H Taylor) Radyr, 6m from Cardiff. On A4119 2m W of Llandaff turn R on B4262 towards Morganstown. From M4 junction 32 on A470 to Taffs Well turn L, then L to B4262 for Radyr. Hillside terraced informal garden with year round colour. TEAS. *Adm £1 Chd free. Suns July 17, Aug 7 (2-5.30)*

Newcastle House Gardens ≪✤ (C D Fraser Jenkins Esq) West Road, Bridgend. From town centre 400yds up Park St turn R up St Leonards Rd, 2nd R into West Rd. Small town garden completely surrounded by walls; tender plants grown in unheated greenhouses; rare trees, shrubs and herbaceous plants. *Adm £1.50 Chd 50p Acc children under 14 free. Private visits only welcome, please* **Tel 0656 766880**

Penllyn Castle &≪ (Mrs Christopher Cory) 3m NW of Cowbridge. From A48 turn N at Pentre Meyrick. Turn first R and at T-junction straight ahead through gate, leaving church on L. Large garden with fine views; old trees and some new planting; spring shrubs (rhododendrons and magnolias) and bulbs. TEA. *Adm £1.50 Chd 50p. Sun March 27 (2-6)*

Pontygwaith Farm &✤ (Mr & Mrs R J G Pearce) Edwardsville. Take A4054 Old Cardiff to Merthyr Rd. Travel N for approx 3m through Quaker's Yard and Edwardsville. 1m out of Edwardsville turn sharp L by old bus shelter. Garden at bottom of hill. Medium-sized garden; surrounding c17 farmhouse adjacent to Trevithick's Tramway; situated in picturesque wooded valley; fish pond, lawns, perennial borders. TEAS. *Adm £1 Chd 50p. Suns July 3, Aug 7 (2-6)*

¶**Springside** ≪✤ (Prof & Mrs Michael Laurence) Dinas Powys. From Cardiff take B4055 to Penarth and Dinas Powys as far as the Leckwith (Cardiff Distributor Rd) roundabout. Then take B4267 to Llandough, up Leckwith Hill past Leckwith Village, take R-hand fork in rd into Pen-y-Turnpike as far as the 30mph sign. Turn R immed. into Springside. Undulating 2-acre garden recently rescued after 30yrs of wilderness. Spacious, with views and newly planted trees: small ponds and old village water supply returned to nature, where children must be supervised; vegetable garden. Parking in the grounds only available in dry weather. TEA. *Adm £1.50 Chd 50p (Share to Dinas Powys Orchestra©). Sun May 29 (2-6)*

¶**Ty Gwyn Gardens** ≪ Penylan, Cardiff. TEAS at 10, Ty Gwyn Rd. *Combined adm £2 Chd free. Sun June 5 (2-6)*

¶**Silver Birches** ✤ (Mrs Cheng) Take Cardiff East turning off A48. Take Cyncoed direction at Moat House roundabout. At top of hill, R at traffic lights, L into Bronwydd Ave. Ty Gwyn Ave is 100yds on R. Approx ¼-acre woodland garden. Small collection of hardy geraniums and other slug resistant plants. *Private visits also welcome, please* **Tel 0222 488339**

¶**The George Thomas Centre for Hospice Care** ✤ (The George Thomas Memorial Trust) N from city centre. Aim for Penylan Hill (nr Roath Park). Ty Gwyn Rd is 2nd turning L past the park; house on R before bend; 'slow' sign on rd. From Silver Birches, down Ty Gwyn Rd about ½m; house on L just after bend. City garden on 2 levels divided by a lovely wisteria. 1st level has an interesting herbaceous bed; 2nd level has a reclaimed bank and some good camellia shrubs; also well established pond

¶**8 Ty Gwyn Rd** (Mr & Mrs Colin Daniel) Next door to George Thomas Centre. Reorganised during 1993; several new trees planted; gazebo planned with new patio; pond with koi carp

19 Westfield Road ≪✤ (Mr & Mrs Brian Dockerill) Glyncoch Pontypridd. From Pontypridd travel 1½m N along B4273 and take L turn by school. At top of hill follow road to L then take first R and R again into Westfield Rd. ½-acre garden divided by hedges and dry stone walls into smaller areas each with a separate character. Differing habitats including pools, rock garden and peat beds allow a wide range of plants to be grown extending the season of interest through the year. TEA. *Adm £1 Chd 50p. Private visits welcome, please* **Tel 0443 402999**

By Appointment Gardens. These owners do not have a fixed opening day usually because they do not like crowds or have insufficient parking space. Owner will often give guided tour.

9 Willowbrook Gardens &⚘ (Dr & Mrs Gallagher) Mayals, 4m W of Swansea on A4067 (Mumbles) rd to Blackpill; take B4436 (Mayals) rd; 1st R leads to Westport Ave along W boundary of Clyne Park; 1st L into cul-de-sac. ½-acre informal garden designed to give natural effect with balance of form and colour between various areas linked by lawns; unusual trees suited to small suburban garden, esp conifers and maples; rock and water garden. TEAS. *Adm £1.20 Chd 30p. Sun May 15 (2-6) also private visits welcome, please* **Tel 0792 403268**

Gwent

Hon County Organiser: Mrs Glynne Clay, Lower House Farm, Nantyderry, Abergavenny NP7 9DP
Tel 0873 880257

Asst Hon County Organiser: Mrs R L Thompson, Llangwilym House, Llanfihangel Gobion, Abergavenny
Tel 0873 840269

DATES OF OPENING

By appointment
For telephone numbers and other details see garden descriptions. Private visits welcomed

Castle House, Usk
The Chain Garden, Abergavenny
Clytha Park, nr Abergavenny
Lower House Farm, Nantyderry
Wern Farm, Glascoed

Regular openings
For details see garden description

Penpergwm Lodge, nr Abergavenny.
    Thurs, Fris & Sats April 1 to Aug 13
Tredegar House & Park, Newport.
    Easter to end of Oct

May 8 Sunday
    Chwarelau Farm, Llanfapley, nr Abergavenny
May 15 Sunday
    Bryngwyn Manor, Raglan
May 21 Saturday
    Traligael, Monmouth
May 22 Sunday
    Clytha Park, nr Abergavenny ‡
    Trostrey Lodge, Bettws Newydd nr Usk ‡
May 29 Sunday
    Lower House Farm, Nantyderry
May 30 Monday
    Lower House Farm, Nantyderry
June 5 Sunday
    The Graig & Box Tree Cottage, nr Raglan
June 12 Sunday
    Llan-y-Nant, Coed Morgan, nr Abergavenny
June 19 Sunday
    Grace Dieu Court, Dingestow
    Wern Farm, Glascoed
June 25 Saturday
    Great Campston, Llanfihangel

    Crucorney
June 26 Sunday
    Great Campston, Llanfihangel
    Crucorney
July 3 Sunday
    Court St Lawrence, nr Usk
July 10 Sunday
    Llanfair Court, nr Abergavenny ‡
    Penpergwm Lodge, nr Abergavenny ‡
July 17 Sunday
    Great Killough, nr Aberavenny
    Tredegar House & Park, Newport
July 24 Sunday
    Brooklands, Mardy, Abergavenny
August 28 Sunday
    Lower House Farm, Nantyderry
August 29 Monday
    Lower House Farm, Nantyderry
September 4 Sunday
    Castle House, Usk
September 11 Sunday
    Tredegar House & Park, Newport
October 9 Sunday
    Llanover, nr Abergavenny

DESCRIPTIONS OF GARDENS

¶**Brooklands** ⚘❀ (Mr & Mrs D G Gordon) Mardy. From Monmouth, Newport and Merthyr, take the A465 rd to Hereford at roundabout 1m S of Abergavenny. Take 1st turning L. Brooklands approx ½m from that junction. Approx 1½ acres; herbaceous, lge rockery garden, woodland walk. **Brooklands Bungalow** (Mr & Mrs G Smith) Small ornamental garden adjacent to the Gavenny R linked to adjoining 3-acre woodland walk by footbridge. TEAS. *Adm £1.50 Chd 75p, 5 and under free. Sun July 24 (2-6)*

Bryngwyn Manor &⚘ (Mr S Inglefield) 2m W of Raglan. Turn S off old A40 (Abergavenny-Raglan rd) at Croes Bychan (Raglan Garden Centre); house ¼m up lane. 3 acres; good trees, mixed borders, spring bulbs. TEAS. *Adm £1.50 Chd under 10 free. Sun May 15 (2-6)*

Castle House ⚘❀ (Mr & Mrs J H L Humphreys) Usk; 200yds from Usk centre; turn up lane by fire station. Medium-sized garden; a flower garden of orderly disorder around ruins of Usk Castle. TEAS. *Adm £1 Chd free. Sun Sept 4 (2-6). Private visits also welcome, please* **Tel 029167 2563**

The Chain Garden ⚘ (Mrs C F R Price) Chapel Rd, 1m N of Abergavenny. Turn off A40 (on Brecon side of town) into Chapel Rd, garden at top of rd. 2 acres with stream; lawns; rhododendrons; shrubs, fruit and vegetables. *Adm £1 Chd free. Private visits welcome April 1 to Sept 30, please* **Tel 0873 853825**

> **By Appointment Gardens.** Avoid the crowds. Good chance of a tour by owner. See garden description for telephone number.

¶Chwarelau Farm ✲❀ (Mr & Mrs Maurice Trowbridge) On B4233 3½m E of Abergavenny. Medium-sized garden with magnificent views, approached down 200yd drive fringed by ornamental trees and shrubs. TEA. *Adm £1 Chd 50p. Sun May 8 (2-6)*

Clytha Park ♿ (R Hanbury-Tenison Esq) ½ way between Abergavenny and Raglan on old rd (not A40). 5 acres; C18 layout; trees, shrubs; lake. Teas at Clytha Arms (200yds walk thorugh garden) *Adm £1 Chd 50p. Sun May 22 (2-6). Private visits also welcome, please* **Tel 0873 840 300**

Court St Lawrence ♿✲❀ (Mrs G D Inkin) Llangovan, 6m SW of Monmouth, 5m NE of Usk, between Pen-y-Clawdd and Llangovan. 5 acres of garden and woodland with trees, shrubs, lake, roses etc. TEAS, plants and produce stalls. *Adm £1 Chd 25p. Sun July 3 (2-6)*

¶Grace Dieu Court ♿✲❀ (Mr & Mrs David McIntyre) Dingestow. 1½m NW of Dingestow Village which is 1m N of old Raglan-Monmouth rd (not dual carriageway). 3-acre open country garden in rolling countryside. Started from scratch in 1986. Mostly roses as shrubs, climbers and hedges; 2 lge ponds; herbaceous border, young specimen trees, shrubs and fine old oaks. TEAS. *Adm £1 Chd 50p. Sun June 19 (2-6)*

The Graig ♿✲❀ (Mrs Rainforth) Pen-y-Clawdd, SW of Monmouth. Turn S from Raglan-Monmouth rd (not Motorway) at sign to Pen-y-Clawdd. Bus: Newport-Monmouth, alight Keen's shop, ½m. Mixed cottage garden with interesting shrubs & roses. TEAS. Also open **Box Tree Cottage** ♿✲❀ (Mr & Mrs A Ward) Dingestow. On old A40 between Mitchel Troy & Raglan; ¾m from The Graig. 1-acre cottage garden; mixed borders, lawn, shrubs, conifers. *Combined adm £1.50 Chd free. Sun June 5 (2-6)*

Great Campston ✲❀ (Mr & Mrs A D Gill) 7m NE of Abergavenny; 2m towards Grosmont off A465 at Llanfihangel Crucorney. Drive on R just before brow of hill. Pretty 2-acre garden set in wonderful surroundings. Designed and planted from scratch by Mrs Gill, a garden designer; wide variety of interesting plants and trees enhanced by lovely stone walls, paving and summer house with fantastic views. The house stands 750ft above sea level on S facing hillside with spring fed stream feeding 2 ponds. TEAS. *Adm £1.50 Chd 50p. Sat, Sun June 25, 26 (2-6)*

Great Killough ♿✲❀ (Mr & Mrs John F Ingledew) Llantilio Crossenny, 6m E of Abergavenny. S of B4233. 3-acre garden created in the 1960s to complement mediaeval house. TEAS. *Adm £1 Chd free (Share to Barnardo's®). Sun July 17 (2-6)*

Llanfair Court ♿ (Sir William Crawshay) 5m SE of Abergavenny. Route old A40 and B4598. Medium-sized garden, herbaceous border, flowering shrubs, roses, water garden; modern sculpture. TEAS. *Adm £1 Chd 50p. Sun July 10 (2-6)*

Regular Openers. See head of county section.

Llanover ♿ (R A E Herbert, Esq) S of Abergavenny. Bus: Abergavenny-Pontypool, alight drive gates. Large water garden; some rare plants, autumn colour. TEAS. *Adm £1.50 Chd 50p. Sun Oct 9 (2-6)*

Llan-y-Nant ♿✲❀ (Mr & Mrs Charles Pitchford) Coed Morgan. 4m from Abergavenny, 5m from Raglan on old A40 (now B4598) Raglan to Abergavenny rd. Turn up lane opp 'Chart House' inn; pass Monmouthshire Hunt Kennels 500yds on R. 3 acres of garden and woodlands. Lawn, beds, shrubs, herbs, alpines and kitchen garden. Small lake with wild life. TEAS. *Adm £1.50 Chd 50p. Sun June 12 (2-6)*

Lower House Farm ✲❀ (Mr & Mrs Glynne Clay) Nantyderry, 7m SE of Abergavenny. From Usk-Abergavenny rd, B4598, turn off at Chain Bridge. Medium-sized garden designed for all year interest; mixed borders, fern island, bog garden, herb bed, paved area, unusual plants. Late flowering perennials. Featured in magazines and on T.V. and in NGS video 2, see page 344. TEAS. *Adm £1.50 Chd 50p. Suns, Mons May 29, 30; Aug 28, 29 (2-6) Private visits also welcome, please* **Tel Nantyderry 880257**

Penpergwm Lodge ♿❀ (Mr & Mrs Simon Boyle) 3m SE of Abergavenny. From Abergavenny take B 4598 towards Usk, after 2½m turn L opp King of Prussia Inn. Entrance 300yds on L. A 3-acre formal garden with mature trees, hedges & lawns; interesting potager with arches of vines & roses, mixed unusual plants & vegetables; rose walk, apple & pear pergola and S-facing terraces with sun-loving plants & special colour themes. Nursery with rare plants, many from the garden, specialising in unusual hardy perennials. Home of Catriona Boyle's School of Gardening, now in its 8th yr. Featured on Welsh TV and in Hortus. TEAS Sats only (Sun July 10 in aid of St Cadoc's Church). *Adm £1 Chd 20p. Thurs, Fris, Sats April 1 to Aug 13 (2-6). Sun July 10 (2-6)*

Traligael (Mr & Mrs E C Lysaght) 4m S of Monmouth via B4293 turn left for Whitebrook, or 3½m from A466 at Bigsweir Bridge past Whitebrook; garden alongside lane. 3-acre garden in woodland setting with water garden; rhododendrons and shrubs. *Adm £1 Chd free. Sat May 21 (2-6)*

Tredegar House & Park ♿✲❀ (Newport Borough Council) 2m SW of Newport Town Centre. Signposted from A48 (Cardiff road) and M4 junction 28. Set in 90 acres of historic parkland surrounding a magnificent late C17 house (also open) are a series of C17 & C18 formal walled gardens. The early C18 Orangery Garden is currently being recreated following extensive archaeological and research work. The orangery is also open. The central Cedar Garden has wide recently revived herbaceous borders. On NGS days the private gardens around the Curator's Cottage and Home Farm Cottage are also open. Away from the house is an Edwardian sunken garden restored mid 1980s. Spectacular rhododendrons border the lake. TEAS. *Adm £1.50 Chd 50p (Share to The Friends of Tredegar House and Park®). For NGS Suns July 17, Sept 11 (11-6). House, Gardens etc open Easter to end of Oct ring for details* **Tel 0633 815880**

Trostrey Lodge ✿✿ (Mr & Mrs R Pemberton) Bettws Newydd. Half way between Raglan and Abergavenny on old road (not A40). Turning to Bettws Newydd opposite Clytha gates, 1m on R. Pretty walled garden and small orchard in fine landscape; interesting plants; bring and buy plant sale in aid of Bettws Newydd Church. Teas at Clytha Arms 1m. *Adm £1 Chd 50p. Sun May 22 (2-6)*

Wern Farm ✿✿ (Mr & Mrs W A Harris) Between Usk and Little Mill on A472. Turn at signpost for Glascoed village, 1m from main rd (Beaufort Inn or Monkswood Garage). 1½-acres completely new garden created since 1984 following natural contours of ground; trees, shrubs, herbaceous plants, alpines, shrub roses; rockery; herbs; veg garden; small aviary; ¼ acre of flowers grown for drying. Demonstration of Bee-keeping by professional keeper and demonstration of wool spinning with organically dyed wool. TEAS. *Adm £1.20 Chd 30p. Sun June 19 (2-6); Private visits also welcome, please* **Tel 0495 785363**

Gwynedd & Anglesey

Hon County Organisers:
(Anglesey & North Gwynedd)

Mrs B S Osborne, Foxbrush, Aber Pwll, Port Dinorwic, Gwynedd LL56 4JZ
Tel 0248 670463

(South Gwynedd)

Mrs W N Jones, Waen Fechan, Islaw'r Dref, Dolgellau LL40 1TS
Tel 0341 423479

DATES OF OPENING

By appointment
For telephone numbers and other details see garden descriptions. Private visits welcomed

Bont Fechan Farm, Llanystumdwy
Bryniau, Boduan
Brynmelin, Ffestiniog
Bryn-y-Bont, Nantmor
Cefn Bere, Dolgellau
Glandderwen, Bontddu
Hafod Garregog, Nantmor
Hen Ysgoldy, Llanfrothen
Foxbrush, Aber Pwll, Port Dinorwic
Pencarreg, Glyn Garth, Menai Bridge
Henllys Lodge, Beaumaris

Regular openings
For details see garden descriptions

Bryn Meifod, Glan Conwy. Thurs in May & Sept, Suns in June & Aug
Coleg Glynllifon, Ffordd Clynnog. Mon to Fri during College terms
Crug Farm, nr Caernarfon. Thurs, Fri, Sat, Suns & Bank Hols Feb 26 to Sept 25
Plas Muriau, Betws-y-Coed. Tues to Sun March 1 to Oct 31
Plas Newydd, Anglesey. Daily except Sats March 30 to Sept 30, Fri & Sun only Oct 2 to Oct 30
Plas Penhelig, Aberdovey. April 1 to mid Oct Wed to Sun incl
Sychnant, Capelulo. Thurs May 6 to Sept 30

March 20 Sunday
Bryniau, Boduan
April 3 Sunday
Bont Fechan Farm, Llanystumdwy
Crug Farm, nr Caernarfon
Foxbrush, Aber Pwll, Port Dinorwic
April 4 Monday
Crug Farm, nr Caernarfon
Foxbrush, Aber Pwll, Port Dinorwic
April 10 Sunday
Bryniau, Boduan
April 24 Sunday
Gilfach, Rowen, nr Conwy
May 1 Sunday
Bryniau, Boduan
Foxbrush, Aber Pwll, Port Dinorwic
May 8 Sunday
Hafod Garregog, Nantmor
May 12 Thursday
Plas Newydd, Anglesey
May 15 Sunday
Bont Fechan Farm, Llanystumdwy
May 21 Saturday
Farchynys Cottage, Bontddu
May 22 Sunday
Bryniau, Boduan
Farchynys Cottage, Bontddu
Maenan Hall, Llanrwst
May 29 Sunday
Bryn Eisteddfod, Glan Conway
Bryn Golygfa, Bontddu ‡
Crug Farm, nr Caernarfon
Farchynys Cottage, Bontddu ‡
Glandderwen, Bontddu ‡
Penrhyn Castle, nr Bangor
Pen-y-Parc, Beaumaris

May 30 Monday
Bryn Golygfa, Bontddu ‡
Crug Farm, nr Caernarfon
Glandderwen, Bontddu ‡
June 12 Sunday
Bryniau, Boduan
June 18 Saturday
Henllys Lodge, Beaumaris
June 19 Sunday
Gilfach, Rowen, nr Conwy
Henllys Lodge, Beaumaris
June 26 Sunday
Foxbrush, Aber Pwll, Port Dinorwic
The Herb Garden, Pentre Berw
June 29 Wednesday
Bryn Bras Castle, Llanrug
July 3 Sunday
Bont Fechan Farm, Llanystumdwy
Bryniau, Boduan
July 10 Sunday
Gwyndy Bach, Llandrygarn
July 17 Sunday
Crug Farm, nr Caernarfon
July 24 Sunday
Bryniau, Boduan
August 21 Sunday
Bont Fechan Farm, Llanystumdwy
Gilfach, Rowen, nr Conwy
August 28 Sunday
Crug Farm, nr Caernarfon
Maenan Hall, Llanrwst
August 29 Monday
Crug Farm, nr Caernarfon
September 4 Sunday
Bryniau, Boduan

DESCRIPTIONS OF GARDENS

Bont Fechan Farm ও৳✿✿ (Mr & Mrs J D Bean) Llanystumdwy. 2 m from Criccieth on the A487 to Pwllheli on the L-hand side of the main rd. Small garden with rockery, pond, herbaceous border, steps to river, large variety of plants. Nicely planted tubs. Tea. *Adm 50p Chd 25p. Suns April 3, May 15, July 3, Aug 21 (11-5). Private visits welcome, please* **Tel 0766 522604**

¶**Bryn Bras Castle** ✕ (Mr & Mrs Neville E Gray-Parry) LLanrug. 4m E of Caernarfon, ½m off the main Caernarfon to Llanberis rd, A4086. Signposted. The castle, Grade II, was built in 1830 in the Romanesque style on an earlier structure. There are fine examples of stained glass, panelling, interesting ceilings and richly carved furniture. 32-acre extensive and tranquil landscaped gardens of natural beauty, with much wild life, gradually merge into the Snowdonian foothills. They incl peaceful lawns, herbaceous borders, roses, walled knot garden, stream and pools, woodland walks and a ¼m mountain walk with magnificent panoramic views of Snowdon, Anglesey and the sea. Tea-room & picnic area. TEAS. *Adm garden & castle £3.50 Chd £1.75. Wed June 29 (1-5)*

Bryn Eisteddfod ও (Dr Michael Senior) Glan Conwy. 3½m SE Llandudno 3m W Colwyn Bay; up the hill (Bryn-y-Maen direction) from Glan Conwy Corner where A470 joins A55. 8 acres of landscaped grounds incl mature shrubbery, arboretum, old walled 'Dutch' garden, large lawn with ha-ha. Extensive views over Conwy Valley, Snowdonia National Park, Conwy Castle, town and estuary. TEA. *Adm £1 Chd 50p. Sun May 29 (2-5)*

Bryn Golygfa ✕ (Mrs K & Mr R Alexander) Dolgellau. 5m W of Dolgellau. Take A496 to Bontddu; garden is N 100yds past Bontddu Hall Hotel. Small garden on steep hillside; mixed planting incl rhododendrons and alpines. *Adm 50p Chd 25p. Sun, Mon May 29, 30 (11-5). Private visits welcome mid-May to mid-Aug, please* **Tel 0341 49260**

Bryniau ✿ (P W Wright & J E Humphreys) Boduan. ½m down lane opp. St Buan's Church, Boduan, which is halfway between Nefyn and Pwllheli on the A497. New garden created since 1988 on almost pure sand. Over 60 types of trees; hundreds of shrubs, many unusual, showing that with a little effort, one can grow virtually anything anywhere. Plants & woodcraft for sale. TEAS. *Adm £1 Chd free. Suns March 20, April 10, May 1, 22, June 12, July 3, 24, Sept 4 (11-6) and private visits welcome, please* **Tel 0758 7213 38**

Bryn Meifod ✕✿ (Dr & Mrs K Lever) Graig Glan Conwy. Just off A470 1½m S of Glan Conwy. Follow signs for Aberconwy Nursery. ¾-acre garden developed over 25yrs but extensively replanted in the last 6yrs. Unusual trees and shrubs, scree and peat beds. Good autumn colours. Wide ranging collection of alpines especially autumn gentians and saxifrages. Extensive views towards Snowdonia and the Carneddau. *Adm £1 Chd 25p. Thurs in May and Sept; Suns in June and Aug (2-5)*

Brynmelyn ✕ (Mr & Mrs A S Taylor) Cymerau Isaf. About 2m SW of Blaenau Ffestiniog, on A496 Maentwrog-Blaenau Ffestiniog Rd. Enter by lower gate in layby opp junction to Manod, by footpath sign. After 100yds leave car at garage and follow small footpath to R of garage, descending to stone bridge and Cymerau Falls. Continue over bridge and up hill, follow footpath L; garden about ¼m from garage. Upland garden surrounded by National Nature Reserve containing wide variety of plants providing interest throughout the season. *Adm £1 Chd 50p (Share to The National Osteoporosis Society®). Private visits welcome April 1 to Oct 15* **Tel Ffestiniog 076 676 2684**. *Please telephone before 9.30 am or after dusk*

Bryn-y-Bont ✿ (The Misses Davis & Entwisle) Nantmor. 2½m S of Beddgelert, turn L over Aberglaslyn Bridge into A4085, 500yds turn L up hill, 2nd house on R. Small garden created since 1978 on S facing wooded hillside over looking Glaslyn Vale (As featured on Radio Wales 'Get Gardening' in 1990). *Adm £1 Chd free. Private visits welcome mid April to mid Sept (11-5pm) Parties welcome, please* **Tel 076 686 448**

Cefn Bere ✕ (Mr & Mrs Maldwyn Thomas) Cae Deintur, Dolgellau. Turn L at top of main bridge on Bala-Barmouth Rd (not the by-pass); turn R within 20yds; 2nd R behind school and up hill. Small garden; extensive collection of alpines, bulbs and rare plants. Tea Dolgellau. *Collecting box. Private visits welcome, spring & summer months, please* **Tel Dolgellau 422768**

Coleg Glynllifon Walled Garden ও৳✿ (Anwen Harman, Special Needs Co-ordinator) Clynnog Road Caernarfon. Situated within Glynllifon college (open during termtime) and part of the facilites for the Special Needs Dept. A section of East Walled garden is being restored with the aid of the Welsh Historic Gardens trust. Self guide tour leaflets available. Garden produce grown by mentally handicapped students on sale. Tea-room Parc Glynllifon. [OS sheet 115 SH 452555]. *Open Mon to Fri Term-time (10-3).* **Tel 0286 830261**

Crug Farm ✕✿ (Mr & Mrs B Wynn-Jones) Griffiths Crossing. 2m NE of Caernarfon ¼m off main A487 Caernarfon to Bangor Road. Follow signs 'Crug Farm Plants'. Plantsman's garden; ideally situated; 2 to 3 acres grounds to old country house. Gardens filled with choice, unusual collections of climbers, and herbaceous plants; over 300 species of hardy geraniums. Featured in 'The Garden' and on BBC TV. Only partly suitable wheelchairs. TEAS in aid of RNLI® and local charities. *Collecting box for walled display garden open Thurs, Fri, Sat, Suns & Bank Hols Feb 26 to Sept 25 (10-6). See calendar for openings of private gardens. Adm £1 Chd 50p. Natural Rock garden only open Suns & Mons April 3, 4, May 29, 30, July 17, Aug 28, 29 (10-6)*

Farchynys Cottage ✕✿ (Mrs G Townshend) Bontddu. On A496 Dolgellau-Barmouth rd; well signed W of Bontddu village. 4 acres; partly well-established garden, with attractive, unusual shrubs and trees; partly natural woodland first extensive planting in 1982, new plantings each year. Silver Cup winner 'Wales in Bloom' 1987 Committee Award 1985, 1986 and 1989. Car park. TEAS. *Adm £1 Chd free.* ▲*For NGS Sat, Sun May 21, 22 (11-5)*

Foxbrush ఉ&❀ (Mr & Mrs B S Osborne) Aber Pwll, Port Dinorwic. On Bangor to Caernarfon Road, entering village opp. layby with Felinheli sign post. Fascinating 3-acre country garden on site of old mill and created around winding river; rare and interesting plants; ponds and small wooded area. Extensive plant collections incl rhododendrons, ferns, primula, alpines, clematis and roses; 45ft long pergola; fan-shaped knot garden with traditional and unusual herbs; coaches welcome. Craft studio with jewellery, gifts. TEA. *Adm £1 Chd free. Suns April 3, 4, May 1, June 26 (11-5). Also private visits welcome, please* Tel 0248 670463

Gilfach ❀ (James & Isoline Greenhalgh) Rowen. At Xrds 100yds E of Rowen (4m S of Conwy) S towards Llanrwst, past Rowen School on L; turn up 2nd drive on L, signposted. 1-acre country garden on S facing slope overlooking Conwy Valley; set in 35 acres farm and woodland; mature shrubs; herbaceous border; small pool. Partly suitable wheelchairs which are welcome. Magnificent views of River Conwy and mountains. TEAS. *Adm £1 Chd 10p. Suns April 24, June 19, Aug 21 (11-5)*

Glandderwen ❀ (A M Reynolds Esq) 5m W of Dolgellau. Take A496 to Bontddu. Garden is on S 100yds past Bontddu Hall Hotel; large white wooden gates. ½-acre on N bank of Mawddach Estuary facing Cader Idris; set amid large oaks; shrubs, trees; steep and rocky nature. *Adm 50p Chd 25p. Sun, Mon, May 29, 30 (11-5). Private visits welcome May 1 to Sept 30* Tel 0341 49229

Gwyndy Bach ఉ&❀ (Keith & Rosa Andrew) Llandrygarn. From Llangefni take the B5109 towards Bodedern, the cottage is exactly 5m out on the L. A ¾-acre artist's garden set amidst rugged Anglesey landscape. Romantically planted in intimate 'rooms' with interesting plants and shrubs, old roses and secluded lily pond. Studio attached. TEAS. *Adm £1 Chd free. Sun July 10 (11-5.30). Also private visits welcome, please* Tel 0407 720651

Hafod Garregog ❀ (Mr & Mrs Hugh Mason) Nantmor, 5m N of Penrhyndeudraeth on A4085 towards Aberglaslyn. Garden in woodland setting with fine mountain views; trees, shrubs, flowers and vegetables; woodland bluebell walk. Shown on BBC's 'Gardener's World'. Home of Rhys Goch Eryri AD 1430. Situated above N Hafod. Parties welcome. New garden being made. TEAS. *Adm £1 Chd free. Sun May 8 (11-5). Private visits welcome April to Sept* Tel 076 686 282

Henllys Lodge ఉ&❀ (Mr & Mrs K H Lane) Beaumaris. Past Beaumaris Castle, ½m turn L, 1st L again. Lodge at entrance to Henllys Hall Hotel drive. Approx 1-acre country garden, planted in traditional cottage style featuring extensive collection of hardy geraniums. Small woodland area. Stunning views across Menai Straits. TEAS. *Adm £1. Sat, Sun June 18, 19 (2-5.30). Also private visits welcome, please* Tel 0248 810106

Hen Ysgoldy ❀ (Mr & Mrs Michael Jenkins) Llanfrothen. From Garreg via B4410, after ½m L; garden 200yds on R. Natural garden with streams and established trees, incl magnolias, eucalyptus and embothrium. Shrubs incl a variety of azaleas and rhododendrons, mixed borders planted for colour and interest most of the year round. *Collecting box. Private visits welcome April 1 to Sept 30* Tel 0766 771231

¶**The Herb Garden, Plant Hunter's Nursery** ❀❀ (Mr & Mrs Tremaine-Stevenson) Pentre Berw. Follow A5 towards Holyhead Herb Garden is 1st R after Holland Arms Hotel. 1m from Gaerwen. Park in Holland Arms Garden Centre, secondary car park. Small pretty cottage garden, planted with many unusual and old-fashioned plants. A mixture of herbs, wild flowers, old roses and perennials mixed with gay abandon. Also stream, moisture plants and camomile lawn. Just under 2 acres in all the most part being plant nursery. Sensible shoes recommended. Teas at the 'Holland Arms' Garden Centre opp. *Adm £1. Sun June 26 (10-6)*

Maenan Hall ❀ (The Hon Christopher McLaren) Exactly 2m N of Llanrwst on E side of A470, ¼m S of Maenan Abbey Hotel. Gardens created since 1956 by the late Christabel, Lady Aberconway and then present owner; 10 acres; lawns, shrub, rose and walled gardens; rhododendron dell; many species of beautiful and interesting plants, shrubs and trees set amongst mature oaks and other hardwoods; fine views of mountains across Conway valley. Home-made TEAS. *Adm £1.50 Chd 50p (Share to Giurconi Orphanage, Romania© Sun May 22 & Margaret Mee Amazon Trust Aug 28©). Suns May 22, Aug 28 (10-5) Last entry 4pm*

Pencarreg ఉ❀ (Miss G Jones) Glyn Garth. 1½m NE of A545 Menai Bridge towards Beaumaris, Glan Y Menai Drive is turning on R, Pencarreg is 100yds on R. Parking in lay-by on main rd, ltd parking on courtyard for small cars & disabled. This beautiful garden, with a wealth of species planted for all-yr interest, has colour, achieved by the use of common & unusual shrubs. A small stream creates another delightful and sympathetically-exploited feature. The garden terminates at the cliff edge & this too has been skilfully planted. The views to the Menai Straits & the Carneddi Mountains in the distance make it obvious why this garden has been featured in two television programmes. *Collecting Box (Share to Rescue Dogs Wales). Private visits welcome all year, please* Tel 0248 713545

Penrhyn Castle ఉ❀ (The National Trust) 3m E of Bangor on A5122. Buses from Llandudno, Caernarvon. Betws-y-Coed; alight: Grand Lodge Gate. Large gardens; fine trees, shrubs, wild garden, good views. Castle was rebuilt in 1830 for 1st Lord Penrhyn, incorporating part of C15 building on C8 site of home of Welsh Princes. Museum of dolls; museum of locomotives and quarry rolling stock. NT Shop. TEAS and light lunches. Guide dogs admitted into Castle. *Adm £2 Chd £1. For NGS Sun May 29 (12-6). Last adm ½ hr prior to closing*

Pen-y-Parc (Mrs E E Marsh) Beaumaris. A545 Menai Bridge-Beaumaris rd; after Anglesey Boatyard 1st left; after Golf Club 1st drive on left. NOT very easy for wheelchairs. 6 acres; beautiful grounds, magnificent views over Menai Strait; azaleas, rhododendrons and heathers; interesting terrain with rock outcrops used to advantage for recently planted conifer and rock gardens; small lake in natural setting; 2 further enclosed gardens. We would like to share the pleasure of this garden. TEA. *Adm £1 Chd 25p. Sun May 29 (11-5)*

Plas Muriau ✿🌢 (Lorna & Tony Scharer) Betws-y-Coed. On A470 approx ¼m N of Waterloo Bridge, Betws-y-Coed; entrance by minor junction to Capel Garmon. Large neglected Victorian garden undergoing restoration and replanting with approx 1 acre open to visitors; emphasis on recreating a structured garden within its woodland setting and magnificent views, using perennials, herbs, native plants, bulbs and roses. Many unusual plants for sale at adjacent nursery. *Collecting Box. Tues to Sun incl March 1 to Oct 31 (11-6)*

Plas Newydd ఉ✿ (The Marquess of Anglesey; The National Trust) Isle of Anglesey. 1m SW of Llanfairpwll and A5, on A4080. Gardens with massed shrubs, fine trees, and lawns sloping down to Menai Strait. Magnificent views to Snowdonia. C18 house by James Wyatt contains Rex Whistler's largest wall painting; also Military Museum. TEAS and light lunches. *Adm house & garden £3.80 Group £3 Chd £1.90, garden only £1.90, Chd 95p, Family Adm £9.50. Sun to Fri March 30-Sept 30, Fri & Sun only, Oct 2-30. For NGS Thurs May 12 (12-5) last entry 4.30pm*

Plas Penhelig ✿🌢 (Mr & Mrs A C Richardson) Aberdovey, between 2 railway bridges. Driveway to hotel by island and car park. 14 acres overlooking estuary, exceptional views. Particularly lovely in spring: bulbs, daffodils, rhododendrons, azaleas; rock and water gardens, mature tree heathers, magnolias, euphorbias; herbaceous borders, rose garden; wild and woodland flowers encouraged in large orchard; walled kitchen garden, large range of greenhouses, peaches, herbs. TEAS. *Adm £1 Chd 50p. Wed to Sun inc: April 1 to mid-Oct (2.30-5.30). Collecting box*

Sychnant ✿🌢 (Chandler & A Williamson) Penmaenmawr. Situated on and 200 metres from the foot of the Sychnant Pass in Dwygyfylchi. Between Conwy and Penmaenmawr. [OS Sheet SH 745768]. Over ½-acre steep terraced dry garden under renovation, containing many rare and unusual plants. Large collection of pinks, geraniums, erodiums and grasses. Flat shoes recommended. Adjacent nursery open. *Collecting Box. Thurs May 5 to Sept 29 (10-6)*

Powys

Hon County Organisers:
(North – Montgomeryshire)
(South – Brecknock & Radnor)
Captain R Watson, Westwinds, Kerry, Newtown, Powys Tel 0686 670605
Mrs C R C Inglis, Llansantffraed House, Bwlch Brecon Tel 0874 87229
Assistant County Organiser:
S. Powys
Miss Shan Egerton, Pen-y-Maes, Hay on Wye, Via Hereford Tel 0497 820423
Hon County Treasurer: North
Elwyn Pugh Esq, Post Office, Kerry, Newtown Tel 0686 670221

DATES OF OPENING

By appointment
For telephone numbers and other details see garden descriptions. Private visits welcomed

Ashford House, Talybont on Usk
The Bushes, Berriew
Craig-y-Bwla, Crickhowell
Diamond Cottage, Buttington
Maenllwyd Isaf, Abermule
The Old Vicarage, Llangorse
The Walled Garden, Knill, nr Knighton

April 17 Sunday
Gliffaes Country House Hotel, Crickhowell

May 1 Sunday
Maesllwch Castle, Glasbury-on-Wye

May 8 Sunday
Penmyarth, Crickhowell

May 15 Sunday
Glanwye, Builth Wells

Trawscoed Hall, Welshpool
May 18 Wednesday
Diamond Cottage, Buttington
May 21 Saturday
Cae Hywel, Llansantffraid-ym-Mechain
May 22 Sunday
Bronhyddon, Llansantffraid-ym-Mechain
Cae Hywel, Llansantffraid-ym-Mechain
Garth House, Garth
Gliffaes Country House Hotel, Crickhowell
May 30 Monday
Llysdinam, Newbridge-on-Wye
May 31 Tuesday
Powis Castle Gardens, Welshpool
June 5 Sunday
Bodynfoel Hall, Llanfechain
The Bushes, Berriew
Gregynog, Tregynon
Lower Cefn Perfa, Kerry, nr Newtown
Tretower House, Crickhowell
June 18 Saturday
Upper Dolley, Dolley Green,

Presteigne
June 19 Sunday
Ashford House, Talybont on Usk
Upper Dolley, Dolley Green, Presteigne
June 22 Wednesday
Ashford House, Talybont on Usk
June 26 Sunday
Carnog, Llanfrynach, Brecon ‡
Manascin, Pencelli, Brecon ‡
June 29 Wednesday
Carrog, Llanfrynach, Brecon ‡
July 3 Sunday
Treberfydd, Nr Bwlch
July 9 Saturday
Argoed Fawr, Llanwrthwl
Upper Dolley, Dolley Green, Presteigne
July 10 Sunday
Argoed Fawr, Llanwrthwl
The Millers House, Welshpool
Pen y Maes, Hay-on-Wye
Upper Dolley, Dolley Green, Presteigne
July 13 Wednesday
Carrog, Llanfrynach

July 17 Sunday
Moor Park, nr Crickhowell

July 27 Wednesday
Diamond Cottage, Buttington

July 31 Sunday
Fraithwen, Tregynon, Newtown

August 7 Sunday
Lonicera, Talybont-on-Usk

August 14 Sunday
Kerry Gardens, Kerry, nr Newtown

August 21 Sunday
Llysdinam, Newbridge-on-Wye

September 4 Sunday
The Bushes, Berriew

September 11 Sunday
Talybont-on-Usk Gardens

October 2 Sunday
Bodynfoel Hall, Llanfechan

DESCRIPTIONS OF GARDENS

Argoed Fawr ⚭❀ (Mr & Mrs M J Maltby) Llanwrthwl. 7m N of Builth Wells on A470. 5m S of Rhayader. ½-acre cultivated garden with small shrubbery; rock garden; pergola; vegetable garden; fruit trees and bushes. Herbaceous border, climbing roses, and clematis, extending to 3 acres of conservation area with stream where new plantings of trees and hedges have been grown to encourage wildlife. Bring and buy plant stall. TEA. *Adm £1 (Share to Hafen Home, Rhayader®). Sat, Sun July 9, 10 (11-5)*

Ashford House ⚭⚭❀ (Mr & Mrs D A Anderson) Brecon. ¾m E of Talybont on Usk on B4558 signed from A40 through village. Walled garden of about 1 acre surrounded by woodland and wild garden approx 4 acres altogether. Mixed shrub and herbaceous borders; new small formal garden; meadow garden and pond; alpine house and beds; vegetables. The whole garden has gradually been restored and developed over the last 12yrs. Bring and buy plant stall. TEAS. *Adm £1.50 Chd free (Share to Action Research®).* ▲*For NGS Sun, Wed June 19, 22 (2-6). Private visits also welcome, please* **Tel 087 487 271**

Bodynfoel Hall ⚭❀ (Maj & Mrs Bonnor-Maurice) Llanfechain, 10m N of Welshpool. Via A490 to Llanfyllin. Take B4393 to Llanfechain, follow signs to Bodynfoel. 3½ acres; gardens and woodland; lakes; young and mature trees; shrub roses and heather bank. TEAS. *Adm £1 OAPs 50p Chd free. Sun June 5 (2-6); Sun Oct 2 (2-5).* **Tel 0691 648486**

Bronhyddon ⚭❀ (Mr & Mrs R Jones-Perrott) Llansantffraid-ym-Mechain. 10m N Welshpool on A495 on E side in centre of village. Long drive; parking in fields below house. Wood having been almost clear felled now planted with choice young trees & shrubs on acid soil on S facing slope. Grass rides have been made and in spring is a mass of bluebells and foxgloves; a mature stand has anemones, snowdrops & primroses. Both areas lead out of small garden in front of house with elegant Regency verandahs & balconies. TEAS. *Adm £1 Chd free. Sun May 22 (2-6)*

¶The Bushes ⚭❀ (Mr & Mrs Hywel Williams) Berriew. 8m Welshpool on B4390 midway Berriew and Manafon. Pretty closely planted cottage garden arranged in 'rooms' on S sloping site. Pools, cobbled and paved areas. Set in picturesque Rhiew valley. TEAS. *Adm £1. Suns June 5, Sept 4 (2-6). Private visits also welcome May to Oct, please* **Tel 0686 650338**

Cae Hywel ❀ (Miss Judith M Jones) Llansantffraid-ym-Mechain, 10m N of Welshpool. On A495; on E (Oswestry) side of village. Car park in village. 1 acre; S facing slope on different levels; rock garden; herb garden; interesting shrubs, trees and plants. Partly suitable for wheelchairs. TEAS. *Adm £1 Chd 10p. Sat, Sun May 21, 22 (2-6)*

¶Carrog ⚭❀ (Lt Col & Mrs R J M Sinnett) Llanfrynach. 3m SE of Brecon. Llanfrynach is signed from A40 flyover, just E of Brecon. The village is just off B4558. ⅔-acre of mixed borders of shrubs, herbaceous plants and roses. Bring and buy plant stall. TEAS. *Adm £1 Chd free. Sun, Wed June 26, 29 (2-6)*

Craig-y-Bwla (Mr & Mrs George Williams) 5m NE Crickhowell on Llanthony to Fforest Coal Pit Road. Signed from Crickhowell Fire Station 30 acres mainly woodland garden. Laburnum arch. Small lakes. River walks. Picnic area. Autumn foliage. *Adm £1.50 Chd free. Private visits welcome May to Oct, please* **Tel 0873 811810 or 0873 810413**

Diamond Cottage ⚭❀ (Mr & Mrs D T Dorril) Buttington. 4½m NE of Welshpool. From Welshpool take A458 Shrewsbury Rd. Turn R into Heldre Lane, R at next junction, R at Xrds up the hill. From Shrewsbury, turn L 100yds past 'Little Chef' into Sale Lane, L at next junction, R at Xrds. Parking in lane above cottage. 1.7-acre garden created since 1988 on N facing slope of Long Mountain at 700ft. Unusual herbaceous plants and shrubs; natural wooded dingle with small stream; large vegetable garden, patio and pool. Extensive views to Berwyn Mountains. TEAS. *Adm £1 Chd free. Weds May 18, July 27 (2-6). Private visits welcome, please* **Tel 0938 570570**

Fraithwen ⚭❀ (Mr & Mrs David Thomas) Tregynon. 6m N of Newtown on B4389 midway between villages of Bettws, Cedewain and Tregynon. 1-acre garden created in the last 10yrs; herbaceous borders, rockeries and ponds packed with interesting, unusual and rare plants and shrubs for colour throughout the year. Also on display antique horse-drawn machinery and implements. TEAS. *Adm £1 Chd free (Share to Bettws Community Hall®). Sun July 31 (2-6)*

Garth House ⚭ (Mr & Mrs F A Wilson) Garth on A483 6m W of Builth Wells. Drive gates in village of Garth by Garth Inn. Large wood with azaleas and rhododendrons; water and shrub garden; herbaceous garden; fine views. Historic connection with Charles Wesley & the Gwynne family. TEAS. *Adm £1 Chd free. Sun May 22 (2-6)*

Glanwye ⚭❀ (Mr & Mrs David Vaughan, G & H Kidston) 2m SE Builth Wells on A470. Large garden, rhododendrons, azaleas; newly sown wild flower meadow; woodland walk with flowers. Good views of R. Wye. Bring and buy plant stall. Cream TEAS. *Adm £1 Chd free (Share to Llanddewi Cwm and Alltmawr Church©). Sun May 15 (2-6)*

Gliffaes Country House Hotel & (Mr & Mrs Brabner) 3m W of Crickhowell on A40. Large garden; spring bulbs; azaleas & rhododendrons, new ornamental pond; heathers; shrubs; ornamental trees; fine maples; autumn colour; fine position high above R. Usk. *April to Dec. For NGS Adm £1 Chd 50p (collecting box). Suns April 17, May 22 (2-5)*

Gregynog &❀ (University of Wales) Tregynon, 7m N of Newtown. A483 Welshpool to Newtown Rd, turn W at B4389 for Bettws Cedewain, 1m through village gates on left. Large garden; fine banks, rhododendrons and azaleas; dell with specimen shrubs; formal garden; colourcoded walks starting from car park. Descriptive leaflet available. Early C19 black and white house; site inhabited since C12. TEAS. *Adm £1 Chd 10p. Sun June 5 (2-6)*

Kerry Gardens && 3m S of Newtown. Take A489 to Craven Arms. Some gardens featured on BBC TV Wales. Start from Kerry Lamb car park. TEAS in aid of village hall. *Combined adm £1 Chd 10p. Sun Aug 14 (2-6)*
   Mar-Jon Dolforgan View (Mrs O Hughes) Interesting garden; wide variety of annuals, plants and shrubs
   Post Office (Mr & Mrs E Pugh) Leeks, spray chrysanthemums and fuchsias grown for exhibition also small colourful garden
   Westwinds (Captain & Mrs R Watson) Colourful garden; rockery, pools, shrubs, flower beds. TEAS

Llysdinam &❀ (Lady Delia Venables-Llewelyn & Llysdinam Charitable Trust) Newbridge-on-Wye, 3W of Llandrindod Wells. Turn W off A479 at Newbridge-on-Wye; right immediately after crossing R Wye; entrance up hill. Large garden. Azaleas; rhododendrons, water garden and herbaceous borders; shrubs; woodland garden; kitchen garden; fine view of Wye Valley. Bring and buy plant stall. TEAS. *Adm £1.50 Chd free (Share to NSPCC®). Mons May 30, Aug 21 (2-6.30)*

Lonicera && (Mr & Mrs G Davies) Talybont-on-Usk. ½m from turning off A40. 6m E of Brecon, signposted Talybont. A garden of varied interest incorporating several small feature gardens extending to approx ¼ acre. These include a modern rose garden; landscaped heather garden with dwarf conifers; herbaceous and woody perennials; colourful summer bedding displays; window boxes, hanging baskets and patio tubs forming extensive house frontage display; greenhouses. Teas at Llansantffraed House. *Adm £1 Chd free. Sun Aug 7 (2-6)*

Lower Cefn Perfa &❀ (Mr & Mrs J Dugdale) Kerry, Newtown. Follow signs off A489. Medium-sized easily maintained garden with R Mule running through it. TEAS in aid of Powys Branch British Red Cross Soc Holiday for the disabled. *Adm £1 Chd free. Sun June 5 (2-6)*

Maenllwyd Isaf && (Mrs Denise Hatchard) Abermule, 5m NE of Newtown & 10m S of Welshpool. On B4368 Abermule to Craven Arms, 1½m from Abermule. 3 acres; unusual shrubs and plants; goldfish pool; 'wild' pool; R. Mule. C16 listed house. *Adm £1 Chd free (Share to Winged Fellowship Trust®). Private visits welcome all year. Gardening clubs etc welcome, please Tel 0686 630204*

Maesllwch Castle (Walter de Winton Esq) Glasbury-on-Wye. Turn off A438 immediately N of Glasbury bridge. Through Glasbury ½m turn R at Church. Medium-sized, garden owner maintained. Exceptional views from terrace across R. Wye to Black Mountains. Old walled garden, woodland walk, fine trees, c18 gingko tree. TEA. *Adm £1.50 Chd free (Share to All Saints Church, Glasbury®). Sun May 1 (2-5)*

Manascin && (Lady Watson) Pencelli. 3m SE of Brecon on B4558 pink house in Pencelli Village. Small garden, many features; small pond with water lilies and fountain; shrubs; roses, lilies and vegetable patch. TEAS at Carrog. *Adm £1 Chd free. Sun June 26 (2-6)*

¶The Millers House &❀ (Mr & Mrs Mark Kneale) Welshpool. About 1¼m NW of Welshpool on rd to Guilsfield A490; turn L into Windmill Lane; 4th cottage on L. 1½-acre country garden begun in 1988. Superb views. Mixed shrub and herbaceous borders, roses, climbers. Ornamental and fruit trees incl a planting of 12 hardy eucalyptus. TEA. *Adm £1 Chd free. Sun July 10 (2-6)*

Moor Park & (Mr & the Hon Mrs L Price) Llanbedr. Turn off A40 at Fire Station in Crickhowell; continue 2m, signed Llanbedr. 5 acres; roses, borders, trees and walled kitchen garden. Lake, water garden under construction; woodland walk. TEAS. *Adm £1 Chd free. Sun July 17 (2-6.30)*

The Old Vicarage, Langorse && (Major & Mrs J B Anderson) 6½m E of Brecon on B4560. Small family garden maintained by owners with interesting herbaceous and shrub borders; lawns, trees and vegetables. Plants usually for sale in aid of NGS. *Private visits welcome Spring to Oct, please Tel 087484 639*

Penmyarth & (Mr & The Hon Mrs Legge-Bourke) Glanusk Park. 2m W of Crickhowell. A40, 12m from Brecon, 8m from Abergavenny. 11-acre rose, rock and wild garden with bluebells, azaleas, rhododendrons and pond. TEAS. *Adm £1. Sun May 8 (2-6)*

Pen-y-Maes &❀ (Miss S Egerton) 1m W of Hay-on-Wye on B4350 towards Brecon. Entrance on L. Small garden, mainly herbaceous with walled potager of geometrically divided beds full of vegetables, herbs and flowers edged with box. Also old roses, lilies and espaliered fruit trees. Featured in Gardens Illustrated Oct 93. Bring and buy plant stall. TEAS. *Adm £1 Chd free. Sun July 10 (2-5)*

Powis Castle Gardens &❀ (The National Trust) Welshpool. Turn off A483 ¾m out of Welshpool, up Red Lane for ¼m. Gardens laid out in 1720 with most famous hanging terraces in the world; enormous yew hedges; lead statuary, large wild garden. Part of garden suitable for wheelchairs, top terrace only. TEA. The date shown below is a *Special opening* for NGS; garden only. *Adm gardens only (Castle closed) £3.50 Chd £1.50 N.T. members also pay.* ▲*Tues May 31 (12-6)*

Talybont-on-Usk Gardens *⚘⚘* Talybont-on-Usk. 6m E of Brecon, signposted Talybont. Teas at Llansantffraed House. *Combined adm £1.50 Chd free. Sun Sept 11 (2-6)*

    6 Maesmawr Close (Miss Mary Arter) Small, owner-maintained garden in housing estate. Shrubs, perennial and herbaceous plants to encourage wild life. Bring and buy plant stall

    The Old Post Office (Mrs Marjorie Brockwell) Reclaimed ¼-acre surrounding an old stone cottage, with permanent planting in borders; island beds of shrubs and colourful herbaceous plants. Raised bed for alpines. 2 ponds with stream and bog garden. Secluded walled garden with interesting climbers. Garden room

Trawscoed Hall *⚘⚘* (Mr & Mrs J T K Trevor) 3m N of Welshpool on Llanfyllin Road. Long drive through woodlands, lovely panoramic views from S facing sloping gardens with interesting plants. 2 acres. Magnificent wisteria covering front of fine Georgian house (not open) built 1777. Granary dating from 1772. Nature trails through prize-winning woodlands. TEAS (in aid of Asthma Research). *Adm £1 Chd free. Sun May 15 (2-6)*

Treberfydd ⚘ (Lt Col & Mrs D Garnons Williams) Bwlch. 2¼m W of Bwlch. From A40 at Bwlch turning marked Llangorse then L for Pennorth. From Brecon, leave A40 at Llanhamlach. 2¼m to sign Llangasty Church but go over cattle grid to house. Large garden; lawns, roses, trees, rock garden. TEAS. *Adm £1 Chd free (Share to Llangasty Church®). Sun July 3 (2-6)*

Tretower House ⚘*⚘⚘* (Lt Col & Mrs P K Cracroft) Leave Crickhowell on A40 towards Brecon. Take R fork for Builth Wells. Garden 1m in Tretower village. 2½-acre family garden maintained by owners. Mainly herbaceous. Views of Black Mountains and Tretower Castle. Bring and buy plant stall. TEAS. *Adm £1 Chd free (Share to Tretower Church®). Sun June 5 (2-6)*

Upper Dolley ⚘*⚘⚘* (Mrs B P Muggleton) Dolley Green. Take B4356 W out of Presteigne towards Whitton. At Dolley Green, 2m from Presteigne, turn L down 'No Through Road' by red brick church; Upper Dolley is 100yds on L. From Knighton take B4355 to turning for Whitton, B4357. Turn L at Whitton B4356 to brick church; turn R. 2-acre country garden with open views of Lugg Valley; variety of borders with many shrub roses and large natural pond; C16 Grade 2 listed house (not open). TEAS weather permitting. *Adm £1 Chd 50p (Share to The Bible Society®). Sats, Suns June 18, 19; July 9, 10 (2-6)*

The Walled Garden ⚘ (Miss C M Mills) Knill, 3m from Kington and Presteigne. Off B4362 Walton-Presteigne rd to Knill village; right over cattle grid; keep right down drive. 3 acres; walled garden; stream; bog garden; primulas; shrub roses. Nr C13 Church in lovely valley. *Adm £1 Chd 50p. Private visits welcome any day (10-7), please* **Tel 0544 267411**

By Appointment Gardens. Avoid the crowds. Good chance of a tour by owner. See garden description for telephone number.

The counties of England and Wales

Avon **32**
Bedfordshire **27**
Berkshire **34**
Buckinghamshire **26**
Cambridgeshire **20**
Cheshire & Wirral **9**
Clwyd **8**
Cornwall **44**
Cumbria **2**
Derbyshire **11**
Devon **41**
Dorset **42**
Durham **3**
Dyfed **22**
Essex **29**
The Glamorgans **30**
Gloucestershire **24**
Greater London **35**
Gwent **31**
Gwynedd & Anglesey **7**
Hampshire **39**
Hereford & Worcester **23**
Hertfordshire **28**
Humberside **5**
Isle of Wight **43**
Kent **37**
Lancashire, Merseyside & Greater Manchester **6**
Leicestershire & Rutland **16**
Lincolnshire **13**
Norfolk **17**

Northamptonshire **19**
Northumberland & Tyne and Wear **1**
Nottinghamshire **12**
Oxfordshire **25**
Powys **14**
Shropshire **15**
Somerset **38**
Staffordshire & part of West Midlands **10**
Suffolk **21**
Surrey **36**
Sussex **40**
Warwickshire & West Midlands **18**
Wiltshire **33**
Yorkshire & Cleveland **4**

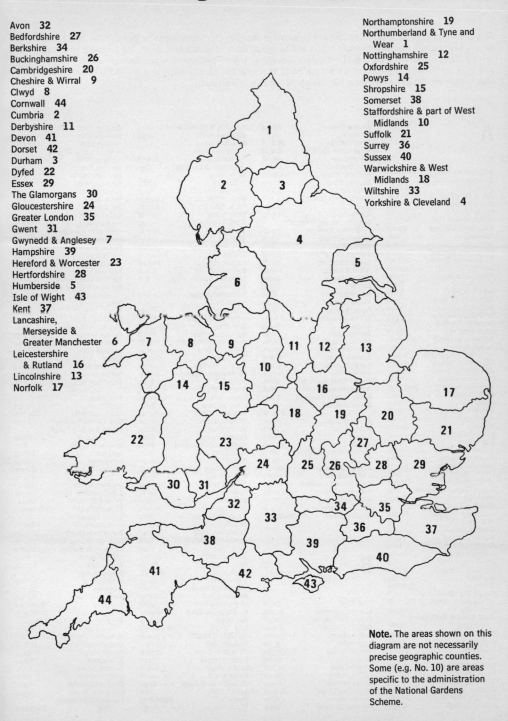

Note. The areas shown on this diagram are not necessarily precise geographic counties. Some (e.g. No. 10) are areas specific to the administration of the National Gardens Scheme.

Index to Gardens

This index lists all gardens alphabetically and gives the counties in which they are to be found. Refer to the relevant county pages where the garden and its details will be found, again in alphabetical order. The following unorthodox county abbreviations are used: C & W—Cheshire and Wirral; L & R—Leicestershire and Rutland; G & A—Gwynedd and Anglesey. An * denotes a garden which will not be in its normal alphabetical order as it is a group garden and will be found under the Group Garden name but still within the county indicated.

Index to Advertisers

Visit our classic country house gardens: so beautiful you might even decide to set up home there.

*T*HE COUNTRY HOUSES ASSOCIATION owns and operates nine superb houses in the south of England, each with extensive and impeccably maintained gardens.

As part of the National Garden Scheme you are welcome to come and visit five of our gems. DANNY, at Hurstpierpoint, nestles amongst trees at the foot of the Sussex Downs. FLETE, near Plymouth, affords splendid views across the Erme estuary. GREAT MAYTHAM HALL stands in 18 acres of grounds at Rolvenden, near Cranbrook in Kent. At SWALLOWFIELD PARK, close by Reading in Berkshire, you can roam 25 acres of glorious parkland. And a special feature, at PYTHOUSE, near Salisbury, is an Orangery restored to its 18th century glory.

All of our properties are living communities; home to active retired people who enjoy a quality of life that is all too rare these days.

So, do come and visit. You might even decide to become a member of the Association – a recognised charity, committed to preserving and maintaining these treasures of our heritage. And, if you really can't bring yourself to leave, we'll be delighted to explain how you could become a resident.

COUNTRY HOUSES *ASSOCIATION*

TO FIND OUT MORE, CONTACT COUNTRY HOUSES ASSOCIATION. FREEPOST, LONDON WC2B 6BR. TELEPHONE 071-836 1624 OR 071-240 1676.

J04

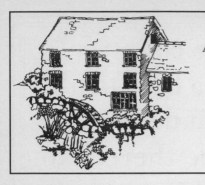

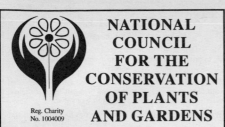

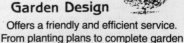

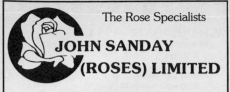

THE SPRING FLOWER SHOW, HARROGATE - 1994

The first great early flower show of the year held in the beautiful setting of the Valley Gardens, Harrogate

Thursday 21st April	9.30 am –	6.00 pm
Friday 22nd April	9.30 am –	6.00 pm
Saturday 23rd April	9.30 am –	6.00 pm
Sunday 24th April	9.30 am –	4.30 pm

GREAT AUTUMN FLOWER SHOW, HARROGATE - 1994

Bringing together in the Exhibition Halls many National Horticultural Societies, Nursery and Sundry exhibitors

Friday 16th September	10.00 am –	7.00 pm
Saturday 17th September	9.30 am –	5.00 pm

Special rates for parties. Information from The North of England Horticultural Society,
4A South Park Road, Harrogate, North Yorkshire HG1 5QU Tel/Fax: 0423-561049

352

Australia's Open Garden Scheme

Going to Australia?

Just as Australian gardeners visiting Britain make straight for the Yellow Book, so visitors to Australia can now plan their holidays with the help of our guidebook.

Gardening is a consuming passion for many Australians. From the exuberance of tropical Queensland to the cool, moist woodlands of Tasmania, our gardens rejoice in a huge diversity of plants and garden styles.

Visit some of our finest private gardens and meet the gardeners who nurture them. *Australia's Open Garden Scheme Guidebook* is published each August by ABC Books and is available from ABC Shops, newsagents and all good bookshops throughout Australia. For further information about the Scheme, please contact our office.

President: *Mrs Malcolm Fraser*
National Executive Officer: *Neil Robertson, Westport, New Gisborne,*
Victoria 3438, Australia   Tel + 61 (54) 28 4557   Fax + 61 (54) 28 4558

Australia's Open Garden Scheme Limited A.C.N. 057 467 553

Merriments Gardens
Hardy Plant Centre

Our personal selection of interesting perennial garden plants, hardy shrubs and grasses available seven days a week throughout the year.

Four acre plantsmen's garden open April to September.

Teas and refreshments.

Only 7 miles from Sissinghurst Castle Gardens.

HAWKHURST ROAD, HURST GREEN
EAST SUSSEX TN19 7RA ENGLAND

TELEPHONE: 0580 860666

SPRING BULBS from GROOMS

Our 48-page fully illustrated Catalogue is now available FREE. Choose your hyacinths, tulips, crocus, lilies and border plants from our wide range.
10 FREE daffodils with your first order.
Write for your copy today to
GROOM BROS LTD (GEW) Pecks Drove Nurseries, Spalding, PE12 6BJ.
Phone: 0775-722421/766006

CREATING A CONSERVATION AREA?

Try native trees, shrubs, wildflowers and bulbs from
BTCV TREES & WILDFLOWERS
Telephone: 021 358 2155 for a FREE catalogue.

Profits from the sale of our plants help fund practical conservation work across England & Wales.

Andrea Jones
~ GARDEN PHOTOGRAPHY ~
COMMERCIAL & PRIVATE COMMISSIONS
Crow Hill Top
Crow, Ringwood   Tel:(0425) 480864
HANTS BH24 3DD   Fax:(0425) 480958

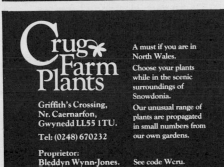

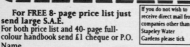

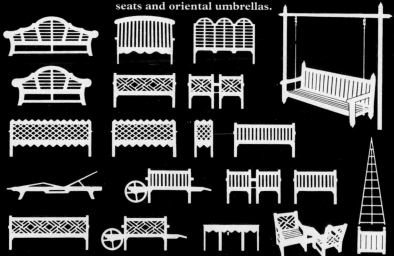

340

342

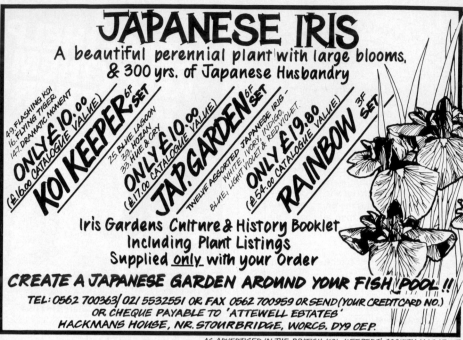

AS ADVERTISED IN THE BRITISH KOI-KEEPERS' SOCIETY MAGAZINE.

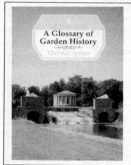

A Glossary of Garden History

by **Michael Symes**   ISBN 0 7478 0223 8   **£6.99**

Explains for garden visitors over 500 terms, from alcove, allée and apiary through gazebo, gazon coupé and gloriette to winter garden, yaird and zigzag. *Over 160 illustrations, 50 in colour.*

Available from booksellers or from Shire Publications (1356), FREEPOST (AHE 135), Princes Risborough, Bucks HP27 8BR. Telephone: 0844 344301

The Gardener's art • Gardening: shrubs and climbers • Garden scenes in Shakespeare • Archaeology and history of Gardens • Gardens in and around Oxford • Gardens in the Severn Valley • Gardens of Argyll • Gardens of the Lake District • Gardens of Le Périgord • Gardens of North Wales • Gardens of Wessex

TIME TO LEARN is an invaluable guide to thousands of study breaks, summer schools, activity courses and study tours in the UK and abroad. Compiled and published biannually by NIACE – the national organisation for adult learning.

April – September 1994 edition **£4.25**
October 1994 – March 1995 edition (available August 1994) **£4.25**
Order from booksellers or from NIACE, 21 De Montfort Street, Leicester LE1 7GE.
(Post free in the UK. Please make cheques payable to NIACE.)
Company number 2603322/Charity number 1002775

Pure Knitted Cotton

☎ 0773 836000

David Nieper

PURE COTTON

Sleep in the luxury of pure knitted jersey cotton. Choice of three feminine nightdresses exclusively designed by David Nieper. Beautifully made in Britain by skilled seamstresses. Generously cut, with specially softened stretch lace. Each in a choice of three lovely shades, cool ivory, warm pink or soft blue. Machine washable. Most attractively priced. Blissfully comfortable.

DAVID NIEPER SAULGROVE HOUSE FREEPOST SOMERCOTES DERBYS. DE55 9BR

STYLE	DESCRIPTION	STATE COLOUR	QTY	S	M	L	XL
F0541 £44.50	Sleeveless N/D Long 54"						
F0540 £42.50 £44.50	Cap Slv N/D Midi 48" Long 54"						
F0543 £47.50	Long Slv N/D Long 54"						

CREDIT CARD NO.

SIGNATURE

EXPIRY DATE — MONTH — YEAR — SWITCH ISSUE No

SPECIAL OFFER £5

Free postage and packing, and an extra £5.00 discount when you buy any two nightdresses

MR/MRS
(Caps please)

ADDRESS

POSTCODE

I WISH TO PAY BY CHEQUE PAYABLE TO DAVID NIEPER

DAYTIME TELEPHONE NUMBER (in case of query):

Delivery within 7 days - max. 28 days
Full refund if returned within 14 days

DAVID NIEPER, FREEPOST, SOMERCOTES DERBYS. DE55 9BR

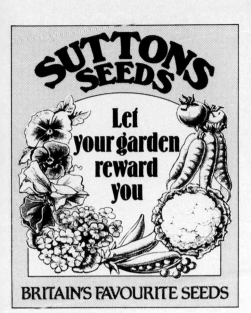

Thompson & Morgan
The Seedsmen. Est. 1855

Since the first seed catalogue in 1855, Thompson & Morgan have been offering to gardeners world wide, some of the most popular, rare and interesting plants from seed. In the latest catalogue, you'll find on offer an extensive range of annuals, perennials, biennials, alpines, house and conservatory plants, cacti, trees, shrubs and vegetables — it's a treasure store of garden gems!

Take the opportunity to browse at your leisure through the world's largest illustrated seed catalogue — almost 2,000 pictures of glorious flowers and mouth watering vegetables. Use the coupon below to request your copy today.

In association with the National Garden Scheme you may deduct £3 OFF the value of your T&M order. Simply cut out the special exclusive voucher on this page and attach to your order.

Michauxia tchihatcheffii

Tomato Sungold — the Sweetest

£3 off

see over page for details

CATALOGUE REQUEST

complete details over page

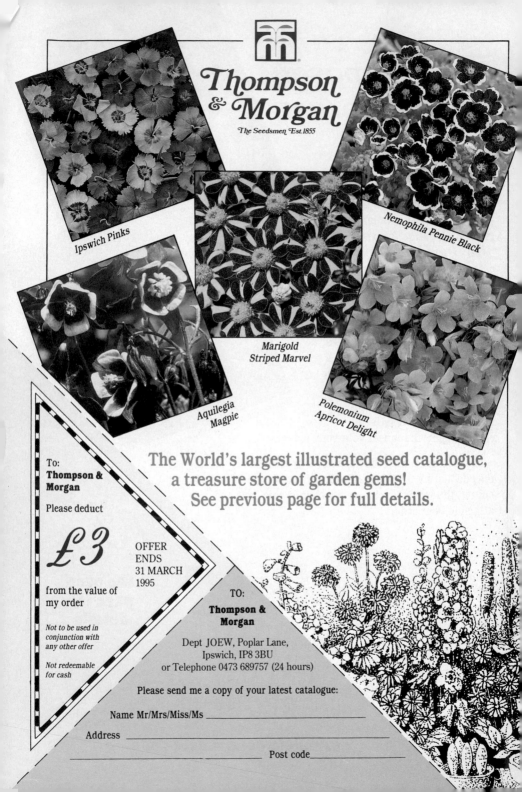

It happened to me...
A new baby came home

Written by
Elizabeth O'Loughlin

Illustrated by
Ellie Dangerfield

First published in the UK in 2005
by PANGOLIN BOOKS
Unit 17, Piccadilly Mill, Lower Street,
Stroud, Gloucestershire, GL5 2HT.

Copyright © 2005 Bookwork Ltd.

A CIP catalogue record for this book is
available from the British Library.

ISBN 1-84493-021-1

Printed in the UK by Goodman Baylis Ltd.

GETTING HELP WHEN A NEW BABY COMES HOME

If you do not like having a new baby at home, it will help if you talk to someone about how you are feeling. You could talk to a friend, like the child in this book does, or to an adult that you trust. Or you can get help from ChildLine or the NSPCC. They will not tell anyone about your call unless you want them to or you are in danger.

Childline (www.childline.org.uk)

If you have a problem, ring ChildLine on 0800 1111 at any time – day or night. Someone there will try to help you find ways to sort things out.

NSPCC (www.nspcc.org.uk)

The NSPCC has a helpline on 0808 800 5000 which never closes. There is always someone there to talk to if you are unhappy, worried or scared about something in your life. You can also e-mail them on help@nspcc.org.uk

Not long ago, there were only
three of us — Me, Dad and Mum.
But now there are four of us.

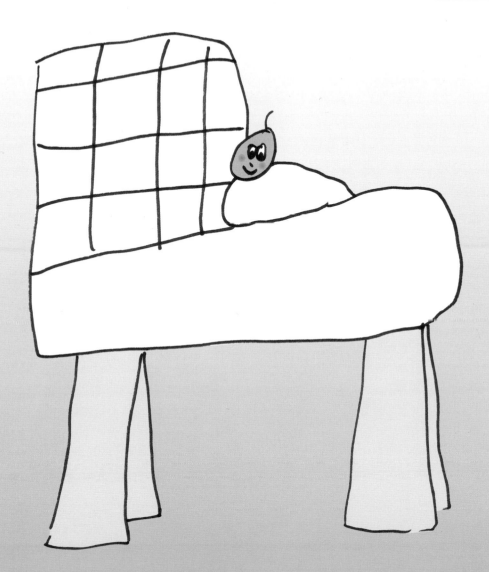

The fourth one is called New Baby.
It has got another name, but I
can't remember what it is.

New Baby was in Mum's tummy. I don't understand how it got there. Dad says he put it there, but I still don't understand and it frightens me a little.

Now New Baby is in our home. I wonder why I am not enough for Mum and Dad. Why do they need somebody else as well?"

Everyone says that I must love New Baby. Sometimes I do, and sometimes I don't.

Sometimes I think it's the best new baby in the world, and sometimes I want to throw it in the dustbin.

Mum often cuddles
New Baby very close.
It makes me feel funny
when I see them.
It makes me feel a
bit like I do when I'm
going to be sick.

Once, when I was watching them, Mum asked me if I was alright. I had to go, because I felt funny. But I said I was ok, and slammed the door.

"My friend Julie has a new baby in her home too, so I talk to her about it.

Julie says that sometimes
she loves her new baby
and sometimes she
doesn't, just like me.

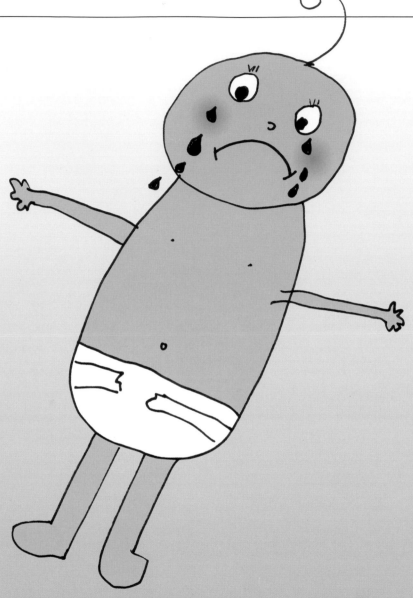

I told Julie that New Baby doesn't even play with me. It just lies around all day and cries or sleeps.

Julie says I will get used to it soon. But I don't want to get used to it soon. I want New Baby to go away so I can be the only one again."

How can I love New Baby when Mum spends all her time with it? She used to spend all her time with me.

And she has changed since New Baby came. She walks very slowly and speaks very quietly. And when I want her to play with me, she says she is too tired. "

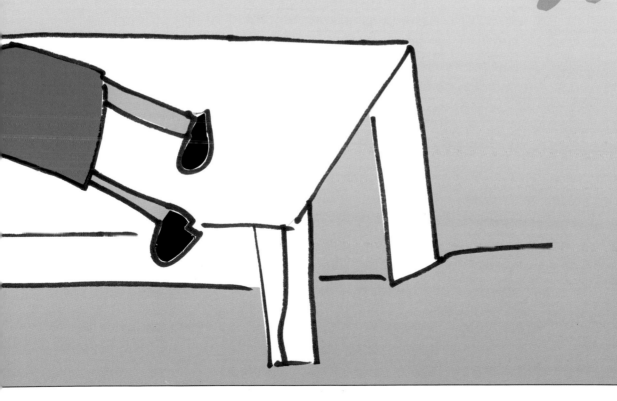

"I want to be New Baby. Then Mum
will spend all her time with me again.
So I cry and climb on Mum's knee.
And I try to be just like New Baby.

Sometimes Mum lets me cuddle up to her, and then I feel a bit better. But often she doesn't let me cuddle up. She says I am too big.

I told Dad it's unfair that Mum is always with New Baby when she used to be always with me. Dad said that Mum was never always with me, because she was with him as well.

I think Mum loves New Baby more than me. Dad says she doesn't, but I don't believe him. I wonder what I can do to make Mum love me best again.

Sometimes I laugh and shout and run very fast so that Mum will look at me and not look at New Baby.

But she tells me
to be quiet because
New Baby has gone
to sleep. She doesn't
understand that I
want to be New Baby
so she won't need
two of us any more. **"**

"Dad says that I was a new baby once, but I don't remember. He says that New Baby will grow up, like I have grown up, and then we will be friends and play together.

I hope we will be friends, but I'm not sure. Perhaps we will be friends, but not all the time. "

"My friend Julie says that she likes having a new baby at home, because now she isn't the smallest.

And she can tell the new baby what to do, like her mum and dad tell her what to do. "

"Julie says it's good to have a new baby at home, because her mum can't watch her and the new baby at the same time. Now she can do some things that her mum doesn't know about. Perhaps my New Baby isn't so bad after all!"

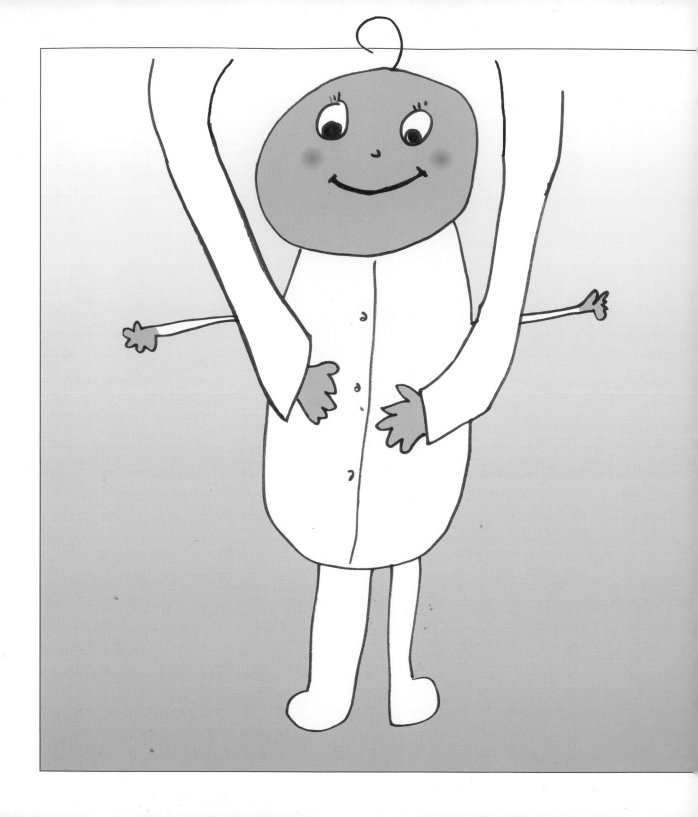

"Today, Mum let me hold New Baby on my lap. He felt all soft and warm, and smelt nice. I liked the way he cuddled into me. And I felt big and strong, like a big bear I saw in my book."

"I've just remembered that
New Baby's name is Dan.
I'll tell Julie tomorrow."